COMPARATIVE CONSTITUTIONAL LAW: A CONTEXTUAL APPROACH

COMPARATIVE CONSTITUTIONAL LAW: A CONTEXTUAL APPROACH

Stephen Ross
Professor of Law
Lewis H. Vovakis Distinguished Faculty Scholar
Penn State Dickinson School of Law

Helen Irving
Professor of Law
Sydney Law School
The University of Sydney

Heinz Klug
Evjue-Bascom Professor of Law
University of Wisconsin Law School
Senior Honorary Research Associate, Law School
University of the Witwatersrand

Print ISBN: 978-0-7698-6649-9
Ebook ISBN: 978-0-3271-9155-1
LL ISBN: 978-1-6304-3601-8

Library of Congress Cataloging-in-Publication Data

Ross, Stephen F., 1955- author.
Constitutional law : a contextual approach / Stephen Ross, Professor of Law, Lewis H. Vovakis Distinguished Faculty Scholar, Penn State Dickinson School of Law, Helen Irving, Professor of Law, Sydney Law School, The University of Sydney, Heinz Klug, Evjue-Bascom Professor of Law, University of Wisconsin Law School, Senior Honorary Research Associate, Law School, University of the Witwatersrand.
p. cm.
Includes index.
ISBN 978-0-7698-6649-9
1. Constitutional law 2. Constitutional law--United States. 3. Constitutional law--Canada. 4. Constitutional law--Australia. 5. Constitutional law--South Africa. I. Irving, Helen, author. II. Klug, Heinz, 1957- author. III. Title.
K3165.R669 2014
342--dc23   2014004374

NOTE TO USERS
To ensure that you are using the latest materials available in this area, please be sure to periodically check the LexisNexis Law School web site for downloadable updates and supplements at www.lexisnexis.com/lawschool.

Editorial Offices
121 Chanlon Rd., New Providence, NJ 07974 (908) 464-6800
201 Mission St., San Francisco, CA 94105-1831 (415) 908-3200
www.lexisnexis.com

MATTHEW◊BENDER

Dedication

Dedicated to our partners, Mary Wujek, Stephen Gaukroger, Gay Seidman, and our children, Elizabeth and Sara (Alex) Ross Kinports, Cressida and Hugh Gaukroger, Benjamin and Matthew Klug

Table of Contents

Introduction   **A FEW THINGS YOU SHOULD KNOW BEFORE TAKING THIS COURSE, AND WHY YOU SHOULD TAKE IT** **1**

I.1.   WHY A COMPARATIVE STUDY OF AUSTRALIAN, CANADIAN, SOUTH AFRICAN AND U.S. CONSTITUTIONAL LAW IS A WORTHY ENDEAVOR 1

I.2.   BRIEF OVERVIEW OF THE ENACTMENT OF EACH NATION'S CONSTITUTION 3

   I.2.1.   The United States of America (1789 and 1860s) 3

   I.2.2.   Canada (1867 and 1982) 5

   I.2.3.   Australia (1900) 6

   I.2.4.   South Africa (1996) 8

I.3.   A FEW BASIC SIMILARITIES AND DIFFERENCES TO UNDERSTAND AT THE OUTSET 13

   I.3.1.   Significant cultural differences 13

   I.3.2.   Constitutional ideology 14

I.4.   BASIC COMPARISONS OF THE LEGISLATIVE PROCESS IN POLITICAL CONTEXT: A BRIEF INTRODUCTION 19

   I.4.1.   United States 19

   I.4.2.   Canada 21

   I.4.3.   Australia 24

   I.4.4.   South Africa 26

I.5.   APPROACHES TO CONSTITUTIONAL INTERPRETATION: A BRIEF SURVEY 29

   I.5.1.   Originalism 30

   I.5.2.   Textualism 30

   I.5.3.   "Living" interpretation 31

   I.5.4.   Pragmatism 31

   I.5.5.   Applying these theories: the "Persons" case 31

      Reference to Meaning of Word "Persons" In Section 24 of British North America Act, 1867 32

   I.5.6.   Interpretation in different countries 38

Chapter 1   **FEDERALISM** **41**

1.1.   THE CONCEPT OF FEDERALISM 42

   1.1.1.   Distinguishing constitutional federalism from efficiency decentralization 42

   1.1.2.   Why federalism? 42

   1.1.3.   Distinguishing co-operative government 43

1.2.   THE FEDERALISM OF THE CONSTITUTIONAL TEXTS 43

Table of Contents

1.2.1.	Canada	43
1.2.2.	United States	45
1.2.3.	Australia	46
1.2.4.	South Africa	47
1.3.	BASIC PRINCIPLES OF CANADIAN FEDERALISM	49
1.3.1.	Early doctrine: narrow construction of the Trade & Commerce power	49
1.3.1.1.	First cases	49
	In re the Board of Commerce Act, 1919, and the Combines and Fair Prices Act, 1919	51
1.3.2.	The modern view of Trade & Commerce	52
	General Motors of Canada Ltd. v. City National Leasing	53
1.3.3.	The limits to the "POGG" and Agriculture power	57
1.3.4.	The breadth of the criminal law power	58
	Morgentaler v. The Queen ("Morgentaler I")	59
1.3.5.	Judicial reasoning in policing Canadian federalism: "Colourability"	61
1.3.6.	Limits on Provincial power	64
	Her Majesty the Queen v. Morgentaler [Morgentaler III]	64
1.4.	BASIC PRINCIPLES OF U.S. FEDERALISM	70
1.4.1.	Scope of deference	70
	McCulloch v. Maryland	71
1.4.2.	Scope of the Commerce Clause	74
	Gibbons v. Ogden	75
	Cooley v. The Board of Wardens of the Port of Philadelphia	77
1.4.3.	Judicial Limits on Federal Legislative Power: the narrowing and broadening of the scope of the Commerce Clause from the *Lochner* era to *Jones & Laughlin*	79
1.4.4.	The rise and fall and rise and fall of the Tenth Amendment as a significant limit on federal legislative power	81
1.4.5.	Lack of requirement that Commerce Clause power be exercised only for commercial regulatory concerns	82
1.4.6.	The pendulum swings back	84
	United States v. Morrison	85
	National Federation of Independent Business v. Sebelius	94
1.4.7.	Limits on state legislative power	103
	Pike v. Bruce Church, Inc.	105
1.5.	BASIC PRINCIPLES OF AUSTRALIAN FEDERALISM	107
1.5.1.	The expansion of federal power via interpretation: *The Engineers Case*	111
1.5.2.	Implied restraint on the scope of federal power: the "Melbourne Corporation doctrine"	112
	Melbourne v. Commonwealth ("Melbourne Corporation Case")	112

Table of Contents

1.5.3.   Further growth in federal power: "external affairs" 115
          Commonwealth v. Tasmania ("Tasmanian Dam Case") 116
1.5.4.   The Trade & Commerce power 119
1.5.5.   Limitations on state power: section 92's requirement that trade and
          commerce must be "absolutely free" 122
1.5.6.   Federal expansion yet again: the "corporations power" and
          Work Choices 123
          NSW v. Commonwealth ("Work Choices Case") 124
1.6.   BASIC PRINCIPLES OF SOUTH AFRICAN CO-OPERATIVE
          GOVERNMENT 125
1.6.1.   The distribution of legislative authority under co-operative
          government 125
1.6.2.   The Constitutional Court's interpretation of the principles of
          Co-operative Government 126
          *Uthukela District Municipality v. The President of the Republic of
          South Africa* 127
1.6.3.   Disputes over the allocation of legislative authority 129
1.6.3.1. Constitutional allocation of legislative power 130
          *The Premier of the Province of the Western Cape v. The President
          of the Republic of South Africa* 131
1.6.3.2. Scope of residual national legislative power 137
          *The Executive Council of the Province of The Western Cape and
          the Executive Council of Kwazulu-Natal v. The President of the
          Republic of South Africa* 137
1.6.3.3. Scope of exclusive Provincial power 142
          *Ex Parte the President of the Republic of South Africain Re:
          Constitutionality of the Liquor Bill* 142
1.7.   CONTRASTING APPROACHES TO FEDERALISM: ADDITIONAL
          COMPARATIVE NOTES AND QUESTIONS 150
1.7.1.   Fiscal federalism and the taxing and spending powers 150
1.7.2.   Active judicial policing of federalism and the national political
          process 153
1.7.3.   Federalism and partisan politics 156
1.7.4.   Originalism awry 158

Chapter 2   **DEFINING THE SCOPE OF CONSTITUTIONAL
                    PROTECTION FOR INDIVIDUAL RIGHTS** **161**

2.1.   INTRODUCTION 162
2.1.1.   Scope of this chapter 162
2.1.2.   A chronological summary 163
2.1.3.   Close judicial scrutiny of interference with fundamental rights 165

Table of Contents

2.1.4.   Interpreting "liberty" in the shadow of *Lochner* 168

     Lochner v. New York 168

     Ferguson v. Skrupa 172

2.2.   CLOSE SCRUTINY OF DEPRIVATIONS OF LIBERTY UNDER THE FOURTEENTH AMENDMENT 174

     Roe v. Wade 178

     Planned Parenthood of Southeastern Pennsylvania v. Casey 184

     Lawrence v. Texas 194

2.3.   CLOSE SCRUTINY OF DEPRIVATIONS OF LIBERTY AND SECURITY OF THE PERSON UNDER SECTION 7 OF THE CANADIAN CHARTER OF RIGHTS AND FREEDOMS 199

     Morgentaler v. The Queen ("Morgentaler II") 202

2.4.   DEFINING THE SCOPE OF BROADLY WORDED PROVISIONS OF THE SOUTH AFRICAN CONSTITUTION AND BILL OF RIGHTS . . 210

     S v. Makwanyane 211

     De Reuck v. Director of Public Prosecutions 215

2.5.   CONSIDERATION OF IMPLIED LIMITS ON GOVERNMENTS TO INFRINGE INDIVIDUAL FREEDOMS IN AUSTRALIA 221

     Australian Capital Television PTY Ltd v. Commonwealth 225

     Lange v. Australian Broadcasting Corporation 230

Chapter 3   **BALANCING THE VALUES OF DIGNITY, EQUALITY, AND FREEDOM** **237**

3.1.   INTRODUCTION 237

3.1.1.   The concept of human dignity and its relation to equality and freedom . 237

3.1.2.   Organization of this chapter 238

3.2.   BASIC APPROACHES TO FREEDOM OF SPEECH AND EXPRESSION 239

3.2.1.   Basic U.S. approach to free speech 239

3.2.1.1.   Circumstances that justify content-based speech restrictions 242

3.2.1.2.   Content-neutral restrictions 245

3.2.2.   Basic Canadian approach to free speech 245

3.2.2.1.   Pre-Charter antecedents 246

3.2.2.2.   Basic Charter principles 246

     Irwin Toy Ltd. v. Quebec (Attorney General) 246

3.2.3.   Basic Australian approach to free speech 253

3.2.3.1.   Overview of the implied freedom of political communication 254

3.2.3.2.   More recent cases 256

3.2.4.   Basic South African approach to free speech 258

3.3.   BALANCING RACIAL EQUALITY AND FREEDOM: HATE SPEECH 259

3.3.1.   Canada 259

Table of Contents

		R. v. Keegstra	259
3.3.2.	United States	270
		R. A. V. v. City of St. Paul, Minnesota	270
3.3.3.	South Africa	277
		The Islamic Unity Convention v. Independent Broadcasting Authority	277
3.3.4.	Australia	282
3.4.	BALANCING GENDER EQUALITY AND FREEDOM: REGULATION OF PORNOGRAPHY	285
3.4.1.	Canada	285
		R. v. Butler	285
3.4.2.	United States	291
		American Booksellers Association, Inc. v. Hudnut	292
3.4.3.	South Africa	297
		De Reuck v. Director of Public Prosecutions (Witwatersrand Local Division)	297
3.4.4.	Australia	298
3.5.	REGULATION OF ELECTION SPENDING	299
3.5.1.	United States	299
		Citizens United v. Federal Election Commission	300
3.5.2.	Canada	308
		Harper v. Canada (Attorney General)	308
3.5.3.	Australia	312
3.5.4.	South Africa	313

Chapter 4	**EQUALITY (GENERALLY)**	**315**
4.1.	BACKGROUND AND OVERVIEW	316
4.1.1.	Origins of constitutional concern about equality	316
4.1.1.1.	Lack of original protection against racial and other forms of discrimination	316
4.1.1.2.	Modern responses to discrimination and inequality	318
4.1.1.2.1.	U.S.: the Civil War amendments	318
4.1.1.2.2.	Canada: the Charter of Rights and Freedoms	319
4.1.1.2.3.	South Africa's new Constitution	319
4.1.1.2.4.	Australia's statutory response	320
4.1.1.3.	Illustration: evolving protection against gender-based discrimination	321
4.1.2.	The fundamental purpose of equality guarantees	323
4.2.	THE PROBLEM OF JUDICIAL SCRUTINY OF LEGISLATIVE CLASSIFICATIONS	324
4.2.1.	Articulating the problem	324

Table of Contents

4.2.2.	Examples of close scrutiny	325
	United States v. Virginia	325
	M. v. H.	330
	The National Coalition for Gay and Lesbian Equality v. The Minister of Home Affairs	338
4.2.3.	The "rational basis" test in American doctrine	341
	Massachusetts Board of Retirement v. Murgia	341
4.3.	WHICH CLASSIFICATIONS WARRANT CLOSE JUDICIAL SCRUTINY?	343
4.3.1.	United States: suspect classifications and fundamental rights	344
	Slaughter-House Cases	344
	United States v. Carolene Products Co.	346
4.3.2.	Canada: substantive discrimination based on enumerated or analogous grounds	350
	Andrews v. Law Society of British Columbia	351
	Law v. Canada (Minister of Employment and Immigration)	357
	R. v. Kapp	361
4.3.3.	South Africa	363
	Prinsloo v. Van Der Linde	364
	Harksen v. Lane	369
4.3.4.	Rationales for the absence of close scrutiny of most economic and social legislation	377
4.4.	INTENTIONAL DISCRIMINATION OR DISPARATE IMPACT	379
	Personnel Administrator of Massachusetts v. Feeney	379
	Eldridge v. British Columbia (Attorney General)	384
4.5.	SAME-SEX MARRIAGE	389
	Minister of Home Affairs v. Fourie	390
	United States v. Windsor	398
Chapter 5	**SOCIAL AND ECONOMIC RIGHTS**	**405**
5.1.	INTRODUCTION	405
5.1.1.	International and American roots	406
5.1.2.	The South African approach: a summary	409
5.1.3.	The significance of the South African approach for comparative analysis	410
5.2.	JUDICIALLY ENFORCEABLE PROTECTION OF SOCIAL AND ECONOMIC RIGHTS UNDER THE SOUTH AFRICAN CONSTITUTION	411
5.2.1.	Allocating scarce resources for health care	411
	Soobramoney v. Minster of Health (Kwazulu-Natal)	411
5.2.2.	Basic right to housing	413

Table of Contents

     The Government of the Republic of South Africa v. Grootboom 414

5.2.3.   Access to essential medicines 417

     Minister of Health v. Treatment Action Campaign 418

5.3.   REASONABLENESS REVIEW 421

     Khosa v. Minister of Social Development 422

     Mazibuko v. City of Johannesburg 425

     City of Johannesburg v. Blue Moonlight Properties 431

5.4.   CONSIDERATION AND REJECTION IN THE UNITED STATES . . . 434

5.4.1.   The possibilities for inclusion through constitutional interpretation . . . 434

5.4.2.   The apex of American recognition of poverty rights 435

     Goldberg v. Kelly 435

5.4.3.   The rejection of social and economic rights 440

     Dandridge v. Williams 440

     San Antonio Independent School District v. Rodriguez 445

5.4.4.   Explanations for the rejection of socio-economic rights in the U.S. . . . 452

5.5.   SOCIAL AND ECONOMIC RIGHTS AS GUARANTEED BY
PROTECTION OF "SECURITY OF THE PERSON" UNDER s. 7 OF
THE CANADIAN CHARTER 453

5.5.1.   General background 453

     Chaoulli v. Attorney General of Quebec 455

5.6.   NON-CONSTITUTIONAL RESPONSE OF THE AUSTRALIAN
GOVERNMENT TO INTERNATIONAL OBLIGATIONS 461

Chapter 6   **THE REGULATION OF PROPERTY** **465**

6.1.   OVERVIEW OF THE RIGHT TO PROPERTY 466

6.1.1.   Textual provisions 466

6.1.2.   The issue of "constitutional jurisprudence" in considering the right to
property 467

6.1.3.   American foundations 468

6.1.4.   Australian foundations 468

6.1.5.   Canadian rejection of a constitutional right to property 470

6.1.6.   The South African compromise 470

6.1.7.   The jurisprudential/doctrinal challenge: distinguishing economic
liberty 470

6.2.   AMERICAN CONSTITUTIONAL PROTECTION OF PROPERTY BUT
NOT ECONOMIC REGULATION 471

6.2.1.   Due Process limits on the use of property 472

     Mugler v. Kansas 472

6.2.2.   The doctrine of regulatory takings 475

     Pennsylvania Coal Company v. Mahon 475

6.2.3.   Distinguishing analysis under the Due Process and Takings Clause
guarantees 480

Table of Contents

	Lingle v. Chevron U.S.A., Inc.	481
6.2.4.	Active or deferential scrutiny	485
6.2.5.	Summary	486
6.3.	COMPULSORY ACQUISITION, JUST TERMS, AND THE AUSTRALIAN CONSTITUTION	487
6.3.1.	What is "property"?	487
6.3.2.	What is an "acquisition of property"?	489
	Commonwealth v. Tasmania ("Tasmanian Dam Case")	490
	JT International SA v. Commonwealth of Australia	496
6.4.	REJECTION OF CANADIAN CONSTITUTIONAL PROTECTION FOR PROPERTY	503
	Irwin Toy Ltd. v. Quebec (Attorney General)	504
	REFERENCE RE SS. 193 AND 195.1(1)(C) OF THE CRIMINAL CODE (MAN.) *"The Prostitution Reference"*	505
6.5.	CANADIAN AND AUSTRALIAN NON-CONSTITUTIONAL PROTECTION FOR PROPERTY	509
6.5.1.	The presumption against expropriation	509
6.5.2.	The requirement of an acquisition for the benefit of the government or the public	511
	Mariner Real Estate Ltd. v. Nova Scotia (Attorney General)	512
6.5.3.	Statutory compensation for 'injurious affection'	518
	Antrim Truck Centre Ltd. v. Ontario (Transportation)	518
6.5.4.	The supremacy of the political process in deliberate and clear expropriations	522
	Durham Holdings Pty Ltd v. New South Wales	522
6.6.	SOUTH AFRICAN CONSTITUTIONAL PROTECTION OF PROPERTY	530
	President of the RSA v. Modderklip Boerdery (Pty) Ltd	532
	First National Bank of SA Ltd T/A Wesbank v. Commissioner, SA Revenue Service	537
6.7.	CONCLUDING NOTE ON THE RELATIONSHIP BETWEEN COMMON LAW RECOGNITION OF PROPERTY RIGHTS AND CONSTITUTIONAL PROTECTION	547
	Lucas v. South Carolina Coastal Council	548
Chapter 7	**UNITARY AND DUAL COURT SYSTEMS AND THE ROLE OF CONSTITUTIONAL VALUES IN PRIVATE LITIGATION**	**555**
7.1.	ORGANIZATION OF THE JUDICIARY	555
7.1.1.	United States	555
7.1.2.	Canada	556
7.1.3.	Australia	557

Table of Contents

7.1.4.   South Africa 558

7.1.5.   Who appoints the judges 558

7.2.   THE CONCEPT OF STATE ACTION 560

          Shelley v. Kraemer 561

          *Retail, Wholesale and Department Store Union, Local 580 v. Dolphin
          Delivery Ltd.* 567

7.3.   CASE STUDY OF CONSTITUTIONAL VALUES AND THE
          COMMON LAW: LIBEL 576

          New York Times Co. v. Sullivan 576

          Hill v. Church of Scientology of Toronto 581

          Grant v. Torstar Corp. 588

          Lange v. Australian Broadcasting Corporation 593

          Khumalo v. Holomisa 604

7.4.   CONSTITUTIONAL VALUES AND THE COMMON LAW 609

7.4.1.   Incorporating values into common law jurisprudence 609

7.4.2.   Legal realism and the constitutionalization of the American common
          law 612

Chapter 8   **ADVISORY OPINIONS, CONSTITUTIONAL
                    CONVENTIONS, AND THE DETERMINATION OF
                    JUDICIAL AUTHORITY** **615**

8.1.   THE CONCEPT OF AN "UNCONSTITUTIONAL" LAW OR
          GOVERNMENT ACT 616

          Marbury v. Madison 616

          Walter L. Nixon v. United States 624

          The State v. Makwanyane 629

          *Ex Parte Chairperson of the Constitutional Assembly: In re Certification
          of the Constitution of the Republic of South Africa (first Certification
          Decision)* 631

8.2.   ADVISORY OPINIONS 636

8.2.1.   United States 636

8.2.2.   Canada 639

          Reference Re Secession of Quebec 639

8.2.3.   Australia 646

          In re Judiciary Act 1903-1920 & In re Navigation Act 1912-1920 . . 646

8.2.4.   South Africa 653

          Tongoane v. Minister of Agriculture 654

8.3.   THE CONCEPT OF CONSTITUTIONAL CONVENTION 660

          Madzimbamuto v. Lardner-Burke 662

8.3.1.   Declaring the existence of conventions 666

8.3.1.1. Constitutional conventions are not judicially-enforceable law 667

          "The Patriation Reference" (Part I) 667

xiii

Table of Contents

8.3.1.2.   The Supreme Court of Canada provides advice on whether a proposed act violates a convention 670

"The Patriation Reference" (Part II) 670

8.3.2.   Distinguishing conventions from long-standing policies 685

8.3.3.   Conventions and crisis in the absence of advisory opinions: The Whitlam Affair 685

8.3.4.   Relationship between conventions and statutes 689

8.3.5.   When constitutional conventions require constitutional amendment . . . 690

8.3.6.   South Africa 690

Ex Parte Chairperson of the Constitutional Assembly: In re Certification of the Constitution of the Republic of South Africa . . . 691

Chapter 9   **HOW ARE DEMOCRACY AND HUMAN RIGHTS BEST PROTECTED?** **693**

9.1.   CHAPTER OVERVIEW 693

9.1.1.   Rights entrenchment versus parliamentary sovereignty 694

9.1.2.   The current rights debate in Australia 696

9.1.3.   Review of alternative ways to protect human rights 698

9.1.4.   Why context matters 699

9.2.   CANADA: JUDICIAL PROTECTION FOR LINGUISTIC MINORITIES 701

9.2.1.   Background on language rights in Canada 701

Paul C. Weiler, Rights and Judges in a Democracy: A New Canadian Version 701

9.2.2.   Background on the Notwithstanding Clause 705

9.2.3.   Judicial protection of Anglophones in Quebec 707

Ford v. Quebec (Attorney-General) 710

9.2.4.   Judicial protection of Francophones in English Canada 716

Barrett v. City of Winnipeg 718

City of Winnipeg v. Barrett 723

9.3.   SEGUE: IS SEPARATE BUT EQUAL INHERENTLY UNEQUAL? . . 727

Brown v. Board of Education of Topeka 727

Mahe v. Alberta 731

9.4.   UNITED STATES: JUDICIAL PROTECTION OF RACIAL MINORITIES 737

9.4.1.   Proof of unconstitutional racial discrimination 737

9.4.2.   Judicial review of race-conscious policies designed to benefit minorities 738

Regents of the University of California v. Bakke 738

Shelby County, Alabama v. Holder 749

9.4.3.   Contrasting Canadian doctrine regarding ameliorative practices 757

Table of Contents

9.3.4.   What is *Brown's legacy?* 759

Parents Involved in Community Schools v. Seattle

School District No. 1 759

9.5.   THE SOUTH AFRICAN EXPERIENCE 770

In re: Dispute Concerning the Constitutionality of Certain Provisions

of the School Education Bill of 1995 770

Mec for Education: Kwazulu-Natal v. Pillay 780

9.6.   LESSONS 787

9.6.1.   Is democracy more secure and political minorities better off with judicial

protection? 787

9.6.2.   Lessons for the current Australian debate 790

Evans v. State of New South Wales 795

9.6.3.   Concluding thoughts 803

TABLE OF CASES TC-1

INDEX I-1

A FEW THINGS YOU SHOULD KNOW BEFORE TAKING THIS COURSE, AND WHY YOU SHOULD TAKE IT

I.1. WHY A COMPARATIVE STUDY OF AUSTRALIAN, CANADIAN, SOUTH AFRICAN AND U.S. CONSTITUTIONAL LAW IS A WORTHY ENDEAVOR

A comparative study naturally allows the student to learn more about other countries. With free trade and the globalized economy, a greater understanding of other major English-speaking trading partners has obvious professional value for lawyers. For those who will be working in the private sector, this has particular relevance as more businesses engage in cross-border ventures, and one's ability to do something other than refer their clients' legal matters to counterparts in the other country will be highly valued. For public lawyers and lawyers-as-citizens, examining the legal institutions and history of a similar country helps us evaluate our own institutions and values to identify areas of improvement, as well as those aspects of our own polity that might render impractical policy initiatives that may seem desirable in the abstract. Most importantly, comparative law helps "to reveal as choices aspects of one's own legal system that appear simply to be 'natural' or 'necessary' practices." Vicki C. Jackson & Mark Tushnet, Comparative Constitutional Law 144 (1999). Recognizing that critical aspects of law and politics are "choices" and not "natural" allows lawyers to better achieve the ideal of well-informed citizens.

From an academic perspective, two quite disparate approaches seem to animate scholars and students of comparative constitutional law. (These are inspired by a categorization by comparative constitutional scholar Mark Tushnet.[1]) One approach, "normative universalism," seeks to study a wide variety of approaches to constitutional issues to identify the "best" practice that its proponents believe should be adopted everywhere (or at least in their own country). In terms of legal pedagogy, such an approach allows advanced students to consider approaches from many countries — just as other seminars or courses might have students delve into journal articles by domestic law professors — all with an aim of reaching an improved normative understanding of what their own constitutional law should be. Tushnet's own casebook in the field, co-authored with the distinguished comparative scholar Vicki Jackson, seems to adopt this approach, as does the other leading

---

[1] Mark Tushnet, *Some Reflections on Method in Comparative Constitutional Law*, Conference on the Migration of Constitutional Ideas, U. Toronto (Oct. 2004).

casebook, DORSEN, ROSENFELD, SAJO AND BAER'S COMPARATIVE CONSTITUTIONALISM: CASES AND MATERIALS (2003).

The second major approach to comparative law is a "contextual" approach. As Tushnet notes, this approach "emphasizes the fact that constitutional law is deeply embedded in the institutional, doctrinal, social, and cultural contexts of each nation, and that we are likely to go wrong if we try to think about any specific doctrine or institution without appreciating the way it is tightly linked to all the contexts within which it exists." Under this approach, the value in studying different countries is neither to preach to them nor to borrow from them, but to understand why it is that Australian, American, South African or Canadian constitutional law has evolved in the way that it has. As we hope to demonstrate in the materials that follow, a study that focuses on those areas of difference in approach to problems addressed by constitutional law reveals three major explanations for the differences:

- (1) there are many significant differences in the **origins of our political and legal institutions**; studying these differences helps expose the historical roots underpinning our respective constitutional doctrines;

- (2) in some important respects, American, Australian, Canadian and South African society reflect **differing dominant cultural values**; studying these differences helps us understand the political ideologies that underlie constitutional judgments by the U.S. and Canadian Supreme Courts, the High Court of Australia, and the South African Constitutional Court;

- (3) the age of a constitution may be significant; the U.S. Constitution was drafted in 1787; Australia's Constitution was drafted in 1897-98; Canada's Charter of Rights and other significant parts of the Canadian Constitution were enacted in 1982, and South Africa's Constitution was adopted in 1996. In some cases, later constitutions reflect the benefit of settled experience with difficult constitutional issues learned from earlier constitutions.

An inquiry seeking primarily to explain *why* doctrines and institutions that may superficially seem natural have been chosen in their particular country is, in our view, best served by a careful study of a limited number of countries, rather than a necessarily thinner study of many. To the extent that legal doctrine is inevitably context-specific, understanding why different countries have followed different paths requires at least a modest understanding of the history, values, and institutions that have created the doctrine. Scientists who seek to explain differences observed in the natural world usually try to focus their inquiry by "controlling" for as many variables as possible. "All else being equal," they can then determine the effect some particular cause may create. The four countries studied here have a common law and English-speaking heritage, a federal system, and a written constitution amenable to judicial review; knowledge of the experiences in the other countries makes it easier to explain differences with some confidence.

A somewhat controversial aspect of comparative constitutional law concerns "constitutional borrowing": the practice of importing doctrines established in other countries. Justice Antonin Scalia is among many who decry this practice. *See, e.g., Printz v. United States*, 521 U.S. 898, 921 (1997) (comparative analysis is "inappropriate to the task of interpreting a constitution, though it was of course quite relevant to the task of writing one"). This seems overstated. When courts seek to create workable legal doctrines to implement broad and evolving concepts such as "freedom of speech," "equal protection," or protection against the deprivation of "property," the actual impact of other nation's judicial decisions interpreting similar phrases is at least relevant. Borrowing can be particularly relevant in rejecting arguments about the effect of proposed constitutional doctrines. For example, a study of the non-constitutional protection of property rights in Canada and within Australian states would seem to cast doubt on claims that a rich and robust interpretation of the Takings Clause of the Fifth Amendment to the U.S. Constitution is necessary to preserve the institution of property. *See, e.g.*, GREGORY S. ALEXANDER, THE GLOBAL DEBATE OVER CONSTITUTIONAL PROPERTY: LESSONS FOR AMERICAN TAKINGS JURISPRUDENCE (2006) (constitutional protections have little bearing on how society treats property). However, without a rich understanding of the context of the decisions, any effort to borrow may not have the consequences intended.

Finally, there is much debate (albeit, to varying degrees in different countries) in constitutional politics over the extent to which judges should be "activists" or, alternatively, exercise "judicial restraint." It is often difficult, however, to focus on this jurisprudential question in a manner distinct from the underlying constitutional issue — a difficulty exacerbated by the fact that many justices betray little consistency in their approach to activism or restraint, depending on the context. Studying issues that may arouse great passion elsewhere but less passion at home may provide some otherwise unavailable insights.

Associated with these differences are varying approaches taken by the courts to the interpretation of their countries' constitution. Although it cannot be claimed that there is national uniformity in interpretation — individual judges on the same court frequently adopt different methods or theories of interpretation — debates about the legitimacy of particular approaches differ from country to country. Knowledge of these differences will assist our understanding of how certain constitutional questions that may appear similar across countries come out differently at the judgment stage. These differences are discussed below.

I.2. BRIEF OVERVIEW OF THE ENACTMENT OF EACH NATION'S CONSTITUTION

I.2.1. The United States of America (1789 and 1860s)

Having declared independence from Britain in 1776 and secured King George III's recognition of this fact in the Treaty of Paris of 1783, the American states labored under a weak form of federal government under an agreement between all thirteen states called the "Articles of Confederation and Perpetual Union." After continuing problems and crises, the legendary and victorious George Washington, commander of the American revolutionary forces, lent his name to the effort to re-craft this governing document, agreeing to chair a convention organized for that purpose. Meeting in secret in Philadelphia, state delegates perhaps went beyond their specific mandate to amend the Articles of Confederation, and created an innovative system of constitutional government, with clearly divided powers between the legislative, executive, and judicial branches, and with powers divided between the federal governments and the states. In addition, compromises between large and small states led to creation of a bi-cameral legislature with a House of Representatives elected for two-year terms based on population and a Senate chosen (until changed in 1913 to popular vote) by state legislatures with two Senators per each state, serving six-year terms. Likewise, compromises between slave and free states led to a 20-year ban on congressional power to stop the slave trade; to census calculations of slaves as 3/5 of a person; and to provisions requiring return of fugitive slaves. The framers addressed the primary defects in the weak Articles of Confederation by providing for a central government that was independently elected, with an elected President serving as commander-in-chief, and with a Congress empowered to pass laws to impose taxes and import duties, and to regulate interstate and foreign commerce.

The Constitution required ratification by 3/4 of the states (although by its own terms, the Articles of Confederation could only be changed unanimously). In arguing for the ratification of the Constitution, Alexander Hamilton famously argued in Federalist Paper No. 78[2] for the benefit of judicial review as a means of protecting the liberty of citizens. This view was confirmed subsequently by the U.S. Supreme Court in the landmark decision in *Marbury v. Madison*, 5 U.S. 137 (1803), where the Court held that the very notion of a written constitution implied that the Constitution was superior to laws or other conduct of legislative and executive branch officers. (This case is discussed below in Chapter 8.) Although the original Constitution (ratified in 1789) included some protection of individual rights (these are discussed in Chapter 2), many complained during the ratification process about the absence of protection for individual rights. Supporters promised to rectify this, and the First Congress proposed and then the states ratified ten amendments to the Constitution to entrench a Bill of Rights, which included provisions barring the federal government from establishing a religion, infringing on freedom of religion or speech, regulating police practices with regard to searches and seizures, protecting property rights, and a variety of other legal rights and limitations on Congressional power.

The major amendment of the original Constitution occurred after the Civil War. From 1865-1870, the requisite states ratified the Thirteenth, Fourteenth, and Fifteenth Amendments, which, among other things, abolished slavery, required states to provide all persons with due process and equal protection, and barred racial discrimination in voting (gender discrimination in voting was outlawed in 1920 with ratification of the Nineteenth Amendment).

---

[2] Ed. Note: After the Philadelphia convention, the U.S. Constitution was submitted to each of the 13 states for ratification. Ratification was controversial; supporters were referred to as "Federalists" and opponents as "Anti-federalists." (This can be somewhat confusing, because after ratification and the emergence of political parties in the United States, those under the leadership of John Adams and Alexander Hamilton who favored a strong central government and creation of a manufacturing base were also called "federalists," in contrast to those under the leadership of Thomas Jefferson and James Madison who favored a weaker government and promotion of an agrarian economy, who were called "republicans.") Three constitutional federalists — Hamilton, Madison, and John Jay — wrote influential arguments in favor of ratification that came to be known as the Federalist Papers. These papers have traditionally been relied on for insights into the original meaning of the Constitution.

I.2.2.   Canada (1867 and 1982)

The settled areas of what we now call Canada were, as of 1867, the colonies of Newfoundland (which did not join the confederation until 1949), New Brunswick, Prince Edward Island, Nova Scotia, and Canada (consisting of modern-day Ontario and Quebec). The maritime colonies had been discussing some form of union, when a broader confederation was proposed by the premier of the colony of Canada, John A. MacDonald. A Tory (conservative), he had organized a "grand coalition" with his arch-rival, Ontario liberal George Brown, and the Quebecois Parti Bleu leader, Georges Cartier. These leaders desired a stronger centralized government to deal with national defence issues in the wake of declining British interest, the withdrawal of free trade by the United States in 1865, and the desirability of assuming provincial debt, and to facilitate the construction of a railway linking the Atlantic maritime provinces with the rest of the country. They also needed to solve ongoing governance problems caused by the Imperial *Act of Union, 1840*. This British statute had re-united predominantly English "Upper Canada" (Ontario) with predominantly French "Lower Canada" (Quebec) in a legislature where each area had equal representation, in spite of population growth in the Anglophone area.

Meetings among colonial leaders led to agreement on confederation under a federal model. Principally focused on the English/French divide, the framers agreed to a federal parliament based entirely on population, but with the assignment to each province of those legislative matters where Quebecois feared Anglophone dominance. Hence, education and the civil law system were assigned to provinces. However, again with an eye to both (Protestant-dominated) Ontario and (Catholic-dominated) Quebec, the rights of Quebec Protestants and Ontario Catholics were specifically protected. In general, the framework was designed to avoid the perceived weakness of the federal government of the United States that Canadians believed had led to the American Civil War; Parliament, based on the British Westminster system of "responsible government" (with members of the Executive, including the Prime Minister, also sitting as elected members of parliament) was given the residual power over all matters not specifically assigned to provinces, and indeed given the power (which fell into disuse by 1900) to disallow provincial laws. All agreed on maintaining strong links with the Queen and the United Kingdom; the Queen (in reality, the Colonial Secretary) retained the power to disallow any provincial or federal law (the British government disavowed use of this power in 1926). Further negotiations in London led to passage by the Imperial Parliament of the *British North America Act* in 1867, and Queen Victoria proclaimed the new country's existence to take effect on July 1 of that year.

[handwritten margin note: opposite of our congress residual power left to the states]

Formally, the statute was an ordinary statute of the UK Parliament, with no provision for amendment other than by that Parliament. With the advent of the constitutional convention (announced in 1926 and codified in the 1931 *Statute of Westminster*) that the British government would not interfere in the domestic affairs of Australia, Canada, South Africa, or other imperial dominions, this machinery became increasingly problematic. On a number of occasions, the Canadian government sought an amendment of the statute, which would be routinely effectuated by the British government. (This is detailed in the *Patriation*

Reference in Chapter 8.) As well, the post-World War II public concern with human rights led to increasing calls for constitutional entrenchment of basic rights. Hence, by the 1970s, there was very strong support for the "repatriation" of the basic constitutional act to Canada.

The push for a Charter of Rights came to fruition under the government of Prime Minister Pierre Elliot Trudeau (1968-1979; 1980-1984). Articulate in both English and French, the former law professor firmly believed that the solution to the duality of Canadian "nationhood" was through legislation making Canada officially bilingual and in entrenching constitutional rights for linguistic minorities (Anglophones in Quebec, Francophones everywhere else). However, while Trudeau saw Canada as a nation of individuals, a number of provincial premiers saw Canada as a nation of provinces. As a Trudeau aide described it:

> . . . the debate leading up to [the constitutional] accord revealed in pristine clarity two compelling visions of Canada. One was a dream of nation-building. Individualism formed the core of this belief. Individual Canadians, possessed of inalienable rights, including linguistic rights, make up a national community in which the people are ultimately sovereign. The other was a paean to province building: parliamentary supremacy is the central concept, diversity and particularism are the emotive forces and sovereignty rests on a provincial compact.

Thomas S. Axworthy, *Colliding Visions: The Debate Over the Canadian Charter of Rights and Freedoms, 1980–81*, 3 J. COMMONWEALTH & COMP. POL. 239 (1986).

In a long process detailed in the *Patriation Reference* case, Trudeau eventually secured agreement with all provincial premiers save the separatist leader of Quebec, René Lévesque, on a document duly submitted and ratified by the UK Parliament in 1982. The *Constitution Act, 1982* not only repatriated the document to Canada, but established a Charter of Rights and Freedoms (subject to a provision permitting reasonable limits on rights, and another provision allowing legislatures to enact statutes "notwithstanding" many of the rights guaranteed in the Charter for a period of five years, as well as entrenched aboriginal rights).

I.2.3. Australia (1900)

Australia's six states emerged from six British colonies that had become self-governing in the 19th century. By the mid-century, all but Western Australia (which achieved self-government in 1890) had democratic parliaments and established judicial systems. As in Canada, they practiced "responsible government," a key feature of British constitutional law that provides that the executive government must be made up of elected members of the legislative branch and enjoy the support of a majority of the elected lower house of the legislature; additionally, power formally vested in the sovereign must always be exercised on the advice of government ministers.[3] Moreover, Australians remained attached to Britain, both sentimentally and legally; after 1865, however, British powers to override all colonial legislation, including Australian, were limited by the *Colonial Laws*

---

[3] This concept is further detailed in section I.4.2.

Validity Act. (Appeals from colonial Supreme Courts to the UK Judicial Committee of the Privy Council were retained, however, in order to keep the common law uniform around the Empire.) Proposals for a federal union of the colonies were first heard in the 1840s, but it took until 1885 for the first concrete step to be taken, with the establishment of the "Federal Council of Australasia" under the *Federal Council of Australasia Act* (UK). As with the American experience under the Articles of Confederation, the powers granted to the Federal Council were weak, and it was to prove unsuccessful as a source of unity. In the 1890s, the process of federating the colonies finally began in earnest. At a Federal Conference in Melbourne in 1890s, representatives of the Australasian colonies (including New Zealand) agreed to several resolutions: that the colonies should federate under the Crown, with a federal scheme based on the United States (not on Canada); that the Federal Council could not serve as the vehicle for federation; and that a full Convention should be held for the purpose of writing a Constitution. Forty-two delegates met in Sydney the following year, and a full draft Constitution, in the form of a bill for an Act, was completed. Like the 1890 Conference, the meeting was open to the press and public, and its Debates were published, verbatim. The Convention concluded with an understanding that the Constitution bill would be adopted by the colonial parliaments and then sent to Britain for enactment. However, for a number of reasons — most dramatically, the world-wide economic Depression that struck in the early 1890s - federation did not proceed.

Within a couple of years, popular pressure forced the colonial premiers to re-start the federation process, leading to their adoption in 1895 of the so-called "Corowa Plan," which entailed the direct, popular election of delegates to a new Convention, the writing of a new Constitution bill, and its adoption by the voters in colonial referendums, before its enactment by the British (Imperial) Parliament. These steps were all followed. An elected Convention of fifty men from five colonies met in early 1897 (New Zealand no longer wished to participate; Queensland was unrepresented, but joined the Commonwealth at the time of federation). The Convention's three sessions spanned a full year, concluding in March 1898. The new draft Constitution was then submitted to the voters in all colonies, and (after some setbacks, and several amendments) approved. It was taken to Britain in 1900, where, it was passed by the British Parliament as the *Commonwealth of Australia Constitution Act 1900* (Imp). The Commonwealth — a name chosen for the new polity in 1891, to signify the "common weal," meaning common good — was inaugurated on 1 January 1901. The High Court of Australia was established two years later.

The Australian Constitution was drafted with a keen eye to both the insights and mistakes of the American project. The framers understood that the judiciary would have the power of judicial review; that is, the power to invalidate laws enacted by either the federal or state parliaments for failure to conform with the Constitution's provisions, although (as in the U.S. Constitution) they did not expressly say this in a constitutional provision. They were reluctant to adopt a comprehensive Bill of Rights, however, but included some rights (including a few individual rights) in the body of the Constitution (these are detailed in Chapter 2). It was anticipated that federalism would be the main ground for judicial review; that is, challenges to constitutional validity would be based on claims that the

Commonwealth parliament had exceeded its powers, or the state parliaments had legislated on a matter exclusive to the Commonwealth or passed laws inconsistent with Commonwealth laws. Federalism challenges remain the principal source of (constitutional) judicial review today. While breaches of the express limitations on the exercise of both Commonwealth and state legislative power (some concerning rights) have also always played an important role in Australia's constitutional case law, claims for breach of implied limitations have grown in recent years.

Although, as in Canada, the Australian Constitution was originally an Act of the Imperial Parliament, unlike in Canada, constitutional amendment was always in the hands of Australians: s 128 of the Constitution provides that amendment can only follow a successful referendum on a proposed alteration that has come via the Commonwealth parliament. For a referendum to succeed, a majority of national votes and a majority of votes in a majority of states have to be achieved. This hurdle was intended to be high, and the Constitution has only been amended eight times (out of 44 attempts) since the first referendum in 1906.

What prompted the federation of the Australian colonies in the 1890s, when all previous proposals had, one after the other, come to nothing? There was no war or other emergency, no struggle for independence, no pressure from outside. A combination of factors must be taken into account: fears that the colonies would be militarily weak without unity; a shared commitment to keeping out "coloured" immigrants; long-standing dissatisfaction with the varied tariff regimes across the colonies; an interest in coordinating services, like the post and telegraph, quarantine, and lighthouses. But these were just the material reasons for federation, and they had always been matters of concern to the colonies. Some historians have argued that federation was prompted primarily by the anticipation of economic advantage: that it was, effectively, a business deal. Others, in contrast, have noted the growing sense of Australian nationalism in the late 1890s, the optimism engendered by the approaching new century, the emergence of a generation of highly skilled leaders, and the fact that by this stage, the majority of the population were now "native-born" and (as a result of the colonial compulsory education Acts which were passed in the 1870s) also literate. The example of the United States also continued to inspire Australians. Many in the colonies wanted to do at the end of the 19th century what the Americans had done at the end of the 18th (albeit without revolution): forge a new constitutional nation, and take their part among the leaders on the international stage.

I.2.4. South Africa (1996)

The 1996 Constitution is South Africa's first legitimate Constitution, following three hundred years of colonialism and forty years of Apartheid rule. While racial segregation was an integral part of colonial rule, the policy of apartheid adopted in 1948 heralded a system of explicitly racist laws that sought to entrench and perpetuate racial domination by the white minority over the majority of black South Africans. Maintaining the apartheid system was only possible through increasing state repression and violence including imposition of repeated states of emergency. Describing the "interim" 1993 Constitution, which enabled the democratic transition, Justice Ismael Mohamed argued in the Constitutional

Court's first major case that South Africa's post-apartheid constitutional order represents less a consensus on national values and aspirations than a rejection of the country's prior history. Contrasting the promise of the constitution with this history Justice Mohamed noted that the Constitution:

> . . . represents a decisive break from, and a ringing rejection of, that part of the past which is disgracefully racist, authoritarian, insular, and repressive and a vigorous identification of and commitment to a democratic, universalistic, caring and aspirationally egalitarian ethos, expressly articulated in the Constitution. The contrast between the past which it repudiates and the future to which it seeks to commit the nation is stark and dramatic. The past institutionalized and legitimized racism. The Constitution expresses in its preamble the need for a "new order.. in which there is equality between . . . people of all races." Chapter 3 [the bill of rights] of the Constitution extends the contrast, in every relevant area of endeavour. . . . The past was redolent with statutes which assaulted the human dignity of persons on the grounds of race and colour alone; section 10 constitutionally protects that dignity. The past accepted, permitted, perpetuated and institutionalized pervasive and manifestly unfair discrimination against women and persons of colour; the preamble, section 8 and the postamble seek to articulate an ethos which not only rejects its rationale but unmistakenly recognizes the clear justification for the reversal of the accumulated legacy of such discrimination. The past permitted detention without trial; section 11(1) prohibits it. The past permitted degrading treatment of persons; section 11(2) renders it unconstitutional. The past arbitrarily repressed the freedoms of expression, assembly, association and movement; sections 15, 16, 17 and 18 accord to these freedoms the status of "fundamental rights." The past limited the right to vote to a minority; section 21 extends it to every citizen. The past arbitrarily denied to citizens on the grounds of race and colour, the right to hold and acquire property; section 26 expressly secures it. Such a jurisprudential past created what the postamble to the Constitution recognizes as a society "characterized by strife, conflict, untold suffering and injustice". . . . [*S v. Makwanyane and Another*, 1995 (3) SA 391, para. 262.]

With the adoption of the 1993 "interim" Constitution, the history of constitutionalism in South Africa might be summarized as the rise and fall of parliamentary sovereignty. However, the democratic era has added an extraordinary chapter in which the government and opposition have accepted — and civil society has relied upon — the constitutional framework to resolve continuing political and social conflict. While constitutional law was a peripheral part of law in the colonial and apartheid eras, since the achievement of democracy in 1994, the Constitution, and its interpretation by the Constitutional Court in particular, have become a central pillar of South African law.

Formally, the *South Africa Act* of 1909, negotiated at a whites only National Convention, brought together four settler colonies[4] into a single Union of South Africa in 1910, but in effect it created a bifurcated state. On the one hand, the Union

---

[4] The Act united the original Cape Colony (settled by the Dutch but colonized by the British in 1806);

Constitution granted parliamentary democracy to the white minority. On the other hand, it subjugated the majority of black South Africans to autocratic administrative rule. When they were excluded from the National Convention, black leaders protested against the Convention's refusal to extend the limited franchise that had been enjoyed by black South Africans in the Cape Colony to the former Boer Republics, but these leaders were rebuffed as not being representative of African society. Instead, African society was presented as essentially "traditional," to be governed separately by chiefs in a system of feudal hierarchy with the Governor-General in Council[5] at its apex. This division of the polity into two separate spheres reflected the fundamentally colonial character of South African legal culture in which "professed legalism with its accompanying rhetoric of justice," co-existed with the "racist abuse of power by the state" (MARTIN CHANOCK, SOUTH AFRICAN LEGAL CULTURE 1902–1936: FEAR, FAVOUR AND PREJUDICE 22 (2001)).

Although the Union Constitution followed the English tradition of parliamentary sovereignty, the legislature was not completely free of external restraints. Until passage of the *Statute of Westminster* by the British Parliament in 1931, the *Colonial Laws Validity Act* of 1865 continued in theory to restrict the sovereignty of the Union Parliament (subjecting it to potential, although limited, override by the British Parliament). Even after the Dominion Parliaments received their independence from Britain, the South African Parliament remained bound, at least procedurally, by the entrenched clauses of the 1910 Union Constitution that protected Cape voters and language rights. While the significance of entrenchment was weakened by the removal of African voters from the common voters roll (Act 12 of 1936), the apartheid government's effort to remove all non-white voters was initially struck down by South African courts, but the government achieved its goals by packing the highest court with new judges, and the Senate with new members, in order to re-pass and re-validate its scheme. The survival of the entrenched language clause, guaranteeing the equality of English and Afrikaans, was more a symbolic restraint than an effective constitutional entrenchment. In effect, equal language rights relied more on a political consensus among whites. The rise of parliamentary sovereignty, over even the limited entrenchment of the Cape franchise, was finally secured with the adoption of the 1961 Republican Constitution (Act 32 of 1961).

In the face of increasing internal resistance and international isolation, the South African government looked in the late 1970s to the political incorporation of the Indian and coloured (mixed-race) communities as a means of broadening its social base. The outcome of this policy shift was the adoption of the 1983 Constitution (Act 110 of 1983), which extended the franchise to "Indians" and "coloureds" in a

---

the eastern colony of Natal (annexed by the British in 1843); and two Afrikaner-created inland colonies, Transvaal and the Orange Free State.

[5] The phrase "Governor-General in Council" is a constitutional term (explicitly used in the *British North America Act* and the Australian Constitution) that implements the constitutional convention of responsible government. Formally, the Governor-General is the Queen's representative in Her Majesty's Dominion. In practice, the Governor-General is a titular figure who exercises formal vice-regal power on advice of the government. The Governor-General in Council refers, effectively, to the decisions of cabinet government, the advice of which the Governor-General is obliged to follow. *See* HELEN IRVING, FIVE THINGS TO KNOW ABOUT THE AUSTRALIAN CONSTITUTION 13 (2004).

tricameral legislature with its jurisdiction distributed according to a vague distinction between "own" and "general" affairs. Two mechanisms ensured, however, that power remained safely in the hands of the dominant white party. First, the running of government was effectively centralized under an executive state president with extraordinary powers in both the executive and legislative arenas. Second, all significant decisions within the legislature — such as the election of the president — would be automatically resolved by the 4:2:1 ratio of white, coloured and Indian representatives, which ensured that even if the "Indian" and "coloured" Houses of Parliament voted in unison, the will of the "white" House would prevail. The exclusion of the African majority from this scheme and resistance from within the targeted Indian and coloured communities meant that the 1983 Constitution was practically stillborn. Its fate was sealed by the escalation of resistance and rebellion that began in late 1984 and led to the imposition of repeated states of emergency from mid-1985.

The continued internal struggles and international pressure that eventually led the National Party (the leading white apartheid party that had governed South Africa) to begin negotiations to move from apartheid to democracy have been well chronicled elsewhere. (For an inspiring version, see *Nelson Mandela, Long Walk to Freedom* (1995)). The democratic transition was achieved through a two-stage process of Constitution-making. The first stage, from approximately February 1990 to April 1994, was buffeted by ongoing violence and protests, yet the process remained ultimately under the control of the main negotiating parties: the National Party government and the African National Congress (ANC) (the leading organization rebelling against apartheid, under the presidency of Nelson Mandela after his release from prison in 1990). In contrast, the second stage, from the time of the elections until the adoption of the "final" Constitution (Act 108 0f 1996) at the end of 1996, was formally constrained by a complex set of constitutional principles contained in the "interim" Constitution (Act 200 of 1993). This stage was driven by an elected Constitutional Assembly made up of a joint-sitting of the National Assembly and the Senate of South Africa's first democratic Parliament (1993 Constitution, section 68). While South Africa's first national elections in April 1994 marked the end of apartheid and the coming into force of the 1993 "interim" Constitution, it took another five years before the 1999 elections swept away the last transitional arrangements at the local level, replacing them with the first democratically elected local governments under the final 1996 Constitution. The 1999 election also marked the setting of the Sunset Clauses, which had provided numerous guarantees to the old order (including a five-year government of national unity and job security for apartheid-era government officials) and facilitated the democratic transition. Even then, the transition effectively took another three years before the amnesty process, initiated by the Promotion of National Unity and Reconciliation Act, formally concluded in March 2002.[6]

---

[6] This statute, signed by President Mandela in 1995, created an internationally recognized Truth and Reconciliation Commission under the co-chairmanship of Nobel peace laureate Archbishop Desmond Tutu and Alex Boraine, to grant amnesty to those who came forward to publicly admit their wrongs perpetrated during the apartheid era. The statute is summarized in *Azapo v. President of the Republic of South Africa*, 1996 (4) SA 562 (CC) (rejecting claims by victims of apartheid that the amnesty process violated their rights for legal redress against their wrongdoers).

The explicit two-stage form of South Africa's Constitution-making process was a key aspect of this historic moment. While all post-conflict transitions have particular phases — often involving cease-fire agreements, constitutional negotiations and elections — a unique aspect of the South African process was the formal adoption of the "interim" Constitution. That document made provisions for the establishment of a Constitutional Assembly and creation of a "final" Constitution that would have to be certified as being consistent with a set of constitutional principles appended as Schedule 4 of the 1993 Constitution.

The interim arrangement guaranteed a Government of National Unity to be formed between the African National Congress and the National Party. Constituted by a joint sitting of the two houses of Parliament — the National Assembly and the Senate — the Constitutional Assembly was given two years, from the first sitting of the National Assembly, to "pass a new Constitutional text" (1993 Constitution, section 73(1)). At its first meeting on 24 May 1994, the Constitutional Assembly, composed of 490 members from seven political parties, elected Cyril Ramaphosa of the ANC as its chairperson and Leon Wessels of the National Party as deputy chairperson. At its second meeting in August 1994 the Constitutional Assembly established a 44-member Constitutional Committee to serve as a steering committee and created an administrative structure to manage the process of Constitution-making. The Constitutional Assembly's administrative team handled support for the Assembly and facilitated other important aspects of the process, including: a public participation program that included both written and electronic submissions; a constitutional education program; a constitutional public meetings program; and a newsletter, Constitutional Talk, devoted to explaining the process. In November 1995, the administrative team distributed four million copies of the working draft, which was approved by the Constitutional Assembly.

The main features of the 1996 Constitution include its founding provisions, the Bill of Rights and the chapter on co-operative government, which structures the relationship among the national, provincial and local spheres of government. In addition, the Constitution — similar to other post-Cold War Constitutions — includes specific chapters on public administration, the security services and finance. The document provides constitutional innovations in chapters on "State Institutions Supporting Constitutional Democracy" and on "Traditional Leaders." While the founding provisions define the nature of the post-apartheid state — emphasizing principles of democracy, human rights and equality — a key feature is the specific provision that this "Constitution is the supreme law of the Republic" and that any "law or conduct inconsistent with it is invalid." The provisions in the chapter on "State Institutions Supporting Constitutional Democracy" reflect this commitment to constitutional democracy. The provisions establish a series of independent constitutional bodies including: Public Protector (an office creating a powerful investigative ombudsperson, appointed by the President, after nomination by a vote of at least 60 percent in the National Assembly, for a single 7-year term); Human Rights Commission; Auditor General; and Electoral Commission. They also establish a Commission for the Promotion of the Rights of Cultural, Religious and Linguistic communities and a Commission for Gender Equality. In contrast to these, the chapter on traditional leaders as well as the general provisions guaranteeing self-determination and the option of adopting additional charters of rights "in order to deepen the culture of democracy," reflect the specific concerns flowing from South Africa's own negotiated transition rather than the global constitutional paradigm of the late 20th century.

I.3. A FEW BASIC SIMILARITIES AND DIFFERENCES TO UNDERSTAND AT THE OUTSET

I.3.1. Significant cultural differences

A detailed comparative sociological analysis is beyond the scope of these legal materials. Current values are better explanators for some areas of doctrinal difference than others. A few very general observations can be made:

- *Religion.* Americans tend to be more religious, and to shape their political and social views based on their religious beliefs, than the other countries studied.

- *Distrust of government.* Current American values retain a significant distrust of government and willingness to tolerate inefficiency as the price for preventing powerful and intrusive government action, while in contrast the majority of South Africans believe that government must take a critical and active role in reshaping a society victimized by years of apartheid. Canadians and Australians tend to be less distrustful of government than Americans, and hew to a more moderate course in this regard.

- *Geographic demography.* Canada features as a country where the overwhelming majority of citizens are English-speaking (either Anglo-Celtic origin or immigrants who learned English and integrated into English-speaking society), but over 80% of the Province of Quebec and about 30% of the Province of New Brunswick are French speaking. In the United States, larger states with urban populations tend to be more demographically-diverse than smaller more rural states, and the American South continues to exhibit significant socio-cultural differences compared to the rest of the country. The South African population is overwhelmingly black African (79.4%), with approximately 9.6% white settlers, descendants of Dutch, Flemish, French and German origin settlers (Afrikaners) with just over a third of Anglo-Celtic descent, 2.6% Indian/Asian, and 8.8% Coloured or "mixed race." Within South Africa, the Western Cape, from which Africans were historically excluded, still has a minority of black African residents. The black African population primarily descends from three principal language groupings: the Nguni languages, including isiZulu, isiXhosa, and siSwati; the Sotho languages, including Sesotho, Sepedi, and Setswana and a variety of distinct languages, Tshivenda and Xitsonga and the Khoi, Nama, and San languages. While these differences play a role in partisan politics, the most significant division in which most isiZulu speakers in the province of KwaZulu-Natal were politically and violently divided between the Inkatha Freedom Party and the African National Congress fell by the wayside with the election of isiZulu-speaking Jacob Zuma as President of the ANC in 2007 and the country in 2009. In contrast, Australia's population is historically more homogenous and monolingually Anglophone (notwithstanding that around 40% of Australians have at least one parent who was born overseas). Although there is some sense that the (demographically) smaller states of South Australia, Western Australia, and Tasmania are more socially conservative, this is shifting. While the populations of all major Australian cities are rapidly becoming more ethnically diverse (due to the repeal, of racially-restrictive immigration laws, and more recently the arrival of refugees from many parts of the world) there are relatively few significant demographic or socio-cultural differences among the states.

• *Living history.* While history plays a significant role in how all people think of their constitutions and the cases that have become the markers of each constitution's progress, in the South African case it is important to realize that the conditions that gave rise to the constitution are still present and while the society has undergone some profound and irreversible changes, the living history of apartheid racism and its legacies of profound inequalities in education, economic opportunity and daily life, continue to dominate the present twenty years after the first democratic election. As a result the constitution serves multiple functions — on the one hand it provides a legal infrastructure for today, empowering government and guaranteeing the rights of individuals and groups, yet at the same time it represents the country's aspirations for a better future in which the substantive rights it promises will hopefully be enjoyed by all.

I.3.2. Constitutional ideology

While reverence for the Constitution in the United States is often described as a secular religion, the four constitutional democracies we explore in this text all share a general commitment to democratic constitutionalism and the rule of law as broad ideological commitments within their political and social systems. Within each of these countries there is of course today a rich variety of political and constitutional ideologies befitting the openness of democratic societies; however within the realm of constitutional law and judicial decision-making specific political orientations produce different approaches to understandings of the constitution as well as the role of judges and other participants in the political system. Even if our focus as lawyers is on judicial decision-making, we must always remember that members of the executive, government bureaucracies as well as members of legislatures are constantly making decisions that require them to interpret and take a view on the meaning of constitutional powers and rights, since their actions are either justified by the powers granted to them or limited by the rights granted to citizens. We will not enter into the debates over whether these co-ordinate branches of government have the authority to independently interpret the constitution, but will instead focus on the judiciary, which at least in constitutional cases, has when it comes to interpretation of the constitution, to some extent or at least formally, the last word.

How judges shape constitutional doctrine inevitably requires a baseline view of political and social life in their country, and of how courts, elected officials, and citizens interact. (These underlying assumptions are not necessarily expressly stated in judicial opinions.) A useful, if partial, analysis is provided by University of Toronto Professor Patrick Macklem, in *Constitutional Ideologies*, 20 Ottawa L. Rev. 117 (1988). Macklem identifies key North American ideologies as (1) Toryism; (2) Classical Liberalism; (3) Pluralist Liberalism; and (4) Socialism.

Understanding the Tory ideology is critical to understanding Canadian law and politics. **Toryism** "sees order necessary to hierarchy and hierarchy necessary to order." *Id.* at 124. (A political scientist described Tory philosophy as "the element of the collective will of the dominant class expressed through the public institutions of the state." Reg Whitaker, *Images of the State in Canada, in* THE CANADIAN STATE: POLITICAL ECONOMY AND POLITICAL POWER 38 (Leo Panitch, ed., 1977).) This is a hierarchical organic vision of the relationship between the individual and the community that "spawns a deferential approach to political life; the rulers of society are figures of authority and, as such, should be treated with trust and respect. In turn, political leaders owe duties to their constituents to act in their best interests and further the common good, which is something more than the sum of the more particular interests of individuals and groups in society." In contrast to the American ideology of, in Lincoln's famous words, a government "of the people, by the people, and for the people," the Tory view is a "government by the ministers of the Crown for the people." Note the distinction between Toryism and modern right-of-centre political parties; Tories might well support a strong social safety net if elites believed this was good for society as a whole. The term "Tory" is still used to describe the Conservative Parties in Britain and Canada. The Australian centre-right parties are the Liberal Party of Australia ("liberal" in the 19th-century sense of being more market- and individualistically-oriented than Labor, but, in the Australian case, not necessarily socially or culturally liberal) and its coalition partner, the rural-based National Party (formerly the Country Party). The principal alternative party of government is the Labor Party, formed out of the union movement in the late 19th century. The dominant Australian view of the relationship between government and individual supports notions of parliamentary supremacy and the collective interest (in particular, in the past, in the sphere of industrial relations), with a weaker view of claims of the individual against the state.

According to Macklem **classical liberalism** imagines society "as an aggregation of rights-bearing individuals, each absolute within his or her sphere of authority." Classical liberals view the judiciary "as a constitutional umpire," drawing a line between conflicting assertions of power to act. They do so by reference to law, which is separate from politics — the latter being the process by which the public interest is articulated, not as something which transcends private interests, but merely as the sum of its parts.

More specifically, this philosophy pictures political life as an arena in which private interests clash with each other in an endless series of struggles between and among individuals, each attempting to use government to serve his or her interests. But classic liberals do not imagine political life as possessing an imminent ordering principle which would contain and check the potential for domination. Thus there is need for exogenously-imposed limits upon political life to protect the individual from the spectre of group tyranny: these limits come from the judiciary. This desire to protect the dignity of the individual and enhance his or her opportunity to realize his or her own individual conception of the good manifests itself in law in the discourse of rights. Rights are viewed as individual trump cards which protect the individual from the collectivity or collectivities in areas most central to the individual's self-definition. In the classical liberal vision, this protection is accorded by law primarily through individual economic activity. The classic argument here is John Locke's *Two Treatises of Government* (1689). This plays out today in an approach that narrowly construes the power of federal governments, and broadly construes individual rights against government intervention, but at the same time narrowly construes rights claims that would require the government to pro-actively adopt measures to solve social problems.

Unlike the classical version, Macklem argues "the **pluralist liberal political vision** pictures social life as complex and highly interdependent, laced together by the competing and overlapping demands of its individual members." While political life is still seen as a competition among individuals and groups seeking to further their interests and conceptions of the good, pluralists reject the view that the marketplace is "the means by which individual initiative and self-reliance will be axiomatically rewarded in a fair and just manner; pluralist liberalism acknowledges that if left on its own, the economic market will generate injustice and inequality." Thus, economic liberty is as much of a threat to, as it is facilitative of, principles of individualism and autonomy. The content of constitutional law at the level of the discourse of rights thus shifts from an emphasis on individual economic liberty to a political inquiry. Constitutional protection of the individual against legislative initiatives is conceived less in terms of an inquiry into the effect of economic redistribution upon an individual's ability to realize his or her conception of the good through property and contract, and more in terms of a need to facilitate and protect the individual's formal ability to enter the political marketplace and participate therein. Among works that, in different ways, seek to implement this version are John Hart Ely's classic *Democracy and Distrust* (1980) (judicial review, Ely argues, should be primarily limited to ways to insure that the democratic political process works) and Jesse Choper's *Judicial Review and the National Political Process* (1980) (courts, Choper argues, should not waste political capital on federalism or separation of powers issues which are politically self-correcting but focus on individual rights violations by majorities). Dominant Australian constitutional principles, which do not offer the range of judicially enforceable rights protections found in North America or South Africa, but do imply judicially enforceable restrictions on government interference with the ability of Australians to elect their government and communicate about political matters, are more consistent with the Ely view.

Finally, Macklem observes that "**socialist discourse**, like toryism, is collectivistic.[7] The individual is imagined not as a self-determining atomistic entity; he or she is seen as a member of a community, with the public good treated as something more than the sum of the parts. . . . But like liberalism, and unlike Toryism, there is a deep commitment in socialist discourse to egalitarian principles. Whereas liberalism sees equality largely in terms of equality of opportunity,

---

[7] *Cf.* Axworthy, *supra*, at 245–46 (noting virtually identical critiques of Trudeau's proposed charter by conservative Manitoba Premier Sterling Lyon and socialist Saskatchewan Premier Allan Blakeney).

facilitating every individual's capacity to further his or her personal conceptions of the good, socialist discourse is rooted in notions of equality of condition."

Thus, socialists tend to view constitutional law instrumentally as part of the assistance in the realization of a more egalitarian and collectivist society. Indeed, there is a great debate among leftist constitutional scholars in Canada, between those who see it as a vehicle for progressive social change, and those who see it as protecting individual rights that are obstacles to such change and therefore limiting the ability of leftist legislatures. As we explore in this text, the tension between liberal protection of individual rights and achievement of significant progress toward rectifying the fundamental inequalities of condition that characterize South African society is played out in the web of constitutional provisions that both protect against government and mandate government action to provide basic social and economic needs.

Apropos of Winston Churchill's famous remark that democracy was the worst system except all the alternatives, except for classical liberalism each of these outlooks assumes that where democracies fail, judicial intervention produces superior results. A critical ideology is **parliamentary sovereignty**. This view was recently articulated by an Australian comparative constitutional law scholar, Jeffrey Goldsworthy, in PARLIAMENTARY SOVEREIGNTY: CONTEMPORARY DEBATES (2010). Professor Goldsworthy rejects the claim that parliamentary sovereigntists naively believe that popular government will never violate the rights of individuals or minority groups. But they do trust that, in appropriate political, social and cultural conditions, clear injustices will be relatively rare, and that in most cases, whether or not the law violates someone's rights will be open to reasonable disagreement. They also trust that over time, the proportion of clear rights violations will diminish, and "that a people, in acting autonomously, will learn how to act rightly." (Quoting ROBERT DAHL, DEMOCRACY AND ITS CRITICS 192 (1989).) Strong democrats hold that where the requirements of justice and human rights are the subject of reasonable disagreement, the opinion of a majority of the people or those elected to represent them, rather than that of a majority of some unelected elite, should prevail. On this view, the price that must be paid for giving judges power to correct the occasional clear injustice by overriding enacted laws, is that they must also be given power to overrule the democratic process in the much greater number of cases where there is reasonable disagreement and healthy debate. For strong democrats, this is too high a price.

We can also identify an approach we might call "**internationalism**" or "cosmopolitanism." This approach promotes constitutional norms, allegiances, and even laws that transcend the nation state. Individuals and courts, from this perspective, are seen as members of a global, humanist community. Internationalists view sovereign states as part of the global community, and a major determinant of each country's public interest as lying in the need to maintain the country's good standing in the global community by adherence to global norms. The cosmopolitan influence in constitutional jurisprudence can be seen in the view that national courts should draw inspiration from the judgments of foreign courts as well as from international law. The former Australian High Court Justice Michael Kirby articulated this position in a 2005 speech to the American Society of International Law. He spoke of the growth of globalization, not only in politics and economics, but also in values and ethics, and he argued that lawyers need to take account of these irreversible trends. He referred to the "memory of the terrible wrongs to human rights" in recent history and the dangers of living in a world without international law. The interaction of international and national law, he said, was one of the greatest challenges facing the legal community, and he urged national courts to respond to this challenge:

> This is a time to acknowledge the role that international law plays, and will increasingly play, in the constitutional jurisprudence of nation states . . . Drawing upon sources found in international law, not as binding rules but as contextual principles, judges of municipal courts in this century will assume an important function in making the principles of international law a reality throughout the world. We cannot leave this function to international courts and tribunals alone. To survive, humanity must globalise and diversify.[8]

Of course, constitutions are not doctoral dissertations in political philosophy, but working political documents. This is especially true in new democracies where constitutions serve not only to structure relations of power but also as the embodiment of these societies' aspirations as they emerge from conflict. This tension is reflected in South Africa where the new institutions created by the Constitution are struggling to both establish their places in the society and to move the country beyond its history of racial conflict and inequality that are apartheid's legacy. To this extent the South African Constitution might be said to reflect a working compromise that brings together many of the ideological arguments set forth above.

On the one hand some South African judges and academics have embraced the notion of a transformative constitutionalism (Karl Klare, *Legal Culture and Transformative Constitutionalism*, 14 SALJ 146 (1998); Pius Langa, *Transformative Constitutionalism*, 17 STELLENBOSCH L. REV. 351) described as "a long-term project of constitutional enactment, interpretation, and enforcement committed . . . to transforming a country's political and social institutions and power relationships in a democratic, participatory and egalitarian direction" (Klare, at 150). These aspirations are reflected in the embrace of substantive equality and the guarantee of social and economic rights that are included in the 1996 Constitution. On the other hand, there are those who once embraced parliamentary sovereignty — although restricted to a racially exclusive electorate that ensured white minority rule — and with the advent of democracy sought entrenched constitutional guarantees (in the form of classic liberal rights) as an essential precondition to their participation in a peaceful transition from apartheid. There is also a section of the ruling African National Congress that now blames the slow pace of social and economic transformation on the constraints the constitution imposes on government action. Expressing this frustration President Jacob Zuma told the National Assembly in November 2011 that:

---

[8] *7th Annual Grotius Lecture*, delivered to the American Society of International Law in Washington on March 30 2005.

[w]e respect the powers and role conferred by our constitution on the legislature and the judiciary. At the same time, we expect the same from these very important institutions of our democratic dispensation. The Executive must be allowed to conduct its administration and policy making work as freely as it possible can. The powers conferred on the courts cannot be regarded as superior to the powers resulting from a mandate given by the people in a popular vote.

Finally, at the extreme there are new political movements and leaders who now campaign against the Constitution which they characterize as the product of an historic compromise that has allowed the white minority to enjoy the spoils of apartheid together with an emergent black elite, but denies the democratic majority the right to redistribute the ill-gotten gains of apartheid and colonialism. In this context the question of constitutional ideology is not merely an academic discussion but becomes a key battleground in the struggle for constitutional democracy itself.

I.4.   BASIC COMPARISONS OF THE LEGISLATIVE PROCESS IN POLITICAL CONTEXT: A BRIEF INTRODUCTION

Any understanding of public law requires some basic appreciation for the process by which a nation establishes its laws. Like substantive legal doctrines, the different processes used to enact legislation in Australia, Canada, South Africa, and the United States reflect each nation's history and values.

I.4.1.   United States

The United States Constitution contains two essential requirements for the enactment of statutes. The legislation must be passed with a majority of a duly constituted quorum of the 435 members of the House of Representatives (elected on the basis of population for 2-year fixed terms of office) and the 100 members of the Senate (two elected from each state for 6-year fixed terms). The legislation must then be approved by either the President (elected nationally[9] for a fixed four-year term and limited to two terms of office) or by a two-thirds "override" of a presidential veto by each house.

Discussion of a particular piece of legislation cannot be divorced from political reality. Passing a bill requires that at least a majority of representatives, a majority of senators, and the President are at least open to persuasion on the issue. The key to understanding the American political process is that it is filled with "veto gates"[10] by which individual legislators or sub-groups can potentially block proposals that may even have strong majority support. The President is clearly the most powerful "lobbyist" in Washington. The President's ability to sign or oppose legislation and to appoint congressional friends to patronage positions gives the

---

[9] Actually, voters in each state select "electors" who formally elect the President. As we now know well, it is possible for a candidate to win a majority of electors but lose in the popular vote.

[10] *See* McNollgast, *Positive Canons: The Role of Legislative Bargains in Statutory Interpretation*, 80 Geo. L.J. 705 (1992).

President strong bargaining leverage with Congressmen (the colloquial name for Members of the House of Representatives) and Senators. And, of course, controversial legislation almost certainly could not pass in the face of a credible Presidential threat to veto the legislation. Moreover, strong support from the relevant cabinet secretary (i.e. minister of state) can provide a bill's supporters with important expertise in drafting the statute, marshaling factual arguments in support of their cause, and providing publicity to create momentum in support of their legislation.

Nonetheless, presidential support is not sufficient to enact legislation. Influential as the President may be, the White House exercises no formal control, and only weak informal control, over the Members of Congress. Indeed, since the end of World War II, the President's party has controlled a majority in both houses only 40% of the time. Moreover, Senators and Representatives usually have their own basis of political support, so that the endorsement and support of a popular President is helpful, but not essential, and the backing of an unpopular President is completely unnecessary.[11] Thus, although it would be a major boost to achieve Presidential support, as long as the President was not unalterably opposed to proposed legislation, advocates would proceed by securing the introduction of legislation by prominent legislators.

Because, even where the President's party is in the majority, individual legislators exercise independent political power, as noted, there are numerous "veto gates" that successful legislation must overcome: (1) the chair of the standing committee of each house to which legislation is almost always referred, who can try to "whip" majority party members to following his or her lead, or can join with minority party members to pass or defeat legislation or amendments; (2) the House Rules Committee, which acts for the Speaker to control the agenda of the House, block undesired legislation passed by committees, and strictly limit the ability to offer and vote on individual amendments; (3) the House floor, where, although individual members are inclined to follow their party leadership, they will not hesitate to vote against their party if their strong personal convictions dictate, or if the vote is particularly unpopular either back home to their constituents or to major political supporters (this is because members will often seek re-election based on their own, rather than their party's, accomplishments, and raise a significant percentage of their campaign funds independently of the party, either from local or other personal supporters, or also from cross-donations from other individually powerful members); (4) similar committee processes in the Senate; (5) a "filibuster" on the Senate floor, where debate can continue, and non-germane amendments be considered,[12] unless and until "cloture" is invoked by the affirmative vote of 60 of the 100 senators. But this also means that a bill's advocates are not as subject to the power of the committee chairs; (6) Presidential approval.

---

[11] *See* McNollgast, *Positive Canons: The Role of Legislative Bargains in Statutory Interpretation*, 80 Geo. L.J. 705 (1992).

[12] In 2000, when the Senate Democrats were stifled by the then-Republican leadership's refusal to consider legislation raising the minimum wage that would probably have attracted a handful of Republican votes sufficient for passage, Sen. Edward Kennedy proposed the minimum wage proposal as an amendment to every single piece of legislation brought to the Senate floor.

I.4.2. Canada

Although the formal requirements for enactment of Canadian law are quite similar to the American system — legislation must pass the House of Commons and the Senate and be approved by the executive — the language of the *Constitution Act, 1867* (before 1982 known as the *British North America Act*), and what is omitted from the Act, reflects important differences with its American counterpart. Most importantly, nations governed by the "Westminster" system of parliamentary democracy developed in Great Britain follow a system of constitutional "conventions": unwritten rules, not to be enforced judicially, that prescribe the way in which legal power is to be exercised. Thus, although the Constitution confers significant power upon the Queen and her personal representative in Canada, the nation follows the British tradition of "responsible government" that this power must always be exercised pursuant to the advice of ministers who are members of the legislative branch and who enjoy the support of a majority of the House of Commons. Thus, there is no real separation of power between the executive and legislative branches, as occurs in the United States. Another significant difference between the Westminster and American systems is the existence of fairly strict party discipline: members of the House of Commons elected under the banner of a political party will follow the party leadership on any significant vote, especially when the party is in the majority and the leadership forms the government.

For this reason, although the most powerful figure in Canadian government is the Prime Minister, who is almost always the leader of the largest party in the House of Commons, there are only two minor references to the Prime Minister in the entire Constitution. Rather, the Prime Minister's power exists through his or her ability to control his or her party to secure necessary support in the House of Commons, and his or her ability to direct the Governor General in how to exercise executive power.

Similarly, the formal role of the Canadian Senate differs sharply from both its conventional (real) role, and from that of the United States Senate. Canadian Senators are appointed based on a formula giving somewhat more weight to smaller provinces than the House of Commons, and serve until a mandatory retirement age of 75. They are appointed by the Governor General pursuant to advice from the governing Prime Minister. The Senate's role in blocking, rather than offering amendments, to government legislation remains contested. Controversial instances of Senate refusals to pass legislation include the Liberal Senate majority's rejection of free trade legislation in 1988, forcing a new election (the Senators acquiesced after the Mulroney government was re-elected); the Conservative Senate majority's rejection of greenhouse gas regulations (the bill had passed the House of Commons when the Tories were running a minority government); Conservative Senators also joined with Liberals to oppose a private member's bill, passed with the support of the Conservative Prime Minister Stephen Harper (but not officially a government bill), to tightly control internal union governance.

The process for considering legislation depends greatly on whether the Prime Minister controls a majority of the Commons, or operates a "minority government" with the acquiescence of one or more opposition parties. Majority governments continue (unless the governing party loses its majority due to defection or lost interim by-elections to fill vacancies) for up to five years, although the Prime Minister may call an election sooner if political calculations warrant. Minority governments continue until either the Prime Minister seeks a new mandate or the opposition parties bring down the government in a no-confidence vote, resulting also in a new election.

With a majority government, legislation will not progress very far without approval of the powerful Prime Minister's Office (PMO). The Prime Minister does not need to rely on the powerful tools of lobbying that the U.S. President must employ — he or she can rely on party discipline to achieve desired ends in the House of Commons. Moreover, legislative supporters do not face the sort of American "veto gates," where individual legislators or sub-groups can block proposals that have strong majority support.

Another major factor in Canadian legislation is the civil service. Canadian ministers have very small staff of political appointees and the major operations of a ministry are conducted under the direction of a career Deputy Minister.[13] Moreover, central cabinet operations are subject to influence both by the political appointees in the PMO as well as by the civil servants in the Privy Council Office (PCO).

Assuming ministers want to move ahead with legislation, they will first present it to a committee within the Cabinet known as the Priority and Planning Committee. Because staffs are smaller and these officials are elected, deliberation in that committee is often vigorous, expert, and substantive. Major objections to proposed legislation may require reevaluation by the Minister proposing the bill and reconsideration; if the bill is unlikely to attract full cabinet support, it might be shelved here. Unlike the American system however, no single objector (save perhaps the Prime Minister) can prevent the proposal's continued progress. With support from this committee, a Memorandum to Cabinet will be proposed. Skilled ministers usually present the cabinet with options and will detail the principles to be included in the legislation. Approval of the cabinet is required before the bill will be formally drafted by ministry experts and introduced in the House of Commons.

Once the legislation has been formally drafted, it would be introduced in the House of Commons and presented for First Reading. The Commons would then vote on whether the legislation should proceed. Because the government controls a majority in Commons, this vote, and a similar one on Second Reading, would be a formality, with one major exception. On important "conscience" issues, the government may permit a "free vote" where members vote according to their consciences regardless of party (this indeed was followed on the actual 1991 vote on abortion legislation). After Second Reading, the bill would be referred to committee.

---

[13] This practice, borrowed from the British, is generally followed in Australia and South Africa as well (the senior civil servants in Australian ministries are called Departmental Secretaries and in South African ministries they are called Directors General). In contrast, in the U.S. Department of Justice, the Deputy Attorney General, the Assistant Attorney General responsible for criminal law, and the Deputy Attorney General responsible for criminal legislation would all be political appointees.

Although there are ways for non-government bills to pass in theory, as a bill originating in the Senate or as a private member's bill, these cannot be passed without the government's approval (either backing or willingness to not use "the whip," i.e., party discipline). In minority governments, private members' bills might move forward, but then the proponents risk forcing a new election if the Prime Minister announces that he or she opposes the bill and considers the vote on passage to be a "confidence vote."

In majority governments, parliamentary committees enjoy far less power than congressional ones. While congressional committees play a vital role in screening out legislation that does not warrant further attention, the full House of Commons fulfills that role in the First and Second Reading votes. It would be extraordinary for a parliamentary committee to fail to report legislation back to the House for Third Reading. Nor does the committee chair have particular power. Indeed, committee chair assignments are the left-overs given to junior or disfavoured members of Parliament (MPs) who have not been chosen to participate in cabinet or to act as parliamentary secretaries (stands-in for ministers in their absence). Committees will conduct a detailed review of legislation, but many problems that are corrected at this point in the American system have already been vetted by the ministry's professional staff. The proceedings are open to the public and sometimes televised, so opposition MPs (who hold seats based on their percentage of the overall House) can offer amendments for political purposes; rarely will these amendments be accepted. The majority of the committee will vote in a disciplined fashion in accord with the Minister's wishes. Significantly, committees are bound to maintain the key principles of each bill; although this standard is not precise, it prevents committees from significantly altering the bill the way American legislators often do.

On the other hand, in minority governments, committees reflect the partisan make-up of the entire House, and American-style individual lobbying and deal-cutting become more prevalent. However, the party leaders must always face the risk that the Prime Minister will assert that any vote is a "confidence" vote, and thus put them to the test of acquiescing in the government's program, or facing a new election. Intra-party disputes, and a seeming public preference for unpopular policies implemented by minority governments rather than the prospect of frequent elections, make this a generally unpleasant prospect for minority parties.

If the bill was initiated in the House, it then proceeds to the Senate. The Senate follows the same procedures used by the House; however convention dictates that the Senate will not obstruct the will of the elected house. The Senate does play an important role, however, in proposing amendments. Realistically, the House can reject the amendments and the Senate will acquiesce, but this comes at a political cost, and well-taken amendments are often accepted by the minister.

After passing both Houses of Parliament, the bill is presented to the Governor General for Royal Assent. As noted earlier, this assent is always going to be given since the bill received the support of the House of Commons.

I.4.3. Australia

Like Canada, Australia has a parliamentary system based on the Westminster model of "responsible" government, meaning that all members of the executive government are also elected members of parliament (this is required by s 64 of the Constitution). Unlike in Canada, however, both of the Australian Houses of Parliament — the House of Representatives and the Senate — are (and have always been) directly elected. Governments are formed by the party or parties that "command the confidence" of the House of Representatives, and the Prime Minister is the leader of the majority party; she or he is (by convention) always a member of the House, and never a Senator. The Australian Constitution has many provisions governing elections, but does not mention the Prime Minister or the Cabinet, or the principle that the government is formed in the House. These are conventions. For a range of reasons, governments often do not control the Senate: the reasons include the fact that the Senate is elected by Proportional Representation whereas members of the House of Representatives are elected in single member constituencies, through a preferential voting system. This often (at least recently) results in the election to the Senate of candidates from small or single-issue parties, and occasionally Independents; sometimes these Senators hold the balance of power in the Senate, and are willing to join with the Opposition to defeat or amend a government bill that has come up from the House of Representatives. It is not at all unusual for bills to be delayed, or amended, or blocked in the Senate.

The Senate is technically a "states house," and cannot be larger than half the size of the House of Representatives (this "nexus" is specified in s 24 of the Constitution); there are 12 Senators per state regardless of population. Senators serve a six year term, with half the Senate being elected every three years (unless, under exceptional circumstances, a "double dissolution" election is held, with all seats in both Houses up for re-election. The grounds and procedure for such an election are set out in s 57 of the Constitution). The regular half-Senate election means that the composition of the Senate may, to some degree, reflect the political climate of the previous election, whereas the House will always be the product of the most recent. With the rare exception of so-called "conscience votes," party discipline is strongly enforced in both Houses (it is required under the rules of the Labor Party, but not the Liberal Party, although it is informally imposed in the latter). Senators almost always vote along party lines, but there is still a sense that they are, in significant but unspecified ways, representatives of their home state, or that they serve an important role in reviewing and restraining government policy. Australian voters will sometimes, even often, vote differently for the Senate from the way they vote for the House, sometimes strategically to "send a message" to the government that they are not happy with its performance, but not yet ready to turn it out and replace it. Voting has been compulsory in Australia since 1924, and this is enforced by law, and supported by a majority of the Australian people who regard it as an Australian institution. The Constitution specifies a maximum three-year term for the House of Representatives (half-Senate terms are also for three years), but the period between general elections is not otherwise fixed, and the actual election date can vary. Early elections (sometimes as soon as eighteen months after the last election) are not uncommon. Each time an election is called, the Prime Minister must seek the Governor-General's assent; this is almost always automatically given, although the Governor-General may require good reasons to be given for a very early election.

Every bill for an Act of parliament must be passed by both Houses. With the exception of revenue bills (known as "money" bills) which cannot originate in or be amended by the Senate (s 53 of the Constitution), bills can be introduced in either House, and must go through three "readings" in each. Contentious bills will often be sent to a Committee for multi-party consideration and sometimes also public submissions and hearings, before being returned for passage. Committees are not powerful, however (although their hearings can attract media attention and generate indirect political pressure on the government); their role is only to review and recommend. Almost all bills come from cabinet, and are presented in the House of Representatives by the relevant Minister. A bill that does not have government support — a so-called "Private Member's Bill" — is very unlikely to be passed. As in Canada, all bills require the assent of the Governor-General to become law. According to the Constitution (s 2), the Governor-General is the Queen's (Queen Elizabeth II) representative in Australia and is commissioned by the Queen, but in practice is always (since 1926) nominated by the Prime Minister. The office these days is popularly regarded as an Australian institution, and the Governor-General is thought to represent the nation. Unlike in Canada, however, the Governor-General does at least have the potential to exercise some independent political power. Although she or he almost always follows government advice to sign bills into law or issue executive orders or proclamations, the prospect remains of a Governor-General's exercising "reserve powers"; that is, acting without, or contrary to, the advice of the government. This occurred, very controversially, in 1975, when the Governor-General dismissed the government because the Senate had failed to pass the government's supply bills, and the Prime Minister had refused to call an election. Future use of the reserve powers has never been ruled out, although politically it is very unlikely. These powers are not codified in the Constitution, and great uncertainty surrounds the desirability, or even possibility, of their being codified.

The Constitution is clear, however, regarding cases where there is a deadlock between the House of Representatives and the Senate over the passage of a bill. Section 57 sets out the procedure that may be followed if the Senate twice refuses to pass a bill within a specified period of time. The Prime Minister may advise the Governor-General to call a "double dissolution" election; both the House and Senate are dissolved, and elections are held for all seats. After the election, a joint sitting of both Houses may (but is not required to) be convened, to vote on the deadlocked bill(s). Such elections are very rare and a joint sitting has only once been held (in 1974). They remain a possibility, however, always hanging over the heads of recalcitrant non-government Senators. The differences in the relationship between the Australian and the Canadian Houses reflect the preference of the framers of Australia's Constitution for an American style of federalism, marrying this with Westminster parliamentary government, in a unique combination that the political scientist, Elaine Thompson famously dubbed the "Washminster

Mutation."[14] Some at the time of federation predicted that the two could never co-exist; that either federalism would kill responsible government, or responsible government would kill federalism. So far, neither has happened.

I.4.4. South Africa

Despite the abandonment of both the "tricameral" legislative structure of the 1983 Constitution and the constituency-based structure of representative democracy that had shaped the legislative branch of government since the introduction of representative government at the Cape in 1854, both the 1993 "interim" and 1996 "final" Constitutions retained South Africa's long-standing parliamentary system. This embrace of an existing institution with long-standing traditions has fundamentally shaped the procedural practices and format of the legislative process.

Parliament is a bicameral institution with the National Assembly (NA) and the National Council of Provinces (NCOP) playing distinct roles in the legislative and oversight functions that are at the core of this branch of government. The National Assembly is composed of between 350 and 400 women and men elected as members. According to the terms of an electoral law framed by three constitutional requirements, the system includes a national common voters' role; minimum voting age of 18 years; and requirement that the process "results, in general, in proportional representation" (1996 Constitution, section 46). The Constitution states that the National Assembly should be elected for a term of five years (section 49) and that it should represent the people and ensure government "by the people under the Constitution . . . by choosing the President, by providing a national forum for public consideration of issues, by passing legislation and by scrutinizing and overseeing executive action" (section 42(3)). The NCOP, in contrast to other parliamentary systems, is not a Senate or upper House, but rather the institutional embodiment of the principles of co-operative government and intergovernmental relations that attempt to mediate among different levels of government without explicitly embracing a federal system of government. The purpose of the NCOP is to integrate the provinces into the national legislative process, thus achieving a level of integrated law-making that is central to the constitutional principle of co-operative government that envisions three spheres of government which are "distinctive, interdependent and interrelated" (section 40(1)).

In this scheme, the NCOP represents the provinces and is composed of provincial delegations appointed by the provinces. While this body has different roles depending on the type of legislation it is considering, its essential function is to represent the interests of the provinces at the national level. Each province is represented by a ten-person delegation made up of four special delegates and six permanent delegates. The permanent delegates come from the different political parties represented in the provincial legislature in proportion to their representation in that legislature and serve until the first meeting of the next elected provincial legislature. The special delegates include the Provincial Premier,

---

[14] Elaine Thompson, *The "Washminster" Mutation*, 15 AUSTRALIAN J. POL. SCI. 32 (1980).

or his or her designated representative, as well as three additional members of the provincial legislature who may be designated from time to time, allowing the legislature to send different delegates depending on the issues to be addressed in the NCOP. In addition to provincial representation, the Constitution also provides for a tenth non-voting delegation to represent organized local government in the NCOP.

The Constitution explicitly distributes legislative authority to all three spheres of government: the national, regional and local. At the same time it ensures that the ultimate law-giving authority is vested in Parliament, which is empowered to override even the exclusive legislative competence of a province if it is necessary to maintain national security, economic unity, essential national standards, minimum standards of service delivery or to prevent "unreasonable action taken by a province" which is prejudicial to the "interests of another province or to the country as a whole" (section 146(3)). It is important to understand, however, that the NCOP, which directly represents provincial governments in the national legislature, is a full participant in the legislative process and therefore plays a central role in the exercise of this override function. Ultimately however, the NCOP cannot prevent the National Assembly from passing legislation affecting the provinces if the legislation is supported by a two-thirds vote in the Assembly. However, such a vote may only take place after a complex procedure in which the legislation is voted on by both houses, submitted to a mediation committee and then if no agreement is reached, either lapses, or is passed by a two-thirds majority in the National Assembly. All other legislation, not directly affecting the provinces as defined in the Constitution, is the preserve of the National Assembly, although the NCOP does have a deliberative role and formally votes on these issues. Voting procedures in the NCOP depend on the subject matter before the Council. In the case of matters affecting the provinces and in the case of constitutional amendments, each provincial delegation has a single vote; while in matters of general interest, in which the NCOP has a primarily deliberative role, the members of the Council cast individual votes.

National legislative action is divided into three categories with related procedural rules: (1) amendments to the Constitution; (2) ordinary bills, including those addressing areas of concurrent provincial and national jurisdiction; and (3) money bills and legislation providing for the "equitable division of revenue . . . among the national, provincial and local spheres of government," which may only be introduced by the Finance Minister. All members and committees of Parliament may introduce legislation, yet in practice, new legislation tends to be introduced by the specific departments of government responsible for the particular subject matter or for implementing the policies or programs the legislation is designed to address. This practice tends, as in many other countries, to shape the law-making agenda of the legislature. While this is not unusual in parliamentary systems, the explicit ring-fencing of money bills, which makes them the sole prerogative of the Ministry of Finance, means that the legislature has limited power over the national purse. In effect, Parliament is simply called upon to vote on the budget as a single package and is unable to exercise its authority over particular spending decisions, unless it is prepared to vote down the budget in toto. Although it has been justified as necessary to maintain financial discipline and also on the grounds that the budget process is just too complicated for most parliamentarians to fully grasp, this provision has come to symbolize the weakness of Parliament in the constitutional scheme.

Frustration among parliamentarians, who have increasingly felt that their inability to seriously challenge the distribution of resources effectively limits their capacity to shape government action, gave impetus to demands that Parliament be given a larger role in defining government expenditures. Moreover, the Constitution, as amended in 2001, provides that procedures for Parliament to amend money bills must be provided for by legislation. This legislation was finally put forward as a bill in July 2008 as part of a wholesale revival of Parliament's authority and autonomy from the executive branch. This political shift was one of the products of the division within the ANC.[15] One of the most significant legislative consequences of this split was the Money Bills Amendment Procedure and Related Matters Act of 2008, which was finally signed into law by South Africa's third President, Kgalema Motlanthe, on 16 April 2009.[16]

The new law requires Parliament to establish separate committees on finance and appropriations in both the National Assembly and in the NCOP, and sets out an elaborate process for the passage of the national budget and related laws. To support this process the law also creates a Parliamentary Budget Office to provide research assistance to the committees as well as "advice and analysis on proposed amendments to the fiscal framework, the Division of Revenues Bill and money Bills and policy proposals with budgetary implications." While this is an important step forward in the empowerment of the legislature, the statute is designed to ensure that the appropriations process remains constrained within a clear budgetary framework. To this end, Parliament is required to first approve a general fiscal framework, which ensures that all subsequent spending proposals remain within the broader economic strategy of the government. Only once there is agreement on the fiscal framework may Parliament tackle both the Division of Revenue Bill, which provides for the distribution of finances between the different spheres of government — national, provincial and local governments — and the Appropriations Bill. Amendments to the Appropriations Bill may only be made after the Division of Revenue Bill has been agreed upon. Finally, the Revenue Bills must be considered and must be consistent with the approved fiscal framework and Division of Revenue bills. While the strict procedural process and the complexity of government finances will constrain members of Parliament, the availability of procedures to approve the overall fiscal framework and to amend and adopt the

---

[15] The post-apartheid ANC, as a political party, was relatively unified under the initial leadership of the first democratically elected President, Nelson Mandela. The December 2007 party conference at Polokwane revealed deep fissures, with Jacob Zuma defeating Mandela's successor, Thabo Mbeki in the election for ANC President. After the conference, power seemed to split between the executive branch, which remained in Mbeki's hands, and Luthuli House (the ANC headquarters in Johannesburg) and Parliament, where the majority of MPs seemed to support Zuma and the ANC policy shifts that were adopted in Polokwane.

[16] President Mbeki resigned under pressure from the ANC's Executive Committee, following a judge's conclusion that Mbeki had improperly abused power by pressuring officials to prosecute his political rival, Zuma, for corruption. The Deputy President of the ANC at the time, Motlanthe, was appointed by Parliament to complete Mbeki's term; Zuma was elected at the next regularly scheduled election.

different aspects of the government's budget holds the promise of fundamentally altering the relationship between the legislature and the executive. At the same time, however, the ANC's continuing domination of Parliament, through its overwhelming electoral support, means that the real power in Parliament continues to reside in the ruling party's parliamentary caucus.

As in legislatures elsewhere, the essential work of Parliament is conducted in the approximately 65 parliamentary committees that exist in both the National Assembly and the NCOP. In the National Assembly there are approximately 30 portfolio committees that track the functional departments of the national government in addition to the specific coordination, oversight and joint committees required by the Constitution. The NCOP is a break from the Westminster tradition, because it is not a second, higher, house but rather a version of the German Bundesrat that represents the provinces in the national legislative process. However, the fact that six of the nine provinces had ANC governments beginning in 1994 and all the provinces were governed by the ANC after the 1999 elections means that the NCOP has never served as a counterbalance to the dominant National Assembly. Even the takeover of the Western Cape government by the opposition after the 2009 elections has not reinvigorated the NCOP.

I.5.   APPROACHES TO CONSTITUTIONAL INTERPRETATION: A BRIEF SURVEY

Policies and legislation in all four countries are shaped by the interplay of these constitutional, institutional, and historical factors. Constitutional law — the product of judicial decisions — is also shaped by such factors. Each country's judiciary is appointed and operates under its own particular procedures and rules. Varying approaches to constitutional interpretation also play an important role in the differences one finds in the respective courts' judgments (also known as "opinions" or "reasons") in which individual constitutional controversies are resolved. It can be difficult to understand these differences without knowing something first about alternative methodologies of interpretation.

It is also important to understand that, in a constitutional dispute, the interpretation of legislation is typically at play in addition to the interpretation of the constitution (sometimes executive acts are challenged on constitutional grounds, but this happens less frequently). Judges have to make a choice about whether or not to interpret legislation/statutes in the same way as they interpret their country's constitution. In the U.S. judicially-created "canons" of statutory interpretation apply; courts in Australia and Canada are guided by Interpretation Acts that set down rules for interpreting statutes as well as common law principles. In South Africa the Constitution provides explicit guidance to the courts on the interpretation of the Bill of Rights (s 39) and the Constitutional Court has in its judgments called for a generous and purposive approach to constitutional interpretation in general. Notwithstanding these small differences, all courts apply a presumption of constitutional validity to the interpretation of statutes. It is assumed that legislatures do not intend to breach the Constitution; so, when faced with a statute that can support more than one interpretation, courts will prefer a meaning that conforms to the constitution over a meaning that does not.

There are many ways to classify the methodologies of constitutional interpretation, but they can be gathered together under four broad headings: "originalism"; "textualism"; "living interpretation," and "pragmatism."

I.5.1. Originalism

"Originalism" is the term used for interpreting constitutional words with the aim of finding out what they meant, historically, at the time they were written. One version of originalism looks for the intention of the constitution's framers: that is, what the men (or, if applicable, women) who framed the constitution had in mind, or intended. This search can be either for what the constitution's framers thought the words meant at the time, and/or what they wanted the words to mean in practice, when applied to future cases. Another version (known as "new originalism") looks for the "public meaning" of the constitution's words: what people generally would have understood the words to mean, at the time they or their representatives approved the whole constitution (for example, through state ratification conventions in the United States; referendums in Australia; or by legislative amendment in Canada and South Africa). Supporters of originalism (either version) argue that this approach is the only way to remain faithful to the intentions and values of those who wrote and approved the constitution. These intentions, they argue, are "contractually" binding, and remain so until the words are changed under the formal procedure for constitutional amendment that itself is set out in the constitution, and must therefore be followed. Originalists maintain that departure from the historical meaning of the constitution gives judges the unauthorized freedom to insert their own values into the constitution and to advance these as the constitution's "meaning"; in other words, it encourages "judicial activism." What the constitution meant when it was written, originalists say, is the only sure guide to what it should mean today.

I.5.2. Textualism

Textualism is often conflated or confused with originalism (textualism is sometimes known as "semantic originalism"), but there are important differences. Textualists argue that it is only the text — the *words* — of a constitution that should be interpreted, not the beliefs or ideas or intentions of the framers, or those of the historical public. Courts, they say, should not look behind the text, but should treat the words themselves as the expression of what the framers wanted to achieve and what they wanted to communicate; whatever went on in their own minds is unknowable and irrelevant. This approach is similar to interpreting legislation (although without considering what the legislators actually had in mind). For textualists, the rules or canons of interpretation are treated as appropriate and, usually, sufficient for interpreting constitutional words or provisions. To the extent that "original" historical sources of meaning are consulted, these are confined to legal dictionaries, treatises of law, and other legal tracts that were in use at the time of the constitution's framing. Textualists promote their approach on similar lines to originalists: they regard departures from the "strict" meaning of the text as an invitation to unconstrained judicial activism.

I.5.3. "Living" interpretation

This approach is also known as "evolutionary interpretation" or "living tree" interpretation (the latter expression comes from a famous UK judgment, *Edwards v. A-G Canada*, [1930] A.C.124, regarding the meaning of words in the Canadian Constitution; it is excerpted below). It treats the constitution as an evolving document, one whose meaning should be modified and adapted in the light of current, progressive values. Sometimes, but not always, these values are identified as lying in international law, or as reflected in widespread practice, and associated judicial attitudes around the developed world. Often they are identified in current community attitudes. Like originalists and textualists, "living" constitutionalists start with the text of the constitution, but they ask what the meaning of the words encompasses today, rather than in the past. They treat the authority of the people who are alive today as having precedence over the authority of those who wrote the constitution. Both originalism and textualism, they argue, bind the living to the wishes of the dead, producing "meanings" that are out-of-date at best, and offensive to current values, at worst. Living constitutionalists see originalists as wanting to cling to the views of the past, and as using the constitution to entrench conservative values.

I.5.4. Pragmatism

Pragmatism is less concerned with the technique of interpretation and is more outcome-oriented. Like all judges, pragmatists start with the constitution's words, but they proceed to weigh up the words' alternative applications against the particular circumstances of the case at hand, and in the light of surrounding sociological factors and the goal of justice. They recognize that judges exercise discretion to choose from a range of available constitutional conclusions, and they maintain that the choice - the preferred meaning given to the words - should be guided by a combination of the text, common sense, the quest for a just outcome, and concern with the broader consequences. They reject the idea, found in other approaches, that an overarching or abstract principle can guide constitutional interpretation, a rejection succinctly captured in 1905 in the words of U.S. Supreme Court Justice Oliver Wendell Holmes: "General propositions do not decide concrete cases."

I.5.5. Applying these theories: the "Persons" case

Each of these theories can be evaluated in the landmark Privy Council decision interpreting the British North America (BNA) Act to permit the appointment of women to the Canadian Senate. Consider the opinion's rhetoric as well as the extent that the judges' opinion can be justified on each of the grounds discussed above.

REFERENCE TO MEANING OF WORD "PERSONS" IN SECTION 24 OF BRITISH NORTH AMERICA ACT, 1867
EDWARDS v. A.G. OF CANADA
[1930] A.C. 124

The judgment of their Lordships was delivered by LORD SANKEY, L.C.:

By sec. 24 of the *British North America Act, 1867*, it is provided that:

> The governor general shall from time to time, in the Queen's name, by instrument under the Great Seal of Canada, summon qualified persons to the Senate; and, subject to the provisions of this Act, every person so summoned shall become and be a member of the Senate and a senator.

The question at issue in this appeal is whether the words "qualified persons" in that section include a woman, and consequently whether women are eligible to be summoned to and become members of the Senate of Canada.

. . . .

On August 29, 1927, the appellants petitioned the Governor-General in Council to refer to the Supreme Court certain questions touching the powers of the Governor-General to summon female persons to the Senate, and upon October 19, 1927, the Governor-General in Council referred to the Supreme Court the aforesaid question. The case was heard before Chief Justice Anglin, Mr. Justice Duff, Mr. Justice Mignault, Mr. Justice Lamont and Mr. Justice Smith, and upon April 24, 1928, the Court answered the question in the negative ([1928] S.C.R. 276); the question being understood to be "Are women eligible for appointment to the Senate of Canada?"

The Chief Justice, whose judgment was concurred in by Mr. Justice Lamont and Mr. Justice Smith, and substantially by Mr. Justice Mignault, came to this conclusion upon broad lines mainly because of the common-law disability of women to hold public office and from a consideration of various cases which had been decided under different statutes as to their right to vote for a member of Parliament.

Mr. Justice Duff, on the other hand, did not agree with this view. He came to the conclusion that women are not eligible for appointment to the Senate upon the narrower ground that upon a close examination of the *British North America Act* of 1867 the word "persons" in sec. 24 is restricted to members of the male sex. The result therefore of the decision was that the Supreme Court was unanimously of opinion that the word "persons" did not include female persons, and that women are not eligible to be summoned to the Senate.

Their Lordships are of opinion that the word "persons" in sec. 24 *does* include women, and that women are eligible to be summoned to and become members of the Senate of Canada.

In coming to a determination as to the meaning of a particular word in a particular Act of Parliament it is permissible to consider two points, viz.: (i) The external evidence derived from extraneous circumstances such as previous legislation and decided cases; (ii) The internal evidence derived from the Act itself.

The exclusion of women from all public offices is a relic of days more barbarous than ours, but it must be remembered that the necessity of the times often forced on man customs which in later years were not necessary. . . .

In England no woman under the degree of a Queen or a Regent, married or unmarried, could take part in the government of the state. A woman was under a legal incapacity to be elected to serve in Parliament and even if a peeress in her own right she was not, nor is, entitled as an incident of peerage to receive a writ of summons to the House of Lords.

. . . .

They were excluded by the common law from taking part in the administration of justice either as Judges or as jurors, with the single exception of inquiries by a jury of matrons upon a suggestion of pregnancy: *Coke*, 2 Inst. 119, 3 Bl. Comm. 362.

. . . .

The passing of *Lord Brougham's Act* in 1850 [*An Act for shortening the Language used in Acts of Parliament*, 13-14 Vict., ch. 21] does not appear to have greatly affected the current of authority. Sec. 4 provided that in all Acts words importing the masculine gender shall be deemed and taken to include female unless the contrary as to gender is expressly provided.

The application and purview of that Act came up for consideration in *Chorlton v. Lings, supra*, where the Court of Common Pleas was required to construe a statute passed in 1861, which conferred the parliamentary franchise on every man possessing certain qualifications and registered as a voter. The chief question discussed was whether by virtue of *Lord Brougham's Act* the words "every man" included women. Chief Justice Bovill, having regard to the subject-matter of the statute and its general scope and language and to the important and striking nature of the departure from the common law involved in extending the franchise to women, declined to accept the view that Parliament had made that change by using the term "man" and held that the word was intentionally used expressly to designate the male sex . . . .

. . . .

Their Lordships now turn for a moment to the special history of the development of Canadian Legislature as bearing upon the matter under discussion. [The Committee reviewed a variety of Imperial and Canadian statutes using the word "persons" to describe office-holders. Their lordships found that the "appeal to history therefore in this particular matter is not conclusive."]

As far back as *Stradling v. Morgan* (1560) 1 Plowd. 199, at 209, 75 E.R. 305, it was laid down that extraneous circumstances may be admitted as an aid to the interpretation of a statute . . . but the argument must not be pushed too far and their Lordships are disposed to agree with Farwell, L.J., in *Rex v. West Riding of Yorkshire County Council*, [1906] 2 K.B. 676, "although it may, perhaps, be legitimate to call history in aid to show what facts existed to bring about a statute the inferences to be drawn therefrom are exceedingly slight:" see *Craies Statute*

Law, 3rd ed., p. 118.

Over and above that, their Lordships do not think it right to apply rigidly to Canada of to-day the decisions and the reasonings therefor which commended themselves, probably rightly, to those who had to apply the law in different circumstances, in different centuries to countries in different stages of development. . . .

Their Lordships now turn to the second point, namely: (ii) The internal evidence derived from the Act itself.

Before discussing the various sections they think it necessary to refer to the circumstances which led up to the passing of the Act.

The communities included within the Britannic system embrace countries and peoples in every stage of social, political and economic development and undergoing a continuous process of evolution.

His Majesty the King in Council is the final Court of Appeal from all these communities and this Board must take great care therefore not to interpret legislation meant to apply to one community by a rigid adherence to the customs and traditions of another. Canada had its difficulties both at home and with the mother country, but soon discovered that union was strength. Delegates from the three maritime provinces met in Charlottetown on September 1, 1864, to discuss proposals for a maritime union. A delegation from the coalition government of that day proceeded to Charlottetown and placed before the maritime delegates their schemes for a union embracing the Canadian provinces. As a result the Quebec conference assembled on October 10, continued in session till October 28 and framed a number of resolutions. These resolutions as revised by the delegates from the different provinces in London in 1866 were based upon a consideration of the rights of others and expressed in a compromise which will remain a lasting monument to the political genius of Canadian statesmen. Upon those resolutions the *British North America Act* of 1867 was framed and passed by the Imperial Legislature. The Quebec resolutions dealing with the Legislative Council, viz., Nos. 6-24, even if their Lordships are entitled to look at them, do not shed any light on the subject under discussion. They refer generally to the "members" of the Legislative Council.

The *British North America Act* planted in Canada a living tree capable of growth and expansion within its natural limits. The object of the Act was to grant a Constitution to Canada. Like all written constitutions it has been subject to development through usage and convention. [*Canadian Constitutional Studies, Sir Robert Borden* (1922) p. 55.]

Their Lordships do not conceive it to be the duty of this Board — it is certainly not their desire — to cut down the provisions of the Act by a narrow and technical construction, but rather to give it a large and liberal interpretation so that the Dominion to a great extent, but within certain fixed limits, may be mistress in her own house, as the provinces to a great extent, but within certain fixed limits, are mistresses in theirs. "The Privy Council, indeed, has laid down that Courts of law must treat the provisions of the *British North America Act* by the same methods of construction and exposition which they apply to other statutes. But there are statutes and statutes; and the strict construction deemed proper in the case, for example, of a penal or taxing statute or one passed to regulate the affairs of an English parish, would be often subversive of Parliament's real intent if applied to an Act passed to ensure the peace, order and good government of a British Colony." See *Clement's Canadian Constitution*, ed. 3, p. 347.

The learned author of that treatise quotes from the argument of Mr. Mowat and Mr. Edward Blake before the Privy Council in *St. Catharine's Milling and Lbr. Co. v. Reg.* (1888) 14 App. Cas. 46, at 50, 58 L.J.P.C. 54: The Act should be on all occasions interpreted in a large, liberal and comprehensive spirit, considering the magnitude of the subjects with which it purports to deal in very few words.

With that their Lordships agree, but as was said by the Lord Chancellor in *Brophy v. Atty.-Gen. for Man.*, [1895] A.C. 202, at 216, 64 L.J.P.C. 70, the question is not what may be supposed to have been intended, but what has been said.

It must be remembered, too, that their Lordships are not here considering the question of the legislative competence either of the Dominion or its provinces which arise under secs. 91 and 92 of the Act providing for the distribution of legislative powers and assigning to the Dominion and its provinces their respective spheres of government.

Their Lordships are concerned with the interpretation of an Imperial Act, but an Imperial Act which creates a constitution for a new country. Nor are their Lordships deciding any question as to the rights of women but only a question as to their eligibility for a particular position. No one either male or female has a right to be summoned to the Senate. The real point at issue is whether the Governor-General has a right to summon women to the Senate.

. . . .

It is in sec. 11 that the word "persons" which is used repeatedly in the Act, occurs for the first time.

It provides that the persons who are members of the Privy Council shall be from time to time chosen and summoned by the Governor-General.

The word "person" as above mentioned may include members of both sexes, and to those who ask why the word should include females, the obvious answer is why should it not.

In these circumstances the burden is upon those who deny that the word includes women to make out their case.

. . . .

It will be observed that sec. 21 provides that the Senate shall consist of 72 members who shall be styled senators. The word "member" is not in ordinary English confined to male persons. Sec. 24 provides that the Governor-General shall summon qualified persons to the Senate.

As already pointed out, "persons" is not confined to members of the male sex, but what effect does the adjective "qualified" before the word "persons" have?

In their Lordships' view it refers back to the previous section, which contains the qualifications of a senator. Subsecs. 2 and 3 appear to have given difficulties to the Supreme Court. Subsec. 2 provides that the qualification of a senator shall be that he shall be either a natural born subject of the Queen naturalized by an Act of Parliament of Great Britain or of one of the provincial Legislatures before the Union or of the Parliament of Canada after the Union. The Chief Justice in dealing with this says that it does not include those who become subjects by marriage, a provision which one would have looked for had it been intended to include women as being eligible.

. . . .

The reasoning of the Chief Justice [of Canada, in the decision below] would compel their Lordships to hold that the word "persons" as used in sec. 11 relating to the constitution of the Privy Council for Canada was limited to "male persons" with the resultant anomaly that a woman might be elected a member of the House of Commons but could not even then be summoned by the Governor-General as a member of the Privy Council.

. . . .

So far with regard to the sections dealing especially with the Senate — Are there any other sections in the Act which shed light upon the meaning of the word "persons"?

Their Lordships think that there are. For example, sec. 41 refers to the qualifications and disqualifications of persons to be elected or to sit or vote as members of the House of Assembly or Legislative Assembly and by a proviso it is said that until the Parliament of Canada otherwise provides at any election for a member of the House of Commons for the district of Algoma in addition to persons qualified by the law of the province of Canada to vote every male British subject aged 21 years or upwards being a householder shall have a vote. This section shows a distinction between "persons" and "males." If persons excluded females it would only have been necessary to say every person who is a British subject aged 21 years or upwards shall have a vote.

Again in sec. 84 referring to Ontario and Quebec a similar proviso is found stating that every male British subject in contra-distinction to "person" shall have a vote.

Again in sec. 133 it is provided that either the English or the French language may be used by any person or in any pleadings in or issuing from any Court of Canada established under this Act and in or from all of any of the Courts of Quebec. The word "person" there must include females as it can hardly have been supposed that a man might use either the English or the French language but a woman might not.

If Parliament had intended to limit the word "persons" in sec. 24 to male persons it would surely have manifested such intention by an express limitation as it has done in secs. 41 and 84. The fact that certain qualifications are set out in sec. 23 is not an argument in favour of further limiting the class, but is an argument to the contrary because it must be presumed that Parliament has set out in sec. 23 all the qualifications deemed necessary for a senator and it does not state that one of the qualifications is that he must be a member of the male sex.

. . . .

The history of these sections and their interpretation in Canada is not without interest and significance.

From Confederation to date both the Dominion Parliament and the provincial Legislatures have interpreted the word "persons" in secs. 41 and 84 of the *British North America Act* as including female persons and have legislated either for the inclusion or exclusion of women from the class of persons entitled to vote and to sit in the Parliament and Legislature respectively, and this interpretation has never been questioned. From Confederation up to 1916 women were excluded from the class of persons entitled to vote in both Federal and provincial elections.

From 1916 to 1922 various Dominion and provincial Acts were passed to admit women to the franchise and to the right to sit as members in both Dominion and provincial legislative bodies.

At the present time women are entitled to vote and to be candidates: (1) At all Dominion elections on the same basis as men; (2) At all provincial elections save in the province of Quebec.

From the date of the enactment of the *Interpretation Acts* in the province of Canada, Nova Scotia and New Brunswick prior to Confederation and in the Dominion of Canada since Confederation and until the franchise was extended, women have been excluded by express enactment from the right to vote.

Neither is it without interest to record that when upon May 20, 1867, the *Representation of the People Bill* came before a committee of the House of Commons, John Stuart Mill moved an amendment to secure women's suffrage and the amendment proposed was to leave out the word "man" in order to insert the word "person" instead thereof. See *Hansard*, 3rd series, vol. 187, column 817.

A heavy burden lies on an appellant who seeks to set aside a unanimous judgment of the Supreme Court, and this Board will only set aside such a decision after convincing argument and anxious consideration, but having regard

1. To the object of the Act, viz., to provide a constitution for Canada, a responsible and developing state;

2. that the word "person" is ambiguous and may include members of either sex;

3. that there are sections in the Act above referred to which show that in some cases the word "person" must include females;

4. that in some sections the words "male persons" is expressly used when it is desired to confine the matter in issue to males, and

5. to the provisions of the *Interpretation Act*;

their Lordships have come to the conclusion that the word "persons" in sec. 24 includes members both of the male and female sex and that, therefore, the question propounded by the Governor-General must be answered in the affirmative and that women are eligible to be summoned to and become members of the Senate of

Canada, and they will humbly advise His Majesty accordingly.

I.5.6.   Interpretation in different countries

In real life, it is rare for judges to stick rigidly to a particular methodology. Most judges tend to blend the different approaches, sometimes throughout their judicial lifetime, sometimes in the same judgment. Cases that come before a country's highest constitutional court are typically complex: the facts themselves are likely to be complicated; non-constitutional questions may be implicated or merged with constitutional questions; the relevant constitutional provisions themselves may clash (free speech versus freedom of religious worship, for example). This, in practice, makes constitutional interpretation a multifaceted task. For this reason, and because precedent — "stare decisis" — is a core principle in applying the law, almost all judges will follow a type of common law approach even in constitutional interpretation, in addition to their individual preferences for a particular interpretive methodology. They will look at the reasoning and the conclusions in similar-fact or analogous cases handed down in the past. They will be guided by these earlier cases, and will hesitate to depart from them. "Overruling" a prior judgment requires major justification and weighty reasons; it is done rarely. All courts that work within a common law system (including the courts we study here) adhere to these principles. There are, nevertheless, discernible differences between individual judges, between constitutional courts, and between constitutional "eras" in the same country. The lines of division tend to be clearer around the question of whether unwritten meanings should be found by implication; that is, derived indirectly from the words of the constitution. Originalists and textualists are adamantly opposed to "finding" constitutional meanings (especially constitutional rights) by implication. Living constitutionalists and pragmatists are open to going beyond the limited words of the constitution, and will ask what these words may imply or whether unwritten meanings may lie in them.

In the United States constitutional interpretation is a major topic of academic and judicial debate, attracting much greater attention than in other countries. Originalism is commonly the focus of these debates, and there are outspoken proponents and opponents of originalism on the current U.S. Supreme Court. In contrast, the Supreme Court of Canada tends to favor the "living" approach, and originalism attracts less attention in discussions of interpretive methodologies. Canadian Charter of Rights decisions will often speak, somewhat confusingly to outsiders, of a "purposive" approach, where judges seek to apply a provision in light of the "interests [that the guarantee] was meant to protect." *R. v. Big M Drug Mart, Ltd.*, [1985] 1 S.C.R. 295. But the failure to seriously inquire as to the original understandings of the drafters suggest that Canadian judges really are applying living interpretation to the Charter as well. In Australia, it is rare (although not unknown) for justices of the High Court to declare that they adhere to a particular methodology in constitutional interpretation; the Court tends to proceed, pragmatically, from case to case, rather than applying an overarching methodology. In the last 60 years or so (after a period broadly characterized by originalism, followed by a period of applying — or, at least, declaring that it was applying — principles of statutory interpretation to the constitution), the Court began to accept that some unwritten limitations on governmental power may be found, by implication from the text and structure, in the Australian Constitution. In the 1990s, it expanded this approach, and, although initially controversial, it has now become established. Despite the fact that the South African Constitution includes explicit guidelines for interpreting the Bill of Rights as well as various principles to guide interpretation of other clauses, the Constitutional Court of South Africa describes its approach to interpretation as "generous" and "purposive" and it has explicitly rejected originalism or simple textualism. To this extent it too has embraced a "living" interpretation of the Constitution.

The constitutional courts of Australia, Canada, and South Africa are all open to exploring what the courts of other countries have done, when similar constitutional questions have come before them (the South African Constitution expressly authorizes its court to look at foreign courts' judgments, and requires it to take guidance from international law in constitutional interpretation). This does not, however, mean that these courts are bound to follow other countries' judgments; but it does mean that a discussion of what another court has done is not infrequently found in their judgments. In the United States, in striking contrast, reference to foreign courts (and international law) is controversial; although it has occurred on some occasions, it is regarded by some people as illegitimate, and is rarely practiced by the Supreme Court.

Chapter 1

FEDERALISM

In a federal system, governmental power is constitutionally distributed between the national (federal) centre and regional parts (states or provinces). The parts are self-governing and semi-autonomous, but their laws apply only within their own territory. Laws made at the federal level apply across the whole nation. The specific history and constitutional politics of each nation leads framers of a federal system to devise general principles that determine when national majorities may not impose their will on dissenting citizens whose views may be in the majority in a state or province. Co-operative governance is based on the idea that governmental power is distributed according to the principle that the level of government at which a particular decision should be made is that level at which it would be most appropriate to make it. However, in contrast to federalism, co-operative governance allocates power based on the availability of information, expertise, and other relevant resources in the specific context, and provides mechanisms to achieve consensus.

KEY CONCEPTS FOR THE CHAPTER

- VIRTUALLY ALL FEDERAL SYSTEMS HAVE CONSTITUTIONAL PROVISIONS TO THE EFFECT THAT VALID LEGISLATION ENACTED BY THE FEDERAL LEGISLATURE TRUMPS CONTRARY OR INCONSISTENT LEGISLATION ENACTED BY STATE OR PROVINCIAL LEGISLATURES;

- THUS, THE KEY *CONSTITUTIONAL* ISSUES WITH REGARD TO FEDERALISM ARE:

  — WHEN SHOULD THERE BE A CONSTITUTIONAL LIMIT ON THE ABILITY OF THE FEDERAL LEGISLATURES TO ENACT STATUTES THAT FEDERAL LAWMAKERS BELIEVE REFLECT SOUND PUBLIC POLICY?

  — WHEN SHOULD THERE BE A CONSTITUTIONAL LIMIT ON THE ABILITY OF STATE/ PROVINCIAL LEGISLATURES TO ENACT STATUTES — IN THE ABSENCE OF CONTRADICTORY FEDERAL LAW — THAT THESE SUB-NATIONAL LAWMAKERS BELIEVE REFLECT SOUND PUBLIC POLICY?

- IN REVIEWING THESE MATERIALS, CONSIDER THE FOLLOWING:

  — WHAT DOES THE CONCEPT OF "STATES' RIGHTS" OR "PROVINCIAL RIGHTS" MEAN? ARE THERE POLICIES THAT YOU WOULD WANT TO BE ENACTED LOCALLY BUT NOT NATIONALLY?

  — WHY DO VARIOUS SUPREME COURTS GIVE BROADER CONSTRUCTION TO SOME POWERS AND NARROWER CONSTRUCTION TO OTHERS?

  — FOR EACH COUNTRY STUDIED, WOULD ACTIVE JUDICIAL SCRUTINY OF LEGISLATION TO ENSURE CENTRAL AND REGIONAL GOVERNMENTS MAINTAIN THEIR PROPER ROLE BEST ACHIEVE THE GOALS OF THE DESIRED CONSTITUTIONAL STRUCTURE? IS THE PROCESS-BASED APPROACH OF CO-OPERATIVE GOVERNANCE

BETTER SUITED TO SOME COUNTRIES AND NOT OTHERS? CAN SOME COUNTRIES RELY ON ORDINARY POLITICAL PROCESSES TO MAINTAIN THE DESIRED STRUCTURE?

1.1. THE CONCEPT OF FEDERALISM

Australia, Canada, and the United States are unusual (though not unique) among the world's nations in their birth as a federation of formerly independent colonies. (In contrast, for example, when South Americans united under Simon Bolivar achieved independence from Spain, they created independent nations roughly corresponding to the boundaries of Spanish imperial administrative districts.) As a result, unlike many nations, the *United States Constitution Act, 1787*, the *British North America Act, 1867*, the *Commonwealth of Australia Constitution Act, 1900* all create a national government with sovereign power constitutionally limited to specified subjects of legislative power, while some matters are constitutionally earmarked for the states or provinces. In contrast the *Constitution of the Republic of South Africa Act, 1996*, creates a government constituted by three distinct spheres, the "national, provincial and local spheres of government which are distinctive, interdependent and interrelated." Art. 40(1). As a result, the existence of nine provinces is only slightly more significant than the existence of six "category A" municipalities (metropolitan areas that contain the majority of the population and have authority over the provision of services and development within their jurisdictions).

1.1.1. Distinguishing constitutional federalism from efficiency decentralization

In considering these issues, it is important to distinguish carefully between constitutionally-mandated federalism, and the sort of decentralization or delegation of powers that occur in unitary states like France or in the delegation by state or provincial governments to local or regional units of government: federal constitutionalism precludes the federal legislature from exercising certain powers, even if federal officials think it would be better if it could do so. It typically implies judicial review of legislation on the ground that the enacting legislature overstepped its authority.

1.1.2. Why federalism?

The key details of this division of power differ in some significant ways from country to country: (1) precisely which matters are assigned to the federal or state/provincial level of government; (2) the role of courts in policing the divisions; and (3) the effect of modern values about national or regional solutions to social problems. Each country's founders chose a system of constitutional federalism for historically-specific reasons. Because the constitutional texts discussed below are broadly worded, judges over time have interpreted these texts in ways that incorporate, to varying degrees, current attitudes toward maintenance of a federal structure. Consider both the history and differing values of each country as you review the different texts and their judicial interpretation.

1.1.3. Distinguishing co-operative government

South Africa's 1996 final Constitution is unlike traditional forms of federalism, which assume the relative autonomy of different political units — either formerly sovereign entities or newly created subdivisions — and their exercise of certain specified powers. South Africa's Constitution creates a structure in which powers are simultaneously allocated and shared among different levels of government. A key aspect of this arrangement is a complex procedure for the resolution of conflicts over governance — between the respective legislative competencies, executive powers, and in relation to other branches and levels of government. Unlike the earlier Indian and Canadian examples, which retained central authority while allocating regional powers, South Africa's Constitution follows more closely in the footsteps of the German Constitution, placing less emphasis on geographic autonomy and more on the integration of geographic jurisdictions into separate functionally determined roles in the continuum of governance over specifically defined issues. Provision is made for some exclusive regional powers, but these are, by and large, of minor significance. All important and contested issues are included in the category of concurrent competence.

1.2. THE FEDERALISM OF THE CONSTITUTIONAL TEXTS

1.2.1. Canada

The basic principles of Canadian federalism are set forth in Part VI of the *BNA Act*. Provinces may only legislate regarding areas enumerated in ss. 92, 92A, 93, and 95. In cases of ambiguity, provinces may not legislate in areas deemed to be within federal jurisdiction under s. 91. In cases of overlap, legislation that is within the federal power under s. 91 is paramount over inconsistent provincial legislation. In addition, s. 91 provides that Parliament may legislate with regard to the "Peace Order, and good Government of Canada, in relation to all Matters not coming within the Classes of Subjects by this Act assigned exclusively to the Legislatures of the Provinces."

Three assignments of power are most significant for purposes of this chapter. Section 91(2) assigns jurisdiction for legislation relating to "trade and commerce" to Parliament. Section 91(27) assigns the criminal law to Parliament as well. Section 92(13) assigns "property and civil rights" to the provinces. An appreciation of Canadian federalism requires a brief historic overview of the significance of the concept of "property and civil rights." The phrase includes all laws governing the relationships between individuals (most generally covered by the law of property, contracts, and torts), as opposed to laws governing the relationship between citizens and government. The term first appeared in s. 8 of the *Quebec Act, 1774,* which restored French civil law as the private law in Canada.[1] The phrase was used

---

[1] This concession to civil law in an English colony, combined with unprecedented recognition of the Catholic Church and political and religious rights for practicing Catholics, was widely understood as a significant factor in the British success in keeping Quebec from joining with the colonies to the south in

again, following the British Parliament's division of "Canada" into a predominantly English-speaking Upper Canada (roughly Ontario) and a predominantly French-speaking Lower Canada in the *Constitutional Act, 1791*, by the first Act of the elected assembly of Upper Canada, which declared that "in all matters of controversy relative to property and civil rights, resort shall be had to the laws of England as the rule for the decision of the same." Accordingly, when the framers of Confederation divided powers between the federal and provincial governments and, in s. 91(13), assigned "property and civil rights" to the exclusive jurisdiction of the provinces, they were consciously continuing a constitutional bargain that had been present at the beginning of the concept of a Canadian nation to permit Quebec to use civil law. The evolution of judicial interpretation of that phrase, and its intersection with the broad textual grant of authority to the federal government under s. 91(2) to regulate "trade and commerce," is discussed in the *City National Leasing* case excerpted below.

It is essential to appreciate the historic compromise reflected in the assignment of powers between the federal and provincial governments. Prior imperial legislation had united Upper and Lower Canada, but with a parliament that assured equality of representation between the two. As Upper Canada grew larger, there was increasing demand for representation by population. However, the idea of a single population-based legislature for "the two Canadas" was completely unacceptable to the Quebecois, who believed that it would put "our civil law and religious institutions at the mercy of the fanatics." By creating a separate province of Quebec, the *BNA Act* "puts under the exclusive control of Lower Canada [Quebec] those questions which we did not want the fanatical partisans of [George Brown, the Liberal leader in Ontario] to deal with."[2] Modern scholars agree that "Quebec has been granted a mix of concurrent and exclusive jurisdiction over a wide range of policy areas that gives it the tools to ensure the survival of a francophone society." Sujit Choudhry, *Does the World Need More Canada? The Politics of the Canadian Model in Constitutional Politics and Political Theory, in* CONSTITUTIONAL DESIGN FOR DIVIDED SOCIETIES 147 (Sujit Choudhry ed., 2008).

Although the restoration of French *civil* law was seen as an essential element in maintaining the loyalty of French Canadians to the British crown, there was little opposition to the importation of English *criminal* law in the 18th Century. English law was seen as more lenient and certain, while French law at the time included features such as the preclusion of circumstantial evidence although it allowed use of confessions secured by torture. While Blackstone praised the genius of the

---

the Revolutionary War. Among the "Facts" to be "submitted to a candid world" to demonstrate that King George III's rule was a history of "repeated Injuries and Usurpations, all having in direct Object the Establishment of an absolute Tyranny over these States," the Declaration of Independence noted that he had combined with the British Parliament for acts of "pretended Legislation," include one "abolishing the free System of English Laws in a neighbouring Province, establishing therein an arbitrary Government, and enlarging its Boundaries, so as to render it at once an Example and fit Instrument for introducing the same absolute Rule in these colonies."

   [2] *See* A.I. SILVER, THE FRENCH-CANADIAN IDEA OF CONFEDERATION, 1864–1900, at 40 (1982) (*quoting Réponses aux censeurs de la Confédération* (St-Hyancinthe: Le Courrier 1867)). Note other provisions of the constitutional text have fallen into disuse, and (*see* Chapter 7) it would now be considered in violation of a constitutional convention for them to be revived. Most notably, this includes the power granted to Parliament in s. 90 of the *BNA Act* to disallow provincial legislation.

English common law of crime, Voltaire and other enlightenment figures criticized the French system. Thus, the English conquest ended the application of French criminal law in North America. At confederation, this division between criminal and civil law was continued, so that, while s. 92(13) gave Quebec the right to continue to use the French civil code, s. 91(27) maintained English criminal law by assigning this matter to Parliament.

1.2.2.   United States

The United States Constitution deals with federalism in a sparser and more implicit way. Article 1, Section 8 sets forth a list of powers authorized to the federal Congress. For purposes of this chapter, the most significant authorized power is the one to "regulate commerce with foreign nations, and among the several states, and with the Indian tribes." Sections 9 and 10 of that Article limit the power of both Congress and state legislatures. The Tenth Amendment provides that "powers not delegated to the United States by the Constitution, nor prohibited by it to the states, are reserved to the states respectively, or to the people."

In addition, several of the rights-creating constitutional amendments (most notably the "Civil War Amendments" that abolished slavery, required states to provide equal protection of the laws and due process to its citizens, and prohibited racial discrimination in voting) each contain provisos that authorize Congress to enforce the amendment by "appropriate legislation." This basis of congressional authority has no counterpart in Canada or Australia — the federal legislatures in those countries have no special power (perhaps with the exception of an emergency declaration under the Canadian POGG power, discussed in Part III-D below) to protect citizens against constitutional deprivations by provincial or state governments. Obviously, the difference is a legacy of the American Civil War. With the exception of linguistic rights specifically protected in ss. 16–19 and s. 23 of the Canadian Charter (we discuss this below in Chapter Five), there is no reason to believe that the Canadian federal government will be more or less hospitable to the rights of citizens than provincial governments. In contrast, the Civil War Amendments clearly reflect the view that the rebel states could not be trusted to protect the rights of former slaves.

Another reason for federal legislation to enforce constitutional rights is the dual court system in the United States. The most visible example today of the use of congressional power in this regard is 42 U.S.C. § 1983, which creates a federal cause of action (a tort claim) for violations of constitutional or federal statutory rights by those acting under color of state law. Absent this exercise of congressional power under §5 of the Fourteenth Amendment, constitutional torts would have to be litigated in state courts, by elected judges or those appointed by local officials. The ability to bring constitutional tort claims before federal judges with life tenure is a critical aspect in protecting constitutional liberties in the United States

The Congressional power to enforce constitutional rights has been recently circumscribed by the Supreme Court. An earlier decision suggested that this congressional power was indeed broad. The Voting Rights Act of 1965, for example, included a section that barred those with at least a 6th-grade education from

Puerto Rican schools from being denied the right to vote because of an inability to speak English. English literacy tests had been previously upheld against a challenge that this violated the equal protection rights of those unable to pass such tests. But in *Katzenbach v. Morgan*, 384 U.S. 641 (1966), the Court upheld the power of Congress to condemn that which the Court had previously upheld, under its broad power to enforce § 5 of the Fourteenth Amendment. More recently, though, the Court has trimmed back on this authority. *See, e.g., City of Boerne v. Flores*, 521 U.S. 507 (1997) (striking down Religious Freedom Restoration Act provisions imposing heavier burden on state government to sustain laws of general applicability that "substantially burden" the exercise of religion that the Court held was required under the First Amendment); *Kimel v. Florida Bd. of Regents*, 528 U.S. 62 (2000) (striking down provisions of the Age Discrimination in Employment Act imposing a heavier burden on employers to justify discriminatory treatment of workers on the basis of age, as applied to state and local government, than the Court held was required under the Equal Protection Clause of the Fourteenth Amendment). In a case we discuss in Chapter 9, the Court recently struck down key portions of the Voting Rights Act in *Shelby County v. Holder*, 133 S. Ct. 2612 (2013).

1.2.3.   Australia

The federation of the Australian colonies under the *Commonwealth of Australia Constitution Act, 1900* (Imp)[3] was the culmination of many years of inter-colonial initiatives, plus a final decade of formal steps. By 1890, all the colonies were self-governing, independent of each other, and protective of their autonomy. Once they began seriously to consider federating, there was no prospect of their agreeing to a unitary state, or to a powerful federal government; the political leaders whose support was essential included colonial premiers and other politicians who had no intention of giving up their own political power base. The Australian Constitution's approach to federalism was, thus, based on the model found in the United States. The Constitution's framers shared Canada's commitment to parliamentary government under the Crown, but they rejected Canada's version of federalism. The majority were advocates of "States rights" and did not consider the *British North American Act* to be adequate for the protection of the existing colonies when these were transformed into States. They believed the Canadian federal legislature to be too powerful, and the Canadian system of government over-centralized.

As in the United States, the Australia Constitution expressly allocates powers to the federal legislature (the Commonwealth Parliament). Section 51 sets down a list of specifically enumerated powers that the Commonwealth parliament may exercise. Most Commonwealth powers were intended to be "concurrent" (that is, exercisable at both the national and the state parliamentary level), albeit subject to the supremacy provision, s 109, which provides for Commonwealth laws to prevail over inconsistent state laws where these are on the same subject. Unlike the

---

[3] The parenthetical refers to the legislature enacting the statute. "Imp" refers to the British parliament acting in its imperial power for now-former colonies. "Cth" refers to the Australian federal parliament; Australia and its national government are constitutionally called the "Commonwealth."

Canadian model, Australia's Constitution does not enumerate the powers of the state arms of government, nor does it expressly restrict state powers (except via certain limitations on the exercise of legislative power, and a small number of powers that are exclusive to the Commonwealth). There is no provision in the Australian Constitution analogous to the U.S. Tenth Amendment, though it was assumed by the Constitution's framers that the enumeration of Commonwealth legislative powers meant a limitation on Commonwealth power and, by implication, that the states were free to exercise any residual powers. An implied protection of state government has, however, been read into the Constitution's guarantee of a federal system, and this has led to the invalidation of Commonwealth laws on more than one occasion (see the "Melbourne Corporation" doctrine, below).

1.2.4.   South Africa

Conflict over the distribution of power between the different levels of government among the parties negotiating South Africa's democratic transition was both contentious and at times intractable. There were however significant changes in the understanding of the issues as claims for "federalism" and local autonomy gave way to debates over the allocation of power and shared responsibilities of governance between different spheres of government. With the re-imagining of the ANC's initial demand for a unitary state as a claim of national sovereignty over the 1910 boundaries of South Africa, rather than a central government with pre-emptive power over regional authorities, the debate became centred around the allocation and interaction of authority between the three levels of government. With this new emphasis, the issue of federalism — which the ANC had initially rejected because of its historic association in South Africa with the white opposition Democratic Party and the emasculation of governmental powers — became, under the guise of regionalism or co-operative government, a central feature of the constitutional debate.

The adoption of the language of "strong regionalism" by both the ANC and the National Party government also reflected the National Party's acceptance that the absolute veto powers of the upper house of the legislature would be limited to regional matters and its notion of political party-based consociationalism (a form of government based on guaranteed group representation, often associated with guaranteed power-sharing) would be formally restricted to local government structures. However, unlike the ANC and the National Party, the Inkatha Freedom Party (IFP) (a rival black political party founded by a Zulu tribal chieftain) refused to concede its claim to regional autonomy, and its alliance with white pro-apartheid parties continued to threaten to disrupt the democratic transition. Although factions of the IFP seemed ready to contest the elections for the KwaZulu-Natal regional government, the party's leader Chief Gatsha Buthelezi interpreted his party's poor showing in pre-election polls as cause to promote an even more autonomous position: encouraging and supporting King Goodwill Zwelethini in his demand for the restoration of the 19th-century Zulu monarchy with territorial claims beyond even the borders of present-day KwaZulu-Natal.

Although supporters of a federal solution advocated for a national government of limited powers, the interim Constitution instead allocated enumerated powers to the provinces. This allocation of regional powers was included in a set of criteria incorporated into the constitutional guidelines and in those sections of the Constitution dealing with the legislative powers of the provinces. The IFP, however, rejected this solution, on the grounds that the Constitution failed to guarantee the autonomy of the provinces. Despite the ANC's protestations that the provincial powers guaranteed by the Constitution could not be withdrawn, the IFP pointed to the fact that the allocated powers were only concurrent powers and that the national legislature could supersede local legislation by establishing a national legislative framework covering any subject matter. This tension between provincial autonomy and the ANC's assertion of the need to establish national frameworks guaranteeing minimum standards and certain basic equalities led to an amendment to the 1993 Constitution before the Constitution even came into force. This amendment granted exclusive powers to the provinces in those areas in which they exercised legislative authority. In addition, the amendment granted exclusive jurisdiction to provincial legislatures in the following areas: agriculture; gambling; cultural affairs; education at all levels except tertiary; environment; health; housing; language policy; local government; nature conservation; police; state media; public transport; regional planning and development; road traffic regulation; roads; tourism; trade and industrial promotion; traditional authorities; urban and rural development and welfare services. Difficulty arose in distinguishing the exact limits of a region's exclusive powers and the extent to which the national legislature was able to pass general laws affecting rather broad areas of governance.

The outcome was a complete reframing of regionalism in the Constitutional Assembly that met to draft the final constitutional document, and the adoption of co-operative government as the basis for government at all levels from the local to the national. Chapter 3 of the 1996 Constitution lays out the constitutional scheme of co-operative government. Most Constitutions rely either on the very structure of the Constitution to establish a "federal" relationship between different regional units or provide specifically for a hierarchy of governments in which the national government allocates powers to the regions or the regions enjoy a degree of autonomy. South Africa's system of co-operative governance is unique in the way it defines different spheres of government and tries to constitutionally regulate their relative roles to facilitate intergovernmental relations across the different loci of governance in the country. Section 40(1) states that the "government is constituted as national, provincial and local spheres of government which are distinctive, interdependent and interrelated." The principles of co-operative government and intergovernmental relations listed in sections 41(1) (a)–(h) and 41 (2)–(4) go on to define the specific duties that each level of government owes to the other as well as the duty of the legislature to adopt legislation creating institutions and mechanisms to facilitate intergovernmental relations and to resolve disputes between different levels of government. At the same time, the Final Constitution adopted a rough division of legislative power: Schedule 4 lists functional areas of concurrent legislative competence, embracing key issues including health services and housing; Schedule 5 lists areas that are presumptively the domain of provincial and local governments; residual matters not listed are reserved exclusively for the national legislature.

Apart from the general commitments to preserve peace and national unity, secure the well-being of the people and provide "effective, transparent, accountable and coherent government," the key boundaries laid down in section 41 of the Constitution require each level of government to "respect the constitutional status, institutions, powers and functions of government in the other spheres," and not to "assume any power or function except those conferred on them in terms of the Constitution." These boundaries also require the different levels of government to "exercise their powers and perform their functions in a manner that does not encroach on the geographical, functional or institutional integrity" of other governing authorities. Instead, s. 41(1)(h) of the Constitution seeks to promote an ethos of co-operation based on "mutual trust and good faith." Finally, s. 41(3) of the Constitution requires an organ of state "involved in an intergovernmental dispute," to make "every reasonable effort to settle the dispute . . . [and] exhaust all other remedies before it approaches a court to resolve the dispute." This last element is strengthened by s. 41(4), providing that a court may refer a dispute back to parties involved if it is not satisfied that they have exhausted all non-legal remedies or made every reasonable effort to settle the dispute by other means.

1.3.   BASIC PRINCIPLES OF CANADIAN FEDERALISM

This Part reviews the basic doctrines of Canadian federalism. Several things become apparent after this review. The early and controversial holdings come from the body that was the final interpreter of Canadian law until 1949, the Judicial Committee of the British Privy Council. These holdings have two prominent features — a narrow interpretation of the federal power to regulate "trade & commerce" and a broad interpretation of the provincial power over "property & civil rights." Even as these holdings have been modified, we see that Canadian courts still actively engage in review of legislative material to ensure that a fair federal/provincial balance is maintained.

1.3.1.   Early doctrine: narrow construction of the Trade & Commerce power

1.3.1.1.   First cases

The first Privy Council case to shape Canadian federalism by limiting federal power related to an Ontario regulatory statute, which was challenged on the grounds that the matter related to trade and commerce and thus was exclusively within the jurisdiction of the federal Parliament. In *Citizens Insurance Co. v. Parsons,* 7 App. Cas. 96 (1881), the Privy Council established some early principles. First, their Lordships (the judges) acknowledged that in real life there was no "sharp and definite distinction" between the powers assigned to Parliament by s. 91 of the *BNA Act* and those assigned to provincial legislatures by s. 92 of the Act. Second, the court held that the framers could not have intended the federal powers to broadly trump any provincial power; the court reasoned that the federal power over marriage and divorce in s. 91 (26) had to be read in conjunction with s. 92 (12)'s assignment of the "solemnization of marriage" to the provinces. Thus:

In these cases it is the duty of the Courts, however difficult it may be, to ascertain in what degree, and to what extent, authority to deal with matters falling within these classes of subjects exists in each legislature, and to define in the particular case before them the limits of their respective powers. It could not have been the intention that a conflict should exist; and, in order to prevent such a result, the two sections must be read together, and the language of one interpreted, and, where necessary, modified, by that of the other. In this way it may, in most cases, be found possible to arrive at a reasonable and practical construction of the language of the sections, so as to reconcile the respective powers they contain, and give effect to all of them. In performing this difficult duty, it will be a wise course for those on whom it is thrown, to decide each case which arises as best they can, without entering more largely upon an interpretation of the statute than is necessary for the decision of the particular question in hand.

Third, the Lords established the principle of narrow construction of the Trade & Commerce power (s. 91(2)) and the broad construction of the Property & Civil Rights power (s. 92(13)). The "fair and ordinary meaning" of "civil rights" included rights arising from contract, and the Lords noted that the assignment of authority relating to a host of commercially-related topics in s. 91 would be superfluous if these fell within the federal Trade & Commerce authority. Most significantly, the Lords added an important historical reason for this principle:

> If, however, the narrow construction of the words "civil rights," contended for by the appellants were to prevail, the dominion parliament could, under its general power, legislate in regard to contracts in all and each of the provinces and as a consequence of this the province of Quebec, though now governed by its own Civil Code, founded on the French law, as regards contracts and their incidents, would be subject to have its law on that subject altered by the dominion legislature, and brought into uniformity with the English law prevailing in the other three provinces, notwithstanding that Quebec has been carefully left out of the uniformity section of the Act.

Given the paramountcy of federal law, broad construction of provincial authority was not enough; the federal power had to be limited to "political arrangements in regard to trade requiring the sanction of parliament, regulation of trade in matters of inter-provincial concern, and it may be that they would include general regulation of trade affecting the whole dominion."

The next case confirmed the limited federal role.

IN RE THE BOARD OF COMMERCE ACT, 1919, AND THE COMBINES AND FAIR PRICES ACT, 1919

PRIVY COUNCIL

[1922] 1 A.C. 191

[Before VISCOUNT HALDANE, LORD BUCKMASTER, VISCOUNT CAVE, LORD PHILLIMORE, and LORD CARSON]

The judgment of their Lordships was delivered by VISCOUNT HALDANE.

*   *   *

The second of these statutes, the *Combines and Fair Prices Act*, enables the Board established by the first statute to restrain and prohibit the formation and operation of such trade combinations for production and distribution in the Provinces of Canada as the Board may consider to be detrimental to the public interest. The Board may also restrict, in the cases of food, clothing and fuel, accumulation of these necessaries of life beyond the amount reasonably required, in the case of a private person, for his household, not less than in the case of a trader for his business. The surplus is in such instances to be offered for sale at fair prices. Certain persons only, such as farmers and gardeners, are excepted. Into the prohibited cases the Board has power to inquire searchingly, and to attach what may be criminal consequences to any breach it determines to be improper. An addition of a consequential character is thus made to the criminal law of Canada.

[The Court put aside the question whether such a statute could be enacted "to meet special conditions in wartime."] It is to the Legislatures of the Provinces that the regulation and restriction of their civil rights have in general been exclusively confided, and as to these the Provincial Legislatures possess quasi-sovereign authority. It can, therefore, be only under necessity in highly exceptional circumstances, such as cannot be assumed to exist in the present case, that the liberty of the inhabitants of the Provinces may be restricted by the Parliament of Canada, and that the Dominion can intervene in the interests of Canada as a whole in questions such as the present one. For normally, the subject-matter to be dealt with in the case would be one falling within s. 92. Nor do the words in s. 91, the "Regulation of trade and commerce," if taken by themselves, assist the present Dominion contention. It may well be, if the Parliament of Canada had, by reason of an altogether exceptional situation, capacity of interfere, that these words would apply so as to enable that Parliament to oust the exclusive character of the Provincial powers under s. 92.

*   *   *

As their Lordships have already indicated, the jurisdiction attempted to be conferred on the new Board of Commerce appears to them to be *ultra vires* for the reasons now discussed. [Ed. note: Because Canada's constitutional scheme of federalism contained in ss. 91 and 92 of the *British North America Act* divides legislative matters between the federal and provincial governments, Canadian courts use the term "*intra vires*" (within the power) to describe legislation properly enacted under one of the constitutionally-delegated powers, and *"ultra vires"* (beyond the power) to describe legislation whose subject matter has been allocated elsewhere.]***

*   *   *

Legislation setting up a Board of Commerce with such powers appears to their Lordships to be beyond the powers conferred by s. 91. *** For throughout the provisions of [the *BNA Act*] there is apparent the recognition that subjects which would normally belong exclusively to a specifically assigned class of subject may, under different circumstances and in another aspect, assume a further significance. Such an aspect may conceivably become of paramount importance, and of dimensions that give rise to other aspects. This is a principle which, although recognized in earlier decisions, such as that of *Russell v. The Queen*, both here and in the Courts of Canada, has always been applied with reluctance, and its recognition as relevant can be justified only after scrutiny sufficient to render it clear that the circumstances are abnormal. [Ed. note: *Russell* upheld a federal law authorizing local governments to ban alcohol; it has subsequently been distinguished as within the federal authority because of the "emergency" facing the country because of the "evils" of alcohol, a distinction that many today find unpersuasive.] In the case before them, however important it may seem to the Parliament of Canada that some such policy as that adopted in the two Acts in question should be made general throughout Canada, their Lordships do not find any evidence that the standard of necessity referred to has been reached, or that the attainment of the end sought is practicable, in view of the distribution of legislative powers enacted by the Constitution Act, without the cooperation of the Provincial Legislatures. ***But even this consideration affords no justification for interpreting the words of s. 91, sub-s. 2, in a fashion which would, as was said in the argument on the other side, make them confer capacity to regulate particular trades and businesses.

1.3.2.   The modern view of Trade & Commerce

The Privy Council's jurisprudence narrowing the power of the new central government was sufficiently contrary to what scholars believe were the expectations of the Canadian drafters of the *BNA Act* that one scholar referred to the Judges of the Privy Council as the "wicked stepfathers of Confederation." Hogg, § 5.3(c) (quoting constitutional scholar E. A. Forsey).[4] The notion that this early jurisprudence may have reflected a refusal or inability of British Lords to appreciate the special Canadian circumstances is hinted at in this modern reappraisal by a Supreme Court of Canada no longer answerable to Westminster.

---

[4] The reference is to Peter Hogg's treatise, CONSTITUTIONAL LAW OF CANADA. The work is available in libraries in a comprehensive loose-leaf edition, and also a one-volume paperback "student edition." The section references are the same in both versions (although the student edition omits some chapters).

The term "framers" is a bit more complex in the context of the *BNA Act* than in the context of the American or Australian Constitution. The legislation was originally drafted by leading Canadian politicians in meetings at Quebec and Charlottetown, but the final version of the Act was tinkered with by British drafters before its eventual adoption by the UK Parliament in 1867. A focus on "original intent" usually looks at the views of the Canadians.

GENERAL MOTORS OF CANADA LTD. v. CITY NATIONAL LEASING

SUPREME COURT OF CANADA
[1989] 1 S.C.R. 641

[Before DICKSON C.J. and BEETZ, MCINTYRE, LAMER, LE DAIN, LA FOREST and L'HEUREUX-DUBE JJ. LE DAIN J. took no part in the judgment.]

The judgment of the Court was delivered by

THE CHIEF JUSTICE — The principal issue in this appeal is the constitutional validity of s. 31.1 of the *Combines Investigation Act*, R.S.C. 1970, c. C-23. Section 31.1 creates a civil cause of action for certain infractions of the *Combines Investigation Act*. It is this fact which makes the section constitutionally suspect: a civil cause of action is within the domain of the provinces to create. [The legislation permits damage recovery for any "person who has suffered loss or damage as a result of conduct" that is illegal under Part V of the *Combines Investigation Act*. Part V prohibits price fixing, bid-rigging, and, relevant to this case, price discrimination — sales at different prices. In this case the plaintiff City National Leasing ("CNL") alleged that General Motors ("GM") illegally provided discriminatory support for low-interest car loans to CNL's competitors, in violation of the price discrimination provisions of the Act. The civil cause of action is basically a tort remedy: providing money damages for those injured by wrongful conduct. Jurisdiction over torts is quintessentially an aspect of "property and civil rights" within provincial jurisdiction.] The essential question raised by this appeal is whether s. 31.1 can, nevertheless, be upheld as constitutionally valid by virtue of its relationship with the *Combines Investigation Act*. Answering this question requires addressing two issues: first, is the Act valid under the federal trade and commerce power, expressed in s. 91(2) of the *Constitution Act*, 1867; and second, is s. 31.1 integrated with the Act in such a way that it too is *intra vires* under s. 91(2).

For the reasons which follow, I have found s. 31.1 to be *intra vires* the federal Parliament. ***

IV

The General Trade and Commerce Power

* * *

[Here, Dickson, C.J., re-affirmed critical principles established by the Privy Council in *Citizens' Insurance Company of Canada v. Parsons*. He secured majority support for reasons he had previously set forth in a separate opinion in *Attorney General of Canada v. Canadian National Transportation*, 2 S.C.R. 206, 258 (1983), reading *Parsons* as having established three important propositions with regard to the federal trade and commerce power:

". . . (i) it does not correspond to the literal meaning of the words "regulation of trade and commerce"; (ii) it includes not only arrangements

with regard to international and interprovincial trade but "it may be that
. . . (it) would include general regulation of trade affecting the whole
dominion"; (iii) it does not extend to regulating the contracts of a particular
business or trade."]

. . . .

The treatment of the general trade and commerce power in the cases just
mentioned was no doubt strongly influenced by earlier Privy Council decisions on s.
91(2) and in particular what Anglin C.J. referred to in *The King v. Eastern
Terminal Elevator Co.*, [(1925) S.C.R. 434, 441], as ". . . their Lordships' emphatic
and reiterated allocation of 'the regulation of trade and commerce' to . . . [a]
subordinate and wholly auxiliary function . . . ." As Professor McDonald observed
in his article "Constitutional Aspects of Canadian Anti-Combines Law Enforcement" (1969), 47 Can. Bar Rev. 161, at p. 189:

> "The *British North America Act* was framed with a greater interest in
> central control than motivated the constitutional fathers to the south.
> Reaction in the founding provinces to the consequences of decentralized
> control in the United States has been well documented. The broad and
> unqualified language of section 91(2) reflected the basic interest that
> strength from economic unity replace the floundering provincial economies.
> Yet, as the American courts broadened their commerce clause until it
> meant essentially what the Fathers of Confederation had sought for
> Canada, so have the Privy Council and the Canadian courts reacted against
> the hopes of the framers of their constitution and have decentralized
> commercial control.

> At least until relatively recently the history of interpretation of the trade
> and commerce power has almost uniformly reinforced the federal paralysis
> which resulted from a series of Privy Council decisions in the years
> 1881-1896. The predominant view was that section 91(2) did not in any way
> go to either general commerce, contracts, particular trades or occupations,
> or commodities so far as those things might be intraprovincial. The test for
> the local nature of a transaction was abstractly legal, divorced from
> commercial effect."

Since 1949 and the abolition of appeals to the Privy Council, the trade and
commerce power has, I think it fair to say, enjoyed an enhanced importance . . . .

In examining cases which have considered s. 91(2), it is evident that courts have
been sensitive to the need to reconcile the general trade and commerce power of the
federal government with the provincial power over property and civil rights.
Balancing has not been easy. ***

The true balance between property and civil rights and the regulation of trade
and commerce must lie somewhere between an all pervasive interpretation of s.
91(2) and an interpretation that renders the general trade and commerce power to
all intents vapid and meaningless.

[Dickson then proceeded to set for a modern standard for the exercise of
Parliament's Trade and Commerce Power under s. 91(2), borrowing from the

majority opinion in *MacDonald v. Vapor Canada Ltd.*, [1977] 2 S.C.R. 134 (upholding most provisions of the *Trade Marks Act* but struck down as *ultra vires* a catch-all provision that prohibited anyone from adopting "any other business practice contrary to honest industrial or commercial usage in Canada") and his own minority opinion in *Canadian National Transportation, supra*.] First, the impugned legislation must be part of a general regulatory scheme. Second, the scheme must be monitored by the continuing oversight of a regulatory agency. Third, the legislation must be concerned with trade as a whole rather than with a particular industry. ***

[Fourth], the legislation should be of a nature that the provinces jointly or severally would be constitutionally incapable of enacting; and [fifth] the failure to include one or more provinces or localities in a legislative scheme would jeopardize the successful operation of the scheme in other parts of the country. These [requirements] serve to ensure that federal legislation does not upset the balance of power between federal and provincial governments. In total, the five factors provide a preliminary check-list of characteristics, the presence of which in legislation is an indication of validity under the trade and commerce power. These indicia do not, however, represent an exhaustive list of traits that will tend to characterize general trade and commerce legislation. Nor is the presence or absence of any of these five criteria necessarily determinative.

*   *   *

V

Approach to Determining Constitutionality

*   *   *

In determining the proper test it should be remembered that in a federal system it is inevitable that, in pursuing valid objectives, the legislation of each level of government will impact occasionally on the sphere of power of the other level of government; overlap of legislation is to be expected and accommodated in a federal state. Thus a certain degree of judicial restraint in proposing strict tests which will result in striking down such legislation is appropriate. [T]he question in this appeal of how far federal legislation may validly impinge on provincial powers is one part of the general notion of the "pith and substance" of legislation; i.e., the doctrine that a law which is federal in its true nature will be upheld even if it affects matters which appear to be a proper subject for provincial legislation (and vice versa). On page 334 of his book Constitutional Law of Canada, supra, Professor Hogg explains this in the following way:

> "The pith and substance doctrine enables a law that is classified as "in relation to" a matter within the competence of the enacting body to have incidental or ancillary effects on matters outside the competence of the enacting body."

*   *   *

The steps in the analysis may be summarized as follows. First, the court must determine whether the impugned provision can be viewed as intruding on provincial powers, and if so to what extent (if it does not intrude, then the only possible issue is the validity of the act). Second, the court must establish whether the act (or a severable part of it) is valid; in cases under the second branch of s. 91(2) this will normally involve finding the presence of a regulatory scheme and then ascertaining whether that scheme meets the requirements articulated in *Vapor Canada, supra,* and in *Canadian National Transportation, supra.* If the scheme is not valid, that is the end of the inquiry. If the scheme of regulation is declared valid, the court must then determine whether the impugned provision is sufficiently integrated with the scheme that it can be upheld by virtue of that relationship. This requires considering the seriousness of the encroachment on provincial powers, in order to decide on the proper standard for such a relationship. If the provision passes this integration test, it is *intra vires* Parliament as an exercise of the general trade and commerce power. If the provision is not sufficiently integrated into the scheme of regulation, it cannot be sustained under the second branch of s. 91(2). ***

[The Court then examined the Act and concluded that, although it did encroach on the significant provincial power to establish civil actions under s. 92(13), it was a permissible encroachment in light of the limited remedy to specific violations of federal law. The Court next found that the Act's regulation of anti-competitive activities operates under the watchful gaze of a regulatory agency, and it is quite clearly concerned with the regulation of trade in general, rather than with the regulation of a particular industry or commodity. Finally, the Court emphasized that Canada was a single marketplace and thus competition law was a "genre of legislation that could not practically or constitutionally be enacted by a provincial government."].

———

Note that the modern Canadian courts continue to limit federal regulation of commercial activities to those areas that practically escape provincial regulation. This concept was reaffirmed in the *Securities Act Reference*, [2011] 2 S.C.R. 837, striking down comprehensive federal securities regulation because the federal government failed to demonstrate why each part of the Act could not be accomplished provincially. In this regard, a leading Canadian political scientist has defended the "stepfathers" in their narrowing of federal power arguably in ways inconsistent with original intent. *See* Alan Cairns, *The Judicial Committee and its Critics,* 4 CAN. J. POL. SCI. 301 (1971). Cairns argues that increased regional diversity as Canada expanded from four to ten provinces, and partisan disputes between Conservative federal Prime Minister John A. Macdonald and Liberal Ontario Premier Oliver Mowat, resulted in an "increasingly federal society." Once the federal government had built railroads and developed the continental nation, Canadians saw a greater need for policymaking at the provincial level. *See also* PIERRE ELLIOT TRUDEAU, FEDERALISM AND THE FRENCH CANADIANS 198(1968), (if law lords had not favoured provinces, Quebec separatism might have occurred).

1.3.3. The limits to the "POGG" and Agriculture power

The effort to protect the broad provincial power over "property & civil rights" might also have been significantly evaded had Canadian courts permitted Parliament a wide berth in passing legislation under their residual power to legislate, in regard to matters not expressly assigned to the provinces, "to make laws for the peace, order, and good government of Canada, in relation to all matters not coming within the classes of subjects by this Act assigned exclusively to the Legislatures of the provinces." (The expression "peace, order, and good government" does not suggest an evaluation of the quality of the laws passed by the parliament, or establish any grounds for judicial review of a statute. Rather, it is a traditional formula used in British constitutional enactments (used also in the Australian Constitution) that merely signifies that the parliament has plenary power.) To preserve significant limits on federal power, the POGG power has been limited to three areas. First, Parliament may legislate in areas unspecified by the distribution of powers in ss. 91 and 92. Examples include legislation mandating bilingualism in the federal government and regulation of offshore minerals beyond provincial boundaries. Second, Parliament may exercise its POGG power in emergencies, even when intruding on matters of provincial concern. Thus, wartime price and rent controls have been sustained, and, more controversially, legislative controls to limit the inflationary spiral of the 1970s were also upheld. The latter is seemingly difficult to reconcile with the "New Deal" cases, discussed in Hogg, § 17.4(a), where the Privy Council held that measures taken during the Great Depression could not be sustained under POGG.

Finally, the modern era has seen growing recognition of Parliament's power to legislate regarding matters of "national concern." The leading precedent is one of the last major constitutional decisions from the Privy Council, *A.-G. Ontario v. Canada Temperance Federation*, [1946] A.C. 193, 206: the POGG power extends to legislation "if it is such that it goes beyond local or provincial concern or interests and must *from its inherent nature* be the concern of the Dominion as a whole." (emphasis added). Examples include aeronautics, regulation of the national capital region (Ottawa and its environs are fully part of the provinces of Ontario and Quebec, unlike Washington, DC), and marine pollution. As a general matter, these involve topics where provincial governments are deemed unable — either because of formal limits or practical politics — to legislate.

Significantly for comparative purposes, although the precise contours of the national concern test are unclear, Professor Hogg suggests, § 17.3(b), that the POGG power exists to permit legislation when national uniformity is not only desirable but essential, in that the problem cannot be dealt with at a provincial level. Thus, an essential aspect of a federal system is that some laws will be non-uniform even if a national majority prefers a uniform rule, but there are circumstances when provinces have an insufficient incentive to act because legislation is needed to solve a problem where the mischief is felt primarily extra-territorially. Thus, the inability of Quebec and Ontario to cooperate in the well-planned development of the national capital region around Ottawa would have harmed the national interest. Environmental protection is a critical area in this regard (and a source of significant practical and theoretical controversy in the

United States): provinces will not seriously consider the environmental harm beyond their own territory in requiring sacrifices and increased costs for industry. In both these situations, the POGG power applies. Of course, any national government has to have the power to act when problems cannot be dealt with at a decentralized level. Consider later how Americans, South Africans and Australians try to resolve this problem.

The Court's desire to protect unfettered provincial control over all local trade also led to substantial judicially-created limits on the textually-broad declaration in s. 95 of the *BNA Act* that "the Parliament of Canada may from Time to Time make Laws in relation to Agriculture in all or any of the Provinces" and that provincial laws relating to agriculture are only effective "as long and as far only as [they are] not repugnant to any Act of the Parliament of Canada." Yet in the *Margarine Reference*, [1949] S.C.R. 1, 52, Rand, J. struck down a federal law banning manufacturing of margarine as unrelated to agriculture; rather, the legislation was deemed to relate to "a product of agriculture" and thus beyond federal jurisdiction.

1.3.4. The breadth of the criminal law power

As noted above in section 3.1, federal power over criminal law dates to the 1774 compromise permitting civil law to remain in Quebec while English criminal law was substituted for the French without opposition. The plenary authority of Parliament to regulate anti-social conduct through criminal law has been consistently upheld. Thus, although regulation of anti-consumer business practices under the Trade & Commerce power was struck down in *Board of Commerce, supra*, when Parliament criminalized price fixing and monopolization it was upheld under the criminal law power. *Proprietary Articles Trade Ass'n v. A.-G. for Canada*, [1931] A.C. 310 (P.C.). Their Lordships held that s. 91(27) included "the criminal law in its widest sense" so would be upheld as long as "Parliament genuinely determines that commercial activities which can be so described are to be suppressed in the public interest."

> Criminal law connotes only the quality of such acts or omissions as are prohibited under appropriate penal provisions by authority of the State. The criminal quality of an act cannot be discerned by intuition; nor can it be discovered by reference to any standard but one: Is the act prohibited with penal consequences? Morality and criminality are far from co-extensive; nor is the sphere of criminality necessarily part of a more extensive field covered by morality - unless the moral code necessarily disapproves all acts prohibited by the State, in which case the argument moves in a circle. It appears to their Lordships to be of little value to seek to confine crimes to a category of acts which by their very nature belong to the domain of "criminal jurisprudence"; for the domain of criminal jurisprudence can only be ascertained by examining what acts at any particular period are declared by the State to be crimes, and the only common nature they will be found to possess is that they are prohibited by the State and that those who commit them are punished.*** The contrast is with matters which are merely attempts to interfere with Provincial rights, and are sought to be justified under the head of "criminal law" colourably and

merely in aid of what is in substance an encroachment. The Board
considered that the *Combines and Fair Prices Act of 1919* came within the
latter class, and was in substance an encroachment on the exclusive power
of the Provinces to legislate on property and civil rights.***

MORGENTALER v. THE QUEEN (" *Morgentaler I*")
SUPREME COURT OF CANADA
[1976] 1 S.C.R. 616

[Before LASKIN, C.J.C., MARTLAND, JUDSON, RITCHIE, SPENCE, PIGEON, DICKSON,
BEETZ and DE GRANDPRE, JJ.]

[Ed. note: The Anglo tradition is to list the Justices' opinion in the order of their
seniority, regardless of whether the senior-authored opinion is in the majority. This
may appear confusing for American readers.]

LASKIN, C.J.C. (dissenting) :This appeal, which is before this Court as of right under
s. 618(2) of the *Criminal Code*, presents the highly unusual, if not the singularly
exceptional, situation of an appellate Court itself entering a conviction after setting
aside a jury verdict of acquittal.[5] The appellant, Dr. Henry Morgentaler, was
acquitted on the verdict of a jury of unlawfully procuring the miscarriage of a
female person, contrary to s. 251 of the *Criminal Code*. That verdict was set aside
and a conviction was entered by the Quebec Court of Appeal which found it
unnecessary to send the case back for a new trial.

[Ed. note: Section 251 of the *Criminal Code* is discussed in detail in Chapter 2.
It provided for life imprisonment for anyone to intentionally cause an abortion, and
for two years imprisonment for a woman to intentionally obtain an abortion.
However, the proscription did not apply to any doctor or patient if permission for an
abortion was first obtained from a hospital committee who determined that a
continued pregnancy would endanger the woman's life or health.]

[First, rejecting the claim that the statute unconstitutionally interfered with the
provincial authority contained in s. 92(7) over hospitals, the Court concluded that
this argument would not suffice if the legislation constituted the valid exercise of
Parliament's criminal law power.]

[Next, the Court reaffirmed the "wide scope" of the federal criminal law power.
Those opposed to the exercise of broad power must turn to the political process]
unless it is made plain to the Court that the use of the penal sanction was a

---

[5] [Ed. note: Canadian practice permits the prosecutor (referred to as "the Crown") to appeal from
acquittals of criminal defendants, just as defendants can appeal from convictions. This was not changed
by the double jeopardy provision of *Charter of Rights and Freedoms*, s. 11(*h*), which guarantees
defendants the right, "if *finally* acquitted of the offense, not to be tried for it again" (emphasis added),
and this has been held to preserve the Crown's right of appeal. Following *Morgentaler I*, Parliament
amended s. 686(4)(b)(ii) of the *Criminal Code*, which governs Crown appeals of verdicts favorable to the
accused, to permit the court of appeal to enter a verdict of guilty only where the acquittal was from a
bench trial. Where the accused was acquitted by a jury, a meritorious appeal would result in a new trial.]

colourable or evasive means of drawing into the orbit of the federal criminal law measures that did not belong there, either because they were essentially regulatory of matters within exclusive provincial competence or were otherwise within such exclusive competence.]

[The Court rejected the appellant's argument that original anti-abortion legislation was based on the dangers to women's health and that new procedures alleviate this concern. The Court rejected the argument that health protection was Parliament's exclusive concern.]

*** What is patent on the face of the prohibitory portion of s. 251 is that Parliament has in its judgment decreed that interference by another, or even by the pregnant woman herself, with the ordinary course of conception is socially undesirable conduct subject to punishment. That was a judgment open to Parliament in the exercise of its plenary criminal law power, and the fact that there may be safe ways of terminating a pregnancy or that any woman or women claim a personal privilege to that end, becomes immaterial. I need cite no authority for the proposition that Parliament may determine what is not criminal as well as what is, and may hence introduce dispensations or exemptions in its criminal legislation. It has done this in respect of gaming and betting by prescribing for lawful operation of pari-mutuel systems (s. 188), by exempting agricultural fairs or exhibitions from certain of the prohibitions against lotteries and games of chance (s. 189(3)) and by expressly permitting lotteries under stated conditions (s. 190). I point also to the *Lord's Day Act*, R.S.C. 1970, c. L-13, as an illustration of a federal statute drawing its validity from the criminal law power which contains various exemptions.

*   *   *

[Nonetheless, Laskin would allow the appeal, set aside the conviction registered by the Quebec Court of Appeal and restore the jury's verdict of acquittal, based on his judgment that the jury reasonably concluded that the accused established the statutory defense under the Act and the common law defense of necessity.]

MARTLAND, J., concurs with PIGEON and DICKSON, JJ.

JUDSON, J., concurs with LASKIN, C.J.C.

RITCHIE, J., concurs with PIGEON and DICKSON, JJ.

SPENCE, J., concurs with LASKIN, C.J.C.

PIGEON, J.: — [Justice Pigeon did not address the constitutional issue discussed by Laskin, other than to note that the Court unanimously agreed that this issue did not even merit hearing oral argument from the Crown. He then discussed why the accused, who admitted performing abortions without consulting with the appropriate committee per s. 251(4) of the Act, was guilty as a matter of law and why the statute permitted a judgment of guilt to be imposed by the appellate court. Finally, the justice noted: "Since writing the above, I have had the advantage of reading the reasons written by Mr. Justice Dickson and wish to add that I agree with the further views he has expressed on the merits of this case."]

[DICKSON, J., wrote separately, to note that, for purposes of this pre-Charter case, so that the "the values we must accept for the purposes of this appeal are those expressed by Parliament which holds the view that the desire of a woman to be relieved of her pregnancy is not, of itself, justification for performing an abortion." The same doctor successfully invoked Charter protections to invalidate the statute in a subsequent case, which is excerpted below in Chapter 2.]

BEETZ and DE GRANDPRE, JJ., concur with PIGEON and DICKSON, JJ.

Appeal dismissed.

1.3.5. Judicial reasoning in policing Canadian federalism: "Colourability"

The complexities of modern society make it impossible to unambiguously categorize legislation as having only one topic. As illustrated by *Parsons* and *Board of Commerce*, many areas of government regulation of business could constitute "Trade & Commerce" subject to federal jurisdiction as well as "Property & Civil Rights" subject to provincial authority; *Morgentaler I* could arguably fall within federal "Criminal Law" power or the provincial "Hospital" power. Judges in some cases resolved this issue simply by declaring one power (*e.g.*,Trade & Commerce) to be narrower; in other cases they found that as long as the authority fell within the designated assignment, it was permissible. The more typical Canadian practice, however, is to resolve the federalism issue by identifying the "pith and substance" of the legislation and then placing the legislation into a single category.

The path-marking case is *Reference as to the Validity of Section 5(a) of the Dairy Industry Act (Margarine Reference)*, [1949] S.C.R. 1. The Court considered a federal criminal statute prohibiting the manufacture, importation, or sale of margarine. The import ban was upheld under the Trade & Commerce power to regulate international commerce, but this power, under its narrow scope, could not be used to prohibit domestic manufacture. The Court rejected the use of the criminal law power in this manner. It noted that margarine was originally barred explicitly on health grounds.

> Is the prohibition then enacted with a view to a public purpose which can support it as being in relation to criminal law? Public peace, order, security, health, morality: these are the ordinary though not exclusive ends served by that law, but they do not appear to be the object of the parliamentary action here. That object, as I must find it, is economic and the legislative purpose, to give trade protection to the dairy industry in the production and sale of butter; to benefit one group of persons as against competitors in business in which, in the absence of the legislation, the latter would be free to engage in the provinces. To forbid manufacture and sale for such an end is prima facie to deal directly with the civil rights of individuals in relation to particular trade within the provinces.

The public interest in this regulation lies obviously in the trade effects: it is annexed to the legislative subject matter and follows the latter in its allocation to the one or other legislature. But to use it as a support for the legislation in the aspect of criminal law would mean that the Dominion under its authority in that field, by forbidding the manufacture or sale of particular products, could, in what it considered a sound trade policy, not only interdict a substantial part of the economic life of one section of Canada but do so for the benefit of that of another. Whatever the scope of the regulation of interprovincial trade, it is hard to conceive a more insidious form of encroachment on a complementary jurisdiction.

* * *

Then undoubtedly the dairy industry has an aspect of concern to this country as a whole, but . . . if the fact of such an interest or that the matter touched the peace, order and good government of Canada was sufficient to attach the jurisdiction of Parliament, "there is hardly a subject enumerated in sec. 92 upon which it might not legislate, to the exclusion of the provincial legislatures." There is nothing before us from which it can be inferred that the industry has attained a national interest, as distinguished from the aggregate of local interests, of such character as gives it a new and pre-eminent aspect. Until that state of things appears, the constitutional structure of powers leaves the regulation of the civil rights affected to the legislative judgment of the province.

What was critical to the Court's conclusion was not just that it questioned whether margarine posed genuine risks to Canadian consumers, but that the lack of apparent harm suggested another, illegitimate legislative purpose to protect dairy farmers, which is the sort of political issue assigned to provinces. This point is illustrated by *Reference re the Firearms Act*, [2000] 1 S.C.R. 783, upholding a federal requirement for firearms registration under the criminal law power.

[16] The first task is to determine the "pith and substance" of the legislation. To use the wording of ss. 91 and 92, what is the "matter" of the law? What is its true meaning or essential character, its core? To determine the pith and substance, two aspects of the law must be examined: the purpose of the enacting body, and the legal effect of the law.

[17] A law's purpose is often stated in the legislation, but it may also be ascertained by reference to extrinsic material such as Hansard [the published transcript of legislative debates — in the U.S. called Congressional Record] and government publications: see *Morgentaler, supra, at pp. 483-84*. While such extrinsic material was at one time inadmissible to facilitate the determination of Parliament's purpose, it is now well accepted that the legislative history, Parliamentary debates, and similar material may be quite properly considered as long as it is relevant and reliable and is not assigned undue weight. Purpose may also be ascertained by considering the "mischief" of the legislation — the problem which Parliament sought to remedy.

[18] Determining the legal effects of a law involves considering how the law will operate and how it will affect Canadians. The Attorney General of Alberta states that the law will not actually achieve its purpose. Where the legislative scheme is relevant to a criminal law purpose, he says, it will be ineffective (e.g., criminals will not register their guns); where it is effective it will not advance the fight against crime (e.g., burdening rural farmers with pointless red tape). These are concerns that were properly directed to and considered by Parliament.[6] Within its constitutional sphere, Parliament is the judge of whether a measure is likely to achieve its intended purposes; efficaciousness is not relevant to the Court's division of powers analysis: *Morgentaler, supra, at pp. 487-88*, and *Reference re Anti-Inflation Act, [1976] 2 S.C.R. 373*. Rather, the inquiry is directed to how the law sets out to achieve its purpose in order to better understand its "total meaning": W. R. Lederman, Continuing Canadian Constitutional Dilemmas (1981), at pp. 239-40. In some cases, the effects of the law may suggest a purpose other than that which is stated in the law. In other words, a law may say that it intends to do one thing and actually do something else. Where the effects of the law diverge substantially from the stated aim, it is sometimes said to be "colourable."

[Concluding that the Act's focus was criminal and not related to property, the Court noted that what] the law does not require also shows that the operation of the scheme is limited to ensuring safety. For instance, the Act does not regulate the legitimate commercial market for guns. It makes no attempt to set labour standards or the price of weapons. There is no attempt to protect or regulate industries or businesses associated with guns (see *Pattison*, at para. 22). Unlike provincial property registries, the registry established under the Act is not concerned with prior interests, and unlike some provincial motor vehicle schemes, the Act does not address insurance. In short, the effects of the law suggest that its essence is the promotion of public safety through the reduction of the misuse of firearms, and negate the proposition that Parliament was in fact attempting to achieve a different goal such as the total regulation of firearms production, trade, and ownership. We therefore conclude that, viewed from its purpose and effects, the Firearms Act is in "pith and substance" directed to public safety.

Finally, the Court rejected the argument that the law was an undue intrusion into provincial authority. The only intrusion is to eliminate the ability of provinces to choose to have no regulation of firearms, which the Court found to be "an inherent feature of the 'double aspect' doctrine" that "permits both levels of government to legislate in one jurisdictional field for two different purposes." Similarly, where the federal government has a real concern about safety, and the provincial government has a real concern about health, both may regulate heroin addiction, the former by criminalizing possession and sale of an illicit drug under the Criminal Law power, and the latter by compelling addicts to receive treatment, even if it includes

---

[6] [Ed. note: In contrast, the efficacy of legislation *is* considered when a statute is constitutionally challenged as impairing a right guaranteed by the Charter. This is discussed in later chapters.]

detention in a treatment centre. *Schneider v. The Queen*, [1982] 2 S.C.R. 112.

1.3.6. Limits on Provincial power

Given the breadth of several subsections of s. 92, such as the authorization for provinces to adopt legislation with regard to "Property & Civil Rights," "Local Works and Undertakings," and "all Matters of a merely local or private Nature in the province," almost any legislation contemplated by a province could arguably be *intra vires*.[7] The pith and substance approach does most of the work in establishing judicial limits on provincial power.

HER MAJESTY THE QUEEN v. MORGENTALER
[*Morgentaler III*]
SUPREME COURT OF CANADA
[1993] 3 S.C.R. 463

[Before LAMER C.J. and LA FOREST, L'HEUREUX-DUBE, SOPINKA, GONTHIER, CORY, MCLACHLIN, IACOBUCCI and MAJOR JJ.]

The judgment of the Court was delivered by

SOPINKA J.

Introduction

The question in this appeal is whether the *Nova Scotia Medical Services Act*, R.S.N.S. 1989, c. 281, and the regulation made under the Act, N.S. Reg. 152/89, are *ultra vires* the province of Nova Scotia on the ground that they are in pith and substance criminal law. The Act and regulation make it an offence to perform an abortion outside a hospital.

* * *

Facts and Legislation

In January 1988, this Court ruled that the Criminal Code provisions relating to abortion were unconstitutional because they violated women's *Charter* guarantee of security of the person: *R. v. Morgentaler*, [1988] 1 S.C.R. 30 [Ed. note: This case is called *Morgentaler II* — excerpted in Chapter 2]. At the same time the Court reaffirmed its earlier decision that the provisions were a valid exercise of the federal

---

[7] Section 121 of the *BNA Act* requires that "all articles of the growth, produce or manufacture of any one of the provinces shall . . . be admitted free into each of the other provinces." Although this text resembles that of s 92 of the Australian Constitution, discussed below in section 1.5.5, this section has been construed only to prohibit customs duties and not non-fiscal impediments to interprovincial trade. *See Gold Seal v. A.-G. Alta.*, (1921) 62 S.C.R. 424. Canadian precedents regarding production quotas and other aspects of marketing is enormously confusing, and in several cases have required identical statutes to be enacted by federal and all provincial governments to ensure that the legislation was *intra vires.See, e.g., Re Agricultural Products Marketing Act*, [1979] 1 S.C.R. 42.

criminal law power: *Morgentaler v. The Queen*, [1976] 1 S.C.R. 616 (*Morgentaler I* (1975)). The 1988 decision meant that abortion was no longer regulated by the criminal law. It was no longer an offence to obtain or perform an abortion in a clinic such as those run by the respondent. A year later, in January 1989, it was rumoured in Nova Scotia that the respondent intended to establish a free-standing abortion clinic in Halifax. Subsequently, the respondent publicly confirmed his intention to do so.

[T]he Nova Scotia government took action to prevent Dr. Morgentaler from realizing his intention. *** [The response culminated in passage of the *Medical Services Act*. The Act stated its purpose as to "prohibit the privatization of the provision of certain medical services in order to maintain a single high-quality health-care delivery system for all Nova Scotians," and prohibited the provision of "designated medical services" other than in a hospital. Shortly thereafter, the government issued regulations authorized by the Act, designating the following medical services for the purposes of the Act: "(a) Arthroscopy; (b) Colonoscopy (which, for greater certainty, does not include flexible sigmoidoscopy); (c) Upper Gastro-Intestinal Endoscopy; (d) Abortion, including a therapeutic abortion, but not including emergency services related to a spontaneous abortion or related to complications arising from a previously performed abortion; (e) Lithotripsy; (f) Liposuction; (g) Nuclear Medicine; (h) Installation or Removal of Intraocular Lenses; (i) Electromyography, including Nerve Conduction Studies"]

*   *   *

[Despite these actions, Dr. Morgentaler opened his clinic in Halifax as predicted. He was charged with 14 counts of unlawfully performing a designated medical service, to wit, an abortion, other than in a hospital approved as such under the *Hospitals Act*, contrary to s. 6 of the *Medical Services Act*. The respondent challenged the constitutionality of the statute as *ultra vires* the province of Nova Scotia. He argued that abortion regulation was exclusively the province of the federal Parliament under the criminal law power; Nova Scotia argued that it could regulate abortions under its jurisdiction over Hospitals, Property & Civil Rights, and "Matters of a merely local or private Nature." He was acquitted at trial after the trial judge held that the legislation under which he was charged was beyond the province's legislative authority to enact because it was in pith and substance criminal law. This decision was upheld by the Nova Scotia Court of Appeal.]

Analysis

*   *   *

B. *Classification of Laws*

(1) "What's the 'Matter'?"

Classification of a law for purposes of federalism involves first identifying the "matter" of the law and then assigning it to one of the "classes of subjects" in respect to which the federal and provincial governments have legislative authority under ss. 91 and 92 of the *Constitution Act*, 1867. This process of classification is "an interlocking one, in which the *British North America Act* and the challenged legislation react on one another and fix each other's meaning": B. Laskin, "Tests for the Validity of Legislation: What's the 'Matter'?" (1955), 11 U.T.L.J. 114, at p. 127. Courts apply considerations of policy along with legal principle; the task requires "a nice balance of legal skill, respect for established rules, and plain common sense. It is not and never can be an exact science": F.R. Scott, *Civil Liberties and Canadian Federalism* (1959), at p. 26.

A law's "matter" is its leading feature or true character, often described as its pith and substance. There is no single test for a law's pith and substance. The approach must be flexible and a technical, formalistic approach is to be avoided. See Hogg, *Constitutional Law of Canada* (3rd ed. 1992), vol. 1, at p. 15-13. While both the purpose and effect of the law are relevant considerations in the process of characterization, [citations omitted] it is often the case that the legislation's dominant purpose or aim is the key to constitutional validity.

(2) Purpose and Effect

*   *   *

(a) *"Legal Effect" or Strict Legal Operation*

*   *   *

The analysis of pith and substance is not, however, restricted to the four corners of the legislation. Thus the court "will look beyond the direct legal effects to inquire into the social or economic purposes which the statute was enacted to achieve," its background and the circumstances surrounding its enactment and, in appropriate cases, will consider evidence of the second form of "effect," the actual or predicted practical effect of the legislation in operation. The ultimate long-term, practical effect of the legislation will in some cases be irrelevant.

(b) *The Use of Extrinsic Materials*

In determining the background, context and purpose of challenged legislation, the court is entitled to refer to extrinsic evidence of various kinds provided it is relevant and not inherently unreliable. This clearly includes related legislation (such as, in this case, the March regulations and the former s. 251 of the *Criminal Code*), and evidence of the "mischief" at which the legislation is directed: *Alberta Bank Taxation Reference*, [Attorney-General for Alberta v. Attorney-General for Canada) [1939] A.C. 117], at pp. 130. It also includes legislative history, in the sense of the events that occurred during drafting and enactment; as Ritchie J., concurring in *Reference re Anti-Inflation Act*, [[1976] 2 S.C.R. 373] wrote at p. 437, it is "not only permissible but essential" to consider the material the legislature had before it when the statute was enacted.

*   *   *

I would therefore hold, as did Freeman J.A. in the Court of Appeal, that the excerpts from Hansard were properly admitted by the trial judge in this case. In a nutshell, this evidence demonstrates that members of all parties in the House understood the central feature of the proposed law to be prohibition of Dr. Morgentaler's proposed clinic on the basis of a common and almost unanimous opposition to abortion clinics per se. I will return to the evidence below.

*   *   *

(3) Scope of the Applicable Heads of Power

The issue we face in the present case is whether Nova Scotia has, by the present legislation, regulated the place for delivery of a medical service with a view to controlling the quality and nature of its health care delivery system, or has attempted to prohibit the performance of abortions outside hospitals with a view to suppressing or punishing what it perceives to be the socially undesirable conduct of abortion. The former would place the legislation within provincial competence; the latter would make it criminal law.

*   *   *

C. *Application of the Principles to the Case at Bar*

*   *   *

(2) Beyond the Four Corners

(a) *Duplication of Criminal Code Provisions*

*   *   *

Provincial legislation has been held invalid when it employs language "virtually indistinguishable" from that found in the *Criminal Code*. However, even when the legal effect of federal and provincial legislation is virtually identical this does not necessarily determine validity, since the provinces can enact provisions with the same legal effect as federal legislation provided this is done in pursuit of a provincial head of power.[8] The duplication of *Criminal Code* language may raise an inference that the province has stepped into the realm of the criminal law; the more exact the reproduction, the stronger the inference that this is the dominant purpose of the enactment.

The guiding principle is that the provinces may not invade the criminal field by attempting to stiffen, supplement or replace the criminal law (*Reference re Freedom of Informed Choice (Abortions) Act* (1985), 44 Sask. R. 104 (C.A.)) or to fill perceived defects or gaps therein. The legal effect of s. 251 and the present legislation, each taken as a whole, is quite different: among other things, s. 251 made it an offence for a woman to obtain an abortion, and prescribed the burdensome "therapeutic abortion committee" system and the "life or health" criterion for a legal abortion, none of which are present in the Act and regulation; and the present legislation prohibits other services besides abortion and directly concerns public health insurance coverage. Freeman J.A. was clearly right, however, that in so far as it prohibits abortion clinics the legal effect of the medical services legislation is completely embraced by s. 251 and, had the latter provision not been struck down,

---

[8] [Ed note: Section 92(15) gives provinces the power to impose criminal punishment for the purposes of enforcing an otherwise valid provincial statute. Thus, if the Court determined that the challenged statute was *intra vires* because it related to health and not criminal law, the fact that the statute contained criminal provisions not be significant.]

the present legislation would have been redundant in that respect. Section 251 is now, of course, inoperative. The absence of operative federal legislation does not enlarge provincial jurisdiction, though. It simply means that if the provincial legislation is found to be *intra vires*, no problem of paramountcy arises.

In my opinion the overlap of legal effects between the now defunct criminal provision and the Nova Scotia legislation is capable of supporting an inference that the legislation was designed to serve a criminal law purpose. It is a piece in the puzzle which along with the other evidence may demonstrate the true purpose of the legislation.

(b) *Background and Surrounding Circumstances*

The events leading up to and including the enactment of the Act and regulation do not support the appellant's assertions that the pith and substance of the legislation relate to provincial jurisdiction over health. On the contrary, they strengthen the inference that the impugned Act and regulation were designed to serve a criminal law purpose.

(i) The Course of Events

It is clear that the catalyst for government action was the rumour and later announcement of Dr. Morgentaler's intention to open his clinic. [First, the government responded by issuing regulations which prohibited abortions outside hospitals and "de-insured" such services. The direct and exclusive aim of this action was to stop the Morgentaler clinic and no one disputes that. These were challenged in court by an abortion-rights group. Shortly before the hearing on that litigation, and days before the end of the annual legislative session, the government introduced and rushed the challenged Act through the House of Assembly.]

(ii) Hansard

I have reviewed the evidence of the legislative debates on the *Medical Services Act*, and have concluded that they give a clear picture of what the members of the House, both government and opposition, saw as being in issue. Both the trial judge and Freeman J.A. referred extensively to excerpts from Hansard. [The court quoted the Liberal Opposition Health critic in reaffirming her party's agreement with the Health Minister that "the Morgentaler clinic should not be set up in this province. I want to make that point very clear. (Applause)." The Liberals' equivocation about the specifics of the legislation were criticized by the Conservative Health Minister as "the most weak-kneed, weak-hearted support for the question of the control of free-standing abortion clinics that I heard yet in this entire session of the Legislature." In contrast, he made his position clear: "as the Minister of Health and I, as an MLA, am not supportive of free-standing abortion clinics. (Applause)." He pledged to "do everything in our effort to stop" abortion clinics.]

The Hansard evidence demonstrates both that the prohibition of Dr. Morgentaler's clinic was the central concern of the members of the legislature who spoke, and that there was a common and emphatically expressed opposition to free-standing abortion clinics per se. The Morgentaler clinic was viewed, it appears, as a public evil which should be eliminated. The concerns to which the appellant submits the legislation is primarily directed — privatization, cost and quality of health care, and a policy of preventing a two-tier system of access to medical services — were conspicuously absent throughout most of the legislative proceedings. They were emphasized by the Minister, Mr. Nantes, on moving second reading of the bill on June 12, 1989. This does not, however, in my view, detract significantly from the overall impression left by the debates.

*   *   *

(iii) Searching for Provincial Objectives

At trial the appellant presented evidence that the Act's objectives were to prevent privatization and the consequent development of a two-tier system of medical service delivery, to ensure the delivery of high-quality health care, and to rationalize the delivery of medical services so as to avoid duplication and reduce public costs. ***

[The court rejected the argument that the impugned legislation furthered objectives related to these legitimate matters of provincial concern. First, there was no evidence that in-hospital abortions are safer. Second, the Throne Speech delivered earlier in the year made no mention of government policy with regard to privatazation. A commissioner report, indeed, has recommended moving as many services as possible out of hospitals to reduce costs. Third, there was no increase in public costs in reimbursing Dr. Morgentaler: the fee is the same paid to a hospital. Finally, although the Court did not weigh this heavily, the Court took note of the severe penalties for violating a public health-oriented regulation.]

If the means employed by a legislature to achieve its purported objectives do not logically advance those objectives, this may indicate that the purported purpose masks the legislation's true purpose. In *Westendorp v. The Queen*, [[1983] 1 S.C.R. 43], Laskin C.J. held that it was specious to regard a by-law which prohibited street prostitution as relating to control of the streets, since if that were its true purpose, "it would have dealt with congregation of persons on the streets or with obstruction, unrelated to what the congregating or obstructing persons say or otherwise do" (at p. 51). Here, one would expect that if the province's policy were to prohibit the performance of any surgical procedures outside hospitals, the legislation would have simply done so.

*   *   *

. . . The primary objective of the legislation was to prohibit abortions outside hospitals as socially undesirable conduct, and any concern with the safety and security of pregnant women or with health care policy, hospitals or the regulation of the medical profession was merely ancillary . . . .

———————

Thus, the "watertight compartments" that had in the early years been used by the Privy Council to restrain Ottawa are now being used to limit the provinces. A note of dissent in this regard was voiced in a related abortion case. New Brunswick's response to Dr. Morgentaler, seeking to legislate squarely within the provincial authority to regulate hospitals and the traditional provincial power to regulate trades and professions, was to enact legislation suspending the license of a physician who performed an abortion outside a hospital. The Court of Appeal held the statute *ultra vires* under the authority of *Morgentaler III*. *Morgentaler v. New Brunswick (Attorney-general)*, 121 D.L.R. (4th) 431(1995). Rice, J.A., dissented, though. He argued:

> That the legislators may have perceived the practice of abortion as having moral overtones and that it may have to a certain extent triggered these amendments to the *Medical Act* does not in my view ipso facto invalidate the legislation.

> In a "co-operative federal system" . . . legislation will overlap on certain subjects and so will purposes and concerns which prompted the legislation. It is not always possible in these overlapping legislations to segregate the objectives of the legislators so that one can say that the concern was solely related to the purpose commensurate to the head of powers the legislators purport to exercise. Criminal law in the circumstances of this case had established that performing abortions outside of a hospital was a crime and expressed Canadians' repulsion at the practice. It would be ludicrous to say that the legislators did not treat that activity as a socially undesirable thing. It had been so declared by Parliament and was the law of the land. However, it is another thing to say that by amending the *Medical Act* as they did, the legislators were creating, establishing, stiffening or supplementing a power exclusively assigned to the domain of criminal law. That proposition, in my view, would render impossible any exercise of provincial powers which affects the practice of abortion.

The failure of logic, and the necessity of policymaking, in characterizing legislation as appropriately national or provincial is noted in less controversial areas as well. As a leading Canadian scholar explained, logic cannot determine whether the law that an unmarried person's will is voided on marriage is legislation with regard to marriage (federal under s. 91(26)) or property and civil rights (provincial under s. 92(13)). *See, e.g.,* W. R. LEDERMAN, CONTINUING CANADIAN CONSTITUTIONAL DILEMMAS (1981), *reprinted in* CONSTITUTIONAL LAW GROUP, CANADIAN CONSTITUTIONAL LAW 211 (4th ed. 2001). The best Professor Lederman could do is to conclude that "a rule of law for purposes of the distribution of legislative powers is to be classified by that feature of its meaning which is judged the most important one in that respect," and that "the question must be asked, Is it better for the people that this thing be done on a national level or a provincial level?" *Id.* at 213.

1.4. BASIC PRINCIPLES OF U.S. FEDERALISM

1.4.1. Scope of deference

Article I, § 8 authorizes Congress to legislate with regard to a number of enumerated matters, and also provides legislative authority for "all Laws which shall be necessary and proper for carrying to Execution the foregoing powers . . . ." From the outset, this authority provided the basis for controversy over constitutional federalism. The ascendant Federalists, led by Alexander Hamilton, advocated broad use of this power to solve federal problems. The Republicans advanced the claim that federal powers must be construed narrowly to include only those specifically listed.

In particular, Thomas Jefferson targeted the unlimited potential of the Necessary and Proper Clause to expand the scope of the federal government. Referring to proposed legislation to grant a federal charter to a mining business, Jefferson complained that a broad reading of what he called "the sweeping clause" allowed such an expansion, since a corporate charter was necessary for mining which was necessary for copper needed for ships needed for national defense. *See* 1 CHARLES WARREN, THE SUPREME COURT IN UNITED STATES HISTORY 501 (1926). This view was championed by Republicans, who slipped in influence in the Washington Administration and lost power in the 1796 defeat of Thomas Jefferson by John Adams. However, Chief Justice Marshall's landmark decision endorsed such a broad interpretation.

McCULLOCH v. MARYLAND
SUPREME COURT OF THE UNITED STATES
17 U.S. (4 Wheat.) 316 (1819)

[This landmark case arose as a challenge to a State tax imposed on bank notes, made particularly questionable because the tax was higher on notes of the federally-chartered Bank of the United States. McCulloch, the cashier of the Bank, refused to pay these taxes and (presumably financed by the Bank) hired U.S. Senator and legendary advocate Daniel Webster to represent him. In a holding not relevant here, the U.S. Supreme Court held that this state tax was unconstitutional if the Bank of the United States had been lawfully created by Congress. The excerpt below provides the Court's reasoning for its conclusion that the legislation creating the Bank was within the federal legislative authority conferred by the Constitution, even though the Constitution did not expressly authorize the creation of the bank or, for that matter, the chartering of any federal corporation.]

[Before MARSHALL, C.J., and WASHINGTON, JOHNSON, LIVINGSTON, TODD, DUVALL and STORY, JJ.]

MR. CHIEF JUSTICE MARSHALL delivered the opinion of the Court.

. . . .

Among the enumerated powers, we do not find that of establishing a bank or creating a corporation. But there is no phrase in the instrument which, like the articles of confederation, excludes incidental or implied powers; and which requires that everything granted shall be expressly and minutely described. Even the 10th amendment, which was framed for the purpose of quieting the excessive jealousies which had been excited, omits the word "expressly," and declares only that the powers "not delegated to the United States, nor prohibited to the States, are reserved to the States or to the people;" thus leaving the question, whether the particular power which may become the subject of contest has been delegated to the one government, or prohibited to the other, to depend on a fair construction of the whole instrument. The men who drew and adopted this amendment had experienced the embarrassments resulting from the insertion of this word in the articles of confederation,[9] and probably omitted it to avoid those embarrassments. A constitution, to contain an accurate detail of all the subdivisions of which its great powers will admit, and of all the means by which they may be carried into execution, would partake of the prolixity of a legal code, and could scarcely be embraced by the human mind. *** It is also, in some degree, warranted by their having omitted to use any restrictive term which might prevent its receiving a fair and just interpretation. In considering this question, then, we must never forget, that it is a constitution we are expounding.

Although, among the enumerated powers of government, we do not find the word "bank" or "incorporation," we find the great powers to lay and collect taxes; to borrow money; to regulate commerce; to declare and conduct a war; and to raise and support armies and navies. The sword and the purse, all the external relations, and no inconsiderable portion of the industry of the nation, are entrusted to its government. It can never be pretended that these vast powers draw after them others of inferior importance, merely because they are inferior. Such an idea can never be advanced. But it may with great reason be contended, that a government, entrusted with such ample powers, on the due execution of which the happiness and prosperity of the nation so vitally depends, must also be entrusted with ample means for their execution. The power being given, it is the interest of the nation to facilitate its execution. It can never be their interest, and cannot be presumed to have been their intention, to clog and embarrass its execution by withholding the most appropriate means. Throughout this vast republic, from the St. Croix to the Gulph of Mexico, from the Atlantic to the Pacific, revenue is to be collected and expended, armies are to be marched and supported. The exigencies of the nation may require that the treasure raised in the north should be transported to the south, that raised in the east conveyed to the west, or that this order should be reversed. Is that construction of the constitution to be preferred which would render these operations difficult, hazardous, and expensive? Can we adopt that construction, (unless the words imperiously require it,) which would impute to the framers of that instrument, when granting these powers for the public good, the intention of impeding their exercise by withholding a choice of means? If, indeed, such be the mandate of the constitution, we have only to obey; but that instrument does not profess to enumerate the means by which the powers it confers may be executed; nor does it prohibit the creation of a corporation, if the existence of such a being be essential to the beneficial exercise of those powers. It is, then, the subject of fair inquiry, how far such means may be employed.

[Significantly, the Court rejected Maryland's argument that the Bank of the United States was not constitutional, because the final clause in Art. I, § 8's conferral of federal legislative authority empowered Congress to "make all laws which shall be necessary and proper for carrying into execution the foregoing

---

[9] [Ed. note: Article II of the *Articles of Confederation*, the document governing the original confederation of the thirteen states forming the U.S., provides: "Each state retains its sovereignty, freedom and independence, and every power, jurisdiction, and right, which is not by this confederation *expressly* delegated to the United States, in Congress assembled." (emphasis added).]

powers," and the Bank was not *necessary* to accomplish these goals. (Indeed, the need for such a bank was a major political controversy in the United States dating back to original proposals in the Washington administration for the Bank made by Secretary of the Treasury Alexander Hamilton and fervently opposed by Secretary of State Thomas Jefferson.) Marshall, C.J., employed a variety of interesting interpretive tools, concluding that read in context the word "necessary" did not mean essential.][10]

. . . To have prescribed the means by which government should, in all future time, execute its powers, would have been to change, entirely, the character of the instrument, and give it the properties of a legal code. It would have been an unwise attempt to provide, by immutable rules, for exigencies which, if foreseen at all, must have been seen dimly, and which can be best provided for as they occur. To have declared that the best means shall not be used, but those alone without which the power given would be nugatory, would have been to deprive the legislature of the capacity to avail itself of experience, to exercise its reason, and to accommodate its legislation to circumstances. If we apply this principle of construction to any of the powers of the government, we shall find it so pernicious in its operation that we shall be compelled to discard it. . . .

. . . .

But the argument which most conclusively demonstrates the error of the construction contended for by the counsel for the State of Maryland, is founded on the intention of the Convention, as manifested in the whole clause. To waste time and argument in proving that, without it, Congress might carry its powers into execution, would be not much less idle than to hold a lighted taper to the sun. As little can it be required to prove, that in the absence of this clause, Congress would have some choice of means. That it might employ those which, in its judgment, would most advantageously effect the object to be accomplished. That any means adapted to the end, any means which tended directly to the execution of the constitutional powers of the government, were in themselves constitutional. This clause, as construed by the State of Maryland, would abridge, and almost annihilate this useful and necessary right of the legislature to select its means. That this could not be intended, is, we should think, had it not been already controverted, too apparent for controversy. We think so for the following reasons:

1st. The clause is placed among the powers of Congress, not among the limitations on those powers.

---

[10] [Ed. note: As counsel for McCulloch, Daniel Webster argued that "necessary and proper" were synonymous terms meaning "suitable and fitted to the object." Thus, the "question is not whether a bank be necessary, or useful, but whether Congress may not constitutionally judge of that necessity or utility." Webster characterized the argument by counsel for Maryland that branches of banks were unnecessary as insisting on a requirement that the power of establishing such a monied corporation should be indispensably necessary to the execution of any of the specified powers of the government. An interpretation of this clause of the constitution so strict and literal, would render every law which could be passed by Congress unconstitutional: for of no particular law can it be predicated, that it is absolutely and indispensably necessary to carry into effect any of the specified powers; since a different law might be imagined, which could be enacted tending to the same object, though not equally well adapted to attain it. 20 L.Ed. at 53–54.]

2nd. Its terms purport to enlarge, not to diminish the powers vested in the government. In purports to be an additional power, not a restriction on those already granted. No reason has been, or can be assigned for thus concealing an intention to narrow the discretion of the national legislature under words which purport to enlarge it. The framers of the constitution wished its adoption, and well knew that it would be endangered by its strength, not by its weakness. *** Had the intention been to make this clause restrictive, it would unquestionably have been so in form as well as in effect.

. . . .

We admit, as all must admit, that the powers of the government are limited, and that its limits are not to be transcended. But we think the sound construction of the constitution must allow to the national legislature that discretion, with respect to the means by which the powers it confers are to be carried into execution, which will enable that body to perform the high duties assigned to it, in the manner most beneficial to the people. Let the end be legitimate, let it be within the scope of the constitution, and all means which are appropriate, which are plainly adapted to that end, which are not prohibited, but consist with the letter and spirit of the constitution, are constitutional.

———————

McCulloch is particularly significant for a doctrinal analysis of the enumerated powers granted to Congress in Art. I, § 8 in the context of judicially-umpired federalism. The interpretation of specific powers is very much affected by how close judges will scrutinize the necessity and propriety of federal legislation. Had Chief Justice Marshall held, for example, that federal authority to regulate "interstate commerce" or spending for the "general welfare" depended on its lawyers' ability to persuade federal judges that the regulations were indeed necessary and proper, the need to develop doctrinal limits on those enumerated powers would vary sharply.

1.4.2. Scope of the Commerce Clause

The powers enumerated in Art. I, § 8, are often recognized as efforts by the Framers' expert Committee on Detail to specify those areas that the Convention had generally designated as appropriate for the national legislature: "to legislate in all cases to which the separate States are incompetent, or in which the harmony of the United States may be interrupted by exercise of individual legislation." *See* JOHN E. NOWAK & RONALD D. ROTUNDA, CONSTITUTIONAL LAW § 3.1 (8th ed. 2010) (hereafter "NOWAK & ROTUNDA"); JACK N. RAKOVE, ORIGINAL MEANINGS: POLITICS AND IDEAS IN THE MAKING OF THE CONSTITUTION CHAPTER VII (1996). The Framers did not, however, expressly grant Congress an inherent right to act on subject matters thought to promote the health, safety, or welfare of the people across the nation (Americans refer to plenary legislative power as "the police power," although it is far broader than that which refers to local law enforcement officials). Nor did they confer a power, akin to the "Peace, Order & Good Government" authority given to the Canadian Parliament, to enact laws when national solutions are required. Throughout American history, when important national legislation was enacted, it was justified as part of Congress' authority to "regulate Commerce . . . among the several States," generally referred to as "interstate commerce."

For almost a century, there was little judicial attention to the scope of congressional power over interstate commerce. Rather, like the first Privy Council case involving the Canadian Parliament's Trade & Commerce power (*Parsons, supra*), the landmark American precedent arose in the context of a challenge to a state statute as *ultra vires*. The following landmark decision established a very different approach to interpreting Art. I, § 8 of the U.S. Constitution than we saw from the Privy Council's interpretation of s. 91(2) of the BNA Act (conferring on Parliament power over "Trade & Commerce").

GIBBONS v. OGDEN
SUPREME COURT OF THE UNITED STATES
22 U.S. (9 Wheat.) 1 (1824)

[Before MARSHALL, C.J., and WASHINGTON, JOHNSON, TODD, DUVALL, STORY, and THOMPSON, JJ.]

[Ogden was the assignee of rights originally granted by the New York state legislature to famed inventors Robert Livingston and Robert Fulton for the exclusive right to navigate steam-fired boats within New York state waters. Gibbons ran a rival steam-fired ferry from Elizabeth, New Jersey, to New York City. Ogden sued and obtained desired relief in New York courts; Gibbons hired Daniel Webster, who again secured a reversal from the U.S. Supreme Court. Gibbons' defense was that the New York grant was contrary to a valid federal statute under which he had a right to operate his ferry service. Such a statute, if valid, trumped the New York law under the Supremacy Clause in Article VI, which provides that laws of the United States made pursuant to the Constitution "shall be the supreme law of the land" binding state and federal judges, "anything in the Constitution or laws of any State to the contrary notwithstanding." Thus, the Court had to decide whether Congress could regulate transportation within the territorial waters of a state.]

The subject to be regulated is commerce; and our constitution being, as was aptly said at the bar, one of enumeration, and not of definition, to ascertain the extent of the power, it becomes necessary to settle the meaning of the word. The counsel for the appellee would limit it to traffic, to buying and selling, or the interchange of commodities, and do not admit that it comprehends navigation. This would restrict a general term, applicable to many objects, to one of its significations. Commerce, undoubtedly, is traffic, but it is something more: it is intercourse. It describes the commercial intercourse between nations, and parts of nations, in all its branches, and is regulated by prescribing rules for carrying on that intercourse. The mind can scarcely conceive a system for regulating commerce between nations, which shall exclude all laws concerning navigation, which shall be silent on the admission of the vessels of the one nation into the ports of the other, and be confined to prescribing rules for the conduct of individuals, in the actual employment of buying and selling, or of barter.

. . . .

The subject to which the power is next applied, is to commerce "among the several States." The word "among" means intermingled with. A thing which is among others, is intermingled with them. Commerce among the States, cannot stop at the external boundary line of each State, but may be introduced into the interior.

It is not intended to say that these words comprehend that commerce, which is completely internal, which is carried on between man and man in a State, or between different parts of the same State, and which does not extend to or affect other States. Such a power would be inconvenient, and is certainly unnecessary.

Comprehensive as the word "among" is, it may very properly be restricted to that commerce which concerns more States than one. The phrase is not one which would probably have been selected to indicate the completely interior traffic of a State, because it is not an apt phrase for that purpose; and the enumeration of the particular classes of commerce, to which the power was to be extended, would not have been made, had the intention been to extend the power to every description. The enumeration presupposes something not enumerated; and that something, if we regard the language or the subject of the sentence, must be the exclusively internal commerce of a State. The genius and character of the whole government seem to be, that its action is to be applied to all the external concerns of the nation, and to those internal concerns which affect the States generally; but not to those which are completely within a particular State, which do not affect other States, and with which it is not necessary to interfere, for the purpose of executing some of the general powers of the government. The completely internal commerce of a State, then, may be considered as reserved for the State itself.

We are now arrived at the inquiry — What is this power?

It is the power to regulate; that is, to prescribe the rule by which commerce is to be governed. This power, like all others vested in Congress, is complete in itself, may be exercised to its utmost extent, and acknowledges no limitations, other than are prescribed in the constitution. These are expressed in plain terms, and do not affect the questions which arise in this case, or which have been discussed at the bar. If, as has always been understood, the sovereignty of Congress, though limited to specified objects, is plenary as to those objects, the power over commerce with foreign nations, and among the several States, is vested in Congress as absolutely as it would be in a single government, having in its constitution the same restrictions on the exercise of the power as are found in the constitution of the United States. The wisdom and the discretion of Congress, their identity with the people, and the influence which their constituents possess at elections, are, in this, as in many other instances, as that, for example, of declaring war, the sole restraints on which they have relied, to secure them from its abuse. They are the restraints on which the people must often rely solely, in all representative governments.

Having read the Canadian cases, what is of course striking about *Gibbons* is the absence of any notion that the scope of the Commerce Clause should be interpreted in light of the Tenth Amendment's express reservation of power to states. While the *BNA Act*'s grant of federal authority over Trade & Commerce was narrowly construed in order to accommodate the provincial Property & Civil Rights power, John Marshall declared that Congress' power of interstate commerce is the same as that vested in a unitary, non-federal government. (As we will see below, the High Court of Australia initially adopted a states' "reserved powers" doctrine that interpreted Commonwealth power narrowly to preserve state power, but then reversed course in the landmark *Engineers* case.)

The *Gibbons* decision avoided the question whether commerce that was inter-state was beyond the reach of state legislation when Congress had not specifically legislated on the subject. The Court rejected the "water-tight compartment" approach in the following case.

COOLEY v. THE BOARD OF WARDENS OF THE PORT OF PHILADELPHIA

SUPREME COURT OF THE UNITED STATES

53 U.S. 299 (1852)

MR. JUSTICE CURTIS delivered the opinion of the court.

[The excerpted opinion below discusses the constitutionality of a Pennsylvania statute requiring ships using the Port of Philadelphia to use a local pilot, or to pay half the pilotage fee "for the use of the society for the relief of distressed and decayed pilots and their families." In this opinion, the court rejects the claim that the state law is invalid in light of the constitutional assignment to Congress of the regulation of interstate commerce. The Court quickly established that Congress had the authority to regulate navigation into a major international port, and that this authority included regulatory authority over pilots. What made the case interesting was that the relevant federal statute did not directly regulate pilots, nor did it simply incorporate by reference existing state laws, but in addition required pilots to conform to "such laws as the States may respectively hereafter enact."]

If the States were divested of the power to legislate on this subject by the grant of the commercial power to Congress, it is plain this act could not confer upon them power thus to legislate. If the Constitution excluded the States from making any law regulating commerce, certainly Congress cannot regrant, or in any manner reconvey to the States that power. And yet this act of 1789 gives its sanction only to laws enacted by the States. This necessarily implies a constitutional power to legislate; for only a rule created by the sovereign power of a State acting in its legislative capacity, can be deemed a law, enacted by a State; and if the State has so limited its sovereign power that it no longer extends to a particular subject, manifestly it cannot, in any proper sense, be said to enact laws thereon. Entertaining these views we are brought directly and unavoidably to the consideration of the question, whether the grant of the commercial power to Congress, did per se deprive the States of all power to regulate pilots. This question has never been decided by this court, nor, in our judgment, has any case depending upon all the considerations which must govern this one, come before this court. The grant of commercial power to Congress does not contain any terms which expressly exclude the States from exercising an authority over its subject-matter. If they are excluded it must be because the nature of the power, thus granted to Congress, requires that a similar authority should not exist in the States. If it were conceded on the one side, that the nature of this power, like that to legislate for the District of Columbia, is absolutely and totally repugnant to the existence of similar power in the States, probably no one would deny that the grant of the power to Congress, as effectually and perfectly excludes the States from all future legislation on the subject, as if express words had been used to exclude them. And on the other hand, if it were admitted that the existence of this power in Congress, like the power of taxation, is compatible with the existence of a similar power in the States, then it would be in conformity with the contemporary exposition of the Constitution, (Federalist, No. 32) and with the judicial construction, given from time to time by this court, after the most deliberate consideration, to hold that the mere grant of such a power to Congress, did not imply a prohibition on the States to exercise the same power; that it is not the mere existence of such a power, but its exercise by Congress, which may be incompatible with the exercise of the same power by the States, and that the States may legislate in the absence of congressional regulations. [citations omitted].

The diversities of opinion, therefore, which have existed on this subject, have arisen from the different views taken of the nature of this power. But when the nature of a power like this is spoken of, when it is said that the nature of the power requires that it should be exercised exclusively by Congress, it must be intended to refer to the subjects of that power, and to say they are of such a nature as to require exclusive legislation by Congress. Now the power to regulate commerce, embraces a vast field, containing not only many, but exceedingly various subjects, quite unlike in their nature; some imperatively demanding a single uniform rule, operating equally on the commerce of the United States in every port; and some, like the subject now in question, as imperatively demanding that diversity, which alone can meet the local necessities of navigation.

Either absolutely to affirm, or deny that the nature of this power requires exclusive legislation by Congress, is to lose sight of the nature of the subjects of this power, and to assert concerning all of them, what is really applicable but to a part. Whatever subjects of this power are in their nature national, or admit only of one uniform system, or plan of regulation, may justly be said to be of such a nature as to require exclusive legislation by Congress. That this cannot be affirmed of laws for the regulation of pilots and pilotage is plain. The act of 1789 contains a clear and authoritative declaration by the first Congress, that the nature of this subject is such, that until Congress should find it necessary to exert its power, it should be left to the legislation of the States; that it is local and not national; that it is likely to be the best provided for, not by one system, or plan of regulations, but by as many as the legislative discretion of the several States should deem applicable to the local peculiarities of the ports within their limits.

Viewed in this light, so much of this act of 1789 as declares that pilots shall continue to be regulated "by such laws as the States may respectively hereafter enact for that purpose," instead of being held to be inoperative, as an attempt to confer on the States a power to legislate, of which the Constitution had deprived them, is allowed an appropriate and important signification. It manifests the understanding of Congress, at the outset of the government, that the nature of this subject is not such as to require its exclusive legislation. The practice of the States, and of the national government, has been in conformity with this declaration, from the origin of the national government to this time; and the nature of the subject when examined, is such as to leave no doubt of the superior fitness and propriety, not to say the absolute necessity, of different systems of regulation, drawn from local knowledge and experience, and conformed to local wants. . . .

How then can we say, that by the mere grant of power to regulate commerce, the States are deprived of all the power to legislate on this subject, because from the nature of the power the legislation of Congress must be exclusive.

Mr. Justice McLean and Mr. Justice Wayne dissented; and Mr. Justice Daniel, although he concurred in the judgment of the court, yet dissented from its reasoning. [These decisions are omitted.]

1.4.3. Judicial Limits on Federal Legislative Power: the narrowing and broadening of the scope of the Commerce Clause from the *Lochner* era to *Jones & Laughlin*

The cases presented to date suggest a broad grant of authority to Congress, while recognizing that states maintain plenary police power over matters solely within their territories. Judicial review of federal legislative power has seen a remarkable ebb and flow in American legal history. As Nowark & Rotunda detail, §§ 4.5–4.7, from 1888–1936, the Supreme Court used the Tenth Amendment as a tool to limit congressional power. Several early cases distinguished "commerce" subject to federal regulation from "production," "manufacturing," or "mining" that were exclusively subject to state legislation. The Court also developed a distinction between commercial activities that "directly" affected interstate commerce, and those with only an "indirect" effect that could not be regulated by Congress. An illustrative case was *United States v. E.C. Knight Co.*, 156 U.S. 1 (1895). The Court held that the federal antitrust laws could not constitutionally apply to monopolization of the manufacturing and sale of sugar, because manufacturing was not interstate commerce. Distinguishing between commerce and manufacturing was essential to maintain our federal system, Fuller, C.J., reasoned:

> If it be held that the term includes the regulation of all such manufactures as are intended to be the subject of commercial transactions in the future, it is impossible to deny that it would also include all productive industries that contemplate the same thing. The result would be that Congress would be invested, to the exclusion of the States, with the power to regulate, not only manufactures, but also agriculture, horticulture, stock raising, domestic fisheries, mining — in short, every branch of human industry. For is there one of them that does not contemplate, more or less clearly, an interstate or foreign market? Does not the wheat grower of the Northwest or the cotton planter of the South, plaint, cultivate, and harvest his crop with an eye on the prices at Liverpool, New York, and Chicago? The power being vested in Congress and denied to the States, it would follow as an inevitable result that the duty would devolve on Congress to regulate all of these delicate, multiform and vital interests — interests which in their nature are and must be local in all the details of their successful management.

Id. (quoting *Kidd v. Pearson*, 128 U.S. 1, 20).

In a series of 5-4 decisions, the Court struck down New Deal legislation to deal with the economic crisis of the Great Depression. *Railroad Retirement Bd. v. Alton Railroad Co.*, 295 U.S. 330 (1935) struck down a statute requiring and regulating pensions for railroad employees. Prior cases upholding federal regulation or the railroad industry were distinguished because these were designed for safety or efficiency aspects of commerce. The majority held, in contrast, that pensions were designed only to help "the social welfare of the worker, and therefore [is] remote from any regulation of commerce." *Id.* at 368. Likewise, in *Carter v. Carter Coal Co.*, 298 U.S. 238 (1936), that federal legislation regulating the wages and hours of coal miners was outside the Commerce power as well as an intrusion into a "purely local activity" reserved for states.

These cases led to what historians call the "Crisis of 1937." Frustrated by the invalidation of New Deal legislation, President Franklin Delano Roosevelt proposed (to a Congress that was overwhelmingly Democratic and supportive of the New Deal) an infamous plan to pack the Court with additional justices.[11] In what has been called the "switch in time that saved nine," Justice Owen Roberts reversed his previous position and voted to uphold the National Labor Relations Act in *National Labor Relations Board v. Jones & Laughlin Steel Corp.*, 301 U.S. 1 (1937). Departing from prior cases, the new Court majority held that intrastate activities that "have such a close and substantial relation to interstate commerce that their control is essential or appropriate to protect that commerce from burdens and obstructions" are within Congress' power to regulate." *Id.* at 37. The Court effectively overruled *E. C. Knight & Co.* several years later, in *Mandeville Island Farms, Inc. v. American Crystal Sugar Co.*, 334 U.S. 219 (1948), applying the federal antitrust laws to anticompetitive conduct among sugar refiners. Within a few years, the elderly conservative justices now in the minority retired from the bench and Roosevelt was able to appoint a solid majority that would uphold modern social and economic regulation.[12] Perhaps the apex of judicial support for broad congressional power over commerce came in *Wickard v. Filburn*, 317 U.S. 111 (1942), upholding the constitutionality of a federal statute that regulated the production and consumption of wheat grown by a farmer for his family's personal use. The Court observed that the cumulative economic effect of wheat grown by American farmers for personal consumption had the requisite impact on interstate commerce. The Court reasoned:

> Even if appellee's activity be local and though it may not be regarded as commerce, it may still, whatever its nature, be reached by Congress if it

---

[11] Unlike justices of the Supreme Court of Canada, the High Court of Australia, and the South African Constitutional Court, who face mandatory retirement, American justices serve as long as they choose to do so. Ironically, although President Roosevelt's unprecedented four terms in office allowed him to eventually appoint a record number of Supreme Court justices, during his first 4½ years in office no justice left office, locking in a majority in favor of active judicial restraint on federal power.

[12] The decisions in 1937 signaled an end to a period of jurisprudence — the so-called "*Lochner* era" — where the Supreme Court frequently invalidated progressive social welfare legislation, both on federalism grounds discussed in text above but also for interfering with what was then a constitutionally-protected economic liberty of freedom-of-contract. The scope of constitutional protection for economic rights is considered below in Chapter Six.

exerts a substantial economic effect on interstate commerce, and this irrespective of whether such effect is what might at some earlier time have been defined as "direct" or "indirect."

Id. at 125.

1.4.4. The rise and fall and rise and fall of the Tenth Amendment as a significant limit on federal legislative power

The *Lochner* era (carefully considered with regard to the question of economic liberty in Chapters 2 and 6, below) featured active use of the Tenth Amendment to invalidate federal legislation. In *Hammer v. Dagenhart*, 247 U.S. 251 (1917), the Court held that the regulation of child labor was within the powers reserved to the states under the Amendment, so that Congress could not regulate the sale of goods in interstate commerce that were otherwise unobjectionable except that they had been manufactured by child labor. Congress' effort to narrowly read this decision as simply limiting its Commerce Clause power, by imposing a tax on goods made with child labor, was likewise struck down. *Bailey v. Drexel Furniture Co.*, 259 U.S. 20 (1922). And, as part of the New Deal crisis, in *United States v. Butler*, 297 U.S. 1, 73 (1936), the Court found it unnecessary to determine if Art. I, §8 authorized legislation for payments to farmers reducing their production, because agricultural production was a subject "reserved to the states."

This approach was explicitly and unanimously overruled in *United States v. Darby*, 312 U.S. 100 (1941). Having concluded, consistent with *Jones & Laughlin* and contrary to *Hammer v. Dagenhart*, which it overruled, that the Commerce Clause permitted Congress to bar goods in interstate commerce produced by labor that did not meet federal standards, the Court explicitly reversed the reasoning of earlier decisions that the Tenth Amendment operated to narrow the scope of Congressional power, declaring that congressional power to regulate commerce "is unaffected by the Tenth Amendment." *Id.* at 123–24. Rather, that Amendment's purpose was simply "to allay fears that the new national government might seek to exercise powers not granted, and that the states might not be able to exercise fully their reserved powers." Likewise, in *Maryland v. Wirtz*, 392 U.S. 183 (1968), upholding the application of federal employment legislation to state employees, the Court rejected as "not tenable" the claim that otherwise valid regulatory legislation might exceed constitutional authorization because of the need to protect matters of state concern. Justice Harlan expressly rejected the notion that there is a general "doctrine implied in the Federal Constitution that the two governments, national and state, are each to exercise its powers so as not to interfere with the free and full exercise of the powers of the other." *Id.* at 195 (quoting *Case v. Bowles*, 327 U.S. 92, 101 (1946)). *See also Lake Shore & Michigan Southern R. Co. v. Ohio*, 173 U.S. 285, 297–298 (1899) ("When Congress acts with reference to a matter confided to it by the Constitution, then its statutes displace all conflicting local regulations touching that matter, although such regulations may have been established in pursuance of a power not surrendered by the States to the General Government.").

Although *Darby* put an end to the use of the Tenth Amendment to preclude Congress from regulating private matters also subject to state regulation, the ability of federal legislation to regulate activities of state governments (particularly with regard to state and local employees) provided another revealing opportunity for the Supreme Court to determine the degree to which it would actively seek to protect "states' rights." In *National League of Cities v. Usery*, 426 U.S. 833 (1976), a 5-4 majority held that the power of state and local governments to determine employee wages was an "attribute" of sovereignty that was "essential" to the separate and independent existence of states. Hence, the Tenth Amendment precluded Congress' ability to regulate labor relations between states and their employees under the Commerce Clause. Several subsequent decisions and a plethora of lower court decisions sought to apply doctrines designed to distinguish matters that were "indisputably attributes of state sovereignty" or impaired a state's ability to "structure integral operations in areas of traditional functions," but the Court did not strike down another federal law and lower courts were "all over the map." NOWAK & ROTUNDA § 4.10.

Nineteen years later, in *Garcia v. San Antonio Metro. Transit Auth.*, 469 U.S. 528 (1985), the Court overruled *National League of Cities* (the four original dissenters were joined by Justice Harry Blackmun, whose majority opinion explained why he changed his mind). He emphasized the difficulty of finding judicially manageable standards to police federalism as intended in the earlier case: "We find it difficult, if not impossible, to identify an organizing principle" to distinguish traditional government functions from others. *Id.* at 538. Likewise, developing Tenth Amendment doctrines to distinguish between state activities that were proprietary and thus subject to regulation and those that were not had proven "unworkable." *Id.* at 543. He expressed doubt that "courts ultimately can identify principled constitutional limitations on the scope of Congress' Commerce Clause powers over the States." *Id.* at 548.

Rather, *Garcia* concluded that the framers "chose to rely on a federal system in which special restraints on federal power over the States inhered principally" in the national political process. *Id.* at 551. (Indeed, following the decision, Congress responded to state governmental lobbying by amending federal law to permit state agencies to provide compensatory time in lieu of otherwise mandated overtime to their employees.)

1.4.5.   Lack of requirement that Commerce Clause power be exercised only for commercial regulatory concerns

One other issue raised by Canadian jurisprudence remains to be explored — the doctrine of "colourability." *Alton* had held that the Commerce power could not be used when Congress' purpose was "social welfare" (pensions for railroad workers) instead of "safety" or "efficiency." Here too, the post-1937 doctrine reversed course. In *United States v. Darby, supra*, the defendant argued that the purpose of the statute was not to regulate the goods in commerce (as in prior cases upholding federal bans on noxious or stolen goods), but rather to exclude non-objectionable goods simply because they were made by labor under employment conditions Congress deemed undesirable, although local employment was a matter for state rather than federal regulation. The Court rejected this argument:

> The motive and purpose of the present regulation are plainly to make effective the Congressional conception of public policy that interstate commerce should not be made the instrument of competition in the distribution of goods produced under substandard labor conditions, which competition is injurious to the commerce and to the states from and to which the commerce flows. The motive and purpose of a regulation of interstate commerce are matters for the legislative judgment upon the exercise of which the Constitution places no restriction and over which the courts are given no control. "The judicial cannot prescribe to the legislative department of the government limitations upon the exercise of its acknowledged power." *Veazie Bank v. Fenno*, 8 Wall. 533. Whatever their motive and purpose, regulations of commerce which do not infringe some constitutional prohibition are within the plenary power conferred on Congress by the Commerce Clause. Subject only to that limitation, presently to be considered, we conclude that the prohibition of the shipment interstate of goods produced under the forbidden substandard labor conditions is within the constitutional authority of Congress. 312 U.S. at 115.

> [Explaining its decision to overrule *Hammer v. Dagenhart*, 247 U.S. 251 (1918), the Court explained that the] thesis of the opinion that the motive of the prohibition or its effect to control in some measure the use or production within the states of the article thus excluded from the commerce can operate to deprive the regulation of its constitutional authority has long since ceased to have force.

Congressional authority to invoke its Commerce Clause power when motivated by non-commercial ends was graphically re-affirmed in *Heart of Atlanta Motel, Inc. v. United States*, 379 U.S. 241 (1964), which upheld the constitutionality of Title II of the Civil Rights Act of 1964, prohibiting racial discrimination in public accommodations, including hotels serving five or more guests. The appellant owned a motel in downtown Atlanta, readily accessible to several major interstate highways. Successfully soliciting guests through magazines and billboards, approximately 75% of its registered guests were from out of state. Noting congressional findings about the significant adverse effect of racial discrimination on the ability of millions of African Americans to travel interstate, the Court had no difficulty concluding that the regulated activity had the requisite substantial effect on interstate commerce. Since the Senate Commerce Committee, in its report on the legislation, made it clear that the fundamental purpose of this title was to vindicate "the deprivation of personal dignity that surely accompanies denials of equal access to public establishments," the Court next turned to Congress' motive.

> That Congress was legislating against moral wrongs in many of [the statutes previously upheld under the Commerce Clause] rendered its enactments no less *valid*. In framing Title II of this Act Congress was also dealing with what it considered a moral problem. But that fact does not detract from the overwhelming evidence of the disruptive effect that racial discrimination has had on commercial intercourse. It was this burden which empowered Congress to enact appropriate legislation, and, given this basis

for the exercise of its power, Congress was not restricted by the fact that the particular obstruction to interstate commerce with which it was dealing was also deemed a moral and social wrong.

As Justice Black noted in a concurring opinion, the Court had frequently upheld the use of the commerce power to advance other ends not entirely commercial.[13]

In a related case, the Court held upheld the application of the Civil Rights Act to a segregated local barbecue shop in Alabama patronized by few if any interstate customers, based on a finding that significant portions of food was purchased from out-of-state suppliers (again, regardless of the actual congressional motivation for the statute). *Katzenbach v. McClung*, 379 U.S. 294 (1964). The Court found that Congress had a rational basis for concluding that more food would flow in interstate commerce if segregated local restaurants opened their doors to minority race customers.

1.4.6.   The pendulum swings back

Within the last decade, the pendulum has begun to swing back. In *United States v. Lopez*, 514 U.S. 549 (1995), the Court struck down a federal prohibition on possessing a gun near a school, finding the link between gun possession and interstate commerce too tenuous. In *United States v. Morrison*, 529 U.S. 598 (2000), the Court struck down a provision of the Violence Against Women Act creating a federal cause of action for tortious assaults that were gender-related. Again, the majority found the logic linking domestic and gender-related violence to interstate commerce to create an unduly expansive federal power. And most famously in *Nat'l Fed'n of Indep. Businesses v. Sebelius*, 132 S. Ct. 2566 (2012), the majority held that Congress could not regulate interstate commerce by requiring individuals to purchase health insurance (although Congress could accomplish the same result through taxation). In all three cases, 5-4 majorities emphasized the need to reject arguments for federal power that had no limiting principle, and the extent to which these statutes intruded in traditional areas of state domain: general criminal law, general tort law, and educational policies. The debate and reasoning is explained in these excerpts from *Morrison* and *Sebelius*.

---

[13] For example: United States v. Darby, 312 U.S. 100 (1941) (Fair Labor Standards Act); United States v. Miller, 307 U.S. 174 (1939) (National Firearms Act); Gooch v. United States, 297 U.S. 124 (1936) (Federal Kidnaping Act); Brooks v. United States, 267 U.S. 432 (1925) (National Motor Vehicle Theft Act); United States v. Simpson, 252 U.S. 465 (1920) (Act forbidding shipment of liquor into a "dry" State); Caminetti v. United States, 242 U.S. 470 (1917) (White-Slave Traffic (Mann) Act); Hoke v. United States, 227 U.S. 308 (1913) (White-Slave Traffic (Mann) Act); Hipolite Egg Co. v. United States, 220 U.S. 45 (1911) (Pure Food and Drugs Act); Lottery Case, 188 U.S. 321 (1903) (Act forbidding interstate shipment of lottery tickets).

UNITED STATES v. MORRISON
SUPREME COURT OF THE UNITED STATES
529 U.S. 598 (2000)

REHNQUIST, C. J., delivered the opinion of the Court, in which O'CONNOR, SCALIA, KENNEDY, and THOMAS, JJ., joined.

[The majority held unconstitutional the portions of the federal Violence Against Women Act of 1994 (VAWA) that create a federal cause of action for compensatory and punitive damages against any person "who commits a crime of violence motivated by gender." The court thus dismissed a federal claim brought by a female student at Virginia Tech who alleged that Morrison and a co-defendant, both members of the football team, had brutally raped her, and that Morrison later bragged about his desire "to get girls drunk and [here the Court simply referred to "boasting, debased remarks . . . that cannot fail to shock and offend."] After the plaintiff learned via the school newspaper that Virginia Tech's provost had over-turned the school's punishment against Morrison, she dropped out of the University, later filing an action against Morrison under VAWA and against the University under another federal statute prohibiting universities receiving federal funds from discriminating on the basis of sex. The court of appeal dismissed the VAWA claim on constitutional grounds.]

[The Court began its analysis of whether VAWA was a proper exercise of federal legislative authority under the Commerce Clause by adverting to its prior historical exegesis in *Lopez*. The majority there wrote:

> We start with first principles. The Constitution creates a Federal Government of enumerated powers. See Art. I, § 8. As James Madison wrote, "the powers delegated by the proposed Constitution to the federal government are few and defined. Those which are to remain in the State governments are numerous and indefinite." The Federalist No. 45, pp. 292-293 (C. Rossiter ed. 1961). This constitutionally mandated division of authority "was adopted by the Framers to ensure protection of our fundamental liberties." *Gregory v. Ashcroft*, 501 U.S. 452, 458, 111 S. Ct. 2395, 115 L. Ed. 2d 410 (1991) (internal quotation marks omitted). "Just as the separation and independence of the coordinate branches of the Federal Government serve to prevent the accumulation of excessive power in any one branch, a healthy balance of power between the States and the Federal Government will reduce the risk of tyranny and abuse from either front." *Ibid.*]

[*Lopez* had acknowledged that the New Deal decisions "ushered in an era of Commerce Clause jurisprudence that greatly expanded the previously defined authority of Congress under that Clause." This reflected both a recognition of the increasing amount of interstate commerce, so that previously local activities "had become national in scope," and partly "reflected a view that earlier Commerce Clause cases artificially had constrained the authority of Congress to regulate interstate commerce." However, *Lopez* explicitly noted that Congressional power was still subject to "outer limits."]

[In *Lopez*, the government defended the statute as within the Congressional power to regulate "those activities intrastate which so affect interstate commerce or the exercise of the power of Congress over it as to make regulation of them appropriate means to the attainment of a legitimate end." *United States v. Darby*, 312 U.S. 100, 118 (1941). The government argued that gun possession leads to violent crime, which costs money throughout the economy; it reduces the willingness of individuals to travel to unsafe areas; gun violence near schools harms the quality of education which results in a less economically-productive citizenry. The majority definitively rejected these arguments. First, in a key footnote the Court emphasized, citing several prior precedents, that in "our federal system, the " 'States possess primary authority for defining and enforcing the criminal law.' " Thus, when "Congress criminalizes conduct already denounced as criminal by the States, it effects a " 'change in the sensitive relation between federal and state criminal jurisdiction.' " The majority also quoted a signing statement by President George H.W. Bush complaining that this provision "inappropriately overrides legitimate State firearms laws with a new and unnecessary Federal law. The policies reflected in these provisions could legitimately be adopted by the States, but they should not be imposed upon the States by the Congress." Second, the Court explained why the causal impact of gun possession on the economy was insufficient to fall within congressional power to regulate activities that "substantially affect" interstate commerce:

We pause to consider the implications of the Government's arguments. The Government admits, under its "costs of crime" reasoning, that Congress could regulate not only all violent crime, but all activities that might lead to violent crime, regardless of how tenuously they relate to interstate commerce. See Tr. of Oral Arg. 8-9. Similarly, under the Government's "national productivity" reasoning, Congress could regulate any activity that it found was related to the economic productivity of individual citizens: family law (including marriage, divorce, and child custody), for example. Under the theories that the Government presents in support of § 922(q), it is difficult to perceive any limitation on federal power, even in areas such as criminal law enforcement or education where States historically have been sovereign. Thus, if we were to accept the Government's arguments, we are hard pressed to posit any activity by an individual that Congress is without power to regulate.

. . . .

To uphold the Government's contentions here, we would have to pile inference upon inference in a manner that would bid fair to convert congressional authority under the Commerce Clause to a general police power of the sort retained by the States. Admittedly, some of our prior cases have taken long steps down that road, giving great deference to congressional action. The broad language in these opinions has suggested the possibility of additional expansion, but we decline here to proceed any further. To do so would require us to conclude that the Constitution's enumeration of powers does not presuppose something not enumerated, cf. *Gibbons v. Ogden*, supra, at 195, and that there never will be a distinction between what is truly national and what is truly local, cf. *Jones & Laughlin*

Steel, supra, at 30. This we are unwilling to do.]

[In this case, the Court rejected congressional findings about the economic impact of gender-motivated violence on victims and their families, concluded that Congress relied "so heavily on a method of reasoning that we have already rejected as unworkable if we are to maintain the Constitution's enumeration of powers." As in *Lopez,* the majority found that its concern "that Congress might use the Commerce Clause to completely obliterate the Constitution's distinction between national and local authority seems well founded."]

Petitioners' reasoning, moreover, will not limit Congress to regulating violence but may, as we suggested in *Lopez,* be applied equally as well to family law and other areas of traditional state regulation since the aggregate effect of marriage, divorce, and childrearing on the national economy is undoubtedly significant. Congress may have recognized this specter when it expressly precluded § 13981 from being used in the family law context. See 42 U.S.C. § 13981(e)(4). Under our written Constitution, however, the limitation of congressional authority is not solely a matter of legislative grace.[14] We accordingly reject the argument that Congress may regulate noneconomic, violent criminal conduct based solely on that conduct's aggregate effect on interstate commerce. The Constitution requires a distinction between what is truly national and what is truly local. *Lopez,* 514 U.S. at 568 (citing *Jones & Laughlin Steel,* 301 U.S. at 30). In recognizing this fact we preserve one of the few principles that has been consistent since the Clause was adopted. The regulation and punishment of intrastate violence that is not directed at the instrumentalities, channels, or goods involved in interstate commerce has always been the province of the States. *See, e.g., Cohens v. Virginia,* 19 U.S. 264, 5 L. Ed. 257, 6 Wheat. 264, 426, 428 (1821) (Marshall, C. J.) (stating that Congress "has no general right to punish murder committed within any of the States," and that it is "clear . . . that congress cannot punish felonies generally"). Indeed, we can think of no better example of the police power, which the Founders denied the National Government and reposed in the States, than the suppression of violent crime and vindication of its victims. See, e.g., *Lopez,* 514 U.S. at 566 ("The Constitution . . . withholds from Congress a plenary police power"); *id.,* at 584-585 (Thomas, J., concurring) ("We always have rejected readings of the Commerce Clause and the scope of federal power that would permit Congress to exercise a police power"), 596-597, and n. 6 (noting that the first Congresses did not enact nationwide punishments for criminal conduct under the Commerce Clause).

. . . .

IV

Petitioner Brzonkala's complaint alleges that she was the victim of a brutal assault. But Congress' effort in § 13981 to provide a federal civil remedy can be sustained neither under the Commerce Clause nor under § 5 of the Fourteenth Amendment. If the allegations here are true, no civilized system of justice could fail

---

[14] [Ed. note: In footnote 7 of its opinion, the majority explicitly discussed and rejected Justice Souter's political process argument in dissent. This footnote is summarized in the narrative following this case.]

to provide her a remedy for the conduct of respondent Morrison. But under our federal system that remedy must be provided by the Commonwealth of Virginia, and not by the United States. The judgment of the Court of Appeals is affirmed.

JUSTICE THOMAS, concurring.

The majority opinion correctly applies our decision in *United States v. Lopez*, 514 U.S. 549, 115 S. Ct. 1624, 131 L. Ed. 2d 626 (1995), and I join it in full. I write separately only to express my view that the very notion of a "substantial effects" test under the Commerce Clause is inconsistent with the original understanding of Congress' powers and with this Court's early Commerce Clause cases. By continuing to apply this rootless and malleable standard, however circumscribed, the Court has encouraged the Federal Government to persist in its view that the Commerce Clause has virtually no limits. Until this Court replaces its existing Commerce Clause jurisprudence with a standard more consistent with the original understanding, we will continue to see Congress appropriating state police powers under the guise of regulating commerce.

[In *Lopez*, Justice Thomas set out his views in greater detail. There, he argued that Congress should not have the authority to regulate intrastate matters "affecting" interstate commerce. He concluded that when the Constitution was drafted, "commerce" consisted of selling, buying, and bartering, as well as transporting for these purposes, in contrast to productive activities such as manufacturing and agriculture. He made several other textual arguments to support his view that "commerce" denoted sale and/or transport rather than business generally. For example, he noted that the Court's understanding of congressional power under the Commerce and Necessary & Proper clauses rendered many of Congress' other enumerated powers under Art. I, § 8, wholly superfluous if the Commerce Clause included the power to regulate intrastate activities "affecting" interstate commerce. Moreover, he argued that the breadth of the post-New Deal scope of the Commerce Clause comes close to "turning the Tenth Amendment on its head."]

JUSTICE SOUTER, with whom JUSTICE STEVENS, JUSTICE GINSBURG, and JUSTICE BREYER join, dissenting.

[Noting the voluminous data that Congress assembled to show the adverse economic effect of violence against women, the dissent concluded that VAWA] would have passed muster at any time between *Wickard* in 1942 and *Lopez* in 1995, a period in which the law enjoyed a stable understanding that congressional power under the Commerce Clause, complemented by the authority of the Necessary and Proper Clause, Art. I. § 8 cl. 18, extended to all activity that, when aggregated, has a substantial effect on interstate commerce. . . .

. . . .

The premise that the enumeration of powers implies that other powers are withheld is sound; the conclusion that some particular categories of subject matter are therefore presumptively beyond the reach of the commerce power is, however, a *non sequitur*. From the fact that Art. I, § 8, cl. 3 grants an authority limited to regulating commerce, it follows only that Congress may claim no authority under that section to address any subject that does not affect commerce. It does not at all follow that an activity affecting commerce nonetheless falls outside the commerce power, depending on the specific character of the activity, or the authority of a State to regulate it along with Congress.[15] My disagreement with the majority is not, however, confined to logic, for history has shown that categorical exclusions have proven as unworkable in practice as they are unsupportable in theory.

A

[In Justice Souter's view, the "attempt to distinguish between primary activities affecting commerce in terms of the relatively commercial or noncommercial character of the primary conduct proscribed comes with the pedigree of near-tragedy" that the Court had previously caused.] In the half century following the modern activation of the commerce power with passage of the Interstate Commerce Act in 1887, this Court from time to time created categorical enclaves beyond congressional reach by declaring such activities as "mining," "production," "manu-facturing," and union membership to be outside the definition of "commerce" and by limiting application of the effects test to "direct" rather than "indirect" commercial consequences. [citing cases].

. . . .

Why is the majority tempted to reject the lesson so painfully learned in 1937? An answer emerges from contrasting *Wickard* with one of the predecessor cases it superseded. It was obvious in *Wickard* that growing wheat for consumption right on the farm was not "commerce" in the common vocabulary, but that did not matter constitutionally so long as the aggregated activity of domestic wheat growing affected commerce substantially. Just a few years before *Wickard*, however, it had certainly been no less obvious that "mining" practices could substantially affect commerce, even though [*Carter v. Carter Coal Co.*, 298 U.S. 238 (1936)] had held mining regulation beyond the national commerce power. When we try to fathom the difference between the two cases, it is clear that they did not go in different directions because the *Carter Coal* Court could not understand a causal connection that the *Wickard* Court could grasp; the difference, rather, turned on the fact that the Court in *Carter Coal* had a reason for trying to maintain its categorical, formalistic distinction, while that reason had been abandoned by the time *Wickard* was decided. The reason was laissez-faire economics, the point of which was to keep government interference to a minimum. The Court in *Carter Coal* was still trying to create a laissez-faire world out of the 20th-century economy, and formalistic

---

[15] [FN 12] To the contrary, we have always recognized that while the federal commerce power may overlap the reserved state police power, in such cases federal authority is supreme. See, e.g., *Lake Shore & Michigan Southern R. Co. v. Ohio*, 173 U.S. 285, 297-298, 19 S. Ct. 465, 43 L. Ed. 702 (1899) ("When Congress acts with reference to a matter confided to it by the Constitution, then its statutes displace all conflicting local regulations touching that matter, although such regulations may have been established in pursuance of a power not surrendered by the States to the General Government"); *United States v. California*, 297 U.S. 175, 185, 56 S. Ct. 421, 80 L. Ed. 567 (1936) ("We look to the activities in which the states have traditionally engaged as marking the boundary of the restriction upon the federal taxing power. But there is no such limitation upon the plenary power to regulate commerce").

commercial distinctions were thought to be useful instruments in achieving that object. The Court in *Wickard* knew it could not do any such thing and in the aftermath of the New Deal had long since stopped attempting the impossible. Without the animating economic theory, there was no point in contriving formalisms in a war with Chief Justice Marshall's conception of the commerce power.

. . . .

B

The Court finds it relevant that the statute addresses conduct traditionally subject to state prohibition under domestic criminal law, a fact said to have some heightened significance when the violent conduct in question is not itself aimed directly at interstate commerce or its instrumentalities. Again, history seems to be recycling, for the theory of traditional state concern as grounding a limiting principle has been rejected previously, and more than once. *** The effort to carve out inviolable state spheres within the spectrum of activities substantially affecting commerce was, of course, just as irreconcilable with *Gibbons's* explanation of the national commerce power as being as "absolute as it would be in a single government," 9 Wheat. at 197.[16]

The objection to reviving traditional state spheres of action as a consideration in commerce analysis, however, not only rests on the portent of incoherence, but is compounded by a further defect just as fundamental. The defect, in essence, is the majority's rejection of the Founders' considered judgment that politics, not judicial review, should mediate between state and national interests as the strength and legislative jurisdiction of the National Government inevitably increased through the expected growth of the national economy. Whereas today's majority takes a leaf from the book of the old judicial economists in saying that the Court should somehow draw the line to keep the federal relationship in a proper balance, Madison, Wilson, and Marshall understood the Constitution very differently.

. . . .

---

[16] [FN 14] The Constitution of 1787 did, in fact, forbid some exercises of the commerce power. Article I, § 9, cl. 6, barred Congress from giving preference to the ports of one State over those of another. More strikingly, the Framers protected the slave trade from federal interference, see Art. I, § 9, cl. 1, and confirmed the power of a State to guarantee the chattel status of slaves who fled to another State, see Art. IV, § 2, cl. 3. These reservations demonstrate the plenary nature of the federal power; the exceptions prove the rule. Apart from them, proposals to carve islands of state authority out of the stream of commerce power were entirely unsuccessful. Roger Sherman's proposed definition of federal legislative power as excluding "matters of internal police" met Gouverneur Morris's response that "the internal police . . . ought to be infringed in many cases" and was voted down eight to two. 2 Records of the Federal Convention of 1787, pp. 25-26 (M. Farrand ed. 1911) (hereinafter Farrand). The Convention similarly rejected Sherman's attempt to include in Article V a proviso that "no state shall . . . be affected in its internal police." 5 Elliot's Debates 551-552. Finally, Rufus King suggested an explicit bill of rights for the States, a device that might indeed have set aside the areas the Court now declares off-limits. 1 Farrand 493 ("As the fundamental rights of individuals are secured by express provisions in the State Constitutions; why may not a like security be provided for the Rights of States in the National Constitution"). That proposal, too, came to naught. In short, to suppose that enumerated powers must have limits is sensible; to maintain that there exist judicially identifiable areas of state regulation immune to the plenary congressional commerce power even though falling within the limits defined by the substantial effects test is to deny our constitutional history.

Politics as the moderator of the congressional employment of the commerce power was the theme many years later in *Wickard*, for after the Court acknowledged the breadth of the *Gibbons* formulation it invoked Chief Justice Marshall yet again in adding that "he made emphatic the embracing and penetrating nature of this power by warning that effective restraints on its exercise must proceed from political rather than judicial processes." *Wickard*, 317 U.S. at 120 (citation omitted). Hence, "conflicts of economic interest . . . are wisely left under our system to resolution by Congress under its more flexible and responsible legislative process. Such conflicts rarely lend themselves to judicial determination. And with the wisdom, workability, or fairness, of the plan of regulation we have nothing to do." *Id.*, at 129 (footnote omitted). [Justice Souter proceeded to refer to *Garcia v. San Antonio Metropolitan Transit Authority*, 469 U.S. 528 (1985), rejecting an argument that the Tenth Amendment limited Congress' ability to regulate relations between states and their employees.]

. . . .

C

[Justice Souter concluded by calling the majority's reliance on traditional state regulation "odd" in light of the overwhelming support of the VAWA by state attorneys general and their support for the conclusion that state remedies for dealing with violence against women were inadequate.]

JUSTICE BREYER, with whom JUSTICE STEVENS joins, and with whom JUSTICE SOUTER and JUSTICE GINSBURG join as to Part I-A, dissenting.

[Justice Breyer's dissent begins with a critique of the difficulty applying the economic/noneconomic distinction created by the majority. Thus, he argued that] Congress, not the courts, must remain primarily responsible for striking the appropriate state/federal balance. Congress is institutionally motivated to do so. Its Members represent state and local district interests. They consider the views of state and local officials when they legislate, and they have even developed formal procedures to ensure that such consideration takes place. See, e.g., Unfunded Mandates Reform Act of 1995, Pub. L. 104-4, 109 Stat. 48 (codified in scattered sections of 2 U.S.C.). Moreover, Congress often can better reflect state concerns for autonomy in the details of sophisticated statutory schemes than can the judiciary, which cannot easily gather the relevant facts and which must apply more general legal rules and categories. Not surprisingly, the bulk of American law is still state law, and overwhelmingly so.

———

One of the key arguments in Justice Souter's dissent — that the political process will adequately ensure that the federal/state balance is preserved in American politics — was sharply disputed by justices in the majority in *Lopez* and *Morrison*. Concurring in *Lopez*, Justice Kennedy (joined by Justice O'Connor) explicitly rejected this argument:

[T]he absence of structural mechanisms to require those officials to undertake this principled task, and the momentary political convenience often attendant upon their failure to do so, argue against a complete renunciation of the judicial role. [T]he federal balance is too essential a part of our constitutional structure and plays too vital a role in securing freedom for us to admit inability to intervene when one or the other level of Government has tipped the scales too far.

Specifically, Justice Kennedy averted to the reduced political accountability if the federal government took over "entire areas of traditional state concern." In footnote 7 of his *Morrison* opinion, Chief Justice Rehnquist was even more explicit in rejecting Justice Souter's argument. This "remarkable" argument "undermines this central principle of our constitutional system. As we have repeatedly noted, the Framers crafted the federal system of government so that the people's rights would be secured by the division of power." The political branches "have a role in interpreting and applying the Constitution, but ever since *Marbury* this Court has remained the ultimate expositor of the constitutional text." The majority concluded that *Gibbons* did not exempt the commerce power from this cardinal rule of constitutional law. Justice Souter's assertion that, from *Gibbons* on, public opinion has been the only restraint on the congressional exercise of the commerce power is true only insofar as it contends that political accountability is and has been the only limit on Congress' exercise of the commerce power within that power's outer bounds. The majority believed that the language surrounding that relied upon by Justice Souter made clear that Chief Jusice Marshall did not remove from this Court the authority to define that boundary.

These issues were again considered in *Gonzales v. Raich*, 545 U.S. 1 (2005), where a 6-3 majority upheld federal legislation prohibiting the local cultivation and use of marijuana for medical purposes in compliance with state law. Justice Stevens relied on *Wickard* in finding that Congress had a rational basis to conclude that failure to regulate medical marijuana could affect, via diversion to illegal channels, interstate commerce in the controlled substance. In contrast to *Lopez*, the marijuana ban was an "essential part of a larger regulation of economic activity." Justice O'Connor, joined by Rehnquist, C.J., and Thomas, J., dissented. She wrote:

> We enforce the "outer limits" of Congress' Commerce Clause authority not for their own sake, but to protect historic spheres of state sovereignty from excessive federal encroachment and thereby to maintain the distribution of power fundamental to our federalist system of government. One of federalism's chief virtues, of course, is that it promotes innovation by allowing for the possibility that "a single courageous State may, if its citizens choose, serve as a laboratory; and try novel social and economic experiments without risk to the rest of the country." *New State Ice Co.* v. *Liebmann*, 285 U.S. 262, 311, 52 S. Ct. 371, 76 L. Ed. 747 (1932) (Brandeis, J., dissenting).

> This case exemplifies the role of States as laboratories. The States' core police powers have always included authority to define criminal law and to protect the health, safety, and welfare of their citizens. Exercising those powers, California (by ballot initiative and then by legislative codification)

has come to its own conclusion about the difficult and sensitive question of whether marijuana should be available to relieve severe pain and suffering. Today the Court sanctions an application of the federal Controlled Substances Act that extinguishes that experiment, without any proof that the personal cultivation, possession, and use of marijuana for medicinal purposes, if economic activity in the first place, has a substantial effect on interstate commerce and is therefore an appropriate subject of federal regulation

545 U.S. at 42–43. Justice O'Connor emphasized that "because fundamental structural concerns about dual sovereignty animate our Commerce Clause cases, it is relevant that this case involves the interplay of federal and state regulation in areas of criminal law and social policy, where 'States lay claim by right of history and expertise.'" She criticized the majority for using "a dictionary definition of economics to skirt the real problem of drawing a meaningful line between 'what is national and what is local.'" *Id.* at 48–49. Writing separately, Justice Thomas concluded: "One searches the Court's opinion in vain for any hint of what aspect of American life is reserved to the States." *Id.* at 70.

In one of the most publicized cases in a generation, the latest word from the U.S. Supreme Court on constitutional federalism arose in the context of a challenge to the Affordable Care Act (or, in political speak, "Obamacare"), comprehensive federal legislation designed to reduce health care costs and to sharply minimize the number of Americans who lacked health insurance. Among the key provisions in the 900-page bill were requirements for minimum coverage in all health insurance policies and a ban on limiting coverage for, or imposing higher premiums on, consumers with pre-existing medical conditions. Two provisions sparked a constitutional challenge: Americans above a designated income level who did not receive health insurance coverage from existing government programs or through their employer (the principal means by which most Americans obtain health insurance) were required to purchase health insurance (the bill set up state-operated clearing houses to facilitate these purchases). Those who failed to do so paid an income-based penalty on their tax return. The individual mandate was justified by its supporters as necessary to insure that the costs of health care were spread widely among all Americans, and to prevent a serious problem, estimated to cost each insured $1,000 per year, of medical coverage for those without health insurance and without the ability to pay cash who actually required health care each year. States were also required, as a condition of receiving massive federal funding for their Medicaid program of assistance to poorer residents, to expand coverage to middle-income residents as well. [Ed. note: the Court's holding that it was an unconstitutional exercise of Congress' Spending Power to condition the receipt of any Medicaid funding on acceptance of Medicaid expansion is considered below in Section 1.7.1.]

NATIONAL FEDERATION OF INDEPENDENT BUSINESS v. SEBELIUS

SUPREME COURT OF THE UNITED STATES

132 S. Ct. 2566 (2012)

CHIEF JUSTICE ROBERTS announced the judgment of the Court and delivered the opinion of the Court with respect to Parts I, II, and III-C, an opinion with respect to Part IV, in which JUSTICE BREYER and JUSTICE KAGAN join, and an opinion with respect to Parts III-A, III-B, and III-D.

[ROBERTS, C.J., began by reciting prior holdings that federal powers and enumerated and limited, and that state sovereignty is not an end in itself but rather a means to secure "to citizens the liberties that derive from the diffusion of sovereign power." *New York v. United States*, 505 U.S. 144, 181 (1992).]

This case concerns two powers that the Constitution does grant the Federal Government, but which must be read carefully to avoid creating a general federal authority akin to the police power. [He noted that precedents authorizing Congress to regulate "activities that substantially affect interstate commerce can be expansive."] That power has been held to authorize federal regulation of such seemingly local matters as a farmer's decision to grow wheat for himself and his livestock, and a loan shark's extortionate collections from a neighborhood butcher shop. See *Wickard v. Filburn*, 317 U.S. 111(1942); *Perez v. United States*, 402 U.S. 146 (1971).

Congress may also "lay and collect Taxes, Duties, Imposts and Excises, to pay the Debts and provide for the common Defence and general Welfare of the United States." U.S. Const., Art. I, § 8, cl. 1. Put simply, Congress may tax and spend. This grant gives the Federal Government considerable influence even in areas where it cannot directly regulate. The Federal Government may enact a tax on an activity that it cannot authorize, forbid, or otherwise control. See, *e.g., License Tax Cases*, 72 U.S. 462, 5 Wall. 462, 471 (1867). And in exercising its spending power, Congress may offer funds to the States, and may condition those offers on compliance with specified conditions. See, *e.g., College Savings Bank v. Florida Prepaid Postsecondary Ed. Expense Bd.*, 527 U.S. 666, 686 (1999). These offers may well induce the States to adopt policies that the Federal Government itself could not impose. See, *e.g., South Dakota v. Dole*, 483 U.S. 203, 205-206 (1987) (conditioning federal highway funds on States raising their drinking age to 21).

The reach of the Federal Government's enumerated powers is broader still because the Constitution authorizes Congress to "make all Laws which shall be necessary and proper for carrying into Execution the foregoing Powers." Art. I, '8, cl. 18. We have long read this provision to give Congress great latitude in exercising its powers: "Let the end be legitimate, let it be within the scope of the constitution, and all means which are appropriate, which are plainly adapted to that end, which are not prohibited, but consist with the letter and spirit of the constitution, are constitutional." *McCulloch, 4 Wheat.*, at 421.

Our permissive reading of these powers is explained in part by a general reticence to invalidate the acts of the Nation's elected leaders. "Proper respect for a coordinate branch of the government" requires that we strike down an Act of Congress only if "the lack of constitutional authority to pass [the] act in question is clearly demonstrated." *United States v. Harris*, 106 U.S. 629, 635 (1883). Members of this Court are vested with the authority to interpret the law; we possess neither the expertise nor the prerogative to make policy judgments. Those decisions are entrusted to our Nation's elected leaders, who can be thrown out of office if the people disagree with them. It is not our job to protect the people from the consequences of their political choices.

Our deference in matters of policy cannot, however, become abdication in matters of law. "The powers of the legislature are defined and limited; and that those limits may not be mistaken, or forgotten, the constitution is written." *Marbury v. Madison*, 5 U.S. 137, 1 Cranch 137, 176 (1803). Our respect for Congress's policy judgments thus can never extend so far as to disavow restraints on federal power that the Constitution carefully constructed. "The peculiar circumstances of the moment may render a measure more or less wise, but cannot render it more or less constitutional." Chief Justice John Marshall, A Friend of the Constitution No. V, Alexandria Gazette, July 5, 1819, in John Marshall's Defense of *McCulloch* v. *Maryland* 190-191 (G. Gunther ed. 1969). And there can be no question that it is the responsibility of this Court to enforce the limits on federal power by striking down acts of Congress that transgress those limits. *Marbury v. Madison, supra*, at 175-176.

. . . .

III

. . . .

A

The Government's first argument is that the individual mandate is a valid exercise of Congress's power under the *Commerce Clause* and the Necessary and Proper Clause. According to the Government, the health care market is characterized by a significant cost-shifting problem. [Here, Roberts, C.J., summarized the problem that hospitals must provide care to those without insurance or the ability to pay, which is passed on in the form of higher insurance premiums, and exacerbated because of provisions barring insurance companies from denying or charging higher premiums to those with preexisting conditions or living in communities characterized by higher health costs.]

. . .

The individual mandate was Congress's solution to these problems. By requiring that individuals purchase health insurance, the mandate prevents cost-shifting by those who would otherwise go without it. In addition, the mandate forces into the insurance risk pool more healthy individuals, whose premiums on average will be higher than their health care expenses. This allows insurers to subsidize the costs of covering the unhealthy individuals the reforms require them to accept. The Government claims that Congress has power under the Commerce and Necessary and Proper Clauses to enact this solution.

1

. . .

Given its expansive scope, it is no surprise that Congress has employed the commerce power in a wide variety of ways to address the pressing needs of the time. But Congress has never attempted to rely on that power to compel individuals not engaged in commerce to purchase an unwanted product. Legislative novelty is not necessarily fatal; there is a first time for everything. But sometimes "the most telling indication of [a] severe constitutional problem . . . is the lack of historical precedent" for Congress's action. *Free Enterprise Fund v. Public Company Accounting Oversight Bd.*, 561 U.S. ___, ___ (2010). At the very least, we should "pause to consider the implications of the Government's arguments" when confronted with such new conceptions of federal power. *Lopez, supra,* at 564.

. . . .

The Constitution grants Congress the power to "*regulate* Commerce." Art. I, § 8, cl. 3 (emphasis added). The power to *regulate* commerce presupposes the existence of commercial activity to be regulated. If the power to "regulate" something included the power to create it, many of the provisions in the Constitution would be superfluous. For example, the Constitution gives Congress the power to "coin Money," in addition to the power to "regulate the Value thereof." *Id.,* cl. 5. And it gives Congress the power to "raise and support Armies" and to "provide and maintain a Navy," in addition to the power to "make Rules for the Government and Regulation of the land and naval Forces." *Id.,* cls. 12-14. If the power to regulate the armed forces or the value of money included the power to bring the subject of the regulation into existence, the specific grant of such powers would have been unnecessary. The language of the Constitution reflects the natural understanding that the power to regulate assumes there is already something to be regulated. See *Gibbons, 9 Wheat.,* at 188 ("[T]he enlightened patriots who framed our constitution, and the people who adopted it, must be understood to have employed words in their natural sense, and to have intended what they have said").

. . .

The individual mandate, however, does not regulate existing commercial activity. It instead compels individuals to *become* active in commerce by purchasing a product, on the ground that their failure to do so affects interstate commerce. Construing the *Commerce Clause* to permit Congress to regulate individuals precisely *because* they are doing nothing would open a new and potentially vast domain to congressional authority. Every day individuals do not do an infinite number of things. In some cases they decide not to do something; in others they simply fail to do it. Allowing Congress to justify federal regulation by pointing to the effect of inaction on commerce would bring countless decisions an individual could *potentially* make within the scope of federal regulation, and — under the Government's theory — empower Congress to make those decisions for him.

. . . .

Indeed, the Government's logic would justify a mandatory purchase to solve almost any problem . . . . To consider a different example in the health care market, many Americans do not eat a balanced diet. That group makes up a larger percentage of the total population than those without health insurance. The failure of that group to have a healthy diet increases health care costs, to a greater extent than the failure of the uninsured to purchase insurance. . . . Under the Government's theory, Congress could address the diet problem by ordering everyone to buy vegetables. . . .

. . . .

That is not the country the Framers of our Constitution envisioned. James Madison explained that the *Commerce Clause* was "an addition which few oppose and from which no apprehensions are entertained." The Federalist No. 45, at 293. While Congress's authority under the *Commerce Clause* has of course expanded with the growth of the national economy, our cases have "always recognized that the power to regulate commerce, though broad indeed, has limits." *Maryland v. Wirtz*, 392 U.S. 183, 196 (1968). The Government's theory would erode those limits, permitting Congress to reach beyond the natural extent of its authority, "everywhere extending the sphere of its activity and drawing all power into its impetuous vortex." The Federalist No. 48, at 309 (J. Madison). . . .

. . . .

2

[Turning to the Government's contention that Congress has the power under the Necessary and Proper Clause to enact the individual mandate, Roberts, C.J. noted that] we have been very deferential to Congress's determination that a regulation is "necessary." We have thus upheld laws that are " 'convenient, or useful' or 'conducive' to the authority's 'beneficial exercise.' " But we have also carried out our responsibility to declare unconstitutional those laws that undermine the structure of government established by the Constitution. . . . *Comstock* (Kennedy, J., concurring in judgment) ("It is of fundamental importance to consider whether essential attributes of state sovereignty are compromised by the assertion of federal power under the Necessary and Proper Clause . . .").

Applying these principles, the individual mandate cannot be sustained under the Necessary and Proper Clause as an essential component of the insurance reforms. Each of our prior cases upholding laws under that Clause involved exercises of authority derivative of, and in service to, a granted power. . . . The individual mandate, by contrast, vests Congress with the extraordinary ability to create the necessary predicate to the exercise of an enumerated power.

. . . .

B

[Nonetheless, the individual mandate provisions were upheld "as within Congress's enumerated power to "lay and collect Taxes." Art. I, '8, cl. 1." Although the "most straightforward reading of the mandate is that it commands individuals to purchase insurance," Roberts, C.J. held that a "fairly possible" interpretation of the mandate was that "it only imposes a tax on those without insurance." Under

Supreme Court precedent, "every reasonable construction must be resorted to, in order to save a statute from unconstitutionality." *Hooper v. California*, 155 U.S. 648, 657 (1895).]

. . . .

JUSTICE GINSBURG, with whom JUSTICE SOTOMAYOR joins, and with whom JUSTICE BREYER and JUSTICE KAGAN join as to Parts I, II, III, and IV, concurring in part, concurring in the judgment in part, and dissenting in part.

. . . .

I

The provision of health care is today a concern of national dimension, just as the provision of old-age and survivors' benefits was in the 1930s. In the Social Security Act, Congress installed a federal system to provide monthly benefits to retired wage earners and, eventually, to their survivors. Beyond question, Congress could have adopted a similar scheme for health care. Congress chose, instead, to preserve a central role for private insurers and state governments. According to the Chief Justice, the *Commerce Clause* does not permit that preservation. This rigid reading of the Clause makes scant sense and is stunningly retrogressive.

Since 1937, our precedent has recognized Congress' large authority to set the Nation's course in the economic and social welfare realm. . . . See *United States v. Darby*, 312 U.S. 100, 115 (1941) (overruling *Hammer v. Dagenhart*, 247 U.S. 251 (1918*)*, and recognizing that "regulations of commerce which do not infringe some constitutional prohibition are within the plenary power conferred on Congress by the *Commerce Clause*"); *NLRB v. Jones & Laughlin Steel Corp.*, 301 U.S. 1, 37 (1937) ("[The commerce]power is plenary and may be exerted to protect interstate commerce no matter what the source of the dangers which threaten it." (internal quotation marks omitted)). The Chief Justice's crabbed reading of the *Commerce Clause* harks back to the era in which the Court routinely thwarted Congress' efforts to regulate the national economy in the interest of those who labor to sustain it. See, *e.g.*, *Railroad Retirement Bd. v. Alton R. Co.*, 295 U.S. 330, 362, 368 (1935) (invalidating compulsory retirement and pension plan for employees of carriers subject to the Interstate Commerce Act; Court found law related essentially "to the social welfare of the worker, and therefore remote from any regulation of commerce as such"). It is a reading that should not have staying power.

. . . .

[The dissent noted the immense size of the national market for healthcare products and services, involving $2.5 trillion in expenditures, accounting for 17.6% of our Nation's economy. It also noted the distinctive nature of the market for medical care as "one in which all individuals inevitably participate." Also distinctive is that, unlike other markets, "the inability to pay for care does not mean that an uninsured individual will receive no care. Federal and state law, as well as professional obligations and embedded social norms, require hospitals and physicians to provide care when it is most needed, regardless of the patient's ability to pay." Ginsburg, J., noted that medical-care providers deliver significant amounts of care to the uninsured for which the providers receive no payment, totaling $43 billion in 2008, passed on in insurance premium increases averaging over $1,000 a year. Moreover, failure of individuals to acquire insurance lessens access to cost-saving preventive care.]

C

States cannot resolve the problem of the uninsured on their own. Like Social Security benefits, a universal health-care system, if adopted by an individual State, would be "bait to the needy and dependent elsewhere, encouraging them to migrate and seek a haven of repose." *Helvering v. Davis*, 301 U.S. 619, 644 (1937). See also Brief for Commonwealth of Massachusetts as *Amicus Curiae* in No. 11-398, p. 15 (noting that, in 2009, Massachusetts' emergency rooms served thousands of uninsured, out-of-state residents). An influx of unhealthy individuals into a State with universal health care would result in increased spending on medical services. To cover the increased costs, a State would have to raise taxes, and private health-insurance companies would have to increase premiums. Higher taxes and increased insurance costs would, in turn, encourage businesses and healthy individuals to leave the State.

States that undertake health-care reforms on their own thus risk "placing themselves in a position of economic disadvantage as compared with neighbors or competitors." *Davis*, 301 U.S., at 644. See also Brief for Health Care for All, Inc., et al. as *Amici Curiae* in No. 11-398, p. 4 ("[O]ut-of-state residents continue to seek and receive millions of dollars in uncompensated care in Massachusetts hospitals, limiting the State's efforts to improve its health care system through the elimination of uncompensated care."). Facing that risk, individual States are unlikely to take the initiative in addressing the problem of the uninsured, even though solving that problem is in all States' best interests. Congress' intervention was needed to overcome this collective-action impasse.

. . . .

II

A

The *Commerce Clause*, it is widely acknowledged, "was the Framers' response to the central problem that gave rise to the Constitution itself." *EEOC v. Wyoming*, 460 U.S. 226, 244, 245, n. 1 (1983) (Stevens, J., concurring) (citing sources). Under the Articles of Confederation, the Constitution's precursor, the regulation of commerce was left to the States. This scheme proved unworkable, because the individual States, understandably focused on their own economic interests, often failed to take actions critical to the success of the Nation as a whole. . . .

. . . .

What was needed was a "national Government . . . armed with a positive & compleat authority in all cases where uniform measures are necessary." See Letter from James Madison to Edmund Randolph (Apr. 8, 1787), in 9 Papers of James

Madison 368, 370 (R. Rutland ed. 1975). See also Letter from George Washington to James Madison (Nov. 30, 1785), in 8 *id.*, at 428, 429 ("We are either a United people, or we are not. If the former, let us, in all matters of general concern act as a nation, which ha[s] national objects to promote, and a national character to support."). The Framers' solution was the *Commerce Clause*, which, as they perceived it, granted Congress the authority to enact economic legislation "in all Cases for the general Interests of the Union, and also in those Cases to which the States are separately incompetent." Records of the Federal Convention of 1787, pp. 131-132, P8 (M. Farrand rev. 1966). See also *North American Co. v. SEC*, 327 U.S. 686, 705 (1946) ("[The commerce power] is an affirmative power commensurate with the national needs.").

. . . .

B

Consistent with the Framers' intent, we have repeatedly emphasized that Congress' authority under the *Commerce Clause* is dependent upon "practical" considerations, including "actual experience." *Jones & Laughlin Steel Corp.*, 301 U.S., at 41-42. . . We afford Congress the leeway "to undertake to solve national problems directly and realistically." *American Power & Light Co. v. SEC*, 329 U.S. 90, 103 (1946).

[The dissent proceeded to criticize Chief Justice Roberts' "newly minted constitutional doctrine" because uninsured Americans are engaged in commerce because they will seek medical services. Ginsburg, J., distinguished markets for cars or broccoli where individuals may well never make a purchase, and where if they wanted to without funds, society would not obligate sellers to provide them with the desired goods.]

. . . .

At bottom, the Chief Justice's and the joint dissenters' view that an individual cannot be subject to Commerce Clause regulation absent voluntary, affirmative acts that enter him or her into, or affect, the interstate market expresses a concern for individual liberty that [is] more redolent of Due Process Clause arguments." *Seven-Sky*, 661 F. 3d, at 19. . . .

2

[Justice Ginsburg suggested that the restriction of regulation to active partici- pants in a commercial market was guided by a fear that the Commerce Clause power would otherwise be unlimited. In her view, this concern was "unfounded." She noted the unique attributes of the health care market. She emphasized that *Lopez/Morrison* preclude regulation of noneconomic conduct with an attenuated effect on interstate commerce where subject to traditional state regulation.]

Supplementing these legal restraints is a formidable check on congressional power: the democratic process. See *Raich*, 545 U.S., at 33; *Wickard*, 317 U.S., at 120 (repeating Chief Justice Marshall's "warning that effective restraints on [the commerce power's] exercise must proceed from political rather than judicial processes" (citing *Gibbons v. Ogden*, 9 Wheat. 1, 197 (1824)). As the controversy surrounding the passage of the Affordable Care Act attests, purchase mandates are likely to engender political resistance. This prospect is borne out by the behavior of state legislators. Despite their possession of unquestioned authority to impose mandates, state governments have rarely done so. See Hall, *Commerce Clause* Challenges to Health Care Reform, 159 U. Pa. L. Rev. 1825, 1838 (2011).

. . . .

III

A

[Justice Ginsburg explained why in her view the individual mandate was valid under the Necessary & Proper Clause to achieve the wholly legitimate regulatory goal of eliminating the insurance industry's practice of charging higher prices or denying coverage to individuals with preexisting medical conditions.]

. . . .

In failing to explain why the individual mandate threatens our constitutional order, the Chief Justice disserves future courts. How is a judge to decide, when ruling on the constitutionality of a federal statute, whether Congress employed an "independent power," or merely a "derivative" one. Whether the power used is "substantive," or just "incidental"? The instruction the Chief Justice, in effect, provides lower courts: You will know it when you see it.

[She rejected the argument that the individual mandate improperly intruded on an area of law where States historically had been sovereign, noting the lead role of the federal government as a subsidizer and regulator of health care.]

Second, and perhaps most important, the minimum coverage provision, along with other provisions of the ACA, addresses the very sort of interstate problem that made the commerce power essential in our federal system. The crisis created by the large number of U.S. residents who lack health insurance is one of national dimension that States are "separately incompetent" to handle. Far from trampling on States' sovereignty, the ACA attempts a federal solution for the very reason that the States, acting separately, cannot meet the need. Notably, the ACA serves the general welfare of the people of the United States while retaining a prominent role for the States.[17]

---

[17] [FN 11] In a separate argument, the joint dissenters contend that the minimum coverage provision is not necessary and proper because it was not the "only . . . way" Congress could have made the guaranteed-issue and community-rating reforms work. [Justice Ginsburg rejected their arguments that alternatives were workable.]

. . . .

But even assuming there were "practicable" alternatives to the minimum coverage provision, "we long ago rejected the view that the Necessary and Proper Clause demands that an Act of Congress be 'absolutely necessary' to the exercise of an enumerated power." *Jinks v. Richland County*, 538 U.S. 456, 462, 123 S. Ct. 1667, 155 L. Ed. 2d 631 (2003) (quoting *McCulloch v. Maryland*, 17 U.S. 316, 4 Wheat. 316, 414-415, 4 L. Ed. 579 [*167] (1819)). Rather, the statutory provision at issue need only be "conducive" and

. . . .

JUSTICE SCALIA, JUSTICE KENNEDY, JUSTICE THOMAS, and JUSTICE ALITO, dissenting.

. . . .

. . . Whatever may be the conceptual limits upon the *Commerce Clause* and upon the power to tax and spend, they cannot be such as will enable the Federal Government to regulate all private conduct and to compel the States to function as administrators of federal programs.

. . . .

I

The Individual Mandate

. . . .

[Using contemporary dictionaries, the dissent argued that the original meaning of the word "regulate"] can mean to direct the manner of something but not to direct that something come into being. There is no instance in which this Court or Congress (or anyone else, to our knowledge) has used "regulate" in that peculiar fashion. If the word bore that meaning, Congress' authority "[t]o make Rules for the Government and Regulation of the land and naval Forces," U.S. Const., Art. I, § 8, cl. 14, would have made superfluous the later provision for authority "[t]o raise and support Armies," *id.*, § 8, cl. 12, and "[t]o provide and maintain a Navy," *id.*, § 8, cl. 13.

. . . .

A

. . . .

With the present statute, by contrast, there are many ways other than this unprecedented Individual Mandate by which the regulatory scheme's goals of reducing insurance premiums and ensuring the profitability of insurers could be achieved. For instance, those who did not purchase insurance could be subjected to a surcharge when they do enter the health insurance system. Or they could be denied a full income tax credit given to those who do purchase the insurance.

The Government was invited, at oral argument, to suggest what federal controls over private conduct (other than those explicitly prohibited by the *Bill of Rights* or other constitutional controls) could *not* be justified as necessary and proper for the carrying out of a general regulatory scheme. It was unable to name any. . . .

"[reasonably] adapted" to the goal Congress seeks to achieve. *Jinks, 538 U.S., at 462* (internal quotation marks omitted). The minimum coverage provision meets this requirement.

B

[The dissent also rejected the claim that the individual mandate regulates commerce because everyone eventually consumes health care services.] Such a definition of market participants is unprecedented, and were it to be a premise for the exercise of national power, it would have no principled limits.

. . . .

C

. . . .

. . . The dissent treats the Constitution as though it is an enumeration of those problems that the Federal Government can address-among which, it finds, is "the Nation's course in the economic and social welfare realm, and more specifically "the problem of the uninsured." The Constitution is not that. It enumerates not federally soluble *problems*, but federally available *powers*. The Federal Government can address whatever problems it wants but can bring to their solution only those powers that the Constitution confers, among which is the power to regulate commerce. None of our cases say anything else. Article I contains no whatever-it-takes-to-solve-a-national-problem power.

. . . .

II

The Taxing Power

. . . .

. . . In a few cases, this Court has held that a "tax" imposed upon private conduct was so onerous as to be in effect a penalty. But we have never held- *never*-that a penalty imposed for violation of the law was so trivial as to be in effect a tax. . . .

. . . .

Justice Thomas, dissenting [reiterated his view in that the "substantial affects" test established in prior precedents for Commerce Clause jurisprudence should be overruled].

1.4.7. Limits on state legislative power

The text of the U.S. Constitution does not provide an exclusive grant of authority for state legislation. Rather, subject to a few explicit exceptions contained in Article I, §10, states enjoy a plenary "police power" to enact legislation. State authority is subject to the supremacy of federal legislation, so that, for example, Congress can enact bankruptcy law that has the effect of pre-empting state debtor-creditor law. There is a rich body of constitutional doctrine in each country concerning when a validly enacted state/provincial law is overridden by a validly enacted federal law. The basic concepts are the same: if a federal statute is valid and if it appears as a matter of statutory interpretation that Congress/Parliament meant to pre-empt a challenged state/provincial law, the latter is struck down or rendered inoperative. However, at different times in different countries, justices may be more or less willing to infer a conflict when the federal legislature does not explicitly preclude conflicting state/provincial law. *See generally* HOGG chapter 16; NOWAK & ROTUNDA chapter 9; Victoria Bronstein, *Conflicts, in* WOOLMAN ET AL., CONSTITUTIONAL LAW OF SOUTH AFRICA, ch. 16 (2d ed. 2006); SARAH JOSEPH & MELISSA CASTAN, FEDERAL CONSTITUTIONAL LAW: A CONTEMPORARY VIEW ch. 7 (2d ed. 2006).[18] When the Supremacy Clause is combined with the broad congressional power under the Commerce Clause, many areas of business regulation are preempted by federal law. (We've seen this already in *Gibbons v. Ogden*, finding New York's monopoly steamship grant preempted by a valid federal statute.)

The authority of American states is also significantly limited by to two judicially-created doctrines interpreting the Commerce Clause. We saw in *Cooley v. Board of Wardens, supra,* that states can regulate and even discriminate with regard to interstate commerce when doing so pursuant to a valid federal statute. The Constitution provides no textual limits to the extent of a state's regulation of commerce that is not solely internal to that state when Congress has not legislated. As Nowark & Rotunda detail, §11.1, the Court could have held that federal power is exclusive, and that congressional silence is indicative of a federal design to leave commerce unregulated. Or, alternatively, the Court could have inferred an intent to defer to state regulation from congressional inaction. Instead, the Court has steered an intermediate course. *Cooley* bars state action in an area of commerce where national uniformity is essential. Otherwise, states can legislate. Thus, while Congress could clearly regulate (and pre-empt conflicting state laws) concerning when and where passenger trains are required to take on and discharge passengers, the U.S. Supreme Court held that an Ohio law to this effect was legitimate absent conflict federal regulation. *Lake Shore & M.S. Ry. v. State of Ohio*, 173 U.S. 285 (1899): "This power in the states is entirely distinct from any power granted to the general government, although, when exercised, it may sometimes reach subjects over which national legislation can be constitutionally extended." (Note that this sort of provincial legislation would be clearly unconstitutional in Canada, because s. 92(10)(a) specifically exempts railways from provincial regulation.)

The U.S. Supreme Court has recognized that American states could significantly disrupt interstate commerce by enacting legislation that discriminates against out-

---

[18] In Australia, Commonwealth laws may be held to "cover the field" (that is, the Commonwealth law allows no room for concurrent state laws) even where they do not explicitly express an intention to do so. This may arise when a Commonwealth law includes highly detailed regulatory provisions, or when the subject matter of the law requires national uniformity. For example, in *Viskauskas v. Niland* (1983) 153 CLR 280, 292, the High Court held that the Commonwealth's Race Discrimination Act 1975 necessarily covered the field: in legislating to give effect to the United Nations Convention on the Elimination of All Forms of Racial Discrimination, the Court said, the Commonwealth "can only fulfill the obligation cast upon it by the Convention if its enactment operates equally and without discrimination in all the States." This meant that the New South Wales state Anti-Discrimination Act 1977 (at issue in the case) was inoperative. The Commonwealth did not intend this result, and was forced to amend its legislation to make it clear that no pre-emption was intended.

of-state products or firms. Absent congressional approval, courts will invalidate such legislation under the "dormant" commerce clause. Nowak & Rotunda identify a key underlying principle of the "inner political check." §11.11:

> The Court recognizes that if a state regulation is designed so that its burdens fall primarily on those interests or persons who reside outside of the state, there is a greater reason for a more active judicial review, because the state's internal political processes do not provide an adequate internal check on legislative excesses. In contrast, if the burden of regulation falls principally on those who live within the state . . . the regulation is more likely to be checked by inner political restraints that ordinarily can be expected to bring about the repeal of undesirable legislation.

PIKE v. BRUCE CHURCH, INC.
SUPREME COURT OF THE UNITED STATES
397 U.S. 137 (1970)

[Before BURGER, C.J., and BLACK, DOUGLAS, HARLAN, BRENNAN, STEWART, WHITE, and MARSHALL, JJ.]

MR. JUSTICE STEWART delivered the opinion of the Court.

The appellee is a company engaged in extensive commercial farming operations in Arizona and California. The appellant is the official charged with enforcing the Arizona Fruit and Vegetable Standardization Act. A provision of the Act requires that, with certain exceptions, all cantaloupes grown in Arizona and offered for sale must "be packed in regular compact arrangement in closed standard containers approved by the supervisor . . . ." Invoking his authority under that provision, the appellant issued an order prohibiting the appellee company from transporting uncrated cantaloupes from its Parker, Arizona, ranch to nearby Blythe, California, for packing and processing. The company then brought this action in a federal court to enjoin the order as unconstitutional.

[The appellee spent over $3 million developing Arizona farmland, and its cantaloupes are considered to be of higher quality than elsewhere in Arizona. Highly perishable, cantaloupes must be immediately harvested, processed, packed, and shipped. The appellee efficiently accomplished this by transporting the cantaloupes in bulk to its plant in Blythe, California, 31 miles away from its farm. The district court found that to comply with the challenged Arizona law would practically require the appellee to spend over $200,000 to construct packing facilities in Arizona to duplicate the Blythe facilities. The district court enjoined enforcement of the Arizona law as an "unlawful burden on interstate commerce."]

[The appellant argued that a statute regulating goods prior to their introduction into interstate commerce could not interfere with such commerce.] If the appellant's theory were correct, then statutes expressly requiring that certain kinds of processing be done in the home State before shipment to a sister State would be immune from constitutional challenge. Yet such statutes have been consistently invalidated by this Court under the Commerce Clause. Thus it is clear that the appellant's order does affect and burden interstate commerce, and the question then becomes whether it does so unconstitutionally. Although the criteria for determining the validity of state statutes affecting interstate commerce have been variously stated, the general rule that emerges can be phrased as follows: Where the statute regulates even-handedly to effectuate a legitimate local public interest, and its effects on interstate commerce are only incidental, it will be upheld unless the burden imposed on such commerce is clearly excessive in relation to the putative local benefits. *Huron Cement Co. v. Detroit, 362 U.S. 440, 443.* [The Court in that case upheld a statute requiring federally-licensed seagoing vessels to meet local water pollution standards.] If a legitimate local purpose is found, then the question becomes one of degree. And the extent of the burden that will be tolerated will of course depend on the nature of the local interest involved, and on whether it could be promoted as well with a lesser impact on interstate activities. Occasionally the Court has candidly undertaken a balancing approach in resolving these issues, *Southern Pacific Co. v. Arizona,* 325 U.S. 761,[19] but more frequently it has spoken in terms of "direct" and "indirect" effects and burdens.

At the core of the Arizona Fruit and Vegetable Standardization Act are the requirements that fruits and vegetables shipped from Arizona meet certain standards of wholesomeness and quality, and that they be packed in standard containers in such a way that the outer layer or exposed portion of the pack does not "materially misrepresent" the quality of the lot as a whole. The impetus for the Act was the fear that some growers were shipping inferior or deceptively packaged produce, with the result that the reputation of Arizona growers generally was being tarnished and their financial return concomitantly reduced. It was to prevent this that the Act was passed in 1929. The State has stipulated that its primary purpose is to promote and preserve the reputation of Arizona growers by prohibiting deceptive packaging.

We are not, then, dealing here with "state legislation in the field of safety where the propriety of local regulation has long been recognized," or with an Act designed to protect consumers in Arizona from contaminated or unfit goods. Its purpose and design are simply to protect and enhance the reputation of growers within the State. These are surely legitimate state interests. We have upheld a State's power to require that produce packaged in the State be packaged in a particular kind of receptacle, *Pacific States Box & Basket Co. v. White,* 296 U.S. 176. And we have recognized the legitimate interest of a State in maximizing the financial return to an industry within it. *Parker v. Brown,* 317 U.S. 341. Therefore, as applied to Arizona growers who package their produce in Arizona, we may assume the constitutional validity of the Act. We may further assume that Arizona has full constitutional power to forbid the misleading use of its name on produce that was grown or packed

---

[19] [FN 21] In *Southern Pacific,* the Court struck down an Arizona law prohibiting long trains from operating within the state. Noting that over 90% of train traffic was interstate and this would seriously burden the Southern Pacific, the practical effect of the law would be to "control the length of passenger trains all the way from Los Angeles to El Paso." Although the state justified the law on safety grounds, the Court looked at the facts and concluded that fewer, longer trains were actually safer. In contrast, though, the Court had a few years earlier upheld a South Carolina law prohibiting very large trucks from operating on its highways. *South Carolina State Highway Dep't v. Barnwell Bros., Inc.,* 303 U.S. 177, 58 S. Ct. 510 (1938). Here, the Court looked at the record and decided that safety concerns were legitimate.

elsewhere. And, to the extent the Act forbids the shipment of contaminated or unfit produce, it clearly rests on sure footing. For, as the Court has said, such produce is "not the legitimate subject of trade or commerce, nor within the protection of the commerce clause of the Constitution."

But application of the Act through the appellant's order to the appellee company has a far different impact, and quite a different purpose. The cantaloupes grown by the company at Parker are of exceptionally high quality. The company does not pack them in Arizona and cannot do so without making a capital expenditure of approximately $200,000. It transports them in bulk to nearby Blythe, California, where they are sorted, inspected, packed, and shipped in containers that do not identify them as Arizona cantaloupes, but bear the name of their California packer. The appellant's order would forbid the company to pack its cantaloupes outside Arizona, not for the purpose of keeping the reputation of its growers unsullied, but to enhance their reputation through the reflected good will of the company's superior produce. The appellant, in other words, is not complaining because the company is putting the good name of Arizona on an inferior or deceptively packaged product, but because it is not putting that name on a product that is superior and well packaged. As the appellant's brief puts the matter, "It is within Arizona's legitimate interest to require that interstate cantaloupe purchasers be informed that this high quality Parker fruit was grown in Arizona."

Although it is not easy to see why the other growers of Arizona are entitled to benefit at the company's expense from the fact that it produces superior crops, we may assume that the asserted state interest is a legitimate one. But the State's tenuous interest in having the company's cantaloupes identified as originating in Arizona cannot constitutionally justify the requirement that the company build and operate an unneeded $200,000 packing plant in the State. The nature of that burden is, constitutionally, more significant than its extent. For the Court has viewed with particular suspicion state statutes requiring business operations to be performed in the home State that could more efficiently be performed elsewhere. Even where the State is pursuing a clearly legitimate local interest, this particular burden on commerce has been declared to be virtually per se illegal.

. . . .

. . . If the Commerce Clause forbids a State to require work to be done within its jurisdiction to promote local employment, then surely it cannot permit a State to require a person to go into a local packing business solely for the sake of enhancing the reputation of other producers within its borders.

1.5.   BASIC PRINCIPLES OF AUSTRALIAN FEDERALISM

Section 51 of the Australian Constitution is the principal source of federal (Commonwealth) power. Forty "placita" (numbered paragraphs) list the subjects with respect to which the Parliament may make laws for the "peace, order, and good government of the Commonwealth." The States can make laws with respect to any subject on, or outside this list, provided that it is not a subject exclusive or otherwise allocated to the Commonwealth. However, in the case of an inconsistency between otherwise valid Commonwealth and state laws on the same subject, the Commonwealth law prevails (s 109). In addition, an implied Commonwealth power — known loosely as the "Nationhood power" — arises from the Executive power (s 61), with the ancillary "incidental power" (s 51(xxxix)) and permits the Commonwealth to make laws for large national projects that the States are, singly or collectively, incapable of undertaking. The power remains imprecise and, to some extent, controversial, and has been applied in only a very small number of cases (although many national projects, such as the massive Snowy Mountains Hydro-Electric scheme, begun in 1949, which presumably relied upon this power, have never been challenged). The Commonwealth also has power, under s 96, to give grants to the States "on such terms and conditions as the Parliament thinks fit"; this is an extremely important source of power, allowing the Commonwealth to direct national policy regarding subjects over which it does not have another source of power (for example, universities), by making grants conditional on putting Commonwealth policy into effect. Additionally, s 51(xxxvii) gives a state or states the power to "refer," or hand over to the Commonwealth Parliament, any matter over which the Commonwealth does not have another source of power, provided both levels of government agree. This power has been used in many cases to relieve one or more of the States of legislative responsibilities for which they are ill-equipped, or where a uniform national law is considered desirable (for example, with respect to civil aviation, crimes of terrorism, the incorporation of companies, and the application of federal family law to custody disputes over children whose parents are not legally married).

Exclusive Commonwealth powers are found in ss 52 and 90 of the Constitution.[20] The former concerns matters only of significance to the Commonwealth (such as Commonwealth places), and has had little impact on case law. In contrast, the latter, giving the power to impose customs or excise duties exclusively to the Commonwealth, has been of major importance in the development of fiscal federalism in Australia, discussed in section 1.7.1 below. The Commonwealth has also significantly expanded its legislative powers through the use of s 51(xxix) — the "external affairs" power. This power has been used to pass laws giving effect, among other things, to international treaties and conventions to which Australia is a party (See also Chapter 4 on Equality Rights).

Section 51(i) gives the Commonwealth power to make laws with respect to "Trade and commerce with other countries, and among the States." The High Court has interpreted this power narrowly, compared to the U.S. Supreme Court's approach to the U.S. " commerce clause." The Court has rejected the American doctrine permitting national regulation of commercial activities that may "substantially affect" interstate commerce, and has interpreted "among" effectively to mean "between"; it has consistently upheld the limitation on laws respecting inter-state trade, ruling out Commonwealth laws that purport to regulate intra-state trade or commerce, and upholding laws that affect intra-state trade or manufacturing or production only if these are "incidental" to the regulation of inter-state or international trade or commerce. Relatively recently, however, the Commonwealth has successfully relied on s 51(xx), the "corporations power," to legislate with

---

[20] In addition, ss 114–15 effectively gives the Commonwealth exclusive control over national defense and coinage of money, respectively.

respect to trading and commercial matters that do not have an inter-state or international character and would otherwise be outside the reach of Commonwealth power. The expansion of the reach of the corporations power has, effectively, neutralized the limitations in s 51(i), and has arguably made the latter power relatively unimportant.

As noted, s 51(xxxvii) of the Constitution has also contributed to the expansion of Commonwealth power, as was anticipated by the Constitution's framers, although the power cannot be used without federal cooperation. The expansion of Commonwealth power has also been assisted by a limited number of successful referendums changing the Constitution: the most significant were in 1946 (adding a Commonwealth power — s 51(xxiii)(A) — over a wide range of social welfare subjects), and 1967 (deleting part of s 51(xxvi) that restricted Commonwealth powers to make special laws for the Aboriginal people).

The key constitutional question asked in Australia about federalism rarely concerns policy — either about which level of government is best suited to regulate a particular field or about which function the federal legislature should be constrained from performing. These question were only asked during the framing of the Constitution, when a type of "categorical" approach was adopted for identifying the powers that should be allocated to the federal level; that is, some fields or functions were treated as "naturally" national, and others as belonging naturally, or inherently, to the states. Occasional debate surrounding proposals to amend the Constitution, or during referendum campaigns, has seen these questions raised again, given that the majority of referendums have been about proposals to increase the Commonwealth's power by creating a new head of federal power or removing a limitation on Commonwealth power. (The 1946 and 1967 referendums are striking, but rare examples of successful "re-categorisation" of federal powers.) The High Court of Australia very rarely engages in an explicit discussion about public policy, or whether there *should be* constitutional limits on either the Commonwealth or the states to enact statutes that they believe to reflect sound public policy. These are treated as political questions. Unlike in the U.S., the main HCA approach to federalism involves doctrinal questions about the scope and limits of power, and also about *characterization*.

Characterization is a process (or the name for a process) of asking about the "character" of a statute, with respect to a constitutional power. The question is this: is the "impugned" or challenged law a law on a subject listed among the Commonwealth's heads of power? If a law is characterized as being on a constitutional subject, so long as it does not breach an implied or express limitation on the exercise of legislative power, it will be held valid. In the exercise of characterization, the Court distinguishes between certain types of power. The subject of some powers is simple to identify: for example, s 51(vii) "Lighthouses, lightships, and beacons and buoys" or s 51(xxiii) "Invalid and old-age pensions." Others are less "concrete," but still lend themselves to relatively straightforward characterization; for example, s 51(ii) "Taxation . . . ," or s 51(xx) "Foreign corporations, and trading or financial corporations . . ." Such powers are known as "subject powers." The characterization of these powers is done by determining what the actual operation of the law does:

> [I]n creating, changing, regulating or abolishing rights, duties, powers or privileges, and then . . . consider[ing] whether that which [it] does falls in substance within the relevant authorized subject matter, or whether it touches it only incidentally, or whether it is really an endeavor, by purporting to use one power, to make a law upon a subject which is beyond power" (Latham CJ, *Bank of NSW v. Commonwealth* (1948) 76 CLR 1, at 187).

Some powers, however, do not refer to a subject, but to a *purpose*. The s 51(vi) power to make laws with respect to "The naval and military defence of the Commonwealth and the several States . . ." does not refer to a "thing" — one cannot point at something and identify it as "defence." Rather, defence is a purpose, and the type of laws required to fulfill the purpose of national defence cannot be defined with precision or in the abstract. Defence laws must meet the particular strategic needs of the country at a particular time, and these needs will vary, depending on whether Australia is at peace or at war, or in between. So, for example, laws regulating the wool industry during the Second World War were held to be valid under the Defence power, because the Commonwealth needed a regular wool supply for the manufacture of military uniforms. "Purposive powers" (as such powers are known) are subject to a characterization test of proportionality: that is, the Court asks whether the law in question is appropriate and adapted to the particular purpose. During wars (including the "war on terror"), the High Court has been generally deferential to the Parliament's determination about what laws are appropriate and adapted to defence. (The characterization of laws supported by the "incidental" power — laws or regulations necessary to give effect to the main subject of the law — also rests on a proportionality test). Some other powers fall in between "subject" and "purpose" and the characterization of laws that purport to rely on these powers is far from precise. For example, section 51(xxi) gives the Commonwealth the power to pass laws with respect to "Marriage." This power appears clear on its face, but challenges have arisen in the past regarding laws that purported to deem non-traditional relationships "marriages"; more recently, controversy has arisen over whether the power permits the Commonwealth to legalise same-sex marriages. The established methods of characterization do not supply the answer. It is now clear that "marriage" is a flexible legislative subject, defined by the Commonwealth parliament.

In regard to characterization, the High Court's approach has been considered "formalistic" or "legalistic," but, as we will see, it has been applied to permit expansive interpretations both by Labor governments (laws barring racial discrimination and protecting the environment) and Liberal governments (laws weakening union-negotiated industrial awards). Like in the U.S. and unlike in Canada, the actual purposes behind the exercise of Commonwealth legislative power does not feature in the characterization process (except for "purposive" powers). *See, e.g., Fairfax v. Federal Commissioner of Taxation* (1965) 114 CLR 1 (elimination of tax exemption for retirement funds which did not invest in designated "public securities" was held to be a law "with respect to taxation" under s 51(ii) even though the legislative purpose was to redirect investment incentives); *Murphyores Inc. Pty. Ltd. v. Commonwealth* (1976) 136 CLR 1 (a bar on exports of sand from an environmentally sensitive beach was characterized as a law "with respect to foreign commerce" under s 51(i) even though the Minister's purpose was environmental protection and not commercial regulation of exports).

1.5.1. The expansion of federal power via interpretation: *The Engineers Case*

The growth of Commonwealth power was considerably facilitated by a High Court decision in 1920 regarding the interpretation of the Constitution. The so-called "Engineers Case" — *Amalgamated Society of Engineers v. Adelaide Steamship Co. Ltd.* (1920) 28 CLR 129 — concerned whether a law passed under a Commonwealth power (in this case, s 51(xxxv) — the power to make laws with respect to inter-state industrial disputes) could be employed to bind a state Government. Previously, the Court had followed two doctrines which restrained the Commonwealth: the doctrine of intergovernmental immunities, and the doctrine of states' reserved powers. Under these doctrines, Commonwealth laws could not bind the states and state laws could not bind the Commonwealth, and, secondly, a sphere of powers into which the Commonwealth could not intrude was held to be "reserved" to the states. The reasoning was that, prior to becoming states, the Colonies had historically agreed to a "federal compact" which protected their self-government and preserved as much of their sovereignty as was compatible with membership of a federal Commonwealth. The *Engineers Case* dismantled both doctrines.

An engineers' union sought a federal industrial award (specifying the terms and conditions of employment in a particular industry) against several hundred employers, including (among others) the Western Australian state engineering works. Western Australia argued that a state government was immune from Commonwealth laws (in this case, from orders made by the Commonwealth Court of Conciliation and Arbitration). The High Court held the contrary. The immunity of state governments from Commonwealth laws rested on nothing but a non-textual, implied claim about federalism, the Court said. Constitutional powers should not be interpreted to include implications "formed on a vague . . . conception of the spirit of the [federal] compact"; they should be interpreted according to their text, giving the words their full and natural meaning, according to the "settled rules" of statutory construction. Justice Higgins wrote:

> [T]here is not the slightest indication that the power conferred on the Federal Parliament as to legislation on the subject of [section 51 (xxxv)] was to stop short at State industries or activities. The Parliament is there given power "subject to this Constitution . . . to make laws for the peace, order, and good government of the Commonwealth with respect to . . . Conciliation and arbitration for the prevention and settlement of industrial disputes extending beyond the limits of any one State." . . . [I]t is clear that the expression ["industrial disputes"] means the same thing whoever is the employer — person or firm or company or State . . . The fundamental rule of interpretation, to which all others are subordinate, is that a statute is to be expounded according to the intent of the Parliament that made it; and that intention has to be found by an examination of the language used in the statute as a whole. The question is, what does the language mean; and when

we find what the language means, in its ordinary and natural sense, it is our duty to obey that meaning, even if we think the result to be inconvenient or impolitic or improbable . . . Once we find a valid Federal law — say, a law as to trade and commerce with other countries — the Courts and Judges and people of every State must obey it, whatever the State laws may say to the contrary.

Although section 107 of the Constitution preserves the powers of the Colonial parliaments as at the establishment of the Commonwealth (other than powers exclusively granted to the Commonwealth by the Constitution), Justice Isaacs rejected the argument that this section thereby preserves state powers against Commonwealth laws. It is, Isaacs stated,

> . . . [A] fundamental and fatal error to read sec. 107 as reserving any power from the Commonwealth that falls fairly within the explicit terms of an express grant in sec. 51, as that grant is reasonably construed, unless that reservation is as explicitly stated.

1.5.2.   Implied restraint on the scope of federal power: the "Melbourne Corporation doctrine"

Since 1920, the growth of Commonwealth power has appeared at times to be inexorable and unidirectional, but it has not been entirely smooth. In 1947, the High Court elaborated the so-called "Melbourne Corporation Doctrine," according to which the Constitution impliedly prohibits the Commonwealth from making laws that discriminate against a state or states, or impair essential state government functions. The HCA struck down a federal law — the *Banking Act, 1947* (Cth) — barring state treasuries from banking with institutions that had not been approved by the federal government. The HCA reasoned that, in guaranteeing the continued existence of state Constitutions and in its whole scheme for a federal polity, the Constitution impliedly protects Australia's federal system. This doctrine has been evoked on a good number of occasions since 1947, but only successfully in a few, most recently in *Clarke v. Commissioner of Taxation* (2009) 258 ALR 623, in which the HCA struck down a Commonwealth scheme imposing a tax on the superannuation (pension) contributions of Members of state parliaments.

MELBOURNE v. COMMONWEALTH
("Melbourne Corporation case")
HIGH COURT OF AUSTRALIA
(1947) 74 CLR 31

DIXON, J.: The prima-facie rule is that a power to legislate with respect to a given subject enables the Parliament to make laws which, upon that subject, affect the operations of the States and their agencies. That . . . is the effect of the *Engineers' Case* stripped of embellishment and reduced to the form of a legal proposition. It is subject, however, to certain reservations . . . The reservation [upon which this case turns] relates to the use of federal legislative power to make, not a general law which governs all alike who come within the area of its operation whether they are subjects of the Crown or the agents of the Crown in right of a

State, but a law which discriminates against States, or a law which places a particular disability or burden upon an operation or activity of a State, and more especially upon the execution of its constitutional powers. In support of such a use of power the *Engineers' Case* has nothing to say. Legislation of that nature discloses an immediate object of controlling the State in the course which otherwise the Executive Government of the State might adopt, if that Government were left free to exercise its authority. The control may be attempted in connection with a matter falling within the enumerated subjects of federal legislative power. But it does not follow that the connection with the matter brings a law aimed at controlling in some particular the State's exercise of its executive power within the true ambit of the Commonwealth legislative power. Such a law wears two aspects. In one aspect the matter with respect to which it is enacted is the restriction of State action, the prescribing of the course which the Executive Government of the State must take or the limiting of the courses available to it. As the operation of such a law is to place a particular burden or disability upon the State in that aspect it may correctly be described as a law for the restriction of State action in the field chosen. That is a direct operation of the law . . . [If] the law operates directly upon a matter forming an actual part of a subject enumerated among the federal legislative powers, its validity could hardly be denied on the simple ground of irrelevance to a head of power. Speaking generally, once it appears that a federal law has an actual and immediate operation within a field assigned to the Commonwealth as a subject of legislative power, that is enough. It will be held to fall within the power unless some further reason appears for excluding it. That it discloses another purpose and that the purpose lies outside the area of federal power are considerations which will not in such a case suffice to invalidate the law. In the United States much use has been made in this way of the postal power and of the commerce power to legislate in a way calculated to vindicate morality or achieve a social purpose rather than to advance the postal services or promote or regulate inter-state commerce as such. When this is done the result is that laws confined to an existing head of federal power nevertheless reach as a matter of purpose into fields lying under State legislative authority. But it is one thing to say that a federal law may be valid notwithstanding a purpose of achieving some result which lies directly within the undefined area of power reserved to the States. It is altogether another thing to apply the same doctrine to a use of federal power for a purpose of restricting or burdening the State in the exercise of its constitutional powers. The one involves no more than a distinction between the subject of a power and the policy which causes its exercise. The other brings into question the independence from federal control of the State in the discharge of its functions.

In the case of most legislative powers assigned to the Commonwealth some ingenuity would be needed to base a law squarely upon the subject matter of the power and at the same time effect by it a restriction or control of the State in respect of some exercise of its executive authority or for that matter in respect of the working of the judiciary or of the legislature of a State. The difficulty of using most federal powers in that way arises from the character of the subjects of the powers. It is, for instance, difficult to see how any law based on the power with respect to lighthouses, astronomical observations, fisheries, weights and measures, bills of exchange or marriage could be aimed at controlling States in the execution of their functions. But to attempt to burden the exercise of State functions by means of the power to tax needs no ingenuity, and that, no doubt, is why that power occupies such a conspicuous place in the long history both in the United States and here of the question how far federal power may be used to interfere with the States in the exercise of their powers. The doctrine that no exercise of the tax power by Congress could work an interference with State government functions was formerly pushed to extravagant lengths. It was applied artificially to notional and abstract interferences, and, moreover, this led to the making of untenable distinctions. The Supreme Court has now reconsidered the older doctrine. The . . . United States now gives as little countenance to the extreme applications made of the principle of non-interference as does the constitutional law of Australia. But, having cleared much of the ground formerly occupied by this doctrine, the Supreme Court has encountered some difficulty in formulating a test by which the validity of a federal tax falling upon operations of the States may be determined. All agree, however, that a tax cannot be laid on the States "as such," that a State cannot be singled out for taxation or for a special burden of taxation in respect of acts or things when others are not taxed or are not so burdened in respect of the same acts or things, in other words, that a taxing law discriminating against a State is unconstitutional and void.

. . . What is important is the firm adherence to the principle that the federal power of taxation will not support a law which places a special burden upon the States. They cannot be singled out and taxed as States in respect of some exercise of their functions. Such a tax is aimed at the States and is an attempt to use federal power to burden or, may be, to control State action. The objection to the use of federal power to single out States and place upon them special burdens or disabilities does not spring from the nature of the power of taxation. The character of the power lends point to the objection but it does not give rise to it. The federal system itself is the foundation of the restraint upon the use of the power to control the States. The same constitutional objection applies to other powers, if under them the States are made the objects of special burdens or disabilities . . . .

[T]he distinction has been constantly drawn between a law of general application and a provision singling out governments and placing special burdens upon the exercise of powers or the fulfilment of functions constitutionally belonging to them. It is but a consequence of the conception upon which the Constitution is framed. The foundation of the Constitution is the conception of a central government and a number of State governments separately organized. The Constitution predicates their continued existence as independent entities. Among them it distributes powers of governing the country. The framers of the Constitution do not appear to have considered that power itself forms part of the conception of a government. They appear rather to have conceived the States as bodies politic whose existence and nature are independent of the powers allocated to them. The Constitution on this footing proceeds to distribute the power between State and Commonwealth and to provide for their inter-relation . . . .

In the many years of debate over the restraints to be implied against any exercise of power by Commonwealth against State and State against Common-wealth calculated to destroy or detract from the independent exercise of the functions of the one or the other, it has often been said that political rather than legal considerations provide the ground of which the restraint is the consequence.

The Constitution is a political instrument. It deals with government and governmental powers. The statement is, therefore, easy to make though it has a specious plausibility. But it is really meaningless. It is not a question whether the considerations are political, for nearly every consideration arising from the Constitution can be so described, but whether they are compelling.

A truism that has been invoked is that the possibility that a power may be abused is no reason for restricting the power by construction. Doubtless it formed a proper objection to the view now completely discredited that an agency of one government was not in that character amenable in any degree to a power of the other lest some exercise of the power might interfere with the due performance of the functions of the agency. But as an objection it is not in point where the question is whether an actual attempt to restrict or control the State in the exercise of a function forming part of its executive power is or is not permitted by the Constitution.

The considerations I have just mentioned have been used in relation to the question what the federal Government may do with reference to the States and the question of what a State may do with reference to the federal Government. But these are two quite different questions and they are affected by considerations that are not the same. The position of the federal government is necessarily stronger than that of the States. The Commonwealth is a government to which enumerated powers have been affirmatively granted. The grant carries all that is proper for its full effectuation. Then supremacy is given to the legislative powers of the Commonwealth.

. . . [T]he considerations upon which the States' title to protection from Commonwealth control depends arise not from the character of the powers retained by the States but from their position as separate governments in the system exercising independent functions. But, to my mind, the efficacy of the system logically demands that, unless a given legislative power appears from its content, context or subject matter so to intend, it should not be understood as authorizing the Commonwealth to make a law aimed at the restriction or control of a State in the exercise of its executive authority . . . .

1.5.3. Further growth in federal power: "external affairs"

While *Melbourne Corporation* appeared to restrain Commonwealth power and offer some protection to the states against the "creep" of power towards the centre, the evolution of the external affairs power — s 51(xxix) — has shifted the balance in the other direction. In 1982, *Koowarta v. Bjelke-Petersen* (1982) 153 CLR 533 broke new ground (and raised alarm among states' rights advocates) by affirming that the Commonwealth *Race Discrimination Act* of 1975 was validly supported by the external affairs power (as it gave effect to the United Nations Convention on the Elimination of All Forms of Racial Discrimination) and that it could prevail over, or preempt, an inconsistent state law, although the Commonwealth law's primary operation was Australian (not "external") and it was supported by no other Commonwealth head of power. The HCA divided sharply in *Koowarta*, however, leaving unclear whether a law, to be validly supported by s 51(xxix), needed to be on a subject of "international concern," or whether the fact that it gave effect to an international treaty was sufficient. The question was resolved the following year, in the *Tasmanian Dam* case. This case concerned a Commonwealth Act that sought to prevent the Tasmanian government from proceeding with plans for building a hydro-electricity generating dam on the Gordon-below-Franklin River, in a wilderness region in southern Tasmania. Australia was (and remains) a party to the UNESCO Convention for the Protection of the World Cultural and Natural Heritage, and the region had been entered for listing under this Convention. The Commonwealth, relying on s 51(xxix) (among other constitutional provisions), enacted the *World Heritage Properties Conservation Act* of 1983, which had the effect of prohibiting the building of the dam. Tasmania challenged the Act. Among other arguments, it attempted to persuade the Court that the external affairs power could only support legislation on a subject matter "of international concern" or having an "international character." The argument was rejected by a 4-3 majority.

COMMONWEALTH v. TASMANIA
("Tasmanian Dam Case")
High Court of Australia
(1983) 158 CLR 1

MASON, J: [W]hen we have regard to international affairs as they are conducted today [compared with 1900], when the nations of the world are accustomed to discuss, negotiate, cooperate and agree on an ever widening range of topics, it is impossible to enunciate a criterion by which potential for international action can be identified from topics which lack this quality. Among the many instances of the common pursuit by nations of common objectives of a humanitarian, cultural and idealistic kind are the International Covenant on Economic, Social and Cultural Rights, the International Convention on the Elimination of All Forms of Racial Discrimination, the Convention on the Political Rights of Women, the Convention against Discrimination in Education, the Convention concerning Freedom of Association and Protection of the Right to Organize, the Convention concerning Discrimination in respect of Employment and Occupation and the Convention concerning Equal Remuneration for Men and Women Workers for Work of Equal Value, to all of which Australia has become a party. There are so many examples of the common pursuit of humanitarian, cultural and idealistic objectives that we cannot treat subjects of this kind as lacking the requisite international character to support a treaty or convention which will attract the exercise of the power. Indeed, the lesson to be learned from this experience is that there are virtually no limits to the topics which may hereafter become the subject of international cooperation and international treaties or conventions.

It is submitted [by Tasmania] that the suggested requirement that the subject matter must be "of international concern" [and that this] means that it must be international in character in the sense that there is a mutuality of interest or benefit in the observance of the provisions of the convention. Thus, we are invited to say that a convention by which the contracting parties agree to enact domestic laws requiring persons in motor vehicles to wear seat belts does not deal with a matter of international concern because no nation can derive a benefit from the wearing of seat belts in another country. This is by no means self-evident. Drivers and passengers cross international boundaries. They are likely to observe in other countries the practices which they observe at home. International cooperation resulting in a convention insisting on compliance with uniform safety standards may well benefit all countries. The illustration is instructive because it demonstrates how difficult it is to say with accuracy of any treaty or convention that observance of its provisions will not benefit a contracting party.

The point is that if a topic becomes the subject of international cooperation or an international convention it is necessarily international in character - the existence of cooperation and the making of a convention establish that the subject matter is an appropriate vehicle for the creation of international relationships or, in the case of a bilateral treaty, a relationship between the parties to it. And participation in a convention indicates a judgment on the part of participating nations that they will derive a benefit from it. All this indicates an absence of any acceptable criteria or guidelines by which the Court can determine the "international character" of the subject matter of a treaty or convention. The existence of international character or international concern is established by entry by Australia into the convention or treaty.

In any event, as I observed in *Koowarta*, the Court would undertake an invidious task if it were to decide whether the subject matter of a convention is of international character or concern. On a question of this kind the Court cannot substitute its judgment for that of the Executive Government and Parliament. The fact of entry into, and of ratification of, an international convention, evidences the judgment of the Executive and of Parliament that the subject matter of the convention is of international character and concern and that its implementation will be a benefit to Australia. Whether the subject matter as dealt with by the convention is of international concern, whether it will yield, or is capable of yielding, a benefit to Australia, whether non-observance by Australia is likely to lead to adverse international action or reaction, are not questions on which the Court can readily arrive at an informed opinion. Essentially they are issues involving nice questions of sensitive judgment which should be left to the Executive Government for determination. The Court should accept and act upon the decision of the Executive Government and upon the expression of the will of Parliament in giving legislative ratification to the treaty or convention.

The argument . . . by Tasmania is largely based on implications to be drawn from the federal nature of the Constitution, and on predictions that "the federal balance" will be disturbed, indeed shattered, if the validity of the Commonwealth legislation is upheld . . .

In the argument which is presented in this case the expression "the federal balance" seems to mean, not so much the distribution of legislative powers effected by the Constitution , as the content, as it was understood in 1900, of the legislative powers thus distributed . . . It is, of course, possible that the framers of the Constitution thought or assumed that the external affairs power would have a less extensive operation than this development has brought about and that Common-wealth legislation by way of implementation of treaty obligations would be infrequent and limited in scope. The framers of the Constitution would not have foreseen with any degree of precision, if at all, the expansion in international and regional affairs that has occurred since the turn of the century, in particular the cooperation between nations that has resulted in the formation of international and regional conventions. But it is not, and could not be, suggested that by reason of this circumstance the power should now be given an operation which conforms to expectations held in 1900. For one thing it is impossible to ascertain what those expectations may have been. For another the difference between those expectations and subsequent events as they have fallen out seems to have been a difference in the frequency and volume of external affairs rather than a difference in kind. Only if there was a difference in kind could we begin to construct an argument that the expression "external affairs" should receive a construction which differs from the meaning that it would receive according to ordinary principles and interpretation. Even then mere expectations held in 1900 could not form a satisfactory basis for departing from the natural interpretation of words used in the Constitution.

. . . .

[I]t conforms to established principle to say that s. 51 (xxix) was framed as an enduring power in broad and general terms enabling the Parliament to legislate with respect to all aspects of Australia's participation in international affairs and of its relationship with other countries in a changing and developing world and in circumstances and situations that could not be easily foreseen in 1900. This circumstance is often overlooked by those who are preoccupied with the impact that the exercise of the power may have in areas of legislation traditionally regarded by the States as their own.

. . . [I[t is well settled [in the *Engineers Case*] that it is wrong to construe a constitutional power by reference to (1) an assumption that there is some content reserved to the States . . . and (2) imaginary abuses of legislative power . . . The only relevant implication [from *Melbourne Corporation*] that can be gleaned from the Constitution . . . is that the Commonwealth cannot in the exercise of its legislative powers enact a law which discriminates against or "singles out" a State or imposes some special burden or disability upon a State or inhibits or impairs the continued existence of a State or its capacity to function.

GIBBS, C.J. [in dissent]:

. . . .

Four members of the Court in *Koowarta* rejected the notion that s. 51(xxix) empowers the Parliament to give effect in Australia to any international agreement to which Australia is a party, whatever its subject matter and whatever the circumstances. In that case, although Stephen, Mason, Murphy and Brennan JJ. joined in holding the challenged legislation to be valid, Stephen J. differed from the other members of the majority on this question. Mason J. expressed his opinion as follows, at p.651: "Agreement by nations to take common action in pursuit of a common objective evidences the existence of international concern and gives the subject-matter of the treaty a character which is international." The view of Murphy J. was equally wide; see at p.656. Brennan J. expressed a similar view, but suggested a possible qualification. At p.663 he said:"When a particular subject affects or is likely to affect Australia's relations with other international persons, a law with respect to that subject is a law with respect to external affairs." (at p 474).

. . . .

The external affairs power differs from the other powers conferred by s. 51 in its capacity for almost unlimited expansion. As Dixon J. pointed out in Stenhouse v. Coleman [1944] HCA 36; (1944),69 C.L.R. 457, at p.471: "In most of the paragraphs of s. 51 the subject of the power is described either by reference to a class of legal, commercial, economic or social transaction or activity (as trade and commerce, banking, marriage), or by specifying some class of public service (as postal installations, lighthouses), or undertaking or operation (as railway construction with the consent of a State), or by naming a recognized category of legislation (as taxation, bankruptcy)." The boundaries of those categories of power may be wide, but at least they are capable of definition. However, there is almost no aspect of life which under modern conditions may not be the subject of an international agreement, and therefore the possible subject of Commonwealth legislative power. Whether Australia enters into any particular international agreement is entirely a matter for decision by the Executive. The division of powers between the Commonwealth and the States which the Constitution effects could be rendered quite meaningless if the Federal Government could, by entering into treaties with foreign governments on matters of domestic concern, enlarge the legislative powers of the Parliament so that they embraced literally all fields of activity. This result could follow even though all the treaties were entered into in good faith, that is, not solely as a device for the purpose of attracting legislative power. Section 51(xxix) should be given a construction that will, so far as possible, avoid the consequence that the federal balance of the Constitution can be destroyed at the will of the Executive.

The majority's view that the HCA should not police the limits of the External Affairs power was re-affirmed in *Polyukhovich v. Cth* (1991) 172 CLR 501, 531, upholding Commonwealth legislation permitting the criminal prosecution of Australians who had committed war crimes during World War II. Justice Mason concluded that "it is not necessary that the court should be satisfied that Australia has an interest or concern in the subject-matter of the legislation . . . It is enough that Parliament's judgment is that Australia has an interest or concern." The principal test now for whether a law is supported by the External Affairs power is one of "geographical externality." There are few limitations; a law that gives effect to an international Convention or treaty must be *bona fides* (not a colorable attempt to expand Commonwealth power), and the Convention relied upon cannot be too vague or imprecise. But these limitations lie in *obiter dicta*; no law has been struck down for breach of either.

1.5.4.   The Trade & Commerce power

The Trade & Commerce power (s 51(i)) has never been the big federal battleground that the U.S. commerce clause proved to be. Nor has it been drawn upon significantly to expand Commonwealth power. (The Commonwealth has employed other heads, or avenues of power, to achieve the sort of regulation that the commerce clause has permitted in the U.S., particularly the "corporations power": see below). The case of *Airlines of NSW Pty. Ltd. v. State of NSW (No. 2)* (1965) 113 CLR 54, expressly rejected the broader reasoning of American cases.

Pursuant to Commonwealth legislation, a federal official had granted the plaintiff a license for intra-state commercial flights between Sydney and Dubbo (both in the state of New South Wales). New South Wales, however, had its own licensing statute, and state officials determined that the airline did not meet its standards for suitability or need for service. The Commonwealth argued that air travel was so integrated that distinguishing between inter-state and intra-state air travel was unworkable and plenary national regulations were necessary. Chief Justice Barwick rejected this claim (at p. 78):

> This proposition so far as it is placed upon the power given by s. 51 (i.) is demonstrably insupportable. It is a claim that the Commonwealth has in some circumstances power to make laws with respect to some aspects of intra-State trade and commerce as themselves topics of legislative power. But the Commonwealth has not and, without constitutional amendment, cannot obtain such legislative power with respect to any aspect of such trade and commerce, including intra-State commercial air transport as an aspect of intra-State air navigation. No so-called "integration" of inter-State and intra-State air navigation or air transport, commercial or otherwise, no intermingling or commingling of the two to any degree, however "complete," can enlarge the subject matter of Commonwealth legislative power in the relevant field. It remains a power to make laws with respect to inter-State and foreign trade and commerce. This Court has never favoured, in relation to Commonwealth power, the more extensive view of the commerce power under the Constitution of Congress which has at times found expression in decisions of the Supreme Court of the United States.

Although the Commonwealth's power to enact safety procedures designed to make interstate and foreign air commerce secure was sustained, the economic regulation at issue in this case was beyond the scope of s. 51(i). Justice Kitto amplified the comparative differences, taking aim at the American precedents allowing Congress to regulate intrastate activities that substantially affected interstate commerce (at p. 115):

> The establishment of these criteria in the United States has evoked in that country itself criticisms of which we would do well to take notice. It was Frankfurter J. who described them as "less than unwavering bright lines": Baker v. Carr [1962] USSC 48; (1962) 369 US 186, at p 283 (7 Law Ed 2d 663, at p 724). One other quotation will be enough. I take it from the writings of Dr. Bernard Schwartz, Professor of Law at New York University: "Decisions like those just discussed illustrate the extent to which the Supreme Court has departed from the concept of dual federalism which had previously governed its approach to cases involving the relationship of federal and State authority. For the older view that the federal power over commerce could not be exercised over local transactions, which were within the exclusive area of State authority, has been substituted the notion of a plenary power of the national Government over commerce. If wheat production intended by the farmer solely for his domestic consumption can be regulated by Congress because of its possible effect upon interstate commerce, however indirect it may be, there are, in practice, no restrictions

upon federal regulation of even so-called purely local commerce. And, if this is true, the American system is clearly no longer one of dual federalism." American Constitutional Law (1955) p. 170. (at p.115).

The Australian union is one of dual federalism, and until the Parliament and the people see fit to change it, a true federation it must remain. This Court is entrusted with the preservation of constitutional distinctions, and it both fails in its task and exceeds its authority if it discards them, however out of touch with practical conceptions or with modern conditions they may appear to be in some or all of their applications. To import the doctrine of the American cases into the law of the Australian Constitution would in my opinion be an error.

Section 51(i), however, usefully illustrates the "incidental" power (analogous to the U.S. "necessary and proper" provision). The Commonwealth is limited to passing laws with respect only to interstate and overseas trade and commerce. It can, however, regulate intra-state trade (including manufacture and production) where it is necessary "to effectuate the main purpose" of the power, or incidental to its operation.

O'Sullivan v. Noarlunga Meat Ltd. (1954) 92 CLR 565 concerned a Commonwealth law that regulated the conditions of state slaughterhouses "incidentally" to regulating the export trade in meat. The HCA held that the Commonwealth law could reach into intra-state trade, including manufacture or production, if this was necessary or beneficial to support laws with respect to export.

In the words of Justice Fullagar:

It is true that the Commonwealth possesses no specific power with respect to slaughter-houses. But it is undeniable that the power with respect to trade and commerce with other countries includes a power to make provision for the condition and quality of meat or of any other commodity to be exported. Nor can the power, in my opinion, be held to stop there. By virtue of that power all matters which may affect beneficially or adversely the export trade of Australia in any commodity produced or manufactured in Australia must be the legitimate concern of the Commonwealth. Such matters include not only grade and quality of goods but packing, get-up, description, labelling, handling, and anything at all that may reasonably be considered likely to affect an export market by developing it or impairing it. It seems clear enough that the objectives for which the power is conferred may be impossible of achievement by means of a mere prescription of standards for export and the institution of a system of inspection at the point of export. It may very reasonably be thought necessary to go further back, and even to enter the factory or the field or the mine. How far back the Commonwealth may constitutionally go . . . must in any case depend on the particular circumstances attending the production or manufacture of particular commodities. But I would think it safe to say that the power of the Commonwealth extended to the supervision and control of all acts or processes which can be identified as being done or carried out for export. The "slaughter for export" of stock is such an act or process, and, in my opinion, the Commerce (Meat Export)

Regulations are within the legislative power conferred upon the Commonwealth by s. 51 (i.).

1.5.5. Limitations on state power: section 92's requirement that trade and commerce must be "absolutely free"

Over the twentieth century, the balance of federal power has shifted, decisively, towards the centre, albeit with very little formal constitutional alteration. Changing approaches to interpretation, along with changes in international relations and in fiscal and corporate life, have made this virtually inevitable. This was unlikely to have been the intention of the Constitution's framers (few Justices of today's High Court, however, would be swayed by such a concern). However, the framers did not intend state legislative power to be unrestrained. Apart from the limitations lying in the fact that the Commonwealth is empowered to pass laws with respect to a wide range of subjects and that any state laws on these same subjects will be invalid if they are inconsistent with a Commonwealth law, there are several constitutional provisions that expressly limit state legislative power in a way relevant to federal relations (there are other limitations, express and implied, of a non-federal nature: these are considered in later chapters). As noted above, certain powers are exclusive to the Commonwealth (s 90); most importantly, under s 90, the states cannot impose customs or excise duties (There are other exclusive or effectively exclusive Commonwealth powers — ss 52, 114, 115 — but these are of little relevance federally).

Section 92 provides a very important limitation on state power. The trade and commerce power, as we have seen, limits the Commonwealth and it is a rare example of a power which has been subject to little expansion by constitutional interpretation in the course of judicial review, but it cannot be understood separately from s 92, which guarantees "absolutely free" trade and commerce "among the States." This provision (which might be considered a written version of the U.S. "dormant commerce clause" reviewed in section 1.4.7 above) acts as a limitation on the exercise of legislative power. For decades, the HCA's interpretation of s 92 seemed to shift, from a protection of individual commercial rights to, at least for some Justices, a virtual constitutional guarantee of a free market economy. Compare *James v. Cowan* (1930) 43 CLR 386, 418, where Justice Isaacs stated that "[t]he right of inter-State trade and commerce protected by sec 92 . . . *is a personal right attaching to the individual* . . ." (a view reiterated in *Bank of NSW v. Commonwealth* (1948) 76 CLR 1), with *Samuels v. Readers' Digest* (1969) 120 CLR 1, 14, where Chief Justice Barwick stated that "a constitutional provision to prevent at least the members of a federation, which in relation to trade and commerce is what we would now call a common market, from making or so operating laws as to inhibit the freedom of trade and commerce between them is necessary and indeed indispensable." Finally, adopting an interpretive approach unusual for the High Court of Australia, a unanimous Court in *Cole v. Whitfield* (1988) 165 CLR 338, focused on both the framers' understanding of the phrase "free trade" and on the record of the various convention debates, holding that s 92 was to be interpreted specifically to prohibit any law that imposes a discriminatory burden of a protectionist kind on inter-state trade or commerce. This is not always fatal, however, to laws that appear on their face to protect state industry. Laws that restrict inter-state trade and commerce may survive constitutional challenge, if they have a legitimate non-protectionist object and are appropriate and adapted to that object. This occurred in *Cole v. Whitfield, supra*, the leading s 92 case, which settled the provision's meaning. The challenged Tasmanian state law restricted the minimum size of crayfish that could be sold in Tasmania, including crayfish imported from another state where smaller crayfish could be lawfully sold. The law burdened interstate trade but was found not to be anti-competitive or protectionist; it was, rather, appropriate and adapted to the purpose of conserving a fragile natural state resource.

1.5.6. Federal expansion yet again: the "corporations power" and *Work Choices*

The biggest federalism controversy in recent years arose in the 2006 *Work Choices* case. It concerned s 51(xx) which gives the Commonwealth power to make laws with respect to "Foreign corporations, and trading or financial corporations formed within the limits of the Commonwealth." Having been treated very restrictively by the High Court for much of the twentieth century, the power has enjoyed an expansive interpretation in recent decades. The Court has applied an "activities" rather than purpose test for identifying a "constitutional corporation" (that is to say, the Court looks at what the corporate entity does, rather than how it describes itself in its articles of incorporation). It progressively upheld legislation that regulated more than just the trading or financial activities of corporations, that regulated more than private corporations, and that targeted the conduct of third parties having an effect on corporations. The power's potential was also greatly enhanced by the great growth in incorporation in the post-war years. In addition to the traditional business enterprise, governmental, educational, charitable, and religious organisations, among others, are now routinely incorporated under law. Around half of all small business are also incorporated. Any corporation whose "activities" involve a significant element of finance or trading may now come under Commonwealth law. This expansion in the scope of the power has had an important effect on the states, and potentially on the "federal balance." Matters that were previously outside the constitutional powers of the Commonwealth have now been brought within it, so long as corporations are involved. How far could this go? Could the Commonwealth regulate the terms and conditions of employment internal to a corporation, having nothing directly to do with the activities or "corporate" identity of the corporation, as such? The answer proved to be yes.

The *Work Choices case* concerned legislation which gave effect to the policy of a Liberal-National Party government seeking to dismantle the long-standing industrial relations system, in particular, the practice of union-negotiated industrial awards. The *Workplace Relations Amendment (Work Choices) Act 2005* (Cth) included numerous provisions, with key sections that aimed to decentralise and individualise agreements between employers and employees. Its "framework for cooperative workplace relations" rested upon the definition of "employer" and "employee" as employer or employee "of a constitutional corporation." Given the spread of corporations, the majority of Australian employers or employees (an estimated 85 %) would now come under this definition.

If the corporations power extended to regulating effectively anything that could be defined in this way, the reach of federal legislation would potentially be hugely expanded. The High Court, however, does not take hypothetical or future impacts into account in its reasoning. The government's strategy succeeded, with the HCA majority (with two robust dissents) upholding the law.

NSW v. COMMONWEALTH
("WORK CHOICES CASE")
HIGH COURT OF AUSTRALIA
(2006) 229 CLR 1

GLEESON CJ, GUMMOW, HAYNE, HEYDON and CRENNAN JJ:

[R]eliance on the corporations power to support legislation relating to industrial relations matters and terms and conditions of employment in 2005 [is] not novel. At least since 1993, the Parliament has included provisions enacted in reliance on s 51 (xx) in its industrial relations legislation . . . . It is the extent of the reliance that is new . . . .

If, in the exercise of its powers under s 51 (xx), the Commonwealth Parliament can regulate the terms and conditions on which constitutional corporations may deal with their customers, or their suppliers of goods or services, why can it not, in the exercise of the same powers, regulate the terms and conditions on which constitutional corporations may deal with employees, or with prospective employees? If . . . a corporation's dealings with its employees are part of its trading activities, how can it be that the Parliament has power to prohibit constitutional corporations from engaging in some forms of business activities (such as anti-competitive behaviour) but not others (such as engaging in certain industrial practices)? Why is not use of the corporations power to regulate aspects of intra-State trade just as much an incursion into State legislative power as use of the corporations power to regulate aspects of industrial relations? . . .

The arguments of the plaintiffs included a submission that the power conferred by s 51 (xx) was restricted to a power to regulate the dealings of constitutional corporations with persons external to the corporation, but not with employees (or, apparently, prospective employees). It was also submitted that s 51 (xx) should be read down, or restricted in its operation, by reference to . . . s 51 (xxxv). That paragraph confers on the Parliament the power to make laws with respect to "conciliation and arbitration for the prevention and settlement of industrial disputes extending beyond the limits of any one State.". . . Alternatively, it was argued that, even if the presence of s 51 (xxxv) did not affect the general ambit of s 51 (xx), at least it operated to restrict the capacity of the Parliament to enact a law that can be characterised as a law with respect to the prevention and settlement of industrial disputes . . . . Underlying all these arguments there was a theme, much discussed in the authorities on the corporations power, that there is a need to confine its operation because of its potential effect upon the (concurrent) legislative authority of the States . . . . References to the "federal balance" carry a misleading implication of static equilibrium, an equilibrium that is disturbed by changes in constitutional doctrine such as occurred in the *Engineers' Case*, and changes in circumstances as a result of the First World War. The error in implications of that kind has long been recognised . . . .

## 1.6.	BASIC PRINCIPLES OF SOUTH AFRICAN CO-OPERATIVE GOVERNMENT

Chapter 3 of the 1996 Constitution lays out the constitutional scheme of co-operative government. Most Constitutions rely either on the very structure of the Constitution to establish a "federal" relationship between different regional units or provide specifically for a hierarchy of governments in which the national government allocates powers to the regions or the regions enjoy a degree of autonomy. South Africa's system of co-operative governance is unique in the way it defines different spheres of government and tries to constitutionally regulate their relative roles to facilitate intergovernmental relations across the different loci of governance in the country. Section 40(1) states that the "government is constituted as national, provincial and local spheres of government which are distinctive, interdependent and interrelated." The principles of co-operative government and intergovernmental relations listed in s 41(1) go on to define the specific duties that each level of government owes to the other as well as the duty of the legislature to adopt legislation creating institutions and mechanisms to facilitate intergovernmental relations and to resolve disputes between different levels of government.

Apart from the general commitments to preserve peace and national unity, secure the well-being of the people and provide "effective, transparent, accountable and coherent government," the key constitutional boundaries set forth in s 41(1)(a-f) laid down in the Principles require each level of government to "respect the constitutional status, institutions, powers and functions of government in the other spheres," and not to "assume any power or function except those conferred on them in terms of the Constitution." These boundaries also require, in s 41(1)(h), that the different levels of government to "exercise their powers and perform their functions in a manner that does not encroach on the geographical, functional or institutional integrity" of other governing authorities. Instead, the Principles seek to promote an ethos of co-operation based on "mutual trust and good faith." Finally, s 41(3) requires an organ of state "involved in an intergovernmental dispute must make every reasonable effort to settle the dispute . . . and must exhaust all other remedies before it approaches a court to resolve the dispute." This last element is strengthened by s 41(4), providing that a court may refer a dispute back to parties involved if it is not satisfied that they have exhausted all non-legal remedies or made every reasonable effort to settle the dispute by other means.

### 1.6.1.	The distribution of legislative authority under co-operative government

The Constitution explicitly distributes legislative authority to all three spheres of government: the national, regional and local. At the same time it ensures that the ultimate law-giving authority is vested in Parliament: ss 44(2)(a)–(e) empowers the national legislature to override even the exclusive legislative competence of a province if it is necessary to maintain national security, economic unity, essential national standards, minimum standards of service delivery or "to prevent unreasonable action taken by a province which is prejudicial to the interests of another province or to the country as a whole." It is important to understand, however, that the National Council of Provinces (NCOP) (detailed in the introductory chapter), which directly represents provincial governments in the national legislature, is a full participant in the legislative process and therefore plays a central role in the exercise of this override function. Ultimately however, the NCOP cannot prevent the National Assembly from passing legislation affecting the provinces if the legislation is supported by a two-thirds vote in the Assembly. However, such a vote may only take place after a complex procedure set forth in s 76, in which the legislation is voted on by both houses, submitted to a mediation committee and then if no agreement is reached, either lapses, or is passed by a two-thirds majority in the National Assembly. All other legislation, not directly affecting the provinces as defined in the Constitution, is the preserve of the National Assembly, although the NCOP does have a deliberative role and formally votes on these issues. Voting procedures in the NCOP depend on the subject matter before the Council. In the case of matters affecting the provinces and in the case of constitutional amendments, each provincial delegation has a single vote. In matters of general interest, in which the NCOP has a primarily deliberative role, the members of the Council cast individual votes.

1.6.2.   The Constitutional Court's interpretation of the principles of Co-operative Government

While the principles of co-operative government are called upon to play a symbolic and pedagogical role in shaping the behaviour of government departments and officials — both internally and in their relations with other governing units — the Constitutional Court has been called upon to apply them in related cases. Asked to confirm a High Court declaration of unconstitutionality, in a case in which district municipalities claimed they had been excluded from receiving equitable fiscal allotments by the *Division of Revenue Act 1* of 2001, the Constitutional Court reviewed the Constitutional requirements of co-operative government in deciding whether to exercise its discretion to confirm the High Court's decision, despite the parties' settlement of the case. *Uthukela District Municipality v. President of the Republic of South Africa*, CCT 7/02 (2002). In reaching its decision, the Court held that organs of state have a "constitutional duty to foster co-operative government" and that the essence of Chapter 3 of the Constitution is that "disputes should where possible be resolved at a political level rather than through adversarial litigation." *Id.* para 13. In fact, the Court argued, the requirements of co-operative government include a duty to "avoid legal proceedings against one another," a duty the courts must ensure is duly performed. *Id.* More specifically, the Court stated that "apart from the general duty to avoid legal proceedings against one another," a two-fold duty obliges organs of state in an intergovernmental dispute to "make every reasonable effort to settle the dispute by means of mechanisms and procedures provided for" and to "exhaust all other remedies before they approach a court to resolve the dispute." *Id.* para 19. Finally, note that s 150 of the Constitution expressly directs courts to prefer a constitutional or statutory interpretation that avoids a conflict over an alternative that results in a conflict.[21]

UTHUKELA DISTRICT MUNICIPALITY v. THE PRESIDENT OF THE REPUBLIC OF SOUTH AFRICA
CONSTITUTIONAL COURT OF SOUTH AFRICA
2003 (1) SA 678

DU PLESSIS AJ:

[1] Government in the Republic of South Africa "is constituted as national, provincial and local spheres of government which are distinctive, interdependent and interrelated."[22] Municipalities established throughout the territory of the Republic constitute the local sphere of government.[23]

[2] The local sphere of government is structured as

> "(a) self-standing municipalities, (b) municipalities that form part of a comprehensive co-ordinating structure, and (c) municipalities that perform co-ordinating functions."[24]

The Constitution refers to these municipalities respectively as Category A, B and C municipalities.[25] This case concerns the entitlement of category C municipalities to an equitable share of revenue raised nationally.

[3] In terms of section 214(1)(a) of the Constitution, an Act of Parliament must provide for "the equitable division of revenue raised nationally among the national, provincial and local spheres of government." Section 227(1)(a) of the Constitution in turn provides that "local government and each province . . . is entitled to an equitable share of revenue raised nationally to enable it to provide basic services and perform the functions allocated to it."

[4] In order to comply with sections 214(1)(a) and 227(1)(a) of the Constitution, Parliament annually enacts a Division of Revenue Act. At issue in this case is the Division of Revenue Act 1 of 2001 ("the 2001 Act") that dealt with the 2001/2002 financial year. Section 3(1) thereof provided for the division of revenue raised nationally among the national, provincial and local spheres of government. Section 5(1) in turn provided for the allocation to individual municipalities, of their equitable share. The subsection made no provision for the payment to Category C munici-palities of an equitable share of revenue raised nationally.

[5] The three applicants are Category C municipalities whose respective areas of

---

[21] Note the similarity between section 150 and a similar judicially-created principle invoked by Roberts, C.J., in *NFIB v. Sebelius*, to uphold a federal mandate to purchase health insurance under Congress' Taxing Power even though Congress had not actually called the mandate a "tax."

[22] [FN 1] Section 40(1) of the Constitution of the Republic of South Africa.

[23] [FN 2] Section 151(1) of the Constitution.

[24] [FN 3] *Ex Parte Chairperson of the Constitutional Assembly: In re Certification of the Amended Text of the Constitution of the RSA, 1996*, 1997 (2) SA 97 (CC); 1997 (1) BCLR 1 (CC) para 77.

[25] [FN 4] Section 155(1).

jurisdiction fall within the KwaZulu-Natal (KZN) province. In three separate applications they applied to the Natal High Court for orders declaring section 5(1) of the 2001 Act unconstitutional "in its omission to accord Applicant's entitlement to an equitable share of revenue raised nationally allocated to the local sphere of government." The three applications were consolidated and the High Court gave an order declaring section 5(1) unconstitutional and "invalid to the extent that it excludes Category 'C' municipalities from sharing with Category 'A' and 'B' municipalities in the local government allocation of revenue raised nationally." (It is convenient to refer to Category B municipalities as "local municipalities" and to Category C municipalities as "district municipalities.")

. . . .

[13] If parties who may be affected by confirmation proceedings are organs of state,[26] a further important factor must be taken into consideration. Organs of state have the constitutional duty to foster co-operative government as provided for in Chapter 3 of the Constitution. This entails that organs of state must "avoid legal proceedings against one another." The essence of Chapter 3 of the Constitution is that "disputes should where possible be resolved at a political level rather than through adversarial litigation."[27] Courts must ensure that the duty is duly performed. This is apparent from section 41(4) which provides:

> "If a court is not satisfied that the requirements of subsection (3) have been met, it may refer a dispute back to the organs of state involved."

[14] In view of the important requirements of co-operative government, a court, including this Court, will rarely decide an intergovernmental dispute unless the organs of state involved in the dispute have made every reasonable effort to resolve it at a political level. When exercising a discretion whether to deal with confirmation proceedings, this Court must thus bear in mind that Chapter 3 of the Constitution contemplates that organs of state must make every reasonable effort to resolve intergovernmental disputes before having recourse to the courts.

. . . .

Co-operative government

[18] Municipalities are organs of state in the local sphere of government. The first, second and third respondents, are all organs of state in the national sphere.

---

[26] [FN 20] Section 239 of the Constitution defines "organ of state" as:
- (a) any department of state or administration in the national, provincial or local sphere of government; or
- (b) any other functionary or institution —
  - (i)   exercising a power or performing a function in terms of the Constitution or a provincial constitution; or
  - (ii) exercising a public power or performing a public function in terms of any legislation, but does not include a court or a judicial officer;"

[27] [FN 23] *Ex Parte Chairperson of the Constitutional Assembly: In re Certification of the Constitution of the Republic of South Africa, 1996* 1996 (4) SA 744 (CC); 1996 (10) BCLR 1253 (CC) para 291.

[19] Apart from the general duty to avoid legal proceedings against one another, section 41(3) of the Constitution places a two-fold obligation on organs of state involved in an intergovernmental dispute: First, they must make every reasonable effort to settle the dispute by means of mechanisms and procedures provided for. Second, they must exhaust all other remedies before they approach a court to resolve the dispute.

[20] There is a dispute-resolution mechanism in place in the context of fiscal disputes between organs of state in the national and local spheres. Part 2 of the Intergovernmental Fiscal Relations Act[28] (the Fiscal Relations Act) establishes a Local Government Budget Forum (the Forum). The Forum consists[29] of the national minister of finance, the member of the executive council for finance of each province, five representatives nominated by SALGA and one representative nominated by each provincial organisation recognised in terms of the Organised Local Government Act. KWANALOGA, who represents the majority of municipalities in KZN, thus has one representative on the Forum.

. . . .

[23] If municipalities are aggrieved by the omission of district municipalities from the 2001 equitable share, they can and must make use of the dispute-resolution procedures described above. If such municipalities are unable to resolve their grievances, they must approach the relevant national minister directly. The papers before this Court do not suggest that the national organs of state involved are not willing to address, at a political level, problems regarding the 2001 equitable share. From an annexure to an affidavit filed in this Court by the first three respondents it appears that the Minister of Finance, dealing with the present issue, said in Parliament:

> "Our intergovernmental system for dealing with financial and fiscal matters is maturing, and flexible enough to allow us to deal with some of the unintended consequences of section 5(1) of the Division of Revenue Act, 2001."

[24] In the circumstances and in the interest of co-operative government, this Court should not exercise its discretion to decide the confirmation issue. It must first be left to the organs of state to endeavour to resolve at a political level such issues as there may still be.

. . . .

1.6.3.   Disputes over the allocation of legislative authority

The Constitutional Court has addressed three issues central to the question of legislative authority within the context of co-operative government in the Constitution. First, the court was called upon to define the constitutional allocation of legislative power in a case where a province claimed implied legislative powers to define the structure of its own civil service. Second, the court was required to

---

[28]   [FN 30]: Act 97 of 1997.

[29]   [FN 31]: Section 5 of the Fiscal Relations Act.

determine the scope of residual national legislative power in a case where the national government claimed concurrent authority over the establishment of municipal governments — despite the Constitution's simultaneous allocation in this field of specific functions to different institutions and spheres of government. Finally, an attempt by the national government to extensively regulate liquor production, sale and consumption — a field in which the regions were granted at least some exclusive powers under the Constitution — required the court to define the specific content of the exclusive legislative powers of the provinces.

Virtually all disputes over federalism can be characterized as debating when a national majority should be constrained in its ability to enact nationwide legislation when dissenting citizens control a majority of a state or province. To date, post-apartheid South Africa has been characterized by the virtually complete control of national and provincial legislatures by the African National Congress. As a result, the Madisonian notion that federalism would pit the ambitions of federal and state politicians against each other in liberty-protecting ways has been muted in South Africa. It is not a coincidence that the principal cases excerpted below arise out of disputes between the national government and those of the provinces of Kwa-Zulu Natal and Western Cape, where non-ANC parties have won provincial elections.

1.6.3.1. Constitutional allocation of legislative power

One of the very first cases involved a challenge to national legislation that sought to define the structure of the public service, including all provincial public services. This legislation restructured the public service which, under the interim Constitution, was organized at the national and provincial levels, with separate Public Service Commissions in each province in addition to the national Public Service Commission. The final 1996 Constitution reversed this situation, creating a single public service under one Public Service Commission. The Western Cape government, which has been led by parties other than the ANC except for one brief period, felt that the national ANC government, which has controlled the central government in the post-apartheid era, was using this change in the constitution to undermine the authority of the provincial government. In this case, the provincial government objected to provisions of the national statute that assign functions to the provincial Director Generals (a powerful civil servant who reports directly to the provincial premier and to whom all other civil servants report, directly or indirectly) and heads of departments in an unacceptable manner; that it constrains the Premier's executive power to establish or abolish departments of government; and that it empowers the Minister to give directions concerning the transfer of certain functions to and from the provincial administration and its departments. The Western Cape argued that the legislation unconstitutionally infringed the executive power vested in the provinces and detracted from the legitimate autonomy of the provinces. The Western Cape's constitutional attack was multi-faceted. It argued that the power to establish and structure a public service administration for the province was implied in the enumeration in s 125 of the Constitution of the powers of the provincial executive. It argued that s 197, expressly dealing with the public administration, should be construed narrowly to proscribe the challenged national statute. It invoked the general principles of cooperative government entrenched in s 44(1)(g) that constrains the ability of any sphere of government to "encroach on the geographical, functional or institutional integrity of government in another sphere."

Each of these arguments were rejected by the Constitutional Court.

THE PREMIER OF THE PROVINCE OF THE WESTERN CAPE v. THE PRESIDENT OF THE REPUBLIC OF SOUTH AFRICA
CONSTITUTIONAL COURT OF SOUTH AFRICA
1999 (3) SA 657

CHASKALSON P:

Introduction

[1] This case arises out of a dispute between the government of the Western Cape province and the national government relating to the constitutional validity of certain amendments to the Public Service Act, 1994 (the 1994 Act) introduced by the Public Service Laws Amendment Act, 1998 (the 1998 Amendment). The 1998 Amendment is part of a legislative scheme aimed at the structural transformation of the public service.

. . . .

[6] The main contention of the Western Cape government is that it is part of the executive power of a province to structure its own administration, and that national legislation which seeks to impose such a structure on the provinces infringes this provincial power.

[7] Much of the evidence placed before this Court was addressed to the question whether the provisions of the new scheme dealing with the structure and functioning of the public service in the provinces, and specifically in the Western Cape, is likely to be better or worse than the existing scheme according to which control of provincial administrations is centralized and vested in the DGs of the provinces. In the circumstances of the present case, that, however, is not a question that has to be addressed in dealing with this issue. The question is not which scheme is better suited to the conditions in the Western Cape in the circumstances of the present case; it is whether Parliament has the competence to prescribe how provincial administrations in the public service are to be structured . . . .

The executive power of the provinces

[8] The executive authority of provinces is set out in section 125 of the Constitution which provides:

(1)   The executive authority of a province is vested in the Premier of that province.

(2)   The Premier exercises the executive authority, together with the other members of the Executive Council, by —

(a) implementing provincial legislation in the province;

(b) implementing all national legislation within the functional areas listed in schedule 4 or 5 except where the Constitution or an Act of Parliament provides otherwise;

(c) administering in the province, national legislation outside the functional areas listed in schedules 4 and 5, the administration of which has been assigned to the provincial executive in terms of an Act of Parliament;

(d) developing and implementing provincial policy;

(e) co-ordinating the functions of the provincial administration and its departments;

(f) preparing and initiating provincial legislation; and

(g) performing any other function assigned to the provincial executive in terms of the Constitution or an Act of Parliament.

(3) A province has executive authority in terms of subsection 2(b) only to the extent that the province has the administrative capacity to assume effective responsibility. The national government, by legislative and other measures, must assist provinces to develop the administrative capacity required for the effective exercise of their powers and performance of their functions referred in subsection (2).

(4) . . . .

(5) . . . .

(6) The provincial executive must act in accordance with -

(a) the Constitution; and

(b) the provincial constitution, if a constitution has been passed for the province."

[9] Section 125 does not specifically include as an executive power of a province, the power to establish and structure a public service administration for the province. The Western Cape government contended, however, that such a power is implicit in the executive power of a province.

Section 197 of the Constitution

[10] The only provision of the Constitution dealing with the structuring of the public service is section 197 which provides:

(1) Within public administration there is a public service for the Republic, which must function, and be structured, in terms of national legislation, and which must loyally execute the lawful policies of the government of the day.

(2) The terms and conditions of employment in the public service must be regulated by national legislation. Employees are entitled to a fair pension as regulated by national legislation.

(3) No employee of the public service may be favoured or prejudiced only because that person supports a particular political party or cause.

(4)   Provincial governments are responsible for the recruitment, appointment, promotion, transfer and dismissal of members of the public service in their administrations within a framework of uniform norms and standards applying to the public service.

[11] Section 197(1) requires national legislation to address the structure of the public service (the framework within which it will be organized), and the functioning of the public service (how duties will be carried out). A law making provision for the public service to be organized in departments and prescribing the line and reporting functions of heads of departments and other officers and employees would ordinarily be within the purview of such a power.

. . . .

[46] The Constitution requires that one public service be established to implement national and provincial laws. It is presumably for this reason and in order to avoid any dispute thereon that the competence concerning the structure and functioning of the public service is dealt with specifically in the Constitution, and was not left to be dealt with under the general legislative power conferred on parliament by section 44(1)(a). If the Constitution had provided that the structure and control of all aspects of the public service would reside solely at national sphere, personnel would be employed by and answerable to national functionaries, and as was pointed out in the First Certification Judgment, that would have detracted materially from the legitimate autonomy of the provinces. On the other hand, if each province and the national government had the power to structure and control their respective segments of the public service, there would in substance be several public services and the concept of one public service would be a fiction. The compromise struck by the Constitution is that the framework for the public service must be set by national legislation, but employment, transfers etc. are the responsibility of the various administrations of which the public service is composed. . . .. . .

[48] The main attack on the constitutionality of the new scheme must accordingly fail. What remains to be considered is whether the detailed provisions of the new scheme infringe the executive powers of the provinces in any other respect, or whether they "encroach on the geographical, functional or institutional integrity" of provincial governments contrary to the requirements of section 41(1)(g)[30] of the Constitution.

Cooperative government

[49] For the purposes of this part of the judgment it is necessary to consider the provisions of chapter 3 of the Constitution which deal with cooperative government.

[50] The principle of cooperative government is established in section 40 where all spheres of government are described as being "distinctive, inter-dependent and inter-related." This is consistent with the way powers have been allocated between

---

[30] [FN 59] Section 44(1)(g) provides:

"All spheres of government and all organs of state within each sphere must exercise their powers and perform their functions in a manner that does not encroach on the geographical, functional or institutional integrity of government in another sphere."

different spheres of government. Distinctiveness lies in the provision made for elected governments at national, provincial and local levels. The interdependence and interrelatedness flow from the founding provision that South Africa is "one sovereign, democratic state," and a constitutional structure which makes provision for framework provisions to be set by the national sphere of government. These provisions vest concurrent legislative competences in respect of important matters in the national and provincial spheres of government,[31] and contemplate that provincial executives will have responsibility for implementing certain national laws as well as provincial laws.

. . . .

[52] The national legislature is more powerful than other legislatures, having a legislative competence in respect of any matter including the functional areas referred to in schedule 4, though its competence in respect of functional areas listed in schedule 5 is limited to making laws that are necessary for one of the purposes referred to in Section 44(2).[32]

[53] The national government is also given overall responsibility for ensuring that other spheres of government carry out their obligations under the Constitution. In addition to its powers in respect of local government, it may also intervene in the provincial sphere in circumstances where a provincial government "cannot or does not fulfil an executive obligation in terms of legislation or the Constitution."[33] It is empowered in such circumstances to take "any appropriate steps to ensure fulfilment" of such obligations.[34]

. . . .

[57] Section 41(1)(g) is concerned with the way power is exercised, not with whether or not a power exists. That is determined by the provisions of the Constitution. In the present case what is relevant is that the constitutional power to structure the public service vests in the national sphere of government.

[58] Although the circumstances in which section 41(1)(g) can be invoked to defeat the exercise of a lawful power are not entirely clear, the purpose of the section seems to be to prevent one sphere of government using its powers in ways which would undermine other spheres of government, and prevent them from functioning effectively. The functional and institutional integrity of the different spheres of

---

[31] [FN 62] National and provincial legislatures have concurrent powers in respect of the 33 functional areas referred to in schedule 4. These includes matters as important to day-to-day living as education at all but tertiary level, the environment, health services, housing, industrial promotion, public transport, trade, urban and rural development and welfare services. The manner in which conflicts between national and provincial laws are to be resolved is not relevant to this judgment. It is dealt with in sections 146 to 150 of the Constitution.

[32] [FN 69] In terms of section 44(2) the purposes are:

"to maintain national security; to maintain economic unity; to maintain essential national standards; to establish minimum standards required for the rendering of services; or to prevent unreasonable action taken by a province which is prejudicial to the interests of another province or to the country as a whole."

[33] [FN 71] Section 100.

[34] [FN 72] *Id.*

government must, however, be determined with due regard to their place in the constitutional order, their powers and functions under the Constitution, and the countervailing powers of other spheres of government.

[59] I have previously referred to the finding made by this Court in the First Certification Judgment that the [interim Constitutional Principles] contemplated that the national government would have powers that transcend provincial boundaries and competences and that "legitimate provincial autonomy does not mean that the provinces can ignore [the constitutional] framework or demand to be insulated from the exercise of such power." Nor does it mean that provinces have the right to veto national legislation with which they disagree, or to prevent the national sphere of government from exercising its powers in a manner to which they object.

[60] The Constitution provides that provinces shall have exclusive functions as well as functions shared concurrently with the national legislature. The Constitution also requires the establishment of a single public service and gives the power to structure that public service to the national legislature. This power given to the national legislature is one which needs to be exercised carefully in the context of the demands of section 41(1)(g) to ensure that in exercising its power, the national legislature does not encroach on the ability of the provinces to carry out the functions entrusted to them by the Constitution.

[61] The Western Cape government contends that the public service in that province functions effectively under the existing scheme and that there is no need for it to be reorganised in the manner contemplated by the amendments to which it objects. It contends further that the reorganisation will hamper rather than assist it in the execution of its executive functions, and that in all the circumstances the reorganisation of the provincial administration of the public service in the Western Cape, contrary to its wishes encroaches upon its functional or institutional integrity.

. . . .

[72] In the First Certification Judgment what this Court required as protection for the limited "autonomy" of provinces within the larger framework prescribed by the Constitution, was that they should have the ability to employ the personnel in the provincial administrations of the public service. The determination of posts and functions to be performed by the personnel in such posts, provides the framework within which the appointments are to be made. According to the Constitution, as certified, that framework must be determined by national legislation. One of the posts in the framework is that of DG in the Premier's office who, in addition to the administration of that office, is now required to assume responsibility as secretary to the Executive Council, the coordinator of intergovernmental and intragovernmental relations and other functions. These functions are of considerable importance and are not inconsistent with the post of the most senior person in the administration. The province has the competence to appoint the functionary who is to occupy this post, and that is all that the Constitution requires. It cannot be said that there are not valid reasons for having included such functions within the duties of the DG, or that to do so, would prevent the provincial government from carrying out its constitutional duties effectively.

. . . .

[74] It follows that the provisions of the 1998 Amendment dealing with the powers and functions of the DG are not inconsistent with the executive power of the province. It has also not been established that such provisions infringe section 41(1)(g) of the Constitution.

Establishment and abolition of departments

[80] In substance, the premier has the power to establish or abolish provincial departments. This power is limited only to the extent that it must be exercised by way of a request directed to the President . . . .

[83] A procedure requiring the President and the Premier to seek agreement concerning the legality of a proposed restructuring of the public service within a provincial administration, is entirely consistent with the system of cooperative government prescribed by the Constitution, and cannot be said to invade either the executive power vested in the Premier by the Constitution, or the "functional or institutional" integrity of provincial governments.

. . . .

Transfer of functions between departments and between different spheres of government

[The Constitutional Court found that one provision of the national law, which gave a national minister the authority to transfer administration of provincial laws to a national department, unconstitutionally infringed the executive authority of provinces to administer their own laws.]

Does the new scheme contravene section 41 of the Constitution?

[89] With the exception of section 3(3)(b) which infringes the executive power and autonomy of the provinces to the extent referred to in paragraph 86 above, none of the other provisions to which objection is taken can be said on their own to infringe section 41. What remains to be considered is whether, apart from section 3(3)(b), the new scheme as a whole can be said to infringe the functional and institutional integrity of the provinces.

. . . .

[91] The Western Cape government has not been deprived of any power vested in it under the Constitution or the Western Cape Constitution. The Premier of the province has the power to appoint the members of the executive council, to determine what departments should be established within the provincial government, to allocate functions to departments and transfer functions from one department to another. Functionaries in the provincial administration of the public service are appointed by the provincial government, are answerable to it, and can be promoted, transferred or discharged by it. The right of the Premier and Executive Council to coordinate the functions of the provincial administration and its departments has been preserved.

. . . .

[94] In the circumstances, and subject to what has been said concerning section 3(3)(b), the provisions of the 1998 Amendment to which objection is taken, seen alone or cumulatively, do not detract from the executive power of the provinces, nor do they infringe their functional or institutional integrity.

1.6.3.2. Scope of residual national legislative power

Although the Court seemed to come down strongly in favour of national legislative authority — at least when it is explicitly granted in the Constitution — the question of the allocation of legislative authority soon arose again. This time the case involved a dispute between the national government and the regional governments of the Western Cape and KwaZulu-Natal. The provincial governments challenged provisions of the *Local Government: Municipal Structures Act* 117 of 1998, in which the national government claimed residual concurrent powers to determine the structure of local government, despite the provisions of the local government chapter of the Constitution, which set out a comprehensive scheme for the allocation of powers among the national, provincial, and local levels of government.

THE EXECUTIVE COUNCIL OF THE PROVINCE OF THE WESTERN CAPE AND THE EXECUTIVE COUNCIL OF KWAZULU-NATAL v. THE PRESIDENT OF THE REPUBLIC OF SOUTH AFRICA

CONSTITUTIONAL COURT OF SOUTH AFRICA
2000 (1) SA 661

NGCOBO J:

. . . .

The Controlling Provisions of the Constitution

[12] Chapter 7 of the Constitution deals with local government. It makes provision for the establishment of municipalities "for the whole of the territory of the Republic." The objects of local government are, amongst other things, "to provide democratic and accountable government for local communities"; "to ensure the provision of services to communities in a sustainable manner"; and "to promote social and economic development." The executive and legislative authority of municipalities to govern local government affairs of their communities are subject to national and provincial legislation. However, "[t]he national or a provincial government may not compromise or impede" the ability or right of the municipalities to exercise their powers or perform their functions. The national and provincial governments are moreover required to "support and strengthen the capacity of municipalities to manage their own affairs, to exercise their powers and to perform their functions."

[13] Section 155 deals with the establishment of municipalities. It makes provision for three different categories of municipality, namely, category A, self-standing

municipalities, category B, municipalities that form part of a comprehensive co-ordinating structure, and category C, municipalities that perform co-ordinating functions. In addition, it also makes provision for national legislation to define different types of municipality that may be established within each such category. It sets out a scheme for the allocation of powers and functions between the national government, provincial government and the Demarcation Board[35] in relation to the establishment of municipalities. In terms of this scheme: (a) national legislation must establish criteria for determining which category of municipality should be established in a particular area, must define the types of municipality that may be established within each such category, must establish criteria and procedures for the determination of municipal boundaries by an independent authority (which is the Demarcation Board), and must make provision for the division of powers and functions between municipalities with shared powers; (b) the Demarcation Board must determine the municipal boundaries in accordance with the criteria and procedures established by such national legislation; and (c) provincial legislation must determine which types of municipality should be established in its province. In addition, provincial governments "must establish municipalities" in their provinces "in a manner consistent with the legislation enacted in terms of subsections (2) and (3)" of section 155.

[14] In terms of section 156, municipalities have executive authority in respect of matters listed in part B of Schedule 4 and part B of Schedule 5 and "any other matter assigned to [them] by national or provincial legislation." They are empowered to make "by-laws for the effective administration of the matters" which they have the right to administer. However, subject to section 151(4), a by-law which is in conflict with national or provincial legislation is invalid.

. . . .

The Local Government: Municipal Structures Act

. . . .

[17] Mr Olver, the Deputy Director General for Local Government, who deposed to the answering affidavit on behalf of the national government in both applications, deals with the history of local government which, like so much of our history, was characterised by racial discrimination and segregation. Those divisions have left deep scars on our society, and as Mr Olver points out, vast disparities still exist in different local government areas in relation to service infrastructure, tax bases and institutional capacity. That was not and could not be disputed by the provinces.

. . .

[20] The Structures Act provides a detailed framework for the final phase of the transition to democratic local government, which, according to the preamble, is "to be transformed in line with the vision of democratic and developmental local government." Mr Olver explains why the various provisions of the Structures Act are considered by the government to be the best way of dealing with this. That,

[35] [Ed. note: The Constitution and this statute created an agency charged with drawing boundaries for municipalities and other electoral entities.]

however, is not an issue before this Court. The means chosen must be consistent with the requirements of the Constitution. If they are, they are valid. If they are not, they are invalid, even if they are an effective way of dealing with the problems that exist.

[21] Broadly speaking, the Structures Act deals with the definition and creation of municipalities. It establishes the criteria for determining the different categories of municipality; assigns the application of these criteria; defines the types of municipalities that may be established within the different categories of municipality; provides guidelines for selecting types of municipalities; makes provision for the establishment of municipalities; makes provision for internal structures of municipalities, including various committees that may be established; sets out the functions and powers of municipalities; and deals with other miscellaneous matters such as transitional arrangements and regulations.

The Constitutional Challenge

[The provinces argued that the Structures Act unconstitutionally encroached on the powers of the provinces to establish municipalities, and on the constitutional power of municipalities to regulate internal affairs.]

[23] In regard to both these complaints, the national government contended that although the Constitution allocates powers to provinces and municipalities in Chapter 7, it does not deprive Parliament of legislating in relation to the same matters. The broad contention advanced by the national government was that, in terms of section 44(1)(a)(ii) of the Constitution, Parliament has legislative capacity in all fields other than the exclusive powers referred to in Schedule 5. The powers vested in the provinces and municipalities in Chapter 7 of the Constitution are accordingly concurrent with those of the national government, so it was argued. This broad contention shall be considered before I turn to the specific challenges themselves.

The Concurrency Argument

. . . .

[25] The legislative power vested in Parliament by section 44(1)(a)(ii) "to pass legislation with regard to any matter . . . excluding, subject to subsection (2), a matter within a functional area listed in Schedule 5" must be exercised, in terms of subsection (4), "in accordance with, and within the limits of, the Constitution." Thus, where on a proper construction of the Constitution such limits exist, they constrain the residual power of Parliament.

[26] There are a number of such constraints in the Constitution. The most obvious example is the power to pass or amend a provincial constitution which, on a proper construction of section 104(1) of the Constitution, is clearly an exclusive provincial competence. Other provisions of the Constitution also place constraints on the powers of Parliament. A few examples are: the provisions of Chapter 2, the "manner and form" procedures prescribed by the Constitution for the passing of legislation,

the entrenchment of the judicial power in the courts by Chapter 8, the protection given to state institutions protecting democracy by Chapter 9, legislation sanctioning the withdrawal of money from a provincial revenue fund which, apart from the provisions of the Constitution, is an exclusive provincial competence, and the fiscal powers of provinces and municipalities which in terms of Chapter 13 are subject to regulation, but not repeal, by Parliament.

[27] The question then is whether, on a proper construction of Chapter 7 of the Constitution dealing with local government, the provinces are correct in contending that there are certain constraints upon Parliament's powers. If regard is had to the plan for local government set out in Chapter 7, we see that there is indeed a comprehensive scheme set out in the Chapter for the allocation of powers between the national, provincial and local levels of government. That is apparent not only from the way the Chapter is drafted, with the allocation of specific powers and functions to different spheres of government, but also from the provisions of section 164 that:

> "Any matter concerning local government not dealt with in the Constitution may be prescribed by national legislation or by provincial legislation within the framework of national legislation."

[28] The submission that Parliament has concurrent power with the other spheres of government in respect of all powers vested in such spheres by Chapter 7 is inconsistent with the language of the provisions of Chapter 7 itself, and cannot be reconciled with the terms of section 164. If Parliament indeed had full residual power in respect of all matters referred to in Chapter 7, there would have been no need for the reference in section 164 to "any matter not dealt with in the Constitution." . . . It is necessary, therefore, to consider the allocation of powers made in Chapter 7 and to decide whether, on a proper construction of each of those provisions, they constrain Parliament in the manner contended for by the provinces.

[29] Municipalities have the fiscal and budgetary powers vested in them by Chapter 13 of the Constitution, and a general power to "govern" local government affairs. This general power is "subject to national and provincial legislation." The powers and functions of municipalities are set out in section 156 but it is clear from sections 155(7) and 151(3) that these powers are subject to supervision by national and provincial governments, and that national and provincial legislation has precedence over municipal legislation. The powers of municipalities must, however, be respected by the national and provincial governments which may not use their powers to "compromise or impede a municipality's ability or *right* to exercise its powers or perform its functions" (emphasis supplied). There is also a duty on national and provincial governments "by legislative and other measures" to support and strengthen the capacity of municipalities to manage their own affairs and an obligation imposed by section 41(1)(g) of the Constitution on all spheres of government to "exercise their powers and perform their functions in a manner that does not encroach on the geographical, functional or institutional integrity of government in another sphere." The Constitution therefore protects the role of local government, and places certain constraints upon the powers of Parliament to interfere with local government decisions. It is neither necessary nor desirable to attempt to define these constraints in any detail. It is sufficient to say that the

constraints exist, and if an Act of Parliament is inconsistent with such constraints it would to that extent be invalid.

. . . .

Discussion of the Challenges

[32] It will be convenient to consider the constitutional challenges to the Structures Act under the following headings: (a) establishment powers; (b) encroachment on municipal powers; (c) challenge to Chapter 4 and related provisions; and (e) supremacy clause.

A. Establishment Powers

. . . .

[46] The scheme of the allocation of powers and functions which emerges from section 155 of the Constitution is the following: (a) the role of the national government is limited to establishing criteria for determining different categories of municipality, establishing criteria and procedures for determining municipal boundaries, defining different types of municipalities that may be established within each category, and making provision for how powers and functions are to be divided between municipalities with shared powers; (b) the power to determine municipal boundaries vests solely in the Demarcation Board; and (c) the role of the provincial government is limited to determining the types of municipalities that may be established within the province, and establishing municipalities "in a manner consistent with the [national] legislation enacted in terms of subsections (2) and (3)." The question that arises is where the power to apply the criteria to establish categories of municipality naturally falls in this constitutional scheme of powers and functions. In my view, the answer to this question must be sought in the functions required to be performed under this scheme.

. . . .

[The Court found provisions in the legislation allowing a national minister to interfere with the Demarcation Board's determination of the boundaries of municipalities and wards was unconstitutional.]

Section 13

[77] Section 13 provides:

    (1)   The Minister, by notice in the *Government Gazette*, may determine guidelines to assist MECs for local government to decide which type of municipality would be appropriate for a particular area.

    (2)   An MEC for local government must take these guidelines into account when establishing a municipality in terms of section 12 or changing the type of a municipality in terms of section 16(1)(a).

[78] The provinces contended that Parliament has no powers to prescribe to the provinces guidelines which they must take into account in the exercise of their

legislative power to determine the types of municipality that may be established in the provinces.

. . . .

[80] [Various constitutional] provisions underscore the significance of recognising the principle of the allocation of powers between national government and the provincial governments. The Constitution therefore sets out limits within which each sphere of government must exercise its constitutional powers. Beyond these limits, conduct becomes unconstitutional. This principle was given effect to by this Court in *Fedsure* when it said:

> "It seems central to the conception of our constitutional order that the legislature and executive in every sphere are constrained by the principle that they may exercise no power and perform no function beyond that conferred upon them by law."

. . . .

[83] Section 13 of the Structures Act, in peremptory terms, tells the provinces how they must set about exercising a power in respect of a matter which falls outside the competence of the national government. It is true that the MEC is only required to take the guidelines into account, and is not obliged to implement them. That the MEC, having taken the guidelines into account, is not obliged to follow them, matters not. Nor is the fact that the Minister may decide not to lay down any guidelines, of any moment. What matters is that the national government has legislated on a matter which falls outside of its competence.

. . . .

1.6.3.3. Scope of exclusive Provincial power

EX PARTE THE PRESIDENT OF THE REPUBLIC OF SOUTH AFRICA
IN RE: CONSTITUTIONALITY OF THE LIQUOR BILL
CONSTITUTIONAL COURT OF SOUTH AFRICA
2000 (1) SA 732

CAMERON AJ:

INTRODUCTION

[1] The legislation before us is inchoate. Parliament has passed a Bill, but it has not received the assent of the President, who referred it to this Court for a decision on its constitutionality . . .

. . . .

The Challenge to the Constitutionality of the Liquor Bill

. . . .

[31] In his affidavit the Minister of Trade and Industry asserts that the objectives the Bill seeks to attain include—

(a) erasing the history of the use of liquor as an instrument of control over most of the population as part of the policy of apartheid;

(b) making the liquor industry more accessible to historically disadvantaged groups.

It is evident, and relevant to a proper understanding of these proceedings, that liquor licensing has a shameful history in this country's racial past. The manufacture, distribution, sale and use of liquor after the Union of South Africa came into being in 1910 was regulated through the Liquor Act, 30 of 1928 and Native (Urban Areas) Act, 21 of 1923 (for Africans). These statutes together prohibited the supply and delivery to or the possession of liquor by blacks (Africans, coloureds and Indians).[36] Blacks were allowed to be supplied or to be in possession of liquor only for "medical purposes"; for "sacramental purposes"; or if an exemption was granted. Umqombothi or "homebrew," derived from sorghum, was alone treated differently . . . .

[32] It is against the background of this history of overt racism in the control of the manufacturing, distribution and sale of liquor that the Minister contends that the provisions of the Bill constitute a permissible exercise by Parliament of its legislative powers.

. . . .

[34] First, the Bill divides economic activity within the liquor industry into three categories: production (which it terms "manufacturing"), distribution, and retail sales. [In part, this was to address the concentration of economic power in the

---

[36] [FN 39] In terms of section 94 of Act 30 of 1928:

"Save as is otherwise specially provided by this Act, no person shall supply or deliver any liquor to any native, and no native shall obtain or be in possession of, any liquor: Provided that save in any area proclaimed by the Governor General as an area to which the proviso shall not apply, a native may on a written order dated and signed by his *bona fide* employer, and setting forth in legible characters such employer's full name and address, obtain the delivery of liquor for conveyance to such employer, if such employer is not a person to whom it is unlawful to supply liquor.

"This was to be read with section 19(1) of the Natives (Urban Areas) Act, 21 of 1923.

Section 95 provided:

"Save as is otherwise provided by this Act-(a) in the Provinces of the Transvaal and Orange Free State no person shall sell or supply or deliver any liquor to any Asiatic or coloured person, and no Asiatic or coloured person shall obtain or be in possession of liquor; and(b) in the province of Natal no Asiatic shall be supplied with or obtain liquor save for consumption on premises licenced under this Act for the sale thereof, or be in possession of liquor off such premises:Provided that save in any area proclaimed by the Governor-General as an area to which the proviso shall not apply, an Asiatic or coloured person may, on a written order dated and signed by his *bona fide* employer and setting forth in legible characters such employers full name and address, obtain the delivery of liquor for conveyance to such employer, if such employer is not a person to whom it is unlawful to supply liquor."

manufacturing sector, and to open opportunities for new entrants, particularly from historically disadvantaged groups.]

[35] Second, the Bill divides responsibility for these tiers between national and provincial government by effecting a division between manufacture and distribution of liquor on the one hand and retail sale, on the other. The Bill treats manufacture and distribution of liquor as national issues, to be dealt with by the national liquor authority and appeal tribunal, whose members are appointed by the Minister. Retail sales (including sales of liquor at special events) are treated as provincial issues, and are to be dealt with by provincial liquor authorities and provincial panels of appeal. For the establishment of the latter, the Bill imposes an obligation upon the provincial legislature of each province to pass legislation. The national liquor authority is charged with considering whether the statutorily prescribed require-ments for registration as a wholesaler or distributor have been met, and with considering the "merits" of an application, and determining the terms and conditions applicable to the registration that conform with prescribed criteria, norms and standards pertaining, inter alia, to limiting vertical integration, encour-aging diversity of ownership and facilitating the entry of new participants into the industry. Provision is made for objections to applications for registration. The provincial liquor authorities are obliged to consider applications for retail and special event registrations. The public must be enabled to lodge objections.

. . . .

[37] The province's complaint is in essence that the Bill exhaustively regulates the activities of persons involved in the manufacture, wholesale distribution and retail sale of liquor; and that even in the retail sphere the structures the Bill seeks to create reduce the provinces, in an area in which they would (subject to section 44(2)) have exclusive legislative and executive competence, to the role of funders and administrators. The province asserts that the Bill thereby intrudes into its area of exclusive legislative competence.

. . . .

[The Court reviewed relevant constitutional provisions regarding cooperative government, emphasizing several key provisions. Although provincial governments were granted exclusive authority over a variety of subjects in Schedule 5, section 44(2) provides that Parliament may intervene within areas of provincial authority "when it is necessary (a) to maintain national security; (b) to maintain economic unity; (c) to maintain essential national standards; (d) to establish minimum standards required for the rendering of services; or (e) to prevent unreasonable action taken by a province which is prejudicial to the interests of another province or to the country as a whole." In addition, section 44(3) provides that "Legislation with regard to a matter that is reasonably necessary for, or incidental to, the effective exercise of a power concerning any matter listed in Schedule 4 is, for all purposes, legislation with regard to a matter listed in Schedule 4."]

. . . .

[46] By contrast with Schedule 5, the Constitution contains no express itemisation of the exclusive competences of the national legislature. These may be gleaned from individual provisions requiring or authorising "national legislation" regarding

specific matters.[37] They may also be derived by converse inference from the fact that specified concurrent and exclusive legislative competences are conferred upon the provinces, read together with the residual power of the national Parliament, in terms of section 44(1)(a)(ii), to pass legislation with regard to "any matter." This is subject only to the exclusive competences of Schedule 5 which are in turn subordinated to the "override" provision in section 44(2). An obvious instance of exclusive national legislative competence to which the Constitution makes no express allusion is foreign affairs.

. . . .

[49] As pointed out in the first *Certification Judgment,* the introduction into the 1996 Constitution of a category of exclusive powers gave the provinces "more powers" than they had enjoyed under the interim Constitution. This Court found that Parliament's power of intervention in the field of these exclusive powers was "defined and limited" by section 44(2): "Outside that limit the exclusive provincial power remains intact and beyond the legislative competence of Parliament." This Court also held that, if regard is had to the nature of the exclusive competences in Schedule 5 and the requirements of section 44(2), "the occasion for intervention by Parliament is likely to be limited."

. . . .

[51] The constitution-makers' allocation of powers to the national and provincial spheres appears to have proceeded from a functional vision of what was appropriate to each sphere, and accordingly the competences itemised in Schedules 4 and 5 are referred to as being in respect of "functional areas." The ambit of the provinces' exclusive powers must in my view be determined in the light of that vision. It is significant that section 104(1)(b) confers power on each province to pass legislation "for its province" within a "functional area." It is thus clear from the outset that the Schedule 5 competences must be interpreted as conferring power on each province to legislate in the exclusive domain only "for its province." From the provisions of section 44(2) it is evident that the national government is entrusted with overriding powers where necessary to maintain national security, economic unity and essential national standards, to establish minimum standards required for the rendering of services, and to prevent unreasonable action by provinces which is prejudicial to the interests of another province or to the country as a whole. From section 146 it is evident that national legislation within the concurrent terrain of Schedule 4 that applies uniformly to the country takes precedence over provincial legislation in the circumstances contemplated in section 44(2), as well as when it —

    (a)   deals with a matter that cannot be regulated effectively by provincial legislation;

    (b)   provides necessary uniformity by establishing norms and standards, frameworks or national policy;

---

[37] [FN 81] Instances include various matters relating to the judiciary and the courts (Chapter 8), state institutions supporting democracy (Chapter 9), public administration (Chapter 10), national security (which in terms of section 198(d) "is subject to the authority of Parliament and the national executive"), certain financial and revenue matters (Chapter 13), and the approval or tabling of international agreements (section 231).

(c) is necessary for the protection of the common market in respect of the mobility of goods, services, capital and labour, for the promotion of economic activities across provincial boundaries, the promotion of equal opportunity or equal access to government services, or the protection of the environment.

[52] From this it is evident that where a matter requires regulation inter-provincially, as opposed to intra-provincially, the Constitution ensures that national government has been accorded the necessary power, whether exclusively or concurrently under Schedule 4, or through the powers of intervention accorded by section 44(2). The corollary is that where provinces are accorded exclusive powers these should be interpreted as applying primarily to matters which may appropriately be regulated intra-provincially.

[53] It is in the light of this vision of the allocation of provincial and national legislative powers that the inclusion of the functional area "liquor licences" in Schedule 5A must in my view be given meaning. That backdrop includes the express concurrency of national and provincial legislative power in respect of the functional area of "trade" and "industrial promotion" created by Schedule 4.

[54] According to the New Shorter Oxford Dictionary, "trade" in its ordinary signification means the "[b]uying and selling or exchange of commodities for profit, *spec.* between nations; commerce, trading, orig. conducted by passage or travel between trading parties." Nothing in Schedule 4 suggests that the term should be restricted in any way, and the Western Cape government did not contend that Parliament's concurrent competence in regard to "trade" should be limited to cross-border or inter-provincial trade. It follows that in its ordinary signification, the concurrent national legislative power with regard to "trade" includes the power not only to legislate intra-provincially in respect of the liquor trade, but to do so at all three levels of manufacturing, distribution and sale.

[55] The concurrent legislative competence in regard to "industrial promotion" should in my view be given a similarly full meaning as conferring on the national legislature and the provinces the power to initiate, advance and encourage all branches of trade and manufacture. But the exclusive provincial competence to legislate in respect of "liquor licences" must also be given meaningful content, and, as suggested earlier, the constitutional scheme requires that this be done by defining its ambit in a way that leaves it ordinarily distinct and separate from the potentially overlapping concurrent competences set out in Schedule 4.

. . . .

[57] The Western Cape government contended that liquor licences are never an end in themselves, but control and regulate the production, distribution and sale of liquor in pursuit "of yet further social, economic and financial objectives." Accordingly, the Province contended, the authors of the Constitution must have intended the term "liquor licences" in Schedule 5A to encompass all legislative means and ends appurtenant to the liquor trade at all levels of production, manufacture and sale, and that these were intended to be reserved, outside the circumstances envisaged by section 44(2), for the exclusive competence of the provinces. This submission cannot in my view be accepted. In the first place, the field of "liquor

licences" is narrower than the liquor trade. The Schedule does not refer simply to "liquor" or the "liquor trade" or the "liquor industry." Instead it uses the phrase "liquor licences." There is a range of legislation in South Africa regulating the liquor trade. Production, marketing, export and import of wine and spirits is regulated in terms of two important statutes, the Wine and Spirit Control Act, 47 of 1970 and the Liquor Products Act, 60 of 1989. These are primarily concerned with aspects of the liquor trade and industry, and not with liquor licensing itself. Legislation concerning the production of liquor products, including quality control, marketing and import and export of such products would fall within the concurrent competence of trade and/or industrial promotion, rather than within the exclusive competence of liquor licences.

[Although the Court rejected the provincial challenge, the Court rejected an effort to justify the legislation's intrusion on provincial authority as "incidental" to provisions whose "pith and substance" (borrowing from the Canadian approach to allocation of powers) was the radical restructuring of the liquor industry for trade purposes.]

[61] It is not necessary for the purposes of this judgment to consider the utility or applicability of the Canadian "pith and substance" cases to the development of an indigenous South African jurisprudence regarding national and provincial legislative competences. It is sufficient to say that although our Constitution creates exclusive provincial legislative competences, the separation of the functional areas in Schedules 4 and 5 can never be absolute:

> "Whenever a legislature's authority is limited some rule must be adopted to address the possibility that a [single] law may touch upon subject matter [both] within and outside legislative competence."[38]

. . . .

[63] In *Ex Parte Speaker of the KwaZulu-Natal Provincial Legislature: In re KwaZulu-Natal Amakhosi and Iziphakanyiswa Amendment Bill of 1995*,[39] this Court had to determine whether a provincial Bill fell within the legislative competence granted the provinces in Schedule 6 of the interim Constitution. Chaskalson P rejected the argument that the "purpose" of legislation was irrelevant to the constitutionality inquiry:

> "It may be relevant to show that although the legislation purports to deal with a matter within Schedule 6 its true purpose and effect is to achieve a different goal which falls outside the functional areas listed in Schedule 6. In such a case a Court would hold that the province has exceeded its legislative competence. It is necessary, therefore, to consider whether the substance of the legislation, which depends not only on its form but also on its purpose and effect, is within the legislative competence of the KwaZulu-Natal provincial legislature."[40]

---

[38] [FN 92] P Craig and M Walters "The Courts, Devolution and Judicial Review" (1999) *Public Law* 274 at 299.

[39] [FN 94] 1996 (4) SA 653 (CC); 1996 (7) BCLR 903 (CC).

[40] [FN 96] At para 19.

. . . .

[69] The true substance of the Bill is in my view directed at three objectives. These are: (a) the prohibition on cross-holdings between the three tiers involved in the liquor trade, namely producers, distributors and retailers; (b) the establishment of uniform conditions, in a single system, for the national registration of liquor manufacturers and distributors; and, in a further attempt at establishing national uniformity within the liquor trade, (c) the prescription of detailed mechanisms to provincial legislatures for the establishment of retail licensing mechanisms.

[70] Regarding (a): In my view the Bill's prohibition of cross-holdings falls within the national legislature's competence to regulate trade. On any approach, the vertical and horizontal regulation of the liquor trade, and the promotion of racial equity within the trade, are legislative ends which fall within the functional competence Schedule 4 accords the national Parliament under the headings of trade and industrial promotion. I did not understand counsel for the Western Cape government to contest this. The Bill, however, attains this objective by employing a specific means, namely a system of registration which is in all material respects identical to a licensing system. In addition, the Bill accords to national government regulatory functions in regard to liquor licensing in the production and distribution sphere. That the ends the national legislature so seeks to attain fall within its power does not automatically entail that the means it has chosen, namely a system of liquor licensing, are competent. For that conclusion to be reached, the national government must show that the means is "necessary" for one of the purposes specified in section 44(2), or, on one reading of section 44(3), that they are reasonably necessary for, or incidental to the effective exercise of a Schedule 4 power.

[71] Regarding (b) (the national system of registration for producers and wholesalers): Persuasive justification for understanding "liquor licences" more narrowly than the reading advanced by the Western Cape government appears, as indicated earlier, from the scheme of the Constitution. These suggest that the primary purport of the exclusive competences, including "liquor licences," lies in activities that take place within or can be regulated in a manner that has a direct effect upon the inhabitants of the province alone. In relation to "liquor licences," it is obvious that the retail sale of liquor will, except for a probably negligible minority of sales that are effected across provincial borders, occur solely within the province. The primary and most obvious signification of the exclusive competence therefore seems to me to lie in the licensing of retail sale of liquor.

[72] As far as the Bill's "three-tier" structure is concerned, the same considerations suggest that manufacturing or production of liquor was not intended to be the primary field of "liquor licences." The manufacturing and wholesale trades in liquor have a national and also international dimension. Manufacturers and wholesalers ordinarily trade across the nation, and some trade both nationally and internationally. Little, if any, liquor production is directed to an intra-provincial market only. On the contrary, in large measure, the production of liquor — whether brewing of beer (which on the evidence before us occurs largely in the northern provinces), or viticulture and wine production (which occurs "overwhelmingly" within the Western Cape), or the production of vodka, cane spirit and gin (which occurs "mostly" in

KwaZulu-Natal) — is necessarily directed at an extra-provincial or international market.

[73] The same considerations in my view apply in general to the distribution of liquor, where the scale of distribution is likely, in almost all cases, to be inter- as opposed to intra-provincial. The regulation and control of liquor distribution, on this approach, therefore falls outside the primary signification of the exclusive competence. If production and distribution of liquor were to be regulated by each province, manufacturers and distributors would require licences from each province for the purpose of conducting national trading, and possibly a national licence for export.

. . . .

[75] But it is unnecessary to conclude that the competence in regard to "liquor licences" does not extend to intra-provincial production and distribution activities since the national government has in my view in any event shown that, if the exclusive provincial legislative competence in respect of "liquor licences" extends to licensing production and distribution, its interest in maintaining economic unity authorises it to intervene in these areas under section 44(2). "Economic unity" as envisaged in section 44(2) must be understood in the context of our Constitution, which calls for a system of co-operative government, in which provinces are involved largely in the delivery of services and have concurrent legislative authority in everyday matters such as health, housing and primary and secondary education. They are entitled to an equitable share of the national revenue, but may not levy any of the primary taxes, and may not impose any tax which may "materially and unreasonably" prejudice national economic policies, economic activities across provincial boundaries, or the national mobility of goods, services, capital or labour. Our constitutional structure does not contemplate that provinces will compete with each other. It is one in which there is to be a single economy and in which all levels of government are to co-operate with one another. In the context of trade, economic unity must in my view therefore mean the oneness, as opposed to the fragmentation, of the national economy with regard to the regulation of inter-provincial, as opposed to intra-provincial, trade. In that context it seems to follow that economic unity must contemplate at least the power to require a single regulatory system for the conduct of trades which are conducted at a national (as opposed to an intra-provincial) level.

[76] Given the history of the liquor trade, the need for vertical and horizontal regulation, the need for racial equity, and the need to avoid the possibility of multiple regulatory systems affecting the manufacturing and wholesale trades in different parts of the country, in my view the "economic unity" requirement of section 44(2) has been satisfied. Indeed, many of the considerations mentioned earlier in relation to the primary signification of the term "liquor licences" suggest the conclusion that manufacture and distribution of liquor require national, as opposed to provincial, regulation.

. . . .

[However, the Court struck down the provisions dealing with the award of retail licenses. This matter clearly fell within the exclusive jurisdiction of the provinces, and counsel for the national government failed to persuade the Court that the law was necessary under ss. 44(2) or (3).]

[83] The same considerations seem to me to apply to the Bill's provisions regarding micro-manufacturers and manufacturers of sorghum beer, who are permitted to sell the liquor produced by them "directly to the public for consumption on and off the registered premises, as prescribed." In effect, these provisions confer national permission for retail sales in circumstances where it does not seem to me that the national government has made a case under section 44(2) for intervening in the provinces' exclusive legislative competence. The provisions of section 46(2) also require scrutiny. These permit a manufacturer to sell the liquor produced "directly to the public for consumption on and off the registered premises, subject to the terms and conditions that the relevant authority may determine." To the extent that this exempts wine farms, for instance, from the national prohibition on producers holding retail licences, it lies within the competence of national government. But in so far as this provision precludes provinces from also requiring provincial licences for what is in effect retail selling, it too lies beyond the competence of the national legislature.

[84] The provisions of section 44(2) have also not been satisfied in regard to the national regulation of micro-manufacturers of liquor, whose businesses may be essentially provincial in character.

1.7. CONTRASTING APPROACHES TO FEDERALISM: ADDITIONAL COMPARATIVE NOTES AND QUESTIONS

1.7.1. Fiscal federalism and the taxing and spending powers

The practical effect of judicial limits on federal legislative power in each country is substantially constrained because its highest court in each case has granted the federal government broad leeway to strongly influence policy decisions made by, and within the jurisdiction of, the states/provinces. Each court has construed its Constitution to permit the national government broad power over much of its tax base, affording it significant leverage with regard to spending priorities at each level of government.[41] Moreover, each court has allowed the national government to condition the receipt of federal funds by states/provinces on acceptance of a host of federal conditions, even when those conditions relate to matters (constitutionally) solely within local authority. A prominent Canadian example is the *Canada Health Act*, which conditions vast sums of federal money provided to the provinces for health care on the requirement that the provinces adhere to a single-payer government health insurance plan, even though health care is clearly a legislative matter for the provinces. Likewise, the U.S. *No Child Left Behind Act* uses congressional spending to require a host of detailed tests and rules for

---

[41] The High Court of Australia has also construed s 90's grant of exclusive Commonwealth power over "excise duties" to restrict state taxing options. *See, e.g., Ha v. New South Wales* (1997) 189 CLR 465 (invalidating a state "business franchise fee"). The *BNA Act*, § 92(2), limits Canadian provinces' taxing power to "direct taxation."

American schools that receive federal funds. In perhaps the broadest use of this power in terms of effects on fiscal federalism, the High Court of Australia upheld, in the "First Uniform Tax" case — *South Australia v. Commonwealth* (1942) 65 CLR 373 — a Commonwealth legislative scheme that required the States to cease imposing income tax as a condition for the receipt of grants under s 96. This broad approach is most easily justified by the text of s 96, which expressly empowers the federal Parliament to "grant financial assistance to any State on such terms and conditions as the Parliament thinks fit."

The spending power in Canada is not among the express powers granted to the federal and provincial legislatures in ss 91 and 92 of the *BNA Act;* rather, it is implied. In light of the judicial interpretation of the *B.N.A. Act* narrowly construing federal regulatory power, it is somewhat ironic that the Supreme Court of Canada has broadly interpreted federal fiscal powers. The best explanation for this broad interpretation is probably the constitutional reality that almost all parties accept that certain programs seen as essential parts of modern Canada would not be possible without federal funding, and Parliament is politically unwilling to fund significant programs without attaching conditions.

This view has been severely criticized as inconsistent with the very concept of exclusive legislative jurisdiction contained in ss. 91 and 92 of the BNA Act. Two leading constitutional scholars have criticized this approach. One, who reversed course in politics, was Pierre Trudeau, later Prime Minister. *See, e.g.*, Pierre Elliot Trudeau, *Federal Grants to Universities, in* FEDERALISM AND THE FRENCH CANADIANS 79 (1968) (federal spending should be confined to objects within federal legislative competence). Another is Andrew Petter (now President of Simon Fraser University in Vancouver, former Dean of the University of Victoria Faculty of Law and a former minister in the left-wing New Democratic Party government of British Columbia). In *Federalism and the Myth of the Federal Spending Power*, 68 CAN. B. REV. 448 (1989), Petter dissects the doctrinal arguments made in support of federal spending regarding provincial matters, but then raises important values to explain his objection to increasing federal power. Petter begins by articulating the underlying rationale for constitutional federalism: "a belief that while some matters are better decided by the national political community, others should be left to regional political communities." Because Canada is so diverse, regional majorities may have different opinions and priorities, and provincial governments need to be responsive to these concerns. In contrast, "a central government can afford to ignore the preference of a particular region of the country (and may have to do so to garner voter support in other regions." Applied to the scope of the federal spending power, the constitutionality of conditional spending allows the federal government to influence provincial decision-making: "it allows national majorities to set priorities and to determine policy within spheres of influence allocated under the Constitution to regional majorities." Thus Petter argues it is counter to the political goals of the federal system. Finally, Petter dissents from the view that broad federal spending power is necessary to promote and protect new and existing social programs. This wrongly assumes, in Petter's view, that "the central government is better trusted with the social welfare of Canadians than are provincial governments."

A major reason why Petter's critique has not proven persuasive, however, is that perhaps the one government policy to which Canadians have the greatest attachment — national health care — is the result of conditional spending by the federal government.

A similar approach has been traditionally used by the U.S. Supreme Court in interpreting the power granted Congress in Art. I, § 8 to "pay the Debts and provide for the . . . general welfare of the United States." As Chief Justice Roberts explained in the "*Obamacare*" decision, discussed above in section 1.4.6, 132 S. Ct. at 2579:

> Put simply, Congress may tax and spend. This grant gives the Federal Government considerable influence even in areas where it cannot directly regulate. The Federal Government may enact a tax on an activity that it cannot authorize, forbid, or otherwise control. See, *e.g.*, *License Tax Cases*, 72 U.S. 462 (1867). And in exercising its spending power, Congress may offer funds to the States, and may condition those offers on compliance with specified conditions. See, *e.g.*, *College Savings Bank* v. *Florida Prepaid Postsecondary Ed. Expense Bd.*, 527 U.S. 666, 686 (1999). These offers may well induce the States to adopt policies that the Federal Government itself could not impose. See, *e.g.*, *South Dakota* v. *Dole*, 483 U.S. 203, 205-206 (1987) (conditioning federal highway funds on States raising their drinking age to 21).

Yet a 7-2 majority went on to conclude that Congress could not constitutionally condition federal funds for "Medicaid," a cooperative federal-state program of government-paid health care for the poor and disabled, on a state's willingness to expand the program to cover middle-income residents without access to employer-based health care. The majority emphasized the extent to which states relied on federal funding for a major portion of state spending, concluding that the Medicaid expansion program was unduly "coercive." Even here, however, the holding is primarily a process-based determination, rather than a holding that conditional spending can be substantively "coercive." The majority acknowledged that Congress could have constitutionally repealed the entire Medicaid legislative scheme, and reenacted a new expanded scheme covering middle-class as well as poor and disabled residents. However, the majority noted that such a process would have entailed substantial political costs. In the majority's view, if Congress is going to impose such serious conditions on state acceptance of funds, it must do so with clarity and bear all political costs. *Id.* at 2606 n.14.

Fiscal Federalism in South Africa has a very particular character, being at one and the same time more strictly institutionalized — through the creation of a constitutional Financial and Fiscal Commission (sections 220-222) that advises Parliament and Provincial Legislators on the equitable division of revenue between the different spheres of government — and yet less "federal" in that all significant tax revenue is collected by the national government and its allocation is determined by national legislation (sections 213-215). Budgeting authority is vested in the National Assembly and given the nature of concurrent legislative authority there is no real limitation on the spending powers of the national government with respect to the provincial or local spheres of government. The spending powers of provincial and municipal governments are constrained by both their budget allocations (section 215) as well as specific constitutionally mandated national laws that control processes of government procurement (section 217) and financial accountability (section 216) in all spheres of government. While there are some limits on national government's power to withhold funds due to a province (section 216 (3)) it is the national legislature that has the ultimate power over spending (sections 216(4)-(5)).

1.7.2.   Active judicial policing of federalism and the national political process

Justice Souter's dissenting opinions in *Lopez* and *Morrison* suggest that the earlier deference to congressional power (dating back to *Gibbons v. Ogden*) is based on a confidence that the structure of the American political process — especially in the Senate — provided sufficient protection for preserving state prerogatives in the American federal system. This view builds upon an argument by Dean Jesse Choper, spelled out in his book JUDICIAL REVIEW AND THE NATIONAL POLITICAL PROCESS (1980). Choper argues that many aspects of the political process effectively ensure that Congress does not overstep its proper authority and unduly tip the balance of our federal system: (1) most federal legislators move to Congress from service as elected officials in states; (2) the Senate is apportioned on an equal basis among states; (3) state legislative power to reapportion districts for the federal House of Representatives each decade gives them significant power over members of the House of Representatives; (4) each state has an organized "delegation" to represent state interests, and party leaders ensure that committee assignments fairly represent each state (so that often a member serves as his or her state's "representative" on an important committee); (5) (as vindicated by the 2000 election) Presidential elections are fought on a state-by-state basis; (6) Washington lobbying is characterized by a strong presence of organizations representing American governors, mayors, state legislators, and municipal officials. Indeed, he agrees that "far from a national authority that is expansionist by nature, the inherent tendency in our system is precisely the reverse, necessitating the widest support before intrusive measures of importance can receive significant consideration, reacting readily to opposition grounded in resistance within the states." NATIONAL POLITICAL PROCESS at 187 (quoting Herbert Weschler, *The Political Safeguards of Federalism: The Role of the States in the Composition and Selection of the National Government*, 54 COLUM. L. REV. 543, 558 (1954)).

These arguments are not available in Canada. The Canadian Senate, by convention, does not exercise real political power (it is in this respect a more egalitarian version of the British House of Lords). Moreover, parliamentary voting is characterized by strict party discipline, which does not exist in the United States and, in addition to the factors cited by Dean Choper, is a powerful reason why state interests remain strong in Washington. Consider a proposal by the Obama administration that was, in the opinion of Mayor Rahm Emanuel of Chicago, unduly intrusive into state and local control in Illinois. Daley could well prevail on Senator Richard Durbin, a fellow Democrat, to vote against the legislation. In Canada, it would be unthinkable for a Conservative MP from suburban Toronto to vote against a proposal by Prime Minister Stephen Harper regardless of the views of Ontarians or Torontonians. *See also* Jean Leclair, *The Securities Reference:*

The Ghost of Political Representation Comes Knocking at Federalism's Door, at 5, *available at* http://papers.ssrn.com/sol3/papers.cfm?abstract_id=2189661 (2012) ("responsible government has contributed to Parliament's incapacity to give voice to regional demands and aspirations and, in so doing, has buttressed the claim of provincial governments of their being sole interpreters of their province's wishes and desires").

In his outstanding book, THE LAST RESORT (1974), Professor Paul Weiler has suggested that Canadian judges act in a manner analogous to interest dispute labor arbitration (a process that occurs in industries where strikes and lockouts are unacceptable, such as police or firefighters). The result is not supposed to be principled, but rather a last resort against over-reaching:

> The critical cases, the areas where judicial review must justify its existence, occur when a court decides to invalidate challenged legislation on the ground that another jurisdiction has a compelling claim to exclusive control. This is essentially a political controversy . . . . All that a court can really do is act on some intuitive sense that the immediate legislation just goes too far . . . Unfortunately, no one can propose any legal standards to tell us how far is too far. [At p. 174.][42]

Australia provides an example in which the American and the Canadian relationship between the political process and judicial policing is somewhat mixed. Unlike in America, it is relatively unusual for Australian politicians to make a successful transition from state to federal politics. It is even rarer for federal party leaders to emerge from state politics. It is not uncommon for state governments to criticize federal government policy, even where the governments represent the same political party. The Council of Australian Governments (COAG) is a forum in which all state Premiers meet with the Prime Minister sometimes several times a year, in order to discuss matters considered to be of national importance or with respect to which state and federal cooperation is thought desirable. Sometimes these meetings lead to significant agreements and are followed by the adoption of common policy in all the States. Ministerial Councils also provide a regular avenue for policy coordination in specific state and federal portfolios (the enactment of uniform state laws restricting handgun ownership following the Port Arthur massacre in Tasmania in 1996, in which a lone gunman randomly murdered thirty-five people, is an example). Just as often — perhaps more often — the Premiers leave a COAG meeting or the relevant ministers leave a Ministerial Council declaring that their state is opposed to Commonwealth policy (this happens

---

[42] [FN 22] In one respect, the Canadian record on adjudication of federalism disputes tends to undercut one of Jesse Choper's arguments; among the reasons Choper argued for non-justiciability of federalism questions is that the umpiring of federalism disputes involves the Court in political controversies and thus uses up scarce judicial capital that ought be reserved for the Court's more necessary and important function of preserving individual liberties. Canadian constitutional history points in the opposite direction, though: despite a century of unpopular judicial decisions in federalism cases — as we will discuss next chapter, including Privy Council invalidation of the Canadian New Deal during the Depression — Canadians overwhelmingly supported the 1982 enactment of the Charter of Rights and Freedoms, which gave the Supreme Court broad additional power to preserve individual liberty.

less often, but still is not rare, when the Premiers and the Prime Minister are from the same party).

Unlike in Canada, the Australian Senate has real power, and exercises it frequently. The Senate has always been directly elected, and each state has the same numbers of Senators; since 1949, the Senate has been elected by proportional representation, resulting in the frequent election (especially in recent times) of minority party Senators or Independents. These Senators may hold the balance of power, and not infrequently do deals with Government or Opposition either to support or reject a Bill when it comes to the Senate. Sometimes these deals are done in the name of protecting the interests of the individual Senator's state. Party discipline is strong in Australia, as in Canada. In the case of the Labor Party, it is written into party rules. In the case of the Liberal Party (the conservatives) it is almost always followed in practice. Labor politicians who "cross the floor" to vote with the Opposition are liable to expulsion from the party. Liberal politicians are freer, but they risk "de-selection" for their seat when the next general election comes around. Both Parties, however, permit "conscience votes" on matters where deep personal convictions or intractable moral issues are at stake. On these very rare occasions (which are determined by the Party leader), MPs or Senators are free to vote as they wish. Conscience votes have always been permitted for laws regulating abortion or access to abortifacient drugs. More recently, proponents of same-sex marriage have called for conscience votes on legalization of same-sex marriage under the Commonwealth Marriage Act. It is unclear whether the Party leaders will permit this. It is rare — although not unheard of — that contentious issues, where a politician may feel compelled to vote against his or her party, arise over federalism. Lobbying is an important activity in Canberra, but the appearance of organized sub-national government delegations is not a routine or familiar part of Australian federal life.

Since Australia does not have a presidential system, there is no parallel to the state organization of presidential elections. The Prime Minister and all members of Cabinet are elected in their own right, as individual members of electorates (constituencies). Federalism rarely comes into the picture in the choice of Prime Minister, other than in the occasional complaint that the majority of Prime Ministers have come from the east coast (the more populated states). In the allocation of portfolios and the formation of Cabinet, however, it is well understood that a Prime Minister must keep in mind some representation of all the states, if possible, at the risk of alienating state branches of his or her party, or of complaint in the media (and, where the opportunity arises, in parliament) about "neglect" of the small states. While these institutions and processes, formal and informal, do keep a check on the centralizing tendencies of the federal parliament, overall, Choper's theory does not translate well into the Australian context. In the past, the High Court played the more important role in "policing" federalism. It would be a stretch today, however, to maintain that it still does so. Complaints are heard, from time to time, about the predominance of the large states in appointments to the High Court, but this is rarely articulated in federalism "policing" terms. Rather it is represented as a matter of federal fairness and "turn-taking." If there are any concerns about eastern state dominance on the Court, the recent appointment of a Chief Justice (French CJ) from Western Australia should have done much to assuage them. (South Australia and Tasmania, however, have remained unrepresented on the High Court since its establishment in 1903, and this matter is routinely raised in legal circles when a new appointment is pending, but so far Commonwealth Attorneys-General have remained impervious to calls for attention to federal "representation" on the Court.)

While South Africa's constitutionally mandated system of co-operative government does not provide the distinct realms of unconnected power characteristic of classic federalism, the fact that it is a new innovation, based in part on the German Basic Law's integration of the *Lande* into the national legislative process, as well as in the implementation of federal legislation, meant that at least in the early years there was a significant degree of contestation as particularly non-ANC provinces — KwaZulu-Natal and the Western Cape — sought to test the limits of their autonomy. Since the adoption of the final constitution, and its explicit adoption of principles of co-operative government in Chapter 3 of the Constitution, there has been far fewer cases brought to the judiciary than what many assumed. First, with the ANC's electoral victory in KwaZulu-Natal in 1999, it has only been the Western Cape that has not been steadily governed by the ANC. Second, the government has established elaborate mechanisms of consultation as part of the implementation of co-operative government, including inter-ministerial groups involving provincial and national ministers in each functional area, as well as co-ordination between the Presidency and the Premiers of the Provinces. Finally, the Constitution explicitly provides that "all spheres of government and all organs of state within each sphere must — . . . co-operate with one another in mutual trust and good faith by . . . avoiding legal proceedings against one another" (s 41(1)(h)). Furthermore the courts are required to refer disputes back to the relevant organs of state involved if the court is not satisfied that "[a]n organ of state involved in an intergovernmental dispute . . . [has] made every reasonable effort to settle the dispute by means of mechanisms and procedures provided for that purpose," and finally, the organ of state "must exhaust all other remedies before it approaches a court to resolve the dispute" (s 41(3)). The clear constitutional message is that intergovernmental disputes are primarily a matter of political negotiation and only in the extreme case, when all other remedies are exhausted, may they be brought to the judiciary. While the Constitutional Court has not as yet declined jurisdiction on these grounds it seems that judicial resolution of an intergovernmental conflict is to be seen as a matter of last resort.

1.7.3. Federalism and partisan politics

There is another *real politik* dimension to the partisan politics of federalism in Canada and the United States. Although it was a legendary American, Justice Louis D. Brandeis, who famously observed that it "is one of the happy incidents of the federal system that a single courageous state may, if its citizens choose, serve as a laboratory; and try novel social and economic experiments without risk to the rest of the country," *New State Ice Co. v. Liebmann*, 285 U.S. 262 (1932), the record of provincial innovation in Canada is even stronger. As Andrew Petter has observed in his article, *Federalism and the Myth of the Federal Spending Power*, 68 Can. B. Rev. 448 (1989), innovations like medicare, statutory protection for labour unions, anti-discrimination statutes, and bills of rights "were pioneered by innovative provincial regimes before gaining political acceptance across the country." For example, Saskatchewan successfully enacted a scheme for public auto insurance, which led to voter demand for similar legislation in Manitoba, and this positive example made such plans politically popular to voters in British Columbia and Quebec, leading next to broad support for such campaigns in other provinces. Similarly, the move to prohibit discrimination on the basis of sexual orientation began in Quebec and has since spread. Ontario's enactment of pay equity legislation applying to the provincial private sector is already placing pressure on other provincial governments to undertake similar initiatives.

This is because, unlike U.S. politics, Canadian federal politics are "necessarily preoccupied with mediating among competing regional, cultural and linguistic interests." Thus, Petter suggests "it is no coincidence that, while the two mainstream political parties have dominated national politics since Confederation, ideological parties have fared much better at the provincial level." Indeed, the social democratic NDP has formed governments in British Columbia, Saskatchewan, Manitoba, and Ontario, while the Parti Québécois has governed Quebec.

In contrast, Australian politics have been almost exclusively dominated by three (arguably two) political parties, at both Commonwealth and state levels. Since the Second World War, no Commonwealth government has been formed by any party other than the Labor Party or the Liberal Party (in coalition with a rural party, previously the Country Party, now called the National Party). The same pattern has largely been followed in the states. On a couple of occasions in Australia's post-War history, there have been Liberal or Labor governments at the Commonwealth level and in all states. Although one hears frequent complaints that the two mainstream political parties are indistinguishable, the majority of Australian voters still vote for one or the other, and minor parties attract lower levels of support.

Some states have gone alone in experimenting with policy and program initiatives. Queensland introduced a free health care system in the 1940s ahead both of the other states and the Commonwealth. South Australia was known as a reforming state with regard to personal and sexual liberties ahead of the others. Victoria passed a *Charter of Human Rights and Responsibilities Act* in 2006. So far, it remains the only state to have done so (the Australian Capital Territory has a similar Act, but is not a state). But, in the main, major policy innovation has occurred at the Commonwealth government level. Up until the late 1990s, with some exceptions, the Labor Party in government was more expansionist and centralist than the Liberal Party in the exercise of federal powers; this tendency was exemplified in the Labor governments of Prime Ministers Ben Chifley (1945–1949) and Gough Whitlam (1972–1975). However, the Liberal government under Prime Minister John Howard (1996–2007) showed itself willing to use federal powers in a radically centralizing fashion, in particular with the passage of the Workplace Relations Amendment Act 2005 ("Work Choices" — see above), which applied federal regulation to the conditions of employment of all employees of corporations, a sphere of law previously regarded as a matter for the states. The Act proved very unpopular, and the Labor government under Prime Minister Kevin Rudd (elected in 2007) repealed the relevant provisions soon after its election in 2007. The Liberal government, under Tony Abbott (elected in 2013) has undertaken not to reinstate Work Choices. It is uncertain what these events tell us about the parties' respective historical positions. The Labor Party's opposition to the Work Choices legislation did not necessarily indicate a reversal of its view of federalism; in reality, it was more about maintaining a commitment to collective union bargaining and industrial arbitration than defence of state powers again federal overreach. The Liberal Party may perhaps be now more willing to use constitutional powers to take advantage of the general centralizing trends in Australian politics, but this remains to be seen.

In the case of South Africa, the dominance of the national government within the system of co-operative governance as well as the reality of a unipolar democracy in which the electoral majority enjoyed by the African National Congress remains uncontested twenty years after the first democratic elections, means that there is in effect a fairly weak form of federalism. While this weakness narrows the space for regional opposition based on the existence of independent governing powers at the regional level, there have been cases in which policy tensions within the ruling ANC have played out in important ways at the provincial level. The most important instance of this dynamic was in the case of challenges to the national government's HIV/AIDS policies. After activists and NGOs managed to challenge the failure of the national government to provide anti-retroviral medications to prevent mother-to-child transmission of HIV, the ANC-controlled Gauteng Provincial government, under pressure from activists, took the next important step by announcing that it would provide anti-retrovirals in provincial hospitals despite national government resistance. As the wealthiest province dominated by the ANC Gauteng was able to push the national government to implement a policy to provide access to medicines that was being actively resisted by the central government and the Minister of Health Manto Tshabala-Mismang in particular.

1.7.4. Originalism awry

Recent American jurisprudence to the contrary notwithstanding, these cases reveal a somewhat more constrained federal power in Canada than in the United States, especially before the broadening of the trade and commerce power in *City National Leasing*. From either a textualist or an originalist perspective, this is somewhat ironic. Subject to the power of Congress to regulate interstate and foreign commerce, bankruptcy, and a few other specific matters, the Tenth Amendment to the U.S. Constitution reserves all power to the states or the people. In contrast, Canada's Parliament has jurisdiction over all "Trade and Commerce," as well as marriage, banking, criminal law, and regulation over any firm declared to be "for the General Advantage of Canada," while provinces are constitutionally limited in their ability to impose certain taxes. Indeed, Professor Hogg believes that the framers of Canada planned a stronger federal government than their American cousins. *See* § 5.3. The critical difference is that the broad language conferring power on Congress to regulate interstate commerce has been given an extremely broad interpretation by the U.S. Supreme Court, while British and Canadian judges have reserved this broad protection for the provincial power over property and civil rights.

Note that none of the major decisions interpreting ss. 91 and 92 of the British North America Act seems to have seriously sought to capture and apply the bargain between the Quebecois and pro-Confederation Ontarians that those sections represent. As with any compromise, one difficulty is that the partisans' public statements reflected quite differing views. As reflected in A.I. Silver's THE FRENCH-CANADIAN IDEA OF CONFEDERATION, 1864–1900 (1982), Sir John A. Macdonald saw the compromise as a "happy medium" between complete union and a truly federal government, giving the central government broad powers save certain guarantees for francophone "language, nationality, and religion." The pro-Confederation *Bleus* of Quebec saw the document as granting to each legislature "perfect independence within the scope of its own jurisdiction, neither one being able to invade the jurisdiction of the other." A useful standard does emerge, however, from the historic record. A leading *Bleu* pamphlet proclaimed that proposals for a single legislature governed by population would have put "our civil law and religious institutions at the mercy of the fanatics," while the BNA Act provided "a system of government which puts under the exclusive control of [Quebec] those questions which we did not want the fanatical partisans of [Ontario Liberal leader George Brown] to deal with." Historian Silver suggests that federal controversies would divide voters on ideological ground, not as French Canadians or English Canadians. Herein might be a workable original standard: would federal power be the sort that would divide Canadians on linguistic lines or the traditional lines of political economy? The narrow definition of Trade & Commerce should be considered in this light. To be sure, a national commercial code or standard of tort liability — which would clearly meet the American definition of affecting interstate commerce — might be seen in Quebec as direct threat to their Civil Code approach to voluntary obligations and delicts. However, it would be untenable to conclude that a price gouging statute passed in the wake of post-World War I inflation (struck down in *Board of Commerce*, excerpted above) was the sort of issue that Quebecois would despair of delegating to "fanatical" Ontarians, or that the issue of government interference in the free market is an issue which divides Canadians on linguistic or national lines.

In Australia, with some rare exceptions, the High Court has permitted a gradual, but progressive accretion of power from the states to the Commonwealth. The notable exception, as we have seen, is the *Melbourne Corporation* case, where the Court held that the Commonwealth may not discriminate against the states (or a state) and may not exercise its powers so as to undermine the continued existence of the states or their essential capacity to govern. The so-called "Melbourne Corporation" doctrine was said to arise from the Constitution's recognition of the continued existence of the states and from its overall structure as a Constitution for a federation. However, the protection of the federal system has not been a pervasive, or even significant theme in Australian constitutional jurisprudence. Some consider Australian federalism to be seriously threatened by the combined forces of Commonwealth fiscal powers, Commonwealth recourse to the external affairs power, and High Court interpretation (which permits these exercises of power and eschews originalism). The "Work Choices" case was for some, the final nail in the coffin of federalism. This case, as we saw, concerned legislation that aimed to bring the bulk of industrial relations regulation under Commonwealth control, via an Act that rested on the Constitution's Corporations power (s 51(xx), bypassing other constitutional limitations (in particular s 51(xxxv) which limits Commonwealth industrial relations regulation to inter-state disputes). The High Court upheld this law, as a valid application of the Corporations power, but in a dissenting judgment, Justice Callinan deplored both the methodology of the Court majority, and the effect of the judgment, and called for an originalist approach:

> The Constitution should be construed in the light of its history. It should be construed purposively. The founders' intentions and understandings, to the extent that they can be seen to be generally consensual, are relevant. The evidence to be found in the Debates is valuable. The referenda [of the 1890s on the Constitution bill], the results of them, and what was said by informed, legally qualified and knowledgeable legislators . . . are relevant . . . . The Constitution should not be construed to enable the Court to supplant the people's voice under s. 128 of it. The Constitution should not in general be read as if it were intended to confer powers in duplicate. "Originalism" so-called, is no less a proper interpretative tool than any other, and will often be an appropriate one. It is useful here . . . . Sight should never be lost of the verity that the Constitution is a constitution for a federation, and that it provides for a federal balance . . . . The text, indeed the whole structure, of the Constitution clearly mandates the co-existence of the Commonwealth and the States . . . . There is nothing in the text or the structure of the Constitution to suggest that the Commonwealth's powers should be enlarged, by successive decisions of this Court, so that the Parliament of each State is progressively reduced until it becomes no more than an impotent debating society . . . . The potential reach of the corporations power, if it is as extensive as the majority would have it, is enormous . . . . [It] has the capacity to obliterate powers of the State hitherto unquestioned. This Act is an Act of unconstitutional spoliation.

Chapter 2

DEFINING THE SCOPE OF CONSTITUTIONAL PROTECTION FOR INDIVIDUAL RIGHTS

KEY CONCEPTS FOR THE CHAPTER

- U.S. COURTS HAVE HELD THAT THE FIFTH AND FOURTEENTH AMENDMENTS' PROTECTION AGAINST DEPRIVATION OF LIBERTY WITHOUT DUE PROCESS OF LAW HAS TWO COMPONENTS: LIBERTY CANNOT BE DEPRIVED UNLESS CERTAIN PROCEDURES ARE USED BY GOVERNMENT, AND CERTAIN RIGHTS THAT ARE ENCOMPASSED BY "LIBERTY" CANNOT BE DEPRIVED UNLESS THE GOVERNMENT CAN JUSTIFY THE DEPRIVATION. THE LATTER CONCEPT IS KNOWN AS "SUBSTANTIVE DUE PROCESS"

- INDIVIDUAL RIGHTS ARE NOT ABSOLUTE.

  — IN THE U.S., CERTAIN "FUNDAMENTAL" RIGHTS CAN BE LIMITED ONLY IF THE GOVERNMENT PERSUADES JUDGES THAT THERE ARE GOOD REASONS FOR DOING SO; FOR "NON-FUNDAMENTAL" RIGHTS, COURTS DEFER TO LEGISLATIVE JUDGMENTS UNDER THE SO-CALLED "RATIONAL BASIS" TEST

  — IN CANADA, THE CHARTER PROTECTS "FUNDAMENTAL" RIGHTS AND SUBJECTS THEM TO CLOSE SCRUTINY UNDER A 4-PRONG TEST (THE "OAKES" TEST); NON-FUNDAMENTAL RIGHTS ARE SIMPLY DEEMED NOT TO BE PROTECTED BY THE CHARTER

  — IN SOUTH AFRICA, RIGHTS ARE LIKEWISE SUBJECT TO "REASONABLE LIMITS"

- GIVEN THE BREADTH OF THE LANGUAGE OF THE FOURTEENTH AMENDMENT, S. 7 OF THE CANADIAN CHARTER AND MANY RIGHTS IN THE SOUTH AFRICAN BILL OF RIGHTS, IDENTIFICATION OF RIGHTS WORTHY OF ACTIVE JUDICIAL PROTECTION IS A MATTER OF JUDICIAL DISCRETION AND JUDGMENT, CONSIDERING THE TEXT, HISTORY, PRECEDENTS, AND ABILITY OF COURTS TO APPLY JUDICIALLY MANAGEABLE STANDARDS

  — IN PARTICULAR, NORTH AMERICAN JUDGES STRUGGLE TO DISTINGUISH THE PROTECTION OF RIGHTS FROM THE DISCREDITED "LOCHNER ERA," WHICH HISTORY SUGGESTS INVOLVED JUDGES STRIKING DOWN PROGRESSIVE LEGISLATION BECAUSE OF THEIR PERSONAL (RIGHT-WING) POLITICAL VIEWS

- THE AUSTRALIAN FRAMERS INCORPORATED SEVERAL RIGHTS INTO THE CONSTITUTION, BUT (WITH SOME FEW EXCEPTIONS) EXPLICITLY REJECTED OPEN-ENDED CONSTITUTIONAL ENTRENCHMENT OF INDIVIDUAL RIGHTS. THE HIGH COURT OF AUSTRALIA HAS "UNCOVERED" A SMALL NUMBER OF IMPLIED RIGHTS — OR MORE PROPERLY, FREEDOMS — THE MOST SIGNIFICANT OF WHICH PROTECTS POLITICAL COMMUNICATIONS. THE COURT HAS MADE IT CLEAR, HOWEVER, THAT THIS SERVES ONLY AS A LIMITATION ON LEGISLATIVE POWER, AND DOES NOT CONSTITUTE A PERSONAL RIGHT. SOME LIMITED PROTECTION AGAINST DEPRIVATION OF RIGHTS HAS ALSO BEEN FOUND TO ARISE FROM THE CONSTITUTION'S SEPARATION OF POWERS. THIS

INCLUDES AN IMPLIED PROHIBITION ON BILLS OF ATTAINDER, AND A PROHIBITION ON PUNITIVE DETENTION OTHER THAN BY THE ORDER OF A COURT.

2.1. INTRODUCTION

2.1.1. Scope of this chapter

Constitutional Law in a federation concerns a variety of topics, most notably the structure of government, the relationship between the federal and sub-national governments, the scope of powers authorized to different branches and levels of government, and the rights of individuals to judicially-enforceable protection for enumerated or implied rights. Individual rights to expression and association, equal treatment, and property, and social and economic rights are considered in detail in subsequent chapters. Other important individual rights are beyond the scope of this text (most notably individual rights regarding religion, law enforcement and criminal justice).

This chapter focuses on the recognition and definition of the scope of constitutionally protected values, including various, often broadly-worded or broadly-conceptualized individual rights, both in constitutional text and in the decisions of each country's highest court. Identification of rights worthy of *active judicial protection* is a matter of judicial discretion and judgment. As we will see, each nation's high court has taken a different approach.

In general, no constitutional rights considered in this chapter are absolute. The key question is *whether the government's infringement of a judicially-recognized "right" can be challenged in court and sustained only if the government shows sufficient justification for the infringement.* Giving courts the power to strike down laws and policies established by elected representatives because judges find the justifications insufficient is a significant limitation on representative democracy. A principal challenge for any legal doctrine protecting constitutional rights with broadly worded constitutional text is how to appropriately protect recognized individual rights without creating (as Americans now perceive the *Lochner* era did, as we study below) an improper delegation to unelected judges to substitute their own personal policy preferences for those of legislators.

The constitutional texts and judicial interpretations in each of the countries we studied evolved from the historic British system of "parliamentary sovereignty." The unwritten constitutional law of Britain — including statutes and conventions built up over time — limited the monarch but placed no limits on the ability of Parliament to pass legislation. The United States, Australia, Canada, and South Africa have each taken different approaches to the question of explicit or implicit protection of individual rights. These approaches differ in regard to several important variables: (a) explicit and specific text; (b) broadly worded text that judges implicitly interpret to protect individual rights; (c) which rights receive protection, and (d) how the scope of protected rights are defined.

This Chapter considers *why* the four countries studied have taken different approaches to these questions. Certain variables might be conveniently excluded, because they do not significantly vary among the countries: all have similar legal institutions evolving from the precedent-based approach of the English common law, and all have written constitutions. In our methodological approach to comparative constitutional law (see introductory chapter), this leaves historical development and current value differences as the principal explanators of different constitutional doctrine. The principal focus of this chapter is not to compare approaches to the *substance* of specific individual rights (although this issue is considered), but rather to the *method* by which each court reasons to reach the results it has reached. We return to this topic in Chapter Nine, when we consider whether the project of judicial enforcement of individual and equality rights is normatively the best way to ensure that these human aspirations are best achieved.

Parts II and III present leading cases establishing the approach to active judicial scrutiny of unenumerated rights in the U.S. and Canada. Part IV discusses the scope of constitutional protection in South Africa and Part V presents cases establishing the more limited approach used in Australia. In reviewing these materials, students should focus on the following questions:

- Which constitutional rights are worthy of active judicial protection? How do the courts identify these rights?

- Are there principled/meaningful ways to explain the active protection of particular rights, while in some jurisdictions social and economic rights are not deemed worthy of active judicial protection?

- What legitimate justifications can be invoked by the government to permit reasonable restrictions on protected rights?

2.1.2. A chronological summary

One approach that may provide insight into the decisions made by constitutional drafters and interpreting judges is to follow a chronological timeline of key constitutional "moments" relating to each country's current constitution (this is not intended to summarize all important aspects of each nation's constitutional history; for an exegesis of the significance of these "moments," *see* Bruce Ackerman, *Constitutional Politics/ Constitutional Law*, 99 YALE L.J. 453 (1989)).

- *1789 (U.S.)*: Responding to complaints about the original Constitution, the First Congress proposes a Bill of Rights, which includes as part of the Fifth Amendment a provision that "No person shall be . . . deprived of life, liberty, or property, without due process of law." The Bill of Rights (the first ten amendments) is ratified in 1791.

- *1868 (U.S.)*: As part of the resolution of the Civil War and limitations on a host of state powers directed at southern states that had used these powers to maintain the institution of slavery, Congress passes, and the requisite three-fourths of the states ratify, the Fourteenth Amendment, which similarly provides ". . . nor shall any state deprive any person of life, liberty, or property, without due process of law . . ."

- *1900 (Aus.)*: An Australian Federal Convention in 1897-1898 drafts a Constitution for the Commonwealth of Australia Bill which is subsequently approved in referendums by the Australian voters; the British (Imperial) Parliament formally enacts the Constitution. The

Constitution provides for separation of powers, authorization of limited powers to the (federal) Commonwealth parliament, and some explicit protections for individuals with regard to Commonwealth criminal trials, property, religious worship, freedom of movement, and non-discrimination on the basis of state of residence. The framers debate, consider, and reject a version of the American 14th Amendment, opting to preserve generally the British concept of parliamentary supremacy.

- *1937-38 (U.S.)*: Overturning over a half-century of precedents that culminated in a constitutional crisis with a 5:4 Supreme Court majority striking down significant federal and state social welfare legislation, the U.S. Supreme Court ends the so-called "*Lochner* era" and attempts to distinguish "ordinary" social and economic legislation, which will be deferentially scrutinized by the court and upheld without having to persuade judges that the legislative justification is sufficient, from a narrow group of explicit or implied rights for which close judicial scrutiny continues.

- *1973-88 (Aus.)*: Efforts to enact provisions creating broad-based judicially-enforced protections of individual rights become a partisan issue between rights advocates supported by the Labor Party and opponents of bills of rights supported by the Liberal and National Parties (the conservative coalition); constitutional efforts include proposed (unsuccessful) amendments in 1988 that would have provide extended religious, property, and criminal rights protection to individuals against state governments.

- *1982 (Can.)*: The Canadian Parliament proposes, with support from all provincial governments save Quebec, and the British Parliament formally "repatriates" the Canadian Constitution of 1867, adding a Charter of Rights and Freedoms including individual rights protections with regard to expression and religion, rights of the accused, minority language rights, aboriginal rights, equality rights, and a broadly worded section 7 providing that "Everyone has the right to life, liberty and security of the person and the right not to be deprived thereof except in accordance with the principles of fundamental justice."

- *1993-96 (S.A.)*: A process begun through negotiation between the African National Congress and its leader Nelson Mandela and the apartheid regime culminates in the adoption of a new Constitution for post-apartheid South Africa. The document creates a new Constitutional Court and includes a bill of rights including individual rights to human dignity, life, freedom and security of the person, and privacy. Section 1 proclaims that the Republic of South Africa is founded on values including "human dignity, the achievement of equality, and the advancement of human rights and freedoms." Section 39 directs courts interpreting the Bill of Rights to "promote the values that underlie an open and democratic society based on human dignity, equality and freedom."

2.1.3. Close judicial scrutiny of interference with fundamental rights

To recognize individual rights claims under broadly worded constitutional texts, a constitutional court must make at least two determinations. First, the claim must fall within the scope of the text, either explicitly or implicitly. Second, because these rights are not absolute, the government lacks a sufficient justification to infringe on the recognized right.

The landmark Canadian case establishing the methodology for close judicial scrutiny is *R v. Oakes*, [1986] 1 S.C.R. 103, hailed by Professor Hogg as a "brilliant" opinion written for a unanimous court by Chief Justice Brian Dickson.[1] The case involved a challenge to a "reverse onus" provision of the *Narcotic Control Act* requiring those found in possession of illegal drugs to prove that they were not intending to distribute the drugs to others to avoid conviction for narcotics trafficking. The court first determined that the provision contravened Oakes' rights under s. 11(d) of the Charter, guaranteeing a presumption of innocence.[2] Of significance to our analysis, the Court then proceeded to consider whether the statute was a "reasonable limit" on the Charter right to presumed innocence. The Court held that the burden is on the government to justify such limits. First, the government must show that the objective of the provision is a pressing and substantial public need. "The standard must be high in order to ensure that objectives which are trivial or discordant with the principles integral to a free and democratic society do not gain s. 1 protection." *Id.* at 138. These principles include, but are not limited to:

> [R]espect for the inherent dignity of the human person, commitment to social justice and equality, accommodation of a wide variety of beliefs, respect for cultural and group identity, and faith in social and political institutions which enhance the participation of individuals and groups in society.

Id. at 136.

Second, the means chosen to achieve the pressing public need must be proportional to the legislative ends. Although the precise contours of this test "will vary depending on the circumstances," the Court referred to three considerations to determine proportionality: (a) the means chosen to achieve an important objective should be rational, fair, and not arbitrary; (b) the means chosen should impair as little as possible the right or freedom under consideration, and (c) the effects of the limitation upon the relevant right or freedom should not be out of proportion to the objective sought to be achieved. *Id.* at 139. The Court concluded that, while the objective of protecting society from the ills of drug trafficking was

---

[1] Published reports have identified UBC Law Professor Joel Bakan as the clerk who actually drafted the landmark test for Chief Justice Dickson. *See, e.g.*, Beverley Baines, *Book Review, The Charter Revolution and the Court Party by F.L. Morton and Rainer Knopff*, 26 QUEEN'S L.J. 589, 601 (2001).

[2] Similarly, the U.S. Supreme Court has held that the Due Process clauses prohibit the government from shifting the burden of proof for any element of a crime to the defendant and that the government must prove "every ingredient of an offense beyond a reasonable doubt." *Patterson v. New York*, 432 U.S. 197 (1977); *see generally* WAYNE R. LAFAVE, CRIMINAL LAW § 3.4 (4th ed. 2003).

sufficiently important, it was irrational to infer that a person had an intent to traffic on the basis of possession of a very small quantity of narcotics. So the restriction was not reasonable. *Id.* at 142.[3] Although *Oakes* involved an effort to justify a reasonable limit on an enumerated right, *Morgentaler II, infra,* applies practically the same inquiry in determining that an infringement of security of the person under s. 7 is not consistent with principles of fundamental justice.

The South African Constitution built upon *Oakes* jurisprudence. Section 36 explicitly provides:

> The rights in the Bill of Rights may be limited only in terms of a law of general application to the extent that the limitation is reasonable and justifiable in an open and democratic society based on human dignity, equality and freedom, taking into account all relevant factors, including - (a) the nature of the right; (b) the importance of the purpose of the limitation; (c) the nature and extent of the limitation; (d) the relation between the limitation and its purpose; and (e) less restrictive means to achieve the purpose.

The U.S. Supreme Court uses a somewhat different approach to close judicial scrutiny. Since the path-breaking decision in *United States v. Carolene Products Co.,* 304 U.S. 144 (1938) [excerpted in Chapter Four], the U.S. Supreme Court has suggested a different level of judicial scrutiny for due process challenges, depending on the individual rights impinged upon. Where rights are fundamental, the statute is strictly scrutinized: the government must show a "compelling" interest and must select the "least restrictive alternative" to achieve its goals. Where rights are not fundamental, the statute is deferentially reviewed — if "any rational basis" can be conceived to support the bill, the legislation will be upheld. To summarize, under that rational basis test:

- any legitimate interest can support the legislation, whether or not a judge thinks it is important or compelling

- justifications cannot be generally challenged as pretext

- overbroad and underinclusive legislation is permissible, and the legislature is permitted to solve part of a problem without solving all of it

- the legislature is entitled to its own view of a factual dispute, even if evidence in court might lead a judge to believe that the legislature was wrong.

The High Court of Australia does not employ concepts like "levels of scrutiny," or the language of "governmental interest." It comes closest to balancing the protection of rights (or freedoms) against legislative purpose in the "Lange test" (from *Lange v. ABC* (1997) 189 CLR 520 — extracted below) which it applies in determining whether the implied freedom of political communication can be legitimately burdened by legislation.

---

[3] In contrast, by way of example, *see R. v. Whyte,* [1988] 2 S.C.R. 3 (reasonable limit on presumption to require accused, charged with having "care and control" of an automobile when sitting in the driver's seat while intoxicated, to show that he did not intend to operate the car).

Under the "Lange test" (slightly modified in *Coleman v. Power* (2004) 220 CLR 360) the Court asks:

1. Does the law effectively burden freedom of communication about government or political matters either in its terms, operation or effect?

    If the answer is Yes:

2. Is the object of the law "reasonably appropriate and adapted to serve a legitimate end, in a manner compatible with the maintenance of the constitutionally prescribed system of representative and responsible government?"

If the answer is No, the impugned (challenged) legislation is unconstitutional.

If the answer to both 1. and 2. is Yes, the legislation survives challenge.

The Court has insisted that the implied freedom of political communication arises from the text and structure of the Constitution (specifically sections 7 & 24) and is not open-ended: it is specifically attached to, and required by, the constitutional entrenchment of representative government. It does not protect individual speech or personal interests or rights. The Court does not "invite" the government to make a case for, or justify its legislation, and it does not consider the impact of the legislation in any wider context than the protection of political communication. It directs its attention to whether the legislation evinces a "legitimate" purpose or end which is not the suppression of political communication itself. Legislation that is "inappropriate" or "disproportionate" (or excessive) to achieving a legitimate end is unconstitutional. The High Court has not yet settled on a precise test for, or ways of identifying, disproportionate or excessive legislative means of achieving otherwise legitimate ends, nor is it precise about its identification of the latter.

Thus, the constitutionality of many statutes will turn on how they are characterized by reviewing courts. In Canada and South Africa, if the party challenging the statute can demonstrate that his or her liberty or security of the person have been infringed, a fairly rigorous standard applies; if the party cannot, the law will be sustained. This analysis involves a two-stage process which first focuses on whether there has been a violation of the right and then applies a separate "limitations" analysis to decide whether the government can justify limiting the right. In the U.S., the definition of the specific right or "liberty" interest as a fundamental right is the key step. Even if the definition of "liberty" is somewhat broader, the level of analysis will depend on whether the interest is deemed fundamental. If the party challenging the statute demonstrates an infringement of a "fundamental right," then close scrutiny applies; if not, a much more deferential standard applies and the law will usually (albeit not always) be sustained. It is often argued by the U.S. Supreme Court that a fundamental right is one that is "deeply rooted in the history and traditions" of the American people. For these courts, the critical question then is what non-enumerated rights are worthy of non-deferential protection.

2.1.4. Interpreting "liberty" in the shadow of *Lochner*

LOCHNER v. NEW YORK
SUPREME COURT OF THE UNITED STATES
198 U.S. 45 (1905)

MR. JUSTICE PECKHAM delivered the opinion of the Court:

[Defendant was convicted of a misdemeanor violation of a New York statute], in that he wrongfully and unlawfully required and permitted an employee working for him to work more than sixty hours in one week. There is nothing in any of the opinions delivered in this case, either in the Supreme Court or the Court of Appeals of the State, which construes the section, in using the word "required," as referring to any physical force being used to obtain the labor of an employee. It is assumed that the word means nothing more than the requirement arising from voluntary contract for such labor in excess of the number of hours specified in the statute. . . . It is not an act merely fixing the number of hours which shall constitute a legal day's work, but an absolute prohibition upon the employer, permitting, under any circumstances, more than ten hours work to be done in his establishment. The employee may desire to earn the extra money, which would arise from his working more than the prescribed time, but this statute forbids the employer from permitting the employee to earn it.

The statute necessarily interferes with the right of contract between the employer and employees, concerning the number of hours in which the latter may labor in the bakery of the employer. The general right to make a contract in relation to his business is part of the liberty of the individual protected by the Fourteenth Amendment of the Federal Constitution. *Allgeyer* v. *Louisiana*, 165 U.S. 578. Under that provision no State can deprive any person of life, liberty or property without due process of law. The right to purchase or to sell labor is part of the liberty protected by this amendment, unless there are circumstances which exclude the right. There are, however, certain powers, existing in the sovereignty of each State in the Union, somewhat vaguely termed police powers, the exact description and limitation of which have not been attempted by the courts. Those powers, broadly stated and without, at present, any attempt at a more specific limitation, relate to the safety, health, morals and general welfare of the public. Both property and liberty are held on such reasonable conditions as may be imposed by the governing power of the State in the exercise of those powers, and with such conditions the Fourteenth Amendment was not designed to interfere.

The State, therefore, has power to prevent the individual from making certain kinds of contracts, and in regard to them the Federal Constitution offers no protection. If the contract be one which the State, in the legitimate exercise of its police power, has the right to prohibit, it is not prevented from prohibiting it by the Fourteenth Amendment. Contracts in violation of a statute, either of the Federal or state government, or a contract to let one's property for immoral purposes, or to do any other unlawful act, could obtain no protection from the Federal Constitution, as coming under the liberty of person or of free contract. Therefore, when the State, by its legislature, in the assumed exercise of its police powers, has passed an act which seriously limits the right to labor or the right of contract in regard to their means of livelihood between persons who are *sui juris* (both employer and employee), it becomes of great importance to determine which shall prevail — the right of the individual to labor for such time as he may choose, or the right of the State to prevent the individual from laboring or from entering into any contract to labor, beyond a certain time prescribed by the State.

. . . .

It must, of course, be conceded that there is a limit to the valid exercise of the police power by the State. There is no dispute concerning this general proposition. Otherwise the Fourteenth Amendment would have no efficacy and the legislatures of the States would have unbounded power, and it would be enough to say that any piece of legislation was enacted to conserve the morals, the health or the safety of the people; such legislation would be valid, no matter how absolutely without foundation the claim might be. The claim of the police power would be a mere pretext — become another and delusive name for the supreme sovereignty of the State to be exercised free from constitutional restraint. This is not contended for. In every case that comes before this court, therefore, where legislation of this character is concerned and where the protection of the Federal Constitution is sought, the question necessarily arises: Is this a fair, reasonable and appropriate exercise of the police power of the State, or is it an unreasonable, unnecessary and arbitrary interference with the right of the individual to his personal liberty or to enter into those contracts in relation to labor which may seem to him appropriate or necessary for the support of himself and his family? Of course the liberty of contract relating to labor includes both parties to it. The one has as much right to purchase as the other to sell labor.

. . . .

The question whether this act is valid as a labor law, pure and simple, may be dismissed in a few words. There is no reasonable ground for interfering with the liberty of person or the right of free contract, by determining the hours of labor, in the occupation of a baker. There is no contention that bakers as a class are not equal in intelligence and capacity to men in other trades or manual occupations, or that they are not able to assert their rights and care for themselves without the protecting arm of the State, interfering with their independence of judgment and of action. They are in no sense wards of the State. Viewed in the light of a purely labor law, with no reference whatever to the question of health, we think that a law like the one before us involves neither the safety, the morals nor the welfare of the public, and that the interest of the public is not in the slightest degree affected by such an act. The law must be upheld, if at all, as a law pertaining to the health of the individual engaged in the occupation of a baker. It does not affect any other portion of the public than those who are engaged in that occupation. Clean and wholesome bread does not depend upon whether the baker works but ten hours per day or only sixty hours a week. The limitation of the hours of labor does not come within the police power on that ground.

. . . .

We think that there can be no fair doubt that the trade of a baker, in and of itself, is not an unhealthy one to that degree which would authorize the legislature to interfere with the right to labor, and with the right of free contract on the part of the individual, either as employer or employee. In looking through statistics regarding all trades and occupations, it may be true that the trade of a baker does not appear to be as healthy as some other trades, and is also vastly more healthy than still others. *** There must be more than the mere fact of the possible existence of some small amount of unhealthiness to warrant legislative interference with liberty. It is unfortunately true that labor, even in any department, may possibly carry with it the seeds of unhealthiness. But are we all, on that account, at the mercy of legislative majorities? . . . No trade, no occupation, no mode of earning one's living, could escape this all-pervading power, and the acts of the legislature in limiting the hours of labor in all employments would be valid, although such limitation might seriously cripple the ability of the laborer to support himself and his family. . . .

This interference on the part of the legislatures of the several States with the ordinary trades and occupations of the people seems to be on the increase. . . .

It is impossible for us to shut our eyes to the fact that many of the laws of this character, while passed under what is claimed to be the police power for the purpose of protecting the public health or welfare, are, in reality, passed from other motives. We are justified in saying so when, from the character of the law and the subject upon which it legislates, it is apparent that the public health or welfare bears but the most remote relation to the law. The purpose of a statute must be determined from the natural and legal effect of the language employed; and whether it is or is not repugnant to the Constitution of the United States must be determined from the natural effect of such statutes when put into operation, and not from their proclaimed purpose.

It is manifest to us that the limitation of the hours of labor as provided for in this section of the statute under which the indictment was found, and the plaintiff in error convicted, has no such direct relation to and no such substantial effect upon the health of the employee, as to justify us in regarding the section as really a health law. It seems to us that the real object and purpose were simply to regulate the hours of labor between the master and his employees (all being men, *sui juris*), in a private business, not dangerous in any degree to morals or in any real and substantial degree, to the health of the employees. Under such circumstances the freedom of master and employee to contract with each other in relation to their employment, and in defining the same, cannot be prohibited or interfered with, without violating the Federal Constitution.

MR. JUSTICE HARLAN, with whom MR. JUSTICE WHITE and MR. JUSTICE DAY concurred, dissenting.

[Justice Harlan's dissent accepted the existence of a constitutionally guaranteed liberty of contract, but argued that "the rule is universal that a legislative enactment, Federal or state, is never to be disregarded or held invalid unless it be, beyond question, plainly and palpably in excess of legislative power." Under that more deferential standard, the dissenting justices were of the view that, regardless of the economic philosophy of unfair bargaining that may have been held by the

Legislature] the statute must be taken as expressing the belief of the people of New York that, as a general rule, and in the case of the average man, labor in excess of sixty hours during a week in such establishments may endanger the health of those who thus labor. Whether or not this be wise legislation it is not the province of the court to inquire. Under our systems of government the courts are not concerned with the wisdom or policy of legislation. So that in determining the question of power to interfere with liberty of contract, the court may inquire whether the means devised by the State are germane to an end which may be lawfully accomplished and have a real or substantial relation to the protection of health, as involved in the daily work of the persons, male and female, engaged in bakery and confectionery establishments. But when this inquiry is entered upon I find it impossible, in view of common experience, to say that there is here no real or substantial relation between the means employed by the State and the end sought to be accomplished by its legislation.]

[The dissent went on to cite research about health problems among overworked bakers. It found evidence to support the conclusion that labor in excess of 10 hours per day was a danger to health.]

If such reasons exist that ought to be the end of this case, for the State is not amenable to the judiciary, in respect of its legislative enactments, unless such enactments are plainly, palpably, beyond all question, inconsistent with the Constitution of the United States. . . .

. . . .

The judgment in my opinion should be affirmed.

MR. JUSTICE HOLMES dissenting.

I regret sincerely that I am unable to agree with the judgment in this case, and that I think it my duty to express my dissent.

This case is decided upon an economic theory which a large part of the country does not entertain. If it were a question whether I agreed with that theory I should desire to study it further and long before making up my mind. But I do not conceive that to be my duty, because I strongly believe that my agreement or disagreement has nothing to do with the right of a majority to embody their opinions in law. It is settled by various decisions of this court that state constitutions and state laws may regulate life in many ways which we as legislators might think as injudicious or if you like as tyrannical as this, and which equally with this interfere with the liberty to contract. Sunday laws and usury laws are ancient examples. A more modern one is the prohibition of lotteries. The liberty of the citizen to do as he likes so long as he does not interfere with the liberty of others to do the same, which has been a shibboleth for some well-known writers, is interfered with by school laws, by the Post Office, by every state or municipal institution which takes his money for purposes thought desirable, whether he likes it or not. The Fourteenth Amendment does not enact Mr. Herbert Spencer's Social Statics.[4] [Justice Holmes cited cases

---

[4] [Ed. note: This 1850 text by an English philosopher was a powerful argument for economic

upholding state vaccination laws, state and federal antitrust laws, securities regulation, and miners' labor.] Some of these laws embody convictions or prejudices which judges are likely to share. Some may not. But a constitution is not intended to embody a particular economic theory, whether of paternalism and the organic relation of the citizen to the State or of *laissez faire*. It is made for people of fundamentally differing views, and the accident of our finding certain opinions natural and familiar or novel and even shocking ought not to conclude our judgment upon the question whether statutes embodying them conflict with the Constitution of the United States.

General propositions do not decide concrete cases. The decision will depend on a judgment or intuition more subtle than any articulate major premise. But I think that the proposition just stated, if it is accepted, will carry us far toward the end. Every opinion tends to become a law. I think that the word liberty in the Fourteenth Amendment is perverted when it is held to prevent the natural outcome of a dominant opinion, unless it can be said that a rational and fair man necessarily would admit that the statute proposed would infringe fundamental principles as they have been understood by the traditions of our people and our law. It does not need research to show that no such sweeping condemnation can be passed upon the statute before us . . . .

FERGUSON v. SKRUPA
SUPREME COURT OF THE UNITED STATES
372 U.S. 726 (1963)

MR. JUSTICE BLACK delivered the opinion of the Court.

[A three-judge District Court enjoined enforcement of a Kansas statute making it a misdemeanor for any person to engage "in the business of debt adjusting" except as an incident to "the lawful practice of law in this state." The statute defines "debt adjusting" as "the making of a contract, express, or implied with a particular debtor whereby the debtor agrees to pay a certain amount of money periodically to the person engaged in the debt adjusting business who shall for a consideration distribute the same among certain specified creditors in accordance with a plan agreed upon." The three-judge court heard evidence by Skrupa tending to show the usefulness and desirability of his business and evidence by the state officials tending to show that "debt adjusting" lends itself to grave abuses against distressed debtors, particularly in the lower income brackets.]

[The district court] relied heavily on *Adams v. Tanner*, 244 U.S. 590 (1917), which held that the Due Process Clause forbids a State to prohibit a business which is "useful" and not "inherently immoral or dangerous to public welfare."

. . . [T]he philosophy of *Adams v. Tanner*, and cases like it, [is] that it is the province of courts to draw on their own views as to the morality, legitimacy, and usefulness of a particular business in order to decide whether a statute bears too heavily upon that business and by so doing violates due process. Under the system

---

libertarianism, and was one of the key works that influenced a philosophy of "social Darwinism" that preached that society would improve by the survival of the economically prosperous.]

of government created by our Constitution, it is up to legislatures, not courts, to decide on the wisdom and utility of legislation. There was a time when the Due Process Clause was used by this Court to strike down laws which were thought unreasonable, that is, unwise or incompatible with some particular economic or social philosophy. In this manner the Due Process Clause was used, for example, to nullify laws prescribing maximum hours for work in bakeries, *Lochner v. New York*, 198 U.S. 45 (1905), outlawing "yellow dog" contracts [provisions where workers agreed not to join unions as a condition of employment], *Coppage v. Kansas*, 236 U.S. 1 (1915), setting minimum wages for women, *Adkins v. Children's Hospital*, 261 U.S. 525 (1923), and fixing the weight of loaves of bread, *Jay Burns Baking Co. v. Bryan*, 264 U.S. 504 (1924). This intrusion by the judiciary into the realm of legislative value judgments was strongly objected to at the time, particularly by Mr. Justice Holmes and Mr. Justice Brandeis. ***

The doctrine that prevailed in *Lochner, Coppage, Adkins, Burns*, and like cases — that due process authorizes courts to hold laws unconstitutional when they believe the legislature has acted unwisely — has long since been discarded. We have returned to the original constitutional proposition that courts do not substitute their social and economic beliefs for the judgment of legislative bodies, who are elected to pass laws. . . .

. . . Unquestionably, there are arguments showing that the business of debt adjusting has social utility, but such arguments are properly addressed to the legislature, not to us. We refuse to sit as a "superlegislature to weigh the wisdom of legislation," and we emphatically refuse to go back to the time when courts used the Due Process Clause "to strike down state laws, regulatory of business and industrial conditions, because they may be unwise, improvident, or out of harmony with a particular school of thought." Nor are we able or willing to draw lines by calling a law "prohibitory" or "regulatory." Whether the legislature takes for its textbook Adam Smith, Herbert Spencer, Lord Keynes, or some other is no concern of ours.[5] The Kansas debt adjusting statute may be wise or unwise. But relief, if any be needed, lies not with us but with the body constituted to pass laws for the State of Kansas.

Reversed.

MR. JUSTICE HARLAN concurs in the judgment on the ground that this state measure bears a rational relation to a constitutionally permissible objective. See *Williamson v. Lee Optical Co.*, 348 U.S. 483, 491.

––––––––––

Professor Hogg expounds upon *Lochner's* effect in Canada, at § 44.7(b).: "All this happened in the United States, but the *Lochner* era casts its shadow over Canada as well. The framers of Canada's Charter of Rights deliberately omitted any reference to property in s. 7,[6] and they also omitted any guarantee of the obligation of contracts." This was "intended to banish *Lochner* from Canada. The product is a

––––––––––

[5] [FN 13] "The Fourteenth Amendment does not enact Mr. Herbert Spencer's Social Statics." *Lochner v. New York*, 198 U.S. 45, 74, 75 (1905) (Holmes, J., dissenting).

[6] [Ed. note: This issue is addressed in Chapter 6, below.]

s. 7 in which liberty must be interpreted as not including property, as not including freedom of contract, and, in short, as not including *economic* liberty."

2.2. CLOSE SCRUTINY OF DEPRIVATIONS OF LIBERTY UNDER THE FOURTEENTH AMENDMENT

Although, post-*Lochner*, the United States Supreme Court has cautioned against the use of active judicial scrutiny in most cases, a variety of non-enumerated rights are protected by active judicial scrutiny. The Court has found that the right to procreate, vote, travel, divorce, determine whether to continue a pregnancy, live with grandchildren, and engage in intimate private personal relations with another person of the same sex all require heightened governmental justifications. Professors Rotunda and Nowak, at § 11.7, conclude that

> [T]here was no real break in the use of a subjective test for finding individual rights and liberties following the 1937 renouncement of substantive due process as a control over economic and social welfare legislation. [Because the justices] were deprived of the natural law-substantive due process language to describe the process by which they identified and enforced these fundamental rights . . . the justices have attempted to give different justifications for actions that were simply a form of substantive due process.

The rights warranting close judicial scrutiny all relate to a general concept of a right to individual privacy. The landmark *post-Carolene Products* case recognizing such a right was *Griswold v. Connecticut*, 381 U.S. 479 (1965). The appellants were officials of the Planned Parenthood League of Connecticut and were convicted of providing information, instruction, and medical advice to married persons regarding contraceptives. They were convicted of a misdemeanor violation of a Connecticut law prohibiting the distribution or use of any "drug, medicinal article or instrument for the purpose of preventing conception." The Court held that the statute was unconstitutional.

The majority opinion disavowed any return to *Lochner v. New York*. "We do not sit as a super-legislature to determine the wisdom, need, and propriety of laws that touch economic problems, business affairs, or social conditions. This law, however, operates directly on an intimate relation of husband and wife and their physician's role in one aspect of that relation."

Acknowledging the lack of an express right to privacy or marital relations in the Constitution, the Court noted earlier precedents establishing the right to educate a child in a school of the parents' choice, whether public or private or parochial, *Pierce v. Society of Sisters*, 268 U.S. 510 (1925), and the right to study any particular subject or any foreign language, *Meyer v. Nebraska*, 262 U.S. 390 (1923). These cases, the Court held, indicate that:

> [S]pecific guarantees in the Bill of Rights have penumbras, formed by emanations from those guarantees that help give them life and substance. See *Poe v. Ullman*, 367 U.S. 497, 516–522 (dissenting opinion). Various guarantees create zones of privacy. The right of association contained in the

penumbra of the First Amendment is one, as we have seen. The Third Amendment in its prohibition against the quartering of soldiers "in any house" in time of peace without the consent of the owner is another facet of that privacy. The Fourth Amendment explicitly affirms the "right of the people to be secure in their persons, houses, papers, and effects, against unreasonable searches and seizures." The Fifth Amendment in its Self-Incrimination Clause enables the citizen to create a zone of privacy which government may not force him to surrender to his detriment. The Ninth Amendment provides: "The enumeration in the Constitution, of certain rights, shall not be construed to deny or disparage others retained by the people."

. . ~ .

The present case, then, concerns a relationship lying within the zone of privacy created by several fundamental constitutional guarantees. And it concerns a law which, in forbidding the *use* of contraceptives rather than regulating their manufacture or sale, seeks to achieve its goals by means having a maximum destructive impact upon that relationship. Such a law cannot stand in light of the familiar principle, so often applied by this Court, that a "governmental purpose to control or prevent activities constitution-ally subject to state regulation may not be achieved by means which sweep unnecessarily broadly and thereby invade the area of protected freedoms." *NAACP v. Alabama*, 377 U.S. 288, 307. Would we allow the police to search the sacred precincts of marital bedrooms for telltale signs of the use of contraceptives? The very idea is repulsive to the notions of privacy surrounding the marriage relationship.

We deal with a right of privacy older than the Bill of Rights — older than our political parties, older than our school system. Marriage is a coming together for better or for worse, hopefully enduring, and intimate to the degree of being sacred. It is an association that promotes a way of life, not causes; a harmony in living, not political faiths; a bilateral loyalty, not commercial or social projects. Yet it is an association for as noble a purpose as any involved in our prior decisions.

In a concurring opinion, Justice Goldberg (joined by Warren, C.J., and Brennan, J.), added the view "that the concept of liberty protects those personal rights that are fundamental, and is not confined to the specific terms of the Bill of Rights." He concluded that the right to liberty protected by the Fifth and Fourteenth Amendments required close scrutiny of government action impinging on the unenumerated "right to marital privacy" is also supported by the Ninth Amendment.

Justice Goldberg noted that the Amendment, the work of chief constitutional drafter James Madison as a leading member of the first House of Representatives, was intended to respond to fears that a bill of specifically enumerated rights could not be sufficiently broad to cover all essential rights and that the specific mention of certain rights would be interpreted as a denial that others were protected.

The Ninth Amendment to the Constitution may be regarded by some as a recent discovery and may be forgotten by others, but since 1791 it has been a basic part of the Constitution which we are sworn to uphold. To hold that a right so basic and fundamental and so deep-rooted in our society as the right of privacy in marriage may be infringed because that right is not guaranteed in so many words by the first eight amendments to the Constitution is to ignore the Ninth Amendment and to give it no effect whatsoever. Moreover, a judicial construction that this fundamental right is not protected by the Constitution because it is not mentioned in explicit terms by one of the first eight amendments or elsewhere in the Constitution would violate the Ninth Amendment, which specifically states that "the enumeration in the Constitution, of certain rights, shall not be *construed* to deny or disparage others retained by the people." (Emphasis added.)

Again heeding the concerns about the *Lochner* experience, Justice Goldberg made clear his view that "judges are not left at large to decide cases in light of their personal and private notions."

Rather, they must look to the "traditions and [collective] conscience of our people" to determine whether a principle is "so rooted [there] . . . as to be ranked as fundamental." *Snyder v. Massachusetts*, 291 U.S. 97, 105. The inquiry is whether a right involved "is of such a character that it cannot be denied without violating those 'fundamental principles of liberty and justice which lie at the base of all our civil and political institutions' . . . ." *Powell v. Alabama*, 287 U.S. 45, 67. "Liberty" also "gains content from the emanations of . . . specific [constitutional] guarantees" and "from experience with the requirements of a free society." *Poe v. Ullman*, 367 U.S. 497, 517 (dissenting opinion of Mr. Justice Douglas).

I agree fully with the Court that, applying these tests, the right of privacy is a fundamental personal right, emanating "from the totality of the constitutional scheme under which we live." *Id.*, at 521.

. . . .

The logic of the dissents would sanction federal or state legislation that seems to me even more plainly unconstitutional than the statute before us. Surely the Government, absent a showing of a compelling subordinating state interest, could not decree that all husbands and wives must be sterilized after two children have been born to them. Yet by their reasoning such an invasion of marital privacy would not be subject to constitutional challenge because, while it might be "silly," no provision of the Constitution specifically prevents the Government from curtailing the marital right to bear children and raise a family. While it may shock some of my Brethren that the Court today holds that the Constitution protects the right of marital privacy, in my view it is far more shocking to believe that the personal liberty guaranteed by the Constitution does not include protection against such totalitarian limitation of family size, which is at complete variance with our constitutional concepts. Yet, if upon a showing of a slender basis of rationality, a law outlawing voluntary birth control by married persons is valid, then, by the same reasoning, a law requiring compulsory birth control also would seem to be valid. In my view, however, both types of law would unjustifiably intrude upon rights of marital privacy which are constitutionally protected.

Justices Black (joined by Justice Stewart) dissented. Although noting his personal opposition to the challenged law, he wrote: "I like my privacy as well as the next one, but I am nevertheless compelled to admit that government has a right to invade it unless prohibited by some specific constitutional provision." Black noted that the two cases relied upon by those voting to strike down the law involving family privacy, *Pierce* and *Meyer*, were both decided in opinions by Justice McReynolds which elaborated the same natural law due process philosophy found in *Lochner v. New York*.

> The Due Process Clause with an "arbitrary and capricious" or "shocking to the conscience" formula was liberally used by this Court to strike down economic legislation in the early decades of this century, threatening, many people thought, the tranquility and stability of the Nation. See, *e. g., Lochner v. New York*, 198 U.S. 45. That formula, based on subjective considerations of "natural justice," is no less dangerous when used to enforce this Court's views about personal rights than those about economic rights. I had thought that we had laid that formula, as a means for striking down state legislation, to rest once and for all in [post-New Deal] cases ***.

>   . . . .

> In 1798, when this Court was asked to hold another Connecticut law unconstitutional, Justice Iredell said:

>> "It has been the policy of all the *American* states, which have, individually, framed their state constitutions since the revolution, and of the people of the *United States*, when they framed the Federal Constitution, to define with precision the objects of the legislative power, and to restrain its exercise within marked and settled boundaries. If any act of Congress, or of the Legislature of a state, violates those constitutional provisions, it is unquestionably void; though, I admit, that as the authority to declare it void is of a delicate and awful nature, the Court will never resort to that authority, but in a clear and urgent case. If, on the other hand, the Legislature of the Union, or the Legislature of any member of the Union, shall pass a law, within the general scope of their constitutional power, the Court cannot pronounce it to be void, merely because it is, in their judgment, contrary to the principles of natural justice. The ideas of natural justice are regulated by no fixed standard: the ablest and the purest men have differed upon the subject; and all that the Court could properly say, in such an event, would be, that the Legislature (possessed of an equal right of opinion) had passed an act which, in the opinion of the judges, was inconsistent with the abstract principles of natural justice." *Calder v. Bull*, 3 Dall. 386, 399 (emphasis in original).

Justice Stewart, joined by Justice Black, separately dissented in rejecting Justice Goldberg's reliance on the Ninth Amendment. In his view, that provision was designed simply to make clear that the adoption of the Bill of Rights did not alter the plan that the *Federal* Government was to be a government of express and limited powers, and that all rights and powers not delegated to it were retained by the people and the individual States. In Stewart's view: "Until today no member of this Court has ever suggested that the Ninth Amendment meant anything else, and the idea that a federal court could ever use the Ninth Amendment to annul a law passed by the elected representatives of the people of the State of Connecticut would have caused James Madison no little wonder."

In the years following *Griswold*, the U.S. Supreme Court has recognized a variety of fundamental liberties relating to personal and family life. Detailed in Rotunda & Nowak, §§18.26-18.30, these decisions require careful judicial scrutiny over state law involving:

- sterilization
- abortion
- contraception (regardless of marital status)
- freedom of choice in marriage, including the ability of the poor to marry or to obtain a divorce
- sexuality
- procedural and substantive ability of parents to defend against termination of parental rights
- control by custodial parents over visitation by others
- [perhaps] the decision of a competent person to refuse life sustaining medical treatment (But not an affirmative right to receive assistance in suicide.)

ROE v. WADE
SUPREME COURT OF THE UNITED STATES
410 U.S. 113 (1973)

MR. JUSTICE BLACKMUN delivered the opinion of the Court.

. . . .

I

The Texas statutes that concern us here are Arts. 1191-1194 and 1196 of the State's Penal Code. These make it a crime to "procure an abortion," as therein defined, or to attempt one, except with respect to "an abortion procured or attempted by medical advice for the purpose of saving the life of the mother." Similar statutes are in existence in a majority of the States.

. . . .

V

The principal thrust of appellant's attack on the Texas statutes is that they improperly invade a right, said to be possessed by the pregnant woman, to choose to terminate her pregnancy. Appellant would discover this right in the concept of personal "liberty" embodied in the Fourteenth Amendment's Due Process Clause; or in personal, marital, familial, and sexual privacy said to be protected by the Bill of Rights or its penumbras; or among those rights reserved to the people by the Ninth Amendment. Before addressing this claim, we feel it desirable briefly to survey, in several aspects, the history of abortion, for such insight as that history may afford us, and then to examine the state purposes and interests behind the criminal abortion laws.

. . . .

VII

[First, the Court summarily dismissed the argument, not made by counsel in these cases, that these laws were the product of a Victorian social concern to discourage illicit sexual conduct. Second was the concern that when most criminal abortion laws were first enacted, the procedure was a hazardous one for the woman. The Court, however, observed that improvements in medicine are such that medical data indicate that abortion is now safe and, in some cases, safer than carrying a child to term.]

The third reason is the State's interest — some phrase it in terms of duty — in protecting prenatal life. Some of the argument for this justification rests on the theory that a new human life is present from the moment of conception. The State's interest and general obligation to protect life then extends, it is argued, to prenatal life. Only when the life of the pregnant mother herself is at stake, balanced against the life she carries within her, should the interest of the embryo or fetus not prevail. Logically, of course, a legitimate state interest in this area need not stand or fall on acceptance of the belief that life begins at conception or at some other point prior to live birth. In assessing the State's interest, recognition may be given to the less rigid claim that as long as at least potential life is involved, the State may assert interests beyond the protection of the pregnant woman alone.

It is with these interests, and the weight to be attached to them, that this case is concerned.

VIII

The Constitution does not explicitly mention any right of privacy. In a line of decisions, however, going back perhaps as far as *Union Pacific R. Co.* v. *Botsford*, 141 U.S. 250, 251 (1891), the Court has recognized that a right of personal privacy, or a guarantee of certain areas or zones of privacy, does exist under the Constitution. In varying contexts, the Court or individual Justices have, indeed, found at least the roots of that right in the First Amendment; in the Fourth and Fifth Amendments, in the penumbras of the Bill of Rights; in the Ninth Amendment; or in the concept of liberty guaranteed by the first section of the Fourteenth

Amendment. These decisions make it clear that only personal rights that can be deemed "fundamental" or "implicit in the concept of ordered liberty," *Palko v. Connecticut*, 302 U.S. 319, 325 (1937), are included in this guarantee of personal privacy. They also make it clear that the right has some extension to activities relating to marriage, *Loving v. Virginia*, 388 U.S. 1, 12 (1967); procreation, *Skinner v. Oklahoma*, 316 U.S. 535, 541–542 (1942); contraception, *Eisenstadt v. Baird*, 405 U.S., at 453–454; id., at 460, 463–465 (White, J., concurring in result); family relationships, *Prince v. Massachusetts*, 321 U.S. 158, 166 (1944); and child rearing and education, *Pierce v. Society of Sisters*, 268 U.S. 510, 535 (1925), *Meyer v. Nebraska, supra*. This right of privacy, whether it be founded in the Fourteenth Amendment's concept of personal liberty and restrictions upon state action, as we feel it is, or, as the District Court determined, in the Ninth Amendment's reservation of rights to the people, is broad enough to encompass a woman's decision whether or not to terminate her pregnancy. The detriment that the State would impose upon the pregnant woman by denying this choice altogether is apparent. Specific and direct harm medically diagnosable even in early pregnancy may be involved. Maternity, or additional offspring, may force upon the woman a distressful life and future. Psychological harm may be imminent. Mental and physical health may be taxed by child care. There is also the distress, for all concerned, associated with the unwanted child, and there is the problem of bringing a child into a family already unable, psychologically and otherwise, to care for it. In other cases, as in this one, the additional difficulties and continuing stigma of unwed motherhood may be involved. All these are factors the woman and her responsible physician necessarily will consider in consultation.

On the basis of elements such as these, appellant and some *amici* argue that the woman's right is absolute and that she is entitled to terminate her pregnancy at whatever time, in whatever way, and for whatever reason she alone chooses. With this we do not agree. Appellant's arguments that Texas either has no valid interest at all in regulating the abortion decision, or no interest strong enough to support any limitation upon the woman's sole determination, are unpersuasive. The Court's decisions recognizing a right of privacy also acknowledge that some state regulation in areas protected by that right is appropriate. As noted above, a State may properly assert important interests in safeguarding health, in maintaining medical standards, and in protecting potential life. At some point in pregnancy, these respective interests become sufficiently compelling to sustain regulation of the factors that govern the abortion decision. The privacy right involved, therefore, cannot be said to be absolute. In fact, it is not clear to us that the claim asserted by some *amici* that one has an unlimited right to do with one's body as one pleases bears a close relationship to the right of privacy previously articulated in the Court's decisions. The Court has refused to recognize an unlimited right of this kind in the past. *Jacobson v. Massachusetts*, 197 U.S. 11 (1905) (vaccination); *Buck v. Bell*, 274 U.S. 200 (1927) (sterilization).

. . . .

Where certain "fundamental rights" are involved, the Court has held that regulation limiting these rights may be justified only by a "compelling state interest," and that legislative enactments must be narrowly drawn to express only the legitimate state interests at stake.

. . . .

IX

[The Court held that it need not resolve "the difficult question of when life begins," but noted that legal protections afforded to "persons" generally does not apply to fetuses. "In short," the Court concluded, "the unborn have never been recognized in the law as persons in the whole sense."]

X

In view of all this, we do not agree that, by adopting one theory of life, Texas may override the rights of the pregnant woman that are at stake. We repeat, however, that the State does have an important and legitimate interest in preserving and protecting the health of the pregnant woman, whether she be a resident of the State or a nonresident who seeks medical consultation and treatment there, and that it has still another important and legitimate interest in protecting the potentiality of human life. These interests are separate and distinct. [The majority concluded that the state's interest in reasonable regulations regarding abortion designed to protect a woman's health becomes sufficiently "compelling" at the end of the first trimester, because at that point abortions become more medically risky than childbirth. With respect to the state's "important and legitimate" interest in "potential life," the "compelling" point is when the fetus is viable. With regard to first-trimester abortions, "the attending physician, in consultation with his patient, is free to determine, without regulation by the State, that, in his medical judgment, the patient's pregnancy should be terminated."]

. . . .

[The concurring opinions of MR. CHIEF JUSTICE BURGER and MR. JUSTICE DOUGLAS are omitted.]

MR. JUSTICE STEWART, concurring.

In 1963, this Court, in *Ferguson v. Skrupa*, 372 U.S. 726, purported to sound the death knell for the doctrine of substantive due process, a doctrine under which many state laws had in the past been held to violate the Fourteenth Amendment. As Mr. Justice Black's opinion for the Court in *Skrupa* put it: "We have returned to the original constitutional proposition that courts do not substitute their social and economic beliefs for the judgment of legislative bodies, who are elected to pass laws." *Id.*, at 730.

Barely two years later, in *Griswold v. Connecticut*, 381 U.S. 479, the Court held a Connecticut birth control law unconstitutional. In view of what had been so recently said in *Skrupa*, the Court's opinion in *Griswold* understandably did its best to avoid reliance on the Due Process Clause of the Fourteenth Amendment as the ground for decision. Yet, the Connecticut law did not violate any provision of the Bill of Rights, nor any other specific provision of the Constitution.[7] So it was clear to me then, and it is equally clear to me now, that the *Griswold* decision can be rationally understood only as a holding that the Connecticut statute substantively invaded the "liberty" that is protected by the Due Process Clause of the Fourteenth Amendment. As so understood, *Griswold* stands as one in a long line of pre-*Skrupa* cases decided under the doctrine of substantive due process, and I now accept it as such.

"In a Constitution for a free people, there can be no doubt that the meaning of 'liberty' must be broad indeed." *Board of Regents v. Roth*, 408 U.S. 564, 572. The Constitution nowhere mentions a specific right of personal choice in matters of marriage and family life, but the "liberty" protected by the Due Process Clause of the Fourteenth Amendment covers more than those freedoms explicitly named in the Bill of Rights.

. . . .

Several decisions of this Court make clear that freedom of personal choice in matters of marriage and family life is one of the liberties protected by the Due Process Clause of the Fourteenth Amendment. . . . .

Clearly, therefore, the Court today is correct in holding that the right asserted by Jane Roe is embraced within the personal liberty protected by the Due Process Clause of the Fourteenth Amendment.

. . . .

MR. JUSTICE REHNQUIST, dissenting.

The Court's opinion brings to the decision of this troubling question both extensive historical fact and a wealth of legal scholarship. While the opinion thus commands my respect, I find myself nonetheless in fundamental disagreement with those parts of it that invalidate the Texas statute in question, and therefore dissent.

. . . .

II

[First, the dissent rejected the conclusion that any right of "privacy" was involved in the case. The statute barred a medical procedure by a state-licensed physician.] A transaction resulting in an operation such as this is not 'private' in the ordinary usage of that word. Nor is the "privacy" that the Court finds here even a distant relative of the freedom from searches and seizures protected by the Fourth Amendment to the Constitution, which the Court has referred to as embodying a right to privacy. *Katz v. United States*, 389 U.S. 347 (1967).

---

[7] [FN 2] There is no constitutional right of privacy, as such. "[The Fourth] Amendment protects individual privacy against certain kinds of governmental intrusion, but its protections go further, and often have nothing to do with privacy at all. Other provisions of the Constitution protect personal privacy from other forms of governmental invasion. But the protection of a person's general right to privacy — his right to be let alone by other people — is, like the protection of his property and of his very life, left largely to the law of the individual States." *Katz v. United States*, 389 U.S. 347, 350–351 (footnotes omitted).

If the Court means by the term "privacy" no more than that the claim of a person to be free from unwanted state regulation of consensual transactions may be a form of "liberty" protected by the Fourteenth Amendment, there is no doubt that similar claims have been upheld in our earlier decisions on the basis of that liberty. I agree with the statement of Mr. Justice Stewart in his concurring opinion that the "liberty," against deprivation of which without due process the Fourteenth Amendment protects, embraces more than the rights found in the Bill of Rights. But that liberty is not guaranteed absolutely against deprivation, only against deprivation without due process of law. The test traditionally applied in the area of social and economic legislation is whether or not a law such as that challenged has a rational relation to a valid state objective. *Williamson v. Lee Optical Co.,* 348 U.S. 483, 491 (1955). . . .

While the Court's opinion quotes from the dissent of Mr. Justice Holmes in *Lochner v. New York,* 198 U.S. 45, 74 (1905), the result it reaches is more closely attuned to the majority opinion of Mr. Justice Peckham in that case. As in *Lochner* and similar cases applying substantive due process standards to economic and social welfare legislation, the adoption of the compelling state interest standard will inevitably require this Court to examine the legislative policies and pass on the wisdom of these policies in the very process of deciding whether a particular state interest put forward may or may not be "compelling." The decision here to break pregnancy into three distinct terms and to outline the permissible restrictions the State may impose in each one, for example, partakes more of judicial legislation than it does of a determination of the intent of the drafters of the Fourteenth Amendment.

The fact that a majority of the States reflecting, after all, the majority sentiment in those States, have had restrictions on abortions for at least a century is a strong indication, it seems to me, that the asserted right to an abortion is not "so rooted in the traditions and conscience of our people as to be ranked as fundamental." *Snyder v. Massachusetts,* 291 U.S. 97, 105 (1934). Even today, when society's views on abortion are changing, the very existence of the debate is evidence that the "right" to an abortion is not so universally accepted as the appellant would have us believe.

To reach its result, the Court necessarily has had to find within the scope of the Fourteenth Amendment a right that was apparently completely unknown to the drafters of the Amendment. As early as 1821, the first state law dealing directly with abortion was enacted by the Connecticut Legislature. Conn. Stat., Tit. 20, §§ 14, 16. By the time of the adoption of the Fourteenth Amendment in 1868, there were at least 36 laws enacted by state or territorial legislatures limiting abortion. While many States have amended or updated their laws, 21 of the laws on the books in 1868 remain in effect today. Indeed, the Texas statute struck down today was, as the majority notes, first enacted in 1857 and "has remained substantially unchanged to the present time."

There apparently was no question concerning the validity of this provision or of any of the other state statutes when the Fourteenth Amendment was adopted. The only conclusion possible from this history is that the drafters did not intend to have the Fourteenth Amendment withdraw from the States the power to legislate with respect to this matter.

MR. JUSTICE WHITE, with whom MR. JUSTICE REHNQUIST joins, dissenting:

[This opinion was a combined dissent to the Court's judgment in *Roe* and a companion case, *Doe v. Bolton*].

. . . .

With all due respect, I dissent. I find nothing in the language or history of the Constitution to support the Court's judgment. The Court simply fashions and announces a new constitutional right for pregnant mothers and, with scarcely any reason or authority for its action, invests that right with sufficient substance to override most existing state abortion statutes. The upshot is that the people and the legislatures of the 50 States are constitutionally disentitled to weigh the relative importance of the continued existence and development of the fetus, on the one hand, against a spectrum of possible impacts on the mother, on the other hand. As an exercise of raw judicial power, the Court perhaps has authority to do what it does today; but in my view its judgment is an improvident and extravagant exercise of the power of judicial review that the Constitution extends to this Court.

The Court apparently values the convenience of the pregnant mother more than the continued existence and development of the life or potential life that she carries. Whether or not I might agree with that marshaling of values, I can in no event join the Court's judgment because I find no constitutional warrant for imposing such an order of priorities on the people and legislatures of the States. In a sensitive area such as this, involving as it does issues over which reasonable men may easily and heatedly differ, I cannot accept the Court's exercise of its clear power of choice by interposing a constitutional barrier to state efforts to protect human life and by investing mothers and doctors with the constitutionally protected right to exterminate it. This issue, for the most part, should be left with the people and to the political processes the people have devised to govern their affairs.

PLANNED PARENTHOOD OF SOUTHEASTERN PENNSYLVANIA v. CASEY
SUPREME COURT OF THE UNITED STATES
505 U.S. 833 (1992)

JUSTICE O'CONNOR, JUSTICE KENNEDY, and JUSTICE SOUTER announced the judgment of the Court and delivered the opinion of the Court with respect to Parts I, II, III, V-A, V-C, and VI, an opinion with respect to Part V-E, in which JUSTICE STEVENS joins, and an opinion with respect to Parts IV, V-B, and V-D.

I

. . . .

At issue in these cases are five provisions of the Pennsylvania Abortion Control

Act of 1982, as amended in 1988 and 1989. . . . The Act requires that a woman seeking an abortion give her informed consent prior to the abortion procedure, and specifies that she be provided with certain information at least 24 hours before the abortion is performed. § 3205. For a minor to obtain an abortion, the Act requires the informed consent of one of her parents, but provides for a judicial bypass option if the minor does not wish to or cannot obtain a parent's consent. § 3206. Another provision of the Act requires that, unless certain exceptions apply, a married woman seeking an abortion must sign a statement indicating that she has notified her husband of her intended abortion. § 3209. The Act exempts compliance with these three requirements in the event of a "medical emergency," which is [interpreted to include any significant threat to the woman's health]. In addition to the above provisions regulating the performance of abortions, the Act imposes certain reporting requirements on facilities that provide abortion services.

. . . .

   . . . [W]e find it imperative to review once more the principles that define the rights of the woman and the legitimate authority of the State respecting the termination of pregnancies by abortion procedures. After considering the fundamental constitutional questions resolved by *Roe*, principles of institutional integrity, and the rule of *stare decisis*, we are led to conclude this: the essential holding of *Roe v. Wade* should be retained and once again reaffirmed.

   It must be stated at the outset and with clarity that *Roe's* essential holding, the holding we reaffirm, has three parts. First is a recognition of the right of the woman to choose to have an abortion before viability and to obtain it without undue interference from the State. Before viability, the State's interests are not strong enough to support a prohibition of abortion or the imposition of a substantial obstacle to the woman's effective right to elect the procedure. Second is a confirmation of the State's power to restrict abortions after fetal viability, if the law contains exceptions for pregnancies which endanger the woman's life or health. And third is the principle that the State has legitimate interests from the outset of the pregnancy in protecting the health of the woman and the life of the fetus that may become a child. These principles do not contradict one another; and we adhere to each.

II

. . . .

   The most familiar of the substantive liberties protected by the Fourteenth Amendment are those recognized by the Bill of Rights. We have held that the Due Process Clause of the Fourteenth Amendment incorporates most of the Bill of Rights against the States. See, e. g., *Duncan v. Louisiana*, 391 U.S. 145, 147–148 (1968). It is tempting, as a means of curbing the discretion of federal judges, to suppose that liberty encompasses no more than those rights already guaranteed to the individual against federal interference by the express provisions of the first eight Amendments to the Constitution. But of course this Court has never accepted that view. It is also tempting, for the same reason, to suppose that the Due Process Clause protects only those practices, defined at the most specific level, that were protected against government interference by other rules of law when the Fourteenth Amendment was ratified. But such a view would be inconsistent with our law. It is a promise of the Constitution that there is a realm of personal liberty which the government may not enter. We have vindicated this principle before. Marriage is mentioned nowhere in the Bill of Rights and interracial marriage was illegal in most States in the 19th century, but the Court was no doubt correct in finding it to be an aspect of liberty protected against state interference by the substantive component of the Due Process Clause in *Loving v. Virginia*, 388 U.S. 1, 12 (1967) (relying, in an opinion for eight Justices, on the Due Process Clause). Neither the Bill of Rights nor the specific practices of States at the time of the adoption of the Fourteenth Amendment marks the outer limits of the substantive sphere of liberty which the Fourteenth Amendment protects. See U.S. Const., Amdt. 9. As the second Justice Harlan recognized:

> "The full scope of the liberty guaranteed by the Due Process Clause cannot be found in or limited by the precise terms of the specific guarantees elsewhere provided in the Constitution. This 'liberty' is not a series of isolated points pricked out in terms of the taking of property; the freedom of speech, press, and religion; the right to keep and bear arms; the freedom from unreasonable searches and seizures; and so on. It is a rational continuum which, broadly speaking, includes a freedom from all substantial arbitrary impositions and purposeless restraints, . . . and which also recognizes, what a reasonable and sensitive judgment must, that certain interests require particularly careful scrutiny of the state needs asserted to justify their abridgment." *Poe v. Ullman, supra*, at 543 (opinion dissenting from dismissal on jurisdictional grounds) [this was a challenge to a ban on contraceptive use later struck down in *Griswold v. Connecticut*].

. . . .

Our law affords constitutional protection to personal decisions relating to marriage, procreation, contraception, family relationships, child rearing, and education. . . . These matters, involving the most intimate and personal choices a person may make in a lifetime, choices central to personal dignity and autonomy, are central to the liberty protected by the Fourteenth Amendment. At the heart of liberty is the right to define one's own concept of existence, of meaning, of the universe, and of the mystery of human life. Beliefs about these matters could not define the attributes of personhood were they formed under compulsion of the State.

These considerations begin our analysis of the woman's interest in terminating her pregnancy but cannot end it, for this reason: though the abortion decision may originate within the zone of conscience and belief, it is more than a philosophic exercise. Abortion is a unique act. It is an act fraught with consequences for others: for the woman who must live with the implications of her decision; for the persons who perform and assist in the procedure; for the spouse, family, and society which must confront the knowledge that these procedures exist, procedures some deem nothing short of an act of violence against innocent human life; and, depending on one's beliefs, for the life or potential life that is aborted. Though abortion is conduct, it does not follow that the State is entitled to proscribe it in all instances. That is because the liberty of the woman is at stake in a sense unique to the human condition and so unique to the law. The mother who carries a child to full term is subject to anxieties, to physical constraints, to pain that only she must bear. That these sacrifices have from the beginning of the human race been endured by woman with a pride that ennobles her in the eyes of others and gives to the infant a bond of love cannot alone be grounds for the State to insist she make the sacrifice. Her suffering is too intimate and personal for the State to insist, without more, upon its own vision of the woman's role, however dominant that vision has been in the course of our history and our culture. The destiny of the woman must be shaped to a large extent on her own conception of her spiritual imperatives and her place in society.

III

[The opinion then discusses at length the reasons for adhering to *Roe* for reasons of *stare decisis*, concluding]:

The Court's duty in the present cases is clear. In 1973, it confronted the already-divisive issue of governmental power to limit personal choice to undergo abortion, for which it provided a new resolution based on the due process guaranteed by the Fourteenth Amendment. Whether or not a new social consensus is developing on that issue, its divisiveness is no less today than in 1973, and pressure to overrule the decision, like pressure to retain it, has grown only more intense. A decision to overrule *Roe's* essential holding under the existing circumstances would address error, if error there was, at the cost of both profound and unnecessary damage to the Court's legitimacy, and to the Nation's commitment to the rule of law. It is therefore imperative to adhere to the essence of *Roe's* original decision, and we do so today.

IV

[While adhering to *Roe's* recognition "of a woman's right to terminate her pregnancy before viability," the plurality emphasized that *Roe* had also recognized the State's "important and legitimate interest in protecting the potentiality of human life." This interest, the plurality concluded, had been given too little weight in post-*Roe* decisions enforcing a rigid "trimester" framework permitting state regulation in the final trimester, forbidding almost all regulation in the first trimester, and permitting regulations to protect a woman's health in the second trimester. The plurality rejected this framework, adopting instead an "undue burden" standard, which they declared to be "a shorthand for the conclusion that a state regulation has the purpose or effect of placing a substantial obstacle in the path of a woman seeking an abortion of a nonviable fetus." The following "guiding principles" were set forth: (a) an "undue burden exists, and therefore a provision of law is invalid, if its purpose or effect is to place a substantial obstacle in the path of a woman seeking an abortion before the fetus attains viability"; (b) throughout pregnancy the State may legislate to ensure women make informed choices and may seek to persuade women to choose childbirth over abortion; (c) health regulations are measured by whether they have the purpose or effect of presenting a substantial obstacle to abortion; (d) the ultimate choice must remain the woman's; (e) the state may regulate or proscribe abortion after the fetus is viable except for the preservation of the life and health of the mother.]

[Applying the undue burden standard to the facts of the case, the plurality upheld, as not unduly burdensome, the statute's requirements of a 24-hour waiting period, that a physician (and not another health care professional) inform the woman of the nature of the procedure, the health risks involved, and the probable gestational age of the "unborn child," that the woman be informed of various social welfare and adoption services and child support requirements, and that the woman certifies in writing that she has been so informed. Although they found "troubling in some respects" the district court's findings that the practical effect of the statute will be to require many women to make at least two visits to the doctor, and that multiple visits will increase the exposure of women seeking abortions to "the harassment and hostility of anti-abortion protestors demonstrating outside a clinic," the plurality ultimately concluded that it would reserve for later specific cases specific challenges to the statute as applied to individual women. The plurality also rejected as "insufficient" the District Court's reasoning that the waiting period was "particularly burdensome" for poor women, those who must travel long distances, and those who have difficulty explaining their whereabouts to husband, employers, or others.]

[At the same time, the plurality voted to invalidate provisions barring abortions for married women without a statement that her husband was notified (subject to exceptions for assault, where the husband is not the man who impregnated her, or where the woman believes that notifying her husband will cause him or someone else to inflict bodily injury upon her). Noting that "there are millions of women in this country who are the victims of regular physical and psychological abuse at the hands of their husbands" and these women "may have very good reasons for not wishing to inform their husbands of their decision to obtain an abortion," including fear of abuse to the family's children or psychological abuse to themselves as well as other harms beyond bodily injury, the plurality concluded that the "spousal notification requirement is thus likely to prevent a significant number of women from obtaining an abortion. It does not merely make abortions a little more difficult or expensive to obtain; for many women, it will impose a substantial obstacle."]

D

[The plurality adhered to prior cases upholding requirements that a minor obtain parental consent, as long as there exists a procedure allowing the minor to obtain on an individualized basis judicial dispensation from the requirement.]

JUSTICE STEVENS, concurring in part and dissenting in part:

[The opinion began by endorsing the plurality's *stare decisis* analysis, noting that of the 15 justices who have sat in review of the issues since *Roe v. Wade*, "11 have voted as the majority does today: Chief Justice Burger, Justices Douglas, Brennan, Stewart, Marshall, and Powell, and Justices Blackmun, O'Connor, Kennedy, Souter, and myself. Only four — all of whom happen to be on the Court today — have reached the opposite conclusion." Next, Stevens observed that the State's interest must be secular; consistent with the First Amendment the State may not promote a theological or sectarian interest. He identified two such interests: the minimization of the offense that many Americans take at what they believe to be an unacceptable disrespect for potential human life, and a broader interest in expanding the population, that "the potential human lives might include the occasional Mozart or Curie." In counterpoise is the woman's constitutional interest in liberty, which includes a right to bodily integrity and her freedom to decide matters of the highest privacy and the most personal nature, because the "authority to make such traumatic and yet empowering decisions is an element of basic human dignity."]

JUSTICE BLACKMUN, concurring in part, concurring in the judgment in part, and dissenting in part.

. . . .

Three years ago, in *Webster v. Reproductive Health Services*, 492 U.S. 490, (1989), four Members of this Court appeared poised to "cast into darkness the hopes and visions of every woman in this country" who had come to believe that the Constitution guaranteed her the right to reproductive choice. *Id.*, at 557 (Blackmun, J., dissenting). All that remained between the promise of *Roe* and the darkness of the plurality was a single, flickering flame. Decisions since *Webster* gave little reason to hope that this flame would cast much light. But now, just when so many expected the darkness to fall, the flame has grown bright.

I do not underestimate the significance of today's joint opinion. Yet I remain steadfast in my belief that the right to reproductive choice is entitled to the full protection afforded by this Court before *Webster*. And I fear for the darkness as four Justices anxiously await the single vote necessary to extinguish the light.

. . . .

II

[Justice Blackmun observed that restrictions on abortion "force women to endure physical invasions far more substantial than those this Court has held to violate the constitutional principle of bodily integrity in other contexts," such as surgical removal of bullet from murder suspect or pumping the stomach of a drug suspect. He also addressed an argument, considered in Chapter Four, that abortion restrictions "also implicate constitutional guarantees of gender equality."]

[Applying the strict scrutiny standard he believed to be more appropriate, Justice Blackmun concluded that requirements that information be provided by a doctor were "not narrowly tailored to serve the Commonwealth's interest in protecting maternal health," nor was the 24-hour waiting period tailored to legitimate state ends.]

III

. . . .

Even more shocking than the Chief Justice's cramped notion of individual liberty is his complete omission of any discussion of the effects that compelled childbirth and motherhood have on women's lives. The only expression of concern with women's health is purely instrumental — for the Chief Justice, only women's psychological health is a concern, and only to the extent that he assumes that every woman who decides to have an abortion does so without serious consideration of the moral implications of her decision. *Post*, 505 U.S. at 967–968. In short, the Chief Justice's view of the State's compelling interest in maternal health has less to do with health than it does with compelling women to be maternal.

. . .

But, we are reassured, there is always the protection of the democratic process. While there is much to be praised about our democracy, our country since its founding has recognized that there are certain fundamental liberties that are not to be left to the whims of an election. A woman's right to reproductive choice is one of those fundamental liberties. Accordingly, that liberty need not seek refuge at the ballot box.

. . . .

CHIEF JUSTICE REHNQUIST, with whom JUSTICE WHITE, JUSTICE SCALIA, and JUSTICE THOMAS join, concurring in the judgment in part and dissenting in part.

. . . .

I

. . . .

In *Roe v. Wade*, the Court recognized a "guarantee of personal privacy" which "is broad enough to encompass a woman's decision whether or not to terminate her pregnancy." 410 U.S. at 152–153. We are now of the view that, in terming this right fundamental, the Court in *Roe* read the earlier opinions upon which it based its decision much too broadly. Unlike marriage, procreation, and contraception, abortion "involves the purposeful termination of a potential life." *Harris v. McRae*, 448 U.S. 297, 325, (1980). The abortion decision must therefore "be recognized as *sui generis*, different in kind from the others that the Court has protected under the rubric of personal or family privacy and autonomy." *Thornburgh v. American College of Obstetricians and Gynecologists, supra*, at 792 (White, J., dissenting). One cannot ignore the fact that a woman is not isolated in her pregnancy, and that the decision to abort necessarily involves the destruction of a fetus. See *Michael H. v. Gerald D., supra, at 124, n.4* (To look "at the act which is assertedly the subject of a liberty interest in isolation from its effect upon other people [is] like inquiring whether there is a liberty interest in firing a gun where the case at hand happens to involve its discharge into another person's body").

Nor do the historical traditions of the American people support the view that the right to terminate one's pregnancy is "fundamental." . . . On this record, it can scarcely be said that any deeply rooted tradition of relatively unrestricted abortion in our history supported the classification of the right to abortion as "fundamental" under the Due Process Clause of the Fourteenth Amendment.

II

[The opinion then discusses why *stare decisis* does not require reaffirmation of *Roe*, concluding]:

The sum of the joint opinion's labors in the name of *stare decisis* and "legitimacy" is this: *Roe v. Wade* stands as a sort of judicial Potemkin Village, which may be pointed out to passers-by as a monument to the importance of adhering to precedent. But behind the facade, an entirely new method of analysis, without any roots in constitutional law, is imported to decide the constitutionality of state laws regulating abortion. Neither stare decisis nor "legitimacy" are truly served by such an effort.

We have stated above our belief that the Constitution does not subject state abortion regulations to heightened scrutiny. Accordingly, we think that the correct analysis is that set forth by the plurality opinion in *Webster*. A woman's interest in having an abortion is a form of liberty protected by the Due Process Clause, but States may regulate abortion procedures in ways rationally related to a legitimate state interest. *Williamson v. Lee Optical of Oklahoma, Inc.*, 348 U.S. 483, 491 (1955). . . .

JUSTICE SCALIA, with whom THE CHIEF JUSTICE, JUSTICE WHITE, and JUSTICE THOMAS join, concurring in the judgment in part and dissenting in part.

. . . .

The States may, if they wish, permit abortion on demand, but the Constitution does not require them to do so. The permissibility of abortion, and the limitations upon it, are to be resolved like most important questions in our democracy: by citizens trying to persuade one another and then voting. As the Court acknowledges, "where reasonable people disagree the government can adopt one position or the other." The Court is correct in adding the qualification that this "assumes a state of affairs in which the choice does not intrude upon a protected liberty," *ibid.* — but the crucial part of that qualification is the penultimate word. A State's choice between two positions on which reasonable people can disagree is constitutional even when (as is often the case) it intrudes upon a "liberty" in the absolute sense. Laws against bigamy, for example — with which entire societies of reasonable people disagree — intrude upon men and women's liberty to marry and live with one another. But bigamy happens not to be a liberty specially "protected" by the Constitution.

That is, quite simply, the issue in these cases: not whether the power of a woman to abort her unborn child is a "liberty" in the absolute sense; or even whether it is a liberty of great importance to many women. Of course it is both. The issue is whether it is a liberty protected by the Constitution of the United States. I am sure it is not. I reach that conclusion not because of anything so exalted as my views concerning the "concept of existence, of meaning, of the universe, and of the mystery of human life." Rather, I reach it for the same reason I reach the conclusion that bigamy is not constitutionally protected — because of two simple facts: (1) the Constitution says absolutely nothing about it, and (2) the longstanding traditions of American society have permitted it to be legally proscribed.

. . . .

The emptiness of the "reasoned judgment" that produced *Roe* is displayed in plain view by the fact that, after more than 19 years of effort by some of the brightest (and most determined) legal minds in the country, after more than 10 cases upholding abortion rights in this Court, and after dozens upon dozens of amicus briefs submitted in these and other cases, the best the Court can do to explain how it is that the word "liberty" must be thought to include the right to destroy human fetuses is to rattle off a collection of adjectives that simply decorate a value judgment and conceal a political choice. *** Those adjectives might be applied, for example, to homosexual sodomy, polygamy, adult incest, and suicide, all of which are equally "intimate" and "deeply personal" decisions involving "personal autonomy and bodily integrity," and all of which can constitutionally be proscribed because it is our unquestionable constitutional tradition that they are proscribable. It is not reasoned judgment that supports the Court's decision; only personal predilection. . . .

The Court's abortion jurisprudence may well reflect the replacement of Justice Sandra Day O'Connor by Justice Samuel Alito. In *Stenberg v. Carhart*, 530 U.S. 914 (2000), a 5-4 majority struck down a Nebraska statute outlawing certain types of "partial birth" abortion procedures as imposing an "undue burden" on a woman's reproductive rights, principally on the ground that the statute lacked an exception for the use of such procedures when necessary to preserve the health of the mother. The Court accepted the district court's factual findings rejecting the state's claim that safe alternatives existed. The Court also faulted the statute for being too overbroad in potentially including in its prohibition aspects of more typical and widespread abortion procedures. In *Gonzales v. Carhart*, 127 S. Ct. 1610 (2007), a 5-4 majority upheld a more carefully drafted federal statute.[8]

The majority began by observing that 3 of its members strongly dissented from *Casey*, but that "[w]hatever one's views concerning the Casey joint opinion, it is evident a premise central to its conclusion — that the government has a legitimate and substantial interest in preserving and promoting fetal life — would be repudiated were the Court now to affirm the judgments of the Courts of Appeals." The majority observed that Congress found that the prohibited abortion procedures had a "disturbing similarity to the killing of a newborn infant "and that the government may use its voice and its regulatory authority to show its profound respect for the life within the woman," and that it was "self-evident" that mothers who regret their choice to abort will suffer more to learn about the details of the proscribed abortion procedures. The Court concluded that a statute is not "invalid on its face where there is uncertainty over whether the barred procedure is ever necessary to preserve a woman's health, given the availability of other abortion procedures considered to be safe alternatives.

---

[8] The prior majority, *sans* Justice O'Connor, all dissented, while the prior dissenters, with Chief Justice Rehnquist replaced by Chief Justice Roberts and Justice O'Connor replaced by Justice Alito, formed the majority.

The dissent was authored by Justice Ginsburg. She viewed *Roe v. Wade* as focusing "in considerable measure" on vindicating the right of a physician to administer medical treatment in accordance with his professional judgment, *id.* at 1641 n.2, while *Casey* "described more precisely" the "centrality of the decision whether to bear a child to a woman's dignity and autonomy, her personhood and destiny, and her conception of her place in society." *Id.* (quotations and citations omitted). Ginsburg continued:

> As *Casey* comprehended, at stake in cases challenging abortion restrictions is a woman's "control over her [own] destiny." 505 U.S., at 869. "There was a time, not so long ago," when women were "regarded as the center of home and family life, with attendant special responsibilities that precluded full and independent legal status under the Constitution." *Id.*, at 896-897. Those views, this Court made clear in *Casey*, "are no longer consistent with our understanding of the family, the individual, or the Constitution." 505 U.S., at 897. Women, it is now acknowledged, have the talent, capacity, and right "to participate equally in the economic and social life of the Nation." *Id.*, at 856. Their ability to realize their full potential, the Court recognized, is intimately connected to "their ability to control their reproductive lives." *Ibid.* Thus, legal challenges to undue restrictions on abortion procedures do not seek to vindicate some generalized notion of privacy; rather, they center on a woman's autonomy to determine her life's course, and thus to enjoy equal citizenship stature. See, *e.g.*, Siegel, Reasoning from the Body: A Historical Perspective on Abortion Regulation and Questions of Equal Protection, 44 Stan. L. Rev. 261 (1992); Law, Rethinking Sex and the Constitution, 132 U. Pa. L. Rev. 955, 1002–1028 (1984).

She criticized the majority's emphasis on "moral concerns" that "could yield prohibitions on any abortion." She added:

> Revealing in this regard, the Court invokes an antiabortion shibboleth for which it concededly has no reliable evidence: Women who have abortions come to regret their choices, and consequently suffer from "severe depression and loss of esteem." Because of women's fragile emotional state and because of the "bond of love the mother has for her child," the Court worries, doctors may withhold information about the nature of the [prohibited] procedure. The solution the Court approves, then, is *not* to require doctors to inform women, accurately and adequately, of the different procedures and their attendant risks. Instead, the Court deprives women of the right to make an autonomous choice, even at the expense of their safety.

> This way of thinking reflects ancient notions about women's place in the family and under the Constitution — ideas that have long since been discredited.

Taking note of the changed precedent, she concluded, at 1652–53:

> Though today's opinion does not go so far as to discard *Roe* or *Casey*, the Court, differently composed than it was when we last considered a restrictive abortion regulation, is hardly faithful to our earlier invocations

of "the rule of law" and the "principles of *stare decisis*." Congress imposed a ban despite our clear prior holdings that the State cannot proscribe an abortion procedure when its use is necessary to protect a woman's health. Although Congress' findings could not withstand the crucible of trial, the Court defers to the legislative override of our Constitution-based rulings. A decision so at odds with our jurisprudence should not have staying power.

LAWRENCE v. TEXAS
SUPREME COURT OF THE UNITED STATES
539 U.S. 558 (2003)

KENNEDY, J:

Liberty protects the person from unwarranted government intrusions into a dwelling or other private places. In our tradition the State is not omnipresent in the home. And there are other spheres of our lives and existence, outside the home, where the State should not be a dominant presence. Freedom extends beyond spatial bounds. Liberty presumes an autonomy of self that includes freedom of thought, belief, expression, and certain intimate conduct. The instant case involves liberty of the person both in its spatial and more transcendent dimensions.

I

The question before the Court is the validity of a Texas statute making it a crime for two persons of the same sex to engage in certain intimate sexual conduct. [The appellant was convicted of a misdemeanor for engaging in anal sex with another man. These offenses are rarely prosecuted; the arrest occurred because police entered their apartment because of a reported weapons disturbance. The petitioners were adults at the time of the alleged offense. Their conduct was in private and consensual.]

II

We conclude the case should be resolved by determining whether the petitioners were free as adults to engage in the private conduct in the exercise of their liberty under the Due Process Clause of the Fourteenth Amendment to the Constitution. For this inquiry we deem it necessary to reconsider the Court's holding in *Bowers*[*v. Hardwick*, 478 U.S. 186 (1986) where a 5-4 majority rejected a constitutional change to a similar Georgia statute.].

. . . .

The Court began its substantive discussion in *Bowers* as follows: "The issue presented is whether the Federal Constitution confers a fundamental right upon homosexuals to engage in sodomy and hence invalidates the laws of the many States that still make such conduct illegal and have done so for a very long time." *Id.*, at 190. That statement, we now conclude, discloses the Court's own failure to appreciate the extent of the liberty at stake. To say that the issue in *Bowers* was simply the right to engage in certain sexual conduct demeans the claim the individual put forward, just as it would demean a married couple were it to be said marriage is simply about the right to have sexual intercourse. The laws involved in *Bowers* and here are, to be sure, statutes that purport to do no more than prohibit a particular sexual act. Their penalties and purposes, though, have more far-reaching consequences, touching upon the most private human conduct, sexual behavior, and in the most private of places, the home. The statutes do seek to control a personal relationship that, whether or not entitled to formal recognition in the law, is within the liberty of persons to choose without being punished as criminals.

This, as a general rule, should counsel against attempts by the State, or a court, to define the meaning of the relationship or to set its boundaries absent injury to a person or abuse of an institution the law protects. It suffices for us to acknowledge that adults may choose to enter upon this relationship in the confines of their homes and their own private lives and still retain their dignity as free persons. When sexuality finds overt expression in intimate conduct with another person, the conduct can be but one element in a personal bond that is more enduring. The liberty protected by the Constitution allows homosexual persons the right to make this choice.

[The court took issue with *Bowers* claim that proscriptions against homosexual sexual activities had "ancient roots," arguing instead that "there is no longstanding history in this country of laws directed at homosexual conduct as a distinct matter." Rather, traditionally sodomy was illegal regardless of the sex of those involved. Historically, the court suggested that the vast majority of sodomy prosecutions did not involve relations between consenting adults, which the Court understood to be motivated in part by strict evidentiary rules making it difficult to prove rape.]

[The majority observed that the "most relevance" should be given to "our laws and traditions in the past half century," which showed "an emerging awareness that liberty gives substantial protection to adult persons in deciding how to conduct their private lives in matters pertaining to sex." Kennedy, J., stated that "History and tradition are the starting point but not in all cases the ending point of the substantive due process inquiry." Thus, the majority took note of the decriminalization of consensual sexual relations in the 1955 Model Penal Code, the 1957 British parliamentary committee recommendation of similar action, taken by Parliament in 1967, a 1981 decision of the European Court of Human rights, the reduction since *Bowers* from 25 to 13 of anti-sodomy laws, and the strong pattern of non-enforcement in those remaining states, including Texas.]

[The majority relied upon an equal protection case, *Romer v. Evans*, 517 U.S. 620 (1996), where the Court struck down class-based legislation directed at homosexuals as a violation of the Equal Protection Clause. *Romer* concluded that the provision was "born of animosity toward the class of persons affected" and further that it had no rational relation to a legitimate governmental purpose. *Id.*, at 634.]

[The majority rejected an alternative argument to strike the statute down on equal protection grounds. Kennedy, J., reasoned that criminalizing conduct without regard to sexual orientation would continue as] an invitation to subject homosexual persons to discrimination both in the public and in the private spheres. The central holding of *Bowers* has been brought in question by this case, and it should be addressed. Its continuance as precedent demeans the lives of homosexual persons.

. . . .

[The Court then explained that *stare decisis* did not require adherence to *Bowers* because later events, including five state court decisions rejecting the reasoning on state constitutional grounds, and the lack of reliance on the precedent.]

The present case does not involve minors. It does not involve persons who might be injured or coerced or who are situated in relationships where consent might not easily be refused. It does not involve public conduct or prostitution. It does not involve whether the government must give formal recognition to any relationship that homosexual persons seek to enter. The case does involve two adults who, with full and mutual consent from each other, engaged in sexual practices common to a homosexual lifestyle. The petitioners are entitled to respect for their private lives. The State cannot demean their existence or control their destiny by making their private sexual conduct a crime. Their right to liberty under the Due Process Clause gives them the full right to engage in their conduct without intervention of the government. "It is a promise of the Constitution that there is a realm of personal liberty which the government may not enter." *Casey, supra,* at 847. The Texas statute furthers no legitimate state interest which can justify its intrusion into the personal and private life of the individual.

Had those who drew and ratified the Due Process Clauses of the Fifth Amendment or the Fourteenth Amendment known the components of liberty in its manifold possibilities, they might have been more specific. They did not presume to have this insight. They knew times can blind us to certain truths and later generations can see that laws once thought necessary and proper in fact serve only to oppress. As the Constitution endures, persons in every generation can invoke its principles in their own search for greater freedom.

The judgment of the Court of Appeals for the Texas Fourteenth District is reversed, and the case is remanded for further proceedings not inconsistent with this opinion.

JUSTICE O'CONNOR, concurring in the judgment.

[Justice O'Connor, who joined *Bowers*, declined to vote to overrule, concluding instead that the Texas statute unconstitutionally discriminated against same-sex couples in violation of the Equal Protection Clause. Equality is discussed in Chapter Four.]

JUSTICE SCALIA, with whom the CHIEF JUSTICE and JUSTICE THOMAS join, dissenting.

[The dissenters complained that the majority's decision was incoherent in refusing to finding that engaging in intimate homosexual relations was a fundamental right and then applying "an unheard-of form of rational-basis review that will have far-reaching implications beyond this case." First, Justice Scalia strongly criticized the majority's willingness to overrule *Bowers* in light of the plurality opinion in *Casey*, joined by Justice Kennedy, that refused to overrule *Roe v. Wade*. Second, the dissent argued that the restraints on liberty imposed by the sodomy law should be constitutionally analyzed in the same way as laws "prohibiting prostitu-tion, recreational use of heroin, and, for that matter, working more than 60 hours per week in a bakery. But there is no right to "liberty" under the Due Process Clause, though today's opinion repeatedly makes that claim." Rather, the Consti-tution "*expressly allows* States to deprive their citizens of "liberty," *so long as "due process of law" is provided.*"]

[The dissent found that the criminalization of sodomy by many states demon-strated that "that homosexual sodomy is not a right 'deeply rooted in our Nation's history and tradition.' " Scalia, J., rejected the argument that an "emerging awareness" of liberty's application to private consensual conduct does not establish a fundamental right and was factually false in light of the many states that continue to criminalize prostitution, adultery, obscenity, and adult incest. Moreover, the dissent noted that the Model Penal Code's rejection of criminalization of sodomy was rejected by most states. He continued:]

In any event, an "emerging awareness" is by definition not "deeply rooted in this Nation's history and traditions," as we have said "fundamental right" status requires. Constitutional entitlements do not spring into existence because some States choose to lessen or eliminate criminal sanctions on certain behavior. Much less do they spring into existence, as the Court seems to believe, because *foreign nations* decriminalize conduct. The *Bowers* majority opinion *never* relied on "values we share with a wider civilization," *ante*, at 156 L Ed 2d, at 524, but rather rejected the claimed right to sodomy on the ground that such a right was not " 'deeply rooted in *this Nation's* history and tradition.' " *** The Court's discussion of these foreign views (ignoring, of course, the many countries that have retained criminal prohibi-tions on sodomy) is therefore meaningless dicta. Dangerous dicta, however, since "this Court . . . should not impose foreign moods, fads, or fashions on Americans." *Foster* v. *Florida*, 537 U.S. 990, 537 U.S. 990, 154 L. Ed. 2d 359, 123 S. Ct. 470470 (2002) (Thomas, J., concurring in denial of certiorari).

IV

I turn now to the ground on which the Court squarely rests its holding: the contention that there is no rational basis for the law here under attack. This proposition is so out of accord with our jurisprudence — indeed, with the jurisprudence of *any* society we know — that it requires little discussion.

The Texas statute undeniably seeks to further the belief of its citizens that certain forms of sexual behavior are "immoral and unacceptable," *Bowers, supra*, at 196 — the same interest furthered by criminal laws against fornication, bigamy, adultery, adult incest, bestiality, and obscenity. *Bowers* held that this *was* a legitimate state interest. The Court today reaches the opposite conclusion. The Texas statute, it says, "furthers *no legitimate state interest* which can justify its intrusion into the personal and private life of the individual," *ante*, at 156 L Ed 2d, at 526 (emphasis added). The Court embraces instead Justice Stevens' declaration in his *Bowers* dissent, that "the fact that the governing majority in a State has traditionally viewed a particular practice as immoral is not a sufficient reason for upholding a law prohibiting the practice," *ante*, at 156 L Ed 2d, at 525. This effectively decrees the end of all morals legislation. If, as the Court asserts, the promotion of majoritarian sexual morality is not even a *legitimate* state interest, none of the above-mentioned laws can survive rational-basis review.

. . . .

Today's opinion is the product of a Court, which is the product of a law-profession culture, that has largely signed on to the so-called homosexual agenda, by which I mean the agenda promoted by some homosexual activists directed at eliminating the moral opprobrium that has traditionally attached to homosexual conduct. . . .

One of the most revealing statements in today's opinion is the Court's grim warning that the criminalization of homosexual conduct is "an invitation to subject homosexual persons to discrimination both in the public and in the private spheres." It is clear from this that the Court has taken sides in the culture war, departing from its role of assuring, as neutral observer, that the democratic rules of engagement are observed. Many Americans do not want persons who openly engage in homosexual conduct as partners in their business, as scoutmasters for their children, as teachers in their children's schools, or as boarders in their home. They view this as protecting themselves and their families from a lifestyle that they believe to be immoral and destructive. The Court views it as "discrimination" which it is the function of our judgments to deter. So imbued is the Court with the law profession's anti-anti-homosexual culture, that it is seemingly unaware that the attitudes of that culture are not obviously "mainstream"; that in most States what the Court calls "discrimination" against those who engage in homosexual acts is perfectly legal; that proposals to ban such "discrimination" under Title VII have repeatedly been rejected by Congress, that in some cases such "discrimination" is *mandated* by federal statute, see 10 U.S.C. § 654(b)(1) (mandating discharge from the armed forces of any service member who engages in or intends to engage in homosexual acts); and that in some cases such "discrimination" is a constitutional right, see *Boy Scouts of America* v. *Dale*, 530 U.S. 640 (2000).

JUSTICE THOMAS, dissenting, [omitted].

———————

Whatever one's views of the result in *Lawrence*, it seems difficult to quibble with Justice Scalia's claim that the majority was not really applying the highly deferential "rational basis" test of *Carolene Products*. Indeed, from a comparative perspective, it seems that Justice Kennedy's opinion resembles the "pith and substance" approach to Canadian federalism we studied in Chapter 1. Compare *Carolene Products* (refusing to consider whether banned "filled milk" was less safe than other dairy products) with *Margarine Reference* (ban on margarine manufacture cannot be justified on safety grounds so exceeds the legislature's criminal law power). Once the majority makes clear that animus against gay men and lesbians is not a legitimate interest, judges necessarily must determine the "real" purpose of a challenged statute. (A similar approach was used by an earlier court in *City of Cleburne* v. *Cleburne Living Ctr.*, 473 U.S. 432 (1985) (striking down ban on zoning barring housing for disabled)). It is too soon to tell whether this approach signals a slight but significant shift in deferential scrutiny, or is a *sui generis* transition stage toward active scrutiny of laws targeting same-sex couples. Two recent cases failed to provide a definitive word on marriage rights. In *United States v. Windsor*, 133 S. Ct. 2675 (2013), the Supreme Court struck down provisions of the federal Defense of Marriage Act that deprived federal benefits to a same-sex couples whose marriage was recognized under New York law. However, the Court's analysis emphasized federalism (state autonomy to recognize marriages) and equal protection (we discuss this issue below in Chapter 4). However, the Court did follow the approach of *City of Cleburne* and *Lawrence* in declaring that "no legitimate purpose overcomes the purpose and effect to disparage and to injure those whom the State, by its marriage laws, sought to protect in personhood and dignity." *Id.* at 2696. In *Hollingsworth v. Perry*, 133 S. Ct. 2652 (2013), discussed in Chapter 4, the Court refused to review an appellate court decision holding unconstitutional, on equal protection grounds, an initiative adopted by California voters that provided that marriage was solely between a man and a woman. The Court held that there was no case or controversy because the state government had refused to defend the provision.

2.3. CLOSE SCRUTINY OF DEPRIVATIONS OF LIBERTY AND SECURITY OF THE PERSON UNDER SECTION 7 OF THE CANADIAN CHARTER OF RIGHTS AND FREEDOMS

As noted by Professor Hogg (see Part I-D, above), among many others, the text of section 7 was written with a clear design to avoid the wholesale judicial invalidation of statutes infringing on liberty. The text was deliberately changed from that of the Fourteenth Amendment, by omitting property and adding "security of the person" and by changing "due process" to "principles of fundamental justice." Indeed, the legislative history shows that both the professional and ministerial drafters of s. 7, including former Prime Minister Jean Chretien, envisioned s. 7 as limited to ensuring procedural fairness, and providing no means for judicial protection for rights not otherwise enumerated in the Charter. A leading constitutional scholar (and later appellate judge), Walter Tarnopolsky, testified before the Special Joint Committee of the Senate and House of Commons on the Constitution of Canada that:

> [T]here is no doubt that the due process clause has come in academic circles to mean more and more the over-all penumbra of fairness in the administration of justice. However, our courts have not yet adopted that interpretation, and there remains a fear in many circles that any reference to a due process clause, even without reference to property in this clause, could reintroduce the substantive "due process" interpretation in the United States.

The principal drafter of the Charter, Mr. Barry Strayer, Q.C., the Assistant Deputy Minister, Public Law of the Department of Justice (and now a retired Federal Court judge) stated:

> Due process would certainly include the concept of procedural fairness that we think is covered by fundamental justice, but we think that "due process" would have the danger of going well beyond procedural fairness and to deal

with substantive fairness which raises the possibility of the courts second guessing Parliaments or legislatures on the policy of the law as opposed to the procedure by which rights are to be dealt with. That has been the experience at times in the United States in the interpretation of the term "due process."

In contrast, Strayer concluded that the phrase "fundamental justice" meant:

[T]he same thing as what is called procedural due process, that is the meaning of due process in relation to requiring fair procedure. However, it in our view does not cover the concept of what is called substantive due process, which would impose substantive requirements as to policy of the law in question.

This has been most clearly demonstrated in the United States in the area of property, but also in other areas such as the right to life. The term due process has been given the broader concept of meaning both the procedure and substance. Natural justice or fundamental justice in our view does not go beyond the procedural requirements of fairness.

Responding to a leading conservative MP, Minister of Justice Jean Chretien stated:

The point, Mr. Crombie, that it is important to understand the difference is that we pass legislation here on abortion, criminal code, and we pass legislation on capital punishment; Parliament has the authority to do that, and the court at this moment, because we do not have the due process of law written there, cannot go and see whether we made the right decision or the wrong decision in Parliament. If you write down the words, "due process of law" here, the advice I am receiving is the court could go behind our decision and say that their decision on abortion was not the right one, their decision on capital punishment was not the right one, and it is a danger, according to legal advice I am receiving, that it will very much limit the scope of the power of legislation by the Parliament and we do not want that; and it is why we do not want the words "due process of law." These are the two main examples that we should keep in mind. You can keep speculating on all the things that have never been touched, but these are two very sensitive areas that we have to cope with as legislators and my view is that Parliament has decided a certain law on abortion and a certain law on capital punishment, and it should prevail and we do not want the courts to say that the judgment of Parliament was wrong in using the constitution.[9]

The Supreme Court of Canada, however, has refused to read s. 7 so restrictively. In the *B.C. Motor Vehicle Reference*, [1985] 2 S.C.R. 486, the Court wrote:

[T]he simple fact remains that the Charter is not the product of a few individual public servants, however distinguished, but of a multiplicity of individuals who played major roles in the negotiating, drafting and adoption of the Charter. How can one say with any confidence that within this enormous multiplicity of actors, without forgetting the role of the

---

[9] The foregoing quotations are taken from the decision in *R. v. Morgentaler*, 22 D.L.R. (4th) 641 (O.C.A. 1985), which was reversed in the *Morgentaler II* case excerpted below.

provinces, the comments of a few federal civil servants can in any way be determinative?

Were this Court to accord any significant weight to this testimony, it would in effect be assuming a fact which is nearly impossible of proof, i.e., the intention of the legislative bodies which adopted the Charter. In view of the indeterminate nature of the data, it would in my view be erroneous to give these materials anything but minimal weight.

Another danger with casting the interpretation of s. 7 in terms of the comments made by those heard at the Special Joint Committee Proceedings is that, in so doing, the rights, freedoms and values embodied in the Charter in effect become frozen in time to the moment of adoption with little or no possibility of growth, development and adjustment to changing societal needs. Obviously, in the present case, given the proximity in time of the Charter debates, such a problem is relatively minor, even though it must be noted that even at this early stage in the life of the Charter, a host of issues and questions have been raised which were largely unforeseen at the time of such proceedings. If the newly planted "living tree" which is the Charter is to have the possibility of growth and adjustment over time, care must be taken to ensure that historical materials, *** do not stunt its growth. ***

Accordingly, the Court crafted a broader scope for s. 7. Sections 8 to 14 of the Charter (primarily providing protections for the accused) are "illustrative of the meaning, in criminal or penal law, of 'principles of fundamental justice'; they represent principles which have been recognized by the common law, the international conventions and by the very fact of entrenchment in the Charter, as essential elements of a system for the administration of justice which is founded upon the belief in the dignity and worth of the human person and the rule of law." Although "many of the principles of fundamental justice are procedural in nature," (here, the Court quotes American Justice Felix Frankfurter's observation in *McNabb v. United States*, 318 U.S. 332, 347 (1943) that "the history of liberty has largely been the history of observance of procedural safeguards"), this

[I]s not to say, however, that the principles of fundamental justice are limited solely to procedural guarantees. Rather, the proper approach to the determination of the principles of fundamental justice is quite simply one in which, as Professor L. Tremblay has written, "future growth will be based on historical roots" (*Section 7 of the Charter: Substantive Due Process?*, 18 U. B.C. L. Rev. 201 (1984)).

Whether any given principle may be said to be a principle of fundamental justice within the meaning of s. 7 will rest upon an analysis of the nature, sources, rationale and essential role of that principle within the judicial process and in our legal system, as it evolves.

Consequently, those words cannot be given any exhaustive content or simple enumerative definition, but will take on concrete meaning as the courts address alleged violations of s. 7.

MORGENTALER v. THE QUEEN (*"Morgentaler II"*)
SUPREME COURT OF CANADA
1 S.C.R. 30 (1988)

DICKSON C.J.C. [Lamer J concurred with Dickson CJC's opinion]:

The principal issue raised by this appeal is whether the abortion provisions of the *Criminal Code* infringe the "right to life, liberty and security of the person and the right not to be deprived thereof except in accordance with the principles of fundamental justice" as formulated in s. 7 of the *Canadian Charter of Rights and Freedoms.* ***

* * *

[The challenged statute provided for life imprisonment for anyone to intentionally cause an abortion, and for two years imprisonment for a woman to intentionally obtain an abortion. However, the proscription did not apply to any doctor or patient if permission for an abortion was first obtained from a hospital committee who determined that a continued pregnancy would endanger the woman's life or health. The case, like *Morgentaler I*, arose from the decision of the Court of Appeal allowing the Crown's appeal from a jury verdict of acquittal.]

IV

SECTION 7 OF THE *CHARTER*

[Initially, Dickson, C.J.C., explained why "it is neither necessary nor wise in this appeal" to ground it in liberty in the manner of *Roe v. Wade.*] I do not think it would be appropriate to attempt an all-encompassing explication of so important a provision as s. 7 so early in the history of *Charter* interpretation. The court should be presented with a wide variety of claims and factual situations before articulating the full range of s. 7 rights. I will therefore limit my comments to some interpretive principles already set down by the court and to an analysis of only two aspects of s. 7, the right to "security of the person" and "the principles of fundamental justice."

* * *

B. *Security of the person*

The law has long recognized that the human body ought to be protected from interference by others. At common law, for example, any medical procedure carried out on a person without that person's consent is an assault. Only in emergency circumstances does the law allow others to make decisions of this nature. Similarly, art. 19 of the Civil Code of Lower Canada [*i.e.* the civil law in Quebec] provides that "[t]he human person is inviolable" and that "[n]o person may cause harm to the person of another without his consent or without being authorized by law to do so." ***

* * *

The case-law leads me to the conclusion that state interference with bodily integrity and serious state-imposed psychological stress, at least in the criminal law context, constitute a breach of security of the person. It is not necessary in this case to determine whether the right extends further, to protect either interests central to personal autonomy, such as a right to privacy, or interests unrelated to criminal justice. ***

At the most basic, physical and emotional level, every pregnant woman is told by the section that she cannot submit to a generally safe medical procedure that might be of clear benefit to her unless she meets criteria entirely unrelated to her own priorities and aspirations. Not only does the removal of decision making power threaten women in a physical sense; the indecision of knowing whether an abortion will be granted inflicts emotional stress. Section 251 clearly interferes with a woman's bodily integrity in both a physical and emotional sense. ***

Although this interference with physical and emotional integrity is sufficient in itself to trigger a review of s. 251 against the principles of fundamental justice, the operation of the decision-making mechanism set out in s. 251 creates additional glaring breaches of security of the person. The evidence indicates that s. 251 causes a certain amount of delay for women who are successful in meeting its criteria. In the context of abortion, any unnecessary delay can have profound consequences on the woman's physical and emotional well-being.

*　　*　　*

C. *The principles of fundamental justice*

*　　*　　*

[The opinion focused on the complex procedures the statute required to secure approval from a "therapeutic abortion committee" of an "accredited or approved hospital." The opinion detailed the difficulty with these procedures, including the lack of four physicians in almost 1/4 of all Canadian hospitals, accrediting requirements precluding over 1/3 of hospitals from performing the procedure, that only 1/5 of hospitals had actually set up the required committee, etc. In addition, the lack of a consistent standard for whether an abortion would harm the woman's health led to widely differing approaches by hospital committees.]

The combined effect of all of these problems with the procedure stipulated in s. 251 for access to therapeutic abortions is a failure to comply with the principles of fundamental justice. In *Reference re s. 94(2) of Motor Vehicle Act*, Lamer J. held, that "the principles of fundamental justice are to be found in the basic tenets of our legal system." One of the basic tenets of our system of criminal justice is that when Parliament creates a defence to a criminal charge, the defence should not be illusory or so difficult to attain as to be practically illusory. The criminal law is a very special form of governmental regulation, for it seeks to express our society's collective disapprobation of certain acts and omissions. When a defence is provided, especially a specifically-tailored defence to a particular charge, it is because the legislator has determined that the disapprobation of society is not warranted when the conditions of the defence are met.

* * *

. . . In the present case, the structure — the system regulating access to therapeutic abortions — is manifestly unfair. It contains so many potential barriers to its own operation that the defence it creates will in many circumstances be practically unavailable to women who would prima facie qualify for the defence, or at least would force such women to travel great distances at substantial expense and inconvenience in order to benefit from a defence that is held out to be generally available.

* * *

V

[Chief Justice Dickson proceeded to consider whether the breach of fundamental justice was nonetheless a "reasonable limit" under section 1, by applying the *Oakes* test set forth in Part I-C of these teaching materials. He read s. 251 as expressing Parliament's intent that foetal interests are not to be protected where the "life or health" of the woman is threatened. At the same time, he agreed that protection of foetal interests was a valid objective, and thus balancing these goals was sufficiently important to meet the first prong of the *Oakes* test.]

I am equally convinced, however, that the means chosen to advance the legislative objectives of s. 251 do not satisfy any of the three elements of the proportionality component of *R. v. Oakes*. [Because "the procedures and administrative structures created by s. 251 are often arbitrary and unfair," he concluded that] many women whom Parliament professes not to wish to subject to criminal liability will nevertheless be forced by the practical unavailability of the supposed defence to risk liability or to suffer other harm such as a traumatic late abortion caused by the delay inherent in the s. 251 system. Finally, the effects of the limitation upon the s. 7 rights of many pregnant women are out of proportion to the objective sought to be achieved. Indeed, to the extent that s. 251(4) is designed to protect the life and health of women, the procedures it establishes may actually defeat that objective. The administrative structures of s. 251(4) are so cumbersome that women whose health is endangered by pregnancy may not be able to gain a therapeutic abortion, at least without great trauma, expense and inconvenience.

* * *

BEETZ J. [with whose opinion ESTEY, J., concurred, agreed with DICKSON, C.J.C. that the statute was invalid].

I find it convenient to outline at the outset the steps which lead me to this result:

I — Before the advent of the *Charter*, Parliament recognized, in adopting s. 251(4) of the *Criminal Code*, that the interest in the life or health of the pregnant woman takes precedence over the interest in prohibiting abortions, including the interest of the state in the protection of the foetus, when "the continuation of the pregnancy of such female person would or would be likely to endanger her life or health." In my view, this standard in s. 251(4) became entrenched at least as a minimum when the "right to life, liberty and security of the person" was enshrined in the *Canadian Charter of Rights and Freedoms* at s. 7.

II — "Security of the person" within the meaning of s. 7 of the *Charter* must include a right of access to medical treatment for a condition representing a danger to life or health without fear of criminal sanction. If an Act of Parliament forces a pregnant woman whose life or health is in danger to choose between, on the one hand, the commission of a crime to obtain effective and timely medical treatment and, on the other hand, inadequate treatment or no treatment at all, her right to security of the person has been violated.

III — According to the evidence, the procedural requirements of s. 251 of the *Criminal Code* significantly delay pregnant women's access to medical treatment resulting in an additional danger to their health, thereby depriving them of their right to security of the person.

IV — The deprivation referred to in the preceding proposition does not accord with the principles of fundamental justice. [Beetz, J., found that legitimate procedures to assure a "reliable, independent and medically sound opinion" as to the "life or health" of the pregnant woman in order to protect the state interest in the foetus, and while any such statutory mechanism will inevitably result in some delay, the specific procedural requirements of s. 251 of the *Criminal Code* were "manifestly unfair," because they were "unnecessary in respect of Parliament's objectives" and "result in additional risks to the health of pregnant women."]

V — The primary objective of s. 251 of the *Criminal Code* is the protection of the foetus. The protection of the life and health of the pregnant woman is an ancillary objective. The primary objective does relate to concerns which are pressing and substantial in a free and democratic society and which, pursuant to s. 1 of the *Charter*, justify reasonable limits to be put on a woman's right. However, rules unnecessary in respect of the primary and ancillary objectives which they are designed to serve, such as some of the rules contained in s. 251, cannot be said to be rationally connected to these objectives under s. 1 of the *Charter*. Consequently, s. 251 does not constitute a reasonable limit to the security of the person. [However, he concluded that a properly structured and narrowly tailored requirement that a hospital committee determine that a medical standard based on danger to a woman's life or health be met, before an abortion would be non-criminal, would not offend the principles of fundamental justice.]

*   *   *

V — Section 1 of the *Charter*

[Justice Beetz's application of the *Oakes* test differed from Chief Justice Dickson's in finding that the Parliamentary objective was not a balancing of foetal interests with those of pregnant women but rather protecting the foetus. He found such an interest to be sufficiently pressing and substantial to justify a proportionate limit on *Charter* rights. However, he found that the variety of limits and delays set forth in the statute were not even rationally related to a goal of foetal protection, and thus the statute could not be justified under s. 1.]

*   *   *

McIntyre J. (dissenting) [LaForest, J., concurred with McIntyre]: — ***

Section 251 of the *Criminal Code*

[The opinion notes that many Canadians find s. 251 to be unacceptable, either as overly restrictive of the right of women to control their own bodies or an inadequate protection for the inherent right to life of the unborn child. It quotes opinion polls showing about 20% of Canadians adopting each view with about 60% of Canadians favouring prohibition in some circumstances.]***

*   *   *

Scope of judicial review under the *Charter*

[Justice McIntyre quoted at length from American dissents by Justice Holmes and more recent majority opinions, such as *Ferguson v. Skrupa, supra,* of the dangers of the use of due process to strike down legislation.]

Holmes J. wrote in 1927, but his words have retained their force in American jurisprudence. In my view, although written in the American context, the principle stated is equally applicable in Canada.

It is essential that this principle be maintained in a constitutional democracy. The court must not resolve an issue such as that of abortion on the basis of how many judges may favour "pro-choice" or "pro-life." To do so would be contrary to sound principle and the rule of law affirmed in the preamble to the *Charter* which must mean that no discretion, including a judicial discretion, can be unlimited. But there is a problem, for the court must clothe the general expression of rights and freedoms contained in the *Charter* with real substance and vitality. How can the courts go about this task without imposing at least some of their views and predilections upon the law? This question has been the subject of much discussion and comment. Many theories have been postulated but few have had direct reference to the problem in the Canadian context. In my view, this court has offered guidance in this matter. In [several cases], it has enjoined what has been termed a "purposive approach" in applying the *Charter* and its provisions. I take this to mean that the courts should interpret the *Charter* in a manner calculated to give effect to its provisions, not to the idiosyncratic view of the judge who is writing. This approach marks out the limits of appropriate *Charter* adjudication. It confines the content of *Charter* guaranteed rights and freedoms to the purposes given expression in the *Charter*. Consequently, while the courts must continue to give a fair, large and liberal construction to the *Charter* provisions, this approach prevents the court from abandoning its traditional adjudicatory function in order to formulate its own conclusions on questions of public policy, a step which this court has said on numerous occasions it must not take. That *Charter* interpretation is to be purposive necessarily implies the converse: it is not to be "non-purposive." A court is not entitled to define a right in a manner unrelated to the interest which the right in question was meant to protect.***

*   *   *

The right to abortion and s. 7 of the *Charter*

[Here, McIntyre, J. notes his disagreement with the opinions of Dickson, C.J.C. and Wilson J that s. 7 confers a right to an abortion. In particular, he disagreed with the claim that laws that interfere with individual priorities and aspirations implicate s. 7 protections, because almost all laws do so. In his view, "For the appellants to succeed here, then, they must show more than an interference with priorities and aspirations; they must show the infringement of a right which is included in the concept of security of the person."]

The proposition that women enjoy a constitutional right to have an abortion is devoid of support in the language of s. 7 of the *Charter* or any other section. *** Furthermore, it would appear that the history of the constitutional text of the *Charter* affords no support for the appellants' proposition. [Here, the dissent refers to the legislative history set forth in the materials, above.]

It cannot be said that the history, traditions and underlying philosophies of our society would support the proposition that a right to abortion could be implied in the *Charter*. ***

*   *   *

Procedural fairness

*   *   *

. . . I would suggest it is apparent that the court's role is not to second-guess Parliament's policy choice as to how broad or how narrow the defence should be. The determination of when "the disapprobation of society is not warranted" is in Parliament's hands. The court's role when the enactment is attacked on the basis that the defence is illusory is to determine whether the defence is available in the circumstances in which it was intended to apply. Parliament has set out the conditions, in s. 251(4), under which a therapeutic abortion may be obtained, free from criminal sanction. It is patent on the face of the legislation that the defence is circumscribed and narrow. It is clear that this was the Parliamentary intent and it was expressed with precision. I am not able to accept the contention that the defence has been held out to be generally available. It is, on the contrary, carefully tailored and limited to special circumstances. Therapeutic abortions may be performed only in certain hospitals and in accordance with certain specified provisions. It could only be classed as illusory or practically so if it could be found that it does not provide lawful access to abortions in circumstances described in the section. No such finding should be made upon the material before this court. The evidence will not support the proposition that significant numbers of those who meet the conditions imposed in s. 251 of the *Criminal Code* are denied abortions.

*   *   *

Wilson J.: — ***

With all due respect, I think that the court must tackle the primary issue first. A consideration as to whether or not the procedural requirements for obtaining or performing an abortion comport with fundamental justice is purely academic if such requirements cannot as a constitutional matter be imposed at all. If a pregnant woman cannot, as a constitutional matter, be compelled by law to carry the foetus to term against her will, a review of the procedural requirements by which she may be compelled to do so seems pointless. Moreover, it would, in my opinion, be an exercise in futility for the legislature to expend its time and energy in attempting to remedy the defects in the procedural requirements unless it has some assurance that this process will, at the end of the day, result in the creation of a valid criminal offence. I turn, therefore, to what I believe is the central issue that must be addressed.

1. The right of access to abortion

*   *   *

(a) The right to liberty

The *Charter* and the right to individual liberty guaranteed under it are inextricably tied to the concept of human dignity. [She cited the work of University of Edinburgh Professor Neil MacCormick, *Legal Right and Social Democracy: Essays in Legal and Political Philosophy*, defining liberty as "a condition of human self-respect and of that contentment which resides in the ability to pursue one's own conception of a full and rewarding life." She also quoted from an earlier dissent she had written embracing philosopher John Stuart Mill's principle that individuals should be able to pursue their own good in their own way as long as they do not deprive others of their own ability to do so.]

[Justice Wilson then embraced American substantive due process jurisprudence.]

The question then becomes whether the decision of a woman to terminate her pregnancy falls within this class of protected decisions. I have no doubt that it does. This decision is one that will have profound psychological, economic and social consequences for the pregnant woman. The circumstances giving rise to it can be complex and varied and there may be, and usually are, powerful considerations militating in opposite directions. It is a decision that deeply reflects the way the woman thinks about herself and her relationship to others and to society at large. It is not just a medical decision; it is a profound social and ethical one as well. Her response to it will be the response of the whole person.

It is probably impossible for a man to respond, even imaginatively, to such a dilemma not just because it is outside the realm of his personal experience (although this is, of course, the case) but because he can relate to it only by objectifying it, thereby eliminating the subjective elements of the female psyche which are at the heart of the dilemma. As Noreen Burrows, Lecturer in European Law, University of Glasgow, has pointed out in her essay on *International Law and Human Rights: the Case of Women's Rights*, 81-2 *in* HUMAN RIGHTS: FROM RHETORIC TO REALITY, the history of the struggle for human rights from the 18th century on has been the history of men struggling to assert their dignity and common humanity against an overbearing state apparatus. The more recent struggle for women's rights has been a struggle to eliminate discrimination, to achieve a place for women in a man's world, to develop a set of legislative reforms in order to place women in the same position as men. It has not been a struggle to define the rights of women in relation to their special place in the societal structure and in relation to the biological distinction between the two sexes. Thus, women's needs and aspirations are only now being translated into protected rights. The right to reproduce or not to reproduce which is in issue in this case is one such right and is properly perceived as an integral part of modern woman's struggle to assert her dignity and worth as a human being.

*　　*　　*

[Wilson J next suggested that the deprivation of rights in this case offends s. 2(a) of the Charter, because the decision to terminate a pregnancy is essentially a moral decision and freedom of conscience is guaranteed by s. 2(a). Finally, agreeing with Crown counsel that the state's interests in imposing reasonable limits increased in light of the developing foetus, Wilson J adopted the trimester framework from *Roe v. Wade* as the appropriate test for when reasonable limits could be imposed under s. 1.]

Two other important decisions further developing s. 7 jurisprudence warrant specific mention in these comparative materials. In *Rodriguez v. British Columbia (Attorney General)*, [1993] 3 S.C.R. 519, the Court rejected a challenge to Canada's criminalization of assisting suicides in a case brought by a terminally-ill woman with ALS (Lou Gehrig's Disease). Although the 5-4 majority found that the statute affected her right to security of the person under s. 7, Justice Sopinka concluded that the statute did not do so in a manner that violation principles of fundamental justice. He wrote:

> The principles of fundamental justice cannot be created for the occasion to reflect the court's dislike or distaste of a particular statute. While the principles of fundamental justice are concerned with more than process, reference must be made to principles which are "fundamental" in the sense that they would have general acceptance among reasonable people. From the review that I have conducted above, I am unable to discern anything approaching unanimity with respect to the issue before us. Regardless of one's personal views as to whether the distinctions drawn between withdrawal of treatment and palliative care, on the one hand, and assisted suicide on the other are practically compelling, the fact remains that these distinctions are maintained and can be persuasively defended. To the extent that there is a consensus, it is that human life must be respected and we must be careful not to undermine the institutions that protect it.

Id. at 607–08. In reaching this conclusion, the majority relied upon, *inter alia*, societal rejection of capital punishment, opposition to decriminalizing suicide by major medical associations, and most importantly by the continuing widespread prohibition on suicide throughout the world.

Suresh v. Canada (Minister of Citizenship and Immigration), [2002] 1 S.C.R. 3, concerned the deportation to Sri Lanka of an alleged member of the Tamil Tigers.

The government claimed that Suresh was a threat to Canada and a member of a terrorist organization. Suresh sought refugee status on the ground that he would be tortured by the Sri Lankan government, with whom the Tamil Tigers have been waging a civil war for over two decades. The Court rejected the deportation order on procedural grounds, but upheld the constitutionality of the statutory framework permitting the Minister to deport dangerous aliens even in circumstances where torture was foreseeable:

> Determining whether deportation to torture violates the principles of fundamental justice requires us to balance Canada's interest in combatting terrorism and the Convention refugee's interest in not being deported to torture. Canada has a legitimate and compelling interest in combatting terrorism. But it is also committed to fundamental justice. The notion of proportionality is fundamental to our constitutional system. Thus we must ask whether the government's proposed response is reasonable in relation to the threat. In the past, we have held that some responses are so extreme that they are per se disproportionate to any legitimate government interest. We must ask whether deporting a refugee to torture would be such a response.

2.4. DEFINING THE SCOPE OF BROADLY WORDED PROVISIONS OF THE SOUTH AFRICAN CONSTITUTION AND BILL OF RIGHTS

Deciding what rights are worthy of active judicial protection would seem to be a less complicated task in a constitutional order that includes a highly developed and specific bill of rights, as is the case in Chapter 2 of South Africa's 1996 Constitution. As a more recent post-cold war process, the constitution-makers were fully aware of both comparative constitutional experiences and the history of post-World War II human rights struggles, to which the struggle against apartheid was integral. Given this history Chapter 2 includes a more specific cataloging of rights as well as the embrace of a wider range of rights than the other jurisdictions we cover in this course. Furthermore, Section 7 describes the bill of rights as "a cornerstone of democracy in South Africa" and tasks the state with the duty to "respect, protect, promote and fulfill the rights in the Bill of Rights." At the same time however Section 7(3) states that the rights in the bill of rights are "subject to the limitations contained or referred to in section 36, or elsewhere in the Bill."

While the bill of rights contains a detailed list of specific rights, it is in the realm of limitations on those rights as well as the broader structural features of the Constitution that provide the conditions for deciding the scope of active judicial protection. The scope of judicial protection of constitutional rights in South Africa is thus defined by a number of issues, including: the two-step analysis of rights violations adopted from Canadian jurisprudence and then explicitly included by South Africa's constitution-makers in Section 36 of the 1996 Constitution; the place of the foundational principles contained in Section 1 of the Constitution; and, debates over the role of the constitutional principles contained in the "interim" 1993 Constitution and subsequent references to the basic structure doctrine. Constitutional recognition of the fact that rights are not absolute and that their application often involves conflicts between different rights as well as tensions with necessary public policies, places the "limitation" of rights at the center of the constitutional adjudication of rights.

While not strictly a problem of an "unenumerated" right, the Constitutional Court was faced in its first major case in 1995 with an issue, the death penalty, which the constitution-makers had failed to resolve even though it had been part of the negotiations in the democratic transition. With no explicit statement on the death penalty, the Constitutional Court was left to decide on its constitutionality based on the inclusions in the 1993 and 1996 constitutions of both a right to life as well as prohibitions on cruel, inhuman, and degrading punishment. Central to the Constitutional Courts task in addressing the question of the death penalty would be the question of the justifiable limitation of these specific, enumerated rights.

At the beginning of South Africa's democratic transition in 1990 there were over 400 individuals awaiting execution on death row, including a number of individuals who had been sentenced to death for their part in resisting apartheid. The first major case to be decided by the newly established Constitutional Court in 1995 was *S v Makwanyane* which held the death penalty unconstitutional.(Note: this case was decided under the 1993 Interim Constitution.)

S v. MAKWANYANE
CONSTITUTIONAL COURT OF SOUTH AFRICA
1995 (3) SA 391

CHASKALSON P:

[1] The two accused in this matter were convicted in the Witwatersrand Local Division of the Supreme Court on four counts of murder, one count of attempted murder and one count of robbery with aggravating circumstances. They were sentenced to death on each of the counts of murder and to long terms of imprisonment on the other counts.

. . . .

[5] It would no doubt have been better if the framers of the Constitution had stated specifically, either that the death sentence is not a competent penalty, or that it is permissible in circumstances sanctioned by law. This, however, was not done and it has been left to this Court to decide whether the penalty is consistent with the provisions of the Constitution . . .

. . . .

[26] Death is the most extreme form of punishment to which a convicted criminal can be subjected. Its execution is final and irrevocable. It puts an end not only to the right to life itself, but to all other personal rights which had vested in the deceased under Chapter Three of the Constitution. It leaves nothing except the memory in others of what has been and the property that passes to the deceased's heirs. In the ordinary meaning of the words, the death sentence is undoubtedly a cruel punishment. Once sentenced, the prisoner waits on death row in the company of other prisoners under sentence of death, for the processes of their appeals and the

procedures for clemency to be carried out. Throughout this period, those who remain on death row are uncertain of their fate, not knowing whether they will ultimately be reprieved or taken to the gallows. Death is a cruel penalty and the legal processes which necessarily involve waiting in uncertainty for the sentence to be set aside or carried out, add to the cruelty. It is also an inhuman punishment for it

". . . involves, by its very nature, a denial of the executed person's humanity," and it is degrading because it strips the convicted person of all dignity and treats him or her as an object to be eliminated by the state. The question is not, however, whether the death sentence is a cruel, inhuman or degrading punishment in the ordinary meaning of these words but whether it is a cruel, inhuman or degrading punishment within the meaning of section 11(2) of our Constitution . . . .

. . . .

[95] The carrying out of the death sentence destroys life, which is protected without reservation under section 9 of our Constitution, it annihilates human dignity which is protected under section 10, elements of arbitrariness are present in its enforcement and it is irremediable. Taking these factors into account, as well as the assumption that I have made in regard to public opinion in South Africa, and giving the words of section 11(2) the broader meaning to which they are entitled at this stage of the enquiry, rather than a narrow meaning, I am satisfied that in the context of our Constitution the death penalty is indeed a cruel, inhuman and degrading punishment.

[96] The question that now has to be considered is whether the imposition of such punishment is nonetheless justifiable as a penalty for murder in the circumstances contemplated by sections 277(1)(a), 316A and 322(2A) of the Criminal Procedure Act.

. . . .

[100] Our Constitution deals with the limitation of rights through a general limitations clause. As was pointed out by Kentridge AJ in Zuma's case, this calls for a "two-stage" approach, in which a broad rather than a narrow interpretation is given to the fundamental rights enshrined in Chapter Three, and limitations have to be justified through the application of section 33. In this it differs from the Constitution of the United States, which does not contain a limitation clause, as a result of which courts in that country have been obliged to find limits to constitutional rights through a narrow interpretation of the rights themselves. Although the "two-stage" approach may often produce the same result as the "one-stage" approach, this will not always be the case.

. . . .

[103] The criteria prescribed by section 33(1) for any limitation of the rights contained in section 11(2) are that the limitation must be justifiable in an open and democratic society based on freedom and equality, it must be both reasonable and necessary and it must not negate the essential content of the right.

[104] The limitation of constitutional rights for a purpose that is reasonable and necessary in a democratic society involves the weighing up of competing values, and

ultimately an assessment based on proportionality. This is implicit in the provisions of section 33(1). The fact that different rights have different implications for democracy, and in the case of our Constitution, for "an open and democratic society based on freedom and equality," means that there is no absolute standard which can be laid down for determining reasonableness and necessity. Principles can be established, but the application of those principles to particular circumstances can only be done on a case by case basis. This is inherent in the requirement of proportionality, which calls for the balancing of different interests. In the balancing process, the relevant considerations will include the nature of the right that is limited, and its importance to an open and democratic society based on freedom and equality; the purpose for which the right is limited and the importance of that purpose to such a society; the extent of the limitation, its efficacy, and particularly where the limitation has to be necessary, whether the desired ends could reasonably be achieved through other means less damaging to the right in question. In the process regard must be had to the provisions of section 33(1), and the underlying values of the Constitution, bearing in mind that, as a Canadian Judge has said, "the role of the Court is not to second-guess the wisdom of policy choices made by legislators.

. . . .

[144] The rights to life and dignity are the most important of all human rights, and the source of all other personal rights in Chapter Three. By committing ourselves to a society founded on the recognition of human rights we are required to value these two rights above all others. And this must be demonstrated by the State in everything that it does, including the way it punishes criminals. This is not achieved by objectifying murderers and putting them to death to serve as an example to others in the expectation that they might possibly be deterred thereby.

[145] In the balancing process the principal factors that have to be weighed are on the one hand the destruction of life and dignity that is a consequence of the implementation of the death sentence, the elements of arbitrariness and the possibility of error in the enforcement of capital punishment, and the existence of a severe alternative punishment (life imprisonment) and, on the other, the claim that the death sentence is a greater deterrent to murder, and will more effectively prevent its commission, than would a sentence of life imprisonment, and that there is a public demand for retributive justice to be imposed on murderers, which only the death sentence can meet.

[146] Retribution cannot be accorded the same weight under our Constitution as the rights to life and dignity, which are the most important of all the rights in Chapter Three. It has not been shown that the death sentence would be materially more effective to deter or prevent murder than the alternative sentence of life imprisonment would be. Taking these factors into account, as well as the elements of arbitrariness and the possibility of error in enforcing the death penalty, the clear and convincing case that is required to justify the death sentence as a penalty for murder, has not been made out. The requirements of section 33(1) have accordingly not been satisfied, and it follows that the provisions of section 277(1)(a) of the Criminal Procedure Act, 1977 must be held to be inconsistent with section 11(2) of the Constitution.

The *Makwanyane* case is excerpted because it illustrates the SACC's approach to interpreting individual rights guaranteed by the South African Constitution. For comparative purposes, however, we note the approach of the other highest courts to the constitutionality of the death penalty:

- In *Furman v. Georgia*, 408 U.S. 238 (1972), the U.S. Supreme Court found that the death penalty was generally administered in an arbitrary and random manner and was therefore "cruel and unusual punishment" precluded by the Eighth and Fourteenth Amendments. Over 35 states responded by re-enacting death penalty provisions designed to meet the Court's concerns, and *Gregg v. Georgia*, 428 U.S. 153 (1976), upheld Georgia's response as constitutional. Subsequently, the Court has held that the death penalty cannot be constitutionally imposed where the offender was a juvenile at the time of the offense, *Roper v. Simmons*, 543 U.S. 551 (2005) and for crimes other than intentional murder, *Kennedy v. Louisiana*, 554 U.S. 407 (2008).

- Because Canadian criminal law is federal, Parliament has sole power to impose a death penalty. Parliament abolished the death penalty for murder, treason, and piracy in 1976, and the remaining capital offenses (espionage, mutiny with violence, and war crimes) in 1998. Although the SCC has thus not had occasion to rule on the constitutionality of the death penalty per se, in *United States v. Burns*, [2001] 1 S.C.R. 283, it found that extradition to face the death penalty in the United States was not in accordance with principles of fundamental justice and thus was inconsistent with s. 7 of the Charter.

- Each Australian state legislatively abolished the death penalty during the 20th Century (the last execution took place in Victoria, in 1967). The Commonwealth abolished capital punishment for federal offenses in 1973, signed an international covenant committing Australia to the abolition of the death penalty in 1990, and in 2010 implemented the covenant by enacting legislation barring any state from re-imposing the death penalty.

Describing the Constitutional Court's analysis of the limitations clause as a balancing approach, the Court in *S v. Bhulwana* 1996 (1) SA 388 (CC), a case challenging the presumption, in an anti-drug trafficking statute, that an individual caught in possession of more than a specific amount of marijuana is guilty of the offence of dealing, rather than merely possession, stated that it:

> [18] . . . [P]laces the purpose, effects and importance of the infringing legislation on one side of the scales and the nature and effect of the infringement caused by the legislation on the other. The more substantial the inroad into fundamental rights, the more persuasive the grounds of justification must be.

Taking its lead from the Constitutional Court, the Constitutional Assembly modified the language of the limitations clause so that Section 36(1) now states:

> The rights in the Bill of Rights may be limited only in terms of a law of general application to the extent that the limitation is reasonable and

justifiable in an open and democratic society based on human dignity, equality and freedom, taking into account all the relevant factors, including:

(a) the nature of the right;

(b) the importance of the purpose of the limitation;

(c) the nature and extent of the limitation;

(d) the relation between the limitation and its purpose; and

(e) less restrictive means to achieve the purpose.

While the Constitutional Court's approach to the interpretation of the limitations clause of the 1993 Constitution, including the Court's concerns about the inclusion of language prohibiting violation of the "essential content of the right," shaped the direction taken by the Constitutional Assembly, the Constitutional Court is still challenged with determining the relationship between the values that must shape the scope of the limitation on rights, and the application of the specific factors contained in Section 36. Highlighting the difficulty of this task Denise Meyerson (in her book *Rights Limited: Freedom of Expression, Religion and the South African Constitution*, Juta 1997) concludes that "the limitations clause imposes an ideal of neutrality on the state's justifications for limiting a constitutionally protected right." Despite criticism that the two-stage approach is too crude or that the Constitutional Court's balancing approach lacks specificity (see Woolman, *Limitations, in* Woolman et al. 2d ed, 2006), the Constitutional Court has developed an approach based on proportionality that was well demonstrated by former Chief Justice Pius Langa in *De Reuck v. Director of Public Prosecutions*, a case in which a conviction under a new child pornography statute was challenged on the grounds that the statute violated the accused's constitutional rights to freedom of expression, privacy and equality. [Note that pornography is discussed further in Chapter 3.]

DE REUCK v. DIRECTOR OF PUBLIC PROSECUTIONS
CONSTITUTIONAL COURT OF SOUTH AFRICA
2004 (1) SA 406

LANGA DCJ:

INTRODUCTION

[This case arose after the appellant, a film producer, was charged under section 27(1) of the Films and Publications Act 65 of 1996 (the Act), a provision which relates to child pornography. Early in the proceedings, the applicant raised objections regarding the constitutional validity of certain of the provisions of the Act on which the charges were based.]

. . . .

[5] The applicant's case in both the High Court and this Court was that the provisions of section 27(1) read with the definition of child pornography in section 1 of the Act, constituted a limitation of the constitutional rights to privacy, freedom of expression and equality. He contended that the limitation was not justifiable, in

particular because the provisions in question were not only overbroad, but were also vague. The respondents denied that any of the rights mentioned above were limited by the impugned provisions. In the alternative, they contended that if the provisions were found to be a limitation of the rights concerned, such limitation was justified and therefore constitutionally valid.

. . . .

LIMITATION ANALYSIS

[56] I proceed to the limitation analysis of the two rights limited by section 27(1), namely, freedom of expression and privacy . . . . It is well established that courts applying section 36(1) are required to undertake a proportionality enquiry, in the course of which they consider factors including, but not limited to, those listed in sub-paragraphs (a)-(e).

[57] The first question is whether section 27(1), read with the definition of child pornography, is a "law of general application" as required by section 36(1). This Court has held that this requirement derives from an important principle of the rule of law, namely that "rules be stated in a clear and accessible manner". The applicant's complaint concerned clarity: he submitted that the definition of "child pornography" in section 1 was too vague to satisfy this requirement. Having analysed and considered that definition above, I am satisfied that it is sufficiently clear and does constitute a law of general application.

LIMITATION ANALYSIS: FREEDOM OF EXPRESSION

[58] The applicant accepts that the legislature may, consistently with the Constitution, prohibit the possession, importation, creation and production of child pornography in certain circumstances. The question this Court has to answer is whether the limitation occasioned by section 27(1) is justifiable. To do so, the nature of the right and the extent of the limitation, on the one hand, and the purpose of the limitation on the other need to be considered.

THE NATURE AND EXTENT OF THE LIMITATION

[59] Freedom of expression is an important right in our Bill of Rights. It

". . . lies at the heart of a democracy. It is valuable for many reasons, including its instrumental function as a guarantor of democracy, its implicit recognition and protection of the moral agency of individuals in our society and its facilitation of the search for truth by individuals and society generally. The Constitution recognises that individuals in our society need to be able to hear, form and express opinions and views freely on a wide range of matters . . .". [footnotes omitted]

Seen from this perspective, the limitation of the right caused by section 27(1) does not implicate the core values of the right. Expression that is restricted is, for the most part, expression of little value which is found on the periphery of the right and is a form of expression that is not protected as part of the freedom of expression in many democratic societies.

[60] The applicant did not suggest that the prevention of the creation and possession of child pornography was not a legitimate government purpose. He contended, however, that the statute in the present case goes further than is necessary for this purpose. I deal with this when I consider the relationship between the limitation and its purpose. But first it is necessary to address the purpose of the legislation.

The Purpose of the Legislation

[61] In determining the importance of section 27(1) of the Act, it is necessary to examine its objective as a whole. The purpose of the legislation is to curb child pornography which is seen as an evil in all democratic societies. Child pornography is universally condemned for good reason. It strikes at the dignity of children, it is harmful to children who are used in its production, and it is potentially harmful because of the attitude to child sex that it fosters and the use to which it can be put in grooming children to engage in sexual conduct. I will deal with each of these in turn.

[62] Dignity is a founding value of our Constitution. It informs most if not all of the rights in the Bill of Rights and for that reason is of central significance in the limitations analysis. As this Court held in *Dawood*:

"The value of dignity in our Constitutional framework cannot therefore be doubted. The Constitution asserts dignity to contradict our past in which human dignity for black South Africans was routinely and cruelly denied. It asserts it too to inform the future, to invest in our democracy respect for the intrinsic worth of all human beings. Human dignity therefore informs constitutional adjudication and interpretation at a range of levels. It is a value that informs the interpretation of many, possibly all, other rights. This Court has already acknowledged the importance of the constitutional value of dignity in interpreting rights such as the right to equality, the right not to be punished in a cruel, inhuman or degrading way, and the right to life. Human dignity is also a constitutional value that is of central significance in the limitations analysis. Section 10, however, makes it plain that dignity is not only a value fundamental to our Constitution, it is a justiciable and enforceable right that must be respected and protected. In many cases, however, where the value of human dignity is offended, the primary constitutional breach occasioned may be of a more specific right such as the right to bodily integrity, the right to equality or the right not to be subjected to slavery, servitude or forced labour." [footnotes omitted].

[63] Similarly, article 1 of the Universal Declaration of Human Rights stresses the importance of human dignity. It states: "All human beings are born free and equal in dignity and rights." Children merit special protection by the state and must be protected by legislation which guards and enforces their rights and liberties. This is recognised in section 28 of our Constitution. Children's dignity rights are of special importance. The degradation of children through child pornography is a

serious harm which impairs their dignity and contributes to a culture which devalues their worth.

. . . .

Society has recognised that childhood is a special stage in life which is to be both treasured and guarded. The state must ensure that the lives of children are not disrupted by adults who objectify and sexualise them through the production and possession of child pornography. There is obvious physical harm suffered by the victims of sexual abuse and by those children forced to yield to the demands of the paedophile and pornographer, but there is also harm to the dignity and perception of all children when a society allows sexualised images of children to be available. The chief purpose of the statutory prohibitions against child pornography is to protect the dignity, humanity and integrity of children.

. . . .

[66] The question of reasonable apprehension of harm was considered in S v Jordan. In that case it was argued, in the context of a limitation of the right to privacy, that some of the harm was caused not by prostitution itself but by its criminalisation, and that legalisation or regulation could lead to a net reduction of such harm. Although the state did not empirically refute these claims, the Court nevertheless found that the state was entitled to criminalise prostitution as a reasonable means of combating the harm. The harm of child abuse is real and ongoing and the state is under a constitutional obligation to combat it. To hold otherwise would place the state in jeopardy of having to close the gate, as it were, after the horse has bolted and might signal a breach by the state of its obligation towards children.

[67] I conclude that the state has established three legitimate objectives which the limitation aims to serve, namely, protecting the dignity of children, stamping out the market for photographs made by abusing children and preventing a reasonable risk that images will be used to harm children.

[68] I turn now to the question whether there are less restrictive means available to the state to achieve these purposes. Statutes dealing with child pornography in the United Kingdom and Germany penalise the possession of photographs and "pseudophotographs" only.

[69] These may amount to less restrictive means. The English and German statutes would exclude any imaginative image which is not a photograph or a pseudophotograph. This requires presiding officers to ask the question "Is it a photograph or a pseudophotograph?" rather than "Is it art?" On the other hand, what precisely is a pseudophotograph may be difficult to determine. Section 27 has adopted instead a test whereby a judge is required to consider whether the material would, from the perspective of a reasonable viewer, have as its predominant purpose the stimulation of erotic feeling. I am not persuaded that this approach is significantly more invasive of the right to freedom of expression than the approach adopted in the United Kingdom and Germany.

[70] I am however persuaded that the relatively narrow infringement of expression is outweighed by the important legislative purposes performed by

section 27, together with the legislative safeguards provided, as well as the difficulty of legislating in this area at all.

. . . .

LIMITATION ANALYSIS: RIGHT TO PRIVACY

[89] The next question is whether the limitation of the right to privacy is justifiable. Once again the applicant argued that the limitation was not justifiable.

[90] Although possession and consumption of child pornography often takes place in the inner sanctum of the home, the legislative purposes identified above remain of great importance. It should not be overlooked that many of the resultant acts of abuse against children take place in private. In other words, where the reasonable risk of harm to children is likely to materialise in private, some intrusion by the law into the private domain is justified. Moreover, since child pornography is frequently being imported via the Internet and possessed on computers, the ease with which such possessors may become distributors at the touch of a button, as it were, should be taken into account. This exacerbates the risk of harm and further justifies the intrusion of the Act into the private sphere.

[91] For these reasons and for those given in my consideration of the justifiability of the limitation of the right to freedom of expression, I find that the limitation of the right to privacy is also justifiable.

There exist a number of other constitutional sources of authority from which claims for judicial protection of rights or constitutional principles of democracy or the rule of law may be asserted. First among these were the constitutional principles contained in Schedule 4 of the "interim" Constitution. While the constitutional principles may have formed an integral part of the supreme law of the Constitution during the transitional period, the adoption of the "final" Constitution and its certification by the Constitutional Court terminated the legally significant role of those principles. Although there is no formal place for the principles some have argued that since they served as the basis for the creation and certification of the 1996 Constitution they remain at the core of the Constitution (*see* Francois Venter, *Requirements for a New Constitutional Text: The Imperatives of the Constitutional Principles*, 112 SALJ 32, 1995). However, it was the express inclusion of a set of founding provisions in Chapter 1 of the Constitution that provides the most explicit source of the principles underlying the 1996 Constitution.

Chapter 1 begins with a description of the State — the Republic of South Africa — as "one, sovereign, democratic state founded" on a particular set of values. Section 1, subsections (a)-(d) describes the founding values as including: "human dignity, the achievement of equality and the advancement of human rights and freedoms; non-racialism and non-sexism; supremacy of the constitution and the rule of law; as well as the basic principles of an electoral democracy, universal adult suffrage, a national common voters role, regular elections and a multi-party system of democratic government to ensure accountability, responsiveness and openness." The status of these founding provisions in the constitutional order is enhanced by their entrenchment. Section 1 may only be amended by a 75 percent majority of the National Assembly, supported by six of the nine provinces in the National Council of Provinces — a level of political agreement that is hard to imagine.

Any violation of the core meanings of these founding values would clearly be unconstitutional, yet it is unclear exactly how these values may be raised by litigants and applied in litigation. In *Minister of Home Affairs v. National Institute for Crime Prevention and the Re-Integration of Offenders (NICRO) & Others*, 2005 (3) SA 280 (CC), the Constitutional Court declared that while the "values enunciated in section 1 of the Constitution are of fundamental importance," they are not the basis of justiciable rights. *Id.* para. 21. Instead the Court argued that they "inform and give substance to all the provisions of the Constitution," but "do not . . . give rise to discrete and enforceable rights in themselves". *Id.* This is a significant qualification since the highly entrenched founding values are presumably not subject to the limitation clause analysis of section 36.

This proposition was put to the test when the United Democratic Movement (UDM), a small parliamentary opposition party, challenged a series of constitutional amendments and related legislation that allowed elected representatives to switch political parties without losing their seats.[10] Claiming that these changes undermined minority parties and therefore violated the founding values of South Africa's multi-party democracy and the rule of law, the UDM argued that they should be struck down as unconstitutional and could not be justified in terms of the limitation clause analysis. The Court rejected both the claim that floor-crossing undermined democracy and the rule of law and while it recognized that the founding values "inform the interpretation of the Constitution and other law, and set positive standards with which all law must comply to be valid," the court refused to elevate these rights above other rights in the bill of rights based on their status as foundational values (*United Democratic Movement v. President of the Republic of South Africa & Others*, 2003 (1) SA 678, [19]).

Chapter 1 also includes a provision guaranteeing the supremacy of the Constitution, declaring that "law or conduct inconsistent with [the Constitution] is invalid," (Section 2), however, it does not claim to exhaust all the principles the constitution encompasses nor are all the founding provisions in Chapter 1 equivalent in form and status to constitutional principles (see, section 4 [national anthem] or section 5 [national flag]. Instead, the Constitutional Court has repeatedly made reference to the Constitution embodying an "objective, normative value system," which is in many ways a broader conception of underlying constitutional principles than either the specific clauses of section 1 or the original constitutional principles contained in Schedule 4 of the "interim" Constitution. This notion of an "objective, normative value system," has been articulated most often in relation to the interpretation of constitutional rights and even with explicit reference to the role this notion plays in the German Constitutional system as a "guiding principle" for all levels of the constitutional order — the legislature, executive and judiciary.

---

[10] [Ed. note: Recall from the Introductory chapter that the South African Parliament is based on principles of proportional representation.]

Finally, the heightened entrenchment of the founding values in Section 1 has led to discussion about the applicability of the "basic structure" doctrine in South Africa. This doctrine, which originates in German and Indian constitutional jurisprudence, is the idea that even procedurally perfect constitutional amendments may be challenged as being incompatible with the implicit framework or basic structure of the constitution and therefore may be struck down by the courts. The South African Constitutional Court first made reference to the "basic structure doctrine" in a challenge by KwaZulu-Natal to amendments made to the "interim" Constitution in 1995 (*Premier KwaZulu-Natal & Others v. President of the Republic of South Africa & Others*, 1996 (1) SA 769 (CC)). In that case the Court made reference to the possibility that "a purported amendment to the Constitution, following the formal procedures prescribed by the Constitution, but radically and fundamentally restructuring and reorganizing the fundamental premises of the Constitution, might not qualify as an 'amendment' at all." *Id.* para. 47. Despite this statement, on the two occasions when the Court has had the opportunity to invoke the doctrine it has declined to apply it, or to even decide whether it would be applicable in the South Africa constitutional context (see the *UDM* and *NICRO* cases discussed above).

This has led some commentators to argue that the idea of a "basic structure doctrine'" is clearly not "coterminous with the special protection given to the foundational values" in section 1 of the Constitution. Christopher Roederer, *Founding Provisions, in* Constitutional Law of South Africa ch. 13, at 16 (Woolman, Stuart, Theunis Roux, Michael Bishop & Anthony Stein ed., 2d ed., Original Service 2006). The Constitutional Courts refusal to find the constitutional amendments at stake in the *UDM* case in tension with the founding principle of democracy has led these same commentators to conclude that "the threshold for the deployment of the foundational values to protect the basic structure of the South African constitutional legal order is very high and that only extraordinary amendments to that order will trigger the protection afforded by," *id.* at 17, section 1 of the Constitution.

2.5. CONSIDERATION OF IMPLIED LIMITS ON GOVERNMENTS TO INFRINGE INDIVIDUAL FREEDOMS IN AUSTRALIA

As we have gathered, the Australian Constitution, which includes a small number of rights-protecting provisions but lacks a Bill or Charter of Rights, has not generated a large body of case law concerning rights, either enumerated or unenumerated. However, in some key cases, the High Court of Australia has identified rights and freedoms as implications arising from the text and structure of the Constitution. The Court has made clear that these rights or freedoms derive from the Constitution's textual provisions for parliamentary government, representative democracy, and (arguably) the rule of law. It has not addressed questions such as whether there is an implied right to privacy, or to marry, or for a woman to have an abortion, or other rights concerning personal choice or intimate relations. Such issues (with the exception of marriage and divorce over which the Commonwealth has legislative power) are constitutionally a matter for the states, and are regulated by state law. However, at the federal level, there is a wide range of anti-discrimination legislation, most of these passed by the Commonwealth parliament to give effect to international covenants or conventions. These include: the *Racial Discrimination Act* (1975); *Sex Discrimination Act* (1984); *Privacy Act* (1988); *Disability Discrimination Act* (1992); *Human Rights (Sexual Conduct) Act* (1994); *Age Discrimination Act* (2004). Likewise, as we saw, the Commonwealth Parliament has enacted legislation barring states (which all have legislatively outlawed the death penalty) from re-instituting a death penalty, pursuant to an international covenant to this effect. Presumably, the Commonwealth could enact related statutes with regard to due process or individual liberties, if it so chose, to effectuate international obligations. Constitutional issues concerning such laws would only concern whether they genuinely or validly gave effect to an international obligation on the relevant subject (and were therefore characterized as laws with respect to "external affairs"), and not whether the Constitution itself protected persons against the relevant form of discrimination.

In the framing of the Constitution, the delegates at the Federal Conventions of the 1890s considered the inclusion of a provision similar to the U.S. Fourteenth Amendment. The first draft Constitution indeed included the provision: "A State shall not make or enforce any law abridging any privilege or immunity of citizens of other States of the Commonwealth, nor shall a State deny to any person, within its jurisdiction, the equal protection of the laws." At the 1897-98 Convention, Andrew Inglis Clark, Tasmanian Attorney-General, proposed that the section be struck out, and replaced with: "The citizens of each State, and all other persons owing allegiance to the Queen and residing in any territory of the Commonwealth, shall be citizens of the Commonwealth, and shall be entitled to all the privileges and immunities of citizens of the Commonwealth in the several States; and a State shall not make or enforce any law abridging any privilege or immunity of citizens of the Commonwealth; nor shall a State deprive any person of life, liberty, or property, without due process of law, or deny to any person within its jurisdiction the equal protection of its laws."[11] The Convention considered Clark's proposal, but rejected it. They inserted, in its place, the provision that is now s 117 of the Constitution prohibiting out-of-State residency discrimination. The framers' reasons were multiple. They considered the Fourteenth Amendment to be a uniquely American response to the history of slavery and the denial of citizenship to African Americans; they were reluctant to insert the expression "citizen" in the Constitution, because "citizenship" had no meaning under Australian law (at the time, in common with all members of the British Empire, Australians were British Subjects and, furthermore, subject status was, at that time, a matter for common law rather than legislation); they did not want the Constitution to interfere unnecessarily in matters they regarded as belonging to the states; they were reluctant to go beyond the prohibitions and rights protections found in the common law; they also wanted the states to be free to enact laws that were discriminatory, in particular with respect to the employment of Chinese immigrants.

Over the twentieth century, a number of attempts were made to extend the range of rights protected by the Constitution or, as an alternative strategy, to enact a

---

[11] *See* JOHN M. WILLIAMS, THE AUSTRALIAN CONSTITUTION: A DOCUMENTARY HISTORY 208–10 (2005).

legislative Bill of Rights. All were unsuccessful. The 1944 referendum on Post-War Reconstruction and Democratic Rights asked a single question with fourteen proposed constitutional changes, including an express guarantee of freedom of speech, the extension of freedom of religion to state laws, and safeguards against the abuse of delegated legislative power. A referendum in 1988 proposed extending to the states some of the rights or freedoms in the Constitution that bind only the Commonwealth. It proposed "To alter the Constitution to extend the right to trial by jury, to extend freedom of religion, and to ensure fair terms for persons whose property is acquired by any government." Statutory Bills of Rights were introduced in 1973 into the Commonwealth parliament by Labor Attorney-General, Lionel Murphy (later to be appointed to the High Court), and in 1985 by Labor Attorney-General, Lionel Bowen. Facing a parliamentary filibuster and loss of political will, neither Bill proceeded to a vote.

In 2004, the legislature of the Australian Capital Territory (ACT) adopted a Human Rights Act; in 2006, the Victorian Parliament adopted the *Charter of Human Rights and Responsibilities Act.* These Acts of course only apply in the relevant jurisdiction; however, combined with international pressures, their adoption generated renewed enthusiasm among proponents of a national Bill of Rights, and stimulated a new campaign. In 2008 (on the 60th anniversary of the Universal Declaration of Human Rights), the new Labor Attorney-General, Robert McClelland, announced a "National Consultation" on the protection of human rights in Australia. The debate quickly became focused on whether Australia should adopt a Bill (or Charter). The Committee established to administer this Consultation handed down its report in October 2009; it recommended, among other things, the adoption of a "Human Rights Act," to be modeled on the Victorian Act (which was modeled on the UK *Human Rights Act* 1998). (The Committee's terms of reference ruled out recommending constitutional change.) This proposed Act would have permitted High Court to make a "declaration of inconsistency" between challenged legislation and one or more of the rights protected under the Act. This type of judicial review — labeled "weak form" by Mark Tushnet[12] — does not permit courts to strike down legislation for breach of the Constitution, but merely to inform the executive government and/or parliament if a breach is found. The recommendation, however, proved controversial and generated much heated debate. In April 2010, the government issued its response — it decided not to proceed with a Human Rights Act, but instead to pass an Act requiring governments to attach a statement of rights "compatibility" to all proposed legislation, and empowering the courts to interpret legislation in light of the rights protected under international law. The *Human Rights (Parliamentary Scrutiny) Act* was accordingly passed by the Commonwealth parliament in late 2011.

The last few decades of the twentieth century saw various challenges to Commonwealth laws, based on claims for implied constitutional rights or freedoms. In *A-G (NSW); Ex rel McKinlay v. Commonwealth* (1975) 135 CLR 1 it was argued that the words "directly chosen by the people" in section 24 of the Constitution included an implied equality in voting power; that is, that the provision mandated adherence to the principle of "one vote, one value," and therefore that disparities in

---

[12] Mark Tushnet, *Alternative Forms of Judicial Review*, 101 MICH. L. REV. 2781 (2003).

electorate (constituency) sizes were unconstitutional. The Court rejected this argument, although one dissenting judge, Justice Lionel Murphy, found it persuasive. "Great rights are often expressed in simple phrases," Murphy J declared (a phrase suggestive of a wide scope for implied or unenumerated rights). He also quoted from the U.S. case of *Wesberry v. Sanders* [376 US 1] in which similar words in the American Constitution had been found to imply equal representation in the House of Representatives for equal numbers of people. Stephen J, while joining the majority, suggested in *obiter dicta* that the words of s 24 were indeed capacious: "Three great principles, representative democracy, . . . direct popular election, and the national character of the lower House, may each be discerned in the opening words of s 24." The spectrum of political institutions characteristic of representative democracy, he said, "has finite limits and in a particular instance there may be absent some quality which is regarded as so essential to representative democracy as to place that instance outside those limits altogether." No formula for knowing when this point had been reached was proposed, however. Two decades later, a similar claim regarding electorate size malapportionment was made, also unsuccessfully, in *McGinty v. Western Australia* (1996) 186 CLR 140. The renewed effort had been encouraged by indications that the Court was now willing to find specific implications in s 24. In 1992 the Court had identified an implied freedom of political communication lying in the words of section 24 (and its companion, s 7, which provides that Senators as well as MHRs shall be "directly chosen by the people").

The implied freedom of political communication (IFPC) cases had a dramatic impact on Australian constitutional jurisprudence. Until that time, implications had been held only to arise either from the constitutional text under ordinary principles of statutory interpretation (by "necessary intendment") or for the protection of Australia's federal system (see the discussion of the "Melbourne Corporation doctrine" in Chapter 1). The IFPC, in striking contrast, concerned the rights or freedoms of individuals. Two cases were handed down on the same day: *Nationwide News Pty Ltd v. Wills* (1992) 177 CLR 1, and *Australian Capital Television Pty Ltd v. Commonwealth* (1992) 177 CLR 106. In the first case (which concerned a law making it an offence to use words calculated to bring a member of the Industrial Relations Commission into disrepute), four Justices enunciated the new freedom and the grounds upon which it rested. In the second case (which concerned a law restricting commercial political advertising in the electronic media), the Court (with one dissent) adopted and applied the IFPC. This second case — the "political advertising case" — quickly emerged as the more important of the two.

In a judgment which traversed the history of the framing of the Constitution and the evolution of Australian sovereignty, as well as challenging the "orthodox" approach to constitutional interpretation, the Chief Justice set out his reasons.

AUSTRALIAN CAPITAL TELEVISION PTY LTD v. COMMONWEALTH
HIGH COURT OF AUSTRALIA
(1992) 177 CLR 106

MASON CJ:

. . . Sir Owen Dixon [former Chief Justice of the HCA] noted that, following the decision in *Amalgamated Society of Engineers v. Adelaide Steamship Co. Ltd.* ("the Engineers' Case") ((52) (1920) 28 CLR 129), the notion seemed to gain currency that no implications could be made in interpreting the Constitution ((53) *West v. Commissioner of Taxation (N.S.W.)* (1937) 56 CLR 657, at p 681). The Engineers' Case certainly did not support such a Draconian and unthinking approach to constitutional interpretation . . . Sir Owen expressed his own opposition to that approach when he said (ibid., at p 681): "Such a method of construction would defeat the intention of any instrument, but of all instruments a written constitution seems the last to which it could be applied."

Later, he was to say . . . "We should avoid pedantic and narrow constructions in dealing with an instrument of government and I do not see why we should be fearful about making implications."

Subsequently, Windeyer J., in a passage in which he referred to that statement, remarked (*Victoria v. The Commonwealth* ("the Payroll Tax Case") 122 CLR 353, at pp 401-402) "implications have a place in the interpretation of the Constitution" and "our avowed task is simply the revealing or uncovering of implications that are already there".

In conformity with this approach, the Court has drawn implications from the federal structure prohibiting the Commonwealth from exercising its legislative and executive powers in such a way as to impose upon a State some special disability or burden unless the relevant power authorized that imposition or in such a way as to threaten the continued existence of a State as an independent entity or its capacity to function as such (*Queensland Electricity Commission v. The Commonwealth* (1985) 159 CLR 192 . . .). But there is no reason to limit the process of constitutional implication to that particular source.

Of course, any implication must be securely based. Thus, it has been said that "ordinary principles of construction are applied so as to discover in the actual terms of the instrument their expressed or necessarily implied meaning" (*The Engineers' Case* (1920) 28 CLR, per Knox C.J., Isaacs, Rich and Starke JJ. at p 155) . . . This statement is too restrictive because, if taken literally, it would deny the very basis — the federal nature of the Constitution — from which the Court has implied restrictions on Commonwealth and State legislative powers . . . That the statement is too restrictive is evident from the remarks of Dixon J. in *Melbourne Corporation v. The Commonwealth* (1947) 74 CLR, at p 83) where his Honour stated that "the efficacy of the system logically demands" the restriction which has been implied and that "an intention of this sort is . . . to be plainly seen in the very frame of the Constitution".

It may not be right to say that no implication will be made unless it is necessary. In cases where the implication is sought to be derived from the actual terms of the Constitution it may be sufficient that the relevant intention is manifested according to the accepted principles of interpretation. However, where the implication is structural rather than textual it is no doubt correct to say that the term sought to be implied must be logically or practically necessary for the preservation of the integrity of that structure.

It is essential to keep steadily in mind the critical difference between an implication and an unexpressed assumption upon which the framers proceeded in drafting the Constitution . . . The former is a term or concept which inheres in the instrument and as such operates as part of the instrument, whereas an assumption stands outside the instrument. Thus, the founders assumed that the Senate would protect the States but in the result it did not do so. On the other hand, the principle of responsible government — the system of government by which the executive is responsible to the legislature — is not merely an assumption upon which the actual provisions are based; it is an integral element in the Constitution . . .

THE IMPLICATION OF FUNDAMENTAL RIGHTS

The adoption by the framers of the Constitution of the principle of responsible government was perhaps the major reason for their disinclination to incorporate in the Constitution comprehensive guarantees of individual rights . . . They refused to adopt a counterpart to the Fourteenth Amendment to the Constitution of the United States. Sir Owen Dixon said (Sir Owen Dixon, "Two Constitutions Compared," Jesting Pilate, (1965), p 102):

> (they) were not prepared to place fetters upon legislative action, except and in so far as it might be necessary for the purpose of distributing between the States and the central government the full content of legislative power. The history of their country had not taught them the need of provisions directed to control of the legislature itself.

The framers of the Constitution accepted, in accordance with prevailing English thinking, that the citizen's rights were best left to the protection of the common law in association with the doctrine of parliamentary supremacy (Sir Anthony Mason, "The Role of a Constitutional Court in a Federation," (1986) 16 Federal Law Review 1, at p 8).

So it was that Professor Harrison Moore, writing in 1901, was able to say of the Constitution ((68) The Constitution of the Commonwealth of Australia, 1st ed. (1902), p 329): "The great underlying principle is, that the rights of individuals are sufficiently secured by ensuring, as far as possible, to each a share, and an equal share, in political power."

In the light of this well recognized background, it is difficult, if not impossible, to establish a foundation for the implication of general guarantees of fundamental rights and freedoms. To make such an implication would run counter to the prevailing sentiment of the framers that there was no need to incorporate a comprehensive Bill of Rights in order to protect the rights and freedoms of citizens.

That sentiment was one of the unexpressed assumptions on which the Constitution was drafted.

However, the existence of that sentiment when the Constitution was adopted and the influence which it had on the shaping of the Constitution are no answer to the case which the plaintiffs now present. Their case is that a guarantee of freedom of expression in relation to public and political affairs must necessarily be implied from the provision which the Constitution makes for a system of representative government. The plaintiffs say that, because such a freedom is an essential concomitant of representative government, it is necessarily implied in the prescription of that system.

* * *

[The Chief Justice then described the Constitution's provisions for representative government, and the principles upon which representation rest. He concluded]:

The point is that the representatives who are members of Parliament and Ministers of State are not only chosen by the people but exercise their legislative and executive powers as representatives of the people. And in the exercise of those powers the representatives of necessity are accountable to the people for what they do and have a responsibility to take account of the views of the people on whose behalf they act. Freedom of communication as an indispensable element in representative government

Indispensable to that accountability and that responsibility is freedom of communication, at least in relation to public affairs and political discussion. Only by exercising that freedom can the citizen communicate his or her views on the wide range of matters that may call for, or are relevant to, political action or decision. Only by exercising that freedom can the citizen criticize government decisions and actions, seek to bring about change, call for action where none has been taken and in this way influence the elected representatives. By these means the elected representatives are equipped to discharge their role so that they may take account of and respond to the will of the people. Communication in the exercise of the freedom is by no means a one-way traffic, for the elected representatives have a responsibility not only to ascertain the views of the electorate but also to explain and account for their decisions and actions in government and to inform the people so that they may make informed judgments on relevant matters. Absent such a freedom of communication, representative government would fail to achieve its purpose, namely, government by the people through their elected representatives; government would cease to be responsive to the needs and wishes of the people and, in that sense, would cease to be truly representative.

Freedom of communication in relation to public affairs and political discussion cannot be confined to communications between elected representatives and candidates for election on the one hand and the electorate on the other. The efficacy of representative government depends also upon free communication on such matters between all persons, groups and other bodies in the community. That is because individual judgment, whether that of the elector, the representative or the candidate, on so many issues turns upon free public discussion in the media of the views of all interested persons, groups and bodies and on public participation in, and access to, that discussion.

. . . .

The fundamental importance, indeed the essentiality, of freedom of communication, including freedom to criticize government action, in the system of modern representative government has been recognized by courts in many jurisdictions.

. . . .

Freedom of communication in the sense just discussed is so indispensable to the efficacy of the system of representative government for which the Constitution makes provision that it is necessarily implied in the making of that provision. . . .

The concept of freedom to communicate with respect to public affairs and political discussion does not lend itself to subdivision. Public affairs and political discussion are indivisible and cannot be subdivided into compartments that correspond with, or relate to, the various tiers of government in Australia. Unlike the legislative powers of the Commonwealth Parliament, there are no limits to the range of matters that may be relevant to debate in the Commonwealth Parliament or to its workings. The consequence is that the implied freedom of communication extends to all matters of public affairs and political discussion . . . ."

———

(We consider the evolution of the IFPC, including the identification of legitimate legislative limits in Chapter 3.)

This case raised many hopes and gave rise to a series of challenges to laws in which arguments were made for the further identification of unenumerated or implied rights. With some few exceptions, the excitement generated by the political advertising case did not last. The exceptions, however, are not unimportant. Some people have sought to find implications in the Constitution's provision for separation of powers, specifically for the judicial power to be exclusively exercisable by the High Court, Federal Courts and State Courts invested with federal jurisdiction (s 71) — i.e., "Chapter III Courts." These cases include elements of due process protection.

Kable v. Director of Public Prosecutions (NSW) (1996) 189 CLR 51 concerned a New South Wales Act directed specifically at a named individual, Gregory Kable, who had served a period of imprisonment for the manslaughter of his wife, and whose date of release was approaching. While in detention, Kable had written letters threatening members of his late wife's family and undertaking to carry out these threats when free (had the letters been posted they would have breached federal postal laws, but they were intercepted by prison authorities). The media learned of this and there was a public outcry against Kable's release. The NSW Parliament responded with the *Community Protection Act 1994* (NSW) which provided for the Supreme Court of NSW, on the application of the NSW Director of Public Prosecutions, to make orders, renewable on six-monthly basis, for Kable's continued incarceration. Kable argued that the Act constituted a legislative interference with the judicial power of the Commonwealth, and thus a breach of the constitutional separation of powers. The High Court upheld Kable's claim. The reasoning in this case is very complex, and several of the judgments (opinions) appear to have a different *ratio*. We can summarise the conclusion, however: Because the Supreme Court of NSW (like other state courts) is invested with federal jurisdiction (under s 77 (iii) of the Constitution), it is a Chapter III Court and is protected by the separation of powers provided for in the Commonwealth Constitution. This prohibits legislative interference in the exercise of judicial power. It is "incompatible" with the exercise of the judicial power of the Commonwealth for judges to order detention at the behest of the parliament. Non-punitive or preventive detention is beyond judicial power and cannot be ordered by Chapter III Courts (*Chu Kheng Lim v Minister for Immigration* (1992) 176 CLR 1). Furthermore, an Act targeting a named-individual — a "Bill of Attainder" — amounts to legislative imprisonment, and breaches the separation of powers.

In the words of Justice Toohey (at p. 98):

> Preventive detention . . . is not an incident of the exclusively judicial function of adjudging and punishing criminal guilt. It is not part of a system of . . . detention with appropriate safeguards, consequent upon or ancillary to the adjudication of guilt . . . [T]he Act requires the Supreme Court to exercise the judicial power of the Commonwealth in a manner which is inconsistent with traditional judicial process.

> The extraordinary character of the legislation and of the functions it requires the Supreme Court to perform is highlighted by the operation of the statute upon one named person only.

In 2007, the High Court once again entered the arena of implied democratic rights. *Roach v. Electoral Commissioner* (2007) 233 CLR 162 concerned an amendment to the Commonwealth *Electoral Act* which purported to disqualify all prisoners currently serving sentences of any length in state prisons (there are no federal prisons in Australia). Previously, the Act had disenfranchised prisoners serving sentences of three years or more. Vicki Roach was serving a sentence of six years. She challenged the Act on the footing that it breached an implied right to vote, guaranteed in the Constitution's mandate that the Parliament must be "directly chosen by the people." The High Court upheld the challenge to the amendment (it left the original Act intact, thus making no alteration to Roach's own right to vote.) The reasoning of the majority of the Court is captured in the words of Chief Justice Gleeson:

> [B]ecause of changed historical circumstances including legislative history, [the words of ss 7 and 24 of the Constitution], have come to be a constitutional protection of the right to vote. That, however, leaves open for debate the nature and extent of the exceptions. The Constitution leaves it to Parliament to define those exceptions, but its power to do so is not unconstrained. Because the franchise is critical to representative government, and lies at the centre of our concept of participation in the life of the community, and of citizenship, disenfranchisement of any group of adult citizens on a basis that does not constitute a substantial reason for exclusion from such participation would not be consistent with choice by the people. To say that, of course, raises questions as to what constitutes a

substantial reason, and what, if any, limits there are to Parliament's capacity to decide that matter . . .

An arbitrary exception would be inconsistent with choice by the people. There would need to be some rationale for the exception; the definition of the excluded class or group would need to have a rational connection with the identification of community membership or with the capacity to exercise free choice.

. . . .

What is the rationale for the exclusion of prisoners? . . . [T]he rationale for the exclusion must be that serious offending represents such a form of civic irresponsibility that it is appropriate for Parliament to mark such behaviour as anti-social and to direct that physical separation from the community will be accompanied by symbolic separation in the form of loss of a fundamental political right.

. . . .

The adoption of the criterion of serving a sentence of imprisonment as the method of identifying serious criminal conduct for the purpose of satisfying the rationale for treating serious offenders as having severed their link with the community, a severance reflected in temporary disenfranchisement, breaks down at the level of short-term prisoners. They include a not insubstantial number of people who, by reason of their personal characteristics (such as poverty, homelessness, or mental problems), or geographical circumstances, do not qualify for, or, do not qualify for a full range of, non-custodial sentencing options. At this level, the method of discriminating between offences, for the purpose of deciding which are so serious as to warrant disenfranchisement and which are not, becomes arbitrary.

The step that was taken by Parliament in 2006 of abandoning any attempt to identify prisoners who have committed serious crimes by reference to either the term of imprisonment imposed or the maximum penalty for the offence broke the rational connection necessary to reconcile the disenfranchisement with the constitutional imperative of choice by the people.

LANGE v. AUSTRALIAN BROADCASTING CORPORATION
HIGH COURT OF AUSTRALIA
(1997) 189 CLR 520

THE COURT:

. . . .

The case stated arises out of a defamation action brought in the Supreme Court of New South Wales by Mr David Lange, a former Prime Minister of New Zealand (the plaintiff), against the Australian Broadcasting Corporation (the defendant).

The defendant has relied on the decisions of this court in *Theophanous v Herald & Weekly Times Ltd*[13] and *Stephens v West Australian Newspapers Ltd*[14] to plead a defence against an action brought by the plaintiff in respect of matters published when he was a member of the New Zealand Parliament. [Based on these precedents, the ABC alleged that the matter complained of was published "pursuant to a freedom guaranteed by the Commonwealth Constitution" to publish material "in the course of discussion of government and political matters" relating to the plaintiffs as a public official and "in circumstances such that: (i) if the matter was false (which is not admitted) the defendant was unaware of its falsity; (ii) the defendant did not publish the matter recklessly, that is, not caring whether the material was true or false; (iii) the publication was reasonable."]

. . . .

THEOPHANOUS

In *Theophanous*,[15] this court by majority . . . declared that:

There is implied in the Commonwealth Constitution a freedom to publish material:

(a) discussing government and political matters;

(b) of and concerning members of the Parliament of the Commonwealth of Australia which relates to the performance by such members of their duties as members of the Parliament or parliamentary committees;

(c) in relation to the suitability of persons for office as members of the Parliament.

By the same majority, the court [also held that] . . .

A publication that attracts the freedom implied in the Commonwealth Constitution can also be described as a publication on an occasion of qualified privilege. Whether a federal election is about to be called is not a relevant consideration.

. . . .

STEPHENS

On the same day that judgment was delivered in *Theophanous*, the court delivered judgment in *Stephens*. By the same majority, the court held that defences based on the Constitution of the Commonwealth and the Constitution Act 1889 (WA) were good defences to an action brought by a State member of parliament in respect of a publication that criticised an overseas trip being made by a six-member committee of the Legislative Council of Western Australia, of which the plaintiff was a member.

. . . .

[The court did not view these precedents as binding, however, because of the lack of a clear majority opinion.]

---

[13] [FN 2] (1994) 182 CLR 104; 124 ALR 1.

[14] [FN 3] (1994) 182 CLR 211; 124 ALR 80.

[15] [FN 4] (1994) 182 CLR 104 at 208; 124 ALR 1, at 26.

However, for the reasons set out below, *Theophanous* and *Stephens* should be accepted as deciding that in Australia the common law rules of defamation must conform to the requirements of the Constitution . . .

. . . .

Having regard to the foregoing discussion, the appropriate course is to examine the correctness of the defences pleaded in the present case as a matter of principle and not of authority. The starting point of that examination must be the terms of the Constitution illuminated by the assistance which is to be obtained from *Theophanous* and the other authorities which have dealt with the question of "implied freedoms" under the Constitution.

REPRESENTATIVE AND RESPONSIBLE GOVERNMENT

Sections 7 and 24 of the Constitution, read in context, require the members of the Senate and the House of Representatives to be directly chosen at periodic elections by the people of the States and of the Commonwealth respectively. This requirement embraces all that is necessary to effectuate the free election of representatives at periodic elections. What is involved in the people directly choosing their representatives at periodic elections, however, can be understood only by reference to the system of representative and responsible government to which ss 7 and 24 and other sections of the Constitution give effect.

. . . .

Other sections of the Constitution establish a formal relationship between the executive government and the parliament and provide for a system of responsible ministerial government, a system of government which, "prior to the establishment of the Commonwealth of Australia in 1901 . . . had become one of the central characteristics of our polity". . . .

The requirement that the parliament meet at least annually, the provision for control of supply by the legislature, the requirement that ministers be members of the legislature, the privilege of freedom of speech in debate, and the power to coerce the provision of information provide the means for enforcing the responsibility of the executive to the organs of representative government . . . .

Reference should also be made to s 128 which ensures that the Constitution shall not be altered except by a referendum passed by a majority of electors in the States and in those Territories with representation in the House of Representatives, taken together, and by the electors in a majority of States.

FREEDOM OF COMMUNICATION

Freedom of communication on matters of government and politics is an indispensable incident of that system of representative government which the Constitution creates by directing that the members of the House of Representatives and the Senate shall be "directly chosen by the people" of the Commonwealth and the States, respectively.

. . . .

Communications concerning political or government matters between the electors and the elected representatives, between the electors and the candidates for election and between the electors themselves were central to the system of representative government, as it was understood at federation. While the system of representative government for which the Constitution provides does not expressly mention freedom of communication, it can hardly be doubted, given the history of representative government and the holding of elections under that system in Australia prior to federation, that the elections for which the Constitution provides were intended to be free elections . . . Furthermore, because the choice given by ss 7 and 24 must be a true choice with "an opportunity to gain an appreciation of the available alternatives," as Dawson J pointed out in *Australian Capital Television Pty Ltd v. Commonwealth*,[16] legislative power cannot support an absolute denial of access by the people to relevant information about the functioning of government in Australia and about the policies of political parties and candidates for election.

That being so, ss 7 and 24 and the related sections of the Constitution necessarily protect that freedom of communication between the people concerning political or government matters which enables the people to exercise a free and informed choice as electors. Those sections do not confer personal rights on individuals. Rather they preclude the curtailment of the protected freedom by the exercise of legislative or executive power. As Deane J said in *Theophanous*,[17] they are "a limitation or confinement of laws and powers [which] gives rise to a pro tanto immunity on the part of the citizen from being adversely affected by those laws or by the exercise of those powers rather than to a 'right' in the strict sense." In *Cunliffe v. Commonwealth*,[18] Brennan J pointed out that the freedom confers no rights on individuals and, to the extent that the freedom rests upon implication, that implication defines the nature and extent of the freedom. His Honour said: "The implication is negative in nature: it invalidates laws and consequently creates an area of immunity from legal control, particularly from legislative control."

If the freedom is to effectively serve the purpose of ss 7 and 24 and related sections, it cannot be confined to the election period. Most of the matters necessary to enable "the people" to make an informed choice will occur during the period between the holding of one, and the calling of the next, election. If the freedom to receive and disseminate information were confined to election periods, the electors would be deprived of the greater part of the information necessary to make an effective choice at the election.

. . . .

Similarly, those provisions which prescribe the system of responsible government necessarily imply a limitation on legislative and executive power to deny the electors and their representatives information concerning the conduct of the executive branch of government throughout the life of a federal parliament. Moreover, the conduct of the executive branch is not confined to ministers and the public service. It includes the affairs of statutory authorities and public utilities which are obliged

---

[16] [FN 44] (1992) 177 CLR 106 at 187; 108 ALR 577.

[17] [FN 45] (1994) 182 CLR 104 at 168; see also 146-8; 124 ALR 1 at 48.

[18] [FN 46] (1994) 182 CLR 272 at 326; 124 ALR 120.

to report to the legislature or to a minister who is responsible to the legislature . . . . Whatever the scope of the implications arising from responsible government and the amendment of the Constitution may be, those implications cannot be confined to election periods relating to the Federal Parliament.

However, the freedom of communication which the Constitution protects is not absolute. It is limited to what is necessary for the effective operation of that system of representative and responsible government provided for by the Constitution. The freedom of communication required by ss 7 and 24 and reinforced by the sections concerning responsible government and the amendment of the Constitution operates as a restriction on legislative power. However, the freedom will not invalidate a law enacted to satisfy some other legitimate end if the law satisfies two conditions. The first condition is that the object of the law is compatible with the maintenance of the constitutionally prescribed system of representative and responsible government or the procedure for submitting a proposed amendment to the Constitution to the informed decision of the people which the Constitution prescribes. The second is that the law is reasonably appropriate and adapted to achieving that legitimate object or end. Different formulae have been used by members of this court in other cases to express the test whether the freedom provided by the Constitution has been infringed. Some judges have expressed the test as whether the law is reasonably appropriate and adapted to the fulfilment of a legitimate purpose. Others have favoured different expressions, including proportionality. In the context of the questions raised by the case stated, there is no need to distinguish these concepts. For ease of expression, throughout these reasons we have used the formulation of reasonably appropriate and adapted.

. . . .

[T]he New South Wales law of defamation cannot be said to place an undue burden on those communications that are necessary to give effect to the choice in federal elections given by ss 7 & 24 and the freedom of communication implied by those sections and ss 64 and 128 of the Constitution. It is true that the law of defamation in that State effectively places a burden on those communications although it does not prohibit them. Nevertheless, having regard to the necessity to protect reputation, the law of New South Wales goes no further than is reasonably appropriate and adapted to achieve the protection of reputation once it provides for the extended application of the law of qualified privilege. Moreover, even without the common law extension . . . the Defamation Act ensures that the New South Wales law of defamation does not place an undue burden on communications falling within the protection of the Constitution. This is because s 22 [of the NSW Act] protects [qualified privilege, namely] matter published to any person where the recipient had an interest or apparent interest in having information on a subject, the matter was published in the course of giving information on that subject to the recipient, and the conduct of the publisher in publishing the matter was reasonable in the circumstances.

In so far as the Amended Defence in the present case rests on the claim that the defamatory matter was published pursuant to a freedom guaranteed by the Constitution of the Commonwealth, the defence fails. For the reasons that we have given, the Constitution itself confers no private right of defence and the New South

Wales law of defamation action places no undue burden on the freedom of communication required by the Constitution . . . .

Chapter 3

BALANCING THE VALUES OF DIGNITY, EQUALITY, AND FREEDOM

KEY CONCEPTS FOR THE CHAPTER

- WESTERN DEMOCRACIES HAVE ALWAYS STRUGGLED WITH THE TWIN ASPIRATIONS OF FREEDOM AND EQUALITY: THE DECLARATION OF INDEPENDENCE RECOGNIZES THAT WE ARE ALL "CREATED EQUAL" WITH THE INALIENABLE RIGHT TO LIBERTY; THE FRENCH REVOLUTION PROCLAIMED "LIBERTÉ, EGALITÉ, FRATERNITÉ."

- BOTH FREE EXPRESSION AND THE RIGHT TO BE FREE FROM DISCRIMINATION ARE INTERESTS THAT COURTS HAVE FOUND TO BE SUFFICIENTLY IMPORTANT TO WARRANT CLOSE JUDICIAL SCRUTINY, BUT REACH DIFFERENT RESULTS BECAUSE OF DIFFERENT VIEWS ABOUT WHAT LEGITIMATE REASONS EXIST TO LIMIT THE LEGISLATURE'S ABILITY TO PROSCRIBE DEEPLY OFFENSIVE SPEECH.

- THE HIGH COURT OF AUSTRALIA CLOSELY PROTECTS ONLY EXPRESSION RELATED TO POLITICAL SPEECH; AUSTRALIAN LEGISLATORS ARE ABLE TO PROHIBIT OTHER FORMS OF SPEECH, SUCH AS RACIAL VILIFICATION AND PORNOGRAPHY WITHOUT THE NEED TO SECURE FEDERAL JUDICIAL APPROVAL. THE COMMONWEALTH (FEDERAL LEGISLATURE), HOWEVER, HAS LIMITED LEGISLATIVE POWERS FOR RESTRICTING SPEECH OR EXPRESSION. ANY ACTS THAT PURPORT TO REGULATE A PARTICULAR FORM OF SPEECH WOULD NEED TO BE SUPPORTED BY A CONSTITUTIONAL HEAD OF CONSTITUTIONAL POWER.

3.1. INTRODUCTION

3.1.1. The concept of human dignity and its relation to equality and freedom

Democratic societies strive, in various forms and in various contexts, to achieve human dignity, equality, and freedom for their citizens. Because of its specific history and the benefit of its constitution-drafting most recently of the countries studied in this text, South Africans have codified these aspirations as constitutional goals. Each country, however, continues to consider the extent to which its Constitution facilitates, prohibits, or in other ways affects the interaction of government actions with these constitutional aspirations.

In many cases, these aspirations are strongly complementary. When, for example, the (1948-1994) apartheid-era South African government significantly curtailed the political rights of the black majority, this oppression simultaneously, and in an interconnected manner, harmed the human dignity of all South Africans, facilitated their unequal treatment and inhibited their efforts to seek more equality, and severely limited their freedom. In other cases, courts find that these aspirations can conflict. Freedom and racial equality conflict when governments seek to ban hate speech; freedom and gender equality conflict when governments seek to ban pornography; freedom and economic equality conflict when governments seek to regulate and limit election campaign spending.

The term "human dignity" is constitutionally enshrined only in South Africa; there are five specific references to that concept in the 1996 Constitution. Section 1(a) provides that the Republic of South Africa is founded on values that include "human dignity, the achievement of equality and the advancement of human rights and freedoms." There are four separate references to human dignity within the Bill of Rights: s 7 (requiring the state to respect the Bill of Rights, which explicitly "affirms the democratic values of human rights, equality, and freedom"), s 10 (expressly declaring that "everyone has inherent dignity and the right to have their dignity respected and protected"), s 35(2)(e) (granting prisoners "conditions of detention that are consistent with human dignity"), and s 36(1) (noting that rights may be reasonably limited, but only if justified "in an open and democratic society based on human dignity, equality and freedom).

The foundational status of human dignity means it both operates as an independent constitutional concept[1] and also as a background principle in the interpretation of other constitutional rights, including equality and freedom. The Constitutional Court has expressly held that constitutional equality is intended to protect against "treating persons differently in a way which impairs their fundamental dignity as human beings, who are inherently equal indignity." *Prinsloo v. Van der Linde* 1997 (3) SA 1012 [¶ 31]. As we discuss in Chapter Seven, the Constitutional Court endorsed a common law rule developed by the Supreme Court of Appeals allowing public officials to use defamation law to protect their dignity while allowing a defence of "reasonable publication." *Khumalo v. Bantubonke Harrington Holomisa* CCT 53/01 (2002).

3.1.2.   Organization of this chapter

This chapter details three examples of conflict between constitutional aspirations, in the context of potential government limits on the freedom of speech or expression. To facilitate consideration of the ways in which courts balance the concepts of dignity, equality, and freedom when they conflict, we first turn to a basic outline of the constitutional concept of the freedom of expression. This is briefly dealt with here, because the substantive differences with regard to "core" political speech are, relatively speaking, less significant among Australia, Canada, South Africa, and the United States than the way in which the concepts are applied in conflict. Next, the three areas of hate speech, pornography, and political speech are considered.

---

[1] Human dignity features most significantly in the area of criminal sanctions, notably in the landmark decision of *S v. Makwanyane* 1995 (3) SA 391 (CC), striking down the death penalty.

3.2.   BASIC APPROACHES TO FREEDOM OF SPEECH AND EXPRESSION

All democracies necessarily protect (albeit in various forms and degrees) the ability of citizens to express themselves. Freedom of speech is, of course, the anchor to American constitutional rights, enshrined (not accidentally) in the First Amendment to the Constitution. As is evident in the decisions excerpted below, the Supreme Court of Canada has drawn heavily on American jurisprudence in giving effect to the right of free expression enshrined in section 2(b) of the Charter. This freedom is not absolute, but courts have created a relative hierarchy of speech, with governmental limits on political speech subject to the closest scrutiny. In South Africa, this right is entrenched in s 16(1) of the Constitution, but s 16(2) expressly provides that the right does not extend to war propaganda, incitement of imminent violence, or "advocacy of hatred that is based on race, ethnicity, gender or religion, and that constitutes incitement to cause harm." Courts in these nations allow greater restraints on commercial speech, which is nonetheless protected. As we saw in Chapter 2, the High Court of Australia has found an implied freedom of political communication in the Australian Constitution. It is confined, however, to speech or expression concerned with political matters ("political" is, however, defined very broadly). In Australia, neither commercial speech (as such) nor pornography is constitutionally protected.

3.2.1.   Basic U.S. approach to free speech

Freedom of speech, protected by the First Amendment, is the topic of an entire course in many U.S. law schools and represents one-half of an entire volume in the five-volume Rotunda & Nowak treatise. The following is intended merely to provide the reader with the very basics.

Free speech is obviously a fundamental constitutional right. Thus, as we saw in Chapter Two, restrictions on this right are subject to careful judicial scrutiny. The Court's decision in *Terminiello v. City of Chicago*, 337 U.S. 1 (1949) articulates some of the principles underlying American free speech jurisprudence. The case arose after Father Arthur Terminiello was successfully prosecuted for breach of the peace after a vitriolic anti-communist speech where, according to the Court, he "vigorously, if not viciously, criticized various political and racial groups whose activities he denounced as inimical to the nation's welfare." The Court took particular exception to jury instructions defining the statutory violation to include speech that "stirs the public to anger, invites dispute, brings about a condition of unrest, or creates a disturbance." The Court found that this instruction impermissibly led to the punishment of constitutionally-protected speech. A key function of free speech "is to invite dispute," and indeed speech may "serve its high purpose when it induces a condition of unrest, creates dissatisfaction with conditions as they are, or even stirs people to anger." Accordingly, although "freedom of speech, though not absolute, is nevertheless protected against censorship or punishment, unless shown likely to produce a clear and present danger of a serious substantive evil that rises far above public inconvenience, annoyance, or unrest. There is no room under our Constitution for a more restrictive view. For the alternative would lead to standardization of ideas either by legislatures, courts, or dominant political or community groups." 337 U.S. at 4.

Although the text of the First Amendment speaks in absolute terms ("Congress shall make *no law* . . . abridging the freedom of speech") — in contrast with the Fourth Amendment's ban on *unreasonable* searches and seizures — the U.S. Supreme Court has rejected the idea of an absolute ban on any governmental limits on expression. Even the "great dissenters," Justices Oliver Wendell Holmes, Jr., and Louis D. Brandeis, whose views on free speech were vindicated by later Courts, recognized that restraints on speech would pass constitutional muster where they posed a "clear and present danger." However, the government must not only have a substantial need to inhibit expression, but the government must select a means least restrictive of expression to accomplish valid objectives. For example, in *Shelton v. Tucker*, 364 U.S. 479 (1960), the Court invalidated an Arkansas statute requiring all public school teachers to disclose all their organizational memberships, because many of these relationships "could have no possible bearing upon the teacher's occupational competence or fitness," and the disclosures were not confidential. The Court declared:

> In a series of decisions this Court has held that, even though the governmental purpose be legitimate and substantial, that purpose cannot be pursued by means that broadly stifle fundamental personal liberties when the end can be more narrowly achieved. The breadth of legislative abridgment must be viewed in the light of less drastic means for achieving the same basic purpose.

The legislature's ability to limit speech sparked an important debate in *Konigsberg v. State Bar of California*, 366 U.S. 36 (1961), challenging the state's power to refuse admission to the Bar to an applicant who refused to answer questions related to membership in the Communist Party. The majority found that this refusal was not protected by the First Amendment:

> At the outset we reject the view that freedom of speech and association, as protected by the First and Fourteenth Amendments, are "absolutes," not only in the undoubted sense that where the constitutional protection exists it must prevail, but also in the sense that the scope of that protection must be gathered solely from a literal reading of the First Amendment. Throughout its history this Court has consistently recognized at least two ways in which constitutionally protected freedom of speech is narrower than an unlimited license to talk. On the one hand, certain forms of speech, or speech in certain contexts, has been considered outside the scope of constitutional protection. On the other hand, general regulatory statutes, not intended to control the content of speech but incidentally limiting its unfettered exercise, have not been regarded as the type of law the First or Fourteenth Amendment forbade Congress or the States to pass, when they have been found justified by subordinating valid governmental interests, a prerequisite to constitutionality which has necessarily involved a weighing of the governmental interest involved. It is in the latter class of cases that this Court has always placed rules compelling disclosure of prior association as an incident of the informed exercise of a valid governmental function. Whenever, in such a context, these constitutional protections are

asserted against the exercise of a valid governmental powers a reconciliation must be effected, and that perforce requires an appropriate weighing of the respective interests involved. With more particular reference to the present context of a state decision as to character qualifications, it is difficult, indeed, to imagine a view of the constitutional protections of speech and association which would automatically and without consideration of the extent of the deterrence of speech and association and of the importance of the state function, exclude all reference to prior speech or association on such issues as character, purpose, credibility, or intent. On the basis of these considerations we now judge petitioner's contentions in the present case.

Justice Black, joined by Warren, C.J. and Douglas, J., dissented, setting forth a more absolutist view:

The recognition that California has subjected "speech and association to the deterrence of subsequent disclosure" is, under the First Amendment, sufficient in itself to render the action of the State unconstitutional unless one subscribes to the doctrine that permits constitutionally protected rights to be "balanced" away whenever a majority of this Court thinks that a State might have interest sufficient to justify abridgment of those freedoms. As I have indicated many times before, I do not subscribe to that doctrine for I believe that the First Amendment's unequivocal command that there shall be no abridgment of the rights of free speech and assembly shows that the men who drafted our Bill of Rights did all the "balancing" that was to be done in this field. The history of the First Amendment is too well known to require repeating here except to say that it certainly cannot be denied that the very object of adopting the First Amendment, as well as the other provisions of the Bill of Rights, was to put the freedoms protected there completely out of the area of any congressional control that may be attempted through the exercise of precisely those powers that are now being used to "balance" the Bill of Rights out of existence.

The Court attempts to justify its refusal to apply the plain mandate of the First Amendment in part by reference to the so-called "clear and present danger test" forcefully used by Mr. Justice Holmes and Mr. Justice Brandeis, not to narrow but to broaden the then prevailing interpretation of First Amendment freedoms. I think very little can be found in anything they ever said that would provide support for the "balancing test" presently in use. Indeed, the idea of "balancing" away First Amendment freedoms appears to me to be wholly inconsistent with the view, strongly espoused by Justices Holmes and Brandeis, that the best test of truth is the power of the thought to get itself accepted in the competition of the market. The "clear and present danger test" was urged as consistent with this view in that it protected speech in all cases except those in which danger was so imminent that there was no time for rational discussion. The "balancing test," on the other hand, rests upon the notion that some ideas are so dangerous that Government need not restrict itself to contrary arguments as a means of opposing them even where there is ample time to do so. Thus here, where there is not a semblance of a "clear and present danger," and where there is more than ample time in which to combat by discussion any idea which may be involved, the majority permits the State of California to adopt measures calculated to suppress the advocacy of views about governmental affairs.

. . . .

. . . But I fear that the creation of "tests" by which speech is left unprotected under certain circumstances is a standing invitation to abridge it. This is nowhere more clearly indicated than by the sudden transformation of the "clear and present danger test" in *Dennis v. United States* [341 U.S. 494 (1951)]. In that case, this Court accepted Judge Learned Hand's "restatement" of the "clear and present danger test": "In each case [courts] must ask whether the gravity of the 'evil,' discounted by its improbability, justifies such invasion of free speech as is necessary to avoid the danger." After the "clear and present danger test" was diluted and weakened by being recast in terms of this "balancing" formula, there seems to me to be much room to doubt that Justices Holmes and Brandeis would even have recognized their test. And the reliance upon that weakened "test" by the majority here, without even so much as an attempt to find either a "clear" or a "present" danger, is only another persuasive reason for rejecting all such "tests" and enforcing the First Amendment according to its terms.

Justice Black rejected any speech limits based on a fear that Americans might be alienated from "our form of government" by "the talk of zealots," because:

[T]he loyalty and patriotism of the American people toward our own free way of life are too deeply rooted to be shaken by mere talk or argument from people who are wedded to totalitarian forms of government. It was this kind of faith in the American people that brought about the adoption of the First Amendment, which was expressly designed to let people say what they wanted to about government — even against government if they were so inclined. The idea underlying this then revolutionary idea of freedom was that the Constitution had set up a government so favorable to individual liberty that arguments against that government would fall harmless at the feet of a satisfied and happy citizenship. Thomas Jefferson voiced this idea with simple eloquence on the occasion of his first inauguration as President of the United States: "If there be any among us who would wish to dissolve this Union or to change its republican form, let them stand undisturbed as monuments of the safety with which error of opinion may be tolerated where reason is left free to combat it."

3.2.1.1. Circumstances that justify content-based speech restrictions

Popular support for the right of free expression makes it difficult for political leaders in functioning democracies to enact legislation suppressing dissent. Three episodes in American history have tested the limits of democratic self-control, and have led to the development of First Amendment standards.

In 1798, faced with increasing hostility from supporters of France and harsh and unprecedented (in the short history of the Republic) partisan criticism by Jeffersonians, Federalist supporters of President John Adams enacted the Sedition Act, prohibiting "publishing any false, scandalous and malicious writing or writings against the government of the United States, or either house of Congress . . . or the President . . . with intent to defame.. or to bring them . . . into contempt or disrepute . . . ." The Supreme Court later explained the Act's ignominious end — *New York Times Co. v. Sullivan*, 376 U.S. 254, 276 (1964) (citations omitted):

> Although the Sedition Act was never tested in this Court [the Act expired by its terms in 1801], the attack upon its validity has carried the day in the court of history. Fines levied in its prosecution were repaid by Act of Congress on the ground that it was unconstitutional. [Legendary Senator John C.] Calhoun, reporting to the Senate on February 4, 1836, assumed that its invalidity was a matter "which no one now doubts." Jefferson, as President, pardoned those who had been convicted and sentenced under the Act and remitted their fines, stating: "I discharged every person under punishment or prosecution under the sedition law, because I considered, and now consider, that law to be a nullity, as absolute and as palpable as if Congress had ordered us to fall down and worship a golden image." The invalidity of the Act has also been assumed by Justices of this Court. See Holmes, J., dissenting and joined by Brandeis, J., in Abrams v. United States, 250 U.S. 616, 630; Jackson, J., dissenting in Beauharnais v. Illinois, 343 U.S. 250, 288–289. These views reflect a broad consensus that the Act, because of the restraint it imposed upon criticism of government and public officials, was inconsistent with the First Amendment.

Rotunda & Nowak, § 20.13(a), catalog the second significant failure of democracy during and shortly after World War I to protect free expression. Communist successes in Russia and central Europe and the activities of a few bomb-throwing anarchists in the United States and a radical workers group led to a "Red scare" highlighted by mass arrests without benefit of *habeas corpus*, hasty prosecutions, and mass deportation of radicals by President Wilson's Attorney General, A. Mitchell Palmer. Congress responded as well with the Espionage Act of 1917 and the Sedition Act of 1918. In *Schenck v. United States*, 249 U.S. 47 (1919), the Court upheld a conviction of the general secretary of the Socialist Party for mailing leaflets to draft-eligible men asserting that the draft violated the Thirteenth Amendment. Writing his famous line, Justice Holmes stated in dissent:

> We admit that in many places and in ordinary times the defendants in saying all that was said in the circular would have been within their constitutional rights. But the character of every act depends upon the circumstances in which it is done. The most stringent protection of free speech would not protect a man in falsely shouting fire in a theatre and causing a panic. It does not even protect a man from an injunction against uttering words that may have all the effect of force. The question in every case is whether the words used are used in such circumstances and are of such a nature as to create a clear and present danger that they will bring about the substantive evils that Congress has a right to prevent. It is a question of proximity and degree. When a nation is at war many things that

might be said in time of peace are such a hindrance to its effort that their utterance will not be endured so long as men fight and that no Court could regard them as protected by any constitutional right. *Id.* at 51 (citations omitted).

Holmes and Brandeis went on in other cases to object to convictions on lesser standards of threatened harm. *See, e.g., Abrams v. United States*, 250 U.S. 616 (1919) (twenty year sentences for distributing leaflets critical of American involvement in effort to crush Russia's new communist government affirmed by majority because of the "bad tendency" of speech).

The next example from history of litigated Supreme Court cases came during the McCarthy era of the 1950s, when Congress again passed anti-communist legislation. *Dennis v. United States*, 341 U.S. 494 (1951), upheld convictions for organizing the Communist Party of the United States. Congress found that the goal of the Party was the violent overthrow of the government. A plurality of the Court, in an opinion by Chief Justice Vinson, adopted the verbal formulation of the clear and present danger standard, but reasoned that this "cannot mean that before the Government may act, it must wait until the *putsch* is about to be executed." The Court adopted a new formulation announced by the court of appeals in the case: "in each case [courts] must ask whether the gravity of the 'evil,' discounted by its improbability, justifies such invasion of free speech as is necessary to avoid danger." *Id.* at 510 (quoting from 183 F.2d 201, 212 (2d Cir. 1950) (Hand, J.).

Finally, the Court "signaled a major shift," Rotunda & Nowak §20.15, to ensure that the protections of the clear and present danger test would not be diluted. In *Brandenburg v. Ohio*, 395 U.S. 444 (1969), the Court reversed a conviction of a Ku Klux Klan member who had organized a rally, attended only by 12 Klan members and a few invited reporters, under the state Criminal Syndicalism statute that barred advocacy of "the duty, necessity, or propriety of crime, sabotage, violence, or unlawful methods of terrorism as a means of accomplishing industrial or political reform" and for "voluntarily assembl[ing] with any society, group, or assemblage of persons formed to teach or advocate the doctrines of criminal syndicalism." Speeches derogatory of African Americans and Jews were made, and the defendant, in Klan robes, proclaimed that "We're not a revengent organization, but if our President, our Congress, our Supreme Court, continues to suppress the white, Caucasian race, it's possible that there might have to be some revengeance taken." In reversing the conviction, the Court expressly overruled an earlier precedent upholding a similar statute, *Whitney v. California*, 274 U.S. 357 (1927).

The Court read more recent precedents as establishing the "principle that the constitutional guarantees of free speech and free press do not permit a State to forbid or proscribe advocacy of the use of force or of law violation except where such advocacy is directed to inciting or producing imminent lawless action and is likely to incite or produce such action." The Ohio conviction was reversed because the prosecution had not "refined the statute's bald definition of the crime in terms of mere advocacy not distinguished from incitement to imminent lawless action."

Finally, the Court returned to the issue in upholding a provision of the post-9/11 Patriot Act making it a crime to "materially assist" an entity designated as a "foreign terrorist organization." *Holder v. Humanitarian Law Project*, 130 S. Ct.

2705 (2010). Noting that the statute did not prohibit membership in organizations nor independent advocacy of an organization's goals, the majority credited congressional findings that material support for legitimate and peaceful activities still enabled the terrorist organization to free other resources for terrorist and illegal activities. The Court rejected the government's claim that the statute regulated conduct, not speech, but found under careful scrutiny that the provision did not offend the First Amendment.

3.2.1.2.   Content-neutral restrictions

The prior cases, all involving government restrictions on expressive activity based on the content of the expression (political associations, hate speech, obscenity), demonstrate the very demanding scrutiny that American courts give to content-based restrictions on free speech. Many government regulations, however, have some effect on speech or expression — for example a city ordinance prohibiting loud noises in the late evening or a prosecution of littering involving leaflets. These regulations are evaluated under a distinct standard. In *United States v. O'Brien*, 391 U.S. 367 (1968), the Court affirmed the defendant's conviction for burning his draft card (a common form of protest against the War in Vietnam). When speech and conduct combine, "a sufficiently important governmental interest in regulating the nonspeech element can justify incidental limitations on First Amendment freedoms." *Id.* at 376. To pass muster, the regulation must (1) further an important or substantial governmental interest, which must (2) be unrelated to the suppression of free expression; and (3) the incidental restriction on alleged First Amendment freedoms can be no greater than is essential to the furtherance of that interest. *Id.* at 377. The statute was upheld as fulfilling the smooth operation of the military draft system.

3.2.2.   Basic Canadian approach to free speech

Canadian courts recognized the importance of speech to a functioning democracy long before the Charter. The SCC struck down an Alberta statute requiring newspapers to publish government reply to criticism of government policies in *Re Alberta Statutes*, [1938] S.C.R. 100 (the *Alberta Press* case). Duff, C.J., reasoned from the BNA Act's declaration that the constitution of Canada was to be similar in principle to that of the United Kingdom that Canada's constitution featured "a parliament working under the influence of public opinion and public discussion." Thus, "this right of free public discussion of public affairs, notwithstanding its incidental mischiefs, is the breadth of life for parliamentary institutions." *Id.* at 133. Accordingly, not only could Parliament affirmatively legislate to protect public expressions, but legislation abrogating the right was beyond the legislative competence of the provinces.

With the enactment of the Charter, freedom of expression became constitutionally entrenched. As detailed in *Irwin Toy*, excerpted below, the Court has adopted a very broad interpretation of the scope of the guarantee set forth in s. 2(b). In contrast to the pre-Charter view that protected expression necessary for a functioning democracy, Canadian doctrine today is that all expressive activity is protected, but then subject to reasonable limits under s. 1. This approach significantly differs from the Court's interpretation of other sections. Most notably, as we will see in Chapter Four, the SCC rejected the idea in *Andrews v. Law Society of B.C.*, [1989] 1 S.C.R. 143, that s. 15's guarantee of equality should be construed to encompass any differential treatment and could then be justified under s. 1. (Professor Hogg, who initially advocated this approach, discusses the topic in *Constitutional Law of Canada*, § 55.8(a).)

Thus, almost any limits on expressive activity can be challenged in Canadian courts. They will use the *Oakes* test to determine if the limit is reasonable.

3.2.2.1. Pre-Charter antecedents

In *Switzman v. Elbling*, [1957] S.C.R. 285, the Court invalidated a Quebec statute making it illegal to use a house "to propagate Communism." Although a leading Quebecois justice, Robert Taschereau, defended the statute as a regulation of property, the other justices held that the statute was *ultra vires* the Quebec National Assembly. The majority held that the law was tantamount to the creation of a new crime, exclusively assigned to Parliament. The concurrence held that the law's pith and substance was in relation to speech. This meant that speech could only be regulated by Parliament under the POGG power, based on the earlier *Alberta Press* decision, [1938] S.C.R. 100 These opinions emphasized how free expression was "essential to the working of a parliamentary democracy," [1957] S.C.R. at 369 (Abbott, J.), and that parliamentary government required "the condition of a virtually unobstructed access to and diffusion of ideas." *Id.* at 358 (Rand, J.).

More limited use of federalism principles was at work in *Nova Scotia Board of Censors v. McNeil*, [1978] 2 S.C.R. 662, upholding the provincial censorship of films as the regulation of business or a local matter. However, the court narrowly construed the unbound discretion of the censor board to exclude censorship of political or religious ideas.

3.2.2.2. Basic Charter principles

IRWIN TOY LTD. v. QUEBEC (ATTORNEY GENERAL)
SUPREME COURT OF CANADA
[1989] 1 S.C.R. 927

[Before DICKSON, CJC, BEETZ, MCINTYRE, LAMER, and WILSON, JJ.]

THE CHIEF JUSTICE and LAMER AND WILSON JJ. — This appeal raises questions concerning the constitutionality, under ss. 91 and 92 of the *Constitution Act*, 1867, and ss. 2(b) and 7 of the *Canadian Charter of Rights and Freedoms*, of ss. 248 and 249 of the *Quebec Consumer Protection Act*, R.S.Q., c. P-40.1, respecting the prohibition of television advertising directed at persons under thirteen years of age.

[Section 248 generally prohibits commercial advertising directed at children 12 and under. To determine if the advertisement is directed at children, s. 249 requires consideration of the nature and purpose of the goods, the manner of the ad, and the time and placement are considered. The fact that the ad appears in material, or broadcast on a program intended for an older audience is not presumptive. Commercial advertising to children is permitted, however, if it appears in ordinary periodicals or in store displays and meets a variety of criteria set forth in s. 91 of the statute. Even here, advertising is significantly restricted, prohibiting many standard advertising techniques considered "puffing" in commercial lexicon, to "directly incite a child to buy or urge another person to buy goods or services," to use cartoon characters, etc.]

[First, the Court rejected a federalism challenge, holding that the advertising regulations were *intra vires* the Legislature of the Province of Quebec. Because their focus is on advertising, not broadcasting, they do not fall within the latter's exclusive federal sphere, they were not pre-empted by federal broadcast regulations, nor did they invade the federal criminal law power.]

VI — Whether ss. 248 and 249 Limits Freedom of Expression as Guaranteed by the Canadian and Quebec Charters

[Initially, the Court concluded that the constitutional guarantee of freedom of expression applied to commercial expression.]

B. *The First Step: Was the Plaintiff's Activity Within the Sphere of Conduct Protected by Freedom of Expression?*

[The Court noted that "not all activity is protected by freedom of expression, and governmental action restricting this form of advertising only limits the guarantee if the activity in issue was protected in the first place." For example, a previous case had held that freedom of association did not include the right to strike. The first step "is to discover whether the activity which the plaintiff wishes to pursue may properly be characterized as falling within 'freedom of expression'."]

"Expression" has both a content and a form, and the two can be inextricably connected. Activity is expressive if it attempts to convey meaning. That meaning is its content. Freedom of expression was entrenched in our Constitution and is guaranteed in the Quebec Charter so as to ensure that everyone can manifest their thoughts, opinions, beliefs, indeed all expressions of the heart and mind, however unpopular, distasteful or contrary to the mainstream. Such protection is, in the words of both the Canadian and Quebec Charters, "fundamental" because in a free, pluralistic and democratic society we prize a diversity of ideas and opinions for their inherent value both to the community and to the individual. ***

We cannot, then, exclude human activity from the scope of guaranteed free expression on the basis of the content or meaning being conveyed. Indeed, if the activity conveys or attempts to convey a meaning, it has expressive content and prima facie falls within the scope of the guarantee. Of course, while most human activity combines expressive and physical elements, some human activity is purely physical and does not convey or attempt to convey meaning. It might be difficult to characterize certain day-to-day tasks, like parking a car, as having expressive content. To bring such activity within the protected sphere, the plaintiff would have to show that it was performed to convey a meaning. For example, an unmarried person might, as part of a public protest, park in a zone reserved for spouses of government employees in order to express dissatisfaction or outrage at the chosen method of allocating a limited resource. If that person could demonstrate that his activity did in fact have expressive content, he would, at this stage, be within the protected sphere and the s. 2(b) challenge would proceed.

*   *   *

Thus, the first question remains: Does the advertising aimed at children fall within the scope of freedom of expression? Surely it aims to convey a meaning, and cannot be excluded as having no expressive content. ***

C. *The Second Step: Was the Purpose or Effect of the Government Action to Restrict Freedom of Expression?*

*   *   *

a. *Purpose*

*   *   *

If the government's purpose is to restrict the content of expression by singling out particular meanings that are not to be conveyed, it necessarily limits the guarantee of free expression. If the government's purpose is to restrict a form of expression in order to control access by others to the meaning being conveyed or to control the ability of the one conveying the meaning to do so, it also limits the guarantee. On the other hand, where the government aims to control only the physical consequences of certain human activity, regardless of the meaning being conveyed, its purpose is not to control expression. ***

Thus, for example, a rule against handing out pamphlets is a restriction on a manner of expression and is "tied to content," even if that restriction purports to control litter. The rule aims to control access by others to a meaning being conveyed as well as to control the ability of the pamphleteer to convey a meaning. To restrict this form of expression, handing out pamphlets, entails restricting its content. By contrast, a rule against littering is not a restriction "tied to content." It aims to control the physical consequences of certain conduct regardless of whether that conduct attempts to convey meaning. To restrict littering as a "manner of expression" need not lead inexorably to restricting content. Of course, rules can be framed to appear neutral as to content even if their true purpose is to control attempts to convey a meaning. For example, in *Saumur v. City of Quebec*, [1953] 2 S.C.R. 299, a municipal by-law forbidding distribution of pamphlets without prior authorization from the Chief of Police was a colourable attempt to restrict expression.

*   *   *

b. *Effects*

Even if the government's purpose was not to control or restrict attempts to convey a meaning, the Court must still decide whether the effect of the government action was to restrict the plaintiff's free expression. Here, the burden is on the plaintiff to demonstrate that such an effect occurred. In order so to demonstrate, a plaintiff must state her claim with reference to the principles and values underlying the freedom.

We have already discussed the nature of the principles and values underlying the vigilant protection of free expression in a society such as ours. They were also discussed by the Court, and can be summarized as follows: (1) seeking and attaining the truth is an inherently good activity; (2) participation in social and political decision-making is to be fostered and encouraged; and (3) the diversity in forms of individual self-fulfillment and human flourishing ought to be cultivated in an essentially tolerant, indeed welcoming, environment not only for the sake of those who convey a meaning, but also for the sake of those to whom it is conveyed. In showing that the effect of the government's action was to restrict her free expression, a plaintiff must demonstrate that her activity promotes at least one of these principles. It is not enough that shouting, for example, has an expressive element. If the plaintiff challenges the effect of government action to control noise, presuming that action to have a purpose neutral as to expression, she must show that her aim was to convey a meaning reflective of the principles underlying freedom of expression. The precise and complete articulation of what kinds of activity promote these principles is, of course, a matter for judicial appreciation to be developed on a case by case basis. But the plaintiff must at least identify the meaning being conveyed and how it relates to the pursuit of truth, participation in the community, or individual self-fulfillment and human flourishing.

c. Sections 248 and 249

[The Court restated its finding that the challenged provisions were designed to restrict content and forms of expression in the name of protecting children. Indeed, Quebec's arguments justifying the restriction under s. 1 of the Canadian Charter and s. 9.1 of the Quebec Charter acknowledged that "the purported mischief at which the Act and regulations were directed was the harm caused by the message itself."]

VII — Whether the Limit on Freedom of Expression Imposed by ss. 248 and 249 Is Justified Under s. 9.1 of the Quebec Charter or s. 1 of the Canadian Charter

[Ed. note: The law was challenged under the free expression provisions of both the Canadian Charter and a Quebec statute, the *Quebec Charter of Human Rights and Freedoms*, originally enacted in 1975, seven years before the federal Charter. Like its federal counterpart, the Quebec charter has a provision, s. 9.1, that permits limits on fundamental rights in appropriate circumstances. The Supreme Court of Canada's determination that s. 9.1 has the same meaning as s. 1 of the federal charter (*i.e.*, the *Oakes* test applies), is discussed in connection with the *Ford* case in Chapter 9.]

D. *Whether the s. 1 and s. 9.1 Materials Justify Banning Commercial Advertising Directed at Persons Under Thirteen Years of Age*

It is now well established that the onus of justifying the limitation of a right or freedom rests with the party seeking to uphold the limitation, in this case the Attorney General of Quebec, and that the analysis to be conducted is that set forth by Dickson C.J. in *R. v. Oakes, supra.* [This case is discussed in Chapter 2.]

a. *Pressing and Substantial Objective*

*   *   *

In our view, the Attorney General of Quebec has demonstrated that the concern which prompted the enactment of the impugned legislation is pressing and substantial and that the purpose of the legislation is one of great importance. The concern is for the protection of a group which is particularly vulnerable to the techniques of seduction and manipulation abundant in advertising . . . .

In establishing the factual basis for this generally identified concern, the Attorney General relied heavily upon the U.S. Federal Trade Commission (FTC) Final Staff Report and Recommendation, *In the Matter of Children's Advertising,* which contains a thorough review of the scientific evidence on the subject as at 1981. The Report emerged from a rulemaking proceeding initiated by the FTC. The Report's assessment both of children's cognitive ability to evaluate television advertising directed at them and of the possible remedies to mitigate the adverse effects of such advertising are relevant here. One of its principal conclusions is that young children (2-6) cannot distinguish fact from fiction or programming from advertising and are completely credulous when presented with advertising messages (at pp. 34-35).

*   *   *

The Report thus provides a sound basis on which to conclude that television advertising directed at young children is per se manipulative. Such advertising aims to promote products by convincing those who will always believe.

*   *   *

[The Court upheld the legislative choice of 13 as the upper age limit for the protected group.] Where the legislature mediates between the competing claims of different groups in the community, it will inevitably be called upon to draw a line marking where one set of claims legitimately begins and the other fades away without access to complete knowledge as to its precise location. If the legislature has made a reasonable assessment as to where the line is most properly drawn, especially if that assessment involves weighing conflicting scientific evidence and allocating scarce resources on this basis, it is not for the court to second guess. That would only be to substitute one estimate for another. In dealing with inherently heterogeneous groups defined in terms of age or a characteristic analogous to age, evidence showing that a clear majority of the group requires the protection which the government has identified can help to establish that the group was defined reasonably. Here, the legislature has mediated between the claims of advertisers and those seeking commercial information on the one hand, and the claims of children and parents on the other. There is sufficient evidence to warrant drawing a line at age thirteen, and we would not presume to re-draw the line. We note that in *Ford*, *supra*, at pp. 777–79, the Court also recognized that the government was afforded a margin of appreciation to form legitimate objectives based on somewhat inconclusive social science evidence.

b. *Means Proportional to the Ends*

[The Court restated the next three prongs in the *Oakes* test for active judicial review, all of which concern whether the means chosen by the government are proportional to its objective: (2) "the limiting measures must be carefully designed, or rationally connected, to the objective; (3) they must impair the right as little as possible; and (4) their effects must not so severely trench on individual or group rights that the legislative objective, albeit important, is nevertheless outweighed by the abridgement of rights." The court found that the advertising ban is rationally connected to protecting children from advertising. With regard to the "minimal impairment" test, the Court interpreting *Oakes* requirement that the means chosen impair the right "as little as possible" as varying "depending on the government objective and the means available to it."]

Thus, in matching means to ends and asking whether rights or freedoms are impaired as little as possible, a legislature mediating between the claims of competing groups will be forced to strike a balance without the benefit of absolute certainty concerning how that balance is best struck. Vulnerable groups will claim the need for protection by the government whereas other groups and individuals will assert that the government should not intrude. In *Edwards Books and Art Ltd.*, *supra*, Dickson C.J. expressed an important concern about the situation of vulnerable groups (at p. 779):

> "In interpreting and applying the Charter I believe that the courts must be cautious to ensure that it does not simply become an instrument of better situated individuals to roll back legislation which has as its object the improvement of the condition of less advantaged persons."

When striking a balance between the claims of competing groups, the choice of means, like the choice of ends, frequently will require an assessment of conflicting scientific evidence and differing justified demands on scarce resources. Democratic institutions are meant to let us all share in the responsibility for these difficult choices. Thus, as courts review the results of the legislature's deliberations, particularly with respect to the protection of vulnerable groups, they must be mindful of the legislature's representative function . . . .

In other cases, however, rather than mediating between different groups, the government is best characterized as the singular antagonist of the individual whose right has been infringed. For example, in justifying an infringement of legal rights enshrined in ss. 7 to 14 of the Charter, the state, on behalf of the whole community, typically will assert its responsibility for prosecuting crime whereas the individual will assert the paramountcy of principles of fundamental justice. There might not be any further competing claims among different groups. In such circumstances, and indeed whenever the government's purpose relates to maintaining the authority and impartiality of the judicial system, the courts can assess with some certainty whether the "least drastic means" for achieving the purpose have been chosen, especially given their accumulated experience in dealing with such questions: see *Sunday Times v. United Kingdom* (1979), 2 E.H.R.R. 245, at p. 276. The same degree of certainty may not be achievable in cases involving the reconciliation of claims of competing individuals or groups or the distribution of scarce government resources.

* * *

In sum, the evidence [primarily the FTC staff report] sustains the reasonableness of the legislature's conclusion that a ban on commercial advertising directed to children was the minimal impairment of free expression consistent with the pressing and substantial goal of protecting children against manipulation through such advertising. While evidence exists that other less intrusive options reflecting more modest objectives were available to the government, there is evidence establishing the necessity of a ban to meet the objectives the government had reasonably set. This Court will not, in the name of minimal impairment, take a restrictive approach to social science evidence and require legislatures to choose the least ambitious means to protect vulnerable groups. There must nevertheless be a sound evidentiary basis for the government's conclusions. ***

* * *

The reasons of BEETZ and McINTYRE JJ. were delivered by

McINTYRE J. (dissenting):

[The dissent agreed that the challenged provisions infringed free expression protection in s. 2(b) of the *Canadian Charter* and s. 3 of the *Quebec Charter*, but did not find them to be justified under s. 1 of the Canadian Charter or s. 9.1 of the Quebec Charter. The dissent found] no case has been made that children are at risk. Furthermore, even if I could reach another conclusion, I would be of the view that the restriction fails on the issue of proportionality. A total prohibition of advertising aimed at children below an arbitrarily fixed age makes no attempt at the achievement of proportionality.[2]

In conclusion, I would say that freedom of expression is too important to be lightly cast aside or limited. It is ironic that most attempts to limit freedom of expression and hence freedom of knowledge and information are justified on the

---

[2] [Ed. note: Justice McIntyre omitted an interesting fact: neither the FTC nor the U.S. Congress ever enacted limits on advertising directed toward children following issuance of the staff report relied upon by the majority. Indeed, it was the subject to vitriolic criticism in Washington. *See, e.g., The FTC as National Nanny* (Editorial), WASH. POST, Mar. 1, 1978, at A22:

. . . what are the children to be protected from? The candy and sugar-coated cereals that lead to tooth decay? Or the inability or refusal of parents to say no? . . . the proposal, in reality, is designed to protect children from the weaknesses of their parents — and the parents from the wailing insistence of their children. That, traditionally, is one of the roles of a governess — if you can afford one. It is not a proper role of government.]

basis that the limitation is for the benefit of those whose rights will be limited. It was this proposition that motivated the early church in restricting access to information, even to prohibiting the promulgation and reading of the scriptures in a language understood by the people. The argument that freedom of expression was dangerous was used to oppose and restrict public education in earlier times. The education of women was greatly retarded on the basis that wider knowledge would only make them dissatisfied with their role in society. I do not suggest that the limitations imposed by ss. 248 and 249 are so earth shaking or that if sustained they will cause irremediable damage. I do say, however, that these limitations represent a small abandonment of a principle of vital importance in a free and democratic society and, therefore, even if it could be shown that some child or children have been adversely affected by advertising of the kind prohibited, I would still be of the opinion that the restriction should not be sustained. Our concern should be to recognize that in this century we have seen whole societies utterly corrupted by the suppression of free expression. We should not lightly take a step in that direction, even a small one.

*   *   *

Because of the presence of section 1, Canadian courts do not need to draw the distinction between content-based infringements of speech and other regulation that Americans would say does not "abridge" but only "incidentally regulates" speech. In the U.S., laws limiting anti-abortion protesters have been the subject of considerable controversy, with the Supreme Court carefully reviewing court injunctions and a statute banning picketing at health care facilities to assure that the regulations were content-neutral and minimally impaired free speech rights. *See, e.g., Madsen v. Women's Health Clinic, Inc.*, 512 U.S. 753 (1994). In British Columbia, a similar statute was upheld as a reasonable limit. *R. v. Lewis*, 139 D.L.R. (4th) 480 (B.C.S.C. 1996) (case dismissed on appeal because the accused had died). To pass constitutional muster, the British Columbia legislature did not need to draft a content-neutral statute. Rather, it enacted the *Access to Abortion Services Act* specifically to facilitate access to abortion services. The court conceded that the statute was not content neutral, but that did "not fatally taint the legislation as [it might have] in the United States of America, which does not have the equivalent of s. 1 of the *Charter* to allow a balancing of rights." *Id.* at 508. While U.S. courts have found an 8-foot buffer zone acceptable but a 15-foot zone not, the statute created a 50-metre access free zone, which the court upheld as within the range that minimally impaired the rights of the protesters. (A uniquely Canadian aspect of the analysis was the court's observation that because abortion is a lawful medical service, and because the Canada Health Act requires health care to be "universal and accessible," it then "follows that the government has an obligation to provide generally equal access to this controversial service." *Id.* at 509.)

3.2.3.   Basic Australian approach to free speech

The Australian Constitution does not include a generalized guarantee of "free speech." It protects *political* speech or communication specifically, via an implied constitutional limitation on legislative power. Australia has a long history of restricting speech of three kinds: obscene speech, defamatory speech, and speech that is regarded as dangerous to democratic institutions or values. Australia's once-strict obscenity laws have been wound-back or liberalized since the 1970s. Defamation laws (modernized in 2006) still allow a person to sue in tort for defamation; successful actions are relatively common (although defences of truth, privilege, and honest opinion apply). Laws targeting seditious speech have long been in force; their most famous application was the prosecution of several Communist Party members for seditious speech during the Cold War years (there were few convictions, however, and an attempt to ban the Communist Party of Australia was ruled unconstitutional in 1951). In 2005, the Commonwealth modernized the sedition laws to encompass new (post 9/11) types of inflammatory or politically dangerous speech, at the same time as offering a more modern range of defences. Additionally, as discussed below, laws restricting hate speech and speech that vilifies vulnerable minority groups have been passed in all Australian jurisdictions in recent decades. These laws, although extending to political speech, have not been challenged for breach of the implied freedom of political communication; it is generally accepted that the High Court would find them valid, as serving a legitimate governmental purpose under the "Lange test" (see below).

In contrast, in countries with enumerated free speech provisions in their constitutions, such laws are less likely to survive judicial review. Advocates of a Bill of Rights for Australia treat this conclusion as evidence that further rights protection is needed. Opponents reach the opposite conclusion, and point to the obstacles that entrenched free speech may create for the regulation of politically harmful speech (such as speech that gives encouragement to terrorism). On the merits of restricting hate speech, however, advocates and opponents tend to reason conversely. Few Australians would argue that speech should be entirely "free" of any regulation.

In December 2013, the Commonwealth Attorney-General, George Brandis, announced a review by the Australian Law Reform Commission of Australia's laws, with the purpose of identifying those that "encroach upon traditional [common law] rights, freedoms, and privileges", including laws that "interfere" with free speech. Brandis, an opponent of a Bill of Rights, has previously questioned the desirability of anti-vilification and hate speech laws. If his reform agenda is followed, Australia's protection of free speech may (perhaps paradoxically) be extended further, albeit by legislative reform, rather than constitutional means.

3.2.3.1.   Overview of the implied freedom of political communication

We saw in Chapter 2 the foundations of the implied freedom of political communication [IFPC], as identified in the High Court of Australia in 1992, in *Nationwide News Pty Ltd v. Wills* (1992) 177 CLR 1 and *Australian Capital Television Pty Ltd v. Commonwealth* (1992) 177 CLR 106. These cases established the principle that the freedom of communication concerning what people need to know in order freely to choose their representatives was protected by the words of the Constitution which, in ss. 7 & 24, mandate that the Parliament is to be "directly chosen by the people." In these early cases, the Court had not yet settled on a number of related issues:

- Where, exactly in the Constitution, did the implied freedom lie?
- Did the freedom extend to the states?
- Did the freedom extend to acts (expressive conduct) as well as speech?
- Did it protect speech or communication about foreign matters?
- Did it create a new defence for defamation?
- What is meant by "political"?
- What is the test for legitimate legislative limits on the implied freedom?

Over the course of many subsequent cases, the Court answered these questions: The implied freedom lies in the text and structure of the Constitution, specifically in ss. 7 & 24, and not in the Constitution's overall scheme for democratic government or liberty. The freedom extends to the states. It protects expressive conduct — like protesting or demonstrating (*Levy v. Victoria* (1997) 189 CLR 579). It is not confined to discussion or communication about Australian political matters. In *Theophanous v. Herald & Weekly Times Ltd* (1994) 182 CLR 104, the High Court ruled that the IFPC created a new defence for defamation, where the publication complained of concerned a public figure (Mr Theophanous was a Member of Parliament and Minister of State). However, in *Lange v. Australian Broadcasting Corporation* (1997) 189 CLR 520, the Court reversed and overruled *Theophanous* on this point. The IFPC, the Court said (unanimously) did not create a new defence, or a personal right. It served only as a limitation on legislative power. In *Lange*, the Court also settled on the test for legitimate limitations on this freedom. As we saw in Chapter 2, the Court must ask of impugned (challenged) legislation:

(1)   "Does the law effectively burden freedom of communication about government or political matters either in its terms, operation or effect?"

(2)   If it does, "Is the law reasonably appropriate and adapted to serve a legitimate end the fulfillment of which is compatible with the maintenance of the constitutionally prescribed system of representative and responsible government?"

If the answer to the first question is "yes" and to the second is "no," then the law is invalid. *Lange* is now the leading case on the IFPC. In *Lange*, the Court concluded that New South Wales' defamation law did burden the freedom of communication, but it was reasonably appropriate and adapted to a legitimate purpose. (A significant part of the court's analysis concerned the relationship between the implied constitutional right and the common law. This aspect of the opinion is discussed in Chapter Seven, below.)

In a case note, *Lange, Levy and the Direction of the Freedom of Political Communication under the Australian Constitution*, 21 UNSW L.J. 117 (1998), Professor Adrienne Stone explained the Court's reasoning in a companion case of *Levy v. State of Victoria* (1997) 189 CLR 579. The case resulted in six separate judgments by the HCA, although all the justices agreed that the IFPC did not preclude Victoria from prohibiting political activist Lawrie Levy from entering a hunting area without a license in order to protest against duck hunting. One issue was whether the IFPC applied to conduct, as well as speech. As Professor Stone explained (at p. 128), it was clear from *Levy* that it did. She noted Chief Justice Brennan's comment that:

> . . . unlike the United States where free speech law is governed by the text of the First Amendment, in Australia there is no need to categorise communicative conduct as "speech" in order to attract the freedom. The only question is whether the relevant law restricts communication necessary to preserve the system of representative and responsible government that the Constitution prescribes[:] "[a] law which simply denied an opportunity make . . . a protest about an issue relevant to the government or politics of the Commonwealth would be as offensive to the constitutionally implied freedom as a law which banned speech making on the issue."

The other justices also included non-verbal conduct within the IFPC. However, the Court splintered on whether discussion of state political matters fell within the IFPC. As McHugh J noted, *Levy, supra*, at 625:

> It is not easy to see a connection between the message that the protesters wished to send to the public of Victoria and the freedom of communication protected by the Constitution. It seems remote from choosing members of the Senate or House of Representatives or the conduct of the federal government.

Stone notes that the Court also divided on whether Victoria's regulations violated the *Lange* requirement that the law be "reasonably appropriate" if overly restrictive. Brennan CJ rejected the claim: the IFPC did not give courts the "power to determine that some more limited restriction than that imposed by an impugned law could suffice to achieve a legitimate purpose." In this regard, Stone notes that Brennan specifically rejected a parallel American case (refusing to follow *Schenck v. Pro-Choice Network of Western New York*, 519 U.S. 357 (1997), invalidating restrictions on anti-abortion protesters because they were greater than necessary to achieve their purpose). The other justices, however, all indicated that they believed that the regulations did not impose a "greater curtailment" than necessary. In Professor Stone's view, this signals the survival of prior precedents suggesting a "two tiered" approach, requiring a showing that a law is necessary to achieve an overriding public purpose when its "direct purpose" is to restrict communication, but a more deferential "reasonably appropriate" standard should be used when the regulation "only incidentally" restricted political communication.

3.2.3.2. More recent cases

A significant number of cases have come before the High Court in the last ten years, in which the IFPC has been argued, although there has been little development in its scope. In 2004, in *Coleman v. Power* (2004) 220 CLR 1, the question of whether the IFPC protects insulting language or "fighting words" was considered. The challenge was the first to succeed after *Lange*, albeit without a decisive answer.

The case concerned the conviction of a political activist under a Queensland state law which made it an offence to use "threatening, abusive, or insulting words to any person" in or near a public place. The activist, Patrick Coleman, had been handing out leaflets in a shopping mall protesting against official corruption; he was arrested for shouting out that a passing police officer was "corrupt." Coleman challenged the law as inconsistent with the implied freedom of political communication. The Court upheld his appeal; its reasoning, however, was complex. As Adrienne Stone and Simon Evans explain in *Australia: Freedom of Speech and Insult in the High Court of Australia*, 4 INT'L J. OF CONSTITUTIONAL L. 677 (2006):

> Three justices held that the law was valid, but the freedom at issue was such that the law had to be read so narrowly as not to apply to the facts of Coleman's case . . . A fourth justice held that the law could not be read down in this way and was, therefore, invalid. The three dissenting justices held that the law ought not to be read narrowly but, nonetheless, validly applied to the facts of Coleman's case . . . The Court's decision . . . confirm[ed] the survival of the freedom of political communication . . .

The remaining question — what is meant by "political"? — still awaits clear jurisprudential guidelines. The Federal Court of Australia considered this question in 1998, in *Brown v. Classification Review Board of the Office of Film and Literature Classification* (1998) 154 ALR 67. The case was an appeal against an adverse decision of the Classification Review Board regarding an issue of *Rabelais*, the La Trobe University students' newspaper (the decision had the effect that the publication could not be distributed). The particular issue included an article entitled "The Art of Shoplifting," styled as a "step by step guide to shoplifting." The Federal Court dismissed the appeal. Justice Heerey said:

> In the present case, the article does not concern "political or government matters." The author is not advocating the repeal of the law of theft, either generally or in respect of theft from shops owned by large corporations. The article says nothing, expressly or by implication, about the conduct of holders of elected or appointed public office or the policies which should be followed by them. The article is not addressed to readers in their capacity as fellow-citizens and voters. The article does not even advocate breaking one law as a means of securing the repeal of another law perceived as bad, as with draft card burning in protest against conscription for Vietnam . . . The appellants' counsel point out in their submission that writers have from time to time advocated theft as an appropriate means of reallocation of resources (Oscar Wilde in *The Soul of Man Under Socialism*), or of political dissent ("On Maoism: An Interview with Jean-Paul Sartre" in Telos, Summer 1973), or as a central tenet of Anarchist theory (Proudhon, "Qu'est-ce que la propriété?"). . . All this may be in one sense politics, but the constitutional freedom of political communication assumes — indeed exists to support, foster and protect — representative democracy and the rule of law. The advocacy of law breaking falls outside this protection and is antithetical to it.
>
> It follows that in my opinion United States decisions like *Brandenburg v. Ohio* 395 U.S. 444 (1969) and the line of cases which follow it are not applicable to the implied freedom under the Australian Constitution. There is no constitutional protection for speech which is "mere advocacy" or abstract teaching of the necessity or propriety of criminal or violent

conduct. The reason is simple. Such conduct is not part of the system of representative and responsible government or of the political and democratic process.

Justice French (now Chief Justice French of the High Court) did not reject the argument that the article was "political," and that the restriction on its publication burdened the implied freedom of political communication. Nevertheless, he said, the restriction was legitimate:

> There is much to be said for the conclusion that "The Art of Shoplifting" falls outside the scope of political discussion. But, inelegant, awkward and unconvincing as is its attempt to justify its practical message about shoplifting by reference to the evils of capitalism, it is arguable that in some aspects it would fall within a broad understanding of political discussion. That characterization, however, will not invalidate the effective operation upon it of a law which is enacted for a legitimate end, is compatible with representative and responsible government and is reasonably appropriate and adapted to achieving that end . . .

The decision was not appealed to the High Court.

3.2.4.   Basic South African approach to free speech

The South African Constitution explicitly protects freedom of expression and not only freedom of speech. In addition to a broad right to freedom of expression, the clause includes specific references to freedom of the press, artistic creativity, academic freedom and the right to receive and impart information or ideas. At the same time, the clause includes explicit internal limitations on the freedom of expression, including propaganda for war, incitement to imminent violence as well as advocacy of hatred based on race, ethnicity, gender or religion when this hatred constitutes incitement to cause harm. In addition to these specific limitations which specifically preclude such expression from constitutional protection, protected expression remains subject to the Constitution's limitations clause which allows for regulation so long as the resulting limitation on the right is reasonable and justifiable in an open and democratic society based on human dignity, equality, and freedom.

The Constitutional Court has responded to this framework by recognizing the importance of free expression in a democratic society and by adopting a generous interpretation of the rights guaranteed. In one of its earliest cases the Constitutional Court struck down the Indecent or Obscene Photographic Matter Act of 1967 on the grounds that its definition of indecent material was too broad. In the decision Justice Mogoro argued that "We must understand [freedom of expression] . . . not in isolation, but as part of a web of mutually supporting rights enumerated in the Constitution, including the right to 'freedom of conscience, religion, thought, belief and opinion', the right to privacy, and the right to dignity. Ultimately, all of these rights together may be conceived as underpinning an entitlement to participate in an ongoing process of communicative interaction that is of both instrumental and intrinsic value." *Case and Another v. Minister of Safety and Security*, 1996 (3) SA 617 (CC) para 27. Elaborating on this view in a case involving the right of members of the defence force to engage in public protest and to form a trade union, Justice O'Regan stated that "freedom of expression lies at the heart of a democracy," *South African National Defence Union v. Minister of Defence*, 1999 (4) SA 469 (CC) para 7, and that this:

> [W]eb of mutually supporting rights taken together protect the rights of individuals not only individually to form and express opinions, of whatever nature, but to establish associations and groups of like-minded people to foster and propagate such opinions. The rights implicitly recognise the importance, both for a democratic society and for individuals personally, of the ability to form and express opinions, whether individually or collectively, even where those views are controversial. The corollary of the freedom of expression and its related rights is tolerance by society of different views. Tolerance, of course, does not require approbation of a particular view. In essence, it requires the acceptance of the public airing of disagreements and the refusal to silence unpopular views (para 8).

3.3. BALANCING RACIAL EQUALITY AND FREEDOM: HATE SPEECH

3.3.1. Canada

R. v. KEEGSTRA

SUPREME COURT OF CANADA

[1990] 3 S.C.R. 697, 61 C.C.C. (3d) 1

The judgment of DICKSON C.J. and WILSON, L'HEUREUX-DUBE and GONTHIER JJ. was delivered by DICKSON C..J.—

. . . .

I. FACTS

Mr. James Keegstra was a high school teacher in Eckville, Alberta from the early 1970s until his dismissal in 1982. In 1984 Mr. Keegstra was charged under s. 319(2) . . . with unlawfully promoting hatred against an identifiable group by communicating anti-semitic statements to his students. He was convicted by a jury in a trial before McKenzie J. of the Alberta Court of Queen's Bench.

Mr. Keegstra's teachings attributed various evil qualities to Jews. He thus described Jews to his pupils as "treacherous," "subversive," "sadistic," "money-loving," "power hungry" and "child killers." He taught his classes that Jewish people seek to destroy Christianity and are responsible for depressions, anarchy, chaos, wars and revolution. According to Mr. Keegstra, Jews "created the Holocaust to gain sympathy" and, in contrast to the open and honest Christians, were said to be deceptive, secretive and inherently evil. Mr. Keegstra expected his students to reproduce his teachings in class and on exams. If they failed to do so, their marks suffered.

* * *

III. Relevant Statutory and Constitutional Provisions

The relevant legislative . . . provisions are set out below:

"*Criminal Code* s. 319. . . .

(2) Every one who, by communicating statements, other than in private conversation, wilfully promotes hatred against any identifiable group is guilty of

    (a) an indictable offence and is liable to imprisonment for a term not exceeding two years; or

    (b) an offence punishable on summary conviction.

(3) No person shall be convicted of an offence under subsection (2)

    (a) if he establishes that the statements communicated were true;

    (b) if, in good faith, he expressed or attempted to establish by argument an opinion on a religious subject;

    (c) if the statements were relevant to any subject of public interest, the discussion of which was for the public benefit, and if on reasonable grounds he believed them to be true; or

    (d) if, in good faith, he intended to point out, for the purpose of removal, matters producing or tending to produce feelings of hatred toward an identifiable group in Canada.

    . . . .

(6) No proceeding for an offence under subsection (2) shall be instituted without the consent of the Attorney General.

    318. . . .

(4) In this section, "identifiable group" means any section of the public distinguished by colour, race, religion or ethnic origin."

* * *

V. The History of Hate Propaganda Crimes in Canada

[The Court traced the history of attempts to prevent the propagation of scurrilous statements about particular groups to the 1275 creation of the offence of *De Scandalis Magnatum*, prohibiting "any false News or Tales, whereby discord, or occasion of discord or slander may grow between the King and his People, or the Great Men of the Realm." Although rarely employed and abolished in England in 1877, its legacy is *Criminal Code* s. 181, which makes it an offence to spread knowingly false news that is likely to cause injury or mischief to a public interest. That statute had been used to prosecute distribution of anti-semitic material, although it had been construed narrowly. In the 1930s, provinces began to act against Nazi propaganda. Following the Second World War and revelation of the Holocaust, in Canada and throughout the world a desire grew to protect human rights, and especially to guard against discrimination. This led to several international instruments against hate propaganda. In Canada, growing concern resulted in a special study committee, chaired by Justice Minister Guy Favreau. The Favreau report led to enactment of the challenged statute. The Report's Preface emphasized "the power of words to maim, and what it is that a civilized society can do about it." Although a free society must be heavily biased "in favour of the maximum of rhetoric whatever the cost and consequences," the report concluded that this "bias stops this side of injury to the community itself and to individual members or identifiable groups innocently caught in verbal cross-fire that goes beyond legitimate debate."]

*   *   *

VI. Section 2(b) of the *Charter* — Freedom of Expression

[The Court applied the *Irwin Toy* test to conclude that the challenged legislation infringed] the freedom of expression guarantee of s. 2(b). Communications which wilfully promote hatred against an identifiable group without doubt convey a meaning, and are intended to do so by those who make them. Because *Irwin Toy* stresses that the type of meaning conveyed is irrelevant to the question of whether s. 2(b) is infringed, that the expression covered by s. 319(2) is invidious and obnoxious is beside the point. It is enough that those who publicly and wilfully promote hatred convey or attempt to convey a meaning, and it must therefore be concluded that the first step of the *Irwin Toy* test is satisfied.

*   *   *

VII. Section 1 Analysis of Section 319(2)

*   *   *

B. *The Use of American Constitutional Jurisprudence*

*   *   *

[The SCC observed that American courts have grappled with this issue under the First Amendment. Although the U.S. Supreme Court upheld a criminal statute forbidding certain types of group defamation in *Beauharnais v. Illinois*, 343 U.S. 250 (1952), Dickson, CJ observed that this decision] appears to have been weakened by later pronouncements of the Supreme Court. The trend reflected in many of these pronouncements is to protect offensive, public invective as long as the speaker has not knowingly lied and there exists no clear and present danger of violence or insurrection.

In the wake of subsequent developments in the Supreme Court, on several occasions *Beauharnais* has been distinguished and doubted by lower courts. Of the judgments expressing a shaken faith in *Beauharnais*, *Collin v. Smith*, 578 F.2d 1197 (7th Cir. 1978), *certiorari denied*, 439 U.S. 916 (1978), is of greatest relevance to this appeal. In *Collin*, the Court of Appeal for the Seventh Circuit invalidated a municipal ordinance prohibiting public demonstrations inciting "violence, hatred, abuse or hostility toward a person or group of persons by reason of reference to religious, racial, ethnic, national or regional affiliation," and thereby allowed members of the American Nazi Party to march through Skokie, Illinois, home to a large number of Jewish Holocaust survivors.

The question that concerns us in this appeal is not, of course, what the law is or should be in the United States. But it is important to be explicit as to the reasons why or why not American experience may be useful in the s. 1 analysis of s. 319(2) of the *Criminal Code*. In the United States, a collection of fundamental rights has been constitutionally protected for over two hundred years. The resulting practical and theoretical experience is immense, and should not be overlooked by Canadian courts. On the other hand, we must examine American constitutional law with a critical eye, and in this respect La Forest J. has noted in *R. v. Rahey*, [1987] 1 S.C.R. 588, at p. 639:

> "While it is natural and even desirable for Canadian courts to refer to American constitutional jurisprudence in seeking to elucidate the meaning of Charter guarantees that have counterparts in the United States Constitution, they should be wary of drawing too ready a parallel between constitutions born to different countries in different ages and in very different circumstances . . . ."

. . . .

[Dickson, CJC, noted "important differences between Canadian and American constitutional perspectives." First, Canadian rights are subject to reasonable limits under s. 1, which has no American counterpart. Although he noted that American courts do permit some limits on expression, section 1's focus on "a uniquely Canadian vision of a free and democratic society" is a second major difference, with Canada's different focus on its international commitments to eradicate hate propaganda and its constitutional commitment to equality and multiculturalism.]

C. *Objective of Section 319(2)*

I now turn to the specific requirements of the *Oakes* approach in deciding whether the infringement of s. 2(b) occasioned by s. 319(2) is justifiable in a free and democratic society. * * *

(i) *Harm Caused by Expression Promoting the Hatred of Identifiable Groups*

[The majority cited another parliamentary committee, speaking in 1965, that "found that the incidence of hate propaganda in Canada was not insignificant." On this basis, the Court found that "the presence of hate propaganda in Canada is sufficiently substantial to warrant concern." The opinion distinguished between offensiveness and "very real harm" of two sorts. First, it "is indisputable that the emotional damage caused by words may be of grave psychological and social consequence," resulting in humiliation and degradation, resulting in a] severely negative impact on the individual's sense of self-worth and acceptance. This impact may cause target group members to take drastic measures in reaction, perhaps avoiding activities which bring them into contact with non-group members or adopting attitudes and postures directed towards blending in with the majority. Such consequences bear heavily in a nation that prides itself on tolerance and the fostering of human dignity through, among other things, respect for the many racial, religious and cultural groups in our society. ***

A second harmful effect of hate propaganda which is of pressing and substantial concern is its influence upon society at large. The Cohen Committee noted that individuals can be persuaded to believe "almost anything" if information or ideas are communicated using the right technique and in the proper circumstances. [The committee acknowledged that "we are less confident in the 20th century that the critical faculties of individuals will be brought to bear on the speech and writing which is directed at them. Thus, in contrast to Milton's confidence that truth and falsehood should "grapple," because "who ever knew truth put to the worse in a free and open encounter," the Committee noted that the "successes of modern advertising, the triumphs of impudent propaganda such as Hitler's, have qualified sharply our belief in the rationality of man."]

*   *   *

(ii) *International Human Rights Instruments*

*   *   *

Generally speaking, the international human rights obligations taken on by Canada reflect the values and principles of a free and democratic society, and thus those values and principles that underlie the *Charter* itself. ***

*   *   *

[The Court noted the U.N.'s adoption of and Canada's signature on the International Convention on the Elimination of All Forms of Racial Discrimination, Can. T.S. 1970 No. 28 (hereineafter "CERD"), which obliges countries to "adopt all necessary measures for speedily eliminating racial discrimination in all its forms and manifestations, and to prevent and combat racist doctrines and practices in order to promote understanding between races and to build an international community free from all forms of racial segregation and racial discrimination." In particular, Art. 4 of the Convention provides that signatory parties "condemn all propaganda and all organizations" that "attempt to justify or promote racial hatred," and specifically pledge to "declare an offence punishable by law all dissemination of ideas based on racial superiority or hatred, incitement to racial discrimination, as well as all acts of violence or incitement to such acts against any race or group of persons of another colour or ethnic origin, and also the provision of any assistance to racist activities, including the financing thereof."]

*   *   *

(iii) *Other Provisions of the Charter*

. . . .

Most importantly for the purposes of this appeal, ss. 15 and 27 represent a strong commitment to the values of equality and multiculturalism, and hence underline the great importance of Parliament's objective in prohibiting hate propaganda.

[The Court expressed its agreement with an intervenor's submission that s. 15 requires special constitutional consideration of government action against group hate.] In light of the *Charter* commitment to equality, and the reflection of this commitment in the framework of s. 1, the objective of the impugned legislation is enhanced in so far as it seeks to ensure the equality of all individuals in Canadian society. The message of the expressive activity covered by s. 319(2) is that members of identifiable groups are not to be given equal standing in society, and are not human beings equally deserving of concern, respect and consideration. The harms caused by this message run directly counter to the values central to a free and democratic society, and in restricting the promotion of hatred Parliament is therefore seeking to bolster the notion of mutual respect necessary in a nation which venerates the equality of all persons.

[Turning to s. 27's directive to interpret the *Charter* "in a manner consistent with the preservation and enhancement of the multicultural heritage of Canadians," Dickson, C.J., noted that s. 27 and the commitment to a multicultural vision of our nation "bear notice in emphasizing the acute importance of the objective of eradicating hate propaganda from society." He quoted with approval the opinion of Justice Cory when the latter was a lower court judge: "Multiculturalism cannot be preserved let alone enhanced if free rein is given to the promotion of hatred against identifiable cultural groups." *R. v. Andrews* (1988), 65 O.R. (2d) 161, 181.]

D. *Proportionality*

*   *   *

(i) *Relation of the Expression at Stake to Free Expression Values*

. . . .

From the outset, I wish to make clear that in my opinion the expression prohibited by s. 319(2) is not closely linked to the rationale underlying s. 2(b). ***

At the core of freedom of expression lies the need to ensure that truth and the common good are attained, whether in scientific and artistic endeavors or in the process of determining the best course to take in our political affairs. Since truth and the ideal form of political and social organization can rarely, if at all, be identified with absolute certainty, it is difficult to prohibit expression without impeding the free exchange of potentially valuable information. * * * There is very little chance that statements intended to promote hatred against an identifiable group are true, or that their vision of society will lead to a better world. To portray such statements as crucial to truth and the betterment of the political and social milieu is therefore misguided.

. . . .

The suppression of hate propaganda undeniably muzzles the participation of a few individuals in the democratic process, and hence detracts somewhat from free expression values, but the degree of this limitation is not substantial. I am aware that the use of strong language in political and social debate — indeed, perhaps even language intended to promote hatred — is an unavoidable part of the democratic process. Moreover, I recognize that hate propaganda is expression of a type which would generally be categorized as "political," thus putatively placing it at the very heart of the principle extolling freedom of expression as vital to the democratic process. Nonetheless, expression can work to undermine our commitment to democracy where employed to propagate ideas anathemic to democratic values. Hate propaganda works in just such a way, arguing as it does for a society in which the democratic process is subverted and individuals are denied respect and dignity simply because of racial or religious characteristics. This brand of expressive activity is thus wholly inimical to the democratic aspirations of the free expression guarantee.

*   *   *

(ii) *Rational Connection*

[Dickson, CJC, found a rational connection between criminalizing hate speech and "legitimate Parliamentary objective of protecting target group members and fostering harmonious social relations in a community dedicated to equality and multiculturalism." The suppression of "hate propaganda reduces the harm such expression does to individuals who belong to identifiable groups and to relations between various cultural and religious groups in Canadian society." The majority responded to arguments that the statute was an irrational means of eradicating hatred, because the statute could increase media attention on hate-mongers and fulfill their self-perception as martyrs or the public's suspicion of government could lead to a perception that hate speech has elements of truth.]

If s. 319(2) can be said to have no impact in the quest to achieve Parliament's admirable objectives, or in fact works in opposition to these objectives, then I agree that the provision could be described as "arbitrary, unfair or based on irrational considerations." (*Oakes, supra*). I recognize that the effect of s. 319(2) is impossible to define with exact precision — the same can be said for many laws, criminal or otherwise. In my view, however, the position that there is no strong and evident connection between the criminalization of hate propaganda and its suppression is unconvincing. [First, he noted that the media attention for s. 319(2) prosecutions "serves to illustrate to the public the severe reprobation with which society holds messages of hate directed towards racial and religious groups. Thus, "many, many Canadians who belong to identifiable groups surely gain a great deal of comfort from the knowledge that the hate-monger is criminally prosecuted and his or her ideas rejected. Equally, the community as a whole is reminded of the importance of diversity and multiculturalism in Canada, the value of equality and the worth and dignity of each human person being particularly emphasized." Second, he found it "very doubtful" that prosecutions will engender sympathy for hate propagators.]

(iii) *Minimal Impairment of the Section 2(b) Freedom*

The criminal nature of the impugned provision, involving the associated risks of prejudice through prosecution, conviction and the imposition of up to two years imprisonment, indicates that the means embodied in hate propaganda legislation should be carefully tailored so as to minimize impairment of the freedom of expression. ***

*   *   *

266 BALANCING THE VALUES OF DIGNITY, EQUALITY, AND FREEDOM CH. 3

[The majority proceeded to interpret s. 319(2) in a manner designed to minimally impair expressive rights. Noting the *mens rea* requirement of willfulness, the Court adopted the approach of Martin J.A. in *R. v. Buzzanga and Durocher* (1979), 49 C.C.C. (2d) 369 (Ont. C.A.), requiring proof that the accused "subjectively desires the promotion of hatred or foresees such a consequence as certain or substantially certain to result from an act done in order to achieve some other purpose."[3] Although the Court rejected an interpretation requiring proof that the criminalized speech resulted in actual hatred toward the target group as insufficiently narrow to achieve Parliament's aim, it interpreted the phrase "promotes hatred against any identifiable group" to indicate "active support or instigation." [Here, the Court notes that the French version of the offence uses the verb *"fomenter,"* which in English means to foment or stir up. The Court further defined "hatred" as an "emotion of an intense and extreme nature that is clearly associated with vilification and detestation." Finally, although acknowledging that the "danger that a trier will improperly infer hatred from statements he or she personally finds offensive cannot be dismissed lightly," the majority instructed that trial judges should expressly mention to jurors "the need to avoid finding that the accused intended to promote hatred merely because the expression is distasteful. If such a warning is given, the danger referred to above will be avoided and the freedom of expression limited no more than is necessary." The Court also noted that the danger of overbreadth was "significantly reduced" by defenses of good faith contained in subsections (b), (c), and (d) of s. 319(3). The Court suggested that the statutory defense of truth went farther than necessary under the *Charter*, because in its view Parliament could ban factually accurate statements if "used for no other purpose than to stir up hatred against a racial or religious group."]

[The Court acknowledged that it was "surely worrying" that in the past authorities had used s. 319(2) to "restrict expression offering valuable contributions to the arts, education or politics in Canada," referring to "overzealous" authorities arrested individuals calling on Americans to leave the country or temporarily barring the importation of a film about Nelson Mandela and Salman Rushdie's novel, *The Satanic Verses*. However, the Court hoped that the interpretation in this case would avoid future abuses.]

c. *Alternative Modes of Furthering Parliament's Objective*

[Finally, the Court rejected claims that non-criminal responses, like information and education programmes and civil remedies under human rights statutes, can more effectively combat the harm caused by hate propaganda.]

In assessing the proportionality of a legislative enactment to a valid governmental objective, however, s. 1 should not operate in every instance so as to force the government to rely upon only the mode of intervention least intrusive of a *Charter* right or freedom. It may be that a number of courses of action are available in the furtherance of a pressing and substantial objective, each imposing a varying degree of restriction upon a right or freedom. In such circumstances, the government may

---

[3] [Ed. note: The judgment resulted in dismissal of charges against two francophones who had disseminated anti-French literature in hopes of provoking a government reaction in favour of demands for construction of a French-language school in Essex County in western Ontario (about 30 minutes from Detroit/Windsor).]

legitimately employ a more restrictive measure, either alone or as part of a larger programme of action, if that measure is not redundant, furthering the objective in ways that alternative responses could not, and is in all other respects proportionate to a valid s. 1 aim.

*   *   *

(iv) *Effects of the Limitation*

The third branch of the proportionality test entails a weighing of the importance of the state objective against the effect of limits imposed upon a *Charter* right or guarantee. Even if the purpose of the limiting measure is substantial and the first two components of the proportionality test are satisfied, the deleterious effects of a limit may be too great to permit the infringement of the right or guarantee in issue.

[The opinion repeated its conclusion that the majority did not see the restriction as a serious infringement on the sort of expression that s. 2(b) is designed to protect, while the dissipation of racism was a central concept to a free and democratic society.]

*   *   *

La Forest J. (dissenting) — [omitted; indicates agreement with McLachlin, J, below]

The reasons of Sopinka and McLachlin JJ. were delivered by McLachlin J. (dissenting)—

*   *   *

Analysis

I. Background

[The dissent noted the classic argument set forth by Alexander Meiklejohn in *Free Speech and its Relation to Self-Government* (1948), that the free flow of ideas is essential to political democracy and the functioning of democratic institutions. This theory postulates that only political speech is protected, but that it must be absolutely protected. However, *Irwin Toy* gives far broader protection. Second, the dissent took note of the argument — dating back at least to Milton's *Areopagitica* in 1644 — that free expression is essential in the search for truth, or to use Justice Holmes' famous phrase, that it promotes a "marketplace of ideas." See *Abrams v. United States*, 250 U.S. 616 (1919) (dissenting op.). Acknowledging that history demonstrates that this "marketplace" does not guarantee that truth will prevail, at least in the short run, "to confine the justification for guaranteeing freedom of expression to the promotion of truth is arguably wrong, because however important truth may be, certain opinions are incapable of being proven either true or false. Many ideas and expressions which cannot be verified are valuable. Such considerations convince me that freedom of expression can be justified at least in part on the basis that it promotes the 'marketplace of ideas' and hence a more relevant, vibrant and progressive society." Third, a significant argument for expression articulated in

T. I. Emerson, "Toward a General Theory of the First Amendment" (1963), 72 Yale L.J. 877, is that the right to form and express ideas "is an integral part of the development of ideas, of mental exploration and of the affirmation of self." Under this theory, free expression is worth preserving for its own intrinsic value.]

Arguments based on intrinsic value and practical consequences are married in the thought of F. Schauer (*Free Speech: A Philosophical Enquiry* (1982)). Rather than evaluating expression to see why it might be worthy of protection, Schauer evaluates the reasons why a government might attempt to limit expression. Schauer points out that throughout history, attempts to restrict expression have accounted for a disproportionate share of governmental blunders — from the condemnation of Galileo for suggesting the earth is round to the suppression as "obscene" of many great works of art. Professor Schauer explains this peculiar inability of censoring governments to avoid mistakes by the fact that, in limiting expression, governments often act as judge in their own cause. They have an interest in stilling criticism of themselves, or even in enhancing their own popularity by silencing unpopular expression. These motives may render them unable to carefully weigh the advantages and disadvantages of suppression in many instances. That is not to say that it is always illegitimate for governments to curtail expression, but government attempts to do so must prima facie be viewed with suspicion.

. . . .

II. The Scope of Section 2(B) of the Charter

*   *   *

B. *The Construction Arguments*

These submissions urge that s. 2(b) of the *Charter* should not be construed as extending to statements which offend s. 319(2) of the *Criminal Code*. The arguments are founded on three distinct considerations: s. 15 of the *Charter*; s. 27 of the *Charter*; and Canada's international obligations.

[McLachlin, J. rejected each of these arguments. In her view, there is no conflict between guarantees of free expression and equality, because s. 15 is limited to "discrimination effected by the state," not from individuals. She viewed the commitment to multiculturalism as "inherently vague and to some extent a matter of personal opinion," and questioned whether, under the majority's approach, suggestions that immigration from certain countries be limited might be banned. Finally, although recognizing the relevance of international law, she concluded: "The provisions of the *Charter*, though drawing on a political and social philosophy shared with other democratic societies, are uniquely Canadian. As a result, considerations may point, as they do in this case, to a conclusion regarding a rights violation which is not necessarily in accord with those international covenants."]

*   *   *

IV. The Analysis Under Section 1

[In a significant portion of her dissent, McLachlin, J., argued that legislation that "takes away a measure of one's constitutional freedom" cannot be reasonably and demonstrably justified under s. 1 "unless there is some likelihood that it will further the objective upon which its justification rests." She noted concerns that undue media attention and sympathy may hamper, rather than achieve, the statute's goals.]

The argument that criminal prosecutions for this kind of expression will reduce racism and foster multiculturalism depends on the assumption that some listeners are gullible enough to believe the expression if exposed to it. But if this assumption is valid, these listeners might be just as likely to believe that there must be some truth in the racist expression because the government is trying to suppress it. Theories of a grand conspiracy between government and elements of society wrongly perceived as malevolent can become all too appealing if government dignifies them by completely suppressing their utterance. It is therefore not surprising that the criminalization of hate propaganda and prosecutions under such legislation have been subject to so much controversy in this country.

*   *   *

(c) *Minimum Impairment*

*   *   *

The real answer to the debate about whether s. 319(2) is overbroad is provided by the section's track record. [Here, she cites a number of examples of abuses of the statute.]

Even where investigations are not initiated or prosecutions pursued, the vagueness and subjectivity inherent in s. 319(2) of the *Criminal Code* give ground for concern that the chilling effect of the law may be substantial. The more vague the language of the prohibition, the greater the danger that right-minded citizens may curtail the range of their expression against the possibility that they may run afoul of the law. [Thus, n]ovelists may steer clear of controversial characterizations of ethnic characteristics, such as Shakespeare's portrayal of Shylock in *The Merchant of Venice*. Scientists may well think twice before researching and publishing results of research suggesting difference between ethnic or racial groups. Given the serious consequences of criminal prosecution, it is not entirely speculative to suppose that even political debate on crucial issues such as immigration, educational language rights, foreign ownership and trade may be tempered. These matters go to the heart of the traditional justifications for protecting freedom of expression.

*   *   *

Moreover, it is arguable whether criminalization of expression calculated to promote racial hatred is necessary. [She cited with approval A. A. Borovoy, *When Freedoms Collide: The Case for our Civil Liberties* (1988), which argued that administrative proceedings had proven more successful in getting voluntary change in conduct.]

(d) *Importance of the Right versus Benefit Conferred*

[Here the dissent concludes that the "tenuous" benefits from criminalizing speech do not outweigh the infringement on expression.]

———————

A unanimous Supreme Court revisited the issue in a recent civil decision, *Saskatchewan (Human Rights Comm'n) v. Whatcott*, 2013 SCC 11 (Feb. 27, 2013). The Court upheld the constitutionality of most impugned civil and administrative provisions of hate speech provisions of a provincial human rights statute. The Court upheld a tribunal's determination that several homophobic leaflets exposed persons to hatred and ridicule because of their sexual orientation. The respondents were enjoined from further distribution of the leaflets and ordered to pay compensation totaling $17,500 to four complainants. In finding that the statute was a reasonable limit on free expression, the Court repeated many of the arguments set forth by the majority in *Keegstra*. However, the Court invalidated statutory provisions barring expression that "ridicules, belittles or otherwise affronts the dignity of" persons belonging to protected classes. The Court reasoned that this standard is not rationally connected to the legislative purpose of addressing systemic discrimination of protected groups, nor tailored to minimally impair freedom of religion. The Court rejected the respondent's argument that the leaflets were political speech (urging that homosexuality be illegal and homosexual teachers be fired). It reasoned hate speech, by inciting ridicule and hatred, is antithetical to political speech by making it difficult for members of the protected group to respond.

3.3.2. United States

R. A. V. v. CITY OF ST. PAUL, MINNESOTA
SUPREME COURT OF THE UNITED STATES
505 U.S. 377 (1992)

SCALIA, J., delivered the opinion of the Court, in which REHNQUIST, C J., and KENNEDY, SOUTER, and THOMAS, JJ., joined.

In the predawn hours of June 21, 1990, petitioner and several other teenagers allegedly assembled a crudely made cross by taping together broken chair legs. They then allegedly burned the cross inside the fenced yard of a black family that lived across the street from the house where petitioner was staying. Although this conduct could have been punished under any of a number of laws,[4] one of the two provisions under which respondent city of St. Paul chose to charge petitioner (then a juvenile) was the St. Paul Bias-Motivated Crime Ordinance, St. Paul, Minn., Legis. Code § 292.02 (1990), which provides:

———————

[4] [FN 6] The conduct might have violated Minnesota statutes carrying significant penalties. See, e. g., Minn. Stat. § 609.713(1) (1987) (providing for up to five years in prison for terroristic threats); § 609.563 (arson) (providing for up to five years and a $10,000 fine, depending on the value of the property intended to be damaged); § 609.595 (Supp. 1992) (criminal damage to property) (providing for up to one year and a $3,000 fine, depending upon the extent of the damage to the property).

"Whoever places on public or private property a symbol, object, appellation, characterization or graffiti, including, but not limited to, a burning
cross or Nazi swastika, which one knows or has reasonable grounds to know
arouses anger, alarm or resentment in others on the basis of race, color,
creed, religion or gender commits disorderly conduct and shall be guilty of
a misdemeanor."

Petitioner moved to dismiss this count on the ground that the St. Paul ordinance
was substantially overbroad and impermissibly content based and therefore facially
invalid under the First Amendment. The trial court granted this motion, but the
Minnesota Supreme Court reversed. That court rejected petitioner's overbreadth
claim because, as construed in prior Minnesota cases, the modifying phrase
"arouses anger, alarm or resentment in others" limited the reach of the ordinance
to conduct that amounts to "fighting words," i. e., "conduct that itself inflicts injury
or tends to incite immediate violence . . . ," *In re Welfare of R. A. V.*, 464 N.W.2d
507, 510 (Minn. 1991) (citing *Chaplinsky v. New Hampshire*, 315 U.S. 568, 572
(1942)), and therefore the ordinance reached only expression "that the first
amendment does not protect," 464 N.W.2d at 511. The court also concluded that the
ordinance was not impermissibly content based because, in its view, "the ordinance
is a narrowly tailored means toward accomplishing the compelling governmental
interest in protecting the community against bias-motivated threats to public safety
and order." *Ibid.* We granted certiorari.

I

In construing the St. Paul ordinance, we are bound by the construction given to
it by the Minnesota court.

The First Amendment generally prevents government from proscribing speech,
or even expressive conduct, because of disapproval of the ideas expressed. Content-
based regulations are presumptively invalid. From 1791 to the present, however, our
society, like other free but civilized societies, has permitted restrictions upon the
content of speech in a few limited areas, which are "of such slight social value as a
step to truth that any benefit that may be derived from them is clearly outweighed
by the social interest in order and morality." *Chaplinsky*, 315 U.S. at 572. We have
recognized that "the freedom of speech" referred to by the First Amendment does
not include a freedom to disregard these traditional limitations. See, e. g., *Roth v.
United States*, 354 U.S. 476 (1957) (obscenity); *Beauharnais v. Illinois*, 343 U.S. 250
(1952) (defamation); *Chaplinsky v. New Hampshire, supra* (" 'fighting' words"). Our
decisions since the 1960's have narrowed the scope of the traditional categorical
exceptions for defamation, but a limited categorical approach has remained an
important part of our First Amendment jurisprudence. We have sometimes said
that these categories of expression are "not within the area of constitutionally
protected speech," or that the "protection of the First Amendment does not extend"
to them. Such statements must be taken in context, however, and are no more
literally true than is the occasionally repeated shorthand characterizing obscenity
"as not being speech at all," Sunstein, *Pornography and the First Amendment*, 1986
Duke L. J. 589, 615, n.46.What they mean is that these areas of speech can,
consistently with the First Amendment, be regulated because of their constitution-

ally proscribable content (obscenity, defamation, etc.) — not that they are categories of speech entirely invisible to the Constitution, so that they may be made the vehicles for content discrimination unrelated to their distinctively proscribable content. Thus, the government may proscribe libel; but it may not make the further content discrimination of proscribing only libel critical of the government . . . .

. . . .

In other words, the exclusion of "fighting words" from the scope of the First Amendment simply means that, for purposes of that Amendment, the unprotected features of the words are, despite their verbal character, essentially a "nonspeech" element of communication. Fighting words are thus analogous to a noisy sound truck. . . .

II

Applying these principles to the St. Paul ordinance, we conclude that, even as narrowly construed by the Minnesota Supreme Court, the ordinance is facially unconstitutional. Although the phrase in the ordinance, "arouses anger, alarm or resentment in others," has been limited by the Minnesota Supreme Court's construction to reach only those symbols or displays that amount to "fighting words," the remaining, unmodified terms make clear that the ordinance applies only to "fighting words" that insult, or provoke violence, "on the basis of race, color, creed, religion or gender." Displays containing abusive invective, no matter how vicious or severe, are permissible unless they are addressed to one of the specified disfavored topics. Those who wish to use "fighting words" in connection with other ideas — to express hostility, for example, on the basis of political affiliation, union membership, or homosexuality — are not covered. The First Amendment does not permit St. Paul to impose special prohibitions on those speakers who express views on disfavored subjects.

In its practical operation, moreover, the ordinance goes even beyond mere content discrimination, to actual viewpoint discrimination. Displays containing some words — odious racial epithets, for example — would be prohibited to proponents of all views. But "fighting words" that do not themselves invoke race, color, creed, religion, or gender — aspersions upon a person's mother, for example — would seemingly be usable *ad libitum* in the placards of those arguing in favor of racial, color, etc., tolerance and equality, but could not be used by those speakers' opponents. One could hold up a sign saying, for example, that all "anti-Catholic bigots" are misbegotten; but not that all "papists" are, for that would insult and provoke violence "on the basis of religion." St. Paul has no such authority to license one side of a debate to fight freestyle, while requiring the other to follow Marquis of Queensberry rules.

. . . One must wholeheartedly agree with the Minnesota Supreme Court that "it is the responsibility, even the obligation, of diverse communities to confront such notions in whatever form they appear," but the manner of that confrontation cannot consist of selective limitations upon speech . . . .

. . . .

Finally, St. Paul and its *amici* defend the conclusion of the Minnesota Supreme Court that, even if the ordinance regulates expression based on hostility towards its protected ideological content, this discrimination is nonetheless justified because it is narrowly tailored to serve compelling state interests. Specifically, they assert that the ordinance helps to ensure the basic human rights of members of groups that have historically been subjected to discrimination, including the right of such group members to live in peace where they wish. We do not doubt that these interests are compelling, and that the ordinance can be said to promote them. But the "danger of censorship" presented by a facially content-based statute, requires that that weapon be employed only where it is "necessary to serve the asserted [compelling] interest." The existence of adequate content-neutral alternatives thus "undercuts significantly" any defense of such a statute, casting considerable doubt on the government's protestations that "the asserted justification is in fact an accurate description of the purpose and effect of the law." The dispositive question in this case, therefore, is whether content discrimination is reasonably necessary to achieve St. Paul's compelling interests; it plainly is not. An ordinance not limited to the favored topics, for example, would have precisely the same beneficial effect. In fact the only interest distinctively served by the content limitation is that of displaying the city council's special hostility towards the particular biases thus singled out. That is precisely what the First Amendment forbids. The politicians of St. Paul are entitled to express that hostility — but not through the means of imposing unique limitations upon speakers who (however benightedly) disagree.

Let there be no mistake about our belief that burning a cross in someone's front yard is reprehensible. But St. Paul has sufficient means at its disposal to prevent such behavior without adding the First Amendment to the fire.

JUSTICE WHITE, with whom JUSTICE BLACKMUN and JUSTICE O'CONNOR join, and with whom JUSTICE STEVENS joins except as to Part I-A, concurring in the judgment.

I agree with the majority that the judgment of the Minnesota Supreme Court should be reversed. However, our agreement ends there. [The concurrence concluded that the ordinance was "fatally overbroad because it criminalizes not only unprotected expression but expression protected by the First Amendment."]

I

A

. . . .

Today, however, the Court announces that earlier Courts did not mean their repeated statements that certain categories of expression are "not within the area of constitutionally protected speech." *Roth*, 354 U.S. at 483. See ante, 505 U.S. at 383, citing *Beauharnais v. Illinois*, 343 U.S. 250, 266 (1952); *Chaplinsky*, 315 U.S. at 571–572; The present Court submits that such clear statements "must be taken in context" and are not "literally true."

To the contrary, those statements meant precisely what they said: The categorical approach is a firmly entrenched part of our First Amendment jurisprudence. Indeed, the Court in *Roth* reviewed the guarantees of freedom of expression in effect at the time of the ratification of the Constitution and concluded, "In light of this history, it is apparent that the unconditional phrasing of the First Amendment was not intended to protect every utterance." 354 U.S. at 482–483.

. . . .

II

. . . .

[Nonetheless, the concurring justices agreed that the ordinance criminalized expressive conduct that causes only "hurt feelings, offense, or resentment," which is protected by the First Amendment. This renders the ordinance "fatally overbroad and invalid on its face."]

JUSTICE BLACKMUN, concurring in the judgment. [omitted]

JUSTICE STEVENS, with whom JUSTICE WHITE and JUSTICE BLACKMUN join as to Part I, concurring in the judgment.

Conduct that creates special risks or causes special harms may be prohibited by special rules. Lighting a fire near an ammunition dump or a gasoline storage tank is especially dangerous; such behavior may be punished more severely than burning trash in a vacant lot. Threatening someone because of her race or religious beliefs may cause particularly severe trauma or touch off a riot, and threatening a high public official may cause substantial social disruption; such threats may be punished more severely than threats against someone based on, say, his support of a particular athletic team. There are legitimate, reasonable, and neutral justifications for such special rules.

. . . .

Although the Court has, on occasion, declared that content-based regulations of speech are "never permitted," *Police Dept. of Chicago v. Mosley*, 408 U.S. 92, 99 (1972), such claims are overstated. Indeed, in *Mosley* itself, the Court indicated that Chicago's selective proscription of nonlabor picketing was not per se unconstitutional, but rather could be upheld if the city demonstrated that nonlabor picketing was "clearly more disruptive than [labor] picketing." *Id.*, at 100. Contrary to the broad dicta in *Mosley* and elsewhere, our decisions demonstrate that content-based distinctions, far from being presumptively invalid, are an inevitable and indispensable aspect of a coherent understanding of the First Amendment.

This is true at every level of First Amendment law. In broadest terms, our entire First Amendment jurisprudence creates a regime based on the content of speech. The scope of the First Amendment is determined by the content of expressive activity: Although the First Amendment broadly protects "speech," it does not protect the right to "fix prices, breach contracts, make false warranties, place bets with bookies, threaten, [or] extort." Schauer, *Categories and the First Amendment: A Play in Three Acts*, 34 Vand. L. Rev. 265, 270 (1981). . . .

Our First Amendment decisions have created a rough hierarchy in the constitutional protection of speech. Core political speech occupies the highest, most protected position; commercial speech and nonobscene, sexually explicit speech are regarded as a sort of second-class expression; obscenity and fighting words receive the least protection of all. Assuming that the Court is correct that this last class of speech is not wholly "unprotected," it certainly does not follow that fighting words and obscenity receive the same sort of protection afforded core political speech. Yet in ruling that proscribable speech cannot be regulated based on subject matter, the Court does just that. Perversely, this gives fighting words greater protection than is afforded commercial speech. If Congress can prohibit false advertising directed at airline passengers without also prohibiting false advertising directed at bus passengers and if a city can prohibit political advertisements in its buses while allowing other advertisements, it is ironic to hold that a city cannot regulate fighting words based on "race, color, creed, religion or gender" while leaving unregulated fighting words based on "union membership . . . or homosexuality."

The Court today turns First Amendment law on its head: Communication that was once entirely unprotected (and that still can be wholly proscribed) is now entitled to greater protection than commercial speech — and possibly greater protection than core political speech.

Perhaps because the Court recognizes these perversities, it quickly offers some ad hoc limitations on its newly extended prohibition on content-based regulations. Just as Congress may determine that threats against the President entail more severe consequences than other threats, so St. Paul's City Council may determine that threats based on the target's race, religion, or gender cause more severe harm to both the target and to society than other threats. This latter judgment — that harms caused by racial, religious, and gender-based invective are qualitatively different from that caused by other fighting words — seems to me eminently reasonable and realistic.

. . . .

III

. . . .

Contrary to the suggestion of the majority, the St. Paul ordinance does not regulate expression based on viewpoint. The Court contends that the ordinance requires proponents of racial intolerance to "follow the Marquis of Queensberry rules" while allowing advocates of racial tolerance to "fight freestyle." The law does no such thing.

The Court writes:

> "One could hold up a sign saying, for example, that all 'anti-Catholic bigots' are misbegotten; but not that all 'papists' are, for that would insult and provoke violence 'on the basis of religion.' " *Ante*, 505 U.S. at 391–392.

This may be true, but it hardly proves the Court's point. The Court's reasoning is asymmetrical. The response to a sign saying that "all [religious] bigots are misbegotten" is a sign saying that "all advocates of religious tolerance are misbegotten." Assuming such signs could be fighting words (which seems to me extremely unlikely), neither sign would be banned by the ordinance for the attacks were not "based on . . . religion" but rather on one's beliefs about tolerance. Conversely (and again assuming such signs are fighting words), just as the ordinance would prohibit a Muslim from hoisting a sign claiming that all Catholics were misbegotten, so the ordinance would bar a Catholic from hoisting a similar sign attacking Muslims.

The St. Paul ordinance is evenhanded. In a battle between advocates of tolerance and advocates of intolerance, the ordinance does not prevent either side from hurling fighting words at the other on the basis of their conflicting ideas, but it does bar both sides from hurling such words on the basis of the target's "race, color, creed, religion or gender." To extend the Court's pugilistic metaphor, the St. Paul ordinance simply bans punches "below the belt" — by either party. It does not, therefore, favor one side of any debate. * * *

In *United States v. McDermott*, 822 F. Supp. 582 (N.D. Iowa 1993), the court distinguished *R.A.V. v. St. Paul* in a case where the defendants had burned a cross and engaged in other activities in a public park with intent to threaten or intimidate African Americans not to use the park. The court emphasized the need for the government to prove a specific intent to threaten or intimidate in order to secure a conviction.

To some degree, Canadian and American differences may reflect a heightened American commitment to classic liberalism's overriding concern with preserving individual autonomy and maintaining a clear distinction between private and public domains, and Canadians' greater commitment to the state as a benign mediator among groups and promoter of collective aspirations. Consider the variety of collective values incorporated into the Canadian Charter: s. 6(3)(b) (social services); s. 6(4) (unemployment benefits); s. 15(2) (affirmative action); ss. 16-22 (language rights); s. 23 (minority language education); s. 25 (aboriginal rights); s. 27 (multiculturalism as interpretive guidepost); s. 28 (gender equality as interpretive guidepost); s. 29 (denominational schools); and s. 33 (legislative override of judiciary). None of these provisions have any constitutional counterpart in the United States.

Consider also the extent to which Canada's history and politics also reflect a more modest view of the government as a threat to individual liberty than the view from south of the border. The Progressive Conservative party (now merged with a more libertarian western Canadian party which dropped the adjective) traditionally was a strong believer in the positive use of government to maintain peace, order, and social stability. The New Democratic Party is a social democratic party that strongly advocates government support for working people and the poor. The Bloc Québécois has strong social democratic roots and primarily advocates the use of government to achieve the collective aspirations of French Canadians. The two dominant churches — Catholic and Anglican — are hierarchical with strong ties with the government. The government has often been seen by Canadians not as the principal threat to their liberty but as their principal protector — initially to promote law and order and more recently as against the U.S.

### 3.3.3.	South Africa

THE ISLAMIC UNITY CONVENTION v. INDEPENDENT BROADCASTING AUTHORITY
CONSTITUTIONAL COURT OF SOUTH AFRICA
2002 (4) SA 294 (CC)

LANGA DCJ:

Introduction

[1] The applicant, the Islamic Unity Convention, runs a community radio station known as Radio 786 under a broadcasting licence issued to it by the first respondent, the Independent Broadcasting Authority (the IBA). On 8 May 1998 the station broadcast a programme entitled "Zionism and Israel: An in-depth analysis" in which an interview with one Dr Yaqub Zaki, described as an historian and author, was featured. In the interview, Dr Zaki dealt with the historical, political, social and economic factors which, according to him, played a role in the establishment of the state of Israel. He expressed views which, among other things, questioned the legitimacy of the state of Israel and Zionism as a political ideology, asserted that Jewish people were not gassed in concentration camps during the Second World War but died of infectious diseases, particularly typhus and that only a million Jews had died.

[2] Following the broadcast, fourth respondent, the South African Jewish Board of Deputies (the Board), lodged a formal complaint with the second respondent, the Head: Monitoring and Complaints Unit, claiming that the material that had been broadcast contravened clause 2(a) of the Code of Conduct for Broadcasting Services (the Code), in that it was "likely to prejudice relations between sections of the population, i.e. Jews and other communities." The Code is contained in Schedule 1 to the Independent Broadcasting Authority Act (the Act).

. . . .

[26] This Court has held that—

". . . freedom of expression is one of a 'web of mutually supporting rights' in the Constitution. It is closely related to freedom of religion, belief and opinion (s 15), the right to dignity (s 10), as well as the right to freedom of association (s 18), the right to vote and to stand for public office (s 19), and the right to assembly (s 17) . . . The rights implicitly recognise the importance, both for a democratic society and for individuals personally, of the ability to form and express opinions, whether individually or collectively, even where those views are controversial." [*South African National*

Defence Union v. Minister of Defence and Another 1999 (6) BCLR 615 (CC); 1999 (4) SA 469 (CC) para 8.]

As to its relevance to a democratic state, the Court has pointed out that freedom of expression —

". . . lies at the heart of a democracy. It is valuable for many reasons, including its instrumental functions as a guarantor of democracy, its implicit recognition and protection of the moral agency of individuals in our society and its facilitation of the search for truth by individuals and society generally. The Constitution recognises that individuals in our society need to be able to hear, form and express opinions and views freely on a wide range of matters . . . ." [footnotes omitted.] and in *S v Mamabolo* (E TV, Business Day and the Freedom of Expression Institute Intervening) the following was said—

"Freedom of expression, especially when gauged in conjunction with its accompanying fundamental freedoms, is of the utmost importance in the kind of open and democratic society the Constitution has set as our aspirational norm. Having regard to our recent past of thought control, censorship and enforced conformity to governmental theories, freedom of expression — the free and open exchange of ideas — is no less important than it is in the United States of America. It could actually be contended with much force that the public interest in the open market-place of ideas is all the more important to us in this country because our democracy is not yet firmly established and must feel its way. Therefore we should be particularly astute to outlaw any form of thought control, however respectably dressed."

[27] Notwithstanding the fact that the right to freedom of expression and speech has always been recognised in the South African common law, we have recently emerged from a severely restrictive past where expression, especially political and artistic expression, was extensively circumscribed by various legislative enactments. The restrictions that were placed on expression were not only a denial of democracy itself, but also exacerbated the impact of the systemic violations of other fundamental human rights in South Africa. Those restrictions would be incompatible with South Africa's present commitment to a society based on a "constitutionally protected culture of openness and democracy and universal human rights for South Africans of all ages, classes and colours." As pointed out by Kriegler J in Mamabolo—

". . . freedom to speak one's mind is now an inherent quality of the type of society contemplated by the Constitution as a whole and is specifically promoted by the freedoms of conscience, expression, assembly, association and political participation protected by sections 15 to 19 of the Bill of Rights."

. . . .

[29] The pluralism and broadmindedness that is central to an open and democratic society can, however, be undermined by speech which seriously threatens democratic pluralism itself. Section 1 of the Constitution declares that South Africa is founded on the values of "human dignity, the achievement of equality and the

advancement of human rights and freedoms." Thus, open and democratic societies permit reasonable proscription of activity and expression that pose a real and substantial threat to such values and to the constitutional order itself. Many societies also accept limits on free speech in order to protect the fairness of trials. Speech of an inflammatory or unduly abusive kind may be restricted so as to guarantee free and fair elections in a tranquil atmosphere.

[30] There is thus recognition of the potential that expression has to impair the exercise and enjoyment of other important rights, such as the right to dignity, as well as other state interests, such as the pursuit of national unity and reconciliation. The right is accordingly not absolute; it is, like other rights, subject to limitation under section 36(1) of the Constitution. Determining its parameters in any given case is therefore important, particularly where its exercise might intersect with other interests. Thus in Mamabolo, the following was said in the context of the hierarchical relationship between the rights to dignity and freedom of expression:

> "With us the right to freedom of expression cannot be said automatically to trump the right to human dignity. The right to dignity is at least as worthy of protection as the right to freedom of expression. How these two rights are to be balanced, in principle and in any particular set of circumstances, is not a question that can or should be addressed here. What is clear though and must be stated, is that freedom of expression does not enjoy superior status in our law." [footnote omitted.]

[31] Section 16 is in two parts. Subsection (1) is concerned with expression that is protected under the Constitution. It is clear that any limitation of this category of expression must satisfy the requirements of the limitations clause to be constitutionally valid. Subsection (2) deals with expression that is specifically excluded from the protection of the right.

[32] How is section 16(2) to be interpreted? The words "[t]he right in subsection (1) does not extend to . . ." imply that the categories of expression enumerated in section 16(2) are not to be regarded as constitutionally protected speech. Section 16(2) therefore defines the boundaries beyond which the right to freedom of expression does not extend. In that sense, the subsection is definitional. Implicit in its provisions is an acknowledgment that certain expression does not deserve constitutional protection because, among other things, it has the potential to impinge adversely on the dignity of others and cause harm. Our Constitution is founded on the principles of dignity, equal worth and freedom, and these objectives should be given effect to.

[33] Three categories of expression are enumerated in section 16(2). They are expressed in specific and defined terms. Section 16(2)(a) and (b) are respectively concerned with "propaganda for war" and "incitement of imminent violence." Section 16(2)(c) is directed at what is commonly referred to as hate speech. What is not protected by the Constitution is expression or speech that amounts to "advocacy of hatred" that is based on one or other of the listed grounds, namely race, ethnicity, gender or religion and which amounts to "incitement to cause harm." There is no doubt that the state has a particular interest in regulating this type of expression because of the harm it may pose to the constitutionally mandated objective of building the non-racial and non-sexist society based on human dignity and the

achievement of equality. There is accordingly no bar to the enactment of legislation that prohibits such expression. Any regulation of expression that falls within the categories enumerated in section 16(2) would not be a limitation of the right in section 16.

[34] Where the state extends the scope of regulation beyond expression envisaged in section 16(2), it encroaches on the terrain of protected expression and can do so only if such regulation meets the justification criteria in section 36(1) of the Constitution.

[35] The prohibition against the broadcasting of material that is "likely to prejudice relations between sections of the population" self-evidently limits the right in section 16 of the Constitution. The phrase "section of the population" in this part of clause 2(a) is less specific than "race, ethnicity, gender or religion" as spelt out in section 16(2)(a). The prohibition clearly goes beyond the categories of expression enumerated in section 16(2). It does not, for instance, require that the material prohibited should amount to advocacy of hatred, least of all hatred based on race, ethnicity, gender or religion, nor that it should have any potential to cause harm.

[36] Whilst, on the one hand, the categories of speech referred to in section 16(2)(c), are carefully circumscribed, no such tailoring is evident in the relevant portion of clause 2(a). There is no doubt that each of the forms of expression listed in section 16(2) could produce the result envisaged in clause 2(a). Expression that makes propaganda for war (section 16(2)(a)) may, depending on the circumstances, threaten relations between sections of the population, or produce a situation where these are likely to be prejudiced. The converse is however not true. Not every expression or speech that is likely to prejudice relations between sections of the population would be "propaganda for war," or "incitement of imminent violence" or "advocacy of hatred" that is not only based on race, ethnicity, gender or religion, but that also "constitutes incitement to cause harm." There may well be instances where the prohibition in clause 2(a) coincides with what is excluded from the protection of the right. The real question though is whether the clause, in prohibiting that which is not excluded from the protection of section 16(1), does so in a manner which is constitutionally impermissible. It is to that enquiry that I now turn.

The justification enquiry

[37] The responsibility for the regulation of broadcasting in South Africa stems from section 192 of the Constitution which provides that —

> "National legislation must establish an independent authority to regulate broadcasting in the public interest, and to ensure fairness and a diversity of views broadly representing South African society."

In fulfilling this regulatory function the broadcasting authority is bound to respect the provisions of the Bill of Rights while the legislation may limit the protected rights only as permitted by the Constitution. In the context of broadcasting, freedom of expression will have special relevance. It is in the public interest that people be free to speak their minds openly and robustly, and, in turn, to receive information, views and ideas. It is also in the public interest that reasonable limitations be applied, provided that they are consistent with the Constitution.

[38] Section 36(1) of the Constitution sets out the criteria for the limitation of rights. The limitation must be by means of a law of general application and determining what is fair and reasonable is an exercise in proportionality, involving the weighing up of various factors in a balancing exercise to determine whether or not the limitation is reasonable and justifiable in an open and democratic society founded on human dignity, equality and freedom. No grounds for justification have been provided by either the IBA or the Fifth Respondent, the Minister of Communications, who was joined in the proceedings at the instance of the applicant. On the contrary and consistent with its view that the clause is constitutionally objectionable, the IBA has set a process in train for the relevant legislation and the Code to be revised.

[39] The relevant part of clause 2(a) prohibits licensees from broadcasting any material of the nature which it describes. Applicant has argued that the prohibition is unreasonable and unjustifiable and accordingly inconsistent with the Constitution. The Board denies this and contends that, on a proper interpretation of the prohibition, the limitation is justifiable and therefore consistent with the Constitution. The Board submitted that if the prohibition against the broadcasting of material "likely to prejudice relations between sections of the population" were given a narrow interpretation, it is reasonably capable of a meaning which renders it justifiable in terms of section 36(1).

[40] In *Investigating Directorate, Serious Economic Offences and Others v Hyundai Motor Distributors (Pty) Ltd and Others* [2001 (1) SA 545 (CC)] this Court held that if there is an interpretation of the impugned provision that is reasonably capable of being read consistently with the Constitution, such interpretation should be adopted. The interpretation must however not be unduly strained. Furthermore, a balance must be struck between the duty of a judicial officer to interpret legislation in conformity with the Constitution in so far as it is reasonably possible, and the duty of the legislature to pass legislation that is reasonably clear and precise, enabling citizens to understand what is expected of them. The question in the present case is whether the relevant portion of clause 2(a) is capable of a meaning that is consistent with the Constitution, while at the same time being sufficiently clear and precise to enable the IBA (ICASA) and the BMCC to handle complaints in a consistent manner.

[41] The Board's suggestion is that the relevant part of the clause should be interpreted to mean that only broadcasts which will probably cause material damage to relations between readily identifiable sections of the population are hit by the proscription. In order to cause legally cognizable prejudice to relations between sections of society, so the argument goes, the broadcast must promote prejudice and stereotyping or the demonizing of a target victim group by violating their dignity in such a way that—

a. other defined groups within society (as opposed to individuals) will be sufficiently moved by the stereotyping or demonizing to regard the target victim group with contempt or hatred or to inflict harm on that target victim group; and

b. the offensive content of the broadcast is viewed by the target victim group as being the collective responsibility of a different section of society ("the perpetrator group") and not the work or responsibility merely of individuals, and is sufficiently offensive to a sufficient number of members of the target victim group that it moves them as a group, as opposed to individuals drawn from that group, to regard the perpetrator group with contempt or hatred or to want to inflict harm on that perpetrator group.

[42] Thus a breakdown of the phrase "likely to prejudice relations between sections of the population" would go something like this: "likely to prejudice" would be interpreted to refer to material that would "probably cause material damage" and "sections of the population" would be understood to refer to such sections as are identifiable on the basis of race, ethnicity, gender and religion. According to the argument, "relations" would be used in the context of there being a target victim group on the one hand, and a defined perpetrator group on the other, whose expression moves other defined groups to demonise or stereotype the victim group, and the victim group must, in turn, blame the perpetrator group for this.

[43] It is obvious that the interpretation contended for would entail a complicated exercise of interpreting the very wide language of the relevant part of clause 2(a) in the light of the very concise and specific provisions of section 16(2)(c). Whilst this process might assist in determining whether particular expression can be regarded as hate speech, I fail to see how its meaning can coincide with that of the impugned clause on any reasonable interpretation, without being unduly strained. This segment of the clause is accordingly not reasonably capable of being read to give the meaning which is favoured by the Board.

. . . .

Conclusion of justification enquiry

[51] There is no doubt that the inroads on the right to freedom of expression made by the prohibition on which the complaint is based are far too extensive and outweigh the factors considered by the Board as ameliorating their impact. As already stated, no grounds of justification have been advanced by the IBA and the Minister for such a serious infraction of the right guaranteed by section 16(1) of the Constitution. It has also not been shown that the very real need to protect dignity, equality and the development of national unity could not be adequately served by the enactment of a provision which is appropriately tailored and more narrowly focussed. I find therefore that the relevant portion of clause 2(a) impermissibly limits the right to freedom of expression and is accordingly unconstitutional.

3.3.4. Australia

In Australia, notwithstanding the constitutional protection of political communication and speech, anti-vilification laws are in force. The first law was introduced in New South Wales in 1989 (as an amendment to the NSW *Anti-Discrimination Act* of 1977). Under this law, prosecution of the offence of serious vilification requires the consent of the Attorney-General, and carries penalties of fines and imprisonment (up to a maximum of six months). One other state and the Australian Capital Territory have similar legislation; other states rely on both civil and criminal laws. Western Australia has only criminal sanctions (up to 2 years imprisonment), but confines its definition of vilification to written or pictorial material, and does not including verbal comment. Some jurisdictions also include "religious" vilification in their laws; the NSW *Anti-Discrimination Act* refers to "ethno-religious" discrimination (which may extend to Jews, Sikhs, and Muslims).

The 1975 Commonwealth *Racial Discrimination Act* (which gives effect to the United Nations International Convention on the Elimination of All Forms of Racial Discrimination) was amended in 1995, to include a prohibition on racist speech: Section 18C makes it unlawful to publish material that offends or insults a person or group because "of the race, colour or national or ethnic origin of the person or of some or all of the people in the group." In 2010, nine indigenous Australians brought an action in the Federal Court against a journalist, Andrew Bolt, and the newspaper which employed him, over several of Bolt's blog posts; these had suggested that prominent "fair-skinned people" with mixed racial ancestry chose to identify as black in order to gain political or career advantages. The plaintiffs sought an apology, legal costs, and an injunction against the posts' re-publication. Bolt was found by the Federal Court to have contravened the Act. (Following the change of government in September 2013, the new Commonwealth Attorney-General announced his government's intention to repeal s 18C. In his words, "you cannot have a situation in a liberal democracy in which the expression of an opinion is rendered unlawful because somebody else . . . finds it offensive or insulting".)

In 1995, the *Racial Discrimination Act* was extended to incorporate the *Racial Hatred Act*. Under the Act, complaints of racial hatred may be lodged with the Human Rights Commission (HRC). HRC undertakes arbitration or conciliation of disputes where these can be settled (to give one example, between complainants and a newspaper in which articles derogatory of English tourists were published). As a federal tribunal cannot exercise judicial power, prosecutions and enforcement are the domain of the Federal Courts.

The HRC describes the aim of the *Racial Hatred Act* as being "to strike a balance between two valued rights: the right to communicate freely and the right to live free from vilification. This Act makes public acts unlawful if they are "done, in whole or part, because of the race, colour, or national or ethnic origin of a person or group AND [are] reasonably likely in all the circumstances to offend, insult, humiliate or intimidate that person or group." It includes defences of reasonableness and good faith, including for artistic works or performance, academic and scientific publications, discussion or debate, fair and accurate reporting of a matter of public interest, and fair comment as an expression of a person's genuine belief. A public place is defined under the Act as "any place to which the public have access as of right or by invitation, whether express or implied and whether or not a charge is made for admission." "Public" incorporates acts done in virtual public space, including the internet and electronic media. Private acts or private conversations are not unlawful, and trivial impacts or "mere slights" are not actionable. Only an aggrieved person may lodge a complaint; a third party, who is not from a targeted group that is offended, insulted, humiliated or intimidated because of race, cannot complain on another's behalf.

In introducing the bill into parliament in 1994, the then Attorney-General emphasized that the law was intended to apply only to "extreme" racist behavior, and to fill a gap in state and territory laws that punish the perpetrators of violence, without adequately dealing with "conduct that is a pre-condition of racial violence." Since the adoption of this law, several hundred complaints (mostly about the media, neighborhood disputes, employment, personal conflict, and public debate) have been lodged with the HRC, and a number of cases have proceeded to the court. In several cases, the defenses of artistic freedom or good faith have been successful.

The most publicized cases have involved, first, the publication of material on the internet denying the Holocaust and vilifying the Jewish people;[5] and secondly, public statements made by the leader of a Christian Church organization about the Koran and Muslims.[6] The first is the only case to date dealing with publication on the internet. It began with a successful complaint to the HRC in 2000, followed by an application to the Federal Court for enforcement of the Commission's determination by the complainant, the President of the Executive Council of Australian Jewry. The judge in this instance issued an injunction ordering the removal of the offending material from the website.[7] The respondent then appealed to the full Federal Court.

In his appeal, Dr Fredrick Toben, representing the Adelaide Institute, challenged (among other things) the constitutional validity of the amended *Racial Discrimination Act* as an Act giving effect to the International Convention on the Elimination of all Forms of Racial Discrimination. The Court acknowledged that the Act did not fully implement the relevant part of the Convention, but held that it was nevertheless consistent with the Convention, including in its intention that a State Party should "nip in the bud" racially-motivated public acts before they "can grow into incitement or promotion of racial hatred or discrimination."[8] The defense of reasonableness and good faith were argued, but were unsuccessful. A judge of the Court, Justice Kiefel (now a Justice of the High Court of Australia) emphasized that the provision in the Act "does not render unlawful insensitive statements or those made in poor taste" and recognized that in some cases "in pursuing an historical or other discourse, offence cannot be avoided." Surprisingly, the compatibility of the law with the implied freedom of political communication was not raised. However, Justice Allsop adverted briefly to this freedom, and to United States jurisprudence in which, he stated, "even in circumstances of the clearest constitutional guarantee of freedom of speech . . . [the Supreme Court] recognizes the powerful effect of deeply entrenched symbols and habits of intimidation."

For a general exploration, *see* Nicholas Aroney, *The Constitutional (In)validity of Religious Vilification Laws: Implications for Their Interpretation*, 34 FED. L. REV. 287 (2006).

---

[5] *Toben v. Jones* (2003) 129 FCR 515.

[6] *Islamic Council of Victoria v. Catch the Fire Ministries Inc* [2005] VCAT 1159 (first hearing).

[7] The defendant had already been imprisoned in Germany for publishing similar material.

[8] *Toben v. Jones* (2003) 129 FCR 515 (Carr J).

3.4. BALANCING GENDER EQUALITY AND FREEDOM: REGULATION OF PORNOGRAPHY

3.4.1. Canada

R. v. BUTLER
SUPREME COURT OF CANADA
[1992] 1 S.C.R. 452

The judgment of LAMER C.J. and LA FOREST, SOPINKA, CORY, McLACHLIN, STEVENSON and IACOBUCCI JJ. was delivered by

SOPINKA J. —

[This appeal calls into question the constitutionality under s. 2(b) of the *Charter* of the obscenity provisions of the *Criminal Code*, R.S.C., 1985, c. C-46, s. 163, which proscribes the making or possession with intent to distribute "any obscene matter," or who "knowingly, without lawful justification or excuse," sells or publicizes obscene matter. However, s. 163(3) provides a defence if the person "establishes that the public good was served by the acts that are alleged to constitute the offence and that the acts alleged did not extend beyond what served the public good. Most significantly, s. 163(8) specifies that "any publication a dominant characteristic of which is the undue exploitation of sex, or of sex and any one or more of the following subjects, namely, crime, horror, cruelty and violence, shall be deemed to be obscene."]

4. Analysis

*   *   *

A. *Legislative History*

[The Court concluded that s. 163(8) provided a definition of obscenity that effectively replaced the traditional test formulated by Cockburn C.J. in *R. v. Hicklin* (1868), L.R. 3 Q.B. 360, at p. 371: ". . . whether the tendency of the matter charged as obscenity is to deprave and corrupt those whose minds are open to such immoral influences, and into whose hands a publication of this sort may fall."]

B. *Judicial Interpretation of s. 163(8)*

The first case to consider the current provision was *Brodie v. The Queen*, [1962] S.C.R. 681. The majority of this Court found in that case that D. H. Lawrence's novel, *Lady Chatterley's Lover*, was not obscene within the meaning of the Code. The *Brodie* case lay the groundwork for the interpretation of s. 163(8) by setting out the principal tests which should govern the determination of what is obscene for the purposes of criminal prosecution. [The first test is the ""Community Standard of Tolerance." In *Towne Cinema Theatres Ltd. v. The Queen*, [1985] 1 S.C.R. 494. Dickson C.J. reviewed the case law and found (at pp. 508–9):

"The cases all emphasize that it is a standard of *tolerance* not taste, that is relevant. What matters is not what Canadians think is right for themselves to see. What matters is what Canadians would not abide other Canadians seeing because it would be beyond the contemporary Canadian standard of tolerance to allow them to see it.

Since the standard is tolerance, I think the audience to which the allegedly obscene material is targeted must be relevant. The operative standards are those of the Canadian community as a whole, but since what matters is what other people may see, it is quite conceivable that the Canadian community would tolerate varying degrees of explicitness depending upon the audience and the circumstances." [Emphasis in original.]

* * *

[The second test is the "Degradation or Dehumanization" Test. The court noted "a growing recognition in recent cases that material which may be said to exploit sex in a 'degrading or dehumanizing' manner will necessarily fail the community standards test."]

Among other things, degrading or dehumanizing materials place women (and sometimes men) in positions of subordination, servile submission or humiliation. They run against the principles of equality and dignity of all human beings. In the appreciation of whether material is degrading or dehumanizing, the appearance of consent is not necessarily determinative. Consent cannot save materials that otherwise contain degrading or dehumanizing scenes. Sometimes the very appearance of consent makes the depicted acts even more degrading or dehumanizing.

This type of material would, apparently, fail the community standards test not because it offends against morals but because it is perceived by public opinion to be harmful to society, particularly to women. While the accuracy of this perception is not susceptible of exact proof, there is a substantial body of opinion that holds that the portrayal of persons being subjected to degrading or dehumanizing sexual treatment results in harm, particularly to women and therefore to society as a whole. It would be reasonable to conclude that there is an appreciable risk of harm to society in the portrayal of such material. * * *

[Indeed, *Towne Cinema* suggested that degrading pornography would be obscene even if it did not offend the community standard of tolerance]:

. . . No one should be subject to the degradation and humiliation inherent in publications which link sex with violence, cruelty, and other forms of dehumanizing treatment. It is not likely that at a given moment in a society's history, such publications will be tolerated . . . .

* * *

[The third test is the "Artistic Defence" Test. As explained in *Brodie*, obscenity involves]

. . . excessive emphasis on the theme for a base purpose. But I do not think that there is undue exploitation if there is no more emphasis on the theme than is required in the serious treatment of the theme of a novel with honesty and uprightness. That the work under attack is a serious work of fiction is to me beyond question. It has none of the characteristics that are often described in judgments dealing with obscenity — dirt for dirt's sake, the leer of the sensualist, depravity in the mind of an author with an obsession for dirt, pornography, an appeal to a prurient interest, etc. The section recognizes that the serious-minded author must have freedom in the production of a work of genuine artistic and literary merit and the quality of the work, as the witnesses point out and common sense indicates, must have real relevance in determining not only a dominant characteristic but also whether there is undue exploitation."

*   *   *

Pornography can be usefully divided into three categories: (1) explicit sex with violence, (2) explicit sex without violence but which subjects people to treatment that is degrading or dehumanizing, and (3) explicit sex without violence that is neither degrading nor dehumanizing. Violence in this context includes both actual physical violence and threats of physical violence. Relating these three categories to the terms of s. 163(8) of the Code, the first, explicit sex coupled with violence, is expressly mentioned. Sex coupled with crime, horror or cruelty will sometimes involve violence. Cruelty, for instance, will usually do so. But, even in the absence of violence, sex coupled with crime, horror or cruelty may fall within the second category. As for category (3), subject to the exception referred to below, it is not covered.

Some segments of society would consider that all three categories of pornography cause harm to society because they tend to undermine its moral fibre. Others would contend that none of the categories cause harm. Furthermore there is a range of opinion as to what is degrading or dehumanizing. Because this is not a matter that is susceptible of proof in the traditional way and because we do not wish to leave it to the individual tastes of judges, we must have a norm that will serve as an arbiter in determining what amounts to an undue exploitation of sex. That arbiter is the community as a whole.

The courts must determine as best they can what the community would tolerate others being exposed to on the basis of the degree of harm that may flow from such exposure. Harm in this context means that it predisposes persons to act in an anti-social manner as, for example, the physical or mental mistreatment of women by men, or, what is perhaps debatable, the reverse. Anti-social conduct for this purpose is conduct which society formally recognizes as incompatible with its proper functioning. The stronger the inference of a risk of harm the lesser the likelihood of tolerance. The inference may be drawn from the material itself or from the material and other evidence. Similarly evidence as to the community standards is desirable but not essential.

In making this determination with respect to the three categories of pornography referred to above, the portrayal of sex coupled with violence will almost always constitute the undue exploitation of sex. Explicit sex which is degrading or dehumanizing may be undue if the risk of harm is substantial. Finally, explicit sex that is not violent and neither degrading nor dehumanizing is generally tolerated in our society and will not qualify as the undue exploitation of sex unless it employs children in its production.

. . . .

D. *Is s. 163 Justified Under s. 1 of the Charter?*

. . . .

(b) Objective

. . . .

I agree with Twaddle J.A. of the Court of Appeal that [the traditional legislative objective of prohibiting "immoral influences" of obscenity, thus advancing a particular conception of morality] is no longer defensible in view of the *Charter*. To impose a certain standard of public and sexual morality, solely because it reflects the conventions of a given community, is inimical to the exercise and enjoyment of individual freedoms, which form the basis of our social contract. D. Dyzenhaus, "Obscenity and the Charter: Autonomy and Equality" (1991), 1 C.R. (4th) 367, at p. 370, refers to this as "legal moralism," of a majority deciding what values should inform individual lives and then coercively imposing those values on minorities. The prevention of "dirt for dirt's sake" is not a legitimate objective which would justify the violation of one of the most fundamental freedoms enshrined in the *Charter*.

On the other hand, I cannot agree with the suggestion of the appellant that Parliament does not have the right to legislate on the basis of some fundamental conception of morality for the purposes of safeguarding the values which are integral to a free and democratic society. As Dyzenhaus, supra, at p. 376, writes: "Moral disapprobation is recognized as an appropriate response when it has its basis in *Charter* values."

*   *   *

In my view, however, the overriding objective of s. 163 is not moral disapprobation but the avoidance of harm to society. [The Court cited the Report on Pornography by the Standing Committee on Justice and Legal Affairs (MacGuigan Report) (1978), at p. 18:4, which concluded that obscenity reinforces "male-female stereotypes to the detriment of both sexes. It attempts to make degradation, humiliation, victimization, and violence in human relationships appear normal and acceptable. A society which holds that egalitarianism, non-violence, consensualism, and mutuality are basic to any human interaction, whether sexual or other, is clearly justified in controlling and prohibiting any medium of depiction, description or advocacy which violates these principles."]

In reaching the conclusion that legislation proscribing obscenity is a valid objective which justifies some encroachment on the right to freedom of expression, I am persuaded in part that such legislation may be found in most free and democratic societies. * * *

The enactment of the impugned provision is also consistent with Canada's international obligations (Agreement for the Suppression of the Circulation of

Obscene Publications and the Convention for the Suppression of the Circulation of and Traffic in Obscene Publications).

. . . .

(c) Proportionality

. . . .

The values which underlie the protection of freedom of expression relate to the search for truth, participation in the political process, and individual self-fulfilment. The Attorney General for Ontario argues that of these, only "individual self-fulfilment," and only in its most base aspect, that of physical arousal, is engaged by pornography. On the other hand, the civil liberties groups argue that pornography forces us to question conventional notions of sexuality and thereby launches us into an inherently political discourse. In their factum, the British Columbia Civil Liberties Association adopts a passage from R. West, "The Feminist-Conservative Anti-Pornography Alliance and the 1986 Attorney General's Commission on Pornography Report" (1987), 4 Am. Bar Found. Res. J. 681, at p. 696:

> "Good pornography has value because it validates women's will to pleasure. It celebrates female nature. It validates a range of female sexuality that is wider and truer than that legitimated by the non-pornographic culture. Pornography (when it is good) celebrates both female pleasure and male rationality."

A proper application of the test should not suppress what West refers to as "good pornography." The objective of the impugned provision is not to inhibit the celebration of human sexuality. However, it cannot be ignored that the realities of the pornography industry are far from the picture which the British Columbia Civil Liberties Association would have us paint. Shannon J., in *R. v. Wagner*, [(1985) 43 C.R.(3d) 318] described the materials more accurately when he observed:

> "Women, particularly, are deprived of unique human character or identity and are depicted as sexual playthings, hysterically and instantly responsive to male sexual demands. They worship male genitals and their own value depends upon the quality of their genitals and breasts."

In my view, the kind of expression which is sought to be advanced does not stand on an equal footing with other kinds of expression which directly engage the "core" of the freedom of expression values.

This conclusion is further buttressed by the fact that the targeted material is expression which is motivated, in the overwhelming majority of cases, by economic profit. This Court held in *Rocket v. Royal College of Dental Surgeons of Ontario*, [1990] 2 S.C.R. 232, at p. 247, that an economic motive for expression means that restrictions on the expression might "be easier to justify than other infringements."

[The Court then found the statute proportional under *Oakes*. Acknowledging "inconclusive social science evidence" on the risk of harm to society, the Court applied *Irwin Toy* to determine that "it is sufficient that Parliament had a reasonable basis" to find harm. With regard to minimal impairment, the Court emphasized that "it is not necessary that the legislative scheme be the 'perfect' scheme, but that it be appropriately tailored in the context of the infringed right." In this regard, the Court noted that the statute did not proscribe explicit erotic "violence that is not degrading or dehumanizing," that it likewise excluded works that have "scientific, artistic or literary merit," and that prior efforts to enact more specific legislation were found to be unsuccessful. The Court also noted that private viewing of obscenity was largely uncovered.]

It is also submitted that there are more effective techniques to promote the objectives of Parliament. For example, if pornography is seen as encouraging violence against women, there are certain activities which discourage it - counselling rape victims to charge their assailants, provision of shelter and assistance for battered women, campaigns for laws against discrimination on the grounds of sex, education to increase the sensitivity of law enforcement agencies and other governmental authorities. In addition, it is submitted that education is an under-used response.

It is noteworthy that many of the above suggested alternatives are in the form of responses to the harm engendered by negative attitudes against women. The role of the impugned provision is to control the dissemination of the very images that contribute to such attitudes. Moreover, it is true that there are additional measures which could alleviate the problem of violence against women. However, given the gravity of the harm, and the threat to the values at stake, I do not believe that the measure chosen by Parliament is equalled by the alternatives which have been suggested. Education, too, may offer a means of combating negative attitudes to women, just as it is currently used as a means of addressing other problems dealt with in the Code. However, there is no reason to rely on education alone. It should be emphasized that this is in no way intended to deny the value of other educational and counselling measures to deal with the roots and effects of negative attitudes. Rather, it is only to stress the arbitrariness and unacceptability of the claim that such measures represent the sole legitimate means of addressing the phenomenon. Serious social problems such as violence against women require multi-pronged approaches by government. Education and legislation are not alternatives but complements in addressing such problems. There is nothing in the *Charter* which requires Parliament to choose between such complementary measures.

(iv) *Balance Between Effects of Limiting Measures and Legislative Objective*

The final question to be answered in the proportionality test is whether the effects of the law so severely trench on a protected right that the legislative objective is outweighed by the infringement. [The Court concluded that the proscribed material "lies far from the core of the guarantee of freedom of expression. It appeals only to the most base aspect of individual fulfilment, and it is primarily economically motivated." On the other hand, the objective of protecting women and children "is of fundamental importance in a free and democratic society."]

*   *   *

The reasons of L'HEUREUX-DUBE and GONTHIER J J. were delivered by

Gonthier J. —

[Justice Gonthier agreed with the majority that Parliament may constitutionally prohibit pornography that contains explicit sex with violence and explicit sex that is degrading or dehumanizing. He disagrees with the view that explicit sex that is neither violent, degrading, nor dehumanizing must be protected. As an example, he cites an explicit portrayal of consensual sexual intercourse displayed on a billboard.]

3.4.2. United States

The U.S. Supreme Court's treatment of obscenity experienced considerable uncertainty in the middle third of the 20th century, finally settling on some relatively clear standards. In *Roth v. United States*, 354 U.S. 476 (1957), the Court sustained a conviction under a federal statute punishing the mailing of "obscene, lewd, lascivious or filthy . . ." materials. The key to that holding was the Court's rejection of the claim that obscene materials were protected by the First Amendment.

In *Miller v. California*, 413 U.S. 15 (1973), the Court sustained a conviction for knowingly distributing obscene matter. The defendant had sent pornographic direct mail advertisements to a variety of recipients, many of whom had not requested the materials. The Court emphasized the unwilling receipt of offensive materials. Recognizing the "inherent dangers of undertaking to regulate any form of expression," the court "carefully limited" the scope of permissible regulation:

> State statutes designed to regulate obscene materials must be carefully limited. As a result, we now confine the permissible scope of such regulation to works which depict or describe sexual conduct. That conduct must be specifically defined by the applicable state law, as written or authoritatively construed. A state offense must also be limited to works which, taken as a whole, appeal to the prurient interest in sex, which portray sexual conduct in a patently offensive way, and which, taken as a whole, do not have serious literary, artistic, political, or scientific value.

Examples of material that could be constitutionally regulated included, according to the Court,

(a) Patently offensive representations or descriptions of ultimate sexual acts, normal or perverted, actual or simulated.

(b) Patently offensive representations or descriptions of masturbation, excretory functions, and lewd exhibition of the genitals. Sex and nudity may not be exploited without limit by films or pictures exhibited or sold in places of public accommodation any more than live sex and nudity can be exhibited or sold without limit in such public places. At a minimum, prurient, patently offensive depiction or description of sexual conduct must have serious literary, artistic, political, or scientific value to merit First Amendment protection.

The court rejected Justice Brennan's approach, in dissent, that would only permit regulation of obscenity narrowly tailored to avoid exposure to unconsenting adults and juveniles, as unworkable. Concluding that it was "neither realistic nor constitutionally sound to read the First Amendment as requiring that the people of Maine or Mississippi accept public depiction of conduct found tolerable in Las Vegas, or New York City," the Court concluded that "the requirement that the jury evaluate the materials with reference to 'contemporary standards of the State of California' serves this protective purpose and is constitutionally adequate." Finally, responding to what it characterized as the dissent's "alarm of repression," the Court observed the absence of evidence that the stern censorship that prevailed in the 19th Century "in any way limited or affected expression of serious literary, artistic, political, or scientific ideas."

Justice Douglas vigorously dissented, arguing that civil censorship proceedings were less restrictive alternatives and thus criminalizing the sale of obscene materials was necessarily overbroad as well as having an impermissible chilling effect on speech, compared to civil proceedings. He took particular umbrage at the claim that the First Amendment permits punishment for ideas that are "offensive."

> The First Amendment was not fashioned as a vehicle for dispensing tranquilizers to the people. Its prime function was to keep debate open to "offensive" as well as to "staid" people. The tendency throughout history has been to subdue the individual and to exalt the power of government. The use of the standard "offensive" gives authority to government that cuts the very vitals out of the First Amendment.

Justices Brennan, Stewart, and Marshall also dissented, concluding that no verbal formula could reduce the problem of vague standards to a tolerable level, especially in light of the conclusion that state interests in preventing consenting adults from purchasing obscene materials cannot justify the restraint on constitutional rights.

AMERICAN BOOKSELLERS ASSOCIATION, INC. v. HUDNUT

UNITED STATES COURT OF APPEALS FOR THE SEVENTH CIRCUIT

771 F.2d 323 (1985)

CUDAHY and EASTERBROOK, CIRCUIT JUDGES, and SWYGERT, SENIOR CIRCUIT JUDGE. SWYGERT, SENIOR CIRCUIT JUDGE, concurring.

EASTERBROOK, CIRCUIT JUDGE.

Indianapolis enacted an ordinance defining "pornography" as a practice that discriminates against women. "Pornography" is to be redressed through the administrative and judicial methods used for other discrimination. The City's definition of "pornography" is considerably different from "obscenity," which the Supreme Court has held is not protected by the First Amendment.

To be "obscene" under *Miller v. California*, 413 U.S. 15 (1973), "a publication must, taken as a whole, appeal to the prurient interest, must contain patently offensive depictions or descriptions of specified sexual conduct, and on the whole have no serious literary, artistic, political, or scientific value." Offensiveness must be assessed under the standards of the community. Both offensiveness and an appeal to something other than "normal, healthy sexual desires" are essential elements of "obscenity."

"Pornography" under the ordinance is "the graphic sexually explicit subordination of women, whether in pictures or in words, that also includes one or more of the following:

(1) Women are presented as sexual objects who enjoy pain or humiliation; or

(2) Women are presented as sexual objects who experience sexual pleasure in being raped; or

(3) Women are presented as sexual objects tied up or cut up or mutilated or bruised or physically hurt, or as dismembered or truncated or fragmented or severed into body parts; or

(4) Women are presented as being penetrated by objects or animals; or

(5) Women are presented in scenarios of degradation, injury abasement, torture, shown as filthy or inferior, bleeding, bruised, or hurt in a context that makes these conditions sexual; or

(6) Women are presented as sexual objects for domination, conquest, violation, exploitation, possession, or use, or through postures or positions of servility or submission or display."

Indianapolis Code § 16-3(q). The statute provides that the "use of men, children, or transsexuals in the place of women in paragraphs (1) through (6) above shall also constitute pornography under this section." The ordinance as passed in April 1984 defined "sexually explicit" to mean actual or simulated intercourse or the uncovered exhibition of the genitals, buttocks or anus. An amendment in June 1984 deleted this provision, leaving the term undefined.

The Indianapolis ordinance does not refer to the prurient interest, to offensiveness, or to the standards of the community. It demands attention to particular depictions, not to the work judged as a whole. It is irrelevant under the ordinance whether the work has literary, artistic, political, or scientific value. The City and many *amici* point to these omissions as virtues. They maintain that pornography influences attitudes, and the statute is a way to alter the socialization of men and women rather than to vindicate community standards of offensiveness. And as one of the principal drafters of the ordinance has asserted, "if a woman is subjected, why should it matter that the work has other value?" Catharine A. MacKinnon, *Pornography, Civil Rights, and Speech*, 20 Harv. Civ. Rts. — Civ. Lib. L. Rev. 1, 21 (1985).

Civil rights groups and feminists have entered this case as *amici* on both sides. Those supporting the ordinance say that it will play an important role in reducing the tendency of men to view women as sexual objects, a tendency that leads to both unacceptable attitudes and discrimination in the workplace and violence away from it. Those opposing the ordinance point out that much radical feminist literature is explicit and depicts women in ways forbidden by the ordinance and that the ordinance would reopen old battles. It is unclear how Indianapolis would treat works from James Joyce's Ulysses to Homer's Iliad; both depict women as submissive objects for conquest and domination.

We do not try to balance the arguments for and against an ordinance such as this. The ordinance discriminates on the ground of the content of the speech. Speech treating women in the approved way — in sexual encounters "premised on equality" (MacKinnon, supra, at 22) — is lawful no matter how sexually explicit. Speech treating women in the disapproved way — as submissive in matters sexual or as enjoying humiliation — is unlawful no matter how significant the literary, artistic, or political qualities of the work taken as a whole. The state may not ordain preferred viewpoints in this way. The Constitution forbids the state to declare one perspective right and silence opponents.

. . . .

III

"If there is any fixed star in our constitutional constellation, it is that no official, high or petty, can prescribe what shall be orthodox in politics, nationalism, religion, or other matters of opinion or force citizens to confess by word or act their faith therein." *West Virginia State Board of Education v. Barnette*, 319 U.S. 624 (1943). Under the First Amendment the government must leave to the people the evaluation of ideas. Bald or subtle, an idea is as powerful as the audience allows it to be. A belief may be pernicious — the beliefs of Nazis led to the death of millions, those of the Klan to the repression of millions. A pernicious belief may prevail. Totalitarian governments today rule much of the planet, practicing suppression of billions and spreading dogma that may enslave others. One of the things that separates our society from theirs is our absolute right to propagate opinions that the government finds wrong or even hateful.

. . . .

Under the ordinance graphic sexually explicit speech is "pornography" or not depending on the perspective the author adopts. Speech that "subordinates" women and also, for example, presents women as enjoying pain, humiliation, or rape, or even simply presents women in "positions of servility or submission or display" is forbidden, no matter how great the literary or political value of the work taken as a whole. Speech that portrays women in positions of equality is lawful, no matter how graphic the sexual content. This is thought control. It establishes an "approved" view of women, of how they may react to sexual encounters, of how the sexes may relate to each other. Those who espouse the approved view may use sexual images; those who do not, may not.

[The Court accepted the legislation's premise that "depictions of subordination tend to perpetuate subordination. The subordinate status of women in turn leads to affront and lower pay at work, insult and injury at home, battery and rape on the streets." The Court also agreed that counter-speech may not be effective in countering this social harm.]

Yet this simply demonstrates the power of pornography as speech. All of these unhappy effects depend on mental intermediation. Pornography affects how people see the world, their fellows, and social relations. If pornography is what pornography does, so is other speech. Hitler's orations affected how some Germans saw Jews. Communism is a world view, not simply a Manifesto by Marx and Engels or a set of speeches. Efforts to suppress communist speech in the United States were based on the belief that the public acceptability of such ideas would increase the likelihood of totalitarian government. Religions affect socialization in the most pervasive way. The opinion in *Wisconsin v. Yoder*, 406 U.S. 205 (1972), shows how a religion can dominate an entire approach to life, governing much more than the relation between the sexes. Many people believe that the existence of television, apart from the content of specific programs, leads to intellectual laziness, to a penchant for violence, to many other ills. The Alien and Sedition Acts passed during the administration of John Adams rested on a sincerely held belief that disrespect for the government leads to social collapse and revolution — a belief with support in the history of many nations. Most governments of the world act on this empirical regularity, suppressing critical speech. In the United States, however, the strength of the support for this belief is irrelevant. Seditious libel is protected speech unless the danger is not only grave but also imminent.

. . . .

Much of Indianapolis's argument rests on the belief that when speech is "unanswerable," and the metaphor that there is a "marketplace of ideas" does not apply, the First Amendment does not apply either. The metaphor is honored; Milton's *Aeropagitica* and John Stewart Mill's *On Liberty* defend freedom of speech on the ground that the truth will prevail, and many of the most important cases under the First Amendment recite this position. The Framers undoubtedly believed it. As a general matter it is true. But the Constitution does not make the dominance of truth a necessary condition of freedom of speech. To say that it does would be to confuse an outcome of free speech with a necessary condition for the application of the amendment.

A power to limit speech on the ground that truth has not yet prevailed and is not likely to prevail implies the power to declare truth. At some point the government must be able to say (as Indianapolis has said): "We know what the truth is, yet a free exchange of speech has not driven out falsity, so that we must now prohibit falsity." If the government may declare the truth, why wait for the failure of speech? Under the First Amendment, however, there is no such thing as a false idea, so the government may not restrict speech on the ground that in a free exchange truth is not yet dominant.

. . . .

The Supreme Court has rejected the position that speech must be "effectively answerable" to be protected by the Constitution. For example, in *Buckley v. Valeo*, 424 U.S. 1, 39–54 (1976), the Court held unconstitutional limitations on expenditures that were neutral with regard to the speakers' opinions and designed to make it easier for one person to answer another's speech. In *Mills v. Alabama*, 384 U.S. 214 (1966), the Court held unconstitutional a statute prohibiting editorials on election day — a statute the state had designed to prevent speech that came too late for answer. In cases from *Eastern Railroad Presidents Conference v. Noerr Motor Freight, Inc.*, 365 U.S. 127 (1961), through *NAACP v. Claiborne Hardware Co.*, 458 U.S. 886 (1982), the Court has held that the First Amendment protects political stratagems — obtaining legislation through underhanded ploys and outright fraud in *Noerr*, obtaining political and economic ends through boycotts in *Clairborne*

Hardware — that may be beyond effective correction through more speech.

[Finally, the Court rejected the argument that pornography is "low value" speech, on two grounds. First, the failure to immunize pornography with literary, artistic, political, or scientific value meant that some "high value" speech was also condemned. Secondly, the First Amendment does not permit condemnation of some speech based on its viewpoint.]

SWYGERT, SENIOR CIRCUIT JUDGE, concurring. [omitted]

———————

Consistent with these cases, the American and Canadian courts have reached different results regarding depictions of child pornography where children are not used in production. In *Ashcroft v. Free Speech Coalition*, 535 U.S. 234 (2002), the U.S. Supreme Court invalidated portions of the federal Child Pornography Prevention Act of 1996 involving computer-generated imagery or with adult actors portraying children that was not obscene under the *Miller* standard. As in *Hudnut*, the Court rejected the claim that the proscribed material was low value speech, holding that the appropriate test for that speech was *Miller*. It further rejected the argument that speech could be suppressed because its dissemination would "whet the appetite" of pedophiles for criminal activity. Justice Kennedy noted for the majority:

> This rationale cannot sustain the provision in question. The mere tendency of speech to encourage unlawful acts is not a sufficient reason for banning it. The government "cannot constitutionally premise legislation on the desirability of controlling a person's private thoughts." *Stanley v. Georgia*, 394 U.S. 557, 566 (1969).

R. v. Sharpe, [2001] 1 S.C.R. 45, by contrast, upheld most of the *Criminal Code*'s proscriptions on possession of child pornography, only limiting its scope by interpreting the statute to create exceptions for private material created by the accused. Unlike the U.S. Supreme Court, the Supreme Court of Canada found that possession of pornography (including material involving adult actors or drawings) was a reasonable limit (per s. 1) on rights to free expression that were infringed (per s. 2(b)). Parliament's "reasoned apprehension" that a vibrant market for all forms of child pornography facilitated the seduction of victims and broke down inhibitions among pedophiles was held sufficient to justify the reasonable limit.

REGULATION OF PORNOGRAPHY

3.4.3. South Africa

DE REUCK v. DIRECTOR OF PUBLIC PROSECUTIONS (WITWATERSRAND LOCAL DIVISION)
CONSTITUTIONAL COURT OF SOUTH AFRICA
2004 (3) SA 345
[see excerpt in Chapter 2 above for additional details]

LANGA DCJ:

Introduction

[1] The applicant, a film producer, appeared in the Randburg Regional Court where he was charged under section 27(1) of the Films and Publications Act 65 of 1996 (the Act), a provision which relates to child pornography . . . .

[5] The applicant's case in both the High Court and this Court was that the provisions of section 27(1) read with the definition of child pornography in section 1 of the Act, constituted a limitation of the constitutional rights to privacy, freedom of expression and equality . . . .

[38] I now summarise my approach to the question whether an image constitutes child pornography for the purposes of section 27(1). The overarching enquiry, objectively viewed, is whether the purpose of the image is to stimulate sexual arousal in the target audience. This entails considering the context of the publication or film in which the image occurs as a visual presentation or scene. The court conducts the enquiry from the perspective of the reasonable viewer. The image will not be child pornography unless one or more of the four prohibited acts listed below is explicitly depicted for this purpose. The person "who is shown as being under the age of eighteen years" in the image may be real or imaginary. The prohibited acts are:

  (a) a child engaged in sexual conduct;

  (b) a child engaged in a display of genitals;

  (c) a child participating in sexual conduct; and

  (d) a child assisting another person to engage in sexual conduct.

. . . .

[46] The applicant argued that section 27(1) of the Act infringed both the right to freedom of expression and the right to privacy as protected by the Constitution.

. . . .

[48] The respondents dispute that child pornography, as defined by the Act, is expression. Relying on the approach of the United States Supreme Court where certain categories of expression are unprotected forms of speech, the respondents argued such materials do not serve any of the values traditionally considered as underlying freedom of expression, namely, truth-seeking, free political activity and

self-fulfillment. This argument must fail. In this respect, our Constitution is different from that of the United States of America. Limitations of rights are dealt with under section 36 of the Constitution and not at the threshold level. Section 16(1) expressly protects the freedom of expression in a manner that does not warrant a narrow reading. Any restriction upon artistic creativity must satisfy the rigours of the limitation analysis.

. . . .

[50] The criminalisation of the creation, production, importation, distribution and possession of the material that falls within the definition of child pornography, as discussed above, limits the right to freedom of expression. Whether the limitation is justifiable remains to be considered under a limitation analysis.

. . . .

[52] In *Case* [1996 (3) SA 617 (CC)], all the members of this Court held that the crime of possessing "indecent or obscene photographic matter" (a much wider range of materials than those at issue in the present case) violated the right to privacy under the interim Constitution. The majority of the Court in that matter, however, agreed that a law prohibiting possession of a narrower category of erotic materials would limit the right to privacy, but could be upheld if it satisfied the requirements of the limitation clause. It flows from this decision that the impugned provisions infringe the right to privacy and their constitutionality will depend on whether the requirements of the limitation clause in section 36 of the Constitution are fulfilled.

. . . .

[For limitations analysis see excerpt in Chapter 2 above]

[67] I conclude that the state has established three legitimate objectives which the limitation aims to serve, namely, protecting the dignity of children, stamping out the market for photographs made by abusing children and preventing a reasonable risk that images will be used to harm children.

3.4.4. Australia

In Australia, until the 1970s, laws prohibiting the publication or distribution of material classified as obscene were strenuously enforced, and there were celebrated "obscenity trials." Although Australian law and culture has become considerably more liberal and permissive in recent decades, some states' Summary Offences Acts still include offences relating to the display of obscene, indecent or offensive material. Tests for what is "obscene" etc tend to follow imprecise criteria such as community standards or capacity to "deprave and corrupt." Regulation of such material, for the most part, occurs via Commonwealth classifications applied to films, publications, video and computer games. These classifications restrict access based on age groups; sometimes the classifications can be so restrictive as effectively to prevent distribution (see the *Rabelais Case* discussed above.) *Rabelais* concerned a publication deemed to be a "guide" to committing an offence (shoplifting). It did not concern whether material was obscene or pornographic. The constitutional protection of political speech or communication has never been raised with respect to such material, and a challenge against a prosecution or classification on this footing is unlikely to succeed.

3.5.   REGULATION OF ELECTION SPENDING

The permissibility of governmental restrictions on election spending obviously raises many different issues than those that arise in the context of hate speech and pornography. The harms that electoral restraints seek to address are thought to result in an inferior process, a disaffected electorate, or skewed public policy; it is more difficult to point directly to "victims" than in the first two contexts we've studied. On the flip side of this equation, the type of expression restrained — political speech — has always been considered to be the most highly valued and essential to our democracy. Nonetheless, there are important similarities. Campaign finance restrictions designed to minimize the disproportionate influence of those with greater wealth involve the intrusion of the government on behalf of equality concerns at the expense of the individual liberty of those restrained. The way that each country's highest court balances dignity, equality, and freedom affects the legal doctrines developed in this area. This topic also reveals the significant interconnections between constitutional law and ordinary politics. In the United States, contributions from private individuals, corporations, and other entities provide most of the funds for political campaigns. In Canada, political parties receive substantial public funding, but rely extensively on private contributions as well, and privately-funded third-party campaigns have had a significant effect on political contests.

3.5.1.   United States

American campaign law is a complex mix of statutory and administrative regulation, judicial interpretation of these statutes, and judicial limits on regulation based on the First Amendment. In *Buckley v. Valeo*, 424 U.S. 1 (1976), the Supreme Court, in the wake of the excesses by President Richard Nixon's re-election campaign contributing to the Watergate scandal and his subsequent impeachment, upheld a statute restricting the amount individuals or political committees could contribute to candidates for federal elective office, and the total amount any individual could contribute to all candidates. The Court, however, struck down provisions that also limited contributions to independent campaign organizations "relative to a clearly identified candidate" and the amount that individuals could spend on their own campaigns. The upheld provisions were constitutional as necessary to prevent the actual or perceived influence of large financial contributions on candidates' positions and actions. The Court specifically rejected equal access concerns that went beyond protecting the political process from the appearance of corruption, *Buckley*, 424 U.S. at 48:

> It is argued, however, that the ancillary governmental interest in equalizing the relative ability of individuals and groups to influence the outcome of elections serves to justify the limitation on express advocacy of the election or defeat of candidates imposed by § 608 (e)(1)'s expenditure ceiling. But the concept that government may restrict the speech of some elements of our society in order to enhance the relative voice of others is

wholly foreign to the First Amendment, which was designed "to secure 'the widest possible dissemination of information from diverse and antagonistic sources,'" and "'to assure unfettered interchange of ideas for the bringing about of political and social changes desired by the people.'" *New York Times Co. v. Sullivan*, 376 U.S. 254, 266, 269 (1964).

Shortly thereafter, in *First Nat'l Bank of Boston v. Bellotti*, 435 U.S. 765, 790 (1978), the Court recognized that the First Amendment applies to corporations' political speech. Having done so, the Court considered and rejected the following argument in invalidating a bar on corporate spending in referendum campaigns. The state's arguments that corporate participation in discussion of a referendum endangered state interests:

> [H]inge upon the assumption that such participation would exert an undue influence on the outcome of a referendum vote, and — in the end — destroy the confidence of the people in the democratic process and the integrity of government. According to appellee, corporations are wealthy and powerful and their views may drown out other points of view. If appellee's arguments were supported by record or legislative findings that corporate advocacy threatened imminently to undermine democratic processes, thereby denigrating rather than serving First Amendment interests, these arguments would merit our consideration. But there has been no showing that the relative voice of corporations has been overwhelming or even significant in influencing referenda in Massachusetts, or that there has been any threat to the confidence of the citizenry in government.

But see Daniel H. Lowenstein, *Campaign Spending and Ballot Propositions: Recent Experience, Public Choice Theory and the First Amendment*, 29 UCLA L. Rev. 505 (1982) ("one-sided" corporate spending generally effective in defeating voter-initiated referenda). Corporations and labor unions remained subject, however, to extensive regulation with regard to specific candidates for office. Although these entities were permitted to establish separate "political action committees" funded by individual donations from employees, shareholders, or members, they could not use general treasury funds for an "electioneering communication" that expressly advocated the election or defeat of a candidate. In the following case, the Court overruled earlier precedent to hold that the First Amendment barred limits on the ability of corporations to fund a documentary critical of 2008 presidential candidate Hillary Clinton.

CITIZENS UNITED v. FEDERAL ELECTION COMMISSION
SUPREME COURT OF THE UNITED STATES
558 U.S. 310 (2010)

JUSTICE KENNEDY delivered the opinion of the Court.

. . . .

III

The law before us is an outright ban, backed by criminal sanctions. Section 441b makes it a felony for all corporations — including nonprofit advocacy corporations — either to expressly advocate the election or defeat of candidates or to broadcast electioneering communications within 30 days of a primary election and 60 days of a general election. Thus, the following acts would all be felonies under § 441b: The Sierra Club runs an ad, within the crucial phase of 60 days before the general election, that exhorts the public to disapprove of a Congressman who favors logging in national forests; the National Rifle Association publishes a book urging the public to vote for the challenger because the incumbent U.S. Senator supports a handgun ban; and the American Civil Liberties Union creates a Web site telling the public to vote for a Presidential candidate in light of that candidate's defense of free speech. These prohibitions are classic examples of censorship.

[The Court explained why requiring corporations to create political action committees (PACs) was an unduly burdensome and ineffective alternative.]

. . . .

[Because of its importance in a democracy,] political speech must prevail against laws that would suppress it, whether by design or inadvertence. Laws that burden political speech are "subject to strict scrutiny," which requires the Government to prove that the restriction "furthers a compelling interest and is narrowly tailored to achieve that interest." . . .

. . . .

Quite apart from the purpose or effect of regulating content, moreover, the Government may commit a constitutional wrong when by law it identifies certain preferred speakers. By taking the right to speak from some and giving it to others, the Government deprives the disadvantaged person or class of the right to use speech to strive to establish worth, standing, and respect for the speaker's voice. The Government may not by these means deprive the public of the right and privilege to determine for itself what speech and speakers are worthy of consideration. The First Amendment protects speech and speaker, and the ideas that flow from each.

. . . .

A

[In extending First Amendment protection to corporations, the] Court has thus rejected the argument that political speech of corporations or other associations should be treated differently under the First Amendment simply because such associations are not "natural persons." [In reviewing precedents, Kennedy J. noted dissents and concurrences arguing that any " 'undue influence' " generated by a speaker's "large expenditures" was outweighed "by the loss for democratic processes resulting from the restrictions upon free and full public discussion." *United States v. CIO*, 335 U.S. 106, 143 (1948).]

B

[The Court overruled its holding in *Austin v. Michigan Chamber of Commerce*, 494 U.S. 652 (1990), upholding the distinction between corporate and individual campaign expenditures.]

. . . *Austin* sought to defend the antidistortion rationale as a means to prevent corporations from obtaining " 'an unfair advantage in the political marketplace' " by using " 'resources amassed in the economic marketplace.' " 494 U.S. at 659. But *Buckley* rejected the premise that the Government has an interest "in equalizing the relative ability of individuals and groups to influence the outcome of elections." 424 U.S. at 48. *Buckley* was specific in stating that "the skyrocketing cost of political campaigns" could not sustain the governmental prohibition. 424 U.S. at 26. The First Amendment's protections do not depend on the speaker's "financial ability to engage in public discussion." *Id.* at 49.

. . . .

Either as support for its antidistortion rationale or as a further argument, the *Austin* majority undertook to distinguish wealthy individuals from corporations on the ground that "[s]tate law grants corporations special advantages — such as limited liability, perpetual life, and favorable treatment of the accumulation and distribution of assets." 494 U.S. at 658–659. This does not suffice, however, to allow laws prohibiting speech. "It is rudimentary that the State cannot exact as the price of those special advantages the forfeiture of First Amendment rights." *Id.* at 680 (Scalia, J., dissenting).

It is irrelevant for purposes of the First Amendment that corporate funds may "have little or no correlation to the public's support for the corporation's political ideas." *Id*, at 660. All speakers, including individuals and the media, use money amassed from the economic marketplace to fund their speech. The First Amendment protects the resulting speech, even if it was enabled by economic transactions with persons or entities who disagree with the speaker's ideas . . . .

Austin's antidistortion rationale would produce the dangerous, and unacceptable, consequence that Congress could ban political speech of media corporations . . . .

. . . .

There is simply no support for the view that the First Amendment, as originally understood, would permit the suppression of political speech by media corporations. The Framers may not have anticipated modern business and media corporations. Yet television networks and major newspapers owned by media corporations have become the most important means of mass communication in modern times. The First Amendment was certainly not understood to condone the suppression of political speech in society's most salient media. It was understood as a response to the repression of speech and the press that had existed in England and the heavy taxes on the press that were imposed in the colonies . . . . The Framers may have been unaware of certain types of speakers or forms of communication, but that does not mean that those speakers and media are entitled to less First Amendment protection than those types of speakers and media that provided the means of communicating political ideas when the Bill of Rights was adopted.

. . . .

The purpose and effect of this law is to prevent corporations, including small and nonprofit corporations, from presenting both facts and opinions to the public. This makes *Austin*'s antidistortion rationale all the more an aberration . . . . Corporate executives and employees counsel Members of Congress and Presidential administrations on many issues, as a matter of routine and often in private . . . . When that phenomenon is coupled with § 441b, the result is that smaller or nonprofit corporations cannot raise a voice to object when other corporations, including those with vast wealth, are cooperating with the Government. That cooperation may sometimes be voluntary, or it may be at the demand of a Government official who uses his or her authority, influence, and power to threaten corporations to support the Government's policies. Those kinds of interactions are often unknown and unseen. The speech that § 441b forbids, though, is public, and all can judge its content and purpose. References to massive corporate treasuries should not mask the real operation of this law. Rhetoric ought not obscure reality.

Even if § 441b's expenditure ban were constitutional, wealthy corporations could still lobby elected officials, although smaller corporations may not have the resources to do so. And wealthy individuals and unincorporated associations can spend unlimited amounts on independent expenditures. See, *e.g.*, *WRTL*, 551 U.S. at 503–504 (opinion of Scalia, J.) ("In the 2004 election cycle, a mere 24 individuals contributed an astounding total of $142 million to [26 U.S.C. § 527 organizations]"). Yet certain disfavored associations of citizens — those that have taken on the corporate form — are penalized for engaging in the same political speech.

When Government seeks to use its full power, including the criminal law, to command where a person may get his or her information or what distrusted source he or she may not hear, it uses censorship to control thought. This is unlawful. The First Amendment confirms the freedom to think for ourselves.

[The Court concluded that *Buckley*'s rejection of limits on independent expenditures by individuals applied also to corporations. It noted that when "*Buckley* identified a sufficiently important governmental interest in preventing corruption or the appearance of corruption, that interest was limited to *quid pro quo* corruption." Quoting his individual opinion in *McConnell v. FEC*, 540 U.S. 93, 297 (2003):

> Favoritism and influence are not . . . avoidable in representative politics. It is in the nature of an elected representative to favor certain policies, and, by necessary corollary, to favor the voters and contributors who support those policies. It is well understood that a substantial and legitimate reason, if not the only reason, to cast a vote for, or to make a contribution to, one candidate over another is that the candidate will respond by producing those political outcomes the supporter favors. Democracy is premised on responsiveness.

Reliance on a "generic favoritism or influence theory . . . is at odds with standard *First Amendment* analyses because it is unbounded and susceptible to no limiting principle." *Id.*, at 296.

The appearance of influence or access, furthermore, will not cause the electorate to lose faith in our democracy. By definition, an independent expenditure is political speech presented to the electorate that is not coordinated with a candidate. See *Buckley, supra*, at 46. The fact that a corporation, or any other speaker, is willing to spend money to try to persuade voters presupposes that the people have the ultimate influence over elected officials. This is inconsistent with any suggestion that the electorate will refuse " 'to take part in democratic governance' " because of additional political speech made by a corporation or any other speaker. *McConnell, supra*, at 144.

. . . .

[The court also rejected the government's argument that corporate independent expenditures can be limited because of its interest in protecting dissenting shareholders from being compelled to fund corporate political speech, and that any interest in preventing foreign influence could not justify the overbroad ban on all corporate expenditures.]

IV

[The Court, however, upheld the requirements that televised electioneering communications funded by anyone other than a candidate must include a disclaimer that identifying who is responsible for the advertising. Similar disclaimers had been upheld in the past "on the ground that they would help citizens " 'make informed choices in the political marketplace.' "]

CHIEF JUSTICE ROBERTS, with whom JUSTICE ALITO joins, concurring [explained why the decision was consistent with *stare decisis* and judicial restraint.]

JUSTICE SCALIA, with whom JUSTICE ALITO joins, and with whom JUSTICE THOMAS joins in part, concurring [explained his disagreement with Stevens J's argument that the decision was not supported by the original understanding of the First Amendment. He rejected the claim that the right of Englishmen to free speech did not include the freedom to speak in association with other individuals, including association in the corporate form. Although at the time, corporations could pursue only the objectives set forth in their charters [and those charters were typically more limited], but there was no evidence that their speech in the pursuit of those objectives could be censored.

. . . The Framers didn't like corporations, the dissent concludes, and therefore it follows (as night the day) that corporations had no rights of free speech. Of course the Framers' personal affection or disaffection for corporations is relevant only insofar as it can be thought to be reflected in the understood meaning of the text they enacted — not, as the dissent suggests, as a freestanding substitute for that text . . . .

. . . .

Even if we thought it proper to apply the dissent's approach of excluding from *First Amendment* coverage what the Founders disliked, and even if we agreed that the Founders disliked founding-era corporations; modern corporations might not qualify for exclusion. Most of the Founders' resentment towards corporations was directed at the state-granted monopoly privileges that individually chartered corporations enjoyed . . . .

   . . . .

JUSTICE STEVENS, with whom JUSTICES GINSBURG, BREYER, and SOTOMAYOR join, concurring in part and dissenting in part.

   . . . .

In the context of election to public office, the distinction between corporate and human speakers is significant. Although they make enormous contributions to our society, corporations are not actually members of it. They cannot vote or run for office. Because they may be managed and controlled by nonresidents, their interests may conflict in fundamental respects with the interests of eligible voters. The financial resources, legal structure, and instrumental orientation of corporations raise legitimate concerns about their role in the electoral process. Our lawmakers have a compelling constitutional basis, if not also a democratic duty, to take measures designed to guard against the potentially deleterious effects of corporate spending in local and national races.

The majority's approach to corporate electioneering marks a dramatic break from our past. Congress has placed special limitations on campaign spending by corporations ever since the passage of the Tillman Act in 1907, ch. 420, 34 Stat. 864. We have unanimously concluded that this "reflects a permissible assessment of the dangers posed by those entities to the electoral process," *FEC v. National Right to Work Comm.*, 459 U.S. 197 (1982) (NRWC), and have accepted the "legislative judgment that the special characteristics of the corporate structure require particularly careful regulation," *id.*, at 209–210. . . .

I

The Court's ruling threatens to undermine the integrity of elected institutions across the Nation. The path it has taken to reach its outcome will, I fear, do damage to this institution . . . .

   . . . .

III

[The dissent claimed that no speech was "banned" and that the frequent use of the word in the majority's opinion was "highly misleading." The opportunity to speak through PACs is significant, in the dissent's view.]

[The dissent also took issue to view that the First Amendment bars identity-based distinctions, noting cases upholding speech limits on students, prisoners, soldiers, foreigners, and court employees.]

[As noted in Scalia J's concurrence, the dissent argued that the original understanding of the First Amendment would uphold the challenged statute.] This is not only because the Framers and their contemporaries conceived of speech more narrowly than we now think of it, see Bork, *Neutral Principles and Some First Amendment Problems*, 47 Ind. L.J. 1, 22 (1971), but also because they held very different views about the nature of the First Amendment right and the role of corporations in society. Those few corporations that existed at the founding were authorized by grant of a special legislative charter. [These corporations, resulting often from specific legislation, were highly regulated.]

. . . In light of these background practices and understandings, it seems to me implausible that the Framers believed "the freedom of speech" would extend equally to all corporate speakers, much less that it would preclude legislatures from taking limited measures to guard against corporate capture of elections.

[The dissent detailed its view that the majority's decision was unfaithful to the legislative and judicial understandings of First Amendment tradition.]

. . . .

IV

. . . .

. . . Corruption can take many forms. Bribery may be the paradigm case. But the difference between selling a vote and selling access is a matter of degree, not kind. And selling access is not qualitatively different from giving special preference to those who spent money on one's behalf. Corruption operates along a spectrum, and the majority's apparent belief that *quid pro quo* arrangements can be neatly demarcated from other improper influences does not accord with the theory or reality of politics. It certainly does not accord with the record Congress developed in passing BCRA, a record that stands as a remarkable testament to the energy and ingenuity with which corporations, unions, lobbyists, and politicians may go about scratching each other's backs — and which amply supported Congress' determination to target a limited set of especially destructive practices.

. . .

It is with regret rather than satisfaction that I can now say that time has borne out my concerns. The legislative and judicial proceedings relating to BCRA generated a substantial body of evidence suggesting that, as corporations grew more and more adept at crafting "issue ads" to help or harm a particular candidate, these nominally independent expenditures began to corrupt the political process in a very direct sense. The sponsors of these ads were routinely granted special access after the campaign was over; "candidates and officials knew who their friends were," *McConnell*, 540 U.S., at 129.

. . . .

The fact that corporations are different from human beings might seem to need no elaboration, except that the majority opinion almost completely elides it. *Austin* set forth some of the basic differences. Unlike natural persons, corporations have "limited liability" for their owners and managers, "perpetual life," separation of ownership and control, "and favorable treatment of the accumulation and distribution of assets . . . that enhance their ability to attract capital and to deploy their resources in ways that maximize the return on their shareholders' investments." 494 U.S., at 658–659. . . .

It might also be added that corporations have no consciences, no beliefs, no feelings, no thoughts, no desires. Corporations help structure and facilitate the activities of human beings, to be sure, and their "personhood" often serves as a useful legal fiction. But they are not themselves members of "We the People" by whom and for whom our Constitution was established.

. . . .

It is an interesting question "who" is even speaking when a business corporation places an advertisement that endorses or attacks a particular candidate. Presumably it is not the customers or employees, who typically have no say in such matters. It cannot realistically be said to be the shareholders, who tend to be far removed from the day-to-day decisions of the firm and whose political preferences may be opaque to management. Perhaps the officers or directors of the corporation have the best claim to be the ones speaking, except their fiduciary duties generally prohibit them from using corporate funds for personal ends. Some individuals associated with the corporation must make the decision to place the ad, but the idea that these individuals are thereby fostering their self-expression or cultivating their critical faculties is fanciful. It is entirely possible that the corporation's electoral message will *conflict* with their personal convictions. Take away the ability to use general treasury funds for some of those ads, and no one's autonomy, dignity, or political equality has been impinged upon in the least. Corporate expenditures are distinguishable from individual expenditures in this respect . . . .

. . . .

In addition to . . . drowning out of noncorporate voices, there may be deleterious effects that follow soon thereafter. Corporate "domination" of electioneering, *Austin*, 494 U.S., at 659, can generate the impression that corporations dominate our democracy. When citizens turn on their televisions and radios before an election and hear only corporate electioneering, they may lose faith in their capacity, as citizens, to influence public policy. A Government captured by corporate interests, they may come to believe, will be neither responsive to their needs nor willing to give their views a fair hearing. The predictable result is cynicism and disenchantment: an increased perception that large spenders " 'call the tune' " and a reduced " 'willingness of voters to take part in democratic governance.' " *McConnell*, 540 U.S., at 144. . . .

. . . .

. . . If individuals in our society had infinite free time to listen to and contemplate every last bit of speech uttered by anyone, anywhere; and if broadcast advertisements had no special ability to influence elections apart from the merits of their arguments (to the extent they make any); and if legislators always operated with nothing less than perfect virtue; then I suppose the majority's premise would be sound. In the real world, we have seen, corporate domination of the airwaves prior to an election may decrease the average listener's exposure to relevant viewpoints, and it may diminish citizens' willingness and capacity to participate in the democratic process.

Justice Thomas, concurring in part and dissenting in part [objected to the disclosure requirements].

•••••

3.5.2.   Canada

HARPER v. CANADA (ATTORNEY GENERAL)
Supreme Court of Canada
[2004] 1 S.C.R. 827

[Before Mclachlin C.J. and Iacobucci, Major, Bastarache, Binnie, Arbour, Lebel, Deschamps and Fish JJ.]

[Stephen Harper — now the Prime Minister — was at the time of the suit the head of the National Citizens Council, a pro-business lobbying group. He challenged several provisions of the *Canada Elections Act* that limit the spending by third parties to $3,000 per riding and $150,000 nationally and bars advertising on election day. The statute specifically proscribes spending "incurred to promote or oppose the election of one or more candidates in a given electoral district, including by (a) naming them; (b) showing their likenesses; (c) identifying them by their respective political affiliations; or (d) taking a position on an issue with which they are particularly associated." As the majority noted, the statute thus does not apply to advertising prior to a statutory period during which active campaigning takes place — usually about six weeks [Ed. note: in contrast to the seemingly perennial campaigning in the United States) nor does it apply to advertising promoting an issue not associated with a candidate or political party.]

The judgment of Iacobucci, Arbour, Bastarache, Lebel, Deschamps and Fish JJ. was delivered by

Bastarache J. —

*   *   *

V. Analysis

A. *Third Party Electoral Advertising Regime*

Numerous groups and organizations participate in the electoral process as third parties. They do so to achieve three purposes. First, third parties may seek to influence the outcome of an election by commenting on the merits and faults of a particular candidate or political party. In this respect, the influence of third parties is most pronounced in electoral districts with "marginal seats," in other words, in electoral districts where the incumbent does not have a significant advantage. Second, third parties may add a fresh perspective or new dimension to the discourse surrounding one or more issues associated with a candidate or political party. While third parties are true electoral participants, their role and the extent of their participation, like candidates and political parties, cannot be unlimited. Third, they may add an issue to the political debate and in some cases force candidates and political parties to address it.

*   *   *

[The majority next repeated the key legal principles applicable to the regulation of election spending derived from *Libman v. Quebec (Attorney General)*, [1997] 3 S.C.R. 569.] They include (at paras. 47-50):

[1] If the principle of fairness in the political sphere is to be preserved, it cannot be presumed that all persons have the same financial resources to communicate with the electorate. To ensure a right of equal participation in democratic government, laws limiting spending are needed to preserve the equality of democratic rights and ensure that one person's exercise of the freedom to spend does not hinder the communication opportunities of others. *Owing to the competitive nature of elections, such spending limits are necessary to prevent the most affluent from monopolizing election discourse and consequently depriving their opponents of a reasonable opportunity to speak and be heard.*

[2] Spending limits are also necessary to guarantee *the right of electors to be adequately informed of all the political positions* advanced by the candidates and by the various political parties.

[3] For spending limits to be fully effective, *they must apply to all possible election expenses*, including those of independent individuals and groups.

[4] The actions of independent individuals and groups can [either] directly or indirectly support one of the parties or candidates, thereby resulting in an imbalance in the financial resources each candidate or political party is permitted . . . . "At elections, *the advocacy of issue positions inevitably has consequences for election discourse and thus has partisan implications, either direct or indirect*: voters cast their ballots for candidates and not for issues."

[5] It is also important to *limit independent spending more strictly than spending by candidates or political parties* . . . . [O]wing to their numbers, the impact of such spending on one of the candidates or political parties to the detriment of the others could be disproportionate.

The Court's conception of electoral fairness as reflected in the foregoing principles is consistent with the egalitarian model of elections adopted by Parliament as an essential component of our democratic society. This model is premised on the notion that individuals should have an equal opportunity to participate in the electoral process. Under this model, wealth is the main obstacle to equal participation; see C. Feasby, "*Libman v. Quebec (A.G.)* and the Administration of the Process of Democracy under the *Charter*: The Emerging Egalitarian Model" (1999), 44 *McGill L.J.* 5. Thus, the egalitarian model promotes an electoral process that requires the wealthy to be prevented from controlling the electoral process to the detriment of others with less economic power. The state can equalize participation in the electoral process in two ways; see O. M. Fiss, *The Irony of Free Speech* (1996), at p. 4. First, the State can provide a voice to those who might otherwise not be heard. The Act does so by reimbursing candidates and political parties and by providing broadcast time to political parties. Second, the State can restrict the voices which dominate the political discourse so that others may be heard as well. In Canada, electoral regulation has focussed on the latter by regulating electoral spending through comprehensive election finance provisions. These provisions seek to create a level playing field for those who wish to engage in the electoral discourse. This, in turn, enables voters to be better informed; no one voice is overwhelmed by another. In contrast, the libertarian model of elections favours an electoral process subject to as few restrictions as possible.

* * *

The question, then, is whether the spending limits set out in s. 350 interfere with the right of each citizen to play a meaningful role in the electoral process. In my view, they do not. The trial judge found that the advertising expense limits allow third parties to engage in "modest, national, informational campaigns" as well as "reasonable electoral district informational campaigns" but would prevent third parties from engaging in an "effective persuasive campaign" (para. 78). He did not give sufficient attention to the potential number of third parties or their ability to act in concert. Meaningful participation in elections is not synonymous with the ability to mount a media campaign capable of determining the outcome. In fact, such an understanding of "meaningful participation" would leave little room in the political discourse for the individual citizen and would be inimical to the right to vote. Accordingly, there is no infringement of s. 3 in this case and no conflict between the right to vote and freedom of expression.

(3) The s. 1 Justification Applicable to the Infringement of Freedom of Expression

The central issue at this stage of the analysis is the nature and sufficiency of the evidence required for the Attorney General to demonstrate that the limits imposed on freedom of expression are reasonable and justifiable in a free and democratic society. The Attorney General of Canada alleges that the lower courts erred in requiring scientific proof that harm had actually occurred and, specifically, by requiring conclusive proof that third party advertising influences voters and election outcomes rendering them unfair.

* * *

The legislature is not required to provide scientific proof based on concrete evidence of the problem it seeks to address in every case. Where the court is faced with inconclusive or competing social science evidence relating the harm to the Legislature's measures, the court may rely on a reasoned apprehension of that harm.

[In addition to the cases previously discussed in these materials, the Court took note of *RJR-MacDonald v. Canada (Attorney General)*, [1995] 3 S.C.R. 199, at para. 137, upholding advertising bans and package warnings for tobacco in the absence of direct scientific evidence showing a causal link between advertising bans and a decrease in tobacco consumption/use. In this case, the Court observed that "the nature of the harm and the efficaciousness of Parliament's remedy in this case is difficult, if not impossible, to measure scientifically." The harm of "electoral unfairness" was virtually impossible to measure "because of the subtle ways in which advertising influences human behaviour; the influence of other factors such as the media and polls; and the multitude of issues, candidates and independent parties involved in the electoral process."]

[In determining whether the restriction was a reasonable limit under s. 1, the Court proceeded to find that the parliamentary objectives were pressing and substantial. The Lortie Commission report that led to the legislation was based in part on research suggesting that third-party spending had affected the outcome of the 1988 federal election. In that election, Prime Minister Brian Mulroney's Progressive Conservative Party was re-elected on a specific pledge to institute a free trade agreement with the United States; the Liberals and New Democrats strongly opposed free trade; significant third party spending by business groups in favour of free trade supported the Tories. The Court held that the finding was valid, notwithstanding substantial political science research suggesting that the third party spending did not alter the outcome of the election. In addition to avoiding outcome-determinative spending, the Court found three other pressing and substantial objectives: (i) promoting equality in political discourse; (ii) protecting the integrity of finance limits on parties and candidates; and (iii) maintaining public confidence in the electoral process.]

*   *   *

Certainly, one can conceive of less impairing limits. Indeed, any limit greater than $150,000 would be less impairing. Nevertheless, s. 350 satisfies this stage of the Oakes analysis. The limits allow third parties to inform the electorate of their message in a manner that will not overwhelm candidates, political parties or other third parties. The limits preclude the voices of the wealthy from dominating the political discourse, thereby allowing more voices to be heard. The limits allow for meaningful participation in the electoral process and encourage informed voting. The limits promote a free and democratic society.

*   *   *

The reasons of McLachlin C.J., Major and Binnie JJ. were delivered by The Chief Justice and Major J. (dissenting in part) —

[The dissent took particular issue with the level of the spending limit, in light of the approximate cost of $425,000 for a one-time full-page advertisement in all major Canadian newspapers.]

*   *   *

The *Canada Elections Act* undercuts the right to listen by withholding from voters an ingredient that is critical to their individual and collective deliberation: substantive analysis and commentary on political issues of the day. The spending limits impede the ability of citizens to communicate with one another through public fora and media during elections and curtail the diversity of perspectives heard and assessed by the electorate. Because citizens cannot mount effective national television, radio and print campaigns, the only sustained messages voters see and hear during the course of an election campaign are from political parties.

It is clear that the right here at issue is of vital importance to Canadian democracy. In the democracy of ancient Athens, all citizens were able to meet and discuss the issues of the day in person. In our modern democracy, we cannot speak personally with each of our co-citizens. We can convey our message only through methods of mass communication. Advertising through mail-outs and the media is one of the most effective means of communication on a large scale. We need only look at the reliance of political parties on advertising to realize how important it is to actually reaching citizens — in a word, to effective participation. The ability to speak in one's own home or on a remote street corner does not fulfill the objective of the guarantee of freedom of expression, which is that each citizen be afforded the opportunity to present her views for public consumption and attempt to persuade her fellow citizens. Pell J.'s observation could not be more apt: "Speech without effective communication is not speech but an idle monologue in the wilderness"; see *United States v. Dellinger*, 472 F.2d 340 (7th Cir. 1972), at p. 415.

[Although the dissent agreed that the objective of the legislation was pressing and substantial, and rationally connected to the expenditure limits, it concluded that the restrictions went too far, flunking the minimal impairment and proportionality tests.]

Here the concern of the Alberta courts that the Attorney General had not shown any real problem requiring rectification becomes relevant. The dangers posited are wholly hypothetical. The Attorney General presented no evidence that wealthier Canadians — alone or in concert — will dominate political debate during the electoral period absent limits. It offered only the hypothetical possibility that, without limits on citizen spending, problems could arise. If, as urged by the Attorney General, wealthy Canadians are poised to hijack this country's election process, an expectation of some evidence to that effect is reasonable. Yet none was presented. This minimizes the Attorney General's assertions of necessity and lends credence to the argument that the legislation is an overreaction to a non-existent problem.

3.5.3. Australia

In Australia, since 1984, under the Commonwealth *Electoral* Act public funding is available for election campaign expenses for registered parties. Prosecutions may follow — and have done — where claims for funding have been made fraudulently. Private donations — with disclosure stipulations — are also permitted. These schemes (especially the disclosure threshold) have been controversial. The registration requirements have been subject to constitutional challenges, in both the Federal Court, and the High Court, the latter in *Mulholland v Australian Electoral Commission* (2004) 220 CLR 181. In *Mullholland*, the Court held that the requirement that a registered party have at least 500 members did not breach the implied freedom of political communication. The justices emphasised that the Constitution "does not mandate any particular electoral system" (McHugh J) and although "the overriding requirement that senators and members of the House of Representatives are to be 'directly chosen by the people' . . . imposes a basic condition of democratic process . . . [it] leaves substantial room for parliamentary choice" (Gleeson CJ).

Public funding for political candidates was introduced with the goal of reducing parties' reliance on private donations. The apportionment of funds is calculated on the basis of a percentage of first preference votes received in an election. As explained by the Australian Electoral Commission, candidates for the House of Representatives and Senate who receive 4% or more of the formal first preference votes in an electorate in a federal election or by-election are entitled to receive public election funding. The funding entitlement is calculated by multiplying the number of formal first preference votes received by the funding rate. The basefunding rate of $1.50 (set in 1995) is adjusted each six months in line with changes in the consumer price index. The states also have similar schemes for state elections.

As noted, private donations — whether from corporations, unions, or individuals — are permitted (and are tax deductible), but donations over a certain threshold ($12,000 in 2013) must be publicly disclosed. Disclosure is intended to achieve transparency, and to discourage wealthy donors from appearing to seek political favouritism or advantage. The system has proven controversial, however, and various governmental inquiries have looked at ways of further regulating donations. An attempt in by the former Commonwealth Labor government to reduce the disclosure threshold to $1,000 was blocked by the Opposition in the Senate (the Labor Party applies this threshold voluntarily to the election donations it receives).

3.5.4.   South Africa

While the Public Funding of Represented Political Parties Act of 1997 provides funding for political parties represented in South Africa's legislature, the parties are prohibited from using these funds for electoral purposes within 21 days of an election. The outcome is that electoral spending and party funding remain uncontrolled.

Chapter 4

EQUALITY (GENERALLY)

KEY CONCEPTS FOR THE CHAPTER

- ALTHOUGH MUCH GOVERNMENT ACTION AND LEGISLATION CLASSIFIES INDIVIDUALS, TREATING THEM DIFFERENTLY, THERE IS A WIDESPREAD CONSENSUS THAT EVERY LAW NEED NOT BE DEMONSTRABLY JUSTIFIED IN COURT AND THAT LINE-DRAWING IS A NECESSARY LEGISLATIVE TASK

- IN THE U.S., COURTS GENERALLY USE THE "RATIONAL BASIS" TEST, WHICH IS HIGHLY DEFERENTIAL TO THE LEGISLATURE, UNLESS A CLASSIFICATION IS BASED ON A "SUSPECT" CLASS OR INVOLVES A "FUNDAMENTAL RIGHT," IN WHICH CASE STRICTER JUDICIAL REVIEW IS APPLIED.

- IN CANADA THE EQUALITY PROVISIONS OF THE CHARTER — WHICH TRIGGER CLOSE JUDICIAL SCRUTINY — ONLY APPLY TO DISCRIMINATION BASED ON A GROUND ENUMERATED IN S. 15 OR ON A GROUND "ANALOGOUS" TO AN ENUMERATED GROUND

- IN AUSTRALIA, THE CONSTITUTION'S FRAMERS REJECTED A GENERAL EQUALITY PROVISION MODELED ON THE AMERICAN 14TH AMENDMENT, AND ADOPTED A PROVISION PROHIBITING DISCRIMINATION ONLY AGAINST RESIDENTS (OR "SUBJECTS OF THE QUEEN") OF OTHER AUSTRALIAN STATES

- THE U.S. SUPREME COURT HAS CHARACTERIZED THE PURPOSE OF THE 14TH AMENDMENT'S EQUAL PROTECTION CLAUSE AS A MANDATE THAT "THE STATE MUST GOVERN IMPARTIALLY"

  — THIS DOCTRINE DOES NOT EXTEND TO FACIALLY NON-DISCRIMINATORY LAWS (THAT IS, LAWS THAT ARE EXPRESSLY DISCRIMINATORY ON THE FACE OF THE TEXT) UNLESS THEY WERE INTENDED TO DISCRIMINATE AGAINST A PROTECTED GROUP

- THE SUPREME COURT OF CANADA HAS CHARACTERIZED THE PURPOSE OF S. 15 AS TO "PREVENT THE VIOLATION OF ESSENTIAL HUMAN DIGNITY" THROUGH "THE IMPOSITION OF DISADVANTAGE, STEREOTYPING, OR POLITICAL OR SOCIAL PREJUDICE"

  — CANADIAN DOCTRINE EXTENDS TO LAWS THAT DISPROPORTIONATELY IMPACT PROTECTED GROUPS

  — CANADIAN DOCTRINE ONLY APPLIES WHERE A LAW CONSTITUTES A "SUBSTANTIVE DISCRIMINATION": FORMAL DIFFERENCES IN TREATMENT ARE INSUFFICIENT TO INVOKE S. 15

- THE STRUGGLE FOR EQUALITY LIES AT THE CENTER OF SOUTH AFRICA'S POST-APARTHEID CONSTITUTIONAL ORDER

— SOUTH AFRICAN DOCTRINE PROVIDES A CLEAR STEP BY STEP ANALYSIS FOR ADDRESSING CLAIMS OF DISCRIMINATION AND JUSTIFICATION OF REMEDIAL ACTION

— NOT ONLY DOES THE CONSTITUTION PROTECT AGAINST DISCRIMINATION BUT IT ALSO PROVIDES A BASIS FOR ADDRESSING THE LEGACIES OF APARTHEID AND ADVANCING THE GOAL AND VALUE OF SUBSTANTIVE EQUALITY

• IN AUSTRALIA, THE PARLIAMENT HAS PASSED A NUMBER OF STATUTES PROHIBITING SPECIFIC FORMS OF DISCRIMINATION, GIVING EFFECT TO OBLIGATIONS THAT AUSTRALIA HAS INCURRED AS A SIGNATORY TO A NUMBER OF INTERNATIONAL CONVENTIONS. THE PARLIAMENT RELIES ON THE CONSTITUTION'S "EXTERNAL AFFAIRS" POWER TO PASS THESE ACTS. THE PROVISIONS OF THESE ACTS ARE APPLIED BY TRIBUNALS AND COURTS IN THE COURSE OF ORDINARY LAW ENFORCEMENT; THAT IS TO SAY, THEY ARE NOT CONSTITUTIONAL AND DO NOT AUTHORISE JUDICIAL REVIEW OF OTHER LEGISLATION.

4.1. BACKGROUND AND OVERVIEW

4.1.1. Origins of constitutional concern about equality

4.1.1.1. Lack of original protection against racial and other forms of discrimination

The U.S. Constitution originally contained no broad provision barring discrimination against minorities. Indeed, the U.S. Constitution barred *congressional limitation* of the slave trade until 1808 and specifically protected the rights of slaveholders against those who sought their freedom.[1] And, in *Dred Scott v. Sandford*, 60 U.S. (19 How.) 393 (1857), the Supreme Court held that slaves were not citizens, and that neither non-slave states nor the federal government could grant them citizenship. Indeed, any legislation limiting slaveholders "rights" (such as the Missouri Compromise of 1820, invalidated by that decision, that had admitted certain states on condition that slavery was banned) constituted an improper taking of property without due process.[2]

---

[1] Art. IV, §2, clause 3 provides: "No person held to service or labor in one state, under the laws thereof, escaping into another, shall, in consequence of any law or regulation therein, be discharged from such service or labor, but shall be delivered up on claim of the party to whom such service or labor may be due."

[2] This decision was not foreordained. The majority could have avoided the contentious issue entirely: if Scott was not a citizen of Missouri, then the federal court there lacked jurisdiction. Justice Curtis wrote a powerful dissent, vindicated by the judgment of history, that the Court's conclusions were erroneous, even based on the pre-Civil War text of the Constitution. *See generally* Rotunda & Nowak, § 18.6. Scott was a slave who had traveled with his owner into the Territory of Minnesota and the free state of Illinois, then returning with his owner to the slave state of Missouri. He filed a common law claim of trespass in Missouri federal court, arguing that the act of transporting him into non-slave territories resulted in his freedom. Although no questions of federal law were raised by Scott's claim, he filed it in federal court based on the constitutional grant of federal court jurisdiction based on diversity of citizenship. (Sanford was executor of his now-deceased owner's estate, and was a citizen of New York.) Justice Curtis argued that freed slaves had often been recognized as citizens at the time of the adoption of the Constitution, and so if, on the merits, Dred Scott was free, then he was a citizen of Missouri and

In Canada, provincial laws discriminating against Indians and aliens were constrained by provisions of the *British North America Act* (1867) that declared these laws *ultra vires* because the federal power in that regard was exclusive. Otherwise, the founding document did not address equality issues.

South Africa's political and legal system was premised on inequality, the product of a history of colonialism and apartheid. While it is often argued that the principle of legal equality was a fundamental tenet of South Africa's Roman-Dutch "common law," racial oppression and discrimination have been at the core of South African legal culture since the beginning of colonial rule in 1652 (see MARTIN CHANOCK, THE MAKING OF SOUTH AFRICAN LEGAL CULTURE 1902–1936 (2001)). While slavery was officially abolished in the Cape Colony by Ordinance 50 of 1828, colonial imperatives and later scientific racism would dominate the law, producing first, a bifurcated state in which the African majority was governed under a system of administrative authoritarianism in the Union of South Africa from 1910, and second, apartheid, an explicit system of racial domination under law, as government policy after 1948 and as the basic constitutional structure of the "white" Republic of South Africa from 1961. The demise of apartheid led to the first democratic election in 1994 under a negotiated constitution with a bill of rights that guaranteed equality. The Constitutional Assembly that produced the "final" 1996 Constitution declared the "achievement of equality" to be one of the founding values of the Constitution which articulates a vision of substantive equality as the appropriate means to overcome the legacies of colonialism and apartheid.

The framers of the Australian Constitution considered incorporating a provision resembling the Fourteenth Amendment. The 1891 draft, completed at the first Federal Convention, included the provision: "A State shall not make or enforce any law abridging any privilege or immunity of citizens of other States of the Commonwealth, nor shall a State deny to any person, within its jurisdiction, the equal protection of the laws," and the draft Bill completed in 1897 in the middle of the second Convention retained this section. In his Memorandum of Proposed Amendments to the Bill, Andrew Inglis Clark (Tasmanian Attorney-General) proposed that the section be replaced with: "The citizens of each State, and all other persons owing allegiance to the Queen and residing in any territory of the Commonwealth, shall be citizens of the Commonwealth, and shall be entitled to all the privileges and immunities of citizens of the Commonwealth in the several States; and a State shall not make or enforce any law abridging any privilege or immunity of citizens of the Commonwealth; nor shall a State deprive any person of life, liberty, or property, without due process of law, or deny to any person within its jurisdiction the equal protection of its laws." In the event, however, neither version was adopted. At the completion of the second Federal Convention, in 1898, the framers settled for a simpler formula, now s 117 of the Constitution (note: the term "subject[s] of the Queen" was the expression used in British common law at the time, to refer to people we would today call "citizens"):

---

jurisdiction was proper. On the merits, Curtis argued that Congress enjoyed plenary power over territories and that, as slavery was against natural law, it could only be imposed by specific local acts; thus, Congress had the constitutional power to ban slavery in new territories. An excellent summary of *Dred Scott* can be found in Carl B. Swisher, 5 THE OLIVER WENDELL HOMES DEVISE OF THE SUPREME COURT OF THE UNITED STATES: THE TANEY PERIOD (1974).

A subject of the Queen, resident in any State, shall not be subject in any other State to any disability or discrimination which would not be equally applicable to him if he were a subject of the Queen resident in such other States.

Why did Australia's founders end up prohibiting only "out-of-State residency" discrimination? The framers had several reservations about the Fourteenth Amendment. Some regarded it as a product of uniquely American history, with no relevance for Australia. In the words of Victorian delegate, Isaac Isaacs (later, Justice and Chief Justice of the High Court of Australia, and Governor-General of Australia), the Fourteenth Amendment "was put in the American Constitution immediately after the Civil War, because the Southern States refused to concede to persons of African descent the rights of citizenship. The object of the amendment was purely to insure to the black population that they should not be deprived of the suffrage and various rights of citizenship in the Southern States." Some believed that the equal protection of the laws was already guaranteed by English common law, and did not need to be stated in the Constitution. Others did not want the equal protection to extend to all "citizens" (or subjects) because they wanted the states to remain free to discriminate on racial grounds with respect, in particular, to employment laws (the main minority group targeted was the Chinese). Many were convinced, in any case, that the only relevant "mischief" the Fourteenth Amendment was designed to overcome was discrimination against "citizens" (that is, not specifically minorities).[3]

4.1.1.2.   Modern responses to discrimination and inequality

4.1.1.2.1.   U.S.: the Civil War amendments

Following the Civil War, Congress passed and the states ratified the Thirteenth, Fourteenth, and Fifteenth Amendments. The Thirteenth Amendment abolished slavery and empowered Congress to enact legislation to fully implement abolition. The Fourteenth Amendment specifically provided that all persons born or naturalized in the United States are citizens, and enacted a general prohibition against states denying to "any person within its jurisdiction the equal protection of the laws."[4] The Supreme Court has subsequently interpreted the Due Process Clause of the Fifth Amendment to apply the same standards to actions of the federal government. *Bolling v. Sharpe*, 347 U.S. 497 (1954) (applying the *Brown v. Board of Education* desegregation decision to District of Columbia schools). The Fifteenth Amendment outlawed racial discrimination in voting.

---

[3] Section 117, which is the product of this debate, has been used only rarely to strike down relevantly discriminatory laws. *See, e.g., Street v. Qld Bar Association* (1989) 168 CLR 461 (striking down discriminatory treatment of out-of-state applicants for admission to practice law).

[4] The Fourteenth Amendment also bars state laws that "abridge the privileges or immunities of citizens of the United States." In *Slaughter-House Cases*, 83 U.S. (16 Wall.) 36 (1873), the Court narrowly construed this clause, rejecting claims that it protects citizens against state incursions of rights guaranteed by the Bill of Rights or elsewhere; the clause only protects uniquely federal rights such as the right to vote in federal elections or to travel in interstate commerce.

4.1.1.2.2.   Canada: the Charter of Rights and Freedoms

When Canadians sought to constitutionalize their basic human rights, the Charter was drafted to include several provisions that limit discrimination. Section 15(1) provides that "Every individual is equal before and under the law and has the right to the equal protection and equal benefit of the law without discrimination and, in particular, without discrimination based on race, national or ethnic origin, color, religion, sex, age or mental or physical disability." In addition, s. 27 of the Charter requires its construction in a manner "consistent with the preservation and enhancement of the multicultural heritage of Canadians," and s. 28 provides Charter rights are "guaranteed equally to male and female persons."

Section 15 guarantees four types of equalities. The first clause constitutionally enshrines the right to "equality before the law" that had been previously guaranteed by the statutory *Canadian Bill of Rights* (1960). The Charter's drafters added the phrase "equality under the law" because pre-Charter courts had held that the *Bill of Rights* only concerned itself with discriminatory administration of law, not the substance of the law itself. "Equal benefit of the law" was added because prior cases had excluded government benefit programs from the scope of the pre-Charter equality provision. "Equal protection of the law" sought to add, to the extent appropriate, jurisprudence developed in the U.S. under the Fourteenth Amendment.

4.1.1.2.3.   South Africa's new Constitution

The equality clause of South Africa's 1996 Constitution is a core element of the project to address apartheid's legacy. Section 9 includes three distinct approaches to protect and further the goal of equality.

First, section 9(1) guarantees everyone formal equality both before and under the law. This clause ensures that the law, in its form, substance and application meets the basic requirements of rationality.

Second, section 9(2) provides the basis for the advancement of substantive equality under the constitution. This is the constitutional basis of the goal of addressing the legacies of exclusion, discrimination and impoverishment that are the consequence of the colonial and apartheid history the constitution seeks to overcome. This section protects "affirmative action" through "legislative and other measures designed to advance persons, or categories of persons, disadvantaged by unfair discrimination."

Finally, sections 9(3)-(5) provide a constitutional framework to tackle discrimination, whether public or private. Section 9(3) prohibits discrimination on multiple grounds, including but not limited to, "race, gender, sex, pregnancy, marital status, ethnic or social origin, colour, sexual orientation, age, disability, religion, conscience, belief, culture, language and birth." Section 9(4) extends the prohibition of discrimination to private actors but requires national legislation to "prevent or prohibit unfair discrimination." Significantly, section 9(5) completes the prohibition on discrimination by shifting the burden for justifying discrimination, requiring any discrimination based on the listed or analogous grounds in section

9(3) to be shown to be fair or to be presumed to be unlawful discrimination.

South Africa's constitutional provisions have been implemented through a series of statutes designed to address discrimination in different social and economic contexts, including the *Employment Equity Act 55 of 1998* and the *Promotion of Equality and the Prevention of Unfair Discrimination Act 4 of 2000.*

4.1.1.2.4.   Australia's statutory response

Despite a constitutional "lacuna," Australia now has many statutes prohibiting discrimination against minorities or historically disadvantaged groups. These give effect to international conventions or treaties to which Australia is a party, and they put the obligations Australia has undertaken into domestic legislation. These laws include, among others: the *Racial Discrimination Act* 1975 (giving effect to the United Nations Convention on the Elimination of All Forms of Racial Discrimination); the *Sex Discrimination Act* 1984 (giving effect to the United Nations Convention on the Elimination of All Forms of Discrimination Against Women — CEDAW); the *Disability Discrimination Act* 1992 (giving effect to the International Labor Organisation [ILO] Discrimination (Employment and Occupation) Convention 1958); the *Human Rights (Sexual Conduct) Act* 1994 (giving effect to the Article 17 of the United Nations International Covenant on Civil and Political Rights — ICCPR.); the *Age Discrimination Act* 2004 (giving effect to, among others, the ILO Discrimination (Employment and Occupation) Convention, 1958). Of these, only the *Racial Discrimination Act* extends to other laws; that is, it overrides other laws that are inconsistent with it. The other Acts prohibit discriminatory conduct only on the part of persons or agencies: official, private, or corporate.

Two sub-national jurisdictions in Australia have comprehensive rights protection legislation. The Australian Capital Territory (ACT) has the *Human Rights Act 2004*; Victoria has the *Charter of Human Rights and Responsibilities Act 2006.* Section 8 of the Victorian Charter states the broad principles of equality under which it operates: (1) Every person has the right to recognition as a person before the law. (2) Every person has the right to enjoy his or her human rights without discrimination. (3) Every person is equal before the law and is entitled to the equal protection of the law without discrimination and has the right to equal and effective protection against discrimination.(4) Measures taken for the purpose of assisting or advancing persons or groups of persons disadvantaged because of discrimination do not constitute discrimination. The Act includes a sweeping list of protected rights and freedoms: Right to life; protection from torture and cruel, inhuman or degrading treatment; freedom from forced work; freedom of movement; privacy and reputation; freedom of thought, conscience, religion, belief, and expression; right to peaceful assembly and freedom of association; protection of families and children; right to take part in public life; cultural rights; property rights; right to liberty and security of person; humane treatment when deprived of liberty; protection of children in the criminal process; right to a fair hearing; rights in criminal proceedings; right not to be tried or punished more than once; prohibition of retrospective criminal laws (other than under international law).

Both the ACT and the Victorian Act allow only judicial "declarations" of incompatibility or inconsistency between a law and a protected right; that is, they do not permit judicial invalidation of laws.

4.1.1.3. Illustration: evolving protection against gender-based discrimination

Constitutional law during the first century following the ratification of the Fourteenth Amendment provided little protection for women. In *Goesaert v. Cleary*, 335 U.S. 464 (1948), for example, the Court upheld differential treatment of female bartenders (who only could be licensed in Michigan if they were the wife or daughter of the male owner).[5] These decisions led to efforts to amend the Constitution to expressly guarantee equal rights for women. The so-called "Equal Rights Amendment" (first proposed in 1923) was passed by 2/3 majorities in the Senate and House in 1972 but not ratified by the requisite 3/4 of the states. However, as demonstrated by the cases below, most notably *United States v. Virginia*, much of the doctrinal benefits that women would derive from a constitutional amendment have subsequently been achieved by judicial interpretation of the Fourteenth Amendment. Indeed, Justice Ruth Bader Ginsburg, one of the principal architects of the ERA and the cases enhancing judicial scrutiny of gender discrimination, and the author of that opinion, has declared that there "is no practical difference between what has evolved and the ERA."[6]

In contrast to the unsuccessful effort to add the ERA to the United States Constitution, Section 28 was explicitly added to the Canadian Charter to supplement the prohibition on sex discrimination in section 15. Among the reasons for a supplemental provision were to clearly reject Supreme Court of Canada decisions interpreting the equality provisions of the *Canadian Bill of Rights* in a way that would render them ineffectual against a host of discriminatory practices. In addition, after the successful demand by a number of provincial premiers for a provision that allows the provinces to enact legislation "notwithstanding" the Charter (this provision, s. 33, is discussed in Chapter 9), women's advocacy groups demanded a separate provision that would not be subject (as section 15 is) to legislative opt-out.

After inclusion of a special provision recognizing multiculturalism in Canada (section 27), women's groups wanted to ensure that practices that discriminated against women could not be justified by links to traditional cultural practices of particular ethnic or racial groups. Although a full analysis of the reasons why specific constitutional protection for women's equality rights prevailed in Canada but not in the United States is beyond the scope of an introductory note,[7] one factor

---

[5] Even more offensive to modern conceptions was the decision, under the Privileges and Immunities Clause, in *Bradwell v. Illinois*, 83 U.S. (16 Wall.) 130 (1873), upholding the state's refusal to license the petitioner to practice law, especially the concurring opinion finding that differential treatment of women was mandated by "the law of the creator" and admission to the bar was inconsistent with Bradwell's "paramount destiny" to be a wife and mother.

[6] Jeffrey Rosen, *The New Look of Liberalism on the Court*, N.Y. TIMES MAG., Oct. 1, 1997, 6, at 60.

[7] *Cf.* Catharine A. MacKinnon, *Unthinking ERA Thinking*, 54 U. CHI. L. REV. 759 (1987) (reviewing JANE MANSBRIDGE, WHY WE LOST THE ERA (1986) ("when women's demands for good sex equality guarantees in the proposed Charter of Rights and Freedoms were not met . . . Canadian women

may have been the need for the Trudeau government to get political support from women's groups and others in their battle with provincial premiers over a Charter perceived to constitute a limitation on provincial prerogatives.

Debate and struggles over gender equality played a significant role in the constitutional negotiations in South Africa. In a unique effort, a Women's National Coalition was formed by women from all the parties involved in the negotiations coming together and insisting that women be at the negotiating table. As a result the "interim" and "final" Constitutions included significant recognition of women's rights, including the establishment of a Gender Commission as one of the Chapter 9 institutions supporting constitutional democracy. Despite these gains there was constant concern that the recognition of traditional authority and customary law in the Constitution would undermine women's rights; however the recognition of customary law in Chapter 12 of the Constitution specifies that "courts must apply customary law when that law is applicable, subject to the Constitution." While the acceptance that customary law is subject to the Constitution is an important principle, this only sets the stage for a much longer struggle to resolve the contradictions between the lives of the majority of women, whether under custom- ary law or not, and the task of achieving substantive gender equality in law and practice in South Africa. As cases have made their way to the Constitutional Court there have been significant victories for gender equality, including the rejection of the principle of primogeniture in the customary law of inheritance (see, *Bhe v. Magistrate Khayelitsha* 2005 (1) SA 580 (CC)) as well as holding that customary law is a living law recognizing a "traditional community's authority to development their customs so as to promote gender equality in the succession of traditional leadership, in accordance with the Constitution" (see *Shilubana v. Nwamitwa*, 2009 (2) SA 66 (CC)).

Less successful, and consistent with a persistent division in the jurisprudence of the Constitutional Court, has been the failure of the majority of the Court to recognize the consequences of discrimination that flow from indirect discrimination (see Albertyn & Goldblatt, *Equality*, ch. 35, at 47 *in* WOOLMAN ET AL. (2d ed. 2007). This limitation was most evident in the Constitutional Court's rejection of a claim that the criminalization of sex work was not gender neutral as claimed by the state (see *Jordan v. The State*, 2002 (6) SA 642 (CC)), which has been criticized as reflecting the majority's "inability to understand the social context of sex work and the unequal gender relations in society that shape this occupation" (Albertyn & Goldblatt, *id.*).

As noted above, although Australia lacks a constitutional provision protecting against sex discrimination, in 1984 the Commonwealth Parliament adopted the *Sex Discrimination Act* (giving effect under the External Affairs head of power, s 51(xxix) to the United Nations Convention on the Elimination of All Forms of Discrimination Against Women [CEDAW]). It prohibits discrimination on the ground of sex, marital status, and pregnancy or potential pregnancy, in employ- ment, education, accommodation, the provision of services, facilities, the disposal of land, the activities of clubs, and the administration of Commonwealth laws and

---

spontaneously rebelled nationwide" while "American women, a majority of whom were said to have wanted it, let ERA go so quietly").

programs. It also aims to promote recognition and acceptance within the community of the principle of the equality of men and women. (There are counterpart laws in the states.)

Australia's Constitution contains no specific equality provisions and there have been no official proposals that it should incorporate gender equality (the Preamble that was proposed as a constitutional amendment, defeated in a referendum in 1999, included broad statements of equality, but, to the dismay of some, did not include a reference to the equality of men and women). Notwithstanding this, (white) Australian women have had equal political rights at the national level — to vote and stand for political office — for the whole of the 20th century (since the first Commonwealth Franchise Act, 1902). Like their counterparts in many modern countries, however, it was not until the 1960s that women's disadvantage and inequality in other spheres began to gain official recognition. The principle of equal pay was accepted (if not fully achieved); the requirement for women to resign from the public service on marriage or pregnancy was ended. In 1999 the *Equal Opportunity for Women in the Workplace Act (Cth)* was passed, also giving effect to CEDAW (as well as drawing on the "Corporations power," s 51 (xx) of the Constitution). Its principal objects are stated as: (a) to promote the principle that employment for women should be dealt with on the basis of merit; and (b) to promote, amongst employers, the elimination of discrimination against, and the provision of equal opportunity for, women in relation to employment matters; and (c) to foster workplace consultation between employers and employees on issues concerning equal opportunity for women in relation to employment.

4.1.2.   The fundamental purpose of equality guarantees

In addition to grants of power, one of the fundamental purposes of a constitution is, at least in certain respects, to limit the ability of elected officials to act in ways that they might, in the moment, deem politically desirable. To illustrate this point, both the U.S. Constitution (Art. VI, cl. 3) and the Australian Constitution (s 116) prohibit a religious test as a qualification for holding federal office; the purpose is to bar such a test, even if Congress or Parliament thinks it desirable.

With regard to equality, the related question is *why elected officials should be constrained in their ability to treat people differently, if they deem it appropriate to do so.* Each country's answer to this question reveals some key and different foundational philosophies about equality.

In the United States, the governing principle is that **"the state must govern impartially."** *New York City Transit Authority v. Beazer*, 440 U.S. 568, 588 (1979). All governmental classifications are thus within the scope of the equality principle, although, as we shall see, American courts review some allegedly partial state action more closely than others.

The Canadian equality provision has not been construed to create a general and judicially enforceable requirement of government impartiality. Rather, the purposes of s. 15, and its relationship to the section 1 general authorization for reasonably justified limits on rights, reveals that the fundamental purpose of the provision, as explained in *Law v. Canada (Minister of Employment and*

Immigration), [1999] 1 S.C.R. 497, is "to prevent the violation of essential human dignity and freedom through the imposition of disadvantage, stereotyping, or political or social prejudice."

As former Chief Justice of South Africa Arthur Chaskalson observed, when the Constitution for South Africa was adopted in 1996, the nation was "one of the most unequal societies in the world," where the "great majority of our people had been the victims of a vicious system of racial discrimination and repression which had affected them deeply in almost all aspects of their lives."[8] Thus, s 1(a) of the Constitution describes the new nation as grounded in the values of "human dignity, the achievement of equality and the advancement of human rights, non-racialism and non-sexism." The Constitutional Court has recognized a mandate to view the Constitution as "a commitment to transform our society." *Minister of Finance v. Van Heerden*, 2004 (6) SA 121 (CC) at para 22. In contrast to an American focus on formally equal treatment of individuals presuming that any differential treatment on arbitrary grounds is irrational and the result of prejudice, South African jurisprudence focuses on **substantive equality: "a credible and abiding process of reparation for past exclusion, dispossession and indignity."** *Id.* at para 25. It does not presuppose "the elimination or suppression of difference" but "equal concern and respect across difference." *Minister of Home Affairs v. Fourie*, 2006 (1) SA 525 (CC) at para 60.

Because Australia has no over-arching bar on discrimination but a series of specific statutes, articulating a fundamental purpose is a bit more speculative. All federal anti-discrimination statutes are enacted pursuant to the Commonwealth's external affairs power, as a means of implementing international anti-discrimination conventions which Australia has ratified. So it might be fairly said that the fundamental purpose is a commitment to adhering to and enforcing domestically those equality norms recognized as a matter of international human rights law. These norms embrace principles of both formal and substantive equality, as well as "moral" guidelines concerning human dignity and the inherent worth of all persons. Their implementation in Australian legislation is guided by these norms, but in practice is substantially pragmatic.

4.2. THE PROBLEM OF JUDICIAL SCRUTINY OF LEGISLATIVE CLASSIFICATIONS

4.2.1. Articulating the problem

A critical doctrinal problem in the three countries with general constitutional limits on laws that discriminate is that virtually all government action classifies individuals, treating them differently. How to draw a workable line between appropriately differential treatment of individuals and illegal discrimination is a topic resulting in significant litigation. Courts have interpreted constitutional provisions to, in effect, exclude some classifications from the scope of the relevant provisions. In Australia, specific statutes provide much of the line-drawing that

---

[8] Quoted in Catherine Albertyn & Beth Goldblatt, Equality, *in* 2 CONSTITUTIONAL LAW OF SOUTH AFRICA 35-2 (2d ed.).

must be judicially created under broader constitutional provisions.

4.2.2.   Examples of close scrutiny

When constitutional doctrine requires close scrutiny, this typically means that the government must offer (1) a strong justification for the classification and that the classification not be (2) based on pretext; (3) based on stereotypes; or (4) significantly overbroad or underinclusive. Several examples follow.

UNITED STATES v. VIRGINIA

SUPREME COURT OF THE UNITED STATES

518 U.S. 515 (1996)

GINSBURG, J., delivered the opinion of the Court, in which STEVENS, O'CONNOR, KENNEDY, SOUTER, and BREYER, JJ., joined.

Virginia's public institutions of higher learning include an incomparable military college, Virginia Military Institute (VMI). The United States maintains that the Constitution's equal protection guarantee precludes Virginia from reserving exclusively to men the unique educational opportunities VMI affords. We agree.

I

Founded in 1839, VMI is today the sole single-sex school among Virginia's 15 public institutions of higher learning. VMI's distinctive mission is to produce "citizen-soldiers," men prepared for leadership in civilian life and in military service. VMI pursues this mission through pervasive training of a kind not available anywhere else in Virginia. Assigning prime place to character development, VMI uses an adversative method modeled on English public schools and once characteristic of military instruction. VMI constantly endeavors to instill physical and mental discipline in its cadets and impart to them a strong moral code. The school's graduates leave VMI with heightened comprehension of their capacity to deal with duress and stress, and a large sense of accomplishment for completing the hazardous course.

* * *

II

* * *

C

[The opinion describes an alternative "parallel" program for women, a leadership institute that would share VMI's mission of producing "citizen-soldiers" but would be located at Mary Baldwin College, a private liberal arts school for women. Justice Ginsburg noted that Mary Baldwin students average 100 points lower on the SAT, their faculty is lower-paid and has fewer Ph.Ds, and offers no degrees in sciences and engineering, and even after state and VMI contributions, would have an endowment a fraction of VMI's size.].

IV

We note, once again, the core instruction of this Court's pathmarking decisions in *J. E. B. v. Alabama ex rel. T. B.*, 511 U.S. 127, 136–137, and n. 6 (1994), and *Mississippi Univ. for Women*, 458 U.S.[718, 724 (1982)]: Parties who seek to defend gender-based government action must demonstrate an "exceedingly persuasive justification" for that action.

Today's skeptical scrutiny of official action denying rights or opportunities based on sex responds to volumes of history. As a plurality of this Court acknowledged a generation ago, "our Nation has had a long and unfortunate history of sex discrimination." *Frontiero v. Richardson*, 411 U.S. 677, 684 (1973). Through a century plus three decades and more of that history, women did not count among voters composing "We the People"; not until 1920 did women gain a constitutional right to the franchise. *Id.*, at 685. And for a half century thereafter, it remained the prevailing doctrine that government, both federal and state, could withhold from women opportunities accorded men so long as any "basis in reason" could be conceived for the discrimination. See, e. g., *Goesaert v. Cleary*, 335 U.S. 464, 467 (1948) (rejecting challenge of female tavern owner and her daughter to Michigan law denying bartender licenses to females — except for wives and daughters of male tavern owners; Court would not "give ear" to the contention that "an unchivalrous desire of male bartenders to . . . monopolize the calling" prompted the legislation).

* * *

Without equating gender classifications, for all purposes, to classifications based on race or national origin, the Court, in post-*Reed* decisions, has carefully inspected official action that closes a door or denies opportunity to women (or to men). See *J. E. B.*, 511 U.S. at 152 (Kennedy, J., concurring in judgment) (case law evolving since 1971 "reveal[s] a strong presumption that gender classifications are invalid"). To summarize the Court's current directions for cases of official classification based on gender: Focusing on the differential treatment or denial of opportunity for which relief is sought, the reviewing court must determine whether the proffered justification is "exceedingly persuasive." The burden of justification is demanding and it rests entirely on the State. The State must show "at least that the [challenged] classification serves 'important governmental objectives and that the discriminatory means employed' are 'substantially related to the achievement of those objectives.'" The justification must be genuine, not hypothesized or invented post hoc in response to litigation. And it must not rely on overbroad generalizations about the different talents, capacities, or preferences of males and females.

* * *

"Inherent differences" between men and women, we have come to appreciate, remain cause for celebration, but not for denigration of the members of either sex or for artificial constraints on an individual's opportunity. Sex classifications may be used to compensate women "for particular economic disabilities [they have] suffered," *Califano v. Webster*, 430 U.S. 313, 320 (1977) (per curiam), to "promote equal employment opportunity," see *California Fed. Sav. & Loan Assn. v. Guerra*, 479 U.S. 272, 289 (1987), to advance full development of the talent and capacities of our Nation's people.[9] But such classifications may not be used, as they once were, see *Goesaert*, 335 U.S. at 467, to create or perpetuate the legal, social, and economic inferiority of women.

*   *   *

V

*   *   *

In sum, we find no persuasive evidence in this record that VMI's male-only admission policy "is in furtherance of a state policy of 'diversity.'" No such policy, the Fourth Circuit observed, can be discerned from the movement of all other public colleges and universities in Virginia away from single-sex education. That court also questioned "how one institution with autonomy, but with no authority over any other state institution, can give effect to a state policy of diversity among institutions." A purpose genuinely to advance an array of educational options, as the Court of Appeals recognized, is not served by VMI's historic and constant plan — a plan to "afford a unique educational benefit only to males." However "liberally" this plan serves the Commonwealth's sons, it makes no provision whatever for her daughters. That is not equal protection.

B

Virginia next argues that VMI's adversative method of training provides educational benefits that cannot be made available, unmodified, to women. *** Men would be deprived of the unique opportunity currently available to them; women would not gain that opportunity because their participation would "eliminate the very aspects of [the] program that distinguish [VMI] from . . . other institutions of higher education in Virginia."

---

[9] [FN 7] Several amici have urged that diversity in educational opportunities is an altogether appropriate governmental pursuit and that single-sex schools can contribute importantly to such diversity. Indeed, it is the mission of some single-sex schools "to dissipate, rather than perpetuate, traditional gender classifications." See Brief for Twenty-six Private Women's Colleges as Amici Curiae 5. We do not question the Commonwealth's prerogative evenhandedly to support diverse educational opportunities. We address specifically and only an educational opportunity recognized by the District Court and the Court of Appeals as "unique," see 766 F. Supp., at 1413, 1432; 976 F.2d, at 892, an opportunity available only at Virginia's premier military institute, the Commonwealth's sole single-sex public university or college. Cf. *Mississippi Univ. for Women v. Hogan*, 458 U.S. 718, 720, n. 1 (1982) ("Mississippi maintains no other single-sex public university or college. Thus, we are not faced with the question of whether States can provide 'separate but equal' undergraduate institutions for males and females.").

* * *

In support of its initial judgment for Virginia, a judgment rejecting all equal protection objections presented by the United States, the District Court made "findings" on "gender-based developmental differences." These "findings" restate the opinions of Virginia's expert witnesses, opinions about typically male or typically female "tendencies." For example, "males tend to need an atmosphere of adversativeness," while "females tend to thrive in a cooperative atmosphere." "I'm not saying that some women don't do well under [the] adversative model," VMI's expert on educational institutions testified, "undoubtedly there are some [women] who do"; but educational experiences must be designed "around the rule," this expert maintained, and not "around the exception."

The United States does not challenge any expert witness estimation on average capacities or preferences of men and women. Instead, the United States emphasizes that time and again since this Court's turning point decision in *Reed v. Reed*, 404 U.S. 71 (1971), we have cautioned reviewing courts to take a "hard look" at generalizations or "tendencies" of the kind pressed by Virginia, and relied upon by the District Court. See O'Connor, Portia's Progress, 66 N. Y. U. L. Rev. 1546, 1551 (1991). State actors controlling gates to opportunity, we have instructed, may not exclude qualified individuals based on "fixed notions concerning the roles and abilities of males and females." *Mississippi Univ. for Women*, 458 U.S. at 725; see *J. E. B.*, 511 U.S. at 139, n. 11 (equal protection principles, as applied to gender classifications, mean state actors may not rely on "overbroad" generalizations to make "judgments about people that are likely to . . . perpetuate historical patterns of discrimination").

*   *   *

[Justice Ginsburg observed that VMI's argument was "a prediction hardly different" from those "once routinely used to deny rights or opportunities." For example, she noted that a 1925 report counseled against admission of women to Columbia Law School (Justice Ginsburg's alma mater) because "then the choicer, more manly and red-blooded graduates of our great universities would go to the Harvard Law School!" *The Nation*, Feb. 18, 1925, p. 173. Similar forecasts preceded admission of women to federal military academies and medical schools. She also noted that VMI successfully managed another notable change — the 1968 admission of African American cadets.]

*   *   *

JUSTICE THOMAS took no part in the consideration or decision of this case.

CHIEF JUSTICE REHNQUIST, concurring in the judgment. [The Chief Justice wrote that it was "unfortunate" for the Court to change prior formulations of the test for sex-based discrimination by demanding an "exceedingly persuasive justification," but under other precedents requiring that gender classifications serve "important governmental interests" and be "substantially related" to those objectives, he found that Virginia's claim to promote diversity in educational opportunity was "problematic" because the diversity benefitted only one sex. He also demurred as to whether admitting women to VMI was the only appropriate remedy, suggesting that Virginia might constitutionally comply by offering a women-only institution with strengths in areas demanded by women.]

* * *

JUSTICE SCALIA, dissenting.

Today the Court shuts down an institution that has served the people of the Commonwealth of Virginia with pride and distinction for over a century and a half. To achieve that desired result, it rejects (contrary to our established practice) the factual findings of two courts below, sweeps aside the precedents of this Court, and ignores the history of our people. As to facts: It explicitly rejects the finding that there exist "gender-based developmental differences" supporting Virginia's restriction of the "adversative" method to only a men's institution, and the finding that the all-male composition of the Virginia Military Institute (VMI) is essential to that institution's character. As to precedent: It drastically revises our established standards for reviewing sex-based classifications. And as to history: It counts for nothing the long tradition, enduring down to the present, of men's military colleges supported by both States and the Federal Government.

Much of the Court's opinion is devoted to deprecating the closed-mindedness of our forebears with regard to women's education, and even with regard to the treatment of women in areas that have nothing to do with education. Closedminded they were — as every age is, including our own, with regard to matters it cannot guess, because it simply does not consider them debatable. The virtue of a democratic system with a First Amendment is that it readily enables the people, over time, to be persuaded that what they took for granted is not so, and to change their laws accordingly. That system is destroyed if the smug assurances of each age are removed from the democratic process and written into the Constitution. So to counterbalance the Court's criticism of our ancestors, let me say a word in their praise: They left us free to change. The same cannot be said of this most illiberal Court, which has embarked on a course of inscribing one after another of the current preferences of the society (and in some cases only the countermajoritarian preferences of the society's law-trained elite) into our Basic Law. Today it enshrines the notion that no substantial educational value is to be served by an all-men's military academy — so that the decision by the people of Virginia to maintain such an institution denies equal protection to women who cannot attend that institution but can attend others. Since it is entirely clear that the Constitution of the United States — the old one — takes no sides in this educational debate, I dissent.

I

* * *

I have no problem with a system of abstract tests such as rational basis, intermediate, and strict scrutiny (though I think we can do better than applying strict scrutiny and intermediate scrutiny whenever we feel like it). Such formulas are essential to evaluating whether the new restrictions that a changing society constantly imposes upon private conduct comport with that "equal protection" our society has always accorded in the past. But in my view the function of this Court is to preserve our society's values regarding (among other things) equal protection, not to revise them; to prevent backsliding from the degree of restriction the Constitution imposed upon democratic government, not to prescribe, on our own authority, progressively higher degrees. For that reason it is my view that, whatever abstract tests we may choose to devise, they cannot supersede — and indeed ought to be crafted so as to reflect — those constant and unbroken national traditions that embody the people's understanding of ambiguous constitutional texts. More specifically, it is my view that "when a practice not expressly prohibited by the text of the Bill of Rights bears the endorsement of a long tradition of open, widespread, and unchallenged use that dates back to the beginning of the Republic, we have no proper basis for striking it down." *Rutan v. Republican Party of Ill.*, 497 U.S. 62, 95, 110 S. Ct. 2729, 111 L. Ed. 2d 52 (1990) (SCALIA, J., dissenting). The same applies, *mutatis mutandis*, to a practice asserted to be in violation of the post-Civil War Fourteenth Amendment.

The all-male constitution of VMI comes squarely within such a governing tradition. ***

*   *   *

M. v. H.
Supreme Court of Canada
[1999] 2 S.C.R. 3, 171 D.L.R. 4th 577

Cory and Iacobucci JJ. (Lamer C.J.C., L'Heureux-Dube, McLachlin and Binnie JJ. Concurring):

I. Introduction and Overview

[Ontario's *Family Law Act* creates special support obligations toward one's spouse. In Part II, the statute sets forth a variety of rights and responsibilities of married couples to each other. In addition, Part III of the Act provides spousal and child support obligations applicable both to married couples as well as to "a man and woman who are not married to each other and have cohabited" for three continuous years. This litigation was brought by M., a woman who had cohabited with another woman, H., for almost a decade. She alleged that the distinction between same-sex and opposite-sex conjugal relationships violated s. 15(1) of the Charter.]

[3] The crux of the issue is that this differential treatment discriminates in a substantive sense by violating the human dignity of individuals in same-sex relationships.[10]

[4] This infringement is not justified under s. 1 of the Charter because there is no rational connection between the objectives of the spousal support provisions and

---

10 [Ed. note: The Canadian test for substantive discrimination is discussed in *Nancy Law v. Canada (Minister of Employment and Immigration)*, below in this chapter.]

the means chosen to further this objective. The objectives were accurately identified by Charron J.A., in the court below, as providing for the equitable resolution of economic disputes when intimate relationships between financially interdependent individuals break down, and alleviating the burden on the public purse to provide for dependent spouses. Neither of these objectives is furthered by the exclusion of individuals in same-sex couples from the spousal support regime. If anything, these goals are undermined by this exclusion.

* * *

V. Analysis

* * *

B. *Does* s. *29 of the FLA Infringe* s. *15(1) of the Charter?*

* * *

[The Court emphasized that, although "women in common law relationships often tended to become financially dependent on their male partners because they raised their children and because of their unequal earning power," the "legislature drafted s. 29 to allow either a man or a woman to apply for support, thereby recognizing that financial dependence can arise in an intimate relationship in a context entirely unrelated either to child-rearing or to any gender-based discrimination existing in our society." The Court also emphasized that "the special situation of financial dependence potentially created by procreation is specifically addressed in s. 29(b)" concerning child support, while this appeal only relates to what was traditionally called alimony under s. 29(a), which the Court found to be "aimed at remedying situations of dependence in intimate relationships without imposing any limitation relating to the circumstances that may give rise to that dependence."]

[The Court found facially differential treatment because members "of same-sex couples are denied access to this system entirely on the basis of their sexual orientation."]

[Next, the Court re-affirmed its conclusion that sexual orientation is an analogous ground.] In addition, a majority of this Court explicitly recognized that gays, lesbians and bisexuals, "whether as individuals or couples, form an identifiable minority who have suffered and continue to suffer serious social, political and economic disadvantage" (at para. 175 per Cory J.; at para. 89 per L'Heureux-Dubé J.).]

* * *

C. *Is Section 29 of the FLA Justified Under Section 1 of the Charter?*

[Here, the Court applied the 4-part *Oakes* test, set forth in Chapter 2, adopted to implement section 1's provision that rights guaranteed by the Charter may be limited to the extent demonstrably justified in a free and democratic society.]

* * *

3. Pressing and Substantial Objective

[Justice Iacobucci found that the best description of the objective of the current version of the FLA is provided by the Ontario Law Reform Commission ("OLRC") — "to provide for the equitable resolution of economic disputes that arise when intimate relationships between individuals who have been financially interdependent break down." Although the legislature recognized that married women tend to become economically dependent upon their partners owing to the traditional division of labour between husbands and wives, the 1978 FLRA abandoned a statutory spousal support regime under which only a wife could oblige her husband to pay support in favour of one which imposed mutual support obligations on both men and women. Indeed, "the thrust of the OLRC's 1975 remarks which preceded the new legislation emphasize the importance of a gender-neutral scheme."]

[The opinion noted that the statute] is silent with respect to the economic vulnerability of heterosexual women, their tendency to take on primary responsibility for parenting, the greater earning capacity of men, and systemic sexual inequality. In the face of this clearly gender-neutral scheme, the fact that a significant majority of the spousal support claimants are women does not, in my view, establish that the goal of Part III of the FLA is to address the special needs of women in opposite-sex relationships.

* * *

[98] As to the goal of reducing the strain on the public purse, members of the legislature have complained publicly about the number of dependent people who turn to the welfare rolls upon the breakdown of their relationships. The notion that the spousal support provisions of the FLA and its predecessors were in large part aimed at shifting the financial burden away from the government and on to those partners with the capacity to provide support for dependent spouses has been voiced several times in legislative debates. * * *

* * *

4. Proportionality Analysis

(a) *Rational Connection*

* * *

[110] Although there is evidence to suggest that same-sex relationships are not typically characterized by the same economic and other inequalities which affect opposite-sex relationships (see, e.g., M.S. Schneider, "The Relationships of Cohabiting Lesbian and Heterosexual Couples: A Comparison," Psychology of Women Quarterly, 10 (1986), 234–239, at p. 237, and J.M. Lynch and M.E. Reilly, "Role Relationships: Lesbian Perspectives," Journal of Homosexuality, 12(2) (Winter 1985/86), 53–69, at pp. 53–54, 66), this does not, in my mind, explain why the right to apply for support is limited to heterosexuals. As submitted by LEAF, the

infrequency with which members of same-sex relationships find themselves in circumstances resembling those of many heterosexual women is no different from heterosexual men who, notwithstanding that they tend to benefit from the gender-based division of labour and inequality of earning power, have as much right to apply for support as their female partners.

* * *

[113] Even if I were to accept that the object of the legislation is the protection of children, I would have to conclude that the spousal support provisions in Part III of the FLA are simultaneously underinclusive and overinclusive. They are overinclusive because members of opposite-sex couples are entitled to apply for spousal support irrespective of whether or not they are parents and regardless of their reproductive capabilities or desires. Thus, if the legislation was meant to protect children, it would be incongruous that childless opposite-sex couples were included among those eligible to apply for and to receive the support in question.

[114] The impugned provisions are also underinclusive. An increasing percentage of children are being conceived and raised by lesbian and gay couples as a result of adoption, surrogacy and donor insemination. Although their numbers are still fairly small, it seems to me that the goal of protecting children cannot be but incompletely achieved by denying some children the benefits that flow from a spousal support award merely because their parents were in a same-sex relationship. As Cory J. and I noted in *Egan, supra*, at para. 191, "[i]f there is an intention to ameliorate the position of a group, it cannot be considered entirely rational to assist only a portion of that group."

* * *

(b) *Minimal Impairment*

[Here, the Court rejected the claim that the existence of alternative remedies is available where economic dependence occurs in same-sex relationships. The court analyzed and demonstrated the inadequacies of contract or constructive trust doctrines. The Court observed that] if these remedies were considered satisfactory there would have been no need for the spousal support regime, or its extension to unmarried, opposite-sex couples. It must also be remembered that the exclusion of same-sex partners from this support regime does not simply deny them a certain benefit, but does so in a manner that violates their right to be given equal concern and respect by the government. The alternative regimes just outlined do not address the fact that exclusion from the statutory scheme has moral and societal implications beyond economic ones, as discussed by my colleague, Cory J., at paras. 71-72. Therefore the existence of these remedies fails to minimize sufficiently the denial of same-sex partners' constitutionally guaranteed equality rights.

* * *

[128] In addition, the deferential approach is not warranted, as submitted by the appellant, on the basis that Part III of the FLA and s. 29 thereof are steps in an incremental process of reform of spousal support. As this Court noted in *Vriend, supra*, government incrementalism, or the notion that government ought to be

accorded time to amend discriminatory legislation, is generally an inappropriate justification for Charter violations. However, even if I were to accept that such a justification might be suitable in the present case, it seems to me that its application to the facts of the case at bar cannot legitimize the continued exclusion of same-sex couples from the FLA's spousal support regime.

*   *   *

[130] Moreover, in contrast to *Egan, supra*, where Sopinka J. relied in part on incrementalism in upholding [discriminatory pension] legislation under s. 1 of the Charter, there is no concern regarding the financial implications of extending benefits to gay men and lesbians in the case at bar. As already pointed out, rather than increasing the strain on the public coffers, the extension will likely go some way toward alleviating those concerns because same-sex couples as a group will be less reliant on government welfare if the support scheme is available to them. Thus, I conclude that government incrementalism cannot constitute a reason to show deference to the legislature in the present case.

*   *   *

VI. REMEDY

[The Court's discussion of remedy is omitted. In the court below, the words "a man and woman" were read out of the definition of "spouse" in s. 29 of the FLA and replaced with the words "two persons." The application of the order was suspended for a period of one year. The Supreme Court concluded that this result wreaked too much havoc with the overall statutory scheme. Thus, the Court ruled that severing s. 29 of the Act such that it alone is declared of no force or effect is the most appropriate remedy in the present case. This remedy should be temporarily suspended for a period of six months to give the Ontario provincial legislature time to re-enact non-discriminatory legislation.]

[The basic approach in Canadian and American cases concerning the issue of remedy when a statute is under-inclusive appears to be similar. The Court considers a variety of circumstances that, in sum, attempt to determine whether the legislature, once apprised of the inability to discriminate, would prefer to provide benefits to all or deny them to all. The leading cases are *Schacter v. Canada*, [1992] 2 S.C.R. 679 and *Califano v. Westcott*, 443 U.S. 76, 99 S. Ct. 2655 (1979).]

GONTHIER J. (Dissenting):

[The dissent found that the purpose of the statute was to] recognize the specific social function of opposite-sex couples in society, and to address a dynamic of dependence unique to both men and women in opposite-sex couples that flows from three basic realities. First, this dynamic of dependence relates to the biological reality of the opposite-sex relationship and its unique potential for giving birth to children and its being the primary forum for raising them. Second, this dynamic relates to a unique form of dependence that is unrelated to children but is specific to heterosexual relationships. And third, this dynamic of dependence is particularly acute for women in opposite-sex relationships, who suffer from pre-existing economic disadvantage as compared with men. Providing a benefit (and concomitantly imposing a burden) on a group that uniquely possesses this social function, biological reality and economic disadvantage, in my opinion, is not discriminatory. Although the legislature is free to extend this benefit to others who do not possess these characteristics, the Constitution does not impose such a duty on that sovereign body.

[The dissent complained that the majority "ascribes to the impugned legislation a purpose that bears little relation to the actual statute, its structure, or its history. It comes as no surprise that, having ascribed to the FLA a purpose that its language does not bear, my colleague then strikes down the legislation for failing to fulfill a purpose never intended by the Legislative Assembly." In his view, the gender-neutral language chosen because of "the tenor of the times" did not detract from the expectation that the vast majority of claimants would be women and that the statute was enacted because of the unequal economic dependence of women on husbands. Focusing on the key role of stereotype in s. 15 analysis, he noted that a "description is unlikely to be a stereotype when it is an accurate account of the characteristic being described."]

* * *

[243] The evidence before us also indicates that partners in a lesbian couple are more likely to each pursue a career and to work outside the home than are partners in an opposite-sex couple: ibid., at pp. 183–84; N. S. Eldridge and L. A. Gilbert, "Correlates of Relationship Satisfaction in Lesbian Couples," Psychology of Women Quarterly, 14 (1990), 43–62, at p. 44. As members of same-sex couples are, obviously, of the same sex, they are more likely than members of opposite-sex couples to earn similar incomes, because no male-female income differential is present. For the same reason, the gendered division of domestic and child-care responsibilities that continues to characterize opposite-sex relationships simply has no purchase in same-sex relationships.

* * *

[249] I pause to underline that nothing in my reasons should be taken as suggesting that same-sex couples are incapable of forming enduring relationships of love and support, nor do I wish to imply that individuals living in same-sex relationships are less deserving of respect. To this end, I reiterate the position that the Court recently adopted in Vriend, supra, where I concurred with the majority reasons of Cory and Iacobucci JJ., that discrimination on the basis of sexual orientation is abhorrent and corrosive of our values. However, the difference between this case and Vriend is that in this case the Legislative Assembly has not discriminated on the basis of arbitrary distinctions or stereotypes. In Vriend, the stated purpose of the legislation was to address comprehensively discrimination in several contexts such as employment and housing. By failing to include sexual orientation as one of the protected grounds, the legislation was thus found to be "underinclusive," having regard to its stated purpose. Unlike those listed in the legislation, homosexuals were denied access to the remedial procedures specifically designed to redress discrimination. Whereas in Vriend, the target of the legislation was those individuals who suffered discrimination in these contexts, the legislation

here is entirely different. Here, we are asked whether the legislature violates the Charter by imposing a special support regime on individuals who are in a particular type of relationship that fulfills a special social function, and has special needs, without extending that support regime to other types of relationships which do not, as a group, fulfil a similar role or exhibit those needs. Considering all of the contextual factors, I believe that the question must be answered in the negative. While discrimination on the basis of sexual orientation is abhorrent, mere distinction that takes into account the actual circumstances of the claimant and comparison group in a manner which does not violate the claimant's human dignity is not.

*   *   *

[279] MAJOR J.: [omitted].

[285] BASTARACHE J.:

*   *   *

[322] Determining legislative purpose is theoretically and practically a difficult task. As Professor Hogg has remarked (*Constitutional Law of Canada* (looseleaf ed.), vol. 2, at p. 35–17):

> At the practical level, the objective of the legislators in enacting the challenged law may be unknown. To be sure, the courts will now willingly receive the legislative history of the law, but this is often silent or unclear with respect to the provision under attack. Courts have not been troubled by this difficulty as much as one might expect. They usually assume that the statute itself reveals its objective, and they may pronounce confidently on the point even if there is no supporting evidence.

Despite these obstacles, the search for legislative intention has been laid as the cornerstone of the s. 1 analysis. It has even been suggested that "how the Court characterizes the objective of the impugned legislation essentially determines whether legislation should be struck down or upheld" (E. P. Mendes, "The Crucible of the Charter: Judicial Principles v. Judicial Deference in the Context of Section 1" in G. A. Beaudoin and E. Mendes, *The Canadian Charter of Rights and Freedoms*, 3rd ed. (1996), at p. 3–14). Given the particular difficulties surrounding the determination of the legislative purpose in this case, it may be necessary at this point to sound some of the theoretical underpinnings of this approach, and to define precisely the nature of the task.

[323] The search for legislative purpose as a method of statutory interpretation is not a novel concept. In *Heydon's Case* (1584), 3 Co. Rep. 7a, 76 E.R. 637, Lord Coke reports, at p. 638:

> And it was resolved by them, that for the sure and true interpretation of all statutes in general . . . four things are to be discerned and considered:

> 1st. What was the common law before the making of the Act.

2nd. What was the mischief and defect for which the common law did not provide.

3rd. What remedy the Parliament hath resolved and appointed to cure the disease of the commonwealth.

And, 4th. The true reason of the remedy; and then the office of all the judges is always to make such construction as shall suppress the mischief . . . according to the true intent of the makers of the Act . . . [Emphasis added.]

* * *

[In Justice Bastarache's view, the purpose of Part III of the FLA was "to impose support obligations upon partners in relationships in which they have consciously signaled a desire to be so bound (i.e., through marriage); and upon those partners in relationships of sufficient duration to indicate permanence and seriousness, and which involve the assumption of household responsibilities, or other career or financial sacrifices, by one partner for the common benefit of the couple, and which cause or enhance an economic disparity between the partners." Under this view, the distinction was not supported.]

———————

Another example of legislation surviving active judicial scrutiny is *Newfoundland (Treasury Board) v. Newfoundland and Labrador Assn. of Public and Private Employees (N.A.P.E.)*, [2004] 3 S.C.R. 381. The Court upheld a provision of the province's *Public Sector Restraint Act*, passed in 1991 to respond to an unprecedented fiscal crisis caused by a $130 million reduction in federal transfer payments at a time when the traditionally-poor province was still reeling from the dramatic loss of much of the North Atlantic fishery due to international over-fishing. The challenged provision erased an agreement with public sector employees to spend $24 million over three years to provide pay equity for workers in traditionally-female job categories.

The Court first determined that the effect of the challenged law was to affirm a policy of gender discrimination which the provincial government had itself denounced three years previously. The Act draws a clear formal distinction between those who were entitled to benefit from pay equity, and everyone else. The appropriate comparator group consists of men in male-dominated classifications performing work of equal value. That group was not similarly targeted. They were paid according to their contractual entitlement. The adverse impact of the legislation therefore fell disproportionately on women, who were already at a disadvantage relative to male-dominated jobs as they earned less money.

The Court thus distinguished this case from *Ferrell v. Ontario (Attorney General)* (1998), 42 O.R. (3d) 97 (C.A.), which upheld the authority of the Conservative Ontario government to repeal an affirmative action provision in the *Employment Equity Act, 1993*, put in place by the previous NDP government, on the ground that the repealed statute went beyond what was constitutionally required. Both the prior policy of pay inequity and the 1991 repealer "perpetuated and reinforced the idea that women could be paid less for no reason other than the fact they are women."

However, the Court concluded that the legislation was a reasonable limit under section 1. First, the Court found that the government was indeed in the midst of a fiscal crisis. Second, the Court limited language in a prior opinion that suggested that financial purposes "can never" serve as a justification under s. 1. While "normal budgetary considerations" could always justify delays in *Charter* compliance, and hence could not be invoked, the legislation here, the Court found, avoided the layoff of 1,300 permanent employees and 700 part-time and seasonal workers, and avoided a costly loss of credit rating. Noting that the legislation reflected the government's role as mediating between claims of many stakeholders, the Court noted that "a legislature must be given reasonable room to manoeuvre to meet these conflicting pressures."

At the same time, the Court reaffirmed its active scrutiny, expressly rejecting the reasoning of the Newfoundland & Labrador Court of Appeal that the non-deferential scrutiny mandated by *Oakes* did not reflect a proper regard for separation of powers. The Court reasoned that legislatures generally think that their own work is reasonable, so section 1 would be superfluous if it did not contemplate an independent, non-deferential judicial review. And the minimal impairment test was justified by wondering "how a court could satisfy itself that a particular legislative limit is 'reasonable' if it is blinkered from considering whether other less limiting measures were available."

THE NATIONAL COALITION FOR GAY AND LESBIAN EQUALITY v. THE MINISTER OF HOME AFFAIRS
CONSTITUTIONAL COURT OF SOUTH AFRICA
1999 (1) SA 6

ACKERMANN J:

. . . .

[14] I shall for the moment deal only with sodomy which takes place in private between consenting males. The long history relating to the ways in which the South African criminal common law differentiated in its treatment of gays as opposed to its treatment of heterosexuals and lesbians, prior to the passing of the interim Constitution, has already been dealt with in at least three judgments of the High Court. The conclusions can be briefly stated. The offence of sodomy, prior to the coming into force of the interim Constitution, was defined as "unlawful and intentional sexual intercourse per anum between human males," consent not depriving the act of unlawfulness, "and thus both parties commit the crime." Neither anal nor oral sex in private between a consenting adult male and a consenting adult female was punishable by the criminal law. Nor was any sexual act, in private, between consenting adult females so punishable.

[15] In what follows I will proceed on the assumption that the equality jurisprudence and analysis developed by this Court in relation to section 8 of the interim Constitution is applicable equally to section 9 of the 1996 Constitution, notwith-

standing certain differences in the wording of these provisions. It is relevant to mention at this point that Mr Davis, who appeared for the amicus curiae, submitted that a more substantive interpretation should be given to the provisions of section 9(1) of the 1996 Constitution than this Court has given to the provisions of section 8(1) of the interim Constitution . . .

[16] Neither section 8 of the interim Constitution nor section 9 of the 1996 Constitution envisages a passive or purely negative concept of equality; quite the contrary. In *Brink v Kitshoff NO*, O'Regan J, with the concurrence of all the members of the Court, stated:

> "Section 8 was adopted then in the recognition that discrimination against people who are members of disfavoured groups can lead to patterns of group disadvantage and harm. Such discrimination is unfair: it builds and entrenches inequality amongst different groups in our society. The drafters realised that it was necessary both to proscribe such forms of discrimination and to permit positive steps to redress the effects of such discrimination. The need to prohibit such patterns of discrimination and to remedy their results are the primary purposes of section 8 and, in particular, subsections (2), (3) and (4)."

[17] In *Prinsloo* and in *Harksen* a multi-stage enquiry was postulated as being necessary when an attack of constitutional invalidity was based on section 8 of the interim Constitution . . .

[18] This does not mean, however, that in all cases the rational connection inquiry of stage (a) must inevitably precede stage (b). The stage (a) rational connection inquiry would be clearly unnecessary in a case in which a court holds that the discrimination is unfair and unjustifiable. I proceed with the enquiry as to whether the differentiation on the ground of sexual orientation constitutes unfair discrimination. Being a ground listed in section 9(3) it is presumed, in terms of section 9(5), that the differentiation constitutes unfair discrimination "unless it is established that the discrimination is fair." Although nobody in this case contended that the discrimination was fair, the Court must still be satisfied, on a consideration of all the circumstances, that fairness has not been established.

[19] Although, in the final analysis, it is the impact of the discrimination on the complainant or the members of the affected group that is the determining factor regarding the unfairness of the discrimination, the approach to be adopted, as appears from the decision of this Court in Harksen, is comprehensive and nuanced.

. . . .

[21] The concept "sexual orientation" as used in section 9(3) of the 1996 Constitution must be given a generous interpretation of which it is linguistically and textually fully capable of bearing. It applies equally to the orientation of persons who are bi-sexual, or transsexual and it also applies to the orientation of persons who might on a single occasion only be erotically attracted to a member of their own sex.

[22] The desire for equality is not a hope for the elimination of all differences.

> "The experience of subordination - of personal subordination, above all - lies behind the vision of equality."

To understand "the other" one must try, as far as is humanly possible, to place oneself in the position of "the other."

"It is easy to say that everyone who is just like 'us' is entitled to equality. Everyone finds it more difficult to say that those who are 'different' from us in some way should have the same equality rights that we enjoy. Yet so soon as we say any . . . group is less deserving and unworthy of equal protection and benefit of the law all minorities and all of . . . society are demeaned. It is so deceptively simple and so devastatingly injurious to say that those who are handicapped or of a different race, or religion, or colour or sexual orientation are less worthy."

[23] The discriminatory prohibitions on sex between men reinforces already existing societal prejudices and severely increases the negative effects of such prejudices on their lives . . . .

. . . .

[25] The impact of discrimination on gays and lesbians is rendered more serious and their vulnerability increased by the fact that they are a political minority not able on their own to use political power to secure favourable legislation for themselves. They are accordingly almost exclusively reliant on the Bill of Rights for their protection.

[26] I turn now to consider the impact which the common law offence of sodomy has on gay men in the light of the approach developed by this Court and referred to in paragraph 19 above:

(a) The discrimination is on a specified ground. Gay men are a permanent minority in society and have suffered in the past from patterns of disadvantage. The impact is severe, affecting the dignity, personhood and identity of gay men at a deep level. It occurs at many levels and in many ways and is often difficult to eradicate.

(b) The nature of the power and its purpose is to criminalise private conduct of consenting adults which causes no harm to anyone else. It has no other purpose than to criminalise conduct which fails to conform with the moral or religious views of a section of society.

(c) The discrimination has, for the reasons already mentioned, gravely affected the rights and interests of gay men and deeply impaired their fundamental dignity.

[27] The above analysis confirms that the discrimination is unfair. There is nothing which can be placed in the other balance of the scale. The inevitable conclusion is that the discrimination in question is unfair and therefore in breach of section 9 of the 1996 Constitution.

———

The Australian statutory approach is somewhat different. Statutes provide a somewhat detailed definition of prohibited "discrimination." Conduct that is considered "direct discrimination" is either outlawed, or protected by specific exemptions. Conduct considered "indirect discrimination" (principally, practices that have a disparate and adverse impact on protected groups: see Part 4 of this Chapter) can be justified if it is "reasonable in the circumstances."[11] Both ends and means are considered. Courts inquire as to whether practice has been adopted for the purpose of achieving a legitimate goal, whether the chosen means for adopting the end is efficient, effective, appropriate, and adapted to the activity, and whether there is a less discriminatory alternative way of achieving the goal that would not impose excessive hardship on the respondent. *See, e.g., Waters v. Public Transport Corp.,* (1991) 173 CLR 349 at 378 (Brennan, J.) The respondent's financial situation and the cost of alternative measures are considered, typically by an administrative agency assigned by the statute to consider these issues.

4.2.3.   The "rational basis" test in American doctrine

Government could hardly function if any person adversely affected by government action could seek judicial or administrative review of each decision on grounds that their treatment, in comparison to some other group, was not fully justified as required by the cases discussed above. The approach in most countries is to limit the scope of the constitutional or statutory limits on equality, so that government action, other than that which discriminates against protected groups, is simply not within the scope of the relevant provision. Thus, the Supreme Court of Canada did not require any justification or scrutiny of a statute denying a tort remedy to persons injured in the course of employment, while preserving a tort remedy for other injured parties. As detailed in Part 3 below, discrimination based on the context of an injury was regarded as not analogous to those prohibited grounds for discrimination set forth in s. 15 of the Charter. *Workers' Compensation Reference,* [1989] 1 S.C.R. 922. The following case illustrates the need to develop additional doctrinal approaches in the U.S., given the broad language of the Equal Protection Clause and the "formal equality" interpretation it has been given by the U.S. Supreme Court.

MASSACHUSETTS BOARD OF RETIREMENT v. MURGIA
SUPREME COURT OF THE UNITED STATES
427 U.S. 307 (1976)

[Before BURGER, C.J., and BRENNAN, STEWART, WHITE, MARSHALL, BLACKMUN, POWELL, and REHNQUIST, JJ.]

PER CURIAM.

This case presents the question whether the provision of Mass. Gen. Laws Ann. c. 32, § 26(3)(a) (1966), that a uniformed state police officer "shall be retired . . . upon his attaining age fifty," denies appellee police officer equal protection of the laws in violation of the Fourteenth Amendment.

*   *   *

---

[11] *See* Belinda Smith, *Anti-discrimination Law in* C. SAPPIDEEN, P. O'GRADY, J RILEY, G. WARBURTON, MACKEN'S LAW OF EMPLOYMENT (Lawbook Co.: Sydney, 7th ed. 2011).

I

We need state only briefly our reasons for agreeing that strict scrutiny is not the proper test for determining whether the mandatory retirement provision denies appellee equal protection. *San Antonio School District v. Rodriguez*, 411 U.S. 1, 16 (1973), reaffirmed that equal protection analysis requires strict scrutiny of a legislative classification only when the classification impermissibly interferes with the exercise of a fundamental right[12] or operates to the peculiar disadvantage of a suspect class.[13] Mandatory retirement at age 50 under the Massachusetts statute involves neither situation.

This Court's decisions give no support to the proposition that a right of governmental employment *per se* is fundamental. See *San Antonio School District v. Rodriguez, supra; Lindsey v. Normet*, 405 U.S. 56, 73 (1972); *Dandridge v. Williams, supra*, at 485. Accordingly, we have expressly stated that a standard less than strict scrutiny "has consistently been applied to state legislation restricting the availability of employment opportunities." *Ibid.*

Nor does the class of uniformed state police officers over 50 constitute a suspect class for purposes of equal protection analysis. *Rodriguez, supra*, at 28, observed that a suspect class is one "saddled with such disabilities, or subjected to such a history of purposeful unequal treatment, or relegated to such a position of political powerlessness as to command extraordinary protection from the majoritarian political process." While the treatment of the aged in this Nation has not been wholly free of discrimination, such persons, unlike, say, those who have been discriminated against on the basis of race or national origin, have not experienced a "history of purposeful unequal treatment" or been subjected to unique disabilities on the basis of stereotyped characteristics not truly indicative of their abilities. The class subject to the compulsory retirement feature of the Massachusetts statute consists of uniformed state police officers over the age of 50. It cannot be said to discriminate only against the elderly. Rather, it draws the line at a certain age in middle life. But even old age does not define a "discrete and insular" group, *United States v. Carolene Products Co.*, 304 U.S. 144, 152–153, n. 4 (1938), in need of "extraordinary protection from the majoritarian political process." Instead, it marks a stage that each of us will reach if we live out our normal span. Even if the statute could be said to impose a penalty upon a class defined as the aged, it would not impose a distinction sufficiently akin to those classifications that we have found suspect to call for strict judicial scrutiny. Under the circumstances, it is unnecessary to subject the State's resolution of competing interests in this case to the degree of critical examination that our cases under the Equal Protection Clause recently have characterized as "strict judicial scrutiny."

---

[12] [FN 3] *E.g., Roe v. Wade*, 410 U.S. 113 (1973) (right of a uniquely private nature); *Bullock v. Carter*, 405 U.S. 134 (1972) (right to vote); *Shapiro v. Thompson*, 394 U.S. 618 (1969) (right of interstate travel); *Williams v. Rhodes*, 393 U.S. 23 (1968) (rights guaranteed by the First Amendment); *Skinner v. Oklahoma ex rel. Williamson*, 316 U.S. 535 (1942) (right to procreate).

[13] [FN 4] *E.g., Graham v. Richardson*, 403 U.S. 365 (1971) (alienage); *McLaughlin v. Florida*, 379 U.S. 184 (1964) (race); *Oyama v. California*, 332 U.S. 633 (1948) (ancestry).

II

We turn then to examine this state classification under the rational-basis standard. This inquiry employs a relatively relaxed standard reflecting the Court's awareness that the drawing of lines that create distinctions is peculiarly a legislative task and an unavoidable one. Perfection in making the necessary classifications is neither possible nor necessary. *Dandridge v. Williams, supra,* at 485. Such action by a legislature is presumed to be valid.

In this case, the Massachusetts statute clearly meets the requirements of the Equal Protection Clause, for the State's classification rationally furthers the purpose identified by the State. [The Court noted that mandatory retirement removed those whose fitness had "presumptively has diminished with age." The State's decision to adopt a generalization rather than adopt individualized fitness testing might well demonstrate that "the State perhaps has not chosen the best means to accomplish this purpose."] But where rationality is the test, a State "does not violate the Equal Protection Clause merely because the classifications made by its laws are imperfect." *Dandridge v. Williams,* 397 U.S., at 485.

We do not make light of the substantial economic and psychological effects premature and compulsory retirement can have on an individual; nor do we denigrate the ability of elderly citizens to continue to contribute to society. The problems of retirement have been well documented and are beyond serious dispute. But "[w]e do not decide today that the [Massachusetts statute] is wise, that it best fulfills the relevant social and economic objectives that [Massachusetts] might ideally espouse, or that a more just and humane system could not be devised." *Id.,* at 487. We decide only that the system enacted by the Massachusetts Legislature does not deny appellee equal protection of the laws.

4.3.   WHICH CLASSIFICATIONS WARRANT CLOSE JUDICIAL SCRUTINY?

The puzzle for courts in protecting constitutional principles of equality is to create judicially manageable standards to implement these grand principles. Professor Hogg, at § 52.6, catalogues the challenge. Every statute or regulation classifies persons in some way, so a rule of absolute equality can't possibly be required by the Fourteenth Amendment or s. 15. Aristotle's definition of equality — "persons who are equal should have assigned to them equal things" — sounds great, but as Hogg concludes, this idea is stated at too high a level of generality to be useful. Most significantly, it fails to identify who is similarly situated to whom. As McIntyre, J. observed in *Andrews,* the Nazi Nuremberg Laws could have been upheld by racist judges on the grounds that all Jews were treated alike. At the other end of the spectrum, in attempting to give some meaning to these important constitutional provisions, courts in the three countries that constitutionalize equality have also recognized that a standard that sustains any classification the legislature itself considers "reasonable" or "pursue[s] a valid federal objective" (the standard under Canada's 1960 statutory *Bill of Rights*) would be insufficient to protect people against discrimination.[14] The solution, implemented in different ways, is to carefully scrutinize certain kinds of classifications and provide minimal or no scrutiny of others. In Australia, (with few exceptions) the courts are not concerned with whether "classifications" in laws are "reasonable," but with what sort of conduct (individual, corporate, or official) warrants active judicial or administrative scrutiny. The decision is made by the Commonwealth Parliament; the parliament, as we have seen, has enacted laws against race, sex, disability, sexual orientation, and age discrimination, among others.

4.3.1.   United States: suspect classifications and fundamental rights

SLAUGHTER-HOUSE CASES
SUPREME COURT OF THE UNITED STATES
83 U.S. 36, 16 Wall. 36 (1873)

MR. JUSTICE MILLER delivered the opinion of the Court.

[This litigation challenged a Louisiana statute that created a corporation and gave it the exclusive right for 25 years to maintain slaughter-houses and ancillary facilities for slaughtering cattle within the New Orleans metropolitan area. The Court quickly rejected a claim that the Thirteenth Amendment's ban on slavery was implicated, although the statute's effect was to require all New Orleans workers in this industry to seek employment from the single authorized slaughter-house. The Court also considered and rejected three separate challenges based on the Fourteenth Amendment made by those either put out of work by this monopoly, or who objected to being subject to the economic power of the monopoly. First, the Court narrowly construed the Privileges and Immunities Clause to not apply to the right to conduct a lawful business. Next, the Court disposed of the claim that the statute denied the plaintiffs their property or liberty without due process of law by construing the Due Process Clause to only provide procedural protection. Last, the Court considered the claim that, by exempting the favored corporation from a general ban on slaughter-houses in New Orleans, the statute violated the Equal Protection Clause of the 14th Amendment. The Court wrote, in that regard]:

In the light of the history of these amendments, and the pervading purpose of them, which we have already discussed, it is not difficult to give a meaning to this clause. The existence of laws in the States where the newly emancipated negroes resided, which discriminated with gross injustice and hardship against them as a class, was the evil to be remedied by this clause, and by it such laws are forbidden.

If, however, the States did not conform their laws to its requirements, then by the fifth section of the article of amendment Congress was authorized to enforce it by suitable legislation. We doubt very much whether any action of a State not directed by way of discrimination against the negroes as a class, or on account of

---

[14]   Indeed, the legislative history of s. 15 makes it clear that the Charter's drafters expressly rejected this deferential approach.

their race, will ever be held to come within the purview of this provision. It is so clearly a provision for that race and that emergency, that a strong case would be necessary for its application to any other. But as it is a State that is to be dealt with, and not alone the validity of its laws, we may safely leave that matter until Congress shall have exercised its power, or some case of State oppression, by denial of equal justice in its courts, shall have claimed a decision at our hands. We find no such case in the one before us, and do not deem it necessary to go over the argument again, as it may have relation to this particular clause of the amendment.

In the early history of the organization of the government, its statesmen seem to have divided on the line which should separate the powers of the National government from those of the State governments, and though this line has never been very well defined in public opinion, such a division has continued from that day to this.

The adoption of the first eleven amendments to the Constitution so soon after the original instrument was accepted, shows a prevailing sense of danger at that time from the Federal power. And it cannot be denied that such a jealousy continued to exist with many patriotic men until the breaking out of the late civil war. It was then discovered that the true danger to the perpetuity of the Union was in the capacity of the State organizations to combine and concentrate all the powers of the State, and of contiguous States, for a determined resistance to the General Government.

Unquestionably this has given great force to the argument, and added largely to the number of those who believe in the necessity of a strong National government.

But, however pervading this sentiment, and however it may have contributed to the adoption of the amendments we have been considering, we do not see in those amendments any purpose to destroy the main features of the general system. Under the pressure of all the excited feeling growing out of the war, our statesmen have still believed that the existence of the States with powers for domestic and local government, including the regulation of civil rights — the rights of person and of property — was essential to the perfect working of our complex form of government, though they have thought proper to impose additional limitations on the States, and to confer additional power on that of the Nation.

But whatever fluctuations may be seen in the history of public opinion on this subject during the period of our national existence, we think it will be found that this court, so far as its functions required, has always held with a steady and an even hand the balance between State and Federal power, and we trust that such may continue to be the history of its relation to that subject so long as it shall have duties to perform which demand of it a construction of the Constitution, or of any of its parts.

MR. JUSTICE FIELD, dissenting:

[Justice Field wrote a lengthy historical argument contending that the 14th Amendment protected all United States citizens against abridgement of those privileges and immunities "which of right belong to the citizens of all free governments," and which include the right to make and enforce contracts, to sue, give evidence in court, inherit and alienate property, and to the same limitations on the right to labor as all other citizens in the community.]

I am authorized by the CHIEF JUSTICE, MR. JUSTICE SWAYNE, and MR. JUSTICE BRADLEY, to state that they concur with me in this opinion.

MR. JUSTICE BRADLEY, also dissenting:

* * *

It is futile to argue that none but persons of the African race are intended to be benefited by this amendment. They may have been the primary cause of the amendment, but its language is general, embracing all citizens, and I think it was purposely so expressed.

The mischief to be remedied was not merely slavery and its incidents and consequences; but that spirit of insubordination and disloyalty to the National government which had troubled the country for so many years in some of the States, and that intolerance of free speech and free discussion which often rendered life and property insecure, and led to much unequal legislation. The amendment was an attempt to give voice to the strong National yearning for that time and that condition of things, in which American citizenship should be a sure guaranty of safety, and in which every citizen of the United States might stand erect on every portion of its soil, in the full enjoyment of every right and privilege belonging to a freeman, without fear of violence or molestation.

[Justice Bradley acknowledged that such a broad interpretation of congressional power could lead to widespread federal legislation "interfering with the internal affairs of the States" and "abolishing the State governments in everything but name," but he dismissed these fears because the basic privileges and immunities of all citizens would be relatively narrow and that increased federal litigation could be met by increased numbers of courts.]

MR. JUSTICE SWAYNE, dissenting: [This dissent responded to objections that a broad congressional power was "novel and large" by noting that "the novelty was known and the measure deliberately adopted." The majority's judgment was "much too narrow." As Swayne, J., observed, the pre-Civil War Constitution gave "ample protection" against oppression by the federal government "but little was given against wrong and oppression by the States. That want was intended to be supplied by this amendment."]

UNITED STATES v. CAROLENE PRODUCTS CO.
SUPREME COURT OF THE UNITED STATES
304 U.S. 144 (1938)

MR. JUSTICE STONE delivered the opinion of the Court.

[The appellee was indicted for violating a federal statute banning the shipment in interstate commerce of "filled milk," i.e. skimmed milk with other fat or cream added. The statute declared that these products were injurious to public health and misled the public. The appellee argued that the statute was invalid on due process and equal protection grounds.]

Appellee raises no valid objection to the present statute by arguing that its prohibition has not been extended to oleomargarine or other butter substitutes in which vegetable fats or oils are substituted for butter fat. The Fifth Amendment has no equal protection clause, and even that of the Fourteenth, applicable only to the states, does not compel their legislatures to prohibit all like evils, or none. A legislature may hit at an abuse which it has found, even though it has failed to strike at another.

Third. We may assume for present purposes that no pronouncement of a legislature can forestall attack upon the constitutionality of the prohibition which it enacts by applying opprobrious epithets to the prohibited act, and that a statute would deny due process which precluded the disproof in judicial proceedings of all facts which would show or tend to show that a statute depriving the suitor of life, liberty or property had a rational basis. But such we think is not the purpose or construction of the statutory characterization of filled milk as injurious to health and as a fraud upon the public. There is no need to consider it here as more than a declaration of the legislative findings deemed to support and justify the action taken as a constitutional exertion of the legislative power, aiding informed judicial review, as do the reports of legislative committees, by revealing the rationale of the legislation. Even in the absence of such aids the existence of facts supporting the legislative judgment is to be presumed, for regulatory legislation affecting ordinary commercial transactions is not to be pronounced unconstitutional unless in the light of the facts made known or generally assumed it is of such a character as to preclude the assumption that it rests upon some rational basis within the knowledge and experience of the legislators.[15] The present statutory findings affect appellee no more than the reports of the Congressional committees; and since in the absence of

---

[15] [Ed. note: this is the famous "footnote 4"] There may be narrower scope for operation of the presumption of constitutionality when legislation appears on its face to be within a specific prohibition of the Constitution, such as those of the first ten amendments, which are deemed equally specific when held to be embraced within the Fourteenth. See *Stromberg v. California*, 283 U.S. 359, 369–370; *Lovell v. Griffin*, 303 U.S. 444, 452.

It is unnecessary to consider now whether legislation which restricts those political processes which can ordinarily be expected to bring about repeal of undesirable legislation, is to be subjected to more exacting judicial scrutiny under the general prohibitions of the Fourteenth Amendment than are most other types of legislation. On restrictions upon the right to vote, see *Nixon v. Herndon*, 273 U.S. 536; *Nixon v. Condon*, 286 U.S. 73; on restraints upon the dissemination of information, see *Near v. Minnesota ex rel. Olson*, 283 U.S. 697, 713–714, 718–720, 722; *Grosjean v. American Press Co.*, 297 U.S. 233; *Lovell v. Griffin, supra*; on interferences with political organizations, see *Stromberg v. California, supra*, 369; *Fiske v. Kansas*, 274 U.S. 380; *Whitney v. California*, 274 U.S. 357, 373–378; *Herndon v. Lowry*, 301 U.S. 242; and see Holmes, J., in *Gitlow v. New York*, 268 U.S. 652, 673; as to prohibition of peaceable assembly, see *De Jonge v. Oregon*, 299 U.S. 353, 365.

Nor need we enquire whether similar considerations enter into the review of statutes directed at particular religious, *Pierce v. Society of Sisters*, 268 U.S. 510, or national, *Meyer v. Nebraska*, 262 U.S. 390; *Bartels v. Iowa*, 262 U.S. 404; *Farrington v. Tokushige*, 273 U.S. 284, or racial minorities, *Nixon v. Herndon, supra*; *Nixon v. Condon, supra:* whether prejudice against discrete and insular minorities may be a special condition, which tends seriously to curtail the operation of those political processes ordinarily to be relied upon to protect minorities, and which may call for a correspondingly more searching judicial inquiry. Compare *McCulloch v. Maryland*, 4 Wheat. 316, 428; *South Carolina v. Barnwell Bros.*, 303 U.S. 177, 184, n. 2, and cases cited.

the statutory findings they would be presumed, their incorporation in the statute is no more prejudicial than surplusage.

Where the existence of a rational basis for legislation whose constitutionality is attacked depends upon facts beyond the sphere of judicial notice, such facts may properly be made the subject of judicial inquiry, and the constitutionality of a statute predicated upon the existence of a particular state of facts may be challenged by showing to the court that those facts have ceased to exist. Similarly we recognize that the constitutionality of a statute, valid on its face, may be assailed by proof of facts tending to show that the statute as applied to a particular article is without support in reason because the article, although within the prohibited class, is so different from others of the class as to be without the reason for the prohibition, though the effect of such proof depends on the relevant circumstances of each case, as for example the administrative difficulty of excluding the article from the regulated class. But by their very nature such inquiries, where the legislative judgment is drawn in question, must be restricted to the issue whether any state of facts either known or which could reasonably be assumed affords support for it. Here the demurrer challenges the validity of the statute on its face and it is evident from all the considerations presented to Congress, and those of which we may take judicial notice, that the question is at least debatable whether commerce in filled milk should be left unregulated, or in some measure restricted, or wholly prohibited. As that decision was for Congress, neither the finding of a court arrived at by weighing the evidence, nor the verdict of a jury can be substituted for it.

The prohibition of shipment in interstate commerce of appellee's product, as described in the indictment, is a constitutional exercise of the power to regulate interstate commerce. As the statute is not unconstitutional on its face the demurrer should have been overruled and the judgment will be

Reversed.

Mr. Justice BLACK concurs in the result and in all of the opinion except the part marked "Third."

Mr. Justice MCREYNOLDS thinks that the judgment should be affirmed.

Mr. Justice CARDOZO and Mr. Justice REED took no part in the consideration or decision of this case.

[Mr. Justice BUTLER concurred, emphasizing that the appellee was free to introduce at trial evidence to show that the declaration of the Act that the described product is injurious to public health and that the sale of it is a fraud upon the public are without any substantial foundation.]

As Rotunda and Nowak observe, § 18.3(b), in the three decades after the end of the *Lochner* era, "it appeared that any classification would be upheld if it was subjected only to the rational relationship test." And *Carolene Products, supra,* makes clear that under this deferential test courts were not going to sit in judgment as to whether Congress was really concerned about the health effects of filled milk or were simply trying to protect dairy farmers. However, Rotunda & Nowak's comprehensive analysis identifies cases governing at least three different non-suspect classifications where the Court has invalidated statutes despite its refusal to acknowledge that it was engaging in close judicial scrutiny. The Court has on several occasions struck down statutes where it determined that the only state interest is one of favoring long-time residents or local businesses. *See, e.g., Metropolitan Life Ins. Co. v. Ward,* 470 U.S. 869 (1985) (higher tax on out-of-state insurance companies); *Williams v. Vermont,* 472 U.S. 14 (1985) (sales tax exemption for car purchases only for buyers who were residents of Vermont at time of purchase); *Hooper v. Bernalillo County Assessor,* 472 U.S. 612 (1985) (property tax exemption available only to those in residents prior to certain date); *Zobel v. Williams,* 457 U.S. 55 (1982) (retroactive distribution of state money to residents based on length of residency). In another well-known case, the Court invalidated a city zoning ordinance that prohibited operation of a group home for the mentally retarded in a residential area while permitting other group homes (like fraternities). *City of Cleburne v. Cleburne Living Center,* 473 U.S. 432 (1985). In two more recent cases, the Court concluded that the challenged statutes were designed solely out of animus directed at gay men and lesbians. And in *Lawrence v. Texas,* 539 U.S. 558 (2003), the Court struck down a state sodomy law prohibiting specified sexual practices between persons of the same sex, again noting the absence of any legitimate state interest other than antipathy toward homosexuals. In each case, the Court declared that the statute lacked a rational basis.

Although these decisions may superficially appear to reflect an erosion in the *Carolene Products* two-tier approach that has dominated post-*Lochner* jurisprudence, on reflection they appear to be better explained as careful exceptions that are faithful to *Carolene Products* reasoning. As specifically articulated in *Vance v. Bradley* (discussed below in section 3.4), the Court assumes that unfair or improvident discrimination against slaughterhouse operators, filled milk sellers, methadone users, older police or foreign service officers, residents of low-wealth school districts, or poor tenants is likely to be corrected by the political process. As with women, non-residents, the mentally retarded, and gays may not meet the requisite qualifications to officially merit strict scrutiny, but the justices are apparently not sufficiently trusting of ordinary politics to completely foreclose closer scrutiny in these cases, at least to the extent of assuring the existence of a real, legitimate, and non-pretextual justification for any disadvantaging legislation.

A related case with potentially farther-reaching implications is *Romer v. Evans,* 517 U.S. 620 (1996), where the Court invalidated a state law enacted by voter initiative that prevented municipalities from proscribing discrimination on the basis of sexual orientation. Justice Kennedy began by quoting from Justice John Marshall Harlan's famous dissent in *Plessy v. Ferguson* (discussed more extensively in Chapter Five) that "the constitution 'neither knows nor tolerates classes among citizens.'" He emphasized that the state law did not simply preempt particular local statutes. Rather, it preserved broad powers for local governments in other areas, including the authority to prevent discrimination against other classes of people. In contrast, gay men and lesbians "by state decree, are put in a solitary class with respect to transactions and relations in both the private and governmental spheres. The amendment withdraws from homosexuals, but no others, specific legal protection from the injuries caused by discrimination, and it forbids reinstatement of these laws and policies." *Id.* at 627.

The Court held that precedents calling for active judicial scrutiny did not apply, but that the challenged initiative failed to pass the deferential standard requiring the court to "uphold the legislative classification so long as it bears a rational relation to some legitimate end." The majority reached this conclusion by finding that "its sheer breadth is so discontinuous with the reasons offered for it that the amendment seems inexplicable by anything but animus toward the class it affects; it lacks a rational relationship to legitimate state interests." *Id.* at 631–32. The initiative, by "making a general announcement that gays and lesbians shall not have any particular protections from the law, inflicts on them immediate, continuing, and real injuries that outrun and belie any legitimate justifications that may be claimed for it." Justice Scalia, joined by Chief Justice Rehnquist and Justice Thomas, dissented, arguing that

> The Court has mistaken a Kulturkampf for a fit of spite. The constitutional amendment before us here is not the manifestation of a " 'bare . . . desire to harm' " homosexuals, but is rather a modest attempt by seemingly tolerant Coloradans to preserve traditional sexual mores against the efforts of a politically powerful minority to revise those mores through use of the laws.

Id. at 636.

Romer has significant implications because, while obviously not requiring that laws adversely treating gay men and lesbians be justified and necessary for a compelling state interest, it does require some degree of closer judicial scrutiny to determine whether any purported state justification is not a pretext for unadulterated homophobic animus.

4.3.2. Canada: substantive discrimination based on enumerated or analogous grounds

If the differential treatment challenged in the litigation is based on one of the grounds enumerated in s. 15, or a ground found by the courts to be "analogous" to these grounds, then the Charter applies. (As noted below, the plaintiff must still demonstrate that the differential treatment constitutes "substantive discrimination" and the government can still demonstrate that the discrimination constitutes a reasonable limit.) If the classification is based on a ground neither enumerated nor analogous, s. 15 simply isn't applicable.

ANDREWS v. LAW SOCIETY OF BRITISH COLUMBIA
SUPREME COURT OF CANADA
[1989] 1 S.C.R. 143, 56 D.L.R. (4th) 1

[The litigation challenged a British Columbia statute that barred the plaintiff, an Oxford-trained lawyer with permanent residency in Canada who was otherwise qualified, from practicing law because he was not a Canadian citizen. In the British tradition, the opinions are listed in order of the seniority of the justice, rather than the majority following by concurrences and dissents. First, we see Justice McIntyre's individual view that the challenged statute infringed Andrews' equality rights under s. 15 but that it was a reasonable limit under s. 1. Three justices (Wilson, Dickson and L'Heureux-Dube) adopted McIntyre, J.'s s. 15 analysis but found the statute unreasonable and thus invalid. For his own reasons, LaForest, J., also voted to strike down the statute.]

McINTYRE J. (dissenting in part):

* * *

THE CONCEPT OF EQUALITY

* * *

McLachlin J.A. in the Court of Appeal expressed the view, at p. 605, that:

> ". . . the essential meaning of the constitutional requirement of equal protection and equal benefit is that persons who are "similarly situated be similarly treated" and conversely, that persons who are "differently situated be differently treated" . . . ."

In this, she was adopting and applying as a test a proposition which seems to have been widely accepted with some modifications in both trial and appeal court decisions throughout the country on s. 15(1) of the Charter. The reliance on this concept appears to have derived, at least in recent times, from J. T. Tussman and J. tenBroek, "The Equal Protection of Laws" (1949), 37 Calif. L. Rev. 341. The similarly situated test is a restatement of the Aristotelian principle of formal equality — that "things that are alike should be treated alike, while things that are unalike should be treated unalike in proportion to their unalikeness" (*Ethica Nichomacea*, trans. W. Ross, Book V3, at p. 1131a-6 (1925)).

The test as stated, however, is seriously deficient in that it excludes any consideration of the nature of the law. If it were to be applied literally, it could be used to justify the Nuremberg laws of Adolf Hitler. Similar treatment was contemplated for all Jews. The similarly situated test would have justified the formalistic separate but equal doctrine of *Plessy v. Ferguson*, 163 U.S. 537 (1896), a doctrine that incidentally was still the law in the United States at the time that Professor Tussman and J. tenBroek wrote their much cited article. ***

This approach was rejected in this Court by Ritchie J. in *R. v. Drybones*, [1970] S.C.R. 282, in a similar case involving a provision of the *Indian Act* making it an offence for an Indian to be intoxicated off a reserve. He said, at p. 297:

". . . I cannot agree with this interpretation pursuant to which it seems to me that the most glaring discriminatory legislation against a racial group would have to be construed as recognizing the right of each of its individual members "to equality before the law," so long as all the other members are being discriminated against in the same way."

*   *   *

[Next, McIntyre, J. reviewed the unsatisfactory history of judicial interpretation of the equality provision of the pre-Charter, statutory *Canadian Bill of Rights*, which was narrowly construed to protect only "equality before the law" and hence was held not to cover challenged legislation that discriminated against First Nations women (but not men) who married non-Indians, and held that the denial of unemployment insurance benefits to women because they were pregnant did not violate the guarantee of equality before the law, because any inequality in the protection and benefit of the law was "not created by legislation but by nature."[16]]

It must be recognized, however, as well that the promotion of equality under s. 15 has a much more specific goal than the mere elimination of distinctions. If the Charter was intended to eliminate all distinctions, then there would be no place for sections such as 27 (multicultural heritage); 2(a) (freedom of conscience and religion); 25 (aboriginal rights and freedoms); and other such provisions designed to safeguard certain distinctions. Moreover, the fact that identical treatment may frequently produce serious inequality is recognized in s. 15(2), which states that the equality rights in s. 15(1) do "not preclude any law, program or activity that has as its object the amelioration of conditions of disadvantaged individuals or groups . . . ."

DISCRIMINATION

The right to equality before and under the law, and the rights to the equal protection and benefit of the law contained in s. 15, are granted with the direction contained in s. 15 itself that they be without discrimination. Discrimination is unacceptable in a democratic society because it epitomizes the worst effects of the denial of equality, and discrimination reinforced by law is particularly repugnant. The worst oppression will result from discriminatory measures having the force of

---

16 [Ed. note: Consistent with this view of s. 15 as correcting some defects in prior jurisprudence, the Supreme Court of Canada held in *Brooks v. Canada Safeway Ltd.*, [1989] 1 S.C.R. 1219, that an employer's insurance plan that disentitled pregnant women from certain benefits was illegal sex discrimination. The United States Supreme Court held that differential treatment of pregnant women was neither unconstitutional under the 14th Amendment, *Geduldig v. Aiello*, 417 U.S. 484 (1974), nor illegal under anti-discrimination legislation, *General Electric Co. v. Gilbert*, 429 U.S. 125. The Court concluded that the classification was not based on gender but between two groups — pregnant women and nonpregnant persons. *Geduldig*, 417 U.S. at 497. The court reasoned that, while only women can become pregnant, "pregnancy is an objectively identifiable physical condition with unique characteristics. Absent a showing that distinctions involving pregnancy are mere pretexts designed to effect an invidious discrimination against the members of one sex or the other, lawmakers are constitutionally free to include or exclude pregnancy from the coverage of legislation such as this on any reasonable basis, just as with respect to any other physical characteristic." *Id.*, 417 U.S. at 497 n.20. Congress subsequently overturned the latter interpretation by statutory amendment.]

law. It is against this evil that s. 15 provides a guarantee.

Discrimination as referred to in s. 15 of the Charter must be understood in the context of pre-Charter history. Prior to the enactment of s. 15(1), the Legislatures of the various provinces and the federal Parliament had passed during the previous fifty years what may be generally referred to as Human Rights Acts. With the steady increase in population from the earliest days of European emigration into Canada and with the consequential growth of industry, agriculture and commerce and the vast increase in national wealth which followed, many social problems developed. The contact of the European immigrant with the indigenous population, the steady increase in immigration bringing those of neither French nor British background, and in more recent years the greatly expanded role of women in all forms of industrial, commercial and professional activity led to much inequality and many forms of discrimination. In great part these developments, in the absence of any significant legislative protection for the victims of discrimination, called into being the Human Rights Acts. In 1944, the *Racial Discrimination Act, 1944*, S.O. 1944, c. 51, was passed, to be followed in 1947 by *The Saskatchewan Bill of Rights Act, 1947*, S.S. 1947, c. 35, and in 1960 by the *Canadian Bill of Rights*. Since then every jurisdiction in Canada has enacted broadranging Human Rights Acts which have attacked most of the more common forms of discrimination found in society. This development has been recorded and discussed by Walter Tarnopolsky, now Tarnopolsky J.A., in *Discrimination and the Law* (2nd ed. 1985).

What does discrimination mean? [Here, McIntyre, J., draws upon the interpretation of that concept in statutory Human Rights Acts, and notes that these rulings focuses on the *effects* of a challenged rule on a victimized group entitled to protection under s. 15. He noted that Supreme Court in statutory cases had expressly held] that no intent was required as an element of discrimination, for it is in essence the impact of the discriminatory act or provision upon the person affected which is decisive in considering any complaint. ***

[McIntyre also noted a key statutory precedent, *Canadian National Railway Co. v. Canada (Canadian Human Rights Commission)*, [1987] 1 S.C.R. 1114 (better known as the *Action Travail des Femmes* case), where Dickson, C.J. quoted from a report by now-Justice Rosalie Abella:

> Discrimination . . . means practices or attitudes that have, whether by design or impact, the effect of limiting an individual's or a group's right to the opportunities generally available because of attributed rather than actual characteristics . . . .

> It is not a question of whether this discrimination is motivated by an intentional desire to obstruct someone's potential, or whether it is the accidental by-product of innocently motivated practices or systems. If the barrier is affecting certain groups in a disproportionately negative way, it is a signal that the practices that lead to this adverse impact may be discriminatory."]

*   *   *

The Court in the case at bar must address the issue of discrimination as the term is used in s. 15(1) of the Charter. In general, it may be said that the principles which have been applied under the Human Rights Acts are equally applicable in considering questions of discrimination under s. 15(1). [At the same time, the Court noted certain differences: Human Rights Acts applied to private as well as government discrimination; they specified categories of prohibited discrimination; and they contain a variety of exemptions or defences, while similar issues would be resolved in Charter litigation by claiming that the challenged law was a reasonable limit under s. 1.]

RELATIONSHIP BETWEEN S. 15(1) AND S. 1 OF THE CHARTER

[McIntyre J held that the Charter requires a two-step inquiry. First, the court inquires into whether an infringement of the rights guaranteed by s. 15 have occurred. Second, and analytically distinct, the inquiry turns to whether the discrimination is reasonable. To determine if an infringement occurred, McIntyre adopted the "enumerated or analogous grounds," which is that s. 15(1) is designed to prevent discrimination based on these grounds enumerated in the text, and other grounds analogous to the ones enumerated. McIntyre cited with approval the judgment of Hugessen J.A. in *Smith, Kline & French Laboratories Ltd. v. Canada (Attorney General)*, [[1987] 2 F.C. 359, 367–69]:

> As far as the text of section 15 itself is concerned, one may look to whether or not there is "discrimination," in the pejorative sense of that word, and as to whether the categories are based upon the grounds enumerated or grounds analogous to them. The inquiry, in effect, concentrates upon the personal characteristics of those who claim to have been unequally treated. Questions of stereotyping, of historical disadvantagement, in a word, of prejudice, are the focus and there may even be a recognition that for some people equality has a different meaning than for others."]

[The opinion concluded that "a legislative distinction has been made by s. 42 of the *Barristers and Solicitors Act* between citizens and non-citizens with respect to the practice of law," and that by requiring non-citizens to wait three years to qualify as permanent residents to be called to the bar, the distinction is "discriminatory."]

The rights guaranteed in s. 15(1) apply to all persons whether citizens or not. A rule which bars an entire class of persons from certain forms of employment, solely on the grounds of a lack of citizenship status and without consideration of educational and professional qualifications or the other attributes or merits of individuals in the group, would, in my view, infringe s. 15 equality rights. Non-citizens, lawfully permanent residents of Canada, are — in the words of the U.S. Supreme Court in *United States v. Carolene Products Co.*, 304 U.S. 144 (1938), at pp. 152–53, n. 4, subsequently affirmed in *Graham v. Richardson*, 403 U.S. 365 (1971), at p. 372 — a good example of a "discrete and insular minority" who come within the protection of s. 15.[17]

---

[17] [Ed. note: Applying the language of strict judicial scrutiny from *Graham*, a requirement of citizenship for admission to the bar was rejected in *Application of Griffiths*, 394 U.S. 618 (1969). Since that time, the U.S. Supreme Court has used different standards for review of alienage cases, demanding compelling justifications for state or local denial of economic benefits on the basis of citizenship,

SECTION 1

[Here, McIntyre, J. disagreed with his colleagues. He noted that when "making distinctions between groups and individuals to achieve desirable social goals, it will rarely be possible to say of any legislative distinction that it is clearly the right legislative choice or that it is clearly a wrong one." In "seeking to achieve a goal that is demonstrably justified in a free and democratic society, therefore, a legislature must be given reasonable room to manoeuvre to meet these conflicting pressures." He therefore concluded that the limitation on bar membership was reasonable.]

LA FOREST J.: ***

*** I am convinced that it was never intended in enacting s. 15 that it become a tool for the wholesale subjection to judicial scrutiny of variegated legislative choices in no way infringing on values fundamental to a free and democratic society. Like my colleague, I am not prepared to accept that all legislative classifications must be rationally supportable before the courts. Much economic and social policy-making is simply beyond the institutional competence of the courts: their role is to protect against incursions on fundamental values, not to second guess policy decisions.

I realize that it is no easy task to distinguish between what is fundamental and what is not and that in this context this may demand consideration of abstruse theories of equality. For example, there may well be legislative or governmental differentiation between individuals or groups that is so grossly unfair to an individual or group and so devoid of any rational relationship to a legitimate state purpose as to offend against the principle of equality before and under the law as to merit intervention pursuant to s. 15. For these reasons I would think it better at this stage of Charter development to leave the question open. I am aware that in the United States, where Holmes J. has referred to the equal protection clause there as the "last resort of constitutional arguments" (*Buck v. Bell*, 274 U.S. 200 (1927), at p. 208), the courts have been extremely reluctant to interfere with legislative judgment. Still, as I stated, there may be cases where it is indeed the last constitutional resort to protect the individual from fundamental unfairness. Assuming there is room under s. 15 for judicial intervention beyond the traditionally established and analogous policies against discrimination discussed by my colleague, it bears repeating that considerations of institutional functions and resources should make courts extremely wary about questioning legislative and governmental choices in such areas.

*   *   *

While it cannot be said that citizenship is a characteristic which "bears no relation to the individual's ability to perform or contribute to society" (*Frontiero v. Richardson*, 411 U.S. 677 (1973), at p. 686), it certainly typically bears an attenuated sense of relevance to these. That is not to say that no legislative conditioning of benefits (for example) on the basis of citizenship is acceptable in the free and democratic society that is Canada, merely that legislation purporting to do so ought

---

reasonable tailoring to meet state interests in allocating political power to citizens, and deferring to federal judgments. See Nowak & Rotunda, § 14.12, at 754.]

to be measured against the touchstone of our Constitution. It requires justification.
***

WILSON, J., (joined by DICKSON, C.J., and L'HEUREUX-DUBÉ, J:

[These justices joined McIntyre, J.'s analysis of the s. 15 infringement, but concluded that the statute was not a reasonable limit under s. 1.]

Before turning to s. 1, I would like to add a brief comment to what my colleague has said concerning non-citizens permanently resident in Canada forming the kind of "discrete and insular minority" to which the Supreme Court of the United States referred in *United States v. Carolene Products Co.*, 304 U.S. 144 (1938), at pp. 152–53, n. 4.

Relative to citizens, non-citizens are a group lacking in political power and as such vulnerable to having their interests overlooked and their rights to equal concern and respect violated. They are among "those groups in society to whose needs and wishes elected officials have no apparent interest in attending": see J. H. Ely, *Democracy and Distrust* (1980), at p. 151. Non-citizens, to take only the most obvious example, do not have the right to vote. Their vulnerability to becoming a disadvantaged group in our society is captured by John Stuart Mill's observation in Book III of Considerations on Representative Government that "in the absence of its natural defenders, the interests of the excluded is always in danger of being overlooked . . . ." I would conclude therefore that non-citizens fall into an analogous category to those specifically enumerated in s. 15. I emphasize, moreover, that this is a determination which is not to be made only in the context of the law which is subject to challenge but rather in the context of the place of the group in the entire social, political and legal fabric of our society. While legislatures must inevitably draw distinctions among the governed, such distinctions should not bring about or reinforce the disadvantage of certain groups and individuals by denying them the rights freely accorded to others.

I believe also that it is important to note that the range of discrete and insular minorities has changed and will continue to change with changing political and social circumstances. For example, Stone J. writing in 1938, was concerned with religious, national and racial minorities. In enumerating the specific grounds in s. 15, the framers of the Charter embraced these concerns in 1982 but also addressed themselves to the difficulties experienced by the disadvantaged on the grounds of ethnic origin, colour, sex, age and physical and mental disability. It can be anticipated that the discrete and insular minorities of tomorrow will include groups not recognized as such today. It is consistent with the constitutional status of s. 15 that it be interpreted with sufficient flexibility to ensure the "unremitting protection" of equality rights in the years to come.

* * *

Likewise, in *Egan v. Canada*, [1995] 2 S.C.R. 513, 528–29, the Court employed this approach in finding that s. 15 protected against discrimination based on sexual orientation:

The appellants' claim before this Court is that the Act contravenes s. 15 of the Charter in that it discriminates on the basis of sexual orientation. To establish that claim, it must first be determined that s. 15's protection of equality without discrimination extends to sexual orientation as a ground analogous to those specifically mentioned in the section. This poses no great hurdle for the appellants; the respondent Attorney General of Canada conceded this point. While I ordinarily have reservations about concessions of constitutional issues, I have no difficulty accepting the appellants' contention that whether or not sexual orientation is based on biological or physiological factors, which may be a matter of some controversy, it is a deeply personal characteristic that is either unchangeable or changeable only at unacceptable personal costs, and so falls within the ambit of s. 15 protection as being analogous to the enumerated grounds. As the courts below observed, this is entirely consistent with a number of cases on the point. Indeed, there is a measure of support for this position in this Court. In *Canada (Attorney General) v. Ward*, [1993] 2 S.C.R. 689, at pp. 737–39, speaking for my colleagues as well, I observed that the analogous grounds approach in s. 15 was appropriate to a consideration of the character of "social groups" subject to protection as Convention refugees. These, I continued, encompass groups defined by an innate or unchangeable characteristic which, I added, would include sexual orientation.[18]

It is necessary but not sufficient for a classification to be based on an enumerated or analogous ground. The challenged provision must also operate to discriminate in a substantive way. *Andrews, supra*, concluded that the use of the word "discrimination" in the text of s. 15 limited "those distinctions which are forbidden by the section to those which involve prejudice or disadvantage." This was spelled out in more detail in the following pathmarking case:

LAW v. CANADA (MINISTER OF EMPLOYMENT AND IMMIGRATION)

SUPREME COURT OF CANADA
[1999] 1 S.C.R. 497, 170 D.L.R. 4th 1

[Before LAMER C.J.C., L'HEUREUX-DUBE, GONTHIER, CORY, McLACHLIN, IACOBUCCI, MAJOR, BASTARACHE and BINNIE JJ.]

The judgment of the court was delivered by IACOBUCCI J.:

[The claimant, who was 30 years old at the time of her spouse's death, challenged provisions of the Canada Pension Plan that deny the usual survivor's pension to non-disabled surviving spouses under the age of 35.]

---

[18] [Ed. note: Almost all the enumerated grounds in s. 15 are immutable, in that they cannot be changed by the choice of the individual, with the exception of religion. Thus, *Andrews, supra*, created the doctrine that citizenship was analogous to religion because it could not be changed "except on the basis of unacceptable costs." In *Egan*, the Court found the same to be true of sexual orientation.]

I. INTRODUCTION AND OVERVIEW

. . . .

[2] Section 15 of the Charter guarantees to every individual the right to equal treatment by the state without discrimination. It is perhaps the Charter's most conceptually difficult provision. In this Court's first s. 15 case, *Andrews v. Law Society of British Columbia*, [1989] 1 S.C.R 143 at p. 164, 56 D.L.R. (4th) 1, McIntyre J. noted that, as embodied in s. 15(1) of the Charter, the concept of equality is "an elusive concept," and that "more than any of the other rights and freedoms guaranteed in the Charter, it lacks precise definition." Part of the difficulty in defining the concept of equality stems from its exalted status. The quest for equality expresses some of humanity's highest ideals and aspirations, which are by their nature abstract and subject to differing articulations. The challenge for the judiciary in interpreting and applying s. 15(1) of the Charter is to transform these ideals and aspirations into practice in a manner which is meaningful to Canadians and which accords with the purpose of the provision.

. . . .

VI. ANALYSIS

A. *Approach to s. 15(1)*

. . . .

[39] [Synthesizing the prior case law, Justice Iacobucci held that] a court that is called upon to determine a discrimination claim under s. 15(1) should make the following three broad inquiries. First, does the impugned law (a) draw a formal distinction between the claimant and others on the basis of one or more personal characteristics, or (b) fail to take into account the claimant's already disadvantaged position within Canadian society resulting in substantively differential treatment between the claimant and others on the basis of one or more personal characteristics? If so, there is differential treatment for the purpose of s. 15(1). Second, was the claimant subject to differential treatment on the basis of one or more of the enumerated and analogous grounds? And third, does the differential treatment discriminate in a substantive sense, bringing into play the purpose of s. 15(1) of the Charter in remedying such ills as prejudice, stereotyping, and historical disadvantage? The second and third inquiries are concerned with whether the differential treatment constitutes discrimination in the substantive sense intended by s. 15(1).

B. *The Purpose of s. 15(1)*

[The current SCC view is discussed in the *Kapp* excerpt following this case.]

C. *The Comparative Approach*

[56] As discussed above, McIntyre J. emphasized in *Andrews, supra*, that the equality guarantee is a comparative concept. Ultimately, a court must identify

differential treatment as compared to one or more other persons or groups. Locating the appropriate comparator is necessary in identifying differential treatment and the grounds of the distinction. Identifying the appropriate comparator will be relevant when considering many of the contextual factors in the discrimination analysis.

. . . .

D. *Establishing Discrimination in a Purposive Sense: Contextual Factors*

. . . .

(a) *Pre-existing Disadvantage*

[63] As has been consistently recognized throughout this Court's jurisprudence, probably the most compelling factor favouring a conclusion that differential treatment imposed by legislation is truly discriminatory will be, where it exists, pre-existing disadvantage, vulnerability, stereotyping, or prejudice experienced by the individual or group. These factors are relevant because, to the extent that the claimant is already subject to unfair circumstances or treatment in society by virtue of personal characteristics or circumstances, persons like him or her have often not been given equal concern, respect, and consideration. It is logical to conclude that, in most cases, further differential treatment will contribute to the perpetuation or promotion of their unfair social characterization, and will have a more severe impact upon them, since they are already vulnerable.

[64] One consideration which the Court has frequently referred to with respect to the issue of pre-existing disadvantage is the role of stereotypes. A stereotype may be described as a misconception whereby a person or, more often, a group is unfairly portrayed as possessing undesirable traits, or traits which the group, or at least some of its members, do not possess. In my view, probably the most prevalent reason that a given legislative provision may be found to infringe s. 15(1) is that it reflects and reinforces existing inaccurate understandings of the merits, capabilities and worth of a particular person or group within Canadian society, resulting in further stigmatization of that person or the members of the group or otherwise in their unfair treatment.***

[The court stressed, however, that proof of membership in a disadvantaged group was not essential to establish a s. 15(1) violation, especially where discrimination is based on an enumerated ground.]

(b) *Relationship Between Grounds and the Claimant's Characteristics or Circumstances*

[In a discussion somewhat superseded by *Kapp, infra*, Iacobucci J observed that "legislation which takes into account the actual needs, capacity, or circumstances of the claimant and others with similar traits in a manner that respects their value as human beings and members of Canadian society will be less likely to have a negative effect on human dignity" and the "fact that the impugned legislation may achieve a valid social purpose for one group of individuals cannot function to deny an equality claim where the effects of the legislation upon another person or group conflict with the purpose of the s. 15(1) guarantee."]

. . . .

F. *Application to the Case at Bar*

[Here, Justice Iacobucci applied the three-part analysis to the statute providing reduced benefits to younger surviving spouses. First, he concluded that this benefit reduction constituted a denial of "equal benefit of the law" under the first step of the equality analysis. Then he agreed that the distinction was based on age, which is an enumerated ground in s. 15(1), satisfying the second prong. Ultimately, however, the Court concluded that the applicant failed to establish that the age-based distinction constituted the sort of discrimination violating essential human dignity and freedom that s. 15(1) was designed to prevent. The Court explained that adults under the age of 45 have not been consistently and routinely subjected to the sorts of discrimination faced by some of Canada's discrete and insular minorities. The appellant specifically challenged as faulty the stereotype that younger widows and widowers have a greater ability to enter or re-enter the workforce following their spouse's death. She challenged this stereotype as unsupported by evidence, thus demeaning the dignity of under-45 adults as less worthy. She noted that the minister responsible for the enactment of the Canada Pension Plan remarked to Parliament in 1964 that "Young widows in their twenties and early thirties usually have little difficulty in finding employment, and of course many of them remarry": see House of Commons Debates (November 16, 1964), at p. 10122. The Court noted that the purpose and function of the impugned CPP provisions is not to remedy the immediate financial need experienced by widows and widowers, but rather to enable older widows and widowers to meet their basic needs during the longer term. Because of the "greater flexibility and opportunity of younger people without dependent children or disabilities to achieve long-term security absent their spouse," the "differential treatment does not reflect or promote the notion that they are less capable or less deserving of concern, respect, and consideration, when the dual perspectives of long-term security and the greater opportunity of youth are considered. Nor does the differential treatment perpetuate the view that people in this class are less capable or less worthy of recognition or value as human beings or as members of Canadian society."]

[106] Under these circumstances, the fact that the legislation is premised upon informed statistical generalizations which may not correspond perfectly with the long-term financial need of all surviving spouses does not affect the ultimate conclusion the legislation is consonant with the human dignity and freedom of the appellant. Parliament is entitled, under these limited circumstances at least, to premise remedial legislation upon informed generalizations without running afoul of s. 15(1) of the Charter and being required to justify its position under s. 1. I emphasize, though, that under other circumstances a more precise correspondence will undoubtedly be required in order to comply with s. 15(1). In particular, a more precise correspondence will likely be important where the individual or group which is excluded by the legislation is already disadvantaged or vulnerable within Canadian society.

. . . .

[109] In finding that the impugned legislative provisions do not infringe s. 15(1) of the Charter, I do not wish in any way to minimize the emotional and economic upset which affects surviving dependents when a spouse dies. My analysis herein is not meant to suggest that young people do not suffer following the death of a loved one, but only that the impugned CPP provisions are not discriminatory between younger and older adults within the purpose and meaning of s. 15(1) of the Charter.

. . . .

The SCC subsequently sharpened and clarified the post-*Law* doctrine regarding substantive discrimination in the following case. The accused were non-aboriginal fishers, convicted of unlawful fishing during a time in which the Aboriginal Communal Fishing Licences Regulations that gave fishers designated by First Nation bands an exclusive right to fish. The appellants argued that the program implemented by the federal government, the communal fishing licence, and the related legislation violated their equality rights under s. 15(1) of the Charter in a manner that was not justified by s. 1. A Provincial Court judge of British Columbia agreed with the accused. He found that B.C. commercial fishers were a distinctive community whose identity was invested in the fishery, and their testimony of how they were "left sitting on the beach" while aboriginal fishers caught salmon "rang true" as an "attack on their worthiness as fishers." Although the trial judge agreed that the accused were not victims of stereotype or prejudice, he found that their human dignity had been impaired because they had been to feel "less capable or worthy of recognition or as a member of Canadian society, equally deserving of concern, respect and consideration." 2003 BCPC 279 (CanLII), [2003] 4 C.N.L.R. 238.

R. v. KAPP
SUPREME COURT OF CANADA
[2008] 2 S.C.R. 483

McLACHLIN C.J. and BASTARACHE, BINNIE, LEBEL, DESCHAMPS, FISH, ABELLA, CHARRON and ROTHSTEIN JJ.

[The SCC upheld the conviction, finding that the appellants' claim was not subject to s. 15(1) because it was an ameliorative program that was exempted by s. 15(2); this aspect of the case is discussed at Chapter 9.4.3. First, the Court used the case to revisit the basic purposes of Canada's equality guarantee.]

The judgment of McLACHLIN C.J. and BINNIE, LEBEL, DESCHAMPS, FISH, ABELLA, CHARRON and ROTHSTEIN JJ. was delivered by

McLACHLIN C.J. and ABELLA J.: —

. . . .

C. *Analysis*

. . . .

1. The Purpose of Section 15

. . . .

[15] Substantive equality, as contrasted with formal equality, is grounded in the idea that: "The promotion of equality entails the promotion of a society in which all are secure in the knowledge that they are recognized at law as human beings equally deserving of concern, respect and consideration": *Andrews*, at p. 171, *per* McIntyre J., for the majority on the s. 15 issue. Pointing out that the concept of equality does not necessarily mean identical treatment and that the formal "like treatment" model of discrimination may in fact produce inequality, McIntyre J. stated (at p. 165):

> To approach the ideal of full equality before and under the law — and in human affairs an approach is all that can be expected — the main consideration must be the impact of the law on the individual or the group concerned. Recognizing that there will always be an infinite variety of personal characteristics, capacities, entitlements and merits among those subject to a law, there must be accorded, as nearly as may be possible, an equality of benefit and protection and no more of the restrictions, penalties or burdens imposed upon one than another. In other words, the admittedly unattainable ideal should be that a law expressed to bind all should not because of irrelevant personal differences have a more burdensome or less beneficial impact on one than another.

While acknowledging that equality is an inherently comparative concept (p. 164), McIntyre J. warned against a sterile similarly situated test focussed on treating "likes" alike. An insistence on substantive equality has remained central to the Court's approach to equality claims.

. . . .

[18] In *Andrews*, McIntyre J. viewed discriminatory impact through the lens of two concepts: (1) the perpetuation of prejudice or disadvantage to members of a group on the basis of personal characteristics identified in the enumerated and analogous grounds; and (2) stereotyping on the basis of these grounds that results in a decision that does not correspond to a claimant's or group's actual circumstances and characteristics. *Andrews*, for example, was decided on the second of these concepts; it was held that the prohibition against non-citizens practising law was based on a stereotype that non-citizens could not *properly* discharge the responsibilities of a lawyer in British Columbia - a view that denied non-citizens a privilege, not on the basis of their merits and capabilities, but on the basis of what the Royal Commission Report on *Equality in Employment* (1984), referred to as "attributed rather than actual characteristics" (p. 2). Additionally, McIntyre J. emphasized that a finding of discrimination might be grounded in the fact that the impact of a particular law or program was to perpetuate the disadvantage of a group defined by enumerated or analogous s. 15 grounds. In this context, he said (at p. 174):

I would say then that discrimination may be described as a distinction, whether intentional or not but based on grounds relating to personal characteristics of the individual or group, which has the effect of imposing burdens, obligations, or disadvantages on such individual or group not imposed upon others, or which withholds or limits access to opportunities, benefits, and advantages available to other members of society.

[19] A decade later, in *Law*, this Court suggested that discrimination should be defined in terms of the impact of the law or program on the "human dignity" of members of the claimant group, having regard to four contextual factors: (1) pre-existing disadvantage, if any, of the claimant group; (2) degree of correspondence between the differential treatment and the claimant group's reality; (3) whether the law or program has an ameliorative purpose or effect; and (4) the nature of the interest affected (paras. 62–75).

. . . .

[21] At the same time, several difficulties have arisen from the attempt in *Law* to employ human dignity *as a legal test*. There can be no doubt that human dignity is an essential value underlying the s. 15 equality guarantee. In fact, the protection of all of the rights guaranteed by the *Charter* has as its lodestar the promotion of human dignity . . . .

[22] But as critics have pointed out, human dignity is an abstract and subjective notion that, even with the guidance of the four contextual factors, cannot only become confusing and difficult to apply; it has also proven to be an *additional* burden on equality claimants, rather than the philosophical enhancement it was intended to be . . . .

. . . .

[25] The central purpose of combatting discrimination, as discussed, underlies both s. 15(1) and s. 15(2). Under s. 15(1), the focus is on *preventing* governments from making distinctions based on the enumerated or analogous grounds that: have the effect of perpetuating group disadvantage and prejudice; or impose disadvantage on the basis of stereotyping . . . .

. . . .

4.3.3. South Africa

Similar to the Canadian approach, the South African Constitution enumerates a number of grounds or categories upon which discrimination would be constitutionally prohibited, "including race, gender, sex, pregnancy, marital status, ethnic or social origin, colour, sexual orientation, age, disability, religion, conscience, belief, culture, language and birth." This is not a closed list and thus the courts may define differentiation on analogous grounds to be prohibited as unfair discrimination. The Constitutional Court has laid out a clear methodology for deciding whether differentiation along these or analogous grounds amounts to unfair discrimination and thus is prohibited.

PRINSLOO v. VAN DER LINDE

CONSTITUTIONAL COURT OF SOUTH AFRICA
1997 (3) SA 1012

ACKERMANN J, O'REGAN J and SACHS J:

[1] Much of South Africa is tinder dry. Veld, forest and mountain fires sweep across the land, causing immense damage to property and destroying valuable forest, flora and fauna. The Forest Act 122 of 1984 (the "Act") has as one of its principal objects the prevention and control of such fires. A major method of achieving this is to create various fire control areas where schemes of compulsory fire control are established, with special emphasis on the clearing and maintenance of fire belts between neighbouring properties. Landowners in areas outside of such fire control areas are, on the other hand, encouraged but not required to embark on similar fire control measures. A number of provisions prescribe criminal penalties for landowners in fire control areas who fail to fulfil their statutory obligations. In addition, an offence is created in respect of persons who are wilfully or negligently responsible for fires "in the open air," while it is an offence for any landowner in any area to fail to take such steps as are under the circumstances reasonably necessary to prevent the spread of fires.

[2] [The court noted that section 84 presumes negligence when fires occur on land outside fire control areas. The suit was for injury to land resulting from a fire on a neighbour's property.]

[Initially, the SACC rejected the claim that civil cases fell within the constitutional presumption of innocence. The Court found this applied only to criminal proceedings.]

. . . .

[16] In his written argument, counsel pointed to the differentiation between defendants in veld fire cases and those in other delictual matters. According to him, this differentiation had no rational basis, because the apparent object that the legislature sought to achieve by reversing the general rule regarding the incidence of onus that whoever avers must prove, could have been, and, indeed, already was, accomplished by means of common law aids to proof. He referred in particular to the concept of res ipsa loquitur and the practice of triers of fact to require less evidence to establish a prima facie case if the facts in issue are peculiarly within the knowledge of the opposing party. A second differentiation which was raised by first respondent, relates to the fact that the presumption of negligence applies only in respect of fires in non-controlled areas, and not to those spreading in controlled areas, which at first blush appears to be incongruous. The challenge to constitutionality in both cases would be based either on a breach of the right to equality as guaranteed in section 8(1) or on a violation of the prohibition of discrimination contained in section 8(2). To determine whether either challenge in terms of section 8 is correct, it is necessary to consider first the proper approach to be taken to sections 8(1) and (2).

[17] If each and every differentiation made in terms of the law amounted to unequal treatment that had to be justified by means of resort to section 33, or else

constituted discrimination which had to be shown not to be unfair, the courts could be called upon to review the justifiability or fairness of just about the whole legislative programme and almost all executive conduct. As Hogg puts it:

> "What is meant by a guarantee of equality? It cannot mean that the law must treat everyone equally. The Criminal Code imposes punishments on persons convicted of criminal offences; no similar burdens are imposed on the innocent. Education Acts require children to attend school; no similar obligation is imposed on adults. Manufacturers of food and drugs are subject to more stringent regulations than the manufacturers of automobile parts. The legal profession is regulated differently from the accounting profession. The Wills Act prescribes a different distribution of the property of a person who dies leaving a will from that of a person who dies leaving no will. The Income Tax Act imposes a higher rate of tax on those with high incomes than on those with low incomes. Indeed, every statute or regulation employs classifications of one kind or another for the imposition of burdens or the grant of benefits. Laws never provide the same treatment for everyone."

> The courts would be compelled to review the reasonableness or the fairness of every classification of rights, duties, privileges, immunities, benefits or disadvantages flowing from any law. Accordingly, it is necessary to identify the criteria that separate legitimate differentiation from differentiation that has crossed the border of constitutional impermissibility and is unequal or discriminatory "in the constitutional sense."

[18] Even a cursory summary of international experience indicates that there are no universally accepted bright lines for determining whether or not an equality or non-discrimination right has been breached. The varying emphases given in different countries depend on a combination of the texts to be interpreted, modes of doctrinal articulation, historical backgrounds and evolving standards. Questions of institutional function and competence might play a role when reviewing, for example, legislation of a social and economic character.

[19] In relation to the text and context of the interim Constitution, it would therefore seem that a simplistic transplantation from other countries into our equality jurisprudence of formulae, modes of classification or degrees of scrutiny, might create more problems than it solved. At the same time, we must be mindful of section 35(1) which states:

> 35. (1) In interpreting the provisions of this Chapter a court of law shall promote the values which underlie an open and democratic society based on freedom and equality . . . ."

[20] Our country has diverse communities with different historical experiences and living conditions. Until recently, very many areas of public and private life were invaded by systematic legal separateness coupled with legally enforced advantage and disadvantage. The impact of structured and vast inequality is still with us despite the arrival of the new constitutional order. It is the majority, and not the minority, which has suffered from this legal separateness and disadvantage. While our country, unfortunately, has great experience in constitutionalising inequality, it

is a newcomer when it comes to ensuring constitutional respect for equality. At the same time, South Africa shares patterns of inequality found all over the globe, so that any development of doctrine relating to section 8 would have to take account both of our specific situation and of the problems which our country shares with the rest of humanity. All this reinforces the idea that this Court should be astute not to lay down sweeping interpretations at this stage but should allow equality doctrine to develop slowly and, hopefully, surely. This is clearly an area where issues should be dealt with incrementally and on a case by case basis with special emphasis on the actual context in which each problem arises.

. . . .

[23] The idea of differentiation (to employ a neutral descriptive term) seems to lie at the heart of equality jurisprudence in general and of the section 8 right or rights in particular. Taking as comprehensive a view as possible of the way equality is treated in section 8, we would suggest that it deals with differentiation in basically two ways: differentiation which does not involve unfair discrimination and differentiation which does involve unfair discrimination. This needs some elaboration. We deal with the former first.

[24] It must be accepted that, in order to govern a modern country efficiently and to harmonise the interests of all its people for the common good, it is essential to regulate the affairs of its inhabitants extensively. It is impossible to do so without differentiation and without classifications which treat people differently and which impact on people differently. It is unnecessary to give examples which abound in everyday life in all democracies based on equality and freedom. Differentiation which falls into this category very rarely constitutes unfair discrimination in respect of persons subject to such regulation, without the addition of a further element. What this further element is will be considered later.

[25] It is convenient, for descriptive purposes, to refer to the differentiation presently under discussion as "mere differentiation." In regard to mere differentiation the constitutional state is expected to act in a rational manner. It should not regulate in an arbitrary manner or manifest "naked preferences" that serve no legitimate governmental purpose, for that would be inconsistent with the rule of law and the fundamental premises of the constitutional state. The purpose of this aspect of equality is, therefore, to ensure that the state is bound to function in a rational manner. This has been said to promote the need for governmental action to relate to a defensible vision of the public good, as well as to enhance the coherence and integrity of legislation. In Mureinik's celebrated formulation, the new constitutional order constitutes "a bridge away from a culture of authority . . . to a culture of justification." Etienne Mureinik, *A Bridge to Where? Introducing the Interim Bill of Rights*, 10 S.Afr. J. on Human Rights 31 (1994).

[26] Accordingly, before it can be said that mere differentiation infringes section 8 it must be established that there is no rational relationship between the differentiation in question and the governmental purpose which is proffered to validate it. In the absence of such rational relationship the differentiation would infringe section 8. But while the existence of such a rational relationship is a necessary condition for the differentiation not to infringe section 8, it is not a sufficient condition; for the differentiation might still constitute unfair discrimination if that

further element, referred to above, is present.

[27] It is to section 8(2) that one must look in order to determine what this further element is. For reasons which will subsequently emerge it is unnecessary to consider the precise ambit or limits of this subsection. It is, however, clearly a section which deals not with all differentiation or even all discrimination but only with unfair discrimination. It does so by distinguishing between two forms of unfair discrimination and dealing with them differently.

[28] The first form relates to certain specifically enumerated grounds ("specified grounds") on the basis whereof no person may unfairly be discriminated against. The specified grounds are race, gender, sex, ethnic or social origin, colour, sexual orientation, age, disability, religion, conscience, belief, culture or language. When there is prima facie proof of discrimination on these grounds it is presumed, in terms of subsection (4), that unfair discrimination has been sufficiently proved, until the contrary is established. These are not the only grounds which would constitute unfair discrimination. The words "without derogating from the generality of this provision," which introduce the specified grounds, make it clear that the specified grounds are not exhaustive. The second form is constituted by unfair discrimination on grounds which are not specified in the subsection. In regard to this second form there is no presumption in favour of unfairness.

[29] The question arises as to what grounds of discrimination this second form includes. A purely literal reading and application of the phrase "without derogating from the generality of this provision" would lead to the conclusion that discrimination on any ground whatsoever is proscribed, provided it is unfair. Such a reading would provide no guidance as to what unfair meant in regard to this second form of discrimination. It would provide very little, if any, guidance in deciding when a differentiation which passed the rational relationship threshold constituted unfair discrimination. It also seems unlikely that the content of the concept unfair discrimination would be left to unguided judicial judgment. We are of the view, however, that when read in its full historical and evolutionary context and in the light of the purpose of section 8 as a whole, and section 8(2) in particular, the second form of unfair discrimination cannot be given such an extremely wide and unstructured meaning.

[30] Proper weight must be given to the use of the word "discrimination" in subsection (2). The drafters of section 8 did not, for example, follow the model of the Fourteenth Amendment to the Constitution of the United States which, in paragraph 1 thereof, refers only to the denial of "the equal protection of the laws." Section 8(1) certainly positively enacts the encompassing and important right to "equality before the law and to equal protection of the law," but section 8 does not stop there. It goes further and in section 8(2) proscribes "unfair discrimination" in the two forms we have mentioned.

[31] The proscribed activity is not stated to be "unfair differentiation" but is stated to be "unfair discrimination." Given the history of this country we are of the view that "discrimination" has acquired a particular pejorative meaning relating to the unequal treatment of people based on attributes and characteristics attaching to them. We are emerging from a period of our history during which the humanity of the majority of the inhabitants of this country was denied. They were treated as not

having inherent worth; as objects whose identities could be arbitrarily defined by those in power rather than as persons of infinite worth. In short, they were denied recognition of their inherent dignity. Although one thinks in the first instance of discrimination on the grounds of race and ethnic origin one should never lose sight in any historical evaluation of other forms of discrimination such as that which has taken place on the grounds of sex and gender. In our view unfair discrimination, when used in this second form in section 8(2), in the context of section 8 as a whole, principally means treating persons differently in a way which impairs their fundamental dignity as human beings, who are inherently equal in dignity.

[32] In Dworkin's words, the right to equality means the right to be treated as equals, which does not always mean the right to receive equal treatment. We find support for the approach we advocate in the following passage from the judgment of this Court in *The President of the Republic of South Africa and Another v. Hugo*:

> "At the heart of the prohibition of unfair discrimination lies a recognition that the purpose of our new constitutional and democratic order is the establishment of a society in which all human beings will be accorded equal dignity and respect regardless of their membership of particular groups. The achievement of such a society in the context of our deeply inegalitarian past will not be easy, but that that is the goal of the Constitution should not be forgotten or overlooked."

and in which the following passage from *Egan v. Canada* was quoted with approval:

> "This court has recognized that inherent human dignity is at the heart of individual rights in a free and democratic society . . . More than any other right in the Charter, s. 15 gives effect to this notion . . . Equality, as that concept is enshrined as a fundamental human right within s. 15 of the Charter, means nothing if it does not represent a commitment to recognizing each person's equal worth as a human being, regardless of individual differences. Equality means that our society cannot tolerate legislative distinctions that treat certain people as second-class citizens, that demean them, that treat them as less capable for no good reason, or that otherwise offend fundamental human dignity."

. . . .

[35] Turning now to the case before us, it is necessary in the first place to enquire whether the necessary rational relationship exists between the purpose sought to be achieved by section 84 of the Act and the means sought to achieve it. The objectives of the Act as set out in the long title, are "[t]o provide for . . . the prevention and combating of veld, forest and mountain fires; . . . and matters connected therewith." In essence, applicant contended that section 84 lacked rationality because it did not use the least onerous means of achieving its objectives. This approach, however, is based on two misconceptions. First, the applicant is prematurely importing a criterion for justification into a test to be applied at the infringement enquiry (definitional or threshold) stage. The question of whether the legislation could have been tailored in a different and more acceptable way is relevant to the issue of justification, but irrelevant to the question of whether there is a sufficient relationship between the means chosen and the end sought, for

purposes of the present enquiry. Second, underlying the argument is an assumption that somehow there should be a "presumption of innocence" in civil matters as weighty and untouchable as that in criminal cases, so that a reverse onus in a civil matter should be as vulnerable to impeachment as one in a criminal trial.

[36] In regard to the first misconception, a person seeking to impugn the constitutionality of a legislative classification cannot simply rely on the fact that the state objective could have been achieved in a better way. As long as there is a rational relationship between the method and object it is irrelevant that the object could have been achieved in a different way. In any civil case, one of the parties will have to bear the onus on each of the factual matters material to the adjudication of the dispute. So, in the case of an aquilian claim for damages[19] arising from a veld fire, one of the parties will bear the onus concerning negligence. As long as the imposition of the onus is not arbitrary, there will be no breach of section 8(1). In rare circumstances, it may be that the allocation of onus will impair other constitutional rights and a challenge will then arise. That is not the case here.

. . . .

[41] This does not end the matter, because despite the existence of the aforementioned rational relationship between means and purpose, the particular differentiation might still constitute unfair discrimination under the second form of unfair discrimination mentioned in section 8(2). The regulation effected by section 84 in the present case differentiates between owners and occupiers of land in fire control areas and those who own or occupy land outside such areas.

Such differentiation cannot, by any stretch of the imagination, be seen as impairing the dignity of the owner or occupier of land outside the fire control area. There is likewise no basis for concluding that the differentiation in some other invidious way adversely affects such owner or occupier in a comparably serious manner. It is clearly a regulatory matter to be adjudged according to whether or not there is a rational relationship between the differentiation enacted by section 84 and the purpose sought to be achieved by the Act. We have decided that such a relationship exists. Accordingly, no breach of section 8(1) or (2) has been established.

HARKSEN v. LANE
CONSTITUTIONAL COURT OF SOUTH AFRICA
1998 (1) SA 300 (CC)

GOLDSTONE J:

[1] In this case the constitutionality of certain provisions of the Insolvency Act 24 of 1936, as amended ("the Act"), comes before us by way of a referral from Farlam J in the Cape of Good Hope Provincial High Court made in terms of section 102(1) of the Constitution of the Republic of South Africa Act 200 of 1993 ("the interim Constitution").

---

[19] [Ed. note: An aquilium claim arises under the South African law of delict, which roughly corresponds to the common law of torts. It results when the defendant has taken some wrongful and positive action that has caused economic loss.]

[2] The referral came about in consequence of the sequestration of the estate of Mr Jürgen Harksen ("Mr Harksen"). The final sequestration order was granted in the Cape of Good Hope Provincial Division of the Supreme Court (as it then was) on 16 October 1995. The applicant in these proceedings, Mrs Jeanette Harksen ("Mrs Harksen"), was at that time married out of community of property to Mr Harksen.[20] The first and second respondents are the trustees in the insolvent estate of Mr Harksen ("the trustees") . . . .

. . . .

[7] In this case the sections of the Act which are impugned are sections 21, 64 and 65. They are alleged to be inconsistent with certain provisions of the bill of rights to the extent that they impact on the property and affairs of a solvent spouse upon the sequestration of the estate of an insolvent spouse . . . ..

[8] In terms of section 20(1) of the Act, the effect of the sequestration of the estate of an insolvent is to divest the insolvent of his or her estate and to vest it in the Master until a trustee has been appointed. Thereafter the estate vests in the trustee . . . .

. . . .

[24] Pursuant to the statutory vesting of her property in the Master and then the trustees, the latter caused the property of Mrs Harksen to be attached. According to her statement of affairs, that property has a value of R6 120 352,50 [in 1998, approximately US$1 million]. None of it has been released by the trustees to Mrs Harksen and it would appear that no application for such release has been made by her.

[25] Mrs Harksen was summoned, under sections 64 and 65 of the Act, to subject herself to interrogation at the first meeting of the creditors in the insolvent estate of Mr Harksen, and to produce at the meeting: "all documentation relating to [her] financial affairs and the financial affairs of Jürgen Harksen." For reasons not now pertinent, the magistrate who presided at the meeting of creditors set aside the summons. However, on 9 December 1996, Farlam J set aside the ruling of the magistrate and directed Mrs Harksen to subject herself to the interrogation and to produce the documents referred to in the summons. That order precipitated the present proceedings impugning the constitutionality of section 21 of the Act and those portions of sections 64 and 65 that provide for enquiries into the estate, business, affairs or property of the spouse of an insolvent person.

. . . .

[40] It was further submitted on behalf of Mrs Harksen that the provisions of section 21 of the Act were in violation of the equality clause of the interim Constitution. More particularly it was contended that the vesting provision constitutes unequal treatment of solvent spouses and discriminates unfairly against

---

[20] [Ed. note: The default family law for South African marriages is community property (similar to that used in Quebec and various American states from California to Florida whose original European settlement was French or Spanish). However, couples who properly file an Antenuptial Contract are married "out of community of property." Among the significant differences is that community property is automatically subject to recovery by creditors of either spouse.]

them; and that its effect is to impose severe burdens, obligations and disadvantages on them beyond those applicable to other persons with whom the insolvent had dealings or close relationships or whose property is found in the possession of the insolvent . . . . Counsel for Mrs Harksen suggested that the provisions of section 21 constituted a violation of both sections 8(1) (a denial of equality before the law and equal protection of the law) and 8(2) (unfair discrimination).

. . . .

[42] Where section 8 is invoked to attack a legislative provision or executive conduct on the ground that it differentiates between people or categories of people in a manner that amounts to unequal treatment or unfair discrimination, the first enquiry must be directed to the question as to whether the impugned provision does differentiate between people or categories of people. If it does so differentiate, then in order not to fall foul of section 8(1) of the interim Constitution there must be a rational connection between the differentiation in question and the legitimate governmental purpose it is designed to further or achieve. If it is justified in that way, then it does not amount to a breach of section 8(1).

. . . .

[44] If the differentiation complained of bears no rational connection to a legitimate governmental purpose which is proffered to validate it, then the provision in question violates the provisions of section 8(1) of the interim Constitution. If there is such a rational connection, then it becomes necessary to proceed to the provisions of section 8(2) to determine whether, despite such rationality, the differentiation none the less amounts to unfair discrimination.

[45] The determination as to whether differentiation amounts to unfair discrimination under section 8(2) requires a two stage analysis. Firstly, the question arises whether the differentiation amounts to "discrimination" and, if it does, whether, secondly, it amounts to "unfair discrimination" . . . .

[46] Section 8(2) contemplates two categories of discrimination. The first is differentiation on one (or more) of the fourteen grounds specified in the subsection (a "specified ground"). The second is differentiation on a ground not specified in subsection (2) but analogous to such ground (for convenience hereinafter called an "unspecified" ground) which we formulated as follows in *Prinsloo*: "The second form is constituted by unfair discrimination on grounds which are not specified in the subsection. In regard to this second form there is no presumption in favour of unfairness." Given the history of this country we are of the view that 'discrimination' has acquired a particular pejorative meaning relating to the unequal treatment of people based on attributes and characteristics attaching to them . . . . [U]nfair discrimination, when used in this second form in section 8(2), in the context of section 8 as a whole, principally means treating persons differently in a way which impairs their fundamental dignity as human beings, who are inherently equal in dignity.

* * *

Where discrimination results in treating persons differently in a way which impairs their fundamental dignity as human beings, it will clearly be a breach of section 8(2).

Other forms of differentiation, which in some other way affect persons adversely in a comparably serious manner, may well constitute a breach of section 8(2) as well.

There will be discrimination on an unspecified ground if it is based on attributes or characteristics which have the potential to impair the fundamental dignity of persons as human beings, or to affect them adversely in a comparably serious manner.

[47] The question whether there has been differentiation on a specified or an unspecified ground must be answered objectively. In the former case the enquiry is directed at determining whether the statutory provision amounts to differentiation on one of the grounds specified in section 8(2). Similarly, in the latter case the enquiry is whether the differentiation in the provision is on an unspecified ground (as explained in para 46 above). If in either case the enquiry leads to a negative conclusion then section 8(2) has not been breached and the question falls away. If the answer is in the affirmative, however, then it is necessary to proceed to the second stage of the analysis and determine whether the discrimination is "unfair." In the case of discrimination on a specified ground, the unfairness of the discrimination is presumed, but the contrary may still be established. In the case of discrimination on an unspecified ground, the unfairness must still be established before it can be found that a breach of section 8(2) has occurred.

[48] Before proceeding to the second stage of the enquiry, it is necessary to comment briefly on one aspect of the specified and unspecified grounds of differentiation which constitute discrimination. In the above quoted passage from *Prinsloo* it was pointed out that the pejorative meaning of "discrimination" related to the unequal treatment of people "based on attributes and characteristics attaching to them." For purposes of that case it was unnecessary to attempt any comprehensive description of what "attributes and characteristics" would comprise.

[49] It is also unnecessary for purposes of the present case, save that I would caution against any narrow definition of these terms. What the specified grounds have in common is that they have been used (or misused) in the past (both in South Africa and elsewhere) to categorize, marginalise and often oppress persons who have had, or who have been associated with, these attributes or characteristics. These grounds have the potential, when manipulated, to demean persons in their inherent humanity and dignity. There is often a complex relationship between these grounds. In some cases they relate to immutable biological attributes or characteristics, in some to the associational life of humans, in some to the intellectual, expressive and religious dimensions of humanity and in some cases to a combination of one or more of these features. The temptation to force them into neatly self-contained categories should be resisted. Section 8(2) seeks to prevent the unequal treatment of people based on such criteria which may, amongst other things, result in the construction of patterns of disadvantage such as has occurred only too visibly in our history.

[50] The nature of the unfairness contemplated by the provisions of section 8 was considered in paras 41 and 43 of the majority judgment in the *Hugo* case. The following was stated:

"The prohibition on unfair discrimination in the interim Constitution seeks not only to avoid discrimination against people who are members of disadvantaged groups. It seeks more than that. At the heart of the prohibition of unfair discrimination lies a recognition that the purpose of our new constitutional and democratic order is the establishment of a society in which all human beings will be accorded equal dignity and respect regardless of their membership of particular groups. The achievement of such a society in the context of our deeply inegalitarian past will not be easy, but that that is the goal of the Constitution should not be forgotten or overlooked.

. . . .

To determine whether that impact was unfair it is necessary to look not only at the group who has been disadvantaged but at the nature of the power in terms of which the discrimination was effected and, also at the nature of the interests which have been affected by the discrimination."

In para 41 dignity was referred to as an underlying consideration in the determination of unfairness. The prohibition of unfair discrimination in the Constitution provides a bulwark against invasions which impair human dignity or which affect people adversely in a comparably serious manner. However, as L'Heureux-Dubé J acknowledged in *Egan v. Canada*, "Dignity [is] a notoriously elusive concept . . . it is clear that [it] cannot, by itself, bear the weight of s. 15's task on its shoulders. It needs precision and elaboration." It is made clear in para 43 of *Hugo* that this stage of the enquiry focuses primarily on the experience of the "victim" of discrimination. In the final analysis it is the impact of the discrimination on the complainant that is the determining factor regarding the unfairness of the discrimination.

[51] In order to determine whether the discriminatory provision has impacted on complainants unfairly, various factors must be considered. These would include:

(a) the position of the complainants in society and whether they have suffered in the past from patterns of disadvantage, whether the discrimination in the case under consideration is on a specified ground or not;

(b) the nature of the provision or power and the purpose sought to be achieved by it. If its purpose is manifestly not directed, in the first instance, at impairing the complainants in the manner indicated above, but is aimed at achieving a worthy and important societal goal, such as, for example, the furthering of equality for all, this purpose may, depending on the facts of the particular case, have a significant bearing on the question whether complainants have in fact suffered the impairment in question. In *Hugo*, [in which President Mandela's pardon of prisoners excluding able bodied men was challenged, ed.] for example, the purpose of the Presidential Act was to benefit three groups of prisoners, namely, disabled prisoners, young people and mothers of young children, as an act of mercy. The fact that all these groups were regarded as being particularly vulnerable in our society, and that in the case of the disabled and the young mothers, they belonged to groups who had been victims of discrimination in the past, weighed with the Court in concluding that the discrimination was not unfair;

(c)   with due regard to (a) and (b) above, and any other relevant factors, the extent to which the discrimination has affected the rights or interests of complainants and whether it has led to an impairment of their fundamental human dignity or constitutes an impairment of a comparably serious nature.

These factors, assessed objectively, will assist in giving "precision and elaboration" to the constitutional test of unfairness. They do not constitute a closed list. Others may emerge as our equality jurisprudence continues to develop. In any event it is the cumulative effect of these factors that must be examined and in respect of which a determination must be made as to whether the discrimination is unfair.

[52] If the discrimination is held to be unfair then the provision in question will be in violation of section 8(2). One will then proceed upon the final leg of the enquiry as to whether the provision can be justified under section 33 of the interim Constitution, the limitations clause. This will involve a weighing of the purpose and effect of the provision in question and a determination as to the proportionality thereof in relation to the extent of its infringement of equality.

[53] At the cost of repetition, it may be as well to tabulate the stages of enquiry which become necessary where an attack is made on a provision in reliance on section 8 of the interim Constitution. They are:

(a)   Does the provision differentiate between people or categories of people? If so, does the differentiation bear a rational connection to a legitimate government purpose? If it does not then there is a violation of section 8(1). Even if it does bear a rational connection, it might nevertheless amount to discrimination.

(b)   Does the differentiation amount to unfair discrimination? This requires a two stage analysis:

(b)(i)   Firstly, does the differentiation amount to "discrimination"? If it is on a specified ground, then discrimination will have been established. If it is not on a specified ground, then whether or not there is discrimination will depend upon whether, objectively, the ground is based on attributes and characteristics which have the potential to impair the fundamental human dignity of persons as human beings or to affect them adversely in a comparably serious manner.

(b)(ii)   If the differentiation amounts to "discrimination," does it amount to "unfair discrimination"? If it has been found to have been on a specified ground, then unfairness will be presumed. If on an unspecified ground, unfairness will have to be established by the complainant. The test of unfairness focuses primarily on the impact of the discrimination on the complainant and others in his or her situation.

If, at the end of this stage of the enquiry, the differentiation is found not to be unfair, then there will be no violation of section 8(2).

(c)   If the discrimination is found to be unfair then a determination will have to be made as to whether the provision can be justified under the limitations clause (section 33 of the interim Constitution).

[54] I turn now to consider the constitutionality of section 21 of the Act in the light of the foregoing analysis.

[55] That section 21 differentiates between the solvent spouse of an insolvent and other persons who might have had dealings with the insolvent is patent. It becomes necessary, therefore, to consider the governmental purpose of the section, whether that purpose is a legitimate one and, if so, whether the differentiation does have a rational connection to that purpose.

. . . .

[57] Since the introduction of the section 21 provision in 1926, the position of women in our society has changed radically . . . . More and more women have become economically active and contribute out of their own income or investments to the property of a common household. The consequence is that nowadays, in the case of honest spouses, who are married out of community of property, it is not infrequently a matter of complexity for the spouses themselves to determine which property in their possession belongs to each of them; or, indeed, which is held in co-ownership because both contributed to the purchase price. Having regard to the close identity of interests between many married couples, they do not always make nice calculations and keep accurate records of their respective contributions to property they acquire. If it is difficult for them to do so, then so much more difficult and complex is it for a trustee who comes as a complete stranger to the financial affairs of the spouses. The provisions of section 21 thus assist a trustee in the important determination of which property in the possession of "spouses" belongs to the insolvent estate, not only in cases of collusion but also in the case of honest partners to a marriage or similar close relationship. This statutory mechanism is an appropriate and effective one.

. . . .

[60] For reasons set out above there can be no doubt as to the existence of a rational connection between the differentiation created by section 21 of the Act and the legitimate governmental purpose behind its enactment. Moreover, in my opinion, reasonable procedures were introduced to safeguard the interests of the solvent spouse in his or her property. It follows that section 21 does not violate the provisions of section 8(1) of the interim Constitution.

[61] The next question is whether the differentiation between solvent spouses and other persons who had dealings with insolvents constitutes discrimination. The differentiation is not on one of the specified grounds. Whether it constitutes discrimination on one of the unspecified grounds is an objective enquiry. In my opinion, this enquiry yields an affirmative result. Other persons who had dealings with the insolvent or whose property is found in the possession of an insolvent are not affected in the same way. Their property does not become vested in the Master or the trustee and they are not burdened with the onus of proving what is their property before it is released to them. They are not prevented from disposing of their property unless and until they prove their ownership either to the satisfaction of a trustee or a court of competent jurisdiction. The differentiation does arise from their attributes or characteristics as solvent spouses, namely their usual close relationship with the insolvent spouse and the fact that they usually live together in

a common household. These attributes have the potential to demean persons in their inherent humanity and dignity. In this regard it might also be mentioned that they have a relationship with the insolvent spouse similar to that of children or other persons who live under the same roof. The disadvantages of section 21 do not apply to the last mentioned categories. It follows that the provisions of section 21 of the Act do discriminate against the solvent spouse of an insolvent.

[62] The discrimination complained of by Mrs Harksen does not fall within the fourteen specified grounds contained in section 8(2). Mrs Harksen thus bears the onus of persuading us on a balance of probabilities that the discrimination is unfair and hence outlawed by section 8(2). In the determination as to whether that onus has been discharged we must have regard to the considerations referred to in para 51 above. I shall consider each in turn.

[63] The group here affected, namely solvent spouses, is not one which has suffered discrimination in the past and is not a vulnerable one. To adopt the words of O'Regan J in the Hugo case, they are not a "vulnerable . . . group adversely affected by . . . discrimination."

[64] In this case the power was exercised by Parliament which has the right and duty to protect the public interest. In the Act, the legislature gave effect to that duty by protecting the rights of the creditors of insolvent estates. That is the purpose of section 21. That purpose is not inconsistent with the underlying values protected by section 8(2).

[65] In the consideration of the effect of section 21 one must assume that Masters and trustees will act reasonably and honestly and not wish to claim for insolvent estates that which solvent spouses are able to establish belongs to them. One must also assume that in an appropriate case the courts will intervene where they do not so act. It must also be borne in mind that the statutory vesting of the property of the solvent spouse does not have as a consequence that such property is necessarily removed from the possession of the solvent spouse. It is attached by the sheriff of the magistrate's court or by a deputy sheriff. They, as it were, place the hand of the law on the property and, of course, it may not be alienated or burdened by the solvent spouse prior to its release. Where the solvent spouse claims property as his or hers and fails to adduce evidence to establish that claim on a balance of probabilities then the insolvent estate is entitled to the property. The legal presumption is that property was owned by the insolvent and not by the solvent spouse. The effect is hence that the solvent spouse has not been divested of what was her or his property. And one must remember that the facts in issue will be peculiarly within the knowledge of the spouses themselves.

[66] In the event that the solvent spouse has to resort to litigation, there is inconvenience and a degree of potential embarrassment to the extent that the litigation may become public. There is also inconvenience and a burden in that the solvent spouse will usually require legal assistance. Some solvent spouses may not have the funds to employ a lawyer and in that way suffer further potential prejudice. But that is an inevitable consequence of a dispute between a trustee of an insolvent estate and a solvent spouse as to ownership of property.

[67] In my judgment the cumulative effect of these criteria, and in particular the

impact of the inconvenience or prejudice on solvent spouses in the context of the Act, and having regard to the underlying values protected by section 8(2), does not justify the conclusion that section 21 of the Act constitutes unfair discrimination. Looked at from the perspective of solvent spouses, it is the kind of inconvenience and burden that any citizen may face when resort to litigation becomes necessary. Indeed it could arise whenever a vindicatory claim (whether justified or not) is brought against a person in possession of property. Again, the inconvenience and burden of having to resist such a claim does not lead to an impairment of fundamental dignity or constitute an impairment of a comparably serious nature.

[68] It follows, in my opinion, that Mrs Harksen has not established that the provisions of section 21 of the Act, especially in its context, constitute unfair discrimination.

[JUSTICES O'REGAN and SACHS dissented. They agreed with JUSTICE GOLDSTONE's legal approach but not with his application of the law to the facts of this case].

The Constitutional Court has subsequently argued that the approach it took in interpreting the equality clause of the 1993 "interim" Constitution in *Harksen v. Lane* NO applies equally to the equality clause of the "final" 1996 Constitution, despite some differences in the formulation of the right in the two constitutions. The three differences of any note are first, the addition of three additional specified grounds of presumptively unfair discrimination — birth, marital status, and pregnancy. Second, the protection of affirmative measures is given a more positive formulation, in which restitutionary or remedial measures are considered an inherent aspect of equality, rather than merely non-prejudicial to equality, and, finally, the right not to be discriminated against is extended to protect against not only state action but also private action.

4.3.4. Rationales for the absence of close scrutiny of most economic and social legislation

The general theory that close judicial scrutiny is not appropriate for most legislative classifications is often based on a trust in the political process to work out these problems. The Court explained this in *Vance v. Bradley*, 440 U.S. 93 (1979), upholding mandatory retirement at age 60 for foreign service officers.

Appellees have not suggested that the statutory distinction between Foreign Service personnel over age 60 and other federal employees over that age burdens a suspect group or a fundamental interest; and in cases where these considerations are absent, courts are quite reluctant to overturn governmental action on the ground that it denies equal protection of the laws. The Constitution presumes that, absent some reason to infer antipathy, even improvident decisions will eventually be rectified by the democratic process and that judicial intervention is generally unwarranted no matter how unwisely we may think a political branch has acted. Thus, we will not overturn such a statute unless the varying treatment of different groups or persons is so unrelated to the achievement of any combination of legitimate purposes that we can only conclude that the legislature's actions were irrational.

The Supreme Court of Canada initially nodded in the same direction in *R. v. Turpin*, [1989] 1 S.C.R. 1296. Although in 1985 the *Criminal Code* was amended to allow the Crown and accused to agree to waive a jury trial in serious criminal cases, prior to that time a strange provision required juries for serious crimes except in Alberta. Turpin, accused in Ontario of murder, challenged her inability to waive a jury trial on constitutional equality grounds. The Court rejected the challenge, finding that the differential treatment did not constitute discrimination, and thus did not infringe Turpin's rights under s. 15. It would "be stretching the imagination to characterize persons accused of one of the crimes listed in s. 427 of the Criminal Code in all the provinces except Alberta as members of a 'discrete and insular minority'." The SCC later retreated from a rigid limit on s. 15 to the politically powerless. In *R. v. Hess*, [1990] 2 S.C.R. 906, 943, the court rejected an effort to summarily dismiss a s. 15 challenge by a man accused of a criminal code provision (since repealed) criminalizing sexual intercourse between a man of any age and a girl under the age of fourteen, noting that the arguments "take the language in *Turpin* further than is justified." Today, the law seems to focus particularly on whether the challenged classification is based on stereotype or disadvantage. *See, e.g., Kapp, supra*. Although not articulated in the same way, the Supreme Court of Canada seems to be adopting an approach similar to that expressed by the U.S. Supreme Court in *Vance v. Bradley, supra*. Legislative classifications that adversely affect disadvantaged groups and that are based on stereotype are those that require careful judicial scrutiny. Where legislation adversely affects a group not subject to disadvantage, or classifies in a tailored way that is not based on stereotype, then the political process can be relied upon to remedy any unfairness.

Because the Australian statutory approach, at the Commonwealth level, is grounded in fulfilling the nation's international human rights obligations, the groups that are protected are those identified under international conventions which Australia has ratified. This is not to say that all such groups automatically receive protection from discrimination under Australian law: the UN Convention on the Rights of the Child, for example, has been ratified by Australia but not yet incorporated into specific legislation (the fact of ratification, however, has been invoked by the High Court in a controversial case concerning the deportation of a non-citizen, the father of Australian children, as a background fact to which an administrative decision-making should pay attention in making a determination: *Minister for Immigration and Ethnic Affairs v. Teoh* (1995) 183 CLR 273)).

The Commonwealth parliament has also recently passed a general *Human Rights (Parliamentary Scrutiny) Act* 2010 which, among other things, requires executive and legislation attention to whether legislation is compatible with the rights protected under the seven principal United Nations Conventions, regardless of whether these have been domestically incorporated, and also empowers the courts to draw on these Conventions in interpreting statutes.

The absence of equality provisions in the Constitution does not mean a shortage of debate in Australia about the rights, either current or proposed, of minority groups. Debates about whether persons of the same sex should be permitted to marry are as robust in Australia as elsewhere, and these have a constitutional dimension: the High Court has recently decided that parliament's power to pass laws with respect to "marriage" (section 51(xxi) of the Constitution) extends to an amendment to Australia's current *Marriage Act* which would authorise same-sex marriage, were such an amendment passed. Current High Court jurisprudence suggests that the parliament does not have the power to define "marriage" to mean just anything it wants. However, the scope of "marriage," in the sense of what makes something a "marriage" in the first place, would appear to be open.

In 2012, an Expert Panel on Constitutional Recognition of Aboriginal and Torres Strait Islander Peoples, appointed by the Commonwealth government, handed down a report proposing constitutional amendments including, among other things, the insertion of a provision prohibiting discrimination "on the grounds of race, colour or ethnic or national origin," as well as provisions recognising the historical place of Australia's indigenous peoples and empowering the parliament to make laws for their "advancement." The government has undertaken to respond to these proposals after they have been publicly discussed.

4.4. INTENTIONAL DISCRIMINATION OR DISPARATE IMPACT

Canadian and American courts have taken sharply different paths in this regard, as the following two cases demonstrate. Keep in mind the distinction between statutory and constitutional prohibitions. As this Part shows, the Canadian approach has been followed by South Africa as a matter of constitutional law (see *Harksen v. Lane NO* above), Australia as a matter of statute, and the United States as a matter of implementing administrative regulations.

PERSONNEL ADMINISTRATOR OF MASSACHUSETTS v. FEENEY

SUPREME COURT OF THE UNITED STATES
442 U.S. 256 (1979)

STEWART, J., delivered the opinion of the Court, in which BURGER, C.J., and WHITE, POWELL, BLACKMUN, REHNQUIST, and STEVENS, JJ., joined.

This case presents a challenge to the constitutionality of the Massachusetts veterans' preference statute, Mass. Gen. Laws Ann., ch. 31, § 23, on the ground that it discriminates against women in violation of the Equal Protection Clause of the Fourteenth Amendment. Under ch. 31, § 23, all veterans who qualify for state civil service positions must be considered for appointment ahead of any qualifying nonveterans. The preference operates overwhelmingly to the advantage of males.

The appellee Helen B. Feeney is not a veteran. She brought this action pursuant to 42 U.S.C. § 1983, alleging that the absolute-preference formula established in ch. 31, § 23, inevitably operates to exclude women from consideration for the best Massachusetts civil service jobs and thus unconstitutionally denies them the equal protection of the laws.[21] The three-judge District Court agreed, one judge dissenting.

The District Court found that the absolute preference afforded by Massachusetts to veterans has a devastating impact upon the employment opportunities of women. Although it found that the goals of the preference were worthy and legitimate and that the legislation had not been enacted for the purpose of discriminating against women, the court reasoned that its exclusionary impact upon women was nonetheless so severe as to require the State to further its goals through a more limited form of preference. Finding that a more modest preference formula would readily accommodate the State's interest in aiding veterans, the court declared ch. 31, § 23, unconstitutional and enjoined its operation.

Upon an appeal taken by the Attorney General of Massachusetts, this Court vacated the judgment and remanded the case for further consideration in light of our intervening decision in *Washington v. Davis*, 426 U.S. 229. *Massachusetts v. Feeney*, 434 U.S. 884. The *Davis* case held that a neutral law does not violate the Equal Protection Clause solely because it results in a racially disproportionate impact; instead the disproportionate impact must be traced to a purpose to discriminate on the basis of race. 426 U.S., at 238–244.

* * *

I

[The Court noted the widespread practice of providing hiring preferences to veterans, although Massachusetts' preference is particularly generous. It applies to all veterans, male or female. However, at time of suit over 98% of veterans were male.]

II

* * *

A

The equal protection guarantee of the Fourteenth Amendment does not take from the States all power of classification. Most laws classify, and many affect certain groups unevenly, even though the law itself treats them no differently from all other members of the class described by the law. When the basic classification is rationally based, uneven effects upon particular groups within a class are ordinarily of no constitutional concern. The calculus of effects, the manner in which a particular law reverberates in a society, is a legislative and not a judicial responsi-

---

[21] [FN 13] No statutory claim was brought under Title VII of the Civil Rights Act of 1964 [which has been interpreted to bar employment practices that have a disproportionate impact on race or sex unless justified by "business necessity."] Section 712 of the Act, 42 U. S. C. § 2000e-11, provides that "[nothing] contained in this subchapter shall be construed to repeal or modify any Federal, State, territorial or local law creating special rights or preference for veterans." The parties have evidently assumed that this provision precludes a Title VII challenge.

bility. In assessing an equal protection challenge, a court is called upon only to measure the basic validity of the legislative classification. When some other independent right is not at stake, see, e. g., *Shapiro v. Thompson*, 394 U.S. 618, [involving the right to travel] and when there is no "reason to infer antipathy," *Vance v. Bradley*, 440 U.S. 93, 97, it is presumed that "even improvident decisions will eventually be rectified by the democratic process . . . ." *Ibid.* Certain classifications, however, in themselves supply a reason to infer antipathy. Race is the paradigm. A racial classification, regardless of purported motivation, is presumptively invalid and can be upheld only upon an extraordinary justification. *Brown v. Board of Education*, 347 U.S. 483; *McLaughlin v. Florida*, 379 U.S. 184. This rule applies as well to a classification that is ostensibly neutral but is an obvious pretext for racial discrimination. But, as was made clear in *Washington v. Davis*, 426 U.S. 229, and *Arlington Heights v. Metropolitan Housing Dev. Corp.*, 429 U.S. 252, even if a neutral law has a disproportionately adverse effect upon a racial minority, it is unconstitutional under the Equal Protection Clause only if that impact can be traced to a discriminatory purpose. [*Davis* upheld a job-related employment test that white people passed in proportionately greater numbers than black applicants, for there had been no showing that racial discrimination entered into the establishment or formulation of the test. *Arlington Heights* upheld a zoning board decision that tended to perpetuate racially segregated housing patterns, since, apart from its effect, the board's decision was shown to be nothing more than an application of a constitutionally neutral zoning policy.]

Classifications based upon gender, not unlike those based upon race, have traditionally been the touchstone for pervasive and often subtle discrimination. This Court's recent cases teach that such classifications must bear a close and substantial relationship to important governmental objectives, *Craig v. Boren*, 429 U.S. 190, 197, and are in many settings unconstitutional. Although public employment is not a constitutional right, and the States have wide discretion in framing employee qualifications, these precedents dictate that any state law overtly or covertly designed to prefer males over females in public employment would require an exceedingly persuasive justification to withstand a constitutional challenge under the Equal Protection Clause of the Fourteenth Amendment.

B

The cases of *Washington v. Davis, supra,* and *Arlington Heights v. Metropolitan Housing Dev. Corp., supra,* recognize that when a neutral law has a disparate impact upon a group that has historically been the victim of discrimination, an unconstitutional purpose may still be at work. But those cases signaled no departure from the settled rule that the Fourteenth Amendment guarantees equal laws, not equal results. *** When a statute gender-neutral on its face is challenged on the ground that its effects upon women are disproportionably adverse, a twofold inquiry is thus appropriate. The first question is whether the statutory classification is indeed neutral in the sense that it is not gender based. If the classification itself, covert or overt, is not based upon gender, the second question is whether the adverse effect reflects invidious gender-based discrimination. ***

It is against this background of precedent that we consider the merits of the case before us.

III

A

[Ms. Feeney conceded that the veterans preference was neither established for the purpose of discriminating against women, nor was a pretext for gender discrimination; rather, the state created the preference for a legitimate and worthy purpose, although she argued the absolute preference went too far.]

If the impact of this statute could not be plausibly explained on a neutral ground, impact itself would signal that the real classification made by the law was in fact not neutral. See *Washington v. Davis*, 426 U.S. at 242; *Arlington Heights v. Metropolitan Housing Dev. Corp., supra*, at 266. But there can be but one answer to the question whether this veteran preference excludes significant numbers of women from preferred state jobs because they are women or because they are nonveterans. Apart from the facts that the definition of "veterans" in the statute has always been neutral as to gender and that Massachusetts has consistently defined veteran status in a way that has been inclusive of women who have served in the military, this is not a law that can plausibly be explained only as a gender-based classification. Indeed, it is not a law that can rationally be explained on that ground. Veteran status is not uniquely male. Although few women benefit from the preference, the nonveteran class is not substantially all female. To the contrary, significant numbers of nonveterans are men, and all nonveterans — male as well as female — are placed at a disadvantage. Too many men are affected by ch. 31, § 23, to permit the inference that the statute is but a pretext for preferring men over women.

* * *

B

* * *

1

[The Court rejected the argument that the State had incorporated prior federal law discriminating against women in regard to military service. The concession that the discrimination was not intentional meant that the preference was not adopted with the *intent* to incorporate prior discrimination. Moreover, it is inconsistent with Feeney's concession that some more modest veterans' preference would be acceptable.] Invidious discrimination does not become less so because the discrimination accomplished is of a lesser magnitude.[22] Discriminatory intent is simply not

---

[22] [FN 23] This is not to say that the degree of impact is irrelevant to the question of intent. But it is to say that a more modest preference, while it might well lessen impact and, as the State argues, might lessen the effectiveness of the statute in helping veterans, would not be any more or less "neutral" in the constitutional sense.

amenable to calibration. It either is a factor that has influenced the legislative choice or it is not. The District Court's conclusion that the absolute veterans' preference was not originally enacted or subsequently reaffirmed for the purpose of giving an advantage to males as such necessarily compels the conclusion that the State intended nothing more than to prefer "veterans." Given this finding, simple logic suggests that an intent to exclude women from significant public jobs was not at work in this law. To reason that it was, by describing the preference as "inherently nonneutral" or "gender-biased," is merely to restate the fact of impact, not to answer the question of intent.

*   *   *

2

The appellee's ultimate argument rests upon the presumption, common to the criminal and civil law, that a person intends the natural and foreseeable consequences of his voluntary actions. ***

"Discriminatory purpose," however, implies more than intent as volition or intent as awareness of consequences. See *United Jewish Organizations v. Carey*, 430 U.S. 144, 179 (concurring opinion). It implies that the decisionmaker, in this case a state legislature, selected or reaffirmed a particular course of action at least in part "because of," not merely "in spite of," its adverse effects upon an identifiable group.[23] Yet nothing in the record demonstrates that this preference for veterans was originally devised or subsequently re-enacted because it would accomplish the collateral goal of keeping women in a stereotypic and predefined place in the Massachusetts Civil Service.

[Mr. Justice Stevens, with whom Mr. Justice White joins, concurred, finding that] the fact that the number of males disadvantaged by Massachusetts' veterans' preference (1,867,000) is sufficiently large — and sufficiently close to the number of disadvantaged females (2,954,000) — to refute the claim that the rule was *intended* to benefit males as a class over females as a class.

Mr. Justice Marshall, with whom Mr. Justice Brennan joins, dissenting.

[The dissent found purposeful discriminatio that was not substantially related to a legitimate governmental objective. It notes that judges cannot ascertain the sole or dominant purpose behind a statute, because lawmakers frequently act for a variety of reasons. "Thus, the critical constitutional inquiry is not whether an illicit consideration was the primary or but-for cause of a decision, but rather whether it

---

[23] [FN 25] This is not to say that the inevitability or foreseeability of consequences of a neutral rule has no bearing upon the existence of discriminatory intent. Certainly, when the adverse consequences of a law upon an identifiable group are as inevitable as the gender-based consequences of ch. 31, § 23, a strong inference that the adverse effects were desired can reasonably be drawn. But in this inquiry — made as it is under the Constitution — an inference is a working tool, not a synonym for proof. When, as here, the impact is essentially an unavoidable consequence of a legislative policy that has in itself always been deemed to be legitimate, and when, as here, the statutory history and all of the available evidence affirmatively demonstrate the opposite, the inference simply fails to ripen into proof.

had an appreciable role in shaping a given legislative enactment." The key, citing *Arlington Heights* at 265–66, is "proof that a discriminatory purpose has been a motivating factor in the decision." In Marshall, J.'s view, where "the foreseeable impact of a facially neutral policy is so disproportionate, the burden should rest on the State to establish that sex-based considerations played no part in the choice of the particular legislative scheme."]

Clearly, that burden was not sustained here. The legislative history of the statute reflects the Commonwealth's patent appreciation of the impact the preference system would have on women, and an equally evident desire to mitigate that impact only with respect to certain traditionally female occupations. Until 1971, the statute and implementing civil service regulations exempted from operation of the preference any job requisitions "especially calling for women." 1954 Mass. Acts, ch. 627, § 5. See also 1896 Mass. Acts, ch. 517, § 6; 1919 Mass. Acts, ch. 150, § 2; 1945 Mass. Acts, ch. 725, § 2 (e); 1965 Mass. Acts, ch. 53; ante, at 266 nn. 13, 14. In practice, this exemption, coupled with the absolute preference for veterans, has created a gender-based civil service hierarchy, with women occupying low-grade clerical and secretarial jobs and men holding more responsible and remunerative positions.

Thus, for over 70 years, the Commonwealth has maintained, as an integral part of its veterans' preference system, an exemption relegating female civil service applicants to occupations traditionally filled by women. Such a statutory scheme both reflects and perpetuates precisely the kind of archaic assumptions about women's roles which we have previously held invalid. Particularly when viewed against the range of less discriminatory alternatives available to assist veterans [only four states have such a generous veterans preference], Massachusetts' choice of a formula that so severely restricts public employment opportunities for women cannot reasonably be thought gender-neutral. The Court's conclusion to the contrary — that "nothing in the record" evinces a "collateral goal of keeping women in a stereotypic and predefined place in the Massachusetts Civil Service," ante, at 279 — displays a singularly myopic view of the facts established below.[24]

ELDRIDGE v. BRITISH COLUMBIA (ATTORNEY GENERAL)
Supreme Court of Canada
[1997] 3 S.C.R. 624

[Before: Lamer C.J. and La Forest, L'Heureux-Dube, Sopinka, Gonthier, Cory, McLachlin, Iacobucci and Major JJ.]

The judgment of the Court was delivered by

[1] La Forest J. — This appeal raises the question whether a provincial government's failure to provide funding for sign language interpreters for deaf persons

---

[24] [FN 2] Although it is relevant that the preference statute also disadvantages a substantial group of men, it is equally pertinent that 47% of Massachusetts men over 18 are veterans, as compared to 0.8% of Massachusetts women. Given this disparity, and the indicia of intent noted supra, at 284-285, the absolute number of men denied preference cannot be dispositive, especially since they have not faced the barriers to achieving veteran status confronted by women.

when they receive medical services violates s. 15(1) of the Canadian Charter of Rights and Freedoms. The appellants assert that, because of the communication barrier that exists between deaf persons and health care providers, they receive a lesser quality of medical services than hearing persons. The failure to pay for interpreters, they contend, infringes their right to equal benefit of the law without discrimination based on physical disability.

[2] Medical care in British Columbia is delivered through two primary mechanisms. Hospital services are funded by the government through the *Hospital Insurance Act*, which reimburses hospitals for the medically required services they provide to the public. Funding for medically required services delivered by doctors and other health care practitioners is provided by the province's Medical Services Plan, which is established and regulated by the [statute] now known as the *Medicare Protection Act*. Neither of these programs pays for sign language interpretation for the deaf.

*   *   *

[At trial, appellants presented testimony about their need for medical services and the difficulty in obtaining services without a sign language interpreter. The respondents presented evidence relating to the budgetary process of the Ministry of Health and the structure of the Medical Services Plan. Hospitals in British Columbia are funded through lump sum "global" payments that they are for the most part free to allocate as they see fit. They are rarely ordered by government to provide specific services. Under the *Medicare Protection Act*, all persons resident in British Columbia for three months are entitled to benefits including "medically required services."]

[The Court next noted that, as deaf persons, the appellants belong to an enumerated group under s. 15(1) — the physically disabled.]

[56] It is an unfortunate truth that the history of disabled persons in Canada is largely one of exclusion and marginalization. Persons with disabilities have too often been excluded from the labour force, denied access to opportunities for social interaction and advancement, subjected to invidious stereotyping and relegated to institutions; see generally M. David Lepofsky, "A Report Card on the Charter's Guarantee of Equality to Persons with Disabilities after 10 Years — What Progress? What Prospects?" (1997), 7 N.J.C.L. 263. This historical disadvantage has to a great extent been shaped and perpetuated by the notion that disability is an abnormality or flaw. As a result, disabled persons have not generally been afforded the "equal concern, respect and consideration" that s. 15(1) of the Charter demands. Instead, they have been subjected to paternalistic attitudes of pity and charity, and their entrance into the social mainstream has been conditional upon their emulation of able-bodied norms; see Sandra A. Goundry and Yvonne Peters, *Litigating for Disability Equality Rights: The Promises and the Pitfalls* (1994), at pp. 5-6. One consequence of these attitudes is the persistent social and economic disadvantage faced by the disabled. Statistics indicate that persons with disabilities, in comparison to non-disabled persons, have less education, are more likely to be outside the labour force, face much higher unemployment rates, and are concentrated at the lower end of the pay scale when employed; see Minister of Human Resources Development, *Persons with Disabilities: A Supplementary Paper* (1994),

at pp. 3–4, and Statistics Canada, *A Portrait of Persons with Disabilities* (1995), at pp. 46-49.

*   *   *

[61] This Court has consistently held that s. 15(1) of the Charter protects against [adverse effects] discrimination. In *Andrews, supra,* McIntyre J. found that facially neutral laws may be discriminatory. "It must be recognized at once," he commented, at p. 164, ". . . that every difference in treatment between individuals under the law will not necessarily result in inequality and, as well, that identical treatment may frequently produce serious inequality." Section 15(1), the Court held, was intended to ensure a measure of substantive, and not merely formal equality.

[The Court expressly noted that "a discriminatory purpose or intention is not a necessary condition of a s. 15(1) violation." Rather, it "is sufficient if the effect of the legislation is to deny someone the equal protection or benefit of the law."] As McIntyre J. stated in *Andrews,* at p. 165, "to approach the ideal of full equality before and under the law . . . the main consideration must be the impact of the law on the individual or the group concerned." In this the Court has staked out a different path than the United States Supreme Court, which requires a discriminatory intent in order to ground an equal protection claim under the Fourteenth Amendment of the Constitution.

[63] This Court first addressed the concept of adverse effects discrimination in the context of provincial human rights legislation. In [*Ontario Human Rights Commission v. Simpsons-Sears Ltd.,* [1985] 2 S.C.R. 536], the Court was faced with the question of whether a rule requiring employees to be available for work on Friday evenings and Saturdays discriminated against those observing a Saturday Sabbath. Though this rule was neutral on its face in that it applied equally to all employees, the Court nevertheless found it to be discriminatory.* * *

I note that in *Andrews,* McIntyre J. made it clear that the equality principles developed by the Court in human rights cases are equally applicable in s. 15(1) cases. ***

[64] Adverse effects discrimination is especially relevant in the case of disability. The government will rarely single out disabled persons for discriminatory treatment. More common are laws of general application that have a disparate impact on the disabled. This was recognized by the Chief Justice in his dissenting opinion in *Rodriguez, supra,* where he held that the law criminalizing assisted suicide violated s. 15(1) of the Charter by discriminating on the basis of physical disability. There, a majority of the Court determined, inter alia, that the law was saved by s. 1 of the Charter, assuming without deciding that it infringed s. 15(1). While I refrain from commenting on the correctness of the Chief Justice's conclusion on the application of s. 15(1) in that case, I endorse his general approach to the scope of that provision, which he set out as follows, at p. 549:

> "Not only does s. 15(1) require the government to exercise greater caution in making express or direct distinctions based on personal characteristics, but legislation equally applicable to everyone is also capable of infringing the right to equality enshrined in that provision, and so of having to be justified in terms of s. 1. Even in imposing generally applicable provisions,

the government must take into account differences which in fact exist between individuals and so far as possible ensure that the provisions adopted will not have a greater impact on certain classes of persons due to irrelevant personal characteristics than on the public as a whole. In other words, to promote the objective of the more equal society, s. 15(1) acts as a bar to the executive enacting provisions without taking into account their possible impact on already disadvantaged classes of persons."

*   *   *

[65] The Court elaborated upon this principle in its recent decision in *Eaton [v. Brant County Board of Education*, [1997] 1 S.C.R. 241]. Although *Eaton* involved direct discrimination [the plaintiff, a disabled student, had been excluded from mainstream classes], Sopinka J. observed that in the case of disabled persons, it is often the failure to take into account the adverse effects of generally applicable laws that results in discrimination. [Unlike other forms of discrimination, *Eaton* held that discrimination against the disabled lies not in the attribution of untrue characteristics but rather "the failure to make reasonable accommodation, to fine-tune society so that its structures and assumptions do not result in the relegation and banishment of disabled persons from participation."]

[66] Unlike in *Simpsons-Sears* and *Rodriguez*, in the present case the adverse effects suffered by deaf persons stem not from the imposition of a burden not faced by the mainstream population, but rather from a failure to ensure that they benefit equally from a service offered to everyone. It is on this basis that the trial judge and the majority of the Court of Appeal found that the failure to provide medically related sign language interpretation was not discriminatory. Their analyses presuppose that there is a categorical distinction to be made between state-imposed burdens and benefits, and that the government is not obliged to ameliorate disadvantage that it has not helped to create or exacerbate.

*   *   *

[The Court explained why an interpreter was essential to effective medical treatment, and rejected the claim that "governments should be entitled to provide benefits to the general population without ensuring that disadvantaged members of society have the resources to take full advantage of those benefits."]

[73] In my view, this position bespeaks a thin and impoverished vision of s. 15(1). It is belied, more importantly, by the thrust of this Court's equality jurisprudence. It has been suggested that s. 15(1) of the Charter does not oblige the state to take positive actions, such as provide services to ameliorate the symptoms of systemic or general inequality. *** Whether or not this is true in all cases, and I do not purport to decide the matter here, the question raised in the present case is of a wholly different order. This Court has repeatedly held that once the state does provide a benefit, it is obliged to do so in a non-discriminatory manner. In many circumstances, this will require governments to take positive action, for example by extending the scope of a benefit to a previously excluded class of persons. ***

[74] The same principle has been applied by this Court in its interpretation of the equality provisions of provincial human rights legislation. In *Brooks v. Canada*

Safeway Ltd., [1989] 1 S.C.R. 1219, the Court found that an employer's accident and sickness insurance plan, which disentitled pregnant women from receiving benefits for any reason during a certain period, discriminated on the basis of pregnancy and hence sex. In so holding, it resoundingly rejected the reasoning of *Bliss v. Attorney General of Canada*, [1979] 1 S.C.R. 183, at p. 190, which had held that the inequality resulting from a similar benefit program was "not created by legislation but by nature."

* * *

[78] The principle that discrimination can accrue from a failure to take positive steps to ensure that disadvantaged groups benefit equally from services offered to the general public is widely accepted in the human rights field. In *Re Saskatchewan Human Rights Commission and Canadian Odeon Theatres Ltd.* (1985), 18 D.L.R. (4th) 93 (Sask. C.A.), leave to appeal refused, [1985] 1 S.C.R. vi, the court found that the failure of a theatre to provide a disabled person a choice of place from which to view a film comparable to that offered to the general public was discriminatory. Similarly, in *Howard v. University of British Columbia* (1993), 18 C.H.R.R. D/353, it was held that the university was obligated to provide a deaf student with a sign language interpreter for his classes. "Without interpreters," the Human Rights Council held, at p. D/358, "the complainant did not have meaningful access to the service." And in *Centre de la communaute sourde du Montreal metropolitain inc. v. Regie du logement*, [1996] R.J.Q. 1776, the Quebec Tribunal des droits de la personne determined that a rent review tribunal must accommodate a deaf litigant by providing sign language interpretation. Moreover, the principle underlying all of these cases was affirmed in *Haig, supra*, where a majority of this Court wrote, at p. 1041, that "a government may be required to take positive steps to ensure the equality of people or groups who come within the scope of s. 15."

[79] It is also a cornerstone of human rights jurisprudence, of course, that the duty to take positive action to ensure that members of disadvantaged groups benefit equally from services offered to the general public is subject to the principle of reasonable accommodation. The obligation to make reasonable accommodation for those adversely affected by a facially neutral policy or rule extends only to the point of "undue hardship." In my view, in s. 15(1) cases this principle is best addressed as a component of the s. 1 analysis. Reasonable accommodation, in this context, is generally equivalent to the concept of "reasonable limits." It should not be employed to restrict the ambit of s. 15(1).

* * *

[81] I acknowledge that the standard I have set is a broad one. Given the nature of the evidentiary record before this Court, however, it would not be appropriate to elaborate it in any detail. Some guidance can be provided, however (and I stress that it is guidance — not authoritative pronouncement), by the experience in the United States under the *Rehabilitation Act*, 29 U.S.C. § 794 (1997), and the *Americans with Disabilities Act*, 42 U.S.C. §§ 12182–12189 (1997). [Under U.S. law, the Court suggests that hospitals would have to provide interpreters for deaf patients.]

* * *

[The Court then explained that the failure to provide interpreters was not a reasonable limit under s. 1, basically finding a lack of "reasonable accommodation."]

4.5.   SAME-SEX MARRIAGE

In the wake of Supreme Court of Canada decisions holding sexual orientation to be an analogous ground under s. 15, a number of lower Canadian courts held that the federal law limiting marriage to opposite-sex couples violated the Charter (recall that, under s. 91(26), marriage and divorce are matters of federal legislation in Canada). Parliament responded by amending the statute to permit gay marriages. (A discussion of the history is summarized in *Reference re Same-Sex Marriage*, [2004] 3 S.C.R. 698.)

In Australia, same-sex marriage has also emerged as an issue in recent years. The Commonwealth exercises constitutional power over marriage and divorce, ss. 51(xxi) & (xxii). Although this is a concurrent, not an exclusive power, Commonwealth law has applied (through the force of the inconsistency — or supremacy — section, s. 109), since the first Commonwealth *Marriage Act* in 1961. The 1961 Act did not make any reference to the gender of married persons (heterosexual marriage was assumed). In 2004, it was amended to state expressly that "*marriage means the union of a man and a woman* . . . ." The amendment also stated that same-sex marriages recognised under the law of another country *must not* be recognised in Australian law. Although these amendments were made by a conservative (Liberal Party) government, they were not altered or repealed by the non-conservative Labor government (2007-2013). However, in 2008, the Commonwealth passed laws recognising the legal rights of same-sex couples, similar to the rights of unmarried heterosexual couples, in areas such as taxation, social security and health, aged care, and employment. (This law was welcomed by Justice Michael Kirby of the High Court of Australia, an openly gay judge, who is said to have waited for its passage before retiring from the Court, ahead of his constitutionally required retirement age of 70.) In 2006, the Commonwealth government also used its constitutional "Territories power" (s. 122) to disallow the *Civil Unions Act* passed by the Australian Capital Territory [ACT], an Act purporting to recognize same-sex partnerships. In late 2013, the ACT legislature passed the *Marriage Equality (Same-Sex) Act*. The Act purported to extend only to same-sex marriages within the jurisdiction. It was immediately challenged by the Commonwealth and struck down by the High Court on the ground of inconsistency with the Commonwealth's *Marriage Act*. The Court held, however, that the Commonwealth is constitutionally empowered to legalize same-sex marriage, if and when the Parliament decides.

The Commonwealth *Marriage Act* is currently considered to "cover the field" of marriage (that is to say, under the s 109 inconsistency test, it overrides any inconsistent state laws). The Commonwealth is, however, constitutionally unable to prevent the recognition of civil unions under state laws. Tasmania was the first state to legislate, in 2003, to recognise same-sex unions. Discrimination on the ground of sexuality had been prohibited by the previous Labor government in 1994, with the passage of the *Human Rights (Sexual Conduct) Act Cth*. This Act relies on the right to privacy provision of the United Nations International Covenant on Civil and

Political Rights, and does not extend to marriage rights (international law recognizes the human right to marry and found a family, but does not extend this right to same-sex couples). In 1997, the High Court heard a challenge to a long-standing Tasmanian law that criminalized "carnal knowledge of any person against the order of nature" and "indecent practices between male persons." The state law had not been enforced for many years, but the plaintiff, a gay Tasmanian man, claimed that he remained susceptible to prosecution; he sought a declaration that the law was inconsistent with the Commonwealth Act. Tasmania attempted, unsuccessfully, to have the action set aside for lack of a "matter" (a concrete, justiciable controversy), *Croome v. Tasmania* (1997) 191 CLR 119. The likelihood was very high that the Court, having accepted the case, would find an inconsistency between the two laws (and with that, the invalidation of the Tasmanian law); Tasmania repealed its law before the case proceeded further.

In South Africa the Constitutional Court ruled in *Minister of Home Affairs v. Fourie* that "the failure of the common law and the *Marriage Act* to provide the means whereby same-sex couples can enjoy the same status, entitlements and responsibilities accorded to heterosexual couples through marriage, constitutes an unjustifiable violation of their right to equal protection of the law under section 9(1), and not to be discriminated against unfairly in terms of section 9(3) of the Constitution." At the same time the Court gave Parliament, the national legislature, one year to adopt legislation that would "ensure that same-sex couples are brought in from the legal cold." In response Parliament adopted and the President signed into law the *Civil Union Act 17 of 2006* which defines a civil union as "the voluntary union of two persons who are both 18 years of age or older which is solemnized and registered by way of either a marriage or a civil partnership in accordance with the procedures proscribed in this Act to the exclusion while it lasts of all others." The result is that anyone may marry under the Civil Union law which provides the same legal status as the *Marriage Act*; however only heterosexual couples may marry under the old *Marriage Act* which remains in force for those who choose to use it.

MINISTER OF HOME AFFAIRS v. FOURIE

CONSTITUTIONAL COURT OF SOUTH AFRICA

2006 (1) SA 524

SACHS J:

[1] Finding themselves strongly attracted to each other, two people went out regularly and eventually decided to set up home together. After being acknowledged by their friends as a couple for more than a decade, they decided that the time had come to get public recognition and registration of their relationship, and formally to embrace the rights and responsibilities they felt should flow from and attach to it. Like many persons in their situation, they wanted to get married. There was one impediment. They are both women.

[2] Ms Marié Adriaana Fourie and Ms Cecelia Johanna Bonthuys are the applicants in the first of two cases that were set down for hearing on the same day in this Court. Their complaint has been that the law excludes them from publicly celebrating their love and commitment to each other in marriage. Far from enabling

them to regularise their union, it shuts them out, unfairly and unconstitutionally, they claim.

[3] They contend that the exclusion comes from the common law definition which states that marriage in South Africa is "a union of one man with one woman, to the exclusion, while it lasts, of all others." The common law is not self-enforcing, and in order for such a union to be formalised and have legal effect, the provisions of the Marriage Act have to be invoked. This, as contended for in the second case, is where the further level of exclusion operates. The Marriage Act provides that a minister of religion who is designated as a marriage officer may follow the marriage formula usually observed by the religion concerned. In terms of section 30(1) other marriage officers must put to each of the parties the following question:

> " 'Do you, A.B., declare that as far as you know there is no lawful impediment to your proposed marriage with C.D. here present, and that you call all here present to witness that you take C.D. as your lawful wife (or husband)?', and thereupon the parties shall give each other the right hand and the marriage officer concerned shall declare the marriage solemnized in the following words: 'I declare that A.B. and C.D. here present have been lawfully married.' "

The reference to wife (or husband) is said to exclude same-sex couples. It was not disputed by any of the parties that neither the common law nor statute provide for any legal mechanism in terms of which Ms Fourie and Ms Bonthuys and other same-sex couples could marry.

[4] In the pre-democratic era same-sex unions were not only denied any form of legal protection, they were regarded as immoral and their consummation by men could attract imprisonment. Since the interim Constitution came into force in 1994, however, the Bill of Rights has dramatically altered the situation.

. . . .

[32] [Summarizing the divided Supreme Court of Appeals judgements below Justice Sachs states] both judgments were in agreement that the SCA could and should rule that the common law definition discriminated unfairly against same-sex couples. The majority judgment by Cameron JA held, however, that although the common law definition should be developed so as to embrace same-sex couples, the Marriage Act could not be read in such a way as to include them. In the result, the only way the parties could marry would be under the auspices of a religious body that recognised same-sex marriages, and whose marriage formula was approved by the Minister of Home Affairs. The right of same-sex couples to celebrate a secular marriage would have to await a challenge to the Marriage Act. The minority judgment of Farlam JA, on the other hand, held both that the common law should be developed and that the Marriage Act could and should be read there and then in updated form so as to permit same-sex couples to pronounce the vows. In his view, however, the development of the common law to bring it into line with the Constitution should be suspended to enable Parliament to enact appropriate legislation. In support of an order of suspension he pointed out that the SALRC had indicated that there were three possible legislative responses to the unconstitution-

ality, and, in his view, it should be Parliament and not the judiciary that should choose.

[33] None of the parties to the litigation were satisfied with the outcome. The state noted an appeal on several grounds, revolving mainly around the proposition that it was not appropriate for the judiciary to bring about what it regarded as a momentous change to the institution of marriage, something, it contended, that should be left to Parliament. The applicants for their part were unhappy because although the newly developed definition of the common law included them in its terms, they were still prevented from getting married by the phrasing of the marriage vows in the Marriage Act. The only possible route enabling them to marry under the Act was a tenuous one, namely, to find a sympathetic religious denomination with an inclusive marriage vow that was approved by the Minister of Home Affairs. In their application to cross-appeal they accordingly supported the reasoning of Farlam JA regarding updating the Marriage Act, while objecting to his suspension of the development of the common law. At the same time they supported Cameron JA's finding that immediate relief should be granted to them, but objected to his decision that the Marriage Act barred them from taking the vows except in the limited circumstances to which he referred. The overall result was that the state has sought leave to appeal against the SCA's decision on the basis that it went too far, while the applicants have sought leave to cross-appeal on the grounds that it did not go far enough. It was common cause that the application in the Fourie matter by the state for leave to appeal and by the applicants for leave to cross-appeal, raise questions of considerable constitutional significance and social importance. It is in the interests of justice that they both be granted.

. . . .

[44] In essence the enquiry into the common law definition of marriage and the constitutional validity of section 30(1) of the Marriage Act is the same. Are gay and lesbian people unfairly discriminated against because they are prevented from achieving the status and benefits coupled with responsibilities which heterosexual couples acquire from marriage? If they are, both the common law definition as well as section 30(1) must have the effect of limiting the rights contained in section 9 of the Constitution. If not, both will be good. It must be emphasised that it is not possible for one of the two provisions concerning marriage that are under attack in this case to be consistent with the Constitution, and for the other to be constitutionally invalid. In the circumstances, a refusal to consider both together would amount to no more than technical nicety. In the circumstances of this case, therefore, it is clearly in the interests of justice that the application for direct access be granted and that the Fourie and the Equality Project matters be heard together.

[45] At the hearing two broad and interrelated questions were raised: The first was whether or not the failure by the common law and the Marriage Act to provide the means whereby same-sex couples can marry, constitutes unfair discrimination against them. If the answer was that it does, the second question arose, namely, what the appropriate remedy for the unconstitutionality should be. These are the central issues in this matter, and I will start with the first.

[46] Counsel for the Minister of Justice argued that the Constitution did not protect the right to marry. It merely guaranteed to same-sex couples the right to establish

their own forms of family life without interference from the state. This was a negative liberty, not to be equated with a right to be assimilated into the institution of marriage, which in terms of its historic genesis and evolution, was heterosexual by nature. International law recognised and protected marriage as so understood. Same-sex couples accordingly had no constitutional right to enter into or manipulate that institution. If their form of family life suffered from particular disadvantages, then these should be dealt with by appropriate legal remedies in response to each of the identified problems, not by entry into the global set of rights and entitlements established by marriage. Marriage law appropriately confined itself to marriage, it was contended, and not to all forms of family relationship.

[47] The initial proposition of the state's argument is undoubtedly correct inasmuch as the Bill of Rights does not expressly include a right to marry. It does not follow, however, that the Constitution does nothing to protect that right, and with it, the concomitant right to be treated equally and with dignity in the exercise of that right. Explaining why the right to marry had not been expressly included in the text of the Constitution as produced by the Constitutional Assembly, this Court in the First Certification case pointed out that families are constituted, function and are dissolved in such a variety of ways, and the possible outcomes of constitutionalising family rights are so uncertain, that Constitution-makers appear frequently to prefer not to regard the right to marry or to pursue family life as a fundamental right that is appropriate for definition in constitutionalised terms. This avoids questions that relate to the history, culture and special circumstances of each society. At the same time, the provisions of the constitutional text would clearly prohibit any arbitrary state interference with the right to marry or to establish and raise a family. The text enshrined the values of human dignity, equality and freedom. However these words might come to be interpreted in the future, the judgment said, it was evident that laws or executive action resulting in enforced marriages, or oppressive prohibitions on marriage or the choice of spouses, would not survive constitutional challenge.

[48] The way the words dignity, equality and privacy later came to be interpreted by this Court showed that they in fact turned out to be central to the way in which the exclusion of same-sex couples from marriage came to be evaluated. In a long line of cases, most of which were concerned with persons unable to get married because of their sexual orientation, this Court highlighted the significance for our equality jurisprudence of the concepts and values of human dignity, equality and freedom. It is these cases that must serve as the compass that guides analysis in the present matter, rather than the references made in argument to North American polemical literature or to religious texts.

[49] Although the Sodomy case, which was the first in the series, did not deal with access to marriage as such, it highlighted the seriously negative impact that societal discrimination on the ground of sexual orientation has had, and continues to have, on gays and same-sex partnerships. It concluded that gay men are a permanent minority in society and have suffered in the past from patterns of disadvantage.

. . . .

[59] This Court has thus in five consecutive decisions highlighted at least four unambiguous features of the context in which the prohibition against unfair

discrimination on grounds of sexual orientation must be analysed. The first is that South Africa has a multitude of family formations that are evolving rapidly as our society develops, so that it is inappropriate to entrench any particular form as the only socially and legally acceptable one. The second is the existence of an imperative constitutional need to acknowledge the long history in our country and abroad of marginalisation and persecution of gays and lesbians, that is, of persons who had the same general characteristics as the rest of the population, save for the fact that their sexual orientation was such that they expressed erotic desire and affinity for individuals of their own sex, and were socially defined as homosexual. The third is that although a number of breakthroughs have been made in particular areas, there is no comprehensive legal regulation of the family law rights of gays and lesbians. Finally, our Constitution represents a radical rupture with a past based on intolerance and exclusion, and the movement forward to the acceptance of the need to develop a society based on equality and respect by all for all. Small gestures in favour of equality, however meaningful, are not enough. In the memorable words of Mahomed J:

> "In some countries, the Constitution only formalises, in a legal instrument, a historical consensus of values and aspirations evolved incrementally from a stable and unbroken past to accommodate the needs of the future. The South African Constitution is different: it retains from the past only what is defensible and represents a decisive break from, and a ringing rejection of, that part of the past which is disgracefully racist, authoritarian, insular, and repressive, and a vigorous identification of and commitment to a democratic, universalistic, caring and aspirationally egalitarian ethos expressly articulated in the Constitution. The contrast between the past which it repudiates and the future to which it seeks to commit the nation is stark and dramatic." [*S v. Makwanyane and Another* 1995 (3) SA 391 (CC)]

[60] A democratic, universalistic, caring and aspirationally egalitarian society embraces everyone and accepts people for who they are. To penalise people for being who and what they are is profoundly disrespectful of the human personality and violatory of equality. Equality means equal concern and respect across difference. It does not presuppose the elimination or suppression of difference. Respect for human rights requires the affirmation of self, not the denial of self. Equality therefore does not imply a levelling or homogenisation of behaviour or extolling one form as supreme, and another as inferior, but an acknowledgement and acceptance of difference. At the very least, it affirms that difference should not be the basis for exclusion, marginalisation and stigma. At best, it celebrates the vitality that difference brings to any society. The issue goes well beyond assumptions of heterosexual exclusivity, a source of contention in the present case. The acknowledgement and acceptance of difference is particularly important in our country where for centuries group membership based on supposed biological characteristics such as skin colour has been the express basis of advantage and disadvantage. South Africans come in all shapes and sizes. The development of an active rather than a purely formal sense of enjoying a common citizenship depends on recognising and accepting people with all their differences, as they are. The Constitution thus acknowledges the variability of human beings (genetic and socio-cultural), affirms the right to be different, and celebrates the diversity of the

nation. Accordingly, what is at stake is not simply a question of removing an injustice experienced by a particular section of the community. At issue is a need to affirm the very character of our society as one based on tolerance and mutual respect. The test of tolerance is not how one finds space for people with whom, and practices with which, one feels comfortable, but how one accommodates the expression of what is discomfiting.

. . . .

[70] Marriage law thus goes well beyond its earlier purpose in the common law of legitimising sexual relations and securing succession of legitimate heirs to family property. And it is much more than a mere piece of paper. As the SALRC Paper comments, the rights and obligations associated with marriage are vast. Besides other important purposes served by marriage, as an institution it was (at the time the SALRC Paper was produced) the only source of socio-economic benefits such as the right to inheritance, medical insurance coverage, adoption, access to wrongful death claims, spousal benefits, bereavement leave, tax advantages and post-divorce rights.

[71] The exclusion of same-sex couples from the benefits and responsibilities of marriage, accordingly, is not a small and tangential inconvenience resulting from a few surviving relics of societal prejudice destined to evaporate like the morning dew. It represents a harsh if oblique statement by the law that same-sex couples are outsiders, and that their need for affirmation and protection of their intimate relations as human beings is somehow less than that of heterosexual couples. It reinforces the wounding notion that they are to be treated as biological oddities, as failed or lapsed human beings who do not fit into normal society, and, as such, do not qualify for the full moral concern and respect that our Constitution seeks to secure for everyone. It signifies that their capacity for love, commitment and accepting responsibility is by definition less worthy of regard than that of heterosexual couples.

. . . .

[78] Sections 9(1) and 9(3) [the equality clauses] cannot be read as merely protecting same-sex couples from punishment or stigmatisation. They also go beyond simply preserving a private space in which gay and lesbian couples may live together without interference from the state. Indeed, what the applicants in this matter seek is not the right to be left alone, but the right to be acknowledged as equals and to be embraced with dignity by the law. Their love that was once forced to be clandestine, may now dare openly to speak its name. The world in which they live and in which the Constitution functions, has evolved from repudiating expressions of their desire to accepting the reality of their presence, and the integrity, in its own terms, of their intimate life. Accordingly, taking account of the decisions of this Court, and bearing in mind the symbolic and practical impact that exclusion from marriage has on same-sex couples, there can only be one answer to the question as to whether or not such couples are denied equal protection and subjected to unfair discrimination. Clearly, they are, and in no small degree. The effect has been wounding and the scars are evident in our society to this day. By both drawing on and reinforcing discriminatory social practices, the law in the past failed to secure for same-sex couples the dignity, status, benefits and responsibilities that it accords

to heterosexual couples. Although considerable progress has been made in specific cases through constitutional interpretation, and, as will be seen, by means of legislative intervention, the default position of gays and lesbians is still one of exclusion and marginalisation. The common law and section 30(1) of the Marriage Act continue to deny to same-sex couples equal protection and benefit of the law, in conflict with section 9(1) of the Constitution, and taken together result in same-sex couples being subjected to unfair discrimination by the state in conflict with section 9(3) of the Constitution.

[79] At the very least, then, the applicants in both matters are entitled to a declaration to the effect that same-sex couples are denied equal protection of the law under section 9(1), and subjected to unfair discrimination under section 9(3) of the Constitution, to the extent that the law makes no provision for them to achieve the dignity, status, benefits and responsibilities available to heterosexual couples through marriage . . . .

. . . .

[114] I conclude that the failure of the common law and the Marriage Act to provide the means whereby same-sex couples can enjoy the same status, entitlements and responsibilities accorded to heterosexual couples through marriage, constitutes an unjustifiable violation of their right to equal protection of the law under section 9(1), and not to be discriminated against unfairly in terms of section 9(3) of the Constitution. Furthermore, and for the reasons given in Home Affairs, such failure represents an unjustifiable violation of their right to dignity in terms of section 10 of the Constitution. As this Court said in that matter, the rights of dignity and equality are closely related. The exclusion to which same-sex couples are subjected, manifestly affects their dignity as members of society.

. . . .

[118] As I have already concluded, the common law and section 30(1) of the Marriage Act are inconsistent with sections 9(1) and 9(3) and 10 of the Constitution to the extent that they make no provision for same-sex couples to enjoy the status, entitlements and responsibilities it accords to heterosexual couples. In terms of section 172(1)(a) of the Constitution, this Court must that declare any law inconsistent with the Constitution is invalid to that extent. Under section 172(1)(b) it is then open to the Court to make any order that is just and equitable. Such order may include suspending the declaration of invalidity to give the legislature time to cure the defect.

. . . .

[122] In deciding on the appropriate remedy in the present matter the possibility of altering the common law through legislative action so as to bring it into line with the Bill of Rights becomes highly relevant. Having heard the Fourie matter together with the Equality Project matter, we can take account of the impact that any correction to the Act, or enactment of a separate statute, would automatically have on the common law. Thus a legislative intervention which had the effect of enabling same-sex couples to enjoy the status, entitlements and responsibilities that heterosexual couples achieve through marriage, would without more override any discriminatory impact flowing from the common law definition standing on its own.

Thus corrected, the Marriage Act would then have to be interpreted and applied in a manner consistent with the constitutional requirement that same-sex couples be treated with the same concern and respect as that accorded to heterosexual couples. The effect would be that formal registration of same-sex unions would automatically extend the common law and statutory legal consequences to same-sex couples that flow to heterosexual couples from marriage.

[123] The Equality Project in fact urged us to adopt the simple corrective statutory strategy of reading in the words "or spouse" after the reference to husband and wife in section 30(1) of the Marriage Act. The state and the amici argued forcibly against this contention. In their view, to accept it would not merely modify a well-established institution to bring it into line with constitutional values. It would completely restructure and possibly even destroy it as an institution. Their argument was three-fold: first, that time should be given for the public to be involved in an issue of such great public interest and importance; second, that it was neither competent nor appropriate for the Court itself to restructure the institution of marriage in such a radical way; and third, that only Parliament had the authority to create such a radical remedy, so that if the Court should declare the Marriage Act to be invalid because of its under-inclusive nature, the declaration of invalidity should be suspended to enable Parliament to correct the defect.

[124] I start with the argument that the Court should not undertake what was said to be a far-reaching and radical change without the general public first having had an opportunity to have its say.

. . . .

[132] Having concluded that the law of marriage as it stands is inconsistent with the Constitution and invalid to the extent outlined above, an appropriate declaration of invalidity needs to be made. The question that arises is whether this Court is obliged to provide immediate relief in the terms sought by the applicants and the Equality Project, or whether it should suspend the order of invalidity to give Parliament a chance to remedy the defect. The test is what is just and equitable, taking account of all the circumstances.

. . . .

[137] The claim by the applicants in Fourie of the right to get married should, in my view, be seen as part of a comprehensive wish to be able to live openly and freely as lesbian women emancipated from all the legal taboos that historically have kept them from enjoying life in the mainstream of society. The right to celebrate their union accordingly signifies far more than a right to enter into a legal arrangement with many attendant and significant consequences, important though they may be. It represents a major symbolical milestone in their long walk to equality and dignity. The greater and more secure the institutional imprimatur for their union, the more solidly will it and other such unions be rescued from legal oblivion, and the more tranquil and enduring will such unions ultimately turn out to be.

[138] This is a matter that touches on deep public and private sensibilities. I believe that Parliament is well-suited to finding the best ways of ensuring that same-sex couples are brought in from the legal cold. The law may not automatically and of itself eliminate stereotyping and prejudice. Yet it serves as a great teacher,

establishes public norms that become assimilated into daily life and protects vulnerable people from unjust marginalisation and abuse. It needs to be remembered that not only the courts are responsible for vindicating the rights enshrined in the Bill of Rights. The legislature is in the frontline in this respect. One of its principal functions is to ensure that the values of the Constitution as set out in the Preamble and section 1 permeate every area of the law.

. . . .

[156] As I have shown, Parliament has already undertaken a number of legislative initiatives which demonstrate its concern to end discrimination on the ground of sexual orientation. Aided by the extensive research and specific proposals made by the SALRC, there is no reason to believe that Parliament will not be able to fulfil its responsibilities in the light of this judgment within a relatively short time. As was pointed out in argument, what is in issue is not a fundamental new start in legislation but the culmination of a process that has been underway for many years. In the circumstances it would be appropriate to give Parliament one year from the date of the delivery of this judgment to cure the defect.

. . . .

[161] In keeping with this approach it is necessary that the orders of this Court, read together, make it clear that if Parliament fails to cure the defect within twelve months, the words "or spouse" will automatically be read into section 30(1) of the Marriage Act. In this event the Marriage Act will, without more, become the legal vehicle to enable same-sex couples to achieve the status and benefits coupled with responsibilities which it presently makes available to heterosexual couples.

The U.S. Supreme Court continues to side-step the question whether sexual orientation is a suspect class. The use of a variant of rational basis, discussed earlier in Chapter 2, was used to strike down a federal statute differentially treating same-sex marriages recognized by the individual's state of domicile.

UNITED STATES v. WINDSOR
SUPREME COURT OF THE UNITED STATES
133 S. Ct. 2675 (2013)

[The State of New York recognizes the marriage of New York residents Edith Windsor and Thea Spyer, who wed in Ontario, Canada, in 2007. When Spyer died in 2009, she left her entire estate to Windsor. Windsor sought to claim the federal estate tax exemption for surviving spouses, but was barred from doing so by §3 of the federal Defense of Marriage Act (DOMA), which amended the Dictionary Act — a law providing rules of construction for over 1,000 federal laws and the whole realm of federal regulations — to define "marriage" and "spouse" as excluding same-sex partners. Windsor brought this refund suit, contending that DOMA violates the principles of equal protection incorporated in the Fifth Amendment.]

JUSTICE KENNEDY delivered the opinion of the Court.

. . . .

I

In 1996, as some States were beginning to consider the concept of same-sex marriage, *see, e.g., Baehr v. Lewin*, 852 P. 2d 44 (1993), and before any State had acted to permit it, Congress enacted the Defense of Marriage Act (DOMA), 110 Stat. 2419. DOMA contains two operative sections: Section 2, which has not been challenged here, allows States to refuse to recognize same-sex marriages performed under the laws of other States. See 28 U.S.C. § 1738C. Section 3 is at issue here. It amends the Dictionary Act in Title 1, §7, of the United States Code to provide a federal definition of "marriage" and "spouse." Section 3 of DOMA provides as follows:

> "In determining the meaning of any Act of Congress, or of any ruling, regulation, or interpretation of the various administrative bureaus and agencies of the United States, the word 'marriage' means only a legal union between one man and one woman as husband and wife, and the word 'spouse' refers only to a person of the opposite sex who is a husband or a wife."

. . . .

III

[As noted in Chapter Two, the majority here emphasized the long American tradition of state law determination of marriage and divorce.]

IV

DOMA seeks to injure the very class New York seeks to protect. By doing so it violates basic due process and equal protection principles applicable to the Federal Government. See U.S. Const., Amdt. 5; *Bolling v. Sharpe*, 347 U.S. 497 (1954). The Constitution's guarantee of equality "must at the very least mean that a bare congressional desire to harm a politically unpopular group cannot" justify disparate treatment of that group. *Department of Agriculture v. Moreno*, 413 U.S. 528, 534–535 (1973). In determining whether a law is motived by an improper animus or purpose, " '[d]iscriminations of an unusual character' " especially require careful consideration. DOMA cannot survive under these principles. The responsibility of the States for the regulation of domestic relations is an important indicator of the substantial societal impact the State's classifications have in the daily lives and customs of its people. DOMA's unusual deviation from the usual tradition of recognizing and accepting state definitions of marriage here operates to deprive same-sex couples of the benefits and responsibilities that come with the federal recognition of their marriages. This is strong evidence of a law having the purpose and effect of disapproval of that class. The avowed purpose and practical effect of the law here in question are to impose a disadvantage, a separate status, and so a stigma upon all who enter into same-sex marriages made lawful by the unquestioned authority of the States.

. . . .

DOMA's principal effect is to identify a subset of state-sanctioned marriages and make them unequal. The principal purpose is to impose inequality, not for other reasons like governmental efficiency. Responsibilities, as well as rights, enhance the dignity and integrity of the person. And DOMA contrives to deprive some couples married under the laws of their State, but not other couples, of both rights and responsibilities. By creating two contradictory marriage regimes within the same State, DOMA forces same-sex couples to live as married for the purpose of state law but unmarried for the purpose of federal law, thus diminishing the stability and predictability of basic personal relations the State has found it proper to acknowledge and protect. By this dynamic DOMA undermines both the public and private significance of state-sanctioned same-sex marriages; for it tells those couples, and all the world, that their otherwise valid marriages are unworthy of federal recognition. This places same-sex couples in an unstable position of being in a second-tier marriage. The differentiation demeans the couple, whose moral and sexual choices the Constitution protects, see *Lawrence*, and whose relationship the State has sought to dignify. And it humiliates tens of thousands of children now being raised by same-sex couples. The law in question makes it even more difficult for the children to understand the integrity and closeness of their own family and its concord with other families in their community and in their daily lives.

. . . .

DOMA also brings financial harm to children of same-sex couples. It raises the cost of health care for families by taxing health benefits provided by employers to their workers' same-sex spouses. And it denies or reduces benefits allowed to families upon the loss of a spouse and parent, benefits that are an integral part of family security.

. . . .

CHIEF JUSTICE ROBERTS, dissenting [omitted, largely agreeing with SCALIA, J.]

JUSTICE SCALIA, with whom JUSTICE THOMAS joins, and with whom THE CHIEF JUSTICE joins as to Part I, dissenting.

. . . .

I

[The dissent found this case not appropriate for Supreme Court review.]

II

. . . .

A

. . . .

Moreover, if this is meant to be an equal-protection opinion, it is a confusing one. The opinion does not resolve and indeed does not even mention what had been the central question in this litigation: whether, under the Equal Protection Clause, laws restricting marriage to a man and a woman are reviewed for more than mere rationality . . . . In accord with my previously expressed skepticism about the Court's "tiers of scrutiny" approach, I would review this classification only for its rationality. See *United States v. Virginia*. As nearly as I can tell, the Court agrees with that; its opinion does not apply strict scrutiny, and its central propositions are taken from rational-basis cases like *Moreno*. But the Court certainly does not apply anything that resembles that deferential framework. See *Heller v. Doe*, 509 U.S. 312, 320 (1993) (a classification " 'must be upheld . . . if there is any reason- ably conceivable state of facts' " that could justify it).

The majority opinion need not get into the strict-vs.-rational-basis scrutiny question, and need not justify its holding under either, because it says that DOMA is unconstitutional as "a deprivation of the liberty of the person protected by the Fifth Amendment of the Constitution," *ante*, at 25; that it violates "basic due process" principles, ante, at 20; and that it inflicts an "injury and indignity" of a kind that denies "an essential part of the liberty protected by the Fifth Amendment," *ante*, at 19. The majority never utters the dread words "substantive due process," perhaps sensing the disrepute into which that doctrine has fallen, but that is what those statements mean. Yet the opinion does not argue that same-sex marriage is "deeply rooted in this Nation's history and tradition," *Washington v. Glucksberg*, 521 U.S. 702–721 (1997) [a case recognizing grandparents' visitation rights as constitutionally protected], a claim that would of course be quite absurd . . . .

. . . .

B

. . . .

However, even setting aside traditional moral disapproval of same-sex marriage (or indeed same-sex sex), there are many perfectly valid — indeed, downright boring — justifying rationales for this legislation. Their existence ought to be the end of this case. For they give the lie to the Court's conclusion that only those with hateful hearts could have voted "aye" on this Act. And more importantly, they serve to make the contents of the legislators' hearts quite irrelevant: "It is a familiar principle of constitutional law that this Court will not strike down an otherwise constitutional statute on the basis of an alleged illicit legislative motive." *United States v. O'Brien*, 391 U.S. 367, 383 (1968). Or at least it was a familiar principle. By holding to the contrary, the majority has declared open season on any law that (in the opinion of the law's opponents and any panel of like-minded federal judges) can be characterized as mean-spirited.

The majority concludes that the only motive for this Act was the "bare . . . desire to harm a politically unpopular group." Ante, at 20. Bear in mind that the object of this condemnation is not the legislature of some once-Confederate Southern state (familiar objects of the Court's scorn, *see, e.g., Edwards v. Aguillard*, 482 U.S. 578 (1987)), but our respected coordinate branches, the Congress and Presidency of the United States. Laying such a charge against them should require the most extraordinary evidence, and I would have thought that every attempt would be made to indulge a more anodyne explanation for the statute. The majority does the opposite — affirmatively concealing from the reader the arguments that exist in justification. It makes only a passing mention of the "arguments put forward" by the Act's defenders, and does not even trouble to paraphrase or describe them. I imagine that this is because it is harder to maintain the illusion of the Act's supporters as unhinged members of a wild-eyed lynch mob when one first describes their views as they see them.

To choose just one of these defenders' arguments, DOMA avoids difficult choice-of-law issues that will now arise absent a uniform federal definition of marriage . . . .

> . . . .

By formally declaring anyone opposed to same-sex marriage an enemy of human decency, the majority arms well every challenger to a state law restricting marriage to its traditional definition. Henceforth those challengers will lead with this Court's declaration that there is "no legitimate purpose" served by such a law, and will claim that the traditional definition has "the purpose and effect to disparage and to injure" the "personhood and dignity" of same-sex couples . . . .

> . . . .

In the majority's telling, this story is black-and-white: Hate your neighbor or come along with us. The truth is more complicated. It is hard to admit that one's political opponents are not monsters, especially in a struggle like this one, and the challenge in the end proves more than today's Court can handle. Too bad. A reminder that disagreement over something so fundamental as marriage can still be politically legitimate would have been a fit task for what in earlier times was called the judicial temperament. We might have covered ourselves with honor today, by promising all sides of this debate that it was theirs to settle and that we would respect their resolution. We might have let the People decide.

> . . . .

JUSTICE ALITO, with whom JUSTICE THOMAS joins as to Parts II and III, dissenting.

Our Nation is engaged in a heated debate about same-sex marriage. That debate is, at bottom, about the nature of the institution of marriage. Respondent Edith Windsor, supported by the United States, asks this Court to intervene in that debate, and although she couches her argument in different terms, what she seeks is a holding that enshrines in the Constitution a particular understanding of marriage under which the sex of the partners makes no difference. The Constitution, however, does not dictate that choice. It leaves the choice to the people, acting through their elected representatives at both the federal and state levels. I would therefore hold that Congress did not violate Windsor's constitutional rights by enacting § 3 of the Defense of Marriage Act (DOMA), 110 Stat. 2419, which defines the meaning of marriage under federal statutes that either confer upon married persons certain federal benefits or impose upon them certain federal obligations.

. . . .

II

. . . .

The family is an ancient and universal human institution. Family structure reflects the characteristics of a civilization, and changes in family structure and in the popular understanding of marriage and the family can have profound effects. Past changes in the understanding of marriage — for example, the gradual ascendance of the idea that romantic love is a prerequisite to marriage — have had far-reaching consequences. But the process by which such consequences come about is complex, involving the interaction of numerous factors, and tends to occur over an extended period of time.

. . . .

At present, no one — including social scientists, philosophers, and historians — can predict with any certainty what the long-term ramifications of widespread acceptance of same-sex marriage will be. And judges are certainly not equipped to make such an assessment. The Members of this Court have the authority and the responsibility to interpret and apply the Constitution. Thus, if the Constitution contained a provision guaranteeing the right to marry a person of the same sex, it would be our duty to enforce that right. But the Constitution simply does not speak to the issue of same-sex marriage. In our system of government, ultimate sovereignty rests with the people, and the people have the right to control their own destiny. Any change on a question so fundamental should be made by the people through their elected officials.

. . . .

Chapter 5

SOCIAL AND ECONOMIC RIGHTS

KEY CONCEPTS FOR THE CHAPTER

- ALL COUNTRIES WE STUDY FEATURE A NUMBER OF GOVERNMENT PROGRAMS TO PROVIDE ITS PEOPLE WITH SUPPORT FOR BASIC FOOD, HOUSING, WATER, AND FINANCIAL SECURITY CONSISTENT WITH THE FINANCIAL RESOURCES AVAILABLE TO THE GOVERNMENT. THE FOCUS OF THIS CHAPTER IS ON WHETHER GOVERNMENT POLICIES WITH REGARD TO BASIC SOCIAL AND ECONOMIC NEEDS ARE PURELY A MATTER OF "ORDINARY POLITICS" OR WHETHER THERE ARE EXTERNAL REQUIREMENTS, PERHAPS ENFORCED BY COURTS, ON GOVERNMENT POLICY.

- EACH COUNTRY TAKES A DIFFERENT APPROACH:

  — SOUTH AFRICA'S CONSTITUTION FEATURES PIONEERING JUDICIALLY ENFORCEABLE RIGHTS TO BASIC SOCIAL AND ECONOMIC NEEDS

  — CANADIAN COURTS HAVE HELD THAT GOVERNMENT ACTION THAT LIMITS INDIVIDUALS' ABILITY TO CONTRACT FOR BASIC RIGHTS CAN POTENTIALLY INFRINGE RIGHTS INCONSISTENT WITH "PRINCIPLES OF FUNDAMENTAL JUSTICE" IN VIOLATION OF THE CANADIAN CHARTER

  — ALTHOUGH THERE IS NO AUSTRALIAN CONSTITUTIONAL PROVISION GRANTING SOCIAL AND ECONOMIC RIGHTS, AUSTRALIA IS A PARTY TO AN INTERNATIONAL COVENANT UNDERTAKING TO PROVIDE SUCH RIGHTS

  — THE UNITED STATES IS NOT A PARTY TO INTERNATIONAL SOCIAL/ECONOMIC RIGHTS AGREEMENTS, AND THE U.S. SUPREME COURT HAS REJECTED CLAIMS FOR JUDICIAL RECOGNITION OF ENFORCEABLE SOCIAL AND ECONOMIC RIGHTS

5.1. INTRODUCTION

It is not surprising to find that different constitutional options reflect continuing ideological and political alternatives for different societies. Since World War II, these ideological responses have included domestic protection for international human rights following the Nazi atrocities, a post-communist concern with state intervention to permit creation of a neo-liberal economic and cultural order, concerns about the anti-democratic implications of constitutional review, and new movements pressing for independent judiciaries to police many political institutions in order to limit the destabilizing impact of politics.

Although the majority of states undergoing constitutional change with the end of the Cold War seemed to accept the liberal paradigm of individual human rights and multiparty democracy, this did not preclude the simultaneous inclusion of other elements, including socio-economic and cultural rights. In this regard, the age-old tension between aspirations for liberty and for equality (which we considered specifically in Chapter 3) appears in regard to concerns about whether the government is viewed principally as (1) a threat to liberty that needs to be constrained by a judicially-enforced constitution, or (2) an essential actor in reconstituting society on more equal terms, with judges authorized if necessary to force the government to perform this role to ensure that it provides a minimum to its citizens.[1]

5.1.1. International and American roots

By early 1944, World War II was turning sharply in favor of the Allied forces, and public attention around the world turned to the conditions of a future peace. This was the context for U.S. President Franklin Delano Roosevelt's annual "State of the Union" speech to Congress. The speech focused on future security, not just military but "economic security, social security, moral security."[2] Roosevelt argued that, although the nation had grown "under the protection of certain inalienable political rights" (referring to the Bill of Rights), "we have come to a clear realization of the fact that true individual freedom cannot exist without economic security and independence." In his view, "necessitous men are not free men" and the hungry and jobless "are the stuff out of which dictatorships are made."

In the same era, the idea of the "Welfare State" was emerging in other Western countries, especially Britain. This expressed the notion that governments had responsibility for the economic and social well-being of their national populations, from birth to old age ("cradle to grave"). It emerged in particular as a response to the destitution and misery in the Great Depression of the 1930s. The celebrated 1942 "Beveridge Report" (*Social Insurance and Allied Services*) on plans for post-war reconstruction in Britain pointed to five "giants on the road": want, disease, ignorance, squalor, and idleness. It recommended a comprehensive, integrated social insurance scheme for Britain to combat these giants. The Report's conclusions were embraced (and enlarged) by Prime Minister Clement Atlee's Labour government, elected in 1945 (the establishment of the still-functioning National Health Service is the best known product of this era).

In Australia, the idea also took on and in 1946, the Prime Minister Ben Chifley's Labor government held a referendum seeking the voters' approval to add a section to the Constitution (s 51 (xxiiiA)) to empower the Commonwealth parliament to pass laws with respect to "the provision of maternity allowances, widows' pensions, child endowment, unemployment, pharmaceutical, sickness and hospital benefits, medical and dental services . . . ." As the price of support for the referendum from the opposition Liberal Party, however, the section rules out the establishment of a national health service ("civil conscription" in medical services is not permitted). The referendum was successful, and the Commonwealth government has had responsibility for most Australian social welfare since.

---

[1] For a broader analysis of these themes, see HEINZ KLUG, CONSTITUTING DEMOCRACY: LAW, GLOBALISM AND SOUTH AFRICA'S POLITICAL RECONSTRUCTION ch. 1 (2000).

[2] The speech is detailed in CASS SUNSTEIN, THE SECOND BILL OF RIGHTS: FDR'S UNFINISHED REVOLUTION AND WHY WE NEED IT MORE THAN EVER ch. 1 (2004).

In the United States, President Roosevelt set forth his "Second Bill of Rights" as follows:

> In our day these economic truths have become accepted as self-evident. We have accepted, so to speak, a second Bill of Rights under which a new basis of security and prosperity can be established for all — regardless of station, race, or creed.

Among these are:

> The right to a useful and remunerative job in the industries or shops or farms or mines of the nation;

> The right to earn enough to provide adequate food and clothing and recreation;

> The right of every farmer to raise and sell his products at a return which will give him and his family a decent living;

> The right of every businessman, large and small, to trade in an atmosphere of freedom from unfair competition and domination by monopolies at home or abroad;

> The right of every family to a decent home;

> The right to adequate medical care and the opportunity to achieve and enjoy good health;

> The right to adequate protection from the economic fears of old age, sickness, accident, and unemployment;

> The right to a good education.

> All of these rights spell security. And after this war is won we must be prepared to move forward, in the implementation of these rights, to new goals of human happiness and well-being. America's own rightful place in the world depends in large part upon how fully these and similar rights have been carried into practice for all our citizens. For unless there is security here at home there cannot be lasting peace in the world.

A short historical re-telling of the saga of the Second Bill of Rights has two salient features. First, Roosevelt never intended the Second Bill to have the legal force of constitutional entrenchment, like the "first" Bill of Rights. Rather, having endured the historic battle with the Supreme Court over the New Deal, Roosevelt viewed the judiciary as hostile to, rather than an ally for, progressive social reform. FDR envisioned his Second Bill to have the same aspirational effect as the Declaration of Independence, and to use it to motivate Congress to implement the Bill's goals through legislation. Second, the Bill was never formally enacted or endorsed, but has been partially implemented through a variety of legislative reform programs.

President Roosevelt's call for a Second Bill of Rights was one of the influences on international recognition of social and economic rights as well. In 1948, the United National General Assembly adopted a non-binding Universal Declaration of Human Rights, based on the belief that freedom, justice, and peace require "recognition of the inherent dignity and of the equal and inalienable rights of all members of the human family." The Declaration contained several provisions relating to social and economic rights:

- Everyone, as a member of society, has the right to social security and is entitled to realization, through national effort and international co-operation and in accordance with the organization and resources of each State, of the economic, social and cultural rights indispensable for his dignity and the free development of his personality (Art. 22)

- (1) Everyone has the right to work, to free choice of employment, to just and favourable conditions of work and to protection against unemployment. (2) Everyone, without any discrimination, has the right to equal pay for equal work. (3) Everyone who works has the right to just and favourable remuneration ensuring for himself and his family an existence worthy of human dignity, and supplemented, if necessary, by other means of social protection. (4) Everyone has the right to form and to join trade unions for the protection of his interests. (Art. 23).

- Everyone has the right to rest and leisure, including reasonable limitation of working hours and periodic holidays with pay. (Art. 24).

- (1) Everyone has the right to a standard of living adequate for the health and well-being of himself and of his family, including food, clothing, housing and medical care and necessary social services, and the right to security in the event of unemployment, sickness, disability, widowhood, old age or other lack of livelihood in circumstances beyond his control. (2) Motherhood and childhood are entitled to special care and assistance. All children, whether born in or out of wedlock, shall enjoy the same social protection. (Art. 25).

- (1) Everyone has the right to education. Education shall be free, at least in the elementary and fundamental stages. Elementary education shall be compulsory. Technical and professional education shall be made generally available and higher education shall be equally accessible to all on the basis of merit. (2) Education shall be directed to the full development of the human personality and to the strengthening of respect for human rights and fundamental freedoms. It shall promote understanding, tolerance and friendship among all nations, racial or religious groups, and shall further the activities of the United Nations for the maintenance of peace. (3) Parents have a prior right to choose the kind of education that shall be given to their children. (Art. 26).

In 1966, the General Assembly adopted another document, the International Covenant on Economic, Social and Cultural Rights. Unlike the non-binding declaration, this covenant contained binding commitments and therefore required accession by individual countries as signatories. The Covenant provides that signatory states will recognize the right to:

- work, with fair and equal wages and safe working conditions and the right to organize collectively;

- social security, including social insurance;

- protection against exploitation of child labor;

- an adequate standard of living, including foot, clothing, housing, and a continuous improvement of living conditions;

- the enjoyment of the highest attainable standard of physical and mental health;

- education, including compulsory and free primary education and higher education equally accessible to all

To enforce these rights, each signatory is required to furnish reports to the U.N. Economic and Social Council regarding their nation's progress toward implementation. Australia's Labor Prime Minister Gough Whitlam secured ratification of the covenant in 1975, and Canada ratified in 1976. The United States and South Africa have both signed the agreement but it has not been ratified. As of 2012, 160 nations have ratified the covenant.

5.1.2. The South African approach: a summary

The South African constitutional approach shares a foundation with the Rooseveltian notion that socio-economic and civil/political rights are interdependent, embracing the notion that "human rights should be treated holistically in order to protect human welfare." Unlike Roosevelt, who did not favor judicially-enforceable rights, the inclusion of justiciable socio-economic rights forecloses the privileging of civil and political rights that serve to protect existing distributions of power and wealth. Sandra Liebenberg, *The Interpretation of Socio-Economic Rights, in* 2 CONSTITUTIONAL LAW OF SOUTH AFRICA § 33.1. In addition to the South African Constitution's provisions granting a right of restitution or secure tenure to those individuals or communities whose land was dispossessed or whose tenure remains insecure as a result of "past racially discriminatory laws" (s 25(7) and (6)), the Constitution expressly provides for a number of social and economic rights, including the right to:

- equitable access to land (s 25(5));

- housing (s 26);

- access to health care, social security, food, and water (s 27);

- basic nutrition, shelter, and health care and social services for children (s 28);

- education (s 29)

The Constitution does create somewhat of a hierarchy of rights, however. The rights to housing, health care services, food, water, and social security require the state to "achieve progressive realization" of these rights through "reasonable legislative and other measures, within its available resources." "Basic" rights to basic nutrition, shelter, health care and social services for children, basic education for children and adults, and minimal conditions consistent with human dignity for detained persons, are not constrained by reasonable measures or resource constraints. Liebenberg, at § 33.2(c)(i).

The Constitutional Court's interpretation of these provisions might be fairly described as expansive yet moderate. The Court has recognized that these rights have both a negative and positive component. Thus, in a case excerpted below, the

Court held that the government had a negative duty to refrain from action that deprived squatters of shelter, and a positive duty to address needs for emergency shelter. *Government of the Rep. of South Africa v. Grootboom*, 2001 (1) SA 46 (CC). However, the Court pleaded sensitivity to the primacy of the political branches in making policy decisions to implement these rights. Thus, the Court has rejected calls to establish a "minimal essential level" for these enumerated social and economic rights. *See, e.g., Mazibuko v. City of Johannesburg*, 2010 (4) SA 1 (CC) (O'Regan, J.). Although the Court has specifically rejected close judicial scrutiny, of the sort typical in dealing with civil rights, of "whether other more desirable or favourable measures could have been adopted, or whether public money could have been better spent," *Grootboom, supra,* ¶ [41], it has found constitutional violations where the government's failure to act was deemed "unreasonable." *See, e.g., Grootboom, supra,* ¶ [44] (failure to respond to the needs of the most desperate for emergency shelter); *Minister of Health v. Treatment Action Campaign (2)*, 2002 (5) SA 721 (CC) (failure to provide mothers and newborns with an antiretroviral drug that reduces by 50% the rate of mother-to-child transmission of HIV).

5.1.3.   The significance of the South African approach for comparative analysis

The inclusion of justiciable socio-economic rights in the South African Constitution has been heralded internationally as a mark of the extraordinary nature of the post-apartheid project in South Africa. Consistent with the comparative method of this book, the factors that led to the entrenchment of these rights in South Africa is also revealing when we consider why North American courts have declined to use broad phrases in the American and Canadian constitutional texts to provide similar protection, and why Australians have rejected any entrenchment of these rights. In addition, the court decisions interpreting these rights provide insights for all nations as to the extent that court-protected entrenched rights can meaningfully address vast socio-economic inequalities in an era a significantly limited governmental capacity.

The reasoning of ANC constitutional experts in insisting on the inclusion of socio-economic rights is also instructive for comparative analysis. As one of us has noted elsewhere,

> Given a history of racially structured deprivation, the ANC recognized during the democratic transition that a commitment to constitutionally enshrined civil rights would merely entrench the economic distributions of apartheid unless it was supplemented with a commitment to at least the basic guarantees of socio-economic rights.

HEINZ KLUG, THE CONSTITUTION OF SOUTH AFRICA: A CONTEXTUAL ANALYSIS 135 (2010). Consider the implications of the converse of the ANC's logic: if a country's history, traditions, and current values preclude entrenching social and economic rights, should those concerned with unequal economic distributions oppose entrenching civil rights, or at least a right to property, as well?

5.2. JUDICIALLY ENFORCEABLE PROTECTION OF SOCIAL AND ECONOMIC RIGHTS UNDER THE SOUTH AFRICAN CONSTITUTION

Responding to concerns about the justiciability of socio-economic rights in the *First Certification* case (*In re Certification of the Constitution for the Republic of South Africa,* 1996, 1996 (4) SA 744 (CC)) the Constitutional Court rejected the rigid distinction between different types of rights and instead argued that:

> [W]e are of the view that these rights are, at least to some extent, justiciable. As we have stated in the previous paragraph, many of the civil and political rights entrenched in the [1996 Constitution] will give rise to similar budgetary implications without compromising their justiciability. The fact that socio-economic rights will almost inevitably give rise to such implications does not seem to us to be a bar to their justiciability. At the very minimum, socio-economic rights can be negatively protected from improper invasion.

The cases below illustrate the way in which the South African Constitutional Court has engaged in judicial reasoning to effectuate the rights granted by the Constitution.

5.2.1. Allocating scarce resources for health care

The 1996 Constitution's introduction of a constitutional right to health (s 27(1), in a context of vast inequality and limited resources, soon produced a tragic confrontation between the health authorities and a patient who required access to renal dialysis in order to prolong his life. When Thiagraj Soobramoney reached the Constitutional Court, the Court denied his claim, drawing a distinction between the right not to be refused emergency medical treatment in terms of section 27(3) of the Constitution[3] and the progressive realisation of the right to health care guaranteed in section 27(2).

SOOBRAMONEY v. MINSTER OF HEALTH (KWAZULU-NATAL)
Constitutional Court of South Africa
1998 (1) SA 765

Chaskalson P:

[1] The appellant, a 41 year old unemployed man, is a diabetic who suffers from ischaemic heart disease and cerebro-vascular disease which caused him to have a stroke during 1996. In 1996 his kidneys also failed. Sadly his condition is irreversible and he is now in the final stages of chronic renal failure. His life could be prolonged

---

[3] Although, as noted in Section 5.3, American constitutional law does not extend to health care, on this particular point a federal statute does require hospitals that maintain an emergency department to provide on request examination or treatment of an emergency medical condition to any individual, regardless of ability to pay. 42 U.S.C. § 1395dd.

by means of regular renal dialysis. He has sought such treatment from the renal unit of the Addington state hospital in Durban. The hospital can, however, only provide dialysis treatment to a limited number of patients. The renal unit has 20 dialysis machines available to it, and some of these machines are in poor condition. Each treatment takes four hours and a further two hours have to be allowed for the cleaning of a machine, before it can be used again for other treatment. Because of the limited facilities that are available for kidney dialysis the hospital has been unable to provide the appellant with the treatment he has requested.

[3] Because of the shortage of resources the hospital follows a set policy in regard to the use of the dialysis resources. Only patients who suffer from acute renal failure, which can be treated and remedied by renal dialysis are given automatic access to renal dialysis at the hospital. Those patients who, like the appellant, suffer from chronic renal failure which is irreversible are not admitted automatically to the renal programme. A set of guidelines has been drawn up and adopted to determine which applicants who have chronic renal failure will be given dialysis treatment. According to the guidelines the primary requirement for admission of such persons to the dialysis programme is that the patient must be eligible for a kidney transplant. A patient who is eligible for a transplant will be provided with dialysis treatment until an organ donor is found and a kidney transplant has been completed.

[4] The guidelines provide that an applicant is not eligible for a transplant unless he or she is [f]ree of significant vascular or cardiac disease. The medical criteria set out in the guidelines also provide that an applicant must be

> Free of significant disease elsewhere e.g. ischaemic heart disease, cerebro-vascular disease, peripheral vascular disease, chronic liver disease, chronic lung disease.

The appellant suffers from ischaemic heart disease and cerebro-vascular disease and he is therefore not eligible for a kidney transplant.

[8] We live in a society in which there are great disparities in wealth. Millions of people are living in deplorable conditions and in great poverty. There is a high level of unemployment, inadequate social security, and many do not have access to clean water or to adequate health services. These conditions already existed when the Constitution was adopted and a commitment to address them, and to transform our society into one in which there will be human dignity, freedom and equality, lies at the heart of our new constitutional order. For as long as these conditions continue to exist that aspiration will have a hollow ring.

[28] The appellant's case must be seen in the context of the needs which the health services have to meet, for if treatment has to be provided to the appellant it would also have to be provided to all other persons similarly placed. Although the renal clinic could be kept open for longer hours, it would involve additional expense in having to pay the clinic personnel at overtime rates, or in having to employ additional personnel working on a shift basis. It would also put a great strain on the existing dialysis machines which are already showing signs of wear. It is estimated that the cost to the state of treating one chronically ill patient by means of renal dialysis provided twice a week at a state hospital is approximately R60 000

[approximately US$6600] per annum. If all the persons in South Africa who suffer from chronic renal failure were to be provided with dialysis treatment and many of them, as the appellant does, would require treatment three times a week, the cost of doing so would make substantial inroads into the health budget. And if this principle were to be applied to all patients claiming access to expensive medical treatment or expensive drugs, the health budget would have to be dramatically increased to the prejudice of other needs which the state has to meet.

[29] The provincial administration which is responsible for health services in KwaZulu-Natal has to make decisions about the funding that should be made available for health care and how such funds should be spent. These choices involve difficult decisions to be taken at the political level in fixing the health budget, and at the functional level in deciding upon the priorities to be met. A court will be slow to interfere with rational decisions taken in good faith by the political organs and medical authorities whose responsibility it is to deal with such matters.

[31] One cannot but have sympathy for the appellant and his family, who face the cruel dilemma of having to impoverish themselves in order to secure the treatment that the appellant seeks in order to prolong his life. The hard and unpalatable fact is that if the appellant were a wealthy man he would be able to procure such treatment from private sources; he is not and has to look to the state to provide him with the treatment. But the state's resources are limited and the appellant does not meet the criteria for admission to the renal dialysis programme. Unfortunately, this is true not only of the appellant but of

many others who need access to renal dialysis units or to other health services. There are also those who need access to housing, food and water, employment opportunities, and social security. These too are aspects of the right to

A . . . human life: the right to live as a human being, to be part of a broader community, to share in the experience of humanity. [O'Regan J in *S v Makwanyane*, 1995 (3) SA 391, para 326]

The state has to manage its limited resources in order to address all these claims. There will be times when this requires it to adopt a holistic approach to the larger needs of society rather than to focus on the specific needs of particular individuals within society.

. . . .

[36] The state has a constitutional duty to comply with the obligations imposed on it by section 27 of the Constitution. It has not been shown in the present case, however, that the state's failure to provide renal dialysis facilities for all persons suffering from chronic renal failure constitutes a breach of those obligations. In the circumstances the appellant is not entitled to the relief that he seeks in these proceedings and his appeal . . . must fail.

5.2.2. Basic right to housing

In its first positive socio-economic rights case the Constitutional Court was required to review a local government's action in evicting squatters from private land that was to be used for low-income housing. In the process of eviction, the homes the squatters had erected were destroyed and much of their personal possessions and building material had also been deliberately destroyed. While the Constitutional Court upheld the claim that the municipality's action violated the negative obligation — the duty not to deprive them of shelter — owed to them under section 26(1), the Court proceeded to extrapolate on the positive duties placed on the state under section 26(2). Although the government was able to present a well-documented national housing policy that met the obligation to "take reasonable legislative and other measures, within its available resources, to achieve the progressive realization of this right," the Court found that the failure to have a policy to address the needs for emergency shelter meant that the policy failed "to respond to the needs of those most desperate" and thus was unreasonable.

THE GOVERNMENT OF THE REPUBLIC OF SOUTH AFRICA v. GROOTBOOM
CONSTITUTIONAL COURT OF SOUTH AFRICA
2001 (1) SA 46

Yacoob J:

[1] The people of South Africa are committed to the attainment of social justice and the improvement of the quality of life for everyone. The Preamble to our Constitution records this commitment. The Constitution declares the founding values of our society to be "[h]uman dignity, the achievement of equality and the advancement of human rights and freedoms." This case grapples with the realisation of these aspirations for it concerns the state's constitutional obligations in relation to housing: a constitutional issue of fundamental importance to the development of South Africa's new constitutional order.

. . . .

[35] A right of access to adequate housing also suggests that it is not only the state who is responsible for the provision of houses, but that other agents within our society, including individuals themselves, must be enabled by legislative and other measures to provide housing. The state must create the conditions for access to adequate housing for people at all economic levels of our society. State policy dealing with housing must therefore take account of different economic levels in our society.

[37] The state's obligation to provide access to adequate housing depends on context, and may differ from province to province, from city to city, from rural to urban areas and from person to person. Some may need access to land and no more; some may need access to land and building materials; some may need access to finance; some may need access to services such as water, sewage, electricity and roads. What might be appropriate in a rural area where people live together in communities engaging in subsistence farming may not be appropriate in an urban area where people are looking for employment and a place to live.

[38] Subsection (2) speaks to the positive obligation imposed upon the state. It requires the state to devise a comprehensive and workable plan to meet its obligations in terms of the subsection. However subsection (2) also makes it clear

that the obligation imposed upon the state is not an absolute or unqualified one. The extent of the state's obligation is defined by three key elements that are considered separately: (a) the obligation to "take reasonable legislative and other measures"; (b) "to achieve the progressive realisation" of the right; and (c) "within available resources."

[41] The measures must establish a coherent public housing programme directed towards the progressive realisation of the right of access to adequate housing within the state's available means. The programme must be capable of facilitating the realisation of the right. The precise contours and content of the measures to be adopted are primarily a matter for the legislature and the executive. They must, however, ensure that the measures they adopt are reasonable. In any challenge based on section 26 in which it is argued that the state has failed to meet the positive obligations imposed upon it by section 26(2), the question will be whether the legislative and other measures taken by the state are reasonable. A court considering reasonableness will not enquire whether other more desirable or favourable measures could have been adopted, or whether public money could have been better spent. The question would be whether the measures that have been adopted are reasonable. It is necessary to recognise that a wide range of possible measures could be adopted by the state to meet its obligations. Many of these would meet the requirement of reasonableness. Once it is shown that the measures do so, this requirement is met.

[42] The state is required to take reasonable legislative and other measures. Legislative measures by themselves are not likely to constitute constitutional compliance. Mere legislation is not enough. The state is obliged to act to achieve the intended result, and the legislative measures will invariably have to be supported by appropriate, well-directed policies and programmes implemented by the executive. These policies and programmes must be reasonable both in their conception and their implementation. The formulation of a programme is only the first stage in meeting the state's obligations. The programme must also be reasonably implemented. An otherwise reasonable programme that is not implemented reasonably will not constitute compliance with the state's obligations.

[44] Reasonableness must also be understood in the context of the Bill of Rights as a whole. The right of access to adequate housing is entrenched because we value human beings and want to ensure that they are afforded their basic human needs. A society must seek to ensure that the basic necessities of life are provided to all if it is to be a society based on human dignity, freedom and equality. To be reasonable, measures cannot leave out of account the degree and extent of the denial of the right they endeavour to realise. Those whose needs are the most urgent and whose ability to enjoy all rights therefore is most in peril, must not be ignored by the measures aimed at achieving realisation of the right. It may not be sufficient to meet the test of reasonableness to show that the measures are capable of achieving a statistical advance in the realisation of the right. Furthermore, the Constitution requires that everyone must be treated with care and concern. If the measures, though statistically successful, fail to respond to the needs of those most desperate, they may not pass the test.

[45] The extent and content of the obligation consist in what must be achieved, that

is, "the progressive realisation of this right." . . . The term "progressive realisation" shows that it was contemplated that the right could not be realised immediately. But the goal of the Constitution is that the basic needs of all in our society be effectively met and the requirement of progressive realisation means that the state must take steps to achieve this goal. It means that accessibility should be progressively facilitated: legal, administrative, operational and financial hurdles should be examined and, where possible, lowered over time. Housing must be made more accessible not only to a larger number of people but to a wider range of people as time progresses. The phrase is taken from international law and Article 2.1 of the Covenant [International Covenant discussed in section 5.1.1, above] in particular.

[66] The national government bears the overall responsibility for ensuring that the state complies with the obligations imposed upon it by section 26. The nationwide housing programme falls short of obligations imposed upon national government to the extent that it fails to recognise that the state must provide for relief for those in desperate need. They are not to be ignored in the interests of an overall programme focussed on medium and long-term objectives. It is essential that a reasonable part of the national housing budget be devoted to this, but the precise allocation is for national government to decide in the first instance.

[67] This case is concerned with the Cape Metro and the municipality. The former has realised that this need has not been fulfilled and has put in place its land programme in an effort to fulfil it. This programme, on the face of it, meets the obligation which the state has towards people in the position of the respondents in the Cape Metro. Indeed, the amicus accepted that this programme "would cater precisely for the needs of people such as the respondents, and, in an appropriate and sustainable manner." However, as with legislative measures, the existence of the programme is a starting point only. What remains is the implementation of the programme by taking all reasonable steps that are necessary to initiate and sustain it. And it must be implemented with due regard to the urgency of the situations it is intended to address.

[85] Consideration is now given to whether the state action (or inaction) in relation to the respondents met the required constitutional standard. [The Court described the context of this litigation: the housing shortage in the area of the Cape Town Metropolitan area in general and in the municipality of Oostenberg in particular had reached crisis proportions. An informal settlement, Wallacedene, "was obviously bursting and it was probable that people in desperation were going to find it difficult to resist the temptation to move out of the shack settlement onto unoccupied land in an effort to improve their position." Respondents moved out of the Wallacedene settlement into an unoccupied area called New Rust.]

[86] Whether the conduct of Mrs Grootboom and the other respondents constituted a land invasion was disputed on the papers. There was no suggestion however that the respondents' circumstances before their move to New Rust was anything but desperate. There is nothing in the papers to indicate any plan by the municipality to deal with the occupation of vacant land if it occurred. If there had been such a plan the appellants might well have acted differently.

[88] There is, however, no dispute that the municipality funded the eviction of the respondents. The magistrate who ordered the ejectment of the respondents

directed a process of mediation in which the municipality was to be involved to identify some alternative land for the occupation for the New Rust residents. Although the reason for this is unclear from the papers, it is evident that no effective mediation took place. The state had an obligation to ensure, at the very least, that the eviction was humanely executed. However, the eviction was reminiscent of the past and inconsistent with the values of the Constitution. The respondents were evicted a day early and to make matters worse, their possessions and building materials were not merely removed, but destroyed and burnt. I have already said that the provisions of section 26(1) of the Constitution burdens the state with at least a negative obligation in relation to housing. The manner in which the eviction was carried out resulted in a breach of this obligation.

[93] This case shows the desperation of hundreds of thousands of people living in deplorable conditions throughout the country. The Constitution obliges the state to act positively to ameliorate these conditions. The obligation is to provide access to housing, health-care, sufficient food and water, and social security to those unable to support themselves and their dependants. The state must also foster conditions to enable citizens to gain access to land on an equitable basis. Those in need have a corresponding right to demand that this be done.

[94] I am conscious that it is an extremely difficult task for the state to meet these obligations in the conditions that prevail in our country. This is recognised by the Constitution which expressly provides that the state is not obliged to go beyond available resources or to realise these rights immediately. I stress however, that despite all these qualifications, these are rights, and the Constitution obliges the state to give effect to them. This is an obligation that courts can, and in appropriate circumstances, must enforce.

[95] Neither section 26 nor section 28 entitles the respondents to claim shelter or housing immediately upon demand . . . . However, section 26 does oblige the state to devise and implement a coherent, co-ordinated programme designed to meet its section 26 obligations. The programme that has been adopted and was in force in the Cape Metro at the time that this application was brought, fell short of the obligations imposed upon the state by section 26(2) in that it failed to provide for any form of relief to those desperately in need of access to housing.

## 5.2.3.	Access to essential medicines

Faced with an HIV/AIDS pandemic — in which an estimated 19.6 % of the population or approximately 4.7 million people were thought to be HIV-positive as the country approached its first decade of freedom — the debate about what to do covered a wide range of options: Some people remained in denial, while others dreamed of local vaccine breakthroughs. Still others, such as activists of the Treatment Action Campaign (TAC), engaged in public acts of lawbreaking, such as importing generic pharmaceuticals from Thailand in defiance of the patent rights guaranteed under South African law. The TAC brought its first legal challenge by demanding that the government provide mothers and their newborn babies access to Nevirapine, an antiretroviral that more than halved the rate of mother-to-child transmission of HIV when it was administered to both mother and child during birth and shortly thereafter. Applying the legal arguments that were developed in the *Grootboom* case in the area of health and in the context of HIV/AIDS in particular, posed a major problem for the courts.

In the *Treatment Action Campaign case*, the Court was asked to require the government to provide Nevirapine to HIV-positive women in childbirth and their newborn babies — and not merely to have a reasonable policy to address the overwhelming HIV/AIDS pandemic within the confines of the state's resources. The Court decided to require the government to provide Nevirapine, marking an important extension of the principles laid out in *Grootboom* and an extraordinary reversal in the Court's approach to health rights, which only a short time earlier had seemed frozen by the combination of medical prerogatives and resource scarcity. Consider the extent to which the case marks the differential treatment of claims that the government has a "negative duty" to refrain from action that actually makes things worse for the poor, in contrast to, for example, *Soobramoney*'s claim that the government had a "positive duty" to provide sufficient resources to allow for adequate health care, or whether it demonstrates the intertwined nature of these obligation.

MINISTER OF HEALTH v. TREATMENT ACTION CAMPAIGN

CONSTITUTIONAL COURT OF SOUTH AFRICA

2002 (5) SA 721

THE COURT:

Introduction

[1] The HIV/AIDS pandemic in South Africa has been described as 'an incomprehensible calamity' and 'the most important challenge facing South Africa since the birth of our new democracy' and government's fight against 'this scourge' as 'a top priority.' It 'has claimed millions of lives, inflicting pain and grief, causing fear and uncertainty, and threatening the economy.' These are not the words of alarmists but are taken from a Department of Health publication in 2000 and a ministerial foreword to an earlier departmental publication.

[2] This appeal is directed at reversing orders made in a high court against government because of perceived shortcomings in its response to an aspect of the HIV/AIDS challenge. The court found that government had not reasonably addressed the need to reduce the risk of HIV-positive mothers transmitting the disease to their babies at birth. More specifically the finding was that government had acted unreasonably in (a) refusing to make an antiretroviral drug called nevirapine available in the public health sector where the attending doctor considered it medically indicated and (b) not setting out a timeframe for a national programme to prevent mother-to-child transmission of HIV.

[12] Nevirapine had been registered in 1998 by the Medicines Control Council, a specialist body created by the Medicines and Related Substances Control Act 101 of 1965 to determine the safety of drugs before their being made available in South Africa. In terms of this Act registration of a drug by definition entails a positive

finding as to its quality, safety and efficacy. In January 2001 the World Health Organization recommended the administration of the drug to mother and infant at the time of birth in order to combat HIV and between November 2000 and April 2001 the Medicines Control Council settled the wording of the package insert dealing with such use. The insert was formally approved by the Council in April 2001 and the parties treated that as the date of approval of the drug for the prevention of mother-to-child transmission of HIV.

[50] The implementation of a comprehensive programme to combat mother-to-child transmission of HIV, such as that provided at the research and training sites, is no doubt the ideal. The real dispute between the parties on this aspect of the case is not, however, whether this optimum was feasible but whether it was reasonable to exclude the use of nevirapine for the treatment of mother-to-child transmission at those public hospitals and clinics where testing and counselling are available and where the administration of nevirapine is medically indicated.

[51] In substance four reasons were advanced in the affidavits for confining the administration of nevirapine to the research and training sites . . . .

[57] First, the concern about efficacy. It is clear from the evidence that the provision of nevirapine will save the lives of a significant number of infants even if it is administered without the full package and support services that are available at the research and training sites. Mother-to-child transmission of HIV can take place during pregnancy, at birth and as a result of breastfeeding. The programme in issue in this case is concerned with transmission at or before birth. Although there is no dispute about the efficacy of nevirapine in materially reducing the likelihood of transmission at birth, the efficacy of the drug as a means of combating mother-to-child transmission of HIV is nevertheless challenged.

[59] As far as resistance is concerned, the only relevance is the possible need to treat the mother and/or the child at some time in the future. Although resistant strains of HIV might exist after a single dose of nevirapine, this mutation is likely to be transient. At most there is a possibility of such resistance persisting, and although this possibility cannot be excluded, its weight is small in comparison with the potential benefit of providing a single tablet of nevirapine to the mother and a few drops to her baby at the time of birth. The prospects of the child surviving if infected are so slim and the nature of the suffering so grave that the risk of some resistance manifesting at some time in the future is well worth running.

[60] The evidence shows that safety is no more than a hypothetical issue. The only evidence of potential harm concerns risks attaching to the administration of nevirapine as a chronic medication on an ongoing basis for the treatment of HIV-positive persons. There is, however, no evidence to suggest that a dose of nevirapine to both mother and child at the time of birth will result in any harm to either of them. According to the current medical consensus, there is no reason to fear any harm from this particular administration of nevirapine. That is why its use is recommended without qualification for this purpose by the World Health Organization.

[63] In any event the main thrust of government's case was that nevirapine should be administered in circumstances in which it would be most effective, not that it

should not be administered because it is dangerous . . . .

[64] It is this that lies at the heart of government policy. There are obviously good reasons from the public health point of view to monitor the efficacy of the 'full package' provided at the research and training sites and determine whether the costs involved are warranted by the efficacy of the treatment. There is a need to determine whether bottle-feeding will be implemented in practice when such advice is given and whether it will be implemented in a way that proves to be more effective than breastfeeding, bearing in mind the cultural problems associated with bottle-feeding, the absence of clean water in certain parts of the country and the fact that breastfeeding provides immunity from other hazards that infants growing up in poor households without access to adequate nutrition and sanitation are likely to encounter. However, this is not a reason for not allowing the administration of nevirapine elsewhere in the public health system when there is the capacity to administer it and its use is medically indicated.

[71] The cost of nevirapine for preventing mother-to-child transmission is not an issue in the present proceedings. It is admittedly within the resources of the state. The relief claimed by the applicants on this aspect of the policy, and the order made by the High Court in that regard, contemplate that nevirapine will only be administered for the prevention of mother-to-child transmission at those hospitals and clinics where testing and counselling facilities are already in place. Therefore this aspect of the claim and the orders made will not attract any significant additional costs.

[73] The administration of nevirapine is a simple procedure. Where counselling and testing facilities exist, the administration of nevirapine is well within the available resources of the state and, in such circumstances, the provision of a single dose of nevirapine to mother and child where medically indicated is a simple, cheap and potentially lifesaving medical intervention.

[80] Government policy was an inflexible one that denied mothers and their newborn children at public hospitals and clinics outside the research and training sites the opportunity of receiving a single dose of nevirapine at the time of the birth of the child. A potentially lifesaving drug was on offer and where testing and counselling facilities were available it could have been administered within the available resources of the state without any known harm to mother or child. In the circumstances we agree with the finding of the High Court that the policy of government in so far as it confines the use of nevirapine to hospitals and clinics which are research and training sites constitutes a breach of the state's obligations under section 27(2) read with section 27(1)(a) of the Constitution.

[81] Implicit in this finding is that a policy of waiting for a protracted period before taking a decision on the use of nevirapine beyond the research and training sites is also not reasonable within the meaning of section 27(2) of the Constitution.

[122] In the present case we have identified aspects of government policy that are inconsistent with the Constitution. The decision not to make nevirapine available at hospitals and clinics other than the research and training sites is central to the entire policy. Once that restriction is removed, government will be able to devise and implement a more comprehensive policy that will give access to health care

services to HIV-positive mothers and their newborn children, and will include the administration of nevirapine where that is appropriate. The policy as reformulated must meet the constitutional requirement of providing reasonable measures within available resources for the progressive realisation of the rights of such women and newborn children. This may also require, where that is necessary, that counsellors at places other than at the research and training sites be trained in counselling for the use of nevirapine. We will formulate a declaration to address these issues.

[123] Three of the nine provinces have publicly announced programmes to realise progressively the rights of pregnant women and their newborn babies to have access to nevirapine treatment. As for the rest, no programme has been disclosed by either the Minister or any of the other six [provincial health ministers], this notwithstanding the pertinent request from the TAC in July 2001 and the subsequent lodging of hundreds of pages of affidavits and written legal argument. This is regrettable. The magnitude of the HIV/AIDS challenge facing the country calls for a concerted, co-ordinated and co-operative national effort in which government in each of its three spheres and the panoply of resources and skills of civil society are marshalled, inspired and led. This can be achieved only if there is proper communication, especially by government. In order for it to be implemented optimally, a public health programme must be made known effectively to all concerned, down to the district nurse and patients. Indeed, for a public programme such as this to meet the constitutional requirement of reasonableness, its contents must be made known appropriately.

[131] We do not underestimate the nature and extent of the problem facing government in its fight to combat HIV/AIDS and, in particular, to reduce the transmission of HIV from mother to child. We also understand the need to exercise caution when dealing with a potent and a relatively unknown drug. But the nature of the problem is such that it demands urgent attention. Nevirapine is a potentially lifesaving drug. Its safety and efficacy have been established. There is a need to assess operational challenges for the best possible use of nevirapine on a comprehensive scale to reduce the risk of mother-to-child transmission of HIV. There is an additional need to monitor issues relevant to the safety and efficacy of and resistance to the use of nevirapine for this purpose. There is, however, also a pressing need to ensure that where possible loss of life is prevented in the meantime.

[132] Government policy is now evolving. Additional sites where nevirapine is provided with a 'full package' to combat mother-to-child transmission of HIV are being added. In the Western Cape, Gauteng and KwaZulu-Natal, programmes have been adopted to extend the supply of nevirapine for such purpose throughout the province. What now remains is for the other provinces to follow suit. The order that we make will facilitate this.

5.3. REASONABLENESS REVIEW

The Constitutional Court's socio-economic rights jurisprudence has coalesced around a standard of reasonableness. The standard of reasonableness is clearly drawn from the language of the socio-economic rights clauses of the Constitution, which explicitly frame the state's positive obligations in terms of a duty to "take reasonable legislative and other measures, within its available resources, to achieve the progressive realization" of the particular right; and the Court has held that both the legislative scheme and the implementation of any measures adopted by the government must be reasonable. Although the Court states clearly in its *Grootboom* decision that it will grant wide discretion to both the legislature and the executive when it comes to the means they adopt to achieve these goals, the government still has a burden to justify its decisions and the Court has demonstrated its willingness to scrutinise and even reject the government's approach if the Court finds it to be unreasonable — as it did in the *TAC* case. The Court has also incorporated other approaches within its analysis of socio-economic rights — as in *Khosa* in which non-citizen permanent residents challenged the denial of social welfare benefits. In that case, the Court adopted an analysis of intersecting rights that brought together the Court's concerns for equality and access to social resources. Yet the Court's ongoing reliance on a form of reasonableness review in this area has continued to draw critical concern.

KHOSA v. MINISTER OF SOCIAL DEVELOPMENT
Constitutional Court of South Africa
2004 (6) SA 505

Mokgoro J:

[1] These two cases concern a constitutional challenge to certain provisions of the Social Assistance Act 59 of 1992 (the Act) . . . .

[2] The applicants in both matters are Mozambican citizens who have acquired permanent residence status in South Africa in terms of exemptions granted to them under the now repealed Aliens Control Act 96 of 1991. All of the applicants in both matters, save for the second applicant in the *Khosa* matter, fled Mozambique in the 1980s as a result of the outbreak of civil war and sought refuge in South Africa. They integrated into the local community in the former Gazankulu territory in what is now known as Limpopo Province. The second applicant in the Khosa matter came to South Africa to work for the then National Parks Board at Skukuza until his retirement in May 1992. He, like the other applicants in this case, is also a permanent resident.

[3] All of the applicants in both matters are destitute and would qualify for social assistance under the Act but for the fact that they are not South African citizens . . . .

[40] The socio-economic rights in our Constitution are closely related to the founding values of human dignity, equality and freedom. Yacoob J observed in *Government of the Republic of South Africa and Others v Grootboom and Others* that the proposition that rights are inter-related and are all equally important, has immense human and practical significance in a society founded on these values.

[41] In this case we are concerned with these intersecting rights which reinforce one another at the point of intersection. The rights to life and dignity, which are intertwined in our Constitution, are implicated in the claims made by the applicants. This Court in *Dawood* said:

"Human dignity . . . informs constitutional adjudication and interpretation at a range of levels. It is a value that informs the interpretation of many, possibly all, other rights . . . . Section 10, however, makes it plain that dignity is not only a value fundamental to our Constitution it is a justiciable and enforceable right that must be respected and protected. In many cases, however, where the value of human dignity is offended, the primary constitutional breach occasioned may be of a more specific right such as the right to bodily integrity, the right to equality or the right not to be subjected to slavery, servitude or forced labour."

[42] Equality is also a foundational value of the Constitution and informs constitutional adjudication in the same way as life and dignity do. Equality in respect of access to socio-economic rights is implicit in the reference to "everyone" being entitled to have access to such rights in section 27. Those who are unable to survive without social assistance are equally desperate and equally in need of such assistance.

[44] When the rights to life, dignity and equality are implicated in cases dealing with socio-economic rights, they have to be taken into account along with the availability of human and financial resources in determining whether the state has complied with the constitutional standard of reasonableness. This is, however, not a closed list and all relevant factors have to be taken into account in this exercise. What is relevant may vary from case to case depending on the particular facts and circumstances. What makes this case different to other cases that have previously been considered by this Court is that, in addition to the rights to life and dignity, the social-security scheme put in place by the state to meet its obligations under section 27 of the Constitution raises the question of the prohibition of unfair discrimination.

[50] The state did not suggest that the exclusion of permanent residents was a temporary measure, nor did it argue that the exclusion was an incident of attempts by it progressively to realise everyone's right of access to social security. The state's case is rather that non-citizens have no legitimate claim of access to social security and it therefore excluded them from the scheme that it put in place. It is that proposition that has to be tested against the constitutional standard of reasonableness demanded by section 27(2).

[52] The right of access to social security, including social assistance, for those unable to support themselves and their dependants is entrenched because as a society we value human beings and want to ensure that people are afforded their basic needs. A society must seek to ensure that the basic necessities of life are accessible to all if it is to be a society in which human dignity, freedom and equality are foundational.

[53] It is necessary to differentiate between people and groups of people in society by classification in order for the state to allocate rights, duties, immunities, privileges, benefits or even disadvantages and to provide efficient and effective delivery of social services. However, those classifications must satisfy the constitutional requirement of "reasonableness" in section 27(2). In this case, the state has chosen to differentiate between citizens and non-citizens. That differentiation, if it is to pass constitutional muster, must not be arbitrary or irrational nor must it manifest a naked preference. There must be a rational connection between that

differentiating law and the legitimate government purpose it is designed to achieve. A differentiating law or action which does not meet these standards will be in violation of section 9(1) and section 27(2) of the Constitution.

[58] I accept that the concern that non-citizens may become a financial burden on the country is a legitimate one and I accept that there are compelling reasons why social benefits should not be made available to all who are in South Africa irrespective of their immigration status. The exclusion of all noncitizens who are destitute, however, irrespective of their immigration status, fails to distinguish between those who have become part of our society and have made their homes in South Africa, and those who have not. It also fails to distinguish between those who are being supported by sponsors who arranged their immigration and those who acquired permanent residence status without having sponsors to whom they could turn in case of need.

[79] It is now necessary to weigh up the competing considerations taking into account the intersecting rights that are involved in the present case. Of crucial importance to this analysis is the fact that the Constitution provides that "everyone" has the right to have access to social security if they are unable to support themselves and their dependants. We are concerned here with a scheme that has been put in place by the state to provide access to social security to persons unable to support themselves and their dependants. The only challenge to the scheme is that it denies access to non-citizens. There is no suggestion that the scheme is otherwise inappropriate or inconsistent with the Constitution.

[80] I have already indicated that the exclusion of permanent residents from the scheme is discriminatory and unfair and I am satisfied that this unfairness would not be justifiable under section 36 of the Constitution. The relevant considerations have been traversed above and need not be repeated. What is of particular importance in my view, however, and can be stressed again, is that the exclusion of permanent residents from the scheme is likely to have a severe impact on the dignity of the persons concerned, who, unable to sustain themselves, have to turn to others to enable them to meet the necessities of life and are thus cast in the role of supplicants.

[82] In my view the importance of providing access to social assistance to all who live permanently in South Africa and the impact upon life and dignity that a denial of such access has, far outweighs the financial and immigration considerations on which the state relies. For the same reasons, I am satisfied that the denial of access to social grants to permanent residents who, but for their citizenship, would qualify for such assistance does not constitute a reasonable legislative measure as contemplated by section 27(2) of the Constitution.

[85] The Constitution vests the right to social security in "everyone." By excluding permanent residents from the scheme for social security, the legislation limits their rights in a manner that affects their dignity and equality in material respects. Dignity and equality are founding values of the Constitution and lie at the heart of the Bill of Rights. Sufficient reason for such invasive treatment of the rights of permanent residents has not been established. The exclusion of permanent residents is therefore inconsistent with section 27 of the Constitution.

Some academic critics, activists and public interest lawyers have called upon the Court to adopt an approach to socio-economic rights similar to the United Nations Committee on Economic, Social and Cultural Rights, which monitors state compliance with the International Covenant on Economic, Social and Cultural Rights of 1966. In its General Comment 3, on the nature of the member state's obligations under the Covenant, the Committee has advocated for a "minimum core" approach, which would require states to achieve "minimum essential levels" of these rights. The Constitutional Court has made clear its resistance to these calls to define the "minimum core" of these rights in the Constitution, although this rejection was initially framed in terms of the availability of contextual evidence and not as a matter of principle. As a result, activists continued to assert that the inclusion of these rights in the Constitution would be meaningless unless they supported some substantive content. When Judge Tsoka of the South Gauteng High Court struck down Johannesburg's policy of installing pre-paid water meters in Phiri (a neighborhood in the Soweto township), and issued an order in April 2008 that required the city to provide each resident with 50 liters of free water each day, it seemed as if the idea of a minimum core had finally been accepted (*Mazibuko and Others v. City of Johannesburg and Others (Centre on Housing Rights and Evictions as amicus curiae)* (2008) 4 SA 471 (W)). And when the Supreme Court of Appeals essentially upheld Judge Tsoka's decision — while reducing the minimum supply of free water to 42 liters — and the City of Johannesburg appealed to the Constitutional Court, the question of whether the right to water required the supply of a specific minimum amount was placed squarely before the Court.

It is also important to note that the Constitutional Court has repeatedly held that "where legislation has been enacted to give effect to a right, a litigant should rely on that legislation in order to give effect to the right or alternatively challenge the legislation as being inconsistent with the Constitution" (Mazibuko, 2010 (4) SA 1 (CC) para 73), see also *Bato Star Fishing (Pty) Ltd v. Minister of Environmental Affairs and Tourism and Others*, 2004 (4) SA 490 (CC) at paras 22–6; *MEC for Education, KwaZulu Natal and Others v. Pillay*, 2008 (1) SA 474 (CC) at para 40; and *South African National Defence Union v. Minister of Defence and Others*, 2007 (5) SA 400 (CC), at para 52.

MAZIBUKO v. CITY OF JOHANNESBURG
CONSTITUTIONAL COURT OF SOUTH AFRICA
2010 (4) SA 1

O'REGAN J:

[1] This application for leave to appeal against a judgment of the Supreme Court of Appeal raises, for the first time in this Court, the proper interpretation of section 27(1)(b) of the Constitution which provides that everyone has the right to have access to sufficient water. Cultures in all parts of the world acknowledge the importance of water. Water is life. Without it, nothing organic grows. Human beings need water to drink, to cook, to wash and to grow our food. Without it, we will die.

It is not surprising then that our Constitution entrenches the right of access to water.

[6] The case concerns two major issues: the first is whether the City's policy in relation to the supply of free basic water, and particularly, its decision to supply 6 kilolitres of free water per month to every accountholder in the city (the Free Basic Water policy) is in conflict with section 27 of the Constitution or section 11 of the Water Services Act. The second major issue is whether the installation of pre-paid water meters by the first and second respondents in Phiri was lawful.

[9] After careful consideration of the issues, this judgment finds that the City's Free Basic Water policy falls within the bounds of reasonableness and therefore is not in conflict with either section 27 of the Constitution or with the national legislation regulating water services. The installation of pre-paid meters in Phiri is found to be lawful. Accordingly, the orders made by the Supreme Court of Appeal and the High Court are set aside.

[31] In regard to the Free Basic Water policy, the applicants argue that the Supreme Court of Appeal erred in determining that the sufficient amount of water required by section 27 is 42 litres per person per day, rather than 50 litres per person. They also assert that the Supreme Court of Appeal should have made an order declaring that the City was obliged to provide this amount of water free of charge to all the residents of Phiri who cannot afford to pay for their own water.

[47] Traditionally, constitutional rights (especially civil and political rights) are understood as imposing an obligation upon the state to refrain from interfering with the exercise of the right by citizens (the so-called negative obligation or the duty to respect). As this Court has held, most notably perhaps in *Jaftha v Schoeman*, [2005 (2) SA 140 CC] social and economic rights are no different. The state bears a duty to refrain from interfering with social and economic rights just as it does with civil and political rights.

[48] The primary question in this case, though, is the extent of the state's positive obligation under section 27(1)(b) and section 27(2). This issue has been addressed by this Court in at least two previous decisions: *Grootboom* and *Treatment Action Campaign No 2*. In *Grootboom*, the Court had to consider whether section 26 (the right to housing) entitles citizens to approach a court to claim a house from the state. Such an interpretation of section 26 would imply a directly enforceable obligation upon the state to provide every citizen with a house immediately.

[49] This Court concluded that section 26 does not impose such an obligation. Instead, the Court held that the scope of the positive obligation imposed upon the state by section 26 is carefully delineated by section 26(2). Section 26(2) provides explicitly that the state must take reasonable legislative and other measures progressively to realise the right of access to adequate housing within available resources. . .

[50] Applying this approach to section 27(1)(b), the right of access to sufficient water, coupled with section 27(2), it is clear that the right does not require the state upon demand to provide every person with sufficient water without more; rather it requires the state to take reasonable legislative and other measures progressively

to realise the achievement of the right of access to sufficient water, within available resources.

[51] The applicants argued that the Court should determine the content of the right in section 27(1)(b) by quantifying the amount of water sufficient for dignified life, and urged that the appropriate amount is 50 litres per person per day. They further contended that the Court should hold that this is the content of the section 27(1)(b) right which the Court should declare and that the Court should then determine whether the state acted reasonably in seeking to achieve the progressive realisation of this right.

[52] This argument is similar to that advanced in earlier cases in this Court asserting that every social and economic right has a minimum core, a basic content which must be provided by the state. In international law, the concept of — minimum core. originates in General Comment 3 (1990) of the United Nations Committee on Economic, Social and Cultural Rights . . . .

[53] In *Grootboom*, this Court rejected the argument that the social and economic rights in our Constitution contain a minimum core which the state is obliged to furnish, the content of which should be determined by the courts . . . .

[56] The applicants' argument that this Court should determine a quantity of water which would constitute the content of the section 27(1)(b) right is, in effect, an argument similar to a minimum core argument though it is more extensive because it goes beyond the minimum. The applicants' argument is that the proposed amount (50 litres per person per day) is what is necessary for dignified human life; they expressly reject the notion that it is the minimum core protection required by the right. Their argument is thus that the Court should adopt a quantified standard determining the content of the right not merely its minimum content. The argument must fail for the same reasons that the minimum core argument failed in *Grootboom* and *Treatment Action Campaign No 2*.

[57] Those reasons are essentially twofold. The first reason arises from the text of the Constitution and the second from an understanding of the proper role of courts in our constitutional democracy. As appears from the reasoning in both *Grootboom* and *Treatment Action Campaign No 2*, section 27(1) and (2) of the Constitution must be read together to delineate the scope of the positive obligation to provide access to sufficient water imposed upon the state. That obligation requires the state to take reasonable legislative and other measures progressively to achieve the right of access to sufficient water within available resources. It does not confer a right to claim —sufficient water — from the state immediately.

[59] At the time the Constitution was adopted, millions of South Africans did not have access to the basic necessities of life, including water. The purpose of the constitutional entrenchment of social and economic rights was thus to ensure that the state continue to take reasonable legislative and other measures progressively to achieve the realisation of the rights to the basic necessities of life. It was not expected, nor could it have been, that the state would be able to furnish citizens immediately with all the basic necessities of life. Social and economic rights empower citizens to demand of the state that it acts reasonably and progressively to ensure that all enjoy the basic necessities of life. In so doing, the social and

economic rights enable citizens to hold government to account for the manner in which it seeks to pursue the achievement of social and economic rights.

[60] Moreover, what the right requires will vary over time and context. Fixing a quantified content might, in a rigid and counter-productive manner, prevent an analysis of context. The concept of reasonableness places context at the centre of the enquiry and permits an assessment of context to determine whether a government programme is indeed reasonable.

[61] Secondly, ordinarily it is institutionally inappropriate for a court to determine precisely what the achievement of any particular social and economic right entails and what steps government should take to ensure the progressive realisation of the right. This is a matter, in the first place, for the legislature and executive, the institutions of government best placed to investigate social conditions in the light of available budgets and to determine what targets are achievable in relation to social and economic rights. Indeed, it is desirable as a matter of democratic accountability that they should do so for it is their programmes and promises that are subjected to democratic popular choice.

[66] The Constitution envisages that legislative and other measures will be the primary instrument for the achievement of social and economic rights. Thus it places a positive obligation upon the state to respond to the basic social and economic needs of the people by adopting reasonable legislative and other measures. By adopting such measures, the rights set out in the Constitution acquire content, and that content is subject to the constitutional standard of reasonableness.

[67] Thus the positive obligations imposed upon government by the social and economic rights in our Constitution will be enforced by courts in at least the following ways. If government takes no steps to realise the rights, the courts will require government to take steps. If government's adopted measures are unreasonable, the courts will similarly require that they be reviewed so as to meet the constitutional standard of reasonableness. From *Grootboom*, it is clear that a measure will be unreasonable if it makes no provision for those most desperately in need. If government adopts a policy with unreasonable limitations or exclusions, as in *Treatment Action Campaign No 2*, the Court may order that those are removed. Finally, the obligation of progressive realisation imposes a duty upon government continually to review its policies to ensure that the achievement of the right is progressively realised.

[71] A reasonableness challenge requires government to explain the choices it has made. To do so, it must provide the information it has considered and the process it has followed to determine its policy. This case provides an excellent example of government doing just that. Although the applicants complained about the volume of material lodged by the City and Johannesburg Water in particular, which covered all aspects of the formulation of the City's water policy, the disclosure of such information points to the substantial importance of litigation concerning social and economic rights. If the process followed by government is flawed or the information gathered is obviously inadequate or incomplete, appropriate relief may be sought. In this way, the social and economic rights entrenched in our Constitution may contribute to the deepening of democracy. They enable citizens to hold government

accountable not only through the ballot box but also, in a different way, through litigation.

[94] The Constitution requires that the state adopt reasonable measures progressively to realise the right of access to sufficient water. Although the free water policy did not contain any provision for flexibility when it was introduced in 2001, the record makes plain that the City was continually reconsidering its policy and investigating ways to ensure that the poorest inhabitants of the City gained access not only to water, but also to other services, such as electricity, sanitation and refuse removal. The extremely informative and candid answering affidavits lodged by the City make it plain that for the City the task was a challenging one, both administratively and financially.

[96] It may well be, as the applicants urge, that the City's comprehensive and persistent engagement has been spurred by the litigation in this case. If that is so, it is not something to deplore. If one of the key goals of the entrenchment of social and economic rights is to ensure that government is responsive and accountable to citizens through both the ballot box and litigation, then that goal will be served when a government respondent takes steps in response to litigation to ensure that the measures it adopts are reasonable, within the meaning of the Constitution. The litigation will in that event have attained at least some of what it sought to achieve.

[160] The purpose of litigation concerning the positive obligations imposed by social and economic rights should be to hold the democratic arms of government to account through litigation. In so doing, litigation of this sort fosters a form of participative democracy that holds government accountable and requires it to account between elections over specific aspects of government policy.

[161] When challenged as to its policies relating to social and economic rights, the government agency must explain why the policy is reasonable. Government must disclose what it has done to formulate the policy: its investigation and research, the alternatives considered, and the reasons why the option underlying the policy was selected. The Constitution does not require government to be held to an impossible standard of perfection. Nor does it require courts to take over the tasks that in a democracy should properly be reserved for the democratic arms of government. Simply put, through the institution of the courts, government can be called upon to account to citizens for its decisions. This understanding of social and economic rights litigation accords with the founding values of our Constitution and, in particular, the principles that government should be responsive, accountable and open.

[162] Not only must government show that the policy it has selected is reasonable, it must show that the policy is being reconsidered consistent with the obligation to progressively realise social and economic rights in mind. A policy that is set in stone and never revisited is unlikely to be a policy that will result in the progressive realisation of rights consistently with the obligations imposed by the social and economic rights in our Constitution.

[163] This case illustrates how litigation concerning social and economic rights can exact a detailed accounting from government and, in doing so, impact beneficially on the policy-making process. The applicants, in argument, rued the fact that the City

had continually amended its policies during the course of the litigation. In fact, that consequence of the litigation (if such it was) was beneficial. Having to explain why the Free Basic Water policy was reasonable shone a bright, cold light on the policy that undoubtedly revealed flaws. The continual revision of the policy in the ensuing years has improved the policy in a manner entirely consistent with an obligation of progressive realisation.

[165] It is true that litigation of this sort is expensive and requires great expertise. South Africa is fortunate to have a range of non-governmental organisations working in the legal arena seeking improvement in the lives of poor South Africans. Long may that be so. These organisations have developed an expertise in litigating in the interests of the poor to the great benefit of our society. The approach to costs in constitutional matters means that litigation launched in a serious attempt to further constitutional rights, even if unsuccessful, will not result in an adverse costs order. The challenges posed by social and economic rights litigation are significant, but given the benefits that it can offer, it should be pursued.

[169] I have thus concluded that neither the Free Basic Water policy nor the introduction of pre-paid water meters in Phiri as a result of Operation Gcin'amanzi constitute a breach of section 27 of the Constitution. Accordingly, the respondents' appeals succeed and the order made by the Supreme Court of Appeal should be set aside, as should the High Court order.

In enforcing socio-economic rights, courts are challenged to ensure that limited resources are allocated to progressively implement rights in a manner subject to s 9's bar on unequal treatment. An example is *Nokotyana v. Ehurhuleni Metro. Municipality*, [2010 (4) BCLR 312 (CC)] where a municipality's refusal to provide additional pit latrines for an informal settlement was challenged in the face of the national and provincial governments' offer to finance the toilets. The Constitutional Court accepted the municipality's justification that providing improved sanitation for this particular settlement but not others would be unequal treatment: "It would not be just and equitable to make an order that would benefit only those who approached a court and caused sufficient embarrassment to provincial and national authorities to motivate them to make a once-off offer of this kind." *Id.* at ¶ 54.

Finally, the Constitutional Court has recently considered the interaction between private actions, in which private owners have obtained court orders evicting occupiers of buildings in Johannesburg and the duty of the City of Johannesburg to provide emergency housing to the people left homeless by the legal eviction [see *Residents of Bon Vista Mansions v. So Metro Local Council*, 2001(6) BCLR 625 (W), holding that water service cannot be discontinued when consumer satisfactorily demonstrates an inability to pay].

CITY OF JOHANNESBURG v. BLUE MOONLIGHT PROPERTIES
CONSTITUTIONAL COURT OF SOUTH AFRICA
2012 (2) SA 104

VAN DER WESTHUIZEN J [MOSENEKE DCJ, CAMERON J, FRONEMAN J, JAFTA J, KHAMPEPE J, MOGOENG J, NKABINDE J, SKWEYIYA J and YACOOB J concurring]:

Introduction

[1] This matter concerns the fate of 86 people (Occupiers), who are poor and unlawfully occupy a property called — Saratoga Avenue in Berea in the City of Johannesburg (property). The property comprises old and dilapidated commercial premises with office space, a factory building and garages. The case deals with the rights of the owner of the property, Blue Moonlight Properties 39 (Pty) Ltd (Blue Moonlight) and with the obligation of the City of Johannesburg Metropolitan Municipality (City) to provide housing for the Occupiers if they are evicted. Ultimately we must decide whether the eviction of the Occupiers is just and equitable.

[2] Seventeen years into our democracy, a dignified existence for all in South Africa has not yet been achieved. The quest for a roof over one's head often lies at the heart of our constitutional, legal, political and economic discourse on how to bring about social justice within a stable constitutional democracy. In view of prevailing socio-economic conditions, this is understandable. An estimated 423 249 households in Johannesburg alone are, for example, without adequate housing. Approximately 1,8 million households in the country were living in informal housing by 2001. The present number may be higher.

[3] The practical questions to be answered in this case are whether the Occupiers must be evicted to allow the owner to fully exercise its rights regarding its property and, if so, whether their eviction must be linked to an order that the City provide them with accommodation. The City's position is that it is neither obliged nor able to provide accommodation in these circumstances. The owner wishes to exercise its right to develop its property and wants no part in the dispute about the City's responsibilities or the plight of the Occupiers. And the Occupiers do not want to end up homeless on the street. All parties rely on the Constitution, statutory law giving effect to the Constitution and judgments of this Court.

[6] The Occupiers comprise 81 adults and five children. One child is a person with disability, two adults are pensioners and a number of the households are headed by women. The average income per household is R940 per month [approximately US$135]. Many of the Occupiers send a portion of their income to family members in other parts of the country. Most of them do not have formal employment and make their living in the informal sector[4] in the central business district. The location

---

4 [Ed. note: the phrase "informal sector" refers to economic activity outside of formal employment or registered business activity e.g., selling goods or food on the side-walk or on street corners, among many other activities.]

of the building is crucial to the Occupiers' income. The majority of them say that they would not be able to afford the transport costs necessitated by living elsewhere. The Occupiers, relying on expert evidence, also state that if they were to be evicted, they would have to sleep on the street as they would not be able to find affordable accommodation.

[8] In 2004 Blue Moonlight purchased the property with the hope of redeveloping it. The Occupiers allege that they paid rent to an individual and into two bank accounts until the end of 2005, but Blue Moonlight contends that it never received payments.

[9] The condition of the property has deteriorated over the years. In 2000 and 2002 — while their occupation was presumably still lawful — the Occupiers laid two complaints with the Housing Tribunal, but nothing came of them. In 2005 the City issued two notices warning Blue Moonlight to remedy the fire safety and the health and sanitation conditions on the property. It is not disputed that the current conditions are abysmal.

[10] On 28 June 2005 Blue Moonlight posted a notice to vacate the property by 31 July 2005. This notice also purported to cancel any lease that may have existed. Another notice, to the same effect, was posted on 6 January 2006 with a deadline of 5 February 2006.

[33] In determining whether the eviction of the Occupiers will be just and equitable, it is necessary to address —

(a) the rights of the owner in a constitutional and PIE era;[5]

(b) the obligations of the City to provide accommodation;

(c) the sufficiency of the City's resources;

(d) the constitutionality of the City's emergency housing policy; and

(e) an appropriate order to facilitate justice and equity in the light of the conclusions on the earlier issues.

[34] The South African constitutional order recognises the social and historical context of property and related rights. The protection against arbitrary deprivation of property in section 25 of the Constitution is balanced by the right of access to adequate housing in section 26(1) and the right not to be evicted arbitrarily from one's home in section 26(3). This Court noted in FNB:

> The purpose of section 25 has to be seen both as protecting existing private property rights as well as serving the public interest, mainly in the sphere of land reform but not limited thereto, and also as striking a proportionate balance between these two functions. [2002 (4) SA 768 para 50.]

[70] The City's Housing Report states that it is urgently relocating people from identified dangerous buildings to temporary accommodation due to the threat to

---

[5] [Ed. note: The PIE is the Prevention of Illegal Eviction from and Unlawful Occupation of Land Act 19 of 1998, which fundamentally changed the existing property law to prevent summary eviction of people from land despite their not having formal legal rights to the property.]

their safety, but that the City does not have alternative accommodation available to temporarily or permanently accommodate those who face homelessness as a result of eviction by private property owners.

[80] The City's housing policy differentiates between those relocated by the City and those whose eviction is sought by private landowners. Persons relocated at the instance of the City are housed in temporary accommodation in one of the buildings made available by the City for this purpose. Persons evicted by private landowners are however not so housed.

[88] In the area of the right of access to adequate housing, of which the provision of temporary or emergency accommodation is a part, the question is essentially one of reasonableness. The availability of resources is an important factor in determining the reasonableness of the measures employed to achieve the progressive realisation of the right. This does not mean that the state may arbitrarily decide which measures to implement. The measures taken must be reasonable. While there will be a range of possible measures that may be reasonable and the Court will not set aside a policy for the mere reason that other measures may have been more desirable or favourable, the enquiry must still take place.

[92] By drawing a rigid line between persons relocated by the City and those evicted by private landowners, the City excludes from the assessment, whether emergency accommodation should be made available, the individual situations of the persons at risk and the reason for the eviction. Affected individuals may include children, elderly people, people with disability or women-headed households, for whom the need for housing is particularly great or for whom homelessness would result in particularly disastrous consequences. Individuals may have a range of incomes — some may be able to afford subsidised housing while others may be completely destitute. In the present case, the Occupiers have a myriad of personal circumstances to be taken into account in considering their eligibility for housing. Furthermore, it cannot necessarily be assumed that the City evicts or relocates mainly for reasons of safety whilst private property owners do so only for commercial reasons. Once an emergency of looming homelessness is created, it in any event matters little to the evicted who the evictor is. The policy does not meaningfully and reasonably allow for the needs of those affected to be taken into account.

[95] As a result, I find that whereas differentiation between emergency housing needs and housing needs that do not constitute an emergency might well be reasonable, the differentiation the City's policy makes is not. To the extent that eviction may result in homelessness, it is of little relevance whether removal from one's home is at the instance of the City or a private property owner.

[96] The findings are briefly summarised. To the extent that it is the owner of the property and the occupation is unlawful, Blue Moonlight is entitled to an eviction order. All relevant circumstances must be taken into account though to determine whether, under which conditions and by which date, eviction would be just and equitable. The availability of alternative housing for the Occupiers is one of the circumstances. The eviction would create an emergency situation in terms of Chapter 12. The City's interpretation of Chapter 12 as neither permitting nor obliging them to take measures to provide emergency accommodation, after having

been refused financial assistance by the province, is incorrect. The City is obliged to provide temporary accommodation. The finding of the Supreme Court of Appeal that the City had not persuaded the Court that it lacks resources to do so has not been shown to be incorrect and must stand.

[97] The City's housing policy is unconstitutional in that it excludes people evicted by a private landowner from its temporary housing programme, as opposed to those relocated by the City. Blue Moonlight cannot be expected indefinitely to provide free housing to the Occupiers, but its rights as property owner must be interpreted within the context of the requirement that eviction must be just and equitable. Eviction of the Occupiers would be just and equitable under the circumstances, if linked to the provision of temporary accommodation by the City.

5.4. CONSIDERATION AND REJECTION IN THE UNITED STATES

5.4.1. The possibilities for inclusion through constitutional interpretation

In his analysis in THE SECOND BILL OF RIGHTS: FDR'S UNFINISHED REVOLUTION AND WHY WE NEED IT MORE THAN EVER (2004), Professor Cass Sunstein notes the breadth of constitutional provisions such as the Fourteenth Amendment guarantee against deprivation of "liberty" without due process and of "equal protection of the laws," and he catalogues numerous examples of how the broad provisions of the U.S. Constitution had changed over time. At one time, it was clear that the Constitution permitted racial segregation, sex discrimination, government suppression of political dissent that had a dangerous tendency, government regulation of commercial speech, prohibited maximum hour and minimum wage laws, and did not protect the right of same-sex couples to sexual intimacy. Today, the opposite doctrines are all established in American constitutional law. SECOND BILL OF RIGHTS, supra, at 123. (For an argument that the evolution of constitutional doctrine is fully consistent with a theory of constitutional interpretation that resembles common law reasoning in property, tort, or contract cases, see DAVID STRAUSS, THE LIVING CONSTITUTION (2010).)

The groundwork for recognition of social and economic rights was laid after World War II, in a series of Supreme Court decisions concerning the rights of the poor. Thus, in *Griffin v. Illinois*, 351 U.S. 12 (1956), the Court held that the Equal Protection Clause required states to provide trial transcripts to poor defendants appealing their criminal convictions. The Court noted that in "criminal cases a State can no more discriminate on account of poverty than on account of religion, race, or color." *Id.* at 17. In one of the most famous decisions in American law, *Gideon v. Wainwright*, 372 U.S. 335 (1963), the Court interpreted the Sixth Amendment's right to counsel to require that in the case of indigent defendants the state must provide for defense counsel.

These rights were extended beyond the criminal law context in *Boddie v. Connecticut*, 401 U.S. 371 (1971), requiring the state to pay an indigent's courts fees and costs in a divorce case. The court noted the importance of marriage, and that in some cases resort to courts was the only legitimate means to resolve disputes.

Expressly noting that notions of equality "do change," the Court in *Harper v. Virginia Board of Elections*, 383 U.S. 663 (1966), held that the Equal Protection Clause did not permit the state to impose a poll tax as a prerequisite to voting. The court noted that "wealth, like race, creed, and color, is not germane to one's ability to participate intelligently in the electoral process," and that lines "drawn on the basis of wealth or property, like those of race, [are] disfavored." *Id.* at 668. Although formally relying on an unenumerated right to travel, the Court in *Shapiro v. Thompson*, 394 U.S. 618 (1969), expanded equal treatment for the poor by holding unconstitutional a state statute that limited welfare benefits to those resident in the state for one year. Using classic common law reasoning, the Court extended this reasoning to nonemergency medical case in *Memorial Hospital v. Maricopa County*, 415 U.S. 250 (1974).

5.4.2.   The apex of American recognition of poverty rights

GOLDBERG v. KELLY
SUPREME COURT OF THE UNITED STATES
397 U.S. 254 (1970)

[Residents of New York City who were receiving financial aid under state or federally assisted welfare programs instituted actions in the United States District Court for the Southern District of New York, alleging that state and city welfare officials had terminated, or were about to terminate, such aid without prior notice and hearing in violation of due process. After the welfare authorities modified their procedures to include an informal discussion with a caseworker, 7 days' notice of proposed termination of payments, review by a higher official with a written statement from the recipient, and a right to appear personally at a post-termination hearing before an independent hearing officer, where the recipient could appear personally, offer oral evidence, confront and cross-examine witnesses, and have a record made of the hearing, the plaintiffs challenged the constitutional adequacy of such procedures.]

MR. JUSTICE BRENNAN delivered the opinion of the Court.

I

The constitutional issue to be decided, therefore, is the narrow one whether the Due Process Clause requires that the recipient be afforded an evidentiary hearing *before* the termination of benefits. The District Court held that only a pre-termination evidentiary hearing would satisfy the constitutional command, and rejected the argument of the state and city officials that the combination of the post-termination "fair hearing" with the informal pre-termination review disposed of all due process claims. The court said: "While post-termination review is relevant, there is one overpowering fact which controls here. By hypothesis, a welfare recipient is destitute, without funds or assets . . . . Suffice it to say that to cut off a welfare recipient in the face of . . . 'brutal need' without a prior hearing of some sort is unconscionable, unless overwhelming considerations justify it." *Kelly v. Wyman*, 294 F. Supp. 893, 899, 900 (1968). The court rejected the argument that the need to protect the public's tax revenues supplied the requisite "overwhelming consideration." "Against the justified desire to protect public funds must be weighed the individual's overpowering need in this unique situation not to be wrongfully deprived of assistance . . . . While the problem of additional expense must be kept in mind, it does not justify denying a hearing meeting the ordinary standards of due process. Under all the circumstances, we hold that due process requires an adequate hearing before termination of welfare benefits, and the fact that there is a later constitutionally fair proceeding does not alter the result." *Id.*, at 901 . . . . We affirm.

Appellant does not contend that procedural due process is not applicable to the termination of welfare benefits. Such benefits are a matter of statutory entitlement for persons qualified to receive them.[6] Their termination involves state action that adjudicates important rights. The constitutional challenge cannot be answered by an argument that public assistance benefits are "a 'privilege' and not a 'right.' " *Shapiro v. Thompson*, 394 U.S. 618, 627 n. 6 (1969). Relevant constitutional restraints apply as much to the withdrawal of public assistance benefits as to disqualification for unemployment compensation, *Sherbert v. Verner*, 374 U.S. 398 (1963); or to denial of a tax exemption, *Speiser v. Randall*, 357 U.S. 513 (1958); or to discharge from public employment, *Slochower v. Board of Higher Education*, 350 U.S. 551 (1956). The extent to which procedural due process must be afforded the recipient is influenced by the extent to which he may be "condemned to suffer grievous loss," *Joint Anti-Fascist Refugee Committee v. McGrath*, 341 U.S. 123, 168 (1951) (Frankfurter, J., concurring), and depends upon whether the recipient's interest in avoiding that loss outweighs the governmental interest in summary adjudication . . . .

It is true, of course, that some governmental benefits may be administratively terminated without affording the recipient a pre-termination evidentiary hearing. But we agree with the District Court that when welfare is discontinued, only a pre-termination evidentiary hearing provides the recipient with procedural due process. For qualified recipients, welfare provides the means to obtain essential

---

[6] [FN 8] It may be realistic today to regard welfare entitlements as more like "property" than a "gratuity." Much of the existing wealth in this country takes the form of rights that do not fall within traditional common-law concepts of property. It has been aptly noted that

> "society today is built around entitlement. The automobile dealer has his franchise, the doctor and lawyer their professional licenses, the worker his union membership, contract, and pension rights, the executive his contract and stock options; all are devices to aid security and independence. Many of the most important of these entitlements now flow from government: subsidies to farmers and businessmen, routes for airlines and channels for television stations; long term contracts for defense, space, and education; social security pensions for individuals. Such sources of security, whether private or public, are no longer regarded as luxuries or gratuities; to the recipients they are essentials, fully deserved, and in no sense a form of charity. It is only the poor whose entitlements, although recognized by public policy, have not been effectively enforced."

Reich, *Individual Rights and Social Welfare: The Emerging Legal Issues*, 74 Yale L.J. 1245, 1255 (1965). See also Reich, *The New Property*, 73 Yale L.J. 733 (1964).

food, clothing, housing, and medical care. Thus the crucial factor in this context —
a factor not present in the case of the blacklisted government contractor, the
discharged government employee, the taxpayer denied a tax exemption, or virtually
anyone else whose governmental entitlements are ended — is that termination of
aid pending resolution of a controversy over eligibility may deprive an *eligible*
recipient of the very means by which to live while he waits. Since he lacks
independent resources, his situation becomes immediately desperate. His need to
concentrate upon finding the means for daily subsistence, in turn, adversely affects
his ability to seek redress from the welfare bureaucracy.[7]

Moreover, important governmental interests are promoted by affording recipients a pre-termination evidentiary hearing. From its founding the Nation's basic
commitment has been to foster the dignity and well-being of all persons within its
borders. We have come to recognize that forces not within the control of the poor
contribute to their poverty. This perception, against the background of our
traditions, has significantly influenced the development of the contemporary public
assistance system. Welfare, by meeting the basic demands of subsistence, can help
bring within the reach of the poor the same opportunities that are available to
others to participate meaningfully in the life of the community. At the same time,
welfare guards against the societal malaise that may flow from a widespread sense
of unjustified frustration and insecurity. Public assistance, then, is not mere charity,
but a means to "promote the general Welfare, and secure the Blessings of Liberty
to ourselves and our Posterity." The same governmental interests that counsel the
provision of welfare, counsel as well its uninterrupted provision to those eligible to
receive it; pre-termination evidentiary hearings are indispensable to that end.

We agree with the District Court, however, that [the interest in conserving fiscal
and administrative resources] are not overriding in the welfare context. The
requirement of a prior hearing doubtless involves some greater expense, and the
benefits paid to ineligible recipients pending decision at the hearing probably
cannot be recouped, since these recipients are likely to be judgment-proof. But the
State is not without weapons to minimize these increased costs. Much of the drain
on fiscal and administrative resources can be reduced by developing procedures for
prompt pre-termination hearings and by skillful use of personnel and facilities.
Indeed, the very provision for a post-termination evidentiary hearing in New York's
Home Relief program is itself cogent evidence that the State recognizes the
primacy of the public interest in correct eligibility determinations and therefore in
the provision of procedural safeguards. Thus, the interest of the eligible recipient in
uninterrupted receipt of public assistance, coupled with the State's interest that his
payments not be erroneously terminated, clearly outweighs the State's competing
concern to prevent any increase in its fiscal and administrative burdens. As the
District Court correctly concluded, "the stakes are simply too high for the welfare
recipient, and the possibility for honest error or irritable misjudgment too great, to
allow termination of aid without giving the recipient a chance, if he so desires, to be
fully informed of the case against him so that he may contest its basis and produce

---

[7] [FN 12] His impaired adversary position is particularly telling in light of the welfare bureaucracy's
difficulties in reaching correct decisions on eligibility. See Comment, *Due Process and the Right to a
Prior Hearing in Welfare Cases*, 37 Ford. L. Rev. 604, 610–611 (1969).

evidence in rebuttal." 294 F. Supp. at 904–905.

II

[The court affirmed the District Court's determination that a quasi-judicial trial was not required. The sole function of the mandated pre-termination hearing was to protect against an erroneous determination of benefits, not to facilitate judicial review and precedent. Although efficiency and cost considerations did not justify denial of any hearing, they did factor in to the Court's conclusion that only minimum procedural safeguards were required.] We wish to add that we, no less than the dissenters, recognize the importance of not imposing upon the States or the Federal Government in this developing field of law any procedural requirements beyond those demanded by rudimentary due process.

[The court concluded that due process required that a recipient have timely and adequate notice detailing the reasons for a proposed termination, and an effective opportunity to defend by confronting any adverse witnesses and by presenting his own arguments and evidence orally. It rejected reliance purely on writing submissions, which "are an unrealistic option for most recipients, who lack the educational attainment necessary to write effectively and who cannot obtain professional assistance. Moreover, written submissions do not afford the flexibility of oral presentations; they do not permit the recipient to mold his argument to the issues the decision maker appears to regard as important." The court further held that, due to our traditional adversary process, welfare recipients must be given an opportunity to confront and cross-examine the witnesses relied on by the department. Although the court did not hold that recipients had a right to counsel, it did hold that counsel must be permitted if retained by the recipient (or, as had become more prevalent, legal aid attorneys). And the Court required that the decision maker to state the reasons for the determination and indicate the evidence relief on.]

MR. JUSTICE BLACK, dissenting.

In the last half century the United States, along with many, perhaps most, other nations of the world, has moved far toward becoming a welfare state, that is, a nation that for one reason or another taxes its most affluent people to help support, feed, clothe, and shelter its less fortunate citizens. The result is that today more than nine million men, women, and children in the United States receive some kind of state or federally financed public assistance in the form of allowances or gratuities, generally paid them periodically, usually by the week, month, or quarter. Since these gratuities are paid on the basis of need, the list of recipients is not static, and some people go off the lists and others are added from time to time. These ever-changing lists put a constant administrative burden on government and it certainly could not have reasonably anticipated that this burden would include the additional procedural expense imposed by the Court today.

The dilemma of the ever-increasing poor in the midst of constantly growing affluence presses upon us and must inevitably be met within the framework of our democratic constitutional government, if our system is to survive as such. It was largely to escape just such pressing economic problems and attendant government repression that people from Europe, Asia, and other areas settled this country and formed our Nation. Many of those settlers had personally suffered from persecutions of various kinds and wanted to get away from governments that had unrestrained powers to make life miserable for their citizens. It was for this reason, or so I believe, that on reaching these new lands the early settlers undertook to curb their governments by confining their powers within written boundaries, which eventually became written constitutions. They wrote their basic charters as nearly as men's collective wisdom could do so as to proclaim to their people and their officials an emphatic command that: "Thus far and no farther shall you go; and where we neither delegate powers to you, nor prohibit your exercise of them, we the people are left free."

[Black, J. accused the majority of using judicial powers for legislative purposes.]

The more than a million names on the relief rolls in New York, and the more than nine million names on the rolls of all the 50 States were not put there at random. The names are there because state welfare officials believed that those people were eligible for assistance. Probably in the officials' haste to make out the lists many names were put there erroneously in order to alleviate immediate suffering, and undoubtedly some people are drawing relief who are not entitled under the law to do so. Doubtless some draw relief checks from time to time who know they are not eligible, either because they are not actually in need or for some other reason. Many of those who thus draw undeserved gratuities are without sufficient property to enable the government to collect back from them any money they wrongfully receive. But the Court today holds that it would violate the Due Process Clause of the Fourteenth Amendment to stop paying those people weekly or monthly allowances unless the government first affords them a full "evidentiary hearing" even though welfare officials are persuaded that the recipients are not rightfully entitled to receive a penny under the law. In other words, although some recipients might be on the lists for payment wholly because of deliberate fraud on their part, the Court holds that the government is helpless and must continue, until after an evidentiary hearing, to pay money that it does not owe, never has owed, and never could owe. I do not believe there is any provision in our Constitution that should thus paralyze the government's efforts to protect itself against making payments to people who are not entitled to them.

Particularly do I not think that the Fourteenth Amendment should be given such an unnecessarily broad construction. That Amendment came into being primarily to protect Negroes from discrimination, and while some of its language can and does protect others, all know that the chief purpose behind it was to protect ex-slaves. The Court, however, relies upon the Fourteenth Amendment and in effect says that failure of the government to pay a promised charitable installment to an individual deprives that individual of *his own property*, in violation of the Due Process Clause of the Fourteenth Amendment. It somewhat strains credulity to say that the government's promise of charity to an individual is property belonging to that individual when the government denies that the individual is honestly entitled to receive such a payment.

Although the majority attempts to bolster its decision with limited quotations from prior cases, it is obvious that today's result does not depend on the language of the Constitution itself or the principles of other decisions, but solely on the collective judgment of the majority as to what would be a fair and humane procedure in this case.

This decision is thus only another variant of the view often expressed by some members of this Court that the Due Process Clause forbids any conduct that a majority of the Court believes "unfair," "indecent," or "shocking to their consciences." Neither these words nor any like them appear anywhere in the Due Process Clause. If they did, they would leave the majority of Justices free to hold any conduct unconstitutional that they should conclude on their own to be unfair or shocking to them. Had the drafters of the Due Process Clause meant to leave judges such ambulatory power to declare laws unconstitutional, the chief value of a written constitution, as the Founders saw it, would have been lost. In fact, if that view of due process is correct, the Due Process Clause could easily swallow up all other parts of the Constitution. And truly the Constitution would always be "what the judges say it is" at a given moment, not what the Founders wrote into the document . . . .

5.4.3.   The rejection of social and economic rights

DANDRIDGE v. WILLIAMS
SUPREME COURT OF THE UNITED STATES
397 U.S. 471 (1970)

MR. JUSTICE STEWART delivered the opinion of the Court.

This case involves the validity of a method used by Maryland, in the administration of an aspect of its public welfare program, to reconcile the demands of its needy citizens with the finite resources available to meet those demands. Like every other State in the Union, Maryland participates in the Federal Aid to Families With Dependent Children (AFDC) program, which originated with the Social Security Act of 1935. Under this jointly financed program, a State computes the so-called "standard of need" of each eligible family unit within its borders. Some States provide that every family shall receive grants sufficient to meet fully the determined standard of need. Other States provide that each family unit shall receive a percentage of the determined need. Still others provide grants to most families in full accord with the ascertained standard of need, but impose an upper limit on the total amount of money any one family unit may receive. Maryland, through administrative adoption of a "maximum grant regulation," has followed this last course. This suit was brought by several AFDC recipients to enjoin the application of the Maryland maximum grant regulation on the ground that it is in conflict with the Social Security Act of 1935 and with the Equal Protection Clause of the Fourteenth Amendment. A three-judge District Court convened pursuant to 28 U.S.C. § 2281, held that the Maryland regulation violates the Equal Protection Clause. 297 F. Supp. 450.

I

[Statutory interpretation of federal welfare law omitted.]

II

Although a State may adopt a maximum grant system in allocating its funds available for AFDC payments without violating the Act, it may not, of course, impose a regime of invidious discrimination in violation of the Equal Protection Clause of the Fourteenth Amendment. Maryland says that its maximum grant regulation is wholly free of any invidiously discriminatory purpose or effect, and that the regulation is rationally supportable on at least four entirely valid grounds. The regulation can be clearly justified, Maryland argues, in terms of legitimate state interests in encouraging gainful employment, in maintaining an equitable balance in economic status as between welfare families and those supported by a wage-earner, in providing incentives for family planning, and in allocating available public funds in such a way as fully to meet the needs of the largest possible number of families. The District Court, while apparently recognizing the validity of at least some of these state concerns, nonetheless held that the regulation "is invalid on its face for overreaching," 297 F. Supp., at 468 — that it violates the Equal Protection Clause "because it cuts too broad a swath on an indiscriminate basis as applied to the entire group of AFDC eligibles to which it purports to apply . . . ." 297 F. Supp., at 469.

If this were a case involving government action claimed to violate the First Amendment guarantee of free speech, a finding of "overreaching" would be significant and might be crucial. For when otherwise valid governmental regulation sweeps so broadly as to impinge upon activity protected by the First Amendment, its very overbreadth may make it unconstitutional. See, e.g., Shelton v. Tucker, 364 U.S. 479. But the concept of "overreaching" has no place in this case. For here we deal with state regulation in the social and economic field, not affecting freedoms guaranteed by the Bill of Rights, and claimed to violate the Fourteenth Amendment only because the regulation results in some disparity in grants of welfare payments to the largest AFDC families. For this Court to approve the invalidation of state economic or social regulation as "overreaching" would be far too reminiscent of an era when the Court thought the Fourteenth Amendment gave it power to strike down state laws "because they may be unwise, improvident, or out of harmony with a particular school of thought." Williamson v. Lee Optical Co., 348 U.S. 483, 488. That era long ago passed into history. Ferguson v. Skrupa, 372 U.S. 726.

In the area of economics and social welfare, a State does not violate the Equal Protection Clause merely because the classifications made by its laws are imperfect. If the classification has some "reasonable basis," it does not offend the Constitution simply because the classification "is not made with mathematical nicety or because in practice it results in some inequality." Lindsley v. Natural Carbonic Gas Co., 220 U.S. 61, 78. "The problems of government are practical ones and may justify, if they do not require, rough accommodations — illogical, it may be, and unscientific." Metropolis Theatre Co. v. City of Chicago, 228 U.S. 61, 69–70. "A statutory discrimination will not be set aside if any state of facts reasonably may be conceived to justify it." McGowan v. Maryland, 366 U.S. 420, 426.

To be sure, the cases cited, and many others enunciating this fundamental standard under the Equal Protection Clause, have in the main involved state regulation of business or industry. The administration of public welfare assistance, by contrast, involves the most basic economic needs of impoverished human beings. We recognize the dramatically real factual difference between the cited cases and this one, but we can find no basis for applying a different constitutional standard.[8] And it is a standard that is true to the principle that the *Fourteenth Amendment* gives the federal courts no power to impose upon the States their views of what constitutes wise economic or social policy.

We do not decide today that the Maryland regulation is wise, that it best fulfills the relevant social and economic objectives that Maryland might ideally espouse, or that a more just and humane system could not be devised. Conflicting claims of morality and intelligence are raised by opponents and proponents of almost every measure, certainly including the one before us. But the intractable economic, social, and even philosophical problems presented by public welfare assistance programs are not the business of this Court. The Constitution may impose certain procedural safeguards upon systems of welfare administration, *Goldberg* v. *Kelly, ante*, p. 254. But the Constitution does not empower this Court to second-guess state officials charged with the difficult responsibility of allocating limited public welfare funds among the myriad of potential recipients.

Mr. Justice Black, with whom The Chief Justice joins, concurring, and Mr. Justice Harlan, concurring [omitted].

Mr. Justice Douglas, dissenting.

On the basis of the inconsistency of the Maryland maximum grant regulation with the Social Security Act, I would affirm the judgment below.

Mr. Justice Marshall, whom Mr. Justice Brennan joins, dissenting.

More important in the long run than this misreading of a federal statute, however, is the Court's emasculation of the Equal Protection Clause as a constitutional principle applicable to the area of social welfare administration. The Court holds today that regardless of the arbitrariness of a classification it must be sustained if any state goal can be imagined that is arguably furthered by its effects. This is so even though the classification's underinclusiveness or overinclusiveness clearly demonstrates that its actual basis is something other than that asserted by the State, and even though the relationship between the classification and the state interests which it purports to serve is so tenuous that it could not seriously be maintained that the classification tends to accomplish the ascribed goals.

The Court recognizes, as it must, that this case involves "the most basic economic needs of impoverished human beings," and that there is therefore a "dramatically

---

[8] [FN 17] It is important to note that there is no contention that the Maryland regulation is infected with a racially discriminatory purpose or effect such as to make it inherently suspect. Cf. *McLaughlin v. Florida*, 379 U.S. 184.

real factual difference" between the instant case and those decisions upon which the Court relies. The acknowledgment that these dramatic differences exist is a candid recognition that the Court's decision today is wholly without precedent. I cannot subscribe to the Court's sweeping refusal to accord the Equal Protection Clause any role in this entire area of the law, and I therefore dissent from both parts of the Court's decision.

II

Having decided that the injunction issued by the District Court was proper as a matter of statutory construction, I would affirm on that ground alone. However, the majority has of necessity passed on the constitutional issues. I believe that in overruling the decision of this and every other district court that has passed on the validity of the maximum grant device, the Court both reaches the wrong result and lays down an insupportable test for determining whether a State has denied its citizens the equal protection of the laws.

This classification process effected by the maximum grant regulation produces a basic denial of equal treatment. Persons who are concededly similarly situated (dependent children and their families), are not afforded equal, or even approximately equal, treatment under the maximum grant regulation. Subsistence benefits are paid with respect to some needy dependent children; nothing is paid with respect to others. Some needy families receive full subsistence assistance as calculated by the State; the assistance paid to other families is grossly below their similarly calculated needs.

In the instant case, the only distinction between those children with respect to whom assistance is granted and those children who are denied such assistance is the size of the family into which the child permits himself to be born.

The cases relied on by the Court, in which a "mere rationality" test was actually used, e.g., *Williamson v. Lee Optical Co.*, 348 U.S. 483 (1955), are most accurately described as involving the application of equal protection reasoning to the regulation of business interests. The extremes to which the Court has gone in dreaming up rational bases for state regulation in that area may in many instances be ascribed to a healthy revulsion from the Court's earlier excesses in using the Constitution to protect interests that have more than enough power to protect themselves in the legislative halls. This case, involving the literally vital interests of a powerless minority — poor families without breadwinners — is far removed from the area of business regulation, as the Court concedes. Why then is the standard used in those cases imposed here? We are told no more than that this case falls in "the area of economics and social welfare," with the implication that from there the answer is obvious.

Vital to the employment-incentive basis found by the Court to sustain the regulation is, of course, the supposition that an appreciable number of AFDC recipients are in fact employable. For it is perfectly obvious that limitations upon assistance cannot reasonably operate as a work incentive with regard to those who cannot work or who cannot be expected to work. In this connection, Maryland candidly notes that "only a very small percentage of the total universe of welfare recipients are employable." The State, however, urges us to ignore the "total universe" and to concentrate attention instead upon the heads of AFDC families. Yet the very purpose of the AFDC program since its inception has been to provide assistance for dependent *children*. The State's position is thus that the State may deprive certain needy children of assistance to which they would otherwise be entitled in order to provide an arguable work incentive for their parents. But the State may not wield its economic whip in this fashion when the effect is to cause a deprivation to needy dependent children in order to correct an arguable fault of their parents.

Finally, it should be noted that, to the extent there is a legitimate state interest in encouraging heads of AFDC households to find employment, application of the maximum grant regulation is also grossly *underinclusive* because it singles out and affects only large families. No reason is suggested why this particular group should be carved out for the purpose of having unusually harsh "work incentives" imposed upon them. Not only has the State selected for special treatment a small group from among similarly situated families, but it has done so on a basis — family size — that bears no relation to the evil that the State claims the regulation was designed to correct. There is simply no indication whatever that heads of large families, as opposed to heads of small families, are particularly prone to refuse to seek or to maintain employment.

However, these asserted state interests, which are not insignificant in themselves, are advanced either not at all or by complete accident by the maximum grant regulation. Clearly they could be served by measures far less destructive of the individual interests at stake. Moreover, the device assertedly chosen to further them is at one and the same time both grossly underinclusive — because it does not apply at all to a much larger class in an equal position — and grossly overinclusive — because it applies so strongly against a substantial class as to which it can rationally serve no end. Were this a case of pure business regulation, these defects would place it beyond what has heretofore seemed a borderline case, see, *e. g.,* *Railway Express Agency v. New York,* 336 U.S. 106 (1949), and I do not believe that the regulation can be sustained even under the Court's "reasonableness" test.

In any event, it cannot suffice merely to invoke the spectre of the past and to recite from *Lindsley* v. *Natural Carbonic Gas Co.* and *Williamson* v. *Lee Optical Co.* to decide the case. Appellees are not a gas company or an optical dispenser; they are needy dependent children and families who are discriminated against by the State. The basis of that discrimination — the classification of individuals into large and small families — is too arbitrary and too unconnected to the asserted rationale, the impact on those discriminated against — the denial of even a subsistence existence — too great, and the supposed interests served too contrived and attenuated to meet the requirements of the Constitution. In my view Maryland's maximum grant regulation is invalid under the Equal Protection Clause of the Fourteenth Amendment.

I would affirm the judgment of the District Court.

SAN ANTONIO INDEPENDENT SCHOOL DISTRICT v. RODRIGUEZ

SUPREME COURT OF THE UNITED STATES

411 U.S. 1 (1973)

[A class action on behalf of certain Texas school children was instituted against state school authorities in the United States District Court for the Western District of Texas, the plaintiffs challenging the constitutionality, under the equal protection clause of the Fourteenth Amendment, of the state's statutory system for financing public education which authorizes an ad valorem tax by each school district on property within the district to supplement educational funds received by each district from the state, and which thus results in substantial interdistrict disparities in per-pupil expenditures attributable chiefly to the differences in amounts received through local property taxation because of variations in the amount of taxable properties within each district. The three-judge District Court held that the Texas school financing system discriminated on the basis of wealth and was unconstitutional under the equal protection clause, ruling that (1) wealth was a suspect classification, and education was a fundamental interest, thus requiring the state to show, under the strict judicial scrutiny test, a compelling state interest for its system, which the state had failed to do, and (2) in any event, the state had failed to establish even a reasonable basis for its system (337 F. Supp. 280).]

MR. JUSTICE POWELL delivered the opinion of the Court.

This suit attacking the Texas system of financing public education was initiated by Mexican-American parents whose children attend the elementary and secondary schools in the Edgewood Independent School District, an urban school district in San Antonio, Texas. They brought a class action on behalf of school children throughout the State who are members of minority groups or who are poor and reside in school districts having a low property tax base.

I

The first Texas State Constitution, promulgated upon Texas' entry into the Union in 1845, provided for the establishment of a system of free schools. Early in its history, Texas adopted a dual approach to the financing of its schools, relying on mutual participation by the local school districts and the State. [The decision reviews increasing state aid because of disparities caused by reliance on property tax revenues.]

[A] comparison between the least and most affluent districts in the San Antonio area serves to illustrate the manner in which the dual system of finance operates and to indicate the extent to which substantial disparities exist despite the State's impressive progress in recent years. [Edgewood is an inner-city district with little commercial or industrial property; 90% of the students are Mexican-American; property value per pupil is $5,960. As a result, even with the area's highest tax *rate*, local taxes contributed $26/child, combined with state and local funds for a budget total of $256/child in 1967-68. Alamo Heights is the most affluent school district in San Antonio. The students are 81% "Anglo," the property value per pupil exceeds

$49,000; with a lower rate, in contributed $333/child which combined with state and federal funding to allow the district to spent $594/child.]

Texas virtually concedes that its historically rooted dual system of financing education could not withstand the strict judicial scrutiny that this Court has found appropriate in reviewing legislative judgments that interfere with fundamental constitutional rights or that involve suspect classifications. If, as previous decisions have indicated, strict scrutiny means that the State's system is not entitled to the usual presumption of validity, that the State rather than the complainants must carry a "heavy burden of justification," that the State must demonstrate that its educational system has been structured with "precision," and is "tailored" narrowly to serve legitimate objectives and that it has selected the "less drastic means" for effectuating its objectives, the Texas financing system and its counterpart in virtually every other State will not pass muster. The State candidly admits that "[n]o one familiar with the Texas system would contend that it has yet achieved perfection." Apart from its concession that educational financing in Texas has "defects" and "imperfections," the State defends the system's rationality with vigor and disputes the District Court's finding that it lacks a "reasonable basis."

II

The District Court's opinion does not reflect the novelty and complexity of the constitutional questions posed by appellees' challenge to Texas' system of school financing. In concluding that strict judicial scrutiny was required, that court relied on decisions dealing with the rights of indigents to equal treatment in the criminal trial and appellate processes,[9] and on cases disapproving wealth restrictions on the right to vote.[10] Those cases, the District Court concluded, established wealth as a suspect classification. Finding that the local property tax system discriminated on the basis of wealth, it regarded those precedents as controlling. It then reasoned, based on decisions of this Court affirming the undeniable importance of education, that there is a fundamental right to education and that, absent some compelling state justification, the Texas system could not stand.

A

[In finding unconstitutional wealth discrimination, the District Court found unconstitutional wealth discrimination because some poorer people receive less expensive educations than more affluent people.] This approach largely ignores the hard threshold questions, including whether it makes a difference for purposes of consideration under the Constitution that the class of disadvantaged "poor" cannot be identified or defined in customary equal protection terms, and whether the relative — rather than absolute — nature of the asserted deprivation is of significant consequence. Before a State's laws and the justifications for the classifications they create are subjected to strict judicial scrutiny, we think these

---

[9] [FN 45] E.g., *Griffin v. Illinois*, 351 U.S. 12 (1956); *Douglas v. California*, 372 U.S. 353 (1963).

[10] [FN 46] *Harper v. Virginia Bd. of Elections*, 383 U.S. 663 (1966); *McDonald v. Board of Election Comm'rs*, 394 U.S. 802 (1969); *Bullock v. Carter*, 405 U.S. 134 (1972); *Goosby v. Osser*, 409 U.S. 512 (1973).

threshold considerations must be analyzed more closely than they were in the court below.

The precedents of this Court provide the proper starting point. The individuals, or groups of individuals, who constituted the class discriminated against in our prior cases shared two distinguishing characteristics: because of their impecunity they were completely unable to pay for some desired benefit, and as a consequence, they sustained an absolute deprivation of a meaningful opportunity to enjoy that benefit.

[The majority suggested that prior precedents did not apply because the plaintiffs had not demonstrated that the challenged plan operates to the peculiar disadvantage of any class fairly definable as indigent, or as composed of persons whose incomes are beneath any designated poverty level. Indeed, there is reason to believe that the poorest families are not necessarily clustered in the poorest property districts . . . .

Second, neither appellees nor the District Court addressed the fact that, unlike each of the foregoing cases, lack of personal resources has not occasioned an absolute deprivation of the desired benefit. The argument here is not that the children in districts having relatively low assessable property values are receiving no public education; rather, it is that they are receiving a poorer quality education than that available to children in districts having more assessable wealth. Apart from the unsettled and disputed question whether the quality of education may be determined by the amount of money expended for it, a sufficient answer to appellees' argument is that, at least where wealth is involved, the Equal Protection Clause does not require absolute equality or precisely equal advantages. Nor, indeed, in view of the infinite variables affecting the educational process, can any system assure equal quality of education except in the most relative sense. Texas asserts that the Minimum Foundation Program provides an "adequate" education for all children in the State. By providing 12 years of free public-school education, and by assuring teachers, books, transportation, and operating funds, the Texas Legislature has endeavored to "guarantee, for the welfare of the state as a whole, that all people shall have at least an adequate program of education. This is what is meant by 'A Minimum Foundation Program of Education.' " The State repeatedly asserted in its briefs in this Court that it has fulfilled this desire and that it now assures "every child in every school district an adequate education." No proof was offered at trial persuasively discrediting or refuting the State's assertion.

However described, it is clear that appellees' suit asks this Court to extend its most exacting scrutiny to review a system that allegedly discriminates against a large, diverse, and amorphous class, unified only by the common factor of residence in districts that happen to have less taxable wealth than other districts. The system of alleged discrimination and the class it defines have none of the traditional indicia of suspectness: the class is not saddled with such disabilities, or subjected to such a history of purposeful unequal treatment, or relegated to such a position of political powerlessness as to command extraordinary protection from the majoritarian political process.

We thus conclude that the Texas system does not operate to the peculiar disadvantage of any suspect class. But in recognition of the fact that this Court has never heretofore held that wealth discrimination alone provides an adequate basis for invoking strict scrutiny, appellees have not relied solely on this contention. They also assert that the State's system impermissibly interferes with the exercise of a "fundamental" right and that accordingly the prior decisions of this Court require the application of the strict standard of judicial review. *Graham v. Richardson*, 403 U.S. 365, 375–376 (1971); *Kramer v. Union School District*, 395 U.S. 621 (1969); *Shapiro v. Thompson*, 394 U.S. 618 (1969). It is this question — whether education is a fundamental right, in the sense that it is among the rights and liberties protected by the Constitution — which has so consumed the attention of courts and commentators in recent years.

B

In *Brown v. Board of Education*, 347 U.S. 483 (1954), a unanimous Court recognized that "education is perhaps the most important function of state and local governments." *Id.* at 493. What was said there in the context of racial discrimination has lost none of its vitality with the passage of time: "Compulsory school attendance laws and the great expenditures for education both demonstrate our recognition of the importance of education to our democratic society. It is required in the performance of our most basic public responsibilities, even service in the armed forces. It is the very foundation of good citizenship. Today it is a principal instrument in awakening the child to cultural values, in preparing him for later professional training, and in helping him to adjust normally to his environment. In these days, it is doubtful that any child may reasonably be expected to succeed in life if he is denied the opportunity of an education. Such an opportunity, where the state has undertaken to provide it, is a right which must be made available to all on equal terms." *Ibid.*

Nothing this Court holds today in any way detracts from our historic dedication to public education. We are in complete agreement with the conclusion of the three-judge panel below that "the grave significance of education both to the individual and to our society" cannot be doubted. But the importance of a service performed by the State does not determine whether it must be regarded as fundamental for purposes of examination under the Equal Protection Clause. Mr. Justice Harlan, dissenting from the Court's application of strict scrutiny to a law impinging upon the right of interstate travel, admonished that "[v]irtually every state statute affects important rights." *Shapiro v. Thompson*, 394 U.S. at 655, 661. In his view, if the degree of judicial scrutiny of state legislation fluctuated depending on a majority's view of the importance of the interest affected, we would have gone "far toward making this Court a 'super-legislature.'" *Ibid.* We would, indeed, then be assuming a legislative role and one for which the Court lacks both authority and competence. But Mr. Justice Stewart's response in *Shapiro* to Mr. Justice Harlan's concern correctly articulates the limits of the fundamental-rights rationale employed in the Court's equal protection decisions:

> The Court today does not 'pick out particular human activities, characterize them as "fundamental," and give them added protection . . .' To the contrary, the Court simply recognizes, as it must, an established constitutional right, and gives to that right no less protection than the Constitution itself demands." *Id.* at 642.

[The opinion restates *Shapiro*'s holding that the right to travel interstate was a long-recognized independent constitutional right.]

Lindsey v. Normet, 405 U.S. 56 (1972), decided only last Term, firmly reiterates that social importance is not the critical determinant for subjecting state legislation to strict scrutiny. The complainants in that case, involving a challenge to the procedural limitations imposed on tenants in suits brought by landlords under Oregon's Forcible Entry and Wrongful Detainer Law, urged the Court to examine the operation of the statute under "a more stringent standard than mere rationality." *Id.* at 73. The tenants argued that the statutory limitations implicated "fundamental interests which are particularly important to the poor," such as the " 'need for decent shelter' " and the " 'right to retain peaceful possession of one's home.' " *Ibid.* Mr. Justice White's analysis, in his opinion for the Court, is instructive:

> We do not denigrate the importance of decent, safe, and sanitary housing. But the Constitution does not provide judicial remedies for every social and economic ill. We are unable to perceive in that document any constitutional guarantee of access to dwellings of a particular quality or any recognition of the right of a tenant to occupy the real property of his landlord beyond the term of his lease, without the payment of rent . . . Absent constitutional mandate, the assurance of adequate housing and the definition of landlord-tenant relationships are legislative, not judicial, functions." *Id.* at 74.

The lesson of these cases [including *Dandrige v. Williams*, excerpted above] in addressing the question now before the Court is plain. It is not the province of this Court to create substantive constitutional rights in the name of guaranteeing equal protection of the laws. Thus, the key to discovering whether education is "fundamental" is not to be found in comparisons of the relative societal significance of education as opposed to subsistence or housing. Nor is it to be found by weighing whether education is as important as the right to travel. Rather, the answer lies in assessing whether there is a right to education explicitly or implicitly guaranteed by the Constitution.

[The court rejected an effort to find an implicit right to education because of it relationship to excerize First Amendment freedoms or the right to vote. Although the most effective speech and informed electoral choice are "indeed goals to be pursued by a people whose thoughts and beliefs are freed from governmental interference," they "are not values to be implemented by judicial intrusion into otherwise legitimate state activities."]

Furthermore, the logical limitations on appellees' nexus theory are difficult to perceive. How, for instance, is education to be distinguished from the significant personal interests in the basics of decent food and shelter? Empirical examination might well buttress an assumption that the ill-fed, ill-clothed, and ill-housed are among the most ineffective participants in the political process, and that they derive the least enjoyment from the benefits of the First Amendment. If so, appellees' thesis would cast serious doubt on the authority of *Dandridge v. Williams, supra,* and *Lindsey v. Normet, supra.*

We need not rest our decision, however, solely on the inappropriateness of the strict-scrutiny test. A century of Supreme Court adjudication under the Equal Protection Clause affirmatively supports the application of the traditional standard of review, which requires only that the State's system be shown to bear some rational relationship to legitimate state purposes. This case represents far more than a challenge to the manner in which Texas provides for the education of its children. We have here nothing less than a direct attack on the way in which Texas has chosen to raise and disburse state and local tax revenues. We are asked to condemn the State's judgment in conferring on political subdivisions the power to tax local property to supply revenues for local interests. In so doing, appellees would have the Court intrude in an area in which it has traditionally deferred to state legislatures. This Court has often admonished against such interferences with the State's fiscal policies under the Equal Protection Clause.

Thus, we stand on familiar ground when we continue to acknowledge that the Justices of this Court lack both the expertise and the familiarity with local problems so necessary to the making of wise decisions with respect to the raising and disposition of public revenues . . . . [The opinion also demurred to the judiciary's lack of "specialized knowledge and experience" with regard to educational policy, and noted that ruling for the plaintiffs would fundamentally affect the federal/state balance.]

[In Parts III and IV, the majority noted the complexity of the school finance issue, given both wealth disparities throughout the state and the strong political attachment to local control of education, and how the judgment of the lower court and dissenters would result in an "unprecedented upheaval in public education.]

Mr. Justice Stewart, concurring.

The method of financing public schools in Texas, as in almost every other State, has resulted in a system of public education that can fairly be described as chaotic and unjust. It does not follow, however, and I cannot find, that this system violates the Constitution of the United States. I join the opinion and judgment of the Court because I am convinced that any other course would mark an extraordinary departure from principled adjudication under the Equal Protection Clause of the Fourteenth Amendment. The uncharted directions of such a departure are suggested, I think, by the imaginative dissenting opinion my Brother Marshall has filed today.

MR. JUSTICE BRENNAN, dissenting [omitted].

MR. JUSTICE WHITE, with whom MR. JUSTICE DOUGLAS and MR. JUSTICE BRENNAN join, dissenting [concluded that the Texas system was so irrational as to violate the minimum rationality standard applied to most classifications by the Equal Protection Clause.]

MR. JUSTICE MARSHALL, with whom MR. JUSTICE DOUGLAS concurs, dissenting.

In my judgment, the right of every American to an equal start in life, so far as the provision of a state service as important as education is concerned, is far too vital to permit state discrimination on grounds as tenuous as those presented by this record. Nor can I accept the notion that it is sufficient to remit these appellees to the vagaries of the political process which, contrary to the majority's suggestion, has proved singularly unsuited to the task of providing a remedy for this discrimination . . . .

[As a foundation, Marshall, J. contended that the spending inequalities directly harmed the equal educational opportunities of poor students, and as a legal matter, at the least the burden should be placed on Texas to demonstrate that the disparities did not result in unequal education.]

[As a constitutional matter, the dissent rejected the claim that provision of a minimally adequate education immunized the state against an equal protection challenge.] But this Court has never suggested that because some "adequate" level of benefits is provided to all, discrimination in the provision of services is therefore constitutionally excusable. The Equal Protection Clause is not addressed to the minimal sufficiency but rather to the unjustifiable inequalities of state action. It mandates nothing less than that "all persons similarly circumstanced shall be treated alike." *F.S. Royster Guano Co. v. Virginia*, 253 U.S. 412, 415 (1920).

The majority today concludes, however, that the Texas scheme is not subject to such a strict standard of review under the Equal Protection Clause. Instead, in its view, the Texas scheme must be tested by nothing more than that lenient standard of rationality which we have traditionally applied to discriminatory state action in the context of economic and commercial matters. [citations omitted.] By so doing, the Court avoids the telling task of searching for a substantial state interest which the Texas financing scheme, with its variations in taxable district property wealth, is necessary to further. I cannot accept such an emasculation of the Equal Protection Clause in the context of this case.

I would like to know where the Constitution guarantees the right to procreate, *Skinner v. Oklahoma*, 316 U.S. 535, 541 (1942), or the right to vote in state elections, e.g., *Reynolds v. Sims*, 377 U.S. 533 (1964), or the right to an appeal from a criminal conviction, e.g., *Griffin v. Illinois*, 351 U.S. 12 (1956). These are instances in which, due to the importance of the interests at stake, the Court has displayed a strong concern with the existence of discriminatory state treatment. But the Court has never said or indicated that these are interests which independently enjoy full-blown constitutional protection. [Here, he cites cases barring discrimination regarding forced sterilization, marriage, and abortion.]

[Marshall, J. rejected "the view that the process need necessarily degenerate into an unprincipled, subjective 'picking-and-choosing'." Indeed, he suggested that several cases striking down statutes discriminating against women or children born to unmarried parents as "irrational" were more likely to create a perception of the Court as super-legislature.]

The disability of the disadvantaged class in this case extends as well into the political processes upon which we ordinarily rely as adequate for the protection and promotion of all interests. Here legislative reallocation of the State's property wealth must be sought in the face of inevitable opposition from significantly advantaged districts that have a strong vested interest in the preservation of the status quo, a problem not completely dissimilar to that faced by underrepresented districts prior to the Court's intervention in the process of reapportionment, see *Baker v. Carr*, 369 U.S. 186, 191–192 (1962).

5.4.4. Explanations for the rejection of socio-economic rights in the U.S.

In his detailed treatment of the issue in THE SECOND BILL OF RIGHTS, Professor Sunstein seeks to explain why the courts rejected a constitutional interpretation to include these rights. He offers and then rejects three possible explanations. CASS SUNSTEIN, THE SECOND BILL OF RIGHTS: FDR'S UNFINISHED REVOLUTION AND WHY WE NEED IT MORE THAN EVER 105–08 (2004). These explanations are worth considering most directly in the American and South African contexts, where explicitly different choices were made, but also for other countries.

First, Professor Sunstein notes that these rights are 20thCentury creations, and the U.S. Constitution is significantly older. He finds this unpersuasive because in many respects the U.S. Constitution has, with judicial interpretation, changed over time. Second is the hypothesis that "American culture is especially hostile" to these rights. He acknowledges that historically, a hostility to special attention to those in economic distress raised difficult questions of race. However, he notes that one of Roosevelt's central claims was that economic rights could be justified in the name of individualism itself, and be completely consistent with capitalist institutions. Third, he notes that while some nation's constitutions are seen as aspirational and symbolic, the U.S. Constitution is seen principally as a legal document to be enforced by judges. If Americans believe that judges cannot meaningfully enforce rights, then Americans think those rights should not be entrenched in the Constitution. He rebuts this claim by noting that "courts can in fact enforce social and economic rights, at least to a degree." *Id.* at 107. Indeed, if we consider the central claims in the cases excerpted above, there was a very strong argument in *Dandridge* that the Maryland welfare scheme violated the federal statute conditioning federal funding for welfare, and the U.S. Supreme Court has indeed, as Justice Marshall observed, required more than "rational basis" for a wide variety of classifications.

Sunstein's concluding hypothesis is political. In his view, the Supreme Court under Chief Justice Earl Warren had been creating an evolutionary interpretation of the Fourteenth Amendment (indeed drawing on earlier cases) that could easily have led later courts to embrace closer judicial scrutiny of social and economic rights. However, in the 1968 election, Republican Richard Nixon narrowly defeated Democrat Hubert H. Humphrey, and Nixon was able to promptly appoint four new justices: Warren Burger, William Rehnquist, Lewis Powell, and Harry Blackmun. All four joined the majorities in *Dandridge, Linsdsey v. Normet* (rejecting a right to housing), and *Rodriguez*.

Sunstein's analysis is premised on the view that entrenching socio-economic rights is a good idea. Another explanation for the American rejection of a constitutional requirement that legislation drawing classifications based on wealth or impacting socio-economic rights like housing and education is ideological. Sunstein's former colleague at the University of Chicago Law School, Professor Richard Epstein, offers a different perspective. Epstein calls the Second Bill of Rights "politically dangerous," a "treacherous transformation of human aspirations into enforceable legal rights." Epstein critiques FDR's concept of economic rights. If there is a right to a "decent" job, workers' rights predominate regardless of the harms to employers, shareholders, and the public. Farmers' rights come at the expense of "Roosevelt's deadly double of agricultural subsidies and state-sponsored crop cartels." Who determines a decent price or a remunerative wage is another difficulty. Often, Epstein says, the solution is to fund positive rights by "punitive and self-destructive taxes on the rich." Epstein concludes that "there is no way to translate Roosevelt's — or Sunstein's vision — into sustainable social practices," which is why he believes that the current Bill of Rights, which provides "bloodless protection" to property and contract rights, speech and religion, should not be undermined. *See* Richard Epstein, *Sunstein's Second Bill of Rights*, Forbes.Com, Sept. 15, 2009.

5.5. SOCIAL AND ECONOMIC RIGHTS AS GUARANTEED BY PROTECTION OF "SECURITY OF THE PERSON" UNDER s. 7 OF THE CANADIAN CHARTER

5.5.1. General background

The authority over "property and civil rights" in s. 92(13) gives Canada's provinces the right to regulate economic aspects of trades related to health. In addition, the authority to make laws regarding "all matters of a merely local or private nature in the province" in s. 92(16) has been construed to permit regulation of public health. *Schneider v. The Queen*, [1982] 2 S.C.R. 112 (upholding BC Heroin Treatment Act's compulsory treatment of drug addicts). In addition, s. 92(7) authorizes provincial regulation of hospitals.

When drafting the Charter in 1982, the Canadian framers did not follow the course that would be adopted subsequently by countries such as South Africa that explicitly include enforceable economic rights in their Constitution. As we detail in Chapter Six, the Supreme Court of Canada has reaffirmed its aversion to reading economic rights into s. 7 in the context of basic economic needs. However, it has declined to explicitly reject precluding an interpretation of s. 7 broadly. However, several decisions suggest that when the state creates a monopoly in the delivery of health services, it cannot limit these services in a manner that infringes life or security of the person without justification under "principles of fundamental justice."

In *Gosselin v. Quebec (Attorney General)*, [2002] 4 S.C.R. 429, the Court rejected a claim that the Charter required close judicial scrutiny of a provision in the Quebec *Social Aid Act* dramatically reducing welfare benefits to recipients under the age of 30 unless they participated in educational or training activities. The majority expressly rejected the claim by Justice Bastarache, concurring, that s. 7 only concerns itself with deprivations of life, liberty, or security of the person that occur in the administration of justice through courts or government agencies. For a majority, McLachlin, C.J., wrote:

> [81] Nothing in the jurisprudence thus far suggests that s. 7 places a positive obligation on the state to ensure that each person enjoys life, liberty or security of the person. Rather, s. 7 has been interpreted as restricting the state's ability to deprive people of these. Such a deprivation does not exist in the case at bar.
>
> [82] One day s. 7 may be interpreted to include positive obligations. To evoke Lord Sankey's celebrated phrase in *Edwards v. Attorney-General for Canada*, [1930] AC 124, the *Canadian Charter* must be viewed as "living tree capable of growth and expansion within its natural limits." It would be a mistake to regard s. 7 as frozen, or its content as having been exhaustively defined in previous cases . . . . The question therefore is not whether s. 7 has ever been — or will ever be — recognized as creating positive rights. Rather, the question is whether the present circumstances warrant a novel application of s. 7 as the basis for a positive state obligation to guarantee adequate living standards.
>
> [83] I conclude that they do not. With due respect for the views of my colleague Arbour J., I do not believe that there is sufficient evidence in this case to support the proposed interpretation of s. 7. I leave open the possibility that a positive obligation to sustain life, liberty, or security of person may be made out in special circumstances. However, this is not such a case. The impugned program contained compensatory "workfare" provisions and the evidence of actual hardship is wanting. The frail platform provided by the facts of this case cannot support the weight of a positive state obligation of citizen support.

Justice Arbour dissented. She interpreted s. 7 as containing two distinctive rights: the rights to life, liberty and security of the person, and the freedom from impairment of those rights except in accordance with principles of fundamental justice. In her view, "a minimum level of welfare is so closely connected to issues relating to one's basic health (or security of the person), and potentially even to one's survival (or life interest), that it appears inevitable that a positive right to life, liberty and security of the person must provide for it." [¶ 358].

CHAOULLI v. ATTORNEY GENERAL OF QUEBEC
SUPREME COURT OF CANADA
[2005] 1 S.C.R. 791

[In the exercise of its spending powers, the Canadian Parliament enacted the *Canada Health Act*, R.S.C. 1985, c. C-6, which provides significant money to provinces who accepted the Act's conditions for a single-payer system of health insurance in Canada. The primary objective of the federal Act is "to protect, promote and restore the physical and mental well-being of residents of Canada and to facilitate reasonable access to health services without financial or other barriers" (s. 3)." Two Quebec statutes, the *Health Insurance Act* and the *Hospital Insurance Act*, combine to achieve these goals by, *inter alia*, barring insurance for private medical care within Canada.]

[This action was brought by an individual with chronic medical needs who has languished on waiting lists for insured medical services in Quebec, and a doctor who desires to provide private services and seek remuneration from private insurance, but is barred from doing so by Quebec law. They claimed that the statutes were inconsistent with a provision of the Quebec provincial charter protecting the right to life and personal inviolability, and s. 7 of the Canadian Charter, which bars government from interfering with life, liberty, or security of the person in a manner inconsistent with "principles of fundamental justice."]

[English version of the reasons delivered by:]

[1] DESCHAMPS J.: Quebeckers are prohibited from taking out insurance to obtain in the private sector services that are available under Quebec's public health care plan. Is this prohibition justified by the need to preserve the integrity of the plan?

[Deschamps, J. reasoned that (similar to American practice) that courts should first determine legality under provincial charters before assessing the issue under the Canadian Charter. Using an analysis similar to that of McLachlin, C.J. and Major, J, below, she concluded that the ban on private insurance violated the Quebec Charter. Responding to claims that private insurance would threaten the public system, Deschamps wrote that these predictions "described by the experts, many of whom came from outside Quebec, do not appear to me to be very convincing." She emphasized that under the Quebec Charter (the same analysis applies to the Canadian Charter), the "onus was on the Attorney General of Quebec to justify the prohibition," because under each charter "the government is responsible for justifying measures it imposes that impair rights." A comparative analysis showed that "there are a wide range of measures that are less drastic, and also less intrusive in relation to the protected rights."]

[102] MCLACHLIN C.J. and MAJOR J. [joined by BASTARACHE, J.]: We concur in the conclusion of our colleague Deschamps J. that the prohibition against contracting for private health insurance violates [the Quebec *Charter of Human Rights and Freedoms*, R.S.Q., c. C-12] . . . .

[103] The appellants do not seek an order that the government spend more money on health care, nor do they seek an order that waiting times for treatment under the public health care scheme be reduced. They only seek a ruling that because delays

in the public system place their health and security at risk, they should be allowed to take out insurance to permit them to access private services.

[104] The *Charter* does not confer a freestanding constitutional right to health care. However, where the government puts in place a scheme to provide health care, that scheme must comply with the *Charter*. We are of the view that the prohibition on medical insurance in s. 15 of the *Health Insurance Act*, R.S.Q., c. A-29, and s. 11 of the *Hospital Insurance Act*, R.S.Q., c. A-28 (see Appendix), violates s. 7 of the *Charter* because it impinges on the right to life, liberty and security of the person in an arbitrary fashion that fails to conform to the principles of fundamental justice.

[106] . . . The result is a virtual monopoly for the public health scheme. The state has effectively limited access to private health care except for the very rich, who can afford private care without need of insurance. This virtual monopoly, on the evidence, results in delays in treatment that adversely affect the citizen's security of the person. Where a law adversely affects life, liberty or security of the person, it must conform to the principles of fundamental justice. This law, in our view, fails to do so.

[111] The appellants have established that many Quebec residents face delays in treatment that adversely affect their security of the person and that they would not sustain but for the prohibition on medical insurance . . . . Given the ban on insurance, most Quebeckers have no choice but to accept delays in the medical system and their adverse physical and psychological consequences.

[118] The jurisprudence of this Court holds that delays in obtaining medical treatment which affect patients physically and psychologically trigger the protection of s. 7 of the *Charter*. In *R. v. Morgentaler*, [1988] 1 S.C.R. 30, Dickson C.J. concluded that the delay in obtaining therapeutic abortions, which increased the risk of complications and mortality due to mandatory procedures imposed by the state, was sufficient to trigger the physical aspect of the woman's right to security of the person: *Morgentaler*, at p. 59. He found that the psychological impact on women awaiting abortions constituted an infringement of security of the person. Beetz J. agreed with Dickson C.J. that "[t]he delays mean therefore that the state has intervened in such a manner as to create an additional risk to health, and consequently this intervention constitutes a violation of the woman's security of the person": see *Morgentaler*, at pp. 105–6.

[129] It is a well-recognized principle of fundamental justice that laws should not be arbitrary . . .

[130] A law is arbitrary where "it bears no relation to, or is inconsistent with, the objective that lies behind [it]." To determine whether this is the case, it is necessary to consider the state interest and societal concerns that the provision is meant to reflect: *Rodriguez*, at pp. 594–95.

[131] In order not to be arbitrary, the limit on life, liberty and security requires not only a theoretical connection between the limit and the legislative goal, but a real connection on the facts. The onus of showing lack of connection in this sense rests with the claimant. The question in every case is whether the measure is arbitrary in the sense of bearing no real relation to the goal and hence being manifestly unfair. The more serious the impingement on the person's liberty and security, the

more clear must be the connection. Where the individual's very life may be at stake, the reasonable person would expect a clear connection, in theory and in fact, between the measure that puts life at risk and the legislative goals.

[135] The government argues that the interference with security of the person caused by denying people the right to purchase private health insurance is necessary to providing effective health care under the public health system. It argues that if people can purchase private health insurance, they will seek treatment from private doctors and hospitals, which are not banned under the Act. According to the government's argument, this will divert resources from the public health system into private health facilities, ultimately reducing the quality of public care.

[Here, the plurality looked to other countries, and to a Canadian Senate committee report, that] establishes that many western democracies that do not impose a monopoly on the delivery of health care have successfully delivered to their citizens medical services that are superior to and more affordable than the services that are presently available in Canada. This demonstrates that a monopoly is not necessary or even related to the provision of quality public health care.

BINNIE and LEBEL JJ. [joined by FISH, J.] (dissenting):

[161] The question in this appeal is whether the province of Quebec not only has the constitutional authority to establish a comprehensive single-tier health plan, but to discourage a second (private) tier health sector by prohibiting the purchase and sale of private health insurance. The appellants argue that timely access to needed medical service is not being provided in the publicly funded system and that the province cannot therefore deny to those Quebeckers (who can qualify) the right to purchase private insurance to pay for medical services whenever and wherever such services can be obtained for a fee, i.e., in the private sector. This issue has been the subject of protracted debate across Canada through several provincial and federal elections. We are unable to agree with our four colleagues who would allow the appeal that such a debate can or should be resolved as a matter of law by judges. We find that, on the **legal** issues raised, the appeal should be dismissed.

[163] The Court recently held in *Auton (Guardian ad litem of) v. British Columbia (Attorney General)*, [2004] 3 S.C.R. 657, 2004 SCC 78, that the government was not required to fund the treatment of autistic children. It did not on that occasion address in constitutional terms the scope and nature of "reasonable" health services. Courts will now have to make that determination. What, then, are constitutionally required "reasonable health services"? What is treatment "within a reasonable time"? What are the benchmarks? How short a waiting list is short enough? How many MRIs does the Constitution require? The majority does not tell us. The majority lays down no manageable constitutional standard. The public cannot know, nor can judges or governments know, how much health care is "reasonable" enough to satisfy [Charter requirements]. It is to be hoped that we will know it when we see it.

[164] The policy of the *Canada Health Act*, R.S.C. 1985, c. C-6, and its provincial counterparts is to provide health care based on need rather than on wealth or

status. The evidence certainly established that the public health care system put in place to implement this policy has serious and persistent problems. This does not mean that the courts are well placed to perform the required surgery. The resolution of such a complex fact-laden policy debate does not fit easily within the institutional competence or procedures of courts of law. The courts can use s. 7 of the *Canadian Charter* to pre-empt the ongoing public debate only if the current health plan violates an established "principle of fundamental justice." Our colleagues McLachlin C.J. and Major J. argue that Quebec's enforcement of a single-tier health plan meets this legal test because it is "arbitrary." In our view, with respect, the prohibition against private health insurance is a rational consequence of Quebec's commitment to the goals and objectives of the *Canada Health Act*.

[166] The Quebec government views the prohibition against private insurance as essential to preventing the current single-tier health system from disintegrating into a *de facto* two-tier system. The trial judge found, and the evidence demonstrated, that there is good reason for this fear. The trial judge concluded that a private health sector fuelled by private insurance would frustrate achievement of the objectives of the *Canada Health Act*. She thus found no **legal** basis to intervene, and declined to do so. This raises the issue of *who* it is that *should* resolve these important and contentious issues. Commissioner Roy Romanow makes the following observation in his Report:

> Some have described it as a perversion of Canadian values that they cannot use their money to purchase faster treatment from a private provider for their loved ones. I believe it is a far greater perversion of Canadian values to accept a system where money, rather than need, determines who gets access to care.
>
> (Building on Values: The Future of Health Care in Canada: Final Report (2002) ("Romanow Report"), at p. xx)

Whether or not one endorses this assessment, his premise is that the debate is about **social** values. It is not about constitutional law. We agree.

[169] A legislative policy is not "arbitrary" just because we may disagree with it . . . .

[The dissent distinguished *Morgantaler*, as limited to the imposition to criminal penalties for obtaining medical care necessary for health.]

[181] As stated, we accept the finding of the courts below that a two-tier health care system would likely have a negative impact on the integrity, functioning and viability of the public system . . . . [It] cannot be contested that as a matter of *principle*, access to **private** health care based on wealth rather than need contradicts one of the key social policy objectives expressed in the *Canada Health Act*. The state has established its interest in promoting the **equal** treatment of its citizens in terms of health care. The issue of arbitrariness relates only to the validity of the *means* adopted to achieve that policy objective. Counsel for the appellant Zeliotis was not oblivious to the potential danger posed by the re-allocation of health resources to the private sector. [Counsel conceded that "it is perfectly legitimate for the state to make sure that the public system has on a priority basis all the

resources it needs to function. *Thus, we concede that, if this were in fact impossible, our appeal should fail.* [Emphasis added.]"]

[The dissent acknowledged prior precedents rejecting the claim (supported by some strong originalist arguments) that s. 7 should be interpreted to only apply to legal rights enumerated in ss. 8-14 of the Charter, related to adjudicative or administrative proceedings, or to limit s. 7 to what Americans call "procedural due process." Because s. 7 protects basic interests in life, liberty, and security, and thus calls on courts to "adjudicate many difficult moral and ethical issues," the dissent argued that courts need "to proceed cautiously and incrementally."]

[Accepting that, "at least in the cases of **some** individuals on **some** occasions," the statutes "put at risk" individuals' life or security of the person, the dissent rejected the claim that the scheme implicated Quebeckers' liberty.] The argument that "liberty" includes freedom of contract (in this case to contract for private medical insurance) is novel in Canada, where economic rights are not included in the *Canadian Charter* and discredited in the United States. In that country, the liberty of individuals (mainly employers) to contract out of social and economic programs was endorsed by the Supreme Court in the early decades of the 20th century on the theory that laws that prohibited employers from entering into oppressive contracts with employees violated their "liberty" of contract; see, e.g., *Lochner v. New York, 198 U.S. 45 (1905)*, at p. 62. . .

[202] Nor do we accept that s. 7 of the *Canadian Charter* guarantees Dr. Chaoulli the "liberty" to deliver health care in a private context. The trial judge correctly concluded that "*s. 7 of the Canadian charter does not protect a physician's right to practise his or her profession without restrictions.*"

[208] For a principle to be one of fundamental justice, it must count among the basic tenets of our **legal** system: *Re B.C. Motor Vehicle Act*, at p. 503. It must generally be accepted as such among reasonable people. As explained by the majority in *Malmo-Levine*, [[2003] 3 S.C.R. 571] at para. 113:

> The requirement of "general acceptance among reasonable people" enhances the legitimacy of judicial review of state action, and ensures that the values against which state action is measured are not just fundamental "in the eye of the beholder **only**": *Rodriguez*, at pp. 607 and 590 . . . . In short, for a rule or principle to constitute a principle of fundamental justice for the purposes of s. 7, it must be **a legal principle** about which there is **significant societal consensus** that it is fundamental to the way in which **the legal system** ought fairly to operate, and it must be identified with sufficient precision to yield a **manageable standard** against which to measure deprivations of life, liberty or security of the person. [First emphasis in *Rodriguez*; subsequent emphasis added.]

[209] Thus, the formal requirements for a principle of fundamental justice are threefold. First, it must be a **legal** principle. Second, the reasonable person must regard it as vital to our societal notion of justice, which implies a significant **societal consensus**. Third, it must be capable of being **identified with precision** and applied in a manner that yields **predictable results**. These requirements present insurmountable hurdles to the appellants. The aim of "health care of a reasonable

standard within a reasonable time" is not a **legal** principle. There is no "societal consensus" about what it means or how to achieve it. It cannot be "identified with precision."

[234] The accepted definition in *Rodriguez* states that a law is arbitrary only where "it bears no relation to, or is inconsistent with, the objective that lies behind the legislation." To substitute the term "unnecessary" for "inconsistent" is to substantively alter the meaning of the term "arbitrary." "Inconsistent" means that the law logically contradicts its objectives, whereas "unnecessary" simply means that the objective could be met by other means. It is quite apparent that the latter is a much broader term that involves a policy choice. If a court were to declare unconstitutional every law impacting "security of the person" that the court considers unnecessary, there would be much greater scope for intervention under s. 7 than has previously been considered by this Court to be acceptable. (In *Rodriguez* itself, for example, could the criminalization of assisted suicide simply have been dismissed as "unnecessary"? As with health care, many jurisdictions have treated euthanasia differently than does our *Criminal Code*.) The courts might find themselves constantly second-guessing the validity of governments' public policy objectives based on subjective views of the *necessity* of particular means used to advance legitimate government action as opposed to other means which critics might prefer.

[The dissent cited evidence from OECD countries that "shows that an increase in private funding typically leads to a decrease in government funding." Although these conclusions are disputed, "the government's reliance on [this evidence] cannot be dismissed as 'arbitrary.' "]

Notwithstanding the formalized debate over arbitrariness, Professor Hogg concludes that the Supreme Court of Canada has decided that "when the state assumes a monopoly power over the provision of a medical service that affects life or security of the person, it is under a constitutional duty to ensure that the service is provided in a timely fashion." *Constitutional Law of Canada*, § 32.6.

Subsequent case law has found arbitrary deprivations of security of the person, in violation of s. 7, in the reversal by the Harper Government of a Liberal exemption to drug laws that permitted a local NGO to dispense safe hypodermic needles to Vancouver drug addicts. *Canada (Attorney General) v. PHS Community Services Society*, 336 D.L.R. (4th) 385 (Sept. 30, 2011). In that decision, McLachlin CJ acknowledged that the SCC's "jurisprudence on arbitrariness is not entirely settled," noting that three justices asked "whether a limit was 'necessary' to further the state objective while three justices "preferred to avoid the language of necessity and instead approved of the prior articulation of arbitrariness as where '[a] deprivation of a right . . . bears no relation to, or is inconsistent with, the state interest that lies behind the legislation.' " [¶ 133]. And an interesting case for comparative scholars, due to its parallel with the leading South African *Grootboom* case, was the lower court decision in *Victoria (City) v. Adams*, [2008] B.C.J. No. 1935 (BC Sup. Ct. 2008). The judge found that a municipal park bylaw violated s. 7 when it barred homeless people from erecting temporary shelters on public property, although the city did not bar the homeless from sleeping in public places, which evidence showed subjected the homeless to significant health risks.

The willingness of occasional majorities of the Supreme Court of Canada to find that a law arbitrary, as bearing "no relation to" legitimate social objectives (as in *Chaoulli*), even though the legislature and other judges perceive perfectly sound reasons for the legislative choice, extends to other areas of section 7 jurisprudence as well. Thus, in *R. v. Heywood*, [1994] 3 S.C.R. 761, the Court struck down a provision of the Criminal Code that banned convicted sex offenders from loitering near schools, playgrounds, parks, or bathing areas, on the grounds that the statute was overbroad. Although the majority determined that the overbreadth resulted in the unconstitutional restriction of liberty "for no reason," *id.* at 793, Professor Hogg has criticized the decision as raising "serious practical and theoretical difficulties, and confers an exceedingly discretionary power of review on the Court." HOGG, CONSTITUTIONAL LAW OF CANADA, § 47.15.

5.6.   NON-CONSTITUTIONAL RESPONSE OF THE AUSTRALIAN GOVERNMENT TO INTERNATIONAL OBLIGATIONS

As noted above, Australia's Constitution has neither specific provisions guaranteeing social and economic rights as in South Africa, nor broadly-phrased rights guarantees susceptible of judicial interpretation so as to grant some form of social or economic rights, as in North America. Australia is a signatory of the 1966 U.N. International Covenant on Economic, Social and Cultural Rights, and Art. 2(1) of the Covenant requires signatories to take steps, including legislative measures, to achieve "progressive realisation" of the Covenant's recognized rights.

Although the Commonwealth Parliament has enacted a variety of laws, pursuant to the External Affairs power, implementing obligations to which Australia has acceded under other international human rights treaties (most notably against race and sex discrimination), the Parliament has never enacted specific legislation implementing the ICESCR. It has, however, passed many laws under its social welfare powers (section 51 (xxiiiA) of the Constitution — see above), which, among other things, it documents in its regular reports to the U.N. on compliance with its international obligations. (It should also be noted, with respect to the ICESCR's commitments, that public education is provided free in all states, and by far the majority of Australian children are educated in the public system; public hospitals are also free, and are widely used by all sectors of Australian society. The poor health and low educational levels of indigenous Australians compared to the rest of the population remain critical issues, however, and there is much debate about whether the enactment of laws or the entrenchment of rights are possible responses to these problems.)

Some human rights activists have suggested that Parliament's failure to implement the ICESCR demonstrates Australia's lack of commitment to these important rights, as well as underlining why greater rights protection, in the form of constitutional entrenchment or at least a statutory bill of rights, is a necessary corrective. However, even the 2009 National Human Rights Consultation, which recommended enactment of a human rights act (the topic is fully discussed below in

Chapter Nine), did not support the inclusion of socio-economic rights in the proposed act. The Consultation accepted the view that inclusion of these rights would lead to inappropriate judicial involvement in matters such as policy choices and budget priorities. In its Report, it acknowledged that the main concern of most advocates of a bill of rights in Australia was "the realisation of primary economic and social rights such as the rights to education, housing and the highest attainable standard of health." However, it concluded that such rights "would be very difficult, if not impossible, to make . . . matters for determination in the courts." The Consultation Committee's experience at a "roundtable" in a remote community had made it aware, the Report stated, that

> [i]f it came to a choice between the maintenance of the [health] clinic or the primary school, there would be no suitable criteria a judge could apply to make such a determination. If the residents had petitioned the court to maintain the clinic, the judge might not even be apprised of the fact that the school was being maintained.[11]

Moreover, given the constitutional allocation of powers between the Commonwealth and state governments (discussed above in Chapter One), full implementation of the ICESCR under the External Affairs power would unsettle the federal/state balance in Australia. Although, as noted, social welfare or social security schemes (unemployment and disability benefits, supporting parent benefits, family allowances, "Medicare," etc) are federal matters, other matters, for example, housing, education, and hospitals are handled at the state level. Although much federal funding is directed at these state schemes (and in most cases the funds come with conditions determined by federal government policy) significant tension would arise between federal and state governments if a Commonwealth human rights act permitted the High Court to rule on the rights compatibility of state laws.

It is important to note that most cases regarding, broadly, social security entitlements arise in Australia (as in Britain) in the field of administrative law. Administrative or executive decision-makers (including government ministers) are required to accord "procedural fairness" to all persons who are the subjects of their decisions. The requirement includes giving reasons for the decision, lack of bias, taking into account only relevant considerations in reaching the decision, and giving the person the right to a hearing on an adverse decision. So, for example, a decision regarding the denial of a pension or unemployment benefits to an individual is subject to such rules. The requirement to observe procedural fairness is not entrenched in the Constitution, but is considered a core aspect of "natural justice." There are different views regarding the source of the requirement. For some judges, it is the common law. For others, it is implied in legislative intent; legislators are assumed not to intend to abrogate common law rights, unless the contrary intention is expressed clearly and unambiguously in the relevant legislation. Both assumptions are consistent with the views of the framers of Australia's Constitution that rights are broadly best protected by the common law or legislation, rather than by constitutional provisions. These assumptions were reinforced in the 1970s by the

---

[11] National Human Rights Consultation Report, Commonwealth of Australia 365–6 (2009).

creation of a system of administrative review tribunals, from which appeals to courts may be available.

Australia now has a system of tribunals at both federal and state level, which permit "merits review" (regarding the correctness of a decision, including on the facts). For example, the Administrative Appeals Tribunal — the "umbrella" federal tribunal — reviews decisions in cases concerning family assistance, social security, taxation, veterans' affairs, workers' compensation, bankruptcy, child support, citizenship and immigration, among others. Tribunal decisions are, in some cases, able to be appealed to the courts if there is an error of law (they cannot be judicially reviewed on the merits). Legislation governing certain classes of administrative decision has removed the right of appeal from a tribunal to a court, but the High Court cannot be deprived of the power to review administrative or executive decisions, since s 75 (v) of the Constitution confers original jurisdiction on the Court "[i]n all matters . . . in which a writ of Mandamus or prohibition or an injunction is sought against an officer of the Commonwealth." Legislation may also exclude the requirement to follow procedural fairness in certain decisions, but the Court has set very stringent standards for finding a clear intention on the part of legislators to do so.

The case law on judicial review of administrative decisions has developed significantly in recent decades, in particular in the area of migration law. At first the High Court confined the requirement of procedural fairness to cases where statutory "rights" were affected. In 1985, in a case concerning a non-citizen who was subject to an executive deportation order — *Kioa v. West* (1985) 159 CLR 550 — the Court extended the requirement to interests. Justice Mason stated that procedural fairness attached to rights and interests relating to "personal liberty, status, preservation of livelihood and reputation, as well as to proprietary rights and interests"; he found this requirement to lie in the common law. The similarities with the U.S. case of *Goldberg v. Kelly* (discussed above) are striking. Just as striking is the fact that the High Court reached similar conclusions in the absence of a constitutionally protected right to "due process."

Chapter 6

THE REGULATION OF PROPERTY

KEY CONCEPTS FOR THE CHAPTER

- EACH COUNTRY HAS CAREFULLY CONSIDERED THE ENTRENCHMENT OF A CONSTITUTIONAL RIGHT TO PROPERTY

  — SEVERAL PROVISIONS OF THE U.S. CONSTITUTION PROTECT INTERESTS IN PROPERTY;

  — THE CANADIAN CHARTER DELIBERATELY EXCLUDED ANY TEXTUAL PROTECTION OF PROPERTY INTERESTS;

  — THE AUSTRALIAN CONSTITUTION INCLUDES A PROVISION, MODELED ON THE U.S. TAKINGS CLAUSE, REQUIRING THE FEDERAL LEGISLATURE TO OFFER "JUST TERMS" FOR PROPERTY COMPULSORILY ACQUIRED "FOR ANY PURPOSE IN RESPECT OF WHICH THE [FEDERAL] PARLIAMENT HAS POWER TO MAKE LAWS," BUT DOES NOT CONSTITUTIONALLY RESTRAIN STATE GOVERNMENTS

  — PROPERTY RIGHTS AND CLAIMS FOR RESTITUTION WERE AT THE HEART OF THE COMPROMISE THAT RESULTED IN THE SOUTH AFRICAN CONSTITUTION, WITH PROPERTY RIGHTS PROTECTED IN A DETAILED SECTION, BUT SUBJECT TO AFFIRMATIVE GOVERNMENT OBLIGATIONS TOWARD HOUSING AND LAND REFORM

- NONETHELESS, THE ACTUAL DIFFERENCE IN PROTECTION OF PROPERTY INTERESTS AGAINST EXPROPRIATION SHOULD NOT BE EXAGGERATED, BECAUSE ALL CANADIAN JURISDICTIONS AND AUSTRALIAN STATES HAVE ENACTED EXPROPRIATION STATUTES.

- THE GENERAL PRINCIPLE OF THE TAKINGS CLAUSE OF THE FIFTH AMENDMENT — THAT THE GOVERNMENT SHOULD NOT FORCE SOME TO BEAR A PUBLIC BURDEN WHICH SHOULD BE BORNE BY ALL OF SOCIETY — IS SHARED BY ALL COUNTRIES; THE KEY QUESTION IS WHETHER COURTS OR LEGISLATURES SHOULD BE ENTRUSTED WITH ENFORCING THIS PRINCIPLE

- BOTH AMERICAN AND CANADIAN CONSTITUTIONAL JURISPRUDENCE SEEKS TO AVOID THE "GHOST" OF THE *LOCHNER*-ERA IN U.S. JURISPRUDENCE: AMERICAN JUSTICES BY DISTINGUISHING BETWEEN "ECONOMIC" AND "PROPERTY" RIGHTS, AND CANADIAN JUSTICES BY AVOIDING THIS DISTINCTION COMPLETELY. FOR AUSTRALIAN COURTS, PROPERTY RIGHTS ARE DEFINED QUITE BROADLY BUT A KEY DISTINCTION IS DRAWN BETWEEN THE ACQUISITION OF PROPERTY AND THE REGULATION OF PROPERTY. THE DETAILED PROVISIONS OF THE SOUTH AFRICAN CONSTITUTION SEEM DESIGNED TO PROTECT AGAINST ARBITRARY AND UNFAIR EXPROPRIATIONS WHILE PERMITTING PROGRESSIVE WEALTH REDISTRIBUTION

- THE MAJOR SIGNIFICANT DIFFERENCE IN THE REGULATION OF PROPERTY CONCERNS JUDICIAL REVIEW OF ENVIRONMENTAL AND LAND-USE REGULATIONS THAT MAY SIGNIFICANTLY IMPAIR THE ECONOMIC VALUE OF REAL PROPERTY; THESE

465

"REGULATORY TAKINGS" WILL OFTEN REQUIRE COMPENSATION IN THE U.S., WILL SOMETIMES BE CONSIDERED ACQUISITIONS OF PROPERTY IN AUSTRALIA, AND ARE NOT CONSTITUTIONALLY PROTECTED IN CANADA OR SOUTH AFRICA.

6.1. OVERVIEW OF THE RIGHT TO PROPERTY

6.1.1. Textual provisions

One of the fundamental differences between the constitutions that are the focus of these materials concerns protection of interests in property. Article I, § 10 of the U.S. Constitution bars states from passing any law "impairing the Obligation of Contracts," and the Fifth and Fourteenth Amendments to the U.S. Constitution provide that no person shall be deprived of property without due process of law. Section 51(xxxi) of the Australian Constitution authorizes the federal government to acquire property on "just terms," but does not otherwise protect property or economic interests, and this provision does not apply to Australian states. The Canadian Charter contains no express textual protection for property interests. Indeed, great care was taken to avoid such protection in the drafting of s. 7 of the Charter, which provides that "everyone" has the right to "life, liberty, and security of the person" and cannot be deprived of these rights unless "in accordance with the principles of fundamental justice."

The most recent, and nuanced, constitutional provision among those that are the focus of this text is s 25 of the South African Constitution, which specifies the right in a manner much more detailed than its older cousins, with nine subsections:

(1) requires property deprivation only by a law of general application, and bars arbitrary deprivations

(2) limits expropriations to takings by a law of general application, for a public purpose or in the public interest, and subject to compensation

(3) sets forth a variety of factors to determine "just and equitable" compensation

(4) expressly notes that land reform and equitable access to natural resources are in the public interest and property is not limited to land

(5) requires the state to take "reasonable legislative and other measures, within its available resources" to allow equitable access to land

(6) establishes redress to a "person or community" whose land tenure is insecure because of past racially discriminatory laws

(7) permits Parliament to grant restitution or redress for victims of property dispossession after 1913

(8) provides that this section shall not impede legislative land reform, providing action conforms to s 36(1) [permitting reasonable and justifiable limitations on constitutional rights]

(9) requires Parliament to enact legislation re subsection (6)

6.1.2. The issue of "constitutional jurisprudence" in considering the right to property

An oft-cited effort to explain American takings jurisprudence is Frank Michelman, *Property, Utility, and Fairness: Comments on the Ethical Foundations of "Just Compensation" Law*, 80 HARV. L. REV. 1165 (1967) (succinctly explained and analyzed in Michael A. Heller & James E. Krier, *Deterrence and Distribution in the Law of Takings*, 112 HARV. L. REV. 997 (1999)). Michelman frames the issue broadly, at p. 1169:

> When a social decision to redirect economic resources entails painfully obvious opportunity costs, how shall these costs ultimately be distributed among all the members of society? *** Shall the losses be left with the individuals on whom they happen first to fall, or shall they be "socialized?"

Michelman argues that losses should be socialized when it would be either inefficient or unjust to allow the government to take the property without compensation. The principal economic explanation for the compensation requirement is that otherwise the government would take an inefficiently large amount of property — that is, the price system provides an efficient discipline on the state's "consumption" of private property. *See* William A. Fischel & Perry Shapiro, *Takings, Insurance, and Michelman: Comments on Economic Interpretations of "Just Compensation Law,"* 17 J. LEGAL STUD. 269 (1988). Both efficiency and fairness are also invoked to limit the ability of government to expropriate property of politically vulnerable groups and individuals. *See* Saul Levmore, *Just Compensation and Just Politics*, 22 CONN. L. REV. 285 (1990). In his book, THE GLOBAL DEBATE OVER CONSTITUTIONAL PROPERTY: LESSONS FOR AMERICAN TAKINGS JURISPRUDENCE (2006), Gregory S. Alexander argues that economic efficiency is just one goal of constitutionalizing property rights. Others include the creation of a zone of individual autonomy from the state, promoting human dignity, and providing the material conditions for creating and maintaining the proper social order. *Id.* at 220–22. The U.S. Supreme Court has restated these principles in an oft-quoted statement about the meaning of American constitutional protection for property: the Takings Clause prevents the government "from forcing some people to alone bear public burdens which, in all fairness and justice, should be borne by the public as a whole." *Armstrong v. United States*, 364 U.S. 40, 49 (1960).

For constitutional law purposes, however, the question is a bit more specific — when government policy causes tangible economic injury, under what circumstances, if any, should *Courts* require the government to compensate, *even if the legislature believes that the injury is not one that ought to be "socialized"*? For example, Melbourne Professor Simon Evans, quoting Yale Professor Thomas Merrill, suggests that "[c]onstitutional property clauses . . . attempt to mediate 'the perennial' and, I would add, irreducibly moral, 'conflict between the need for stability of entitlements, on the one hand, and the need for flexibility and modification of entitlements in light of changed circumstances, on the other." While Evans is descriptively accurate, the problem for constitutional theory is that Evans has described the inevitable balance in common law reasoning that judges who rule in contract, tort, trusts, and other cases face each day between stability and modern concerns. Evans, *Constitutional Property Rights in Australia, in* PROTECTING

RIGHTS WITHOUT A BILL OF RIGHTS 198 (Campbell, et. al, eds., 2006). *See generally* MELVIN A. EISENBERG, THE NATURE OF THE COMMON LAW (1991). The question here is to what extent these changes in entitlements are constitutionally protected. Each country answers this question differently, based on different histories as well as evolved jurisprudence.[1] The following is a brief summary, in chronological order of constitutional framing.

6.1.3. American foundations

There is strong evidence that the drafters of the U.S. Constitution and Bill of Rights viewed the inalienable right to property as the right most at risk in the nascent American republic. In contemporary terms, property holders would have been considered the leading "discrete and insular minority." As Jennifer Nedelsky (an American-trained political scientist at the University of Toronto) sets forth in her book, PRIVATE PROPERTY AND THE LIMITS OF AMERICAN CONSTITUTIONALISM (1990), the Madisonian constitutional structure of divided powers between the federal and state governments and among the legislative, executive, and judicial branches of the federal government would generally protect against the "tyranny of the majority." However, "the focus on property bred a suspicion of the people — a permanent, fluid, majority of propertyless voters." This was exacerbated by the class divisions of the Revolutionary War, where many of those subject to property deprivation had been loyalist sympathizers. Thus, not only did property have to be protected, as Madison provided, but the protection needed to be judicially enforceable.

It must be noted, however, that the scope of property rights intended for counter-majoritarian protection is not clear. Legal historians have suggested that the framers did not intend to protect what we now call regulatory takings to come within the ambit of the Fifth Amendment's protection, John F. Hart, *Colonial Land Use Law and its Significance for Modern Takings Doctrine*, 109 HARV. L. REV. 1252 (1996), and that most early judicial interpretations of the Fifth Amendment and contemporaneous state constitutional equivalents indicate that "compensation was mandated only when the government physically took property." William Treanor, *The Origins and Significance of the Just Compensation Clause of the Fifth Amendment*, 94 YALE L.J. 694, 798 (1985).

6.1.4. Australian foundations

As Simon Evans has observed, interpretation of the Australian constitutional provision regarding property is "unclear and contested and in some areas close to incoherent." *Constitutional Property Rights in Australia: Reconciling Individual Rights and the Common Good, in* PROTECTING RIGHTS WITHOUT A BILL OF RIGHTS (Tom Campbell, Jeffrey Goldsworthy & Adrienne Stone, eds., 2006). Indeed, it is not clear that the jurisprudential question raised above in 6.1.2 played any role in the original development of the constitutionalized right. The explanation provided by the "classic" commentators, *Quick and Garran* in 1901 in *The Annotated*

---

[1] *See generally* Donna R. Christie, *A Tale of Three Takings: Taking Analysis Inland Use Regulation in the United States, Australia, and Canada*, 12 BROOK. J. INT'L L. 359 (2007).

Constitution of the Commonwealth of Australia[2] was that the Australian framers distinguished the United States, which had unilaterally declared itself to be a sovereign state, from the Commonwealth, which "was a federated community possessing many political powers approaching, and elements resembling, sovereignty, but falling short of it," since it remained subject to the paramount power of the British Parliament (pp. 640–41). Although the Fifth Amendment was therefore a limitation on the implicit sovereign power of the government of the United States, Australia needed an express provision to remove any doubt about the right of the Commonwealth to acquire property for federal purposes. Although Justice Dixon has stated that s 51(xxxi) was based on the Fifth Amendment (*Andrews v. Howell* (1941) 65 CLR 255, 282), there is no direct evidence in the constitutional debates of fears of a democratic government that would redistribute property rights at will. *See* Simon Evans, *Property and the Drafting of the Australian Constitution*, 29 FED. L. REV. 121, 121 (2001). The Constitution's framers, however, were well familiar with statutory limits on the power of eminent domain. All the parliaments of the participating colonies had earlier passed laws, modeled on the UK *Lands Clauses Consolidation Act* 1845, requiring compensation for compulsorily acquired land to take into account more than merely the market price, but also to consider use-value, and the injurious impact on the owner. Indeed, the Australian framers would have recognized that, of those countries adopting the common law of England (including Blackstone's commentary in favor of compensation for expropriation), the American revolutionary experience with seizure of loyalist property was the exception. *See also* R. W. Baker, *The Compulsory Acquisition Powers of the Commonwealth*, in ESSAYS ON THE AUSTRALIAN CONSTITUTION (R. Else-Mitchell ed., 1961).

Moreover, there is clear evidence — inferential and textual — that the framers were influenced by the United States example, and regarded s 51(xxxi) as a limitation on the Commonwealth's power over the individual right to hold property, and not merely a grant of power to the Commonwealth. Furthermore, the High Court of Australia has followed U.S. "just compensation" jurisprudence, and at times has been more influenced by it than scholars previously recognized. This fact, however, must be tempered by the High Court's refusal, in 2012, to embrace certain propositions found in U.S. "takings" jurisprudence, in the "Tobacco Plain Packaging" case, *JT International SA v. Commonwealth of Australia* (extracted below).

Generally, however, the High Court has not set out to develop a consistent property rights jurisprudence, and has tended to proceed (as is characteristic of the Court) on a case by case basis, asking: *what is property?* and *what is an acquisition?* The question *what are just terms?*, which might force the Court to consider the nature of the right to property more closely, has also been raised, but much less frequently.

---

[2] John Quick was a Victorian delegate to the Federal Convention, and Robert Garran was Secretary to the Convention's Drafting Committee. This work is regarded as authoritative, akin to the notes on the U.S. Constitutional Convention prepared by James Madison.

6.1.5. Canadian rejection of a constitutional right to property

When Canadians turned to draft their Charter in 1982, the types of redistributive governmental programs considered acceptable had changed entirely from the view of 18th century politicians, and the notion that owners of property were somehow a discrete and insular minority unable to protect themselves in the political process seemed laughable. Even if s. 7 of the Charter had contained a right to property, its scope would be far narrower than the equivalent provisions of the Fifth and Fourteenth Amendments. In *Irwin Toy*, excerpted below, the Supreme Court of Canada interpreted s. 7's coverage of "everyone" as limited to real people, not corporations. In contrast, shortly after the adoption of the Fourteenth Amendment, the U.S. Supreme Court held the opposite. *See Santa Clara County v. Southern Pacific Railroad Co.*, 118 U.S. 394 (1886); *Mo. Pac. R.R. v. Nebraska*, 164 U.S. 403, 417 (1896) (holding that the takings clause applies to corporations).

Indeed, the Supreme Court of Canada found in *Manitoba Prostitution Reference*, excerpted below, that the purpose behind the deliberate exclusion of property rights from the Canadian Charter was to avoid the undesirable line of American cases prior to the New Deal that struck down progressive social welfare legislation as an unconstitutional deprivation of economic liberty. See part 6.1.7 below.

6.1.6. The South African compromise

The answer to the jurisprudential question posed in 6.1.2 is clear. As detailed in the Introductory Chapter, the peaceful creation of a post-apartheid South Africa was based on a willingness of the white minority to cede power to the black majority with assurances necessary to satisfy a critical mass of white South Africans, as well as the international community, that rights would be protected by a judicially enforced written constitution. The African National Congress signaled its movement, as part of this compromise, from the 1955 Freedom Charter's declaration that "the national wealth of our country . . . shall be restored to the people" and "all the land redivided amongst those who work it" to an acceptance of constitutional protection of property rights. As detailed in HEINZ KLUG, CONSTITUTING DEMOCRACY: LAW, GLOBALISM AND SOUTH AFRICA'S POLITICAL RECONSTRUCTION 124–36 (2000), the detailed provisions of s. 25 of the 1996 Constitution reflect this careful compromise, prohibiting wholesale expropriation and arbitrary deprivations but providing the government with flexibility to address the serious injustices in the distribution of wealth and property that resulted from apartheid.

6.1.7. The jurisprudential/doctrinal challenge: distinguishing economic liberty

In TAKINGS: PRIVATE PROPERTY AND THE POWER OF EMINENT DOMAIN, a leading American proponent of vigorous judicial protection of property rights, Professor Richard Epstein, carefully sets out his view that, in additional to conventional takings of real property, "[a]ll regulations, *all* taxes, and *all* modifications of liability rules are takings of private property prima facie compensable by the state." TAKINGS at 95. Although the Canadian approach seems to share Epstein's view that "the line between regulation and takings is incoherent," American, Australian, and South African courts continue to grapple with this issue in determining what is "property" that is protected and subject to compensation.

Consider the case of *Kaiser Aetna v. United States*, 444 U.S. 164 (1979). The plaintiff secured government permission to dig channels connecting a pond it owned into a Hawaiian bay, thus converting the pond into a lagoon and eventual marina. As a "navigable water" subject to federal jurisdiction, the lagoon thus became subject to regulation by the Army Corps of Engineers, who required public access. The Court held that such a requirement was a taking, based primarily on the plaintiff's investment-backed expectation that its marina would be exclusive. Now consider an alternative scenario: another firm spent the same amount of money as Kaiser Aetna did, in this case on designing and manufacturing boats for marinas like the one at issue in this case, when suddenly the Army Corps of Engineers issued regulations precluding boats of this type from federal navigable waters. It seems reasonably clear that there would be no compensation in this case.

Consider, as you review the American, Australian, and South African materials below, what each nation's court finds is the dividing line between economic regulations that reduce the profit-maximizing potential to which property could be used, and expropriations of property that require compensation.

6.2.   AMERICAN CONSTITUTIONAL PROTECTION OF PROPERTY BUT NOT ECONOMIC REGULATION

Conventional wisdom of judges and commentators is that the Takings Clause of the Fifth Amendment (applied to the states by incorporation into the rights guaranteed by the Fourteenth Amendment) was originally understood to require compensation when the government actually acquired a legal interest in property or physically invaded or took over private property.[3] As we saw in Chapter 2, during the "*Lochner* era," the Due Process Clause of the Fourteenth Amendment was construed to bar economic regulation that judges did not believe were sufficiently justified in the public interest to warrant invading freedom of contract. But this era came to a close during the New Deal, when the Supreme Court adopted a much more deferential approach to legislation that allegedly interfered with economic liberty. During this same era, the Supreme Court, in its landmark *Pennsylvania Coal* decision excerpted below, held that regulation of property that went "too far" would be considered a taking. Ever since, American courts have wrestled with the problem raised in part 6.1.7, *supra* and discussed in detail in Chapter 2: why are

---

[3] *See* William Michael Treanor, *The Original Understanding of the Takings Clause and the Political Process*, 95 COLUM. L. REV. 782, 798 (1995) ("The predecessor clauses to the Fifth Amendment's Takings Clause, the original understanding of the Takings Clause itself, and the weight of early judicial interpretations of federal and state takings clauses all indicate that compensation was mandated only when the government physically took property.").

some kinds of economic regulation subject to deferential scrutiny and no compensation, but not others?

6.2.1.   Due Process limits on the use of property

MUGLER v. KANSAS
SUPREME COURT OF THE UNITED STATES
123 U.S. 623 (1887)

[Before WAITE, C.J., and MILLER, FIELD, BRADLEY, HARLAN, WOODS, GRAY, MATHEWS, BLATCHFORD, JJ.]

MR. JUSTICE HARLAN delivered the opinion of the court.

[Over a period from 1868-85, the Kansas legislature passed a series of statutes outlawing the manufacture of alcoholic beverages and the possession of implements of alcohol manufacture. Mugler and others were convicted under these statutes.]

The buildings and machinery constituting these breweries are of little value if not used for the purpose of manufacturing beer; that is to say, if the statutes are enforced against the defendants the value of their property will be very materially diminished.

*   *   *

Keeping in view these principles, as governing the relations of the judicial and legislative departments of the government with each other, it is difficult to perceive any ground for the judiciary to declare that the prohibition by Kansas of the manufacture or sale, within her limits, of intoxicating liquors for general use there as a beverage, is not fairly adapted to the end of protecting the community against the evils which confessedly result from the excessive use of ardent spirits. There is no justification for holding that the State, under the guise merely of police regulations, is here aiming to deprive the citizen of his constitutional rights; for we cannot shut out of view the fact, within the knowledge of all, that the public health, the public morals, and the public safety, may be endangered by the general use of intoxicating drinks; nor the fact, established by statistics accessible to every one, that the idleness, disorder, pauperism, and crime existing in the country are, in some degree at least, traceable to this evil. If, therefore, a state deems the absolute prohibition of the manufacture and sale, within her limits, of intoxicating liquors for other than medical, scientific, and manufacturing purposes, to be necessary to the peace and security of society, the courts cannot, without usurping legislative functions, override the will of the people as thus expressed by their chosen representatives. They have nothing to do with the mere policy of legislation. Indeed, it is a fundamental principle in our institutions, indispensable to the preservation of public liberty, that one of the separate departments of government shall not usurp powers committed by the Constitution to another department. And so, if, in the judgment of the legislature, the manufacture of intoxicating liquors for the maker's own use, as a beverage, would tend to cripple, if it did not defeat, the effort to guard the community against the evils attending the excessive use of such liquors, it is not for the courts, upon their views as to what is best and safest for the community, to disregard the legislative determination of that question. So far from such a regulation having no relation to the general end sought to be accomplished, the entire scheme of prohibition, as embodied in the constitution and laws of Kansas, might fail, if the right of each citizen to manufacture intoxicating liquors for his own use as a beverage were recognized. Such a right does not inhere in citizenship. Nor can it be said that government interferes with or impairs any one's constitutional rights of liberty or of property, when it determines that the manufacture and sale of intoxicating drinks, for general or individual use, as a beverage, are, or may become, hurtful to society, and constitute, therefore, a business in which no one may lawfully engage. Those rights are best secured, in our government, by the observance, upon the part of all, of such regulations as are established by competent authority to promote the common good. No one may rightfully do that which the law-making power, upon reasonable grounds, declares to be prejudicial to the general welfare.

* * *

The principle, that no person shall be deprived of life, liberty, or property, without due process of law, was embodied, in substance, in the constitutions of nearly all, if not all, of the States at the time of the adoption of the Fourteenth Amendment; and it has never been regarded as incompatible with the principle, equally vital, because essential to the peace and safety of society, that all property in this country is held under the implied obligation that the owner's use of it shall not be injurious to the community. * * *

It is supposed by the defendants that the doctrine for which they contend is sustained by *Pumpelly v. Green Bay Co., 13 Wall. 166.* But in that view we do not concur. That was an action for the recovery of damages for the overflowing of the plaintiff's land by water, resulting from the construction of a dam across a river. The defence was that the dam constituted a part of the system adopted by the State for improving the navigation of Fox and Wisconsin rivers; and it was contended that as the damages of which the plaintiff complained were only the result of the improvement, under legislative sanction, of a navigable stream, he was not entitled to compensation from the State or its agents. The case, therefore, involved the question whether the overflowing of the plaintiff's land, to such an extent that it became practically unfit to be used, was a taking of property, within the meaning of the constitution of Wisconsin, providing that "the property of no person shall be taken for public use without just compensation therefor." This court said it would be a very curious and unsatisfactory result, were it held that, "if the government refrains from the absolute conversion of real property to the uses of the public, it can destroy its value entirely, can inflict irreparable and permanent injury to any extent, can, in effect, subject it to total destruction, without making any compensation, because, in the narrowest sense of that word, it is not taken for the public use. Such a construction would pervert the constitutional provision into a restriction upon the rights of the citizen, as those rights stood at the common law, instead of the government, and make it an authority for the invasion of private right under the pretext of the public good, which had no warrant in the laws or practices of our ancestors." pp. 177, 178.

These principles have no application to the case under consideration. The question in *Pumpelly v. Green Bay Company* arose under the State's power of eminent domain; while the question now before us arises under what are, strictly, the police powers of the State, exerted for the protection of the health, morals, and safety of the people. That case, was an extreme qualification of the doctrine, universally held, that "acts done in the proper exercise of governmental powers, and not directly encroaching upon private property, though these consequences may impair its use," do not constitute a taking within the meaning of the constitutional provision, or entitle the owner of such property to compensation from the State or its agents, or give him any right of action. It was a case in which there was a "permanent flooding of private property," a "physical invasion of the real estate of the private owner, and a practical ouster of his possession." His property was, in effect, required to be devoted to the use of the public, and, consequently, he was entitled to compensation.

As already stated, the present case must be governed by principles that do not involve the power of eminent domain, in the exercise of which property may not be taken for public use without compensation. A prohibition simply upon the use of property for purposes that are declared, by valid legislation, to be injurious to the health, morals, or safety of the community, cannot, in any just sense, be deemed a taking or an appropriation of property for the public benefit. Such legislation does not disturb the owner in the control or use of his property for lawful purposes, nor restrict his right to dispose of it, but is only a declaration by the State that its use by any one, for certain forbidden purposes, is prejudicial to the public interests. Nor can legislation of that character come within the Fourteenth Amendment, in any case, unless it is apparent that its real object is not to protect the community, or to promote the general well-being, but, under the guise of police regulation, to deprive the owner of his liberty and property, without due process of law. The power which the States have of prohibiting such use by individuals of their property as will be prejudicial to the health, the morals, or the safety of the public, is not — and, consistently with the existence and safety of organized society, cannot be — burdened with the condition that the State must compensate such individual owners for pecuniary losses they may sustain, by reason of their not being permitted, by a noxious use of their property, to inflict injury upon the community. The exercise of the police power by the destruction of property which is itself a public nuisance, or the prohibition of its use in a particular way, whereby its value becomes depreciated, is very different from taking property for public use, or from depriving a person of his property without due process of law. In the one case, a nuisance only is abated; in the other, unoffending property is taken away from an innocent owner.

It is true, that, when the defendants in these cases purchased or erected their breweries, the laws of the State did not forbid the manufacture of intoxicating liquors. But the State did not thereby give any assurance, or come under an obligation, that its legislation upon that subject would remain unchanged. Indeed, as was said in *Stone v. Mississippi*, above cited, the supervision of the public health and the public morals is a governmental power, "continuing in its nature," and "to be dealt with as the special exigencies of the moment may require;" and that, "for this purpose, the largest legislative discretion is allowed, and the discretion cannot be parted with any more than the power itself." So in *Beer Co. v. Massachusetts*, 97

U.S. 32: "If the public safety or the public morals require the discontinuance of any manufacture or traffic, the hand of the legislature cannot be stayed from providing for its discontinuance by any incidental inconvenience which individuals or corporations may suffer."

* * *

MR. JUSTICE FIELD delivered the following separate opinion.

[Justice Field dissented on the grounds that Kansas did not have the authority to prohibit the manufacture of alcoholic beverages for export, and that a statutory provision destroying bottles, glasses, and other implements of manufacture was not required to protect the health and morals of Kansans.]

6.2.2.   The doctrine of regulatory takings

PENNSYLVANIA COAL COMPANY v. MAHON
SUPREME COURT OF THE UNITED STATES
260 U.S. 393 (1922)

[Before TAFT, C.J., and MCKENNA, HOLMES, VAN DEVANTER, MCREYNOLDS, BRANDEIS, SUTHERLAND, BUTLER, and SANFORD, JJ.]

MR. JUSTICE HOLMES delivered the opinion of the Court.

This is a bill in equity brought by the defendants in error to prevent the Pennsylvania Coal Company from mining under their property in such way as to remove the supports and cause a subsidence of the surface and of their house. The bill sets out a deed executed by the Coal Company in 1878, under which the plaintiffs claim. The deed conveys the surface, but in express terms reserves the right to remove all the coal under the same, and the grantee takes the premises with the risk, and waives all claim for damages that may arise from mining out the coal. But the plaintiffs say that whatever may have been the Coal Company's rights, they were taken away by an Act of Pennsylvania, approved May 27, 1921, P.L. 1198, commonly known there as the Kohler Act. The Court of Common Pleas found that if not restrained the defendant would cause the damage to prevent which the bill was brought, but denied an injunction, holding that the statute if applied to this case would be unconstitutional. On appeal the Supreme Court of the State agreed that the defendant had contract and property rights protected by the Constitution of the United States, but held that the statute was a legitimate exercise of the police power and directed a decree for the plaintiffs. A writ of error was granted bringing the case to this Court.

The statute forbids the mining of anthracite coal in such way as to cause the subsidence of, among other things, any structure used as a human habitation, with certain exceptions, including among them land where the surface is owned by the owner of the underlying coal and is distant more than one hundred and fifty feet from any improved property belonging to any other person. As applied to this case the statute is admitted to destroy previously existing rights of property and contract. The question is whether the police power can be stretched so far.

Government hardly could go on if to some extent values incident to property could not be diminished without paying for every such change in the general law. As long recognized, some values are enjoyed under an implied limitation and must yield to the police power. But obviously the implied limitation must have its limits, or the contract and due process clauses are gone. One fact for consideration in determining such limits is the extent of the diminution. When it reaches a certain magnitude, in most if not in all cases there must be an exercise of eminent domain and compensation to sustain the act. So the question depends upon the particular facts. The greatest weight is given to the judgment of the legislature, but it always is open to interested parties to contend that the legislature has gone beyond its constitutional power.

This is the case of a single private house. No doubt there is a public interest even in this, as there is in every purchase and sale and in all that happens within the commonwealth. Some existing rights may be modified even in such a case. Rideout v. Knox, 148 Mass. 368. But usually in ordinary private affairs the public interest does not warrant much of this kind of interference. A source of damage to such a house is not a public nuisance even if similar damage is inflicted on others in different places. The damage is not common or public. Wesson v. Washburn Iron Co., 13 Allen, 95, 103. The extent of the public interest is shown by the statute to be limited, since the statute ordinarily does not apply to land when the surface is owned by the owner of the coal. Furthermore, it is not justified as a protection of personal safety. That could be provided for by notice. Indeed the very foundation of this bill is that the defendant gave timely notice of its intent to mine under the house. On the other hand the extent of the taking is great. It purports to abolish what is recognized in Pennsylvania as an estate in land — a very valuable estate — and what is declared by the Court below to be a contract hitherto binding the plaintiffs. If we were called upon to deal with the plaintiffs' position alone, we should think it clear that the statute does not disclose a public interest sufficient to warrant so extensive a destruction of the defendant's constitutionally protected rights.

*   *   *

It is our opinion that the act cannot be sustained as an exercise of the police power, so far as it affects the mining of coal under streets or cities in places where the right to mine such coal has been reserved. As said in a Pennsylvania case, "For practical purposes, the right to coal consists in the right to mine it." Commonwealth v. Clearview Coal Co., 256 Pa. St. 328, 331. What makes the right to mine coal valuable is that it can be exercised with profit. To make it commercially impracticable to mine certain coal has very nearly the same effect for constitutional purposes as appropriating or destroying it. This we think that we are warranted in assuming that the statute does.

It is true that in Plymouth Coal Co. v. Pennsylvania, 232 U.S. 531, it was held competent for the legislature to require a pillar of coal to be left along the line of adjoining property, that, with the pillar on the other side of the line, would be a barrier sufficient for the safety of the employees of either mine in case the other should be abandoned and allowed to fill with water. But that was a requirement for the safety of employees invited into the mine, and secured an average reciprocity of advantage that has been recognized as a justification of various laws.

*   *   *

The general rule at least is, that while property may be regulated to a certain extent, if regulation goes too far it will be recognized as a taking. It may be doubted how far exceptional cases, like the blowing up of a house to stop a conflagration, go — and if they go beyond the general rule, whether they do not stand as much upon tradition as upon principle. In general it is not plain that a man's misfortunes or necessities will justify his shifting the damages to his neighbor's shoulders. We are in danger of forgetting that a strong public desire to improve the public condition is not enough to warrant achieving the desire by a shorter cut than the constitutional way of paying for the change. As we already have said, this is a question of degree — and therefore cannot be disposed of by general propositions. But we regard this as going beyond any of the cases decided by this Court. The late decisions upon laws dealing with the congestion of Washington and New York, caused by the war, dealt with laws intended to meet a temporary emergency and providing for compensation determined to be reasonable by an impartial board. They went to the verge of the law but fell far short of the present act.

We assume, of course, that the statute was passed upon the conviction that an exigency existed that would warrant it, and we assume that an exigency exists that would warrant the exercise of eminent domain. But the question at bottom is upon whom the loss of the changes desired should fall. So far as private persons or communities have seen fit to take the risk of acquiring only surface rights, we cannot see that the fact that their risk has become a danger warrants the giving to them greater rights than they bought.

Decree reversed.

Mr. Justice Brandeis, dissenting.

The Kohler Act prohibits, under certain conditions, the mining of anthracite coal within the limits of a city in such a manner or to such an extent "as to cause the . . . subsidence of any dwelling or other structure used as a human habitation, or any factory, store, or other industrial or mercantile establishment in which human labor is employed." Coal in place is land; and the right of the owner to use his land is not absolute. He may not so use it as to create a public nuisance; and uses, once harmless, may, owing to changed conditions, seriously threaten the public welfare. Whenever they do, the legislature has power to prohibit such uses without paying compensation; and the power to prohibit extends alike to the manner, the character and the purpose of the use. Are we justified in declaring that the Legislature of Pennsylvania has, in restricting the right to mine anthracite, exercised this power so arbitrarily as to violate the Fourteenth Amendment?

Every restriction upon the use of property imposed in the exercise of the police power deprives the owner of some right theretofore enjoyed, and is, in that sense, an abridgment by the State of rights in property without making compensation. But restriction imposed to protect the public health, safety or morals from dangers threatened is not a taking. The restriction here in question is merely the prohibition of a noxious use. The property so restricted remains in the possession of its owner. The State does not appropriate it or make any use of it. The State merely prevents the owner from making a use which interferes with paramount rights of the public. Whenever the use prohibited ceases to be noxious, — as it may because of further change in local or social conditions, — the restriction will have to be removed and the owner will again be free to enjoy his property as heretofore.

The restriction upon the use of this property cannot, of course, be lawfully imposed, unless its purpose is to protect the public. But the purpose of a restriction does not cease to be public, because incidentally some private persons may thereby receive gratuitously valuable special benefits. Thus, owners of low buildings may obtain, through statutory restrictions upon the height of neighboring structures, benefits equivalent to an easement of light and air. Furthermore, a restriction, though imposed for a public purpose, will not be lawful, unless the restriction is an appropriate means to the public end. But to keep coal in place is surely an appropriate means of preventing subsidence of the surface; and ordinarily it is the only available means. Restriction upon use does not become inappropriate as a means, merely because it deprives the owner of the only use to which the property can then be profitably put. The liquor and the oleomargarine cases settled that. Mugler v. Kansas, 123 U.S. 623, 668, 669; Powell v. Pennsylvania, 127 U.S. 678, 682. Nor is a restriction imposed through exercise of the police power inappropriate as a means, merely because the same end might be effected through exercise of the power of eminent domain, or otherwise at public expense. Every restriction upon the height of buildings might be secured through acquiring by eminent domain the right of each owner to build above the limiting height; but it is settled that the State need not resort to that power. If by mining anthracite coal the owner would necessarily unloose poisonous gasses, I suppose no one would doubt the power of the State to prevent the mining, without buying his coal fields. And why may not the State, likewise, without paying compensation, prohibit one from digging so deep or excavating so near the surface, as to expose the community to like dangers? In the latter case, as in the former, carrying on the business would be a public nuisance.

It is said that one fact for consideration in determining whether the limits of the police power have been exceeded is the extent of the resulting diminution in value; and that here the restriction destroys existing rights of property and contract. But values are relative. If we are to consider the value of the coal kept in place by the restriction, we should compare it with the value of all other parts of the land. That is, with the value not of the coal alone, but with the value of the whole property. The rights of an owner as against the public are not increased by dividing the interests in his property into surface and subsoil. The sum of the rights in the parts can not be greater than the rights in the whole. The estate of an owner in land is grandiloquently described as extending ab orco usque ad coelum. But I suppose no one would contend that by selling his interest above one hundred feet from the surface he could prevent the State from limiting, by the police power, the height of structures in a city. And why should a sale of underground rights bar the State's power? For aught that appears the value of the coal kept in place by the restriction may be negligible as compared with the value of the whole property, or even as compared with that part of it which is represented by the coal remaining in place and which may be extracted despite the statute. Ordinarily a police regulation, general in operation, will not be held void as to a particular property, although proof is offered that owing to conditions peculiar to it the restriction could not reasonably be applied. But even if the particular facts are to govern, the statute should, in my opinion, be upheld in this case. For the defendant has failed to adduce any evidence from which it appears that to restrict its mining operations was an unreasonable exercise of the police power. Where the surface and the coal belong to the same person, self-interest would ordinarily prevent mining to such an extent as to cause a subsidence. It was, doubtless, for this reason that the legislature, estimating the degrees of danger, deemed statutory restriction unnecessary for the public safety under such conditions.

*   *   *

A prohibition of mining which causes subsidence of such structures and facilities is obviously enacted for a public purpose; and it seems, likewise, clear that mere notice of intention to mine would not in this connection secure the public safety. Yet it is said that these provisions of the act cannot be sustained as an exercise of the police power where the right to mine such coal has been reserved. The conclusion seems to rest upon the assumption that in order to justify such exercise of the police power there must be "an average reciprocity of advantage" as between the owner of the property restricted and the rest of the community; and that here such reciprocity is absent. Reciprocity of advantage is an important consideration, and may even be an essential, where the State's power is exercised for the purpose of conferring benefits upon the property of a neighborhood, as in drainage projects, or upon adjoining owners, as by party wall provisions. But where the police power is exercised, not to confer benefits upon property owners, but to protect the public from detriment and danger, there is, in my opinion, no room for considering reciprocity of advantage. There was no reciprocal advantage to the owner prohibited from using his oil tanks in 248 U.S. 498; his brickyard, in 239 U.S. 394; his livery stable, in 237 U.S. 171; his billiard hall, in 225 U.S. 623; his oleomargarine factory, in 127 U.S. 678; his brewery, in 123 U.S. 623; unless it be the advantage of living and doing business in a civilized community. That reciprocal advantage is given by the act to the coal operators.

After *Pennsylvania Coal*, the Supreme Court sought to provide further guidance on when a compensable taking occurs without a physical invasion of the landowner's property or the actual conversion of the property to public use; that is, when regulation "goes too far." In *Penn Central Transportation Co. v. New York City*, 438 U.S. 104 (1978), the Court considered a claim that the government had to compensate the owner of Grand Central Station, because the city had rejected permission to construct a large office building over the terminal that would destroy the terminal's historic and aesthetic features in a manner inconsistent with its designation as a historic landmark. The court reaffirmed the view that a taking can occur even if the government does not seek to transfer physical control over land. *Id.* at 123 n.25. For the majority, Justice Brennan acknowledged that while the purpose of the Takings Clause was to prevent the government from forcing some to bear burdens that "in fairness and justice" should be borne by all, "this Court, quite simply, has been unable to develop any 'set formula' for determining when 'justice and fairness' require that economic injuries caused by public action be compensated by the government, rather than remain disproportionately concentrated on a few persons. *Id.* at 124. However, three factors have "particular significance":

(1) "the economic impact of the regulation on the claimant";

(2) "the extent to which the regulation has interfered with distinct investment-backed expectations"; and

(3) "the character of the governmental action."

Considering that New York gave the appellants special rights to develop other properties (these rights could be sold to others for valuable consideration), a consideration of these three factors led the majority to conclude that there was not a compensable taking.

Likewise, the Court held in *Connolly v. Pension Benefit Guaranty Corp.*, 475 U.S. 211 (1986) that mandatory payments to an insurance fund did not constitute a compensable taking of property. Although the Court rejected a claim that the legislative creation of any liability to a private party "if accepted, would prove too much," and that compensation was not required "whenever legislation requires one person to use his or her assets for the benefit of another," *id.* at 222–23, in the end the Court based its judgment on its own conclusion that it was not persuaded "that fairness and justice require the public, rather than the withdrawing employers and other parties to pension plan agreements, to shoulder the responsibility for rescuing plans that are in financial trouble."

Guggenheim v. City of Goleta, 582 F.3d 996 (9th Cir. 2008), applied this doctrine to a rent control statute applying only to mobile-home parks. The property was acquired when the land was subject to a less-restrictive county ordinance, but the property was then annexed by the city. A divided court of appeals held that "to prevail under *Penn Central*, the property owner must demonstrate a loss of value that may be less than 100 percent, but high enough to have "go[ne] too far." *Id.* at 1018, citing *Penn Central.* The majority found that, although the property owners' rate of return was not necessarily less than other real estate investments, the control resulted in a premium of close to 90% of the value of a mobile home tenancy. Acknowledging that an analysis of "investment-backed expectations" was "self-referential, *id.* at 1027, the majority found that the existence of current regulations did not preclude a regulatory takings claim by the property owner. The majority rejected the argument that the "character of governmental action" should focus on whether the act is more akin to a physical invasion of land or instead merely adjusts the benefits and burdens of economic life to promote the common good. Rather, focusing on the impact solely on mobile home property owners, the majority invoked *Armstrong* to conclude that the ordinance improperly imposed a burden on them that should be diffused.

6.2.3. Distinguishing analysis under the Due Process and Takings Clause guarantees

Pennsylvania Coal's iconic status in creating the doctrine of regulatory takings is the result of later Supreme Court decisions, not anything explicit in the decision itself. Although Justice Holmes used the phrase "taking" in several parts of his

Pennsylvania Coal opinion, that decision could be read in historical context as one based on the constitutional prohibition on state impairment of contracts (recall that the Coal Company had originally sold the surface land to residents with the express provision that it retained mining rights even if the mining created subsistence) or that it was a violation of the notions of substantive due process that prevailed during the *Lochner* era: it is clear that, like Justice Peckham's decision in *Lochner* and unlike Justice Harlan's decision in *Mugler*, Justice Holmes found no strong public interest in preventing the Coal Company's mining activity. Recall that the state statute would not have prevented the Coal Company from mining causing widespread subsistence of surface land if the Coal Company owned both the surface and mining rights.

However, *Penn Central* confirms the melding of due process and takings precedents.[4] This presents doctrinal problems, because, as seen in Chapter 2, when state regulation of economic activity unrelated to real property is challenged in the post-*Lochner* era, it is typically sustained under a highly deferential rational basis test. The following case illustrates the confusion at the lower court level and the Supreme Court's effort to clarify doctrine.

LINGLE v. CHEVRON U.S.A., INC.
SUPREME COURT OF THE UNITED STATES
544 U.S. 528 (2005)

JUSTICE O'CONNOR delivered the opinion of the Court.

On occasion, a would-be doctrinal rule or test finds its way into our case law through simple repetition of a phrase — however fortuitously coined. A quarter century ago, in *Agins v. City of Tiburon*, 447 U.S. 255 (1980), the Court declared that government regulation of private property "effects a taking if [such regulation] does not substantially advance legitimate state interests . . . ." 447 U.S., at 260. Through reiteration in a half dozen or so decisions since *Agins*, this language has been ensconced in our *Fifth Amendment* takings jurisprudence.

In the case before us, the lower courts applied *Agins*' "substantially advances" formula to strike down a Hawaii statute that limits the rent that oil companies may charge to dealers who lease service stations owned by the companies. The lower courts held that the rent cap effects an uncompensated taking of private property

---

[4] *See* Jamison E. Colburn, *Does the Earth Belong to the Living? Property and Environmental Law Perspectives on the Rights of Future Generations: Splitting the Atom of Property: Rights Experimentalism as Obligation to Future Generations*, 77 GEO. WASH. L. REV. 1411, 1426 (2009). Colburn observes that in *Penn Central* the Court, after applying the Fifth Amendment through the Fourteenth,

> then proceeded to collapse two nominally different legal doctrines into a single, multi-factor test. Penn Central seemed to assume that the many substantive due process precedents it invoked were actually precedents [applying the Fifth Amendment to the states]. Technically, of course, that is precisely what they were not. And although the two bodies of doctrine approached each other in substance throughout the twentieth century, they were always very different jurisdictionally until 1978. . . . Since 1978, though, there has been little if any explicit or deliberate differentiation between the authorities under challenge or the precise constitutional rights being asserted.

in violation of the *Fifth* and *Fourteenth Amendments* because it does not substantially advance Hawaii's asserted interest in controlling retail gasoline prices. This case requires us to decide whether the "substantially advances" formula announced in *Agins* is an appropriate test for determining whether a regulation effects a *Fifth Amendment* taking. We conclude that it is not.

I

. . . .

To facilitate resolution of the summary judgment motions, the parties jointly stipulated to certain relevant facts. They agreed that Act 257 reduces by about $207,000 per year the aggregate rent that Chevron would otherwise charge on 11 of its 64 lessee-dealer stations. On the other hand, the statute allows Chevron to collect more rent than it would otherwise charge at its remaining 53 lessee-dealer stations, such that Chevron could increase its overall rental income from all 64 stations by nearly $1.1 million per year. The parties further stipulated that, over the past 20 years, Chevron has not fully recovered the costs of maintaining lessee-dealer stations in any State through rent alone. Rather, the company recoups its expenses through a combination of rent and product sales. Finally, the joint stipulation states that Chevron has earned in the past, and anticipates that it will continue to earn under Act 257, a return on its investment in lessee-dealer stations in Hawaii that satisfies any constitutional standard.

[The lower courts ruled in favor of Chevron based on their economic analysis of the effects of the challenged rent cap. Finding Chevron's expert to be "more persuasive" than the State's expert, they concluded that the statute would not actually benefit consumers but rather would simply benefit the favored retail station lease-holders.]

II

A

The *Takings Clause of the Fifth Amendment*, made applicable to the States through the *Fourteenth*, see *Chicago, B. & Q. R. Co. v. Chicago*, 166 U.S. 226 (1897), provides that private property shall not "be taken for public use, without just compensation." As its text makes plain, the *Takings Clause* "does not prohibit the taking of private property, but instead places a condition on the exercise of that power." *First English Evangelical Lutheran Church of Glendale v. County of Los Angeles*, 482 U.S. 304 (1987). In other words, it "is designed not to limit the governmental interference with property rights *per se*, but rather to secure compensation in the event of otherwise proper interference amounting to a taking." 482 U.S., at 315. While scholars have offered various justifications for this regime, we have emphasized its role in "barring Government from forcing some people alone to bear public burdens which, in all fairness and justice, should be borne by the public as a whole." *Armstrong v. United States*, 364 U.S. 40, 49 (1960) . . . .

The paradigmatic taking requiring just compensation is a direct government appropriation or physical nvasion of private property. . . . Indeed, until the Court's watershed decision in *Pennsylvania Coal Co. v. Mahon*, 260 U.S. 393 (1922), "it was generally thought that the *Takings Clause* reached *only* a 'direct appropriation' of property, or the functional equivalent of a 'practical ouster of [the owner's] possession.'" *Lucas v. South Carolina Coastal Council*, 505 U.S. 1003, 1014 (1992); see also 505 U.S., at 1028, n. 15, ("Early constitutional theorists did not believe the *Takings Clause* embraced regulations of property at all").

Beginning with *Mahon*, however, the Court recognized that government regulation of private property may, in some instances, be so onerous that its effect is tantamount to a direct appropriation or ouster — and that such "regulatory takings" may be compensable under the *Fifth Amendment*. In Justice Holmes' storied but cryptic formulation, "while property may be regulated to a certain extent, if regulation goes too far it will be recognized as a taking." 260 U.S., at 415. The rub, of course, has been — and remains — how to discern how far is "too far." In answering that question, we must remain cognizant that "government regulation — by definition — involves the adjustment of rights for the public good," *Andrus v. Allard*, 444 U.S. 51, 65, 100 S. Ct. 318, 62 L. Ed. 2d 210 (1979), and that "Government hardly could go on if to some extent values incident to property could not be diminished without paying for every such change in the general law," *Mahon, supra*, 260 U.S., at 413.

Our precedents stake out two categories of regulatory action that generally will be deemed *per se* takings for *Fifth Amendment* purposes. First, where government requires an owner to suffer a permanent physical invasion of her property — however minor — it must provide just compensation. See *Loretto v. Teleprompter Manhattan CATV Corp.*, 458 U.S. 419 (1982) (state law requiring landlords to permit cable companies to install cable facilities in apartment buildings effected a taking). A second categorical rule applies to regulations that completely deprive an owner of "*all* economically beneficial use" of her property. *Lucas*, 505 U.S., at 1019 (emphasis in original). We held in *Lucas* that the government must pay just compensation for such "total regulatory takings," except to the extent that "background principles of nuisance and property law" independently restrict the owner's intended use of the property. 505 U.S., at 1026-1032.

Outside these two relatively narrow categories . . . regulatory takings challenges are governed by the standards set forth in *Penn Central Transp. Co. v. New York City*, 438 U.S. 104, 98 S. Ct. 2646, 57 L. Ed. 2d 631 (1978). Although our regulatory takings jurisprudence cannot be characterized as unified, these three inquiries (reflected in *Loretto*, *Lucas*, and *Penn Central*) share a common touchstone. Each aims to identify regulatory actions that are functionally equivalent to the classic taking in which government directly appropriates private property or ousts the owner from his domain . . . .

B

. . . .

Although *Agins*' reliance on due process precedents is understandable, the language the Court selected was regrettably imprecise. The "substantially advances" formula suggests a means-ends test: It asks, in essence, whether a regulation of private property is *effective* in achieving some legitimate public purpose. An inquiry of this nature has some logic in the context of a due process challenge, for a regulation that fails to serve any legitimate governmental objective may be so arbitrary or irrational that it runs afoul of the *Due Process Clause*. *See, e.g., County of Sacramento v. Lewis*, 523 U.S. 833, 846 (1998) (stating that the *Due Process Clause* is intended, in part, to protect the individual against "the exercise of power without any reasonable justification in the service of a legitimate governmental objective"). But such a test is not a valid method of discerning whether private property has been "taken" for purposes of the *Fifth Amendment*.

. . . .

Chevron's challenge to the Hawaii statute in this case illustrates the flaws in the "substantially advances" theory. To begin with, it is unclear how significantly Hawaii's rent cap actually burdens Chevron's property rights. . . . In short, Chevron has not clearly argued — let alone established — that it has been singled out to bear any particularly severe regulatory burden. Rather, the gravamen of Chevron's claim is simply that Hawaii's rent cap will not actually serve the State's legitimate interest in protecting consumers against high gasoline prices. Whatever the merits of that claim, it does not sound under the *Takings Clause*. Chevron plainly does not seek compensation for a taking of its property for a legitimate public use, but rather an injunction against the enforcement of a regulation that it alleges to be fundamentally arbitrary and irrational.

Finally, the "substantially advances" formula is not only doctrinally untenable as a takings test — its application as such would also present serious practical difficulties. The *Agins* formula can be read to demand heightened means-ends review of virtually any regulation of private property. If so interpreted, it would require courts to scrutinize the efficacy of a vast array of state and federal regulations — a task for which courts are not well suited. Moreover, it would empower — and might often require — courts to substitute their predictive judgments for those of elected legislatures and expert agencies.

Although the instant case is only the tip of the proverbial iceberg, it foreshadows the hazards of placing courts in this role. To resolve Chevron's takings claim, the District Court was required to choose between the views of two opposing economists as to whether Hawaii's rent control statute would help to prevent concentration and supracompetitive prices in the State's retail gasoline market. Finding one expert to be "more persuasive" than the other, the court concluded that the Hawaii Legislature's chosen regulatory strategy would not actually achieve its objectives. *See* 198 F. Supp. 2d, at 1187-1193. The court determined that there was no evidence that oil companies had charged, or would charge, excessive rents. *See id.*, at 1191. Based on this and other findings, the District Court enjoined further enforcement of Act 257's rent cap provision against Chevron. We find the proceedings below remarkable, to say the least, given that we have long eschewed such heightened scrutiny when addressing substantive due process challenges to government regulation. *See, e.g., Exxon Corp. v. Governor of Maryland*, 437 U.S. 117, 124–125, 98 S. Ct. 2207, 57 L. Ed. 2d 91 (1978); *Ferguson v. Skrupa*, 372 U.S. 726, 730–732, 83 S. Ct. 1028, 10 L. Ed. 2d 93 (1963). The reasons for deference to legislative judgments about the need for, and likely effectiveness of, regulatory actions are by now well established, and we think they are no less applicable here.

. . . .

[JUSTICE KENNEDY's concurring opinion omitted.]

———————

Scholars continue to debate the coherence of American doctrine that applies a different level of judicial review to regulation of land (a taking if it "goes too far") and regulation of other economic activity (permitted if any rational basis to support). *Compare* WILLIAM A. FISCHEL, REGULATOR TAKINGS: LAW, ECONOMICS, AND POLITICS 5, 107 (1995) (political process most likely to malfunction with immobile land and when harm imposed on non-residents or non-owners, as in municipal decisions), *with* William M. Treanor, *Original Understandings, supra*, 95 COLUM. L. REV. at 863–64 and Daniel A. Farber, *Economic Analysis and Just Compensation*, 12 INT'L REV. L. & ECON. 125, 130 (1992) (landowners are politically powerful and can lobby state legislatures to protect their interests adequately).

6.2.4.   Active or deferential scrutiny

In specific land use cases, the Court has found that a compensable taking has occurred when a condition imposed on a landowner to secure development approval is insufficiently related to mitigating any public concerns from the planned development. *See, e.g., Nollan v. California Coastal Comm'n*, 483 U.S. 825 (1987) (easement for beach access unrelated to concern that development would obscure ocean vistas from public highway); *Dolan v. City of Tigard*, 512 U.S. 374 (1994) (conditioning approval of Dolan's building permit on agreement to dedicate a portion of her property for flood control and traffic improvements, specifically part of a bikeway along the flood plain on which she was otherwise prohibited from building, lacked the requisite "rough proportionality" between social harm caused by Dolan's development and the imposition on her property rights).

Although these cases show how courts closely scrutinize government action to determine if property is "taken," and whether compensation is appropriate, the Supreme Court has been much more deferential to legislative judgments about whether the property is being taken (with compensation) "for public use." In *Berman v. Parker*, 348 U.S. 26 (1954), the court upheld an urban renewal scheme where land was expropriated, compensation provided, and the land resold to a developer whose plans removed urban blight. The Court held that any goal that was within Congress' recognized authority over the District of Columbia (or, more broadly, within the state's police power) would justify the use of eminent domain proceedings. In *Hawaii Housing Authority v. Midkiff*, 467 U.S. 229 (1984), the Court likewise upheld a plan to condemn vast landholdings by the few Hawaiians who owned private land, for redistribution to the vast number of homeowners who rented their land. In *Kelo v. City of New London*, 545 U.S. 469 (2005), the Court upheld the forced sale of homes directed by the city so that a shopping mall likely to generate higher tax revenues could be constructed. This particular use of eminent domain is highly controversial in the United States, and the decision provoked a strong reaction. Although no federal response has been passed by Congress, homeowners in 42 states have used the political process to enact legislation that bars or significantly limits the authority of local governments to use the eminent domain power in broad and unfettered ways.

6.2.5. Summary

The cases excerpted and summarized above are sufficiently dense from a doctrinal perspective that the doctrine is worth summarizing:

(1) The Fifth Amendment requires the federal government to provide just compensation to those whose "property"[5] is taken

(2) The Fourteenth Amendment applies this principle to state and local governments

(3) Any physical invasion of property is a taking, no matter how small

(4) Although government may regulate the use of property, when regulation "goes too far," a taking occurs

    a. compensation can be, in some cases, required for excessive regulation of real property in context where similarly excessive regulation of personal property would not be a taking, and where the Due Process clause would not bar the deprivation

    b. the operative principle is whether "fairness and justice" require that society, rather than an individual property owner, bear the burden of the regulation; this has been encapsulated in the three factors set forth in *Penn Central:*

        i. "the economic impact of the regulation on the claimant";

        ii. "the extent to which the regulation has interfered with distinct investment-backed expectations"; and

        iii. "the character of the governmental action."

    c. regulation that denies any economically productive use of the property is a per se taking

    d. a special rule limits government conditions on permit appeals (exactions) to those that are proportionate

(5) Property owners who object to state and local land use regulation must litigate their claims in state court, raising applicable state law claims as well as federal constitutional claims, and the state courts decisions are final unless the U.S. Supreme Court grants discretionary review from the state courts

---

[5] [Ed. note: see section 6.7, *infra,* for a discussion on how courts determine what is "property."]

6.3.   COMPULSORY ACQUISITION, JUST TERMS, AND THE AUSTRALIAN CONSTITUTION

As noted above, the principal questions asked by the High Court over the years concerning the scope of s 51(xxxi) have been: *what is property?* and *what is an acquisition?*

6.3.1.   What is "property"?

The Court has defined property broadly to include "real and personal property, incorporeal hereditaments such as rents and services, rights of way, rights of profit or use in land of another, and *choses in action,*" *Minister of State for the Army v. Dalziel* (1944) 68 CLR 261, and even to include common law causes of action (*Georgiadis v. Australian & Overseas Telecommunications Corporation* (1994) 179 CLR 297). However, the High Court has suggested that regulation which has the effect of adversely altering property rights that are purely the product of statutory schemes does not amount to an acquisition, since statutory schemes are inherently susceptible to adjustment. Even here, the doctrine is not the model of clarity, and some subsequent *obiter dicta* suggests that some statutory property rights may be protected by s 51(xxxi). In *Mutual Pools v. Commonwealth* (1994) 179 CLR 155, Justices Deane and Gaudron stated:

> While there is no set test or formula for determining whether a particular law can or cannot properly be characterized for the purposes of s 51(xxxi) as a law with respect to the acquisition of property for a purpose in respect of which the Parliament has power to make laws, it is possible to identify in general terms some categories of laws which are unlikely to bear the character of a law with respect to the acquisition of property notwithstanding the fact that an acquisition of property may be an incident of their operation or application. One such category consists of laws which provide for the creation, modification, extinguishment or transfer of rights and liabilities as an incident of, or a means for enforcing, some general regulation of the conduct, rights and obligations of citizens in relationships or areas which need to be regulated in the common interest. Another category consists of laws defining and altering rights and liabilities under a government scheme involving the expenditure of government funds to provide social security benefits or for other public purposes. A law falling within either of those categories may, as an incident of its operation or enforcement, adjust, modify or extinguish rights in a way which involves an "acquisition of property" within the wide meaning which that phrase bears for the purposes of s 51(xxxi). Yet, if such a law is of general operation, it is unlikely that it will be susceptible of being properly characterized, for the purposes of s 51 of the Constitution, as a law with respect to the acquisition of property for a purpose in respect of which the Parliament has power to make laws. The reason why that is so is that, even though an "acquisition of property" may be an incident or a consequence of the operation of such a law, it is unlikely that it will constitute an element or aspect which is capable of imparting to it the character of a law with respect to the subject-matter of s 51(xxxi).

On the other hand, the Court stated that

> references to statutory rights as being 'inherently susceptible of change' must not be permitted to mask the fact that "[i]t is too broad a proposition . . . that the contingency of subsequent legislative modification or extinguishment removes all statutory rights and interests from the scope of s 51(xxxi)" [*Attorney-General (NT) v. Chaffey* (2007) 231 CLR 651 at 664]. Instead, analysis of the constitutional issues must begin from an understanding of the practical and legal operation of the legislative provisions that are in issue.

Several cases illustrate these general observations. First, there is a literal taking of property inherent in certain types of legislation authorized by the Constitution, and these powers would be nullified if compensation were owed. The clearest example is a tax authorized under s 51(ii), *McCormick v. FCT* (1984), 158 CLR 622 at 638, 649. Second, when the Constitution grants the Commonwealth Parliament the authority to create or modify property rights, s 51(xxxi) is not implicated. Thus, in *Nintendo v. Centronic* (1994), 181 CLR 134, the Court rejected a claim for compensation when the *Circuit Layouts Act 1989* (Cth), enacted under the power to legislate with regard to copyrights and patents (s 51(xviii)), limited Centronic's prior freedom to use Nintendo's innovations without a licence. Third, compensation is not required for changes in legislation depriving individuals of the ability to collect social benefits. In *Health Insurance Commission v. Peverill* (1994) 179 CLR 226, where Mason CJ, Dean, and Gaudron JJ observed, at 237:

> It is significant that the rights that have been terminated or diminished are statutory entitlements to receive payments from consolidated revenue which were not based on antecedent proprietary rights recognized by the general law. Rights of that kind are inherently susceptible of variation.

A case illustrating the contingent nature of statutory rights is *Telstra Corp Ltd v. Commonwealth* (2008) 234 CLR 210. The Court explained its rejection of Telstra's claim for compensation for legislation licensing other telecommunications carriers to use their network:

> [50] In the particular circumstances of this case it is of especial importance, in undertaking that task of understanding the operation of the relevant provisions, to recognise that the particular provisions . . . that are impugned in this litigation must not be divorced from their statutory context, and must not be understood in isolation from the history of the provision and regulation of telephone and telecommunications services in Australia.

> [51] There are three cardinal features of context and history that bear upon the constitutional issues which are raised. First, the *[public switched telephone network]* PSTN which Telstra now owns (and of which the local loops form part) was originally a public asset owned and operated as a monopoly since Federation by the Commonwealth. Second, the successive steps of corporatisation and privatisation that have led to Telstra now owning the PSTN (and the local loops that are now in issue) were steps which were accompanied by measures which gave competitors of Telstra

access to the use of the assets of that network. In particular, as noted earlier in these reasons, the step of vesting assets of the PSTN in Telstra, in 1992, was preceded by the enactment of the 1991 Telecommunications Act. At all times thereafter Telstra has operated as a carrier, first under the 1991 Telecommunications Act, and later under the 1997 Telecommunications Act, within a regulatory regime by which other carriers have the right to interconnect their facilities to Telstra's network and to obtain access to services supplied by Telstra, and Telstra has like rights with respect to other carriers. Telstra has never owned or operated any of the assets that now comprise the PSTN except under and in accordance with legislative provisions that were directed to "promoting . . . competition in the telecommunications industry generally and among carriers" and sought to achieve this goal by "giving each carrier the right . . . to obtain access to services supplied by the other carriers." And the third feature of context and history which is of cardinal importance is that in 1992, when the assets of the PSTN were vested in Telstra, Telstra was wholly owned by the Commonwealth.

[52] When proper account is taken of these three considerations, it becomes apparent that Telstra's argument that there is an acquisition of its property otherwise than on just terms is, as Dixon J said in *British Medical Association v The Commonwealth* [(1949) 79 CLR 201 at 270], "a synthetic argument, and . . . unreal." The argument is synthetic and unreal because it proceeds from an unstated premise that Telstra has larger and more ample rights in respect of the PSTN than it has. But Telstra's "bundle of rights" in respect of the assets of the PSTN has never been of the nature and amplitude which its present argument assumes. Telstra's bundle of rights in respect of the PSTN has always been subject to the rights of its competitors to require access to and use of the assets. And the engagement of the impugned provisions (ss 152AL(3) and 152AR) does not impair the bundle of rights constituting the property in question in a manner sufficient to attract the operation of s 51(xxxi).

The proposition that the adjustment of statutory property rights is shielded from the application of s 51(xxxi) was questioned in *JT International SA v. Commonwealth of Australia* (HCA 2012), and it may be open to future challenge; but, as is characteristic of the Court, it is reasonable to conjecture that any shift in thinking will depend on the individual case, rather than on the development of jurisprudential principle.

6.3.2.   What is an "acquisition of property"?

The same questions that have perplexed students of American jurisprudence since the debate between Justices Holmes and Brandeis in *Pennsylvania Coal* have been considered in Australia, to interesting effect.

COMMONWEALTH v. TASMANIA ("Tasmanian Dam Case")

HIGH COURT OF AUSTRALIA

(1983) 158 CLR 1

GIBBS, C.J.:

1. The question of immediate practical importance which falls for decision in these three cases is whether it is lawful for the Hydro-Electric Commission of Tasmania (the Commission) to construct a dam on the Gordon River, downstream of its junction with the Franklin River, in south-western Tasmania. The construction of the dam, and of associated works, including a power station, is authorized by the *Gordon River Hydro-Electric Power Development Act 1982* (Tas.), a law of Tasmania which came into force on 12th July, 1982. The construction work commenced on 14th July, 1982. The dam proposed to be constructed will dam the waters of the Gordon River to a maximum depth, at the toe of the dam, of approximately 84 metres, will raise the levels of the Franklin River and other tributaries and will have a storage capacity of about 2,700 million cubic metres. The power station will add about 180 megawatts on average to the capacity of the Tasmanian electricity generating system and will have an installed generator capacity of about 300 megawatts. The Government of Tasmania wishes to proceed with the Gordon below Franklin Scheme (as it is called) since it considers that the ability to generate electricity at low cost by this means is necessary to enable the State to achieve economic growth and to increase the opportunities for employment. However, the Government of the Commonwealth wishes to stop the construction of the dam, which it considers will inundate significant Aboriginal archaeological sites, and will cause damage to a wilderness area which is of great natural significance, and which satisfies the criteria for listing on the World Heritage List maintained under the Convention for the Protection of the World Cultural and Natural Heritage (the Convention). In conformity with the policy of the Government to stop the construction of the dam, the Governor-General, acting in intended exercise of the power conferred by s. 69 of the *National Parks and Wildlife Conservation Act 1975 (Cth)*, has made the *World Heritage (Western Tasmania Wilderness) Regulations* (S.R. Nos. 31 and 66 of 1983) and the Parliament has enacted the *World Heritage Properties Conservation Act 1983* (Cth) (the Act). Either the Regulations or the Act, if valid, will render it unlawful to construct the dam, except with the consent of a Commonwealth Minister. The important legal question that now falls for decision is whether the Regulations and the Act are valid.

2. No lawyer will need to be told that in these proceedings the Court is not called upon to decide whether the Gordon below Franklin Scheme ought to proceed. It is not for the Court to weigh the economic needs of Tasmania against the possible damage that will be caused to the archaeological sites and the wilderness area if the construction of the dam proceeds. The wisdom and expediency of the two competing courses are matters of policy for the Governments to consider, and not for the Court. We are concerned with a strictly legal question - whether the Commonwealth regulations and the Commonwealth statute are within constitutional power.

. . . .

[Gibbs dissented from the decision, excerpted in Chapter 1, that the Commonwealth's legislation was lawful under the External Affairs power in s 51(xix), so he did not deal with the question of compensation under s 51(xxxi). Wilson and Dawson, JJ., reached similar conclusions in their own opinions.]

MASON J:

. . . .

65. At this point it is convenient to deal with the argument that ss. 9, 10, 11 and 17 effect an acquisition of property otherwise than on just terms. Tasmania's submission is that, although the Act does not attempt to divest title from the State to the Commonwealth, it so restricts the rights of the State with respect to its waste lands and confers such rights on the federal Minister with respect to those lands that there has been an acquisition of property. Mr Ellicott, Q.C., points to the distinction between "taking" property and "regulation" of property which has been developed in the United States, a distinction which was discussed by Stephen J. in *Trade Practices Commission v. Tooth & Co. Ltd.* [1979] HCA 47; [1979] HCA 47; (1979), 142 C.L.R. 397, at pp. 413–415. (at p. 494)

66. The proposition, supported by the judgments of Holmes J. and Brandeis J., in *Pennsylvania Coal Co. v. Mahon*, is that a restriction on the use of property deprives the owner of some right previously enjoyed and is therefore an abridgment of rights in property without making compensation. The consequence is that if the regulation of property goes too far it is a "taking". . . .

67. The decisions of the United States Supreme Court have no direct relevance to s. 51(xxxi) of the Constitution. Many of them turn on the Fifth Amendment which is made applicable to the states by the Fourteenth Amendment . . . . The relevant provision in the Fifth Amendment is ". . . nor shall private property be taken for public use, without just compensation." It seems that the Supreme Court has proceeded according to the view that the object of the clause is to prevent government from forcing some people alone to bear public burdens which should be undertaken by the entire public [citing *Armstrong and Penn Central, supra*].

68. The emphasis in s. 51(xxxi) is not on a "taking" of private property but on the acquisition of property for purposes of the Commonwealth. To bring the Constitutional provision into play it is not enough that legislation adversely affects or terminates a pre-existing right that an owner enjoys in relation to his property; there must be an acquisition whereby the Commonwealth or another acquires an interest in property, however slight or insubstantial it may be. . . .

. . . .

70. The effect of [the Commonwealth's legislation] is to prevent any development of the property in question, subject to the Minister's consent, so as to preserve its character as a wilderness area. . . . In terms of its potential for use, the property is sterilized, in much the same way as a park which is dedicated to public purposes or vested in trustees for public purposes, subject, of course, to such use or development as may attract the consent of the Minister. In this sense, the property is "dedicated" or devoted to uses, that is, protection and conservation which, by

virtue of Australia's adoption of the Convention and the legislation, have become purposes of the Commonwealth. However, what is important in the present context is that neither the Commonwealth nor anyone else acquires by virtue of the legislation a proprietary interest of any kind in the property. The power of the Minister to refuse consent under the section is merely a power of veto. He cannot positively authorize the doing of acts on the property. As the State remains in all respects the owner the consent of the Minister does not overcome or override an absence of consent by the State in its capacity as owner. The fact that the Minister has a power of veto of any development of or activity on the property does not amount to a vesting of possession in the Commonwealth. Significantly, the Act contains no provision dealing with possession.

[MURPHY J reached the same conclusion as MASON, J. on this point.]

BRENNAN J:

. . . .

91. Where neither the Commonwealth nor any other person acquires proprietary rights under a law of the Commonwealth, there is no acquisition upon which par. (xxxi) may fasten. And so, in *Trade Practices Commission v. Tooth & Co. Ltd.*(1979), [1979] HCA 47; 142 C.L.R. 397, at p.408, Gibbs J. observed that "not every compulsory divesting of property is an acquisition within s. 51(xxxi)." [Ed. note: this case held that s 51(xxxi) did not apply to a commission order under a competition statute that barred a property owner from refusing to renew a lease on anticompetitive grounds.]

92. In the United States, where the Fifth Amendment directed that private property should not be "taken" without just compensation, the Supreme Court construed the provision as one "designed to bar Government from forcing some people alone to bear public burdens which, in all fairness and justice, should be borne by the public as a whole" (Armstrong v. United States 364 U.S.40 (1960), at p. 49 (4 Law. Ed. 2d 1554, at p. 1561)). If this Court were to construe s. 51(xxxi) so that its limitation applies to laws which regulate or restrict the use and enjoyment of proprietary rights but which do not provide for the acquisition of such rights, it would be necessary to identify a touchstone for applying the limitation to some regulatory laws and not to others. The experience of the Supreme Court of the United States was frankly stated in *Penn Central Transport Co. v. New York City*, 438 U.S. 104 (1978), at p. 124: ". . . this Court, quite simply, has been unable to develop any 'set formula' for determining when 'justice and fairness' require that economic injuries caused by public action be compensated by the government, rather than remain disproportionately concentrated on a few persons."

93. In this Court, the limitation in par. (xxxi) has not been thought hitherto to apply to a regulatory law that did not effect an acquisition of property. In *Tooth's Case*, the distinction between a law that provides for an acquisition of property and a law that does not was clearly drawn. Thus Mason J. said, at p. 428:

"It is one thing to say that a law which is merely regulatory and does not provide for the acquisition of title to property is not a law with respect to acquisition of property. It is quite another thing to say that a law which does provide for the compulsory acquisition of title to property and which also happens to be regulatory is not a law with respect to the acquisition of property."

DEANE J:

. . . .

73. . . . laws which merely prohibit or control a particular use of, or particular acts upon, property plainly do not constitute an "acquisition" of property for purposes of the Commonwealth. Commonly, such laws are of general application and apply to property by reason of its being property of a particular description or by reference to the nature of the use or act prohibited or controlled. While a law which restricts or controls the use or enjoyment of property by means of specific identification of the property effected comes closer to the area of acquisition of property, it is, as a matter of ordinary language, impossible to say that there has been any acquisition of property if all that is involved is restriction of what can be done upon it; see, for example, *Belfast Corporation v. O.D. Cars Ltd.*, (1960) AC 490 The mere extinguishment or deprivation of rights in relation to property does not involve acquisition.

74. Difficult questions can arise when one passes from the area of mere prohibition or regulation into the area where one can identify some benefit flowing to the Commonwealth or elsewhere as a result of the prohibition or regulation. Where the benefit involved represents no more than the adjustment of competing claims between citizens in a field which needs to be regulated in the common interest, such as zoning under a local government statute, it will be apparent that no question of acquisition of property for a purpose of the Commonwealth is involved. Where, however, the effect of prohibition or regulation is to confer upon the Commonwealth or another an identifiable and measurable advantage or is akin to applying the property, either totally or partially, for a purpose of the Commonwealth, it is possible that an acquisition for the purposes of s. 51(xxxi) is involved. The benefit of land can, in certain circumstances, be enjoyed without any active right in relation to the land being acquired or exercised . . . . Thus, if the Parliament were to make a law prohibiting any presence upon land within a radius of 1 kilometre of any point on the boundary of a particular defence establishment and thereby obtain the benefit of a buffer zone, there would, in my view, be an effective confiscation or acquisition of the benefit of use of the land in its unoccupied state notwithstanding that neither the owner nor the Commonwealth possessed any right to go upon or actively to use the land affected.

. . . .

[Deane adopted the approach of Stephen J in *Tooth & Co., supra*, at 414–15:]

"On the one hand, many measures which in one way or another impair an owner's exercise of his proprietary rights will involve no 'acquisition' such as pl. (xxxi) speaks of. On the other hand, far reaching restrictions upon the use of property may in appropriate circumstances be seen to involve such an acquisition. That the American experience should provide guidance in this area is testimony to the universality of the problem sooner or later encountered wherever constitutional regulation of compulsory acquisition is sought to be applied to restraints, short of actual acquisition, imposed upon the free enjoyment of proprietary rights. In each case the particular circumstances must be ascertained and weighed and, as in all questions of degree, it will be idle to seek to draw precise lines in advance."

. . . .

84. In the present case, the Commonwealth has, under Commonwealth Act and Regulations, obtained the benefit of a prohibition, which the Commonwealth alone can lift, of the doing of the specified acts upon the HEC land. The range of the prohibited acts is such that the practical effect of the benefit obtained by the Commonwealth is that the Commonwealth can ensure, by proceedings for penalties and injunctive relief if necessary, that the land remains in the condition which the Commonwealth, for its own purposes, desires to have conserved. In these circumstances, the obtaining by the Commonwealth of the benefit acquired under the Regulations is properly to be seen as a purported acquisition of property for a purpose in respect of which the Parliament has power to make laws. The "property" purportedly acquired consists of the benefit of the prohibition of the exercise of the rights of use and development of the land which would be involved in the doing of any of the specified acts. The purpose for which that property has been purportedly acquired is the "application of the property in or towards carrying out" Australia's obligations under the Convention . . . .The compensation which would represent "just terms" for that acquisition of property would be the difference between the value of the HEC land without and with the restrictions.

———

Consistent with Justice Mason's analysis, note that most environmental protection laws are matters for state legislatures. Unlike the Fourteenth Amendment and s. 25 of the South African Constitution, which apply to all levels of government, the provisions of s 51(xxxi) do not apply to Australian states. (The states have their own statutory provisions regarding compensation for compulsory acquisitions.)

However, although an "acquisition" must include some benefit gained by the Commonwealth, what is acquired does not have to be the same as that which is lost. *Newcrest Mining (WA) Ltd v. Commonwealth* (1997) 190 CLR 513 concerned Commonwealth laws that extended the boundaries of Kakadu National Park (in the Northern Territory),[6] combined with the *Conservation Amendment Act* 1987 (Cth) which prohibited mining in the Park. The result was that certain mining tenements operated by Newcrest were now situated on protected land, and the company could not continue mining. Newcrest challenged the laws, arguing that they amounted to an acquisition of property without just terms. Despite the fact that the Commonwealth did not "acquire" the corresponding right to mine, the High Court held that there had been an acquisition. The law, furthermore, was not based on a statutory scheme, but constituted a modification of the Commonwealth's pre-existing common law (Crown) title to the land. As Justice Gummow explained it:

———

[6] The statute was enacted pursuant to the Commonwealth's plenary Territorial Power under s 122 of the Constitution. *Newcrest Mining* also held that s 122 did not permit the Commonwealth to acquire property without providing just terms as required by s 51 (xxxi).

It is true, as [the Commonwealth] submit[s], that the mining tenements were not, in terms, extinguished. It is true also that Kakadu extended only 1,000 m beneath the surface. But, on the surface and to that depth . . . [the Act] forbade the carrying out of operations for the recovery of minerals. The vesting in the Commonwealth of the minerals to that depth and the vesting of the surface and balance of the relevant segments of the subterranean land in the [Commonwealth] had the effect, as a legal and practical matter, of denying to Newcrest the exercise of its rights under the mining tenements.

As Brennan CJ explained:

. . . the Commonwealth was left in undisturbed possession of the minerals on and under the land included in Kakadu National Park. The Commonwealth's interest in respect of the minerals was enhanced by the sterilisation of Newcrest's interests therein. In my opinion, by force of the impugned proclamations, the Commonwealth acquired property from Newcrest. The property consisted not in a right to possession or occupation of the relevant area of land nor in the bare leasehold interest vested in Newcrest but in the benefit of relief from the burden of Newcrest's rights to carry on "operations for the recovery of minerals."

In 2012, the reach of s 51(xxxi) was further tested in a case that (unusually for Australia) attracted international attention: *JT International SA v. Commonwealth of Australia*. The case concerned the Commonwealth's *Tobacco Plain Packaging Act* 2011 (Cth), the purpose of which was to make cigarette and other tobacco products less attractive (indeed repulsive) to potential purchasers, by requiring their packaging to be in a uniform, drab color, with the tobacco brand and logo in a generic, small font, and graphic images of diseased bodily parts (with the disease attributed to smoking) featuring prominently, along with health warnings and information about services for quitting smoking. The Act was challenged by two international tobacco companies, as a breach of s 51(xxxi).

The Commonwealth's power to pass the legislation was uncontroversial. The Act's stated purposes included giving effect to the World Health Organisation's *Framework Convention on Tobacco Control*; the principal head of power supporting the Act was therefore the External Affairs power, s 51(xxix). Certain other powers, such as the Corporations Power, s 51(xx) and the Territories Power (s 122) also applied.

The challenge was resolved in favor of the Commonwealth along relatively predictable lines, and consistent with previous cases. The Court (with one dissent) accepted that the tobacco companies' intellectual property had been adversely affected by the Act; all the judges then focused on whether an *acquisition* had been effected by the Commonwealth. No acquisition was found; whether there had been a denial of "just terms" was therefore not considered.

This conclusion added little new to existing case law. However, the judgment is interesting for its response to a couple of propositions. Arguments made by both the plaintiffs and the Commonwealth for the development of s 51(xxxi) jurisprudence along Fifth Amendment "takings" lines were dismissed. The Commonwealth's proposition that, as in the United States, "a prohibition on the use of property which is declared by legislation to be injurious to the health, morals or safety of the community cannot be deemed a taking" was not followed (it proved unnecessary, in any case). The tobacco companies' contrary proposition that restrictions on the use and economic value of its property were so extreme as to constitute "regulatory takings" was also dismissed. With each of these propositions, however, the judges stopped short out outright rejection. They emphasized the historical and jurispru-dential differences between s 51(xxxi) and the Fifth Amendment, but effectively left the question open for another day. What the Court made clear, however, was that any future application of s 51(xxxi) would continue to involve close analysis of the indicia of an "acquisition" and conclusions would depend upon whether or not an "acquisition" was made out.

Of further interest is Justice Kiefel's introduction of "proportionality" language: her suggestion appears to be that, at some point, in the taking of property, or indeed the "acquisition" of property, the public benefit might be "balanced" against the degree of impairment or extinguishment of the relevant property rights. The language of "proportionality" is new to the High Court; it is suggestive of an approach more familiar to countries with constitutional Bills of Rights, where the validity of impairing or restricting individual rights and freedoms is subject to a test of degree, and the onus falls on the government to demonstrate that laws are proportional to a justified governmental purpose, and/or "narrowly tailored" to that purpose. Such a direction has not yet been signaled by the Court, but it is something to watch for in future s 51(xxxi) cases, if not more widely in High Court jurisprudence.

JT INTERNATIONAL SA v. COMMONWEALTH OF AUSTRALIA
HIGH COURT OF AUSTRALIA
HCA 43 (Oct. 5, 2012)

FRENCH CJ.

. . . .

Section 51(xxxi) [of the Constitution] confers upon the Commonwealth Parliament the power to make laws with respect to: "[t]he acquisition of property on just terms from any State or person for any purpose in respect of which the Parliament has power to make laws." It uses the term "property" which appears in a number of places in the Constitution. As used in s 51(xxxi) it has long been construed broadly by this Court. It extends to property rights created by statute although the terms of such statutes and the nature of the property rights which they create require examination to determine whether and to what extent that property attracts the protection of s 51(xxxi) . . . . There are and always have been purposive elements reflecting public policy considerations which inform the statutory creation of intellectual property rights . . . .

The observation in [an earlier] case that Australian trade marks law has "mani-fested from time to time a varying accommodation of commercial and the consuming public's interests" has application with varying degrees of intensity to other intellectual property rights created by statute . . . . The statutory purpose, reflected in the character of such rights and in the conditions informing their creation, may be relevant to the question whether and in what circumstances restriction or regulation of their enjoyment by a law of the Commonwealth amounts to acquisition of property for the purposes of s 51(xxxi) of the Constitution.

That is not to say that such rights are, on account of their instrumental character, inherently susceptible to variation and, on that account, not within the protection of s 51(xxxi) . . . .

On the other hand, [this] is not to be taken as support for the proposition that the extinguishment or restriction of a statutory exclusive right, without more, would constitute an acquisition for the purpose of s 51(xxxi) . . . . The property said to have been the subject of acquisition under the TPP Act comprises a mixture of statutory and associated or derivative non-statutory rights.

. . . .

The Commonwealth submitted that the property rights associated with the registered trade marks, design, patents and copyright asserted by JTI and BAT involve "a statutory assurance of exclusive use, not a positive right or authority to use." On that basis the imposition of restrictions on their use would take nothing away from the rights granted. Therefore, it was submitted, no property had been taken by the TPP Act. BAT stigmatised that argument as formalistic, observing that rights of exclusion are of the essence of all proprietary rights. Plainly, not all property rights are defined only by rights of exclusion. In law the term "property" generally refers to "a legal relationship with a thing" and in many cases is helpfully described as "a bundle of rights." However, BAT correctly submitted that rights to exclude others from using property have no substance if all use of the property is prohibited . . . .

Section 51(xxxi) embodies a constitutional guarantee of just terms "and is to be given the liberal construction appropriate to such a constitutional provision." Broad constructions of "property" and "acquisition" were linked by Dixon J in the *Bank Nationalisation case*. Section 51(xxxi) was said to extend to "innominate and anomalous interests" and to include "the assumption and indefinite continuance of exclusive possession and control for the purpose of the Commonwealth of any subject of property." There is, however, an important distinction between a taking of property and its acquisition.

Taking involves deprivation of property seen from the perspective of its owner. Acquisition involves receipt of something seen from the perspective of the acquirer. Acquisition is therefore not made out by mere extinguishment of rights . . . . Mason J said in the *Tasmanian Dam case*:

> "To bring the constitutional provision into play it is not enough that legislation adversely affects or terminates a pre-existing right that an owner enjoys in relation to his property; there must be an acquisition whereby the Commonwealth or another acquires an interest in property, however slight or insubstantial it may be."

Importantly, the interest or benefit accruing to the Commonwealth or another person must be proprietary in character. On no view can it be said that the Commonwealth as a polity or by any authority or instrumentality, has acquired any benefit of a proprietary character by reason of the operation of the TPP Act on the plaintiffs' property rights . . . .

It may also be observed that the negative character of the plaintiffs' property rights leaves something of a logical gap between the restrictions on their enjoyment and the accrual of any benefit to the Commonwealth or any other person. Unlike the *Newcrest case*, there is no expansion in rights, interests, or benefits accruing to the Commonwealth that corresponds to or bears any relationship to the restrictions imposed on the use of the plaintiffs' intellectual property rights. The fact that the restrictions and prohibitions imposed by the TPP Act create the "space" for the application of Commonwealth regulatory requirements as to the textual and graphical content of tobacco product packages does not constitute such an accrual. Rather, it reflects a serious judgment that the public purposes to be advanced and the public benefits to be derived from the regulatory scheme outweigh those public purposes and public benefits which underpin the statutory intellectual property rights and the common law rights enjoyed by the plaintiffs. The scheme does that without effecting an acquisition.

In summary, the TPP Act is part of a legislative scheme which places controls on the way in which tobacco products can be marketed. While the imposition of those controls may be said to constitute a taking in the sense that the plaintiffs' enjoyment of their intellectual property rights and related rights is restricted, the corresponding imposition of controls on the packaging and presentation of tobacco products does not involve the accrual of a benefit of a proprietary character to the Commonwealth which would constitute an acquisition. That conclusion is fatal to the case of both JTI and BAT.

GUMMOW J.

. . . .

The issue . . . is whether the tobacco product requirements of the Packaging Act do not amount to an "acquisition" of the property of the plaintiffs . . . . This presents two questions. The first is whether there is a "taking" or "deprivation" of the property of the plaintiffs and, if so, the second question is whether the Packaging Act effects an "acquisition" of property otherwise than on just terms as proscribed by s 51(xxxi) of the Constitution. The distinction between the two questions appears from the pithy statement of Gibbs CJ, Wilson, Brennan, Deane and Dawson JJ to the effect that rights of property may be extinguished without being acquired. [*R v. Ludeke; Ex parte Australian Building Construction Employees' and Builders Labourers' Federation* (1985) 159 CLR 636 at 653.] The submissions of the plaintiffs, in some instances directly, and in others with more subtlety, sought to displace or diminish the importance of that second question. That attempt was contrary to established authority in this Court.

. . . .

For the reasons which follow, there is sufficient impairment, at least of the statutory intellectual property of the plaintiffs, to amount to a "taking," but there is no acquisition of any property. The result is the plaintiffs' cases for invalidity fail . . . .

In *Wurridjal v. The Commonwealth* Crennan J said of s 51(xxxi):

> It can be significant that rights which are diminished by subsequent legislation are statutory entitlements. Where a right which has no existence apart from statute is one that, of its nature, is susceptible to modification, legislation which effects a modification of that right is not necessarily legislation with respect to an acquisition of property within the meaning of s 51(xxxi). It does not follow, however, that all rights which owe their existence to statute are ones which, of their nature, are susceptible to modification, as the contingency of subsequent legislative modification or extinguishment does not automatically remove a statutory right from the scope of s 51(xxxi).

Putting to one side statutory rights which replace existing general law rights, the extent to which a right created by statute may be modified by subsequent legislation without amounting to an acquisition of property under s 51(xxxi) must depend upon the nature of the right created by statute. It may be evident in the express terms of the statute that the right is subject to subsequent statutory variation. It may be clear from the scope of the rights conferred by the statute that what appears to be a new impingement on the rights was in fact always a limitation inherent in those rights. The statutory right may also be a part of a scheme of statutory entitlements which will inevitably require modification over time.

. . . However, it should be borne in mind that all these items of "property" are, as Higgins J put it, "artificial products of society," not "physical objects" the boundaries of each class of which "are fixed by external nature"; more precisely, as Isaacs J emphasised with respect to trade marks, these are not affirmative rights like the property in goods and are not rights "in gross, or in the abstract."

These considerations direct further attention to the identification of those rights which constitute the property in question in these cases. This is an essential first step in the identification of that of which there has been a deprivation or "taking." It is convenient first to say something respecting the position in the United States.

. . . .

Reference was made in the submissions of various parties and interveners to decisions of the United States Supreme Court upon the "taking" clause of the Fifth Amendment.

Both in this provision and in s 51(xxxi) the term "property" is used with respect to the group of rights inhering in ownership and, as the Supreme Court put it, not in any "vulgar and untechnical sense." In this Court, it has been emphasised that "to characterise something as a proprietary right . . . is not to say that it has all the indicia of other things called proprietary rights" and that "the protection given to property rights varies with the nature of the right"; this understanding of the general law has influenced the interpretation of s 51(xxxi).

. . . .

However, it has been apparent for some time that with respect to "taking" and "acquisition" some important distinctions are to be observed between the United States and Australian Constitutions. . . .

The Fifth Amendment, which also applies to the States by the medium of the Fourteenth Amendment guarantee against the deprivation of property without due process of law, is expressed in the form of a negative, appears with the due process clause, and speaks of private property being "taken" for "public use." On the other hand, s 51(xxxi) is directed to the Parliament and speaks of "acquisition" for any "purpose" in respect of which there is federal legislative power. "Acquisition" is a term which indicates, [that] . . . "not every compulsory divesting of property is an acquisition within s 51(xxxi)."

It should be emphasised that under the Fifth Amendment, even if just compensation be made, the "taking" must be for "public use," that is to say for "the public good, the public necessity or the public utility." In *Kelo v. City of New London*, the Supreme Court ruled that the federal judiciary should not make an independent judgment as to whether a taking of private property is for a "public use"; rather, the question is whether the government authority, federal, State or local, can make a rational argument that the taking resulted in a "public benefit."

The effect of the United States decisions is to accept that the "taking" clause may be engaged without what the decisions in this Court would classify as an "acquisition." However, the greater scope this gives to the Fifth Amendment has been tempered by a doctrine permitting "regulation" which does not amount to a "taking"; "regulation" will amount to a "taking" if the regulatory actions in question are "functionally equivalent to the classic taking in which government directly appropriates private property or ousts the owner from his domain."

. . . .

Whether the law in question sufficiently impairs the group of rights inhering in the property in question as to amount to an involuntary taking of that property, presents questions of substance and degree, rather than merely of form.

. . . .

[T]he TMA, like other trade mark legislation, does not confer on registered owners or authorised users a liberty to use registered trade marks free from restraints found in other statutes. Nevertheless,,, [t]he rights mentioned in respect of registered trade marks are in substance, if not in form, denuded of their value and thus of their utility by the imposition of the regime under the Packaging Act . . . The result is that while the trade marks remain on the face of the register, their value and utility for assignment and licensing is very substantially impaired. The situation is even more drastic as regards the BAT Copyrights, the BAT Patent and the BAT Design at stake in the BAT Matter. Use of the artistic works on retail packaging of tobacco products is denied by the operation of . . . the Packaging Act. Use of the BAT Design would conflict with . . . the Packaging Act and exploitation of the BAT Patent would conflict with . . . the Packaging Regulations.

The circumstances just described are sufficient to render the operation of the Packaging Act a "taking" of these items of intellectual property.

. . . .

In the *Tasmanian Dam Case*, Mason J said of the federal legislation there under challenge:

"In terms of its potential for use, the property is sterilized, in much the same way as a park which is dedicated to public purposes or vested in trustees for public purposes, subject, of course, to such use or development as may attract the consent of the Minister. In this sense, the property is 'dedicated' or devoted to uses, ie, protection and conservation which, by virtue of Australia's adoption of the Convention and the legislation, have become purposes of the Commonwealth. However, what is important in the present context is that neither the Commonwealth nor anyone else acquires by virtue of the legislation a proprietary interest of any kind in the property. The power of the Minister to refuse consent under the section is merely a power of veto. He cannot positively authorize the doing of acts on the property. As the State remains in all respects the owner the consent of the Minister does not overcome or override an absence of consent by the State in its capacity as owner."

Brennan J concluded:

"Unless proprietary rights are acquired, par (xxxi) is immaterial to the validity of the impugned Commonwealth measures. Though the Act conferred a power upon the Minister to consent to the doing of acts which were otherwise prohibited on or in relation to land, that power was not a proprietary right."

These statements exemplify the application of the established doctrine of the Court respecting s 51(xxxi).

The objects of the Packaging Act . . . include the improvement in public health by discouraging people from using tobacco products and from relapsing if they have stopped such use, and by reducing exposure to smoke from tobacco products. Parliament desires to contribute to achievement of those objects by regulating the retail packaging and appearance of tobacco products to reduce their appeal to consumers, increasing the effectiveness of health warnings thereon and reducing the ability of retail packaging to mislead consumers about the harmful effects of using tobacco products.

Another object . . . is the giving of effect to certain obligations upon Australia as a party to the WHO Framework Convention on Tobacco Control, done at Geneva on 21 May 2003.

. . . .

In its submissions Philip Morris contended that it was sufficient that there has been obtained no more than some identifiable benefit or advantage, which, while not of a proprietary character, is at least a benefit or advantage "*relating to* the ownership or use of property" (emphasis added) . . . . Philip Morris then submitted that the Packaging Act conferred such a benefit on the Commonwealth because the statutory regime "controlled" the exploitation of the trade marks on the packaging even though the Commonwealth itself did not exploit the trade marks; it was sufficient that the control related to the use of the trade marks . . . However . . . to characterise as "control" by "the Commonwealth" compliance with federal law which prescribes what can and cannot appear on the retail packaging of tobacco products diverts attention from a fundamental question presented by s 51(xxxi) of the Constitution. Compliance with the federal law does not create a relationship between "the Commonwealth" and the packaging which is proprietary in nature.

. . . .

In oral submissions the Commonwealth placed at the forefront of its arguments first that no "property" had been "taken" and, secondly, that in any event there had been no "acquisition" of "property." The upshot is that the Commonwealth should succeed on the second of these grounds.

That makes it unnecessary to rule upon two further and related submissions by the Commonwealth. The first is that there is no contextual, structural or historical reason to treat every transfer of property as an acquisition to which s 51(xxxi) applies where the transfer is "incidental to regulation in the public interest." The second proposition is that s 51(xxxi) has no operation where the acquisition of property without compensation "is no more than a necessary consequence or incident of a restriction on a commercial trading activity . . . reasonably necessary to prevent or reduce harm caused by that trading activity to members of the public or public health."

These submissions bring to mind remarks by Brandeis J in his dissenting reasons in *Pennsylvania Coal Company v. Mahon*:

> "Every restriction upon the use of property imposed in the exercise of the police power deprives the owner of some right theretofore enjoyed, and is, in that sense, an abridgment by the State of rights in property without making compensation. But restriction imposed to protect the public health, safety or morals from dangers threatened is not a taking."

It is sufficient for present purposes to say that propositions of the width of those put by the Commonwealth have not so far been endorsed by decisions of this Court and that whether such propositions should be accepted would require most careful consideration on an appropriate occasion.

. . . .

The third question — what are "just terms"? — has received relatively little attention. The "justness" of compensation offered by the Commonwealth has only occasionally been at issue. *Grace Brothers Pty Ltd v. Commonwealth* (1946) 72 CLR 269 concerned the amount of compensation offered for a department store that had been occupied during World War II for Defence Force purposes, and then permanently acquired at the end of the war. The question was, among others, whether a compensation scheme based on a calculation of the market rate prior to the date of acquisition was "just." Justice Dixon expressed "justness" in terms of fairness, asking "whether the law amounts to a true attempt to provide fair and just standards of compensating or rehabilitating the individual considered as an owner of property, fair and just as between him and the government of the country." (He, and the majority, concluded that the law did not breach s 51 (xxxi).)

As all of the above suggests, the High Court has tended to proceed on a case-by-case basis in its interpretation of s 51 (xxxi). No single normative principle has emerged from its jurisprudence. The provision, however, has had a life of its own in other quarters — as the "star" of a movie, *The Castle*, a 1997 comedy about a family whose house is about to be compulsory acquired by the Commonwealth for the extension of an airport runway. The family protest — successfully in the end — that *no* money, indeed *nothing*, could serve as "just terms" to compensate for the loss of their modest home. While the conclusion is jurisprudentially very doubtful, accurate reference is made to real case law in the depiction of High Court argument (although the Justices' wearing of wigs and red robes is inaccurate!). The film — perhaps the first to take a constitutional section as its core — has given rise to a now popular expression, *"The Vibe,"* which refers to the principles of fairness and decency, supposedly inherent in the Constitution (and is intended also to indicate an inability on the part of its user to explain anything more precise about the Constitution — Australians, who do not revere their Constitution, find such incompetence very funny) (*see* http://en.wikipedia.org/wiki/The_Castle_(film)). *The Castle* is not only celebrated in Australian popular culture, but has its own entry in *The Oxford Companion to the High Court of Australia* (OUP 2001).

6.4.   REJECTION OF CANADIAN CONSTITUTIONAL PROTECTION FOR PROPERTY

The Charter's framers "clearly wanted to avoid a re-enactment of the extremes that had accompanied early American substantive review of the content of legislation." Jean McBean, *The Implications of Entrenching Property Rights in Section 7 of the Charter of Rights* (1988), 26 ALTA. L. REV. 548. Opposition from several provincial premiers and the leadership of the New Democratic Party led Pierre Trudeau's Liberal government to oppose efforts by the Conservative Party to include in the Charter a right to property. The principal provincial opposition came from those who feared judicial attacks on zoning legislation and limitations on land ownership by non-residents (apparently a significant problem on tiny Prince Edward Island). The NDP opposition was based on its concern with the possible inhibition on public ownership of resource-based industries.

Post-patriation academic work echoes the original intent to prevent the Charter from introducing *Lochner*-like close scrutiny of economic regulation in Canada. As Dean Peter Hogg explained, the principal normative objection to constitutionalizing a right to property is its effect on society's ability to regulate business:

> Most forms of regulation impose costs on those who are regulated, and it would be intolerably costly to compensate them. Moreover, much regulation has a redistributive purpose: it is designed to reduce the rights of one group (manufacturers, employers, for example) and increase the rights of another (consumers, employees, for example). A compensation regime would work at cross-purposes to the purpose of the regulation.

1 CONSTITUTIONAL LAW OF CANADA § 28.5, at 28-10 (Looseleaf edition).

Professor Joel Bakan observes that many of today's statutes reflect efforts "to provide at least some limited safeguards against the most egregious abuses by individuals and corporations of the power they derive from their property rights." *Against Constitutional Property Rights, in* CONSTITUTIONAL POLITICS (D. Cameron & M. Smith, eds., 1992). Bakan suggests that Canadians should be particularly risk-averse to adding an American-style right to property, because of the different social and political framework of the two countries:

> . . . the Canadian state has traditionally been more "interventionist" in the market than has its American counterpart. Parliament and the provincial legislatures have developed over the years a wide range of social programmes and regulation (often at the expense of private property rights) that have no parallel in the United States. Would such programmes have passed constitutional muster in the United States? We will never know because there have been no attempts to introduce them in the United States. Id. at 125.

IRWIN TOY LTD. v. QUEBEC (ATTORNEY GENERAL)
SUPREME COURT OF CANADA
[1989] 1 S.C.R. 927, 58 D.L.R. (4th) 577

THE CHIEF JUSTICE and LAMER and WILSON JJ.

[This decision, also excerpted above in Chapter 3, concerned the constitutionality of a Quebec statute strictly regulating television advertising directed at younger children. In the prior excerpt, the Court explained why the statute constituted a reasonable limit on the right of free expression.]

VIII — Whether ss. 248 and 249 Violate s. 7 of the Canadian *Charter of Rights and Freedoms*

[The plaintiffs further alleged that the statute violated s. 7 of the Charter because the imposition of penal sanctions require an even greater degree of certainty than required by the right of free expression and the statute was too vague to meet this standard.]

In order to put forward a s. 7 argument in a case of this kind where the officers of the corporation are not named as parties to the proceedings, the corporation would have to urge that its own life, liberty or security of the person was being deprived in a manner not in accordance with the principles of fundamental justice. In our opinion, a corporation cannot avail itself of the protection offered by s. 7 of the Charter. First, we would have to conceive of a manner in which a corporation could be deprived of its "life, liberty or security of the person." We have already noted that it is nonsensical to speak of a corporation being put in jail. To say that bankruptcy and winding up proceedings engage s. 7 would stretch the meaning of the right to life beyond recognition. The only remaining argument is that corporations are protected against deprivations of some sort of "economic liberty."

There are several reasons why we are of the view that this argument cannot succeed. It is useful to reproduce s. 7, which reads as follows:

"7. Everyone has the right to life, liberty and security of the person and the right not to be deprived thereof except in accordance with the principles of fundamental justice."

What is immediately striking about this section is the inclusion of "security of the person" as opposed to "property." This stands in contrast to the classic liberal formulation, adopted, for example, in the Fifth and Fourteenth Amendments in the American Bill of Rights, which provide that no person shall be deprived "of life, liberty or property, without due process of law." The intentional exclusion of property from s. 7, and the substitution therefor of "security of the person" has, in our estimation, a dual effect. First, it leads to a general inference that economic rights as generally encompassed by the term "property" are not within the perimeters of the s. 7 guarantee. This is not to declare, however, that no right with an economic component can fall within "security of the person." Lower courts have found that the rubric of "economic rights" embraces a broad spectrum of interests, ranging from such rights, included in various international covenants, as rights to social security, equal pay for equal work, adequate food, clothing and shelter, to traditional property — contract rights. To exclude all of these at this early moment in the history of Charter interpretation seems to us to be precipitous. We do not, at this moment, choose to pronounce upon whether those economic rights fundamental to human life or survival are to be treated as though they are of the same ilk as corporate-commercial economic rights. In so stating, we find the second effect of the inclusion of "security of the person" to be that a corporation's economic rights find no constitutional protection in that section.

. . . .

REFERENCE RE SS. 193 AND 195.1(1)(C) OF THE CRIMINAL CODE (MAN.)
"The Prostitution Reference"
SUPREME COURT OF CANADA
[1990] 1 S.C.R. 1123, 56 C.C.C. (3d) 65

LAMER J. —

* * *

VI. Economic Liberty and s. 7 of the Charter

This case raises an important issue that has been recurring in our jurisprudence under the Charter. Simply stated, the issue centers on the scope of s. 7 of the Charter, more specifically the guarantees of life, liberty and security of the person. The appellants argue that the impugned provisions infringe prostitutes' right to liberty in not allowing them to exercise their chosen profession, and their right to security of the person, in not permitting them to exercise their profession in order to provide the basic necessities of life. I should like to point out at the outset something that may seem obvious to some, or which may come as a surprise to others, but which in any event needs to be kept in mind throughout: prostitution is not illegal in Canada. We find ourselves in an anomalous, some would say bizarre, situation where almost everything related to prostitution has been regulated by the criminal law except the transaction itself. The appellants' argument then, more precisely stated, is that in criminalizing so many activities surrounding the act itself, Parliament has made prostitution *de facto* illegal if not *de jure* illegal.

I now turn to the issue of interpreting the meaning of the rights guaranteed by s. 7 of the Charter, more specifically the right to liberty and security of the person. The appellants in the case at bar rely on an expansive interpretation of the rights guaranteed by s. 7 to argue that carrying on a lawful occupation is protected by the right to liberty. As a basis for this view the following summary of the position taken by the English philosopher John Stuart Mill is relied upon:

> "The only end for which society is warranted in infringing the liberty of action of any individual, he said, is self-protection. Power should be exercised to prevent the individual from doing harm to others, but that is the only part of his conduct for which he should be answerable to society. In every other way he should have freedom."

* * *

One of the earliest U.S. decisions interpreting what has become known as the " due process clause" of the Fourteenth Amendment is *Allgeyer v. Louisiana*, 165 U.S. 578 (1897). The Supreme Court held that a Louisiana statute that purported to regulate a contract formed between parties in Louisiana and New York was unconstitutional. Peckham J., speaking for the court, held that the Fourteenth Amendment protected liberty of contract, and more specifically stated the following at p. 589:

> "The liberty mentioned in that amendment means not only the right of the citizen to be free from the mere physical restraint of his person, as by incarceration, but the term is deemed to embrace the right of the citizen to be free in the enjoyment of all his faculties; to be free to use them in all lawful ways; to live and work where he will; to earn his livelihood by any lawful calling; to pursue any livelihood or avocation, and for that purpose to enter into all contracts which may be proper, necessary and essential to his carrying out to a successful conclusion the purposes above mentioned."

* * *

It should not be overlooked, however, that the American experience with "economic liberty" jurisprudence in particular, has been controversial throughout its history. As I noted above, the case of *Allgeyer v. Louisiana, supra*, was the first to define liberty as including the right to make contracts. But it is the decision in *Lochner v. New York*, 198 U.S. 45 (1905), that firmly established economic liberty as a constitutionally protected interest. In that case a majority of the United States Supreme Court invalidated a New York law that set maximum hours of work for bakers because, at p. 57,

> ". . . there is no reasonable ground for interfering with the liberty of person or the right of free contract, by determining the hours of labor, in the occupation of a baker."

Between *Lochner, supra*, and the start of the Depression, the U.S. Supreme Court invalidated many regulatory measures on the grounds that they intruded upon liberty of contract and property rights: see for example *Adair v. United States*, 208 U.S. 161 (1908), *Coppage v. Kansas*, 236 U.S. 1 (1915), invalidating legislation prohibiting employers from imposing "yellow-dog" contracts (a contract requiring employees to disavow union membership or affiliation as a condition of employment), and *Adkins v. Children's Hospital*, 261 U.S. 525 (1923), invalidating a minimum wage law in the District of Columbia.

The onset of the Depression and President Roosevelt's New Deal initiatives caused a confrontation between the notion of "economic liberty" and the needs of a modern regulatory state. Beginning in 1935 the U.S. Supreme Court rendered a number of decisions invalidating New Deal legislation, one of the most significant being *Morehead v. New York ex rel. Tipaldo*, 298 U.S. 587 (1936), a decision striking down state minimum wage legislation. What ensued was the so-called "Court Crisis" in which President Roosevelt proposed a court reorganization plan. The plan was never put into effect. Significantly, however, the court overruled its decisions in *Morehead* and *Adkins, supra*, in *West Coast Hotel Co. v. Parrish*, 300 U.S. 379 (1937), and adopted a more deferential approach to cases of state regulation of "economic liberty." Indeed, in *United States v. Carolene Products Co.*, 304 U.S. 144 (1938), the court espoused a deferential standard of review on questions of "economic liberty" with more active scrutiny where the state interferes with "civil" liberties: see United States v. Carolene Products Co., *supra*, at pp. 152–53, especially the now famous "Footnote 4." This attitude of deference in respect of "economic liberty" has been reiterated more recently. All of this is to emphasize the difficulties that the United States Supreme Court has faced in dealing with the concept of "economic liberty" as a constitutionally protected freedom, and how much the American experience is linked to its particular historical and social context.

Along these lines, I pause to note that in applying principles developed under a provision of the U.S. Constitution to cases arising under our Charter, the Court must take into account differences in wording and historical foundations of the two documents. As Strayer J.[7] observed in *Smith, Kline & French Laboratories Ltd. v. Attorney General of Canada*, [1986] 1 F.C. 274, at p. 314:

". . . it must be kept in mind that the historical background and social and economic context of the Fourteenth Amendment are distinctly American. Further it must be noted that in the Fourteenth Amendment "liberty" is combined with "property" which gives a different colouration to the former through the introduction of economic values as well as personal values. This is not the case in section 7 of the *Canadian Charter of Rights and Freedoms*."

With this in mind I now propose to examine the Canadian jurisprudence in the area of "economic liberty" and s. 7 of the Charter.

---

[7] [Ed. note: Judge Barry Strayer, now retired from the Federal Court of Appeal, was a professor of constitutional law at the University of Saskatchewan in the 1960s and served from 1974–83, during the period when the *Charter* was drafted, as the Assistant Deputy Minister of Justice. He is generally regarded as the *Charter*'s principal drafter.]

I begin by noting the words of the Chief Justice in *R. v. Edwards Books and Art Ltd.*, [1986] 2 S.C.R. 713, at pp. 785–86:

> "In my opinion "liberty" in s. 7 of the Charter is not synonymous with unconstrained freedom . . . . Whatever the precise contours of "liberty" in s. 7, I cannot accept that it extends to an unconstrained right to transact business whenever one wishes."

Much in the same vein other courts in this country have decided that "liberty" does not generally extend to commercial or economic interests. * * *

In short then I find myself in agreement with the following statement of McIntyre J. in the *Reference Re Public Service Employee Relations Act (Alta.)*, [[1987] 1 S.C.R. 313], at p. 412:

> "It is also to be observed that the Charter, with the possible exception of s. 6(2)(b) (right to earn a livelihood in any province) and s. 6(4), does not concern itself with economic rights."

I therefore reject the application of the American line of cases that suggest that liberty under the Fourteenth Amendment includes liberty of contract. As I stated earlier these cases have a specific historical context, a context that incorporated into the American jurisprudence certain laissez-faire principles that may not have a corresponding application to the interpretation of the Charter in the present day. There is also a significant difference in the wording of s. 7 and the Fourteenth Amendment. The American provision speaks specifically of a protection of property interests while our framers did not choose to similarly protect property rights. This then, is sufficient to dispose of this ground of appeal.

[However, Lamer J went on to quote his previous observation in *B.C. Motor Vehicle Reference*, excerpted in Chapter 2, that "the principles of fundamental justice are to be found in the basic tenets of our legal system. They do not lie in the realm of general public policy but in the inherent domain of the judiciary as guardian of the justice system." He explained that moving beyond "the confinement of individuals against their will, or the restriction of control over their own minds and bodies," meant moving beyond "the judicial domain" into the "realm of general public policy":]

> where the principles of fundamental justice, as they have been developed primarily through the common law, are significantly irrelevant. In the area of public policy what is at issue are political interests, pressures and values that no doubt are of social significance, but which are not "essential elements of a system for the administration of justice," and hence are not principles of fundamental justice within the meaning of s. 7. The courts must not, because of the nature of the institution, be involved the realm of pure public policy; that is the exclusive role of the properly elected representatives, the legislators. To expand the scope of s. 7 too widely would be to infringe upon that role.

* * *

[The judgment of Dickson C.J. and La Forest and Sopinka JJ. concluded that the challenged law had to meet the requirements of fundamental justice because there was a clear infringement of liberty in this case given the possibility of imprisonment.] With regard to the appellants claim that the statute infringed the liberty interest of street prostitutes in not allowing them to exercise their chosen profession, and their right to security of the person, in not permitting them to exercise their profession in order to provide the basic necessities of life, they found it unnecessary to address the question of whether s. 7 liberty is violated in another, "economic," way. ***

The reasons of WILSON and L'HEUREUX-DUBE JJ. were delivered by WILSON J. (dissenting) [omitted].

6.5.   CANADIAN AND AUSTRALIAN NON-CONSTITUTIONAL PROTECTION FOR PROPERTY

Recall that the fundamental constitutional issue is not whether the government should require "some people to alone bear public burdens which, in all fairness and justice, should be borne by the public as a whole," but rather whether the decision about whether a particular judgment that certain burden should be fairly borne by certain owners of property should be made by the courts or the legislatures. In the United States, Takings Clause jurisprudence makes it clear that this decision is made by the courts; in Canada (and in Australia at the state level), the foregoing decisions make it clear that the decision is up to the legislatures.

The Canadian and Australian experience demonstrates that, freed of constitutional limits, there are few expropriations of property without compensation. Although express expropriations are possible, see, e.g., R. v. Appleby (No. 2) (1976) 76 D.L.R. (3d) 110 (N.B.A.D.) (no compensation owed to publisher complying with statutory requirement that two copies of each book be provided "at his own expense" to the National Library); ss. 53(3) and 121(2) of the British Columbia Forest Act (no compensation for taking of less than 5% of total land value for forest roads), statutes and judicial decisions create strong presumptions in favor of compensation for expropriation. At the same time, courts reject efforts to expand statutory expropriation protection to regulatory takings.

Expropriations acts likewise have a "quasi-constitutional" status in Canada and Australia. In case of a conflict between ordinary statutes, courts generally seek an interpretation that accommodates both pieces of legislation. Quasi-constitutional statutes, however, completely trump any prior statute, and any subsequent statute is presumed to have been written subject to the quasi-constitutional statute, unless it explicitly provides to the contrary.

6.5.1.   The presumption against expropriation

Compensation claims for property allegedly taken by Canadian governments are usually based on an *Expropriations Act* enacted by each province and Parliament. *Manitoba Fisheries Ltd. v. The Queen*, [1979] 1 S.C.R. 101, 88 D.L.R. (3d) 462, illustrates the fairly broad protection extended to property owners by statute. The appellant was a private corporation engaged in exporting fish from Manitoba lakes to other provinces and the United States, until May 1, 1969. On that date, the *Freshwater Fish Marketing Act* came into effect, creating a crown corporation with the exclusive right to export fish from Manitoba. This put Manitoba Fisheries out of business. The statute empowered the federal government to compensate the plaintiff for plant and equipment. The government argued since none of the plaintiff's plant or equipment had been taken, no compensation was owed. The plaintiff argued that it had developed substantial goodwill in building its business over many years and this was an asset for which compensation was due. The Supreme Court agreed and reversed.

Justice Ritchie held that "goodwill, although intangible in character is a part of the property of a business just as much as the premises, machinery and equipment employed in the production of the product whose quality engenders that goodwill." He acknowledged that the federal *Expropriation Act* did not expressly provide for compensation for goodwill. However, he invoked a "long-established rule" of broad construction of expropriation statutes.

> The recognized rule for the construction of [these] statutes is that, unless the words of the statute clearly so demand, a statute is not to be construed so as to take away the property of a subject without compensation. (quoting Lord Atkinson in *Attorney-General v. De Keyser's Royal Hotel Ltd.* [[1920] A.C. 508], at p. 542])

> . . . the general principle, accepted by the legislature and scrupulously defended by the courts, [is] that the title to property or the enjoyment of its possession was not to be compulsorily acquired from a subject unless full compensation was afforded in its place. Acquisition of title or possession was "taking." Aspects of this principle are found in the rules of statutory interpretation devised by the courts, which required the presence of the most explicit words before an acquisition could be held to be sanctioned by an Act of Parliament without full compensation being provided, or imported an intention to give compensation and machinery for assessing it into any Act of Parliament that did not positively exclude it. (quoting *Belfast Corp. v. O.D. Cars Ltd.*, [1960] A.C. 490 (H.L. (N.I.))

See also Toronto Area Transit Operating Authority v. Dell Holdings Ltd., [1997] 1 S.C.R. 32, 142 D.L.R. (4th) 206, where the court stressed the need to broadly interpret the provincial *Expropriations Act*. The Court reasoned:

> 20. The expropriation of property is one of the ultimate exercises of governmental authority. To take all or part of person's property constitutes a severe loss and a very significant interference with a citizen's private property rights. It follows that the power of an expropriating authority should be strictly construed in favour of those whose rights have been affected. This principle has been stressed by eminent writers and emphasized in decisions of this Court.[8]

A similarly expansive Australian interpretation resulted in compensation in *Kettering Pty Ltd v. Noosa Shire Council*, 207 ALR 1 (HCA 2004). The plaintiff

---

[8] [Ed. note: Indeed, the specific holding that lost profits caused by the delay in determining where to locate a rapid transit station until Dell's property was eventually acquired provided Dell with more compensation that it would have received in the United States under the Takings Clause.]

sought $9.3 million, claiming that the defendant's Development Control Plan had injuriously affected his land, reducing the potential development from 73 house lots and 132 building units to 24 house lots and 75 units. Compensation was sought pursuant to s 3.5(1) of the *Local Government (Planning and Environment) Act 1990 (Qld)*, which provides for compensation where "a person has an interest in premises within a planning scheme area and the interest is injuriously affected by the coming into force of any provision contained in a planning scheme." The Court noted that s 3.5(5) puts the onus on the local government authority to prove that exceptions to compensation apply. *See also Marshall v. Director-General, Department of Transport* (2001) 205 CLR 603 at 623 [38] (Gaudron, J) ("The right to compensation for injurious affection following upon the resumption of land is an important right of that kind and statutory permit. Certainly, such provisions should not be construed on the basis that the right to compensation is subject to limitations or qualifications which are not found in the terms of the statute.") However, state laws differ on this point: compensation for reduced property value can be required in some circumstances in Western Australia and Queensland, for example, but not New South Wales.

6.5.2. The requirement of an acquisition for the benefit of the government or the public

Critically important, however, is that Expropriations Acts usually require some interest to be acquired for the benefit of the government or the public. As the Court observed in *Steer Holdings Ltd. v. Manitoba*, [1992] 79 Man. R.2d 169, 174–75 (Q.B.), there must be something "conferred on whatever entity the Legislature intended to benefit. Something must not only be taken away, it must be taken over." This is illustrated by two cases, which closely parallel the Australian *Newcrest Mining* decision excerpted above and the American *Lucas* decision excerpted below.

The Queen v. Tener, [1985] 2 S.C.R. 533, concerned the claims of holders of mineral rights granted when Wells Gray Provincial Park had originally been created and designated as a "Class B park" that permitted some mining operations. In 1973, the British Columbia legislature enacted new legislation upgrading the park to a "Class A park" resulting in a denial of mining permit to the Teners. Justice Estey's majority opinion explained why the Teners' claim for compensation would be recognized:

> The denial of access to these lands occurred under the *Park Act* and amounts to a recovery by the Crown of a part of the right granted to the respondents in 1937. This acquisition by the Crown constitutes a taking from which compensation must flow. Such a conclusion is consistent with this Court's judgment in *Manitoba Fisheries Ltd. v. The Queen*, [1979] 1 S.C.R. 101. In that case the province had established a Crown corporation with a commercial monopoly in the export of fish from Manitoba and other participating provinces. The establishment of the Crown corporation had the effect of putting Manitoba Fisheries out of business. This Court held that the province's actions deprived Manitoba Fisheries of its goodwill as a going concern and that the goodwill so taken by the Crown entitled the

company to compensation despite the fact that they retained their physical assets, as those assets had been rendered virtually useless. Similarly in this case, the respondents are left with the minerals. The value of the minerals in such a state depends upon one's assessment of the chances of a reversal of executive policy in the issuance of a removal permit under the *Park Act*. This is relevant to the valuation process and particularly if and when the Crown takes the last step and expropriates the minerals themselves. It has, however, an importance now because the value of the loss of access, the interest which in my view has now been taken from the respondents, must represent the total value of the minerals less whatever value may be attributed to the future possibility of the issuance of a removal permit. All this is for the tribunal charged with determination of compensation, to decide.

This process I have already distinguished from zoning, the broad legislative assignment of land use to land in the community. It is also to be distinguished from regulation of specific activity on certain land, as for example, the prohibition of specified manufacturing processes. This type of regulation is akin to zoning except that it may extend to the entire community. See *Re Bridgman and City of Toronto*, [1951] O.R. 489, at p. 491, for an example of such regulation. Here, the action taken by the government was to enhance the value of the public park. The imposition of zoning regulation and the regulation of activities on lands, fire regulation limits and so on, add nothing to the value of public property. Here the government wished, for obvious reasons, to preserve the qualities perceived as being desirable for public parks, and saw the mineral operations of the respondents under their 1937 grant as a threat to the park. The notice of 1978 took value from the respondents and added value to the park. The taker, the government of the province, clearly did so in exercise of its valid authority to govern. It clearly enhanced the value of its asset, the park. The respondents are left with only the hope of some future reversal of park policy and the burden of paying taxes on their minerals. The notice of 1978 was an expropriation and, in my view, the rest is part of the compensation assessment process.

MARINER REAL ESTATE LTD. v. NOVA SCOTIA (ATTORNEY GENERAL)

NOVA SCOTIA COURT OF APPEAL

178 N.S.R. (2d) 294, 549 A.P.R. 294 (1999)

[The respondents own land at Kingsburg Beach, which was designated as a protected beach under a provincial statute, the *Beaches Act*, R.S.N.S. 1989, c. 32. Pursuant to power conferred by the Act and Regulations made under it, the Minister refused to grant the respondents permission to build single family dwellings on their land. The Minister's letter rejecting respondent's requests to build homes on the beach noted that a commissioned study found that "maintaining the integrity of the present sand dunes is critical to reducing or preventing widespread flooding of the backshore lowland by the sea and to preventing erosion and narrowing of the beach face. Given the sensitive nature of the dune system, no additional development was recommended." The respondents sued, claiming that their lands had, in effect, been expropriated and they were entitled to compensation pursuant to the *Expropriation Act*, R.S.N.S. 1989, c. 56.]

[The right is based on s. 24 of the Act: "Where land is expropriated, the statutory authority shall pay the owner compensation as is determined in accordance with this Act." Section 3(1) of the *Expropriation Act* defines expropriation as ". . . the taking of land without consent of the owner by an expropriating authority in the exercise of its statutory powers . . . ." There is no issue here that the owners did not consent or that the designation was lawful. The question is whether "land" was "taken" "by" an expropriating authority.]

[The trial judge held that the plaintiffs had been deprived of land within the meaning of the *Expropriation Act* because the designation as a "protected beach" was either itself a taking of land, or a taking when combined with the application of regulations flowing from the designation. Second, the trial judge held that the land was taken within the meaning of the *Expropriation Act* because the regulation of the respondents' lands enhanced the value of the provincially owned property from the high watermark seaward. The Court of Appeal reversed on both points.]

III. Analysis:

(a) De Facto Expropriation:

[37] The respondents' claim that what was, in form, a designation of their land under the *Beaches Act* is, in fact, a taking of their land by a statutory authority within the meaning of the *Expropriation Act*. This claim of de facto expropriation, or as it is known in United States constitutional law, regulatory taking, does not have a long history or clearly articulated basis in Canadian law. We were referred to only three Canadian cases in which such a claim was made successfully, only two of which dealt with the expropriation of land.

[38] The scope of claims of de facto expropriation is very limited in Canadian law. They are constrained by two governing principles. The first is that valid legislation (primary or subordinate)[9] or action taken lawfully with legislative authority may very significantly restrict an owner's enjoyment of private land. The second is that the courts may order compensation for such restriction only where authorized to do so by legislation. In other words, the only questions the court is entitled to consider are whether the regulatory action was lawful and whether the *Expropriation Act* entitles the owner to compensation for the resulting restrictions.

[39] De facto expropriation is conceptually difficult given the narrow parameters of the court's authority which I have just outlined. While de facto expropriation is concerned with whether the "rights" of ownership have been taken away, those rights are defined only by reference to lawful uses of land which may, by law, be severely restricted. In short, the bundle of rights associated with ownership carries

---

[9] [Ed. note: "primary" legislation are statutes passed by elected legislatures; "secondary" legislation includes regulations promulgated by administrative agencies pursuant to statute, or orders in council enacted by the cabinet, either pursuant to express statutory delegation or royal prerogative.]

with it the possibility of stringent land use regulation.

[40] I dwell on this point because there is a rich line of constitutional jurisprudence on regulatory takings in both the United States and Australia which is sometimes referred to in the English and Canadian cases dealing with de facto expropriation. The Fifth Amendment to the United States Constitution (which also applies to the States through the Fourteenth Amendment) provides that private property shall not be taken for public use without just compensation. In the Australian Constitution, s. 51(xxxi) prohibits the acquisition of property except upon just terms. While these abundant sources of case law may be of assistance in developing the Canadian law of de facto expropriation, it is vital to recognize that the question posed in the constitutional cases is fundamentally different.

[41] These U.S. and Australian constitutional cases concern constitutional limits on legislative power in relation to private property. As O'Connor, J., said in the United States Supreme Court case of *Eastern Enterprises v. Apfel* (1998), 118 S. Ct. 2131, the purpose of the U.S. constitutional provision (referred to as the " takings clause") is to prevent the government from ". . . forcing some people alone to bear public burdens which, in all fairness and justice, should be borne by the public as a whole." Canadian courts have no similar broad mandate to review and vary legislative judgments about the appropriate distribution of burdens and benefits flowing from environmental or other land use controls. In Canada, the courts' task is to determine whether the regulation in question entitles the respondents to compensation under the *Expropriation Act*, not to pass judgment on the way the Legislature apportions the burdens flowing from land use regulation.

[42] In this country, extensive and restrictive land use regulation is the norm. Such regulation has, almost without exception, been found not to constitute compensable expropriation. It is settled law, for example, that the regulation of land use which has the effect of decreasing the value of the land is not an expropriation . . . . I would refer, as well, to the following from E.C.E. Todd, *The Law of Expropriation in Canada* (2nd 1992), at pp. 22–23:

> "Traditionally the property concept is thought of as a bundle of rights of which one of the most important is that of user. At common law this right was virtually unlimited and subject only to the restraints imposed by the law of public and private nuisance. At a later stage in the evolution of property law the use of land might be limited by the terms of restrictive covenants.

> "Today the principal restrictions on land use arise from the planning and zoning provisions of public authorities. By the imposition, removal or alteration of land use controls a public authority may dramatically increase, or decrease, the value of land by changing the permitted uses which may be made of it. In such a case, in the absence of express statutory provision to the contrary an owner is not entitled to compensation or any other remedy notwithstanding that subdivision approval or rezoning is refused or development is blocked or frozen pursuant to statutory planning powers in order, for example, to facilitate the future acquisition of the land for public purposes . . . .

. . . .

[47] In light of this long tradition of vigorous land use regulation, the test that has developed for applying the *Expropriation Act* to land use restrictions is exacting and, of course, the respondents on appeal as the plaintiffs at trial, had the burden of proving that they met it. In each of the three Canadian cases which have found compensation payable for de facto expropriations, the result of the governmental action went beyond drastically limiting use or reducing the value of the owner's property. In *Tener and Tener v. British Columbia*, [1985] 1 S.C.R. 533; 59 N.R. 82, the denial of the permit meant that access to the respondents' mineral rights was completely negated, or as Wilson, J., put it at p. 552, amounted to total denial of that interest. In *Casamiro Resource Corp. v. British Columbia* (1991), 80 D.L.R.(4th) 1 (B.C.C.A.), which closely parallels *Tener*, the private rights had become "meaningless." In *Manitoba Fisheries v. Canada*, [1979] 1 S.C.R. 101; 23 N.R. 159, the legislation absolutely prohibited the claimant from carrying on its business.

[48] In reviewing the de facto expropriation cases, R.J. Bauman concluded, and I agree, that to constitute a de facto expropriation, there must be a confiscation of ". . . all reasonable private uses of the lands in question": R.J. Bauman, "Exotic Expropriations: Government Action and Compensation" (1994), 54 The Advocate 561, at p. 574. While there is no magic formula for determining (or describing) the point at which regulation ends and taking begins, I think that Marceau, J.'s, formulation in [*Alberta v. Nilsson*, [1999] A.R. TBEd. JN.053; [1999] A.J. No. 645 (Q.B.)] is helpful. The question is whether the regulation is of "sufficient severity to remove virtually all of the rights associated with the property holder's interest." (at para. 48).

[49] Considerations of a claim of de facto expropriation must recognize that the effect of the particular regulation must be compared with reasonable use of the lands in modern Canada, not with their use as if they were in some imaginary state of nature unconstrained by regulation. In modern Canada, extensive land use regulation is the norm and it should not be assumed that ownership carries with it any exemption from such regulation. As stated in *Belfast [Corp. v. O.D. Cars Ltd.,* [1960] A.C. 490 (H.L. (N.I.))], there is a distinction between the numerous "rights" (or the "bundle of rights") associated with ownership and ownership itself. The "rights" of ownership and the concept of reasonable use of the land include regulation in the public interest falling short of what the Australian cases have called deprivation of the reality of proprietorship: see e.g. *Newcrest Mining (W.A.) Ltd. v. Australia (Commonwealth)*, [1996–1997] 190 C.L.R. 513, at p. 633. In other words, what is, in form, regulation will be held to be expropriation only when virtually all of the aggregated incidents of ownership have been taken away. The extent of this bundle of rights of ownership must be assessed, not only in relation to the land's potential highest and best use, but having regard to the nature of the land and the range of reasonable uses to which it has actually been put. It seems to me there is a significant difference in this regard between, for example, environmentally fragile dune land which, by its nature, is not particularly well-suited for residential development and which has long been used for primarily recreational purposes and a lot in a residential subdivision for which the most reasonable use is for residential construction.

[50] Claims of de facto expropriation may be contrasted with administrative law challenges to the legality or appropriateness of planning decisions. For example, zoning bylaws may be attacked as *ultra vires* if they are enacted for a confiscatory or other improper purpose if such purpose is not one authorized by the relevant grant of zoning power . . . .

(b) The Effects of Regulation:

[Here, the court adopted the American practice of looking at the "actual application of the regulatory scheme as opposed simply to its potential for interference with the owner's activities." Thus, the mere act of designating the property as a protected beach was insufficient as a matter of law to find an expropriation.]

(c) Is Loss Of Economic Value Loss Of Land Under The *Expropriation Act*?

[55] The trial judge found that the respondents had been deprived of land. His main conclusion appears to have been that the loss of "virtually all economic value" constituted the loss of an interest in land. He also found, however, that the ". . . fee simple in the [respondents'] lands has been stripped of its whole bundle of rights." Both aspects of his holding are before us in this appeal and, in my respectful view, both are in error.

. . . .

[62] While the term "land" must be given a broad and liberal interpretation, the interpretation must also respect the legislative context and purpose. As I will develop below, the *Expropriation Act* draws a line, on policy grounds, between the sorts of interference with the ownership of land that are compensable under the Act and those which are not. That line, in general, is drawn where land is taken. In interpreting where this line falls, the court must give the term a meaning which is both consistent with the Act's remedial nature but also with appropriate regard to the legal context in which the term was adopted. It is not the court's function, as it would be if applying a constitutional guarantee of rights of private property, to evaluate the legality or fairness of where the legislature has drawn that line, but to interpret and apply it.

. . . .

[71] We have been referred to no Canadian case in which the decline of economic value of land, on its own, has been held to be the loss of an interest in land. Several cases, on the contrary, recognize the distinction between the value of ownership and ownership itself. This suggests that the loss of economic value of land is not the loss of an interest in land within the meaning of the *Expropriation Act*. This conclusion is, in my view, strongly supported by the overall scheme of compensation established by the Act and by judicial interpretation of it.

. . . .

[79] I conclude, therefore, that the learned trial judge erred in holding that the loss of virtually all economic value of the respondents' land, was the loss of an

interest in land within the meaning of the Expropriation Act.

(d) Loss Of The "Bundle Of Rights"

[Although the court acknowledged that "restrictions on the use of land may be so stringent and all-encompassing that they have the effect of depriving the owner of his or her interest in the land, although leaving paper title undisturbed," and that the decline in economic value may be evidence of the loss of an interest in land, the trial judge erred here, because, although residences could not be built on them, there was no evidence that permission for other uses has been refused.]

(e) Acquisition Of Land

[Here, the court emphasized than in prior cases the challenged activity benefitted government land or crown corporation assets.]

[99] I conclude that for there to be a taking, there must be, in effect, as Estey, J., said in *Tener*, an acquisition of an interest in land and that enhanced value is not such an interest.

[100] The respondents further submit that their lands have been effectively pressed into public service and that this is sufficient to constitute an acquisition of land. The judgment of the United States Supreme Court in *Lucas v. South Carolina Coastal Council* (1992), 112 S. Ct. 2886 (U.S. Sup. Ct.), is relied on. I do not think that case assists us here.

[101] The U.S. constitutional law has, on this issue, taken a fundamentally different path than has Canadian law concerning the interpretation of expropriation legislation. In U.S. constitutional law, regulation which has the effect of denying the owner all economically beneficial or productive use of land constitutes a taking of property for which compensation must be paid. Under Canadian expropriation law, deprivation of economic value is not a taking of land, for the reasons I have set out at length earlier. It follows that U.S. constitutional law cases cannot be relied on as accurately stating Canadian law on this point. Moreover, in U.S. constitutional law, as I understand it, deprivation of property through regulation for public purposes is sufficient to bring a case within the constitutional protection against taking for "public use," unlike the situation under the *Expropriation Act* which requires the taking of land. It is not, as I understand it, necessary in U.S. constitutional law to show that the state acquires any title or interest in the land regulated. For these reasons, I conclude that the U.S. takings clause cases are not of assistance in determining whether there has been an acquisition of land within the meaning of the Nova Scotia *Expropriation Act*.

[Although the court found there to be no expropriation, in *dicta* it rejected the government's claim that provision in the *Beaches Act* precluded any compensation. The court found that the express and broad provisions of the *Expropriation Act* trump any inconsistent provisions of the *Beaches Act*, so that compensation would have been owed if an expropriation had occurred.]

* * *

6.5.3. Statutory compensation for 'injurious affection'

The following case appropriately captures the Canadian perspective that entrenching a right to property in the Charter was not necessary to protect individuals against bearing burdens with regard to property that ought to be "socialized," in Professor Michelman's terms.

ANTRIM TRUCK CENTRE LTD. v. ONTARIO (TRANSPORTATION)
Supreme Court of Canada
2013 SCC 13 (Mar. 7, 2013)

[From 1978 until 2004, the appellant owned property on Highway 17 near the hamlet of Antrim where it operated a truck stop complex that included a restaurant and gas bar and enjoyed the patronage of drivers travelling along the highway. In September 2004, the respondent opened a new section of Highway 417 running parallel to Highway 17 near the appellant's property. Highway 17 was significantly altered by the construction of Highway 417 and access to the appellant's land was severely restricted. Motorists travelling on the new highway did not have direct access to the appellant's truck stop and so it was effectively put out of business at that location. The appellant brought a claim for damages for injurious affection before the Ontario Municipal Board under the *Expropriations Act* and was awarded $58,000 for business loss and $335,000 for loss in market value of the land. This decision was upheld on appeal to the Divisional Court. The Court of Appeal set aside the Board's decision, however, finding that its application of the law of private nuisance to the facts was unreasonable.]

The judgment of the Court was delivered by CROMWELL J. —

. . . .

I.   INTRODUCTION

. . . .

[2] The main question on appeal is this: How should we decide whether an interference with the private use and enjoyment of land is unreasonable when it results from construction which serves an important public purpose? The answer, as I see it, is that the reasonableness of the interference must be determined by balancing the competing interests, as it is in all other cases of private nuisance. The balance is appropriately struck by answering the question whether, in all of the circumstances, the individual claimant has shouldered a greater share of the burden of construction than it would be reasonable to expect individuals to bear without compensation. Here, the interference with the appellant's land caused by the construction of the new highway inflicted significant and permanent loss on the appellant; in the circumstances of this case, it was not unreasonable for the Board to conclude that an individual should not be expected to bear such a loss for the greater public good without compensation.

. . . .

II. Legal Context and Issues

[4] The legal framework for the appeal is found in the law concerning injurious affection. Injurious affection occurs when the defendant's activities interfere with the claimant's use or enjoyment of land. Such interference may occur where a portion of an owner's land is expropriated with negative effects on the value of the remaining property. Alternatively, it may arise where, although no land is expropriated, the lawful activities of a statutory authority on one piece of land interfere with the use or enjoyment of another property: E. C. E. Todd, *The Law of Expropriation and Compensation in Canada* (2nd ed. 1992), at pp. 331–33. In this case, the appellant claimed compensation for injurious affection where no land is taken because the highway construction had significantly impeded access to its land.

[5] The Ontario *Expropriations Act*, R.S.O. 1990, c. E.26, provides a right to compensation for injurious affection on certain conditions: s. 21. Where none of the claimant's land is expropriated, the Act provides a right to compensation for "such reduction in the market value of the land to the owner, and . . . such personal and business damages, resulting from the construction and not the use of the works by the statutory authority as the statutory authority would be liable for if the construction were not under the authority of a statute": s. 1(1). Thus, in order to recover under the Act, the claimant has to meet these three statutory requirements, which are often referred to as the requirements of "statutory authority," "actionability" and "construction and not the use." These requirements mean that (i) the damage must result from action taken under statutory authority; (ii) the action would give rise to liability but for that statutory authority; and (iii) the damage must result from the construction and not the use of the works. Where these conditions are present, the Act requires that the complainant be compensated for the amount by which the affected land's market value was reduced because of the interference, and for personal and business damages: ss. 1(1) and 21.

[6] The appellant satisfied the first and third requirements. As for the first, there was never any dispute that the construction of the new section of highway was carried out under statutory authority. With respect to the third, the "construction and not the use" requirement was contested in the earlier proceedings, but it is no longer in issue in this Court. What remains is the question of whether the second requirement is met. That is, whether, if the highway construction had not been done under statutory authority, the appellant could have successfully sued for damages caused by the construction.

[7] The appellant's primary position, which the Board accepted, is that it meets this second requirement because it would be entitled to damages for private nuisance. The Court of Appeal disagreed. While finding no fault in the Board's articulation of the law about private nuisance, the Court of Appeal nonetheless found that the Board had not reasonably applied that law to the facts before it: 2011 ONCA 419, 106 O.R. (3d) 81. Thus, the reviewable error found by the Court of Appeal concerns the application of the legal test for nuisance to the facts.

. . . .

III. Facts, Proceedings and Standard of Review

. . . .

C. *First Question: What Are the Elements of Private Nuisance?*

. . . .

[19] The elements of a claim in private nuisance have often been expressed in terms of a two-part test of this nature: to support a claim in private nuisance the interference with the owner's use or enjoyment of land must be both *substantial* and *unreasonable*. A substantial interference with property is one that is non-trivial. Where this threshold is met, the inquiry proceeds to the reasonableness analysis, which is concerned with whether the non-trivial interference was also unreasonable in all of the circumstances. . . .

. . . .

D. *Second Question: How Is Reasonableness Assessed in the Context of Interference Caused by Projects That Further the Public Good?*

. . . .

[26] In the traditional law of private nuisance, the courts assess, in broad terms, whether the interference is unreasonable by balancing the gravity of the harm against the utility of the defendant's conduct in all of the circumstances: see, e.g., A. M. Linden and B. Feldthusen, *Canadian Tort Law* (9th ed. 2011), at p. 580. . . .

[28] The first point is that there is a distinction between the utility of the conduct, which focuses on its purpose, such as construction of a highway, and the nature of the defendant's conduct, which focuses on how that purpose is carried out. Generally, the focus in nuisance is on whether the *interference suffered by the claimant* is unreasonable, not on whether *the nature of the defendant's conduct* is unreasonable. This point was made by the court in *Jesperson's Brake & Muffler Ltd. v. Chilliwack (District)* (1994), 88 B.C.L.R. (2d) 230 (C.A.). In that case, the construction of an overpass resulted in a 40 percent drop in the market value of the claimant's lands. The statutory authority argued that the claimant had to establish (and had failed to do so) that *the statutory authority* had used *its* land unreasonably. The Court of Appeal correctly rejected that contention. The focus of the reasonableness analysis in private nuisance is on the character and extent of the interference with the claimant's land; the burden on the claimant is to show that the interference is substantial and unreasonable, not to show that the defendant's use of its own land is unreasonable.

. . . .

[30] The second point is that the utility of the defendant's conduct is especially significant in claims against public authorities. Even where a public authority is involved, however, the utility of its conduct is always considered in light of the other relevant factors in the reasonableness analysis; it is not, by itself, an answer to the reasonableness inquiry. Moreover, in the reasonableness analysis, the severity of the harm and the public utility of the impugned activity are not equally weighted

considerations. If they were, an important public purpose would always override even very significant harm caused by carrying it out. As the editors of *Fleming's The Law of Torts* put it, the utility consideration "must not be pushed too far . . . . [A] defendant cannot simply justify his infliction of great harm upon the plaintiff by urging that a greater benefit to the public at large has accrued from his conduct": s. 21.110. The words of McIntyre J.A. in *Royal Anne Hotel/Co. Ltd. v. Village of Ashcroft (1979), 95 D.L.R. (3d) 756]* are apposite:

> There is no reason why a disproportionate share of the cost of such a beneficial service should be visited upon one member of the community by leaving him uncompensated for damage caused by the existence of that which benefits the community at large. [p. 761]

. . . .

[34] *Mandrake Management Consultants Ltd. v. Toronto Transit Commission* (1993), 62 O.A.C. 202, concerned a claim in nuisance on the basis that subway lines caused noise and vibrations affecting the xplaintiffs' enjoyment of their property. In allowing the appeal from an award of damages, the Court of Appeal noted that "where an essential public service is involved the factor of the utility of the defendant's conduct must not be disregarded. Indeed, I think it must be given substantial weight": para. 46. The court noted, however, that "private rights cannot be trampled upon in the name of the public good": para. 46. It also underlined this point by quoting, at para. 19, the following passage with approval: "Liability for damages is imposed in those cases in which the harm or risk to one *is greater than he ought to be required to bear under the circumstances, at least without compensation*": *Schenck v. The Queen* (1981), 34 O.R. (2d) 595 (H.C.J.), *per* Robins J. (as he then was), at p. 603, citing *Restatement of the Law, Second: Torts 2d*, vol. 4 (1979), at § 822 (emphasis added). In other words, the question is not simply whether the broader public good outweighs the individual interference when the two are assigned equal weight. Rather, the question is whether the interference is greater than the individual should be expected to bear in the public interest without compensation.

. . . .

[45] To sum up on this point, my view is that in considering the reasonableness of an interference that arises from an activity that furthers the public good, the question is whether, in light of all of the circumstances, it is unreasonable to expect the claimant to bear the interference without compensation.

. . . .

F. *Fourth Question: Did the Court of Appeal Err in Finding That the Board's Application of the Law of Nuisance to the Facts Was Unreasonable?*

. . . .

[55] The Board's task was to determine whether, having regard to all of the circumstances, it was unreasonable to require the appellant to suffer the interference without compensation. The Board considered the evidence and the leading cases. Although it did not refer to them by name, the Board took into account the

relevant factors in this case. In particular, it considered the extent of the changes to Highway 17, the fact that those changes were considered necessary for public safety, the appellant's knowledge of — and involvement in — the plans to make changes to the highway, and the extent to which the appellant's concerns about the new highway were taken into account by the respondent in its decision making. The Board concluded that the interference resulting from the construction of the highway was serious and would constitute nuisance but for the fact that the work was constructed pursuant to statutory authority: paras. 37–54. There was no reviewable error in this approach.

[56] . . . The Board properly understood that the purpose of the statutory compensation scheme for injurious affection was to ensure that individuals do not have to bear a disproportionate burden of damage flowing from interference with the use and enjoyment of land caused by the construction of a public work. It was reasonable for the Board to conclude that in all of the circumstances, the appellant should not be expected to endure permanent interference with the use of its land that caused a significant diminution of its market value in order to serve the greater public good.

. . . .

6.5.4.   The supremacy of the political process in deliberate and clear expropriations

Although, as noted, Australian states are not subject to the "just terms" requirement imposed on Commonwealth acquisitions of property by s 51(xxxi), they do have their own statutory schemes for the protection of property; for example the *Land Acquisition (Just Terms Compensation) Act* 1991 (NSW). The NSW Act is a "super-statute": it includes a provision (section 8), stating that the Act "prevails, to the extent of any inconsistency, over the provisions of any other Act relating to the acquisition of land by an authority of the State." Notably, this Act protects real property, and does not extend to the very wide types of property defined by the High Court as falling under s. 51 (xxxi). The scope of protection for state governmental takings was the subject of the following case.

DURHAM HOLDINGS PTY LTD v. NEW SOUTH WALES
HIGH COURT OF AUSTRALIA
(2001) 205 CLR 399, 177 A.L.R. 436

[By the operation of s 5 of the *Coal Acquisition Act 1981 (NSW)* (the Act) on 1 January 1982, coal in certain lands in New South Wales was vested in the Crown in right of that state. Pursuant to s 6 of the Act, an instrument was made by the governor providing for payments of compensation described as interim payments (the arrangements). Under this scheme, the applicant would have been entitled to more than $93 million in compensation. However, s 6 was amended by the *Coal Acquisition (Amendment) Act 1990 (NSW)* (the 1990 Act) which added s 6(3). This stated:

"Arrangements under this section may differentiate between the persons to whom compensation is payable as a result of the enactment of this Act by providing that specified persons, or persons of a specified class, are not entitled to be paid more than a specified sum or specified sums of money in respect of coal vested in the Crown by the operation of section 5, irrespective of the amount of coal that they owned immediately before the commencement of this Act."

The result of that provision, and [regulations governing administrative arrangements, made under the Act], was to cap the total amount of compensation payable to the applicant at $23.25m. The applicant contended that cl 22AA(3) of the arrangements was invalid because it was beyond the power conferred by s 6 as amended by the 1990 Act, that s 6 must be read in accordance with the presumption that the legislature did not intend to acquire property without compensation and that the legislation was invalid because the Parliament of New South Wales lacked power to enact laws for the acquisition of property without compensation.

GAUDRON, MCHUGH, GUMMOW and HAYNE JJ.

. . . .

. . . The applicant submits, as it did to the Court of Appeal, that s 6 must be read in accordance with the presumption that the legislature does not intend to acquire property without compensation. The terms of s 6(3) of the Act rebut any operation of the presumption.**

The applicant also contends in this court that the legislation in question is invalid because the Parliament of New South Wales lacks power to enact laws for the acquisition of property without compensation. There are numerous statements in this court which deny that proposition.[10] Moreover, the existence of the presumption referred to above suggests that the power, against the exercise of which the presumption operates, indeed exists.

. . . .

In *Union Steamship Co of Australia Pty Ltd v King*, [(1988) 166 CLR 1 at 10] the court stated that, within the limits of the grant, a power such as that conferred on the New South Wales Parliament by s 5 of the *Constitution Act 1902 (NSW)* to make laws "for the peace, welfare, and good government of New South Wales" is "as ample and plenary as the power possessed by the Imperial Parliament itself." Moreover, at the time of the 1990 Act, *the Australia Act 1986* (Cth) (the Australia Act) was in force. Section 2(2) thereof declared and enacted that the legislative powers of each state parliament included all legislative powers that Westminster might have exercised before the commencement of that Act for the peace, order and good government of the state.

. . . .

[10] [FN 10] *New South Wales v. Commonwealth (the Wheat Case)* (1915) 20 CLR 54 at 66, 77, 98, 105; *P J Magennis Pty Ltd v. Commonwealth* (1949) 80 CLR 382 at 403, 405, 416, 419; *Pye v. Renshaw* (1951) 84 CLR 58 at 78–80; *Minister for Lands (NSW) v. Pye* (1953) 87 CLR 469 at 486; *Mabo v. Queensland* (1988) 166 CLR 186 at 202 83 ALR 14 at 21; *Commonwealth v. WMC Resources Ltd* (1998) 194 CLR 1 at 58 [149] 152 ALR 1 at 43.

In *Union Steamship*, the court added [(1988) 166 CLR 1 at 10; 82 ALR 43 at 48]:

> Just as the courts of the United Kingdom cannot invalidate laws made by the Parliament of the United Kingdom on the ground that they do not secure the welfare and the public interest, so the exercise of its legislative power by the Parliament of New South Wales is not susceptible to judicial review on that score. Whether the exercise of that legislative power is subject to some restraints by reference to rights deeply rooted in our democratic system of government and the common law . . . is another question which we need not explore.

The question that the applicant posed for the Court of Appeal thus was whether or not the right to receive "just" or "properly adequate" compensation is such a "deeply rooted right" as to operate as a restraint upon the legislative power of the New South Wales Parliament. What the Court of Appeal said is true of the application to this court, namely:[11]

> The [applicant] was unable to point to any judicial pronouncements, let alone a decided case, which indicated, at any time, that any such principle existed in the common law of England, or of the colonies of Australasia, or of Australia. It advocated the development of the common law, by the recognition of such a principle for the first time in this case.

The applicant sought to rely upon statements respecting the common law in decisions respecting the powers of several of the states of the United States before the inclusion in those written state constitutions of guarantees respecting the taking of property.[12] However, what would be involved if the applicant's submission were accepted would not be the development of the common law of Australia. Rather, it would involve modification of the arrangements which comprise the constitutions of the states within the meaning of s 106 of the Constitution, and by which the state legislatures are erected and maintained, and exercise their powers.

The applicant must seek to introduce into the constitutional text, in particular s 2(2) of the *Australia Act*, a limitation not found there. Undoubtedly, having regard to the federal system and the text and structure of "[t]he Constitution of each State of the Commonwealth" (the phrase used in s 106 of the Constitution), there are limits to the exercise of the legislative powers conferred upon the parliament which are not spelled out in the constitutional text.[fn deleted] However, the limitation for which the applicant contends is not, as a matter of logical or practical necessity, implicit in the federal structure within which state parliaments legislate. Further, whatever may be the scope of the inhibitions on legislative power involved in the question identified but not explored in *Union Steamship*, the requirement of compensation which answers the description "just" or "properly adequate" falls outside that field of discourse. The Court of Appeal correctly refused to disturb what, since the *Wheat Case*, [(1915) 20 CLR 54] has been taken to be the settled position respecting state legislative power.

---

[11] [FN 14] (1999) 47 NSWLR 340 at 365; 166 ALR 500 at 520–1

[12] [FN 15] See . . . Stoebuck, "A General Theory of Eminent Domain" (1972) 47 *Washington Law Review* 553 at 572–88.

KIRBY J.

. . . .

Normally, in Australia, where property is compulsorily acquired in accordance with law, the property owner is compensated justly for the property so acquired.[fn deleted] Australian society ordinarily attaches importance to protecting ownership rights in property. The present application was brought to test the constitutional right of a parliament and executive government of a state of the Commonwealth to depart from the foregoing norms.

. . . .

The presumption of compensation

It is usually appropriate (and often necessary) to consider any arguments of construction of legislation before embarking on challenges to constitutional validity . . .

The foundation for the applicant's first argument is . . . that, within the Australian legal system, courts will presume that legislation (federal, state or territory), or subordinate laws made under such legislation, do not amend the common law to derogate from important rights enjoyed under that law, except by provisions expressed in clear language. This principle is sometimes described as a "presumption" or as a "[rule] of construction" or as an "intention" which is attributed to the lawmaker. It rests on the imputed aspiration of the law to attain, and not to deny, basic precepts of justice. The presumption, rule of construction or imputed intention certainly applies to the taking of property without compensation. This has been acknowledged by this court in respect both of legislation[13] and delegated lawmaking.[14] Indeed, it has been suggested that "the general rule has added force in its application to common law principles respecting property rights."[15]

In addition to these principles of the common law, the applicant invoked a connected, but different, "presumption." This was that Australian legislation would be construed so as to accord with the basic principles of customary international law.[fn deleted] It submitted that this was particularly so where such law expressed established norms of fundamental human rights. [fn deleted] The applicant argued that the right of an individual, corporation or state in Australia to own property (and thus, by inference, not to be deprived of property by arbitrary process or without just terms) was implicit in contemporary customary international law.[fn deleted] According to the applicant "compensation," in this context, meant "the full money equivalent of the thing of which [the owner] has been deprived."[16]

. . . .

---

[13] [FN 37] Bropho v. Western Australia (1990) 171 CLR 1 at 17–18, 93 ALR 207 at 214–15.

[14] [FN 38] C J Burland Pty Ltd v. Metropolitan Meat Industry Board (1968) 120 CLR 400 at 406–7, 415.

[15] [FN 39] American Dairy Queen (Qld) Pty Ltd v. Blue Rio Pty Ltd (1981) 147 CLR 677 at 683.

[16] [FN 43] Nelungaloo Pty Ltd v. Commonwealth (1948) 75 CLR 495 at 571.

However, any presumption, rule of construction, or imputed intention is subject to valid legislative provisions to the contrary. Judges may decline to read such legislation as having such an effect. The more peremptory, arbitrary and unjust the provisions, the less willing a judge may be to impute such a purpose to an Australian lawmaker. But a point will be reached where the law in question is "clear and unambiguous.". . . Once that point is reached, subject to any constitutional invalidity, the judge has no authority to ignore or frustrate the commands of the lawmaker. To do so would be to abuse judicial power, not to exercise it.

. . . .

A glance at the legislative history of the Act, contained in the parliamentary debates, indicates that a deliberate policy decision was made by the government, and explained to the parliament of the state prior to the enactment of s 6(3) of the Act. This was to impose the limit of $60m on compensation for the three largest claimants, including the applicant.

. . . .

The Court of Appeal was therefore correct to dismiss the construction argument. No occasion arises for this court to disturb that court's judgment on that basis.

Powers of state parliament: the applicant's arguments

This conclusion obliges this court to examine the applicant's second argument. This was that the Act, specifically s 6, construed as above, is outside the legislative powers of the state and, by inference, that the arrangements are likewise unconstitutional.

It is not unusual to have challenges in this court to the constitutional validity of state legislation. Such challenges have arisen ever since the court was established. Provisions in state statutes, including some of great importance to the state, are, from time to time, found constitutionally invalid. But this result ordinarily follows a conclusion that the state law in question is invalid because it is inconsistent with federal law, or with an express prohibition in the Constitution or with an implication drawn from the language and structure of the Constitution. What was unusual about the present application was that, for the most part, the applicant's argument did not rest on an invocation of the federal Constitution. It depended upon contentions about fundamental limitations said to exist in the legislative powers of a parliament of a state to enact a law such as the Act.

In essence, the applicant submitted that the lawmaking powers of the parliament of the state were "largely determined by the common law" and were therefore subject to such restrictions as the common law imposed. The applicant argued that the assumption that a legislature, such as the parliament of the state, was "uncontrolled" and subject to no applicable constitutional limits (within the subjects of lawmaking otherwise open to it) was fundamentally misconceived.

. . . .

[Kirby, J., traced "celebrated instances" when English judges have held that an Act of the English Parliament could be treated as invalid where it conflicted with a

~~basic principle of the common~~ law, *see, e.g., Dr Bonham's case* (1610) and the uncontrolled omnipotence of parliament was rejected by many other prominent jurists. Kirby suggested that this view also led early American courts to hold that state legislatures (at the time, not subject to the Takings Clause by virtue of the Fourteenth Amendment) lacked the power to take property without compensation.[17]].

Secondly, the applicant invoked Sir Owen Dixon's reminder that the principle of parliamentary supremacy is itself a doctrine of the common law.[18] What the judges had recognised for a time to be an omnipotent and unqualified supremacy, they could now recognise to be subject to specified limitations. Such limitations would include controls at least on such gross and discriminatory departures from basic civil rights as were reflected in the Act and the arrangements.

. . . .

Powers of state parliament: authority

In *Union Steamship Co of Australia Pty Ltd v. King* . . . this court left open the question whether, with respect to a parliament of a state, there were any common law rights which were so fundamental as to be beyond legislative power . . . [T]he applicant contended that the legislative powers of the parliament of the state excluded the power to "deprive named persons of their property without just, or any properly adequate, compensation." However, the applicant could not point to any case in England, the colonies of Australasia or modern Australia, to support its argument that this was the kind of "fundamental" common law right that "lay so deep" . . . It could point to no judicial opinion to support its attempt to revive the question reserved in *Union Steamship* and to require its answer in this case.

[Next, Kirby J rejected the notion that the grant of legislative power "to make laws for the peace, welfare, and good government" of the colony (later the state) operate as words of limitation.]

Thirdly, so far as the powers of a parliament of a state of Australia to permit the acquisition of property without the payment of compensation are concerned, a long line of opinions in this court upholds the existence of that power . . . Whereas in the federal Constitution, specific provision had been made requiring the provision of "just terms" as a precondition to the acquisition of property from any state or person by federal law, no equivalent provision was there included in respect of state acquisition laws.

[Kirby J then noted that the HCA had, in *Mabo v. Queensland*, (1988) 166 CLR 186; 83 ALR 14, rejected the argument that the Queensland Parliament lacked

---

[17] [FN 80] Early decisions in the United States held that state legislatures had no power to take property without compensation: Gardner v. Newburgh 2 Johns Ch 161 (NY) (1816) 7 Am Dec 526; Sinnickson v. Johnson 2 Harrison 129 (NJ) (1839) 34 Am Dec 184; Young v. McKenzie 3 Ga 31 at 42 (1847); Parham v. Justices 9 Ga 341 at 349–50 (1851); Pumpelly v. Green Bay Co 80 US 166 (1871); Chicago, Burlington and Quincy Railroad Co v. Chicago 166 U.S. 226 at 236–8 (1897).

[18] [FN 92] Dixon, "The Common Law as an Ultimate Constitutional Foundation" in *Jesting Pilate*, 1965, p. 203 at pp. 206–11.

legislative power to deprive indigenous peoples of property rights without providing compensation.]

. . . .

Powers of state parliament: the theory and reality

Apart from the expositions of judicial authority in the above decisions, considerations of legal policy and political theory reinforce, and to some extent explain, the judicial authority collected in the cases.

Members of a legislature, such as the Parliament of New South Wales, are regularly answerable to the electors, whereas judges in Australia are not. Judges recognise that, whatever the deficiencies of electoral democracy, the necessity of answering to the electorate at regular intervals has a tendency to curb legislative excesses. Many judges reject "the role of a Platonic guardian" and are "pleased to live in a society that does not thrust [that role] upon [them]." Most judges in Australia would probably share this relatively modest conception of their role. In this conception, the duty of obedience to a law made by a parliament of a state derives from the observance of parliamentary procedures and the conformity of the resulting law with the state and federal constitutions. It does not rest upon judicial pronouncements to accord, or withhold, recognition of the law in question by reference to the judge's own notions of fundamental rights, apart from those constitutionally established.

. . . .

One further consideration, to which the Court of Appeal referred, should also be mentioned in answering the applicant's submission that this court should now turn its back on past authority, if necessary overrule its previous holdings, and uphold as a doctrine of the common law an entitlement of judges to invalidate state legislation found to breach fundamental or "deep lying" rights. It is a consideration of particular relevance to the present case. In 1988 a referendum of electors in Australia rejected a proposal to add to the federal Constitution a new provision requiring that, to be valid, a "law of a State" providing for the "acquisition of property from any person" had to afford "just terms."

. . . .

The referendum proposal of 1988, although it was lost, reinforces to some extent the orthodox theory of Australia's legal and political arrangements. Under the Australian Constitution, it is not necessary to depend on judges to prevent, or cure, all injustices, including those of the kind of which the applicant complains. At least in theory, it is open to the electors to do so.

. . . .

———

Politically and constitutionally, a similar case is *Canadian Pacific Railway v. Vancouver (City)*, [2006] 1 S.C.R. 227. The CPR, as with many North American railways, was given vast tracts of land in return for constructing rail lines across the continent.[19] The CPR used a portion of the land grants for actual rail construction and developed the rest of the property. As rail usage decreased, the CPR abandoned the ten kilometer Arbutus Corridor on the west side of Vancouver, but the city' official development plan (ODP) limited its use to a public thoroughfare for rail, transit, bicycles, or pathways. CPR filed suit, claiming that this amounted to an expropriation. The SCC rejected the claim. Consistent with *Mariner Realty*, the SCC held that to establish what it called a "de facto taking," the claimant must establish "(1) an acquisition of a beneficial interest in the property or flowing from it, and (2) removal of all reasonable uses of the property."

Significantly, the Court quickly rejected the argument that compensation was owed because of the strong presumption in favour of application of the provincial *Expropriation Act.*

> [19] . . . the *Vancouver Charter* expressly contemplates the possibility that an ODP may adversely affect land and exempts the City from liability for such effects. This negates the argument that ODPs are simply statements of policy and, to the extent that they may affect land use and values, must be accompanied by plans to acquire the affected land. Section 569 deems that the exercise of the City's power does not constitute a "tak[ing] or injuriou[s] affect[ion]" and that "no compensation shall be payable by the city or any inspector or official thereof." The Legislature clearly contemplated that ODPs could have effects like those found in this case, and went on to hold that the City was not liable for the consequences.

> . . . .

> [35] CPR also argues that the British Columbia *Expropriation Act,* R.S.B.C. 1996, c. 125, requires the City to compensate CPR. Section 1 of the Act defines "expropria[tion]" as "the taking of land by an expropriating authority under an enactment without the consent of the owner," and goes on to define "expropriating authority" as "a person. . . empowered under an enactment to expropriate land." Section 2(1) of the Act provides that "[i]f an expropriating authority proposes to expropriate land, th[e] Act applies to the expropriation, and, if there is an inconsistency between any of the provisions of th[e] Act and any other enactment respecting the expropriation, the provisions of [the *Expropriation Act*] apply." The *Expropriation Act* requires compensation for land expropriated, while the *Vancouver Charter* states the City is not obliged to compensate for adverse effects to land caused by an ODP. CPR argues that this constitutes an inconsistency and that, under s. 2 of the *Expropriation Act*, the requirement of compensation in that Act must prevail.

> [36] This argument rests on the premise that there is an inconsistency between the *Expropriation Act* and the *Vancouver Charter* as applied to the facts in this case. It assumes that the land is "expropriate[d]" or "taken" and that the two statutes impose different obligations in this event

---

[19] Indeed, for a narrative on how the land grants effectively created the city of Vancouver, see Douglas C. Harris, *A Railway, a City, and the Public Regulation of Private Property: CPR v. City of Vancouver,* in CANADIAN PROPERTY LAW STORIES (James Muir, Eric Tucker & Bruce Ziff, eds., 2012).

— compensation in one case, no compensation in the other. In fact, however, the provisions of the *Vancouver Charter* prevent a conflict from ever arising. Section 569 of the *Vancouver Charter* provides that property affected by a by-law "shall be deemed as against the city not to have been taken." The *Expropriation Act* applies only where there has been a "tak[ing]" or "expropriat[ion]." Since by statute there is no taking or expropriation here, there is no inconsistency with the *Expropriation Act* and s. 2(1) cannot apply.

[37] I add this. Even if the facts of this case could be seen to support an inference of *de facto* taking at common law, that inference has been conclusively negated by s. 569 of the *Vancouver Charter*. The Province has the power to alter the common law. Here, by providing that the effects of the ODP by-law cannot amount to a "tak[ing]," it has rendered inapplicable the common law *de facto* taking remedy upon which CPR relies.

6.6. SOUTH AFRICAN CONSTITUTIONAL PROTECTION OF PROPERTY

The role of property rights in the constitutional politics of South Africa cannot be overstated. Some form of protection was necessary to ensure a democratic transition, but many strongly opposed any entrenchment of the maldistribution of wealth and poverty following a century of subjugation of the black majority: over 85% of land was held by the white minority. Genuine fears were expressed for the prospects of a constitutional state if entrenched rights would impede the necessary social and economic reforms facing the country. *See, e.g.*, Hugh Corder et al., A Charter for Social Justice: a Contribution to the South African Bill of Rights Debate 63–64 (Juta Publ. 1992).

The debate over the inclusion of a property rights clause in the South African Constitution is still continuing. Just prior to the beginning of substantive constitutional negotiation in early 1993, the ANC and the National Party government presented dramatically alternative notions of how property should be constitutionally protected. While the ANC was willing to protect the undisturbed enjoyment of personal possessions, property entitlements were to be determined by legislation and provision was to be made for the restoration of land to people dispossessed under Apartheid. The Government's proposals aimed at protecting all property rights and would only allow expropriation for public purposes and subject to cash compensation determined by a court of law according to the market value of the property. In response the ANC suggested that no property clause was necessary. As one commentator has noted, how South Africa "will be able to fully transform itself and completely eradicate all vestiges of its apartheid past is substantially a matter of property." Gregory S. Alexander, The Global Debate Over Constitutional Property: Lessons for American Takings Jurisprudence 12 (2006).

As the negotiations progressed the conflict over the property clause became focused on specific issues. The apartheid government insisted that property rights be included in the constitution and that the measure of compensation include specific reference to the market value of the property. In response the ANC insisted that the property clause not frustrate efforts to address land claims and that the state must have the power to regulate property without obligations to pay compensation unless there was a clear expropriation of the property. The interim 1993 Constitution resolved these conflicts by providing a separate institutional basis for land restitution, which was guaranteed in the corrective action provisions of the equality clause; the interim Constitution's drafters compromised on the question of compensation by including a range of factors the courts would have to consider in determining just and equitable compensation. Despite predictions that there would be very little change in the Constitution during the second phase of the constitution-making process, particularly on such sensitive issues as the property clause and the Bill of Rights, in fact, the property issue once again became one of the points of contention in the Constitutional Assembly.

Although the committee charged with reviewing the Bill of Rights was at first reluctant to change the formulation of the 1993 compromise, challenges centred on the question of land restitution and reform. This forced even those representing long established interests, like the National Party and the South African Agricultural Union, to agree on the need "to rectify past wrongs" and the need for some form of land reform. Disagreement here was over the means. The South African Agricultural Union, for example continued to assert that "it should be done in a way without jeopardising the protection of private ownership," while the National Party now embraced the World Bank's proposals, arguing that land reform should "be accomplished within the parameters of the market and should be demand-driven."

The final property clause guarantees not only the restitution of land taken after 1913, and a right to legally secure tenure for those whose tenure is insecure as a result of racially discriminatory laws or practices, but also includes an obligation on the state to enable citizens to gain access to land on an equitable basis. Furthermore, the state is granted a limited exemption from the protective provisions of the property clause so as to empower it to take "legislative and other measures to achieve land, water and related reform, in order to redress the results of past racial discrimination."

Despite agreement in the Constitutional Assembly, the property clause in the draft final Constitution was challenged in the Constitutional Court as violating the Constitutional Principles of the Interim Constitution, and therefore warranted denial of certification of the Constitution. Two major objections were raised: first, that unlike the interim Constitution, the new clause did not expressly protect the right to acquire, hold and dispose of property; second, the provisions governing expropriation and the payment of compensation were inadequate. The Constitutional Court rejected both of these arguments. First, the Court noted that the test to be applied was whether the formulation of the right met the standard of a "universally accepted fundamental right" as required by Constitutional Principle II. Second the Court surveyed international and foreign sources and observed that "[i]f one looks to international conventions and foreign constitutions, one is immediately struck by the wide variety of formulations adopted to protect the right to property, as well as by the fact that significant conventions and constitutions contain no protection of property at all" (para. 71, *First Certification Case*). In conclusion the Court argued that it could not "uphold the argument that, because the formulation adopted is expressed in a negative and not a positive form and because it does not contain an express recognition of the right to acquire and dispose of property, it fails to meet the prescription of CPII" (para. 72). The second objection met the same fate with the Court concluding that an "examination of international conventions and foreign constitutions suggests that a wide range of criteria for expropriation and the payment of compensation exists," and thus the "approach taken in NT 25 [new text section 25] cannot be said to flout any universally accepted approach to the question" (para 73).

Although it may be argued that the property clause in the final Constitution is unique to South Africa and is the product of South Africa's particular history of dispossession, it is also important to note how resolution of the property question was framed by international options. While the Constitutional Court could argue that the particular formulation of the clause was compatible with global standards — given the variety of formulations in existence — it is also true that those who advocated that there should be no property clause in the Constitution were compelled by the politics of recognition of property rights to accept its inclusion.

Despite this contentious beginning there has been very little litigation based on the property clause of the Constitution. While the socio-economic rights jurisprudence clearly affects property rights at a fundamental level, the only claims under the property clause have involved either the failure of the government to protect property — in a case in which the government failed to act to evict people who had built their homes on private land — and one important case in which a bank challenged the tax departments seizure of automobiles from an import company that had failed to pay taxes — because the bank claimed the seizure of its lien on the automobiles meant that it had been unjustly deprived of its property rights.

PRESIDENT OF THE RSA v. MODDERKLIP BOERDERY (PTY) LTD
CONSTITUTIONAL COURT OF SOUTH AFRICA
2004 (6) SA 40

LANGA ACJ:

[3] The farm Modderklip adjoins Daveyton Township in Benoni [east of Johannesburg]. During the 1990s, because of overcrowded conditions in the township, a number of its residents began settling on the strip of land between the township and Modderklip's farm. The strip became known as the Chris Hani informal settlement. The municipality reacted by evicting the residents of the Chris Hani settlement. In May 2000 about 400 of them moved onto Modderklip's farm where they erected some 50 informal dwellings.

[4] In May 2000, the Benoni City Council alerted Modderklip to the unlawful occupation of its land and gave it notice in terms of section 6(4) of the Prevention of Illegal Eviction from and Unlawful Occupation of Land Act 19 of 1998 (the Act), requiring it to institute eviction proceedings against the unlawful occupiers. Modderklip refused to do so and informed the City Council that it considered it to be the Council's responsibility to evict the occupiers. Modderklip stated however that it would cooperate with the Council to the extent necessary should it take steps

to evict the occupiers. The Council did not respond to this communication, nor did it take any steps as suggested by Modderklip.

[5] Modderklip then laid charges of trespass against the occupiers. Those convicted were given warnings by the court and released. The unlawful occupiers however simply went back to the farm after their release by the court and resumed their occupation. The local head of the prison then requested both Modderklip and representatives of the South African Police Service (the police) not to proceed with further criminal prosecutions as the prison would be hard-pressed to find space to accommodate convicted unlawful occupiers should they be sentenced to prison terms.

[6] For its part, Modderklip continued to search for ways to resolve the problem. It sought assistance from several organs of state, including the police and officials of the Ekurhuleni Metropolitan Municipality (the municipality) into which the Benoni City Council had become subsumed. No help was forthcoming from any of these organs of state. Modderklip also offered to sell to the municipality the portion of the farm that was unlawfully occupied at a negotiable price of R10 000 per hectare. Although the municipality initially showed some interest in the offer, nothing came of it. In the meantime, the number of unlawful occupiers continued to grow. By October 2000 there were approximately 4000 residential units, occupied by some 18 000 persons.

Proceedings in the Johannesburg High Court

[7] In October 2000, still within a period of 6 months of the initial occupation of its property, Modderklip instituted proceedings in the Johannesburg High Court for an eviction order in terms of the Act. The occupiers and the municipality were cited as respondents and the occupiers opposed the application. In April 2001 the High Court granted the eviction order and gave the occupiers two months within which to vacate Modderklip's farm. The court order also authorised the sheriff to enlist the assistance of the police in the eviction or removal of the occupiers and the removal or demolition of their informal dwellings.

[8] The order of the Johannesburg High Court for the eviction of the occupiers was never complied with, nor was an appeal lodged against it at that stage. Instead, the number of the occupiers continued to increase. Later estimates put their number at approximately 40 000 of whom roughly a third were alleged to be illegal immigrants. The settlement has streets and the erven are mostly fenced and numbered. It has shops and other modest commercial ventures. There is one tap from which the occupiers draw water and there are no other services except for pit toilets. The community, which is now fairly settled and has a voluntary form of civic structure, calls itself the Gabon Informal Settlement. About 50 hectares of Modderklip's property are now under illegal occupation.

[9] Pursuant to the judgment and order of the Johannesburg High Court, a writ of execution was issued at Modderklip's instance. The sheriff however indicated that she would have to engage a security firm to assist her in carrying out the evictions and therefore insisted on a deposit of R1,8 million to secure the costs of the evictions. This amount far exceeds the value of the piece of land which is illegally

occupied. Modderklip refused to pay this amount. It instead approached the President and the Ministers of Safety and Security, Agriculture and Land Affairs and of Housing, respectively, for assistance but to no avail. On being requested to enforce the eviction order, the police refused because they regarded the matter as a private civil dispute between Modderklip and the occupiers. They however indicated that they would be prepared to stand by when the evictions were taking place in order to ensure that there was no breach of the peace. Finding itself with an eviction order that it could not enforce, Modderklip then approached the Pretoria High Court for relief.

Proceedings before the Pretoria High Court

[14] In opposing the application, the police contended that the problem was not a police matter but one of land reform. They also pointed to the expense, estimated to be at least R18 million, that would be incurred if the eviction order were to be implemented. In his affidavit articulating the attitude of the police to the application, Assistant Commissioner Van der Westhuizen put his finger on what became one of the central issues of this case. He asked the question where the occupiers, with their possessions, would be accommodated after eviction. He pointed out that if the occupiers were simply thrown onto the street, they would either return to Modderklip's farm or occupy some other property unlawfully. The Assistant Commissioner also questioned the wisdom of prosecuting the occupiers because it would not be possible to identify those who should be prosecuted for contempt of court, or those upon whom the eviction application or the order had been served. Because of the continuing influx of unlawful occupiers onto Modderklip's farm, it would also be difficult to make a distinction between the unlawful occupiers on the one hand and transient visitors on the other.

[15] The relief requested by Modderklip was, to a substantial extent, granted by the Pretoria High Court. It declared that Modderklip's property rights under section 25(1) of the Constitution had been violated by the illegal occupation and the failure of the occupiers to comply with the eviction order. It also held that the state had breached its obligations in terms of sections 26(1) and (2) of the Constitution, read with section 25(5), to take reasonable steps within its available resources to realise the right of the occupiers to have access to adequate housing and land. According to the High Court, this failure by the state effectively amounted to the unlawful expropriation of Modderklip's property and also infringed Modderklip's rights to equality — under sections 9(1) and 9(2) of the Constitution — by requiring it to bear the burden of providing accommodation to the occupiers, a function that should have been undertaken by the state.

[36] The problem of homelessness is particularly acute in our society. It is a direct consequence of apartheid urban planning which sought to exclude African people from urban areas, and enforced this vision through policies regulating access to land and housing which meant that far too little land and too few houses were supplied to African people. The painful consequences of these policies are still with us eleven years into our new democracy, despite government's attempts to remedy them. The frustration and helplessness suffered by many who still struggle against heavy odds to meet the challenge merely to survive and to have shelter can never be

underestimated. The fact that poverty and homelessness still plague many South Africans is a painful reminder of the chasm that still needs to be bridged before the constitutional ideal to establish a society based on social justice and improved quality of life for all citizens is fully achieved.

[42] It is obvious in this case that only one party, the state, holds the key to the solution of Modderklip's problem. There is no possibility of the order of the Johannesburg High Court being carried out in the absence of effective participation by the state. The only question is whether the state is obliged to help in resolving the problem, in other words, whether Modderklip is entitled to any relief from the state.

[43] The obligation on the state goes further than the mere provision of the mechanisms and institutions referred to above. It is also obliged to take reasonable steps, where possible, to ensure that large-scale disruptions in the social fabric do not occur in the wake of the execution of court orders, thus undermining the rule of law. The precise nature of the state's obligation in any particular case and in respect of any particular right will depend on what is reasonable, regard being had to the nature of the right or interest that is at risk as well as on the circumstances of each case.

[44] The position of Modderklip, as a victim of the unlawful occupation of its property on a massive scale, is aggravated by the failure to have the eviction order carried out. Its efforts to extricate itself were frustrated by the ineffectiveness of the mechanisms provided by the state to resolve this specific problem because of the sheer magnitude of the invasion and occupation of Modderklip's property. The judgment in the eviction case and the order granted by the Johannesburg High Court did not provide an answer. The eviction order became unenforceable because the occupiers, in their thousands, would have had nowhere to go when the order to evict them was carried out. The problem was compounded by the inordinate increase in the number of occupiers. Indeed, in the founding affidavit, it is stated that Modderklip found itself in a checkmate position, having followed the correct legal procedures and having obtained a court order, only to find that the organs of state were either unwilling or unable to assist in enforcing it.

[45] It is unreasonable for a private entity such as Modderklip to be forced to bear the burden which should be borne by the state of providing the occupiers with accommodation. Land invasions of this scale are a matter that threatens far more than the private rights of a single property owner. Because of their capacity to be socially inflammatory, they have the potential to have serious implications for stability and public peace. Failure by the state to act in an appropriate manner in the circumstances would mean that Modderklip, and others similarly placed, could not look upon the state and its organs to protect them from invasions of their property. That would be a recipe for anarchy.

[46] The execution of an eviction order does not ordinarily raise problems which cannot be accommodated through the existing mechanisms. They allow for the execution of court orders so that citizens have no justification to take the law into their own hands. Consequently order in society is preserved and inappropriate societal disruptions are prevented. It follows that court orders must be executed in a manner that prevents social upheaval. Otherwise the purpose of the rule of law

would be subverted by the very execution process that ought to uphold it.

[47] The circumstances of this case are extraordinary in that it is not possible to rely on mechanisms normally employed to execute eviction orders. This should have been obvious to the state. It was not a case of one or two or even ten evictions where a routine eviction order would have sufficed. To execute this particular court order and evict tens of thousands of people with nowhere to go would cause unimaginable social chaos and misery and untold disruption. In the circumstances of this case, it would also not be consistent with the rule of law.

[48] The question that needs to be answered is whether the state was, in the circumstances, obliged to do more than it has done to satisfy the requirements of the rule of law and fulfil the section 34 rights of Modderklip. I find that it was unreasonable of the state to stand by and do nothing in circumstances where it was impossible for Modderklip to evict the occupiers because of the sheer magnitude of the invasion and the particular circumstances of the occupiers.

[49] The state is under an obligation progressively to ensure access to housing or land for the homeless. I am mindful of the fact that those charged with the provision of housing face immense problems. Confronted by intense competition for scarce resources from people forced to live in the bleakest of circumstances, the situation of local government officials can never be easy. The progressive realisation of access to adequate housing, as promised in the Constitution, requires careful planning and fair procedures made known in advance to those most affected. Orderly and predictable processes are vital. Land invasions should always be discouraged. At the same time, for the requisite measures to operate in a reasonable manner, they must not be unduly hamstrung so as to exclude all possible adaptation to evolving circumstances. If social reality fails to conform to the best laid plans, reasonable and appropriate responses may be necessary. Such responses should advance the interests at stake and not be unduly disruptive towards other persons. Indeed, any planning which leaves no scope whatsoever for relatively marginal adjustments in the light of evolving reality, may often not be reasonable.

[50] No acceptable reason has been proffered for the state's failure to assist Modderklip. The understandable desire to discourage "queue-jumping" does not explain or justify why Modderklip was left to carry the burden imposed on it to provide accommodation to such a large number of occupiers. No reasons have been given why Modderklip's offer for the state to purchase a portion of Modderklip's farm was not taken up and why no attempt was made to assist Modderklip to extricate itself.

[51] The obligation resting on the state in terms of section 34 of the Constitution was, in the circumstances, to take reasonable steps to ensure that Modderklip was, in the final analysis, provided with effective relief. The state could have expropriated the property in question or provided other land, a course that would have relieved Modderklip from continuing to bear the burden of providing the occupiers with accommodation. The state failed to do anything and accordingly breached Modderklip's constitutional rights to an effective remedy as required by the rule of law and entrenched in section 34 of the Constitution.

FIRST NATIONAL BANK OF SA LTD t/a WESBANK v. COMMISSIONER, SA REVENUE SERVICE
CONSTITUTIONAL COURT OF SOUTH AFRICA
2002 (4) SA 768

ACKERMANN J:

[2] FNB is a financial institution that sells and leases movables. Three motor vehicles of which it is the owner have been detained under the provisions of section 114 of the Act. The first respondent is the Commissioner of the South African Revenue Service (the Commissioner) who is charged under section 2(1) of the Act with its administration. The second respondent is the Minister of Finance (the Minister) under whose aegis the Act falls.

The factual background

[7] FNB, acting in the normal course of its business, leased a Volkswagen Jetta to Lauray Manufacturers CC ("Lauray") in November 1994 and a Volkswagen Golf to Airpark Cold Halaal Storage CC ("Airpark") in November 1995. In January 1996 FNB sold a Mercedes-Benz to Airpark under an installment sale agreement with reservation of ownership until the last instalment was paid. Appellant thus remained the owner of all three vehicles.

[8] On 16 February 1996 the Commissioner detained, and thereby established a lien, over several vehicles on Lauray's premises in terms of section 114 of the Act. One of these vehicles was the Volkswagen Jetta. This was done in order to obtain security for approximately R3, 26m comprising predominantly of outstanding customs duty, penalties and payment in lieu of forfeiture arising out of an alleged fabric smuggling network. Lauray was placed in provisional liquidation on 17 November 1997. On 18 December 1997 the liquidator cancelled the lease. The Commissioner lodged a claim with the liquidator and received an amount of R198 074,96. Appellant did not lodge a claim for the arrears in lease payments since it would have been treated as a concurrent creditor in circumstances where there was no prospect of a dividend for concurrent creditors. The Commissioner has indicated, subject to the outcome of these legal proceedings, that he intends selling the vehicle in order to satisfy the outstanding customs debts of Lauray. Lauray was originally allowed to use the Jetta after detention, but it has been stored in a state warehouse since 27 March 1998.

[9] On 7 April 1997 the Commissioner detained and established a lien over the Volkswagen Golf and the Mercedes-Benz leased and sold respectively by FNB to Airpark. This was done in order to obtain security for customs debts and penalties of R640 571, 32 owed by Airpark. Airpark had removed goods from a customs and excise cold storage warehouse without paying customs duty. The Commissioner has not sought to liquidate Airpark since there would be no benefit to creditors. The Commissioner has however stated his intention to sell the vehicles in an endeavour to recover at least part of Airpark's outstanding debt of R397 920,80. The two vehicles have been stored in the state warehouse since 26 March 1998.

[10] It should further be noted that FNB claims substantial sums to be outstanding with regard to the three vehicles, both in terms of payments which have fallen in arrears and in terms of total outstanding contract payments.

The property challenge

[26] It was contended on behalf of FNB, both in the High Court and in this Court, that the detention and sale by the Commissioner under the provisions of section 114 of the motor vehicles owned by FNB, under circumstances where FNB was not a customs debtor, amounted to an expropriation of the motor vehicles in question for purposes of section 25 of the Constitution. Neither section 114, nor any other provision of the Act provided for the payment of compensation for such expropriation as mandated by section 25(2)(b) of the Constitution. Accordingly, it was submitted, the provisions of section 114 of the Act that authorised such expropriation were inconsistent with section 25(1) of the Constitution and invalid.

. . . .

[46] The following questions arise:

   (a)   Does that which is taken away from FNB by the operation of section 114 amount to "property" for purpose of section 25?

   (b)   Has there been a deprivation of such property by the Commissioner?

   (c)   If there has, is such deprivation consistent with the provisions of section 25(1)?

   (d)   If not, is such deprivation justified under section 36 of the Constitution?

   (e)   If it is, does it amount to expropriation for purpose of section 25(2)?

   (f)   If so, does the deprivation comply with the requirements of section 25(2)(a) and (b)?

   (g)   If not, is the expropriation justified under section 36?

Before turning to these issues it is essential, by way of introduction, to consider the meaning of section 25 more broadly and in a more comprehensive context.

The Meaning of section 25: Introduction

[47] Constitutional property clauses are notoriously difficult to interpret and it is unlikely that the interpretation of section 25 of the Constitution will be wholly spared these problems. A court is therefore fortunate, at this relatively early stage of section 25 jurisprudence, to have at its disposal a considerable body of work produced by South African scholars in the field. In this judgment heavy reliance is placed on such work and the assistance derived therefrom gratefully acknowledged.

[48] Section 25 embodies a negative protection of property and does not expressly guarantee the right to acquire, hold and dispose of property. This was one of the major objections raised against the section and rejected by this Court in the *First Certification* case. After referring to the wide variety of formulations of the right to property in the constitutions and bills of rights of recognised democracies, the Court on that occasion pointed out that no universally recognised formulation of the

right to property exists and held that the "[p]rotection for the holding of property is implicit in [section] 25." Subsection (4)(b) makes plain that for purposes of the section "property is not limited to land."

[49] The subsections which have specifically to be interpreted in the present case must not be construed in isolation, but in the context of the other provisions of section 25 and their historical context, and indeed in the context of the Constitution as a whole. Subsections (4) to (9) all, in one way or another, underline the need for and aim at redressing one of the most enduring legacies of racial discrimination in the past, namely the grossly unequal distribution of land in South Africa. The details of these provisions are not directly relevant to the present case, but ought to be borne in mind whenever section 25 is being construed, because they emphasise that under the 1996 Constitution the protection of property as an individual right is not absolute but subject to societal considerations.

[50] The preamble to the Constitution indicates that one of the purposes of its adoption was to establish a society based, not only on "democratic values" and "fundamental human rights" but also on "social justice." Moreover the Bill of Rights places positive obligations on the state in regard to various social and economic rights. Van der Walt (1997) aptly explains the tensions that exists within section 25:

> "[T]he meaning of section 25 has to be determined, in each specific case, within an interpretative framework that takes due cognisance of the inevitable tensions which characterize the operation of the property clause. This tension between individual rights and social responsibilities has to be the guiding principle in terms of which the section is analysed, interpreted and applied in every individual case."

The purpose of section 25 has to be seen both as protecting existing private property rights as well as serving the public interest, mainly in the sphere of land reform but not limited thereto, and also as striking a proportionate balance between these two functions.

. . . .

The approach to deprivation in the context of section 25

[57] The term "deprive" or "deprivation" is, as Van der Walt (1997) points out, somewhat misleading or confusing because it can create the wrong impression that it invariably refers to the taking away of property, whereas in fact

> "the term 'deprivation' is distinguished very clearly from the narrower term 'expropriation' in constitutional jurisprudence worldwide."

In a certain sense any interference with the use, enjoyment or exploitation of private property involves some deprivation in respect of the person having title or right to or in the property concerned. If section 25 is applied to this wide *genus* of interference, "deprivation" would encompass all species thereof and "expropriation" would apply only to a narrower species of interference. Chaskalson and Lewis, using a slightly different idiom and dealing with both the interim and 1996 Constitutions, put it equally correctly thus:

"Expropriations are treated as a subset of deprivations. There are certain requirements for the validity of all deprivations."

[58] Viewed from this perspective section 25(1) deals with all "property" and all deprivations (including expropriations). If the deprivation infringes (limits) section 25(1) and cannot be justified under section 36 that is the end of the matter. The provision is unconstitutional.

[59] If, however, the deprivation passes scrutiny under section 25(1) (i.e. it does not infringe section 25(1) or, if it does, is a justified limitation) then the question arises as to whether it is an expropriation. If the deprivation amounts to an expropriation then it must pass scrutiny under section 25(2)(a) and make provision for compensation under section 25(2)(b). Various writers, when dealing with the interrelation between deprivations and expropriations under section 25 refer to pre-constitutional judgments on expropriation. This must always be done circumspectly, because such judgments are not necessarily reliable when it comes to interpreting the property clauses under the interim and 1996 Constitutions.

[60] The starting point for constitutional analysis, when considering any challenge under section 25 for the infringement of property rights, must be section 25(1).

The meaning of "arbitrary" in section 25

Introduction

[61] Dispossessing an owner of all rights, use and benefit to and of corporeal movable goods, is a prime example of deprivation in both its grammatical and contextual sense. The infringement issue in relation to section 25(1) is thus really limited to determining whether the deprivation of property enacted by section 114 is "arbitrary," within the meaning of that concept as employed in section 25(1) of the Constitution, because section 114 clearly constitutes a law of general application.

[62] The word "arbitrary," depending on its statutory context, may only impose a low level of judicial scrutiny, requiring nothing more than the absence of bias or bad faith to satisfy such scrutiny. For example, it has been held to mean "capricious or proceeding merely from the will and not based on reason or principle."

[63] But context is all-important; as Lord Steyn observed in *R v Secretary of State for the Home Department, ex parte Daly*:

"The differences in approach between the traditional grounds of review and the proportionality approach may therefore sometimes yield different results . . . This does not mean that there has been a shift to merits review. On the contrary . . . the respective roles of judges and administrators are fundamentally distinct and will remain so . . . Laws LJ (at 847 (para 18)) rightly emphasised in *Mahmood's case* [*R (Mahmood) v Secretary of State for the Home Dept* [2001] 1 WLR 840] 'that the intensity of review in a public law case will depend on the subject matter in hand'. That is so even in a case involving convention rights. In the law context is everything." (Emphasis supplied.)

Context is crucial, both in the sense that the concept "arbitrary" appears in a constitution, and in the sense that it must be construed as part of a comprehensive and coherent Bill of Rights in a comprehensive and coherent constitution. This is certainly all part of the context.

[64] Yet context goes further and would include the particular international jurisprudential context in which the Constitution came into existence and presently functions. Section 39(1) of the Constitution provides that a court, when interpreting the Bill of Rights, "must consider international law" and "may consider foreign law." At the same time one should never lose sight of the historical context in which the property clause came into existence. The background is one of conquest, as a consequence of which there was a taking of land in circumstances which, to this day, are a source of pain and tension. As already mentioned, the purpose of section 25 is not merely to protect private property but also to advance the public interest in relation to property. Thus it is necessary not only to have regard to foreign law, but also to the peculiar circumstances of our own history and the provisions of our Constitution. In the present case all this would be relevant to determining what purpose the word "arbitrary" was intended to serve in a Constitution which has established a constitutional state and in a provision therein dealing with the protection of property against deprivation by the state. It must be construed in a manner that is appropriate to determining whether the section 25(1) protection of property against deprivation for which no compensation is payable has been infringed (limited).

. . . .

[66] In its context "arbitrary," as used in section 25, is not limited to non-rational deprivations, in the sense of there being no rational connection between means and ends. It refers to a wider concept and a broader controlling principle that is more demanding than an enquiry into mere rationality. At the same time it is a narrower and less intrusive concept than that of the proportionality evaluation required by the limitation provisions of section 36. This is so because the standard set in section 36 is "reasonableness" and "justifiability," whilst the standard set in section 25 is "arbitrariness." This distinction must be kept in mind when interpreting and applying the two sections.

[67] It is important in every case in which section 25(1) is in issue to have regard to the legislative context *to which* the prohibition against "arbitrary" deprivation has to be applied; and also to the nature and extent of the deprivation. In certain circumstances the legislative deprivation might be such that no more than a rational connection between means and ends would be required, while in others the ends would have to be more compelling to prevent the deprivation from being arbitrary.

[68] De Waal et al are of the view that a deprivation "is arbitrary" for purposes of section 25(1) "if it follows unfair procedures, if it is irrational, or is for no good reason." The protection against unfair procedure has particular relevance to administrative action — which protection is provided for under section 33 of the Constitution — but it could also apply to legislation and be relevant to determining whether, in the light of any procedure prescribed, the deprivation is arbitrary. Although the learned authors conclude that—

"the substantive element of s 25(1)'s non-arbitrariness requirement probably does not involve a proportionality enquiry,"

their conclusion that deprivation would be arbitrary if it took place "for no good
reason" seems to import a stricter evaluative norm than mere rationality, although
less strict than the proportionality evaluation under section 36.

[69] Chaskalson and Lewis, as well as Budlender, contest the view that "arbitrary"
in section 25(1) of the 1996 Constitution imports anything more than non-rationality
and rely in this regard on this Court's judgment in *Lawrence*. After referring to the
judgment, Chaskalson and Lewis state the following:

"The court stated that legislative measures are arbitrary when they bear no
rational relationship to the legislative goal they are intended to achieve. In
so doing the court equated a 'non-arbitrary' standard of review with the
'rationality review' standard of minimal scrutiny in United States equality
law. It emphasized that the prohibition against arbitrariness did not involve
a proportionality enquiry between means and ends, but only a rationality
enquiry. The proportionality enquiry was excluded in order 'to maintain the
proper balance between the roles of the legislature and the courts': in a
democratic society it is not the function of courts to sit in judgment over the
merits of socio-economic policies of the legislature." (Footnotes omitted.)

In this passage the learned authors seek to extrapolate the dicta in *Lawrence* and
raise them to a level of generality in a manner not warranted by the constitutional
context in which *Lawrence* was decided.

[70] The *Lawrence* case was concerned with certain provisions of the Liquor Act 27
of 1989 that restricted trading in wine under a grocer's wine licence. The
constitutionality of the provisions was challenged, amongst others, on the grounds
that they infringed the right to free economic activity as guaranteed by section 26
of the interim Constitution. The case was not concerned with the meaning of
"arbitrary." That word did not appear in section 26, or in the Liquor Act. What was
an issue in *Lawrence*'s case was the meaning to be given to a proviso to section 26
that excluded certain measures from the protection given by section 26 (1) to free
economic activity if they were "justifiable in an open and democratic society based
on freedom and equality." Chaskalson P held that, in the context of section 26,
measures that were arbitrary would be inconsistent with "values which underlie an
open and democratic society based on freedom and equality" and would not pass
constitutional scrutiny. The judgment went on to hold that if a broad meaning were
to be given to the right to engage freely in economic activity under section 26(1), an
equally broad meaning would have to be given to the power of the State to pass
measures restricting economic activity under section 26(2). In that context, it was
held that the provisions of section 26(2) would be met by measures embodying a
rational relationship between means and ends. Absent such relationship, the
measure would be arbitrary and would not pass constitutional scrutiny. That
decision provides no authority for the manner in which "arbitrary" should be
construed in the context of the property provisions of section 25 of the Constitution.

. . . .

The conclusion reached on the meaning of arbitrary in section 25

[100] Having regard to what has gone before, it is concluded that a deprivation of property is "arbitrary" as meant by section 25 when the "law" referred to in section 25(1) does not provide sufficient reason for the particular deprivation in question or is procedurally unfair. Sufficient reason is to be established as follows:

(a) It is to be determined by evaluating the relationship between means employed, namely the deprivation in question, and ends sought to be achieved, namely the purpose of the law in question.

(b) A complexity of relationships has to be considered.

(c) In evaluating the deprivation in question, regard must be had to the relationship between the purpose for the deprivation and the person whose property is affected.

(d) In addition, regard must be had to the relationship between the purpose of the deprivation and the nature of the property as well as the extent of the deprivation in respect of such property.

(e) Generally speaking, where the property in question is ownership of land or a corporeal moveable, a more compelling purpose will have to be established in order for the depriving law to constitute sufficient reason for the deprivation, than in the case when the property is something different, and the property right something less extensive. This judgment is not concerned at all with incorporeal property.

(f) Generally speaking, when the deprivation in question embraces all the incidents of ownership, the purpose for the deprivation will have to be more compelling than when the deprivation embraces only some incidents of ownership and those incidents only partially.

(g) Depending on such interplay between variable means and ends, the nature of the property in question and the extent of its deprivation, there may be circumstances when sufficient reason is established by, in effect, no more than a mere rational relationship between means and ends; in others this might only be established by a proportionality evaluation closer to that required by section 36(1) of the Constitution.

(h) Whether there is sufficient reason to warrant the deprivation is a matter to be decided on all the relevant facts of each particular case, always bearing in mind that the enquiry is concerned with "arbitrary" in relation to the deprivation of property under section 25.

"Arbitrary" deprivation as applied to section 114 of the Act

[101] The present case is distinguishable from the Australian decisions in *Lawler* and *Airservices Australia*, ... In *Lawler*, factors such as the following were taken into account in holding the forfeiture of the commercial fishing boat to be valid: the protection of the fishing grounds of the nation from foreign exploitation; that this was akin to the protection of the country from smuggling; drastic action in protection of the country's interests was warranted if not expected; the difficulty of enforcing provisions against foreign owners; the difficulty of enforcing compliance

along the length of the Australian coastline called for a stern deterrent; the likelihood of the deliberate intrusion of the foreign boat for purposes of fishing into the declared fishing zone without the complicity of the owner of the boat being small; that the liability to forfeiture enlists the innocent owner's participation in ensuring the observance of the law and precludes the future use of the confiscated vessel in the commission of crime; "in weighing the proportionality of Parliament's response in this particular field the utility of deterrent measures is of paramount importance."

[102] In *Airservices Australia* the considerations that weighed with the Court in upholding the statutory liens can be gleaned from the following passages in the judgment:

> "Aircraft operators, who may incur liability for charges and penalties, may have few assets within a particular jurisdiction at any time except aircraft, and aircraft may leave the jurisdiction very quickly . . . . [C]harges in large sums can accumulate in a short time. The charges are for services related to the safety of aircraft, and those with a proprietary interest, as well as the operators, receive a benefit from those services. They are in some respect akin to necessaries supplied to a ship. The regulatory regimes . . . are likely to be widely known to owners of aircraft . . . ;"

> . . . .

> "[the owners knew] that such aircraft would be flown on routes to, from and within Australia, attracting charges for services and facilities provided to all airline operators.

> . . . [I]t would have been open to [the owners] to protect themselves (by contract, insurance, or facilities for auditing and reporting) against the kind of result that ensued."

> . . . .

> "While there is no 'illegality' in this case . . . the owners and lessors of an aircraft, like the owners of the ship in *Lawler*, cannot be regarded as third parties who have no rational connection with the achievement of the purpose sought to be achieved by the impugned provision."

[103] The Australian High Court judgment in *Burton v Honan*, on which reliance was placed on the Commissioner's behalf both in the High Court and in this Court, is likewise distinguishable. It concerned an imported motor car that was seized in the hands of a purchaser in good faith as goods forfeited to the Crown pursuant to section 229 of the *Customs Act* 1901-1950. The person importing the car had been convicted of the offence of having unlawfully imported the car and under section 229 this resulted in the car in question being forfeited to the Crown. In regard to such forfeiture, section 262 provided that it would have effect as condemnation of the car. The High Court in effect held that such forfeiture and condemnation did not constitute an acquisition under section 51(xxxi) of the Constitution, for which "just terms" would have been necessary, but a valid deprivation under the *Customs Act*. In this regard Dixon CJ said the following:

"It is nothing but forfeiture imposed on all persons in derogation of any rights such persons might otherwise have in relation to the goods, a forfeiture imposed as part of the incidental powers for the purposes of vindicating the Customs laws. It has no more to do with the acquisition of property for a purpose in respect of which the Parliament has power to make laws within s. 51 (xxxi.) than has the imposition of taxation itself, or the forfeiture of goods in the hands of the actual offender."

[104] Dealing with an argument relating to the inequity of the forfeiture in relation to the purchaser in good faith, Dixon CJ said the following:

"In the administration of the judicial power in relation to the Constitution there are points at which matters of degree seem sometimes to bring forth arguments in relation to justice, fairness, morality and propriety, but those are not matters for the judiciary to decide upon. The reason why this appears to be so is simply because a reasonable connection between the law which is challenged and the subject of the power under which the legislature purported to enact it must be shown before the law can be sustained under the incidental power."

What appears to have constituted the "reasonable connection" in that case was that—

". . . the history of English and Australian Customs legislation forfeiture provisions are common, drastic and far-reaching, and that they have been considered a necessary measure to vindicate the right of the Crown and to ensure the strict and complete observance of the Customs laws, which are notoriously difficult of complete enforcement in the absence of strong provisions supporting their administration."

[105] In the present case we are not dealing with the forfeiture of property in the hands of those who have committed offences or assisted in the commission of offences, whether customs or other offences, nor with imported property that has been declared forfeited. In the present case we are also not concerned with property that has been unlawfully smuggled into the country or in respect whereof an offence has been committed in the course of importation, nor where imported property is for such or any other similar reason subject to forfeiture in the hands of third parties. It deals exclusively with the recovery of a customs debt.

[The SACC distinguished a European Court precedent involving a challenge to a Dutch tax statute. That case, the Court noted, approved the seizing of a concrete mixer on the debtor's premises, regarding the interest retained by the company that sold the mixer to debtor as something different from "true" or "ordinary" property; in that case, the European Court found it "apparent that whoever sells goods subject to retention of title is not interested so much in maintaining the link of ownership with the goods themselves as in receiving the purchase price."]

The motor vehicles in the present case did not serve as "furnishings" and there is no evidence to suggest that FNB, by placing the respective customs debtors in possession thereof, induced any belief in the Commissioner which could in any way have been to the latter's detriment, either at the time of the debtors importing the goods in respect whereof they owe the duty or subsequently. For these reasons, the

Gasus case is also distinguishable from the present and, in any event, one is constrained to disagree with the conclusions reached if they are sought to be applied under the South African Constitution.

[108] Here the end sought to be achieved by the deprivation is to exact payment of a customs debt. This is a legitimate and important legislative purpose, essential for the financial well-being of the country and in the interest of all its inhabitants. Section 114, however, casts the net far too wide. The means it uses sanctions the total deprivation of a person's property under circumstances where (a) such *person* has no connection with the *transaction* giving rise to the customs debt; (b) where such *property* also has no connection with the *customs debt*; and (c) where such person has not transacted with or placed the customs debtor in possession of the property under circumstances that have induced the Commissioner to act to her detriment in relation to the incurring of the customs debt.

[109] In the absence of any such relevant nexus, no sufficient reason exists for section 114 to deprive persons other than the customs debtor of their goods. Such deprivation is accordingly arbitrary for purpose of section 25(1) and consequently a limitation (infringement) of such persons' rights.

. . . .

The appropriate relief:

[114] On the basis of the above conclusion regarding FNB's property attack, it is impossible textually to sever the good from the bad in section 114 of the Act without embarking on an extensive redrafting of the section, an action which would impermissibly trespass on the terrain of the legislature and be inappropriate in the present case. Considering only the successful property attack, the appropriate remedy would be an order declaring the provisions of section 114 to be constitutionally invalid to the extent that they provide that the goods of persons other than the customs debtor referred to in the section are subject to a lien, detention and sale; an order analogous to the order made in *Ferreira v Levin*. I would stress that, because of the expansive wording of section 114 and for the reasons mentioned, it is not possible to tailor a narrower order of constitutional invalidity. This must not be taken to imply that there may not be circumstances when the nexus between the third party and the customs debtor, or that between the goods of the third party and the customs debtor or that between the goods of the third party and the customs debt is such that the detention and sale of such goods would pass constitutional muster. There may well be such situations and it may be possible to craft a statutory provision which would limit the detention and sale of the goods of third parties to such circumstances. But that is a task for the legislature and not for this Court.

As Gregory Alexander notes, *Global Debate, supra*, at 170, the step-wise approach to s. 25 announced in *FNB* likely precludes the requirement of compensation that was ordered in *Pennsylvania Coal* when regulation went, in the opinion of the justices, "too far." Under *FNB*, a government act that arbitrarily deprives a person of their property will require compensation, but government regulation that does not arbitrarily deprive a person of property will be valid. Frank Michelman has written that the *FNB* case in South Africa has "[f]rom a US observers standpoint" the effect of depriving "South Africa forever of the possible development of a body of law paralleling that which in the US is known as the doctrine of 'regulatory taking' (and elsewhere is sometimes called 'constructive expropriation')." *See Against Regulatory Taking: In Defense of the Two-stage Inquiry — A Reply to Theunis Roux, in* CONSTITUTIONAL CONVERSATIONS (Stu Woolman & Michael Bishop, eds., 2008).

6.7.   CONCLUDING NOTE ON THE RELATIONSHIP BETWEEN COMMON LAW RECOGNITION OF PROPERTY RIGHTS AND CONSTITUTIONAL PROTECTION

As noted earlier, one of the principal reasons for the Canadian unwillingness to constitutionalize a right to property is the perceived difficulty in distinguishing property rights from other economic rights that Canadians do not want to protect from government regulation. This difficulty could be significantly ameliorated if the right to property were fixed and unchanging. If this were so, the boundaries of the constitutional right would be clear, and government regulation of economic interests that were not within these boundaries could proceed unfettered. But it isn't. As Dean John Cribbet noted in *Concepts in Transition: The Search for a New Definition of Property*, 1989 U. of Ill. L. Rev. 1, "the meaning of the chameleon-like word property constantly changes in time and space."

Cribbet concludes that even with a takings clause it is "still incorrect to say that the judiciary protects property. Rather, the judiciary calls property that which they protect, and that which they protect is forever in transition." *Id.* at 41. As a leading South African scholar has observed, "property is intrinsically created by and therefore open to further democratic redefinition and regulation." Andre van der Walt, *The Constitutional Property Clause: Striking a Balance Between a Guarantee and a Limitation, in* PROPERTY AND THE CONSTITUTION 128 (Janel McLean ed., 1999). The process of defining the right to property is particularly difficult in the United States. The constitutional right is a federal one, determined ultimately by the U.S. Supreme Court. But property rights are generally defined by states (originally under the common law, often today by statute). As the common law right to property evolves, whether the state is "taking" property rights gets very murky.

This is because of the U.S. Supreme Court's focus on "background principles of the State's law of property and nuisance" that may burden property, first articulated in the following case (also useful for comparative analysis because of its factual similarity to the *Mariner Realty* case in Canada). The case involved a landowner who purchased two residential lots on a South Carolina barrier island, intending to build single-family homes such as those on the immediately adjacent parcels. Subsequent to the purchase, the state legislature enacted the *Beachfront Management Act*, which barred the landowner from erecting any permanent habitable structures on his parcels. He filed suit, claiming that, even though the Act may have been a lawful exercise of the State's police power, the ban on construction deprived him of all "economically viable use" of his property and therefore effected a "taking" under the Fifth and Fourteenth Amendments that required the payment of just compensation. As summarized in the *Lingle* case in section 6.2.3, *supra*, the Supreme Court accepted the state trial court's finding that the ban rendered Lucas's parcels "valueless," upheld an award exceeding $1.2 million because compensation was categorically required for any regulation that deprived the landowner of any economic value in the land. Note that many have suggested that these findings were in error and that Lucas' retained significant economic value from his land.[20] The excerpt below discusses the relevance of underlying state property law in determining whether land use restrictions constitute takings.

LUCAS v. SOUTH CAROLINA COASTAL COUNCIL
SUPREME COURT OF THE UNITED STATES
505 U.S. 1003 (1992)

JUSTICE SCALIA delivered the opinion of the Court.

. . . .

III

A

Prior to Justice Holmes's exposition in *Pennsylvania Coal Co. v. Mahon*, 260 U.S. 393, 43 S. Ct. 158, 67 L. Ed. 322 (1922), it was generally thought that the Takings Clause reached only a "direct appropriation" of property, *Legal Tender Cases*, 79 U.S. (12 Wall.) 457, 551, 20 L. Ed. 287 (1871), or the functional equivalent of a "practical ouster of [the owner's] possession," *Transportation Co. v. Chicago*, 99 U.S. 635, 642, 25 L. Ed. 336 (1879). Justice Holmes recognized in *Mahon*, however, that if the protection against physical appropriations of private property was to be meaningfully enforced, the government's power to redefine the range of interests included in the ownership of property was necessarily constrained by constitutional limits. 260 U.S. at 414–415. If, instead, the uses of private property were subject to unbridled, uncompensated qualification under the police power, "the natural tendency of human nature [would be] to extend the qualification more and more until at last private property disappeared." *Id.*, at 415. These considerations gave birth in that case to the oft-cited maxim that, "while property may be regulated to a certain extent, if regulation goes too far it will be recognized as a taking." *Ibid.*

. . . .

---

[20] Indeed, Justice Blackmun dissented on this very ground:

> Petitioner still can enjoy other attributes of ownership, such as the right to exclude others, "one of the most essential sticks in the bundle of rights that are commonly characterized as property." *Kaiser Aetna v. United States*, 444 U.S. 164, 176 (1979). Petitioner can picnic, swim, camp in a tent, or live on the property in a movable trailer. State courts frequently have recognized that land has economic value where the only residual economic uses are recreation or camping. Petitioner also retains the right to alienate the land, which would have value for neighbors and for those prepared to enjoy proximity to the ocean without a house.

B

[The majority rejected the South Carolina Supreme Court's effort to preclude compensation by affirming the legislature's finding that Lucas' construction of homes was a noxious use.] If it were, departure would virtually always be allowed. The South Carolina Supreme Court's approach would essentially nullify *Mahon's* affirmation of limits to the noncompensable exercise of the police power. Our cases provide no support for this: None of them that employed the logic of "harmful use" prevention to sustain a regulation involved an allegation that the regulation wholly eliminated the value of the claimant's land.

Where the State seeks to sustain regulation that deprives land of all economically beneficial use, we think it may resist compensation only if the logically antecedent inquiry into the nature of the owner's estate shows that the proscribed use interests were not part of his title to begin with. This accords, we think, with our "takings" jurisprudence, which has traditionally been guided by the understandings of our citizens regarding the content of, and the State's power over, the "bundle of rights" that they acquire when they obtain title to property. It seems to us that the property owner necessarily expects the uses of his property to be restricted, from time to time, by various measures newly enacted by the State in legitimate exercise of its police powers; "as long recognized, some values are enjoyed under an implied limitation and must yield to the police power." *Pennsylvania Coal Co. v. Mahon*, 260 U.S. at 413. And in the case of personal property, by reason of the State's traditionally high degree of control over commercial dealings, he ought to be aware of the possibility that new regulation might even render his property economically worthless (at least if the property's only economically productive use is sale or manufacture for sale). See *Andrus v. Allard*, 444 U.S. 51, 66–67, 100 S. Ct. 318, 62 L. Ed. 2d 210 (1979) (prohibition on sale of eagle feathers). In the case of land, however, we think the notion pressed by the Council that title is somehow held subject to the "implied limitation" that the State may subsequently eliminate all economically valuable use is inconsistent with the historical compact recorded in the Takings Clause that has become part of our constitutional culture.

Where "permanent physical occupation" of land is concerned, we have refused to allow the government to decree it anew (without compensation), no matter how weighty the asserted "public interests" involved [cases omitted]. We believe similar treatment must be accorded confiscatory regulations, *i.e.*, regulations that prohibit all economically beneficial use of land: Any limitation so severe cannot be newly legislated or decreed (without compensation), but must inhere in the title itself, in the restrictions that background principles of the State's law of property and nuisance already place upon land ownership. A law or decree with such an effect must, in other words, do no more than duplicate the result that could have been achieved in the courts — by adjacent landowners (or other uniquely affected persons) under the State's law of private nuisance, or by the State under its complementary power to abate nuisances that affect the public generally, or otherwise.

*   *   *

The "total taking" inquiry we require today will ordinarily entail (as the application of state nuisance law ordinarily entails) analysis of, among other things, the degree of harm to public lands and resources, or adjacent private property, posed by the claimant's proposed activities, see, *e.g.*, Restatement (Second) of Torts §§ 826, 827, the social value of the claimant's activities and their suitability to the locality in question, see, *e.g.*, *id.*, §§ 828(a) and (b), 831, and the relative ease with which the alleged harm can be avoided through measures taken by the claimant and the government (or adjacent private landowners) alike, see, *e.g.*, *id.*, §§ 827(e), 828(c), 830. The fact that a particular use has long been engaged in by similarly situated owners ordinarily imports a lack of any common-law prohibition (though changed circumstances or new knowledge may make what was previously permissible no longer so, see *id.*, § 827, Comment *g.* So also does the fact that other landowners, similarly situated, are permitted to continue the use denied to the claimant.

It seems unlikely that common-law principles would have prevented the erection of any habitable or productive improvements on petitioner's land; they rarely support prohibition of the "essential use" of land, *Curtin v. Benson*, 222 U.S. 78, 86, 32 S. Ct. 31, 56 L. Ed. 102 (1911). The question, however, is one of state law to be dealt with on remand. We emphasize that to win its case South Carolina must do more than proffer the legislature's declaration that the uses Lucas desires are inconsistent with the public interest, or the conclusory assertion that they violate a common-law maxim such as *sic utere tuo ut alienum non laedas.* As we have said, a "State, by *ipse dixit*, may not transform private property into public property without compensation . . . ." *Webb's Fabulous Pharmacies, Inc. v. Beckwith*, 449 U.S. 155, 164, 101 S. Ct. 446, 66 L. Ed. 2d 358 (1980). Instead, as it would be required to do if it sought to restrain Lucas in a common-law action for public nuisance, South Carolina must identify background principles of nuisance and property law that prohibit the uses he now intends in the circumstances in which the property is presently found. Only on this showing can the State fairly claim that, in proscribing all such beneficial uses, the Beachfront Management Act is taking nothing.

JUSTICE KENNEDY, concurring in the judgment. [Opinion omitted.]

JUSTICE BLACKMUN, dissenting.

. . . .

Ultimately even the Court cannot embrace the full implications of its *per se* rule: It eventually agrees that there cannot be a categorical rule for a taking based on economic value that wholly disregards the public need asserted. Instead, the Court decides that it will permit a State to regulate all economic value only if the State prohibits uses that would not be permitted under "background principles of nuisance and property law."[21]

---

[21] [FN 15] Although it refers to state nuisance and property law, the Court apparently does not mean just any state nuisance and property law. Public nuisance was first a common-law creation, see Newark, The Boundaries of Nuisance, 65 L. Q. Rev. 480, 482 (1949) (attributing development of nuisance to 1535), but by the 1800's in both the United States and England, legislatures had the power to define what is a

Until today, the Court explicitly had rejected the contention that the government's power to act without paying compensation turns on whether the prohibited activity is a common-law nuisance.[22] The brewery closed in *Mugler* itself was not a common-law nuisance, and the Court specifically stated that it was the role of the legislature to determine what measures would be appropriate for the protection of public health and safety. See 123 U.S. at 661. ***

*   *   *

Even more perplexing, however, is the Court's reliance on common-law principles of nuisance in its quest for a valuefree takings jurisprudence. In determining what is a nuisance at common law, state courts make exactly the decision that the Court finds so troubling when made by the South Carolina General Assembly today: They determine whether the use is harmful. Common-law public and private nuisance law is simply a determination whether a particular use causes harm. See Prosser, Private Action for Public Nuisance, 52 Va. L. Rev. 997 (1966) ("*Nuisance* is a French word which means nothing more than harm"). There is nothing magical in the reasoning of judges long dead. They determined a harm in the same way as state judges and legislatures do today. If judges in the 18th and 19th centuries can distinguish a harm from a benefit, why not judges in the 20th century, and if judges can, why not legislators? There simply is no reason to believe that new interpretations of the hoary common-law nuisance doctrine will be particularly "objective" or "value free." ***

*   *   *

JUSTICE STEVENS, dissenting.

*   *   *

The Court's holding today effectively freezes the State's common law, denying the legislature much of its traditional power to revise the law governing the rights and uses of property. Until today, I had thought that we had long abandoned this approach to constitutional law. More than a century ago we recognized that "the great office of statutes is to remedy defects in the common law as they are developed, and to adapt it to the changes of time and circumstances." *Munn v. Illinois*, 94 U.S. 113, 134, 24 L. Ed. 77 (1877). As Justice Marshall observed about a position similar to that adopted by the Court today:

---

public nuisance, and particular uses often have been selectively targeted. See Prosser, Private Action for Public Nuisance, 52 Va. L. Rev. 997, 999–1000 (1966); J. Stephen, A General View of the Criminal Law of England 105–107 (2d ed. 1890). The Court's references to "common-law" background principles, however, indicate that legislative determinations do not constitute "state nuisance and property law" for the Court.

[22] [FN 16] Also, until today the fact that the regulation prohibited uses that were lawful at the time the owner purchased did not determine the constitutional question. The brewery, the brickyard, the cedar trees, and the gravel pit were all perfectly legitimate uses prior to the passage of the regulation. See *Mugler v. Kansas*, 123 U.S. at 654; *Hadacheck v. Sebastian*, 239 U.S. 394, 36 S. Ct. 143, 60 L. Ed. 348 (1915); *Miller*, 276 U.S. at 272; *Goldblatt v. Hempstead*, 369 U.S. 590, 82 S. Ct. 987, 8 L. Ed. 2d 130 (1962). This Court explicitly acknowledged in *Hadacheck* that "[a] vested interest cannot be asserted against [the police power] because of conditions once obtaining. To so hold would preclude development and fix a city forever in its primitive conditions." 239 U.S. at 410 (citation omitted).

"If accepted, that claim would represent a return to the era of *Lochner v. New York*, 198 U.S. 45, 25 S. Ct. 539, 49 L. Ed. 937 (1905), when common-law rights were also found immune from revision by State or Federal Government. Such an approach would freeze the common law as it has been constructed by the courts, perhaps at its 19th-century state of development. It would allow no room for change in response to changes in circumstance. The Due Process Clause does not require such a result." *PruneYard Shopping Center v. Robins*, 447 U.S. 74, 93, 100 S. Ct. 2035, 64 L. Ed. 2d 741 (1980) (concurring opinion).

Arresting the development of the common law is not only a departure from our prior decisions; it is also profoundly unwise. The human condition is one of constant learning and evolution — both moral and practical. Legislatures implement that new learning; in doing so they must often revise the definition of property and the rights of property owners. Thus, when the Nation came to understand that slavery was morally wrong and mandated the emancipation of all slaves, it, in effect, redefined "property." On a lesser scale, our ongoing self-education produces similar changes in the rights of property owners: New appreciation of the significance of endangered species, see, *e. g., Andrus v. Allard*, 444 U.S. 51, 100 S. Ct. 318, 62 L. Ed. 2d 210 (1979); the importance of wetlands, see, *e. g.*, 16 U.S.C. § 3801 *et seq.*; and the vulnerability of coastal lands, see, *e. g.*, 16 U.S.C. § 1451 *et seq.*, shapes our evolving understandings of property rights.

* * *

The Just Compensation Clause "was designed to bar Government from forcing some people alone to bear public burdens which, in all fairness and justice, should be borne by the public as a whole." *Armstrong*, 364 U.S. at 49. Accordingly, one of the central concerns of our takings jurisprudence is "preventing the public from loading upon one individual more than his just share of the burdens of government." *Monongahela Navigation Co. v. United States*, 148 U.S. 312, 325 (1893). We have, therefore, in our takings law frequently looked to the *generality* of a regulation of property.[23]

[Thus, Stevens, J. agreed that so-called "developmental exactions" require close scrutiny because of "the risk that particular landowners might 'be singled out to bear the burden' of a broader problem not of his own making." Likewise, a diminution in value caused by a zoning regulation is far less likely to constitute a taking if it is part of a general and comprehensive land-use plan, while "spot zoning" is far more likely to constitute a taking.]

---

[23] [FN 7] This principle of generality is well rooted in our broader understandings of the Constitution as designed in part to control the "mischiefs of faction." *See* The Federalist No. 10, at 43 (G. Wills ed. 1982) (J. Madison).

An analogous concern arises in First Amendment law. There we have recognized that an individual's rights are not violated when his religious practices are prohibited under a neutral law of general applicability. ***

If such a neutral law of general applicability may severely burden constitutionally protected interests in liberty, a comparable burden on property owners should not be considered unreasonably onerous.

Statement of JUSTICE SOUTER [omitted]

———

See also Stop the Beach Renourishment, Inc. v. Florida Dep't of Environmental Protection, 560 U.S. 702 (2010) (applying *Lucas* to deny compensation for ocean-front landowners when tidal changes added additional land between their property line and the high-tide line, because under common law of property such land was the state's, not theirs).

In important respects, then, *Lucas* can be read to effectively constitutionalize the common law of property in the United States, and to possibly limit the common law's ability to regulate land use to traditional concepts of nuisance. This aspect has provoked a sharp critique:

> In *Lucas* the Supreme Court held firm to the distinction between common law ownership and the statutory rules of the ecological age, as if one were static, neutral, and sound, the other shifting, political, and suspect. With the golden age of the common law long passed, this reasoning rings hollow. Back when courts kept ownership norms up to date, the common law embodied the community's values and aims. In an age when governing power has drifted from courts to regulatory agencies, from states to the federal level, the common law no longer reflects current thinking on right and wrong land use. The latest thinking - indeed, the accumulated wisdom of much of the last century - now resides elsewhere. It is simply not possible to discern the "understanding" of citizens, as *Lucas* would have us do, without paying heed to these positive lawmaking efforts. Only by ignoring statutory law, federal law, and the entire "public" legal realm can one embrace the severely flawed notion that land ownership today means the right to engage in any land use that is not a common law nuisance.

Eric T. Freyfogle, *The Owning and Taking of Sensitive Lands*, 43 U.C.L.A. L. REV. 77, 123–24 (1995).

In this regard, consider one venerable and two recent cases. In *Palmer v. Mulligan*, 3 Cai. R. 307 (N.Y. Sup. Ct. 1805), the court refused to apply traditional concepts of riparian water rights, which barred any use of water that caused any harm to upstream or downstream owners. In permitting the defendant to construct a mill in competition with the plaintiff's mill, the court reasoned, in part, that sound public policy in favor of competition counseled against a rule of law that limited another mill on the river. The traditional rule may have well-fitted life in 17th century England, when low levels of economic activity made land use conflicts rare. With intensive uses accompanying industrialization, the common law evolved. *See generally* ERIC T. FREYFOGLE, THE LAND WE SHARE: PRIVATE PROPERTY AND THE COMMON GOOD 66–70 (2003). State courts have reached conflicting opinions as to whether legislation can protect modern economic activity from traditional nuisance suits. *Compare Bormann v. Bd. of Supervisors*, 584 N.W.2d 309 (Iowa 1998) (because under the Restatement of Property the ability to engage in harmful activity constitutes an easement on the property of the affected owner, compensation required), *with Moon v. N. Idaho Farmers Ass'n*, 96 P.3d 637 (Idaho 2004) (nuisance a creature of state law and subject to legislative re-definition without compensation).

This problem would not arise in Australia because the High Court of Australia is a general court of appeal, as well as a constitutional court. *See, e.g., ICM Agriculture Pty Ltd v. Cth*, (2009) 240 CLR 140 (federally-subsidized state legislation reducing water that can be taken from aquifers not an acquisition requiring compensation because the state always had the power to limit the volume of water to be taken from a natural resource). Because regulation of property is (with some limited exceptions) a state concern in Australia, and states are not subject to the just terms requirements of s 51(xxxi), the states would not be subject to mandatory compensation arising from the common law, if the Court had held otherwise. Individual state legislation could, however, override the common law in the state's own jurisdiction, and, as we saw with *Durham Holdings* would stand, unaffected by the common law or the Commonwealth Constitution. In South Africa all governmental action affecting property is subject to the Constitution while the law of property is defined by both the common law of South Africa, which in the case of property is rooted in Roman-Dutch law, as well as indigenous law, both recognized as equally valid sources of law by the Constitution.

Chapter 7

UNITARY AND DUAL COURT SYSTEMS AND THE ROLE OF CONSTITUTIONAL VALUES IN PRIVATE LITIGATION

KEY CONCEPTS FOR THE CHAPTER

- CONSTITUTIONAL VALUES PLAY A ROLE IN PRIVATE AS WELL AS PUBLIC LITIGATION, BUT THE DOCTRINES DIFFER IN SIGNIFICANT DEGREE BECAUSE OF THE ORGANIZATION OF EACH COUNTRY'S JUDICIARY:

  — THE U.S. SUPREME COURT CAN ONLY DETERMINE FEDERAL CONSTITUTIONAL AND STATUTORY ISSUES, WHILE THE SUPREME COURT OF CANADA AND THE HIGH COURT OF AUSTRALIA ARE GENERAL COURTS OF APPEAL COMPETENT TO HEAR APPEALS FROM LOWER COURTS.

  — MOST COMMON LAW SUITS IN THE UNITED STATES ARE FILED IN STATE COURTS OF GENERAL JURISDICTION, IN MANY CASES BEFORE ELECTED JUDGES; COMMON LAW SUITS IN CANADA MUST BE FILED IN COURTS OF GENERAL JURISDICTION BEFORE FEDERALLY-APPOINTED JUDGES WITH LIFE TENURE; WHILE AUSTRALIAN STATE COURTS ARE OF GENERAL JURISDICTIONS, THEIR JUDGMENTS CAN BE APPEALED TO THE HIGH COURT.

  — THE SOUTH AFRICAN CONSTITUTION EXPLICITLY PROVIDES THAT THE BILL OF RIGHTS APPLIES NOT ONLY TO THE STATE BUT ALSO TO NATURAL OR JURISTIC PERSONS TO THE EXTENT APPLICABLE, TAKING INTO ACCOUNT THE NATURE OF THE RIGHT AND ANY DUTY IMPOSED BY THE RIGHT. IN THE SAME VEIN THE COURTS ARE EMPOWERED TO DEVELOP THE COMMON LAW IN ORDER TO GIVE EFFECT TO THE RIGHT IN THE ABSENCE OF APPLICABLE STATUTORY LAW OR SUITABLE COMMON LAW RULE.

7.1. ORGANIZATION OF THE JUDICIARY

One of the significant structural differences in the administration of law in the United States and Canada concerns the organization of the judiciary. As with other matters, the formal differences can't be fully appreciated without understanding the informal customary practices as well.

7.1.1. United States

The American system features a dual judicial structure. Each state has its own judicial system, usually including inferior courts of limited jurisdiction, superior courts of general jurisdiction, an intermediate appellate court in all but the smallest states, and a supreme court of the state. The powers and authority of state courts are entirely governed by state law, except for the provision in the U.S. Constitution that "the Judges in every State shall be bound" by the Constitution, Laws, and Treaties of the United States, "any Thing in the Constitution or Laws of any State to the Contrary notwithstanding." Art. VI, § 2. State courts handle most litigation in the United States. Litigation over tort, property, or contract law issues, and most criminal prosecutions, occur in state courts. Recall that, under the Tenth Amendment, states enjoy plenary power to enact laws on any subject, except the few specifically denied to them by Art. I, § 10, and (more significantly today) areas of law where Congress, as part of its authority to regulate interstate commerce, regulate bankruptcy, control immigration, etc. has pre-empted state law.

The federal courts of the United States are all formally courts of limited jurisdiction. The federal structure includes district courts, circuit courts of appeal (the country is divided geographically into 12 circuits), and the U.S. Supreme Court. In addition, Congress has created several courts with special jurisdiction (e.g., trial courts for tax and government claims and an appellate court for tax, government contracts, and patent cases, and a nationwide system of bankruptcy judges). Article III of the U.S. Constitution expressly limits the "judicial power of the United States" to "Cases, in Law and Equity, arising under this Constitution, the Laws of the United States, and Treaties made, or which shall be made, under their Authority," to admiralty and maritime cases, and to other special cases based on the identity of the parties. The latter category includes, most notably, litigation where the United States is a party and cases between citizens of different states (this is called "diversity" jurisdiction).

Because Article III's jurisdictional limitation applies to the U.S. Supreme Court, that court's authority to review decisions by state courts is limited to questions of federal law. In addition, under the doctrine established in *Erie R.R. Co. v. Tompkins*, 304 U.S. 64 (1938), even when federal courts are hearing cases of state law pursuant to their diversity jurisdiction, the federal judge is to follow the state court's interpretation of state law issues. As applied, issues arising under the common law, and non-federal modifications of the common law by statute, are determined by each state. It might be fair to say that there is no "common" law of the United States, but rather 51 common laws.

7.1.2. Canada

Canada has a more unitary judicial structure. At confederation, each of the uniting provinces had its own system of courts modeled on the English judiciary. This included inferior courts of limited geographic or subject matter jurisdiction, a superior court of general jurisdiction, a provincial court of appeal, and final appeal to the Privy Council in London. The *British North America Act* expressly continued these courts, and assigned the matter of the "administration of justice" to each province under s. 92(14). This power enables the provinces to vest their courts with jurisdiction over all cases, which includes litigation over the Constitution, federal law, provincial law, or common law. Of particular comparative significance, s. 101 of the *BNA Act* authorized Parliament to create a Supreme Court of Canada to serve as a "general court of appeal for Canada." Thus, all judgments of the provincial courts of appeal are subject to further appeal to the

Supreme Court of Canada.[1]

Canada does have a federal court structure as well. Section 101 of the *BNA Act* authorized Parliament to create a Supreme Court but "any additional courts for the better administration of the laws of Canada." Parliament has created a Federal Court (consisting of a trial and appellate division) to cover a host of specific matters that are the subject of federal statutes, including tax and government claims, intellectual property, admiralty, citizenship, federal agency administrative review, and certain interprovincial commercial claims and claims regarding certain kinds of commercial paper (per s. 91(18)).

7.1.3. Australia

Australia has both a unified judicial system, with a single common law, and a federal judicial system. State courts are jurisdictionally separate from each other, but are linked at the apex of the system by the High Court which has (discretionary) jurisdiction to hear appeals from state Supreme Courts in all classes of matter, civil and criminal. The High Court also exercises jurisdiction over constitutional questions, applications for writs against an Officer of the Commonwealth, and appeals from other federal courts.[2]

There are three other (lower) federal Courts (state courts are also "vested" with federal jurisdiction): The Federal Court of Australia (established in 1976) has jurisdiction in matters invested by Commonwealth (federal) legislation, including bankruptcy, corporations, patents, industrial relations, taxation and trade practices laws. It is also able to hear applications for writs of mandamus, prohibition and injunction against an Officer of the Commonwealth. Panels of Federal Court judges hear appeals from a single judge of the Federal Court, and in some limited cases from state Supreme Courts, concerning matters coming under its statutory jurisdiction. The Family Court of Australia (established 1975) is a court of specialist jurisdiction, exercising both original and appellate jurisdiction with respect to marriage, divorce, and the custody of children. Its power to hear cases concerning the custody of ex-nuptial children has been conferred upon it under Commonwealth law, by a "referral" of state power to the Commonwealth, under s. 51(xxxvii) of the Constitution. The Federal Magistrates Court (established in 2000) shared jurisdiction with the Federal Court and the Family Court, and heard similar, but less complex, disputes; in 2013 it was renamed the Federal Circuit Court of Australia. Its jurisdiction remains similar, but, as its new name suggests,

---

[1] Many Americans are amazed to learn that panels of the Supreme Court of Canada routinely review judgments from the Quebec Court of Appeals on ordinary questions of civil law. Here, like other matters discussed below in text, formality must be combined with custom to understand what is really going on. These cases are generally assigned to panels of five of the nine justices, which will include all three justices that the *Supreme Court Act* requires be appointed from the Quebec bar. The two non-Quebec justices by custom vote to join the result reached by the majority of the Quebecois justices.

[2] The High Court rarely (if ever, these days) exercises original jurisdiction in civil law matters. Section 75 (iv) of the Constitution confers original jurisdiction on it over matters between (among others) "residents of different States" ("resident" is confined to natural, not corporate persons). This form of "diversity jurisdiction" has little application, however, and the High Court will discourage actions by, among other things, exercising its power, under the *Judiciary Act* 1903, to "remit" any matter coming under its original jurisdiction to a lower Court, to avoid hearing trivial matters.

judges also hear cases in regional locations, relieving the travelling costs of non-urban litigants, and (as its website states) "providing access to justice to the people of Australia."

The states typically have three levels of court: Magistrates Courts, which deal with summary offences and some small civil actions; intermediate courts (known variously as "District" or "County Courts") which conduct most criminal trials and civil litigation up to a certain money limit; and Supreme Courts, which exercise both original and appellate jurisdiction, dealing with the most serious criminal and civil cases, and hearing appeals from lower state Courts. As noted, the Supreme Courts are also vested with federal jurisdiction, and can act as federal courts when federal matters arise. Some states also have specialist courts — for example the Land and Environment Court of NSW.

Common law actions for tortious wrongs on the part of a federal (Commonwealth) Officer(s) would be brought in state courts (vested with federal jurisdiction). Federal Court jurisdiction in tort law only arises where this is conferred under a Commonwealth statute.

7.1.4. South Africa

With the adoption of the "final" Constitution in 1996, the previous provincial Supreme Courts were transformed into High Courts while the former Appellate Division of the Supreme Court has become the Supreme Court of Appeal. The Constitutional Court remains the court of final appeal on constitutional matters and must hear and confirm any decision to strike down an Act of Parliament as unconstitutional. While there has been some suggestion that the Supreme Court of Appeal and the Constitutional Court could be amalgamated into a larger supreme court with different panels to hear civil and criminal appeals as well as constitutional cases, this debate remains unresolved. Parliament passed the Superior Courts Act 10 of 2013 which reorganized the various High Courts into a single High Court of South Africa with divisions established in each of the nine provinces. This involves the creation of two new courts (Limpopo and Mpumalanga Divisions) and the designation of a single High Court with jurisdiction over each Province (the main seat of the Division) with additional High Courts (local seats) in a division having jurisdiction over a restricted area. The new statute also put the administration and financial management of the Courts under a newly expanded office of the Chief Justice.

7.1.5. Who appoints the judges

An understanding of the differences in judicial structure must include an appreciation of the formal and informal practices concerning the appointment of judges. In the United States, federal judges enjoy life tenure after being appointed by the President and confirmed by the Senate. The appointment process is highly political. Increasingly, nominees are appointed and sometimes rejected because of their judicial philosophy. In addition, the President relies heavily on the recommendation of Senators from his party when appointing judges in their states. At the circuit court level, there is a customary allocation of seats to the various states that comprise the circuit (and occasionally a customary allocation within a state's geographic regions). Regional balance has not played a significant role in appointments to the U.S. Supreme Court in recent years.[3] The composition of the state judiciary varies widely, but many judges are elected for a term of years, many running with party labels.

In Canada, all but inferior court judges are appointed by the Governor General. They serve until mandatory retirement at age 75. In reality, this means that they are appointed by the Prime Minister in consultation with the Minister of Justice. By law, three of the nine Supreme Court justices must be from Quebec; by custom, three of the others are allocated to Ontario, and one each to British Columbia, the Maritime provinces (New Brunswick, Nova Scotia, Prince Edward Island, and Newfoundland), and the Prairie (Manitoba, Saskatchewan, and Alberta). Within the latter categories, a weaker custom rotates the seat among the provinces. The Minister of Justice extensively consults with the bar. Although partisanship and politics are not insignificant, there are many occasions where a nominee comes from a different party than the government. (The only real political barrier — which is significant — seems to be the inability to obtain an appointment if one is a Quebec separatist.)

Inferior judges are appointed by each province's Lieutenant Governor (i.e., by the provincial cabinet). Provincial custom varies widely — some require an application and review process where the Attorney General is limited to selecting among a small list of nominees approved by a bar committee, while others feature widespread use of the provincial judiciary for political patronage.

Given their broad power to administer the judiciary, provinces could easily evade the constitutional requirement that judges be federally-appointed by expanding the jurisdiction of provincial courts. The Supreme Court has held, however, that any court that exercises jurisdiction over the sort of cases that have traditionally been exercised by the federally-appointed superior court judges (called "s. 96 courts") must conform to the federal appointment requirements. For example, in *Re B.C. Family Relations Act*, [1982] 1 S.C.R. 62, the Court upheld the assignment of guardianship and custody issues to the provincial court, but rejected provisions also conferring provincial court jurisdiction over occupancy and access to the family residence, which was "more conformable to that exercised and exercisable by a s. 96 court."

In Australia, all Federal (including High Court) judges are appointed by the "Governor-General in Council" (s. 72 of the Constitution) — meaning, appointment on the advice of the executive government (in practice, the Attorney-General). The Constitution mandates a minimum of three Justices on the High Court. Since 1913, there have been seven; currently, four men (including the Chief Justice) and three women sit on the Court. State Court judges are, similarly, appointed by the state Governor, on the advice of the state government.

South Africa's enshrining of constitutional supremacy, as one of the founding principles of the post-apartheid state, fundamentally transformed the legal system.

---

[3] Significant attention was paid to President Reagan's nomination of the first woman justice, Sandra Day O'Connor. Very little attention was paid to the fact that this gave the small state of Arizona two of the nine justices.

The acceptance of constitutional review during the constitution-making process brought attention to the structure and staffing of the superior courts. In order to both overcome the legacy of apartheid — in which the vast majority of superior judges were conservative white males — and in order to bolster the legitimacy of the judiciary and courts, the Constitution created a new Constitutional Court which would be placed above the old Appellate Division of the Supreme Court in decisions concerning the interpretation of the Constitution and constitutional review of national legislation. With the new court came a new system of judicial appointment, including public nomination and interviews by a constitutionally established Judicial Service Commission. As part of the political negotiations it was agreed that four justices had to be drawn from among the existing judiciary while the President of the court would be appointed directly by the Head of State (President Mandela) after consultation with the sitting Chief Justice. After a lengthy appointment process, the first eleven justices took the oath of office at the opening of the Constitutional Court in February 1995.

Appointments to the judicial branch are determined by whether the appointment is to the higher courts (Supreme Courts or now High Courts) or to the lower or magistrates courts. While judges of the various divisions of the former Supreme Court always claimed formal independence — despite their appointment by the government — magistrates were until 1992 members of the civil service and were subject, in their appointment, assignment and promotion, to the authority of the Minister of Justice. Since 1994 all judicial appointments have been subject to processes which bring together different parts of the legal profession and government to select candidates for appointment by either the Minister of Justice (in the case of magistrates) or the President, in the case of judges. Appointment of judicial officers is now provided for in the Constitution: judges of the Constitutional Court are to be appointed by the President from a list submitted by the Judicial Service Commission (JSC), while judges of the Supreme Court of Appeal and the High Courts are to be appointed by the President on the advice of the JSC. Exceptions to this process apply in the case of the President and Deputy President of the Constitutional Court as well as the Chief Justice and Deputy Chief Justice, all of whom are appointed by the President after consultation with the JSC and in the case of the Constitutional Court, with the leaders of political parties represented in the National Assembly as well. In practice, most appointments to the higher courts still come from the ranks of advocates with the addition of a number of legal academics who previously could not be considered.

While the ANC had, prior to the beginning of formal negotiations, called for the apartheid judges to be subjected to individual review to determine their fitness to serve as judicial officers in post-apartheid South Africa, in fact there was no such process and all sitting judicial officers were able to retain their posts in the new order.

7.2. THE CONCEPT OF STATE ACTION

The topic of this Chapter is litigation where a private party seeks to invoke the Constitution either to state a claim or provide a defense in litigation with another party. The question is whether the courts should subject private acts to constitutional restrictions. *See* NOWAK & ROTUNDA § 12.1. As we will see, the Supreme Court of Canada finds no "state action" sufficient to directly invoke the Charter, while on similar facts the U.S. Supreme Court finds state action to exist, and it appears that the High Court of Australia has shifted toward its Canadian sister. However, the basic principles are the same. The Canadian Charter applies only to the legislatures and government of Canada and the provinces (s. 32). The original U.S. Constitution only applied to the federal government, and the 14th Amendment's key protection against deprivations of due process or equal protection are textually limited to deprivations by the states. The High Court of Australia has extended the implied right of political communication to all levels of governments while other individual rights or freedoms guaranteed in the Australian Constitution — with the exception of s. 117 (prohibiting out-of-state residency discrimination) and s. 92 (guaranteeing "absolutely free . . . intercourse," or freedom of movement, among the states) — are expressly confined to the federal government. Thus, each country requires an element of "state action" before courts will recognize constitutional rights.

SHELLEY v. KRAEMER
SUPREME COURT OF THE UNITED STATES
334 U.S. 1 (1948)

[Before VINSON, C.J., and BLACK, DOUGLAS, FRANKFURTER, MURPHY, and BURTON, JJ.]

MR. CHIEF JUSTICE VINSON delivered the opinion of the Court.

These cases present for our consideration questions relating to the validity of court enforcement of private agreements, generally described as restrictive covenants, which have as their purpose the exclusion of persons of designated race or color from the ownership or occupancy of real property. Basic constitutional issues of obvious importance have been raised.

[The opinion is for two cases consolidated for judgment. The first comes to the Court on certiorari to the Supreme Court of Missouri. In 1911, thirty out of a total of thirty-nine owners of property fronting both sides of Labadie Avenue between Taylor Avenue and Cora Avenue in the city of St. Louis, signed an agreement, which was subsequently recorded, restricting the use and occupancy of the properties to exclude persons "not of the Caucasian race." Shelley, an African American, received a warranty deed to a parcel subject to the restriction. Kraemer and others brought suit in Missouri state court to restrain Shelley from taking possession for the property, divesting Shelley's title, and revesting it in the immediate grantor or another party. The trial court denied the requested relief on the ground that the restrictive agreement, upon which respondents based their action, had never become final and complete because it was the intention of the parties to that agreement that it was not to become effective until signed by all property owners in the district, and signatures of all the owners had never been obtained. The Supreme Court of Missouri sitting en banc reversed and directed the trial court to grant the relief for which respondents had prayed. That court rejected the trial judge's conclusion about the intent of the parties. The court noted that covenants "restricting property from being transferred to or occupied by negroes have been consistently upheld by the courts of this state as one which the parties have the right to make and which is not contrary to public policy." *Kraemer v. Shelley*, 198 S.W.2d 679, 682 (1946).]

[The second of the cases under consideration came from the Supreme Court of Michigan. The circumstances presented do not differ materially from the Missouri case. The Michigan Court distinguished *In re Wren*, [1945] O.R. 778 (Ont. H.C.), which held, *inter alia*, that a covenant not to sell land to "Jews or persons of objectionable nationality" was too indefinite to be enforceable.[4] Although many states outside the south did not have miscegenation laws, the court wrote that no one "could contend either that persons of the Mongoloid or Negroid races are embraced within the term 'Caucasian,' or that this term does not specifically exclude all other races." *Sipes v. McGhee*, 25 N.W.2d 638, 642 (1947). The Michigan court then considered the claim that the restriction was enforceable as contravening public policy. The court took note of state statutes prohibiting racial discrimination in public schools and public accommodations, mental institutions, and life insurance sales. The court also noted that contract restrictions are valuable property rights that cannot be taken without compensation, and cited state precedents that recognized rules of property "ought not to be overturned without the very best of reasons." *Ibid.* at 643. Thus, the court re-affirmed prior precedents that racially restrictive covenants were not contrary to public policy. *Parmalee v. Morris*, 188 N.W. 330 (1922). The court declined the invitation to reconsider that precedent in light of international declarations of human rights. "So far as the instant case is concerned, these pronouncements are merely indicative or a desirable social trend and an objective devoutly to be desired by all well-thinking peoples. These arguments are predicated upon a plea for justice rather than the application of the settled principles of established law."[5]]

Petitioners have placed primary reliance on their contentions, first raised in the state courts, that judicial enforcement of the restrictive agreements in these cases has violated rights guaranteed to petitioners by the Fourteenth Amendment of the Federal Constitution and Acts of Congress passed pursuant to that Amendment. Specifically, petitioners urge that they have been denied the equal protection of the laws, deprived of property without due process of law, and have been denied privileges and immunities of citizens of the United States. We pass to a consideration of those issues.

I

Whether the equal protection clause of the Fourteenth Amendment inhibits judicial enforcement by state courts of restrictive covenants based on race or color is a question which this Court has not heretofore been called upon to consider.

---

[4] [Ed. note: This case is discussed below.]

[5] [Ed. note: As discussed in the Introductory Notes, these holdings about the enforceability of covenants under the common law in light of public policy were not subject to appeal to the U.S. Supreme Court. That court's jurisdiction was limited to issues arising under federal law. Absent statutory authority, the only federal question was a constitutional one.]

*   *   *

It cannot be doubted that among the civil rights intended to be protected from discriminatory state action by the Fourteenth Amendment are the rights to acquire, enjoy, own and dispose of property. Equality in the enjoyment of property rights was regarded by the framers of that Amendment as an essential pre-condition to the realization of other basic civil rights and liberties which the Amendment was intended to guarantee. Thus, § 1978 of the Revised Statutes, derived from § 1 of the Civil Rights Act of 1866 which was enacted by Congress while the Fourteenth Amendment was also under consideration,[6] provides:

> "All citizens of the United States shall have the same right, in every State and Territory, as is enjoyed by white citizens thereof to inherit, purchase, lease, sell, hold, and convey real and personal property."

*   *   *

It is likewise clear that restrictions on the right of occupancy of the sort sought to be created by the private agreements in these cases could not be squared with the requirements of the Fourteenth Amendment if imposed by state statute or local ordinance. We do not understand respondents to urge the contrary. In the case of *Buchanan v. Warley*, [245 U.S. 60 (1917)] a unanimous Court declared unconstitutional the provisions of a city ordinance which denied to colored persons the right to occupy houses in blocks in which the greater number of houses were occupied by white persons, and imposed similar restrictions on white persons with respect to blocks in which the greater number of houses were occupied by colored persons. During the course of the opinion in that case, this Court stated: "The Fourteenth Amendment and these statutes enacted in furtherance of its purpose operate to qualify and entitle a colored man to acquire property without state legislation discriminating against him solely because of color."

*   *   *

But the present cases, unlike those just discussed, do not involve action by state legislatures or city councils. Here the particular patterns of discrimination and the areas in which the restrictions are to operate, are determined, in the first instance, by the terms of agreements among private individuals. Participation of the State consists in the enforcement of the restrictions so defined. The crucial issue with which we are here confronted is whether this distinction removes these cases from the operation of the prohibitory provisions of the Fourteenth Amendment.

Since the decision of this Court in the *Civil Rights Cases*, 109 U.S. 3 (1883), the principle has become firmly embedded in our constitutional law that the action inhibited by the first section of the Fourteenth Amendment is only such action as may fairly be said to be that of the States. That Amendment erects no shield against merely private conduct, however discriminatory or wrongful.

---

[6] [FN 8] In *Oyama v. California*, 332 U.S. 633, 640 (1948) the section of the Civil Rights Act herein considered is described as the federal statute, "enacted before the Fourteenth Amendment but vindicated by it." The Civil Rights Act of 1866 was reenacted in § 18 of the Act of May 31, 1870, subsequent to the adoption of the Fourteenth Amendment. . . .

We conclude, therefore, that the restrictive agreements standing alone cannot be regarded as violative of any rights guaranteed to petitioners by the Fourteenth Amendment. So long as the purposes of those agreements are effectuated by voluntary adherence to their terms, it would appear clear that there has been no action by the State and the provisions of the Amendment have not been violated.

But here there was more. These are cases in which the purposes of the agreements were secured only by judicial enforcement by state courts of the restrictive terms of the agreements. The respondents urge that judicial enforcement of private agreements does not amount to state action; or, in any event, the participation of the State is so attenuated in character as not to amount to state action within the meaning of the Fourteenth Amendment. Finally, it is suggested, even if the States in these cases may be deemed to have acted in the constitutional sense, their action did not deprive petitioners of rights guaranteed by the Fourteenth Amendment. We move to a consideration of these matters.

II

That the action of state courts and judicial officers in their official capacities is to be regarded as action of the State within the meaning of the Fourteenth Amendment, is a proposition which has long been established by decisions of this Court. That principle was given expression in the earliest cases involving the construction of the terms of the Fourteenth Amendment. Thus, in *Virginia v. Rives*, 100 U.S. 313, 318 (1880), this Court stated: "It is doubtless true that a State may act through different agencies, — either by its legislative, its executive, or its judicial authorities; and the prohibitions of the amendment extend to all action of the State denying equal protection of the laws, whether it be action by one of these agencies or by another." In *Ex parte Virginia*, 100 U.S. 339, 347 (1880), the Court observed: "A State acts by its legislative, its executive, or its judicial authorities. It can act in no other way." In the *Civil Rights Cases*, 109 U.S. 3, 11, 17 (1883), this Court pointed out that the Amendment makes void "State action of every kind" which is inconsistent with the guaranties therein contained, and extends to manifestations of "State authority in the shape of laws, customs, or judicial or executive proceedings." Language to like effect is employed no less than eighteen times during the course of that opinion.

* * *

The action of state courts in imposing penalties or depriving parties of other substantive rights without providing adequate notice and opportunity to defend, has, of course, long been regarded as a denial of the due process of law guaranteed by the Fourteenth Amendment. *Brinkerhoff-Faris Trust & Savings Co. v. Hill, supra.* Cf. *Pennoyer v. Neff*, 95 U.S. 714 (1878).

* * *

But the examples of state judicial action which have been held by this Court to violate the Amendment's commands are not restricted to situations in which the judicial proceedings were found in some manner to be procedurally unfair. It has been recognized that the action of state courts in enforcing a substantive common-law rule formulated by those courts, may result in the denial of rights guaranteed by the Fourteenth Amendment, even though the judicial proceedings in such cases may have been in complete accord with the most rigorous conceptions of procedural due process.[7] Thus, in *American Federation of Labor v. Swing*, 312 U.S. 321 (1941),enforcement by state courts of the common-law policy of the State, which resulted in the restraining of peaceful picketing, was held to be state action of the sort prohibited by the Amendment's guaranties of freedom of discussion. In *Cantwell v. Connecticut*, 310 U.S. 296 (1940), a conviction in a state court of the common-law crime of breach of the peace was, under the circumstances of the case, found to be a violation of the Amendment's commands relating to freedom of religion. In *Bridges v. California*, 314 U.S. 252 (1941), enforcement of the state's common-law rule relating to contempts by publication was held to be state action inconsistent with the prohibitions of the Fourteenth Amendment. And *cf. Chicago, Burlington and Quincy R. Co.* v. *Chicago*, 166 U.S. 226 (1897).

The short of the matter is that from the time of the adoption of the Fourteenth Amendment until the present, it has been the consistent ruling of this Court that the action of the States to which the Amendment has reference includes action of state courts and state judicial officials. Although, in construing the terms of the Fourteenth Amendment, differences have from time to time been expressed as to whether particular types of state action may be said to offend the Amendment's prohibitory provisions, it has never been suggested that state court action is immunized from the operation of those provisions simply because the act is that of the judicial branch of the state government.

III

*   *   *

We have no doubt that there has been state action in these cases in the full and complete sense of the phrase. The undisputed facts disclose that petitioners were willing purchasers of properties upon which they desired to establish homes. The owners of the properties were willing sellers; and contracts of sale were accordingly consummated. It is clear that but for the active intervention of the state courts, supported by the full panoply of state power, petitioners would have been free to occupy the properties in question without restraint.

These are not cases, as has been suggested, in which the States have merely abstained from action, leaving private individuals free to impose such discriminations as they see fit. Rather, these are cases in which the States have made available to such individuals the full coercive power of government to deny to petitioners, on the grounds of race or color, the enjoyment of property rights in premises which petitioners are willing and financially able to acquire and which the grantors are willing to sell. The difference between judicial enforcement and non-enforcement of the restrictive covenants is the difference to petitioners between being denied rights of property available to other members of the community and being accorded full

---

[7] [FN 19] In applying the rule of *Erie R. Co. v. Tompkins*, 304 U.S. 64 (1938), it is clear that the common-law rules enunciated by state courts in judicial opinions are to be regarded as a part of the law of the State.

enjoyment of those rights on an equal footing.

* * *

Respondents urge, however, that since the state courts stand ready to enforce restrictive covenants excluding white persons from the ownership or occupancy of property covered by such agreements, enforcement of covenants excluding colored persons may not be deemed a denial of equal protection of the laws to the colored persons who are thereby affected. This contention does not bear scrutiny. The parties have directed our attention to no case in which a court, state or federal, has been called upon to enforce a covenant excluding members of the white majority from ownership or occupancy of real property on grounds of race or color. But there are more fundamental considerations. The rights created by the first section of the Fourteenth Amendment are, by its terms, guaranteed to the individual. The rights established are personal rights. It is, therefore, no answer to these petitioners to say that the courts may also be induced to deny white persons rights of ownership and occupancy on grounds of race or color. Equal protection of the laws is not achieved through indiscriminate imposition of inequalities.

* * *

The historical context in which the Fourteenth Amendment became a part of the Constitution should not be forgotten. Whatever else the framers sought to achieve, it is clear that the matter of primary concern was the establishment of equality in the enjoyment of basic civil and political rights and the preservation of those rights from discriminatory action on the part of the States based on considerations of race or color. Seventy-five years ago this Court announced that the provisions of the Amendment are to be construed with this fundamental purpose in mind. Upon full consideration, we have concluded that in these cases the States have acted to deny petitioners the equal protection of the laws guaranteed by the Fourteenth Amendment. Having so decided, we find it unnecessary to consider whether petitioners have also been deprived of property without due process of law or denied privileges and immunities of citizens of the United States.

For the reasons stated, the judgment of the Supreme Court of Missouri and the judgment of the Supreme Court of Michigan must be reversed.

———————

As we will see in the next case, the Supreme Court of Canada reached the opposite result concerning the applicability of the Charter to judicial enforcement of common law remedies. Some additional background is required to understand the case. The defendant union was engaged in "secondary picketing." This term means that the union pickets were not targeting their own employer — Purolator Courier — but a sub-contractor from Purolator. Secondary picketing is a desirable strategy when the simple refusal to work does not confer sufficient bargaining leverage on the union, which is particularly true when the employer can outsource work to other firms and their employees to carry on despite the strike. At common law, secondary picketing was held to be an unreasonable restraint of trade and a concerted effort to unjustifiably encourage the plaintiff's workers to break their own employment contracts with Dolphin Delivery in order to get Dolphin to put economic pressure on Purolator to settle with the union. Secondary picketing also violates the *B.C. Labour Code*, as well as the U.S. National Labor Relations Act. There are, however, no provisions of the (federal) *Canada Labour Code* concerning secondary picketing.

The B.C. Labour Code's provisions apply to most secondary picketing in British Columbia, because the *British North America Act* generally assigns labor relations to provincial regulation. (In contrast, Congress has exercised its authority under the Commerce Clause to create a federal scheme of labor law administered by the National Labor Relations Board.) However, there is an exception for national industries such as telecommunications and transportation. These industries are governed by a federal labor relations regime.

Under modern labour statutes, including U.S. and B.C. laws, the common law has been superseded by rulings by a specialized agency. However, the federal labour law in Canada applicable to the transportation industry did not supplement the common law. Hence, this case is one of the few labour issues to arise under the common law.

RETAIL, WHOLESALE AND DEPARTMENT STORE UNION, LOCAL 580 v. DOLPHIN DELIVERY LTD.

SUPREME COURT OF CANADA
[1986] 2 S.C.R. 573, 33 D.L.R. (4th) 174

The judgment of DICKSON C.J. and ESTEY, MCINTYRE, CHOUINARD and LE DAIN JJ. was delivered by

MCINTYRE J. — This appeal raises the question of whether secondary picketing by members of a trade union in a labour dispute is a protected activity under s. 2(b) of the Canadian Charter of Rights and Freedoms and, accordingly, not the proper subject of an injunction to restrain it. In reaching the answer, consideration must be given to the application of the Charter to the common law and as well to its application in private litigation.

The respondent, Dolphin Delivery Ltd. ("Dolphin"), is a company engaged in the courier business in Vancouver and the surrounding area. Its employees are represented by a trade union, not the appellant. A collective agreement is in effect between Dolphin and the union representing its employees, which provides in clause 8: "it shall not be a violation of this agreement or cause for discipline or discharge if an employee refuses to cross a picket line which has been established in full compliance with the British Columbia Labour Code." The appellant trade union is the bargaining agent under a federal certification for the employees of Purolator Courier Incorporated ("Purolator"). That company has a principal place of operations in Ontario but, prior to the month of June, 1981 when it locked out its employees in a labour dispute, it had a place of operations in Vancouver. That dispute is as yet unresolved. Prior to the lock-out, Dolphin did business with Purolator making deliveries within its area for Purolator. Since the lock-out, Dolphin has done business in a similar manner with another company, known as Supercourier Ltd. ("Supercourier"), which is incorporated in Ontario. There is a connection between Supercourier and Purolator, the exact particulars of which are not clearly established in the evidence, but it appears that Dolphin carries on in roughly the same manner with Supercourier as it had formerly done with Purolator and about twenty per cent of its total volume of business originates with Supercourier. This is about the same percentage of business as was done with Purolator before the lock-out.

In October of 1982 the appellant applied to the British Columbia Labour Relations Board for a declaration that Dolphin and Supercourier were allies of Purolator in their dispute with the appellant. A declaration to this effect would have rendered lawful the picketing of the place of business of Dolphin under British Columbia legislation. The Board, however, declined to make the declaration sought, on the basis that it had no jurisdiction because the union's collective bargaining relationship with Purolator and any picketing which might be done were governed by the *Canada Labour Code*, R.S.C. 1970, c. L-1. In the face of this finding it became common ground between the parties that where the *Labour Code of British Columbia*, R.S.B.C. 1979, c. 212, does not apply, the legality of picketing falls for determination under the common law because the *Canada Labour Code* is silent on the question. In November of 1982 the individual appellants, on behalf of the appellant union, advised Dolphin that its place of business in Vancouver would be picketed unless it agreed to cease doing business with Supercourier. An application was made at once for a quia timet injunction to restrain the threatened picketing. No picketing occurred, the application being made before its commencement.

The matter came before Sheppard L.J.S.C. and on November 30 he granted the injunction [pending trial. He rejected the union's claims that Purolator and Dolphin were allies. Thus, the union's secondary picketing was "for the purpose either of the tort of inducing breach of contract, or of the tort of civil conspiracy in that the predominant purpose of the picketing is to injure the plaintiff rather than the dissemination of information and the protection of the defendant's interest. Accordingly, I find that the plaintiff is entitled to an injunction to restrain the picketing."]

[Conducting its own review, the SCC agreed. Although the Court assumed that the picketing would be peaceful, it determined that some employees of the respondent and other trade union members of customers would decline to cross the picket lines, and that the business of the respondent would be disrupted to a considerable extent.]

FREEDOM OF EXPRESSION

[Cataloguing philosophical and precedential support for free speech and the importance of free expression under the Charter, the Court noted that the union argued that picketing is entitled to Charter protection limiting infringements on free expression, and rejecting the American distinction between the concept of speech and that of conduct made in picketing cases.[8] The plaintiff argued that

---

[8] [Ed. note: The U.S. Supreme Court has held that laws against secondary picketing do not violate the First Amendment rights of union workers. Under U.S. labor law, it is illegal for unions to strike a "neutral" company, with which it does not have a direct labor dispute, to pressure the neutral into ceasing to do business with the employer with whom the union does have a dispute. The Court has reasoned that

picketing in a labour dispute is more than mere communication of information. It is also a signal to trade unionists not to cross the picket line. The respect accorded to picket lines by trade unionists is such that the result of the picketing would be to damage seriously the operation of the employer, not to communicate any information. Therefore, it is argued, since the picket line was not intended to promote dialogue or discourse (as would be the case where its purpose was the exercise of freedom of expression), it cannot qualify for protection under the Charter.]

On the basis of the findings of fact that I have referred to above, it is evident that the purpose of the picketing in this case was to induce a breach of contract between the respondent and Supercourier and thus to exert economic pressure to force it to cease doing business with Supercourier. It is equally evident that, if successful, the picketing would have done serious injury to the respondent. There is nothing remarkable about this, however, because all picketing is designed to bring economic pressure on the person picketed and to cause economic loss for so long as the object of the picketing remains unfulfilled. There is, as I have earlier said, always some element of expression in picketing. The union is making a statement to the general public that it is involved in a dispute, that it is seeking to impose its will on the object of the picketing, and that it solicits the assistance of the public in honouring the picket line. Action on the part of the picketers will, of course, always accompany the expression, but not every action on the part of the picketers will be such as to alter the nature of the whole transaction and remove it from Charter protection for freedom of expression. That freedom, of course, would not extend to protect threats of violence or acts of violence. It would not protect the destruction of property, or assaults, or other clearly unlawful conduct. We need not, however, be concerned with such matters here because the picketing would have been peaceful. I am therefore of the view that the picketing sought to be restrained would have involved the exercise of the right of freedom of expression.

Section 1 of the Charter

It is not necessary, in view of the disposition of this appeal that I propose, to deal with the application of s. 1 of the Charter. It was, however, referred to in the Court of Appeal and I will deal with it here. It will be recalled that the Chambers judge in granting the injunction did so on the basis that the picketing involved the commission of two common law torts, that of civil conspiracy to injure and that of inducing a breach of contract. [The opinion discusses these common law claims. McIntyre, J., explained the narrowing, by statute and judicial decision, of the tort of conspiracy to injure, citing with approval a law review article observing that this tort "stands condemned, almost universally, as the vehicle of judicial anti-unionism." For this reason, the sole basis by which the Court considered the claim was for the tort of inducing Dolphin Delivery's workers, who were not in dispute with their own employer, to breach their own collective bargaining agreement to observe the picket lines.]

---

secondary picketing is simply a call for others to perform illegal acts. Thus, it is entitled to no more constitutional protection than a speech urging competitors to fix prices or a solicitation to a safecracker to help rob a bank. *See International Brotherhood of Teamsters v. Vogt, Inc.*, 354 U.S. 945 (1957).]

*   *   *

From the evidence, it may well be said that the concern of the respondent is pressing and substantial. It will suffer economically in the absence of an injunction to restrain picketing. On the other hand, the injunction has imposed a limitation upon a Charter freedom. A balance between the two competing concerns must be found. It may be argued that the concern of the respondent regarding economic loss would not be sufficient to constitute a reasonable limitation on the right of freedom of expression, but there is another basis upon which the respondent's position may be supported. This case involves secondary picketing — picketing of a third party not concerned in the dispute which underlies the picketing. The basis of our system of collective bargaining is the proposition that the parties themselves should, wherever possible, work out their own agreement.

[McIntyre, J., explained why he believed that the union's free speech interests in secondary picketing were entitled to less weight. Quoting a leading labour law scholar, Professor Paul Weiler:] [U]nions should not be permitted to picket the business of a third party. Such a secondary employer is not involved in the primary dispute, it does not have it within its power to make the concessions that will settle the new contract, and thus it should not be the target of a weapon whose legitimate purpose is to extract such economic concessions. [McIntyre, J., added that although this dispute in the transportation industry was beyond the jurisdiction of provincial law, British Columbia labour law also bars secondary picketing, which] shows that the application of s. 1 of the Charter to sustain the limitation imposed by the common law would be consistent with legislative policy in British Columbia. I would say that the requirement of proportionality is also met, particularly when it is recalled that this is an interim injunction effective only until trial when the issues may be more fully canvassed on fuller evidence. It is my opinion then that a limitation on secondary picketing against a third party, that is, a non-ally, would be a reasonable limit in the facts of this case. I would therefore conclude that the injunction is "a reasonable limit prescribed by law which can be demonstrably justified in a free and democratic society."

DOES THE CHARTER APPLY TO THE COMMON LAW?

In my view, there can be no doubt that it does apply. Section 52(1) of the Constitution Act, 1982 provides:

> "52. (1) The Constitution of Canada is the supreme law of Canada, and any law that is inconsistent with the provisions of the Constitution is, to the extent of the inconsistency, of no force or effect.

> 52. (1) La Constitution du Canada est la loi supreme du Canada; elle rend inoperantes les dispositions incompatibles de toute autre regle de droit."

The English text provides that "any law that is inconsistent with the provisions of the Constitution is, to the extent of the inconsistency, of no force or effect". If this language is not broad enough to include the common law, it should be observed as well that the French text adds strong support to this conclusion in its employment of the words "*elle rend inoperantes les dispositions incompatibles de tout autre regle de droit.*" (Emphasis added.) To adopt a construction of s. 52(1) which would exclude from Charter application the whole body of the common law which in great part governs the rights and obligations of the individuals in society, would be wholly unrealistic and contrary to the clear language employed in s. 52(1) of the Act.

DOES THE CHARTER APPLY TO PRIVATE LITIGATION?

This question involves consideration of whether or not an individual may found a cause of action or defence against another individual on the basis of a breach of a Charter right. In other words, does the Charter apply to private litigation divorced completely from any connection with Government? This is a subject of controversy in legal circles and the question has not been dealt with in this Court. One view of the matter rests on the proposition that the Charter, like most written constitutions, was set up to regulate the relationship between the individual and the Government. It was intended to restrain government action and to protect the individual. It was not intended in the absence of some governmental action to be applied in private litigation.

* * *

I am in agreement with the view that the Charter does not apply to private litigation. It is evident from the authorities and articles cited above that that approach has been adopted by most judges and commentators who have dealt with this question. In my view, s. 32 of the Charter, specifically dealing with the question of Charter application, is conclusive on this issue. Section 32 is reproduced hereunder:

"32. (1) This Charter applies

(a) to the Parliament and government of Canada in respect of all matters within the authority of Parliament including all matters relating to the Yukon Territory and Northwest Territories; and

(b) to the legislature and government of each province in respect of all matters within the authority of the legislature of each province.

32. (1) La presente charte s'applique:

a) au Parlement et au gouvernement du Canada, pour tous les domaines relevant du Parlement, y compris ceux qui concernent le territoire du Yukon et les territoires du Nord-Ouest;

b) a la legislature et au gouvernement de chaque province pour tous les domaines relevant de cette legislature."

Section 32(1) refers to the Parliament and Government of Canada and to the legislatures and governments of the Provinces in respect of all matters within their respective authorities. In this, it may be seen that Parliament and the Legislatures are treated as separate or specific branches of government, distinct from the executive branch of government, and therefore where the word 'government' is used in s. 32 it refers not to government in its generic sense — meaning the whole of the governmental apparatus of the state — but to a branch of government. The word 'government', following as it does the words 'Parliament' and 'Legislature', must then, it would seem, refer to the executive or administrative branch of government. This is the sense in which one generally speaks of the Government of Canada or of a province. I am of the opinion that the word 'government' is used in s. 32 of the Charter in the sense of the executive government of Canada and the Provinces. This is the sense in which the words 'Government of Canada' are ordinarily employed in other sections of the *Constitution Act*, 1867. Sections 12, 16, and 132 all refer to the Parliament and the Government of Canada as separate entities. The words 'Government of Canada', particularly where they follow a reference to the word 'Parliament', almost always refer to the executive government.

It is my view that s. 32 of the Charter specifies the actors to whom the Charter will apply. They are the legislative, executive and administrative branches of government. It will apply to those branches of government whether or not their action is invoked in public or private litigation. It would seem that legislation is the only way in which a legislature may infringe a guaranteed right or freedom. Action by the executive or administrative branches of government will generally depend upon legislation, that is, statutory authority. Such action may also depend, however, on the common law, as in the case of the prerogative. To the extent that it relies on statutory authority which constitutes or results in an infringement of a guaranteed right or freedom, the Charter will apply and it will be unconstitutional. The action will also be unconstitutional to the extent that it relies for authority or justification on a rule of the common law which constitutes or creates an infringement of a Charter right or freedom. In this way the Charter will apply to the common law, whether in public or private litigation. It will apply to the common law, however, only in so far as the common law is the basis of some governmental action which, it is alleged, infringes a guaranteed right or freedom.

*   *   *

I find [Prof. Hogg's conclusion that the Charter precludes enforcement of private arrangements in derogation of a guaranteed right to be] troublesome and, in my view, it should not be accepted as an approach to this problem. While in political science terms it is probably acceptable to treat the courts as one of the three fundamental branches of Government, that is, legislative, executive, and judicial, I cannot equate for the purposes of Charter application the order of a court with an element of governmental action. This is not to say that the courts are not bound by the Charter. The courts are, of course, bound by the Charter as they are bound by all law. It is their duty to apply the law, but in doing so they act as neutral arbiters, not as contending parties involved in a dispute. To regard a court order as an element of governmental intervention necessary to invoke the Charter would, it seems to me, widen the scope of Charter application to virtually all private litigation. All cases must end, if carried to completion, with an enforcement order and if the Charter precludes the making of the order, where a Charter right would be infringed, it would seem that all private litigation would be subject to the Charter. In my view, this approach will not provide the answer to the question. A more direct and a more precisely-defined connection between the element of government action and the claim advanced must be present before the Charter applies.

*   *   *

As has been noted above, it is difficult and probably dangerous to attempt to define with narrow precision that element of governmental intervention which will suffice to permit reliance on the Charter by private litigants in private litigation. Professor Hogg has dealt with this question, at p. 677, supra, where he said:

> ". . . the Charter would apply to a private person exercising the power of arrest that is granted to "any one" by the Criminal Code, and to a private railway company exercising the power to make by-laws (and impose penalties for their breach) that is granted to a "railway company" by the Railway Act; all action taken in exercise of a statutory power is covered by the Charter by virtue of the references to "Parliament" and "legislature" in s. 32. The Charter would also apply to the action of a commercial corporation that was an agent of the Crown, by virtue of the reference to "government" in s. 32."

It would also seem that the Charter would apply to many forms of delegated legislation, regulations, orders in council, possibly municipal by-laws, and by-laws and regulations of other creatures of Parliament and the Legislatures. It is not suggested that this list is exhaustive. Where such exercise of, or reliance upon, governmental action is present and where one private party invokes or relies upon it to produce an infringement of the Charter rights of another, the Charter will be applicable. Where, however, private party "A" sues private party "B" relying on the common law and where no act of government is relied upon to support the action, the Charter will not apply. I should make it clear, however, that this is a distinct issue from the question whether the judiciary ought to apply and develop the principles of the common law in a manner consistent with the fundamental values enshrined in the Constitution. The answer to this question must be in the affirmative. In this sense, then, the Charter is far from irrelevant to private litigants whose disputes fall to be decided at common law. But this is different from the proposition that one private party owes a constitutional duty to another, which proposition underlies the purported assertion of Charter causes of action or Charter defenses between individuals.

*   *   *

BEETZ J. [concluded that the secondary picketing was not expression covered by s. 2(b), but even if it was, he agreed with McIntyre, J.'s reasoning about the common law and the charter.]

WILSON J. — I agree with the reasons of my colleague, McIntyre J., with the exception of his reasons dealing with the application of s. 1 of the Charter.

The path-breaking Australian case on the relationship between the common law and the Constitution is *Lange v. Australian Broadcasting Corporation* (1997) 189 CLR 520, which is also a major case in the law of libel against public officials. We consider that case below, but in sum, the High Court of Australia followed the Canadian approach in rejecting an assertion that the application of the common law violated the Constitution, while reconsidering how the common law should actually be applied in Australia in light of constitutional concerns.

Although *Dolphin Delivery* directly contradicts its equivalent American case cited in *Shelley v. Kraemer* (*AFL v. Swing*, 312 U.S. 321, 326 (1941)), the results in some other cases are probably not that different. Suppose Nigel Windsor of Manitoba wishes to host a backyard barbecue for his neighbours; being a bigot, he declines to invite the Lemieux family from across the street, because of their French Canadian background and their Catholic religion. If M. Lemieux sues Mr. Windsor, will a court order Mr. Windsor to invite the Lemieuxs to his party? Suppose the Lemieux family tries to crash the party, and Mr. Windsor calls the police. Can the M. Lemieux be prosecuted for trespass? Could Windsor file a common law tort action for trespass? It would appear that, on both sides of the border, the Lemieuxs can be excluded, and probably can be sued as well as prosecuted for trespass.

Professor John Nowak offers a way to reconcile and make sense out of these cases. *See* Robert Glennon & John Nowak, *A Functional Analysis of the Fourteenth Amendment "State Action" Requirement*, 1976 SUP. CT. REV. 221; NOWAK & ROTUNDA § 12.5. He notes that the aggrieved party in these cases is claiming that the state has unconstitutionally preferred the alleged wrongdoer's challenged practice over the aggrieved party's constitutional rights. (The preference is apparent: otherwise the state would have passed a statute prohibiting the alleged wrongdoer from interfering with the plaintiff's rights.) In each case, the plaintiff's asserted right and the defendant's challenged conduct are incompatible: the issue is whether the Constitution requires the state to prefer one over the other. This inquiry "has nothing to do with finding a minimum quantum of state activity" and thus explains, according to Nowak, why cases where the aggrieved party is challenging racial discrimination almost always find state action. The Court is comparing the plaintiff's right to equal treatment with the defendant's right to exercise a "private" choice to be a racist. Absent extreme examples (like the racist dinner party host), the defendant loses.

The question whether the constitution requires a private defendant to conform its behavior to norms like equality or free expression has provoked considerable controversy in Canada. Consider *McKinney v. University of Guelph*, [1990] 3 S.C.R. 229, 76 D.L.R. (4th) 545, which held that an autonomous university's mandatory retirement age did not violate the Charter's prohibition on age discrimination. (An Ontario age discrimination statute that did apply to private conduct explicitly covered only those under age 65.) Justice LaForest reasoned that the Charter is limited to restraining the government because only the government needs to be restrained to preserve individual rights. This sparked a strong dissent from Wilson, J., suggesting (although the majority denied it) that this reflected a traditional liberal view that "the role of government should be strictly confined" and that "social and economic ordering should be left to the private sector." In her view, the majority's opinion is too reflective of libertarian American ideals to be appropriate for Canadian law. First, she argued that the American Revolution left Americans with a deep distrust of powerful states, and thus enshrined in the U.S. Constitution "the belief that unless the state is strictly controlled it poses a great danger to individual liberty. . . . *Canada does not share this history.*" Indeed, the decision by Canadian colonists not to join the American Revolution, coupled by the mass migration of United Empire Loyalists from the American colonies meant that the Province of Canada, from its inception, had as its core value a trust of the very government from which Americans rebelled. Second, she canvassed the essential role played by the Canadian government in developing the country economically and maintaining a social safety net. She concluded that "regulation has always played a role in the governance of Canadian society and that laissez faire ideology never really took hold in Canada." Third, she notes that "one of the realities of modern life is that 'private' power when left unchecked can and does lead to problems which are incompatible with the Canadian conception of a just society."

Although Wilson, J.'s first point clearly distinguishes the two countries, it is less clear whether the latter two are more descriptive of historical differences or of differences in the dominant political philosophy. The U.S. government, after all, also played a huge role in developing the United States, notwithstanding the myth of laissez faire; many in the United States also share her view that private power can be inconsistent with a just society. The constitutional question is whether private power should be constrained by judicial application of constitutional principles or only to the extent that the legislature regulates the conduct by ordinary legislation.

In South Africa debates over the "horizontal" application of the bill of rights began under the "interim" Constitution and have continued under the "final" Constitution although the express inclusion of provisions in the Constitution addressing the application of the bill of rights to the actions of private individuals and juristic persons has shifted the debate from whether the bill of rights applies to non-state action to discussions over the scope and implications of sections 8(1)-(4) that define the application of the bill of rights.

Section 8(1) states that "[t]he Bill of Rights applies to all law, and binds the legislature, the executive, the judiciary and all organs of state." This clause is understood as describing the direct application of the bill of rights, or what might be called the vertical application of the constitution. Some commentators (see Woolman et al., 2d ed., ch. 31) have argued that the reference to "all law" must mean that the bill of rights applies directly to the common law; however this interpretation has been resisted on the grounds that it would make clauses 8(2) and (3) redundant (see *Khumalo v. Holomisa* below).

Section 8(2) states that "[a] provision of the bill of rights binds a natural or juristic person if, and to the extent that, it is applicable, taking into account the nature of the right and the nature of any duty imposed by the right." Sections 8(3) proceeds to discuss how courts, in applying the bill of rights to natural and juristic persons "must apply, or if necessary develop, the common law to the extent that legislation does not give effect to that right, and may develop rules of the common law to limit the right" so long as it is consistent with the limitations clause. Finally, section 8(4) states that "[a] juristic person is entitled to the rights in the bill of rights" but only in ways that are appropriate to the nature of the juristic person and the relevant right.

Finally, courts or other relevant fora [e.g., the chapter 9 institutions] involved in the interpretation of the bill of rights in South Africa are admonished in section 39(2) that "[w]hen interpreting any legislation, and when developing the common law or customary law [they] must promote the spirit, purport and objects of the Bill of Rights."

7.3. CASE STUDY OF CONSTITUTIONAL VALUES AND THE COMMON LAW: LIBEL

NEW YORK TIMES CO. v. SULLIVAN
Supreme Court of the United States
376 U.S. 254 (1964)

[Before Warren, C.J., and Black, Douglas, Clark, Harlan, Brennan, Stewart, White, Goldberg, JJ.]

Mr. Justice Brennan delivered the opinion of the Court.

We are required in this case to determine for the first time the extent to which the constitutional protections for speech and press limit a State's power to award damages in a libel action brought by a public official against critics of his official conduct.

[Sullivan was an elected Commissioner of the City of Montgomery, Alabama, responsible for supervising the police and fire departments. His] complaint alleged that he had been libeled by statements in a full-page advertisement that was carried in the New York Times on March 29, 1960, discussing civil rights protests in Montgomery appealing for funds to support protesting students and the legal defense of Dr. Martin Luther King, Jr., against a perjury indictment then pending in Montgomery. Although no statement referred to Sullivan by name, he complained that he was libeled by (1) a statement that "truckloads of police armed with shotguns and tear-gas ringed the Alabama State College campus," when in fact police were just deployed near the campus; (2) a statement that the dining hall "was padlocked in an attempt to starve" the entire student body into submission when they refused to register for classes, when in fact only most of the student body had protested by boycotting classes rather than refusing to register and the dining hall was not padlocked; (3) a statement that "southern violators" had assaulted Dr. Martin Luther King, Jr., and arrested him seven times, when the officers denied any assault and he had only been arrested four times. Based on these claims, a jury in the Circuit Court of Montgomery County awarded him damages of $500,000, the full amount claimed, against all the petitioners, and the Supreme Court of Alabama affirmed. 273 Ala. 656, 144 So. 2d 25.

Respondent made no effort to prove that he suffered actual pecuniary loss as a result of the alleged libel. . . .

In affirming the judgment, the Supreme Court of Alabama sustained the trial judge's rulings and instructions in all respects. 273 Ala. 656, 144 So. 2d 25. It held that "where the words published tend to injure a person libeled by them in his reputation, profession, trade or business, or charge him with an indictable offense, or tend to bring the individual into public contempt," they are "libelous per se"; that "the matter complained of is, under the above doctrine, libelous per se, if it was published of and concerning the plaintiff"; and that it was actionable without "proof of pecuniary injury . . . , such injury being implied." *Id.* at 673, 676, 144 So. 2d at 37, 41. It approved the trial court's ruling that the jury could find the statements to have been made "of and concerning" respondent, stating: "We think it common knowledge that the average person knows that municipal agents, such as police and firemen, and others, are under the control and direction of the city governing body, and more particularly under the direction and control of a single commissioner. In measuring the performance or deficiencies of such groups, praise or criticism is usually attached to the official in complete control of the body." *Id.* at 674–675, 144 So. 2d at 39. In sustaining the trial court's determination that the verdict was not excessive, the court said that malice could be inferred from the Times' "irresponsibility" in printing the advertisement while "the Times in its own files had articles already published which would have demonstrated the falsity of the allegations in the advertisement"; from the Times' failure to retract for respondent while retracting for the Governor, whereas the falsity of some of the allegations was then known to the Times and "the matter contained in the advertisement was equally false as to both parties"; and from the testimony of the Times' Secretary that, apart from the statement that the dining hall was padlocked, he thought the two paragraphs were "substantially correct." *Id*, at 686–687, 144 So. 2d at 50–51. The court reaffirmed a statement in an earlier opinion that "There is no legal measure of damages in cases of this character." *Id.* at 686, 144 So. 2d at 50. It rejected petitioners' constitutional contentions with the brief statements that "The First Amendment of the U.S. Constitution does not protect libelous publications" and "The Fourteenth Amendment is directed against State action and not private action." *Id.* at 676, 144 So. 2d at 40. Because of the importance of the constitutional issues involved, we granted the separate petitions for certiorari of the individual petitioners and of the Times. We reverse the judgment. We hold that the rule of law applied by the Alabama courts is constitutionally deficient for failure to provide the safeguards for freedom of speech and of the press that are required by the First and Fourteenth Amendments in a libel action brought by a public official against critics of his official conduct. We further hold that under the proper safeguards the evidence presented in this case is constitutionally insufficient to support the judgment for respondent.

I

[First, the Court disposed of two claims that the judgment was insulated from its review. The application of a state rule or law in a civil action was reaffirmed to constitute "state action" subject to the Fourteenth Amendment under the doctrine announced in *Shelley v. Kraemer*. Second, the fact that the alleged libel took place in a "commercial advertisement" did not preclude application of the First Amendment.]

II

[The Court distinguished prior precedents rejecting constitutional challenges to libel verdicts, which did not involve sanctioning expression critical of the official conduct of public officials. The Court emphasized the First Amendment's role in guaranteeing expression related to public questions.]

That erroneous statement is inevitable in free debate, and that it must be protected if the freedoms of expression are to have the "breathing space" that they "need . . . to survive," *N. A. A. C. P. v. Button*, 371 U.S. 415, 433, was also recognized by the Court of Appeals for the District of Columbia Circuit in *Sweeney v. Patterson*, 128 F.2d 457, 458 (1942), cert. denied, 317 U.S. 678. In that decision, the D.C. Circuit balanced the public interest in free debate and the individual interest of the libeled plaintiff, concluding: "Errors of fact, particularly in regard to a man's mental states and processes, are inevitable. . . . Whatever is added to the field of libel is taken from the field of free debate."

Injury to official reputation affords no more warrant for repressing speech that would otherwise be free than does factual error. Where judicial officers are involved, this Court has held that concern for the dignity and reputation of the courts does not justify the punishment as criminal contempt of criticism of the judge or his decision. This is true even though the utterance contains "half-truths" and "misinformation." Such repression can be justified, if at all, only by a clear and present danger of the obstruction of justice. If judges are to be treated as "men of fortitude, able to thrive in a hardy climate," surely the same must be true of other government officials, such as elected city commissioners. Criticism of their official conduct does not lose its constitutional protection merely because it is effective criticism and hence diminishes their official reputations.

If neither factual error nor defamatory content suffices to remove the constitutional shield from criticism of official conduct, the combination of the two elements is no less inadequate. This is the lesson to be drawn from the great controversy over the Sedition Act of 1798, 1 Stat. 596, which first crystallized a national awareness of the central meaning of the First Amendment. *** [Although the statute criminalizing "false, scandalous, and malicious writing" against the government or federal officials allowed the defense of truth,] the Act was vigorously condemned as unconstitutional in an attack joined in by Jefferson and Madison. . . .

. . . .

Although the Sedition Act was never tested in this Court,[9] the attack upon its validity has carried the day in the court of history. Fines levied in its prosecution were repaid by Act of Congress on the ground that it was unconstitutional. See, e. g., Act of July 4, 1840, c. 45, 6 Stat. 802, accompanied by H. R. Rep. No. 86, 26th Cong., 1st Sess. (1840). Calhoun, reporting to the Senate on February 4, 1836, assumed that its invalidity was a matter "which no one now doubts." Report with Senate bill No. 122, 24th Cong., 1st Sess., p. 3. Jefferson, as President, pardoned those who had been convicted and sentenced under the Act and remitted their fines, stating: "I discharged every person under punishment or prosecution under the sedition law, because I considered, and now consider, that law to be a nullity, as absolute and as palpable as if Congress had ordered us to fall down and worship a golden image." Letter to Mrs. Adams, July 22, 1804, 4 *Jefferson's Works* (Washington ed.), pp. 555, 556. The invalidity of the Act has also been assumed by Justices of this Court. These views reflect a broad consensus that the Act, because of the restraint it imposed upon criticism of government and public officials, was inconsistent with the First Amendment.

. . . .

[9] [FN 16] The Act expired by its terms in 1801.

What a State may not constitutionally bring about by means of a criminal statute is likewise beyond the reach of its civil law of libel. The fear of damage awards under a rule such as that invoked by the Alabama courts here may be markedly more inhibiting than the fear of prosecution under a criminal statute. Alabama, for example, has a criminal libel law which subjects to prosecution "any person who speaks, writes, or prints of and concerning another any accusation falsely and maliciously importing the commission by such person of a felony, or any other indictable offense involving moral turpitude," and which allows as punishment upon conviction a fine not exceeding $500 and a prison sentence of six months. Alabama Code, Tit. 14, § 350. Presumably a person charged with violation of this statute enjoys ordinary criminal-law safeguards such as the requirements of an indictment and of proof beyond a reasonable doubt. These safeguards are not available to the defendant in a civil action. The judgment awarded in this case — without the need for any proof of actual pecuniary loss — was one thousand times greater than the maximum fine provided by the Alabama criminal statute, and one hundred times greater than that provided by the Sedition Act. And since there is no double-jeopardy limitation applicable to civil lawsuits, this is not the only judgment that may be awarded against petitioners for the same publication. Whether or not a newspaper can survive a succession of such judgments, the pall of fear and timidity imposed upon those who would give voice to public criticism is an atmosphere in which the First Amendment freedoms cannot survive. Plainly the Alabama law of civil libel is "a form of regulation that creates hazards to protected freedoms markedly greater than those that attend reliance upon the criminal law." *Bantam Books, Inc., v. Sullivan*, 372 U.S. 58, 70.

The state rule of law is not saved by its allowance of the defense of truth. A defense for erroneous statements honestly made is no less essential here than was the requirement of proof of guilty knowledge which, in *Smith v. California*, 361 U.S. 147, we held indispensable to a valid conviction of a bookseller for possessing obscene writings for sale. We said:

> "For if the bookseller is criminally liable without knowledge of the contents, . . . he will tend to restrict the books he sells to those he has inspected; and thus the State will have imposed a restriction upon the distribution of constitutionally protected as well as obscene literature. . . . And the bookseller's burden would become the public's burden, for by restricting him the public's access to reading matter would be restricted. . . . [His] timidity in the face of his absolute criminal liability, thus would tend to restrict the public's access to forms of the printed word which the State could not constitutionally suppress directly. The bookseller's self-censorship, compelled by the State, would be a censorship affecting the whole public, hardly less virulent for being privately administered. Through it, the distribution of all books, both obscene and not obscene, would be impeded." (361 U.S. 147, 153–154.)

A rule compelling the critic of official conduct to guarantee the truth of all his factual assertions — and to do so on pain of libel judgments virtually unlimited in amount — leads to a comparable "self-censorship." Allowance of the defense of truth, with the burden of proving it on the defendant, does not mean that only false speech will be deterred.[10] Even courts accepting this defense as an adequate safeguard have recognized the difficulties of adducing legal proofs that the alleged libel was true in all its factual particulars. Under such a rule, would-be critics of official conduct may be deterred from voicing their criticism, even though it is believed to be true and even though it is in fact true, because of doubt whether it can be proved in court or fear of the expense of having to do so. They tend to make only statements which "steer far wider of the unlawful zone." The rule thus dampens the vigor and limits the variety of public debate. It is inconsistent with the First and Fourteenth Amendments.

The constitutional guarantees require, we think, a federal rule that prohibits a public official from recovering damages for a defamatory falsehood relating to his official conduct unless he proves that the statement was made with "actual malice" — that is, with knowledge that it was false or with reckless disregard of whether it was false or not. An oft-cited statement of a like rule, which has been adopted by a number of state courts,[11] is found in the Kansas case of *Coleman v. MacLennan*, 78 Kan. 711, 98 P. 281 (1908). . . .

. . . .

Such a privilege for criticism of official conduct[12] is appropriately analogous to the protection accorded a public official when he is sued for libel by a private citizen. . . . The reason for the official privilege is said to be that the threat of damage suits would otherwise "inhibit the fearless, vigorous, and effective administration of policies of government" and "dampen the ardor of all but the most resolute, or the most irresponsible, in the unflinching discharge of their duties." *Barr v. Matteo*, 360 U.S., at 571. Analogous considerations support the privilege for the citizen-critic of government. . . .

---

[10] [FN 19] Even a false statement may be deemed to make a valuable contribution to public debate, since it brings about "the clearer perception and livelier impression of truth, produced by its collision with error." Mill, On Liberty (Oxford: Blackwell, 1947), at 15; see also Milton, Areopagitica, in Prose Works (Yale, 1959), Vol. II, at 561.

[11] [FN 20] *E. g., Ponder v. Cobb*, 257 N. C. 281, 299, 126 S.E.2d 67, 80 (1962); *Lawrence v. Fox*, 357 Mich. 134, 146, 97 N.W.2d 719, 725 (1959); *Stice v. Beacon Newspaper Corp.*, 185 Kan. 61, 65–67, 340 P.2d 396, 400–401 (1959); *Bailey v. Charleston Mail Assn.*, 126 W. Va. 292, 307, 27 S.E.2d 837, 844 (1943); *Salinger v. Cowles*, 195 Iowa 873, 889, 191 N. W. 167, 174 (1922); *Snively v. Record Publishing Co.*, 185 Cal. 565, 571–576, 198 P. 1 (1921); *McLean v. Merriman*, 42 S. D. 394, 175 N. W. 878 (1920). Applying the same rule to candidates for public office, see, e. g., *Phoenix Newspapers v. Choisser*, 82 Ariz. 271, 276–277, 312 P. 2d 150, 154 (1957); *Friedell v. Blakely Printing Co.*, 163 Minn. 226, 230, 203 N. W. 974, 975 (1925). And see *Chagnon v. Union-Leader Corp.*, 103 N. H. 426, 438, 174 A. 2d 825, 833 (1961), *cert. denied*, 369 U.S. 830.

The consensus of scholarly opinion apparently favors the rule that is here adopted. E. g., 1 Harper and James, Torts, § 5.26, at 449–450 (1956); Noel, *Defamation of Public Officers and Candidates*, 49 Col. L. Rev. 875, 891–895, 897, 903 (1949); Hallen, *Fair Comment*, 8 Tex. L. Rev. 41, 61 (1929); Smith, *Charges Against Candidates*, 18 Mich. L. Rev. 1, 115 (1919); Chase, *Criticism of Public Officers and Candidates for Office*, 23 Am. L. Rev. 346, 367–371 (1889); Cooley, Constitutional Limitations (7th ed., Lane, 1903), at 604, 616–628. But see, e. g., American Law Institute, Restatement of Torts, § 598, Comment a (1938) (reversing the position taken in Tentative Draft 13, § 1041 (2) (1936)); Veeder, *Freedom of Public Discussion*, 23 Harv. L. Rev. 413, 419 (1910).

[12] [FN 21] The privilege immunizing honest misstatements of fact is often referred to as a "conditional" privilege to distinguish it from the "absolute" privilege recognized in judicial, legislative, administrative and executive proceedings. See, e. g., Prosser, Torts (2d ed., 1955), § 95.

We conclude that such a privilege is required by the First and Fourteenth Amendments.

. . . .

MR. JUSTICE BLACK, with whom MR. JUSTICE DOUGLAS joins, concurring.

I concur in reversing this half-million-dollar judgment against the New York Times Company and the four individual defendants. . . . "Malice," even as defined by the Court, is an elusive, abstract concept, hard to prove and hard to disprove. The requirement that malice be proved provides at best an evanescent protection for the right critically to discuss public affairs and certainly does not measure up to the sturdy safeguard embodied in the First Amendment. Unlike the Court, therefore, I vote to reverse exclusively on the ground that the Times and the individual defendants had an absolute, unconditional constitutional right to publish in the Times advertisement their criticisms of the Montgomery agencies and officials. . . .

. . . .

MR. JUSTICE GOLDBERG, with whom MR. JUSTICE DOUGLAS joins, concurring in the result.

[The concurring justices agreed with JUSTICE BLACK.]

HILL v. CHURCH OF SCIENTOLOGY OF TORONTO
SUPREME COURT OF CANADA
[1995] 2 S.C.R. 1130, 126 D.L.R. (4th) 129

The judgment of LA FOREST, GONTHIER, CORY, MCLACHLIN, IACOBUCCI and MAJOR JJ. was delivered by CORY J. —

[The litigation surrounding public statements made by appellant Morris Manning, a prominent criminal defence and constitutional rights litigator, accompanied by representatives of the appellant Church of Scientology of Toronto ("Scientology"), commenting on allegations contained in a notice of motion by which Scientology intended to commence criminal contempt proceedings against the respondent Casey Hill, a Crown attorney, alleging that Hill had misled a judge of the Supreme Court of Ontario and had breached orders sealing certain documents belonging to Scientology. The contempt proceedings found the allegations against Hill to be untrue and without foundation. Hill thereupon commenced this action for damages in libel against both Manning and Scientology, resulting in a jury finding of liability, general damages of $300,000 and a judgment against Scientology alone for aggravated damages of $500,000 and punitive damages of $800,000.]

I. Factual Background

[At the time the defamatory statements were made, Casey Hill was employed as counsel with the Crown Law Office, Criminal Division of the Ministry of the Attorney General for the Province of Ontario. He had given advice to the Ontario

Provincial Police ("OPP") regarding a warrant which authorized a search of the premises occupied by Scientology. A massive quantity of documents (900 boxes worth!) were seized. In ensuing litigation, a judge ruled that the solicitor-and-client privilege applied to 232 of the seized documents he had reviewed and ordered that they remain sealed pending further order of the court. A series of bureaucratic snafus resulted in the release of sealed, privileged information to an official in an unrelated ministry. Well-known Toronto criminal attorney Clayton Ruby, who had been litigating the matter for Scientology, was outraged and demanded an explanation within five days. When he was informed by Hill's superior that a response would be delayed, he retained Manning, who advised Scientology to commence contempt proceedings against Hill and others. This was based on second- and third-hand information relayed to Manning about Hill's cavalier attitude toward the release of the sealed documents. Subsequent proceedings demonstrated that Hill had no role or responsibility in the document release.]

[Evidence in the libel trial demonstrated that Scientology had created a file tracking Hill as "Enemy Canada," and that Scientology was aware prior to commencing the proceedings against Hill and making public allegations against him that, although sealed envelopes had been improperly released, they had not been actually opened or seen by any unauthorized persons. During the trial, Scientology continued to attack Hill's character and repeat the libel, even though they knew it to be false.]

. . . .

III. Analysis

. . . .

(A) *Application of the Charter*

. . . .

[68] La Forest J., writing for the majority in *McKinney v. University of Guelph*, [1990] 3 S.C.R. 229, stressed the importance of this limitation on the application of the Charter to the actions of government [found by the Court in *Dolphin Delivery*]. He said this at p. 262:

> "The exclusion of private activity from the Charter was not a result of happenstance. It was a deliberate choice which must be respected. We do not really know why this approach was taken, but several reasons suggest themselves. Historically, bills of rights, of which that of the United States is the great constitutional exemplar, have been directed at government. Government is the body that can enact and enforce rules and authoritatively impinge on individual freedom. Only government requires to be constitutionally shackled to preserve the rights of the individual."

[69] La Forest J. warned that subjecting all private and public action to constitutional review would mean reopening whole areas of settled law and would be "tantamount to setting up an alternative tort system" (p. 263). He expressed the very sage warning that this "could strangle the operation of society" (p. 262).

. . . .

(2) Section 52: Charter Values and the Common Law

(a) Interpreting the Common Law in Light of the Values Underlying the Charter

. . . .

[85] In *R. v. Salituro*, [[1991] 3 S.C.R. 654]; the Crown called the accused's estranged wife as a witness. The common law rule prohibiting spouses from testifying against each other was found to be inconsistent with developing social values and with the values enshrined in the Charter. At page 670, Iacobucci J., writing for the Court, held:

"Judges can and should adapt the common law to reflect the changing social, moral and economic fabric of the country. Judges should not be quick to perpetuate rules whose social foundation has long since disappeared. Nonetheless, there are significant constraints on the power of the judiciary to change the law. As McLachlin J. indicated in *Watkins v. Olafson*, [1989] 2 S.C.R. 750, in a constitutional democracy such as ours it is the legislature and not the courts which has the major responsibility for law reform; and for any changes to the law which may have complex ramifications, however necessary or desirable such changes may be, they should be left to the legislature. The judiciary should confine itself to those incremental changes which are necessary to keep the common law in step with the dynamic and evolving fabric of our society."

Further, at p. 675 this Court held:

"Where the principles underlying a common law rule are out of step with the values enshrined in the Charter, the courts should scrutinize the rule closely. If it is possible to change the common law rule so as to make it consistent with Charter values, without upsetting the proper balance between judicial and legislative action that I have referred to above, then the rule ought to be changed."

[86] [The Court observed that *Salituro* did not] undertake an analysis similar to that which would be required under s. 1 to determine if the Charter breach was justifiable. Rather, it proceeded to balance, in a broad and flexible manner, the conflicting values. The reasons examined the origins of the impugned common law rule and the justifications which had been raised for upholding it. These concerns were weighed against the Charter's recognition of the equality of women and, more specifically, against the concept of human dignity which inspires the Charter. It was held that the values which were set out in the common law rule did not represent the values of today's society which are reflected in the provisions of the Charter.

. . . .

[Next, the Court discussed *R. v. Swain*, [1991] 1 S.C.R. 933, where the accused had challenged the application of a common law rule allowing the Crown to raise an insanity defence over the accused's objection. Rather than proceed to evaluate the rule under *R. v. Oakes*' test for reasonable limits on Charter infringements, the SCC simply altered the common law so it would not conflict with the current Court's view of principles of fundamental justice mandated by s. 7 of the Charter.]

. . . .

[91] It is clear from *Dolphin Delivery, supra,* that the common law must be interpreted in a manner which is consistent with Charter principles. This obligation is simply a manifestation of the inherent jurisdiction of the courts to modify or extend the common law in order to comply with prevailing social conditions and values. As was said in *Salituro, supra,* at p. 678:

> "The courts are the custodians of the common law, and it is their duty to see that the common law reflects the emerging needs and values of our society."

[92] Historically, the common law evolved as a result of the courts making those incremental changes which were necessary in order to make the law comply with current societal values. The Charter represents a restatement of the fundamental values which guide and shape our democratic society and our legal system. It follows that it is appropriate for the courts to make such incremental revisions to the common law as may be necessary to have it comply with the values enunciated in the Charter.

. . . .

[97] When the common law is in conflict with Charter values, how should the competing principles be balanced? In my view, a traditional s. 1 framework for justification is not appropriate. It must be remembered that the Charter "challenge" in a case involving private litigants does not allege the violation of a Charter right. It addresses a conflict between principles. Therefore, the balancing must be more flexible than the traditional s. 1 analysis undertaken in cases involving governmental action cases. Charter values, framed in general terms, should be weighed against the principles which underlie the common law. The Charter values will then provide the guidelines for any modification to the common law which the court feels is necessary.

[98] Finally, the division of onus which normally operates in a Charter challenge to government action should not be applicable in a private litigation Charter "challenge" to the common law. This is not a situation in which one party must prove a prima facie violation of a right while the other bears the onus of defending it. Rather, the party who is alleging that the common law is inconsistent with the Charter should bear the onus of proving both that the common law fails to comply with Charter values and that, when these values are balanced, the common law should be modified. In the ordinary situation, where government action is said to violate a Charter right, it is appropriate that the government undertake the justification for the impugned statute or common law rule. However, the situation is very different where two private parties are involved in a civil suit. One party will have brought the action on the basis of the prevailing common law which may have a long history of acceptance in the community. That party should be able to rely upon that law and should not be placed in the position of having to defend it. It is up to the party challenging the common law to bear the burden of proving not only that the common law is inconsistent with Charter values but also that its provisions cannot be justified.

. . . .

(b) The Nature of Actions for Defamation: The Values to Be Balanced

[100] There can be no doubt that in libel cases the twin values of reputation and freedom of expression will clash. As Edgerton J. stated in *Sweeney v. Patterson*, 128 F.2d 457 (D.C. Cir. 1942), at p. 458, *cert. denied* 317 U.S. 678 (1942), whatever is "added to the field of libel is taken from the field of free debate." The real question, however, is whether the common law strikes an appropriate balance between the two. Let us consider the nature of each of these values.

(i) Freedom of Expression

[The Court emphasized the importance of free speech in a democracy. But it noted that "freedom of expression has never been recognized as an absolute right. The Court next cited several precedents illustrating s.1's requirement of balancing interests, including *Keegstra* (hate speech) and *Butler* (pornography), excerpted above in Chapter 3.]

[106] Certainly, defamatory statements are very tenuously related to the core values which underlie s. 2(b). They are inimical to the search for truth. False and injurious statements cannot enhance self-development. Nor can it ever be said that they lead to healthy participation in the affairs of the community. Indeed, they are detrimental to the advancement of these values and harmful to the interests of a free and democratic society. This concept was accepted in *Globe and Mail Ltd. v. Boland*, [1960] S.C.R. 203, at pp. 208-9, where it was held that an extension of the qualified privilege to the publication of defamatory statements concerning the fitness for office of a candidate for election would be "harmful to that 'common convenience and welfare of society'." Reliance was placed upon the text Gatley on *Libel and Slander in a Civil Action: With Precedents of Pleadings* (4th ed. 1953), at p. 254, wherein the author stated the following:

> "It would tend to deter sensitive and honourable men from seeking public positions of trust and responsibility, and leave them open to others who have no respect for their reputation."

(ii) The Reputation of the Individual

[107] The other value to be balanced in a defamation action is the protection of the reputation of the individual. Although much has very properly been said and written about the importance of freedom of expression, little has been written of the importance of reputation. Yet, to most people, their good reputation is to be cherished above all. A good reputation is closely related to the innate worthiness and dignity of the individual. It is an attribute that must, just as much as freedom of expression, be protected by society's laws. In order to undertake the balancing required by this case, something must be said about the value of reputation.

[108] Democracy has always recognized and cherished the fundamental importance of an individual. That importance must, in turn, be based upon the good repute of a person. It is that good repute which enhances an individual's sense of

worth and value. False allegations can so very quickly and completely destroy a good reputation. A reputation tarnished by libel can seldom regain its former lustre. A democratic society, therefore, has an interest in ensuring that its members can enjoy and protect their good reputation so long as it is merited.

[The Court traced the historic recognition of harm from false statements, from the Biblical injunction against being a false witness to Roman penalties for defamation to the creation of the common law action designed to replace the duel as a means of repairing character assaults.]

. . . .

(c) The Proposed Remedy: Adopting the *New York Times v. Sullivan* "Actual Malice" Rule

. . . .

[123] At the outset, it is important to understand the social and political context of the times which undoubtedly influenced the decision in *New York Times v. Sullivan, supra*. [The Court discussed the critical importance of the challenged advertisement in protesting segregation, the weak case against the defendants there, and the huge jury verdict.]

(d) Critiques of the "Actual Malice" Rule

[The court noted the significant criticism of the *Sullivan* rule by American judges and academic writers. The decision actually increased the number of libel actions and the size of awards, put great pressure on the fact-finding process since courts are now required to make subjective determinations as to who is a public figure and what is a matter of legitimate public concern, increased discovery costs by inquiring into media procedures, and shifted the focus of defamation suits away from deciding upon the truth of the impugned statement to the defendant's negligence. The latter is problematic because it denies "the plaintiff the opportunity to establish the falsity of the defamatory statements and to determine the consequent reputational harm." Moreover, the protection of "the dissemination of falsehoods" is "said to exact a major social cost by deprecating truth in public discourse." The majority cited approvingly a dissenting opinion from Justice White in *Dun & Bradstreet, Inc. v. Greenmoss Builders, Inc.*, 472 U.S. 749, 767–69 (1985)]:

> "In a country like ours, where the people purport to be able to govern themselves through their elected representatives, adequate information about their government is of transcendent importance. That flow of intelligence deserves full First Amendment protection. Criticism and assessment of the performance of public officials and of government in general are not subject to penalties imposed by law. But these First Amendment values are not at all served by circulating false statements of fact about public officials. On the contrary, erroneous information frustrates these values. They are even more disserved when the statements falsely impugn the honesty of those men and women and hence lessen the confidence in government. As the Court said in *Gertz*: "*There is no*

constitutional value in false statements of fact. Neither the intentional lie nor the careless error materially advances society's interest in 'uninhibited, robust, and wide-open' debate on public issues." . . . Yet in *New York Times* cases, the public official's complaint will be dismissed unless he alleges and makes out a jury case of a knowing or reckless falsehood. Absent such proof, there will be no jury verdict or judgment of any kind in his favor, even if the challenged publication is admittedly false. The lie will stand, and the public continue to be misinformed about public matters. . . . Furthermore, when the plaintiff loses, the jury will likely return a general verdict and there will be no judgment that the publication was false, even though it was without foundation in reality. The public is left to conclude that the challenged statement was true after all. Their only chance of being accurately informed is measured by the public official's ability himself to counter the lie, unaided by the courts. That is a decidedly weak reed to depend on for the vindication of First Amendment interests . . .

[The Court noted that the House of Lords had declined to adopt the actual malice standard, as did the Australian High Court. The Australian court noted that under Australian common law, the *Sullivan* standard gave inadequate protection to the reputation of public officials.]

. . . .

(e) *Conclusion: Should the Law of Defamation be Modified by Incorporating the* Sullivan *Principle?*

. . . .

[141] In conclusion, in its application to the parties in this action, the common law of defamation complies with the underlying values of the Charter and there is no need to amend or alter it.

. . . .

(f) *Should the Common Law Defence of Qualified Privilege be Expanded to Comply with Charter Values?*

[The Court explained that when defamatory words are published in privileged circumstances, the *bona fides* of the defendant is presumed. However, the presumption can be rebutted by evidence that the defendant's dominant motive was malicious. For these purposes, malice includes not only spite or ill-will but also an ulterior purpose that conflicts with the sense of duty that justifies the privilege, as well as evidence that the defendant spoke in knowing or reckless disregard for the truth.]

[155] This said, it is my conclusion that Morris Manning's conduct far exceeded the legitimate purposes of the occasion. The circumstances of this case called for great restraint in the communication of information concerning the proceedings launched against Casey Hill. As an experienced lawyer, Manning ought to have taken steps to confirm the allegations that were being made. This is particularly true since he should have been aware of the Scientology investigation pertaining to

access to the sealed documents. In those circumstances he was duty bound to wait until the investigation was completed before launching such a serious attack on Hill's professional integrity. Manning failed to take either of these reasonable steps. As a result of this failure, the permissible scope of his comments was limited and the qualified privilege which attached to his remarks was defeated.

. . . .

The following are the reasons delivered by

[205] L'HEUREUX-DUBE J. — I have had the advantage of reading the reasons of my colleague Justice Cory and, except on one point, generally agree with them as well as with his disposition of this appeal. [L'Heureux-Dube, J., concluded that there is a right to publish details of judicial proceedings before they are heard in open court, but such publication does not enjoy the protection of qualified privilege if it is defamatory. She concluded that no such privilege is necessary if the statements published are true, and no such privilege is desirable if they are not true.]

GRANT v. TORSTAR CORP.
SUPREME COURT OF CANADA
[2009] 3 S.C.R. 640

The judgment of McLACHLIN C.J. and BINNIE, LeBEL, DESCHAMPS, FISH, CHARRON, ROTHSTEIN and CROMWELL JJ. was delivered by McLACHLIN C.J.: —

I. Introduction

[1] Freedom of expression is guaranteed by s. 2(b) of the *Canadian Charter of Rights and Freedoms*. It is essential to the functioning of our democracy, to seeking the truth in diverse fields of inquiry, and to our capacity for self-expression and individual realization.

[2] But freedom of expression is not absolute. One limitation on free expression is the law of defamation, which protects a person's reputation from unjustified assault. The law of defamation does not forbid people from expressing themselves. It merely provides that if a person defames another, that person may be required to pay damages to the other for the harm caused to the other's reputation. However, if the defences available to a publisher are too narrowly defined, the result may be "libel chill," undermining freedom of expression and of the press.

[3] Two conflicting values are at stake — on the one hand freedom of expression and on the other the protection of reputation. While freedom of expression is a fundamental freedom protected by s. 2(b) of the *Charter*, courts have long recognized that protection of reputation is also worthy of legal recognition. The challenge of courts has been to strike an appropriate balance between them in articulating the common law of defamation. In this case, we are asked to consider, once again, whether this balance requires further adjustment.

[4] [Grant sued the *Toronto Star* in defamation for a 2001 article concerning a proposed private golf course development on Grant's lakefront estate.] The story aired the views of local residents who were critical of the development's environ-

mental impact and suspicious that Grant was exercising political influence behind the scenes to secure government approval for the new golf course. The reporter, an experienced journalist named Bill Schiller, attempted to verify the allegations in the article, including asking Grant for comment, which Grant chose not to provide. The article was published, and Grant brought this libel action.

[A trial resulted in a jury verdict for the plaintiff with general, aggravated and punitive damages totalling $ 1.475 million.]

. . . .

[7] For the reasons that follow, I conclude that the common law should be modified to recognize a defence of responsible communication on matters of public interest. In view of this new defence, as well as errors in the jury instruction on fair comment, a new trial should be ordered.

. . . .

V. Analysis

A. *Should the Common Law Provide a Defence Based on Responsible Communication in the Public Interest?*

. . . .

(1) The Current Law

[Canadian defamation law allows the plaintiff to establish a prima facie claim by showing (1) that the impugned words were defamatory, in the sense that they would tend to lower the plaintiff's reputation in the eyes of a reasonable person; (2) that the words in fact referred to the plaintiff; and (3) that the words were published. Falsity and damage are presumed. The onus then shifts to the defendant to advance a defence in order to escape liability. There exist absolute privileges (statements in Parliament and in legal proceedings) and qualified privilege (statements without malice like reference letters or credit reports). In addition, a defense of "fair comment" exists for certain statements of opinion. Other than privilege, the only other defense is one of justification, based on proof that the statement was substantially true. The qualified privileged seldom assists media organizations because it has traditionally been grounded in special relationships characterized by a "duty" to communicate the information and a reciprocal "interest" in receiving it. The press communicates information not to identified individuals with whom it has a personal relationship, but to the public at large.] Another reason is the conservative stance of early decisions, which struck a balance that preferred reputation over freedom of expression. . . .

. . . .

(2) The Case for Changing the Law

. . . .

[41] The fundamental question of principle is whether the traditional defences for defamatory statements of fact curtail freedom of expression in a way that is inconsistent with Canadian constitutional values. Does the existing law strike an appropriate balance between two values vital to Canadian society — freedom of expression on the one hand, and the protection of individuals' reputations on the other? As Binnie J. stated in *WIC Radio*, "An individual's reputation is not to be treated as regrettable but unavoidable road kill on the highway of public controversy, but nor should an overly solicitous regard for personal reputation be permitted to 'chill' freewheeling debate on matters of public interest" (para. 2).[13]

. . . .

[44] The constitutional status of freedom of expression under the *Charter* means that all Canadian laws must conform to it. The common law, though not directly subject to *Charter* scrutiny where disputes between private parties are concerned, may be modified to bring it into harmony with the *Charter*. . . .

. . . .

[46] While *Hill* stands for a rejection of the *Sullivan* approach and an affirmation of the common law of defamation's general conformity with the *Charter*, it does not close the door to further changes in specific rules and doctrines. As Iacobucci J. observed in *R. v. Salituro, [1991] 3 S.C.R. 654, at p. 670*, "[j]udges can and should adapt the common law to reflect the changing social, moral and economic fabric of the country." It is implicit in this duty that the courts will, from time to time, take a fresh look at the common law and re-evaluate its consistency with evolving societal expectations through the lens of *Charter* values.

. . . .

[53] Freedom does not negate responsibility. It is vital that the media act responsibly in reporting facts on matters of public concern, holding themselves to the highest journalistic standards. But to insist on court-established certainty in reporting on matters of public interest may have the effect of preventing communication of facts which a reasonable person would accept as reliable and which are relevant and important to public debate. The existing common law rules mean, in effect, that the publisher must be certain before publication that it can prove the statement to be true in a court of law, should a suit be filed. Verification of the facts and reliability of the sources may lead a publisher to a reasonable certainty of their truth, but that is different from knowing that one will be able to prove their truth in a court of law, perhaps years later. This, in turn, may have a chilling effect on what is published. Information that is reliable and in the public's interest to know may never see the light of day.

---

[13] [Ed. note: *WIC Radio* expanded the Fair Comment defence by changing the traditional requirement from proof that the opinion was one that a "fair-minded" person could hold to one that "anyone could honestly have expressed." Binnie J remarked in that case that in Canada "people have as much right to express outrageous and ridiculous opinions as moderate ones."]

. . . .

[55] Against this, it is argued that false statements cannot advance the purposes of s. 2(b). This contention, however, is belied by the fact the existing defence of privilege concedes: sometimes the public interest requires that untrue statements should be granted immunity, because of the importance of robust debate on matters of public interest (e.g. Parliamentary privilege), or the importance of discussion and disclosure as a means of getting at the truth (e.g. police reports, employment recommendations).

. . . .

[58] This brings me to the competing value: protection of reputation. Canadian law recognizes that the right to free expression does not confer a licence to ruin reputations. . . .

. . . .

[60] The Grant appellants argue that a defence based on the conduct of the defendant devalues the plaintiff's ability to vindicate reputation. A plaintiff's concern, it is said, is with the falsity of the libel, not the responsibility of the journalistic practices that led to its publication. To the extent that a revised defence shifts the focus of the litigation from the truth or falsity of the defamatory statements to the diligence of the defendant in verifying them, the plaintiff's very reason for bringing the suit is obscured.

[61] The answer to this argument lies in the fact that a balanced approach to libel law properly reflects both the interests of the plaintiff and the defendant. The law must take due account of the damage to the plaintiff's reputation. But this does not preclude consideration of whether the defendant acted responsibly, nor of the social value to a free society of debate on matters of public interest. I agree with Sharpe J.A. that the partial shift of focus involved in considering the responsibility of the publisher's conduct is an "acceptable price to pay for free and open discussion" (*Quan*, C.A. reasons, at para. 142).

. . . .

[66] A consideration of the jurisprudence of other common law democracies favours replacing the current Canadian law governing redress for defamatory statements of fact on matters of public interest, with a rule that gives greater scope to freedom of expression while offering adequate protection of reputation. Different countries canvassed have taken different approaches. Most, however, give more weight to the value of freedom of expression and robust public debate than does the traditional Canadian approach.

[67] In *Sullivan*, the United States Supreme Court applied the First Amendment's free speech guarantee to hold that a "public official" cannot recover in defamation absent proof that the defendant was motivated by "actual malice," meaning knowledge of falsity or reckless indifference to truth. In subsequent cases, the "actual malice" rule was extended to apply to all "public figures," not only people formally involved in government or politics: *Curtis Publishing Co. v. Butts*, 388 U.S. 130 (1967). *Sullivan* and its progeny have made it extremely difficult for anyone in the public eye to sue successfully for defamation. In the contest between free

expression and reputation protection, free expression decisively won the day.

[68] Commonwealth courts have rejected the precise balance struck in *Sullivan* between free expression and protection of reputation. However, the law has begun to shift in favour of broader defences for press defendants, most prominently in England, but also in Australia (*Lange v. Australian Broadcasting Corp.* (1997), 145 A.L.R. 96 (H.C.)), New Zealand (*Lange v. Atkinson*, [1998] 3 N.Z.L.R. 424 (C.A.) ("*Lange v. Atkinson No. 1*"); *Lange v. Atkinson*, [2000] 1 N.Z.L.R. 257 (P.C.) ("*Lange v. Atkinson No. 2*"); *Lange v. Atkinson*, [2000] 3 N.Z.L.R. 385 (C.A.) ("*Lange v. Atkinson No. 3*")), and South Africa (*Du Plessis v. De Klerk*, 1996 (3) S.A. 850 (C.C.); *National Media Ltd. v. Bogoshi*, 1998 (4) S.A. 1196 (S.C.A.)).

. . . .

[The opinion summarizes *Lange*, excerpted below, and the *Du Plessis* case discussed in *Khumalo*, excerpted below.]

. . . .

[85] A number of countries with common law traditions comparable to those of Canada have moved in recent years to modify the law of defamation to provide greater protection for communications on matters of public interest. These developments confront us with a range of possibilities. The traditional common law defence of qualified privilege, which offered no protection in respect of publications to the world at large, situates itself at one end of the spectrum of possible alternatives. At the other end is the American approach of protecting all statements about public figures, unless the plaintiff can show malice. Between these two extremes lies the option of a defence that would allow publishers to escape liability if they can establish that they acted responsibly in attempting to verify the information on a matter of public interest. This middle road is the path chosen by courts in Australia, New Zealand, South Africa and the United Kingdom.

[86] In my view, the third option, buttressed by the argument from *Charter* principles advanced earlier, represents a reasonable and proportionate response to the need to protect reputation while sustaining the public exchange of information that is vital to modern Canadian society.

. . . .

[94] The traditional duty/interest framework works well in its established settings of qualified privilege. These familiar categories should not be compromised or obscured by the addition of a broad new privilege based on public interest. Further, qualified privilege as developed in the cases is grounded not in free expression values but in the social utility of protecting particular communicative occasions from civil liability.

[95] I therefore conclude that the proposed change to the law should be viewed as a new defence, leaving the traditional defence of qualified privilege intact.

. . . .

[98] This brings us to the substance of the test for responsible communication. In *Quan*, Sharpe J.A. held that the defence has two essential elements: public interest and responsibility. I agree, and would formulate the test as follows. First, the

publication must be on a matter of public interest. Second, the defendant must show that publication was responsible, in that he or she was diligent in trying to verify the allegation(s), having regard to all the relevant circumstances.

. . . .

[106] Public interest is not confined to publications on government and political matters, as it is in Australia and New Zealand. Nor is it necessary that the plaintiff be a "public figure," as in the American jurisprudence since *Sullivan.* Both qualifications cast the public interest too narrowly. The public has a genuine stake in knowing about many matters, ranging from science and the arts to the environment, religion, and morality. The democratic interest in such wide-ranging public debate must be reflected in the jurisprudence.

. . . .

[The opinion recites relevant factors in determining "whether a defamatory communication on a matter of public interest was responsibly made." These include (i) the seriousness of the allegation, (ii) the public importance of the matter, (iii) the urgency of the matter, (iv) the status and reliability of the source, (v) whether the plaintiff's side of the story was sought and accurately reported, (vi) whether inclusionof the defamatory statement was necessary to communicate on the matter of public interest, (vii) whether the statement's public interest lay in the fact that it was made rather than its truth; that is, to preclude publication of "a scurrilous libel simply by purporting to attribute the allegation to someone else," as well as other considerations.]

. . . .

[Justice Abella agreed with recognition of a responsible communication defence but concluded that the defence should be decided by the trial judge and not jury.]

LANGE v. AUSTRALIAN BROADCASTING CORPORATION
High Court of Australia
(1997) 189 CLR 520

[The former Prime Minister of New Zealand alleged that the ABC had defamed him. The defendant claimed that the news story was constitutionally protected. The Court reaffirmed the existence of an implied right for political communication.[14]]

The Common Law and the Constitution

A person who is defamed must find a legal remedy against those responsible for publishing defamatory matter either in the common law or in a statute which confers a right of action. The right to a remedy cannot be admitted, however, if its exercise would infringe upon the freedom to discuss government and political matters which the Constitution impliedly requires. It is necessary, therefore, to

---

[14] [Ed. note: The High Court's discussion of the scope of the implied freedom for political communication was discussed in an excerpt added to Chapter 2. The following excerpt discusses the application of the implied right to the common law of defamation.]

consider the relationship between the Constitution and the freedom of communication which it requires on the one hand and the common law and the statute law which govern the law of defamation on the other.

It is appropriate to begin with the Parliament at Westminster. To say of the United Kingdom that it has an "unwritten constitution" is to identify an amalgam of common law and statute and to contrast it with a written constitution which is rigid rather than fluid. The common law supplies elements of the British constitutional fabric. Sir Owen Dixon wrote:[15]

> The British conception of the complete supremacy of parliament developed under the common law; it forms part of the common law and, indeed, it may be considered as deriving its authority from the common law rather than as giving authority to the common law. But, after all, the common law was the common law of England. It was not a law of nations. It developed no general doctrine that all legislatures by their very nature were supreme over the law.

With the establishment of the Commonwealth of Australia, as with that of the United States of America, it became necessary to accommodate basic common law concepts and techniques to a federal system of government embodied in a written and rigid constitution. The outcome in Australia differs from that in the United States. There is but one common law in Australia which is declared by this court as the final court of appeal. In contrast to the position in the United States, the common law as it exists throughout the Australian States and Territories is not fragmented into different systems of jurisprudence, possessing different content and subject to different authoritative interpretations.[16] The distinction is important for the present case and may be illustrated as follows.

The First Amendment to the United States Constitution prohibits Congress from making any law abridging "the freedom of speech, or of the press." This privilege or immunity of citizens of the United States may not be abridged by the making or "the enforcement" by any State of "any law." That is the effect of the interpretation placed on the Fourteenth Amendment.[17] A civil lawsuit between private parties brought in a State court may involve the State court in the enforcement of a State rule of law which infringes the Fourteenth Amendment. If so, it is no answer that the law in question is the common law of the State, such as its defamation law. The interaction in such cases between the United States Constitution and the State common laws has been said to produce "a constitutional privilege" against the enforcement of State common law.[18]

This constitutional classification has also been used in the United States to

---

[15] [FN 50] "Sources of Legal Authority," reprinted in *Jesting Pilate* (1965) 198 at 199–200.

[16] [FN 51] *cf Black & White Taxi Co v. Brown & Yellow Taxi Co* 276 U.S. 518 at 533–4 (1928); *Erie Railroad Co v. Tompkins* 304 U.S. 64 at 78–9 (1938).

[17] [FN 52] *New York Times Co v. Sullivan* 376 U.S. 254 at 264–5 (1964); *Time Inc v Hill* 385 U.S. 374 at 387–8, 409–10 (1967); *Time Inc v. Firestone* 424 U.S. 448 at 452–3 (1976); *Dun & Bradstreet Inc v. Greenmoss Builders Inc* 472 U.S. 749 at 755, 765–6 (1985); Tribe, *American Constitutional Law*, 2nd ed (1988) para 18-6.

[18] [FN 54] *Gertz v Robert Welch Inc* 418 U.S. 323 at 327, 330, 332, 342–3 (1974).

support the existence of a federal action for damages arising from certain executive action in violation of "free-standing" constitutional rights, privileges or immunities.[19] On the other hand, in Australia, recovery of loss arising from conduct in excess of constitutional authority has been dealt with under the rubric of the common law, particularly the law of tort.[20]

It makes little sense in Australia to adopt the United States doctrine so as to identify litigation between private parties over their common law rights and liabilities as involving "State law rights." Here, "[w]e act every day on the unexpressed assumption that the one common law surrounds us and applies where it has not been superseded by statute."[21] Moreover, that one common law operates in the federal system established by the Constitution. The Constitution displaced, or rendered inapplicable, the English common law doctrine of the general competence and unqualified supremacy of the legislature. It placed upon the federal judicature the responsibility of deciding the limits of the respective powers of State and Commonwealth governments. The Constitution, the federal, State and territorial laws, and the common law in Australia together constitute the law of this country and form "one system of jurisprudence."[22] Covering cl 5 of the Constitution renders the Constitution "binding on the courts, judges, and people of every State and of every part of the Commonwealth, notwithstanding anything in the laws of any State." Within that single system of jurisprudence, the basic law of the Constitution provides the authority for the enactment of valid statute law and may have effect on the content of the common law.

Conversely, the Constitution itself is informed by the common law. This was explained extra-judicially by Sir Owen Dixon:[23]

> We do not of course treat the common law as a transcendental body of legal doctrine, but we do treat it as antecedent in operation to the constitutional instruments which first divided Australia into separate colonies and then united her in a federal Commonwealth. We therefore regard Australian law as a unit. Its content comprises besides legislation the general common law which it is the duty of the courts to ascertain as best they may . . . The anterior operation of the common law in Australia is not just a dogma of our legal system, an abstraction of our constitutional reasoning. It is a fact of legal history.

*   *   *

Under a legal system based on the common law, "everybody is free to do anything, subject only to the provisions of the law," so that one proceeds "upon an assumption of freedom of speech" and turns to the law "to discover the established

---

[19] [FN 55] *Bivens v Six Unknown Federal Narcotics Agents* 403 U.S. 388 (1971).

[20] [FN 56] *Northern Territory v Mengel* (1995) 185 CLR 307 at 350–3, 372–3 129 ALR 1.

[21] [FN 57] Dixon, "The Common Law as an Ultimate Constitutional Foundation" (1957) 31 *Australian Law Journal* 240 at 241. See also *Western Australia v. Commonwealth* (1995) 183 CLR 373 at 487 128 ALR 1 (*Native Title Act* case).

[22] [FN 59] *McArthur v Williams* (1936) 55 CLR 324 at 347; *cf*; *Thompson v. R* (1989) 169 CLR 1 at 34-5 86 ALR 1.

[23] [FN 60] "Sources of Legal Authority," reprinted in *Jesting Pilate* (1965) 198 at 199.

exceptions to it."[24] The common law torts of libel and slander are such exceptions. However, these torts do not inhibit the publication of defamatory matter unless the publication is unlawful — that is to say, not justified, protected or excused by any of the various defences to the publication of defamatory matter, including qualified privilege. The result is to confer upon defendants, who choose to plead and establish an appropriate defence, an immunity to action brought against them. In that way, they are protected by the law in respect of certain publications and freedom of communication is maintained.

The issue raised by the Constitution in relation to an action for defamation is whether the immunity conferred by the common law, as it has traditionally been perceived, or, where there is statute law on the subject the immunity conferred by statute, conforms with the freedom required by the Constitution. In 1901, when the Constitution of the Commonwealth took effect and when the Judicial Committee was the ultimate court in the judicial hierarchy, the English common law defined the scope of the torts of libel and slander. At that time, the balance that was struck by the common law between freedom of communication about government and political matters and the protection of personal reputation was thought to be consistent with the freedom that was essential and incidental to the holding of the elections and referenda for which the Constitution provided. Since 1901, the common law — now the common law of Australia — has had to be developed in response to changing conditions. The expansion of the franchise, the increase in literacy, the growth of modern political structures operating at both federal and State levels and the modern development in mass communications, especially the electronic media, now demand the striking of a different balance from that which was struck in 1901. To this question we shall presently return.

The factors which affect the development of the common law equally affect the scope of the freedom which is constitutionally required. "[T]he common convenience and welfare of society" is the criterion of the protection given to communications by the common law of qualified privilege.[25] Similarly, the content of the freedom to discuss government and political matters must be ascertained according to what is for the common convenience and welfare of society. That requires an examination of changing circumstances and the need to strike a balance in those circumstances between absolute freedom of discussion of government and politics and the reasonable protection of the persons who may be involved, directly or incidentally, in the activities of government or politics.

Of necessity, the common law must conform with the Constitution. The development of the common law in Australia cannot run counter to constitutional imperatives.[26] The common law and the requirements of the Constitution cannot be at odds. The common law of libel and slander could not be developed inconsistently with the Constitution, for the common law's protection of personal reputation must admit as an exception that qualified freedom to discuss government and politics which is required by the Constitution.

---

[24] [FN 62] *Attorney-General v. Guardian Newspapers Ltd (No 2)* [1990] 1 AC 109 at 283.

[25] [FN 65] *Toogood v. Spyring* (1834) 1 CM & R 181 at 193 149 ER 1044 at 1050.

[26] [FN 67] *Theophanous* (1994) 182 CLR 104 at 140 124 ALR 1.

In any particular case, the question whether a publication of defamatory matter is protected by the Constitution or is within a common law exception to actionable defamation yields the same answer. But the answer to the common law question has a different significance from the answer to the constitutional law question. The answer to the common law question prima facie defines the existence and scope of the personal right of the person defamed against the person who published the defamatory matter; the answer to the constitutional law question defines the area of immunity which cannot be infringed by a law of the Commonwealth, a law of a State or a law of those Territories whose residents are entitled to exercise the federal franchise. That is because the requirement of freedom of communication operates as a restriction on legislative power. Statutory regimes cannot trespass upon the constitutionally required freedom.

However, a statute which diminishes the rights or remedies of persons defamed and correspondingly enlarges the freedom to discuss government and political matters is not contrary to the constitutional implication. The common law rights of persons defamed may be diminished by statute but they cannot be enlarged so as to restrict the freedom required by the Constitution. Statutes which purport to define the law of defamation are construed, if possible, conformably with the Constitution. But, if their provisions are intractably inconsistent with the Constitution, they must yield to the constitutional norm.

The common law may be developed to confer a head or heads of privilege in terms broader than those which conform to the constitutionally required freedom, but those terms cannot be any narrower. Laws made by Commonwealth or State parliaments or the legislatures of self-governing territories which are otherwise within power may therefore extend a head of privilege, but they cannot derogate from the common law to produce a result which diminishes the extent of the immunity conferred by the Constitution.

*   *   *

THE LAW OF DEFAMATION

The law of defamation does not contain any rule that prohibits an elector from communicating with other electors concerning government or political matters relating to the Commonwealth. Nevertheless, in so far as the law of defamation requires electors and others to pay damages for the publication of communications concerning those matters or leads to the grant of injunctions against such publications, it effectively burdens the freedom of communication about those matters. That being so, the critical question in the present case is whether the common law of defamation as it has traditionally been understood, and the New South Wales law of defamation in its statutory form, are reasonably appropriate and adapted to serving the legitimate end of protecting personal reputation without unnecessarily or unreasonably impairing the freedom of communication about government and political matters protected by the Constitution.

The purpose of the law of defamation is to strike a balance between the right to reputation and freedom of speech.[27] It is not to be supposed that the protection of reputation is a purpose that is incompatible with the requirement of freedom of communication imposed by the Constitution. The protection of the reputations of those who take part in the government and political life of this country from false and defamatory statements is conducive to the public good. The constitutionally prescribed system of government does not require — to the contrary, it would be adversely affected by — an unqualified freedom to publish defamatory matter damaging the reputations of individuals involved in government or politics. The question then is whether the common law of defamation, as it has traditionally been understood, and the statute law regulating the publication of defamatory matter are reasonably appropriate and adapted to the protection of reputation having regard to the requirement of freedom of communication about government and political matters required by the Constitution.

Theophanous and *Stephens* decided that in particular respects the law of defamation throughout Australia was incompatible with the requirement of freedom of communication imposed by the Constitution. However, those cases did so without expressly determining whether the law of defamation in its common law and statutory emanations has developed to the point that it is reasonably appropriate and adapted to achieving a legitimate end that is compatible with the system of government prescribed by the Constitution. Because that is so, those cases ought not to be treated as conclusively determining that question, which should be examined afresh. In the present case, however, it is necessary to examine only the effect of the defamation law of New South Wales on government and political matters. This is because the argument in this court was conducted on the footing that the plaintiff's action was to be determined solely by regard to the defamation law of that State. In New South Wales, the principal defences to the publication of defamatory matter concerning government and political matters are truth in respect of a matter that is related to a matter of public interest or an occasion of qualified privilege, fair comment on a matter relating to the public interest, fair report of parliamentary and similar proceedings, common law qualified privilege[28] and the statutory defence of qualified privilege contained in s 22 of the *Defamation Act 1974* (NSW) (the Defamation Act).[29] Without the statutory defence of qualified privilege, it is clear enough that the law of defamation, as it has traditionally been

---

[27] [FN 68] *Theophanous* (1994) 182 CLR 104 at 131–2, 154–5, 178 124 ALR 1.

[28] [FN 76] Section 11 of the Defamation Act 1974 (NSW) states that the provision of a statutory defence "does not of itself vitiate, diminish or abrogate any defence or exclusion of liability available apart from this Act." As a result, the common law defence of qualified privilege still applies in New South Wales.

[29] [FN 77] Section 22 states:

"(1)   Where, in respect of matter published to any person:
   (a)   the recipient has an interest or apparent interest in having information on some subject;
   (b)   the matter is published to the recipient in the course of giving to him information on that subject; and
   (c)   the conduct of the publisher in publishing that matter is reasonable in the circumstances, there is a defence of qualified privilege for that publication.

(2)   "For the purposes of subsection (1), a person has an apparent interest in having information on some subject if, but only if, at the time of the publication in question, the publisher believes on reasonable grounds that that person has that interest.

"(3)   Where matter is published for reward in circumstances in which there would be a qualified

understood in New South Wales, would impose an undue burden on the required freedom of communication under the Constitution. This is because, apart from the statutory defence, the law as so understood arguably provides no appropriate defence for a person who mistakenly but honestly publishes government or political matter to a large audience. In *Lang v Willis*,[30] this court held that election speeches made to large audiences of unidentified persons are not necessarily privileged even if the speeches deal with matters of general interest to the electors. In that respect, the common law as hitherto understood in Australia has simply reflected the English common law.

The basis of this common law rule is that reciprocity of interest or duty is essential to a claim of qualified privilege at common law.[31]

Only in exceptional cases has the common law recognised an interest or duty to publish defamatory matter to the general public.[32] However, the common law doctrine as expounded in Australia must now be seen as imposing an unreasonable restraint on that freedom of communication, especially communication concerning government and political matters, which "the common convenience and welfare of society" now requires. Equally, the system of government prescribed by the Constitution would be impaired if a wider freedom for members of the public to give and to receive information concerning government and political matters were not recognised. The "varying conditions of society" of which Cockburn CJ spoke in *Wason v Walter*[33] now evoke a broadening of the common law rules of qualified privilege. As McHugh J pointed out in *Stephens*,[34] that has come about in a number of ways:

> In the last decade of the twentieth century, the quality of life and the freedom of the ordinary individual in Australia are highly dependent on the exercise of functions and powers vested in public representatives and officials by a vast legal and bureaucratic apparatus funded by public moneys. How, when, why and where those functions and powers are or are not exercised are matters that are of real and legitimate interest to every member of the community. Information concerning the exercise of those functions and powers is of vital concern to the community. So is the performance of the public representatives and officials who are invested with them. It follows in my opinion that the general public has a legitimate interest in receiving information concerning matters relevant to the exercise of public functions and powers vested in public representatives and officials. Moreover, a narrow view should not be taken of the matters about

---

privilege under subsection (1) for the publication if it were not for reward, there is a defence of qualified privilege for that publication notwithstanding that it is for reward."

[30] [FN 79] (1934) 52 CLR 637.

[31] [FN 80] *Adam v. Ward* [1917] AC 309 at 334.

[32] [FN 81] *Duncombe v. Daniell* (1837) 8 Car & P 222 173 ER 470; *Adam v. Ward* [1917] AC 309; *Chapman v. LordEllesmere* [1932] 2 KB 431; *Telegraph Newspaper Co Ltd v. Bedford* (1934) 50 CLR 632; *Lang v. Willis* (1934) 52 CLR 637; *Radio 2UE Sydney Pty Ltd v. Parker* (1992) 29 NSWLR 448; *Stephens* (1994) 182 CLR 211 at 261; 124 ALR 80.

[33] [FN 83] (1868) LR 4 QB 73 at 93.

[34] [FN 84] (1994) 182 CLR 211 at 264; 124 ALR 80 at 114.

which the general public has an interest in receiving information. With the increasing integration of the social, economic and political life of Australia, it is difficult to contend that the exercise or failure to exercise public functions or powers at any particular level of government or administration, or in any part of the country, is not of relevant interest to the public of Australia generally.

Because the Constitution requires "the people" to be able to communicate with each other with respect to matters that could affect their choice in federal elections or constitutional referenda or that could throw light on the performance of ministers of State and the conduct of the executive branch of government, the common law rules concerning privileged communications, as understood before the decision in *Theophanous*, had reached the point where they failed to meet that requirement. However, the common law of defamation can and ought to be developed to take into account the varied conditions to which McHugh J referred. The common law rules of qualified privilege will then properly reflect the requirements of ss 7, 24, 64, 128 and related sections of the Constitution.

Accordingly, this court should now declare that each member of the Australian community has an interest in disseminating and receiving information, opinions and arguments concerning government and political matters that affect the people of Australia. The duty to disseminate such information is simply the correlative of the interest in receiving it. The common convenience and welfare of Australian society are advanced by discussion — the giving and receiving of information — about government and political matters. The interest that each member of the Australian community has in such a discussion extends the categories of qualified privilege. Consequently, those categories now must be recognised as protecting a communication made to the public on a government or political matter. It may be that, in some respects, the common law defence as so extended goes beyond what is required for the common law of defamation to be compatible with the freedom of communication required by the Constitution. For example, discussion of matters concerning the United Nations or other countries may be protected by the extended defence of qualified privilege, even if those discussions cannot illuminate the choice for electors at federal elections or in amending the Constitution or cannot throw light on the administration of federal government.

Similarly, discussion of government or politics at State or Territory level and even at local government level is amenable to protection by the extended category of qualified privilege, whether or not it bears on matters at the federal level. Of course, the discussion of matters at State, Territory or local level might bear on the choice that the people have to make in federal elections or in voting to amend the Constitution, and on their evaluation of the performance of federal ministers and their departments. The existence of national political parties operating at federal, State, Territory and local government levels, the financial dependence of State, Territory and local governments on federal funding and policies, and the increasing integration of social, economic and political matters in Australia make this conclusion inevitable. Thus, the extended category of common law qualified privilege ensures conformity with the requirements of the Constitution. The real question is as to the conditions upon which this extended category of common law qualified privilege should depend.

At common law, once an occasion of qualified privilege is found to exist, the privilege traditionally protects a communication made on that occasion unless the plaintiff is actuated by malice in making the communication.[35] But, apart from a few exceptional cases, the common law categories of qualified privilege protect only occasions where defamatory matter is published to a limited number of recipients. If a publication is made to a large audience, a claim of qualified privilege at common law is rejected unless, exceptionally, the members of the audience all have an interest in knowing the truth. Publication beyond what was reasonably sufficient for the occasion of qualified privilege is unprotected. Because privileged occasions are ordinarily occasions of limited publication — more often than not occasions of publication to a single person — the common law has seen honesty of purpose in the publisher as the appropriate protection for individual reputation. As long as the publisher honestly and without malice uses the occasion for the purpose for which it is given, that person escapes liability even though the publication is false and defamatory. But a test devised for situations where usually only one person receives the publication is unlikely to be appropriate when the publication is to tens of thousands, or more, of readers, listeners or viewers.

No doubt it is arguable that, because qualified privilege applies only when the communication is for the common convenience and welfare of society, a person publishing to tens of thousands should be able to do so under the same conditions as those that apply to any person publishing on an occasion of qualified privilege. But the damage that can be done when there are thousands of recipients of a communication is obviously so much greater than when there are only a few recipients. Because the damage from the former class of publication is likely to be so much greater than from the latter class, a requirement of reasonableness as contained in s 22 of the Defamation Act, which goes beyond mere honesty, is properly to be seen as reasonably appropriate and adapted to the protection of reputation and, thus, not inconsistent with the freedom of communication which the Constitution requires.

Reasonableness of conduct is the basic criterion in s 22 of the Defamation Act which gives a statutory defence of qualified privilege. It is a concept invoked in one of the defences of qualified protection under the Defamation Codes of Queensland and Tasmania. And it was the test of reasonableness that was invoked in the joint judgment in *Theophanous*. Given these considerations and given, also, that the requirement of honesty of purpose was developed in relation to more limited publications, reasonableness of conduct seems the appropriate criterion to apply when the occasion of the publication of defamatory matter is said to be an occasion of qualified privilege solely by reason of the relevance of the matter published to the discussion of government or political matters. But reasonableness of conduct is imported as an element only when the extended category of qualified privilege is invoked to protect a publication that would otherwise be held to have been made to too wide an audience. For example, reasonableness of conduct is not an element of that qualified privilege which protects a member of the public who makes a complaint to a minister concerning the administration of his or her department.

---

[35] [FN 85] *Mowlds v. Fergusson* (1939) 40 SR(NSW) 311 at 327–9; *Horrocks v. Lowe* [1975] AC 135 at 149.

The truth of

Reasonableness of conduct is an element for the judge to consider only when a publication concerning a government or political matter is made in circumstances that, under the English common law, would have failed to attract a defence of qualified privilege.

In *Theophanous*,[36] the joint judgment also required the defendant to prove that it was unaware of the falsity of the matter published and that it did not publish the matter recklessly. That is a requirement that has little practical significance. The defendant must establish that its conduct in making the publication was reasonable in all the circumstances of the case. In all but exceptional cases, the proof of reasonableness will fail as a matter of fact unless the publisher establishes that it was unaware of the falsity of the matter and did not act recklessly in making the publication.

It may be that, if a statutory provision were to require the additional elements of want of knowledge of falsity and absence of recklessness, as required by *Theophanous*, it would not, on that account, infringe the freedom of communication which the Constitution requires. For present purposes, it is necessary only to state that their absence from s 22 of the Defamation Act cannot have the consequence that the provisions of that Act infringe the constitutional freedom. Moreover, these are not requirements of the common law, as it has traditionally been understood, and there is no reason why they should be engrafted on the expanded common law defence of qualified privilege.

Having regard to the interest that the members of the Australian community have in receiving information on government and political matters that affect them, the reputations of those defamed by widespread publications will be adequately protected by requiring the publisher to prove reasonableness of conduct. The protection of those reputations will be further enhanced by the requirement that the defence will be defeated if the person defamed proves that the publication was actuated by common law malice to the extent that the elements of malice are not covered under the rubric of reasonableness. In the context of the extended defence of qualified privilege in its application to communications with respect to political matters, "actuated by malice" is to be understood as signifying a publication made not for the purpose of communicating government or political information or ideas, but for some improper purpose.

In *Theophanous*, the court held that, once the publisher proved it was unaware of the falsity of the material, had not acted recklessly, and had acted reasonably, malice could not defeat the constitutional defence. But once the concept of actuating malice is understood in its application to government and political communications, in the sense indicated, we see no reason why a publisher who has used the occasion to give vent to its ill will or other improper motive should escape liability for the publication of false and defamatory statements. As we have explained, the existence of ill will or other improper motive will not itself defeat the privilege. The plaintiff must prove that the publication of the defamatory matter was *actuated* by that ill will or other improper motive. Furthermore, having regard to the subject matter of government and politics, the motive of causing political damage to the plaintiff or his

---

[36] [FN 90] (1994) CLR 104 at 137; 124 ALR 1.

or her party cannot be regarded as improper. Nor can the vigour of an attack or the pungency of a defamatory statement, without more, discharge the plaintiff's onus of proof of this issue.

Whether the making of a publication was reasonable must depend upon all the circumstances of the case. But, as a general rule, a defendant's conduct in publishing material giving rise to a defamatory imputation will not be reasonable unless the defendant had reasonable grounds for believing that the imputation was true, took proper steps, so far as they were reasonably open, to verify the accuracy of the material and did not believe the imputation to be untrue. Furthermore, the defendant's conduct will not be reasonable unless the defendant has sought a response from the person defamed and published the response made (if any) except in cases where the seeking or publication of a response was not practicable or it was unnecessary to give the plaintiff an opportunity to respond.

Once the common law is developed in this manner, the New South Wales law of defamation cannot be said to place an undue burden on those communications that are necessary to give effect to the choice in federal elections given by ss 7 and 24 and the freedom of communication implied by those sections and ss 64 and 128 of the Constitution. It is true that the law of defamation in that State effectively places a burden on those communications although it does not prohibit them. Nevertheless, having regard to the necessity to protect reputation, the law of New South Wales goes no further than is reasonably appropriate and adapted to achieve the protection of reputation once it provides for the extended application of the law of qualified privilege. Moreover, even without the common law extension, s 22 of the Defamation Act ensures that the New South Wales law of defamation does not place an undue burden on communications falling within the protection of the Constitution. That is because s 22 protects matter published to any person where the recipient had an interest or apparent interest in having information on a subject, the matter was published in the course of giving information on that subject to the recipient, and the conduct of the publisher in publishing the matter was reasonable in the circumstances.

* * *

By reason of matters of geography, history, and constitutional and trading arrangements, however, the discussion of matters concerning New Zealand may often affect or throw light on government or political matters in Australia. That being so, it may be that further and better particulars can be provided which bring the publications within the expanded defence. We express no view as to whether the publication can be brought within that defence, but the possibility should not be regarded as foreclosed by the orders that the court now makes.

KHUMALO v. HOLOMISA
CONSTITUTIONAL COURT OF SOUTH AFRICA
2002 (5) SA 401

O'REGAN J:

[1] . . . The respondent, a well-known South African politician and the leader of a political party, is suing the applicants whom we may assume are responsible for the publication of a newspaper, the Sunday World, for defamation arising out of the publication of an article with their newspaper. In the article it was stated, amongst other things, that the respondent was involved in a gang of bank robbers and that he was under police investigation for this involvement.

. . . .

[4] The [appeal] . . . crisply raised the question whether the common law of defamation as developed by our courts is inconsistent with the Constitution. In particular, it raised the question whether, to the extent that the law of defamation does not require a plaintiff in a defamation action to plead that the defamatory statement is false in any circumstances, the law limits unjustifiably the right to freedom of expression as enshrined in section 16 of the Constitution. The applicants are therefore asserting that the elements of the law of defamation in South Africa should, in certain circumstances, include a requirement that the defamatory statement be false. The applicants are therefore asserting that the right of freedom of expression in section 16 is directly applicable in this case despite the fact that the litigation does not involve the state nor any organ of state. . . .

. . . .

[16] The extent to which the Constitution requires a development of the law of defamation is a question which has been frequently asked. The issue was raised but not answered in an early decision of this Court *Du Plessis and Others v De Klerk and Another* 1996 (3) SA 850 (CC); 1996 (5) BCLR 658 (CC) and has been considered in a considerable number of High Court judgments since. It is also a matter which has received the attention of the Supreme Court of Appeal in *National Media Ltd v Bogoshi* and has also troubled courts in many other jurisdictions. . . . therefore, it seems that it would be in the interests of justice for this Court to consider the appeal. . . .

. . . .

[17] The law of defamation in South Africa is based on the *actio injuriarum*, a flexible remedy arising from Roman Law, which afforded the right to claim damages to a person whose personality rights had been impaired intentionally by the unlawful act of another. One of those personality rights, is the right to reputation or *fama*, and it is this aspect of personality rights that was protected by the law of defamation.

[18] . . . It is not an element of the delict in common law that the statement be false. Once a plaintiff establishes that a defendant has published a defamatory statement concerning the plaintiff, it is presumed that the publication was both unlawful and intentional. A defendant wishing to avoid liability for defamation must then raise a

defence which rebuts unlawfulness or intention. A defendant wishing to avoid liability for defamation must then raise a defence which rebuts unlawfulness or intention. Although not a closed list, the most commonly raised defences to rebut unlawfulness are that the publication was true and in the public benefit; that the publication constituted fair comment and that the publication was made on a privileged occasion. Most recently, a fourth defence rebutting unlawfulness was adopted by the Supreme Court of Appeal in National Media Ltd and Others v Bogoshi. . . .

[19] This fourth defence for rebutting unlawfulness . . . allows media defendants to establish that the publication of a defamatory statement, albeit false, was nevertheless reasonable in all the circumstances.

. . . .

[21] Having sketched the principles of the common law of defamation, it is now necessary to consider section 16 of the Constitution. It is this provision upon which the applicants rely to assert that the existing common law rules are inconsistent with the Constitution. . . .

The importance of the right of freedom of expression in a democracy has been acknowledged on many occasions by this Court, and other South African courts. Freedom of expression is integral to a democratic society for many reasons. It is constitutive of the dignity and autonomy of human beings. Moreover, without it, the ability of citizens to make responsible political decisions and to participate effectively in public life would be stifled.

. . . .

[25] However, although freedom of expression is fundamental to our democratic society, it is not a paramount value. It must be construed in the context of the other values enshrined in our Constitution. In particular, the values of human dignity, freedom and equality.

[26] It has long been recognised in democratic societies that the law of defamation lies at the intersection of the freedom of speech and the protection of reputation or good name . . . Under our new constitutional order, the recognition and protection of human dignity is a foundational constitutional value.

. . . .

[28] The law of defamation seeks to protect the legitimate interest individuals have in their reputation. To this end, therefore, it is one of the aspects of our law which supports the protection of the value of human dignity. When considering the constitutionality of the law of defamation, therefore, we need to ask whether an appropriate balance is struck between the protection of freedom of expression on the one hand, and the value of human dignity on the other.

[29] The applicants' exception relies directly on section 16 of the Constitution, despite the fact that none of the parties to the defamation action is the state, or any organ of state. Section 8 of the Constitution provides that:

"(1) The Bill of Rights applies to all law, and binds the legislature, the executive, the judiciary and all organs of state.

(2) A provision of the Bill of Rights binds a natural or a juristic person if, and to the extent that, it is applicable, taking into account the nature of the right and the nature of any duty imposed by the right.

(3) When applying a provision of the Bill of Rights to a natural or juristic person in terms of subsection (2), a court—

(a) in order to give effect to a right in the Bill, must apply, or if necessary develop, the common law to the extent that legislation does not give effect to that right; and

(b) may develop rules of the common law to limit the right, provided that the limitation is in accordance with section 36(1)."

[30] The applicants argued that because, in terms of section 8(1), the Bill of Rights applies to all law and binds the judiciary, section 16 must be interpreted to have direct application to the common law of defamation. The applicants observed that in this regard the provisions of the 1996 Constitution were distinguishable from the provisions of the interim Constitution in which the provisions of the Bill of Rights were not directly binding on the judiciary. Accordingly, they argued that the conclusion of the majority of this Court in *Du Plessis and Others v De Klerk and Another*, that the right to freedom of expression in that Constitution could have no direct application in a defamation action to which the state was not a party, was no longer applicable. In that case, the Court held that although the interim Constitution did not directly apply to the common law, the principles of common law would nevertheless have to be applied and developed by courts "with due regard to the spirit, purport and objects" of the Bill of Rights in that Constitution.

[31] The applicants' argument cannot succeed. It is clear from sections 8(1) and (2) of the Constitution that the Constitution distinguishes between two categories of persons and institutions bound by the Bill of Rights. Section 8(1) binds the legislature, executive, judiciary and all organs of state without qualification to the terms of the Bill of Rights. Section 8(2) however provides that natural and juristic persons shall be bound by provisions of the Bill of Rights "to the extent that, it is applicable, taking into account the nature of the right and the nature of any duty imposed by the right." Once it has been determined that a natural person is bound by a particular provision of the Bill of Rights, section 8(3) then provides that a court must apply and if necessary develop the common law to the extent that legislation does not give effect to the right. Moreover, it provides that the rules of the common law may be developed so as to limit a right, as long as that limitation would be consistent with the provisions of section 8(3)(b).

[32] Were the applicants' argument to be correct, it would be hard to give a purpose to section 8(3) of the Constitution. For if the effect of sections 8(1) and (2) read together were to be that the common law in all circumstances would fall within the direct application of the Constitution, section 8(3) would have no apparent purpose. We cannot adopt an interpretation which would render a provision of the Constitution to be without any apparent purpose.

[33] In this case, the applicants are members of the media who are expressly identified as bearers of constitutional rights to freedom of expression. There can be no doubt that the law of defamation does affect the right to freedom of expression.

Given the intensity of the constitutional right in question, coupled with the potential invasion of that right which could be occasioned by persons other than the state or organs of state, it is clear that the right to freedom of expression is of direct horizontal application in this case as contemplated by section 8(2) of the Constitution. The first question we need then to determine is whether the common law of defamation unjustifiably limits that right. If it does, it will be necessary to develop the common law in the manner contemplated by section 8(3) of the Constitution.

[34] The next question is whether, to the extent that the common law does not require as an element of the delict of defamation in any circumstances that a defamatory statement be false, and leaves the question of truth to be raised only as an aspect of a defence, it is inconsistent with the Bill of Rights as directly applicable.

[35] The applicants argued that to the extent that the common law of defamation does not require a plaintiff to allege and prove the falsity of a defamatory statement, it is inconsistent with the Constitution. There can be no doubt that the constitutional protection of freedom of expression has at best an attenuated interest in the publication of false statements. As Cory J observed in the Canadian case, *Hill v Church of Scientology of Toronto*:

> "False and injurious statements cannot enhance self-development. Nor can it ever be said that they lead to healthy participation in the affairs of the community. Indeed, they are detrimental to the advancement of these values and harmful to the interests of a free and democratic society."

Similarly, no person can argue a legitimate constitutional interest in maintaining a reputation based on a false foundation.

[36] To the extent, therefore, that the common law of defamation permits a plaintiff to recover damages for a defamatory statement without establishing the falsity of the defamatory statement, it does not directly protect a powerful constitutional freedom of expression interest, for there is no powerful interest in falsehood. Nor does it provide necessary protection for the constitutional value of human dignity. For, in the main, a person's interest in their reputation can only further constitutional values if that reputation is a true reflection of their character.

[37] However, the common law delict of defamation does not disregard truth entirely. It remains relevant to the establishment of one of the defences going to unlawfulness, that is, truth in the public benefit. The common law requires a defendant to establish, once a plaintiff has proved the publication of a defamatory statement affecting the plaintiff, that the publication was lawful because the contents of the statement were true and in the public benefit. The burden of proving truth thus falls on the defendant.

[38] In considering the constitutionality of this rule, it must be realised that it is often difficult, and sometimes impossible, to determine the truth or falsity of a particular statement. . . .

In not requiring a plaintiff to establish falsity, but in leaving the allegation and proof of falsity to a defendant to a defamation charge, the common law chooses to let the risk lie on defendants. After all, it is by definition the defendant who published the statement and thereby caused the harm to the plaintiff.

[39] The difficulty of proving the truth or otherwise of defamatory statements, and the common-law rule which lets the risk of the failure to establish truth lie on defendants, in the absence of a defence of reasonable publication, does cause "a chilling effect" on the publication of information. A publisher will think twice before publishing a defamatory statement where it may be difficult or impossible to prove the truth of that statement and where no other defence to defamation would be available. . . .

. . . .

But this chilling effect is reduced considerably by the defence of reasonable publication established in Bogoshi's case. For it permits a publisher who is uncertain of proving the truth of a defamatory statement, nevertheless to publish where he or she can establish that it is reasonable.

. . . .

[41] In deciding whether the common law rule complained of by the applicants does indeed constitute an unjustifiable limitation of section 16 of the Constitution, sight must not be lost of other constitutional values and in particular, the value of human dignity. To succeed, the applicants need to show that the balance struck by the common law, in excluding from the elements of the delict a requirement that the defamatory statement published be false, an appropriate balance has been struck between the freedom of expression, on the one hand, and the value of human dignity on the other.

[42] Although the applicants are right when they contend that individuals can assert no strong constitutional interest in protecting their reputations against the publication of truthful but damaging statements, the applicants can also not show that publishers have a strong constitutional speech interest in the publication of false material. At the heart of the constitutional dispute lies the difficulty of establishing the truth or falsehood of defamatory statements. Burdening either plaintiffs or defendants with the onus of proving a statement to be true or false, in circumstances where proof one way or the other is impossible, therefore results in a zero-sum game. Either plaintiffs will benefit from the difficulties of proof, as happened previously under common law rules; or defendants will win, as the applicants propose. Such a zero-sum result, in whomsoever's favour, fits uneasily with the need to establish an appropriate constitutional balance between freedom of expression and human dignity.

[43] Were the Supreme Court of Appeal not to have developed the defence of reasonable publication in Bogoshi's case, a proper application of constitutional principle would have indeed required the development of our common law to avoid this result. However, the defence of reasonableness developed in that case does avoid a zero-sum result and strikes a balance between the constitutional interests of plaintiffs and defendants. It permits a publisher who can establish truth in the public benefit to do so and avoid liability. But if a publisher cannot establish the truth, or finds it disproportionately expensive or difficult to do so, the publisher may show that in all the circumstances the publication was reasonable. In determining whether publication was reasonable, a court will have regard to the individual's interest in protecting his or her reputation in the context of the constitutional

commitment to human dignity. It will also have regard to the individual's interest in privacy. In that regard, there can be no doubt that persons in public office have a diminished right to privacy, though of course their right to dignity persists. It will also have regard to the crucial role played by the press in fostering a transparent and open democracy. The defence of reasonable publication avoids therefore a winner-takes-all result and establishes a proper balance between freedom of expression and the value of human dignity. Moreover, the defence of reasonable publication will encourage editors and journalists to act with due care and respect for the individual interest in human dignity prior to publishing defamatory material, without precluding them from publishing such material when it is reasonable to do so.

. . . .

[45] In the circumstances, the applicants have not shown that the common law as currently developed is inconsistent with the provisions of the Constitution and their appeal must fail.

7.4. CONSTITUTIONAL VALUES AND THE COMMON LAW

7.4.1. Incorporating values into common law jurisprudence

The explicit reconsideration of the common law in light of "Charter values" reflected in *Dolphin Delivery* and *Hill* reflects a marked change in Canadian jurisprudence. Racially restrictive covenants are now outlawed by statute, but at the same time that *Shelley v. Kraemer* was being litigated in the United States, the Supreme Court of Canada was only willing to block enforcement of a covenant on technical grounds, expressly refusing to find these agreements offensive to public policy. *Noble v. Alley*, [1951] S.C.R. 64. Historically, Canadian courts took a cautious approach to public policy, invoking it only "in clear cases where the harm to the public is substantially incontestable and does not depend upon the 'idiosyncratic inferences of a few judicial minds.' " *Re Millar*, [1938] S.C.R. 1, 7–8 (Duff, C.J.C.). More recently, *Canada Trust Co. v. Ontario Human Rights Commission* (1990), 74 O.R. (2d) 481, 69 D.L.R. (4th) 321 (C.A.) distinguished these precedents and held that a charitable trust excluding Catholics and Jews was unenforceable as against public policy. The court, however, emphasized the many statutory declarations of public policy in this area.

In light of the constitutional approach in the United States, it is noteworthy to consider the insights of the trial judge, whose approach in refusing to enforce restrictive covenants on public policy grounds was not accepted by the Supreme Court of Canada in *Noble, supra*:

> Ontario and Canada too, may well be termed a province, and a country, of minorities in regard to the religious and ethnic groups which live therein. It appears to me to be a moral duty, at least, to lend aid to all forces of cohesion, and similarly to repel all fissiparous tendencies which would imperil national unity. The common law courts have, by their actions over the years, obviated the need for rigid constitutional guarantees in our policy by their wise use of the doctrine of public policy as an active agent

in the promotion of the public weal. While courts and eminent judges have, in view of the powers of our legislatures, warned against inventing new heads of public policy, I do not conceive that I would be breaking new ground were I to hold the restrictive covenant impugned in this proceeding to be void as against public policy. Rather would I be applying well-recognized principles of public policy to a set of facts requiring their invocation in the interest of the public good.

In re Wren, [1945] O.R. 778, 783 (H.C.).

Although in *Hill* the Supreme Court of Canada re-affirmed the common law of libel after considering Charter values, the common law was required to give way in *Dagenais v. CBC*, [1994] 3 S.C.R. 835. CBC planned to broadcast a fictional account of sexual and physical abuse of children in a Catholic institution. At the time, Dagenais was on trial for sexual and physical abuse of young boys at a Catholic training school. Under the common law, judges are allowed to issue publications bans upon a demonstration that there is a real and substantial risk of interference with the right to free trial, and on that basis the CBC programme was banned during pendency of the trial. According to the majority opinion by Lamer, C.J., the pre-*Charter* common law rule gave unwarranted primacy to the right to a fair trial over the interests in free expression, a balance that "is inconsistent with the principles of the *Charter*, and in particular, the equal status given by the *Charter* to ss. 2(b) [free expression] and 11(d) [fair trial]." *Id.* at 877. Thus, "it is necessary to reformulate the common law rule governing the issuance of publication bans that reflects the principles of the *Charter. Id.* at 878. Applying the substance of the *Oakes* test for assessing legislation under s. 1, the Court held that the new common law rule would permit publication bans only when *necessary* to prevent a risk to fair trial, only where reasonably available alternative measures will not prevent the risk, and only where the benefits outweigh to harms. *Id.*

Similarly, in *R.W.D.S.U., Local 558 v. Pepsi-Cola Canada Beverages (West) Ltd.*, [2002] 1 S.C.R. 156, the court resolved what it described as a conflict among lower courts concerning the common law of picketing by rejecting a well-established Ontario decision that made secondary picketing *per se* illegal, as insufficiently protective of Charter values of free expression.

The reasons given in *Hill* make clear the majority's view that, on the merits, the pre-*Charter* common law of libel need not be altered in light of Charter values. The Ontario Court of Appeal in *Hill* took another approach, however, in rejecting the defendants' claim that the *New York Times v. Sullivan* standard should be adopted by Canadian courts. Initially, the Court observed that the defendants' argument would require "a major alteration to the common law." To do so, the Court reasoned, "would be contrary to the established rule that changes to the common law should be slow and incremental out of deference to the legislature." 114 D.L.R. (4th) 1, 32. The opinion then quoted *Watkins v. Olafson*, [1989] 2 S.C.R. 750, 61 D.L.R. (4th) 577, 583–84 [an opinion regarding the common law of damages in tort]:

> Generally speaking, the judiciary is bound to apply the rules of law found in the legislation and in the precedents. Over time, the law in any given area may change; but the process of change is a slow and incremental one, based largely on the mechanism of extending an existing principle to new

circumstances. While it may be that some judges are more activist than others, the courts have generally declined to introduce major and far-reaching changes in the rules hitherto accepted as governing the situation before them.

There are sound reasons supporting this judicial reluctance to dramatically recast established rules of law. The court may not be in the best position to assess the deficiencies of the existing law, much less problems which may be associated with the changes it might make. The court has before it a single case; major changes in the law should be predicated on a wider view of how the rule will operate in the broad generality of cases. Moreover, the court may not be in a position to appreciate fully the economic and policy issues underlying the choice it is asked to make. Major changes to the law often involve devising subsidiary rules and procedures relevant to their implementation, a task which is better accomplished through consultation between courts and practitioners than by judicial decree. Finally, and perhaps most importantly, there is the long-established principle that in a constitutional democracy it is the legislature, as the elected branch of government, which should assume the major responsibility for law reform.

Even when reviewing the common law to incorporate Charter values, the court of appeal noted that the Supreme Court had previously applied the same amount of caution about reformulating the common law. Caution in changing the common law, even to account for Charter values, has been particularly emphasized where there is evidence that Parliament relied upon its understanding of background common law norms in enacting legislation, so that any change in common law would have a far-reaching effect. *See, e.g., Vancouver Society of Immigrant and Visible Minority Women v. M.N.R.*, [1999] 1 S.C.R. 10 (changes in common law definition of charity rejected in part because of parliamentary reliance on traditional common law test in defining charitable organisations for purposes of *Income Tax Act*).

The role of the Supreme Court of Canada as a general court of appeal even allows it to use constitutional values to affect the interpretation of provincial statutes. An illustration is *British Columbia (Public Service Employee Relations Commission) v. British Columbia Government and Service Employees' Union (B.C.G.S.E.U.)*, [1999] 3 S.C.R. 3, which concerned the legality under the *British Columbia Human Rights Code* of a requirement that forest firefighters be able to run 2.5 km in a specified time, a requirement that disproportionately affected women. The statute prohibits discrimination against a person regarding any condition of employment on the basis of sex, but does not apply to a "bona fide occupational requirement" (BFOR). The Court used the case to reformulate the legal standards regarding this area of employment law, holding that a BFOR requires evidence that a standard challenged as disproportionately affecting a protected class "is reasonably necessary to the accomplishment of that legitimate work-related purpose. To show that the standard is reasonably necessary, it must be demonstrated that it is impossible to accommodate individual employees sharing the characteristics of the claimant without imposing undue hardship upon the employer." *Id.* at ¶ 54. In adopting this standard, the Court abolished a pre-existing distinction the cases interpreting human rights legislation had used between instances of "direct discrimination" and those where facially neutral standards were applied with disproportionately adverse impact to protected classes. Although the Court acknowledged that these initial statutory interpretation decisions (some of which preceded the adoption of the Charter) may have been based on the idea that discrimination in the latter instance was "less deserving of legal censure," the Court noted that its jurisprudence regarding discrimination in violation of the equality provisions of s. 15 of the Charter had rejected this distinction, and applied the same reasoning to the *B.C. Human Rights Code. Id.* at ¶ 49.

Although Australian law is less developed in this area, the High Court of Australia has re-affirmed the need for the common law to develop according to constitutional principles. Thus, citing *Lange*, the court reconsidered prior decisions and held that a uniform federal choice-of-law rule was constitutionally required, so that Australian Capital Territory courts were required to apply New South Wales law to a tort claim where the tort occurred in New South Wales. *John Pfeiffer Pty Ltd v. Rogerson*, (2000) 203 CLR 503; 172 ALR 625.

By way of comparison, although constitutional values may influence the way that the U.S. Supreme Court interprets federal statutes, William N. Eskridge, Jr., *Public Values in Statutory Interpretation*, 137 U. Pa. L. Rev. 1007 (1989), the U.S. Supreme Court has no jurisdiction to review state statutes other than to find them unconstitutional. The final arbiter of the interpretation of Pennsylvania statutes is the Supreme Court of Pennsylvania.

7.4.2. Legal realism and the constitutionalization of the American common law

One way to explain why the U.S. Supreme Court would hold that the U.S. Constitution applied to common law actions is that this was the only means by which the Court could prevent enforcement of racist covenants[37] or prejudicial libel verdicts. In *Shelley v. Kraemer* and *New York Times v. Sullivan*, the U.S. Supreme Court, as a limited court of appeal, was required to accept without further review

---

[37] Actually, this holding was not necessary in *Shelley*, although it might not have been apparent at the time the case was decided. Section 1 of the Civil Rights Act of 1866, codified at 42 U.S.C. § 1982, provides that all citizens "shall have the same right . . . to . . . inherit, purchase, lease, sell, hold, and convey real and personal property, and to full and equal benefit of all laws and proceedings for the security of person and property, as is enjoyed by white citizens . . ." Writing for the court of appeals in *Jones v. Alfred H. Mayer Co.*, 379 F.2d 33 (8th Cir. 1967), Judge Harry A. Blackmun (as he then was) reviewed Supreme Court precedent and concluded that the statute was to be interpreted as enforcing rights guaranteed under the Fourteenth Amendment — thus limiting its scope to state action. In particular, Blackmun, J., relied upon the Court's decision in the *Civil Rights Cases*, 109 U.S. 3, 22–24 (1883), holding that the Thirteenth Amendment was solely concerned with slavery and not "to adjust what may be called the social rights of men and races in the community." In light of the aforementioned limits on the Fourteenth Amendment, Congress therefore did not have the constitutional power to outlaw private racial discrimination. (Note that private discrimination outlawed by the Civil Rights Act of 1964 was upheld based on Congress' power to regulate interstate commerce.) The Supreme Court reversed, 392 U.S. 409 (1968). Justice Stewart's majority opinion carefully sidestepped contrary language in prior precedents as off-point or *dictum*, and read the plain language and legislative history of the Act to conclude that private discrimination was intended to be outlawed by Congress. The Court also declined to follow the *Civil Rights Cases'* restrictive reading of the Thirteenth Amendment, finding that it authorized Congress to outlaw any "badges or incidents" of slavery, which included inability to purchase property.

the determination by the Missouri Supreme Court that racist covenants were not void as against public policy, and by the Alabama Supreme Court that the libel verdict was an appropriate balance of reputational and speech interests. In identical cases, the Supreme Court of Canada or the High Court of Australia, as general courts of appeal, could simply have reversed the judgment.

These two cases are not the only instances where the U.S. Supreme Court has created constitutional doctrines to ensure that the common law adequately balances constitutional values. Professors Jim Pfander and David Meyer suggest several other areas where constitutional law might not have been created were the U.S. Supreme Court a "general court of appeal" like the Supreme Court of Canada or the High Court of Australia. These include:

- The implied cause of action for injuries suffered when federal agents unreasonably searched a home and seized property in a manner inconsistent with the Fourth Amendment. *See Bivens v. Six Unknown Named Agents*, 403 U.S. 388 (1971). In Canada and Australia, police misconduct is typically litigated under common law principles. (Indeed, in *Lange*, the High Court explicitly noted the difference between American and Australian law in this respect.) Pfander suggests that the U.S. Supreme Court was unwilling to subject Americans to the vagaries of state trespass and related doctrines.

- A limit on excessive punitive damages. In *BMW of North America, Inc. v. Gore*, 517 U.S. 559 (1996), the Court held that an award of $4 million for falsely representing that a repainted BMW was "new" (the jury set compensatory damages at $4,000) was so excessive that it constituted a violation of due process. At the same time, the Court expressly refused to "draw a bright line marking the limits of a constitutionally acceptable punitive damage award." 517 U.S. at 571. Subsequently, the Court held that punitive damages based in part on the jury's desire to punish the manufacturer for harming nonparties amounted to a taking of property from the manufacturer without due process, although it was permissible to consider nonparty harm in determining reprehensibility. *Philip Morris USA v. Williams*, 549 U.S. 346 (2007). The constitutional problem was only raised by the court's inability to directly review the judgment of the Alabama Supreme Court in *BMW* and the Oregon Supreme Court in *Philip Morris* that the jury's award was reasonable and proper. *Cf. Whiten v. Pilot Insurance Co.*, [2002] 1 S.C.R. 595, where the Supreme Court of Canada directly reviewed a jury's award of $1 million in punitive damages as well as the antecedent instructions given by the trial judge. Having regard for the "reprehensible" conduct of the defendant in terminating rent payments and withholding claims based on unsupported allegations of arson, the majority concluded that although the award was higher than they would have imposed, it was "within rational limits."

- The law of property. Reconsider the discussion in the Concluding Note of Chapter 6 concerning the constitutionalization of property law in the United States. In *Lucas v. South Carolina Coastal Council*, 505 U.S. 1003 (1992), the majority implied that a change in the common law that deprived owners of the use of their land might well constitute an unconstitutional taking if compensation were not provided. In this context, note that the U.S. Supreme Court is unable, as a limited court of appeal, from simply reversing the lower court's judgment as to the legitimacy of the change in the common law.

• Custodial disputes before family court judges. The U.S. Supreme Court has no general authority to review state court decisions concerning visitation rights for children. In *Troxel v. Granville*, 530 U.S. 57 (2000), the Court found that the Fourteenth Amendment granted custodial parents certain fundamental rights to make decisions concerning their children. The Court thus invalidated, on constitutional grounds, a state court order requiring a mother to grant visitation rights to the children's grandparents (the parents of the children's deceased father). The Court emphasized that the mother's rights were not absolute, but faulted the state court for failing to give any material weight to the mother's views and affording an unwarranted presumption in favor of the grandparents' visitation. Clearly, the justices did not believe that the state court judge had properly exercised discretion, but general review on this ground is not permitted in the American federal system.

Chapter 8

ADVISORY OPINIONS, CONSTITUTIONAL CONVENTIONS, AND THE DETERMINATION OF JUDICIAL AUTHORITY

KEY CONCEPTS FOR THE CHAPTER

- AMERICAN JUSTICES BELIEVE THAT THE POWER OF JUDICIAL REVIEW OF LEGISLATIVE ACTS IS BASED SOLELY ON THE JUDICIARY'S NECESSARY AND ESSENTIAL ROLE IN DECIDING LITIGATED "CASES OR CONTROVERSIES."

- AUSTRALIAN JUSTICES HAVE HELD THAT THE FACT THAT THE AUSTRALIAN CONSTITUTION CONFINES THE JURISDICTION OF THE HIGH COURT TO "MATTERS" BARS ADVISORY OPINIONS.

- DRAWING ON 19TH CENTURY ENGLISH PRACTICE, CANADA ALLOWS REFERENCES TO THE SUPREME COURT OF CANADA ON "IMPORTANT QUESTIONS OF LAW OR FACT CONCERNING ANY MATTER."

- IN THE U.S., IT IS COMMONLY UNDERSTOOD THAT THE ONLY CONSTITUTIONAL LIMITS ON OFFICIAL BEHAVIOR ARE THOSE THAT WILL BE ENJOINED BY JUDGES; THE TRADITION OF THE BRITISH COMMONWEALTH OF "CONSTITUTIONAL CONVENTIONS" IS MORE EXPANSIVE. IT INCLUDES UNWRITTEN TRADITIONS THAT ARE WIDELY UNDERSTOOD AND ACCEPTED, BUT WHERE COURTS WILL NOT PROVIDE ANY LEGAL OR EQUITABLE RELIEF.

- CONVENTIONS SUCH AS PARLIAMENTARY SOVEREIGNTY THAT DOMINATED SOUTH AFRICAN LAW IN THE COLONIAL AND APARTHEID ERA WERE EXPLICITLY REPLACED BY A CONSTITUTION THAT NOT ONLY STATES THAT IT IS THE SUPREME LAW OF THE LAND BUT ALSO GRANTS THE CONSTITUTIONAL COURT THE POWER TO UPHOLD THE CONSTITUTION AND DETERMINE ITS MEANING.

- THE ENSHRINEMENT OF JUDICIAL OR CONSTITUTIONAL REVIEW IN SOUTH AFRICA INCLUDES THE JURISDICTION TO ADJUDICATE ON BOTH CONCRETE CASES AS WELL AS TO OFFER ABSTRACT REVIEW UNDER CERTAIN CONSTITUTIONALLY DETERMINED CIRCUMSTANCES.

- THE SUPREMACY AND ENTRENCHMENT OF THE SOUTH AFRICAN CONSTITUTION IS GUARANTEED THROUGH THE REQUIREMENT THAT ANY AMENDMENTS REQUIRE SPECIAL PROCEDURES AND SPECIAL MAJORITIES YET THE AMENDMENT PROCEDURES ARE FAR MORE FLEXIBLE THAN IN THE U.S. CONSTITUTION.

8.1. THE CONCEPT OF AN "UNCONSTITUTIONAL" LAW OR GOVERNMENT ACT

MARBURY v. MADISON
SUPREME COURT OF THE UNITED STATES
5 U.S. 137, 1 Cranch 137 (1803 terms)

[Ed. note: A bit of historical context may be helpful to the understanding of this landmark case. Although support for George Washington as the first American president was near-unanimous, two political parties quickly developed. One, under the leadership of Washington's Vice President, John Adams, was often called the Federalists. The other, led by his Secretary of State, Thomas Jefferson, were called the Republicans. (Actually, the Jeffersonian faction morphed into "Democrat-Republicans" and then "Democrats" by the time of the election of Andrew Jackson in 1828, the latter day Republican Party being created anew in the 1850s.) Adams defeated Jefferson in the election of 1796, but Jefferson won the re-match in 1800, sweeping in a majority of allies in Congress as well, thus setting up the first peaceful transition of power from one party to another in U.S. history. The transition was not entirely uneventful, however. President-elect Jefferson was not to be sworn in until March 4, 1801. (The Twentieth Amendment changed the inauguration date to January 20.) In January of that year, President Adams nominated, and the lame duck Federalist Senate confirmed, Adams' Secretary of State, John Marshall, as the new Chief Justice. In February, the lame duck Federalist Congress enacted the Judiciary Act of 1801, doubling the number of federal judges, and creating 42 new justices of the peace for the District of Columbia. President Adams sought to fill every possible judicial position with his Federalist allies, rushing their nominations through (with quick confirmation by the lame duck, Federalist-dominated Senate) on the eve of the expiration of his term of office. Adams' principal deputy in this matter was his Secretary of State, John Marshall, who did not take his oath and assume the duties of Chief Justice until shortly before the end of Adams' term. The case arose when President Jefferson's Secretary of State, James Madison, refused to perform the ministerial duty of turning over the commissions of office to those Federalist "midnight appointees" whom the Adams administration was unable to fully invest in office.

The issue of judicial review arose in an interesting political context. The newly elected Republican Congress, outraged by Adams' tactics, repealed the Judiciary Act of 1801. The Federalist minority in Congress objected that such a repeal would be unconstitutional, since the Constitution protected the tenure of judges. In response, the Republican majority denied that the Supreme Court had the power to invalidate unconstitutional legislation. The delay in the decision in *Marbury* was due to legislation that not only repealed the prior judge-creating statute, but eliminated the 1802 term of the Supreme Court!]

MARSHALL, C.J.:

At the last term, viz. December term, 1801, William Marbury, Dennis Ramsay, Robert Townsend Hooe, and William Harper, by their counsel, Charles Lee, esq. late attorney general of the United States [*i.e.*, a member of President Adams' cabinet], severally moved the court for a rule to James Madison, secretary of state of the United States, to show cause why a mandamus should not issue commanding him to cause to be delivered to them respectively their several commissions as justices of the peace in the district of Columbia. This motion was supported by affidavits of the following facts; that notice of this motion had been given to Mr. Madison; that Mr. Adams, the late president of the United States, nominated the applicants to the senate for their advice and consent to be appointed justices of the peace of the district of Columbia; that the senate advised and consented to the appointments; that commissions in the due form were signed by the said president appointing them justices, &c. and that the seal of the United States was in due form affixed to the said commissions by the secretary of state; that the applicants have requested Mr. Madison to deliver them their said commissions, who has not complied with that request; and that their said commissions are withheld from them; that the applicants have made application to Mr. Madison as secretary of state of the United States at his office, for information whether the commissions were signed and sealed as aforesaid; that explicit and satisfactory information has not been given to that enquiry, either by the secretary of state or by any officer of the department of state; that application has been made to the secretary of the Senate for a certificate of the nomination of the applicants, and of the advice and consent of the senate, who has declined giving such a certificate; whereupon a rule was laid to show cause on the 4th day of this term. This rule having been duly served,

Afterwards, on the 24th of February the following opinion of the court was delivered by the chief justice.

At the last term on the affidavits then read and filed with the clerk, a rule was granted in this case, requiring the secretary of state to show cause why a mandamus should not issue, directing him to deliver to William Marbury his commission as a justice of the peace of the county of Washington, in the district of Columbia.

No cause has been shown, and the present motion is for a mandamus. The peculiar delicacy of this case, the novelty of some of its circumstances, and the real difficulty attending the points which occur in it, require a complete exposition of the principles, on which the opinion to be given by the court, is founded.

*   *   *

This is not a proceeding which may be varied, if the judgment of the executive shall suggest one more eligible; but is a precise course accurately marked out by law, and is to be strictly pursued. It is the duty of the secretary of state to conform to the law, and in this he is an officer of the United States, bound to obey the laws. He acts, in this regard, as has been very properly stated at the bar, under the authority of law, and not by the instructions of the President. It is a ministerial act which the law enjoins on a particular officer for a particular purpose.

*   *   *

The discretion of the executive is to be exercised until the appointment has been made. But having once made the appointment, his power over the office is terminated in all cases, where, by law, the officer is not removable by him. The right to the office is then in the person appointed, and he has the absolute, unconditional, power of accepting or rejecting it.

Mr. Marbury, then, since his commission was signed by the President, and sealed by the secretary of state, was appointed; and as the law creating the office, gave the officer a right to hold for five years, independent of the executive, the appointment was not revocable; but vested in the officer legal rights, which are protected by the laws of his country.

To withhold his commission, therefore, is an act deemed by the court not warranted by law, but violative of a vested legal right.

This brings us to the second enquiry; which is,

2dly. If he has a right, and that right has been violated, do the laws of his country afford him a remedy?

The very essence of civil liberty certainly consists in the right of every individual to claim the protection of the laws, whenever he receives an injury. One of the first duties of government is to afford that protection. In Great Britain the king himself is sued in the respectful form of a petition, and he never fails to comply with the judgment of his court.

In the 3d vol. of his commentaries, p. 23, Blackstone states two cases in which a remedy is afforded by mere operation of law.

"In all other cases," he says, "it is a general and indisputable rule, that where there is a legal right, there is also a legal remedy by suit or action at law, whenever that right is invaded."

* * *

The government of the United States has been emphatically termed a government of laws, and not of men. It will certainly cease to deserve this high appellation, if the laws furnish no remedy for the violation of a vested legal right.

If this obloquy is to be cast on the jurisprudence of our country, it must arise from the peculiar character of the case.

* * *

Is it in the nature of the transaction? Is the act of delivering or withholding a commission to be considered as a mere political act, belonging to the executive department alone, for the performance of which, entire confidence is placed by our constitution in the supreme executive; and for any misconduct respecting which, the injured individual has no remedy.

That there may be such cases is not to be questioned; but that every act of duty, to be performed in any of the great departments of government, constitutes such a case is not to be admitted.

By the act concerning invalids, passed in June, 1794, vol. 3. p. 112, the secretary of war is ordered to place on the pension list, all persons whose names are contained in a report previously made by him to congress. If he should refuse to do so, would the wounded veteran be without remedy? Is it to be contended that where the law in precise terms, directs the performance of an act, in which an individual is interested, the law is incapable of securing obedience to its mandate? Is it on account of the character of the person against whom the complaint is made? Is it to be contended that the heads of departments are not amenable to the laws of their country?

Whatever the practice on particular occasions may be, the theory of this principle will certainly never be maintained. No act of the legislature confers so extraordinary a privilege, nor can it derive countenance from the doctrines of the common law. After stating that personal injury from the king to a subject is presumed to be impossible, Blackstone, vol. 3. p. 255, says, "but injuries to the rights of property can scarcely be committed by the crown without the intervention of its officers; for whom, the law, in matters of right, entertains no respect or delicacy; but furnishes various methods of detecting the errors and misconduct of those agents, by whom the king has been deceived and induced to do a temporary injustice."

* * *

It follows then that the question, whether the legality of an act of the head of a department be examinable in a court of justice or not, must always depend on the nature of that act.

If some acts be examinable, and others not, there must be some rule of law to guide the court in the exercise of its jurisdiction.

In some instances there may be difficulty in applying the rule to particular cases; but there cannot, it is believed, be much difficulty in laying down the rule.

By the constitution of the United States, the President is invested with certain important political powers, in the exercise of which he is to use his own discretion, and is accountable only to his country in his political character, and to his own conscience. To aid him in the performance of these duties, he is authorized to appoint certain officers, who act by his authority and in conformity with his orders.

In such cases, their acts are his acts; and whatever opinion may be entertained of the manner in which executive discretion may be used, still there exists, and can exist, no power to control that discretion. The subjects are political. They respect the nation, not individual rights, and being entrusted to the executive, the decision of the executive is conclusive. The application of this remark will be perceived by adverting to the act of congress for establishing the department of foreign affairs. This office, as his duties were prescribed by that act, is to conform precisely to the will of the President. He is the mere organ by whom that will is communicated. The acts of such an officer, as an officer, can never be examinable by the courts.

But when the legislature proceeds to impose on that officer other duties; when he is directed peremptorily to perform certain acts; when the rights of individuals are dependent on the performance of those acts; he is so far the officer of the law; is amenable to the laws for his conduct; and cannot at his discretion sport away the vested rights of others.

The conclusion from this reasoning is, that where the heads of departments are the political or confidential agents of the executive, merely to execute the will of the President, or rather to act in cases in which the executive possesses a constitutional or legal discretion, nothing can be more perfectly clear than that their acts are only politically examinable. But where a specific duty is assigned by law, and individual rights depend upon the performance of that duty, it seems equally clear that the individual who considers himself injured, has a right to resort to the laws of his country for a remedy.

* * *

It is then the opinion of the court,

1st. That by signing the commission of Mr. Marbury, the president of the United States appointed him a justice of peace, for the county of Washington in the district of Columbia; and that the seal of the United States, affixed thereto by the secretary of state, is conclusive testimony of the verity of the signature, and of the completion of the appointment; and that the appointment conferred on him a legal right to the office for the space of five years.

2dly. That, having this legal title to the office, he has a consequent right to the commission; a refusal to deliver which, is a plain violation of that right, for which the laws of his country afford him a remedy.

* * *

Blackstone, in the 3d volume of his commentaries, page 110, defines a mandamus to be, "a command issued in the King's name from the court of King's Bench, and directed to any person, corporation, or inferior court of judicature within the King's dominions, requiring them to do some particular thing therein specified, which appertains to their office and duty, and which the court of King's Bench has previously determined, or at least supposed, to be consonant to right and justice."

* * *

Still, to render the *mandamus* a proper remedy, the officer to whom it is directed, must be one to whom, on legal principles, such writ may be directed; and the person applying for it must be without any other specific and legal remedy.

1st. With respect to the officer to whom it would be directed. The intimate political relation, subsisting between the president of the United States and the heads of departments, necessarily renders any legal investigation of the acts of one of those high officers peculiarly irksome, as well as delicate; and excites some hesitation with respect to the propriety of entering into such investigation. Impressions are often received without much reflection or examination, and it is not wonderful that in such a case as this, the assertion, by an individual, of his legal claims in a court of justice; to which claims it is the duty of that court to attend; should at first view be considered by some, as an attempt to intrude into the cabinet, and to intermeddle with the prerogatives of the executive.

It is scarcely necessary for the court to disclaim all pretensions to such a jurisdiction. An extravagance, so absurd and excessive, could not have been entertained for a moment. The province of the court is, solely, to decide on the rights of individuals, not to enquire how the executive, or executive officers, perform duties in which they have a discretion. Questions, in their nature political, or which are, by the constitution and laws, submitted to the executive, can never be made in this court.

But, if this be not such a question; if so far from being an intrusion into the secrets of the cabinet, it respects a paper, which, according to law, is upon record, and to a copy of which the law gives a right, on the payment of ten cents; if it be no intermeddling with a subject, over which the executive can be considered as having exercised any control; what is there in the exalted station of the officer, which shall bar a citizen from asserting, in a court of justice, his legal rights, or shall forbid a court to listen to the claim; or to issue a mandamus, directing the performance of a duty, not depending on executive discretion, but on particular acts of congress and the general principles of law?

* * *

This, then, is a plain case for a mandamus, either to deliver the commission, or a copy of it from the record; and it only remains to be enquired,

Whether it can issue from this court.

The act to establish the judicial courts of the United States authorizes the Supreme Court "to issue writs of mandamus, in cases warranted by the principles and usages of law, to any courts appointed, or persons holding office, under the authority of the United States."

The secretary of state, being a person holding an office under the authority of the United States, is precisely within the letter of the description; and if this court is not authorized to issue a writ of mandamus to such an officer, it must be because the law is unconstitutional, and therefore absolutely incapable of conferring the authority, and assigning the duties which its words purport to confer and assign.

[The Court proceeded to find that the statutory grant of original jurisdiction to the Supreme Court to issue writs of mandamus was inconsistent with the allocation of judicial power in Article III of the Constitution.]

The question, whether an act, repugnant to the constitution, can become the law of the land, is a question deeply interesting to the United States; but, happily, not of an intricacy proportioned to its interest. It seems only necessary to recognize certain principles, supposed to have been long and well established, to decide it.

That the people have an original right to establish, for their future government, such principles as, in their opinion, shall most conduce to their own happiness, is the basis, on which the whole American fabric has been erected. The exercise of this original right is a very great exertion; nor can it, nor ought it to be frequently repeated. The principles, therefore, so established, are deemed fundamental. And as the authority, from which they proceed, is supreme, and can seldom act, they are designed to be permanent.

This original and supreme will organizes the government, and assigns, to different departments, their respective powers. It may either stop here; or establish certain limits not to be transcended by those departments.

The government of the United States is of the latter description. The powers of the legislature are defined, and limited; and that those limits may not be mistaken, or forgotten, the constitution is written. To what purpose are powers limited, and to what purpose is that limitation committed to writing, if these limits may, at any time, be passed by those intended to be restrained? The distinction between a government with limited and unlimited powers, is abolished, if those limits do not confine the persons on whom they are imposed, and if acts prohibited and acts allowed, are of equal obligation. It is a proposition too plain to be contested, that the constitution controls any legislative act repugnant to it; or, that the legislature may alter the constitution by an ordinary act.

Between these alternatives there is no middle ground. The constitution is either a superior, paramount law, unchangeable by ordinary means, or it is on a level with ordinary legislative acts, and like other acts, is alterable when the legislature shall please to alter it.

If the former part of the alternative be true, then a legislative act contrary to the constitution is not law; if the latter part be true, then written constitutions are absurd attempts, on the part of the people, to limit a power, in its own nature illimitable.

Certainly all those who have framed written constitutions contemplate them as forming the fundamental and paramount law of the nation, and consequently the theory of every such government must be, that an act of the legislature, repugnant to the constitution, is void.

This theory is essentially attached to a written constitution, and is consequently to be considered, by this court, as one of the fundamental principles of our society. It is not therefore to be lost sight of in the further consideration of this subject.

If an act of the legislature, repugnant to the constitution, is void, does it, notwithstanding its invalidity, bind the courts, and oblige them to give it effect? Or, in other words, though it be not law, does it constitute a rule as operative as if it was a law? This would be to overthrow in fact what was established in theory; and would seem, at first view, an absurdity too gross to be insisted on. It shall, however, receive a more attentive consideration.

It is emphatically the province and duty of the judicial department to say what the law is. Those who apply the rule to particular cases, must of necessity expound and interpret that rule. If two laws conflict with each other, the courts must decide on the operation of each.

* * * Could it be the intention of those who gave this power, to say that, in using it, the constitution should not be looked into? That a case arising under the constitution should be decided without examining the instrument under which it arises?

This is too extravagant to be maintained.

In some cases then, the constitution must be looked into by the judges. And if they can open it at all, what part of it are they forbidden to read, or to obey?

There are many other parts of the constitution which serve to illustrate this subject.

It is declared that "no tax or duty shall be laid on articles exported from any state." Suppose a duty on the export of cotton, of tobacco, or of flour; and a suit instituted to recover it. Ought judgment to be rendered in such a case? Ought the judges to close their eyes on the constitution, and only see the law?

The constitution declares that "no bill of attainder or ex post facto law shall be passed."

If, however, such a bill should be passed and a person should be prosecuted under it; must the court condemn to death those victims whom the constitution endeavors to preserve?

"No person," says the constitution, "shall be convicted of treason unless on the testimony of two witnesses to the fame overt act, or on confession in open court."

Here the language of the constitution is addressed especially to the courts. It prescribes, directly for them, a rule of evidence not to be departed from. If the legislature should change that rule, and declare one witness, or a confession out of court, sufficient for conviction, must the constitutional principle yield to the legislative act?

From these, and many other selections which might be made, it is apparent, that the framers of the constitution contemplated that instrument, as a rule for the government of courts, as well as of the legislature.

* * *

Thus, the particular phraseology of the constitution of the United States confirms and strengthens the principle, supposed to be essential to all written constitutions, that a law repugnant to the constitution is void; and that courts, as well as other departments, are bound by that instrument.

The rule must be discharged.

Marbury's holding that all legal rights require legal remedies is non-controversial, but also involves circular reasoning. Where a matter did involve the exercise of political discretion by the Secretary of State, *Marbury's* reasoning would preclude judicial relief, and thus the courts would say that the applicant lacked a "legal right." Where American and British Commonwealth constitutional discourse differs is the significance of the lack of "legal right." For example, if a Canadian were injured and granted a cause of action by legislation passed by Parliament but refused royal assent, in a contra-conventional act, by the Governor General, we would say that they lacked any legal right, but were indeed the victim of unconstitutional behavior. In the U.S., we often seem to think that the absence of legal right relieves the public official of any constraints on crass political conduct. To illustrate, while *Marbury v. Madison* is one of the most widely discussed cases in American legal history, very little time has been spent discussing whether a constitutional system that retains a significant interregnum between elections and inauguration permits the sort of midnight court-packing that the Federalists engaged in, or whether the appropriate constitutional response to such court packing is to refuse a commission to a duly-appointed official.

There is a direct Canadian analogy to *Marbury*, which illustrates the role of constitutional convention discussed in the cases above. In 1896, Sir Charles Tupper — one of Sir John A. MacDonald's chief political lieutenants, the son of a United Empire Loyalist who moved north in 1776, and the only Nova Scotian favoring confederation to be elected to the first parliament — was asked by the Governor General to become Prime Minister after a rebellion in the Conservative cabinet. (Apparently, the majority conservatives were never able to settle on one leader after MacDonald's death in 1891.) After ten weeks, Parliament was dissolved and Tupper's Conservatives were soundly defeated by Wilfred Laurier's Liberals. Before the new Parliament reconvened and the new government was formed, Tupper advised the Governor General to appoint a number of senators and judges. (The convention that a Prime Minister resigned immediately upon losing an election did not develop until the 1920s.) Lord Aberdeen refused to do so, waiting until Laurier was sworn in to make appointments in accordance with the advice of the new Prime Minister.[1]

WALTER L. NIXON v. UNITED STATES
SUPREME COURT OF THE UNITED STATES
506 U.S. 224 (1993)

[A Federal District Court judge was convicted of making false statements before a federal grand jury. When the judge refused to resign from office notwithstanding his conviction and imprisonment, the United States House of Representatives adopted articles of impeachment which charged the judge with giving false testimony before the grand jury. After the articles of impeachment were presented to the United States Senate, the Senate voted to invoke one of its impeachment rules, under which (1) the presiding officer of the Senate is authorized to appoint a committee of senators to receive evidence and take testimony; and (2) the committee so appointed is to report to the Senate, in writing, a transcript of the proceedings and testimony given. The committee appointed presented the full Senate with a complete transcript of the proceeding and a report stating the uncontested facts and summarizing the evidence on the contested facts. Judge Nixon and House impeachment managers submitted final briefs to the full Senate and delivered arguments from the Senate floor during three hours of oral argument which had been set aside. In addition, the judge made a personal appeal, and several senators posed questions directly to the impeachment managers and Judge Nixon. The Senate voted to convict him, and a judgment was entered removing him from office. Thereafter, the judge filed an action in the United States District Court for the District of Columbia, in which he sought a declaratory judgment that his impeachment conviction was void on the ground that the Senate rule under which the committee had been appointed violated the Federal Constitution's impeachment trial clause (Art I, § 3, cl 6), which provides that the Senate has the "sole" power to "try" all impeachments. Lower courts rejected Judge Nixon's attempt to seek judicial review of his impeachment.]

---

[1] Tupper's political career included service as premier of Nova Scotia. He is the last provincial premier to serve as Prime Minister. Since his tenure in 1896, by comparison, the United States has elected seven Presidents who had served as Governor (Woodrow Wilson, Calvin Coolidge, Franklin D. Roosevelt, Ronald Reagan, Jimmy Carter, Bill Clinton, and George W. Bush).

CHIEF JUSTICE REHNQUIST delivered the opinion of the Court.

Petitioner Walter L. Nixon, Jr., asks this Court to decide whether Senate Rule XI, which allows a committee of Senators to hear evidence against an individual who has been impeached and to report that evidence to the full Senate, violates the Impeachment Trial Clause, Art. I, § 3, cl. 6. That Clause provides that the "Senate shall have the sole Power to try all Impeachments." But before we reach the merits of such a claim, we must decide whether it is "justiciable," that is, whether it is a claim that may be resolved by the courts. We conclude that it is not.

* * *

A controversy is nonjusticiable — *i.e.*, involves a political question — where there is "a textually demonstrable constitutional commitment of the issue to a coordinate political department; or a lack of judicially discoverable and manageable standards for resolving it . . . ." *Baker v. Carr*, 369 U.S. 186, 217 (1962). But the courts must, in the first instance, interpret the text in question and determine whether and to what extent the issue is textually committed. As the discussion that follows makes clear, the concept of a textual commitment to a coordinate political department is not completely separate from the concept of a lack of judicially discoverable and manageable standards for resolving it; the lack of judicially manageable standards may strengthen the conclusion that there is a textually demonstrable commitment to a coordinate branch.

In this case, we must examine Art. I, § 3, cl. 6, to determine the scope of authority conferred upon the Senate by the Framers regarding impeachment. It provides:

> "The Senate shall have the sole Power to try all Impeachments. When sitting for that Purpose, they shall be on Oath or Affirmation. When the President of the United States is tried, the Chief Justice shall preside: And no Person shall be convicted without the Concurrence of two thirds of the Members present."

The language and structure of this Clause are revealing. The first sentence is a grant of authority to the Senate, and the word "sole" indicates that this authority is reposed in the Senate and nowhere else. The next two sentences specify requirements to which the Senate proceedings shall conform: The Senate shall be on oath or affirmation, a two-thirds vote is required to convict, and when the President is tried the Chief Justice shall preside.

Petitioner argues that the word "try" in the first sentence imposes by implication an additional requirement on the Senate in that the proceedings must be in the nature of a judicial trial. From there petitioner goes on to argue that this limitation precludes the Senate from delegating to a select committee the task of hearing the testimony of witnesses, as was done pursuant to Senate Rule XI. " 'Try' means more than simply 'vote on' or 'review' or 'judge.' In 1787 and today, trying a case means hearing the evidence, not scanning a cold record." Brief for Petitioner 25. Petitioner concludes from this that courts may review whether or not the Senate "tried" him before convicting him.

There are several difficulties with this position which lead us ultimately to reject it. The word "try," both in 1787 and later, has considerably broader meanings than those to which petitioner would limit it. Older dictionaries define try as "to examine" or "to examine as a judge." See 2 S. Johnson, A Dictionary of the English Language (1785). In more modern usage the term has various meanings. For example, try can mean "to examine or investigate judicially," "to conduct the trial of," or "to put to the test by experiment, investigation, or trial." Webster's Third New International Dictionary 2457 (1971). Petitioner submits that "try," as contained in T. Sheridan, Dictionary of the English Language (1796), means "to examine as a judge; to bring before a judicial tribunal." Based on the variety of definitions, however, we cannot say that the Framers used the word "try" as an implied limitation on the method by which the Senate might proceed in trying impeachments. "As a rule the Constitution speaks in general terms, leaving Congress to deal with subsidiary matters of detail as the public interests and changing conditions may require . . . ."

The conclusion that the use of the word "try" in the first sentence of the Impeachment Trial Clause lacks sufficient precision to afford any judicially manageable standard of review of the Senate's actions is fortified by the existence of the three very specific requirements that the Constitution does impose on the Senate when trying impeachments. ***

Petitioner devotes only two pages in his brief to negating the significance of the word "sole" in the first sentence of Clause 6. As noted above, that sentence provides that "the Senate shall have the sole Power to try all Impeachments." We think that the word "sole" is of considerable significance. Indeed, the word "sole" appears only one other time in the Constitution — with respect to the House of Representatives' "*sole* Power of Impeachment." Art. I, § 2, cl. 5 (emphasis added). The commonsense meaning of the word "sole" is that the Senate alone shall have authority to determine whether an individual should be acquitted or convicted. ***

*   *   *

The history and contemporary understanding of the impeachment provisions support our reading of the constitutional language. The parties do not offer evidence of a single word in the history of the Constitutional Convention or in contemporary commentary that even alludes to the possibility of judicial review in the context of the impeachment powers. See R. Berger, *Impeachment: The Constitutional Problems* 116 (1973). This silence is quite meaningful in light of the several explicit references to the availability of judicial review as a check on the Legislature's power with respect to bills of attainder, *ex post facto* laws, and statutes. See The Federalist No. 78, p. 524 (J. Cooke ed. 1961) ("Limitations . . . can be preserved in practice no other way than through the medium of the courts of justice").

The Framers labored over the question of where the impeachment power should lie. Significantly, in at least two considered scenarios the power was placed with the Federal Judiciary. See 1 Farrand 21-22 (Virginia Plan); *id.* at 244 (New Jersey Plan). Indeed, James Madison and the Committee of Detail proposed that the Supreme Court should have the power to determine impeachments. See 2 *id.* at 551 (Madison); *id.* at 178-179, 186 (Committee of Detail). Despite these proposals, the Convention ultimately decided that the Senate would have "the sole Power to try all Impeachments." Art. I, § 3, cl. 6. According to Alexander Hamilton, the Senate was the "most fit depositary of this important trust" because its Members are representatives of the people. See The Federalist No. 65, p. 440 (J. Cooke ed. 1961).

The Supreme Court was not the proper body because the Framers "doubted whether the members of that tribunal would, at all times, be endowed with so eminent a portion of fortitude as would be called for in the execution of so difficult a task" or whether the Court "would possess the degree of credit and authority" to carry out its judgment if it conflicted with the accusation brought by the Legislature — the people's representative. See *id.* at 441. In addition, the Framers believed the Court was too small in number: "The awful discretion, which a court of impeachments must necessarily have, to doom to honor or to infamy the most confidential and the most distinguished characters of the community, forbids the commitment of the trust to a small number of persons." *Id.* at 441–442.

There are two additional reasons why the Judiciary, and the Supreme Court in particular, were not chosen to have any role in impeachments. First, the Framers recognized that most likely there would be two sets of proceedings for individuals who commit impeachable offenses — the impeachment trial and a separate criminal trial. In fact, the Constitution explicitly provides for two separate proceedings. See Art. I, § 3, cl. 7. The Framers deliberately separated the two forums to avoid raising the specter of bias and to ensure independent judgments:

> "Would it be proper that the persons, who had disposed of his fame and his most valuable rights as a citizen in one trial, should in another trial, for the same offence, be also the disposers of his life and his fortune? Would there not be the greatest reason to apprehend, that error in the first sentence would be the parent of error in the second sentence? That the strong bias of one decision would be apt to overrule the influence of any new lights, which might be brought to vary the complexion of another decision?" The Federalist No. 65, p. 442 (J. Cooke ed. 1961).

Certainly judicial review of the Senate's "trial" would introduce the same risk of bias as would participation in the trial itself.

Second, judicial review would be inconsistent with the Framers' insistence that our system be one of checks and balances. In our constitutional system, impeachment was designed to be the *only* check on the Judicial Branch by the Legislature. On the topic of judicial accountability, Hamilton wrote:

> "The precautions for their responsibility are comprised in the article respecting impeachments. They are liable to be impeached for mal-conduct by the House of Representatives, and tried by the senate, and if convicted, may be dismissed from office and disqualified for holding any other. *This is the only provision on the point, which is consistent with the necessary independence of the judicial character, and is the only one which we find in our own constitution in respect to our own judges.*" *Id.*, No. 79, at 532–533 (emphasis added).

Judicial involvement in impeachment proceedings, even if only for purposes of judicial review, is counterintuitive because it would eviscerate the "important constitutional check" placed on the Judiciary by the Framers. See *id.*, No. 81, at 545. Nixon's argument would place final reviewing authority with respect to impeachments in the hands of the same body that the impeachment process is meant to regulate.

Nevertheless, Nixon argues that judicial review is necessary in order to place a check on the Legislature. Nixon fears that if the Senate is given unreviewable authority to interpret the Impeachment Trial Clause, there is a grave risk that the Senate will usurp judicial power. The Framers anticipated this objection and created two constitutional safeguards to keep the Senate in check. The first safeguard is that the whole of the impeachment power is divided between the two legislative bodies, with the House given the right to accuse and the Senate given the right to judge. *Id.*, No. 66, at 446. This split of authority "avoids the inconvenience of making the same persons both accusers and judges; and guards against the danger of persecution from the prevalency of a factious spirit in either of those branches." The second safeguard is the two-thirds supermajority vote requirement. Hamilton explained that "as the concurrence of two-thirds of the senate will be requisite to a condemnation, the security to innocence, from this additional circumstance, will be as complete as itself can desire." *Ibid.*

* * *

JUSTICE STEVENS, concurring.

For me, the debate about the strength of the inferences to be drawn from the use of the words "sole" and "try" is far less significant than the central fact that the Framers decided to assign the impeachment power to the Legislative Branch. The disposition of the impeachment of Samuel Chase in 1805[2] demonstrated that the Senate is fully conscious of the profound importance of that assignment, and nothing in the subsequent history of the Senate's exercise of this extraordinary power suggests otherwise. Respect for a coordinate branch of the Government forecloses any assumption that improbable hypotheticals like those mentioned by Justice White and Justice Souter will ever occur. Accordingly, the wise policy of judicial restraint, coupled with the potential anomalies associated with a contrary view, see *ante*, at 234–236, provide a sufficient justification for my agreement with the views of The Chief Justice.

JUSTICE WHITE, with whom JUSTICE BLACKMUN joins, concurring in the judgment.

[White's judgement is that impeachment is reviewable, but that the Senate did not err in conducting the impeachment trial by committee.]

JUSTICE SOUTER, concurring in the judgment.

[Souter, J., concurred on the ground that the Court should exercise its discretion to refuse to review the case under the "political question" doctrine, as articulated in

---

[2] [Ed. note: Chase was an outspoken and controversial Federalist justice appointed by John Adams. Republican supporters of President Jefferson impeached him, allegedly for misconduct in trying cases (this is when Supreme Court justices road on circuit individually as trial judges), although his defenders claimed the action was motivated by his pro-Federalist ideology (aided in part by some degree of intemperance and personal disagreeability). A number of Republican senators joined their Federalist opponents to reject conviction. Although the allegations of misconduct were "not devoid of merit," the acquittal established a principle of judicial independence. *See generally* WILLIAM H. REHNQUIST, GRAND INQUESTS: THE HISTORIC IMPEACHMENTS OF JUSTICE SAMUEL CHASE AND PRESIDENT ANDREW JOHNSON (1992).]

Baker v. Carr, 369 U.S. 186, 217 (1962), a decision declaring that reapportionment of state legislative districts did *not* fall into that category. In that case, the Court wrote:

> "Prominent on the surface of any case held to involve a political question is found a textually demonstrable constitutional commitment of the issue to a coordinate political department; or a lack of judicially discoverable and manageable standards for resolving it; or the impossibility of deciding without an initial policy determination of a kind clearly for nonjudicial discretion; or the impossibility of a court's undertaking independent resolution without expressing lack of the respect due coordinate branches of government; or an unusual need for unquestioning adherence to a political decision already made; or the potentiality of embarrassment from multifarious pronouncements by various departments on one question."

[Although this case "does not demand an answer" given the language of the text, Souter, J., suggested that impeachment should be reviewable if the Senate were to act in a manner seriously threatening the integrity of its results, convicting, say, upon a coin toss, or upon a summary determination that an officer of the United States was simply a bad guy.]

The Constitutional Court in South Africa has explicitly discussed its authority and duty to pronounce on the constitutionality of legislation. Its first major case, *S v. Makwanyane*, sought judicial review of the death penalty (the substantive constitutional issue was discussed in Chapter 2) the issue of counter-majoritarianism and public opinion was raised and the Court responded.

THE STATE v. MAKWANYANE
CONSTITUTIONAL COURT OF SOUTH AFRICA
1995 (3) SA 391

CHASKALSON P:

. . . .

[2] *Section* 277(1)(a) of the Criminal Procedure Act No. 51 of 1977 prescribes that the death penalty is a competent sentence for murder. Counsel for the accused was invited by the Appellate Division to consider whether this provision was consistent with the Republic of South Africa Constitution, 1993, which had come into force subsequent to the conviction and sentence by the trial court. He argued that it was not, contending that it was in conflict with the provisions of *sections* 9 and 11(2) of the Constitution.

. . . .

[5] It would no doubt have been better if the framers of the Constitution had stated specifically, either that the death sentence is not a competent penalty, or that it is permissible in circumstances sanctioned by law. This, however, was not done and it has been left to this Court to decide whether the penalty is consistent with the

provisions of the Constitution. That is the extent and limit of the Court's power in this case.

. . . .

[7] The Constitution . . . provides a historic bridge between the past of a deeply divided society characterised by strife, conflict, untold suffering and injustice, and a future founded on the recognition of human rights, democracy and peaceful co-existence and development opportunities for all South Africans, irrespective of colour, race, class, belief or sex.

It is a transitional constitution but one which itself establishes a new order in South Africa; an order in which human rights and democracy are entrenched and in which the Constitution:

. . . shall be the supreme law of the Republic and any law or act inconsistent with its provisions shall, unless otherwise provided expressly or by necessary implication in this Constitution, be of no force and effect to the extent of the inconsistency.

. . . .

[87] The Attorney General argued that what is cruel, inhuman or degrading depends to a large extent upon contemporary attitudes within society, and that South African society does not regard the death sentence for extreme cases of murder as a cruel, inhuman or degrading form of punishment. It was disputed whether public opinion, properly informed of the different considerations, would in fact favour the death penalty. I am, however, prepared to assume that it does and that the majority of South Africans agree that the death sentence should be imposed in extreme cases of murder. The question before us, however, is not what the majority of South Africans believe a proper sentence for murder should be. It is whether the Constitution allows the sentence.

[88] Public opinion may have some relevance to the enquiry, but in itself, it is no substitute for the duty vested in the Courts to interpret the Constitution and to uphold its provisions without fear or favour. If public opinion were to be decisive there would be no need for constitutional adjudication. The protection of rights could then be left to Parliament, which has a mandate from the public, and is answerable to the public for the way its mandate is exercised, but this would be a return to parliamentary sovereignty, and a retreat from the new legal order established by the 1993 Constitution. By the same token the issue of the constitutionality of capital punishment cannot be referred to a referendum, in which a majority view would prevail over the wishes of any minority. The very reason for establishing the new legal order, and for vesting the power of judicial review of all legislation in the courts, was to protect the rights of minorities and others who cannot protect their rights adequately through the democratic process. Those who are entitled to claim this protection include the social outcasts and marginalised people of our society. It is only if there is a willingness to protect the worst and the weakest amongst us, that all of us can be secure that our own rights will be protected.

[89] This Court cannot allow itself to be diverted from its duty to act as an independent arbiter of the Constitution by making choices on the basis that they

will find favour with the public. Justice Powell's comment in his dissent in *Furman v Georgia* bears repetition:

> . . . the weight of the evidence indicates that the public generally has not accepted either the morality or the social merit of the views so passionately advocated by the articulate spokesmen for abolition. But however one may assess amorphous ebb and flow of public opinion generally on this volatile issue, this type of inquiry lies at the periphery - not the core - of the judicial process in constitutional cases. The assessment of popular opinion is essentially a legislative, and not a judicial, function.

So too does the comment of Justice Jackson in *West Virginia State Board of Education v Barnette*:

> The very purpose of a Bill of Rights was to withdraw certain subjects from the vicissitudes of political controversy, to place them beyond the reach of majorities and officials and to establish them as legal principles to be applied by the courts. One's right to life, liberty, and property, to free speech, a free press, freedom of worship and assembly and other fundamental rights may not be submitted to vote; they depend on the outcome of no elections.

In the *Certification Cases*, in which the Constitutional Court was required, by the constitution-making provisions of the "interim" 1993 Constitution, to certify that the Constitutional Assembly had abided by the 34 constitutional principles agreed upon by the negotiating parties and included in Schedule 4 of the 1993 Constitution in making the "final" 1996 Constitution, the Constitutional Court again returned to the issue of its constitutional authority, but this time in respect of this particularly unique function. In the first certification decision the Constitutional Court refused to certify a provision requiring the Constitutional Assembly to reconvene and address the issues raised by the Court. At the same time the Court reaffirmed its authority to declare law "unconstitutional."

EX PARTE CHAIRPERSON OF THE CONSTITUTIONAL ASSEMBLY: IN RE CERTIFICATION OF THE CONSTITUTION OF THE REPUBLIC OF SOUTH AFRICA (FIRST CERTIFICATION DECISION)

CONSTITUTIONAL COURT OF SOUTH AFRICA
1996 (4) SA 744

THE COURT:

[1] The formal purpose of this judgment is to pronounce whether or not the Court certifies that all the provisions of South Africa's proposed new constitution comply with certain principles contained in the country's current constitution. But its underlying purpose and scope are much wider. Judicial "certification" of a constitution is unprecedented and the very nature of the undertaking has to be explained. To do that, one must place the undertaking in its proper historical, political and legal

context; and, in doing so, the essence of the country's constitutional transition, the respective roles of the political entities involved and the applicable legal principles and terminology must be identified and described. It is also necessary to explain the scope of the Court's certification task and the effect of this judgment, not only the extent and significance of the Court's powers, but also their limitations. Only then can one really come to grips with the certification itself.

. . . .

[5] South Africa's past has been aptly described as that of "a deeply divided society characterised by strife, conflict, untold suffering and injustice" which "generated gross violations of human rights, the transgression of humanitarian principles in violent conflicts and a legacy of hatred, fear, guilt and revenge." From the outset the country maintained a colonial heritage of racial discrimination: in most of the country the franchise was reserved for white males and a rigid system of economic and social segregation was enforced. The administration of African tribal territories through vassal "traditional authorities" passed smoothly from British colonial rule to the new government, which continued its predecessor's policy.

[6] At the same time the Montesquieuan principle of a threefold separation of state power - often but an aspirational ideal - did not flourish in a South Africa which, under the banner of adherence to the Westminster system of government, actively promoted parliamentary supremacy and domination by the executive. Multi-party democracy had always been the preserve of the white minority but even there it had languished since 1948. The rallying call of apartheid proved irresistible for a white electorate embattled by the spectre of decolonisation in Africa to the north.

. . . .

[10] . . . After a long history of "deep conflict between a minority which reserved for itself all control over the political instruments of the state and a majority who sought to resist that domination," the overwhelming majority of South Africans across the political divide realised that the country had to be urgently rescued from imminent disaster by a negotiated commitment to a fundamentally new constitutional order premised upon open and democratic government and the universal enjoyment of fundamental human rights . . . .

. . . .

[12] One of the deadlocks, a crucial one on which the negotiations all but foundered, related to the formulation of a new constitution for the country. All were agreed that such an instrument was necessary and would have to contain certain basic provisions. Those who negotiated this commitment were confronted, however, with two problems. The first arose from the fact that they were not elected to their positions in consequence of any free and verifiable elections and that it was therefore necessary to have this commitment articulated in a final constitution adopted by a credible body properly mandated to do so in consequence of free and fair elections based on universal adult suffrage. The second problem was the fear in some quarters that the constitution eventually favoured by such a body of elected representatives might not sufficiently address the anxieties and the insecurities of such constituencies and might therefore subvert the objectives of a negotiated settlement. The government and other minority groups were prepared to relinquish

power to the majority but were determined to have a hand in drawing the framework for the future governance of the country. The liberation movements on the opposition side were equally adamant that only democratically elected representatives of the people could legitimately engage in forging a constitution: neither they, and certainly not the government of the day, had any claim to the requisite mandate from the electorate.

[13] The impasse was resolved by a compromise which enabled both sides to attain their basic goals without sacrificing principle. What was no less important in the political climate of the time was that it enabled them to keep faith with their respective constituencies: those who feared engulfment by a black majority and those who were determined to eradicate apartheid once and for all. In essence the settlement was quite simple. Instead of an outright transmission of power from the old order to the new, there would be a programmed two-stage transition. An interim government, established and functioning under an interim constitution agreed to by the negotiating parties, would govern the country on a coalition basis while a final constitution was being drafted. A national legislature, elected (directly and indirectly) by universal adult suffrage, would double as the constitution-making body and would draft the new constitution within a given time. But - and herein lies the key to the resolution of the deadlock - that text would have to comply with certain guidelines agreed upon in advance by the negotiating parties. What is more, an independent arbiter would have to ascertain and declare whether the new constitution indeed complied with the guidelines before it could come into force.

. . . .

[26] Notwithstanding publication of the directions by the President, in which the issues were identified, there remained considerable misunderstanding about the Court's functions and powers in relation to certification of the [draft of the final constitution, referred to as the new text or "NT."] As a result many objections - and even some of the oral arguments - were misdirected. Apparently, therefore, there is a risk that the tenor and import of this judgment may be misunderstood by some readers unless the more egregious misapprehensions are resolved.

[27] First and foremost it must be emphasised that the Court has a judicial and not a political mandate. Its function is clearly spelt out in [Interim Constitution (IC)] 71(2): to certify whether all the provisions of the NT comply with the [34 basic constitutional principles (CPs) of the IC]. That is a judicial function, a legal exercise. Admittedly a constitution, by its very nature, deals with the extent, limitations and exercise of political power as also with the relationship between political entities and with the relationship between the state and persons. But this Court has no power, no mandate and no right to express any view on the political choices made by the CA in drafting the NT, save to the extent that such choices may be relevant either to compliance or non-compliance with the CPs. Subject to that qualification, the wisdom or otherwise of any provision of the NT is not this Court's business.

. . . .

[30] It should also be emphasised that, provided there is due compliance with the prescripts of the CPs, this Court is not called upon to express an opinion on any gaps in the NT, whether perceived by an objector or real. More specifically, there

can be no valid objection if the NT contains a provision which in principle complies with the requirements of the CPs, or a particular CP, but does not spell out the details, leaving them to the legislature to flesh out appropriately later. Provided the criteria demanded by the CPs are expressed in the NT, it is quite in order to adopt such a course. The subsequent legislation will be justiciable and any of its provisions that do not come up to the constitutionally enshrined criteria will be liable to invalidation. Here it is important to note that the CPs are principles, not detailed prescripts.

. . . .

[149] NT 241(1) provides that the provisions of the [Labour Relations Act (LRA)] shall, despite the provisions of the Constitution, remain valid until they are amended or repealed. This provision of the NT is objected to on the grounds that it is in conflict with CP IV, which provides that the Constitution shall be supreme, and CPs II and VII, which provide that the fundamental rights contained in the Constitution shall be justiciable. The purpose of NT 241(1) seems clear. The provisions of the LRA are to remain valid and not to be subject to constitutional review until they are amended or repealed. This section is in conflict with the CPs. If CPs II, IV and VII are read together, it is plain that statutory provisions must be subject to the supremacy of the Constitution unless they are made part of the Constitution itself. If that route is followed, the provisions must comply with the CPs and must be subject to amendment by special procedures as contemplated by CP XV. This is not the route adopted in NT 241(1). Alternatively, if the provisions are not part of the Constitution, they must be subject to constitutional review as contemplated by CPs II and VII. If this were not the case, the CA would have been entitled to shield any number of statutes from constitutional review. This could not have been the intention of the drafters of the CPs. NT 241(1) clearly intends to protect the provisions of the LRA from constitutional review without making it part of the Constitution. The section is not in compliance with the CPs.

[150] NT sch 6 s 22(1)(b) provides that the provisions of the Promotion of National Unity and Reconciliation Act 34 of 1995, as amended,107 are valid. Although this is a slightly different formulation from that adopted in NT 241(1), it nevertheless seeks to achieve the same goal, exempting the named statute from constitutional review. For the reasons given above, neither is this provision in compliance with the CPs. However, NT sch 6 s 22(1)(a) is not in breach of the CPs. This provision adds the text of the epilogue of the IC to the text of the NT. As such, that provision is rendered part of the NT and subject to constitutional amendment in the ordinary course. It was not argued and it could not have been argued that the text of the epilogue was in breach of the CPs on any other ground.[3]

---

[3] [Ed. note: The epilogue of the "interim" constitution that was included by reference into the 1996 Constitution reads:

National unity and reconciliation

This Constitution provides a historic bridge between the past of a deeply divided society characterized by strife, conflict, untold suffering and injustice, and a future founded on the recognition of human rights, democracy and peaceful co-existence and development opportunities for all South Africans, irrespective of colour, race, class, belief or sex.

The pursuit of national unity, the well-being of all South African citizens and peace require

. . . .

[206] It is the submission of the objector that the omission to make specific provision for the seal of the Republic in the NT compromises the integrity of the Constitution as the supreme law of the Republic.

[207] The relevant principle is CP IV, which requires: "The Constitution shall be the supreme law of the land. It shall be binding on all organs of state at all levels of government."

[208] The objector had not shown any basis for the contention that the absence from the NT of a reference to the seal of the Republic undermines the supremacy of the Constitution. Constitutional supremacy is unambiguously and adequately entrenched in the NT. There is therefore no violation of CP IV on that account.

. . . .

[483] We wish to conclude this judgment with two observations. The first is to reiterate that the CA has drafted a constitutional text which complies with the overwhelming majority of the requirements of the CPs. The second is that the instances of noncompliance which we have listed in the preceding paragraph, although singly and collectively important, should present no significant obstacle to the formulation of a text which complies fully with those requirements.

––––––––––

The SACC's prediction in ¶ 483 above was realized when, pursuant to s. 73A(2) of the Interim Constitution, the Constitutional Assembly reassembled and adopted an amended text for the new constitution, addressing grounds for non-certification set forth in the *First Certification Judgment* and making other editorial and minor changes. In *Certification of the Amended Text of the Constitution of the Republic of South Africa, 1996 (Second Certification decision)*, 1997 (2) SA 97 (CC), the SACC

––––––––––

reconciliation between the people of South Africa and the reconstruction of society.

The adoption of this Constitution lays the secure foundation for the people of South Africa to transcend the divisions and strife of the past, which generated gross violations of human rights, the transgression of humanitarian principles in violent conflicts and a legacy of hatred, fear, guilt and revenge.

These can now be addressed on the basis that there is a need for understanding but not for vengeance, a need for reparation but not for retaliation, a need for Ubuntu but not for victimization.

In order to advance such reconciliation and reconstruction, amnesty shall be granted in respect of acts, omissions and offenses associated with political objectives and committed in the course of the conflicts of the past. To this end, Parliament under this Constitution shall adopt a law determining a firm cut-off date, which shall be a date after 8 October 1990 and before 6 December 1993, and providing for the mechanisms, criteria and procedures, including tribunals, if any, through which such amnesty shall be dealt with at any time after the law has been passed.

With this Constitution and these commitments we, the people of South Africa, open a new chapter in the history of our country.

Nkosi sikelel' iAfrika. God Seen Suid-Afrika

Morena boloka sechaba sa heso. May God bless our country

Mudzimu fhatutshedza Afrika. Hosi katekisa Afrika.]

upheld these revisions, which resulted in the coming into force of the 1996 Final Constitution. One area of controversy concerned the procedure for constitutional amendment. The SACC found that Constitutional Principle XV, required special majorities for amendment. The *First Certification Judgment* had faulted the Initial Constitution for excluding the National Council of Provinces from the process of amending the Bill of Rights. The amended text required approval by 2/3 of the National Assembly and six of the nine provinces. In the SACC's view, this was consistent with agreed-upon constitutional principles and thus the amended text was certified.

8.2. ADVISORY OPINIONS

8.2.1. United States

During President Washington's administration some questions arose on the legality, under principles of international law, of various foreign relations initiatives. Secretary of State Thomas Jefferson attached 29 questions on points of international law to a letter sent to the Supreme Court with the following request for their advice:

GENTLEMEN:

The war which has taken place among the powers of Europe produces frequent transactions within our ports and limits, on which questions arise of considerable difficulty, and of greater importance to the peace of the United States. Their questions depend for their solution on the construction of our treaties, on the laws of nature and nations, and on the laws of the land, and are often presented under circumstances which do not give a cognisance of them to the tribunals of the country. Yet their decision is so little analogous to the ordinary functions of the executive, as to occasion much embarrassment and difficulty to them. The President therefore would be much relieved if he found himself free to refer questions of this description to the opinions of the judges of the Supreme Court of the United States, whose knowledge of the subject would secure us against errors dangerous to the peace of the United States, and their authority insure the respect of all parties. He has therefore asked the attendance of such of the judges as could be collected in time for the occasion, to know, in the first place, their opinion, whether the public may, with propriety, be availed of their advice on these questions? And if they may, to present, for their advice, the abstract questions which have already occurred, or may soon occur, from which they will themselves strike out such as any circumstances might, in their opinion, forbid them to pronounce on. I have the honour to be with sentiments of the most perfect respect, gentlemen,

Your most obedient and humble servant,

Thos. Jefferson

Two days later, Chief Justice Jay and the Associate Justices present at the time responded, asking for time to consult with absent colleagues. When the President politely replied that he would welcome their decision after due consideration, they wrote the following:

SIR:

> We have considered the previous question stated in a letter written by your direction to us by the Secretary of State on the 18th of last month, [regarding] the lines of separation drawn by the Constitution between the three departments of the government. These being in certain respects checks upon each other, and our being judges of a court of the last resort, are considerations which afford strong arguments against the propriety of our extra-judicially deciding the questions alluded to, especially as the power given by the Constitution to the President, of calling on the heads of departments for opinions, seems to have been *purposely* as well as *expressly limited* to the executive departments.

> We exceedingly regret every event that may cause embarrassment to your administration, but we derive consolation from the reflection that your judgment will discern what is right, and that your usual prudence, decision, and firmness will surmount every obstacle to the preservation of the rights, peace, and dignity of the United States.

> We have the honour to be, with perfect respect, sir, your most obedient and most humble servants.

The view that the U.S. Constitution precluded advisory opinions has now been clearly established. The Court's rationale was clearly articulated in *Muskrat v. United States*, 219 U.S. 346 (1911). Congress enacted a statute transferring Cherokee tribal property to individual ownership by citizens of the Cherokee Nation, and also imposed certain restraints on the land's alienation. In a later statute, Congress increased the number of Cherokees permitted to obtain an individual ownership interest, and increased the restraints on alienation. The plaintiffs in this case, Cherokees entitled to individual ownership under the original statute, sought to challenge the later statutes that took away some of their property and added de-valuing restrictions, claiming that these statutes constituted an unconstitutional taking of property.

The plaintiffs' claim could have been lawfully contested in several ways. They could have sued the Secretary of Interior to enjoin him from increasing the enrollments under the later statute. (Actually, they did, and subsequently lost on the merits.) They could have also proceeded to alienate the property inconsistently with the statutory restraints, and then used private litigation to test the validity of the restraints. However, Congress gave them an easier way — a specific statute authorizing them to bring a suit in the Court of Claims (like the Canadian or Australian Federal Courts), with appeal to the Supreme Court, to determine the validity of the statute. The Supreme Court found this latter approach unconstitutional, and refused to rule.

Justice Day took note of an early precedent, *Hayburn's Case*, 2 U.S. (2 Dall.) 408 (1792), where several justices commented in an otherwise mooted case that federal judges could not adjudicate Revolutionary War pensions under a statute that allowed the Secretary of War to overrule the court. The justices concluded that because the Constitution divides the government "into three distinct and independent branches," it thus "is the duty of each to abstain from, and to oppose, encroachments on either." Specifically, "neither the legislative nor the executive branches can constitutionally assign to the judicial any duties but such as are properly judicial, and to be performed in a judicial manner." Any decision subject to political review was not judicial. Justice Day also cited *In re Pacific Ry. Comm'n*, 32 F. 241 (C.C.D. Cal. 1887), where Justice Field explained that Article III's limitation of judicial power to "cases and controversies" was intended to mean "the claims of litigants brought before the courts for determination by such regular proceedings as are established by law or custom for the protection or enforcement of rights, or the prevention, redress, or punishment of wrongs."

The Court harkened back to *Marbury*:

> In that case Chief Justice Marshall, who spoke for the court, was careful to point out that the right to declare an act of Congress unconstitutional could only be exercised when a proper case between opposing parties was submitted for judicial determination; that there was no general veto power in the court upon the legislation of Congress; and that the authority to declare an act unconstitutional sprung from the requirement that the court, in administering the law and pronouncing judgment between the parties to a case, and choosing between the requirements of the fundamental law established by the people and embodied in the Constitution and an act of the agents of the people, acting under authority of the Constitution, should enforce the Constitution as the supreme law of the land. The Chief Justice demonstrated, in a manner which has been regarded as settling the question, that with the choice thus given between a constitutional requirement and a conflicting statutory enactment, the plain duty of the court was to follow and enforce the Constitution as the supreme law established by the people. And the court recognized, in *Marbury v. Madison* and subsequent cases, that the exercise of this great power could only be invoked in cases which came regularly before the courts for determination
>
> . . . .

Professor (later Justice) Felix Frankfurter, writing during the height of the *Lochner* era of conservative judicial activism against progressive social and economic legislation, offered an interesting perspective critical of advisory opinions. Distinguishing commentary that defended the issuance of such advice in the context of international law, Frankfurter wrote that "our national experience makes it clear that it is extremely dangerous to encourage extension of the device of advisory opinions to constitutional controversies, in view of the nature of the crucial constitutional questions and the conditions for their wise adjudication." *A Note on Advisory Opinions*, 37 HARV. L. REV. 1002, 1002 (1924). The most difficult constitutional questions, Frankfurter asserted, concerned broad constitutional terms like the Commerce or Due Process Clauses, and the "stuff of these contests are facts, and judgment upon facts. Every tendency to deal with them abstractedly, to formulate them in terms of sterile legal questions, is bound to result in sterile conclusions unrelated to actualities." *Id.* at 1002–03. He cited three examples of

cases where the Massachusetts Supreme Court had issued advisory opinions
striking down legislation where the U.S. Supreme Court (even under conservative
control) upheld similar statutes when faced with a real challenge. *Id.* at 1006–07.

8.2.2. Canada

The *Supreme Court Act* formally authorizes the Supreme Court to render
advisory opinions. Section 53 provides:

(1) The Governor in Council [*i.e.*, the federal cabinet] may refer to the Court
for hearing and consideration important questions of law or fact
concerning

   (a) the interpretation of the Constitution Acts;

   (b) the constitutionality or interpretation of any federal or provincial
legislation;

   (c) the appellate jurisdiction respecting educational matters, by the
Constitution Act, 1867, or by any other Act or law vested in the
Governor in Council; or

   (d) the powers of the Parliament of Canada, or of the legislatures of the
provinces, or of the respective governments thereof, whether or not
the particular power in question has been or is proposed to be
exercised.

(2) The Governor in Council may refer to the Court for hearing and
consideration important questions of law or fact concerning any matter,
whether or not in the opinion of the Court *ejusdem generis* with the
enumerations contained in subsection (1), with reference to which the
Governor in Council sees fit to submit any such question.

(3) Any question concerning any of the matters mentioned in subsections (1)
and (2), and referred to the Court by the Governor in Council, shall be
conclusively deemed to be an important question.

In addition, most provincial statutes provide that the provincial cabinet may
likewise refer matters to the provincial court of appeal. Because the Supreme
Court of Canada is a general court of appeal for the country, these decisions are
subject to appellate review, as was the case with the *Patriation Reference*
excerpted in Part 8.3.

REFERENCE RE SECESSION OF QUEBEC
Supreme Court of Canada
[1998] 2 S.C.R. 217, 161 D.L.R. (4th) 385

[In 1995, for the second time Quebec held a referendum regarding possible
withdrawal from the Canadian confederation. The sovereigntist Parti Québécois
government put to the voters the question: "Do you agree that Québec should
become sovereign after having made a formal offer to Canada for a new economic
and political partnership . . . ?" In a bitterly fought election, going to the merits of
Quebecois independence as well as the sort of continued association that might
develop, Quebec voters narrowly defeated the proposal. As part of a post-

referendum strategy to make it clear to Quebec voters that independence was undesirable and unacceptable, the federal government sought a judicial declaration that unilateral secession by Quebec was unlawful.]

[Before LAMER C.J. and L'HEUREUX-DUBÉ, GONTHIER, CORY, McLACHLIN, IACOBUCCI, MAJOR, BASTARACHE and BINNIE JJ.]

The following is the judgment delivered by

THE COURT

I. INTRODUCTION

* * *

[2] The questions posed by the Governor in Council by way of Order in Council P.C. 1996-1497, dated September 30, 1996, read as follows:

> "1. Under the Constitution of Canada, can the National Assembly, legislature or government of Quebec effect the secession of Quebec from Canada unilaterally?
>
> 2. Does international law give the National Assembly, legislature or government of Quebec the right to effect the secession of Quebec from Canada unilaterally? In this regard, is there a right to self-determination under international law that would give the National Assembly, legislature or government of Quebec the right to effect the secession of Quebec from Canada unilaterally?
>
> 3. In the event of a conflict between domestic and international law on the right of the National Assembly, legislature or government of Quebec to effect the secession of Quebec from Canada unilaterally, which would take precedence in Canada?"

[3] Before turning to Question 1, as a preliminary matter, it is necessary to deal with the issues raised with regard to this Court's reference jurisdiction.

II. THE PRELIMINARY OBJECTIONS TO THE COURT'S REFERENCE JURISDICTION

[4] The *amicus* curiae[4] argued that s. 101 of the *Constitution Act, 1867* does not give Parliament the authority to grant this Court the jurisdiction provided for in s. 53 of the *Supreme Court Act*, R.S.C., 1985, c. S-26. Alternatively, it is submitted that even if Parliament were entitled to enact s. 53 of the *Supreme Court Act*, the scope of that section should be interpreted to exclude the kinds of questions the Governor in Council has submitted in this Reference. In particular, it is contended that this Court cannot answer Question 2, since it is a question of "pure" international law

---

[4] [Ed. note: The sovereigntist government of Quebec refused to participate in this litigation, which was initiated by the Chrétien government as part of a well-publicized strategy to oppose secession. The Court appointed a leading separatist constitutional lawyer to act as a friend of the court to defend the separatist position.]

over which this Court has no jurisdiction. Finally, even if this Court's reference jurisdiction is constitutionally valid, and even if the questions are within the purview of s. 53 of the Supreme Court Act, it is argued that the three questions referred to the Court are speculative, of a political nature, and, in any event, are not ripe for judicial decision, and therefore are not justiciable.

[5] Notwithstanding certain formal objections by the Attorney General of Canada, it is our view that the *amicus curiae* was within his rights to make the preliminary objections, and that we should deal with them.

A. *The Constitutional Validity of Section 53 of the Supreme Court Act*

[6] In *Re References by Governor-General in Council* (1910), 43 S.C.R. 536, affirmed on appeal to the Privy Council, [1912] A.C. 571 (*sub nom. Attorney-General for Ontario v. Attorney-General for Canada*), the constitutionality of this Court's special jurisdiction was twice upheld. The Court is asked to revisit these decisions. In light of the significant changes in the role of this Court since 1912, and the very important issues raised in this Reference, it is appropriate to reconsider briefly the constitutional validity of the Court's reference jurisdiction.

[7] Section 3 of the *Supreme Court Act* establishes this Court both as a "general court of appeal" for Canada and as an "additional court for the better administration of the laws of Canada." These two roles reflect the two heads of power enumerated in s. 101 of the Constitution Act, 1867. However, the "laws of Canada" referred to in s. 101 consist only of federal law and statute. As a result, the phrase "additional courts" contained in s. 101 is an insufficient basis upon which to ground the special jurisdiction established in s. 53 of the *Supreme Court Act*, which clearly exceeds a consideration of federal law alone (see, e.g., s. 53(2)). Section 53 must therefore be taken as enacted pursuant to Parliament's power to create a "general court of appeal" for Canada.

[8] Section 53 of the Supreme Court Act is *intra vires* Parliament's power under s. 101 if, in "pith and substance," it is legislation in relation to the constitution or organization of a "general court of appeal." Section 53 is defined by two leading characteristics — it establishes an original jurisdiction in this Court and imposes a duty on the Court to render advisory opinions. Section 53 is therefore constitutionally valid only if (1) a "general court of appeal" may properly exercise an original jurisdiction; and (2) a "general court of appeal" may properly undertake other legal functions, such as the rendering of advisory opinions.

(1) May a Court of Appeal Exercise an Original Jurisdiction?

[The Court concluded that there is nothing inherently self-contradictory about an appellate court exercising original jurisdiction on an exceptional basis.]

(2) May a Court of Appeal Undertake Advisory Functions?

[12] The *amicus curiae* submits that

"[TRANSLATION] either this constitutional power [to give the highest court in the federation jurisdiction to give advisory opinions] is expressly provided for by the Constitution, as is the case in India (*Constitution of India*, art. 143), *or it is not provided for therein and so it simply does not exist.* This is what the Supreme Court of the United States has held. [Emphasis added.]

[13] However, the U.S. Supreme Court did not conclude that it was unable to render advisory opinions because no such express power was included in the United States Constitution. Quite the contrary, it based this conclusion on the express limitation in art. III, § 2 restricting federal court jurisdiction to actual "cases" or "controversies." See, e.g., *Muskrat v. United States*, 219 U.S. 346 (1911), at p. 362. This section reflects the strict separation of powers in the American federal constitutional arrangement. Where the "case or controversy" limitation is missing from their respective state constitutions, some American state courts do undertake advisory functions (e.g., in at least two states — Alabama and Delaware — advisory opinions are authorized, in certain circumstances, by statute: see Ala. Code 1975 § 12-2-10; Del. Code Ann. tit. 10, § 141 (1996 Supp.)).

[14] In addition, the judicial systems in several European countries (such as Germany, France, Italy, Spain, Portugal and Belgium) include courts dedicated to the review of constitutional claims; these tribunals do not require a concrete dispute involving individual rights to examine the constitutionality of a new law — an "abstract or objective question" is sufficient. There is no plausible basis on which to conclude that a court is, by its nature, inherently precluded from undertaking another legal function in tandem with its judicial duties.

[15] Moreover, the Canadian Constitution does not insist on a strict separation of powers. Parliament and the provincial legislatures may properly confer other legal functions on the courts, and may confer certain judicial functions on bodies that are not courts. The exception to this rule relates only to s. 96 courts. Thus, even though the rendering of advisory opinions is quite clearly done outside the framework of adversarial litigation, and such opinions are traditionally obtained by the executive from the law officers of the Crown, there is no constitutional bar to this Court's receipt of jurisdiction to undertake such an advisory role. The legislative grant of reference jurisdiction found in s. 53 of the Supreme Court Act is therefore constitutionally valid.

B. *The Court's Jurisdiction Under Section 53*

* * *

[17] It is argued that even if Parliament were entitled to enact s. 53 of the *Supreme Court Act*, the questions submitted by the Governor in Council fall outside the scope of that section.

* * *

[20] The first contention is that in answering Question 2, the Court would be exceeding its jurisdiction by purporting to act as an international tribunal. The simple answer to this submission is that this Court would not, in providing an advisory opinion in the context of a reference, be purporting to "act as" or substitute itself for an international tribunal. In accordance with well accepted

principles of international law, this Court's answer to Question 2 would not purport to bind any other state or international tribunal that might subsequently consider a similar question. The Court nevertheless has jurisdiction to provide an advisory opinion to the Governor in Council in its capacity as a national court on legal questions touching and concerning the future of the Canadian federation.

*   *   *

[23] More importantly, Question 2 of this Reference does not ask an abstract question of "pure" international law but seeks to determine the legal rights and obligations of the National Assembly, legislature or government of Quebec, institutions that clearly exist as part of the Canadian legal order. As will be seen, the *amicus curiae* himself submitted that the success of any initiative on the part of Quebec to secede from the Canadian federation would be governed by international law. In these circumstances, a consideration of international law in the context of this Reference about the legal aspects of the unilateral secession of Quebec is not only permissible but unavoidable.

C. *Justiciability*

[24] It is submitted that even if the Court has jurisdiction over the questions referred, the questions themselves are not justiciable. Three main arguments are raised in this regard:

   (1) the questions are not justiciable because they are too "theoretical" or speculative;

   (2) the questions are not justiciable because they are political in nature;

   (3) the questions are not yet ripe for judicial consideration.

[25] In the context of a reference, the Court, rather than acting in its traditional adjudicative function, is acting in an advisory capacity. The very fact that the Court may be asked hypothetical questions in a reference, such as the constitutionality of proposed legislation, engages the Court in an exercise it would never entertain in the context of litigation. No matter how closely the procedure on a reference may mirror the litigation process, a reference does not engage the Court in a disposition of rights. For the same reason, the Court may deal on a reference with issues that might otherwise be considered not yet "ripe" for decision.

[26] Though a reference differs from the Court's usual adjudicative function, the Court should not, even in the context of a reference, entertain questions that would be inappropriate to answer. However, given the very different nature of a reference, the question of the appropriateness of answering a question should not focus on whether the dispute is formally adversarial or whether it disposes of cognizable rights. Rather, it should consider whether the dispute is appropriately addressed by a court of law. As we stated in *Reference re Canada Assistance Plan (B.C.)*, [1991] 2 S.C.R. 525, at p. 545:

> "While there may be many reasons why a question is non-justiciable, in this appeal the Attorney General of Canada submitted that to answer the questions would draw the Court into a political controversy and involve it in the legislative process. In exercising its discretion whether to determine a

matter that is alleged to be non-justiciable, *the Court's primary concern is to retain its proper role within the constitutional framework of our democratic form of government* . . . . In considering its appropriate role the Court must determine whether the question is purely political in nature and should, therefore, be determined in another forum or *whether it has a sufficient legal component to warrant the intervention of the judicial branch*." [Emphasis added.][5]

Thus the circumstances in which the Court may decline to answer a reference question on the basis of "non-justiciability" include: (i) if to do so would take the Court beyond its own assessment of its proper role in the constitutional framework of our democratic form of government or (ii) if the Court could not give an answer that lies within its area of expertise: the interpretation of law.

[27] As to the "proper role" of the Court, it is important to underline, contrary to the submission of the *amicus curiae*, that the questions posed in this Reference do not ask the Court to usurp any democratic decision that the people of Quebec may be called upon to make. The questions posed by the Governor in Council, as we interpret them, are strictly limited to aspects of the legal framework in which that democratic decision is to be taken. The attempted analogy to the U.S. "political questions" doctrine therefore has no application. The legal framework having been clarified, it will be for the population of Quebec, acting through the political process, to decide whether or not to pursue secession. As will be seen, the legal framework involves the rights and obligations of Canadians who live outside the province of Quebec, as well as those who live within Quebec.

[28] As to the "legal" nature of the questions posed, if the Court is of the opinion that it is being asked a question with a significant extralegal component, it may interpret the question so as to answer only its legal aspects; if this is not possible, the Court may decline to answer the question. In the present Reference the questions may clearly be interpreted as directed to legal issues, and, so interpreted, the Court is in a position to answer them.

[29] Finally, we turn to the proposition that even though the questions referred to us are justiciable in the "reference" sense, the Court must still determine whether it should exercise its discretion to refuse to answer the questions on a pragmatic basis.

[30] Generally, the instances in which the Court has exercised its discretion to refuse to answer a reference question that is otherwise justiciable can be broadly divided into two categories. First, where the question is too imprecise or ambiguous to permit a complete or accurate answer. Second, where the parties have not provided sufficient information to allow the Court to provide a complete or accurate answer.

[31] There is no doubt that the questions posed in this Reference raise difficult issues and are susceptible to varying interpretations. However, rather than refusing

---

[5] [Ed. note: The Court's holding enabled it to avoid a political controversy, rejecting a claim that the government violated a federal statute by reducing funds for welfare. The Court affirmed that the right of Parliament to repeal a statute and the inability of a statute to bind future parliaments meant that there was no basis to claim a "legitimate expectation" of continuing federal financial support.]

to answer at all, the Court is guided by the approach advocated by the majority on the "conventions" issue in *Reference re Resolution to Amend the Constitution*, [1981] 1 S.C.R. 753 (*Patriation Reference*), at pp. 875–76:

> "If the questions are thought to be ambiguous, this Court should not, in a constitutional reference, be in a worse position than that of a witness in a trial and feel compelled simply to answer yes or no. Should it find that a question might be misleading, or should it simply avoid the risk of misunderstanding, the Court is free either to interpret the question . . . or it may qualify both the question and the answer . . . ."

The Reference questions raise issues of fundamental public importance. It cannot be said that the questions are too imprecise or ambiguous to permit a proper legal answer. Nor can it be said that the Court has been provided with insufficient information regarding the present context in which the questions arise. Thus, the Court is duty bound in the circumstances to provide its answers.

The Court declined to answer an advisory opinion in *Reference re Same-Sex Marriage*, [2004] 3 S.C.R. 698. The federal government referred the constitutionality of proposed legislation that would define marriage as "the lawful union of two persons to the exclusion of all others" with a proviso that the law would not affect "the freedom of officials of religious groups to refuse to perform marriages that are not in accordance with their religious beliefs." The Court entertained three reference questions, holding that the bill's authorization of same-sex marriage was within Parliament's authority pursuant to s. 91(26) of the *BNA Act* ("marriage and divorce"), while the proviso respecting religious objections was *ultra vires* as it fell within provincial authority under s. 92(12) ("solemnization of marriage in the province"). The Court further held that the legislation was consistent with the equality provisions of the Charter, rejecting the argument that the law infringed the rights of those who object to same-sex marriage on religious grounds. Although the Court refused to opine as to a potential "collision between rights" if religious officials were compelled to perform same-sex marriages contrary to their beliefs — observing that "Charter decisions should not and must not be made in a factual vacuum" — the opinion noted that "state compulsion on religious officials to perform same-sex marriages contrary to their religious beliefs would violate the guarantee of freedom of religion under s. 2(a) of the Charter" and, "absent exceptional circumstances which we cannot at present foresee, such a violation could not be justified under s. 1 of the Charter." However, the Court rejected a fourth question asking whether the opposite-sex requirement for marriage established by the common law and the Quebec Civil Code was constitutional. The Court noted that five lower courts had held it was not, people had relied on those decisions, and the federal government had pledged to enact legislation to extend marriage to same sex couples regardless of the Court's decision. "Given the government's stated commitment to this course of action, an opinion on the constitutionality of an opposite-sex requirement for marriage serves no legal purpose." *Id.* at 724.

8.2.3. Australia

Sections 75 and 76 of the Constitution provide:

75. In all matters

    (i.)   Arising under any treaty:

    (ii.)   Affecting consuls or other representatives of other countries:

    (iii.)   In which the Commonwealth, or a person suing or being sued on behalf of the Commonwealth, is a party:

    (iv.)   Between States, or between residents of different States, or between a State and a resident of another State:

    (v.)   In which a writ of Mandamus or prohibition or an injunction is sought against an officer of the Commonwealth:

    the High Court shall have original jurisdiction.

76. The Parliament may make laws conferring original jurisdiction on the High Court in any matter

    (i.)   Arising under this Constitution, or involving its interpretation:

    (ii.)   Arising under any laws made by the Parliaments:

    (iii.)   Of Admiralty and maritime jurisdiction:

    (iv.)   Relating to the same subject-matter claimed under the laws of different States.

IN RE JUDICIARY ACT 1903-1920 & IN RE NAVIGATION ACT 1912-1920
HIGH COURT OF AUSTRALIA
(1921) 29 CLR 257

KNOX C.J., GAVAN DUFFY, POWERS, RICH and STARKE JJ.

This was a reference by the Governor-General under sec. 88 of the Judiciary Act for the determination of the question whether, and to what extent, certain sections of the Navigation Act 1912-1920 are valid enactments of the Parliament of the Commonwealth. Mr. Dixon, for the Attorney-General of the State of Victoria, having raised the objection that Part XII. of the Judiciary Act, in which sec. 88 is found, was beyond the powers of the Commonwealth Parliament, the Court heard argument on that question before proceeding to hear and determine the question referred.

In order to decide the preliminary question it is necessary first to ascertain the meaning of the provisions of Part XII., which comprises secs. 88-94. By sec. 88 Parliament purports to confer on this Court "jurisdiction to hear and determine" "any question of law as to the validity of any Act or enactment of the Parliament" which "the Governor-General refers to the High Court for hearing and determination." Sec. 89 provides that any matter so referred shall be heard and determined by a Full Court consisting of all the available Justices. Sec. 90 provides for notice of the hearing to be given to the Attorney-General of each State, and for his right to appear or be represented at the hearing. Sec. 91 empowers the Court to direct that notice be given to other persons, and that they shall be entitled to appear or be represented at the hearing. Sec. 92 empowers the Court to request counsel to argue the matter as to any interest which in the opinion of the Court is affected and as to which counsel does not appear. Sec. 93 provides that the determination of the Court upon the matter shall be final and conclusive and not subject to any appeal. Sec. 94 provides for the making of rules — none have yet been made.

Mr. Leverrier, for the Commonwealth, contended that a determination of the Court pronounced under this Part of the Act was, on the true construction of these sections, merely advisory and not judicial. In our opinion this contention is untenable. After carefully considering the provisions of Part XII., we have come to the conclusion that Parliament desired to obtain from this Court not merely an opinion but an authoritative declaration of the law. To make such a declaration is clearly a judicial function, and such a function is not competent to this Court unless its exercise is an exercise of part of the judicial power of the Commonwealth. If this be so, it is not within our province in this case to inquire whether Parliament can impose on this Court or on its members any, and if so what, duties other than judicial duties, and we refrain from expressing any opinion on that question. What, then, are the limits of the judicial power of the Commonwealth? The Constitution of the Commonwealth is based upon a separation of the functions of government, and the powers which it confers are divided into three classes — legislative, executive and judicial (*New South Wales v. The Commonwealth* (1915) 20 CLR, 54, at p. 88). In each case the Constitution first grants the power and then delimits the scope of its operation. Sec. 71 enacts that the judicial power of the Commonwealth shall be vested in a Federal Supreme Court, to be called the High Court of Australia, and in such other Federal Courts as the Parliament creates, and in such other Courts as it invests with Federal jurisdiction. Secs. 73 and 74 deal with the appellate power of the High Court, and we need make no further reference to those sections as it is not suggested that the duty imposed by Part XII. of the Judiciary Act is within the appellate jurisdiction of this Court. Sec. 75 confers original jurisdiction on the High Court in certain matters. and sec. 76 enables Parliament to confer original jurisdiction on it in other matters. Sec. 77 enables Parliament to define the jurisdiction of any other Federal Court with respect to any of the matters mentioned in secs. 75 and 76, to invest any Court of the States with Federal jurisdiction in respect of any such matters, and to define the extent to which the jurisdiction of any Federal Court shall be exclusive of that which belongs to or is invested in the Courts of the States. This express statement of the matters in respect of which and the Courts by which the judicial power of the Commonwealth may be exercised is, we think, clearly intended as a delimitation of the whole of the original jurisdiction which may be exercised under the judicial power of the Commonwealth, and as a necessary exclusion of any other exercise of original jurisdiction. The question then is narrowed to this: Is authority to be found under sec. 76 of the Constitution for the enactment of Part XII. of the Judiciary Act? Sec. 51 (XXXIX.) does not extend the power to confer original jurisdiction on the High Court contained in sec. 76. It enables Parliament to provide for the effective exercise by the Legislature, the Executive and the Judiciary, of the powers conferred by the Constitution on those bodies respectively, but does not enable it to extend the ambit of any such power. It is said that here is a matter arising under the Constitution or involving its interpretation, and that Parliament by sec. 30 of the Judiciary Act has conferred on this Court original jurisdiction in all matters arising under the Constitution or involving its interpretation. It is true that the answer to the question submitted for our determination does involve the interpretation of the Constitution, but is there a matter within the meaning of sec. 76? We think not. It was suggested in argument that "matter" meant no more than legal proceeding, and that Parliament might at its discretion create or invent a legal proceeding in which this Court might be called on to interpret the Constitution by a declaration at large. We do not accept this contention; we do not think that the word "matter" in sec. 76 means a legal proceeding, but rather the subject matter for determination in a legal proceeding. In our opinion there can be no matter within the meaning of the section unless there is some immediate right, duty or liability to be established by the determination of the Court. If the matter exists, the Legislature may no doubt prescribe the means by which the determination of the Court is to be obtained, and for that purpose may, we think, adopt any existing method of legal procedure or invent a new one. But it cannot authorize this Court to make a declaration of the law divorced from any attempt to administer that law. The word "matter" is used several times in Chapter III. of the Constitution (secs. 73, 74, 75, 76, 77), and always, we think, with the same meaning. The meaning of the expression "in all matters between States" in sec. 75 was considered by this Court in *State of South Australia v. State of Victoria* [[1911] HCA 17; 12 C.L.R., 667.. Griffith C.J. said that it must be a controversy of such a nature that it could be determined upon principles of law, and in this Barton J. agreed. O'Connor J. said that the matter in dispute must be such that it can be determined upon some recognized principle of law. Isaacs J. said that the expression "matters" used with reference to the Judicature, and applying equally to individuals and States, includes and is confined to claims resting upon an alleged violation of some positive law to which the parties are alike subject, and which therefore governs their relations, and constitutes the measure of their respective rights and duties. Higgins J. appeared to think that the expression involved the necessity of the existence of some cause of action in the party applying to the Court for a declaration. He said [12 C.L.R., at p. 742]:—"Even assuming that the State is to be regarded as being substantially the donee of the power, I know of no instance in any Court in which a donee of a power such as this — a power in gross — has obtained by action a declaration that he has the power. Under the Constitution, it is our duty to give relief as between States in cases where, if the facts had occurred as between private persons, we could give relief on principles of law; but not otherwise." All these opinions indicate that a matter under the judicature provisions of the Constitution must involve some right or privilege or protection given by law, or the prevention, redress or punishment of some act inhibited by law. The adjudication of the Court may be sought in proceedings inter partes or ex parte, or, if Courts had the requisite jurisdiction, even in those administrative proceedings with reference to the custody, residence and management of the affairs of infants or lunatics. But we can find nothing in Chapter III. of the Constitution to lend colour to the view that Parliament can confer power or jurisdiction upon the High Court to determine abstract questions of law without the right or duty of any body or person being involved.

During the argument a strenuous attempt was made to show that this Court had, in earlier cases, approved of the exercise of original jurisdiction in circumstances like those of the present case. We have examined the cases relied on in support of this proposition, and we are satisfied that in all of them the use of the judicial power was approved only when it was used for the purpose of effecting or assisting in effecting a settlement of existing claims of right under the law of the Commonwealth.

* * *

HIGGINS, J. [dissenting]:

* * *

Under sec. 51 of the Constitution the Parliament has power to make laws for the peace, order and good government of the Commonwealth "with respect to" many subjects, including trade and commerce with other countries and among the States; and it has also power (pl. xxxix.) to make laws "with respect to matters incidental to the execution of any power vested by this Constitution in the Parliament or in either House thereof, or in the Government of the Commonwealth." Part XII. of the Judiciary Act seems to me to come precisely under these words. The Government must execute the laws so far as valid; and in order to carry out its duty it is enabled by Part XII. to get the highest legal opinion in the country as to the validity of the sections before acting on them. In my opinion, Part XII. is valid, whether our determination is to be treated as mere advice or as a judicial decision.

* * *

That a determination would be an aid to the Government is unquestionable. It would not be a judgment binding all the world, as has been suggested, or binding as res judicata between parties who have not been heard; but it would be an authority of great weight — a decision which, unless overruled, the Courts would follow in actions between parties; just as a decision between A and B is an authority in a subsequent action between C and D. C and D are certainly "affected" by the decision between A and B; but it is open to C or D to satisfy this Court that the law of the decision was wrong. ***

These considerations bring me to say something as to Chapter III. of the Constitution — "The Judicature." It is said that this Court, as a Court, is forbidden by the Constitution to perform any functions which are not within "the judicial power of the Commonwealth," and that the function of determining the validity of an Act except between litigating parties is not within that judicial power. I cannot accept either proposition. To say that Blackacre shall be vested in A (and in A only) does not carry as a corollary that Whiteacre shall not be vested in A; to say that the judicial power of the Commonwealth shall be vested in the High Court (and other Federal Courts and such other Courts as Parliament invests with Federal jurisdiction — sec. 71 of Constitution) does not imply that no other jurisdiction, or power, shall be vested in the High Court or in the other Courts. This is surely obvious, on the mere form of words. There is a great deal of force in the argument, favoured by lawyers, that decisions of a Court where there is no active controversy between interested parties are not so valuable as when there is such controversy;

and that, when a litigated case comes before the Court subsequently, the Court would approach it with prejudiced minds. But this argument is an argument of expediency, and is not for us. It may be that we shall have in the future attempts at preventive law as well as at preventive medicine, and that, on a balance of expediencies, the law-makers may prefer judicial proceedings before acting, rather than to keep all judicial proceedings till after the doubtful step has been taken. The point is that the Constitution does not expressly forbid the vesting of other powers in this Court, and that there is no necessary implication to that effect. In the next place, I think that an application under Part XII. does come (if that is necessary) within the words of sec. 76, "matter arising under this Constitution, or involving its interpretation." Counsel for the State of Victoria says that "matter" in this contest means a "claim of right": but this definition is too broad, I think, in that it omits the idea of some curial proceeding; and too narrow, in that it assumes that there must be a contest between parties. It is not necessary that a "matter" should be between parties. I pass by the fact that in the Judiciary Act itself, "matter" includes any proceeding in a Court "whether between parties or not"; for it may be urged that the Act was not in force at the time of the Constitution. But in the English Judicature Act 1873 the word "matter" is defined as "every proceeding in the Court not in a cause"; and "cause" includes "any action, suit, or other original proceeding between a plaintiff and a defendant." This is the language of the Parliament which enacted our Constitution; and the distinction between "causes" and "matters" or "suits" and "matters" was common in still earlier legislation (15 & 16 Vict. c. 80; 15 & 16 Vict. c. 86; General Orders of 1841). In the Oxford Dictionary the meaning of "matter," as used in law, is "something which is to be tried or proved." It may be that the connotation of words used in the Constitution may not be extended by Parliament; but surely not the denotation. The Constitution does not stereotype the denotation of words for all subsequent time. The States can create new matters. Any State may hereafter adopt the French law of prodigue, under which a wife may apply for an interdict against extravagance on the part of her husband; and if such a law were adopted the High Court would have jurisdiction of the matter (or cause) if it involve in any way the interpretation of the Constitution. What the State can do, the Commonwealth can do — within the ambit of its specific subjects; and if the Commonwealth Parliament see fit to create a new legal proceeding under sec. 51 (XXXIX.), that legal proceeding comes under the High Court jurisdiction to decide matters involving the interpretation of the Constitution (sec. 76).

But, in my opinion, the only real question necessary to decide here is the meaning of sec. 51 in its relation to sec. 61 of the Constitution. Hitherto, this Court has given the widest construction to pl. xxxix. and to the words "with respect to" in the opening words of sec. 51.*** "Matter" does not mean merely legal proceeding, but some legal proceeding is probably implied — not necessarily a proceeding where some immediate right, duty or liability is to be established by the determination of the Court; for under such a limited meaning the High Court could not decide as to the existence of an industrial dispute under sec. 21AA.

Nor is the jurisdiction given to this Court to entertain and give a determination as to law in non-litigious matters anything startling or novel. In the British Act which organized the Judicial Committee of the Privy Council (3 & 4 Will. IV. c. 41) His Majesty was empowered to refer to the Judicial Committee "for hearing or consideration" any matters (other than appeals, &c.) as His Majesty thought fit; and the Committee has to hear or consider the same, and advise His Majesty (sec. 4). It appears that the Judicial Committee, when acting under this section, does not make a pronouncement in a formal reasoned judgment, but merely advises His Majesty (Bentwich's *Privy Council Practice*, p. 241). As Lord Loreburn L.C. said in *Attorney-General for Ontario v. Attorney-General for Canada* [(1912) A.C., 571]), the Judicial Committee exercises most important judicial functions, yet it is bound to answer His Majesty under this section; and there never has been any suggestion of inconvenience or impropriety. In Canada in several successive Acts the Government was enabled to put before the Supreme Court of Canada questions touching the validity of Dominion or Provincial legislation. In the Act of 1906 (sec. 6): "The opinion of the Court upon any such reference although advisory only shall for all purposes of appeal to His Majesty in Council be treated as a final judgment of the said Court between parties." These words imply that for other purposes the opinion is not to be treated as a res judicata between parties, and yet an appeal lies to the Judicial Committee therefrom. Many such appeals have been heard. In this case sec. 6 was held to be valid; although the argument was used that it was an interference with the judicial character of the Supreme Court, and that the Judges would approach litigation with preconceived opinions. That, the Judicial Committee said, was a matter of policy for Parliament to consider. But for the fact that in Canada the residuary powers of legislation belong to the Dominion, not to the Provinces, this case would be a direct authority in favour of Part XII. of our Act. Why should the Canadian Court have jurisdiction to give an opinion that may be the subject of an appeal, and yet the Australian Court be incapable of giving a determination that is not subject to appeal? In both cases, there is no litigation between parties.

It is true that in the United States the Supreme Court has steadfastly refused to advise the Executive on its request. The principle has been recently stated and explained in United States v. Evans. In 1793 Washington, as President, sought to take the opinion of the Supreme Court as to various questions arising under treaties with France; but there was no response. Marshall C.J. thus speaks of the matter in his Life of Washington: "Considering themselves as merely constituting a legal tribunal for the decision of controversies brought before them in legal form, the Judges deemed it improper to enter into the fields of politics by declaring their opinions on questions not arising out of the case before them." But it will be observed that the question put by Washington was a question under a treaty; and, whatever the question was, it was assumed to be a question of politics, as to external relations — a matter for the Executive, or for Congress. No American case has been cited to us in which, under the Constitution of 1789, an Act of Congress has been held to be invalid which purported to give to the Supreme Court jurisdiction to state the interpretation of the Constitution, or to pronounce as to the validity of an Act made as under the Constitution. Probably the difficulty in the way of such an Act is greater than under our Constitution; because in the article of the United States Constitution as to judicial power the words used are not so wide as in our Constitution. Here, the words are "matters arising under this Constitution, or involving its interpretation" (sec. 76); in the United States the words are "all cases in law and equity arising under the Constitution." There must be in the United

States, a case or a controversy, at law or in equity, between litigating parties. The position is very different.

* * *

The separation of the legislative, executive and judicial powers under the Constitution leaves these arms of the Commonwealth interdependent. In Australia executive Ministers must sit in the Legislature (sec. 64) (not as in the United States); and Parliament can regulate the working of the judicial power. There is nothing in the separation of powers that necessarily involves that the High Court cannot be employed to aid the Executive — judicially, at all events.

I much regret to find myself differing from my learned colleagues, but I can see no sufficient ground for holding Part XII. of the Judiciary Act to be invalid.

In contrast to the U.S. and Canadian polar opposite approaches, which are well-settled and relatively uncontroversial in their respective countries, there have been several efforts to overturn this landmark case and empower the HCA to issue advisory opinions. A 1929 Royal Commission endorsed a constitutional amendment to so provide, although the proposal was never referred by Parliament to a referendum. The issue was re-visited during the ongoing Constitutional Convention which ran, pursuant to a statute enacted by the Whitlam Labor government in 1973, periodically until 1985. The 1978 session considered and endorsed a constitutional amendment; however, a Constitutional Commission deliberating between 1986 and 1988 rejected the proposal.

A number of leading Australian legal thinkers continue to seek re-consideration. Justice Michael Kirby called the precedent "rather narrow" and suggested a change "as the Court adapts its process to a modern understanding of its constitutional and judicial functions." *North Ganalanga Aboriginal Corp. v. Queensland* (1996) CLR 595, 666. Professor John Williams argues that rule of law principles require that law must be "open and clear" if it is to be "capable of guiding the behaviour of its subjects," and this principle is undermine by the Court's "refusal to hear and clarify what *is* the law in a situation where a citizen is unsure which of two competing laws he or she must obey." *Re-thinking Advisory Opinions* 7 PUB. L. REV. 205, 206–7 (1996).

One of us has suggested, to the contrary, that advisory opinions "may well create only the illusion of certainty." *See* Helen Irving, *Advisory Opinions, The Rule of Law, and The Separation of Powers*, 4 MACQUARIE L.J. 105 (2004). The High Court will not test and review every law, nor will an opinion necessarily be final. Even Higgins J, dissenting in *In re Judiciary and Navigation Acts*, acknowledged that advisory opinions would not preclude real parties in a real case from re-litigating the issue later. There is also a concern that the independence of the judiciary could suffer, especially if the court were required rather than permitted to offer advice. Moreover, existing procedures, such as suits for declaratory judgment, can present justiciable controversies that allow for early judicial resolution of constitutional questions. Finally, this analysis echoes Justice Frankfurter's concerns about American advisory opinions: the decisions tend to be conservative and sterile.

8.2.4. South Africa

While the South African Constitutional Court does not issue advisory opinions, it does in some cases conduct what might be termed abstract review. There are three forms of abstract review in the South African context. First, if the President is concerned that a law passed by parliament is in violation of the Constitution the President may decline to sign it into law and instead refer it to the Constitutional Court for a determination of facial or abstract constitutionality. Second, the Constitution provides for a very specific procedure allowing members of legislatures, at either the national or the provincial level to challenge the constitutionality of newly adopted legislation through a form of abstract constitutional review. Third, the expansive standing rules for constitutional litigation in South Africa means that in many instances non-government organizations and other activist constituencies can bring constitutional challenges as soon as a statute becomes law, long before specific cases based on particular parties or conflicts might arise. (These opinions may be abstract but they are not advisory since once the Constitutional Court rules that a particular feature of a bill or a new piece of legislation is unconstitutional it is by definition invalid and the declaration of invalidity has the effect of making the particular provision null and void.)

This power is however tempered by the Constitutional Court's practice in relevant circumstances of suspending its own declaration of invalidity and giving the legislature a specific period of time to amend the legislation so as to address its constitutional infirmity, before the declaration of invalidity takes effect (see *Bhe v. Magistrate, Khayalitsha*, paras 101–108 and *Minister of Home Affairs v. Fourie*, paras 132–153).

A classic abstract review case involved a challenge to the newly passed Communal Land Act (CLARA) by four communities who feared that the Act would impact them. In *Tongoane v. Minister of Agriculture*, 2010 (6) SA 214 (CC), the SACC was considering a constitutional challenge to the Act, principally based on the claim that the CLARA undermined the security of tenure of the applicant communities, contrary to ss. 25(6) and (9) (requiring Parliament to address legally unsecure lands due to past discriminatory laws). However, pending resolution of this claim, the Minister filed an affidavit, clarified by government counsel, that CLARA would be repealed *in toto*.

The Court proceeded to render judgment on the procedure that Parliament needed to follow in considering new land tenure legislation to meet Constitutional standards. Section 75 describes "ordinary bills" that do not affect the provinces, requiring consultation with the National Council of Provinces (NCOP) but permitting the National Assembly (NA) to pass the bill anyway. Section 76 describes the process for legislation affecting the provinces, requiring a mediation of the NCOP and NA cannot agree, and then allowing the NA to pass the legislation with a 2/3 vote. On the federalism claim, the SACC refused to be drawn into a dispute as to whether the legislation's "pith and substance" was land tenure (subject to exclusive national legislation) or indigenous law (concurrent jurisdiction with provinces under Schedule 4); rather, the SACC held that because the legislation significantly affected provincial jurisdiction with regard to the latter, the section 76 procedures were mandatory.

However, the Court declined to rule, in advance, with regard to the substantive challenges raised by the communities opposed to the national legislation. Chief Justice Ngcobo wrote "while the applicants ardently wish to have finality regarding the constitutional propriety of the legislation that will be enacted, the invitation to us to express an opinion on provisions in a statute which we have declared invalid in its entirety, and which we have been told will, in any event, be repealed *in toto*, must be declined."

TONGOANE v. MINISTER OF AGRICULTURE
CONSTITUTIONAL COURT OF SOUTH AFRICA
2010 (6) SA 214

NGCOBO CJ:

[1] This case raises important constitutional questions concerning one of the most crucial pieces of legislation enacted in our country since the advent of our constitutional democracy: the Communal Land Rights Act, 2004 (CLARA). This legislation is intended to meet one of the longstanding constitutional obligations of Parliament to enact legislation to provide legally secure tenure or comparable redress to people or communities whose tenure of land is legally insecure as a result of the racist policies of apartheid that were imposed under the colour of the law. The people and communities who were primarily victimised by these laws were African people.

. . . .

[4] Four communities whose land rights are affected by CLARA mounted a two pronged constitutional challenge to this legislation in the North Gauteng High Court, Pretoria (the High Court). One was substantive, challenging CLARA on the ground that its provisions undermine security of tenure. The other was procedural, contending that the manner in which CLARA was enacted was incorrect. This latter challenge was premised on Parliament's decision to pass CLARA as a Bill which does not affect the provinces, under section 75 of the Constitution, instead of as a Bill which affects the provinces, under section 76 of the Constitution.

[The Constitution sets forth specific legislative procedures Parliament must follow, depending on the nature of legislation. Section 74 describes the super-majority vote required for bills amending the Constitution. Section 75 describes "ordinary bills" that do not affect the provinces, requiring consultation with the National Council of Provinces (NCOP) but permitting the National Assembly (NA) to pass the bill anyway. Section 76 describes the process for legislation affecting the provinces, requiring a mediation of the NCOP and NA cannot agree, and then allowing the NA to pass the legislation with a 2/3 vote. Section 77 deals with money bills.]

. . . .

[10] Until 1905, the practice in the former Transvaal or Zuid-Afrikaansche Republic was that ownership of land could not be registered in the name of a "native." This

was justified on the basis of two instruments, namely, the Volksraad Resolution of 14 August 1884 and article 13 of the Pretoria Convention, 1881. The latter provided that: "Natives will be allowed to acquire land, but the grant or transfer of such land will in every case be made to and registered in the name of the Native Location Commission hereinafter mentioned, in trust for such natives."

[11] However, in 1905, and following the decision in *Tsewu v Registrar of Deeds* which held that neither of these instruments had the force of law and that title could be registered in the names of "natives," African people were able to purchase land from white farmers. It is said that subsequent to 1905 and before June 1913, African people purchased some 399 farms. All this changed in June 1913, when the Natives Land Act, 1913 (now the Black Land Act) was enacted.

[12] The Black Land Act and the Native Trust and Land Act, 1936 (now the Development Trust and Land Act) were the key statutes that determined where African people could live. The former contained a schedule which set out areas in which only African people could purchase, hire or occupy land. In terms of section 2(1), the sale of land between whites and African people in respect of land outside of the scheduled areas referred to in the Act was prohibited. The effect of this legislation was to preclude African people from purchasing land in most of South Africa.

. . . .

[14] The Development Trust and Land Act was enacted in 1936 to make provision for the establishment of the South African Native Trust (the Trust) and the release of more land for occupation by African people. In terms of section 6 of this Act, all land "which [was] reserved or set aside for the occupation of natives" and "land within the scheduled native areas, and . . . within the released areas" vested in the Trust . . . .

[Although the land that vested in the Trust was "held for the exclusive use and benefit of natives," the Trustee retained full powers and the Governor-General retained regulatory powers over the land.]

[17] The Bantu Areas Land Regulations recognised two forms of land tenure, namely, quitrent tenure of land and occupation of land under permission to occupy. Although quitrent title was defined to mean a "title deed relating to land," it did not confer full ownership on the holder. This title was subject to strict conditions prescribed in the regulations which included the right of the Bantu Affairs Commissioner. [Among other onerous conditions, the regulations granted the government authority to "enter upon and inspect the land" to ensure compliance with the regulations, a prohibition against transferring title or disposing of land without the consent of the Bantu Affairs Commissioner, cancellation of rights for failure to uphold specified conditions or upon criminal conviction, and that African people could not be absent from the land allotted to them without written permission issued by the Bantu Affairs Commissioner.]

[20] These regulations recognised the application of indigenous law in the areas reserved for African people. This is apparent from provisions of the regulations dealing with succession to land. Succession to land allotted under the regulations was governed by indigenous law. In addition, tribal authorities or, where they did

not exist, traditional leaders played a role in the allocation of arable and residential allotments. To occupy land in these areas, African people required the permission of the Bantu Affairs Commissioner who would grant permission after consultation with the tribal authority having jurisdiction or a traditional leader, as the case may be.

[21] What emerges from these regulations therefore is that (a) the tenure in land which was subject to the provisions of the Black Land Act and Development Trust and Land Act and which was held by African people was precarious and legally insecure; (b) indigenous law governed succession to land in these areas, and the application of indigenous law in relation to land in these areas subject to regulations was recognised; and (c) tribal authorities and traditional leaders played a role in the allotment of land in these areas.

. . . .

[24] The Black Authorities Act gave the State President the authority to establish "with due regard to native law and custom" tribal authorities for African "tribes" as the basic unit of administration in the areas to which the provisions of CLARA apply . . . . It is these tribal authorities that have now been transformed into traditional councils for the purposes of section 28(4) of the Traditional Leadership and Governance Framework Act, 2003 (the Traditional Leadership Act). And in terms of section 21 of CLARA, these traditional councils may exercise powers and perform functions relating to the administration of communal land.

[25] Under apartheid, these steps were a necessary prelude to the assignment of African people to ethnically-based homelands. This commenced with the creation of "legislative assemblies" which would mature into "self-governing territories" and ultimately into "independent states." According to this plan, there would be no African people in South Africa, as all would assume citizenship of one or other of the newly created homelands, where they could enjoy social, economic and political rights. Section 5(1)(b) of the Black Administration Act became the most powerful tool to effect the removal of African people from "white" South Africa into areas reserved for them under this Act and the Development Trust and Land Act. And as we noted in *DVB Behuising*, "[t]hese removals resulted in untold suffering." The forced removals of African people from the land which they occupied to the limited amount of land reserved for them by the apartheid state resulted in the majority of African people being dispossessed of their land. It also left a majority of them without legally secure tenure in land.

. . . .

[28] One of the goals of our Constitution is to reverse all of this. It requires the restoration of land to people and communities that were dispossessed of land by colonial and apartheid laws after 19 June 1913. It also requires that people and communities whose tenure of land is legally insecure as a result of racially discriminatory colonial and apartheid laws be provided with legally secure tenure or comparable redress. CLARA was enacted with the declared purpose to "provide for legal security of tenure."

. . . .

[33] The communities are concerned that their indigenous-law-based system of land administration [which recognised the individual rights of co-owners and their families in respect of particular plots of land which they came to occupy for purposes of residence and cultivation] will be replaced by the new system that CLARA envisages. They are concerned that this will have an impact on the evolving indigenous law which has always regulated the use and occupation of land they occupy. They are further concerned that their land will now be subject to the control of traditional councils which, as is apparent from the record, they consider to be incapable of administering their land for the benefit of the community. All the communities claim that the provisions of CLARA will undermine the security of tenure they presently enjoy in their land, and those who own the land fear that they will be divested of their ownership of the land. While some of these claims are disputed by the government respondents, what is not disputed is that the land occupied by the communities is administered in accordance with indigenous law, and that traditional leaders, in particular the tribal authorities, play a role in the administration of communal land. There is some issue as to the extent to which the role of traditional leaders and tribal authorities accords with indigenous law.

. . . .

[The major constitutional challenge raised by the plaintiffs was that CLARA undermined the security of tenure of the applicant communities, contrary to ss. 25(6) and (9) (requiring Parliament to address legally unsecure lands due to past discriminatory laws). However, pending resolution of this claim, the Minister filed an affidavit, clarified by government counsel, that CLARA would be repealed *in toto*. The remaining constitutional issue was the procedure required for enactment of new legislation.]

. . . .

[49] The communities contended that CLARA should have been classified as a section 76 Bill because it affects the provinces . . . . They submitted that in *Liquor Bill*, this Court formulated the test for the classification of Bills when it held that a "Bill whose provisions in substantial measure fall within a functional area listed in Schedule 4" must be dealt with under section 76. They submitted that the provisions of CLARA in substantial measure deal with "indigenous and customary law" and "traditional leadership" which are functional areas listed in Schedule 4.

[50] In its written argument, Parliament contended that the test for tagging a Bill was the substance of the legislation which was referred to as the "pith and substance" test. The phrase "pith and substance" is borrowed from other jurisdictions and refers to what we term the "substance," the "purpose and effect" or the "subject-matter" of legislation. The "purpose and effect" test was developed by this Court to determine whether the National Assembly or a provincial legislature has the competence to legislate in a particular field. Based on this test, which Parliament contended should also apply to the process of determining the manner in which a Bill should be tagged, Parliament submitted that the "pith and substance" of CLARA was land tenure. Any provision of CLARA that deals with indigenous law or traditional leadership, matters listed in Schedule 4, is incidental to land tenure. These provisions were irrelevant for the purposes of tagging CLARA.

[51] Parliament contended further that there should be no difference between the test for classifying legislation for the purposes of tagging on the one hand, and on the other hand, determining whether legislation falls within the competence of a legislature. This is so, the argument went, because both have the same end in mind, namely, to determine whether the legislation falls within one of the relevant schedules to the Constitution.

[52] However, in response to questions put to counsel for Parliament in the course of oral argument, there was a noticeable shift in Parliament's position. Counsel for Parliament accepted that there is a difference between the test for determining legislative competence and the test for determining how a Bill should be tagged. He also accepted that if a substantial part of a Bill is concerned with a functional area listed in Schedule 4 then the Bill falls to be classified as a section 76 Bill. However, he maintained that no substantial part of CLARA affected the provinces and that CLARA was correctly tagged as a section 75 Bill. This argument suggests that in tagging a Bill, Parliament looks not only at the substance, or purpose and effect, of the Bill but also at the provisions of the Bill in order to determine whether any of its provisions affect a functional area listed in Schedule 4.

. . . .

[60] The test for tagging must be informed by its purpose. Tagging is not concerned with determining the sphere of government that has the competence to legislate on a matter. Nor is the process concerned with preventing interference in the legislative competence of another sphere of government. The process is concerned with the question of how the Bill should be considered by the provinces and in the NCOP, and how a Bill must be considered by the provincial legislatures depends on whether it affects the provinces. The more it affects the interests, concerns and capacities of the provinces, the more say the provinces should have on its content.

. . . .

[69] The tagging of Bills before Parliament must be informed by the need to ensure that the provinces fully and effectively exercise their appropriate role in the process of considering national legislation that substantially affects them. Paying less attention to the provisions of a Bill once its substance, or purpose and effect, has been identified undermines the role that provinces should play in the enactment of national legislation affecting them. The subject-matter of a Bill may lie in one area, yet its provisions may have a substantial impact on the interests of provinces. And different provisions of the legislation may be so closely intertwined that blind adherence to the subject-matter of the legislation without regard to the impact of its provisions on functional areas in Schedule 4 may frustrate the very purpose of classification.

[70] To apply the "pith and substance" test to the tagging question, therefore, undermines the constitutional role of the provinces in legislation in which they should have a meaningful say, and disregards the breadth of the legislative provisions that section 76(3) requires to be enacted in accordance with the section 76 procedure. It does this because it focuses on the substance of a Bill and treats provisions which fall outside its main substance as merely incidental to it and consequently irrelevant to tagging. In so doing, it ignores the impact of those

provisions on the provinces. To ignore this impact is to ignore the role of the provinces in the enactment of legislation substantially affecting them. Therefore the test for determining how a Bill is to be tagged must be broader than that for determining legislative competence.

. . . .

[74] There are two important considerations that must be borne in mind when determining whether the provisions of CLARA in substantial measure fall within the functional area of indigenous law. The first is to recognise that statutes do not ordinarily deal with indigenous law in the abstract. They do so in the context of specific subject matter of indigenous law, such as matrimonial property, intestate succession, or the occupation and use of communal land, as CLARA does. Therefore any legislation with regard to indigenous law will ordinarily and indeed, almost invariably, also be legislation with regard to the underlying subject-matter of the indigenous law in question. The mere fact that a statute that repeals, replaces or amends indigenous law might have a different subject-matter of its own, does not detract from the fact that it also falls within the functional area of indigenous law.

. . . .

[80] It seems to me that once it is accepted, as it must be, that CLARA's purpose is to introduce a new regime that will regulate the use, occupation and administration of communal land, a field presently regulated to a large extent by indigenous law, it follows that CLARA, in substantial measure, deals with indigenous law, a functional area listed in Schedule 4. To the extent that traditional leaders, through traditional councils, will now have wide-ranging powers in relation to the administration of communal land, the Act deals, in substantial measure, with traditional leadership, another functional area listed in Schedule 4. The attempt by CLARA . . . to reclassify the acts of traditional councils when performing the functions and powers of land administration committees as functions in respect of the "administration of land," simply emphasises the conclusion.

. . . .

[109] I have already described in detail the purpose of the section 76 procedure and the importance of the constitutional role that the provinces must play in considering legislation which affects them. Apart from this, the provisions of section 76(3) are couched in peremptory terms. Having regard to this, and the purpose of section 76(3), I consider that enacting legislation that affects the provinces in accordance with the procedure prescribed in section 76 is a material part of the law-making process relating to legislation that substantially affects the provinces. Failure to comply with the requirements of section 76(3) renders the resulting legislation invalid.

[110] For all these reasons, I conclude that CLARA is unconstitutional in its entirety.

. . . .

[122] . . . while the applicants ardently wish to have finality regarding the constitutional propriety of the legislation that will be enacted, the invitation to us to express an opinion on provisions in a statute which we have declared invalid in its

entirety, and which we have been told will, in any event, be repealed in toto, must be declined.

[123] I should note, however, that the substance of the submissions in respect of the Minister's intention to repeal CLARA lies in the real concern that further delay will be occasioned in the process of finalising new legislation. I understand these concerns. African people were deprived of their land by the apartheid legal order. They were confined to areas where they were not given any secure tenure. The Constitution recognises this — for it not only provides for restitution of land to people or communities that were dispossessed of their land as a result of past racially-discriminatory laws and practices, but it also recognises that African people were deprived of any secure tenure of land by reason of racially-discriminatory laws enacted by a white minority government. Against this background, the Constitution envisages that Parliament will enact legislation that will ensure that there is restitution of land to the people and communities that were dispossessed of their land, and that they will be accorded secure land tenure or comparable redress.

[124] This is a constitutional imperative which must be achieved. I accept the magnitude of the problem created by apartheid laws and practices, as well as the amount of time and effort necessary to undo these consequences. The core problem created by colonial and apartheid geography is that millions of African people were forced into labour reserves that were distant from employment opportunities, impoverished and overcrowded. The repressive machinery of apartheid, from the pass laws to forced removals, evolved in a way that restricted those affected to these impoverished zones. African communities were uprooted from their land and dumped onto foreign land. They were denied secure tenure in these areas. While the deep sense of humiliation and untold suffering cannot be fully compensated, at the very least, lost dignity can be partially restored by providing for security of tenure.

[125] Land restitution and security of tenure must be given priority. We are mindful that Parliament's legislative plate is overflowing. These matters have, however, now become pressing and should be treated with the urgency that they deserve.

. . . .

[127] It is now some 13 years since the final Constitution came into effect. By any standard, a 13-year delay is unfortunate. Further delay as a consequence of this judgment and what we are now told is the inevitable repeal of the entire statute is unavoidable. This judgment will, however, provide Parliament with the opportunity to take a second look at the substantive objections raised by the applicants in respect of CLARA when it considers the proper way to give effect to section 25(6) of the Constitution. Suffice it to say that the legislation contemplated by section 25(9) read with section 25(6) must be enacted with a sense of urgency and diligence.

8.3. THE CONCEPT OF CONSTITUTIONAL CONVENTION

The oft-cited definition of a constitutional convention comes from English scholar K.C. Wheare: it is "a binding rule, a rule of behaviour accepted as obligatory by those concerned in the working of the Constitution." SIR KENNETH WHEARE, MODERN CONSTITUTIONS 179 (1951). What distinguishes conventions from constitutional law is that conventions are not judicially enforceable. (Sometimes as discussed below, conventions become enacted into law — then they are enforceable, but are no longer conventions.)

The *British North America Act* illustrates the concept. First, the preamble states that provinces are to be federally united "with a Constitution similar in Principle to that of the United Kingdom." Since the UK has no written constitution, this refers to the body of constitutional conventions accepted by the British. Second, the *BNA Act* confers a variety of powers on the Queen and her representative, the Governor General, including the power to veto in section 55:

> Where a Bill passed by the Houses of the Parliament is presented to the Governor General for the Queen's Assent, he shall declare, according to his Discretion, but subject to the Provisions of this Act and to Her Majesty's Instructions either that he assents thereto in the Queen's Name, or that he withholds the Queen's Assent, or that he reserves the Bill for the Signification of the Queen's Pleasure.

With regard to the Governor General's authority, "it is accepted that, by convention, this power will not be exercised." *See* Hogg, § 1.1.(a). With regard to the Queen's power of disallowance, after 1930 a new convention was agreed to so that the Queen would take no action in regard to a reserved bill contrary to the wishes of the government of the member of the Commonwealth concerned, and that her exercise of the power of disallowance is no longer possible. *See* Hogg, s 9.5(d).

Conventions can also evolve. Thus, Queen Victoria regularly corresponded with fellow monarchs (who often were relatives) independently of the government; today, Queen Elizabeth II would not think of independently writing King Juan Carlos of Spain on a matter of Anglo-Spanish relations without vetting it with the Foreign Ministry. On the other hand, to keep a watchful eye on the still-powerful monarch, a 19th-century convention had developed allowing the Prime Minister to appoint cronies to be the Queen's ladies-in-waiting; David Cameron does not get to select the women who attend to Queen Elizabeth. A more serious example concerns the power to commit foreign troops. Section 68 of the Australian Constitution provides that the "command in chief of the naval and military forces of the Commonwealth is vested in the Governor-General as the Queen's representative." Even in 1900, this didn't mean the monarch herself; at enactment, this was understood to mean that the Governor-General would take instructions from the British government. Even by 1914, however, the decision to commit Australian troops to World War I was made by Australia's Prime Minister, not the British. *See* Helen Irving, Five Things to Know About the Australian Constitution (2004).

Although this concept may seem foreign to Americans, there are several notable examples of American traditions that meet Professor Wheare's definition of an obligatory rule of behavior. For example, the written Constitution provides for the President's cabinet (Art. II, §2 provides that the President "may require the opinion, in writing, of the principal officer in each of the executive departments" and authorizes Congress by legislation to vest the appointment of inferior officers in the "heads of departments") and requires Senate confirmation of cabinet members ("officers of the United States"). Although the Senate occasionally refuses to confirm nominees deemed unfit or unqualified, even when the Senate is controlled by the opposition party, the Senate has traditionally not rejected a President's choice solely on policy grounds. In contrast, under the French Constitution an elected President must present a cabinet that enjoys the confidence of the legislature, and when the President's party does not control the legislature a "cohabitation" agreement must be worked out. Another American convention is that persons elected to the Electoral College will cast their votes for the presidential candidate to whom they are pledged.

MADZIMBAMUTO v. LARDNER-BURKE
Privy Council
[1969] 1 AC 645, [1968] 3 All ER 561

[Before Lord Reid, Lord Morris of Borth-Y-Gest, Lord Pearce, Lord Wilberforce and Lord Pearson]

[The case was a test case by Stells Madzimbamuto, an imprisoned black Rhodesian, against the Minister of Justice of the rebel government in Southern Rhodesia and other rebel officials. The purpose was] to test the status of the government in control (i.e., since the unilateral declaration of independence on Nov. 11, 1965), its capacity to declare states of emergency, to make regulations thereunder and to detain people in terms of those regulations. ***

[By way of historical background, in 1923 Southern Rhodesia was colonized by the United Kingdom. The Southern Rhodesian government practiced apartheid, copied from its neighbour in South Africa, so the government ruled on behalf of a tiny white minority. Pursuant to the Southern Rhodesia Constitution, a state of emergency was validly proclaimed in 1965 in response to an uprising by black Rhodesians. Pursuant to emergency powers, the appellant's husband was detained by the government. Shortly thereafter, Southern Rhodesian Prime Minister Ian Smith and his Ministerial colleagues issued a unilateral declaration of independence. On the same day, the British Governor issued a statement on behalf of Her Majesty that Mr. Smith and other government Ministers and deputy Ministers ceased to hold office and called on all citizens to refrain from acts which would further the objectives of the illegal authorities, but added that it was the duty of all citizens to maintain law and order and to carry out their normal tasks. The British Parliament responded to the unilateral declaration of independence by enacting the *Southern Rhodesia Act 1965*, declaring that it had responsibility and jurisdiction for Southern Rhodesia as theretofore and authorizing the British government "to make such provision as appeared to be necessary or expedient in consequence of any unconstitutional action." The cabinet implemented the statute by issuing The Southern Rhodesia Constitution Order 1965 (the "Order in Council"), declaring that any laws, regulations, or acts of the rebel government were void. The initial declaration of emergency that had been validly issued by the pre-rebellion government expired on its own terms. The appellant's husband remained under detention, however, pursuant to a new declaration of emergency proclaimed by the rebel government.]

[Madzimbabuto claimed that the new emergency declaration was void. The claim was based on the 1961 Southern Rhodesian Constitution, which created a government similar to Canada's, with a Governor as Her Majesty's representative holding formal executive power and a colonial legislature charged with making laws for the peace, order, and good government of Southern Rhodesia. The Constitution also contained a Declaration of Rights. Of particular relevance was s. 58, which provides "(1) No person shall be deprived of his personal liberty save as may be authorised by law," and s. 69 which provides "(1) Nothing contained in any law shall be held to be inconsistent with or in contravention of inter alia s. 58 to the extent that the law in question makes provision with respect to the taking during any period of public emergency of action for the purpose of dealing with any situation arising during that period . . .". Section 72 (2) defines "period of public emergency" as meaning, inter alia, any period not exceeding three months during which a state of emergency is declared to exist "by virtue of a proclamation issued in terms of any law for the time being in force relating to emergency powers, the reasons for the issue thereof having been communicated to the Legislative Assembly as soon as possible after the issue thereof, or by virtue of a further proclamation so issued on a resolution of the Assembly." Section 71 provides methods by which any person alleging contraven-tion of any of the provisions of s. 57 to s. 68 can apply for redress, and sub-sec. (5) provides "Any person aggrieved by any determination of the High Court under this section may appeal therefrom to Her Majesty in Council."[6]

[The Southern Rhodesian government claimed its declaration of independence rendered lawful its own 1965 constitution, by which it declared a lawful emergency that justified the appellant's imprisonment. The rebel government argued that the *Southern Rhodesia Act, 1965* and accompanying Order in Council voiding their regulations was itself invalid, as violating an established constitutional convention that the British Parliament would not legislate with regard to matters in relation to dominions except on request of the dominion's parliament.[7] It argued that the 1961 Southern Rhodesian Constitution had been enacted by the British Parliament pursuant to this convention, which was unwritten as applied to Southern Rhodesia.]

[The Southern Rhodesian judges] held that the 1965 Constitution was not the lawful Constitution and that Mr. Smith's government was not a lawful government. But they held that necessity required that effect should be given to the emergency power regulations and therefore the detention of the appellant's husband was lawful. ***

*   *   *

Their lordships can now turn to the three main questions in this case: 1. What was the legal effect in Southern Rhodesia of the *Southern Rhodesia Act 1965* and the Order in Council which accompanied it? 2. Can the usurping government now in control in Southern Rhodesaia be regarded for any purpose as a lawful government" 3. If not, to what extent, if at all, are the courts of Southern Rhodesia entitled to

---

[6] [Ed. note: The phrase "Her Majesty in Council" is a term of art that evolved from the original sovereign power of the Crown. With regard to executive powers, the phrase refers to the cabinet led by the Prime Minister, meeting with, and advising the Queen or her Representative (in Australia and Canada, the Governor-General). With regard to judicial powers, the phrase refers to the Judicial Committee of the Privy Council — the Law Lords.]

[7] [Ed. note: This convention originated in an agreement reached in 1926 between the British government and the ministers of several dominions, including Canada, Australia, and New Zealand. It was codified in 1931, as to these countries, in the *Statute of Westminster.*]

recognise or give effect to its legislative or administrative acts?

If the Queen in the Parliament of the United Kingdom was Sovereign in Southern Rhodesia in 1965 there can be no doubt that the *Southern Rhodesia Act 1965* and the Order in Council made under it were of full legal effect there. Several of the learned judges have held that sovereignty was divided between the United Kingdom and Southern Rhodesia. Their lordships cannot agree. So far as they are aware it has never been doubted that, when a colony is acquired or annexed following on conquest or settlement, the sovereignty of the United Kingdom Parliament extends to that colony, and its powers over that colony are the same as its powers in the United Kingdom. So in 1923 full sovereignty over the annexed territory of Southern Rhodesia was acquired. That sovereignty was not diminished by the limited grant of self government which was then made. It was necessary to pass the *Statute of Westminster, 1931*, in order to confer independence and sovereignty on the six Dominions therein mentioned, but Southern Rhodesia was not included. Section 4 of that Act provides:

> "No Act of Parliament of the United Kingdom passed after the commencement of this Act shall extend, or be deemed to extend, to a Dominion as part of the law of that Dominion unless it is expressly declared in that Act that that Dominion has requested, and consented to, the enactment thereof."

No similar provision has been enacted with regard to Southern Rhodesia.

*   *   *

The learned judges refer to the statement of the United Kingdom government in 1961, already quoted, setting out the convention that the Parliament of the United Kingdom does not legislate without the consent of the government of Southern Rhodesia on matters within the competence of the legislative assembly. [Ed. note: The British legislation enacting the *Southern Rhodesia Act 1965* and suspending the "rebel" government was inconsistent with this principle, which had been applied in 1925 to Canada and other self-governing colonies.] That was a very important convention but it had no legal effect in limiting the legal power of Parliament.

It is often said that it would be unconstitutional for the United Kingdom Parliament to do certain things, meaning that the moral, political and other reasons against doing them are so strong that most people would regard it as highly improper if Parliament did these things. But that does not mean that is it beyond the power of Parliament to do such things. If Parliament chose to do any of them the courts could not hold the Act of Parliament invalid. It may be that it would have been thought before 1965 that it would be unconstitutional to disregard this convention. But it may also be that the unilateral declaration of independence released the United Kingdom from any obligation to observe the convention. Their lordships in declaring the law are not concerned with these matters. They are only concerned with the legal powers of Parliament.

Finally, on this first question their lordships can find nothing in the 1961 Constitution which could be interpreted as a grant of limited sovereignty. Even assuming that that is possible under the British system, they did not find an indication of an intention to transfer sovereignty or any such clear cut division between what is granted by way of sovereignty and what is reserved as would be necessary if there were to be a transfer of some part of the sovereignty of The Queen in the Parliament of the United Kingdom. They are therefore of opinion that the Act and Order in Council of 1965 had full legal effect in Southern Rhodesia.

* * *

[The Lords declined, in light of the policy of the British government to restore the constitutional order, to find that the rebel government should be recognized *de jure* or *de facto*. The Lords also distinguished American precedents affirming the legality of decisions made by states that had seceded during the American Civil War, on the grounds that those states had enjoyed a measure of sovereignty prior to secession not enjoyed by Southern Rhodesia, and that local domestic laws had not been voided by congressional legislation equivalent to the *Southern Rhodesia Act.*]

The provisions of the Order in Council are drastic and unqualified. With regard to the making of laws for Southern Rhodesia, s. 3(1)(a) provides that no laws may be made by the legislature of Southern Rhodesia and no business may be transacted by the legislative assembly; then s. 3 (1)(c) authorises Her Majesty in Council to make laws for the peace, order and good government of Southern Rhodesia: and s. 6 declares that any law made in contravention of any prohibition imposed by the Order is void and of no effect. This can only mean that the power to make laws is transferred to Her Majesty in Council with the result that no purported law made by any person or body in Southern Rhodesia can have any legal effect, no matter how necessary that purported law may be for the purpose of preserving law and order or for any other purpose. It is for Her Majesty in Council to judge whether any new law is required and to enact such new laws as may be thought necessary or desirable.

*** [It] is not for their lordships to consider how loyal citizens can now carry on with their normal tasks, particularly when those tasks bring them into contact with the usurping regime. Their lordships are only concerned in this case with the position of Her Majesty's judges. Her Majesty's judges have been put in an extremely difficult position. But the fact that the judges among others have been put in a very difficult position cannot justify disregard of legislation passed or authorised by the United Kingdom Parliament, by the introduction of a doctrine of necessity which in their lordships' judgment cannot be reconciled with the terms of the Order in Council. It is for Parliament and Parliament alone to determine whether the maintenance of law and order would justify giving effect to laws made by the usurping government, to such extent as may be necessary for that purpose.

The issue in the present case is whether emergency powers regulations made under the 1965 Constitution can be regarded as having any legal validity, force or effect. Section 2(1) of the Order in Council of 1965 provides:

"It is hereby declared for the avoidance of doubt that any instrument made or other act done in purported promulgation of any Constitution for Southern Rhodesia except as authorised by Act of Parliament is void and of no effect."

The 1965 Constitution, made void by that provision, provides by s. 3 that "There shall be an Officer Administering the Government in and over Rhodesia" — an office hitherto unknown to the law. The emergency powers regulations which were determined by the High Court to be valid were made by the officer Administering the Government. For the reasons already given their lordships are of opinion that that determination was erroneous. And it must follow that any order for detention made under such regulations is legally invalid.

[The dissenting opinion of Lord Pearce is omitted.]

———————

The *Mazimbamuto* case illustrates two key aspects of conventions. First, when they are violated, it is said that the acts are "unconstitutional." Second, there is no judicial remedy. If the Queen or the Governor General were to refuse royal assent to legislation passed by Parliament because they thought the legislation unwise, it would be regarded as a breach of convention, which would be an unconstitutional act. However, the remedy would have to be political, not legal. The legislation would not go into effect, and would not be enforced by courts (although Canada would probably soon become a republic!). In *Mazimbamuto*, when a statute was passed contrary to the convention created by the *Statute of Westminster, 1931* that henceforth the British Parliament would not legislate with regard to former colonies achieving self-governing status, courts will still enforce it.

Because conventions are judicially unenforceable, any judicial declarations with regard to conventions are necessarily advisory. Because neither the U.S. Supreme Court nor the High Court of Australia will render advisory opinions, American and Australian constitutional conventions are not subject to judicial precedents. However, because the Supreme Court of Canada will issue advisory opinions, that is not the case in the True North.

8.3.1. Declaring the existence of conventions

The *Patriation Reference*, excerpted below, is the first case where the Supreme Court of Canada answered a reference with regard to a constitutional convention. The case arose in an extraordinary setting. Throughout recent Canadian history, many efforts had been made to craft a new constitution to supplement or replace the *British North America Act* of 1867, enacted by the British Parliament to establish the country of Canada. The "repatriation" of a Constitution to Canada, with a charter of rights, was a key priority of Prime Minister Pierre Trudeau. In 1981, after lengthy negotiations with provincial premiers failed to produce a consensus on a new constitution, Trudeau announced plans to introduce a resolution in the federal Parliament requesting that the British Parliament amend the *British North America Act* in accordance with his latest draft proposal.

The provinces responded quickly and somewhat negatively. They objected to the draft constitution's limitation on rights (now s. 1), seeking more latitude for challenged legislation. Their unanimous draft counter-proposal also deleted non-discrimination and property rights, and a provision for remedies. Of even greater concern to Trudeau, they demanded a clause permitting provinces to opt-out of federal conditional spending programs and to receive equivalent funding anyway. Trudeau's threat to press forward without their consent set off a constitutional confrontation that was ultimately resolved politically after the Supreme Court of Canada's decision in *The Patriation Reference*. This extraordinary opinion comes in two segments. First, the majority (followed by a dissent from Justices Martland and Richie) conclude that there is no legal basis to enjoin the federal Parliament from seeking any amendment to the *British North America Act* that it might choose. Second, another majority (followed by a dissent from Chief Justice Laskin and Justices Estey and McIntyre) conclude that an unwritten constitutional convention, not directly enforceable in a court of law or equity, required the federal government to obtain consent of all or a substantial number of the provinces before requesting the British parliament to amend the constitution.

8.3.1.1. Constitutional conventions are not judicially-enforceable law

"THE PATRIATION REFERENCE" (PART I)
SUPREME COURT OF CANADA
[1981] 1 S.C.R. 753, 125 D.L.R. (3d) 1

THE CHIEF JUSTICE and DICKSON, BEETZ, ESTEY, McINTYRE, CHOUINARD and LAMER JJ. —

I

. . . . .

[The questions posed in this advisory opinion were:]

"1. If the amendments to the Constitution of Canada sought in the 'Proposed Resolution for a Joint Address to Her Majesty the Queen respecting the Constitution of Canada', or any of them, were enacted, would federal-provincial relationships or the powers, rights or privileges granted or secured by the Constitution of Canada to the provinces, their legislatures or governments be affected, and if so, in what respect or respects?

2. Is it a constitutional convention that the House of Commons and Senate of Canada will not request Her Majesty the Queen to lay before the Parliament of the United Kingdom of Great Britain and Northern Ireland a measure to amend the Constitution of Canada affecting federal-provincial relationships or the powers, rights or privileges granted or secured by the Constitution of Canada to the provinces, their legislatures or governments without first obtaining the agreement of the provinces?

3. Is the agreement of the provinces of Canada constitutionally required for amendment to the Constitution of Canada where such amendment affects federal-provincial relationships or alters the powers, rights or privileges granted or secured by the Constitution of Canada to the provinces, their legislatures or governments?"

. . . .

II

The References in question here were prompted by the opposition of six provinces, later joined by two others [only New Brunswick and Ontario supported the Trudeau plan], to a proposed Resolution which was published on October 2, 1980 and intended for submission to the House of Commons and as well to the Senate of Canada. It contained an address to be presented to Her Majesty the Queen in right of the United Kingdom respecting what may generally be referred to as the Constitution of Canada. The address laid before the House of Commons on October 6, 1980, was in these terms:

"To the Queen's Most Excellent Majesty:

Most Gracious Sovereign:

We, Your Majesty's loyal subjects, the House of Commons of Canada in Parliament assembled, respectfully approach Your Majesty, requesting that you may graciously be pleased to cause to be laid before the Parliament of the United Kingdom a measure containing the recitals and clauses hereinafter set forth:

[The draft legislation provided that the Canadian-passed *Constitution Act, 1981* would be enacted by the UK Parliament and that no subsequent Act of Parliament of the United Kingdom shall extend to Canada as part of its law.]

[All provinces except Ontario, New Brunswick, and Saskatchewan took the position that, both conventionally and legally, the consent of all the provinces was required for the address to go forward to Her Majesty with the appended statutes.]

VII

[The majority held there was no legal bar to the federal Parliament's passage of a resolution asking the British Parliament to enact the *Canada Act* and repatriate a Constitution to Canada. Whether the British Parliament was conventionally required to act in accordance with the request of the Canadian Parliament was not a matter "upon which this Court would presume to pronounce." As to the argument that the *Statute of Westminster* — and specifically a provision in that statute expressly providing that the statute did not affect in any way the British North America Act and provided that the statute applied to both the Canadian Parliament and provincial legislatures, but that each could only enact laws within their own jurisdiction as established in that Act — had rendered the proposed resolution illegal, the Court rejected the notion that absent specific codifying legislation a convention could be transformed into law. Citing *Madzimbamuto v. Lardner-Burke*, the Court found that the proposed resolution would be lawful.]

VIII

* * *

For the moment, it is relevant to point out that even in those cases where an amendment to the *British North America Act* was founded on a resolution of the federal Houses after having received provincial consent, there is no instance, save in the *British North America Act, 1930* where such consent was recited in the resolution. The matter remained, in short, a conventional one within Canada, without effect on the validity of the resolution in respect of United Kingdom action. The point is underscored in relation to the very first amendment directly affecting provincial legislative power, that in 1940 which added "Unemployment Insurance" to the catalogue of exclusive federal powers. Sir William Jowitt, then Solicitor-General, and later Lord Chancellor, was asked in the British House of Commons about provincial consent when the amendment was in course of passage. The question put to him and his answer are as follows (see 362 U.K. Parl. Deb. 5th Series, H.C. 1177–81);

"Mr. Mander . . . In this Bill we are concerned only with the Parliament of Canada, but, as a matter of interest, I would be obliged if the Solicitor-General would say whether the Provincial Canadian Parliaments are in agreement with the proposals submitted by the Dominion Parliament . . . .

The Solicitor-General [Sir William Jowitt]: . . . One might think that the Canadian Parliament was in some way subservient to ours, which is not the fact. The true position is that at the request of Canada this old machinery still survives until something better is thought of, but we square the legal with the constitutional position by passing these Acts only in the form that the Canadian Parliament require and at the request of the Canadian Parliament.

My justification to the House for this Bill — and it is important to observe this — is not on the merits of the proposal, which is a matter for the Canadian Parliament; if we were to embark upon that, we might trespass on what I conceive to be their constitutional position. The sole justification for this enactment is that we are doing in this way what the Parliament of Canada desires to do.

. . . .

In reply to the hon. Member for East Wolverhampton (Mr. Mander), I do not know what the view of the Provincial Parliaments is. I know, however, that when the matter was before the Privy Council some of the Provincial Parliaments supported the Dominion Parliament. It is a sufficient justification for the Bill that we are morally bound to act on the ground that we have here the request of the Dominion Parliament and that we must operate the old machinery which has been left over at their request in accordance with their wishes."

IX

* * *

The stark legal question is whether this Court can enact by what would be judicial legislation a formula of unanimity to initiate the amending process which would be binding not only in Canada but also on the Parliament of the United

Kingdom with which amending authority would still remain. It would be anomalous indeed, overshadowing the anomaly of a constitution which contains no provision for its amendment, for this Court to say retroactively that in law we have had an amending formula all along, even if we have not hitherto known it; or, to say, that we have had in law one amending formula, say from 1867 to 1931, and a second amending formula that has emerged after 1931. No one can gainsay the desirability of federal-provincial accord of acceptable compromise. That does not, however, go to legality. As Sir William Jowitt said, and quoted earlier, we must operate the old machinery perhaps one more time.

*   *   *

MARTLAND and RITCHIE JJ. (dissenting) — ***

The foregoing review shows that the enactment of the *B.N.A. Act* created a federal constitution of Canada which confided the whole area of self-government within Canada to the Parliament of Canada and the provincial legislatures each being supreme within its own defined sphere and area. It can fairly be said, therefore, that the dominant principle of Canadian constitutional law is federalism. The implications of that principle are clear. Each level of government should not be permitted to encroach on the other, either directly or indirectly. The political compromise achieved as a result of the Quebec and London Conferences preceding the passage of the *B.N.A. Act* would be dissolved unless there were substantive and effective limits on unconstitutional action.

[The dissent held that it was beyond the constitutional power of the federal Parliament, in a constitutional system where federalism was enforced by the courts, for it to pass a resolution requesting British parliamentary approval of changes in the *British North America Act* without provincial consent. Such a resolution, the dissent maintained, exceeded the specified powers authorized to the federal Parliament in s.91.]

8.3.1.2.   The Supreme Court of Canada provides advice on whether a proposed act violates a convention

"THE PATRIATION REFERENCE" (PART II)
SUPREME COURT OF CANADA
[1981] 1 S.C.R. 753, 125 D.L.R. (3d) 1

MARTLAND, RITCHIE, DICKSON, BEETZ, CHOUINARD and LAMER JJ.—***

I — THE NATURE OF CONSTITUTIONAL CONVENTIONS

A substantial part of the rules of the Canadian constitution are written. They are contained not in a single document called a constitution but in a great variety of statutes some of which have been enacted by the Parliament at Westminster, such as the *British North America Act*, 1867, 1867 (U.K.), c. 3, (the *B.N.A. Act*) or by the Parliament of Canada, such as *The Alberta Act*, 1905 (Can.), c. 3, *The Saskatchewan*

Act, 1905 (Can.), c. 42, the *Senate and House of Commons Act*, R.S.C. 1970, c. S-8, or by the provincial legislatures, such as the provincial electoral acts. They are also to be found in orders in council like the Imperial Order in Council of May 16, 1871 admitting British Columbia into the Union, and the Imperial Order in Council of June 26, 1873, admitting Prince Edward Island into the Union.

*   *   *

Those parts of the Constitution of Canada which are composed of statutory rules and common law rules are generically referred to as the law of the constitution. In cases of doubt or dispute, it is the function of the courts to declare what the law is and since the law is sometimes breached, it is generally the function of the courts to ascertain whether it has in fact been breached in specific instances and, if so, to apply such sanctions as are contemplated by the law, whether they be punitive sanctions or civil sanctions such as a declaration of nullity. Thus, when a federal or a provincial statute is found by the courts to be in excess of the legislative competence of the legislature which has enacted it, it is declared null and void and the courts refuse to give effect to it. In this sense it can be said that the law of the constitution is administered or enforced by the courts.

But many Canadians would perhaps be surprised to learn that important parts of the constitution of Canada, with which they are the most familiar because they are directly involved when they exercise their right to vote at federal and provincial elections, are nowhere to be found in the law of the constitution. For instance it is a fundamental requirement of the constitution that if the opposition obtains the majority at the polls, the government must tender its resignation forthwith. But fundamental as it is, this requirement of the constitution does not form part of the law of the constitution.

It is also a constitutional requirement that the person who is appointed prime minister or premier by the Crown and who is the effective head of the government should have the support of the elected branch of the legislature; in practice this means in most cases the leader of the political party which has won a majority of seats at a general election. Other ministers are appointed by the Crown on the advice of the prime minister or premier when he forms or reshuffles his cabinet. Ministers must continuously have the confidence of the elected branch of the legislature, individually and collectively. Should they lose it, they must either resign or ask the Crown for a dissolution of the legislature and the holding of a general election. Most of the powers of the Crown under the prerogative are exercised only upon the advice of the prime minister of the cabinet which means that they are effectively exercised by the latter, together with the innumerable statutory powers delegated to the Crown in council.

Yet none of these essential rules of the constitution can be said to be a law of the constitution. It was apparently Dicey who, in the first edition of his *Law of the Constitution*, in 1885, called them the "conventions of the constitution," (see W. S. Holdsworth, "The Conventions of the Eighteenth Century Constitution" (1932), 17 Iowa Law Rev. 161), an expression which quickly became current. What Dicey described under these terms are the principles and rules of responsible government, several of which are stated above and which regulate the relations between the Crown, the prime minister, the cabinet and the two Houses of Parliament. These rules developed in Great Britain by way of custom and precedent during the nineteenth century and were exported to such British colonies as were granted self-government.

* * *

The main purpose of constitutional conventions is to ensure that the legal framework of the constitution will be operated in accordance with the prevailing constitutional values or principles of the period. For example, the constitutional value which is the pivot of the conventions stated above and relating to responsible government is the democratic principle: the powers of the state must be exercised in accordance with the wishes of the electorate; and the constitutional value or principle which anchors the conventions regulating the relationship between the members of the Commonwealth is the independence of the former British colonies.

* * *

The conventional rules of the constitution present one striking peculiarity. In contradistinction to the laws of the constitution, they are not enforced by the courts. One reason for this situation is that, unlike common law rules, conventions are not judge-made rules. They are not based on judicial precedents but on precedents established by the institutions of government themselves. Nor are they in the nature of statutory commands which it is the function and duty of the courts to obey and enforce. Furthermore, to enforce them would mean to administer some formal sanction when they are breached. But the legal system from which they are distinct does not contemplate formal sanctions for their breach.

Perhaps the main reason why conventional rules cannot be enforced by the courts is that they are generally in conflict with the legal rules which they postulate and the courts are bound to enforce the legal rules. The conflict is not of a type which would entail the commission of any illegality. It results from the fact that legal rules create wide powers, discretions and rights which conventions prescribe should be exercised only in a certain limited manner, if at all.

Some examples will illustrate this point.

As a matter of law, the Queen, or the Governor General or the Lieutenant Governor could refuse assent to every bill passed by both Houses of Parliament or by a Legislative Assembly as the case may be. But by convention they cannot of their own motion refuse to assent to any such bill on any ground, for instance because they disapprove of the policy of the bill. We have here a conflict between a legal rule which creates a complete discretion and a conventional rule which completely neutralizes it. But conventions, like laws, are sometimes violated. And if this particular convention were violated and assent were improperly withheld, the courts would be bound to enforce the law, not the convention. They would refuse to recognize the validity of a vetoed bill. This is what happened in *Gallant v. The King* [[1949] 2 D.L.R. 425].[8] The Lieutenant Governor who had withheld assent in *Gallant* apparently did so towards the end of his term of office. Had it been

---

[8] [Ed. note: This somewhat bizarre case arose during the end of the prohibition era. Liquor possession was prohibited with limited exceptions in the Prince Edward Island *Prohibition Act, 1937*, and the exceptions were somewhat expanded by passage of legislation in 1945 known as the "Cullen Amend-

otherwise, it is not inconceivable that his withholding of assent might have produced a political crisis leading to his removal from office which shows that if the remedy for a breach of a convention does not lie with the courts, still the breach is not necessarily without a remedy. The remedy lies with some other institutions of government; furthermore it is not a formal remedy and it may be administered with less certainty or regularity than it would be by a court.

Another example of the conflict between law and convention is provided by a fundamental convention already stated above: if after a general election where the opposition obtained the majority at the polls the government refused to resign and clung to office, it would thereby commit a fundamental breach of convention, one so serious indeed that it could be regarded as tantamount to a coup d'etat. The remedy in this case would lie with the Governor General or the Lieutenant Governor as the case might be who would be justified in dismissing the ministry and in calling on the opposition to form the government. But should the Crown be slow in taking this course, there is nothing the courts could do about it except at the risk of creating a state of legal discontinuity, that is, a form of revolution. An order or a regulation passed by a minister under statutory authority and otherwise valid could not be invalidated on the ground that, by convention, the minister ought no longer be a minister. A writ of quo warranto aimed at ministers, assuming that quo warranto lies against a minister of the Crown, which is very doubtful, would be of no avail to remove them from office. Required to say by what warrant they occupy their ministerial office, they would answer that they occupy it by the pleasure of the Crown under a commission issued by the Crown and this answer would be a complete one at law, for at law the government is in office by the pleasure of the Crown although by convention it is there by the will of the people.

This conflict between convention and law which prevents the courts from enforcing conventions also prevents conventions from crystallizing into laws, unless it be by statutory adoption.

*   *   *

It should be borne in mind however that, while they are not laws, some conventions may be more important than some laws. Their importance depends on that of the value or principle which they are meant to safeguard. Also they form an integral part of the constitution and of the constitutional system. They come within the meaning of the word "Constitution" in the preamble of the *British North America Act, 1867*:

---

ment." Prohibition was replaced by regulation of liquor in legislation that repealed the criminal provisions, but provided that the Lieutenant Governor would not proclaim the repeal to be effective until July 6, 1948, and only then subject to confirmation by a plebiscite on June 28. Gallant was convicted of possessing rum on June 28 (probably celebrating the victory!).

On appeal of his conviction, based on his claim that his conduct was consistent with modified provisions of the Cullen Amendment, Campbell, C.J. determined that the Lieutenant Governor had never given royal assent to the 1945 legislation. Without even discussing the constitutional convention requiring royal assent to be granted on advice of the government, the judge simply noted that the *British North America Act* specifically required royal assent, and thus the 1945 legislation was void. Thus, Gallant's conduct was clearly illegal, since the only valid legislation in place was the original 1937 prohibition law.]

"Whereas the Provinces of Canada, Nova Scotia, and New Brunswick have expressed their Desire to be federally united . . . with a Constitution similar in Principle to that of the United Kingdom:"

That is why it is perfectly appropriate to say that to violate a convention is to do something which is unconstitutional although it entails no direct legal consequence. But the words "constitutional" and "unconstitutional" may also be used in a strict legal sense, for instance with respect to a statute which is found *ultra vires* or unconstitutional. The foregoing may perhaps be summarized in an equation: constitutional conventions plus constitutional law equal the total constitution of the country.

II — WHETHER THE QUESTIONS SHOULD BE ANSWERED

It was submitted by counsel for Canada and for Ontario that the [questions concerning constitutional conventions] ought not be answered because they do not raise a justiciable issue and are accordingly not appropriate for a court. It was contended that the issue whether a particular convention exists or not is a purely political one. The existence of a definite convention is always unclear and a matter of debate. Furthermore conventions are flexible, somewhat imprecise and unsuitable for judicial determination.

*   *   *

[The conventional question] is not confined to an issue of pure legality but it has to do with a fundamental issue of constitutionality and legitimacy. Given the broad statutory basis upon which the Governments of Manitoba, Newfoundland and Quebec are empowered to put questions to their three respective courts of appeal, they are in our view entitled to an answer to a question of this type.

*   *   *

Finally, we are not asked to hold that a convention has in effect repealed a provision of the *B.N.A. Act*, as was the case in the *Reference re Disallowance and Reservation of Provincial Legislation* [[1938] S.C.R. 71]. Nor are we asked to enforce a convention. We are asked to recognize it if it exists. Courts have done this very thing many times in England and the Commonwealth to provide aid for and background to constitutional or statutory construction. Several such cases are mentioned in the reasons of the majority of this Court relating to the question whether constitutional conventions are capable of crystallizing into law. ***

III — WHETHER THE CONVENTION EXISTS

*   *   *

1. *The class of constitutional amendments contemplated by the question*

*   *   *

These proposed amendments present one essential characteristic: they directly affect federal-provincial relationships in changing legislative powers and in providing for a formula to effect such change.

*   *   *

2. *Requirements for establishing a convention*

The requirements for establishing a convention bear some resemblance with those which apply to customary law. Precedents and usage are necessary but do not suffice. They must be normative. We adopt the following passage of Sir W. Ivor Jennings, *The Law and the Constitution* (5th ed. 1959), at p. 136:

> "We have to ask ourselves three questions: first, what are the precedents; secondly, did the actors in the precedents believe that they were bound by a rule; and thirdly, is there a reason for the rule? A single precedent with a good reason may be enough to establish the rule. A whole string of precedents without such a reason will be of no avail, unless it is perfectly certain that the persons concerned regarded them as bound by it."

i) The precedents

*   *   *

[The opinion proceeded to summarize each previous constitutional amendment].

Of these twenty-two amendments or groups of amendments, five directly affected federal-provincial relationships in the sense of changing provincial legislative powers: they are the amendment of 1930 [confirmed the natural resources agreements between the Government of Canada and the Governments of Manitoba, British Columbia, Alberta and Saskatchewan], the *Statute of Westminster, 1931* [granting power to the Parliament of Canada to make laws having extraterritorial effect, and, most importantly, granting both Parliament and the provincial legislatures the authority, within their powers under the *British North America Acts*, to repeal any United Kingdom statute that formed part of the law of Canada, expressly excluding, however, the *BNA Act* itself],and the amendments of 1940 [grant of exclusive federal power to make laws in relation to Unemployment Insurance], 1951 and 1964 [granting concurrent federal and provincial power regarding legislation concerning old age pensions].

*   *   *

These five amendments are the only ones which can be viewed as positive precedents whereby federal-provincial relationships were directly affected in the sense of changing legislative powers.

Every one of these five amendments was agreed upon by each province whose legislative authority was affected.

In negative terms, no amendment changing provincial legislative powers has been made since Confederation when agreement of a province whose legislative powers would have been changed was withheld.

There are no exceptions. [The opinion cited a variety of examples: (i) a 1951 amendment giving provinces limited powers re indirect taxation was blocked after Ontario and Quebec objected; (ii) a 1960 patriation proposal was not pursued when a minority objected to the amending formula; (iii) a 1964 unanimous agreement on an amending formula was not pursued after Quebec reconsidered; and (iv) a 1971 agreement between the federal government and eight of the provinces was not pursued because Quebec objected to the amending formula and a new Saskatch-ewan government did not take a position because it perceived Quebec's objection to be fatal.]

The accumulation of these precedents, positive and negative, concurrent and without exception, does not of itself suffice in establishing the existence of the convention; but it unmistakably points in its direction. Indeed, if the precedents stood alone, it might be argued that unanimity is required.

* * *

[The Court then suggested that five amendments regarding the internal workings and powers of the federal Parliament, submitted to Westminster without provincial consultation, were of a different category. The only relevant precedents, in the Court's view, were those that altered legislative powers or provided a method to effect such change. Two particular precedents received further comment: the amendment of 1907 increasing the scale of financial subsidies to the provinces and the amendment of 1949 confirming the Terms of Union between Canada and Newfoundland.]

It was contended that British Columbia objected to the 1907 amendment which had been agreed upon by all the other provinces.

Even if it were so, this precedent would at best constitute an argument against the unanimity rule.

But the fact is that British Columbia did agree in principle with the increase of financial subsidies to the provinces. It wanted more and objected to the proposed finality of the increase. The finality aspect was deleted from the amendment by the United Kingdom authorities. Mr. Winston Churchill, Under-Secretary of State for the Colonies made the following comment in the House of Commons:

"In deference to the representations of British Columbia the words "final and unalterable" applying to the revised scale had been omitted from the Bill."

(Commons Debates, (U.K.), June 13, 1907, at p. 1617.)

In the end, the Premier of British Columbia did not refuse to agree to the Act being passed (see A. B. Keith, The Constitutional Law of the British Dominions (1933), at p. 109).

[The Court also distinguished Quebec's objections to the 1949 amendment, wherein the Premier of Quebec is reported to have stated at a press conference simply that the province should have been "consulted" or "advised" as a matter of "courtesy." He is not reported as having said that the consent of the province was required.]

* * *

Each of those five constitutional amendments effected a limited change in legislative powers, affecting one head of legislative competence such as unemploy-ment insurance. Whereas, if the proposed Charter of Rights became law, every head of provincial (and federal) legislative authority could be affected. Furthermore, the Charter of Rights would operate retrospectively as well as prospectively with the result that laws enacted in the future as well as in the past, even before Confederation, would be exposed to attack if inconsistent with the provisions of the Charter of Rights. This Charter would thus abridge provincial legislative authority on a scale exceeding the effect of any previous constitutional amendment for which provincial consent was sought and obtained.

*   *   *

The actors treating the rule as binding

*   *   *

The procedures for amending a constitution are normally a fundamental part of the laws and conventions by which a country is governed. This is particularly true if the constitution is embodied in a formal document, as is the case in such federal states as Australia, the United States and Switzerland. In these countries, the amending process forms an important part of their constitutional law.

In this respect, Canada has been in a unique constitutional position. Not only did the *British North America Act* not provide for its amendment by Canadian legislative authority, except to the extent outlined at the beginning of this chapter, but it also left Canada without any clearly defined procedure for securing constitutional amendments from the British Parliament. As a result, procedures have varied from time to time, with recurring controversies and doubts over the conditions under which various provisions of the Constitution should be amended.

Certain rules and principles relating to amending procedures have nevertheless developed over the years. They have emerged from the practices and procedures employed in securing various amendments to the *British North America Act* since 1867. Though not constitutionally binding in any strict sense, they have come to be recognized and accepted in practice as part of the amendment process in Canada.

*   *   *

***The White Paper [Ed. note: A White Paper is a report issued by a cabinet ministry. It reflects the official policy of the government and is normally the prelude to the introduction of legislation. The White Paper referred to in the text was the government paper entitled, "The Amendment of the Constitution of Canada," published in 1965 under the authority of The Hon. Guy Favreau, the federal Minister of Justice, and approved by the provinces.] then goes on to state these principles, at p. 15:

"The first general principle that emerges in the foregoing resume is that although an enactment by the United Kingdom is necessary to amend the *British North America Act*, such action is taken only upon formal request from Canada. No Act of the United Kingdom Parliament affecting Canada is therefore passed unless it is requested and consented to by Canada. Conversely, every amendment requested by Canada in the past has been enacted.

The second general principle is that the sanction of Parliament is required for a request to the British Parliament for an amendment to the *British North America Act*. This principle was established early in the history of Canada's constitutional amendments, and has not been violated since 1895. The procedure invariably is to seek amendments by a joint Address of the Canadian House of Commons and Senate to the Crown.

The third general principle is that no amendment to Canada's Constitution will be made by the British Parliament merely upon the request of a Canadian province. A number of attempts to secure such amendments have been made, but none has been successful. The first such attempt was made as early as 1868, by a province which was at that time dissatisfied with the terms of Confederation.[9] This was followed by other attempts in 1869, 1874 and 1887. The British Government refused in all cases to act on provincial government representations on the grounds that it should not intervene in the affairs of Canada except at the request of the federal government representing all of Canada.

The fourth general principle is that the Canadian Parliament will not request an amendment directly affecting federal-provincial relationships without prior consultation and agreement with the provinces. This principle did not emerge as early as others but since 1907, and particularly since 1930, has gained increasing recognition and acceptance. The nature and the degree of provincial participation in the amending process, however, have not lent themselves to easy definition."

*   *   *

In our view, the fourth general principle equally and unmistakably states and recognizes as a rule of the Canadian constitution the convention referred to in the second question of the Manitoba and Newfoundland References as well as in Question B of the Quebec Reference, namely that there is a requirement for provincial agreement to amendments which change provincial legislative powers.

This statement is not a casual utterance. It is contained in a carefully drafted document which had been circulated to all the provinces prior to its publication and had been found satisfactory by all of them (see Commons Debates, 1965, at p. 11574, and Background Paper published by the Government of Canada, The Role of the United Kingdom in the Amendment of the Canadian Constitution (March 1981), at p. 30). It was published as a white paper, that is as an official statement of government policy, under the authority of the federal Minister of Justice as member of a government responsible to Parliament, neither House of which, so far as we know, has taken issue with it. This statement is a recognition by all the actors in the precedents that the requirement of provincial agreement is a constitutional rule.

*   *   *

Furthermore, the Government of Canada and the governments of the provinces have attempted to reach a consensus on a constitutional amending formula in the course of ten federal-provincial conferences held in 1927, 1931, 1935, 1950, 1960,

---

[9] [Ed. note: The first election held under the new *British North America Act* for the new federal government of Canada was held simultaneously with a provincial election in Nova Scotia. At the time, almost all Nova Scotian MPs elected, as well as the new premier and an overwhelming majority of the new Nova Scotia legislature, were opposed to confederation on the terms of the *BNA Act*. They petitioned the British Parliament to rescind or amend the Act to permit their withdrawal from confederation, a petition that was rejected.]

1964, 1971, 1978, 1979 and 1980 (see Gerald A. Beaudoin, supra, at p. 346). A major issue at these conferences was the quantification of provincial consent. No consensus was reached on this issue. But the discussion of this very issue for more than fifty years postulates a clear recognition by all the governments concerned of the principle that a substantial degree of provincial consent is required.

* * *

It is sufficient for the Court to decide that at least a substantial measure of provincial consent is required and to decide further whether the situation before the Court meets with this requirement. The situation is one where Ontario and New Brunswick agree with the proposed amendments whereas the eight other provinces oppose it. By no conceivable standard could this situation be thought to pass muster. It clearly does not disclose a sufficient measure of provincial agreement. Nothing more should be said about this.

* * *

iii) A reason for the rule

The reason for the rule is the federal principle. Canada is a federal union. ***

The federal principle cannot be reconciled with a state of affairs where the modification of provincial legislative powers could be obtained by the unilateral action of the federal authorities. It would indeed offend the federal principle that "a radical change to . . . [the] constitution [be] taken at the request of a bare majority of the members of the Canadian House of Commons and Senate" (Report of Dominion Provincial Conference, 1931, at p. 3).

* * *

It is true that Canada would remain a federation if the proposed amendments became law. But it would be a different federation made different at the instance of a majority in the Houses of the federal Parliament acting alone. It is this process itself which offends the federal principle.

* * *

The Chief Justice and Estey and McIntyre JJ. (dissenting) — There are different kinds of conventions and usages, but we are concerned here with what may be termed 'constitutional' conventions or rules of the constitution. They were described by Professor Dicey in the tenth edition of his *Law of the Constitution* (1959), at pp. 23-24, in the following passage:

> "The one set of rules are in the strictest sense "laws," since they are rules which (whether written or unwritten, whether enacted by statute or derived from the mass of custom, tradition, or judge-made maxims known as the common law) are enforced by the courts; these rules constitute "constitutional law" in the proper sense of that term, and may for the sake of distinction be called collectively "the law of the constitution.""

* * *

And further, at pp. 30–31, he added:

"With conventions or understandings he [the lawyer and law teacher] has no direct concern. They vary from generation to generation, almost from year to year. Whether a Ministry defeated at the polling booths ought to retire on the day when the result of the election is known, or may more properly retain office until after a defeat in Parliament, is or may be a question of practical importance. The opinions on this point which prevail to-day differ (it is said) from the opinions or understandings which prevailed thirty years back, and are possibly different from the opinions or understandings which may prevail ten years hence. Weighty precedents and high authority are cited on either side of this knotty question; the dicta or practice of Russell and Peel may be balanced off against the dicta or practice of Beaconsfield and Gladstone. The subject, however, is not one of law but of politics, and need trouble no lawyer or the class of any professor of law. If he is concerned with it at all, he is so only in so far as he may be called upon to show what is the connection (if any there be) between the conventions of the constitution and the law of the constitution."

This view has been adopted by Canadian writers, e.g. Professor Peter W. Hogg in *Constitutional Law of Canada* (1977) . . . . At page 8, he said:

"If a convention is disobeyed by an official, then it is common, especially in the United Kingdom, to describe the official's act or omission as "unconstitutional." But this use of the term unconstitutional must be carefully distinguished from the case where a legal rule of the constitution has been disobeyed. Where unconstitutionality springs from a breach of law, the purported act is normally a nullity and there is a remedy available in the courts. But where "unconstitutionality" springs merely from a breach of convention, no breach of the law has occurred and no legal remedy will be available. If a court did give a remedy for a breach of convention, for example, by declaring invalid a statute enacted for Canada by the United Kingdom Parliament without Canada's request or consent, or by ordering an unwilling Governor General to give his assent to a bill enacted by both houses of Parliament, then we would have to change our language and describe the rule which used to be thought of as a convention as a rule of the common law. In other words a judicial decision could have the effect of transforming a conventional rule into a legal rule. A convention may also be transformed into law by being enacted as a statute."

*   *   *

[Conventions such as that limiting the British Parliament's power to legislate for Canada, that the Governor General will act only according to the advice of the Prime Minister, and that a government losing the confidence of the House of Commons must itself resign, or obtain a dissolution] have an historical origin and bind, and have bound, the actors in constitutional matters in Canada for generations. No one can doubt their operative force or the reality of their existence as an effective part of the Canadian constitution.

These then are recognized conventions; they are definite, understandable and understood. They have the unquestioned acceptance not only of the actors in political affairs but of the public at large. Can it be said that any convention having such clear definition and acceptance concerning provincial participation in the amendment of the Canadian Constitution has developed? It is in the light of this comparison that the existence of any supposed constitutional convention must be considered. It is abundantly clear, in our view, that the answer must be no. The degree of provincial participation in constitutional amendments has been a subject of lasting controversy in Canadian political life for generations. It cannot be asserted, in our opinion, that any view on this subject has become so clear and so broadly accepted as to constitute a constitutional convention. It should be observed that there is a fundamental difference between the convention in the Dicey concept and the convention for which some of the provinces here contend. The Dicey convention relates to the functioning of individuals and institutions within a parliamentary democracy in unitary form. It does not qualify or limit the authority or sovereignty of Parliament or the Crown. The convention sought to be advanced here would truncate the functioning of the executive and legislative branches at the federal level. This would impose a limitation on the sovereign body itself within the Constitution. Surely such a convention would require for its recognition, even in the non-legal, political sphere, the clearest signal from the plenary unit intended to be bound, and not simply a plea from the majority of the beneficiaries of such a convention, the provincial plenary units.

*　　*　　*

In examining these amendments it must be borne in mind that all do not possess the same relevance or force for the purpose of this inquiry. Question 2 of the Manitoba and Newfoundland References and the conventional segment of Question B in the Quebec Reference raise the issue of the propriety of non-consensual amendments which affect federal-provincial relationships and the powers, rights and privileges of the provinces. The questions do not limit consideration to those amendments which affected the distribution of legislative powers between the federal Parliament and the provincial legislatures. Since the distribution of powers is the very essence of a federal system, amendments affecting such distribution will be of especial concern to the provinces. Precedents found in such amendments will be entitled to serious consideration. It does not follow, however, that other amendments which affected federal-provincial relationships without altering the distribution of powers should be disregarded in this inquiry. Consideration must be given in according weight to the various amendments, to the reaction they provoked from the provinces. This is surely the real test of relevance in this discussion. On many occasions provinces considered that amendments not affecting the distribution of legislative power were sufficiently undesirable to call for strenuous opposition. The test of whether the convention exists, or has existed, is to be found by examining the results of such opposition. Professor William S. Livingston in *Federalism and Constitutional Change* (Oxford University Press, 1956), made this comment, at p. 62, when considering the 1943 amendment which did not affect the distribution of powers,[10] and the 1940 amendment which did:

---

[10] [Ed. note: The *British North America Act of 1943* amended the Constitution to delay the reapportionment of seats in the Canadian House of Commons among the provinces for the duration of World War II.]

"The important difference between the two amendments lies, of course, in the fact that that of 1940 clearly and significantly altered the distribution of powers, a part of the constitution which, it has been argued, is especially deserving of the protection afforded by the principle of unanimous consent. But the facts themselves demonstrate that at least one of the provinces considered the alteration of 1943 sufficiently important to call for long and bitter protests at the disdainful attitude of the Dominion Government. If unanimity is for the protection of provinces, whether singly or collectively, it is reasonable to think that the provinces should be the ones to judge when it should be invoked. By the very operation of the principle, a province will not protest unless it considers the matter at hand worth protesting about."

The true test of the importance of the various amendments for our purpose is a consideration of the degree of provincial opposition they aroused, for whatever reason, the consideration that such opposition received, and the influence it had on the course of the amendment proceedings.

Prior to the amendment effected by the *B.N.A. Act of 1930* there were at least three amendments, those of 1886, 1907 and 1915, which substantially affected the provinces and which were procured without the consent of all the provinces. The amendment of 1886 gave power to Parliament to provide for parliamentary representation in the Senate and House of Commons for territories not forming part of any province, and therefore altered the provincial balance of representation. That of 1907 changed the basis of federal subsidies payable to the provinces and thus directly affected the provincial interests. That of 1915 redefined territorial divisions for senatorial representation, and therefore had a potential for altering the provincial balance. Those of 1886 and 1915 were passed without provincial consultation or consent, and that of 1907 had the consent of all provinces save British Columbia, which actively opposed its passage both in Canada and in the United Kingdom. The amendment was passed with minor changes. These precedents, it may be said, should by themselves have only a modest influence in the consideration of the question before the Court. It is clear, however, that no support whatever for the convention may be found on an examination of the amendments made up to 1930. None had full provincial approval.

*   *   *

The amendment of 1940 transferring legislative power over unemployment insurance to the federal Parliament also had full provincial consent. It must be observed here, however, that when questioned in the House of Commons on this point Mr. Mackenzie King, then Prime Minister, while acknowledging that consents had been obtained, specifically stated that this course had been followed to avoid any constitutional issue on this point and he disclaimed any necessity for such consent. * * *

*   *   *

In summary, we observe that in the one hundred and fourteen years since Confederation Canada has grown from a group of four somewhat hesitant colonies into a modern, independent state, vastly increased in size, power and wealth, and having a social and governmental structure unimagined in 1867. It cannot be denied that vast change has occurred in Dominion-provincial relations over that period. Many factors have influenced this process and the amendments to the B.N.A. Act — all the amendments — have played a significant part and all must receive consideration in resolving this question. Only in four cases has full provincial consent been obtained and in many cases the federal government has proceeded with amendments in the face of active provincial opposition. In our view, it is unrealistic in the extreme to say that the convention has emerged.

*   *   *

Thus, as a matter of law, Trudeau could have proceeded to enact his proposed constitution as he originally planned. (There were interesting questions about whether, as a matter of convention, the UK Parliament would be obligated to grant his request, and indeed several provinces dispatched officials to lobby British parliamentarians to refuse to do so.) In the event, a compromise was reached between Trudeau and all of the provincial premiers except Quebec's Rene Levesque. Among the key provisions of the deal was deletion of a right to property and the provincial "opt out" power regarding federal spending programs, but the inclusion of a clause that permitted both Parliament and provincial legislatures to declare for a period of 5 years that a law could take affect "notwithstanding" the Charter. (The deal was labeled by the Quebecois as the *Nuit des Longs Couteaux* (Night of the Long Knives, a reference to events in 1934 when Nazis committed a string of political murders, although its roots go back to 5th century political killings by Anglo-Saxon mercenaries.)[11]

The conventional question left unanswered by the *Patriation Reference* — whether unanimous provincial approval was required to repatriate the Constitution — was answered by the Court in *Re Objection by Quebec to Resolution to Amend the Constitution*, [1982] 2 S.C.R. 793, holding that consent of nine of the ten provinces constituted the "substantial measure of provincial agreement" required by convention.

For a suggestion that the Supreme Court justices deciding the *Patriation Reference* were completely political, see MICHAEL MANDEL, THE CHARTER OF RIGHTS AND THE LEGALIZATION OF POLITICS IN CANADA 30 (Toronto: Thompson Educational Publishing, rev. ed. 1994). Noting that the Charter was favored by allies of Trudeau and generally by Ontarians, Mandel observes that the three justices who completely supported the Prime Minister's view that he was under no legal or conventional obligation to get other provinces to approve the Charter were all Trudeau appointees, two of whom were Ontarians and one (McIntyre, from B.C.), was filling a seat conventionally allocated to Ontario lawyers. The only two justices to completely oppose the Trudeau position were appointees of Conservative Prime Minister John Diefenbaker.

The propriety of judicial advice concerning constitutional convention established in the *Patriation Reference* was cabined by the British Columbia Court of Appeal

---

[11] The CBC's news report of these events is archived at http://www.cbc.ca/archives/categories/politics/the-constitution/charting-the-future-canadas-new-consitution/the-kitchen-accord.html

in *Reference re Constitutional Question Act (B.C.)*, 78 D.L.R. (4th) 285 (1991). The case arose in the context of what itself was arguably a breach of constitutional convention. Because Senators serve until age 75, a government that has been in office a long time (as were the Liberals, who with minor exception governed from the early 1960s until 1984) would command an overwhelming majority of the Upper House despite being in opposition. Convention dictated self-restraint by senators from the party in opposition, but Liberal senators acted contra-conventionally in refusing to enact controversial measures proposed by the Progressive Conservative government of Brian Mulroney and passed over heated Liberal opposition in the House of Commons. In 1988, they refused to implement the Free Trade Agreement with the United States, which actually precipitated an election on the issue, although the Liberal senators acquiesced after the Tories were re-elected. With a gradually declining majority, the Liberal-controlled Senate narrowly rejected the Goods and Services Tax Bill in 1990. This led Prime Minister Mulroney to invoke, for the only time in Canadian history, s. 26 of the *British North America Act*, allowing the appointment of eight additional senators (two each from the Maritimes, Quebec, Ontario, and the western provinces).[12] A number of those opposed to this process filed suit. The plaintiffs argued that the original understanding of the section, requiring formal approval by both the Governor General and the Queen, meant that the appointments required the conventional approval of both the Canadian government and the Imperial Privy Council in London. The role of Her Majesty's British advisers was critical, according to those bringing the lawsuit, because the role of the Senate to constrain the elected government could otherwise be overruled by the current majority in Ottawa. Since the Imperial Privy Council was no longer operative in Canada, and modern sensibilities precluded the Queen from exercising independent political discretion, the whole section was assertedly no longer valid. The Court of Appeal rejected these arguments and concluded that the appointments were *legally* proper. The Court refused, however, to consider a declaration that the appointments violated constitutional convention. The Court distinguished the *Patriation Reference* on two grounds. First, the court found the *Patriation Reference* went to the "very heart of a current constitutional issue in Canada," which the case *sub judice* did not, 78 D.L.R. (4th) at 265. Second, the governments litigating the *Patriation Reference* had not established hard and fast positions. Here, the senators were already appointed, and thus the court concluded that it would not intervene "in the political arena by answering on a reference a matter which is not a question of law and where no assistance can be rendered with respect to any contemplated government action." *Id.*; *see also Hogan v. Newfoundland (Attorney General)*, 1999 C.R.D.J. 88 (Nfld. S.C.) (refusing to opine on existence of convention that rights of minority Catholics granted at union with Canada cannot be abridged without their consent); *Re Canada Assistance Plan*, [1991] 2 S.C.R. 525 (refusing to rule, as beyond scope of reference question, on

---

[12] Potential clashes between bi-cameralism and the principle that the government must be responsible to the House of Commons were resolved in 19th Century England by the convention that, in case of a deadlock between Lords and Commons, the Queen would upon advice of the government appoint a sufficient number of additional peers as to permit the government to pass desired legislation. This solution would not work in Canada, where the Senate served to provide a balanced representation among provinces. Thus, the particular solution of s. 26, permitting the appointment of either four or eight senators.

whether breach of federal-provincial agreement regarding welfare spending was contrary to convention).

8.3.2. Distinguishing conventions from long-standing policies

One cannot fully understand the concept of convention without appreciating the distinction between a binding convention and a "mere" usage or tradition of sound public policy. For example, in *Ontario English Catholic Teachers' Assn. v. Ontario (Attorney General)*, [2001] 1 S.C.R. 470, the Court rejected the claim that a constitutional convention preserved the authority of Ontario school boards to levy property taxes. The Court found that there "is no generally accepted principle in Canada as to the design of the public education system." Although the Court acknowledged that local taxation had been the norm for years, this "reflects consistency in public policy. It does not announce the arrival of a new principle of responsible government."

8.3.3. Conventions and crisis in the absence of advisory opinions: The Whitlam Affair

As we have seen, Canada has conventions and advisory opinions; the United States has neither. Australia does not have advisory opinions; it has a combination of constitutional guidelines and Westminster system conventions, but lacks a tribunal providing authoritative guidance as to the latter. An interesting comparison is between the Canadian crisis detailed in *Patriation Reference*, caused by Prime Minister Trudeau's efforts to repatriate the Constitution without reaching a compromise with provincial premiers, and the 1975 crisis between the Australian Labor government of Prime Minister Gough Whitlam and his conservative opponents. (The following is drawn largely from George Winterton, *1975: The Dismissal of the Whitlam Government, in* AUSTRALIAN CONSTITUTIONAL LANDMARKS (H.P. Lee & George Winterton, eds., 2003).)

For the first time in 23 years, a Labor government had narrowly prevailed over a centre-right coalition of the Liberal and National Parties in the 1972 federal election for the House of Representatives.[13] The Senate did not face an election at that time (Senators serve a fixed term of six years, with half the Senate normally elected at a time, but Senate elections do not have to be held at the same time as House of Representatives elections); the upper-house was still controlled by the centre-right coalition. Many conservatives could not accept that Whitlam had prevailed: the Coalition's Senate Leader, Senator Reg Withers, declared that the Labor victory was the result of the "temporary electoral insanity" of voters in Melbourne and Sydney. Thus, among other things, drawing upon a precedent when Labor senators blocked conservative legislation in the 1950s, opponents saw the

---

[13] The term "liberal" came to apply to European political parties in the 19th century and traditionally meant a party supporting free enterprise and limited government, in contrast with a "conservative party" that supported government policies to prop up a landed aristocracy or socialist parties supporting government control of industry to prevent worker exploitation. In North America, it has been applied to centre-left parties, such as the Liberal Party of Canada and the Democratic Party in the United States. In Australia, Liberal Party policies are more likely to find sympathy with Canadian Conservatives and American Republicans.

Senate as the principal vehicle for bringing down the Whitlam government.

First, in arguable violation of a constitutional convention, conservative state Premiers filled vacancies in the Senate created by resignation or death of elected Labor senators with ideological opponents of the Whitlam government. (The convention that casual vacancies must be filled with someone from the same party, which has subsequently been constitutionally entrenched (see below), flows from the principle of electoral choice, and the fact that senators are elected by proportional representation; the whole process would be frustrated if Party A is entitled to 3 senators based on popular vote but then only has 2 because one of their partisans quits and is replaced by someone from another party.) Next, the Senate proceeded to reject more government bills than any in history: over 93 bills were rejected.[14]

Conservatives then escalated the confrontation by announcing that they would refuse to support a budget to operate the government (called "Supply") unless Whitlam agreed to an election for the House to parallel the election that was required for half the Senate in 1975 (public opinion polls suggested that Labor would lose such an election; Whitlam was not required to call a new election until 1977). A resolution conditioning Supply on a House election was passed 30-29, a victory many claim was due to the refusal of the conservative Queensland government to replace a deceased Labor senator.[15] Whitlam refused the demand.

To put this in comparative context, in Britain the convention that the unelected House of Lords would not block Supply was breached in 1912, resulting in new legislation stripping the Lords of any veto (which the Lords themselves passed after Prime Minister Asquith secured King George V's promise to pack the upper house with new Liberal peers if they didn't acquiesce). In the United States, the President does not control either legislative chamber. Indeed, the United States government did indeed shut down for several days in 1995 because of lack of Supply, during a stand-off between Democratic President Bill Clinton and Republican House Speaker Newt Gingrich that was resolved largely in Clinton's favor when public opinion supported him. A similar government shutdown and confrontation between President Barack Obama and Congress occurred in late 2013, with a resolution again largely in the President's favor.

With no budget in sight, a Liberal MHR and former Solicitor-General, Robert Ellicott, publicly called on the Governor-General to demand assurances that Whitlam could secure Supply. If not, he asserted that "it would be within the Governor-General's power and duty to dismiss his Ministers and appoint others." (The quotation comes from Paul Kelly, *November 1975* (Sydney, 1993)). With Whitlam's approval Governor-General John Kerr — former Chief Justice of the New South Wales Supreme Court and a lawyer for trade union clients with strong ties to the ALP, who had been named to the post by Queen Elizabeth on Whitlam's

---

[14] This practice triggered yet another potential violation of convention: an effort by the Whitlam government to create openings for six, rather than five, elected senators from Queensland in a 1975 senate election, by naming a conservative senator (and harsh government critic) as Ambassador to Ireland. The tactic failed when the news leaked and the Queensland Premier promptly filled the vacancy.

[15] For arguments pro and con on this point, see Winterton at 235–6.

recommendation — consulted legal authorities who opined that he was not required to dismiss Whitlam, and also with Liberal leader Malcolm Fraser on whether a compromise could be found. Without Whitlam's approval, Kerr also consulted with the Chief Justice of Australia, Sir Garfield Barwick, who had previously served as Attorney General in a Liberal government. Barwick advised:

> [A] prime minister who cannot ensure supply to the crown [ie, the government], including funds for carrying on the ordinary services of government, must either advise a general election . . . or resign. If, being unable to secure supply, he refuses to take either course, your Excellency has a constitutional authority to withdraw his commission as prime minister.

Based on this advice, Kerr dismissed Whitlam, commissioned Fraser as a caretaker Prime Minister, and then dissolved Parliament.[16]

Professor Winterton's analysis suggests that:

(1) Conservative state premiers violated convention by replacing Labor senators with Whitlam's opponents; Whitlam may well have been able to secure the passage of Supply in the Senate had that not occurred.

(2) The Senate is constitutionally authorized to block Supply but whether it was a convention not to do so is "debatable."

(3) The Barwick-Kerr principle justifying Whitlam's dismissal was novel, and likely contrary to the contemporary view that the principle of responsible government as applied in Australia required the confidence of the House but not the Senate.

(4) The Chief Justice should not have informally advised the Governor-General on this issue.

In the end, Professor Winterton characterises the crisis as "the most dramatic event in Australian political history," profoundly affecting the power of the Senate, the public perception of the office of Governor-General, the role of constitutional conventions, and even the future of the monarchy; it "arguably hardened political behaviour and contributed to the public cynicism regarding government and politicians." Winterton, *1975: The Dismissal of the Whitlam Government*, at 229. At the same time, the lack of consensus among commentators illustrates the difficulties of determining the existence of a convention based on "the conduct and speech of politicians." GEOFFREY SAWER, FEDERATION UNDER STRAIN: AUSTRALIA 1972–75, at 124 (Melbourne: Hill of Content, 1976).

The crisis did have a constitutional effect (whether this was a direct or indirect effect is debatable). In a referendum in 1977, the Australian voters agreed to amend

---

[16] In his memoirs (all of the major players wrote books about this), the Governor-General stated that he deliberately declined to consult or inform the Queen in advance, to shield her from controversy. JOHN KERR, MATTERS FOR JUDGMENT 330 (Melbourne: MacMillan 1978). The Labor House Speaker wrote Her Majesty asking her to restore Whitlam to office. Winterton concludes that she was clearly correct not to intervene, but that Kerr should have been more forthcoming with Whitlam about his novel views of the Governor-General's power, although, had he been candid earlier, Whitlam might have acted to dismiss him.

the Constitution, to alter section 15 which provides for the method of selecting a replacement Senator when a "casual vacancy" occurs (that is, a vacancy outside the regular electoral cycle, caused by resignation or death). Previously, the nomination of a replacement was made by the relevant State Parliament or Governor (acting on executive advice). As noted above, the convention that the replacement should always be chosen from the same Party as the outgoing Senator, had been breached by two state Premiers, thus altering the balance of power in the Senate, crucial to the events of 1975. Section 15 of the Constitution now states that

> Where a vacancy has at any time occurred in the place of a senator chosen by the people of a State and, at the time when he was so chosen, he was publicly recognized by a particular political party as being an endorsed candidate of that party and publicly represented himself to be such a candidate, a person chosen or appointed under this section in consequence of that vacancy . . . shall, unless there is no member of that party available to be chosen or appointed, be a member of that party.

This referendum result indicated, at the very least, that it is not impossible to turn unwritten conventions into constitutional commitments.

As a political matter, the results are also interesting. Fraser won the election despite strong Labor resentment against his part in the crisis. Labor returned to power seven years later, albeit in a politically more moderate form. The most significant legacy, according to Winterton, was the growth of republicanism, which he noted was ironic because Kerr had acted to keep the Queen from controversy. (One of us, on holiday in Yellowstone National Park in 1999, found a group of touring Australian youths, none born during this affair, bearing t-shirts proclaiming "Sack the Queen, Not Whitlam.") Winterton concluded with a comparison between Australia and the United States:

> The U.S. Constitution has no "ultimate constitutional guardian" like the Governor-General, empowered to protect fundamental constitutional principles by forcing the Government to face its ultimate master — the electors. Consequently, the Americans have to resolve political disputes through political means. They have demonstrated how political sense and reluctance to push issues to their ultimate limit operate in a system of checks and balances. In the years since the Dismissal, Australia has done likewise in dealing with the legacy of 1975. That legacy is still with us, and has not run its course.

Subsequent events, including the defeat of the 1999 referendum on the proposal to change Australia from a constitutional monarchy to a republic, combined with declining public support in the twenty-first century for republicanism and growing popularity of the British Royal Family, suggest that Winterton's conclusion was not correct or, if correct, only for a relatively short period in Australian political life. Most commentators in Australia, post-1999, appear to agree that the republic question will not seriously arise again until Queen Elizabeth's reign comes to an end.

8.3.4.   Relationship between conventions and statutes

Occasionally, courts will opine on conventions because they have become codified in law. For example, the Constitution of Western Nigeria had express provisions for the dismissal of the prime minister by the Governor when the former no longer enjoyed the confidence of the legislature. The Prime Minister had not lost a vote of confidence but was dismissed based on a petition to the Governor from a majority of legislators. In *Adegbenro v. Akintola*, [1963] A.C. 614, the Privy Council held this was sufficient.

Sometimes, the interpretation of enacted law is dependent on the understanding of a constitutional convention, which therefore requires the latter's interpretation. For example, consider *A-G Quebec v. Blaikie*, [1981] 1 S.C.R. 312, discussed in Chapter 5 above. There, the Court held that the constitutional requirement in s. 133 of the *BNA Act* that all Quebec legislation be passed in English and French extended to administrative regulations issued by the Lieutenant Governor in Council, because of the convention that these regulations were only issued upon recommendation of the provincial cabinet — i.e. the legislative leadership — and hence were effectively the same as legislation passed by the National Assembly.

The *Madzimbamuto* case excerpted above clearly demonstrates the legislature's power to override convention by legislation. Similarly, in *Penikett v. The Queen*, 43 D.L.R. 4th 324 (Yuk. S.C.), *rev'd on other grounds*, 45 D.L.R. (4th) 108 (Yuk. C.A. 1987), the court found that any convention in favour of increasing self-determination for territories, leading to provincial status, was no longer valid after the *Constitution Act, 1982* expressly required consent of other provinces to change in Yukon's status. Even here, courts will occasionally declare that the convention has no binding effect and, in what is clearly *obiter dicta*, that the convention didn't exist anyway. *See, e.g., Currie v. McDonald*, 29 Nfld. & P.E.I.R. 294 (1949) (rejecting challenge to referendum approving union of Newfoundland and Canada and finding no convention that union would only be instituted after post-World War II reinstatement by the British government of an independent colonial government in Newfoundland).

Finally, to return to the American context, sometimes conventions, once broken, can be re-enacted into law. One classic example is the convention that a President will not seek more than two terms in office. This was scrupulously adhered to after the tradition was created by President Washington; President Franklin D. Roosevelt, elected to four terms, broke the tradition. After Roosevelt's death, Congress proposed and the states ratified the Twenty-Second Amendment legally limiting a person to two terms.[17]

---

[17] The combination of unwritten binding obligations and the enactment of the Twenty-Fifth Amendment (which deals with succession to the Presidency) now provide a major loophole in the Twenty-Second Amendment, which literally provides that "no person *shall be elected* to the office of the President more than twice." If the voters and Congress were so inclined, two Americans could run for, respectively, President and Vice President pledging that, if elected, the Vice President will resign, the President will appoint a former President as Vice President and, upon confirmation, then resign the Presidency. The two-term President could then serve another term since he had only been "elected" to the Presidency twice.

8.3.5. When constitutional conventions require constitutional amendment

As this text goes to press, the Supreme Court of Canada has agreed to hear a reference concerning whether Parliament, by ordinary legislation, can alter the convention by which Senators are appointed. Section 24 of the *BNA Act* provides that Senators are appointed by the Governor General. Under principles of responsible government, this gave rise to two unwritten conventions: (1) the Prime Minster at the time would appoint senators, and (2) not being elected, the Senate was not an equal body and, at most, could oppose government legislation for the purpose of triggering a new election for the House of Commons. (Thus, the Senate has not had the role of equal chamber accorded to the U.S. and Australian Senates). The new legislation proposes to require the Prime Minster, in recommending individuals to be selected by the Governor General, to "consider" names from a current list of nominees selected at a provincial election. Legally, the legislation would not require the Prime Minister to actually nominate the choice of provincial voters, nor would it require the Governor General to follow any particular advice.

Because s. 42(1)(b) of the 1982 Constitution provides that a constitutional amendment "in relation to . . . the powers of the Senate and the method of selecting Senators" requires approval of both Houses of Parliament and 2/3 of the provinces that have at least 50% of the national population, the Quebec Attorney General, among others, have argued that this legislation is unconstitutional. In *Reference Re Bill C-7 Concerning the Reform of the Senate*, 2013 QCCA 1807 (Oct. 24, 2013), the Quebec Court of Appeal agreed. The court initially rejected the claim that the statute unconstitutionally amended the office of the Governor General (which, if accepted, would have required provincial unanimity to amend under s. 41). Citing Professor Hogg's treatise, §1.10, it noted that conventions are entirely based on the conduct of political actors and if these actors are free from judicial restraint in unilaterally acting contrary to convention, they were certainly free from judicial restraint if their acts were altered by ordinary legislation. However, the court agreed that the text of s. 42(1)(b) was to be read in light of the convention that the Governor General followed governmental advice, and so the effect of the legislation was to change the "method of selecting Senators." The federal government has taken the reference to the Supreme Court of Canada.

8.3.6. South Africa

While South African public law in the colonial and apartheid eras was modeled on English public law, including a tradition of constitutional conventions, the post-apartheid constitutions explicitly incorporated and defined the scope of executive authority which was by convention related to the royal prerogatives in the United Kingdom. When it came to the certification process, some of the parties objected to the new Constitution on the grounds that the authority of the President was no longer bound by common law restraints associated with the traditional conventions. The Constitutional Court rejected these objections, explaining that all public authority was now subject to the Constitution and the rule of law.

EX PARTE CHAIRPERSON OF THE CONSTITUTIONAL ASSEMBLY: IN RE CERTIFICATION OF THE CONSTITUTION OF THE REPUBLIC OF SOUTH AFRICA

(First Certification decision)

CONSTITUTIONAL COURT OF SOUTH AFRICA

1996 (4) SA 744

THE COURT:

. . . .

[114] The powers and functions of the President are set out in [the draft text of the final constitution, or new text (NT)] 84(1) and (2). The objection argued on behalf of the objectors concerns the power given to the President in terms of NT 84(2)(j). NT 84 provides in part:

"(1) The President has the powers entrusted by the Constitution and legislation, including those necessary to perform the functions of Head of State and head of the national executive.

(2) The President is responsible for . . . .

(j) pardoning or reprieving offenders and remitting any fines, penalties or forfeitures."

[115] It is alleged that this power offends [Constitutional Principles (CPs)] IV, VI and VII. The basis of the objection is, first, that the exercise of the power is not constrained by any constitutional or common law procedures, or any substantive constitutional criteria or rules, and that no reasons need be given for its exercise or for any refusal to exercise the power. It was contended that the power therefore detracts from the requirements of CP IV, which proclaims the supremacy of the Constitution. Second, it was argued that the responsibility entrusted to the President is an executive and not a judicial power, yet its exercise encroaches upon the judicial terrain and in fact overrules or negates judicial decisions in violation of both the separation of powers requirement of CP IV and the provisions pertaining to judicial functions in CP VII.

[116] The power of the South African head of state to pardon was originally derived from royal prerogatives. It does not, however, follow that the power given in NT 84(2)(j) is identical in all respects to the ancient royal prerogatives. Regardless of the historical origins of the concept, the President derives this power not from antiquity but from the NT itself. It is that Constitution that proclaims its own supremacy. Should the exercise of the power in any particular instance be such as to undermine any provision of the NT, that conduct would be reviewable.

[117] The objection based on CPs VI and VII really amounts to a complaint about a perceived overlap of powers and functions between the President, as a member of the executive, on the one hand and the judiciary on the other. It has never been part of the general functions of the court to pardon and reprieve offenders after justice has run its course. The function itself is one that is ordinarily entrusted to the head of state in many national constitutions, including in countries where the constitution

is supreme and where the doctrine of separation of powers is strictly observed.

Chapter 9

HOW ARE DEMOCRACY AND HUMAN RIGHTS BEST PROTECTED?

KEY CONCEPTS FOR THE CHAPTER

- IN ADOPTING A CONSTITUTION WITH ENTRENCHED RIGHTS, AND IN PARTICULAR WITH THE ADOPTION OF THE CIVIL WAR AMENDMENTS, AMERICANS ACKNOWLEDGED THAT HISTORY DEMONSTRATED THAT THE DEMOCRATIC MAJORITY HAD NOT PROVIDED SUFFICIENT PROTECTION OF THE RIGHTS OF MINORITIES, PARTICULARLY AMERICANS OF AFRICAN DESCENT. LIKEWISE, A NUMBER OF KEY PROVISIONS OF THE CANADIAN CHARTER REFLECT THE INSUFFICIENT PROTECTION AFFORDED TO THE INTERESTS OF CANADIANS OF FRENCH DESCENT.

- THE SOUTH AFRICAN CONSTITUTION PROVIDES A NUMBER OF PROTECTIONS AGAINST MAJORITY WILL THAT PROVIDED SUFFICIENT ASSURANCE TO BOTH THE WHITE MINORITY WHO HELD POWER UNDER APARTHEID AND THOSE CONCERNED WITH THE PROTECTION OF INDIVIDUAL RIGHTS THAT IT FACILITATED THE PEACEFUL TRANSITION FROM APARTHEID TO A DEMOCRATIC STATE.

- UNDERLYING THESE RIGHTS-PROTECTING PROVISIONS IS THE CRITICAL ASSUMPTION THAT RIGHTS ENFORCED BY A JUDICIAL SYSTEM SOMEWHAT INSULATED FROM POLITICS WOULD PROVIDE A SIGNIFICANT DEGREE OF PROTECTION FOR INTERESTS THAT MAY NOT BE REFLECTED IN ORDINARY POLITICS.

- THIS CHAPTER FOCUSES ON A BROAD ISSUE OF CONSTITUTIONAL JURISPRUDENCE: HAVE COURTS BEEN EFFECTIVE IN PROTECTING THE RIGHTS OF MINORITY GROUPS AND INDIVIDUALS? OR DOES ACTIVE JUDICIAL REVIEW HINDER LEGISLATIVE EFFORTS THAT MIGHT BE SUPERIOR WAYS TO ADVANCE THE HUMAN RIGHTS OF ALL?

9.1. CHAPTER OVERVIEW

Having regard for the wide variety of topics covered in previous chapters, our concluding chapter considers the role that that societal recognition of rights plays in promoting the general welfare and creating a more perfect union (to borrow from the U.S. Constitution's preamble). Previous chapters considered **which** rights each society recognizes. The societal recognition of "rights" has the effect of privileging certain claims. Some rights privilege economic claims over social ones (for example, property rights), while some privilege political claims over economic ones (for example, free spending in American political contests).

Another critical question is **how** the rights recognized by each society are best protected? At various points of constitutional history for each of the countries studied, courts, legislators, and citizens grappled with the question of the role of an independent judiciary in securing recognized rights.

9.1.1.   Rights entrenchment versus parliamentary sovereignty

Each of the four countries that are the focus of these materials crafted their written constitution against the background of the British "unwritten constitution," which rests on the concept of parliamentary sovereignty. This concept, which evolved from the long history of struggles for parliamentary authority in England, emerged from the Glorious Revolution and the notion that not only could Parliament make law (as opposed to the King who was the original source of all law by divine right), but that the Parliament represented the people who were the true source of governmental authority (see EDMUND MORGAN, INVENTING THE PEOPLE: THE RISE OF POPULAR SOVEREIGNTY IN ENGLAND AND AMERICA (1988)). Since all the people of the nation could not assemble to make decisions, Parliament, as the representative of the people, became the sole source of legislative authority. It was thus the problem of representation that led to the notion that the representatives assembled in Parliament were collectively the essence of the sovereignty of the people and not "the people" outside of parliament. It would be the American revolutionaries who would reject this notion and assert that sovereignty lay with the people more broadly in the form of popular sovereignty.

While the idea of popular sovereignty would justify the people throwing off the yoke of the King and asserting their right to form their own government (see, United States Declaration of Independence, 1776), it did not solve the problem of representation that had given birth to the notion of parliamentary sovereignty in the first place. If parliamentary sovereignty asserts that the people must have originally entered into a contract to govern themselves through parliament, popular sovereignty allows the people to renew that contract at the people's will. This again raises the question of democratic representation and especially the concern that political minorities, particularly permanent minorities, may find themselves unrepresented and even deliberately excluded. Early American constitutionalists defined this as the problem of faction and resolved it by assuming that from one policy issue to another, and over time, political alliances would shift, thus alleviating the problem. It was concern over the possibility of majorities at the national level imposing decisions on political minorities in the states that led to demands for a national government of limited powers in the United States. From this point it was only a small step to demand that there be an institutional mechanism to assure that the national government, and by implication, national majorities, could not simply impose their will on minority factions.

The American framers implicitly (at least according to Chief Justice John Marshall in *Marbury v. Madison* 1803) distrusted the functioning of the national political process sufficiently to limit the ability of political majorities in specified ways. Canadians (first in the 1860s and then in the 1970s), Australians, and South Africans crafted written constitutions with the explicit understanding that courts would protect against specific, undesirable policy choices that might otherwise result from the political process, and more specifically, the national political process.

The American framers specifically rejected, and none of the other nation's framers even seriously considered, an arrangement where judges would exercise broad discretion to strike down or limit laws generally considered to be unwise.

Rather, the concept of a national government of limited powers, with specific prohibitions on specified legislation or governmental acts, reflects a view that in some areas, but not others, the best way to organize government is to empower judges to protect claims by individuals or minority groups within a society from the choices of political majorities. This view is most obvious with regard to constitutional protection of free expression in the U.S. First Amendment, s. 2(b) of the Canadian Charter, and s. 16 of the South African Constitution (and implied in by the High Court of Australia from the basic structure of the Australian Constitution), or the guarantees of equal protection in the U.S. Fourteenth Amendment, s. 15 of the Canadian Charter, and many general and specific provisions of the South African Constitution.[1]

Somewhat less obvious, but equally important, is the role of the judiciary present in the concept of judicially-enforced federalism. Perhaps the essential foundation in the Canadian federal system was the concern of Quebecois that a national government could enact legislation hostile to the interests and aspirations of the French-speaking minority. Canadian federalism protects groups that constitute national minorities, but are likely to constitute a provincial majority, against legislation reflecting the nation's majority will. A key element of the American federal system at the time of the Constitution's framing was the concern of slave states that a strong federal government would result in an anti-slave majority limiting their prerogatives. Although Australian constitutional discourse has historically been less focused on individualized rights, the Commonwealth's creators doubtless understood that a judicially-enforced constitution was required to prevent temporary national majorities from enacting laws that would impair the rights of specific minorities in specified ways: the prerogative of political majorities in states to legislate within matters reserved to the states, the prerogatives of religious majorities (protected by s 116), the economic aspirations of those who would be adversely affected by limits on free trade that political majorities might from time to time find convenient (reflected in s. 92). As sketched in the introductory chapter, the historic compromise for a peaceful transition from apartheid to constitutional democracy in South Africa included an independent judiciary (albeit with a new court to be appointed by Nelson Mandela) to protect entrenched interests against defined infringement, counterbalanced with affirmative government obligations.

Thus, the project of constitutional entrenchment implies that certain policy decisions should be removed from the ordinary political process, and that decisions by political actors should be policed by the judiciary to enforce this arrangement. This is based on three foundational claims that, with regard to the specific policy choices at issue:

— *Certain claims should be recognized as "rights"*
— *Courts can effectively protect these rights*

[1] The concept of equality is implicit in the concept of human dignity and explicit in the "achievement of equality" included in the "founding values" in s. 1 of the South African Constitution, generalized in s. 9, and implicit in the myriad guarantees of social and economic rights (discussed in Chapter 5) and in limitations on other rights (e.g., explicit removal of constitutional protection for hate speech discussed in chapter 3 and limits on property rights discussed in Chapter 6).

— *Courts do a better job at protecting these rights than the ordinary political process*

In the Civil War Amendments to the United States Constitution, and in the *Constitution Act, 1982*, Americans and Canadians, respectively, acknowledged that each of our histories demonstrated that the democratic majority had not provided sufficient protection of the rights of racial or linguistic minorities, specifically Americans of African descent and Canadians of French descent. As noted earlier in the materials, the historic compromise resulting in the transition to a democratic post-apartheid South Africa reflected the decision by both the National Party government in power (which had clung to parliamentary sovereignty for an electorate excluding the African majority) and the African National Congress (which espoused majority rule) that individual rights protected by the Constitution and enforceable before the courts was the best way to ensure both the rights of individuals and groups within a democratic framework (see KLUG, CONSTITUTING DEMOCRACY (2000)). A critical assumption in these three countries is that the creation of rights, to be enforced by a judicial system somewhat insulated from political processes, would provide a significant degree of protection for those who might otherwise suffer at the hand of temporary or permanent political majorities.

9.1.2.   The current rights debate in Australia

This debate continues in Australia, whose Constitution currently protects rights in relatively few areas. As noted in Chapter Two, the Australian framers rejected open-textured rights-protecting provisions equivalent to the American Fourteenth Amendment; they were influenced *inter alia* by trust in common law principles and parliamentary democracy, as well as a reluctance to limit discriminatory state policies directed, in particular, at Chinese immigrants.

Over many decades, proposals for the enlargement of the range of rights protected by the Constitution or for the adoption of a statutory Bill of Rights have been unsuccessful: these include the 1944 referendum to alter the Constitution with, among others, a proposed express guarantee of freedom of speech and freedom of religion; 1973, a comprehensive human rights Bill introduced into the Commonwealth parliament; 1985, a second comprehensive human rights Bill, put to the parliament; 1988, a referendum to alter the Constitution to extend to the states the existing Commonwealth right to trial by jury, freedom of religion, and just terms for the acquisition of property.

Notably, all of these initiatives occurred under federal Labor governments, as did the establishment of the National Human Rights Consultation in 2009. Many of the Commonwealth anti-discrimination Acts, giving effect to international Conventions, have also been passed when Labor was in power federally: including the *Racial Discrimination Act 1975; Sex Discrimination Act 1984*; *Human Rights (Sexual Conduct) Act 1994; Disability Discrimination Act 1992*. The *Age Discrimination Act 2004*, it may be noted, was passed by a federal Liberal-National Party coalition government. The fact that Labor has been so closely associated with rights initiatives has, it would seem, contributed to a culture of partisanship on rights entrenchment in Australia (although it should also be noted that opponents of the 2009 proposed Human Rights Act included former Liberal-National and state Labor politicians).[2]

Most recently, a 2009 Report, written by the National Human Rights Consultation Committee, again considered whether to afford greater judicial protection to rights than exist currently under Australian constitutional, statutory, and common law. Consideration of amending the Constitution was ruled out by the Committee's terms of reference: given the history of failed attempts at constitutional alteration (including the fact that the 1988 "rights and freedoms" question suffered the worst defeat on record, with no state majority and only 30.79 % of the national vote in favour), it is widely accepted that a referendum on rights would almost certainly be defeated and would, effectively, kill the chances of any type of bill of rights gaining support. The Committee recommended the passage of a "Human Rights Act," a statute that would, among other things, empower the High Court to make "declarations of inconsistency" between a Commonwealth law and a right or rights protected under the Act (an example of what Mark Tushnet calls "weak form" judicial review, discussed below). The recommendation was not adopted. The Commonwealth Labor government's Attorney-General accepted that the proposal was deeply controversial, and stated that "that the enhancement of human rights should be done in a way that, as far as possible, unites rather than divides our community." He announced, as an alternative, a "Human Rights Framework," to include wide-ranging education programs, and legislation requiring an increased level of parliamentary scrutiny of Bills for human rights compatibility, among other measures.

Why was the proposed "Human Rights Act" controversial? Some critics objected because of their view that the political process works best to protect rights. They joined in opposition with lobby-groups and religious leaders who feared that the protection of some rights (such as sexuality rights or gender equality rights) would attract priority over the rights relevant to their group. Some cited, for example, the provision in the 2009 *Abortion Law Reform Act* of Victoria (which has the 2006 state *Charter of Human Rights and Responsibilities Act*) requiring any doctor who conscientiously objects to abortion to refer a woman seeking an abortion to a doctor who does not, as evidence that a Human Rights Act does not in practice protect freedom of conscience or religious belief.[3]

---

[2] The partisan complexion of Australian rights debates is a feature of the issue distinct from those of the other countries' constitutional histories. The American Bill of Rights was enacted in the pre-partisan days of the First Congress, and for a significant portion of American history constitutional politics were muddled because the Democratic Party was a coalition of northern liberals and southern segregationists. In Canada, the original (statutory) Bill of Rights was enacted by the Conservative government of Prime Minister John Diefenbaker, and the Charter of Rights was the product of a bipartisan coalition led by Liberal Prime Minister Pierre Trudeau but with Conservative Ontario Premier William Davis as a close ally. As noted, the South African Constitution was the result of an express agreement between the two leading political parties, the ANC and the National Party.

[3] There were also concerns among constitutional lawyers about whether a Human Rights Act empowering the High Court effectively to "advise" on the rights compatibility of laws would be unconstitutional in attempting to confer advisory opinion jurisdiction on, and therefore a power outside the constitutional jurisdiction of, the Court. In *Momcilovic v. The Queen* (2011) 245 CLR 1, the HCA confirmed that federal Courts could not exercise such a power.

In rejecting the most recent " Bill of Rights" proposal Australia has, once again, confirmed its now-traditional way of protecting rights: through legislative implementation of international human rights conventions, trust in the progressive character of the legislative process, and confidence that the Australian belief in equality and the "fair go" will prevail. Common law rights — historically grounded in the "natural law," and expressed and affirmed in judicial decisions - also play a significant part in Australia's approach to protecting rights (although statutory rights are tending progressively to give them expression or sometimes displace them). Common law rights include, among others, equality before the law, the freedom to do what is not proscribed by law, the presumption of innocence, the right against self-incrimination. The common law also guides aspects of statutory interpretation, including, importantly, the presumption that legislators do not intend to alter common law rights unless the contrary intention is made expressly and unambiguously clear in the relevant legislation. These principles are not unique to Australia. (For an Australian example of this reasoning, see the extract, below, from *Evans v. State of New South Wales* (200) 168 FCR 576.) Common law rights and presumptions operate in other common law countries, including those with a system of entrenched constitutional rights, although they tend to play less of a role in such jurisdictions.

9.1.3.   Review of alternative ways to protect human rights

In *Taking the Constitution Away from the Courts (1999)*, Professor Mark Tushnet usefully distinguishes "weak-form" and "strong-form" judicial review, as well as the "thick constitution" filled with details and the "thin constitution" as reflecting fundamental constitutional values. How these values can be protected can vary. Here is a sampling of alternatives:

- *Pure legislative supremacy*: loosely borrowing from the phrasing of the Canadian Charter, all rights are subject to such reasonable limits as the legislature determines to be appropriate, in their unreviewable discretion. Indeed, to the extent that legislation seems designed to infringe upon rights, courts should effectuate this legislative purpose regardless of their own, or any traditional conception of rights. This was the approach developed by Chief Justice L. C. Steyn of the apartheid South African Appellate Division. (For a description of Steyn's decisions fervently implementing apartheid-era statutes regardless of effect on liberties, see Edwin Cameron, *Legal Chauvinism, Executive-Mindedness and Justice: L.C. Steyn's Impact on South Africa Law*, 99 S.A.L.J. 56 (part V) (1982).

- *Parliamentary supremacy subject to presumptions about Parliament's intent to preserve rights:* This approach formally retains legislative supremacy, but allows judges to create, over time, judicial doctrines that protect rights unless the legislative infringement is explicit. Steyn CJ's rejection of this approach played a major role in the rise of South African apartheid. It has always been part of the British approach, given their lack of any explicit constitutional rights protections. (Indeed, for a criticism of the 1985 decision to refer to ministerial statements in legislative debate as an interpretive aid, because this could weaken the courts' role in rights protection, see David Robertson, *Judicial Discretion in the House of*

Lords 172–76 (Oxford Univ. Press 1998).) As Peter Hogg explains, *Constitutional Law of Canada* § 34.2, at common law a person is free to do anything that is not positively prohibited, and various doctrines narrow what is indeed prohibited. In particular, "statutes which encroach on the rights of the subject, whether as regards person or property, are subject to a 'strict' construction." *A.G. Can. v. Hallet & Carey*, [1952] A.C. 427, 450 (J.C.P.C.).[4] *Evans v. NSW*, (2008) 168 FCR 576 (Fed. Ct.), an important Australian decision implementing this long-standing approach, co-authored by current Chief Justice Robert French, is excerpted below in section 9.6.2.

- *Statutory bills of rights:* This approach creates judicially enforceable rights, but only as a matter of statutory interpretation, and subject to amendment by ordinary legislation. An early experiment with this approach, as a compromise between parliamentary supremacy and constitutional democracy, was tried in Canada with the adoption of the 1960 *Canadian Bill of Rights*. It was generally regarded as a failure due to weak judicial enforcement, and its lack of success led rights-supporters to succeed in securing an entrenched charter. *See* CHRISTOPHER MACLENNAN, TOWARD THE CHARTER (2003). A variety of other nations, including the United Kingdom and New Zealand, have now adopted this approach with more success. For a collection of essays, *see* Mark Tushnet, BILLS OF RIGHTS (2007).

- *Entrenched judicially-protected constitutional rights subject to legislative override:* This describes the Canadian Charter.

- *Entrenched judicially-protected constitutional rights:* This describes the constitutions of the United States and South Africa. Of course, the specific constitutional rights guaranteed by written constitutions will differ. The focus of this chapter is on how to best protect whatever rights a society wants to protect.

9.1.4. Why context matters

This chapter is formally organized to explore, via a case study approach, the experience of Canadian, American, and South African courts in rights protection, with the purpose of determining whether these experiences provide any useful lessons for Australians currently debating whether to entrench rights in their nation. At the same time, this review is designed to allow readers from elsewhere to explore whether other nations' experiences shed light on their own nation's decision to entrench rights.

We have suggested that the broad question of how best to protect human rights requires a focus on three key questions concerning the substance of the rights

---

[4] For a pre-constitutional American example, *see* William N. Eskridge, Jr., *All About Words: Early Understandings of the "Judicial Power" in Statutory Interpretation, 1776–1806*, 101 COLUM. L. REV. 990 (2001) (describing NY trial court decision adopting attorney Alexander Hamilton's argument that a statute had to be construed not to deprive his clients of rights at international law, because legislature did not explicitly provide that statute was to take effect "notwithstanding" the law of nations).

being protected and the relative institutional competences of politically responsive institutions and independent judges to succeed in rights-protection. Consistent with this book's theme, we believe that this focus cannot take place in the abstract, but requires an understanding of the unique histories, institutions, and values of each country. For example, the question of how to protect the collective societal interests of a large ethnic minority with a distinctive language and culture is present in both Canada (Francophones) and South Africa (Afrikaaners). How Canadians would analyze which rights should be recognized to give effect to a minority group's *legitimate* aspirations, and how best to recognize these rights, will likely differ sharply from how South Africans would answer that question. At the same time, analyzing similarities and differences allows citizens of each nation to sharpen their focus on how their own country's unique history, culture, and institutions affects rights protection.

The materials below will hopefully provide readers with insights into the following claims, each of which reflect current constitutional arrangements:

— The ability of French Canadians to flourish in an officially bilingual Canada is best protected by judicial enforcement of linguistic rights in various sections of the Canadian Charter of Rights and Freedoms;

— The rights to liberty and equality for political minorities, and African Americans in particular, are best protected by judicial enforcement of the Fourteenth Amendment to the U.S. Constitution;

— The balance between protecting the internationally-recognized political, social and property rights of individual, particularly white South Africans, with the legitimate aspirations of the historically-oppressed black majority requires judicial oversight, guided by carefully drafted constitutional provisions;

— The limited protections for religious freedom, against interstate discrimination, and property expropriation by the Commonwealth government, combined with the authority of the Commonwealth Parliament to implement international human rights obligations through the External Affairs power, provides sufficient protection for Australian minorities, so that no additional rights-entrenchment is appropriate at this time.

This Chapter proceeds as follows. First, we will explore the treatment of linguistic minorities in Canada, dividing our inquiry between the treatment of Anglophones in Quebec and the treatment of Francophones in English-speaking Canada. We will segue into our consideration of the treatment of American racial minorities by reconsidering the famous U.S. Supreme Court phrase "separate educational facilities are inherently unequal" in the Canadian context, and then explore the evolution over time of judicial and legislative protection for racial minorities in the United States. Third, we review jurisprudence under South Africa's post-apartheid Constitution to consider the question of whether the judicial protection of rights contained in the historic compromise between the apartheid regime and the African National Congress is effectively protecting the legitimate aspirations of all in a post-apartheid South Africa. Finally, we turn to what lessons can be drawn from these experiences for continued judicial interpretation in North America and South Africa and for the adoption of equality provisions in Australia.

9.2. CANADA: JUDICIAL PROTECTION FOR LINGUISTIC MINORITIES

In this section, consider the way in which the Supreme Court of Canada has interpreted relevant constitutional provisions according to (1) the literal text, (2) the clear original intent of the drafters, or (3) the broad public purposes that underlie the relevant provision. It is in this specific context that we also consider a uniquely Canadian constitutional provision, section 33, that permits a legislature to enact law for a maximum of five years, notwithstanding its inconsistency with a variety of Charter protections.[5]

9.2.1. Background on language rights in Canada

Paul C. Weiler, *Rights and Judges in a Democracy: A New Canadian Version*
18 U. Mich. J.L. Ref. 51 (1984)[6]

* * *

Canadians sought a constitutionally entrenched *Charter of Rights* not just for its own sake, but also as part of a larger effort at constitutional renewal. The hope was that such a *Charter* would preserve a united Canada in the face of the serious threat posed by French Canadian nationalism within a potentially independent Quebec. . . .

* * *

I. The Significance of Language Rights

* * *

I will focus on the language issue for it has been as central to the Canadian experience with rights and constitutions as race has been in the United States. In fact, securing minority language rights was the principal motivation for Prime Minister Trudeau's making the *Charter* the centerpiece of his project for constitutional renewal of Canadian federalism.

The peculiar features of the language issue in Canada are vividly illustrated in our most famous civil rights controversy, the Manitoba School Crisis of the 1890's. In that case, the French Catholic minority asserted its right to have "separate but equal" education in its own schools funded out of the public coffers. The French considered oppressive the English-dominated provincial legislature's attempt to force all students, including French Catholics, into a single, "integrated" public

---

[5] Canada's Notwithstanding Clause is discussed in section 9.2.2., *infra*.

[6] Copyright © 1984 by Paul. C. Weiler. Reprinted with permission.

school system. Paradoxically, the Manitoba minority lost that struggle[7] largely because Canada's French Catholic Prime Minister, Wilfred Laurier, considered it essential to defend the principle of provincial autonomy just then emerging within the Canadian federal regime. Laurier believed that this constitutional principle was vital to the Quebecois (the French in Quebec), because it would keep the authority over education and other areas of public life in the hands of the provincial government in Quebec City, the only government in North America whose constituency was predominantly French.

In these fateful events of nearly a century ago lie the seeds of the modern Canadian dilemma. In fact, throughout the 1970's Canada witnessed an eerie replay of the contest between the strategy of individual constitutional rights as the ideal technique for protecting the French Canadian minority — the position of Trudeau and his federal government in Ottawa — and the alternative of provincial rights (or even more radical forms of Quebecois nationalism) — now identified with Quebec Premier René Lévesque and his Parti Quebecois.

The virtues of the individual rights strategy are evident: through a constitutional guarantee of individual language rights, Canada could undo its past injustice towards the French Canadian minority as exemplified by the Manitoba School case. Such measures would, it was hoped, avert the serious threat to Canadian unity posed by the coexistence of two linguistically separate Canadas, the French in Quebec and the English everywhere else.[8] As Trudeau has argued since his days as a constitutional law professor in Montreal,[9] only if effective legal guarantees against unfriendly provincial governments solidify the precarious situation of the French language outside Quebec will the Quebecois be able to consider all of Canada their homeland, throughout which they can travel and live with confidence in governmen-

---

[7] [FN 13] [Ed. note: Under s. 93 of the *Constitution Act, 1867*, the federal Parliament is authorized to enact remedial laws to correct provincial incursions on minority educational rights. It has never been exercised.] Charles Tupper, the English Protestant leader of the then incumbent Canadian Government, introduced legislation in Ottawa to roll back Manitoba's new education policy, but this measure was opposed by Laurier's Liberals. The Liberals forced and won an election on the issue in 1896 and negotiated a compromise with the Manitoba Premier which effectively denied the French-Catholics their own schools in that province.

[8] [FN 15] While French Canadians were 25.7% of the Canadian population in 1971, they were 80% of the population of Quebec, and just 4.4% of the rest of Canada. Indeed, if one views the 190,000 Francophones in Northwest New Brunswick and the 270,000 in Eastern Ontario as part of a single Quebec and "contact regions," Francophones comprise only 1.5% of the rest of Canada (which constitutes two-thirds of the Canadian population as a whole). The population figures in this note and in most of those that follow are drawn from R. Lachapelle & J. Henripin, The Demolinguistic Situation in Canada (1982), in particular the comprehensive census tables in the book's Appendix.

[Ed. note: Data from the 2000 census paints a similar picture. As summarized in J.E. Magnet, *Modern Constitutionalism: Identity, Equality and Democracy* 143:

> Few Canadians are bilingual. Only 17 per cent speak and understand both English and French. Outside of Quebec, 87 per cent of Canadians speak only English. Inside Quebec, 54 per cent of Canadians speak only French. [Where these unilingual populations] meet, bilingual people are found in high concentrations. Most of Canada's bilingual persons live in this "bilingual belt."]]

[9] [FN 16] See his collected essays in P.E. Trudeau, Federalism and the French Canadians (1968). A position paper of his, Government of Canada, A National Understanding (1977), expressed the same point of view.

tal support of their linguistic and cultural heritage. Although entrenchment of his Official Languages policy at the federal level was an important constitutional goal for Trudeau, his major aim was to prod provincial governments to provide education rights to their French Canadian minorities.

It required the election in the late 1970's of a separatist government in Quebec for English Canada finally to accept this position. By that time, though, bitter opposition to these federal remedial measures had emerged within Quebec. Sophisticated Quebecois felt that this legal lifeline had come a century too late to make the French language viable outside their province. They believed that the tug of assimilation in an urban industrialized society would inevitably trump whatever legal rights were written into a constitution.[10] They were also concerned that the price of using a constitution in the quixotic quest for linguistic equality would be reciprocal limitations on the freedom of action of the French inside Quebec.

This issue was not merely symbolic in the 1970's. The Quebecois were alarmed over the incipient decline in the French proportion of the Quebec population, especially in Montreal, the flagship of French Canada.[11] This gloomy trend was attributable to the fact that, given the choice between adopting French or English as a family language, at least twice as many non-English-speaking entrants to Quebec were choosing English. This trend was most pronounced in Montreal. The economic dominance of the Anglophone community in Quebec and the consequent fact that proficiency in English was more advantageous to one's prospects than was proficiency in French[12] made English the preferred language of the newcomers to the province, and their children flocked to the English schools rather than to the French écoles. Thus, although the individual choices were eminently reasonable for each family concerned, cumulatively they posed a profound threat to the continuing existence of French language and culture in what had been considered its sole safe harbor in North America.

From this situation emerged a comprehensive language policy in Quebec which culminated in passage of the Charter of the French Language in 1977.

---

[10] [FN 18] The tug of assimilation became evident in the more elaborate census data of 1971. That year, of 1,421,000 Canadians of French origin living outside of Quebec, 926,000 had the French language as their mother tongue and 676,000 had French as their home language. That meant that more than one-third of the Canadians with French ancestry did not learn French as their first language in their parents' home and, of those who did, more than one-quarter no longer used French in their own home, teaching it to their children. Especially endangered species were those in Western Canada: 11,000 Francophones in British Columbia, 25,000 in Alberta, and 15,000 in Saskatchewan. While there remained 40,000 of French mother tongue in Manitoba, this was only 6.1% of the provincial population, and the same stark process of assimilation had taken place: 8.8% of Manitobans were of French origin, but just 4.0% used it as their home language.

[11] [FN 19] Jacques Henripin, the leading French Canadian demographer, looked at the declining birth rate of the Quebecois and the growing tendency of immigrants to assimilate into the English community in Quebec and projected a drop in the French share of Quebec from 82.5% in 1951 to a range of 71.6%-79.2% by 2001, and in Montreal from 62% in 1961 to a range of 52-62% by 2001. Naturally enough, the concerned Quebecois focused on the lower end of this scale.

[12] [FN 22] Taking the 1970 earnings of the unilingual Francophone as 100, being a bilingual Francophone added 40 points to one's income level. Being bilingual, however, added almost nothing to the Anglophone edge. That figure rose only one point, from 167 to 168.

[The CFL had several important features which will be discussed in this Chapter. One was a restriction of freedom of choice in the language of education. Related, and in Weiler's view more important, was the requirement that French is the normal language of workplace communication, with the goal of inducing immigrants to realize that speaking French is necessary to advancement. A third was a law requiring public signs to be only in French.]

Given the experience in the United States of states' rights (especially in the South) cast in opposition to racial equality, the notion of provincial autonomy as a strategy for protecting a minority group may seem ludicrous to most Americans. The tactic, however, would appear more plausible if, in the United States, ninety-five percent of blacks lived in one large state, where they constituted eighty percent of the population, and if the national constitution prevented the state's government from taking affirmative action to redress what it considered to be the current impact of historic domination by the state's white minority. This hypothetical situation captures the actual situation of Quebec in Canada, giving rise to the major moral ambiguity bedeviling the Canadian quest for a constitutional *Charter of Rights*.

*   *   *

Benoit Aubin, *Bill 101: A Gift We Never Expected*, MACLEANS, Aug. 13, 2007, at 30–31, puts the language law in some perspective. The law's implementation resulted in the exodus of as many as 150,000 affluent, educated Anglophone Montrealers to Toronto. The law's author, Montreal sociologist Camille Laurin, observed that he "wanted to strike a big blow, and produce a shock therapy, powerful enough to change mentalities." But while some of the results were as designed, others were unforeseen by the Parti Quebecois provincial government:

- Although Laurin sought to "make Montreal as French as Toronto is English," Montreal today boasts the highest proportion of tri-lingual people in North America [French, English, and native language];

- Although criticized as "akin to ethnic cleansing," the law "is creating a multicultural melting pot out of the old, homogenous, and claustrophobic *culture québécoise*;

- The law checked the reality that "bilingualism was a one-sided burden for Francophones, and immigrants were assimilating massively into English"; today 66% of Anglophones who remained or migrated since speak French;

- The "language of work" requirement has effectively narrowed the income gap based on language;

- Many jobs have been created by a new language industry based on translation and correction software, terminology banks, linguistic planning, etc.

In short, according to one language expert, "the paradox today is that French has never been stronger and healthier, but English has never been more present and necessary at the same time."

9.2.2. Background on the Notwithstanding Clause

Human rights are never absolute. Roughly speaking, the American model entrenches broadly worded rights in a written constitution which, in John Marshall's words, the Supreme Court then "expounds" to reflect appropriate and justifiable limits. The South African model sets forth founding constitutional principles that inform judicial interpretation, entrenches qualified rights, and specifically authorizes government activity that imposes "reasonable" limits on rights that can be justified before the courts. In addition, the South African model seeks to balance "liberal" or "political" rights of the individual against the state with affirmative "socio-economic rights" that the state must take reasonable steps to implement. The Australian model generally allows the Commonwealth and State parliaments to balance rights (subject to judicial balancing in the context of political communications necessary for democratic government), but would appear to privilege claims that legislators need to enforce rights recognized in international conventions.

The Canadian Charter reflects a somewhat different model. Like their southern neighbors, Canada has entrenched broadly worded rights to be enforced by Canadian courts. The reasonable limits approach adopted by South Africa was borrowed from the Canadian Charter; these provisions (section 1 of the Canadian Charter and section 36 of the South African Constitution) both give courts the discretion to sustain statutes where judges are satisfied that specific circumstances warrant a demonstrable limitation on rights claims. Unlike the U.S. and South Africa, however, the Notwithstanding Clause in section 33 of the Canadian Charter is an extraordinary provision allowing the federal or provincial legislatures to temporarily override constitutional rights. It allows a legislature to declare, for a period of five years, that a law shall remain in effect although a Court has held (or may hold) that it violates of the Charter. Section 33 was seen as a compromise between the British system of parliamentary supremacy and the American system of judicial supremacy. The Notwithstanding Clause is uniquely Canadian.

To date, Parliament has never sought to implement a federal statute notwithstanding the Charter. Nor have seven of the provinces ever invoked the Clause. The Clause has been exercised in only a few instances by provincial legislatures. These include:

(1) Prime Minister Pierre Trudeau brought the *Constitution Act, 1982* into effect with assent of the federal Parliament and all the provinces except for Quebec. The Quebec National Assembly, with a majority from the separatist Parti Quebecois, responded in 1982 with legislation providing that *all* Quebec statutory law took effect notwithstanding ss. 2 and 7-15 of the *Federal Charter of Rights and Freedoms*. Subsequently, the Quebec National Assembly added a "notwithstanding" provision to every single Act it passed during the tenure of Premier René Lévesque's PQ government. Pointedly, to emphasize that it was not seeking to impinge on civil liberties, the Quebec National Assembly did not invoke a similar clause in the Quebec Charter of Human Rights, except on 8 specific occasions.

In 1985, the Parti Quebecois was defeated in provincial elections by the Liberal Party under Premier Robert Bourassa, who did not re-enact the wholesale invocation of the Notwithstanding Clause. This meant that by 1987, all pre-1982 Quebec law was again subject to the federal Charter. Acts passed between 1982 and 1995 became subject to federal constitutional review five years after enactment.

(2)   The Liberal Bourassa government did, however, invoke the Clause to preclude a modification of the sign law — permitting bilingual signs with larger French lettering — that it enacted following the *Ford* decision.

(3)   Saskatchewan invoked the clause following a Saskatchewan Court of Appeals decision that the right to strike was constitutionally protected.

(4)   The Yukon territorial government invoked the clause to address concerns that legislation allocating seats on various land use planning bodies to nominees of the Council for Yukon Indians might violate equality rights (although the statute at issue never came into effect).

(5)   The Alberta *Marriage Act* was amended in 2000 to expressly limit marriage to those of the opposite sex, and the Notwithstanding Clause was invoked to shield the law against equality challenge. (Subsequently, the federal government, exercising its power over "Marriage and Divorce" in s. 91(26) of the *Constitution Act, 1867*, legalized same-sex marriages.)

Some have decried the evolution of a political climate that makes it very difficult for politicians to invoke the Clause. One factor is the significant popular acceptance within Canada of the Charter. Another is that the media, with a vested institutional interest in protecting its own constitutional rights, is quite hostile to any override for fear that it could be turned on the press. The Liberal government of Prime Minister Jean Chrétien rejected the call by opposition and backbench parliamentarians to invoke the Clause after a British Columbia Supreme Court justice struck down *Criminal Code* provisions on child pornography. (Most of these provisions were subsequently upheld by the Supreme Court of Canada in the *Sharpe* case discussed in Chapter Three.) After significant consideration, the conservative Alberta government rejected the call to invoke the Clause after the Supreme Court of Canada held that the province must protect gays and lesbians as well as other listed minority groups in its statutory ban on unlawful employment discrimination; the government announced that henceforth it would reserve the right to call a referendum on whether to invoke the Clause, and as noted above did use the Clause to seek to proscribe same-sex marriages. Earlier, public furor forced the Alberta government to withdraw legislation introduced to invoke the Clause to limit compensation payable to claimants suing the province for unlawful sterilization. One of the principal issues that emerged during the 2004 federal election was the suggestion by Conservative leader Stephen Harper that he would use the Clause in some cases (he cited child pornography as one), while Liberal Prime Minister Paul Martin expressed the fear that the Conservatives would invoke the power to legislate in numerous areas (most notably with regard to abortion) and unequivocally claimed that his Liberal government would never use the Clause "to take away a right that had been enshrined in the Charter. I believe that rights are rights, and the Supreme Court is there to protect them." *See generally* Barbara Billingsley, *Section 33: The Charter's Sleeping Giant*, 21 WINDSOR Y.B. ACCESS JUST. 331 (2002), which in turn draws upon Tsvi Kahana, *The Notwithstanding Mechanism and Public Discussion: Lessons from the Ignored Practice of Section 33 of the Charter*, 44 CAN. PUB. ADMIN. 255. Peter Hogg suggests that the ability, even if never exercised, to override a Supreme Court decision after debate in a public forum about justice and public policy is preferable to the "court-bashing and court-packing that is a staple of federal politics in the United States," which he attributes to the lack of an override power. HOGG, CONSTITUTIONAL LAW OF CANADA, § 39.8.

9.2.3.   Judicial protection of Anglophones in Quebec

The principal litigation concerning the rights of Anglophones in Quebec concerns the *Charter of the French Language* (CFL),also known as Bill 101. The first challenge decided by the Supreme Court of Canada was *A.G. (Quebec) v. Blaikie (Blaikie I)*, [1979] 2 S.C.R. 1016. The Court invalidated provisions of the *Charter of the French Language* that declared (a) French to be the official language of the legislature and the courts in Quebec; (b) artificial persons were required to use French in all judicial or administrative proceedings unless all parties agreed to pleading in English; (c) all judgments of judicial or administrative bodies shall be written or translated into French. A noted federalist attorney challenged the law, arguing that it was inconsistent with s. 133 of the *British North America Act*, which provides:

> Either the English or the French Language may be used by any Person in the Debates of the Houses of the Parliament of Canada and of the Houses of the Legislature of Quebec; and both those Languages shall be used in the respective Records and Journals of those Houses; and either of those Languages may be used by any Person or in any Pleading or Process in or issuing from any Court of Canada established under this Act, and in or from all or any of the Courts of Quebec.

The Supreme Court refused to narrowly interpret s. 133 to limit the scope of its conflict with the Quebec legislation. The Court declared that "the reference in s. 133 to 'any of the Courts of Quebec' ought to be considered broadly as including not only so-called s. 96 Courts but also Courts established by the Province and administered by provincially-appointed Judges." [For comparative purposes, Canadians seem to use the phrase "s. 96 judges" in the same way that Americans use the phrase "Article III" judges and Australians use the phrase "Chapter III" judges (and Courts.)]

In addition, the Court applied s. 133's bilingual mandate to provincial administrative agencies, although these tribunals did not literally fall within the ambit of s. 133's language. The court observed that, given "the rudimentary state of administrative law in 1867, it is not surprising that there was no reference to non-curial adjudicative agencies. Today, they play a significant role in the control of a wide range of individual and corporate activities, subjecting them to various norms of conduct which are at the same time limitations on the jurisdiction of the agencies and on the legal position of those caught by them."

The broad interpretation of s. 133 was justified by two precedents from the Privy Council. In the landmark decision in *Edwards v. Attorney General of Canada* [[1930] A.C. 124] (excerpted above in the Introductory Chapter), the Privy Council held that women were eligible for appointment to the Canadian Senate under s. 24, although such a prospect was not contemplated by the framers, because a constitutional statute like the *British North America Act* needed to be interpreted broadly to account for changing circumstances. Lord Sankey's famous line was that the Act "planted in Canada a living tree capable of growth and expansion within its natural limits." *Id.* at 136. The Court also cited *Attorney General of Ontario v. Attorney General of Canada* [1947] A.C. 127, 154 (the Privy Council Appeals Reference), where Viscount Jowitt wrote that "To such an organic statute the flexible interpretation must be given which changing circumstances require."

In subsequent litigation, [1981] 1 S.C.R. 312 (*Blaikie II*), the Court further expounded on its broad interpretative approach, declaring that the "ordinary meaning of the words 'Acts . . . of the Legislature' in s. 133 must be departed from to prevent the requirements of the section from being frustrated," although the words cannot be "stretched beyond what is necessary to accomplish this purpose." Thus, the Court held that s. 133 applied to Court rules of practice, even though these too were not literally "Acts of the Legislature," based on the continuous use of French and English in Quebec courts since 1774 and the justices' view that "litigants have the fundamental right to choose either French or English and would be deprived of this freedom of choice should such rules and compulsory forms be couched in one language only."

While the *Blaikie* decisions reflected a view that s. 133 is a constitutional mandate requiring a broad and purposive interpretation, an alternative interpretive technique — original intent — was used to vindicate Anglophone rights in *A.G. (Quebec) v. Quebec Protestant School Boards*, [1984] 2 S.C.R. 66, 10 D.L.R. (4th) 321. This case was the first of many challenges to Language of Education provisions of the CFL, enacted to respond to the pressures on Francophones to learn English and immigrants to Quebec to migrate to the Anglophone rather than Francophone communities. These provisions of the CFL had to be reconciled with the Minority Language Education Rights guarantees incorporated in section 23 of the federal Charter of Rights and Freedoms. PQ Premier René Lévesque identified this Charter provision as his government's principal objection to ratifying the Charter of Rights and Freedoms.

Section 23 has multiple provisions. Subsection (1)(a) would grant the right to have children educated in English in Quebec to all Canadian citizens who are Anglophone, but s. 59 of the Charter provides that this section only applies if authorized by the Quebec National Assembly, which has never happened. Subsection (1)(b) grants a more limited right to all parents who are Canadian citizens who themselves were educated in Canada in English, and ss. (2) provides that where one child has received education in the minority language, all siblings can also receive this education. This particular lawsuit challenged a CFL provision that required all new residents of Quebec, whether immigrants or Canadian citizens from other provinces, to send their children to French-language schools; only those parents who attended English schools in Quebec could send their children to these schools.

There was no question that, as to Anglophone Canadians, the provision infringed s. 23 rights. The PQ government defended the statute as a reasonable limit under s. 1 of the Charter,

> . . . in view of factors such as demographic patterns, the physical mobility (migration) and linguistic mobility ("assimilation") of individuals and the regional distribution of interprovincial migrants. It was further argued that other free and democratic societies such as Switzerland and Belgium, which have sociolinguistic situations comparable to that in Quebec, have adopted stricter linguistic measures than Bill 101, and these measures have been held to be reasonable and justified by the Swiss and European courts. Finally, it was argued that the collective right of the Anglophone minority in Quebec to cultural survival is not threatened by Bill 101, which establishes a system providing access to English schooling which is not unreasonable.

The Court refused to even consider whether the statute was a reasonable limit. It found that s. 23 was not a codification of universal rights, but a "unique set of constitutional provisions, quite peculiar to Canada."

> This set of constitutional provisions was not enacted by the framers in a vacuum. When it was adopted, the framers knew, and clearly had in mind the regimes governing the Anglophone and Francophone linguistic minorities in various provinces in Canada so far as the language of instruction was concerned. They also had in mind the history of these regimes, both earlier ones such as Regulation 17, which for a time limited instruction in French in the separate schools of Ontario — *Ottawa Separate Schools Trustees v. Mackell*, [1917] A.C. 62 — as well as more recent ones such as Bill 101 and the legislation which preceded it in Quebec. Rightly or wrongly,— and it is not for the courts to decide,— the framers of the Constitution manifestly regarded as inadequate some — and perhaps all — of the regimes in force at the time the *Charter* was enacted, and their intention was to remedy the perceived defects of these regimes by uniform corrective measures, namely those contained in s. 23 of the *Charter*, which were at the same time given the status of a constitutional guarantee. The framers of the Constitution unquestionably intended by s. 23 to establish a general regime for the language of instruction, not a special regime for Quebec; but in view of the period when the *Charter* was enacted, and especially in light of the wording of s. 23 of the *Charter* as compared with that of ss. 72 and 73 of Bill 101, it is apparent that the combined effect of the latter two sections seemed to the framers like an archetype of the regimes needing reform, or which at least had to be affected, and the remedy prescribed for all of Canada by s. 23 of the *Charter* was in large part a response to these sections.

* * *

Although the fate reserved to the English language as a language of instruction had generally been more advantageous in Quebec than the fate reserved to the French language in the other provinces, Quebec seems nevertheless to have been the only province where there was then this tendency to limit the benefits conferred on the language of the minority. In the other provinces at the time, either the earlier situation had remained unchanged, at least so far as legislation was concerned, as in Newfoundland and British Columbia which have no legislation on the language of instruction, or else relatively recent statutes had been adopted improving the situation of the linguistic minority, as in New Brunswick, Nova Scotia and Prince Edward Island: see Alfred Monnin, then a puisne judge of the Manitoba Court of Appeal, "L'égalité juridique des langues et l'enseignement: les écoles françaises hors-Québec," (1983) 24 C. de D. 157.

Thus, the Court found it clear that this specific statute "was very much in the minds of the framers of the Constitution when they enacted s. 23 of the *Charter*." In these circumstances, the limits on s. 23 rights imposed by Bill 101 "cannot possibly have been regarded by the framers of the Constitution as coming within 'such reasonable limits prescribed by law as can be demonstrably justified in a free and democratic society.'" Departing from the "living tree" approach, the Court effectuated what it believed to be the actual intent of the drafters.[13]

FORD v. QUEBEC (ATTORNEY-GENERAL)
SUPREME COURT OF CANADA
[1988] 2 S.C.R. 712, 54 D.L.R. 4th 577

[Before DICKSON C.J.C., BEETZ, ESTEY, McINTYRE, LAMER, WILSON and LE DAIN JJ. (ESTEY and LE DAIN JJ. did not take part in the judgment.)]

BY THE COURT: — The principal issue in this appeal is whether ss. 58 and 69 of the Quebec *Charter of the French Language*, R.S.Q. 1977, c. C-11, which require that public signs and posters and commercial advertising shall be in the French language only and that only the French version of a firm name may be used, infringe the freedom of expression guaranteed by s. 2(b) of the Canadian *Charter of Rights and Freedoms* and s. 3 of the Quebec *Charter of Human Rights and Freedoms*, R.S.Q. 1977, c. C-12. . . .

[As noted in the prior discussion, the mandate for French-only signs in s. 58 of the CFL was enacted by the Parti Quebecois government along with the invocation of the Notwithstanding Clause, but the government pointedly did not invoke a similar clause in the Quebec Charter. Thus, this litigation concerned a challenge to the statute under the provincial charter.]

[Initially, the Court rejected an interpretation of the Quebec Court of Appeal that the invocation of the notwithstanding Clause was improper because it failed to specific precisely which rights or freedoms the legislation was intended to override.]

---

[13] The concept that Courts can manageably distinguish between "limits" on rights to which s. 1 applies and "denials" to which s. 1 does not apply was sharply criticized, see Hogg § 35.6, and has been effectively overruled in the *Ford* case excerpted below. It is interesting to speculate as to why the Court reached that holding, in light of the decision by the Quebec trial court that the infringement of s. 23(1)(b) — that is, the requirement that Anglophone Canadians who move to Quebec must send their children to French language schools — would make such a trivial contribution to Quebec's cultural and linguistic objectives that it could not be regarded as reasonable under s. 1. *See* (1982) 140 D.L.R. (3d) 33, 71–90 (Que. S.C.).

VII WHETHER THE FREEDOM OF EXPRESSION GUARANTEED BY S. 2(b) OF THE CANADIAN *CHARTER OF RIGHTS AND FREEDOMS* AND BY S. 3 OF THE QUEBEC *CHARTER OF HUMAN RIGHTS AND FREE-DOMS* INCLUDES THE FREEDOM TO EXPRESS ONESELF IN THE LANGUAGE OF ONE'S CHOICE

[First, the Court held that the words "freedom of expression" in s. 2(b) of the Canadian *Charter* ("Everyone has the following fundamental freedoms: . . . freedom of thought, belief, opinion, and expression . . .") and s. 3 of the Quebec *Charter* ("Every person is the possessor of the fundamental freedoms, including freedom of conscience, . . . freedom of opinion, freedom of expression . . .") should be given the same meaning. Second, the Court reaffirmed that Charter-protected expression includes the freedom to express oneself in the language of one's choice. The Court referred, in this regard, to its decision in *Reference re Language Rights under Manitoba Act, 1870* (1985), 19 D.L.R. (4th) 1 at p. 19, [1985] 1 S.C.R. 721, at p. 744]:

> The importance of language rights is grounded in the essential role that language plays in human existence, development and dignity. It is through language that we are able to form concepts; to structure and order the world around us. Language bridges the gap between isolation and community, allowing humans to delineate the rights and duties they hold in respect of one another, and thus to live in society.

[The Court further explained:] Language is so intimately related to the form and content of expression that there cannot be true freedom of expression by means of language if one is prohibited from using the language of one's choice. Language is not merely a means or medium of expression; it colours the content and meaning of expression. It is, as the preamble of the *Charter of the French Language* itself indicates, a means by which a people may express its cultural identity. [The Court then quoted from the Preamble: "Whereas the French language, the distinctive language of a people that is in the majority French-speaking, is the instrument by which that people has articulated its identity . . ."]

[Next, the Court rejected the Quebec Attorney-General's argument that the express guarantees of language rights in s. 133 of the Constitution Act, 1867, and ss. 16 to 23 of the Canadian *Charter of Rights and Freedoms* imply that linguistic expression is not protected by s. 2(b).]

[In part VIII of the decision, the Court concluded that the free expression guarantee extends to commercial expression.]

IX WHETHER THE LIMIT IMPOSED ON FREEDOM OF EXPRESSION BY SS. 58 AND 69 OF THE *CHARTER OF THE FRENCH LANGUAGE* IS JUSTIFIED UNDER S. 9.1 OF THE QUEBEC *CHARTER* OF THE HUMAN RIGHTS AND FREEDOMS AND S. 1 OF THE CANADIAN *CHARTER OF RIGHTS AND FREEDOMS*

. . . .

A. *The meaning of* s. *9.1 of the Quebec Charter of Human Rights and Freedoms*

The issue here is whether s. 9.1 is a justificatory provision similar in its purpose and effect to s. 1 of the Canadian *Charter* and, if so, what is the test to be applied under it. Section 9.1 is worded differently from s. 1, and it is convenient to set out the two provisions again for comparison, as well as the test under s. 1. Section 9.1 of the Quebec *Charter of Human Rights and Freedoms*, which was added to the *Charter* by an *Act to amend the Charter of Human Rights and Freedoms* and entered into force by proclamation on October 1, 1983, reads as follows:

> 9.1. In exercising his fundamental freedoms and rights, a person shall maintain a proper regard for democratic values, public order and the general well-being of the citizens of Quebec. In this respect, the scope of the freedom and rights, and limits to their exercise, may be fixed by law.

Section 1 of the Canadian *Charter* provides:

> 1. The Canadian *Charter of Rights and Freedoms* guarantees the rights and freedoms set out in it subject only to such reasonable limits prescribed by law as can be demonstrably justified in a free and democratic society.

* * *

It was suggested in argument that because of its quite different wording s. 9.1 was not a justificatory provision similar to s. 1 but merely a provision indicating that the fundamental freedoms and rights guaranteed by the Quebec *Charter* are not absolute but relative and must be construed and exercised in a manner consistent with the values, interests and considerations indicated in s. 9.1 — "democratic values, public order and the general well-being of the citizens of Quebec." In the case at bar the Superior Court and the Court of Appeal held that s. 9.1 was a justificatory provision corresponding to s. 1 of the Canadian *Charter* and that it was subject, in its application, to a similar test of rational connection and proportionality. This court agrees with that conclusion. The first paragraph of s. 9.1 speaks of the manner in which a person must exercise his fundamental freedoms and rights. That is not a limit on the authority of government but rather does suggest the manner in which the scope of the fundamental freedoms and rights is to be interpreted. The second paragraph of s. 9.1, however — "In this respect, the scope of the freedoms and rights, and limits to their exercise, may be fixed by law"— does refer to legislative authority to impose limits on the fundamental freedoms and rights. The words "In this respect" refer to the words "maintain a proper regard for democratic values, public order and the general well-being of the citizens of Quebec." Read as a whole, s. 9.1 provides that limits to the scope and exercise of the fundamental freedoms and rights guaranteed may be fixed by law for the purpose of maintaining a proper regard for democratic values, public order and the general well-being of the citizens of Quebec. That was the view taken of s. 9.1 in both the Superior Court and the Court of Appeal. As for the applicable test under s. 9.1, Boudreault J. in the Superior Court quoted with approval from a paper delivered by Raynold Langlois, Q.C., entitled "Les clauses limitatives des Chartes canadienne et québécoise des droits et libertés et le fardeau de la preuve," and published in *Perspectives canadiennes et européennes des droits de la personne* (Cowansville: Yvon Blais Inc. 1986), in which the author expressed the view that under s. 9.1 the government must show that the restrictive law is neither irrational nor arbitrary and that the means chosen are proportionate to the end to be served. In the Court of Appeal, Bisson J.A. adopted essentially the same test. He said that under s. 9.1 the government has the onus of demonstrating on a balance of probabilities that the impugned means are proportional to the object sought. He also spoke of the necessity that the government show the absence of an irrational or arbitrary character in the limit imposed by law and that there is a rational link between the means and the end pursued. We are in general agreement with this approach. The Attorney-General of Quebec submitted that s. 9.1 left more scope to the legislature than s. 1 and only conferred judicial control of "la finalité des lois," which this court understands to mean the purposes or objects of the law limiting a guaranteed freedom or right, and not the means chosen to attain the purpose or object. What this would mean is that it would be a sufficient justification if the purpose or object of legislation limiting a fundamental freedom or right fell within the general description provided by the words "democratic values, public order and the general well-being of the citizens of Quebec." It cannot have been intended that s. 9.1 should confer such a broad and virtually unrestricted legislative authority to limit fundamental freedoms and rights. Rather, it is an implication of the requirement that a limit serve one of these ends that the limit should be rationally connected to the legislative purpose and that the legislative means be proportionate to the end to be served. That is implicit in a provision that prescribes that certain values or legislative purposes may prevail in particular circumstances over a fundamental freedom or right. That necessarily implies a balancing exercise and the appropriate test for such balancing is one of rational connection and proportionality.

B. *Whether the prohibition of the use of any language other than French by* ss. *58 and 69 of the Charter of the French Language is a "limit" on freedom of expression within the meaning of* s. *1 of the Canadian Charter and* s. *9.1 of the Quebec Charter*

[In *Quebec Association of Protestant School Boards, supra,* the Court held that the *Charter of the French Language* could not be defended as a reasonable limit on minority language educational rights created by s. 23 of the Canadian *Charter* because the Quebec law was intended to deny, rather than limit, those rights. Here, the plaintiffs likewise claimed that the sign law was a denial rather than a limit on rights and thus s. 1 did not apply. The Court distinguished the precedent, holding that the prior case was "a rather unique example of truly complete denial of guaranteed rights."]

. . . .

D. *Whether the* s. *1 and* s. *9.1 materials justify the prohibition of the use of any language other than French*

[Here, the Court discusses the materials offered to justify the statute's limitation on expression. The Court acknowledged that "the material amply establishes the importance of the legislative purpose reflected in the *Charter of the French Language* and that it is a response to a substantial and pressing need."] The causal factors for the threatened position of the French language that have generally been identified are: (a) the declining birth rate of Quebec Francophones resulting in a decline in the Quebec Francophone proportion of the Canadian population as a whole; (b) the decline of the Francophone population outside Quebec as a result of assimilation; (c) the greater rate of assimilation of immigrants to Quebec by the Anglophone community of Quebec; and (d) the continuing dominance of English at the higher levels of the economic sector. These factors have favoured the use of the English language despite the predominance in Quebec of a Francophone population. Thus, in the period prior to the enactment of the legislation at issue, the "visage linguistique" of Quebec often gave the impression that English had become as significant as French. This "visage linguistique" reinforced the concern among Francophones that English was gaining in importance, that the French language was threatened and that it would ultimately disappear. It strongly suggested to young and ambitious Francophones that the language of success was almost exclusively English. It confirmed to Anglophones that there was no great need to learn the majority language. And it suggested to immigrants that the prudent course lay in joining the Anglophone community. The aim of such provisions as ss. 58 and 69 of the *Charter of the French Language* was, in the words of its preamble, "to see the quality and influence of the French language assured." The threat to the French language demonstrated to the government that it should, in particular, take steps to assure that the "visage linguistique" of Quebec would reflect the predominance of the French language.

The s. 1 and s. 9.1 materials establish that the aim of the language policy underlying the *Charter of the French Language* was a serious and legitimate one. They indicate the concern about the survival of the French language and the perceived need for an adequate legislative response to the problem. Moreover, they indicate a rational connection between protecting the French language and assuring that the reality of Quebec society is communicated through the "visage linguistique." The s. 1 and s. 9.1 materials do not, however, demonstrate that the requirement of the use of French only is either necessary for the achievement of the legislative objective or proportionate to it. That specific question is simply not addressed by the materials. Indeed, in his factum and oral argument the Attorney-General of Quebec did not attempt to justify the requirement of the exclusive use of French. He submitted that [statutory provisions for administrative exemptions] exceptions to the requirement of the exclusive use of French indicate the concern for carefully designed measures and for interfering as little as possible with commercial expression. The qualifications of the requirement of the exclusive use of French in other provisions of the *Charter of the French Language* and the regulations do not make ss. 58 and 69 any less prohibitions of the use of any language other than French as applied to the respondents. The issue is whether any such prohibition is justified. In the opinion of this court it has not been demonstrated that the prohibition of the use of any language other than French in ss. 58 and 69 of the *Charter of the French Language* is necessary to the defence and enhancement of the status of the French language in Quebec or that it is proportionate to that legislative purpose. Since the evidence put to us by the government showed that the predominance of the French language was not reflected in the "visage linguistique" of Quebec, the governmental response could well have been tailored to meet that specific problem and to impair freedom of expression minimally. Thus, whereas requiring the predominant display of the

French language, even its marked predominance, would be proportional to the goal of promoting and maintaining a French "visage linguistique" in Quebec and therefore justified under s. 9.1 of the Quebec *Charter* and s. 1 of the Canadian *Charter*, requiring the exclusive use of French has not been so justified. French could be required in addition to any other language or it could be required to have greater visibility than that accorded to other languages. Such measures would ensure that the "visage linguistique" reflected the demography of Quebec: the predominant language is French. This reality should be communicated to all citizens and non-citizens alike, irrespective of their mother tongue. But exclusivity for the French language has not survived the scrutiny of a proportionality test and does not reflect the reality of Quebec society. Accordingly, we are of the view that the limit imposed on freedom of expression by s. 58 of the *Charter of the French Language* respecting the exclusive use of French on public signs and posters and in commercial advertising is not justified under s. 9.1 of the Quebec *Charter*. In like measure, the limit imposed on freedom of expression by s. 69 of the *Charter of the French Language* respecting the exclusive use of the French version of a firm name is not justified under either s. 9.1 of the Quebec *Charter* or s. 1 of the Canadian *Charter*.

The critical holding of *Ford v. Quebec* was that the complete prohibition on English language signs was not necessary to achieve the *visage linguistique* sought by the *Charter of the French Language*. The Court's reasoning seems much stronger if the purpose of the bill was simply to create a *visage linguistique* that made it clear that Quebec was a predominantly-French province. Consider, however, an alternative purpose — to recognize the injustice that, to succeed and flourish in North America, Francophone Quebecois needed to learn English, but that, even after seven generations, many Anglophone Quebeckers simply did not need to learn French. As Professor Weiler notes, *supra*, the provisions requiring that French be the language of work significantly eroded this ability of unilingual Anglophones, who had maintained their success despite their linguistic limitations by hiring bilingual Francophones to communicate to their unilingual Francophone workers. Focusing on Anglophones as consumers, the wholesale elimination of English signs might well be necessary and minimally tailored to promote a pressing and substantial interest if that interest were reconceptualized as intending to force all citizens of Quebec to possess at least a minimal knowledge of French sufficient to comprehend public signs and follow up with verbal inquiries in English. On the other hand, it is not clear, since Quebec's government has no interest in requiring Francophones to become bilingual, whether the Court would find such an asymmetrical interest to be legitimate.

We have seen in these cases that judges have employed a variety of interpretive techniques in their reasons for judgment. *Blaikie* gave a broad and purposive interpretation of s. 133 of the BNA Act to expand its bilingualism mandate to government acts not explicitly covered in the text. In *Quebec Protestant School Boards*, the Supreme Court of Canada also went beyond the literal text or broad purposes of the Charter to hold that the Quebec Attorney General could not seek to demonstrate that a statute inconsistent with s. 23 of the Charter was a reasonable limit on Charter rights, reasoning that the drafters of s. 23 specifically intended that the challenged statute would be unconstitutional. Recently, the SCC has seemingly adopted a textualist approach to s. 23. In *Quebec (Recreation, Education and Sports) v. Nguyen*, [2009] 3 S.C.R. 209, the SCC invalidated a Quebec regulation explicitly designed to prevent expansion of the rights granted under s. 23. A number of Canadian citizens residing in Quebec who were not themselves educated in English in Canada (and thus ineligible to send children to English schools) sought to assert s. 23 rights by sending their oldest child to a private English-language school, and then sought to invoke the sibling rights provision of s. 23(2) to send all their children to English schools. When Quebec responded with CFL amendment to preclude this, the SCC held that the amendments were invalid: they violated the parents' s. 23 rights and (reversing *Quebec Protestant School Boards* on the section 1 issue), flunked the *Oakes* test. The Court claimed to be taking a "purposive approach aimed at aimed at identifying the framers' objective at the time of its enactment" [¶ 26]. They recognized that the specific purpose of s. 23(2) would be to allow Canadians who were educating their children in one of the official languages to have the freedom to move throughout Canada and continue that education (thus an immigrant family whose children attended Vancouver English schools could receive English education in Montreal, and an immigrant receiving French-language education in Montreal could assert s. 23 rights in Edmonton) [¶ 27]. But the Court then observed that the text does not distinguish between public and private schools, and thus held that an immigrant arriving in Quebec could assert English-language rights by sending their children to a private school in Quebec. *Id.* Although, in applying the *Oakes* test, the Court acknowledged that the entire structure of s. 23 was designed to permit Quebec to require allophones (those whose native language is neither English nor French) to send their children to French-language schools, the Court carefully reviewed the regulation to determine that it was not proportionate to the specific concerns Quebec had.

9.2.4. Judicial protection of Francophones in English Canada

The next set of decisions interpret minority education provisions of the *Manitoba Act* and the *BNA Act* — which entrench "any right or privilege with respect to denominational schools which any class of persons have" at the time of admission to the Union. Consider whether the courts are using purposive, intentional, or textual reasoning.[14]

It is important to understand the historic context in which the first case arose. Both prior to and after union with Canada, Manitoba's educational system was entirely private and sectarian, albeit state-funded. Taxes supported English Protestant schools and French Catholic schools. The suit challenged Manitoba legislation that created tax-supported public schools, to be taught solely in English,

---

[14] It is worth emphasizing that s. 93 grants are collective or group rights. In contrast, in *Meyer v. Nebraska*, 262 U.S. 390 (1923), the Court held that a state law prohibiting education in a foreign language unconstitutionally violated individual rights of parents with regard to their children's education. (The statute, passed in the wake of World War I, was directed at German immigrants.) Section 93 grants no such rights — only the collective rights of the predominantly Francophone Catholics and the predominantly Anglophone Protestants to maintain pre-existing rights and privileges.

while allowing French Catholics the right to continue to support unsubsidized private schools if they so desired.[15]

Most of the province of Manitoba was previously part of a large area called Rupert's Land, owned outright by the Hudson Bay Company. To foreclose feared western expansion by the U.S., which had just purchased Alaska, Prime Minister Sir John MacDonald arranged to purchase Rupert's Land from the Hudson Bay Co. for $1.5m + 5% of fertile land. When Canadian surveyors along the Red River ignored property rights of Métis Indians, Louis Riel (a Franco-Manitoban) and armed horsemen broke up the party, organized the Métis, prevented the Lt. Governor-designate from entering the province, seized a fort, put down an attempted overthrow by a pro-Canadian group, assumed the provincial presidency, and carried out the death sentence on an Anglo-Protestant rebel who tried to kill him (fueling anti-Catholic sentiment in Ontario). Apparently, the only quick way to send Canadian troops into Manitoba was through the U.S., and because of national pride MacDonald didn't want to get U.S. approval. So he agreed to deal with Riel, who sent a delegation to Ottawa with demands, which were agreed to and incorporated into the *Manitoba Act*. Its provisions creating a bilingual province and expanding upon the denominational schools guarantee applicable to Ontario and Quebec in s. 93 of the BNA Act were seen by Franco-Manitobans as a key element of the bargain on which the rebellion was peaceably ended and the Métis agreed to support the admission of Manitoba into confederation.

In 1871, when Manitoba was admitted to Canada, its population was 5,700 Francophone mixed; 4,000 Anglophone mixed; 1,600 "white" [presumably Anglo]. The 1891 census: 152,500, of whom only 10,000 were Francophone. This led to legislation creating one system of public schools, with education in English. After the bill's passage, Franco-Manitobans implored the federal government to use the

---

[15] The basic issue in *Barrett* was that "a tax to support public education levied on all rate payers made it difficult if not impossible for those who desired denominational education for their children to finance it." Gordon Bale, *Law, Politics and the Manitoba School Question: Supreme Court and Privy Council* (1985), 63 Can. Bar. Rev. 461, 474. The points made by Manitoba Catholics concerning the significant adverse impact of public schools on their ability to instruct their children according to their own religion can also be made by American Catholics. The issue has never been seriously considered by the U.S. Supreme Court however. Direct public aid to religious schools would violate the Establishment Clause of the First Amendment to the U.S. Constitution. Canada, in contrast, has no such constitutional provision. Indeed, s. 93 of the *Constitution Act, 1867* actually requires public funding for Catholic and Protestant denominational schools if, as was the case in Ontario, such funding existed at confederation. Because the U.S. Supreme Court uses separate tests to analyze whether governmental conduct offends the conflicting goals of the Establishment and Free Exercise Clauses of the First Amendment, a serious inquiry into whether the resulting doctrine strikes the appropriate balance between the two clauses has not been made.

Section 116 of the Australian Constitution prohibits laws "for establishing any religion, or for imposing any religious observance, or for prohibiting the free exercise of any religion . . . ." In the only case to date on the establishment "limb," state funding for religious schools was held not to breach s 116 (*Attorney-General (Vic); Ex rel Black v. Commonwealth* (1981) 145 CLR 559), since funding did not amount to elevating a nationally recognised religion. Regarding the "free exercise" limb, the HCA held that compulsory military service did not prohibit the free exercise of a pacifist religion, *Krygger v. Williams* (1912) 15 CLR 366, since "[t]o require a man to do a thing which has nothing at all to do with religion is not prohibiting him from a free exercise of religion." As in the U.S., this test is not related to the "establishment" test. (There is no case law on the "imposing religious observance" limb.)

general disallowance power in the BNA Act. Federal politicians in both parties sought to avoid the exercise of this power: Prime Minister John A. MacDonald (Conservative) wished to avoid antagonizing Protestant voters in Manitoba and Ontario; Opposition Leader Wilfred Laurier (Liberal) was generally a critic of federal disallowance. Franco-Manitobans were persuaded to first launch a legal challenge to the legislation. Following the *Barrett* case, below, they again turned to Parliament to overturn the Manitoba law, using the power specifically provided in the *Manitoba Act*. Conservative leader Charles Tupper, who had just become Prime Minister amidst continuing disarray among the Tories following the long tenure of recently deceased founding P.M. Sir John A. McDonald, was inclined to support the Franco-Manitobans, but before legislation could be passed he had to call an election. Liberal leader Wilfred Laurier, from Quebec, opposed the use of the disallowance power, which he feared would come back to haunt Quebec. A compromise was agreed to between Laurier and Manitoba Premier Greenway in 1896, which allowed some public schools to teach Catholicism in French. This deal was abrogated, with no federal response, in 1916. (Laurier's position is consistent with the traditional view of many Quebec politicians — prior to Pierre Trudeau and his vision of a strong, bilingual, national government — that federal intervention to protect Francophone minorities in English Canada created too grave a risk that Ottawa would then turn its attention to Quebec City and potentially interfere with Quebec's treatment of its Anglophone minority.)

BARRETT v. CITY OF WINNIPEG

SUPREME COURT OF CANADA

(1891) 19 S.C.R. 374

Sir W. J. RITCHIE C.J. — This is an application to quash two by-laws of the municipal corporation of the city of Winnipeg, which were passed for levying a rate for municipal and school purposes in that city for the year 1890, and they assess all real and personal property in the city for such purpose. It is asked that these by-laws be quashed for illegality on the following among other grounds: That because by the said by-laws the amount to be levied for school purposes for the Protestant and Roman Catholic schools are united, and one rate levied upon Protestants and Roman Catholics alike for the whole sum.

[The relevant statute, s. 22 of the *Manitoba Act*, which was the federal statute creating the new province and thus analogous to the American Northwest Ordinance in creating a basic charter for the province, provided that the provincial legislature "may exclusively make laws in relation to education," subject, however, to the condition that "Nothing in any such law shall prejudicially affect any right or privilege with respect to denominational schools which any class of persons have by law or practice in the province at the Union."]

It must be assumed that in legislating with reference to a constitution for Manitoba the Dominion Parliament was well acquainted with the conditions of the country to which it was about to give a constitution, and they must have known full well that at that time there were no schools established by law, religious or secular, public or sectarian. In such a state of affairs, and having reference to the condition of the population, and the deep interest felt and strong opinions entertained on the subject of separate schools, it cannot be supposed that the legislature had not its attention more particularly directed to the educational institutions of Manitoba, and more especially to the schools then in practical operation, their constitution, mode of support and peculiar character in matters of religious instruction. To have overlooked considerations of this kind is to impute to parliament a degree of short-sightedness and indifference which, in view of the discussions relating to separate schools which had taken place in the older provinces, or some of them, and to the extreme vigilance with which educational questions are scanned and the importance attached to them, more particularly by the Catholic Church as testified to by Monseigneur Taché, cannot to my mind be for a moment entertained. Read in the light of considerations such as these must we not conclude that the legislature well weighed its language and intended that every word it used should have force and effect?

The *British North America Act* confers on the local legislature the exclusive power to make laws in relation to education, provided nothing in such laws shall prejudicially affect any right or privilege, with respect to denominational schools, which any class of persons had by law in the province at the union, but the *Manitoba Act* goes much further and declares that nothing in such law shall prejudicially affect any right or privilege with respect to denominational schools which any class of persons had by law or practice in the province at the union. We are now practically asked to reject the words "or practice" and construe the statute as if they had not been used, and to read this restrictive clause out of the statute as being inapplicable to the existing state of things in Manitoba at the union, whereas on the contrary, I think, by the insertion of the words "or practice" it was made practically applicable to the condition at the time of the educational institutions, which were, unquestionably and solely as the evidence shows, of a denominational character. It is clear that at the time of the passing of the Manitoba Act no class of persons had by law any rights or privileges secured to them; so if we reject the words "or practice" as meaningless or inoperative we shall be practically expunging the whole of the restrictive clause from the statute. I know of no rule of construction to justify such a proceeding unless the clause is wholly unintelligible or incapable of any reasonable construction. The words used, in my opinion, are of no doubtful import, but are, on the contrary, plain, certain and unambiguous, and must be read in their ordinary grammatical sense. Effect should be given to all the words in the statute, nothing adding thereto, nothing diminishing therefrom.

* * *

It is a settled canon of construction that no clause, sentence or word, shall be construed superfluous, void or insignificant if it can be prevented.

While it is quite clear that at the time of the passing of this act there were no denominational or other schools established and recognized by law, it is equally clear that there were at that time in actual operation or practice a system of denominational schools in Manitoba well established and the *de facto* rights and privileges of which were enjoyed by a large class of persons. What then was there more reasonable than that the legislature should protect and preserve to such class of persons those rights and privileges they enjoyed in practice, though not theretofore secured to them by law, but which the Dominion Parliament appears to have deemed it just should not, after the coming into operation of the new provincial constitution, be prejudicially affected by the action of the local legislature?

* * *

The only questions, it strikes me, we are now called upon to consider is: Does this Public School Act prejudicially affect the class of persons who in practice enjoyed the rights and privileges of denominational schools at the time of the union? * * *

But it is said that the Catholics as a class are not prejudicially affected by this act. Does it not prejudicially, that is to say injuriously, disadvantageously, which is the meaning of the word "prejudicially," affect them when they are taxed to support schools of the benefit of which, by their religious belief and the rules and principles of their church, they cannot conscientiously avail themselves, and at the same time by compelling them to find means to support schools to which they can conscientiously send the children, or in the event of their not being able to find sufficient means to do both to be compelled to allow their children to go without either religious or secular instruction? In other words, I think the Catholics were directly prejudicially affected by such legislation, but whether directly or indirectly the local legislature was powerless to affect them prejudicially in the matter of denominational schools, which they certainly did by practically depriving them of their denominational schools and compelling them to support schools the benefit of which Protestants alone can enjoy.

In my opinion the *Public Schools Act is ultra vires* and the by-laws of the city of Winnipeg, Nos. 480 and 483, should be quashed and this appeal allowed with costs.

STRONG J.— I have read the judgment prepared by the Chief Justice, and entirely concur in the conclusion at which he has arrived as well as in the reasons he has given therefor. I have nothing to add to what he has said.

FOURNIER, J.: — [Translated.]

* * *

By the Act 53 Vic. C. 38, the system of separate schools, Catholic and Protestant which had been established in accordance with the constitutional Act of Manitoba, 33 Vict. C. 3, was completely abolished after having been in force for nineteen years.

It is important for the decision of this question to carry oneself back to the circumstance which preceded the entrance of that Province into the Canadian confederation. We remember that it was at the close of a rebellion which had thrown the population into a profound and violent agitation, aroused religious and national passions, and occasioned great disorders, necessitating the intervention of the Federal Government. It was with the object of re-establishing public peace and conciliating the population that the Federal government granted to them the constitution which they have until now enjoyed.

The principle of separate schools introduced into the British North America Act by sect. 93 was also introduced into the constitution of Manitoba, and declared to be applicable to the separate schools which existed in fact in this territory before its organization into a Province. The population was then divided almost equally between Catholics and Protestants.

* * *

[In an affidavit, the Catholic] Archbishop asserts that the Church considers the schools established in virtue of the Public Schools Act as unfit for the education of Catholic children, and that the children will not attend them; that rather than encourage these schools the Catholics will prefer to return to the system existing before the Manitoba Act, and will establish and maintain schools in conformity with the principles of their faith; that the Protestants are satisfied with the system of education established by the Public School Act because these schools resemble those which they maintained before the repeal of the former Acts introducing the system of separate schools over which they had absolute control.

* * *

What was the reason for the introduction of that restriction in sect. 93 and for what reasons was it extended to the right which was based only on the practice in Manitoba at the time of the passage of the Act 33 Vict. C. 3?

[Justice Fournier traced the history of constitutional protection of denominational rights. Section 93 clearly applied to Ontario and Quebec, where the law allowed minorities the right to have separate schools. In establishing those schools the minorities were exempt from contributing to the support of the public schools and had a right to a share of the public grant. In New Brunswick, by contrast, there was no legal right to separate state-supported schools. Legislation creating a unified public school system was thus upheld as consistent with s. 93 of the *BNA Act*. Justice Fournier concluded: "the words 'by practice' had been introduced into the *Manitoba Act* in order to prevent the difficulties which had arisen in New Brunswick."]

It would be absurd to pretend that the privilege guaranteed to Catholics by the words "by practice" should be understood as that of having separate schools like private schools supported by themselves. This privilege existing of common right would not require any legislation and the expression "by practice" would be then altogether useless and without any meaning. The Federal Parliament, knowing of the existence in the territory of separate schools and the fact that there was no law authorizing them, while it desired to secure their legal existence after the union understood that the provisions alone of the British North America Act would not suffice for this object. It was without doubt for this reason that sect. 93 was modified by the addition of the words "by practice." It is then a provision which instead of not having any meaning wisely fills an important gap which existed in the organization of the Province. It is in this case proper to apply the rule which requires that when the language of the law admits of two interpretations one of which would be absurd, and the other reasonable and salutary the latter should be adopted as in accordance with the intention of the legislator.

* * *

It is not difficult to see which of these two constructions is the more reasonable and the more just. If the construction of the words "by practice" was not sufficient to give them the right to maintain their separate schools the Catholics would be taxed for schools which they would not be able to attend and of which the Protestants alone would have the benefit. While on the other hand if we give to the words "by practice" their true construction the schools of the Catholics will be recognized by law. These words "by practice" have without doubt been introduced into the *Manitoba Act* only for the purpose of assuring that those who should desire it the right to maintain their separate schools and of sanctioning their legal existence.

* * *

TASCHEREAU, J.: — [Translated.]

* * *

The law of 1890, says the respondent, does, it is true, oblige Catholics to contribute to free schools, but it does not oblige them to send their children to them. It does not forbid them either from having separate schools; it does not then prejudice in any way any of the rights and privileges conferred on them by custom before the union, consequently it is *intra vires*. I think this reasoning altogether erroneous. In fact I should have been disposed not to believe it serious if it had not received the sanction of the provincial tribunal. To what in effect does it amount? To cause to be said by the non-Catholic majority to the Catholic minority: "you have the privilege of having your schools; we leave it to you provided you help us to support ours. You cannot send your children to our schools, but we do not oblige you to do so all that we demand of you is to pay for instructing ours." I seek in vain in the record proof that this was the custom before the union. I find there quite the opposite.

Is it possible moreover to imagine a system like that which the respondent would wish to enforce in Manitoba, and at the same time to recognize the right of the minority to separate schools, a right which the respondent could not deny in face of sect. 22 of the constitutional Act of 1870? It is plain that the legislator foreseeing that in the future one or other of the two classes, Protestant or Catholic must of necessity prevail by number in the projected Province makes by this section an enactment for both cases. They were then almost equally divided, to judge by the first legislation of the new Province on the subject in 1871, when it appears that the board of education was composed equally of Catholics and of Protestants with a superintendent for each of these two classes and with an equal division of the government grant. In that state of things Parliament by sect. 22 of the Act provides for both of these results. The first sub-section which I have cited at length assures to the minority, whether Catholic or Protestant, the rights up to that time conferred on them by practice, and the second sub-section gives them the right of appeal to the Governor-General in Council from all legislation affecting any of their rights in the matter. Had the Protestant population happened to be in the minority they could not have been compelled to contribute to the support of Catholic schools. They would have claimed the same right to their own schools as their co-religionists enjoy in the Province of Quebec complete and unfettered, that is to say, free from taxation for Catholic schools. To-day the Catholics forming the minority claim only the same right and the free exercise of that right. I am of opinion that their claim is well founded. They have a right to their system of schools such as their co-religionists enjoy in Ontario or on the same principle. It is with this object, and with this object alone, at least I am unable to view the matter otherwise, that this special provision relative to separate schools taken from the British North America Act was inserted in the constitutional Act of 1870 with the addition of the words "or by practice," — words rendered necessary as I have said, to fully express the intention of the legislator, and to accomplish his purpose, owing to the well known fact that there did not then exist on the subject in these regions any law,m and that the whole matter was there governed by practice and by practice alone.

* * *

PATTERSON, J. — [opinion omitted]

CITY OF WINNIPEG v. BARRETT
JUDICIAL COMMITTEE OF THE PRIVY COUNCIL
[1892] A.C. 445

The judgment of their Lordships was delivered by—

LORD MACNAGHTEN: —

* * *

The controversy which has given rise to the present litigation is, no doubt, beset with difficulties. The result of the controversy is of serious moment to the province of Manitoba, and a matter apparently of deep interest throughout the Dominion. But in its legal aspect the question lies in a very narrow compass. The duty of this Board is simply to determine as a matter of law whether, according to the true construction of the *Manitoba Act*, 1870, having regard to the state of things which existed in Manitoba at the time of the Union, the provincial legislature has or has not exceeded its powers in passing the *Public Schools Act, 1890*.

[Manitoba initially argued that because, like s. 93 of the *BNA Act*, subsection 3 of the *Manitoba Act* allowed Parliament to disallow provincial legislation that violated section 22, there was no basis for judicial review of the political remedy. The Privy Council first determined that the case was justiciable.]

* * *

Now, if the state of things which the archbishop describes as existing before the Union had been a system established by law, what would have been the rights and privileges of the Roman Catholics with respect to denominational schools? They would have had by law the right to establish schools at their own expense, to maintain their schools by school fees or voluntary contributions, and to conduct them in accordance with their own religious tenets. Every other religious body, which was engaged in a similar work at the time of the Union, would have had precisely the same right with respect to their denominational schools. Possibly this right, if it had been defined or recognized by positive enactment, might have had attached to it as a necessary or appropriate incident the right of exemption from any contribution under any circumstances to schools of a different denomination. But, in their Lordships' opinion, it would be going much too far to hold that the establishment of a national system of education upon an unsectarian basis is so inconsistent with the right to set up and maintain denominational schools that the two things cannot exist together, or that the existence of the one necessarily implies or involves immunity from taxation for the purpose of the other. It has been objected that if the rights of Roman Catholics, and of other religious bodies, in respect of their denominational schools, are to be so strictly measured and limited by the practice which actually prevailed at the time of the Union, they will be reduced to the condition of a "natural right" which "does not want any legislation to protect it." Such a right, it was said, cannot be called a privilege in any proper sense of the word. If that be so, the only result is that the protection which the Act purports to extend to rights and privileges existing "by practice" has no more operation than the protection which it purports to afford to rights and privileges existing "by law." It can hardly be contended that, in order to give a substantial operation and effect to a saving clause expressed in general terms, it is incumbent upon the Court to discover privileges which are not apparent of themselves, or to ascribe distinctive and peculiar features to rights which seem to be of such a common type as not to deserve special notice or require special protection.

* * *

Notwithstanding the Public Schools Act, 1890, Roman Catholics and members of every other religious body in Manitoba are free to establish schools throughout the province; they are free to maintain their schools by school fees or voluntary subscriptions; they are free to conduct their schools according to their own religious tenets without molestation or interference. No child is compelled to attend a public school. No special advantage other than the advantage of a free education in schools conducted under public management is held out to those who do attend. But then it is said that it is impossible for Roman Catholics, or for members of the Church of England (if their views are correctly represented by the Bishop of Rupert's Land, who has given evidence in Logan's case), to send their children to public schools were the education is not superintended and directed by the authorities of their Church, and that therefore Roman Catholics and members of the Church of England who are taxed for public schools, and at the same time feel themselves compelled to support their own schools, are in a less favourable position than those who can take advantage of the free education provided by the Act of 1890. That may be so. But what right or privilege is violated or prejudicially affected by the law? It is not the law that is in fault. It is owing to religious convictions which everybody must respect, and to the teaching of their Church, that Roman Catholics and members of the Church of England find themselves unable to partake of advantages which the law offers to all alike.

* * *

Consider, in a similar vein, the decision in *Ottawa Separate School Trustees v. Mackell*, [1917] A.C. 62, 32 D.L.R. 1 (1916) (P.C.), upholding a regulation issued by the Ontario provincial department of education mandating Catholic education in English. The Court narrowly construed s. 93 to protect the rights of Catholics to attend denominational schools but not the rights of Francophone Catholics to provide the denominational education in French.

Sections 16-20 of the Charter made the federal government and the government of New Brunswick officially bilingual. (It was Pierre Trudeau's fervent wish that all provinces would similarly commit to bilingualism, and s. 43 of the Charter provides a mechanism for other provinces to do so in the future. There has been no recent movement in this regard.) The provisions go further than s. 133 of the *British North America Act* (English in Quebec) and s. 22 of the *Manitoba Act* (French in Manitoba). Specifically, s. 19(2) provides that either English or French may be used in any New Brunswick court. In *Societé des Acadiens v. Association of Parents*, [1986] 1 S.C.R. 549, the Supreme Court of Canada held that s. 19(2) did not disqualify unilingual Anglophone judges from hearing a case, providing that translators were used. The case was entirely manufactured by all parties in order to litigate symbolically important issues,[16] and the result could have been justified under several less controversial approaches. The case was significant, however, because Justice Beetz, for the majority, rejected the "liberal interpretative approach" that, as the dissent noted, is the usual interpretive method in interpreting the Charter. Rather, the majority distinguished language rights:

> Unlike language rights which are based on political compromise, legal rights tend to be seminal in nature because they are rooted in principle. Some of them, such as the one expressed in s. 7 of the *Charter*, are so broad as to call for frequent judicial determination.
>
> Language rights, on the other hand, although some of them have been enlarged and incorporated into the *Charter*, remain nonetheless founded on political compromise.
>
> This essential difference between the two types of rights dictates a distinct judicial approach with respect to each. More particularly, the courts should pause before they decide to act as instruments of change with

---

[16] The interpretation of the Charter's provisions regarding New Brunswick's bilingual status were ancillary to pending litigation over whether the local school board could offer French-immersion programs to Francophone students in English schools. (One suspects the plaintiffs feared that these programs would detract from the popularity and viability of French-language schools that Francophones had the right to attend under s. 23 of the Charter.) The respondent association of Anglophone parents (who presumably favored French-immersion programs to increase the numbers and diversity of English schools as well as to provide stronger opportunities for some Anglophone students to learn French) sought to intervene in the Court of Appeal to defend the controversial program's legality. The three-judge panel hearing the motion included Judge Stuart Stratton, whose knowledge of French was limited. Although a New Brunswick statute gives all Francophones the right to be heard in French in New Brunswick courts, the Supreme Court of Canada decided the Charter issue anyway.

Section 13(1) of the *Official Languages of New Brunswick Act*, R.S.N.B. 1973, c. O-1, provides that a litigant "may be heard in the official language of his choice and such choice is not to place that person at any disadvantage," so the Court could have disposed of the issue on statutory grounds. Even if the Court felt it necessary to reach the Charter issue, the Court could have held that s. 19(2) needed to be construed more narrowly because its wording — "French may be used" — is less sweeping than the language applicable to communications with government bureaucrats in s. 20 of the Charter (granting New Brunswickers the "right to communicate with" a provincial office in French).

respect to language rights. This is not to say that language rights provisions are cast in stone and should remain immune altogether from judicial interpretation. But, in my opinion, the courts should approach them with more restraint than they would in construing legal rights.

The majority also employed an originalist methodology in bolstering its narrow approach to Charter language rights:

It is public knowledge that some provinces other than New Brunswick — and apart from Quebec and Manitoba — were expected ultimately to opt into the constitutional scheme or part of the constitutional scheme prescribed by ss. 16 to 22 of the *Charter*, and a flexible form of constitutional amendment was provided to achieve such an advancement of language rights. But again, this is a form of advancement brought about through a political process, not a judicial one.

If however the provinces were told that the scheme provided by ss. 16 to 22 of the *Charter* was inherently dynamic and progressive, apart from legislation and constitutional amendment, and that the speed of progress of this scheme was to be controlled mainly by the courts, they would have no means to know with relative precision what it was that they were opting into. This would certainly increase their hesitation in so doing and would run contrary to the principle of advancement contained in s. 16(3).

This approach, in turn, was reversed by the Court, again in dicta, in *Beaulac v. The Queen*, [1999] 1 S.C.R. 768. The case did not involve the Charter but rather the interpretation of s. 530(4) of the *Criminal Code*, which gives the accused the right to a trial in his own language, even if not timely requested, if the judges is "satisfied that it is in the best interests of justice." Beaulac was accused of first-degree murder in British Columbia, and his first trial ended in mistrial with the second conviction overturned because of otherwise improper jury instructions. Based on the difficulty of composing a Francophone jury in Vancouver and Beaulac's fluency in English, the trial judge denied his request that his third trial be conducted in French. The majority reversed, construing the statute broadly and rejecting administrative costs as a valid reason to reject the request. Again, this decision could have been based on a variety of sound principles of statutory interpretation, but the majority (over the objection of two justices) expressly rejected the reasoning of *Societe des Acadiens*, holding that language rights "must in all cases be interpreted purposively, in a manner consistent with the preservation and development of official language communities in Canada." Writing for the majority, Justice Michel Bastarache[17] cited with approval a law review article that argued that other Charter rights, including those in ss. 7 and 15, were the result of political compromise and that "there is no basis in the constitutional history of Canada for holding that any such political compromises require a restrictive interpretation of constitutional guarantees." Although *Beaulac* was a matter of statutory interpretation, it's

---

[17] Bastarache, appointed to the Supreme Court of Canada by the Chrétien government in 1997, is a Francophone from New Brunswick (a province that is formally bilingual and has the largest Francophone minority in the country). He argued a number of language rights cases in the Supreme Court of Canada, including the *Manitoba Language Rights* cases cited herein and the *Mahé* case excerpted in Part III of this Chapter, and is the coauthor of a text on language rights in Canada.

teaching that language rights are to be given a "liberal and purposive interpretation" consistent with "the preservation and development of official language communities in Canada" was accepted for purposes of Charter interpretation in *DesRochers v. Canada*, [2009] 1 S.C.R. 194, at ¶ 31.

9.3. SEGUE: IS SEPARATE BUT EQUAL INHERENTLY UNEQUAL?

BROWN v. BOARD OF EDUCATION OF TOPEKA
SUPREME COURT OF THE UNITED STATES
347 U.S. 483 (1954)

MR. CHIEF JUSTICE WARREN delivered the opinion of the Court.

These cases come to us from the States of Kansas, South Carolina, Virginia, and Delaware. They are premised on different facts and different local conditions, but a common legal question justifies their consideration together in this consolidated opinion.[18]

In each of the cases, minors of the Negro race, through their legal representa-

---

[18] [FN 34] In the Kansas case, *Brown v. Board of Education*, the plaintiffs are Negro children of elementary school age residing in Topeka. * * * The three-judge District Court, convened under 28 U.S.C. §§ 2281 and 2284, found that segregation in public education has a detrimental effect upon Negro children, but denied relief on the ground that the Negro and white schools were substantially equal with respect to buildings, transportation, curricula, and educational qualifications of teachers. 98 F. Supp. 797. The case is here on direct appeal under 28 U.S.C. § 1253.

In the South Carolina case, *Briggs v. Elliott*, the plaintiffs are Negro children of both elementary and high school age residing in Clarendon County. They brought this action in the United States District Court for the Eastern District of South Carolina to enjoin enforcement of provisions in the state constitution and statutory code which require the segregation of Negroes and whites in public schools. S. C. Const., Art. XI, § 7; S. C. Code § 5377 (1942). The three-judge District Court, convened under 28 U. S. C. §§ 2281 and 2284, denied the requested relief. The court found that the Negro schools were inferior to the white schools and ordered the defendants to begin immediately to equalize the facilities. But the court sustained the validity of the contested provisions and denied the plaintiffs admission to the white schools during the equalization program. 98 F. Supp. 529 342 U.S. 350.On remand, the District Court found that substantial equality had been achieved except for buildings and that the defendants were proceeding to rectify this inequality as well. 103 F. Supp. 920. The case is again here on direct appeal under 28 U. S. C. § 1253.

[The Virginia case, *Davis v. County School Board*, is substantially similar to the South Carolina case.]

In the Delaware case, *Gebhart v. Belton*, the plaintiffs are Negro children of both elementary and high school age residing in New Castle County. * * * The Chancellor gave judgment for the plaintiffs and ordered their immediate admission to schools previously attended only by white children, on the ground that the Negro schools were inferior with respect to teacher training, pupil-teacher ratio, extracurricular activities, physical plant, and time and distance involved in travel. 87 A. 2d 862. The Chancellor also found that segregation itself results in an inferior education for Negro children (see note 10, infra), but did not rest his decision on that ground. *Id.*, at 865. The Chancellor's decree was affirmed by the Supreme Court of Delaware, which intimated, however, that the defendants might be able to obtain a modification of the decree after equalization of the Negro and white schools had been accomplished. 91 A. 2d 137, 152. The defendants, contending only that the Delaware courts had erred in ordering the immediate admission of the Negro plaintiffs to the white schools, applied to this Court for certiorari. The writ was granted, 344 U.S. 891. The plaintiffs, who were successful below, did not submit a cross-petition.

728 HOW ARE DEMOCRACY AND HUMAN RIGHTS BEST PROTECTED? CH. 9

tives, seek the aid of the courts in obtaining admission to the public schools of their community on a nonsegregated basis. In each instance, they had been denied admission to schools attended by white children under laws requiring or permitting segregation according to race. This segregation was alleged to deprive the plaintiffs of the equal protection of the laws under the Fourteenth Amendment. In each of the cases other than the Delaware case, a three-judge federal district court denied relief to the plaintiffs on the so-called "separate but equal" doctrine announced by this Court in *Plessy v. Ferguson*, 163 U.S. 537. Under that doctrine, equality of treatment is accorded when the races are provided substantially equal facilities, even though these facilities be separate. In the Delaware case, the Supreme Court of Delaware adhered to that doctrine, but ordered that the plaintiffs be admitted to the white schools because of their superiority to the Negro schools.

The plaintiffs contend that segregated public schools are not "equal" and cannot be made "equal," and that hence they are deprived of the equal protection of the laws. Because of the obvious importance of the question presented, the Court took jurisdiction. Argument was heard in the 1952 Term, and reargument was heard this Term on certain questions propounded by the Court.

Reargument was largely devoted to the circumstances surrounding the adoption of the Fourteenth Amendment in 1868. It covered exhaustively consideration of the Amendment in Congress, ratification by the states, then existing practices in racial segregation, and the views of proponents and opponents of the Amendment. This discussion and our own investigation convince us that, although these sources cast some light, it is not enough to resolve the problem with which we are faced. At best, they are inconclusive. The most avid proponents of the post-War Amendments undoubtedly intended them to remove all legal distinctions among "all persons born or naturalized in the United States." Their opponents, just as certainly, were antagonistic to both the letter and the spirit of the Amendments and wished them to have the most limited effect. What others in Congress and the state legislatures had in mind cannot be determined with any degree of certainty.

An additional reason for the inconclusive nature of the Amendment's history, with respect to segregated schools, is the status of public education at that time. In the South, the movement toward free common schools, supported by general taxation, had not yet taken hold. Education of white children was largely in the hands of private groups. Education of Negroes was almost nonexistent, and practically all of the race were illiterate. In fact, any education of Negroes was forbidden by law in some states. Today, in contrast, many Negroes have achieved outstanding success in the arts and sciences as well as in the business and professional world. It is true that public school education at the time of the Amendment had advanced further in the North, but the effect of the Amendment on Northern States was generally ignored in the congressional debates. Even in the North, the conditions of public education did not approximate those existing today. The curriculum was usually rudimentary; ungraded schools were common in rural areas; the school term was but three months a year in many states; and compulsory school attendance was virtually unknown. As a consequence, it is not surprising that there should be so little in the history of the Fourteenth Amendment relating to its intended effect on public education.

In the first cases in this Court construing the Fourteenth Amendment, decided shortly after its adoption, the Court interpreted it as proscribing all state-imposed discriminations against the Negro race.[19] The doctrine of "separate but equal" did not make its appearance in this Court until 1896 in the case of *Plessy v. Ferguson, supra*, involving not education but transportation. American courts have since labored with the doctrine for over half a century. In this Court, there have been six cases involving the "separate but equal" doctrine in the field of public education. In *Cumming v. County Board of Education*, 175 U.S. 528, and *Gong Lum v. Rice*, 275 U.S. 78, the validity of the doctrine itself was not challenged. In more recent cases, all on the graduate school level, inequality was found in that specific benefits enjoyed by white students were denied to Negro students of the same educational qualifications. *Missouri ex rel. Gaines v. Canada, 305 U.S. 337; Sipuel v. Oklahoma, 332 U.S. 631; Sweatt v. Painter, 339 U.S. 629; McLaurin v. Oklahoma State Regents, 339 U.S. 637*. In none of these cases was it necessary to re-examine the doctrine to grant relief to the Negro plaintiff. And in *Sweatt v. Painter, supra*, the Court expressly reserved decision on the question whether *Plessy v. Ferguson* should be held inapplicable to public education.

In the instant cases, that question is directly presented. Here, unlike *Sweatt v. Painter*, there are findings below that the Negro and white schools involved have been equalized, or are being equalized, with respect to buildings, curricula, qualifications and salaries of teachers, and other "tangible" factors. Our decision, therefore, cannot turn on merely a comparison of these tangible factors in the Negro and white schools involved in each of the cases. We must look instead to the effect of segregation itself on public education.

In approaching this problem, we cannot turn the clock back to 1868 when the Amendment was adopted, or even to 1896 when *Plessy v. Ferguson* was written. We must consider public education in the light of its full development and its present place in American life throughout the Nation. Only in this way can it be determined if segregation in public schools deprives these plaintiffs of the equal protection of the laws.

Today, education is perhaps the most important function of state and local governments. Compulsory school attendance laws and the great expenditures for education both demonstrate our recognition of the importance of education to our

---

[19] [FN 5] *Slaughter-House Cases*, 16 Wall. 36, 67–72 (1873); *Strauder v. West Virginia*, 100 U.S. 303, 307–308 (1880):

"It ordains that no State shall deprive any person of life, liberty, or property, without due process of law, or deny to any person within its jurisdiction the equal protection of the laws. What is this but declaring that the law in the States shall be the same for the black as for the white; that all persons, whether colored or white, shall stand equal before the laws of the States, and, in regard to the colored race, for whose protection the amendment was primarily designed, that no discrimination shall be made against them by law because of their color? The words of the amendment, it is true, are prohibitory, but they contain a necessary implication of a positive immunity, or right, most valuable to the colored race, — the right to exemption from unfriendly legislation against them distinctively as colored, — exemption from legal discriminations, implying inferiority in civil society, lessening the security of their enjoyment of the rights which others enjoy, and discriminations which are steps towards reducing them to the condition of a subject race."

democratic society. It is required in the performance of our most basic public responsibilities, even service in the armed forces. It is the very foundation of good citizenship. Today it is a principal instrument in awakening the child to cultural values, in preparing him for later professional training, and in helping him to adjust normally to his environment. In these days, it is doubtful that any child may reasonably be expected to succeed in life if he is denied the opportunity of an education. Such an opportunity, where the state has undertaken to provide it, is a right which must be made available to all on equal terms.

We come then to the question presented: Does segregation of children in public schools solely on the basis of race, even though the physical facilities and other "tangible" factors may be equal, deprive the children of the minority group of equal educational opportunities? We believe that it does.

In *Sweatt v. Painter, supra,* in finding that a segregated law school for Negroes could not provide them equal educational opportunities, this Court relied in large part on "those qualities which are incapable of objective measurement but which make for greatness in a law school." In *McLaurin v. Oklahoma State Regents, supra,* the Court, in requiring that a Negro admitted to a white graduate school be treated like all other students, again resorted to intangible considerations: ". . . his ability to study, to engage in discussions and exchange views with other students, and, in general, to learn his profession." Such considerations apply with added force to children in grade and high schools. To separate them from others of similar age and qualifications solely because of their race generates a feeling of inferiority as to their status in the community that may affect their hearts and minds in a way unlikely ever to be undone. The effect of this separation on their educational opportunities was well stated by a finding in the Kansas case by a court which nevertheless felt compelled to rule against the Negro plaintiffs:

> "Segregation of white and colored children in public schools has a detrimental effect upon the colored children. The impact is greater when it has the sanction of the law; for the policy of separating the races is usually interpreted as denoting the inferiority of the negro group. A sense of inferiority affects the motivation of a child to learn. Segregation with the sanction of law, therefore, has a tendency to [retard] the educational and mental development of negro children and to deprive them of some of the benefits they would receive in a racial[ly] integrated school system."

Whatever may have been the extent of psychological knowledge at the time of *Plessy v. Ferguson,* this finding is amply supported by modern authority. [Numerous social science citations omitted.] Any language in *Plessy v. Ferguson* contrary to this finding is rejected.

We conclude that in the field of public education the doctrine of "separate but equal" has no place. Separate educational facilities are inherently unequal. Therefore, we hold that the plaintiffs and others similarly situated for whom the actions have been brought are, by reason of the segregation complained of, deprived of the equal protection of the laws guaranteed by the Fourteenth Amendment. * * *

MAHE v. ALBERTA
SUPREME COURT OF CANADA
[1990] 1 S.C.R. 342, 68 D.L.R. (4th) 69

[Before DICKSON C.J. and WILSON, LA FOREST, L'HEUREUX-DUBE, SOPINKA, GONTHIER and CORY JJ.]

The judgment of the Court was delivered by THE CHIEF JUSTICE —

[The litigation is an outgrowth of continuing dissatisfaction with the provision of French language education in Alberta, particularly in Edmonton. The appellants desire a French-language elementary school in Edmonton, which would have the following features: (1) it would instruct Francophone children exclusively in the French language and in a totally "French" environment; (2) it would be administered by a Committee of Parents under the structure of an autonomous French School Board; and (3) it would have a programme reflecting the French linguistic culture. Initially, appellants were encouraged to address their concerns to the Edmonton Roman Catholic Separate School Board (which receives state funding) or to the Edmonton Public School Board. The primarily Anglophone Catholic board studied the issue and created a new school under its direction. In this new school, French is the language of instruction and administration, the personnel are all Francophone, and the stated aim of the school is "to primarily reflect the cultural heritage of the French linguistic minority in Alberta."]

At the heart of this appeal is the claim of the appellants that the term "minority language educational facilities" referred to in s. 23(3)(b) includes administration by distinct school boards. [The provision specifically provides that minority linguistic education rights "includes, where the number of those children so warrants, the right to have them receive that instruction in minority language educational facilities provided out of public funds."] The respondent takes the position that the word "facilities" means a school building. The respondent submits that the rights of the Francophone minority in metropolitan Edmonton have not been denied because those rights are being met with current Francophone educational facilities.

*   *   *

ANALYSIS

*   *   *

There are two general questions which must be answered in order to decide this appeal: (1) do the rights which s. 23 mandates, depending upon the number of students, include a right to management and control; and (2) if so, is the number of students in Edmonton sufficient to invoke this right? I will begin with the first question.

*   *   *

(1) The Purpose of s. 23

The general purpose of s. 23 is clear: it is to preserve and promote the two official languages of Canada, and their respective cultures, by ensuring that each language flourishes, as far as possible, in provinces where it is not spoken by the majority of the population. The section aims at achieving this goal by granting minority language educational rights to minority language parents throughout Canada.

My reference to cultures is significant: it is based on the fact that any broad guarantee of language rights, especially in the context of education, cannot be separated from a concern for the culture associated with the language. Language is more than a mere means of communication, it is part and parcel of the identity and culture of the people speaking it. It is the means by which individuals understand themselves and the world around them. ***

* * *

In addition, it is worth noting that minority schools themselves provide community centres where the promotion and preservation of minority language culture can occur; they provide needed locations where the minority community can meet and facilities which they can use to express their culture.

* * *

In my view the appellants are fully justified in submitting that "history reveals that s. 23 was designed to correct, on a national scale, the progressive erosion of minority official language groups and to give effect to the concept of the 'equal partnership' of the two official language groups in the context of education."

The remedial aspect of s. 23 was indirectly questioned by the respondent and several of the interveners in an argument which they put forward for a "narrow construction" of s. 23. [Ed. note: The Court then quoted at length from the language by Beetz J. in *Societé des Acadiens du Nouveau-Brunswick Inc. v. Association of Parents for Fairness in Education* to the effect that language rights should not be given a broad construction in light of the political compromise that underlay these constitutional provisions. Here in *Mahé*, the Court moved away from that comment. As you recall, the Court in *Beaulac* expressly rejected this language.]

(2) The Context of s. 23(3)(b): An Overview of s. 23

[Here, the Court adopted a "sliding scale" approach, whereby linguistic minorities are entitled to increasing rights as numbers increase, ranging from a separate class within a school to complete control of separate facilities.]

(3) Management and Control Under s. 23(3)(b) — Introduction

* * *

Before directly addressing the question of management and control, I wish to dispose briefly of two arguments raised by the parties. The first, advanced by the appellants, is that s. 23 of the *Charter* should be interpreted in light of the words of ss. 15 and 27 of the *Charter*. [Here, the Court holds that s. 23 was a "comprehensive code for minority language educational rights" with "its own method of internal balancing" that constituted, in effect, an exception to ss. 15 and 27 by providing "special status in comparison to all other linguistic groups in Canada," rather than creating individual rights.]

The second argument, which was advanced by the respondent, is that s. 23 should be interpreted in light of the legislative debates leading up to its introduction. This Court has stated that such debates may be admitted as evidence, but it has also consistently taken the view that they are of minimal relevance (see *Re B.C. Motor Vehicle Act*, [1985] 2 S.C.R. 486, at pp. 506–7). In this case, the evidence from the legislative debates contributes little to the task of interpreting s. 23 and, accordingly, I place no weight upon it.[20]

*   *   *

(4) Management and Control — The Text of s. 23(3)(b)

In my view, the words of s. 23(3)(b) are consistent with and supportive of the conclusion that s. 23 mandates, where the numbers warrant, a measure of management and control. Consider, first, the words of subs. (3)(b) in the context of the entire section. Instruction must take place somewhere and accordingly the right to "instruction" includes an implicit right to be instructed in facilities. If the term "minority language educational facilities" is not viewed as encompassing a degree of management and control, then there would not appear to be any purpose in including it in s. 23. This common sense conclusion militates against interpreting "facilities" as a reference to physical structures. Indeed, once the sliding scale approach is accepted it becomes unnecessary to focus too intently upon the word "facilities." Rather, the text of s. 23 supports viewing the entire term "minority language educational facilities" as setting out an upper level of management and control.

I recognize that the English text of subs. (3)(b) is perhaps ambiguous: the phrase "minority language educational facilities" could either mean the facilities of the minority, or the facilities for the minority. The French text, however, is clearer. It has been stated on several occasions by this Court, that where there is an ambiguity in one version of the *Charter*, and the other version is less ambiguous, then the meaning of the less ambiguous version should be adopted. The French version of s. 23(3)(b) reads:

"23. . . .

(3) Le droit . . .

---

20 [Ed. note: The *Motor Vehicle Reference* is discussed in Chapter 2. The casual reference to legislative history made in the text in this case referred to statements made by the Minister of Justice, Jean Chrétien, before the special joint parliamentary committee on the Charter, suggesting that management and control of minority language educational facilities was not contemplated by s. 23(3)(b). The matter was more carefully considered, with the same result reached by the Supreme Court here, in REFERENCE RE EDUCATION ACT OF ONTARIO AND MINORITY LANGUAGE EDUCATION RIGHTS (1984), 10 D.LR. (4th) 491, 529–31 (Ont. C.A.), where the court concluded that these statements should not be given as much weight as the historic context that led to the new provisions, which demonstrated the lack of responsiveness of Anglophone school boards to the needs of the Francophone minority.]

b) comprend, lorsque le nombre de ces enfants le justifie, le droit de les faire instruire dans des *établissements d'enseignement de la minorité linguistique* financés sur les fonds publics." [Emphasis added.]

The underlined phrase in the French text — which utilizes the possessive "de la"— is more strongly suggestive than the English text that the facilities belong to the minority and hence that a measure of management and control should go to the linguistic minority in respect of educational facilities.

*   *   *

(5) Management and Control — The Purpose of s. 23

The foregoing textual analysis of s. 23(3)(b) is strongly supported by a consideration of the overall purpose of s. 23. That purpose, as discussed earlier, is to preserve and promote minority language and culture throughout Canada. In my view, it is essential, in order to further this purpose, that, where the numbers warrant, minority language parents possess a measure of management and control over the educational facilities in which their children are taught. Such management and control is vital to ensure that their language and culture flourish. It is necessary because a variety of management issues in education, e.g., curricula, hiring and expenditures, can affect linguistic and cultural concerns. I think it incontrovertible that the health and survival of the minority language and culture can be affected in subtle but important ways by decisions relating to these issues. To give but one example, most decisions pertaining to curricula clearly have an influence on the language and culture of the minority students.

Furthermore, as the historical context in which s. 23 was enacted suggests, minority language groups cannot always rely upon the majority to take account of all of their linguistic and cultural concerns. Such neglect is not necessarily intentional: the majority cannot be expected to understand and appreciate all of the diverse ways in which educational practices may influence the language and culture of the minority. In commenting on various setbacks experienced by the Francophone minority in Ontario, the Court of Appeal of that province noted that "lack of meaningful participation in management and control of local school boards by the Francophone minority made these events possible" (*Reference Re Education Act of Ontario [and Minority Language Education Rights*, (1984) 10 D.L.R. (4th) 491], at p. 531). A similar observation was made by the Prince Edward Island Court of Appeal in *Reference Re Minority Language Educational Rights (P.E.I.)*, [(1988), 69 Nfld. & P.E.I.R. 263, 259]:

"It would be foolhardy to assume that Parliament intended to . . . leave the sole control of the program development and delivery with the English majority. If such were the case, a majority language group could soon wreak havoc upon the rights of the minority and could soon render such a right worthless."

I agree with the sentiments expressed in these statements. If section 23 is to remedy past injustices and ensure that they are not repeated in the future, it is important that minority language groups have a measure of control over the minority language facilities and instruction.

(6) The Meaning of the Phrase "Management and Control"

[The Court adopted a flexible approach. It cited with approval a concurring opinion below that "the most effective guarantee to prevent assimilation is a facility under the exclusive control" of the linguistic minority, and held that in "some circumstances an independent Francophone school board is necessary to meet the purpose of s. 23." However, when the number of Francophone students is small, the Court observed that the isolation of these students from the physical resources that the majority school district enjoys would frustrate the purposes of s. 23. If control is not exclusive, however, the Court decreed that it was essential that the "minority language group have control over those aspects of education which pertain to or have an effect upon their language and culture." This could be achieved by a variety of governance devices, such as guaranteed minority representation on school boards, delegation to minority representatives of decisions regarding the operation of minority-language instruction, etc. Applying the holding to the case, the Court held that there were sufficient numbers of Franco-Edmontonians to warrant a separate school. However, the Court was not satisfied that the number of students likely to enroll in a Francophone school was sufficient to mandate the establishment of a separate school board.

As a separate issue, provincial educational regulations required at least 20% of classroom instruction to be in English; the plaintiffs sought a declaration that education could entirely be in French. The Court remanded to allow the province to demonstrate, under s. 1 of the Charter, that some period of mandatory English instruction was a reasonable limit on the rights of Francophone parents to control their children's linguistic education.]

———————

Judicial protection for linguistic minorities seems to have come full circle. As the Alberta Court of Appeal noted in the *Mahé* case, 42 D.L.R. (4th) 514, 532, the Privy Council's jurisprudence could "hardly be described as an example of purposive, generous, or 'growing tree' interpretation. Since *Beaulac, supra*, the Supreme Court of Canada embraces a broad and purposive approach to language rights that characterizes its approach to other Charter rights, and Canadian courts have continued to frustrate the traditional answer that "the French always lose" by judicial reasoning protecting Francophone minorities. For example, in *Arsenault-Cameron v. Prince Edward Island*, [2000] 1 SCR 3, 181 DLR (4th) 1, the court, citing *Beaulac*'s call for broad interpretation, held that s. 23's protection of rights "wherever in the province" meant that the French-language school board, rather than Education ministry officials, could determine whether to establish a school in the Summerside area rather than bus Francophone students to an adjoining district. *See also Lalonde v. Ontario (Commission de restructuration des services de sant)* (2001), 56 O.R. (3d) 505, 208 D.L.R. (4th) 577 (C.A.), a successful challenge to the government's decision to close Montfort Hospital, the only hospital in Ontario where services were available full-time in French and where health care professionals were trained in French.

The legacy of *Brown* leads many Americans to look with less favor on the *Mahé* approach, as illustrated by debates over how southern states that had developed segregated universities ought to offer desegregated higher education, in the context where the state typically features one or two flagship and predominantly white universities and other urban, rural, or specialty-focused state colleges that were either historically white or black. In *United States v. Fordice*, 505 U.S. 717 (1992), the Court rejected as constitutionally deficient a policy of race neutrality coupled with greater resources and support at the traditionally white flagship universities. Although the fact that an institution remains disproportionately white or black was not unconstitutional *per se*, the Court declared that "the State may not leave in place policies rooted in its prior officially segregated system that serve to maintain the racial identifiability of its universities if those policies can practically be eliminated without eroding sound educational policies." Responding to the arguments of private intervenors that the state should increase funding to historically-black colleges, the Court remanded for the trial court to consider whether such an increase was necessary "to achieve a full dismantlement" of the prior unlawful segregation. However, the Court rejected support for minority educational facilities:

> If we understand private petitioners to press us to order the upgrading of Jackson State, Alcorn State, and Mississippi Valley State solely so that they may be publicly financed, exclusively black enclaves by private choice, we reject that request. The State provides these facilities for all its citizens and it has not met its burden under *Brown* to take affirmative steps to dismantle its prior de jure system when it perpetuates a separate, but "more equal" one.

Justice Thomas concurred, observing:

> In particular, we do not foreclose the possibility that there exists "sound educational justification" for maintaining historically black colleges as such. Despite the shameful history of state-enforced segregation, these institutions have survived and flourished. Indeed, they have expanded as opportunities for blacks to enter historically white institutions have expanded. Between 1954 and 1980, for example, enrollment at historically black colleges increased from 70,000 to 200,000 students, while degrees awarded increased from 13,000 to 32,000. See S. Hill, National Center for Education Statistics, *The Traditionally Black Institutions of Higher Education* 1860 to 1982, pp. xiv-xv (1985). These accomplishments have not gone unnoticed:
>
> > "The colleges founded for Negroes are both a source of pride to blacks who have attended them and a source of hope to black families who want the benefits of higher learning for their children. They have exercised leadership in developing educational opportunities for young blacks at all levels of instruction, and, especially in the South, they are still regarded as key institutions for enhancing the general quality of the lives of black Americans." Carnegie Commission on Higher Education, From Isolation to Mainstream: Problems of the Colleges Founded for Negroes 11 (1971).
>
> I think it indisputable that these institutions have succeeded in part because of their distinctive histories and traditions; for many, historically black colleges have become "a symbol of the highest attainments of black culture." J. Preer, *Lawyers v. Educators: Black Colleges and Desegregation*

in Public Higher Education 2 (1982). Obviously, a State cannot maintain such traditions by closing particular institutions, historically white or historically black, to particular racial groups. Nonetheless, it hardly follows that a State cannot operate a diverse assortment of institutions — including historically black institutions — open to all on a race-neutral basis, but with established traditions and programs that might disproportionately appeal to one race or another. No one, I imagine, would argue that such institutional diversity is without "sound educational justification," or that it is even remotely akin to program duplication, which is designed to separate the races for the sake of separating the races. *** Although I agree that a State is not constitutionally required to maintain its historically black institutions as such, I do not understand our opinion to hold that a State is forbidden to do so. It would be ironic, to say the least, if the institutions that sustained blacks during segregation were themselves destroyed in an effort to combat its vestiges.

In *Garrett v. Board of Ed. of School Dist. of Detroit*, 775 F. Supp. 1004 (E.D. Mich. 1991), the court enjoined a plan to create all-male schools for inner-city youth. Neither the Afrocentric curriculum nor the expectation that the school would be overwhelmingly if not exclusively comprised of African Americans was at issue. Rather, the suit was brought by the National Organization for Women and the American Civil Liberties Union because of its single-sex composition. The court reasoned that the school board had failed to show "how the exclusion of females from the Academies is necessary to combat unemployment, dropout and homicide rates among urban males. There is no evidence that the educational system is failing urban males because females attend schools with males. In fact, the educational system is also failing females." *Ibid.* at 1007.

9.4.   UNITED STATES: JUDICIAL PROTECTION OF RACIAL MINORITIES

9.4.1.   Proof of unconstitutional racial discrimination

As noted in Chapter Four, the Supreme Court established in *Washington v. Davis*, 426 U.S. 229 (1976), that laws that harm racial minorities can only be challenged under the Fourteenth Amendment with evidence that the legislative intent was to harm minorities. Statutes passed for race-neutral reasons are not unconstitutional.

9.4.2. Judicial review of race-conscious policies designed to benefit minorities

REGENTS OF THE UNIVERSITY OF CALIFORNIA v. BAKKE

SUPREME COURT OF THE UNITED STATES

438 U.S. 265 (1978)

[Allan Bakke is a white male who applied to the Davis Medical School in both 1973 and 1974 and was rejected both times. In both years, applicants were admitted under a special program for "disadvantaged students" with grade point averages, MCAT scores, and benchmark scores significantly lower than Bakke's. The program had resulted in the admission over a two year period of 51 African American and Latino students, while none had been admitted in prior years. Bakke then filed suit alleging that the program illegally operated to exclude him from the school on the basis of his race, in violation of his rights under the Equal Protection Clause, the equivalent provision of the state constitution, and § 601 of the Civil Rights Act of 1964, which bars "discrimination" by recipients of federal funding.]

[In a path-marking but fractured opinion, Justice Powell announced the judgment of the Court. Joined by four others (Burger, C.J., and Stewart, Rehnquist, and Stevens, JJ.), he concluded that the Civil Rights Act barred the creation of a special admission program. Joined by four others (Brennan, White, Marshall, and Blackmun, JJ.), he concluded that race was a factor that could be considered in admissions processes.]

MR. JUSTICE POWELL announced the judgment of the Court.

. . . .

II

[Noting that the concept of "discrimination" was susceptible of varying interpretations, Powell, J. first concluded that the legislative history of Title VI of the Civil Rights Act of 1964, which banned "discrimination" on grounds of "race, color, or national origin" in any program receiving federal financial assistance, was intended by Congress to stop practices that violate "a prohibition of racial discrimination similar to that of the Constitution."]

. . . .

III

A

Petitioner does not deny that decisions based on race or ethnic origin by faculties and administrations of state universities are reviewable under the Fourteenth Amendment. For his part, respondent does not argue that all racial or ethnic classifications are *per se* invalid. The parties do disagree as to the level of judicial scrutiny to be applied to the special admissions program. Petitioner argues that the court below erred in applying strict scrutiny, as this inexact term has been applied in our cases. That level of review, petitioner asserts, should be reserved for classifications that disadvantage "discrete and insular minorities." See *United States v. Carolene Products Co.*, 304 U.S. 144, 152 n. 4 (1938). Respondent, on the other hand, contends that the California court correctly rejected the notion that the degree of judicial scrutiny accorded a particular racial or ethnic classification hinges upon membership in a discrete and insular minority and duly recognized that the "rights established [by the Fourteenth Amendment] are personal rights." *Shelley v. Kraemer*, 334 U.S. 1, 22 (1948).

. . . .

The guarantees of the Fourteenth Amendment extend to all persons. Its language is explicit: "No State shall . . . deny to any person within its jurisdiction the equal protection of the laws." It is settled beyond question that the "rights created by the first section of the Fourteenth Amendment are, by its terms, guaranteed to the individual. The rights established are personal rights," *Shelley v. Kraemer, supra*, at 22. The guarantee of equal protection cannot mean one thing when applied to one individual and something else when applied to a person of another color. If both are not accorded the same protection, then it is not equal. Nevertheless, petitioner argues that the court below erred in applying strict scrutiny to the special admissions program because white males, such as respondent, are not a "discrete and insular minority" requiring extraordinary protection from the majoritarian political process. *Carolene Products Co., supra*, at 152-153, n. 4. This rationale, however, has never been invoked in our decisions as a prerequisite to subjecting racial or ethnic distinctions to strict scrutiny. Nor has this Court held that discreteness and insularity constitute necessary preconditions to a holding that a particular classification is invidious. See, e. g., *Skinner v. Oklahoma ex rel. Williamson*, 316 U.S. 535, 541 (1942); *Carrington v. Rash*, 380 U.S. 89, 94-97 (1965). These characteristics may be relevant in deciding whether or not to add new types of classifications to the list of "suspect" categories or whether a particular classification survives close examination. See, e. g., *Massachusetts Board of Retirement v. Murgia*, 427 U.S. 307, 313 (1976) (age); *San Antonio Independent School Dist. v. Rodriguez*, 411 U.S. 1, 28 (1973) (wealth); *Graham v. Richardson*, 403 U.S. 365, 372 (1971) (aliens). Racial and ethnic classifications, however, are subject to stringent examination without regard to these additional characteristics. We declared as much in the first cases explicitly to recognize racial distinctions as suspect:

"Distinctions between citizens solely because of their ancestry are by their very nature odious to a free people whose institutions are founded upon the doctrine of equality." *Hirabayashi*, 320 U.S., at 100.

"[All] legal restrictions which curtail the civil rights of a single racial group are immediately suspect. That is not to say that all such restrictions are unconstitutional. It is to say that courts must subject them to the most rigid scrutiny." *Korematsu*, 323 U.S., at 216.

The Court has never questioned the validity of those pronouncements. Racial and ethnic distinctions of any sort are inherently suspect and thus call for the most exacting judicial examination.

B

. . . .

[Suggesting that the Equal Protection Clause had not been vigorously enforced shortly after its ratification in the 1860s, Justice Powell stated that] it was no longer possible to peg the guarantees of the Fourteenth Amendment to the struggle for equality of one racial minority. During the dormancy of the Equal Protection Clause, the United States had become a Nation of minorities. Each had to struggle — and to some extent struggles still — to overcome the prejudices not of a monolithic majority, but of a "majority" composed of various minority groups of whom it was said — perhaps unfairly in many cases — that a shared characteristic was a willingness to disadvantage other groups. As the Nation filled with the stock of many lands, the reach of the Clause was gradually extended to all ethnic groups seeking protection from official discrimination. See *Strauder v. West Virginia,* 100 U.S. 303, 308 (1880) (Celtic Irishmen) (dictum); *Yick Wo v. Hopkins,* 118 U.S. 356 (1886) (Chinese); *Truax v. Raich,* 239 U.S. 33, 41 (1915) (Austrian resident aliens); *Korematsu, supra* (Japanese); *Hernandez v. Texas,* 347 U.S. 475 (1954) (Mexican-Americans). The guarantees of equal protection, said the Court in *Yick Wo,* "are universal in their application, to all persons within the territorial jurisdiction, without regard to any differences of race, of color, or of nationality; and the equal protection of the laws is a pledge of the protection of equal laws." 118 U.S., at 369.

. . . .

Petitioner urges us to adopt for the first time a more restrictive view of the Equal Protection Clause and hold that discrimination against members of the white "majority" cannot be suspect if its purpose can be characterized as "benign."[21] The clock of our liberties, however, cannot be turned back to 1868. *Brown v. Board of Education, supra,* at 492; accord, *Loving v. Virginia, supra,* at 9. It is far too late to argue that the guarantee of equal protection to *all* persons permits the

---

[21] [FN 34] In the view of MR. JUSTICE BRENNAN, MR. JUSTICE WHITE, MR. JUSTICE MARSHALL, and MR. JUSTICE BLACKMUN, the pliable notion of "stigma" is the crucial element in analyzing racial classifications. See, *e. g., post,* at 361, 362. The Equal Protection Clause is not framed in terms of "stigma." Certainly the word has no clearly defined constitutional meaning. It reflects a subjective judgment that is standardless. *All* state-imposed classifications that rearrange burdens and benefits on the basis of race are likely to be viewed with deep resentment by the individuals burdened. The denial to innocent persons of equal rights and opportunities may outrage those so deprived and therefore may be perceived as invidious. These individuals are likely to find little comfort in the notion that the deprivation they are asked to endure is merely the price of membership in the dominant majority and that its imposition is inspired by the supposedly benign purpose of aiding others. One should not lightly dismiss the inherent unfairness of, and the perception of mistreatment that accompanies a system of allocating benefits and privileges on the basis of skin color and ethnic origin. Moreover, MR. JUSTICE BRENNAN, MR. JUSTICE WHITE, MR. JUSTICE MARSHALL, and MR. JUSTICE BLACKMUN offer no principle for deciding whether preferential classifications reflect a benign remedial purpose or a malevolent stigmatic classification, since they are willing in this case to accept mere *post hoc* declarations by an isolated state entity — a medical school faculty — unadorned by particularized findings of past discrimination, to establish such a remedial purpose.

recognition of special wards entitled to a degree of protection greater than that accorded others.[22] "The Fourteenth Amendment is not directed solely against discrimination due to a 'two-class theory' — that is, based upon differences between 'white' and Negro." *Hernandez*, 347 U.S., at 478.

Once the artificial line of a "two-class theory" of the Fourteenth Amendment is put aside, the difficulties entailed in varying the level of judicial review according to a perceived "preferred" status of a particular racial or ethnic minority are intractable. The concepts of "majority" and "minority" necessarily reflect temporary arrangements and political judgments. As observed above, the white "majority" itself is composed of various minority groups, most of which can lay claim to a history of prior discrimination at the hands of the State and private individuals. Not all of these groups can receive preferential treatment and corresponding judicial tolerance of distinctions drawn in terms of race and nationality, for then the only "majority" left would be a new minority of white Anglo-Saxon Protestants. There is no principled basis for deciding which groups would merit "heightened judicial solicitude "and which would not.

The breadth of this hypothesis is unprecedented in our constitutional system. The first step is easily taken. No one denies the regrettable fact that there has been societal discrimination in this country against various racial and ethnic groups. The second step, however, involves a speculative leap: but for this discrimination by society at large, Bakke "would have failed to qualify for admission" because Negro applicants — nothing is said about Asians, cf., *e.g.*, *post*, at 374 n. 57— would have made better scores. . . . Courts would be asked to evaluate the extent of the prejudice and consequent harm suffered by various minority groups. Those whose societal injury is thought to exceed some arbitrary level of tolerability then would be entitled to preferential classifications at the expense of individuals belonging to other groups. Those classifications would be free from exacting judicial scrutiny. As these preferences began to have their desired effect, and the consequences of past discrimination were undone, new judicial rankings would be necessary. The kind of variable sociological and political analysis necessary to produce such rankings simply does not lie within the judicial competence — even if they otherwise were politically feasible and socially desirable.[23]

---

[22]   [FN 35] Professor Bickel noted the self-contradiction of that view:

"The lesson of the great decisions of the Supreme Court and the lesson of contemporary history have been the same for at least a generation: discrimination on the basis of race is illegal, immoral, unconstitutional, inherently wrong, and destructive of democratic society. Now this is to be unlearned and we are told that this is not a matter of fundamental principle but only a matter of whose ox is gored. Those for whom racial equality was demanded are to be more equal than others. Having found support in the Constitution for equality, they now claim support for inequality under the same Constitution." A. Bickel, The Morality of Consent 133 (1975).

[23]   [FN 37] Mr. Justice Douglas has noted the problems associated with such inquiries:

"The reservation of a proportion of the law school class for members of selected minority groups is fraught with . . . dangers, for one must immediately determine which groups are to receive such favored treatment and which are to be excluded, the proportions of the class that are to be allocated to each, and even the criteria by which to determine whether an individual is a member of a favored group. [Cf. *Plessy v. Ferguson*, 163 U.S. 537, 549, 552 (1896).] There is no assurance that a common agreement can be reached, and first the schools, and then the

Moreover, there are serious problems of justice connected with the idea of preference itself. First, it may not always be clear that a so-called preference is in fact benign. Courts may be asked to validate burdens imposed upon individual members of a particular group in order to advance the group's general interest. See *United Jewish Organizations v. Carey*, 430 U.S., at 172-173 (Brennan, J., concurring in part). Nothing in the Constitution supports the notion that individuals may be asked to suffer otherwise impermissible burdens in order to enhance the societal standing of their ethnic groups. Second, preferential programs may only reinforce common stereotypes holding that certain groups are unable to achieve success without special protection based on a factor having no relationship to individual worth. See *DeFunis v. Odegaard*, 416 U.S. 312, 343 (1974) (Douglas, J., dissenting). Third, there is a measure of inequity in forcing innocent persons in respondent's position to bear the burdens of redressing grievances not of their making.

. . . .

IV

[In this part, Justice Powell established the applicable equal protection doctrine. Assuring a specified percentage representation of minorities as an end in itself is an illegitimate purpose. Aiding some individuals, at the expense of other "innocent individuals," based on a finding that the beneficiaries belong to a victimized group, is Powell argues improper, "in the absence of judicial, legislative, or administrative findings of constitutional or statutory violations." The goal of improving health-care to underserved areas was rejected because of lack of evidence that admitting more minority race medical students was "either needed or geared to promote that goal." However, Justice Powell agreed with the University that attainment of a diverse student body is a legitimate goal, but later rejected the argument that reservation

---

courts, will be buffeted with the competing claims. The University of Washington included Filipinos, but excluded Chinese and Japanese; another school may limit its program to blacks, or to blacks and Chicanos. Once the Court sanctioned racial preferences such as these, it could not then wash its hands of the matter, leaving it entirely in the discretion of the school, for then we would have effectively overruled *Sweatt v. Painter,* 339 U.S. 629, and allowed imposition of a 'zero' allocation. But what standard is the Court to apply when a rejected applicant of Japanese ancestry brings suit to require the University of Washington to extend the same privileges to his group? The Committee might conclude that the population of Washington is now 2% Japanese, and that Japanese also constitute 2% of the Bar, but that had they not been handicapped by a history of discrimination, Japanese would now constitute 5% of the Bar, or 20%. Or, alternatively, the Court could attempt to assess how grievously each group has suffered from discrimination, and allocate proportions accordingly; if that were the standard the current University of Washington policy would almost surely fall, for there is no Western State which can claim that it has always treated Japanese and Chinese in a fair and evenhanded manner. See, *e. g., Yick Wo v. Hopkins,* 118 U.S. 356; *Terrace v. Thompson,* 263 U.S. 197; *Oyama v. California,* 332 U.S. 633. This Court has not sustained a racial classification since the wartime cases of *Korematsu v. United States,* 323 U.S. 214, and *Hirabayashi v. United States,* 320 U.S. 81, involving curfews and relocations imposed upon Japanese-Americans.

"Nor obviously will the problem be solved if next year the Law School included only Japanese and Chinese, for then Norwegians and Swedes, Poles and Italians, Puerto Ricans and Hungarians, and all other groups which form this diverse Nation would have just complaints." *DeFunis v. Odegaard,* 416 U.S. 312, 337-340 (1974) (dissenting opinion) (footnotes omitted).

of a specific number of seats for designated minorities was the only way to promote diversity.]

Opinion of MR. JUSTICE BRENNAN, MR. JUSTICE WHITE, MR. JUSTICE MARSHALL, and MR. JUSTICE BLACKMUN, concurring in the judgment in part and dissenting in part.

. . . .

I

Our Nation was founded on the principle that "all Men are created equal." Yet candor requires acknowledgment that the Framers of our Constitution, to forge the 13 Colonies into one Nation, openly compromised this principle of equality with its antithesis: slavery. The consequences of this compromise are well known and have aptly been called our "American Dilemma.". . .

. . . .

Against this background, claims that law must be "colorblind" or that the datum of race is no longer relevant to public policy must be seen as aspiration rather than as description of reality. This is not to denigrate aspiration; for reality rebukes us that race has too often been used by those who would stigmatize and oppress minorities. Yet we cannot — and, as we shall demonstrate, need not under our Constitution or Title VI, which merely extends the constraints of the Fourteenth Amendment to private parties who receive federal funds — let color blindness become myopia which masks the reality that many "created equal" have been treated within our lifetimes as inferior both by the law and by their fellow citizens.

. . . .

MR. JUSTICE MARSHALL.

I agree with the judgment of the Court only insofar as it permits a university to consider the race of an applicant in making admissions decisions. I do not agree that petitioner's admissions program violates the Constitution. For it must be remembered that, during most of the past 200 years, the Constitution as interpreted by this Court did not prohibit the most ingenious and pervasive forms of discrimination against the Negro. Now, when a State acts to remedy the effects of that legacy of discrimination, I cannot believe that this same Constitution stands as a barrier.

I

A

Three hundred and fifty years ago, the Negro was dragged to this country in chains to be sold into slavery. Uprooted from his homeland and thrust into bondage for forced labor, the slave was deprived of all legal rights. It was unlawful to teach him to read; he could be sold away from his family and friends at the whim of his master; and killing or maiming him was not a crime. The system of slavery brutalized and dehumanized both master and slave.

The denial of human rights was etched into the American Colonies' first attempts at establishing self-government. When the colonists determined to seek their independence from England, they drafted a unique document cataloguing their grievances against the King and proclaiming as "self-evident" that "all men are created equal" and are endowed "with certain unalienable Rights," including those to "Life, Liberty and the pursuit of Happiness." The self-evident truths and the unalienable rights were intended, however, to apply only to white men. An earlier draft of the Declaration of Independence, submitted by Thomas Jefferson to the Continental Congress, had included among the charges against the King that

"[he] has waged cruel war against human nature itself, violating its most sacred rights of life and liberty in the persons of a distant people who never offended him, captivating and carrying them into slavery in another hemisphere, or to incur miserable death in their transportation thither." Franklin 88.

The Southern delegation insisted that the charge be deleted; the colonists themselves were implicated in the slave trade, and inclusion of this claim might have made it more difficult to justify the continuation of slavery once the ties to England were severed. Thus, even as the colonists embarked on a course to secure their own freedom and equality, they ensured perpetuation of the system that deprived a whole race of those rights. [Justice Marshall catalogued the various provisions of the original constitution perpetuating slavery: counting slaves as 3/5 of a person (Art. I, § 2), barring Congress from ending the slave trade until 1808 (Art. I, § 9), and requiring the return of fugitive slaves (Art. IV, § 2). He concluded that the Framers had "made it plain that 'we the people,' for whose protection the Constitution was designed, did not include those whose skins were the wrong color."]

B

The status of the Negro as property was officially erased by his emancipation at the end of the Civil War. But the long-awaited emancipation, while freeing the Negro from slavery, did not bring him citizenship or equality in any meaningful way. Slavery was replaced by a system of "laws which imposed upon the colored race onerous disabilities and burdens, and curtailed their rights in the pursuit of life, liberty, and property to such an extent that their freedom was of little value." *Slaughter-House Cases*, 16 Wall. 36, 70 (1873). Despite the passage of the Thirteenth, Fourteenth, and Fifteenth Amendments, the Negro was systematically denied the rights those Amendments were supposed to secure. The combined actions and inactions of the State and Federal Governments maintained Negroes in a position of legal inferiority for another century after the Civil War.

. . . .

II

The position of the Negro today in America is the tragic but inevitable consequence of centuries of unequal treatment. Measured by any benchmark of comfort or achievement, meaningful equality remains a distant dream for the Negro. [Justice Marshall detailed data on lower life expectancy, infant mortality, median income, employment rates, salary, and percentage of professions for African Americans.]

In light of the sorry history of discrimination and its devastating impact on the lives of Negroes, bringing the Negro into the mainstream of American life should be a state interest of the highest order. To fail to do so is to ensure that America will forever remain a divided society.

III

. . . .

A

. . . .

It is plain that the Fourteenth Amendment was not intended to prohibit measures designed to remedy the effects of the Nation's past treatment of Negroes. The Congress that passed the Fourteenth Amendment is the same Congress that passed the 1866 Freedmen's Bureau Act, an Act that provided many of its benefits only to Negroes. Act of July 16, 1866, ch. 200, 14 Stat. 173; see *supra*, at 391. Although the Freedmen's Bureau legislation provided aid for refugees, thereby including white persons within some of the relief measures, 14 Stat. 174; see also Act of Mar. 3, 1865, ch. 90, 13 Stat. 507, the bill was regarded, to the dismay of many Congressmen, as "solely and entirely for the freedmen, and to the exclusion of all other persons. . . ." Cong. Globe, 39th Cong., 1st Sess., 544 (1866) (remarks of Rep. Taylor). See also *id.*, at 634-635 (remarks of Rep. Ritter); *id.*, at App. 78, 80-81 (remarks of Rep. Chanler). Indeed, the bill was bitterly opposed on the ground that it "undertakes to make the negro in some respects . . . superior . . . and gives them favors that the poor white boy in the North cannot get." *Id.*, at 401 (remarks of Sen. McDougall). See also *id.*, at 319 (remarks of Sen. Hendricks); *id.*, at 362 (remarks of Sen. Saulsbury); *id.*, at 397 (remarks of Sen. Willey); *id.*, at 544 (remarks of Rep. Taylor). The bill's supporters defended it — not by rebutting the claim of special treatment — but by pointing to the need for such treatment:

"The very discrimination it makes between 'destitute and suffering' negroes, and destitute and suffering white paupers, proceeds upon the distinction that, in the omitted case, civil rights and immunities are already sufficiently protected by the possession of political power, the absence of which in the case provided for necessitates governmental protection." *Id.*, at App. 75 (remarks of Rep. Phelps).

Despite the objection to the special treatment the bill would provide for Negroes, it was passed by Congress. *Id.*, at 421, 688. President Johnson vetoed this bill and also a subsequent bill that contained some modifications; one of his principal objections to both bills was that they gave special benefits to Negroes. 8 Messages and Papers of the Presidents 3596, 3599, 3620, 3623 (1897). Rejecting the concerns of the President and the bill's opponents, Congress overrode the President's second veto. Cong. Globe, 39th Cong., 1st Sess., 3842, 3850 (1866).

Since the Congress that considered and rejected the objections to the 1866 Freedmen's Bureau Act concerning special relief to Negroes also proposed the Fourteenth Amendment, it is inconceivable that the Fourteenth Amendment was intended to prohibit all race-conscious relief measures. It "would be a distortion of the policy manifested in that amendment, which was adopted to prevent state legislation designed to perpetuate discrimination on the basis of race or color," *Railway Mail Assn. v. Corsi*, 326 U.S. 88, 94 (1945), to hold that it barred state action to remedy the effects of that discrimination. Such a result would pervert the intent of the Framers by substituting abstract equality for the genuine equality the Amendment was intended to achieve.

. . . .

MR. JUSTICE BLACKMUN.

*   *   *

I yield to no one in my earnest hope that the time will come when an "affirmative action" program is unnecessary and is, in truth, only a relic of the past. . . .

. . . .

I suspect that it would be impossible to arrange an affirmative-action program in a racially neutral way and have it successful. To ask that this be so is to demand the impossible. In order to get beyond racism, we must first take account of race. There is no other way. And in order to treat some persons equally, we must treat them differently. We cannot — we dare not — let the Equal Protection Clause perpetuate racial supremacy.

*   *   *

MR. JUSTICE STEVENS, with whom THE CHIEF JUSTICE, MR. JUSTICE STEWART, and MR. JUSTICE REHNQUIST join, concurring in the judgment in part and dissenting in part [on the statutory interpretation of the ban on federal funds for programs that discriminate on the ground of race].

———

Although *Bakke*'s holding was technically limited to a statutory violation, the reasoning was followed as a matter of constitutional law in *City of Richmond v. J.A. Croson Co.*, 488 U.S. 469 (1989), which held that a local ordinance requiring that prime contractors award at least 30% of each contract to minority business enterprises violated the Fourteenth Amendment. Justice O'Connor's plurality opinion explained that "the rights established a personal right," that any racial classifications, "benign" or not, "carry a danger of stigmatic harm" and may "in fact promote notions of racial inferiority and lead to a politics of racial hostility." The "watered-down version of equal protection review" advocated in *Bakke* by Brennan,

J. "effectively assures that race will always be relevant in American life, and that the "ultimate goal" of "eliminat[ing] entirely from governmental decisionmaking such irrelevant factors as a human being's race," [*Wygant v. Jackson Bd. of Education*, 476 U.S. 267, 320 (1986) (Stevens, J., dissenting)] will never be achieved."

Justice Powell's judgment in *Bakke* that the maintenance of diversity in educational institution was a compelling state interest was reaffirmed by a majority in an opinion written by Justice O'Connor. *Grutter v. Bollinger*, 539 U.S. 306 (2003). Moreover, in *Fisher v. University of Texas*, 133 S. Ct. 2411 (2013), the Court reversed a lower court decision upholding a university's consideration of race, rejecting the claim that good faith precluded a claim. Rather, the correct standard of strict scrutiny to apply to race-conscious admissions decisions requires the university to show, with regard to its judgment that racial diversity is essential to its educational mission, that the specific program was narrowly tailored to this goal. The reviewing court must be satisfied "that no workable race-neutral alternatives would produce the educational benefits of diversity."

A 5-4 decision exemplifies the continuing division among the justices. In *Shaw v. Reno*, 509 U.S. 630 (1993), the Court struck down a North Carolina reapportionment statute that created two gerrymandered districts where a majority of voters were African American (the state had 12 representatives and approximately 25% of North Carolinians are African American). For the majority, Justice O'Connor remarked that it was "unsettling how closely the North Carolina plan resembles the most egregious racial gerrymanders of the past." She summarized precedents holding that the purpose of the Equal Protection Clause is to "prevent the States from purposefully discriminating between individuals on the basis of race." Discrimination "solely on the basis of race" is, by its very nature, "odious to a free people whose institutions are founded upon the doctrine of equality." Racial classifications "threaten to stigmatize individuals by reason of their membership in a racial group and to incite racial hostility." Thus, explicit racial distinctions as well as "rare" statutes that are facially neutral but are "unexplainable on grounds other than race" require an "extraordinary justification." The majority also expressed hostility to the whole idea of race-based districting:

> The message that such districting sends to elected representatives is equally pernicious. When a district obviously is created solely to effectuate the perceived common interests of one racial group, elected officials are more likely to believe that their primary obligation is to represent only the members of that group, rather than their constituency as a whole. This is altogether antithetical to our system of representative democracy. As Justice Douglas explained in his dissent in *Wright v. Rockefeller*, [376 U.S. 52 (1964)], nearly 30 years ago:
>
> > "Here the individual is important, not his race, his creed, or his color. The principle of equality is at war with the notion that District A must be represented by a Negro, as it is with the notion that District B must be represented by a Caucasian, District C by a Jew, District D by a Catholic, and so on. . . . That system, by whatever name it is called, is a divisive force in a community, emphasizing

differences between candidates and voters that are irrelevant in the constitutional sense . . . .

. . . .

"When racial or religious lines are drawn by the State, the multiracial, multireligious communities that our Constitution seeks to weld together as one become separatist; antagonisms that relate to race or to religion rather than to political issues are generated; communities seek not the best representative but the best racial or religious partisan. Since that system is at war with the democratic ideal, it should find no footing here." 376 U.S. at 66-67.

Justice O'Connor repeated *Croson*'s holding that "equal protection analysis 'is not dependent on the race of those burdened or benefited by a particular classification.'" *Croson*, 488 U.S. at 494 (plurality opinion).

Among the dissenters, Justice Stevens attacked the basic foundations of the majority's opinion. In his view the Equal Protection Clause's mandate

to govern impartially is abused when a group with power over the electoral process defines electoral boundaries solely to enhance its own political strength at the expense of any weaker group. That duty, however, is not violated when the majority acts to facilitate the election of a member of a group that lacks such power because it remains under-represented in the state legislature — whether that group is defined by political affiliation, by common economic interests, or by religious, ethnic, or racial characteristics.

Justice Stevens also objected that the effect of the Court's holding was to single out racial minorities from the many political minority groups whose interests are considered in reapportionment plans. He argued: "If it is permissible to draw boundaries to provide adequate representation for rural voters, for union members, for Hasidic Jews, for Polish Americans, or for Republicans, it necessarily follows that it is permissible to do the same thing for members of the very minority group whose history in the United States gave birth to the Equal Protection Clause. A contrary conclusion could only be described as perverse."

One of the key provisions of the Voting Rights Act of 1965 created a formula based on low voter turnout, which covered a number of southern states, and required that electoral changes in those states must be "pre-cleared" by the federal Justice Department or a federal court in Washington. Recently, the Court held this provision to be unconstitutional.

SHELBY COUNTY, ALABAMA v. HOLDER
SUPREME COURT OF THE UNITED STATES
133 S. Ct. 2612 (2013)

CHIEF JUSTICE ROBERTS delivered the opinion of the Court.

The Voting Rights Act of 1965 employed extraordinary measures to address an extraordinary problem. *Section 5* of the Act required States to obtain federal permission before enacting any law related to voting — a drastic departure from basic principles of federalism. And § 4 of the Act applied that requirement only to some States — an equally dramatic departure from the principle that all States enjoy equal sovereignty. This was strong medicine, but Congress determined it was needed to address entrenched racial discrimination in voting, "an insidious and pervasive evil which had been perpetuated in certain parts of our country through unremitting and ingenious defiance of the Constitution." *South Carolina v. Katzenbach*, 383 U.S. 301, 309, 86 S. Ct. 803, 15 L. Ed. 2d 769 (1966). As we explained in upholding the law, "exceptional conditions can justify legislative measures not otherwise appropriate." *Id.*, at 334, 86 S. Ct. 803, 15 L. Ed. 2d 769. Reflecting the unprecedented nature of these measures, they were scheduled to expire after five years. See Voting Rights Act of 1965, § 4(a), 79 Stat. 438.

Nearly 50 years later, they are still in effect; indeed, they have been made more stringent, and are now scheduled to last until 2031. There is no denying, however, that the conditions that originally justified these measures no longer characterize voting in the covered jurisdictions. By 2009, "the racial gap in voter registration and turnout [was] lower in the States originally covered by § 5 than it [was] nationwide." Since that time, Census Bureau data indicate that African-American voter turnout has come to exceed white voter turnout in five of the six States originally covered by § 5, with a gap in the sixth State of less than one half of one percent.

At the same time, voting discrimination still exists; no one doubts that. The question is whether the Act's extraordinary measures, including its disparate treatment of the States, continue to satisfy constitutional requirements. As we put it a short time ago, "the Act imposes current burdens and must be justified by current needs." *Northwest Austin*, 557 U.S., at 203, 129 S. Ct. 2504, 174 L. Ed. 2d 140.

I

A

The *Fifteenth Amendment* was ratified in 1870, in the wake of the Civil War. It provides that "[t]he right of citizens of the United States to vote shall not be denied or abridged by the United States or by any State on account of race, color, or previous condition of servitude," and it gives Congress the "power to enforce this article by appropriate legislation."

"The first century of congressional enforcement of the *Amendment*, however, can only be regarded as a failure." *Id.*, at 197, 129 S. Ct. 2504, 174 L. Ed. 2d 140. In the

1890s, Alabama, Georgia, Louisiana, Mississippi, North Carolina, South Carolina, and Virginia began to enact literacy tests for voter registration and to employ other methods designed to prevent African-Americans from voting. *Katzenbach*, 383 U.S., at 310, 86 S. Ct. 803, 15 L. Ed. 2d 769. Congress passed statutes outlawing some of these practices and facilitating litigation against them, but litigation remained slow and expensive, and the States came up with new ways to discriminate as soon as existing ones were struck down. Voter registration of African-Americans barely improved. *Id.*, at 313–314, 86 S. Ct. 803, 15 L. Ed. 2d 769.

Inspired to action by the civil rights movement, Congress responded in 1965 with the Voting Rights Act. *Section 2* was enacted to forbid, in all 50 States, any "standard, practice, or procedure . . . imposed or applied . . . to deny or abridge the right of any citizen of the United States to vote on account of race or color." 79 Stat. 437. The current version forbids any "standard, practice, or procedure" that "results in a denial or abridgement of the right of any citizen of the United States to vote on account of race or color." 42 U.S.C. § 1973(a). . . .

Other sections targeted only some parts of the country. At the time of the Act's passage, these "covered" jurisdictions were those States or political subdivisions that had maintained a test or device as a prerequisite to voting as of November 1, 1964, and had less than 50 percent voter registration or turnout in the 1964 Presidential election. Such tests or devices included literacy and knowledge tests, good moral character requirements, the need for vouchers from registered voters, and the like. § 4(c), *id.*, at 438–439. A covered jurisdiction could "bail out" of coverage if it had not used a test or device in the preceding five years "for the purpose or with the effect of denying or abridging the right to vote on account of race or color." § 4(a), *id.*, at 438. In 1965, the covered States included Alabama, Georgia, Louisiana, Mississippi, South Carolina, and Virginia. The additional covered subdivisions included 39 counties in North Carolina and one in Arizona.

In those jurisdictions, § 4 of the Act banned all such tests or devices. Section 5 provided that no change in voting procedures could take effect until [federal authorities in Washington, D. C. — either the Attorney General or a court of three judges — found the state had shown that] the change had neither "the purpose [nor] the effect of denying or abridging the right to vote on account of race or color." [The opinion retraces the multiple times Congress extended these sections, originally intended to expire in 1970.]

. . . .

B

. . . .

II

In *Northwest Austin*, we stated that "the Act imposes current burdens and must be justified by current needs." *557 U.S.*, at 203, 129 S. Ct. 2504, 174 L. Ed. 2d 140. And we concluded that "a departure from the fundamental principle of equal sovereignty requires a showing that a statute's disparate geographic coverage is sufficiently related to the problem that it targets." *Ibid.* These basic principles guide our review of the question before us.

A

[Roberts, CJ noted that the Framers rejected a proposal to allow the federal government to veto state laws, and the Tenth Amendment "preserves the integrity, dignity, and residual sovereignty of the States," *Bond v. United States*, 131 S. Ct. 2355, (2011).Specifically, the Framers intended that States would retain the power to regulate elections. Next, he emphasized the fundamental principle of *equal sovereignty*" among the States," and concluded that the Act "sharply departs from these basic principles."]

B

In 1966, we found these departures from the basic features of our system of government justified. The "blight of racial discrimination in voting" had "infected the electoral process in parts of our country for nearly a century." *Katzenbach*, 383 U.S., at 308, 86 S. Ct. 803, 15 L. Ed. 2d 769. Several States had enacted a variety of requirements and tests "specifically designed to prevent" African-Americans from voting. *Id.*, at 310, 86 S. Ct. 803, 15 L. Ed. 2d 769. Case-by-case litigation had proved inadequate to prevent such racial discrimination in voting, in part because States "merely switched to discriminatory devices not covered by the federal decrees," "enacted difficult new tests," or simply "defied and evaded court orders." *Id.*, at 314, 86 S. Ct. 803, 15 L. Ed. 2d 769. Shortly before enactment of the Voting Rights Act, only 19.4 percent of African-Americans of voting age were registered to vote in Alabama, only 31.8 percent in Louisiana, and only 6.4 percent in Mississippi. *Id.*, at 313, 86 S. Ct. 803, 15 L. Ed. 2d 769. Those figures were roughly 50 percentage points or more below the figures for whites. *Ibid.*

. . . .

C

Nearly 50 years later, things have changed dramatically. . . . In the covered jurisdictions, "[v]oter turnout and registration rates now approach parity. Blatantly discriminatory evasions of federal decrees are rare. And minority candidates hold office at unprecedented levels." *Northwest Austin*, 557 U.S., at 202, 129 S. Ct. 2504, 174 L. Ed. 2d 140. The tests and devices that blocked access to the ballot have been forbidden nationwide for over 40 years. See § 6, 84 Stat. 314; § 102, 89 Stat. 400.

. . . .

There is no doubt that these improvements are in large part *because of* the Voting Rights Act. The Act has proved immensely successful at redressing racial discrimination and integrating the voting process. See § 2(b)(1), 120 Stat. 577. During the "Freedom Summer" of 1964, in Philadelphia, Mississippi, three men were murdered while working in the area to register African-American voters. See *United States v. Price*, 383 U.S. 787, 790, 86 S. Ct. 1152, 16 L. Ed. 2d 267 (1966). On "Bloody Sunday" in 1965, in Selma, Alabama, police beat and used tear gas against hundreds marching in support of African-American enfranchisement. See *Northwest Austin,* *supra*, at 220, n. 3, 129 S. Ct. 2504, 174 L. Ed. 2d 140 (Thomas, J., concurring in judgment in part and dissenting in part). Today both of those towns are governed by African-American mayors. Problems remain in these States and others, but there is no denying that, due to the Voting Rights Act, our Nation has made great strides.

. . . .

Respondents do not deny that there have been improvements on the ground, but argue that much of this can be attributed to the deterrent effect of § 5, which dissuades covered jurisdictions from engaging in discrimination that they would resume should § 5 be struck down. Under this theory, however, § 5 would be effectively immune from scrutiny; no matter how "clean" the record of covered jurisdictions, the argument could always be made that it was deterrence that accounted for the good behavior.

. . . .

III

A

. . . .

Coverage today is based on decades-old data and eradicated practices. . . .

In 1965, the States could be divided into two groups: those with a recent history of voting tests and low voter registration and turnout, and those without those characteristics. Congress based its coverage formula on that distinction. Today the Nation is no longer divided along those lines, yet the Voting Rights Act continues to treat it as if it were.

B

The Government's defense of the formula is limited. First, the Government contends that the formula is "reverse-engineered": Congress identified the jurisdictions to be covered and *then* came up with criteria to describe them. Brief for Federal Respondent 48-49. Under that reasoning, there need not be any logical relationship between the criteria in the formula and the reason for coverage; all that is necessary is that the formula happen to capture the jurisdictions Congress wanted to single out.

. . . .

The Government falls back to the argument that because the formula was relevant in 1965, its continued use is permissible so long as any discrimination remains in the States Congress identified back then — regardless of how that discrimination compares to discrimination in States unburdened by coverage. This argument does not look to "current political conditions," but instead relies on a comparison between the States in 1965. That comparison reflected the different histories of the North and South. It was in the South that slavery was upheld by law until uprooted by the Civil War, that the reign of Jim Crow denied African-Americans the most basic freedoms, and that state and local governments worked tirelessly to disenfranchise citizens on the basis of race. The Court invoked that history — rightly so — in sustaining the disparate coverage of the Voting Rights Act in 1966. See *Katzenbach, supra,* at 308, 86 S. Ct. 803, 15 L. Ed. 2d 769("The constitutional propriety of the Voting Rights Act of 1965 must be judged with reference to the historical experience which it reflects.").

But history did not end in 1965. By the time the Act was reauthorized in 2006, there had been 40 more years of it. In assessing the "current need[ ]" for a preclearance system that treats States differently from one another today, that history cannot be ignored. During that time, largely because of the Voting Rights Act, voting tests were abolished, disparities in voter registration and turnout due to race were erased, and African-Americans attained political office in record numbers. And yet the coverage formula that Congress reauthorized in 2006 ignores these developments, keeping the focus on decades-old data relevant to decades-old problems, rather than current data reflecting current needs.

. . . .

C

[Roberts, CJ reviewed evidence that the Act's supporters assert justifies disparate coverage.] Regardless of how to look at the record, however, no one can fairly say that it shows anything approaching the "pervasive," "flagrant," "widespread," and "rampant" discrimination that faced Congress in 1965, and that clearly distinguished the covered jurisdictions from the rest of the Nation at that time. *Katzenbach, supra,* at 308, 315, 331, 86 S. Ct. 803, 15 L. Ed. 2d 769; *Northwest Austin,* 557 U.S., at 201, 129 S. Ct. 2504, 174 L. Ed. 2d 140.

But a more fundamental problem remains: Congress did not use the record it compiled to shape a coverage formula grounded in current conditions. It instead reenacted a formula based on 40-year-old facts having no logical relation to the present day. . . .

The dissent also turns to the record to argue that, in light of voting discrimination in Shelby County, the county cannot complain about the provisions that subject it to preclearance. *Post,* at 23-30. But that is like saying that a driver pulled over pursuant to a policy of stopping all redheads cannot complain about that policy, if it turns out his license has expired. Shelby County's claim is that the coverage formula here is unconstitutional in all its applications, because of how it selects the jurisdictions subjected to preclearance. The county was selected based on that formula, and may challenge it in court.

D

The dissent treats the Act as if it were just like any other piece of legislation, but this Court has made clear from the beginning that the Voting Rights Act is far from ordinary. . . .

. . . .

JUSTICE THOMAS, concurring [suggested that, apart from the disparate application of § 5, he would find the provision unconstitutional.]

JUSTICE GINSBURG, with whom JUSTICE BREYER, JUSTICE SOTOMAYOR, and JUSTICE KAGAN join, dissenting.

In the Court's view, the very success of § 5 of the Voting Rights Act demands its dormancy. Congress was of another mind. Recognizing that large progress has been made, Congress determined, based on a voluminous record, that the scourge of discrimination was not yet extirpated. The question this case presents is who decides whether, as currently operative, § 5 remains justifiable, this Court, or a Congress charged with the obligation to enforce the post-Civil War Amendments "by appropriate legislation." With overwhelming support in both Houses, Congress concluded that, for two prime reasons, § 5 should continue in force, unabated. First, continuance would facilitate completion of the impressive gains thus far made; and second, continuance would guard against backsliding. Those assessments were well within Congress' province to make and should elicit this Court's unstinting approbation.

I

. . . .

A century after the *Fourteenth* and *Fifteenth Amendments* guaranteed citizens the right to vote free of discrimination on the basis of race, the "blight of racial discrimination in voting" continued to "infec[t] the electoral process in parts of our country." *South Carolina v. Katzenbach*, 383 U.S. 301, 308, 86 S. Ct. 803, 15 L. Ed. 2d 769 (1966). Early attempts to cope with this vile infection resembled battling the Hydra. Whenever one form of voting discrimination was identified and prohibited, others sprang up in its place. This Court repeatedly encountered the remarkable "variety and persistence" of laws disenfranchising minority citizens. *Id.*, at 311. . . .

. . . .

Congress learned from experience that laws targeting particular electoral practices or enabling case-by-case litigation were inadequate to the task [citing experience with earlier civil rights legislation that authorized the Attorney General to seek injunctions against Fifteenth Amendment violations.]

Answering that need, the Voting Rights Act became one of the most consequential, efficacious, and amply justified exercises of federal legislative power in our Nation's his-tory. Requiring federal preclearance of changes in voting laws in the covered jurisdictions — those States and localities where opposition to the Constitution's commands were most virulent — the VRA provided a fit solution for minority voters as well as for States. . . .

After a century's failure to fulfill the promise of the *Fourteenth* and *Fifteenth Amendments*, passage of the VRA finally led to signal improvement on this front.

[The dissent notes the record of significant progress attributed to the VRA.]

. . . .

In response to evidence of [new "second-generation barriers" to voting], Congress reauthorized the VRA for five years in 1970, for seven years in 1975, and for 25 years in 1982. . . .

Congress did not take this task lightly. [The dissent notes the lengthy hearings, floor consideration, passage by the House by a vote of 390-33, unanimous passage by the Senate, and approval by President George W. Bush, who stated that the law recognized "further work . . . in the fight against injustice," and called the reauthorization "an example of our continued commitment to a united America where every person is valued and treated with dignity and respect."]

. . . .

II

. . . .

It cannot tenably be maintained that the VRA, an Act of Congress adopted to shield the right to vote from racial discrimination, is inconsistent with the letter or spirit of the *Fifteenth Amendment*, or any provision of the Constitution read in light of the Civil War Amendments. Nowhere in today's opinion, or in *Northwest Austin*, is there clear recognition of the transformative effect the *Fifteenth Amendment* aimed to achieve. Notably, "the Founders' first successful amendment told Congress that it could 'make no law' over a certain domain"; in contrast, the Civil War Amendments used "language [that] authorized transformative new federal statutes to uproot all vestiges of unfreedom and inequality" and provided "sweeping enforcement powers . . . to enact 'appropriate' legislation targeting state abuses." A. Amar, America's Constitution: A Biography 361, 363, 399 (2005). See also McConnell, Institutions and Interpretation: A Critique of *City of Boerne* v. *Flores*, 111 Harv. L. Rev. 153, 182 *(1997)* (quoting Civil War-era framer that "the remedy for the violation of the *fourteenth* and *fifteenth amendments* was expressly not left to the courts. The remedy was legislative.").

. . . .

Until today, in considering the constitutionality of the VRA, the Court has accorded Congress the full measure of respect its judgments in this domain should garner. *South Carolina* v. *Katzenbach* supplies the standard of review: "As against the reserved powers of the States, Congress may use any rational means to effectuate the constitutional prohibition of racial discrimination in voting." 383 U.S., at 324, 86 S. Ct. 803, 15 L. Ed. 2d 769. . . .

. . . .

III

. . . .

A

[Here, Ginsburg J catalogued the number of instances where the Justice Department had found, in the period between 1982-2004, changes in election laws in covered jurisdictions that it viewed as discriminatory.]

All told, between 1982 and 2006, DOJ objections blocked over 700 voting changes based on a determination that the changes were discriminatory. H. R. Rep. No. 109-478, at 21. Congress found that the majority of DOJ objections included findings of discriminatory intent, *see 679 F.3d, at 867*, and that the changes blocked by preclearance were "calculated decisions to keep minority voters from fully participating in the political process." H. R. Rep. 109-478, at 21. . . .

. . . .

Congress also received evidence that litigation under § 2 of the VRA was an inadequate substitute for preclearance in the covered jurisdictions. . . .

. . . .

True, conditions in the South have impressively improved since passage of the Voting Rights Act. Congress noted this improvement and found that the VRA was the driving force behind it. 2006 Reauthorization § 2(b)(1). But Congress also found that voting discrimination had evolved into subtler second-generation barriers, and that eliminating preclearance would risk loss of the gains that had been made. . . .

B

. . . .

There is no question, moreover, that the covered jurisdictions have a unique history of problems with racial discrimination in voting. Consideration of this long history, still in living memory, was altogether appropriate. The Court criticizes Congress for failing to recognize that "history did not end in 1965." *Ante*, at 20. But the Court ignores that "what's past is prologue." W. Shakespeare, The Tempest, act 2, sc. 1. And "[t]hose who cannot remember the past are condemned to repeat it." 1 G. Santayana, The Life of Reason 284 (1905). . . .

[The dissent cited a study presented to Congress indicating that "that racial discrimination in voting remains "concentrated in the jurisdictions singled out for preclearance." Specifically, while the covered jurisdictions account for less than 25 percent of the country's population, the study revealed that they accounted for 56 percent of successful § 2 litigation since 1982. Other evidence "indicated that voting in the covered jurisdictions was more racially polarized than elsewhere in the country. H. R. Rep. No. 109-478, at 34-35."]

. . .

IV

. . . .

A

. . . .

[The dissent provided examples of racist behavior by Alabama officials] to demonstrate that, at least in Alabama, the "current burdens" imposed by § 5's preclearance requirement are "justified by current needs." *Northwest Austin*, 557 U.S., at 203, 129 S. Ct. 2504, 174 L. Ed. 2d 140. . . .

. . . .

B

. . . .

Today's unprecedented extension of the equal sovereignty principle outside its proper domain — the admission of new States — is capable of much mischief. Federal statutes that treat States disparately are hardly novelties. See, *e.g.*, 28 U.S.C. § 3704 (no State may operate or permit a sports-related gambling scheme, unless that State conducted such a scheme "at any time during the period beginning January 1, 1976, and ending August 31, 1990"); 26 U.S C. § 142(l) (EPA required to locate green building project in a State meeting specified population criteria); 42 U.S. C. § 3796bb (at least 50 percent of rural drug enforcement assistance funding must be allocated to States with "a population density of fifty-two or fewer persons per square mile or a State in which the largest county has fewer than one hundred and fifty thousand people, based on the decennial census of 1990 through fiscal year 1997"); §§ 13925, 13971 (similar population criteria for funding to combat rural domestic violence); § 10136 (specifying rules applicable to Nevada's Yucca Mountain nuclear waste site, and providing that "[n]o State, other than the State of Nevada, may receive financial assistance under this subsection after December 22, 1987"). Do such provisions remain safe given the Court's expansion of equal sovereignty's sway?

. . . .

9.4.3.   Contrasting Canadian doctrine regarding ameliorative practices

Canadian law on affirmative action is, as we saw in Chapter Four, quite the opposite. Not only must petitioners claim that they suffer differential treatment that is "substantively discriminatory" in that it is based on prejudice or stereotype, but s. 15(2) expressly provides that the equality provision "does not preclude any law, program or activity that has as its object the amelioration of conditions of disadvantaged individuals or groups . . ."

Illustrative is *R. v. Kapp*, [2008] 2 SCR 483, which upheld a challenge to a federal government fishing license granted to designees of specific aboriginal bands who were given the exclusive right to fish for salmon in the mouth of the Fraser River for a 24-hour period. As noted in Chapter Four, the Court used the decision as an opportunity to clarify the basic principles of equality protected by s. 15(1), but still had to deal with the problem that the provincial court judge initially had found that the statute had unconstitutionally infringed the human dignity of white men and women seeking fishing licenses. The Court noted that s. 15(2) built upon judicial interpretation of pre-Charter human rights statutes "recognizing that ameliorative programs targeting a disadvantaged group do not constitute discrimination." *Id.* at ¶ 31. In addition, though, *Kapp* held that a reviewing court need not determine whether a practice is substantively discriminatory if the government establishes that the program is "ameliorative" under s. 15(2). In short, a program "does not violate the s. 15 equality guarantee if the government can demonstrate that: (1) the program has an ameliorative or remedial purpose; and (2) the program targets a disadvantaged group identified by the enumerated or analogous grounds." *Id.* at ¶ 41.

Another example of race-neutral American and race-conscious Canadian approaches arises because both countries are plagued by the disproportionate number of racial minorities (African Americans and aboriginals, respectively) in their prison systems. In many areas of the United States, the number of young black men involved in the criminal justice system approaches 1/3. Manitoba's population is 12% aboriginal, but over half the prison inmates are aboriginal. The figure is even more stark in Saskatchewan. *See generally* Michael Jackson, *Locking Up Natives in Canada*, 23 U.B.C. L. REV. 215 (1988–89).

Parliament responded to academic claims that criminal justice would be improved by taking into account aboriginal concepts of "restorative justice" and that sentencing should focus on the needs of the people most closely affected by the crime — the victim, the immediate community, and the offender. *See generally* Michael Jackson, *In Search of Pathways to Justice: Alternative Dispute Resolution in Aboriginal Communities*, 26 U.B.C L. REV. (Special Ed.) 147 (1992). In addition to adding these factors to general sentencing guidelines, Parliament provided in s. 718.2(e) of the *Criminal Code* that "all available sanctions other than imprisonment that are reasonable in the circumstances should be considered for all offenders, with particular attention to the circumstances of aboriginal offenders." In *R. v. Gladue*, [1999] 1 S.C.R. 688, the Supreme Court of Canada directed judges, in sentencing aboriginal offenders, to consider "the broad systemic and background factors affecting aboriginal people, and of the priority given in aboriginal cultures to a restorative approach to sentencing" in order to determine the sanctions "which maybe appropriate in the circumstances for the offender because of his or her particular aboriginal heritage or connection." *Id.* at 738. While the provision did not mean that sentences were to be automatically reduced for aboriginal offenders, or that restorative sentences were necessarily more lenient, the Court expressly noted that "the jail term for an aboriginal offender may in some circumstances be less than the term imposed on a non-aboriginal offender for the same offense." *Id.* at 739.

In part reflecting similar concerns in the United States, the federal Sentencing Commission recommended a change in law that provides for significant incarceration for possession with intent to distribute 5 grams of crack cocaine or 500 grams of powder cocaine, the former being primarily used by African Americans and the latter drug disproportionately used by whites. Congress, however, rejected the Commission's recommendation. Judicial challenges to the distinction have been uniformly unsuccessful. *See United States v. Harding*, 971 F.2d 410 (9th Cir. 1992).

9.3.4.   What is *Brown*'s legacy?

PARENTS INVOLVED IN COMMUNITY SCHOOLS v. SEATTLE SCHOOL DISTRICT NO. 1
SUPREME COURT OF THE UNITED STATES
551 U.S. 701 (2007)

[The Seattle and Louisville school districts voluntarily adopted student assignment plans that rely on race to determine which schools certain children may attend. The Seattle district, which never operated legally segregated schools, classified children as white or nonwhite, and used the racial classifications as a "tiebreaker" to allocate slots in particular high schools. Louisville schools had been desegrated by court order, but in 2000 the District Court dissolved the decree after finding that the district had eliminated the vestiges of prior segregation to the greatest extent practicable. In 2001, Louisville adopted its plan classifying students as black or "other" in order to make certain elementary school assignments and to rule on transfer requests. The petitioners, parents whose children may not have been able to attend their preferred schools because of the race-conscious plans, contended that allocating children to different public schools based solely on their race violates the Fourteenth Amendment's Equal Protection guarantee.]

CHIEF JUSTICE ROBERTS announced the judgment of the Court [in a divided opinion. For reader's convenience, the portions of his opinion commanding a majority are noted below]

III

A

[For the majority]

[Roberts, C.J., cited precedents requiring strict scrutiny to ensure that the challenged plans were "narrowly tailored" to achieve a "compelling" government interest. The court noted that a previously recognized compelling interest in remedying the effects of past intentional discrimination was not available here because Seattle had not intentionally discriminated and Louisville had been found to have remedied its history of segregation. The opinion recalled a major precedent-setting opinion, *Milliken v. Bradley*, 433 U.S. 267, 280, n. 14 (1977), which held that the harm being remedied by mandatory desegregation plans is the harm that is traceable to segregation, rather than segregated housing patterns, and that "the Constitution is not violated by racial imbalance in the schools, without more."]

The second government interest we have recognized as compelling for purposes of strict scrutiny is the interest in diversity in higher education upheld in [*Grutter v. Bollinger*, 539 U.S. 306, 328 (2003)]. [The opinion contrasted *Grutter*, where race was simply one factor in a "highly individualized, holistic review" to those cases where "race is not considered as part of a broader effort to achieve "exposure to widely diverse people, cultures, ideas, and viewpoints" but was "determinative standing alone." Moreover, "the plans here employ only a limited notion of diversity, viewing race exclusively in white/nonwhite terms in Seattle and black/"other" terms in Jefferson County. But see *Metro Broadcasting, Inc. v. FCC*, 497 U.S. 547, 610, 110 S. Ct. 2997, 111 L. Ed. 2d 445 (1990) ("We are a Nation not of black and white alone, but one teeming with divergent communities knitted together with various traditions and carried forth, above all, by individuals") (O'Connor, J., dissenting)." For example, a Seattle school with 50 percent Asian-American students and 50 percent white students but no African-American, Native-American, or Latino students would qualify as balanced, while a school with 30 percent Asian-American, 25 percent African-American, 25 percent Latino, and 20 percent white students would not.]

B

[For ROBERTS, C.J., and SCALIA and ALITO, JJ.]

[The plurality found that the litigants' dispute over the benefits of racial diversity need not be resolved,] because it is clear that the racial classifications employed by the districts are not narrowly tailored to the goal of achieving the educational and social benefits asserted to flow from racial diversity. In design and operation, the plans are directed only to racial balance, pure and simple, an objective this Court has repeatedly condemned as illegitimate. The Court noted that the plans were tied to each district's specific racial demographics, rather than to any pedagogic concept of the level of diversity needed to obtain the asserted educational benefits. The districts did not offer evidence explaining why the level of racial diversity necessary to achieve the asserted educational benefits happens to coincide with the racial demographics of the respective school districts.

Accepting racial balancing as a compelling state interest would justify the imposition of racial proportionality throughout American society, contrary to our repeated recognition that "at the heart of the Constitution's guarantee of equal protection lies the simple command that the Government must treat citizens as individuals, not as simply components of a racial, religious, sexual or national class." *Miller v. Johnson*, 515 U.S. 900, 911, 115 S. Ct. 2475, 132 L. Ed. 2d 762 (1995) (quoting *Metro Broadcasting, 497 U.S.*, at 602, 110 S. Ct. 2997, 111 L. Ed. 2d 445 (O'Connor, J., dissenting). . . .

. . . .

[The plurality rejected Seattle's effort to justify race-conscious school assignments] as necessary to address the consequences of racially identifiable housing patterns. The sweep of the mandate claimed by the district is contrary to our rulings that remedying past societal discrimination does not justify race-conscious government action. . . .

. . . .

C

[For the majority]

. . . .

The districts have also failed to show that they considered methods other than explicit racial classifications to achieve their stated goals. Narrow tailoring requires "serious, good faith consideration of workable race-neutral alternatives," *Grutter, supra, at 339, 123 S. Ct. 2325, 156 L. Ed. 2d 304*, and yet [neither school district appeared to seriously consider alternatives that would not require race-conscious assignments.]

IV

[For the majority]

[Chief Justice Roberts rejected Justice Breyer's effort to justify the challenged plans by relying on precedents that allowed race-conscious remedies for past intentional discrimination. Justice Breyer's approach would obliterate the clear distinction that prior cases had drawn between segregation by state action and racial imbalance caused by other factors, citing *Freeman v. Pitts*, 503 U.S. 467, 495-96 (1992) ("Where resegregation is a product not of state action but of private choices, it does not have constitutional implications"). . . .]

[After explaining why various precedents upon which Justice Breyer relied were distinguishable or pre-dated the Court's reaffirmation of strict scrutiny for all racial classifications, the opinion returned to, and explicitly rejected, his argument that a different standard of review should be applied because the districts use race for beneficent rather than malicious purposes, noting that it had been repeatedly pressed in the past.]

Justice Breyer's position comes down to a familiar claim: The end justifies the means. He admits that "there is a cost in applying 'a state-mandated racial label,'" but he is confident that the cost is worth paying. Our established strict scrutiny test for racial classifications, however, insists on "detailed examination, both as to ends *and as to means.*" *Adarand, supra, at 236* (emphasis added). Simply because the school districts may seek a worthy goal does not mean they are free to discriminate on the basis of race to achieve it, or that their racial classifications should be subject to less exacting scrutiny.

. . . .

[The opinion notes that the deference to local school boards advocated by Breyer, J., was "fundamentally at odds" with strict scrutiny.]

Justice Breyer's dissent ends on an unjustified note of alarm. [The majority expressly rejected the dissent's prediction that this decision threatens "hundreds of state and federal statutes and regulations," and specifically stated that a provision of the No Child Left Behind Act that requires States to set measurable objectives to track the achievement of students from major racial and ethnic groups, 20 U.S.C. § 6311(b)(2)(C)(v) — had "nothing to do with the pertinent issues in these cases." They further noted that they "express no opinion," "even in dicta," about race-conscious decisions with regard to where to construct new schools, how to allocate resources among schools, and which academic offerings to provide to attract students to certain schools, all of which "implicate different considerations than the explicit racial classifications at issue in these cases."]

If the need for the racial classifications embraced by the school districts is unclear, even on the districts' own terms, the costs are undeniable. "Distinctions between citizens solely because of their ancestry are by their very nature odious to a free people whose institutions are founded upon the doctrine of equality." *Adarand*, 515 U.S., at 214, 115 S. Ct. 2097, 132 L. Ed. 2d 158 (internal quotation marks omitted). Government action dividing us by race is inherently suspect because such classifications promote "notions of racial inferiority and lead to a politics of racial hostility," *Croson, supra*, at 493, 109 S. Ct. 706, 102 L. Ed. 2d 854, "reinforce the belief, held by too many for too much of our history, that individuals should be judged by the color of their skin," *Shaw v. Reno*, 509 U.S. 630, 657, 113 S. Ct. 2816, 125 L. Ed. 2d 511 (1993), and "endorse race-based reasoning and the conception of a Nation divided into racial blocs, thus contributing to an escalation of racial hostility and conflict." *Metro Broadcasting*, 497 U.S., at 603, 110 S. Ct. 2997, 111 L. Ed. 2d 445 (O'Connor, J., dissenting). As the Court explained in *Rice v. Cayetano*, 528 U.S. 495, 517, 120 S. Ct. 1044, 145 L. Ed. 2d 1007 (2000), "one of the principal reasons race is treated as a forbidden classification is that it demeans the dignity and worth of a person to be judged by ancestry instead of by his or her own merit and essential qualities."

. . . .

The parties and their *amici* debate which side is more faithful to the heritage of *Brown*, but the position of the plaintiffs in *Brown* was spelled out in their brief and could not have been clearer: "The *Fourteenth Amendment* prevents states from according differential treatment to American children on the basis of their color or race." Brief for Appellants in Nos. 1, 2, and 4 and for Respondents in No. 10 on Reargument in *Brown I*, O. T. 1953, p. 15 (Summary of Argument). What do the racial classifications at issue here do, if not accord differential treatment on the basis of race? As counsel who appeared before this Court for the plaintiffs in *Brown* put it: "We have one fundamental contention which we will seek to develop in the course of this argument, and that contention is that no State has any authority under the equal-protection clause of the *Fourteenth Amendment* to use race as a factor in affording educational opportunities among its citizens." Tr. of Oral Arg. in *Brown I*, p. 7 (Robert L. Carter, Dec. 9, 1952). There is no ambiguity in that statement. And it was that position that prevailed in this Court, which emphasized in its remedial opinion that what was "at stake is the personal interest of the plaintiffs in admission to public schools as soon as practicable *on a nondiscriminatory basis*," and what was required was "determining admission to the public schools *on a nonracial basis*." *Brown II, supra*, at 300-301, 75 S. Ct. 753, 99 L. Ed. 1083 (emphasis added). What do the racial classifications do in these cases, if not determine admission to a public school on a racial basis?

Before *Brown*, schoolchildren were told where they could and could not go to school based on the color of their skin. The school districts in these cases have not carried the heavy burden of demonstrating that we should allow this once again — even for very different reasons. For schools that never segregated on the basis of race, such as Seattle, or that have removed the vestiges of past segregation, such as Jefferson County, the way "to achieve a system of determining admission to the public schools on a nonracial basis," *Brown II*, 349 U.S., at 300–301, 75 S. Ct. 753, 99 L. Ed. 1083, is to stop assigning students on a racial basis. The way to stop discrimination on the basis of race is to stop discriminating on the basis of race.

. . . .

JUSTICE THOMAS, concurring.

. . . .

I

[Thomas, J., rejected the dissent's claim that the school districts are threatened with resegregation, arguing that racial] imbalance is not segregation, and the mere incantation of terms like resegregation and remediation cannot make up the difference.

A

. . . .

Racial imbalance is the failure of a school district's individual schools to match or approximate the demographic makeup of the student population at large. Racial imbalance is not segregation. Although presently observed racial imbalance might result from past *de jure* segregation, racial imbalance can also result from any number of innocent private decisions, including voluntary housing choices. . . .

B

. . . .

2

This Court has carved out a narrow exception to that general rule for cases in which a school district has a "history of maintaining two sets of schools in a single school system deliberately operated to carry out a governmental policy to separate pupils in schools solely on the basis of race." In such cases, race-based remedial measures are sometimes required.[24] [No such extraordinary circumstance occurs

---

[24] [FN 6] As I have explained elsewhere, the remedies this Court authorized lower courts to compel in early desegregation cases like *Green* and *Swann* were exceptional. Sustained resistance to *Brown* prompted the Court to authorize extraordinary race-conscious remedial measures (like compelled racial mixing) to turn the Constitution's dictate to desegregate into reality. Even if these measures were

here, Justice Thomas concluded.]

. . . .

II

. . . .

A

[Next, Thomas, J., rejected the view expressed by Breyer, J., and several lower court judges that a somewhat less strict scrutiny was appropriate where programs were not "aimed at oppressing blacks," do not "seek to give one racial group an edge over another," or were "far from the original evils at which the *Fourteenth Amendment* was addressed."].

Even supposing it mattered to the constitutional analysis, the race-based student assignment programs before us are not as benign as the dissent believes. "Racial paternalism and its unintended consequences can be as poisonous and pernicious as any other form of discrimination." As these programs demonstrate, every time the government uses racial criteria to "bring the races together," someone gets excluded, and the person excluded suffers an injury solely because of his or her race. The petitioner in the Louisville case received a letter from the school board informing her that her *kindergartener* would not be allowed to attend the school of petitioner's choosing because of the child's race. Doubtless, hundreds of letters like this went out from both school boards every year these race-based assignment plans were in operation. This type of exclusion, solely on the basis of race, is precisely the sort of government action that pits the races against one another, exacerbates racial tension, and "provokes resentment among those who believe that they have been wronged by the government's use of race." . . .

amen.

B

. . . .

2

Next, the dissent argues that the interest in integration has an educational element. The dissent asserts that racially balanced schools improve educational outcomes for black children. In support, the dissent unquestioningly cites certain social science research to support propositions that are hotly disputed among social scientists. In reality, it is far from apparent that coerced racial mixing has any educational benefits, much less that integration is necessary to black achievement. [Here, Thomas, J. catalogues the sharp differences among scholars about the effect of integration, citing, *inter alia*, T. Sowell, Education: Assumptions Versus History

---

appropriate as remedies in the face of widespread resistance to *Brown*'s mandate, they are not forever insulated from constitutional scrutiny. Rather, "such powers should have been temporary and used only to overcome the widespread resistance to the dictates of the Constitution."

7-38 (1986) and L. Izumi, They Have Overcome: High-Poverty, High-Performing Schools in California (2002) (chronicling exemplary achievement in predominantly Hispanic schools in California). He found the dissent's approach of validating race-conscious action if "sufficient social science evidence supports" the government's conclusion to be far too deferential, leaving "our equal-protection jurisprudence at the mercy of elected government officials evaluating the evanescent views of a handful of social scientists. To adopt the dissent's deferential approach would be to abdicate our constitutional responsibilities."]

* * *

III

Most of the dissent's criticisms of today's result can be traced to its rejection of the color-blind Constitution. The dissent attempts to marginalize the notion of a color-blind Constitution by consigning it to me and Members of today's plurality.[25] But I am quite comfortable in the company I keep. My view of the Constitution is Justice Harlan's view in *Plessy:* "Our Constitution is color-blind, and neither knows nor tolerates classes among citizens." *Plessy v. Ferguson,* 163 U.S. 537, 559, 16 S. Ct. 1138, 41 L. Ed. 256 (1896) (dissenting opinion). And my view was the rallying cry for the lawyers who litigated *Brown.* See, *e.g.,* Brief for Appellants in *Brown v. Board of Education,* O. T. 1953, Nos. 1, 2, and 4 p. 65 ("That the Constitution is color blind is our dedicated belief"); Brief for Appellants in *Brown v. Board of Education,* O. T. 1952, No. 1, p. 5 ("The *Fourteenth Amendment* precludes a state from imposing distinctions or classifications based upon race and color alone"); see also In Memoriam: Honorable Thurgood Marshall, Proceedings of the Bar and Officers of the Supreme Court of the United States, X (1993) (remarks of Judge Motley) ("Marshall had a 'Bible' to which he turned during his most depressed moments. The 'Bible' would be known in the legal community as the first Mr. Justice Harlan's dissent in *Plessy v. Ferguson,* 163 U.S. 537, 552, 16 S. Ct. 1138, 41 L. Ed. 256 (1896). I do not know of any opinion which buoyed Marshall more in his pre-*Brown* days . . . .").

. . . .

[Justice Thomas' rejected Justice Breyer's call for deference to "a local school board's knowledge, expertise, and concerns," noting that] with equal vigor, the segregationists argued for deference to local authorities. See, *e.g.,* Brief for Kansas on Reargument in *Brown* v. *Board of Education,* O. T. 1953, No. 1, p. 14 ("We advocate only a concept of constitutional law that permits determinations of state and local policy to be made on state and local levels. We defend only the validity of

---

[25] [FN 19] The dissent half-heartedly attacks the historical underpinnings of the color-blind Constitution. I have no quarrel with the proposition that the *Fourteenth Amendment* sought to bring former slaves into American society as full members. What the dissent fails to understand, however, is that the color-blind Constitution does not bar the government from taking measures to remedy past state-sponsored discrimination — indeed, it requires that such measures be taken in certain circumstances. Race-based government measures during the 1860s and 1870s to remedy *state-enforced slavery* were therefore not inconsistent with the color-blind Constitution.

the statute that enables the Topeka Board of Education to determine its own course").

The similarities between the dissent's arguments and the segregationists' arguments do not stop there. Like the dissent, the segregationists repeatedly cautioned the Court to consider practicalities and not to embrace too theoretical a view of the *Fourteenth Amendment*. And just as the dissent argues that the need for these programs will lessen over time, the segregationists claimed that reliance on segregation was lessening and might eventually end.

What was wrong in 1954 cannot be right today.[26] Whatever else the Court's rejection of the segregationists' arguments in *Brown* might have established, it certainly made clear that state and local governments cannot take from the Constitution a right to make decisions on the basis of race by adverse possession. . . .

. . . .

JUSTICE KENNEDY, concurring in part and concurring in the judgment.

[The opinion notes that while the "enduring hope is that race should not matter; the reality is that too often it does." Thus, Kennedy, J., viewed the plurality opinion as implying] an all-too-unyielding insistence that race cannot be a factor in instances when, in my view, it may be taken into account. The plurality opinion is too dismissive of the legitimate interest government has in ensuring all people have equal opportunity regardless of their race. The plurality's postulate that "the way to stop discrimination on the basis of race is to stop discriminating on the basis of race," *ante*, at 40-41, is not sufficient to decide these cases. Fifty years of experience since *Brown v. Board of Education*, 347 U.S. 483, 74 S. Ct. 686, 98 L. Ed. 873 (1954), should teach us that the problem before us defies so easy a solution. School districts can seek to reach *Brown*'s objective of equal educational opportunity. The plurality opinion is at least open to the interpretation that the Constitution requires school districts to ignore the problem of *de facto* resegregation in schooling. I cannot endorse that conclusion. To the extent the plurality opinion suggests the Constitution mandates that state and local school authorities must accept the status quo of racial isolation in schools, it is, in my view, profoundly mistaken.

---

[26] [FN 27] It is no answer to say that these cases can be distinguished from *Brown* because *Brown* involved invidious racial classifications whereas the racial classifications here are benign. How does one tell when a racial classification is invidious? The segregationists in *Brown* argued that their racial classifications were benign, not invidious. See Tr. of Oral Arg. in *Briggs v. Elliott*, O. T. 1953, No. 2, p. 83 ("It [South Carolina] is confident of its good faith and intention to produce equality for all of its children of whatever race or color. It is convinced that the happiness, the progress and the welfare of these children is best promoted in segregated schools"); Brief for Appellees on Reargument in *Davis v. County School Board*, O. T. 1953, No. 3, p. 82-83 ("Our many hours of research and investigation have led only to confirmation of our view that segregation by race in Virginia's public schools at this time not only does not offend the Constitution of the United States but serves to provide a better education for living for the children of both races"); Tr. of Oral Arg. in *Davis v. County School Board*, O. T. 1952, No. 3, p. 71 ("To make such a transition, would undo what we have been doing, and which we propose to continue to do for the uplift and advancement of the education of both races. It would stop this march of progress, this onward sweep"). It is the height of arrogance for Members of this Court to assert blindly that their motives are better than others.

. . . .

JUSTICE STEVENS, dissenting.

While I join Justice Breyer's eloquent and unanswerable dissent in its entirety, it is appropriate to add these words.

There is a cruel irony in The Chief Justice's reliance on our decision in *Brown v. Board of Education*. The first sentence in the concluding paragraph of his opinion states: "Before *Brown*, schoolchildren were told where they could and could not go to school based on the color of their skin." This sentence reminds me of Anatole France's observation: "The majestic equality of the law, forbids rich and poor alike to sleep under bridges, to beg in the streets, and to steal their bread." The Chief Justice fails to note that it was only black schoolchildren who were so ordered; indeed, the history books do not tell stories of white children struggling to attend black schools. In this and other ways, The Chief Justice rewrites the history of one of this Court's most important decisions.

[Stevens, J. noted that the Supreme Court had affirmed a 1967 judgment of the Supreme Judicial Court of Massachusetts in 1967,] upholding a state statute mandating racial integration in that State's school system. See *School Comm. of Boston v. Board of Education, 352 Mass. 693, 227 N.E.2d 729*. Rejecting arguments comparable to those that the plurality accepts today, that court noted: "It would be the height of irony if the racial imbalance act, enacted as it was with the laudable purpose of achieving equal educational opportunities, should, by prescribing school pupil allocations based on race, founder on unsuspected shoals in the *Fourteenth Amendment." Id., at 698, 227 N. E. 2d, at 733* (footnote omitted).

. . . .

The Court has changed significantly since it decided *School Comm. of Boston* in 1968 [by summarily affirming the Massachusetts Supreme Court]. It was then more faithful to *Brown* and more respectful of our precedent than it is today. It is my firm conviction that no Member of the Court that I joined in 1975 would have agreed with today's decision.

JUSTICE BREYER, with whom JUSTICE STEVENS, JUSTICE SOUTER, and JUSTICE GINSBURG join, dissenting.

These cases consider the longstanding efforts of two local school boards to integrate their public schools. The school board plans before us resemble many others adopted in the last 50 years by primary and secondary schools throughout the Nation. All of those plans represent local efforts to bring about the kind of racially integrated education that *Brown v. Board of Education*, 347 U.S. 483, 74 S. Ct. 686, 98 L. Ed. 873 (1954), long ago promised — efforts that this Court has repeatedly required, permitted, and encouraged local authorities to undertake. This Court has recognized that the public interests at stake in such cases are "compelling." We have approved of "narrowly tailored" plans that are no less race-conscious than the plans before us. And we have understood that the Constitution *permits* local communities to adopt desegregation plans even where it does not *require* them to do so.

The plurality pays inadequate attention to this law, to past opinions' rationales, their language, and the contexts in which they arise. As a result, it reverses course and reaches the wrong conclusion. In doing so, it distorts precedent, it misapplies the relevant constitutional principles, it announces legal rules that will obstruct efforts by state and local governments to deal effectively with the growing resegregation of public schools, it threatens to substitute for present calm a disruptive round of race-related litigation, and it undermines *Brown*'s promise of integrated primary and secondary education that local communities have sought to make a reality. This cannot be justified in the name of the *Equal Protection Clause*.

[The dissent observed that these cases arose in the context of back-sliding in the public school integration, with one in six black children attending a school that is almost entirely composed of minority-race students. Justice Breyer identified three aspects of the interests at stake that he found compelling. First is "an interest in setting right the consequences of prior conditions of segregation" not only in schools but also with regard to housing patterns, employment practices, economic conditions, and social attitudes. Second is an interest in overcoming the adverse educational effects produced by and associated with highly segregated schools. Third, there is an interest in producing an educational environment that reflects the "pluralistic society" in which our children will live. It is an interest in helping our children learn to work and play together with children of different racial backgrounds. It is an interest in teaching children to engage in the kind of cooperation among Americans of all races that is necessary to make a land of three hundred million people one Nation. He acknowledged that social science data reached different results as to whether highly segregated schools in fact produce adverse educational effects and whether integrated schools result in graduates with more cooperative attitudes about race.]

If we are to insist upon unanimity in the social science literature before finding a compelling interest, we might never find one. I believe only that the Constitution allows democratically elected school boards to make up their own minds as to how best to include people of all races in one America.

[With regard to narrow tailoring, the dissent found that alternatives suggested by other justices and *amici* are not likely to be as effective in preventing resegregation.]

V

Consequences

. . . .

[Justice Breyer feared that the plurality's approach would result in a "surge of race-based litigation," would threaten widespread integration practices, etc.]

. . . By way of contrast, I do not claim to know how best to stop harmful discrimination; how best to create a society that includes all Americans; how best to overcome our serious problems of increasing *de facto* segregation, troubled inner city schooling, and poverty correlated with race. But, as a judge, I do know that the Constitution does not authorize judges to dictate solutions to these problems. Rather, the Constitution creates a democratic political system through which the people themselves must together find answers. And it is for them to debate how best to educate the Nation's children and how best to administer America's schools to achieve that aim. The Court should leave them to their work. And it is for them to decide, to quote the plurality's slogan, whether the best "way to stop discrimination on the basis of race is to stop discriminating on the basis of race." That is why the Equal Protection Clause outlaws invidious discrimination, but does not similarly forbid all use of race-conscious criteria.

. . . .

And what of law's concern to diminish and peacefully settle conflict among the Nation's people? Instead of accommodating different good-faith visions of our country and our Constitution, today's holding upsets settled expectations, creates legal uncertainty, and threatens to produce considerable further litigation, aggravating race-related conflict.

And what of the long history and moral vision that the *Fourteenth Amendment* itself embodies? The plurality cites in support those who argued in *Brown* against segregation, and Justice Thomas likens the approach that I have taken to that of segregation's defenders. But segregation policies did not simply tell schoolchildren "where they could and could not go to school based on the color of their skin," they perpetuated a caste system rooted in the institutions of slavery and 80 years of legalized subordination. The lesson of history is not that efforts to continue racial segregation are constitutionally indistinguishable from efforts to achieve racial integration. Indeed, it is a cruel distortion of history to compare Topeka, Kansas, in the 1950's to Louisville and Seattle in the modern day — to equate the plight of Linda Brown (who was ordered to attend a Jim Crow school) to the circumstances of Joshua McDonald (whose request to transfer to a school closer to home was initially declined). This is not to deny that there is a cost in applying "a state-mandated racial label" [citing Justice Kennedy's concurring opinion]. But that cost does not approach, in degree or in kind, the terrible harms of slavery, the resulting caste system, and 80 years of legal racial segregation.

. . . .

———————

To emphasize their strong disagreement, dissenting justices often read a portion of their dissent from the bench when the decision is announced. Extraordinarily, Justice Breyer's comments from the bench included remarks not in his printed opinion, taken by reporters as a reference, on the last day of the Term, to many decisions. Breyer's oral comments were reported to be: "It's very rare in the law that so few have changed so much so quickly." (Transcript from NPR's *Fresh Air* interview with New York Times Supreme Court correspondent Linda Greenhouse.)

9.5.   THE SOUTH AFRICAN EXPERIENCE

While claims of group rights, especially ethnic claims, were eventually rejected in the negotiations towards a post-apartheid society in South Africa, recognition of language and cultural rights, particularly in the context of pre-tertiary education, became a central issue. If constitutional rights, framed as individual rights were to be the alternative to group claims, it was also important to recognize that rights to language and culture, while individually held may only be effectively exercised communally. Article 31 of the Bill of Rights explicitly provides that "[p]ersons belonging to a cultural, religious or linguistic community may not be denied the right, with other members of that community . . . to enjoy their culture, practice their religion and use their language, and . . . to form, join and maintain cultural, religious and linguistic associations and other organs of civil society" although these rights may "not be exercised in a manner inconsistent with any provision of the Bill of Rights."

Integration of apartheid's formally racially exclusive schools took place fairly swiftly between 1990 and 1994, despite the continued existence of apartheid laws; however tensions remained and shortly after the implementation of the 1993 'interim' Constitution a case was brought challenging new provincial educational legislation designed to ensure access to public schools. While the Constitutional Court's opinion based on an interpretation of the language of the Constitution was written by Justice Mohamed, two concurring opinions provide significant additional insights into these issues in the South African context. On the one hand, Justice Kriegler's opinion in Afrikaans, in which he clarifies that the right to education in a language of one's choice is limited to the right to maintain private schools at one's own expense so long as race is not used as a criterion of admission, remains to this day the only constitutional court opinion written in any of South Africa's eleven official languages other than English. On the other hand, Justice Sachs's opinion places the debate over language and cultural rights within the context of both South African history and international law.

IN RE: DISPUTE CONCERNING THE CONSTITUTIONALITY OF CERTAIN PROVISIONS OF THE SCHOOL EDUCATION BILL OF 1995

CONSTITUTIONAL COURT OF SOUTH AFRICA

1996 (3) SA 165

[This case arose under a special reference procedure in the 1993 Interim Constitution allowing the Constitutional Court to rule on the constitutionality of a controversial School Education Bill under consideration by the legislature of Gauteng Province. The principal challenge was to section 19, which provided:

"Language and discrimination

19. (1) Language competence testing shall not be used as an admission requirement to a public school.

(2) Learners at public schools shall be encouraged to make use of the range of official languages.

(3) No learner at a public school or a private school which receives a [government subsidy] shall be punished for expressing himself or herself in a language which is not a language of learning of the school concerned."

Petitioners and amicus, including a foundation whose mission was "to support a Christian value system and prescribe to the principle of mother tongue education" and "to promote education in the South African community as a whole with special reference to the Afrikaans medium education," asserted the right of persons to attend schools where language competence testing is permitted as an admission requirement or where the attendance of scholars at religious education classes is compulsory. The provincial government asserted that the bill does not preclude private single-language education, as the statute only regulated public or taxpayer-subsidized private schools. The challengers asserted that section 32(c) of the Constitution creates a positive obligation on the state to accord to every person the right to require the state to establish, where practicable, educational institutions based on a common culture, language or religion as long as there is no discrimination on the grounds of race.]

MAHOMED DP:

[6] Section 32 reads as follows:

"Education

32. Every person shall have the right—

(a) to basic education and to equal access to educational institutions;

(b) to instruction in the language of his or her choice where this is reasonably practicable; and

(c) to establish, where practicable, educational institutions based on a common culture, language or religion, provided that there shall be no discrimination on the ground of race."[27]

[7] The submission that every person can demand from the state the right to have established schools based on a common culture, language or religion is not supported by the language of section 32(c). The section does not say that every person has the right to have established by the state educational institutions based on such a common culture, language or religion. What it provides is that every person shall have the right to establish such educational institutions. Linguistically

Private

---

[27] [Ed. note: The equivalent provision of the Final Constitution, section 29, retains the right to basic education and access, and, in subsection (2), provides that

(2) Everyone has the right to receive education in the official language or languages of their choice in public educational institutions where that education is reasonably practicable. In order to ensure the effective access to, and implementation of, this right, the state must consider all reasonable educational alternatives, including single medium institutions, taking into account-

(a) equity;

(b) practicability; and

(c) the need to redress the results of past racially discriminatory laws and practices.]

Section 29(3) also provides, subject to limitations, a right to "maintain, at their own expense, independent educational institutions."

and grammatically it provides a defensive right to a person who seeks to establish such educational institutions and it protects that right from invasion by the state, without conferring on the state an obligation to establish such educational institutions.

[8] Considered in context, there is no logical force in the construction favoured by the petitioners. If a person has the right to basic education at public expense in terms of subparagraph (a) and if he or she has the right is to be instructed in the language of his or her choice in terms of sub-paragraph (b), why would there be any need to repeat in subparagraph (c) the right to education at public expense through a common language? The object of sub-section (c) is to make clear that while every person has a right to basic education through instruction in the language of his or her choice, those persons who want more than that and wish to have educational institutions based on a special culture, language or religion which is common, have the freedom to set up such institutions based on that commonality, unless it is not practicable. Thus interpreted, section 32(c) is neither superfluous nor tautologous. It preserves an important freedom. The constitutional entrenchment of that freedom is particularly important because of our special history initiated during the fifties, in terms of the system of Bantu education. From that period the state actively discouraged and effectively prohibited private educational institutions from establishing or continuing private schools and insisted that such schools had to be established and administered subject to the control of the state. The execution of those policies constituted an invasion on the right of individuals in association with one another to establish and continue, at their own expense, their own educational institutions based on their own values. Such invasions would now be constitutionally impermissible in terms of section 32(c).

[9] The interpretation of section 32(c) as a defensive right, based on its grammatical and linguistic structure, seems to me also to be supported by its context within section 32 itself. Section 32(a) creates a positive right that basic education be provided for every person and not merely a negative right that such a person should not be obstructed in pursuing his or her basic education. Section 32(b), recognising the diversity of languages in our country, again creates a positive right for every person to instruction in the language of his or her choice, where this is reasonably practicable, not merely a negative right to prevent any obstruction if such person seeks instruction in the language of his or her choice. Section 32(c), by contrast, guarantees a freedom - a freedom to establish educational institutions based on a common culture, language or religion. It is that freedom which is protected by section 32(c). A person can invoke the protection of the court where that freedom is threatened, but the language of section 32(c) does not support a claim that such educational institutions, based on a commonality of culture, language or religion, must be established by the state, or a claim that any person is entitled to demand such establishment, notwithstanding the fact that his or her right to basic education and to instruction in the language of his or her choice is, where practicable, otherwise being satisfied by the state.

. . . .

[13] In the written argument which was lodged on behalf of the petitioners, some reliance was placed on Canadian authority. We were reminded of section 35(1) of the

Constitution which provides that in the interpretation of Chapter 3 of the Constitution, a court of law may, inter alia, have regard to comparable foreign case law and we were referred to various dicta in a number of Canadian cases to the effect that the Canadian Charter of Rights and Freedoms imposed obligations on the Government to provide specific opportunities for the use of English and French in schools.

. . . .

[15] The language and structure of section 23 of the Canadian Charter are wholly distinguishable from section 32(c) of our Constitution. Section 23 of the Canadian Charter is clearly concerned with the obligation of the Government to provide education in the official languages of Canada to linguistic majorities and minorities. It is analogous to section 32(b) of our Constitution, but very different from section 32(c). The interpretation accorded to it by the Canadian courts can therefore be of scant assistance in the proper interpretation of section 32(c) of our Constitution.

. . . .

SACHS J:

[44] A straightforward reading of the text of section 32 of the Constitution runs directly counter to the arguments advanced by counsel for the Petitioners and the amicus curiae. We were urged, however, to approach the section in a broad and generous manner which took account both of cultural realities in this country and of internationally recognised principles relating to the protection of minorities. In view of the importance of the broader questions argued by the Petitioners in relation to minority rights, I propose to follow their argument through to see if applying internationally accepted principles of minority rights protection, would indeed suggest a different result, even if straining against the text. Preliminary though my explorations have to be, I am left in no doubt as to the answer to the above question. Thus, my answer, and the reasons therefor, follow.

I. THE BROAD SOUTH AFRICAN CONTEXT OF THE ENQUIRY

[45] Before touching on the evolution of international law principles in relation to minority rights, I feel it would be appropriate to locate the problem before us in a broad South African historical/ constitutional context. For the purpose of this analysis I will begin by making four assumptions in favour of the Petitioners.

[46] The first assumption is that the "never again" principle, which I feel should be one of our guides to interpretation, applies not only to bitter experiences of former state enforced segregation, but also to those of past compulsory assimilation. This was a major theme at the National Convention held to draft the document which became the Constitution of the Union of South Africa in 1910.

[47] The second assumption is that the Afrikaans language, like all languages, is not simply a means of communication and instruction, but a central element of community cohesion and identification for a distinct community in South Africa. We are accordingly dealing not merely with practical issues of pedagogy, but with intangible factors, that as was said in *Brown v Board of Education of Topeka*, form

an important part of the educational endeavour. In addition, what goes on in schools can have direct implications for the cultural personality and development of groups spreading far beyond the boundary fences of the schools themselves.

[48] The third assumption is that there exists amongst a considerable number of people in this country a genuinely-held, subjective fear that democratic transformation will lead to the down-grading, suppression and ultimate destruction of the Afrikaans language and the marginalisation and ultimate disintegration of the Afrikaans-speaking community as a vital group in South African society.

[49] The fourth assumption is that the Afrikaans language is one of the cultural treasures of South African national life, widely spoken and deeply implanted, the vehicle of outstanding literature, the bearer of a rich scientific and legal vocabulary and possibly the most creole or "rainbow" of all South African tongues. Its protection and development is therefore the concern not only of its speakers but of the whole South African nation. In approaching the question of the future of the Afrikaans language, then, the issue should not be regarded as simply one of satisfying the self-centred wishes, legitimate or otherwise, of a particular group, but as a question of promoting the rich development of an integral part of the variegated South African national character contemplated by the Constitution. Stripped of its association with race and political dominance, cultural diversity becomes an enriching force which merits constitutional protection, thereby enabling the specific contribution of each to become part of the patrimony of the whole.

[50] At the same time, these assumptions have to be located in the context of three important considerations highlighted by the Constitution.

[51] In the first place, similar claims for constitutional regard can be made by ten or more other language communities, claims which could be weaker in some detailed respects than those made on behalf of Afrikaans, and very much stronger in others. It was evident from the intensity with which the matter was presented by some of the Petitioners that it represents an issue of deep meaning to them. One may accept that even abstract questions of law have to be considered in the concrete context of history, and we can not ignore the fact, urged upon us by counsel, that, although the words of the Constitutional text are generalised, they are also suffused with specific and (frequently contradictory) life experiences. Yet, even if the poignancy of history flows through the veins of the Constitution, we must always be guided by the words and spirit of the constitutional text itself, supporting, not this group or that, but the values articulated by the Constitution. In interpreting clause 19 of the Gauteng Education Bill in the light of section 32 of the Constitution, the rights of certain members of the Afrikaans-speaking community, therefore, cannot be considered in isolation from equally valid claims of members of other language groups. The very concept of multi-culturalism has to be looked at in a multi-cultural way.

[52] The second consideration is that immense inequality continues to exist in relation to access to education in our country. At present, the imperatives of equalising access to education are strong, and even although these should not go to the extent of overriding constitutionally protected rights in relation to language and culture, they do represent an important element in the equation. The theme of

reducing the discrepancies in the life chances of all South Africans runs right through the Constitution, from the forceful opening words of the preamble to the reminder of the past contained in the powerful postscript. The very first fundamental right to be specified, preceding even the rights to life and dignity, is the right to equality. We are further enjoined to interpret the whole of Chapter 3, including section 32, in a way which promotes the values of an open and democratic society based on freedom and equality. The theme of diversity has markedly less constitutional pungency. There are express language rights, a general right to use the language or participate in the cultural life of a person's choice, the provision on educational rights under discussion and, looking to the future, Principle XI, which declares that the diversity of language and culture shall be acknowledged and protected, and conditions for their promotion shall be encouraged. Thus, the dominant theme of the Constitution is the achievement of equality, while considerable importance is also given to cultural diversity and language rights, so that the basic problem is to secure equality in a balanced way which shows maximum regard for diversity. In my view, the Constitution should be seen as providing a bridge to accomplish in a principled yet emphatic manner, the difficult passage from State protection of minority privileges, to State acknowledgement and support of minority rights. The objective should not be to set the principle of equality against that of cultural diversity, but rather to harmonise the two in the interests of both. Democracy in a pluralist society should accordingly not mean the end of cultural diversity, but rather its guarantee, accomplished on the secure bases of justice and equity.

. . . .

[54] It is against this background that I propose to look at universally accepted principles of international law to see what bearing, if any, they could have on the interpretation of section 32, more particularly of section 32(c).

. . . .

III. Basic Principles of Minority Protection Law

[69] A rough survey of the current situation in international law suggests that six interrelated principles enter the picture, with varying degrees of relevance and intensity, when the broad concept of protection of minorities comes into play. They are i) the right to existence, ii) non-discrimination, iii) equal rights, iv) the right to develop autonomously within civil society, v) affirmative action, and vi) positive support from the state. The significance of each and the way they are dealt with in our Constitution, with special reference to language rights, will be treated below.

[70] *i) The right to existence*. The United Nations Convention on the Prevention and Punishment of the Crime of Genocide of 1948 clearly acknowledges the right of all national groups to physical existence. It is not so clear, however, whether a right to independent cultural existence is also recognised, that is, whether or not there is a prohibition on what has been called cultural genocide. There is nothing in the present case, however, to suggest that the challenged statutory provisions form part of a programme calculated to physically eliminate members of the Afrikaans speaking community or to wipe out their culture. In South African conditions today,

the group that would appear to have the greatest claim to invoke any such right would be the San/Khoisan population, whose habitats have been taken away from them or else so ecologically despoiled that their survival as a distinct cultural group can be said to be in peril. It would, however, be unwise to express any opinion on the subject, save to say that the present case stems from the situation of a community defending relative affluence and privilege, rather than one combatting marginalisation and the imminence of group annihilation.

[71] *ii) Non-discrimination.* This is the most enduring and powerful principle to have emerged in relation to protection of minorities. Sieghart refers to it as perhaps the strongest principle of all to be found in international human rights law. It is central to the Universal Declaration of Human Rights, the ICCPR, the European Convention for the Protection of Human Rights and Fundamental Freedoms of 1950, and many other conventions. It precludes the State from discriminating on grounds regarded as unfair or unjustifiable, and race, language, religion and culture are invariably contained in definitions of outlawed discrimination. It is to be noted that various international conventions not only oblige states not to discriminate, but impose obligations on them to take steps to end discrimination. In the case of South Africa, section 8(2) of the Constitution expressly itemises language, culture and religion as constituting prima facie examples of unjustifiable grounds of unfair discrimination. Thus, if persons were denied access to school because they spoke Afrikaans, or belonged to a cultural group which identified itself as Afrikaner, they could claim a violation of their constitutional rights. Similarly, any person who was denied access to State facilities because they did not speak Afrikaans or did not belong to the self-constituted Afrikaner community, could allege that their fundamental rights were being infringed.

[72] *iii) Equal rights.* This is the other side of the non-discrimination coin. It could have more affirmative connotations than non-discrimination, however, in that it could deal not merely with protection against exclusion, but with entitlement to equal benefits and equal regard. This becomes particularly important if the objective is to achieve real rather than formal equality. Thus, it is the equality principle rather than the non-discrimination one which becomes the foundation for special legal and other measures to assist groups suffering from de facto rather than de jure disadvantage. In principle there is, of course, no fundamental distinction between the concept of non-discrimination and that of equal rights, and both are embodied in section 8 of our Constitution. As far as members of the Afrikaans-speaking community are concerned, they could complain if the State treated them less advantageously than other groups; their claim to retain a privileged situation, however, would not have the same, or any, force.

. . . .

[74] [Sachs J considered two relevant constitutional provisions: s. 3(9) requires the promotion of the equal use and enjoyment of Afrikaans, the prevention of the use of, say, English for the purposes of domination, and the non-diminution of rights relating to Afrikaans and its status. Section 32(b) gives the right of every person to instruction in their chosen language "where this is reasonably practicable."] Reading these principles together . . . in the manner most favourable to the Petitioners, would mean that the practicability of language instruction in existing

Afrikaans medium schools could, applying the non-diminution principle, be assumed to exist. At the same time, there is nothing in these principles to guarantee the exclusivity of Afrikaans in any school. On the contrary, the promotion of multi-lingualism, even leaving out the factor of equal access to schools, would encourage the establishment of dual- or multiple-medium schools. Whether or not the Afrikaans language would survive better in isolation rather than, as it were, rubbing shoulders with other languages, would not be a matter of constitutionality but one of policy, on which this Court would not wish to pronounce. Similarly, it would not be for us to say whether denying Afrikaans-speaking children the right to study and play with children of other backgrounds would or would not be to their mutual educational and social detriment or advantage.

. . . .

iv) The right to autonomous development in civil society.

. . . .

[76] Section 8(2) provides that no person may be discriminated against on grounds, inter alia, of religion, culture or language. The provision in section 8 (4) to the effect that prima facie proof of discrimination on the grounds specified in section 8(2) shall be presumed to be sufficient proof of unfair discrimination until the contrary is proved, would make all schools based upon a common culture, language or religion liable to attack on the grounds of practising unfair discrimination, particularly if they closed their doors to persons who did not share that common culture, language or religion. Legislation could then be passed prohibiting such discrimination, and such schools would then have no constitutional umbrella to protect them at all. Section 32(c) appears, therefore, to be an explicit, if limited, acknowledgement of the need in certain circumstances to allow for a departure from the general principles of section 8(2) read with section 8(4). The anti-discrimination principle is so powerful, both in international law and in the warp and woof of our Constitution, that any intention to deviate from it would have to be articulated in the clearest possible language.

[77] What appears to be provided for in section 32(c) is not a duty on the state to support discrimination, but a right of people, acting apart from, but in practicable association with the State, to further their own distinctive interests. If the intention were not only to permit discrimination on the grounds of culture, language or religion in state schools, in such cases where it was justified, but to require it in all cases on demand, then one would have expected that such an exemption from the general non-discrimination principle would have been expressed in the clearest possible language. Furthermore, should such a radical departure from the provisions of the equality clause have been contemplated, then it would have been far more logical to have expressed it as a qualification of section 8, than to have left it to be read in as an implied incident of section 32(c).

[78] My view is strengthened by the fact that section 32(c), construed in the manner proposed by Mahomed DP, corresponds precisely to concepts accepted in many international instruments (although by no means universally). It acknowledges that constitutionally guaranteed space should be made available for private individuals to set up and maintain [establish] their own schools if they feel that their special

cultural, language or religious needs are not being sufficiently catered for in the state system. [Sachs cites two European cases consistent with his conclusion.]

. . . .

[80] I would add two more and to my mind, equally compelling reasons, both of which international law principles have alerted me to, for preferring not to adopt the "generously amplified" interpretation of section 32(c) urged upon us by the petitioners. The first is the historical background of enforced school segregation, which was always justified on grounds of cultural incompatibility, and the spirit of which runs directly counter to the explicit values of our constitution.

[81] The second point is that from a cultural or language point of view, there is no clear majority population in South Africa against which minorities need to be protected. Linguistically and culturally speaking, there are only minorities in our country. The problem is to balance out their various interests, rather than to protect any one group against another. From a purely practical point of view, the financial and administrative implications of granting to each language or cultural group a claim, as of right, on the State to establish schools, exclusive to themselves, not to speak of the extreme educational fragmentation involved, seem to be insuperable. Eleven languages are officially recognised. In addition about a dozen further languages are specified in section 3(10)(c) as being languages whose development must be promoted by the Pan South African Language Board (and this is not presented as an exhaustive list). Added to this, it is a matter of public record that our country is blessed with a multiplicity of religious communities, with independent churches alone probably running into the hundreds if not thousands. Could it possibly be that the framers of the Constitution intended that each language group and each religious community in every one of their multiple spatial conglomerations, should have a claim on the State in terms of section 32(c) to establish on their behalf exclusive schools? Writing before the Constitution was adopted, Professor Van der Westhuizen makes the following pertinent remark:

> "Public schools exclusively or specifically for cultural, religious, or linguistic groups would not seem to be acceptable either. Not only would such a state of affairs serve to perpetuate apartheid in disguise with state funding and official blessing, but as a practical matter, it would be extremely difficult to allocate funds and other supporting facilities on an equal basis."

. . . .

v) Affirmative action.

[83] [Citing human rights treaties promoting affirmative action to assure full enjoyment of human rights, Sachs concluded that] these principles would favour those groups seeking admission to Afrikaans medium schools, rather than the present incumbents in their defensive postures. Any claim of Afrikaans community groups to have the State subsidize what, objectively speaking, are privileges in terms of exclusive access to affluent schools would therefore be weak. Their argument that the State should anticipate and obviate possible future disadvantage may well be somewhat stronger, but I do not see how the threat of loss of dominance could legally per se be regarded as threatened disadvantage.

vi) Positive support from the State.

. . . .

[86] It is quite clear that the manner in which these provisions have been applied varies considerably from country to country, depending on local conditions and preoccupation. In Canada, for example, section 23 of the Canadian Charter of Rights and Freedoms establishes an express right to minority language education out of public funds, providing Francophone and Anglophone minorities with special treatment as compared to other cultural and linguistic minorities. In Belgium and Switzerland, on the other hand, the concept of "areas of linguistic security" applies in terms of which each collectivity can protect its "linguistic homogeneity" from "linguistic competition" from other groups within a defined territory. India provides yet another variant. There, Article 30 of the Constitution guarantees religious and linguistic minorities the right to establish and administer educational institutions of their own choice. The State is precluded, in granting aid to educational institutions, from discriminating against any educational institution on the ground that it is under the management of a minority. These are three countries that have made special provision for minority schools. If [a U.N. Report] is any guide, they certainly cannot be regarded as establishing a universal practice. It would seem that each country has the right, in terms of international law, to develop its own rules in this respect, based on its own history and needs.

. . . .

Conclusion

[90] In summary: a reading of our Constitution would be entirely consistent with the principles of international human rights law if it:

— prevented the State from embarking on programmes intended or calculated to destroy the physical existence or to eliminate the cultural existence, of particular groups;

— required the State to uphold the principles of non-discrimination and equal rights in respect of members of minority groups;

— permitted and possibly required the State to take special remedial or preferential action to assist disadvantaged groups to achieve real equality;

— permitted but did not require the State to establish communal schools, or to support such schools already established;

— permitted members of minority groups to establish their own schools.

[91] None of these principles carry the Petitioners' case any further. The papers before us show a need to transform education in South Africa in the light of constitutional precepts which pay due regard to international law. Exactly how the correct balance should be struck between the importance of overcoming systemic inequality inherited from the past, on the one hand, and preventing legally enforced or de facto assimilation of groups wishing to preserve and develop a distinctive identity, on the other, would, in my view, be primarily a matter for democratic resolution in the legislatures of our country, and not in the first instance be one of adjudication by the courts. Provided that such deliberations result in legislation not

transgressing the Constitution, this Court should decline to interpose its own opinion in relation to exactly how best this balance should be achieved.

. . . .

More recently the question of culture and religion arose in the context of a school ban on jewelry as part of its uniform requirements. In this case the Constitutional Court was required to explore the relationship between culture and religion as well as the necessary accommodations that might be required to respect these values in the educational context.

MEC FOR EDUCATION: KWAZULU-NATAL v. PILLAY
CONSTITUTIONAL COURT OF SOUTH AFRICA
2008 (1) SA 474

LANGA CJ:

[1] What is the place of religious and cultural expression in public schools? This case raises vital questions about the nature of discrimination under the provisions of the Promotion of Equality and Prevention of Unfair Discrimination Act 4 of 2000 (the Equality Act) as well as the extent of protection afforded to cultural and religious rights in the public school setting and possibly beyond. At the centre of the storm is a tiny gold nose stud.

. . . .

[4] Sunali applied for admission to DGHS [Durban Girls High School] for the 2002 school year. Her mother signed a declaration in which she undertook to ensure that Sunali complied with the Code of Conduct of the School (the Code). Sunali was admitted to the School.

[5] During the school holidays in September 2004 Ms Pillay gave Sunali permission to pierce her nose and insert a small gold stud. When she returned to School after the holidays on 4 October 2004, Ms Pillay was informed that her daughter was not allowed to wear the nose stud as it was in contravention of the Code. . . .

. . . .

[11] The issue before the Equality Court was whether the School's refusal to permit Sunali to wear the nose stud at school was an act of unfair discrimination in terms of the Equality Act. The evidence presented by Ms Pillay amounted to the following: the practice of wearing the nose stud is a tradition that is some 4000 to 5000 years old, hailing predominantly from the south of India. When a girl comes of age, a stage marked by the onset of her menstrual cycle, the family honours the fact of her becoming a young woman. As part of the ritual, a prayer is performed and her nose is pierced on the left side for the insertion of the nose stud. The ritual also serves the purpose of endowing daughters with jewellery since a woman's dowry in patriarchal society went to her husband and all she could claim as her own was her jewellery. Further, according to Ayurvedic medicine, the medicinal branch of the Vedas, the left side of the nose is directly related to fertility and childbearing. Ms

Pillay stressed that the practice of wearing the nose stud or ring plays an important part in many religions and is not limited to Hinduism. On the other hand, Hinduism has a variety of sects that observe different practices.

[12] Mrs Martin, on behalf of the School, made the point that the Code had been drawn up in consultation with the learners' representative council, parents and the governing body. It is the practice of the School that exemptions, based on religious considerations, are made from the provisions of the Code. Asked why an exemption was not granted to Sunali on the basis of the religious reasons given by Ms Pillay, she stated that Ms Pillay had made it clear in her letter that the nose stud was worn as a personal choice and tradition and not for religious reasons.

. . . .

[14] The Equality Court held that although a prima facie case of discrimination had been made out, the discrimination was not unfair. It characterised the purpose of the Code as being "to promote uniformity and acceptable convention amongst the learners" and accepted Mrs Martin's evidence that undue permissiveness could result in a conflict with the Code, "thereby creating a disorderly environment." In reaching its conclusion the Court took into account several factors namely: Ms Pillay had agreed to the Code when she took Sunali to the School; the Code was devised by the School in consultation with the students, parents and educators; and also that Ms Pillay had failed to consult with the School before sending Sunali to it with the nose stud. The Court held that no impairment to Sunali's dignity or of another interest of a comparably serious nature had occurred and concluded that DGHS had acted reasonably and fairly. In addition, the Court held that any harm that may have been caused "was as a result of [Sunali's] and her mother's own doing." This decision by the Equality Court was taken on appeal by Ms Pillay to the Pietermaritzburg High Court.

. . . .

[17] In reaching the conclusion that the conduct of the School amounted to unfair discrimination, the High Court noted that Sunali was part of a group that had been historically discriminated against and that the School's contention that its rule prohibiting the wearing of jewellery was a general one applicable to every learner served only to prolong that discrimination. It highlighted the vulnerable and marginalised status of Hindus and Indians in South Africa's past and present, the demeaning effect of denying Sunali's religion — and hence her identity — and the systemic nature of the discrimination. It held that the insistence by the School on uniformity or similar treatment was inappropriate as it failed to dismantle structures of discrimination. The Court held further that the desire to maintain discipline in the School was not an acceptable reason for the prohibition as there was no evidence that wearing the nose stud had a disruptive effect on the smooth-running of the School. The High Court found that, in any event, there were less restrictive means to achieve the laudable objectives of the School as it could simply explain to its learners that Sunali's religion or culture entitles her to wear the nose stud.

. . . .

[36] The first question is whether the discrimination complained of by Ms Pillay

flows from the Code or from the decision of the School to refuse an exemption. Ms Pillay specifically identifies the decision of the School as the problem, but the major part of the arguments addressed to the Court by all the other parties focused on the discriminatory nature of the Code. To my mind, it is the combination of the Code and the refusal to grant an exemption that resulted in the alleged discrimination, not the one or the other in isolation.

. . . .

[46] The prohibition of discrimination on the basis of religion or culture in terms of the Equality Act and section 9 of the Constitution is distinct from the protection of religion and culture provided for by sections 15 and 30 of the Constitution. The two rights may overlap, however, where the discrimination in question flows from an interference with a person's religious or cultural practices. Therefore, in order to establish discrimination in this case, Ms Pillay must show that the School in some way interfered with Sunali's participation in or practice or expression of her religion or culture. This inquiry is similar to an inquiry under sections 15 or 30, but it is not identical because the Court must go on to consider whether the discrimination, if any, was unfair.

[47] The alleged grounds of discrimination are religion and/or culture. It is important to keep these two grounds distinct. Without attempting to provide any form of definition, religion is ordinarily concerned with personal faith and belief, while culture generally relates to traditions and beliefs developed by a community. However, there will often be a great deal of overlap between the two; religious practices are frequently informed not only by faith but also by custom, while cultural beliefs do not develop in a vacuum and may be based on the community's underlying religious or spiritual beliefs. Therefore, while it is possible for a belief or practice to be purely religious or purely cultural, it is equally possible for it to be both religious and cultural.

. . . .

[50] . . . Even on the most restrictive understanding of culture, Sunali is part of the South Indian, Tamil and Hindu groups which are defined by a combination of religion, language, geographical origin, ethnicity and artistic tradition. Whether those groups operate together or separately matters not; combined or separate, they are an identifiable culture of which Sunali is a part.

[51] Next, we need to consider the religious and cultural significance of the nose stud. There were two interrelated areas of contention. The first was whether a claim that a practice has religious or cultural significance should be determined subjectively or objectively. . . .

[52] It is accepted both in South Africa and abroad that, in order to determine if a practice or belief qualifies as religious a court should ask only whether the claimant professes a sincere belief. There is however no such consensus concerning cultural practices and beliefs. There was much argument in this Court that because culture is inherently an associative practice, a more objective approach should be adopted when dealing with cultural beliefs or practices. It is unnecessary in this case to engage too deeply in that debate as both the subjective and objective evidence lead to the same conclusion. It is however necessary to make two points.

[53] Firstly, cultural convictions or practices may be as strongly held and as important to those who hold them as religious beliefs are to those more inclined to find meaning in a higher power than in a community of people. The notion that "we are not islands unto ourselves" is central to the understanding of the individual in African thought. It is often expressed in the phrase *umuntu ngumuntu ngabantu* which emphasises "communality and the inter-dependence of the members of a community" and that every individual is an extension of others. According to Gyekye, "an individual human person cannot develop and achieve the fullness of his/her potential without the concrete act of relating to other individual persons." This thinking emphasises the importance of community to individual identity and hence to human dignity. Dignity and identity are inseparably linked as one's sense of self-worth is defined by one's identity. Cultural identity is one of the most important parts of a person's identity precisely because it flows from belonging to a community and not from personal choice or achievement. And belonging involves more than simple association; it includes participation and expression of the community's practices and traditions.

[54] Secondly, while cultures are associative, they are not monolithic. The practices and beliefs that make up an individual's cultural identity will differ from person to person within a culture: one may express their culture through participation in initiation rites, another through traditional dress or song and another through keeping a traditional home. While people find their cultural identity in different places, the importance of that identity to their being in the world remains the same. There is a danger of falling into an antiquated mode of understanding culture as a single unified entity that can be studied and defined from outside. As Martin Chanock warns us:

> "The idea of culture derived from anthropology, a discipline which studied the encapsulated exotic, is no longer appropriate. There are no longer (if there ever were) single cultures in any country, polity or legal system, but many. Cultures are complex conversations within any social formation. These conversations have many voices."

Cultures are living and contested formations. The protection of the Constitution extends to all those for whom culture gives meaning, not only to those who happen to speak with the most powerful voice in the present cultural conversation.

. . . .

[60] In conclusion, the evidence shows that the nose stud is not a mandatory tenet of Sunali's religion or culture; Ms Pillay has admitted as much. But the evidence does confirm that the nose stud is a voluntary expression of South Indian Tamil Hindu culture, a culture that is intimately intertwined with Hindu religion, and that Sunali regards it as such. The question arises whether the nose stud should be classified as a religious or cultural practice, or both. This Court has noted that "the temptation to force [grounds of discrimination] into neatly self-contained categories should be resisted." That is particularly so in this case where the evidence suggests that the borders between culture and religion are malleable and that religious belief informs cultural practice and cultural practice attains religious significance. As noted above, that will not always be the case: culture and religion remain very different forms of human association and individual identity, and often inform

peoples' lives in very different ways. But in this matter, culture and religion sing with the same voice and it is necessary to understand the nose stud in that light — as an expression of both religion and culture.

. . . .

[64] A necessary element of freedom and of dignity of any individual is an "entitlement to respect for the unique set of ends that the individual pursues." One of those ends is the voluntary religious and cultural practices in which we participate. That we choose voluntarily rather than through a feeling of obligation only enhances the significance of a practice to our autonomy, our identity and our dignity.

. . . .

[66] The protection of voluntary practices applies equally to culture and religion. Indeed, it seems to me that it may even be more vital to protect non-obligatory cultural practices. Cultures, unlike religions, are not necessarily based on tenets of faith but on a collection of practices, ideas or ways of being. While some cultures may have obligatory rules which act as conditions for membership of the culture, many cultures, unlike many religions, will not have an authoritative body or text that determines the dictates of the culture. Any single member of a culture will seldom observe all those practices that make up the cultural milieu, but will choose those which she or he feels are most important to her or his own relationship to and expression of that culture. To limit cultural protection to cultural obligations would, for many cultures and their members, make the protection largely meaningless.

. . . .

[68] I therefore find that Sunali was discriminated against on the basis of both religion and culture in terms of section 6 of the Equality Act. I proceed now to consider whether or not that discrimination was fair.

. . . .

[76] The difficult question then is not whether positive steps must be taken, but how far the community must be required to go to enable those outside the "mainstream" to swim freely in its waters. This is an issue which has been debated both in this Court and abroad and different positions have been taken. For instance, although the term "undue hardship" is employed as the test for reasonable accommodation in both the United States and Canada, the United States Supreme Court has held that employers need only incur "a de minimis cost" in order to accommodate an individual's religion, whilst the Canadian Supreme Court has specifically declined to adopt that standard and has stressed that "more than mere negligible effort is required to satisfy the duty to accommodate." The latter approach is more in line with the spirit of our constitutional project which affirms diversity. However, the utility of either of these phrases is limited as ultimately the question will always be a contextual one dependant not on its compatibility with a judicially created slogan but with the values and principles underlying the Constitution. Reasonable accommodation is, in a sense, an exercise in proportionality that will depend intimately on the facts.

. . . .

[78] There may be circumstances where fairness requires a reasonable accommodation, while in other circumstances it may require more or less, or something completely different. It will depend on the nature of the case and the nature of the interests involved. Two factors seem particularly relevant. First, reasonable accommodation is most appropriate where, as in this case, discrimination arises from a rule or practice that is neutral on its face and is designed to serve a valuable purpose, but which nevertheless has a marginalising effect on certain portions of society. Second, the principle is particularly appropriate in specific localised contexts, such as an individual workplace or school, where a reasonable balance between conflicting interests may more easily be struck.

[79] The present case bears both these characteristics and therefore, in my view, fairness required a reasonable accommodation. Whether that required the School to permit Sunali to wear the nose stud depends on the importance of the practice to Sunali on the one hand, and the hardship that permitting her to wear the stud would cause the School. Before I address that question, there were two points raised about the context within which fairness should be determined. These relate to the need for deference and the consultation that went into the making of the Code.

. . . .

[82] In urging that the Code should be respected, the School stressed the fact that it was devised after extensive consultation with parents, educators, staff, and learners, and accordingly represented the combined wisdom of all who participated in its construction and should therefore be respected. There is no doubt that consultation and public participation in local decision-making are good and deserve to be applauded. . . .

[83] This, however, does not immunise the resultant decisions, in effect the opinion of the school community, from constitutional scrutiny and review. The reality is that many individual communities still retain historically unequal power relations or historically skewed population groups which may make it more likely that local decisions will infringe on the rights of disfavoured groups. In sum, while local democratic processes and consultation are important constitutional values in their own right, their role in the evaluation of the substance of decisions, if any, should not be overstated.

. . . .

[87] While it is tempting to consider the objective importance or centrality of a belief to a particular religion or culture in determining whether the discrimination is fair, that approach raises many difficulties. In my view, courts should not involve themselves in determining the objective centrality of practices, as this would require them to substitute their judgement of the meaning of a practice for that of the person before them and often to take sides in bitter internal disputes. This is true both for religious and cultural practices. If Sunali states that the nose stud is central to her as a South Indian Tamil Hindu, it is not for the Court to tell her that she is wrong because others do not relate to that religion or culture in the same way.

. . . .

[95] It is no doubt true that even the most vital practice of a religion or culture can

be limited for the greater good. No belief is absolute, but those that are closer to the core of an individual's identity require a greater justification to limit. The question is whether, considering the importance of the stud to Sunali, allowing her to wear the stud would impose too great a burden on the School.

. . . .

[103] The only confirmed effect of granting Sunali an exemption is that some of the girls might feel it is unfair. While that is unfortunate, neither the Equality Act nor the Constitution require identical treatment. They require equal concern and equal respect. They specifically recognise that sometimes it is fair to treat people differently. In *Christian Education*, this Court held:

> "It is true that to single out a member of a religious community for disadvantageous treatment would, on the face of it, constitute unfair discrimination against that community. The contrary, however, does not hold. To grant respect to sincerely held religious views of a community and make an exception from a general law to accommodate them, would not be unfair to anyone else who did not hold those views."

[104] This reasoning can and should be explained to all the girls in the School. Teaching the constitutional values of equality and diversity forms an important part of education. This approach not only teaches and promotes the rights and values enshrined in the Constitution, it also treats the learners as sensitive and autonomous people who can understand the impact the ban has on Sunali.

. . . .

[112] The discrimination has had a serious impact on Sunali, and, although the evidence shows that uniforms serve an important purpose, it does not show that the purpose is significantly furthered by refusing Sunali her exemption. Allowing the stud would not have imposed an undue burden on the School. A reasonable accommodation would have been achieved by allowing Sunali to wear the nose stud. I would therefore confirm the High Court's finding of unfair discrimination.

[113] It is necessary, however, to add the following: everything on the record indicates that DGHS maintains high academic standards and that it has taken meaningful steps to accommodate diversity in its community. It regularly allows religious exemptions and promotes the expression of culture at various events on the school calendar. It is, in other words, an excellent school. This judgment is not an indictment on DGHS but an indication of the complexities that have to be overcome in order to achieve a fully religiously and culturally sensitive society, not least of all in the schools of our land.

[114] It is worthwhile to explain at this stage, for the benefit of all schools, what the effect of this judgment is, and what it is not. It does not abolish school uniforms; it only requires that, as a general rule, schools make exemptions for sincerely held religious and cultural beliefs and practices. There should be no blanket distinction between religion and culture. There may be specific schools or specific practices where there is a real possibility of disruption if an exemption is granted. Or, a practice may be so insignificant to the person concerned that it does not require a departure from the ordinary uniform. The position may also be different in private

schools, although even in those institutions, discrimination is impermissible. Those cases all raise different concerns and may justify refusing exemption. However, a mere desire to preserve uniformity, absent real evidence that permitting the practice will threaten academic standards or discipline, will not.

9.6. LESSONS

9.6.1. Is democracy more secure and political minorities better off with judicial protection?

The times in which we live, and the study of the four countries that are the focus of these materials, provide significant insights for those who wish to critically consider the relative role of judges and legislators in enforcing rights. Americans, who invented vigorous judicial review of entrenched, but broadly worded, constitutional rights, can look back on a century featuring the rise and fall of active judicial protection of economic liberty (the "*Lochner* era"), the rise and fall of active judicial protection of the poor and minorities (the Warren Court), and the recent rise of renewed activism to strike down progressive social legislation. Canadians can look back on a generation of experience with a Charter of Rights designed as a compromise between British parliamentary supremacy and American judicial review. South Africans are approaching the 20th anniversary of their post-apartheid Constitution, with a rich array of provisions providing active or more deferential judicial review. Australians seem to have decisively rejected a broad American-style entrenchment of constitutional rights, having previously debated whether to adopt a softer form of statutory rights protection.

Americans interested in the progressive realization of rights for underprivileged minorities have again begun to question whether courts or legislatures are better vehicles to improve social justice. Professor John Nowak, in *The Rise and Fall of Supreme Court Concern for Racial Minorities*, 36 Wm. & M. L. Rev. 345, 347 (1995), concludes that "as the membership of the Court has changed, the Court's approach toward protecting racial minorities has also changed." Thus, "the rise and fall of Supreme Court protection for racial minorities simply reflects the political background of the Justices on the Court in each era." According to Nowak, judicial protection of racial minorities was virtually non-existent prior to the New Deal. From the late 1930s through the early 1950s, the Court incrementally changed its rulings concerning equal protection and congressional power to provide greater protection for minorities, followed by grand rhetoric but modest remedies during a period where society was unwilling to accept a more liberal view of civil rights and then a period of active leadership in the protection of racial minorities through its rulings concerning equal protection and an expansive reading of federal civil rights statutes. Since the 1980s, he finds that the Court has turned against racial minorities. This history, Nowak explains, reveals that judges' political affiliations are much more important in judicial decisions than legal theories:

> In the pre-New Deal era, the Court had absolutely no sympathy for racial minorities . . . and was often an active participant in the oppression of racial minorities.. Fifty years ago, a Court composed of Democrats became increasingly concerned with racial equality. Forty years ago [it] took a bold

step toward the protection of racial minorities in the Brown decision. In the 1960s the Court that was dominated by Democratic appointees who attempted to protect minority race persons . . . . The Nixon appointees brought a wavering approach to civil rights. The Reagan . . . narrow[ed] the Court rulings on civil rights cases.

Id. at 471. The lesson Nowak draws from this history is that "the Justices cannot be counted on to protect racial minorities from oppression in our society." While future presidents might appoint justices that will lead the court to protect minority rights, they might not. He concludes that "Congress is likely to remain a stronger defender of racial minorities than the Supreme Court in the foreseeable future." *Id.* at 472.

More generally, scholars including Professor Morton Horwitz argue that American constitutional history is characterized by the ineffectiveness of judicial protection of the rights of the powerless and the predominant use of rights theories to protect the powerful. Rights theory, the argument continues, was developed in the 18th century as a response to revolutionary sentiments in the U.S. and France with the principal effect of protecting private property rights.

These observations lead to some interesting, though largely academic, questions about the future of rights protection in the United States (which seems realistically to be soundly entrenched):

1) Should those who find these arguments persuasive seriously consider a constitutional amendment to add a Notwithstanding Clause? Shouldn't liberal Democrats endorse it so that progressive legislation may be passed without hectoring from Justice Scalia? Shouldn't conservative Republicans endorse it as an insurance policy to prevent a tilt back to the left?

2) Should the Supreme Court revert to the doctrine initially set forth in *The Slaughter-House Cases*, excerpted in Chapter Two, that the Fourteenth Amendment's Equal Protection Clause directly bars only legislation "hostile to" African Americans, plus anything else that Congress wants to add as part of its powers authorized by Section 5 of the Amendment?[28]

Turning north of the border, how do the materials in this Chapter affect your view of the Trudeau-Lévesque divide between claims that rights are best protected by judges interpreting entrenched constitutional rights as opposed to claims that, at least where the national minority is a provincial majority, rights are best protected by political agreements among provincial leaders? Canadian scholar Michael Mandel concurs with the American critics, concluding that a review of constitutional history has demonstrated that judicial review is usually hostile to progressive political activism. Michael Mandel, *Against Constitutional Law (Populist or Otherwise)*, 34 U. RICH. L. REV. 443, 444–46 (2000); *see generally* MICHAEL MANDEL, THE CHARTER OF RIGHTS AND THE LEGALIZATION OF POLITICS IN CANADA (2d ed.

---

[28] The turn in rhetoric among progressives is striking. When conservative professor/judge Robert Bork, a critic of the Warren Court's liberal activism, was nominated to the Supreme Court by President Reagan, liberal Senator Edward Kennedy led the successful opposition, famously opining that "Robert Bork's America" was a "land in which women would be forced into back-alley abortions, blacks would sit at segregated lunch counters, [and] rogue police could break down citizens' doors in midnight raids." 133 CONG REG. S9188 (July 1, 1987).

1994). On the other hand, Peter Hogg and Allison Bushell have written approvingly that both sections 1 (reasonable limits) and 33 (notwithstanding clause) of the Canadian Charter have promoted a balanced role for both courts and legislatures. *The* Charter *Dialogue Between Courts and Legislatures*, 35 Osgoode Hall L.J. 75 (1997). *See also* Kent Roach, The Supreme Court on Trial: Judicial Activism or Democratic Dialogue (2001).

Flying south of the equator, do you believe that the South African experience will mirror Professor Horwitz's fear that entrenched rights are more likely to serve the interests of the rich and powerful? If not, what is it about South African legal and political institutions and current values that would suggest a different outcome? While the South African Constitution is heralded as a uniquely progressive document and many academics have celebrated the role of "transformative constitutionalism" in the jurisprudence of South Africa's Constitutional Court, it is important to reflect on the limits of judicial power and the capacity of the courts, as compared to the legislature and executive branches, to address the vast social and economic problems that characterize post-apartheid South Africa. One way to think about the place of entrenched rights is to consider the institutional choices that they present, since empowering the courts definitely provides an alternative to the democratic process. Is judicial review based on entrenched individual rights an adequate source of protection for communities whose core interests are perpetually in tension with the interests of the majority of citizens? If not can you imagine what role the enforcement of rights by the courts might play, other than serving as a veto on democratic decision-making?

Despite repeated electoral victories by the African National Congress and the party's near complete control of the country's legislative and executive branches South Africa remains one of the most unequal societies on earth nearly 20 years after the fall of apartheid. While there is political freedom and the government has "delivered" far greater social goods than ever before, many — including some senior ANC politicians — blame the Constitution for slowing down the transformation of the society. At the same time social movements have at times been able to use the guarantee of rights and the Constitutional Court to force the government to change policies, such as its disastrous failure to effectively tackle the HIV/AIDS pandemic. In this context it is hard to argue that the constitution and the protection of rights serves only the interests of the rich and powerful; however it is the case that the continuing social conflict driven by corruption, inequality and governmental incompetence is creating a certain amount of what some commentators have referred to as "lawfare" — a situation in which the law and courts are becoming the center of a multitude of conflicts. While the courts may play an important role in mediating social and political conflict it is less clear that they can make up for the weaknesses in the executive and legislative branches, particularly when the courts themselves then become targets of institutional conflict with challenges to the legitimacy of sitting judges and to the Judicial Service Commission which manages the process of judicial appointment.

In reviewing these issues, Professor Mark Tushnet appropriately emphasizes the role of political culture as well as judicial doctrine. Although one might characterize the traditional British constitution as one of "parliamentary supremacy" and the American one as "constrained parliamentarism," a legislature's unlimited legal power might well be constrained by the political culture's recognition of limits. Mark Tushnet, *New Forms of Judicial Review and the Persistence of Rights- and Democracy-Based Worries*, 38 WAKE FOREST L. REV. 813, 816 (2003). This raises yet another question for those seeking a structure that navigates between strong judicial review and parliamentary supremacy: whether what Tushnet calls "weak form judicial review" might either escalate to become "strong-form" review or degenerate into something that does not significantly constrain political invasion of rights.

9.6.2.   Lessons for the current Australian debate

In Australia (as noted in Chapter Three and above) a 2009 "National Human Rights Consultation" concluded with a recommendation for a "superstatutory" Human Rights Act (which would have allowed only "weak form," or "dialogic" judicial review of federal Acts); the Government did not adopt the recommendation. Australian advocates of rights entrenchment continue to argue that Australia needs greater rights protection. However, they rarely promote the American model of a Bill of Rights as a model to follow.

Professor George Williams, a prominent proponent of a Charter of rights, explained in a radio interview in 2004 that he considered the U.S. Bill of Rights to be "a bad model for [Australia] to follow," because he considered it "too vague in its language [and] not based clearly enough on precise rights that are understood by the community." He suggested instead that Australians should look to Canada, the United Kingdom, and New Zealand, which he considered to offer alternative "contemporary examples that have been very successful'.[29]

In 2007 he set out his reasons for promoting a Charter of rights:

> Australia has a human rights problem. This is apparent in our overreaching anti-terror laws, in how we deny prisoners the vote and have made it harder for young people to enrol [to vote], and in the 17 year gap in life expectancy between Aboriginal and other Australians. The problem also extends to how we treat young children.
>
> Until recently, Australia locked up children [asylum seekers] in conditions that caused many of them to become mentally ill. It seems unthinkable that this could have occurred, yet it did. The problem was the law, which said that the detention of people seeking asylum in Australia was mandatory. That law was applied without exception, even to unaccompanied children already suffering trauma. . . . In other nations, it would have been counter-balanced by a bill or charter of rights. Australia is now the only democratic nation in the world without this human rights protection, and so the Australian immigration law went unchecked. In fact, when the immigration law was challenged in the courts it was held to be legally unobjectionable.

---

[29] Interview with Peter Thompson, ABC radio, 1 July 2004.

The High Court of Australia upheld the detention of children in 2004. Another case that year went further, finding that detention remains lawful even where the conditions are harsh or inhumane.

A final High Court decision added that the detention could be indefinite. As an adult, Ahmed Al-Kateb had arrived in Australia by boat in December 2000 without a passport or visa. Taken into detention under the Migration Act, he sought refugee status but was refused. After eighteen months in detention he asked to be deported.

However, Al-Kateb was born in Kuwait of Palestinian parents and the absence of a Palestinian nation left him 'stateless'. The Commonwealth sought unsuccessfully to remove him to Egypt, Jordan, Kuwait and Syria as well as to Palestinian territories.

Faced with this stalemate and no foreseeable end to his detention, Al-Kateb applied to the courts for his release. In nations like the United Kingdom and the United States, judges have found that the law does not permit indefinite detention. Nevertheless, the Australian High Court found by four to three that the Migration Act and the Constitution permit just this.

One of the majority judges, Justice Michael McHugh, conceded that Al-Kateb's situation was 'tragic'. He also noted that 'Eminent lawyers who have studied the question firmly believe that the Australian Constitution should contain a Bill of Rights.' But, in the absence of such a law, he found that 'the justice or wisdom of the course taken by the parliament is not examinable in this or any other domestic court' since 'it is not for courts . . . to determine whether the course taken by Parliament is unjust or contrary to basic human rights.'

With these words, Justice McHugh spelt out what it means for Australia not to have a charter or bill of rights. Without this instrument, there may be no check on laws that violate even the most basic of our freedoms.

Professor Irving has taken an alternative perspective. In a chapter published in a 2009 collection, she set out some of her reasons[30]:

No reasonable person can object to the protection of rights. Those who question the Bill of Rights agenda are rarely contemptuous of rights, or of the law, or the integrity of the judiciary or the judicial system. Most are concerned, rather, about the *best means* of protecting rights. The central issue is whether the best means revolves around judicial review.

. . . .

A system such as Australia's involves three arms of government. Each plays its part in balancing diverse and conflicting interests, in maintaining and protecting our fundamental institutional structures, in developing our standards and values, and in preventing the other arms of government from accumulating or monopolizing power. The problem does not lie in the

---

[30] Irving, H, *A Legal Perspective on Bills of Rights, in* Don't Leave us with the Bill: The Case Against an Australian Bill of Rights (Menzies Research Centre, Julian Leeser & Ryan Haddrick, eds., 2009).

grasping (or even willing) over-reach of judges. It lies in misconstruing the separation of powers. It lies in what Bills of Rights ask judges to do.

. . . There is a common, and popular perception that individual grievances can be simply redressed through access to the courts, and that claims that rights have been breached will invariably be vindicated. The record is that challenges to the validity of laws fail just as often as, if not more often than they succeed.

. . . .

The objection is not to laws protecting rights, but to a Bill (or other type of legal instrument) according to which the validity of the laws, as such, can be challenged. Australia is far from deficient in rights. There is a range of rights-bearing Commonwealth legislation; for example, the *Racial Discrimination Act* 1975; the *Ombudsman Act* 1976; the *Freedom of Information Act* 1982; the *Sex Discrimination Act* 1984; the *HREOC Act* 1986, among many others. These have counterparts in State laws. Australia has a robust common law, and a network of administrative review tribunals.

Australia's record in protecting rights goes beyond the legal sphere. This is commonly overlooked in debates about the merits of a Bill of Rights. A strong democracy and an active civil society are critical in the protection of rights and freedoms. Australia has a democratic political culture, along with practices and institutions that support it. It has a complex democratic infrastructure. To give one example, the Australian Electoral Commission performs numerous democratic functions, including public education. Australia's long-standing system of compulsory voting serves not only to ensure that a genuine majority records its voice at election time. It also requires governments to make active provision for exercising the vote, creating maximum opportunities for every eligible person (including the homeless, those in remote communities, in hospitals, and even prisons) to cast a vote. [Australia's] parliaments have a complex committee system. The Senate Scrutiny of Bills Committee, for example, assesses and regularly reports on proposed legislation with respect to, among other things, whether bills "trespass unduly on personal rights and liberties"; "make rights, liberties or obligations unduly dependent upon insufficiently defined administrative powers"; or "make rights, liberties or obligations unduly dependent upon non-reviewable decisions." Other standing and select parliamentary committees conduct inquiries into the status of rights protection more broadly . . .

In many of these legal and political initiatives, Australia has been a pioneer. Australians did not feel uncomfortable standing alone, or with few companions in the common law or democratic world, when these initiatives were first adopted. [The] record is not perfect, but it is far from the stark picture that is conveyed in the claim that Australia, alone among democratic countries, lacks a Bill of Rights.

. . . .

People are fearful — quite reasonably at times — of the potential for erosion *unless* rights are protected from alteration. This very goal, however, may have perverse effects, taking the struggle for rights out of the political realm, making it uni-dimensional and uni-directional, encouraging the disadvantaged to think primarily in terms of legal avenues for redress. These avenues are costly and uncertain. The vesting of policy, especially with resource implications, in the judiciary is certain to politicize the judicial arm of government. The "dialogic" process [based on the UK, Victorian and ACT models, and favoured by many advocates in Australia] has the potential for creating antagonism between the judiciary and the government, as much as — perhaps even more than — constructive exchange. If so, it cannot fail to have a corrosive effect upon the independence of the judiciary.

That Australia is unique in not having a Bill is held up by proponents as a defect, even a matter for shame. But unless and until Australia's record in protecting rights is manifestly and consistently weaker than in other comparable countries, there is no cause for shame. Currently [Australia has] a robust, complex system of rights protection, and an effective separation of powers. Australians should work on improving them, not supplanting them.

Concerning the *Al-Kateb* case cited above, Professor Irving has commented further (in an unpublished paper):

As Jeremy Waldron [a prominent critic of judicial review] has noted, attitudes to judicial review tend to rest upon the outcome in particular cases. Waldron adds: 'In politics, support for judicial review is sometimes intensely embroiled in support for particular decisions.[31] This, I suggest, well describes the controversy surrounding the Al-Kateb case. It also informs one of the primary concerns about rights-based judicial review. Many claims for a Human Rights Act seem to rest upon an orientation towards institutional design that (either through failure to recognise that the current advantage is likely to be temporary, or in an attempt to 'freeze' current advantage) assumes the permanence of short-term advantage. Good institutional design, in contrast, should work to produce, even optimize, acceptable outcomes when the power holders — in whose hands the temporary advantage lies — change. In other words, good design will anticipate that the "other side" will eventually win and hold power.

Much of the Human Rights advocacy in Australia rests upon an idea of delivering power (over politically non-negotiable rights) to a benevolent judiciary and, in turn, tying the hands of a malign executive/parliament. The short-termism arises, I speculate, from a protracted honeymoon between progressive lawyers/activists and the High Court. The hostility between the progressives and the [conservative Liberal Coalition] Howard government [1996-2007], joined with the memory of the Mason Court's role in (among others) the freedom of political communication cases, the

---

[31] *The Core of the Case Against Judicial Review*, 115 Yale L.J. 1346, 1346–1351 (2006).

Brennan Court's *Mabo* judgment,[32] and the prominence on the High Court of the (now retired) international human rights advocate, Justice Michael Kirby, created an illusion of *institutional* judicial trustworthiness and *institutional* political untrustworthiness. Such an orientation overlooks not only the likelihood of future change, but also the long historical record of conservative judicial resistance to progressive legislative (sprinkled with occasional, but enticing examples of judicial progressivism), in Australia as in other countries . . .

The *Al-Kateb* decision was deeply controversial. Denunciations of both the government and the High Court were loud and widespread. In a response that surprised many, the government yielded to public pressure, allowing Al-Kateb a temporary "bridging" visa and releasing him (and other stateless persons) into the community. Finally, the Minister for Immigration granted Al-Kateb a humanitarian visa, permitting him to stay permanently in Australia. Despite its positive resolution, however, the case grew in stature as a negative exemplar, even an argument clincher, ultimately becoming the icon of the campaign for an Australian human rights act. . . .

The core paradox (of which there are many) of the *Al-Kateb* judgment lies in the fact that it was the Court that reached a negative — rights-denying — conclusion, while the government's response was positive — rights-granting . . . Four Justices concluded that the relevant provisions of the *Migration Act* applied to a stateless person, holding (even stating) that the Act could not be interpreted conformably with a fundamental right. That is, the Court effectively performed the task that a "dialogic" human rights act would have conferred upon it. In other words, the legal conclusion — one which resembled, even modeled - the type of conclusion that would have been reached if a dialogic human rights act were adopted — was transformed by human rights act advocates into a case study of the mischief for which a (dialogic) human rights act was necessary. The positive political conclusion was overlooked, and an argument was advanced that hinged upon distrust of the political arms of government. A deferential judicial outcome had led to a trans-institutional dialogue/debate, but served only to fuel claims for institutionalising a *directive* cross-institutional form of review . . . The *Migration Act* in fact left open a discretionary *governmental* alternative: the grant of a visa. It was this that ended the tragedy.

Another example, often cited by proponents of a Charter of Rights, is the so-called "Northern Territory Intervention," a legislative package covering welfare entitlements, law enforcement, community governance, and other measures, in Northern Territory Aboriginal communities (the measures were incorporated in the *Northern Territory National Emergence Response Bill 2007*). The legislation was introduced by the conservative Liberal-National Party government of Prime Minister, John Howard, as an "emergency" response to findings of widespread sexual abuse and neglect of children in Aboriginal communities. The measures included increased policing in the designated areas, conditional welfare payments, restricted access to alcohol, restrictions on customary law and on use of community

---

[32] *Mabo v. Queensland* (1992) 175 CLR 1.

land, among other laws applying specifically to Aboriginal people and communities. The "Intervention" proved extremely controversial. Charter of Rights advocates regarded it as an egregious example of racism and denial of human rights, illustrating Australia's need for a "superstatute" that would override any such laws. Among the most contentious of the provisions was the exemption of the Bill from the *Racial Discrimination Act 1975* (Cth) which prohibits unequal treatment of persons on the ground of race. Opinions on both the merits of the program and on the desirability and/or necessity of the exemption were deeply divided, including between "white" and Aboriginal spokespersons. In 2011, the United Nations Commissioner for Human Rights raised concerns about the law. At the same time, some prominent Aboriginal leaders, in particular women, declared it to be a necessary and worthwhile response to a terrible situation that had been caused by decades of governmental neglect and wrongheadedness. The debate on the program's merits continues. At issue are, among many other things, clashes between the rights of children, the right to freedom from racism, community self-determination, and the right to governmental protection. What it illustrates with respect to alternative ways of protecting rights under law is the flexibility inherent in legislation, including the possibility of suspending rights-conferring legislation where it is thought necessary. The question is whether such legislation should never be exempted or suspended, even in an "emergency." Advocates of constitutional Bills of Rights may answer "never," but even with a Bill of Rights, it will still be open to the courts to determine whether a challenged law is justified under a constitutional "limitation" clause or judicially-determined standard of review, including with the assessment of governmental reasons for restricting or burdening rights. All the same, in the absence of an overriding Charter or Bill of Rights, legislators can avoid a judicial determination about the justification of laws, and make this assessment themselves. The question remains whether one wants certainty that all laws — even those with which one does not agree and would like to see removed — will be free of judicial override; or whether one prefers the prospect of judicial override — even of laws with which one agrees and wants to retain. Allowing for some exceptions (rights protected in the Constitution), Australians have mostly opted for the second answer.

Consider also the historic role of the common law and principles of administrative law in protecting human right in Australia. The following opinion, notably co-authored by now Chief Justice Robert French, is illustrative:

EVANS v. STATE OF NEW SOUTH WALES
Federal Court of Australia
(2008) 168 FCR 576

French, Branson and Stone, JJ:

Introduction

1. World Youth Day is a major annual gathering of young members of the Catholic Church. It was established by Pope John Paul II in 1986. Every two or three years World Youth Day is taken to an international host city and comprises a week long

series of events attended by the Pope and a large number of young people from around the world. The numbers can run into the hundreds of thousands. In 2008 World Youth Day is being held in Sydney and runs from today to 20 July 2008.

2. Religious beliefs and doctrines frequently attract public debate and sometimes have political consequences reflected in government laws and policies. World Youth Day has attracted the attention of an organisation known as the No to Pope Coalition (the Coalition). It is an unincorporated association of persons and groups which are opposed to the teachings of the Catholic Church on sexuality, contraception and reproductive rights.

. . . .

4. The applicants are concerned that the *World Youth Day Act 2006* (NSW) (the WYD Act) and the *World Youth Day Regulation 2008* (the Regulation) will prevent them from carrying out their planned activities. [Specifically, the regulations limit the ability to sell or distribute articles, and to engage in conduct that causes "annoyance or inconvenience."]

6. For the reasons which we now publish, we are of the opinion that the list of prescribed items subject to control as to their sale and distribution is within the authority conferred by the Act. We are also of the opinion that most of the items that the applicants wish to distribute are not covered by the list of prescribed items. The provisions relating to the control of sale and distribution of prescribed items do not have the effect of preventing the applicants from doing the things that they want to do. No question of the infringement of the implied freedom of political communication therefore arises in relation to s. 46 or cl 4 of the Regulation.

7. The position is different in relation to that part of the Regulation which would empower an authorised person to direct people to cease engaging in conduct that causes annoyance to participants in a World Youth Day event. In so concluding, we have interpreted the WYD Act on the presumption that it was not the intention of Parliament that regulations would be made under the Act preventing or interfering with the exercise of the fundamental freedom of free speech. We have applied a principle of interpretation in favour of that freedom which has been accepted by the Courts of this country since federation and which has its roots deep in the common law inherited from the United Kingdom at the time of colonisation. Clause 7 is invalid to the extent that it seeks to prevent merely annoying conduct. Moreover its scope is uncertain. The other elements of cl 7 seek to prevent risks to public safety, inconvenience to World Youth Day participants and disruption of World Youth Day events. The applicants' challenge to these provisions of the Regulation fail. They do not infringe the implied freedom of political communication because they are directed not to communication, but to public safety and interference with the rights and freedoms of others.

. . . .

STATUTORY PROVISIONS

[The *World Youth Day Act* constitutes a corporation known as the World Youth Day Co-ordination Authority. Section 12(1) of the WYD Act provides that the principal function of the Authority is: "to develop policies, strategies and plans for the delivery of, and to co-ordinate and manage the delivery of, integrated government services for World Youth Day Events." Section 12(6) gives the Authority "such other functions as are conferred or imposed on it by or under this or any other Act." Under Section 3A(1), the Authority designated Darling Harbour, the Domain, Centennial Park, Royal Botanic Gardens, the University of Sydney, Art Gallery of New South Wales, Sydney Harbour Bridge and the Sydney Opera House as Declared Areas, along with approximately 600 designated religious sites, nearly all being either schools or churches, and "Transport sites." The designated transport sites are mainly railway stations. Section 46 of the WYD Act is concerned with the sale and distribution of articles in certain public places, requiring permission from the Authority to sell or distribute articles within the designated areas. Section 58(1) of the WYD Act gives the Governor the conventional power to make regulations, not inconsistent with the Act, for or with respect to any matter that by the Act is required or permitted to be prescribed or that is necessary or convenient to be prescribed for carrying out or giving effect to the Act. Section 58(2) specifically authorises the making of regulations for or with respect to "regulating the use by the public of, and the conduct of the public on, World Youth Day venues and facilities."]

. . . .

27. Clause 7 of the Regulation is concerned with the conduct of members of the public on World Youth Day declared areas. It provides [in part]:

(1) An authorised person may direct a person within a World Youth Day declared area to cease engaging in conduct that:

(a) is a risk to the safety of the person or others, or

(b) causes annoyance or inconvenience to participants in a World Youth Day event, or

(c) obstructs a World Youth Day event.

(2) A person must not, without reasonable excuse, fail to comply with a direction given to the person under subclause (1).

. . . .

(3) A person is not guilty of an offence under this clause unless it is established that the authorised person warned the person that a failure to comply with the direction is an offence. (4)In this clause, *authorised person* means:

(a) a police officer, or

(b) a member of an SES unit (within the meaning of the *State Emergency Service Act 1989*) or a member of the NSW Rural Fire Service, but only if the member is authorised by the Authority in writing for the purposes of this clause.

THE APPLICANTS' PROPOSED CONDUCT

. . . .

32. In particular Ms Evans proposes on 19 July 2008, while in Moore Park on the

Pilgrim Walking Route, to:

(a)   wear a t-shirt bearing the slogan "The Pope was Wrong — Put a Condom On!";

(b)   hand out condoms and stickers bearing slogans;

(c)   hand out flyers and leaflets urging public support for same-sex marriage rights and same-sex couples in Australia and dealing with the matters identified in (d) below;

(d)   speak to, and engage in discussion with, participants in the Pilgrimage Walk to Randwick about matters including the following:

    i.   the teaching of the Pope and the Catholic Church on homosexuality, same-sex marriages, contraception, abortion and use of condoms to prevent HIV;

    ii.   legal discrimination against same-sex couples in Australia in respect of marriage and superannuation entitlements;

    iii.   the role of developed countries such as Australia and the United States in preventing foreign aid from being used to provide access to abortion in developing countries;

    iv.   the criminalisation of abortion in Australian States and Territories;

    v.   the fact that the Federal and State governments are hosting and funding the Pope's visit and World Youth Day 2008; and

    vi.   the importance of ensuring that education curricula do not discriminate on grounds of homosexuality.

33. Ms Pike proposes on 19 July 2008, while at Central Railway Station on the Pilgrim Waling Route, to:

(a)   wear a giant condom costume and hand out condoms to people in the area;

(b)   speak through a mega-phone and hand out leaflets to communicate her views on sexual health, contraception, abortion, homophobia, same-sex marriage, the funding of World Youth Day events and attacks on civil liberties;

(c)   hand out candles to raise public awareness of the fact that same-sex marriage, abortion, birth control and homosexuality are not obstacles to world peace;

(d)   hand out stickers bearing slogans.

THE APPROACH TO RESOLVING CONSTITUTIONAL VALIDITY

. . . .

40. If on its proper construction a statute does not offend against any constitutional limitation or prohibition it is not ordinarily appropriate for the Court to hypothesise a different construction and then test its constitutionality. If a regulation is found to be invalid as not authorised by the statute under which it is said to be made, then it is not for the Court to hypothesise validity under the statute so that it may test for validity under the Constitution. This approach is consistent with, although not

a corollary of, the well-established presumption in favour of the constitutionality of statutes: *Federal Commissioner of Taxation v. Munro* (1926) 38 CLR 153 at 180 (Isaacs J); *Attorney-General (Victoria) v. Commonwealth* (1945) 71 CLR 237 at 267 (Dixon J); *Chu Kheng Lim v. Minister for Immigration Local Government and Ethnic Affairs* (1992) 176 CLR 1 at 14 (Mason CJ).

THE VALIDITY OF SECTION 46(3) OF THE WYD ACT AND CLAUSE 4 OF THE REGULATION

. . . .

48. As is clear from our discussion below of cl 7, we accept the general principle that a regulation should not be interpreted as conferring powers that are repugnant to fundamental rights and freedoms at common law in the absence of clear authority from the Parliament. The applicants submitted that the "excessive reach" of cl 4 falls foul of this principle and observed, in their written submissions:

> For example, the prescription of all "food and drinks" means that a "Good Samaritan" observing a pilgrim walk in an Authority controlled area who wishes to show the Christian charity by distributing food and drink to the pilgrims is caught by the combined operation of s 46 of the Act and clause 4 of the Regulation. It seems extraordinary that such a spontaneous charitable act requires the Good Samaritan to seek and obtain prior written permission from the Authority to avoid the commission of an offence under sub-section 46(3). The relevant excessiveness is to be found primarily in the list of prescribed articles in clause 4 . . .

49. The concept of "distributing food and drink to the pilgrims" involves an element of forethought and system which is at odds with the notion of "a spontaneous charitable act." In our view, the prohibition on the distribution of food and drink would not prohibit the giving of food or water to a pilgrim in distress. Distributing food and drink has the connotation of sharing between a number of people and would not apply to relieving the distress of an individual or individuals.

. . . .

57. In summary, in relation to the condoms, coat-hangers, t-shirts, leaflets, flyers, button badges and stickers that the applicant wishes to distribute, the argument that the reach of cl 4 is excessive fails because the clause does not cover the items in those categories which the applicants wish to distribute. The question whether the reach of cl 4 may be excessive in other respects is not before the Court.

. . . .

THE VALIDITY OF CLAUSE 7 OF THE REGULATION

. . . .

67. Unconstrained by any limiting principle of construction, the power conferred by s 58(2)(b), taken in isolation, could be used to make a regulation enjoining silence at World Youth Day venues and facilities or mandating prayer. However there are constraints. It is difficult to see how such a wide application of the words in s 58(2)(b) would be consistent with the requirement in s 58(1) that the regulations be

"necessary or convenient . . . for carrying out or giving effect to this Act" or within the scope and objects of the Act. In this case however there is an important principle independent of such constraints, which limits the power to regulate conduct.

68. The term "regulating . . . the conduct of the public" is capable of a range of constructions from the regulation of any conceivable conduct to the regulation of conduct relevant to the events on World Youth Day. It may encompass acts and some or all forms of speech and communication. There are constructional choices open. It is an important principle that Acts be construed, where constructional choices are open, so as not to encroach upon common law rights and freedoms. That principle dates back to the statement in *Potter v. Minahan* (1908) 7 CLR 277 in which O'Connor J, quoting from the fourth edition of Maxwell PB, *On the Interpretation of Statutes* (Sweet & Maxwell, London, 1905) (at 304):

> It is in the last degree improbable that the legislature would overthrow fundamental principles, infringe rights, or depart from the general system of law, without expressing its intention with irresistible clearness; and to give any such effect to general words, simply because they have that meaning in their widest, or usual, or natural sense, would be to give them a meaning in which they were not really used.

See also *Bropho v. State of Western Australia* (1990) 171 CLR 1 at 18 and *Coco v R* (1994) 179 CLR 427. In the latter case the High Court said (at 437):

> The courts should not impute to the legislature an intention to interfere with fundamental rights. Such an intention must be clearly manifested by unmistakeable and unambiguous language. General words will rarely be sufficient for that purpose if they do not specifically deal with the question because, in the context in which they appear, they will often be ambiguous on the aspect of interference with fundamental rights.

69. There has been some discussion whether "fundamental principles" constitute a reliable criterion for a principle favouring one statutory construction over another. McHugh J, who joined in the joint judgment in *Coco* 179 CLR 427 from which the above quoted passage is taken, observed in *Malika Holdings Pty Ltd v. Stretton* (2001) 204 CLR 290 (at [28]):

> What is fundamental in one age or place may not be regarded as fundamental in another age or place. When community values are undergoing radical change and few principles or rights are immune from legislative amendment or abolition, as is the case in Australia today, few principles or rights can claim to be so fundamental that it is unlikely that the legislature would want to change them.

. . . .

While acknowledging the validity of that caution we observe that the legislature, through the expert parliamentary counsel who prepare draft legislation, may be taken to be aware of the principle of construction in *Potter* 7 CLR 277 and later authorities such as *Bropho* 171 CLR 1 and *Coco* 179 CLR 427, and the need for clear words to be used before long established (if not "fundamental") rights and freedoms are taken away. The principle was recently restated by the Full Court in *Minister for Immigration and Citizenship v. Haneef* (2007) 243 ALR 606; 163 FCR 414. In one sense it has a constitutional dimension.

. . . .

71. As McHugh J said in *Theophanous v. Herald and Weekly Times Ltd* (1994) 182 CLR 104 (at 196):

> The true meaning of a legal text almost always depends on a background of concepts, principles, practices, facts, rights and duties which the authors of the text took for granted or understood, without conscious advertence, by reason of their common language or culture.

In Australia, the exercise of legislative power, whether primary or delegated, takes place, as it does in England, in the constitutional setting of "a liberal democracy founded on the traditions and principles of the common law": *R v. Secretary of State for Home Department; Ex parte Pierson* [1998] AC 538 at 587. . . . .

72. Whatever debate there may be about particular rights there is little scope, even in contemporary society, for disputing that personal liberty, including freedom of speech, is regarded as fundamental subject to reasonable regulation for the purposes of an ordered society. The freedoms associated with personal liberty are not residual, i.e.what is left beyond the boundaries of legal regulation. . . .

. . . .

This approach to construction has been described in the United Kingdom as a "principle of legality" explained by Lord Hoffman in *R v. Secretary of State for the Home Department; Ex parte Simms* [2000] 2 AC 115 (at 131):

> The principle of legality means that Parliament must squarely confront what it is doing and accept the political cost. Fundamental rights cannot be overridden by general or ambiguous words. This is because there is too great a risk that the full implications of their unqualified meaning may have passed unnoticed in the democratic process. In the absence of express language or necessary implication to the contrary, the courts therefore presume that even the most general words were intended to be subject to the basic rights of the individual.

73. In *Electrolux Home Products Pty Ltd v. Australian Workers Union* (2004) 221 CLR 309, Gleeson CJ . . . said of it (at 329):

> The presumption is not merely a common sense guide to what a parliament in a liberal democracy is likely to have intended; it is a working hypothesis, the existence of which is known both to Parliament and the courts, upon which statutory language will be interpreted. The hypothesis is an aspect of the rule of law.

74. Freedom of speech and of the press has long enjoyed special recognition at common law. Blackstone described it as "essential to the nature of a free State": *Commentaries on the Laws of England*, Vol 4 at 151-152. . . .

. . . .

77. Brennan J in a separate judgment in [*Davis v. Commonwealth* (1988) 166 CLR

79] said (at 116):

> Freedom of speech may sometimes be a casualty of a law of the Common-wealth made under a specific head of legislative power — for example, wartime censorship — or of a law designed to protect the nation — for example, a law against seditious utterances — but freedom of speech can hardly be an incidental casualty of an activity undertaken by the Executive Government to advance a nation which boasts of its freedom.

. . . .

82. Conduct which may attract a direction under cl 7(1)(b) is conduct which "causes annoyance . . . to participants in a World Youth Day event." That is to say it is conduct which actually results in its observers being ruffled, troubled, vexed, disturbed, displeased or slightly irritated. These are responses which depend very much on the individuals concerned. Some may find protests of the kind which are proposed by the applicants mildly amusing. Others may be practising Catholics or Christians who agree with some of the protestors' points and are not troubled by them. There may be others who find the protests irritating and who are, in the relevant sense, annoyed by them. Annoyance to "participants" within the meaning of the Regulation may be annoyance to many or a few. There is no objective criterion to assist the judgment of "an authorised person" in deciding whether to issue a direction under cl 7. There may be circumstances in which it would be difficult if not impossible for a person to whom a direction is given to know whether his or her conduct was such as to authorise the giving of the direction. It is little consolation to the person affected by a direction that he or she could argue the point later in a prosecution in a court of law as the State suggested.

83. In our opinion the conduct regulated by cl 7(1)(b) so far as it relates to "annoyance" may extend to expressions of opinion which neither disrupt nor interfere with the freedoms of others, nor are objectively offensive in the sense traditionally used in State criminal statutes. Breach of this provision as drafted affects freedom of speech in a way that, in our opinion, is not supported by the statutory power conferred by s 58 properly construed. Moreover there is no intelligible boundary within which the "causes annoyance" limb of s 7 can be read down to save it as a valid expression of the regulating power.

. . . .

CONCLUSION

88. For the preceding reasons, the Court will make a declaration that cl 7(1)(b) is invalid to the extent to which it is applied to conduct which causes annoyance to participants in World Youth Day events. There is otherwise in cl 7 a substantial measure of protection against disruptive behaviour, behaviour which causes incon-venience to participants and behaviour which may give rise to a risk to public safety. Over and above these provisions the general criminal laws of the State relating to disorderly and offensive conduct and the like are able to be invoked should that be necessary.

9.6.3.   Concluding thoughts

Edmund Morgan argues in INVENTING THE PEOPLE (1988), that the very premise of government that a minority of people make decisions that determine the fate of the majority in each society, is and has always been based on the creation of necessary fictions — whether the divine right of Kings, or the idea of a sovereign people whose will is performed by a sovereign parliament, or by the representatives of the people. The legitimacy of any particular "fiction" of just government or representation in a democratic system is a matter of historical struggles rooted in both ideas and the material conditions of each age. First colonization and then globalization caused a diffusion of different models of governance — through imposition, imitation, adoption and innovation. Since the Second World War, and particularly after the end of the Cold War, there emerged an international political culture that places human rights and democracy at the center of the notion of legitimate governance, even if understandings of the content of these ideas and how they might be achieved varies widely across different societies and regions of the world.

Given the physical limits on democratic participation — whether through time, place or process — the problem of representation remains intractable and requires the creation of institutional mechanisms through which the people can govern. Even the holding of elections to decide on representatives requires a range of agreements over the process and scope of an election in which the particular electoral system adopted dramatically shapes the nature of representation that flows from it. Participation in elections has itself been the product of dramatic struggles as those who had been historically excluded — including women, colonial peoples and racial minorities — have demanded inclusion. Even then the role of money and electoral fraud continues to plague processes of representation. It is in this context that we can understand the role of constitutional mechanisms designed to check and balance power or protect minority interests from dominant majorities. Here the notion of rights, inherent in individuals or due to communities based on their vulnerability to political domination, serves as an additional and necessary fiction for the advancement of legitimate, and, some might argue, democratic government.

Recognition that representation produces different outcomes depending on the nature of the electoral system as well as the level of government authority involved or that different majorities or even minority interests may dominate different levels of a political system, gives legitimacy to the idea that constitutional democracy, in which a set of institutions and rights is guaranteed from interference by temporary or even permanent majorities, is essential to the protection and sustainability of democracy. While some argue that constitutional democracy, and judicial review in particular, has led to "juristocracy," in which unelected and unrepresentative judges have disproportionate power to decide important social and political questions, the task is for us to understand the outcomes and consequences are of choosing different balances between imperfect institutional alternatives.

In this text we have focused on comparing the constitutions of four countries, all former British colonies that inherited the common law as the basis of their public law — the rules, conventions and practices of governing these societies. Despite this common legal inheritance these four countries have dramatically different constitutional histories that have led to different institutional choices and constitutional practices. By exploring these differences and some of the similarities that are exhibited in the decisions of their highest courts as they address issues that are both contextually different but fundamentally common to the human condition, we hope we have been able to broaden our understanding of both our own constitutional choices and those of others who seem at times to take a different path.

TABLE OF CASES

[References are to pages]

A

Abrams v. United States 243, 244; 267
Adair v. United States 507
Adams v. Tanner 172
Adarand Constructors v. Pena 761, 762
Adkins v. Children's Hospital 173; 507
AFL v. Swing 565; 574
Agins v. City of Tiburon 481
Allgeyer v. Louisiana 168; 506
American Booksellers Asso. v. Hudnut 292
American Power & Light Co. v. SEC 100
Andrus v. Allard 483; 549; 552
Arlington Heights v. Metropolitan Housing Dev.
    Corp. 381, 382; 384
Armstrong v. United States . . . 467; 482; 492; 552
Ashcroft v. Free Speech Coalition 296
Austin v. Michigan Chamber of Commerce.302; 307

B

Baehr v. Lewin 399
Bailey v. Charleston Mail Ass'n 580
Baker v. Carr 120; 452; 625; 629
Bantam Books, Inc. v. Sullivan 579
Barr v. Matteo 580
Bartels v. Iowa 347
Beauharnais v. Illinois 243; 261; 271; 273
Beauharnais, Collin v. Smith 261
Beer Co. v. Massachusetts 474
Belton v. Gebhart 727
Berman v. Parker 485
Bivens v. Six Unknown Federal Narcotics
    Agents 595; 613
Black & White Taxi Co v. Brown & Yellow Taxi
    Co. 594
BMW of North America, Inc. v. Gore 613
Board of Regents v. Roth 182
Boddie v. Connecticut 434
Boerne, City of v. Flores 46
Bolling v. Sharpe 318; 399
Bond v. United States 751
Bormann v. Bd. of Supervisors 553
Bradwell v. Illinois 321
Brandenburg v. Ohio 244; 257
Bridges v. California 565
Briggs v. Elliott 727
Brinkerhoff-Faris Trust & Sav. Co. v. Hill 564
British Columbia v. Tener 515

Brooks v. United States 84
Brown v. Board of Education . . 381; 448; 727; 740;
                                    762, 763; 766; 767
Brown v. Classification Review Board of the Office of
    Film and Literature Classification 257
BSA v. Dale 198
Buchanan v. Warley 563
Buck v. Bell 180; 355
Buckley v. Valeo 295; 299; 304
Bullock v. Carter 342; 446
Butler; United States v. 81

C

Calder v. Bull 177
Califano v. Webster 327
Califano v. Westcott 334
California Federal Sav. & Loan Ass'n v. Guerra . 327
California; United States v. 89
Caminetti v. United States 84
Canada Trust Co. v. Ontario Human Rights
    Commission 609
Cantwell v. Connecticut 565
Carolene Products Co.; United States v. . . . 166; 342;
                              346; 349; 354; 356; 507; 739
Carrington v. Rash 739
Carter v. Carter Coal Co. 80; 89
Case v. Bowles 81
Chagnon v. Union-Leader Corp. 580
Chaplinsky v. New Hampshire 271; 273
Chevron U.S.A., Inc. v. Cayetano 484
Chicago, B. & Q. R. Co. v. Chicago .482; 527; 565
CIO; United States v. 301
Citizens' Insurance Co. of Canada v. Parsons . . .49
Citizens United v. FEC 300
City of (see name of city)
Clarke v. Commissioner of Taxation 112
Clearview Coal Co.; Commonwealth v. 476
Cleburne, City of v. Cleburne Living Ctr. . .198; 349
Cohens v. Virginia 87
Coleman v. MacLennan 580
College Savings Bank v. Florida Prepaid
    Postsecondary Ed. Expense Bd. 94; 152
Commonwealth v. (see name of defendant)
Connolly v. Pension Benefit Guaranty Corp. 480
Cooley v. Board of Wardens 77; 104
Coppage v. Kansas 173; 507

County of (see name of county)
Craig v. Boren 381
Cumming v. County Board of Education 729
Currie v. Macdonald 689
Curtin v. Benson 550
Curtis Publishing Co. v. Butts 591

D

Dandridge v. Williams 342, 343; 440
Darby; United States v. 81, 82; 84; 86; 98
De Jonge v. Oregon 347
DeFunis v. Odegaard 741, 742
Dellinger; United States v. 312
Dennis v. United States 242; 244
Dennis; United States v. 244
Department of Agriculture v. Moreno 399
Dolan v. City of Tigard 485
Douglas v. California 446
Dred Scott v. Sandford 316
Drexel Furniture Co. v. Bailey 81
Dun & Bradstreet, Inc. v. Greenmoss Builders,
    Inc. 586; 594
Duncan v. Louisiana 185

E

E.C. Knight Co.; United States v. 79
Eastern Enterprises v. Apfel 514
Eastern Railroad Presidents Conference v. Noerr
    Motor Freight, Inc. 295
Edwards v. Aguillard 402
Edwards Books and Art Ltd. 251; 264
EEOC v. Wyoming 99, 100
Eisenstadt v. Baird 180
Erie R.R. Co. v. Tompkins 556; 565; 594
Ex parte (see name of relator)
Ex rel. (see name of relator)
Exxon Corp. v. Governor of Maryland 484

F

F.S. Royster Guano Co. v. Virginia 451
Farrington v. Tokushige 347
FEC v. National Right to Work Comm. 305
FEC v. Wis. Right to Life, Inc. 303
Ferguson v. Skrupa 172; 181; 206; 441; 484
Ferrell v. Ontario (Attorney General) 337
First English Evangelical Lutheran Church of
    Glendale v. County of Los Angeles 482
First Nat'l Bank of Boston v. Bellotti 300
Fisher v. University of Texas 747

Fiske v. Kansas 347
Fordice; United States v. 736
Foster v. Florida 197
Freeman v. Pitts 761
Friedell v. Blakely Printing Co. 580
Frontiero v. Richardson 326; 355
Furman v. Georgia 214

G

Gaines, Missouri ex rel. v. Canada 729
Garcia v. San Antonio Metro. Transit Auth. . . .82; 91
Garrett v. Board of Ed. of School Dist. of
    Detroit 737
Gebhart v. Belton 727
Geduldig v. Aiello 352
General Electric Co. v. Gilbert 352
Gertz v. Robert Welch Inc 594
Gibbons v. Ogden 75; 86; 96; 101
Gideon v. Wainwright 434
Gitlow v. New York 347
Goesaert v. Cleary 321; 326; 327
Goldberg v. Kelly 435
Goldblatt v. Hempstead 551
Gong Lum v. Rice 729
Gonzales v. Carhart 192
Gonzales v. Raich 92; 100
Gooch v. United States 84
Goosby v. Osser 446
Graham v. Richardson 342; 354; 448; 739
Gregg v. Georgia 214
Gregory v. Ashcroft 85
Griffin v. Illinois 434; 446; 451
Griswold v. Connecticut 174; 181
Grosjean v. American Press Co 347
Grutter v. Bollinger 747; 759; 761
Guggenheim v. City of Goleta 480

H

Hadacheck v. Sebastian 479; 551
Hammer v. Dagenhart 81; 83; 98
Harding; United States v. 759
Harper v. Virginia Board of Elections 435; 446
Harris v. McRae 190
Harris; United States v. 95
Hawaii Housing Authority v. Midkiff 485
Heart of Atlanta Motel, Inc. v. United States . . .83
Heller v. Doe 401
Helvering v. Davis 99
Hernandez v. Texas 740, 741

[References are to pages]

Herndon v. Lowry 347
Hipolite Egg Co. v. United States 84
Hirabayashi v. United States 739; 741
Hoke v. United States 84
Holder v. Humanitarian Law Project 244
Hollingsworth v. Perry 199
Hooper v. Bernalillo County Assessor 349
Hooper v. California 98
Huron Portland Cement Co. v. Detroit 106

I

In re (see name of party)
In re Welfare of (see name of party)
International Brotherhood of Teamsters v. Vogt,
Inc. 568

J

J.E.B. v. Alabama ex rel. T.B. 326; 328
Jacobson v. Massachusetts 180
Jay Burns Baking Co v. Bryan 173
Jesperson's Brake & Muffler Ltd. v. Chilliwack
(District) 520
Joint Anti-Fascist Refugee Committee v.
McGrath 436
Jones v. Alfred H. Mayer Co. 612

K

Kaiser Aetna v. United States 471; 548
Katz v. United States 182
Katzenbach v. McClung 84
Katzenbach v. Morgan 46
Kelly v. Wyman 436
Kelo v. City of New London 485
Kennedy v. Louisiana 214
Kettering Pty Ltd v. Noosa Shire Council 510
Kidd v. Pearson 79
Kimel v. Florida Bd. of Regents 46
Konigsberg v. State Bar of California 240
Korematsu 739, 740; 741
Kraemer v. Shelley 562
Kramer v. Union School District 448

L

Lake Shore & Michigan Southern R. Co. v.
Ohio 81; 89; 104
Lalonde v. Ontario (Commission de Restructuration
des Services de Sante) 735
Lawrence v. Fox 580
Lawrence v. Texas 194; 197; 349

Legal Tender Cases 548
License Tax Cases 94; 152
Lindsey v. Normet 342; 449
Lindsley v. Natural Carbonic Gas Co. 441
Lingle v. Chevron U.S.A. Inc. 481
Lochner v. New York . 168; 173; 177; 183; 459; 506;
                                                   507; 552
Lopez; United States v. 84; 87; 88; 96
Loretto v. Teleprompter Manhattan CATV Corp . 483
Lottery Case 84
Lovell v. Griffin 347
Loving v. Virginia 180; 186
Lucas v. South Carolina Coastal Council . . 483; 517;
                                                   548; 613

M

Madsen v. Women's Health Clinic, Inc. 253
Mandeville Island Farms, Inc. v. American Crystal
Sugar Co. 80
Mandrake Management Consultants Ltd. v. Toronto
Transit Commission 521
Marbury v. Madison 4; 95; 616
Maryland v. Wirtz 81; 97
Massachusetts v. Feeney 380
Massachusetts Bd. of Retirement v. Murgia . 341; 739
McConnell v. FEC 303, 304; 306; 307
McCulloch v. Maryland 71; 94; 101; 347
McDermott; United States v. 276
McDonald v. Board of Election Comm'rs 446
McGowan v. Maryland 441
McLaughlin v. Florida 342; 381; 442
McLaurin v. Oklahoma State Regents 729, 730
McLean v. Merriman 580
McNabb v. United States 201
Memorial Hospital v. Maricopa County 435
Metro Broadcasting, Inc. v. FCC 760; 762
Metropolis Theatre Co v. City of Chicago 441
Metropolitan Life Ins. Co. v. Ward 349
Meyer v. Nebraska 174; 180; 347; 716
Miller v. California 291, 292
Miller v. Johnson 760
Miller v. Schoene 551
Miller; United States v. 84
Milliken v. Bradley 759
Mills v. Alabama 295
Minister for Immigration and Citizenship v.
Haneef 800
Mississippi Univ. for Women 326, 327; 328
Mo. Pac. R.R. v. Nebraska 470
Monongahela Navigation Co. v. United States . . 552

[References are to pages]

Moon v. N. Idaho Farmers Ass'n 553
Morehead v. New York ex rel. Tipaldo 507
Morrison; United States v. 84, 85
Mugler v. Kansas 472; 478; 479; 551
Munn v. Illinois 551
Murphy v. California. 479
Muskrat v. United States 637; 642

N

N. A. A. C. P. v. Button 578
NAACP v. Alabama 175
NAACP v. Claiborne Hardware Co. 295
Nat'l Fed'n of Indep. Businesses v. Sebelius . 84; 94
National Labor Relations Board v. Jones & Laughlin
     Steel Corp. 80; 86; 87; 98; 100
National League of Cities v. Usery 82
Near v. Minnesota ex rel. Olson. 347
New State Ice Co. v. Liebmann. 92; 156
New York v. United States 94
New York City Transit Authority v. Beazer. . . .323
New York Times Co. v. Sullivan.243; 300; 576; 586;
                                      594
New York Times Co. v. Sullivan 576
Nixon v. Condon. 347
Nixon v. Herndon 347
Nixon v. United States. 624
Nollan v. California Coastal Comm'n. 485
North American Co. v. SEC. 100
Northwest Austin Mun. Util. Dist. No. One v.
     Holder. 749, 750; 751; 752; 753; 757

O

O'Brien; United States v. 245; 401
Oyama v. California 342; 563; 741

P

Pacific Ry. Comm'n, In re. 638
Pacific States Box & Basket Co. v. White 106
Palko v. Connecticut. 180
Palmer v. Mulligan. 553
Parents Involved in Cmty. Sch. v. Seattle Sch. Dist.
     No. 1 759
Parham v. Justices 527
Parker v. Brown 106
Parmalee v. Morris. 562
Patterson v. New York. 165
Penn Central Transportation Co. v. New York
     City. 479; 483; 492

Pennoyer v. Neff. 564
Pennsylvania Coal Co. v. Mahon.475; 483; 548; 549
Perez v. United States. 94
Pers. Adm'r of Massachusetts v. Feeney 379
Philip Morris USA v. Williams 613
Phoenix Newspapers v. Choisser 580
Pierce v. Society of Sisters. 174; 180; 347
Pierce Oil Corp. v. Hope. 479
Pike v. Bruce Church, Inc.. 105
Planned Parenthood v. Casey 184
Plessy v. Ferguson. 351; 728; 729; 741; 765
Plymouth Coal Co. v. Pennsylvania. 476
Poe v. Ullman. 174; 176; 186
Police Dep't of Chicago v. Mosley 274
Ponder v. Cobb. 580
Powell v. Alabama. 176
Powell v. Pennsylvania. 478, 479; 491
Price; United States v. 751
Prince v. Massachusetts 180
Printz v. United States 2
PruneYard Shopping Center v. Robins 552
Pumpelly v. Green Bay Co. 473; 527

R

R. v. Manitoba Fisheries Ltd. 515
R. A. V. v. City of St. Paul 270
R.A.V., In re Welfare of 271
Railroad Retirement Bd. v. Alton Railroad Co. . . 80;
                                      98
Railway Express Agency v. New York 444
Railway Mail Ass'n v. Corsi. 746
Reed v. Reed. 328
Regents of Univ. of Cal. v. Bakke. 738
Reinman v. Little Rock 479
Reynolds v. Sims. 451
Rice v. Cayetano. 762
Richmond, City of v. J.A. Croson Co . 746; 748; 762
Rideout v. Knox 476
Rodriguez v. San Antonio Independent School
     Dist. 445
Roe v. Wade 178; 342
Romer v. Evans. 195; 349
Roper v. Simmons 214
Roth v. United States. 271; 273; 291
Rutan v. Republican Party of Ill. 330

S

Sacramento, County of v. Lewis. 484

Salinger v. Cowles 580

San Antonio School District v. Rodriguez . 342; 386; 445; 739

Santa Clara County v. Southern Pacific Railroad Co.. 470

Schenck v. Pro-Choice Network of Western New York. 256

Schenck v. United States. 243

School Committee of Boston v. Board of Education 767

Selman v. Shirley. 231; 602

Seven-Sky v. Holder. 100

Shapiro v. Thompson . 342; 354; 381; 435; 436; 448

Shaw v. Reno. 747; 762

Shelby County v. Holder. 46; 749; 756

Shelley v. Kraemer. 561; 739

Shelton v. Tucker. 240; 441

Sherbert v. Verner 436

Simpson; United States v.. 84

Sinnickson v. Johnson 527

Sipes v. McGhee. 562

Sipuel v. Board of Regents 729

Skinner v. Oklahoma 180; 342; 451; 739

Slaughter-House Cases 318; 344; 729; 744

Slochower v. Board of Higher Education. 436

Smith v. California. 579

Snively v. Record Publishing Co.. 580

Snyder v. Massachusetts 176; 183

South Carolina v. Katzenbach . . 749; 750; 751; 753; 754

South Carolina State Highway Dep't v. Barnwell Bros., Inc.. . . . . .106; 347

South Dakota v. Dole 94; 152

Southern Pacific Co. v. Arizona. 106

Speiser v. Randall 436

St. Catharines Milling & Lumber Co. v. The Queen. 35

Stanley v. Georgia. 296

Steer Holdings Ltd. v. Manitoba. 511

Stenberg v. Carhart. 192

Stice v. Beacon Newspaper Corp.. 580

Stop the Beach Renourishment, Inc. v. Florida Dep't of Environmental Protection 553

Strauder v. West Virginia. 729; 740

Stromberg v. California 347

Sweatt v. Painter 729, 730; 741

Sweeney v. Patterson. 578; 585

T

Terminiello v. City of Chicago 239

Terrace v. Thompson. 741

Thornburgh v. American College of Obstetricians & Gynecologists. 190

Time Inc v. Firestone 594

Time Inc v. Hill 594

Transportation Co. v. Chicago. 548

Troxel v. Granville. 614

Truax v. Raich 740

U

Union Pacific R. Co. v. Botsford 179

United Jewish Organizations v. Carey. . . .383; 742

United States v. (see name of defendant)

V

Vance v. Bradley 377, 378; 381

Veazie Bank v. Fenno. 83

Virginia v. Rives. 564

Virginia, Ex parte 564

Virginia; United States v. 325

Virginia; United States v. 327

W

Washington v. Davis. 380, 381; 382; 737

Washington v. Glucksberg. 401

Webb's Fabulous Pharmacies, Inc. v. Beckwith. .550

Webster v. Reproductive Health Services. 189

Wesberry v. Sanders 224

Wesson v. Washburn Iron Co 476

West Coast Hotel Co. v. Parrish. 507

West Virginia State Board of Education v. Barnette. 294

Whitney v. California. 244; 347

Wickard v. Filburn 80; 91; 94; 100

Williams v. Dandridge. 440

Williams v. Rhodes. 342

Williams v. Vermont 349

Williamson v. Lee Optical Co . . 173; 183; 191; 441; 443

Windsor; United States v. 199; 398

Wisconsin v. Yoder. 295

Wright v. Rockefeller 747

Wygant v. Jackson Bd. of Education 747

Y

Yick Wo v. Hopkins 740, 741

Young v. McKenzie 527

[References are to pages]

Z

Zobel v. Williams 349

INDEX

[References are to sections.]

A

ADVISORY OPINIONS
Australia . . . 8.2.3
Canada . . . 8.2.2
South Africa . . . 8.2.4
United States . . . 8.2.1

AMERICAN DOCTRINE
"Rational basis" test in . . . 4.2.3

ANGLOPHONES IN QUEBEC
Judicial protection of . . . 9.2.3

AUSTRALIA
Canadian and Australian non-constitutional protection for property (See REGULATION OF PROPERTY, subhead: Non-constitutional protection for property, Canadian and Australian)
Constitution
    Constitutional law comparative study . . . Intro.1
    Enactment of . . . Intro. 2.3
Democracy and human rights, protection of . . . 9.6.2
Election spending, regulation of . . . 3.5.3
Enactment of constitution . . . Intro. 2.3
Federalism (See FEDERALISM, subhead: Australia)
Free speech, approach to (See FREEDOM OF SPEECH AND EXPRESSION, subhead: Australian approach to free speech)
Hate speech . . . 3.3.4
Human rights, protection of democracy and . . . 9.6.2
Implied limits on governments to infringe individual freedoms in . . . 2.5
Legislative process in political context, comparison of . . . Intro. 4.3
Non-constitutional protection for property (See REGULATION OF PROPERTY, subhead: Non-constitutional protection for property, Canadian and Australian)
Non-constitutional response of Australian government to international obligations . . . 5.6
Pornography, regulation of . . . 3.4.4
Right to property: Australian foundations . . . 6.1.4
Statutory response . . . 4.1.1.2.4

B

BILL OF RIGHTS
Provisions of South African Constitution and . . . 2.4

C

CANADA
Anglophones in Quebec, judicial protection of . . . 9.2.3

CANADA—Cont.
Charter of Rights and Freedoms . . . 4.1.1.2.2
Constitution
    Constitutional law comparative study . . . Intro.1
    Enactment of . . . Intro. 2.2
    Right to property, rejection of constitutional . . . 6.1.5
Election spending, regulation of . . . 3.5.2
Enactment of constitution . . . Intro. 2.2
Federalism (See FEDERALISM, subhead: Canada)
Francophones in English Canada, judicial protection of . . . 9.2.4
Free speech, approach to (See FREEDOM OF SPEECH AND EXPRESSION, subhead: Canadian approach to free speech)
Hate speech . . . 3.3.1
Language rights in . . . 9.2.1
Legislative process in political context, comparison of . . . Intro. 4.2
Linguistic minorities, judicial protection for
    Generally . . . 9.2
    Anglophones in Quebec, judicial protection of . . . 9.2.3
    Francophones in English Canada, judicial protection of . . . 9.2.4
    Judicial protection
        Anglophones in Quebec, of . . . 9.2.3
        Francophones in English Canada, of . . . 9.2.4
    Language rights in Canada . . . 9.2.1
    Notwithstanding Clause . . . 9.2.2
Notwithstanding Clause . . . 9.2.2
Pornography, regulation of . . . 3.4.1
Section 7 of Canadian Charter, "security of the person" under . . . 5.5
"Security of the person" under Section 7 of Canadian Charter . . . 5.5; 5.5.1
Substantive discrimination based on enumerated or analogous grounds . . . 4.3.2

CIVIL WAR
Amendments . . . 4.1.1.2.1

CONSTITUTIONAL CONVENTION
Generally . . . 8.3
Advisory opinions, conventions and crisis in absence of . . . 8.3.3
Constitutional amendment, requirement of . . . 8.3.5
Existence of conventions, declaration of
    Generally . . . 8.3.1
    Conventions are not judicially-enforceable law . . . 8.3.1.1
    Proposed act violation of convention, Supreme Court of Canada advise on . . . 8.3.1.2
    Supreme Court of Canada advise on proposed act violation of convention . . . 8.3.1.2
Long-standing policies versus conventions . . . 8.3.2

I-1

[References are to sections.]

CONSTITUTIONAL CONVENTION—Cont.
South Africa . . . 8.3.6
Statutes and conventions, relationship between
  . . . 8.3.4
Whitlam Affair . . . 8.3.3

CONSTITUTIONAL LAW, COMPARATIVE
  (GENERALLY)
Approaches to constitutional interpretation
    Generally . . . Intro. 5; Intro. 5.6
    "Living" interpretation . . . Intro. 5.3
    Originalism . . . Intro. 5.1
    "Persons" case . . . Intro. 5.5
    Pragmatism . . . Intro. 5.4
    Textualism . . . Intro. 5.2
Australian, Canadian, South African and U.S., com-
  parison of . . . Intro.1
Constitutional ideology . . . Intro. 3.2
Cultural differences, significant . . . Intro. 3.1
Enactment of nation's constitution
    Australia (1900) . . . Intro. 2.3
    Canada (1867 and 1982) . . . Intro. 2.2
    South Africa (1996) . . . Intro. 2.4
    United States of America (1789 and 1860s)
      . . . Intro. 2.1
Legislative process in political context, comparison
  of
    Generally . . . Intro. 4
    Australia . . . Intro. 4.3
    Canada . . . Intro. 4.2
    South Africa . . . Intro. 4.4
    United States . . . Intro. 4.1
Political context, comparison of legislative process
  in (See subhead: Legislative process in political
  context, comparison of)

COURT SYSTEMS AND PRIVATE LITIGA-
  TION
Constitutional values and common law
    American common law, constitutionalization of
      . . . 7.4.2
    Jurisprudence, incorporating values into
      . . . 7.4.1
    Legal realism and constitutionalization of
      American common law . . . 7.4.2
    Libel . . . 7.3
Organization of judiciary (See ORGANIZATION
  OF JUDICIARY)
State action, concept of . . . 7.2

D

DEMOCRACY AND HUMAN RIGHTS, PRO-
  TECTION OF
Generally . . . 9.1; 9.1.3; 9.3; 9.6.1; 9.6.3
Australian debate . . . 9.6.2
Canada: judicial protection for linguistic minorities
  (See CANADA, subhead: Linguistic minorities,
  judicial protection for)
Context . . . 9.1.4

DEMOCRACY AND HUMAN RIGHTS, PRO-
TECTION OF—Cont.
Judicial protection
    Linguistic minorities in Canada, for (See
      CANADA, subhead: Linguistic minorities,
      judicial protection for)
    Political minorities . . . 9.6.1
    Racial minorities, of (See UNITED STATES,
      subhead: Racial minorities, judicial protec-
      tion of)
Linguistic minorities in Canada, judicial protection
  for (See CANADA, subhead: Linguistic minori-
  ties, judicial protection for)
Parliamentary sovereignty, rights entrenchment ver-
  sus . . . 9.1.1
Racial minorities in United States, judicial protec-
  tion of (See UNITED STATES, subhead: Racial
  minorities, judicial protection of)
Rights debate in Australia, current . . . 9.1.2
Rights entrenchment versus parliamentary sover-
  eignty . . . 9.1.1
South Africa . . . 9.5
United States: judicial protection of racial minorities
  (See UNITED STATES, subhead: Racial minori-
  ties, judicial protection of)

DIGNITY, EQUALITY, AND FREEDOM
Generally . . . 3.1.2
Election spending, regulation of
    Generally . . . 3.5
    Australia . . . 3.5.3
    Canada . . . 3.5.2
    South Africa . . . 3.5.4
    United States . . . 3.5.1
Expression, freedom of speech and (See FREEDOM
  OF SPEECH AND EXPRESSION)
Freedom of speech and expression (See FREEDOM
  OF SPEECH AND EXPRESSION)
Gender equality and freedom, balancing (See POR-
  NOGRAPHY, REGULATION OF)
Hate speech (See HATE SPEECH)
Human dignity . . . 3.1.1
Pornography, regulation of (See PORNOGRAPHY,
  REGULATION OF)
Racial equality and freedom, balancing (See HATE
  SPEECH)
Speech and expression, freedom of (See FREEDOM
  OF SPEECH AND EXPRESSION)

DISCRIMINATION
Equality (See EQUALITY, subhead: Discrimination
  and inequality, responses to)
    Intentional . . . 4.4
Gender-based discrimination, protection against
  . . . 4.1.1.3
Racial and other discrimination, lack of protection
  against . . . 4.1.1.1

[References are to sections.]

E

ELECTION SPENDING, REGULATION OF
(See DIGNITY, EQUALITY, AND FREEDOM, subhead: Election spending, regulation of)

EQUALITY
Close judicial scrutiny, classifications that warrant
    Generally . . . 4.3
    Canada: substantive discrimination based on enumerated or analogous grounds . . . 4.3.2
    Economic and social legislation, rationales for absence of close scrutiny of . . . 4.3.4
    South Africa . . . 4.3.3
    United States: suspect classifications and fundamental rights . . . 4.3.1
Constitutional concern, origins of
    Discrimination and inequality, responses to (See subhead: Discrimination and inequality, responses to)
    Gender-based discrimination, protection against . . . 4.1.1.3
    Racial and other discrimination, lack of protection against . . . 4.1.1.1
Dignity, equality, and freedom (See DIGNITY, EQUALITY, AND FREEDOM)
Discrimination and inequality, responses to
    Australia's statutory response . . . 4.1.1.2.4
    Canada: Charter of Rights and Freedoms . . . 4.1.1.2.2
    South Africa's new Constitution . . . 4.1.1.2.3
    U.S.: Civil War amendments . . . 4.1.1.2.1
Disparate impact . . . 4.4
Gender-based discrimination, protection against . . . 4.1.1.3
Guarantees, fundamental purpose of . . . 4.1.2
Inequality, responses to discrimination and (See subhead: Discrimination and inequality, responses to)
Intentional discrimination . . . 4.4
Judicial scrutiny of legislative classifications, problem of
    Generally . . . 4.2.1
    Close scrutiny, examples of . . . 4.2.2
    "Rational basis" test in American doctrine . . . 4.2.3
Racial and other discrimination, lack of protection against . . . 4.1.1.1
"Rational basis" test in American doctrine . . . 4.2.3
Same-sex marriage . . . 4.5

EXPRESSION, FREEDOM OF SPEECH AND
(See FREEDOM OF SPEECH AND EXPRESSION)

F

FEDERALISM
Australia
    Generally . . . 1.2.3; 1.5
    "Corporations power" and *work choices* case . . . 1.5.6
    Engineers case . . . 1.5.1

FEDERALISM—Cont.
Australia—Cont.
    External affairs . . . 1.5.3
    Interpretation, expansion of federal power via . . . 1.5.1
    Melbourne Corporation doctrine . . . 1.5.2
    Section 92 . . . 1.5.5
    State power, limitations on . . . 1.5.5
    Trade and commerce power . . . 1.5.4
    Work Choices case . . . 1.5.6
Canada
    Generally . . . 1.2.1
    Agriculture power, limits to . . . 1.3.3
    "Colourability" . . . 1.3.5
    Criminal law power . . . 1.3.4
    Judicial reasoning in policing . . . 1.3.5
    "Peace, order, and good government" (POGG) power, limits to . . . 1.3.3
    Policing, judicial reasoning in . . . 1.3.5
    Provincial power, limits on . . . 1.3.6
    Trade and commerce power
        Generally . . . 1.3.1.2
        Cases . . . 1.3.1.1
Concept of federalism
    Generally . . . 1.1; 1.1.2
    Constitutional federalism versus decentralization . . . 1.1.1
    Co-operative government distinguished . . . 1.1.3
    Decentralization, constitutional federalism versus . . . 1.1.1
Constitutional texts, of
    Australia . . . 1.2.3
    Canada . . . 1.2.1
    South Africa . . . 1.2.4
    United States . . . 1.2.2
South African co-operative government
    Generally . . . 1.2.4; 1.6
    Active judicial policing of federalism . . . 1.7.2
    Constitutional court's interpretation of principles . . . 1.6.2
    Disputes over allocation of legislative authority
        Generally . . . 1.6.3
        Constitutional allocation of legislative power . . . 1.6.3.1
        Provincial power, scope of exclusive . . . 1.6.3.3
        Residual national legislative power, scope of . . . 1.6.3.2
    Federalism and partisan politics . . . 1.7.3
    Fiscal federalism and taxing and spending powers . . . 1.7.1
    Legislative authority
        Disputes over allocation of (See subhead: Disputes over allocation of legislative authority)
        Distribution of legislative authority under co-operative government . . . 1.6.1
    National political process . . . 1.7.2
    Originalism awry . . . 1.7.4
    Partisan politics, federalism and . . . 1.7.3

[References are to sections.]

FEDERALISM—Cont.

South African co-operative government—Cont.

    Principles, constitutional court's interpretation
       of . . . 1.6.2

    Spending powers . . . 1.7.1

United States

    Generally . . . 1.2.2; 1.4.6

    Commerce Clause

       Power exercised for commercial regula-
          tory concerns . . . 1.4.5

       Scope of . . . 1.4.2

    Deference, scope of . . . 1.4.1

    Federal legislative power

       Judicial limits on . . . 1.4.3

       Tenth Amendment as limits on . . . 1.4.4

    Judicial limits on federal legislative power
       . . . 1.4.3

    State legislative power, limits on . . . 1.4.7

FOURTEENTH AMENDMENT

Close scrutiny of deprivations of liberty under
    . . . 2.2

FRANCOPHONES IN ENGLISH CANADA

Judicial protection of . . . 9.2.4

FREEDOM OF SPEECH AND EXPRESSION

Generally . . . 3.2

Australian approach to free speech

    Generally . . . 3.2.3

    Cases . . . 3.2.3.2

    Implied freedom of political communication
       . . . 3.2.3.1

    Political communication, implied freedom of
       . . . 3.2.3.1

Canadian approach to free speech

    Generally . . . 3.2.2

    Charter principles, basic . . . 3.2.2.2

    Pre-charter antecedents . . . 3.2.2.1

South African approach to free speech . . . 3.2.4

U.S. approach to free speech

    Generally . . . 3.2.1

    Content-based speech restrictions . . . 3.2.1.1

    Content-neutral restrictions . . . 3.2.1.2

G

GENDER

Equality and freedom, balancing (See PORNOGRA-
    PHY, REGULATION OF)

Gender-based discrimination, protection against
    . . . 4.1.1.3

H

HATE SPEECH

Australia . . . 3.3.4

Canada . . . 3.3.1

South Africa . . . 3.3.3

United States . . . 3.3.2

**HUMAN RIGHTS, PROTECTION OF DEMOC-
RACY AND** (See DEMOCRACY AND HUMAN
RIGHTS, PROTECTION OF)

I

**INDIVIDUAL RIGHTS, CONSTITUTIONAL
PROTECTION FOR**

Generally . . . 2.1.1; 2.1.2

Australia, implied limits on governments to infringe
    individual freedoms in . . . 2.5

Bill of Rights, provisions of South African Constitu-
    tion and . . . 2.4

Close judicial scrutiny

    Fundamental rights, interference with
       . . . 2.1.3

    Interference with fundamental rights . . . 2.1.3

    Liberty, deprivations of

       Fourteenth Amendment, under . . . 2.2

       Security of person under Section 7 of
          Canadian Charter of Rights and Free-
          doms . . . 2.3

Fourteenth Amendment, close scrutiny of depriva-
    tions of liberty under . . . 2.2

Fundamental rights, close judicial scrutiny of inter-
    ference with . . . 2.1.3

Implied limits on governments to infringe individual
    freedoms in Australia . . . 2.5

Liberty

    Close scrutiny of deprivations of liberty under
       Fourteenth Amendment . . . 2.2

    Interpreting . . . 2.1.4

Provisions of South African Constitution and Bill of
    Rights . . . 2.4

J

JUDICIAL AUTHORITY

Advisory opinions (See ADVISORY OPINIONS)

Constitutional convention (See CONSTITUTIONAL
    CONVENTION)

Government act, concept of . . . 8.1

"Unconstitutional" law, concept of . . . 8.1

JUDICIARY, ORGANIZATION OF (See ORGA-
NIZATION OF JUDICIARY)

L

LINGUISTIC MINORITIES (See CANADA, subhead: Linguistic minorities, judicial protection for)

M

MARRIAGE

Equality in same-sex marriage . . . 4.5

"MELBOURNE CORPORATION DOCTRINE"

Generally . . . 1.5.2

MINORITIES
Canada: judicial protection for linguistic minorities
(See CANADA, subhead: Linguistic minorities,
judicial protection for)
Judicial protection
Linguistic minorities in Canada, of (See
CANADA, subhead: Linguistic minorities,
judicial protection for)
Political minorities, with . . . 9.6.1
Racial minorities in United States, in (See
UNITED STATES, subhead: Racial minori-
ties, judicial protection of)
Political minorities with judicial protection
. . . 9.6.1
United States: judicial protection of racial minorities
(See UNITED STATES, subhead: Racial minori-
ties, judicial protection of)

N

NOTWITHSTANDING CLAUSE
Generally . . . 9.2.2

O

ORGANIZATION OF JUDICIARY
Generally . . . 7.1
Australia . . . 7.1.3
Canada . . . 7.1.2
Person who appoint judges . . . 7.1.5
South Africa . . . 7.1.4
United States . . . 7.1.1

P

POLITICAL MINORITIES
Judicial protection, with . . . 9.6.1

PORNOGRAPHY, REGULATION OF
Australia . . . 3.4.4
Canada . . . 3.4.1
South Africa . . . 3.4.3
United States . . . 3.4.2

**PRIVATE LITIGATION, COURT SYSTEMS
AND** (See COURT SYSTEMS AND PRIVATE
LITIGATION)

PROPERTY, REGULATION OF (See REGULA-
TION OF PROPERTY)

R

RACIAL MINORITIES (See UNITED STATES,
subhead: Racial minorities, judicial protection of)

"RATIONAL BASIS" TEST
American doctrine, in . . . 4.2.3

REGULATION OF PROPERTY
Acquisition of property defined . . . 6.3.2
American constitutional protection of property and
bar to economic regulation
Generally . . . 6.2; 6.2.5

REGULATION OF PROPERTY—Cont.
American constitutional protection of property and
bar to economic regulation—Cont.
Active or deferential scrutiny . . . 6.2.4
Doctrine of regulatory takings . . . 6.2.2
Due process
Limits on use of property . . . 6.2.1
Takings Clause guarantees versus
. . . 6.2.3
Takings Clause guarantees, due process versus
. . . 6.2.3
Australian non-constitutional protection for property
(See subhead: Non-constitutional protection for
property, Canadian and Australian)
Canada
Canadian constitutional protection for property,
rejection of . . . 6.4
Non-constitutional protection for property (See
subhead: Non-constitutional protection for
property, Canadian and Australian)
Protection for property, rejection of Canadian
constitutional . . . 6.4
Common law recognition of property rights and
constitutional protection, relationship between
. . . 6.7
Constitutional protection, relationship between com-
mon law recognition of property rights and
. . . 6.7
Non-constitutional protection for property, Canadian
and Australian
Generally . . . 6.5
Expropriations
Political process in . . . 6.5.4
Presumption against . . . 6.5.1
Government or public, acquisition for benefit
of . . . 6.5.2
Injurious affection, statutory compensation for
. . . 6.5.3
Political process in expropriations . . . 6.5.4
Presumption against expropriation . . . 6.5.1
Statutory compensation for 'injurious affection'
. . . 6.5.3
Property defined . . . 6.3.1
Right to property
American foundations . . . 6.1.3
Australian foundations . . . 6.1.4
Canadian rejection of constitutional right to
property . . . 6.1.5
Constitutional jurisprudence, issues of
. . . 6.1.2
Economic liberty, distinguishing . . . 6.1.7
Jurisprudential/doctrinal challenge . . . 6.1.7
South African compromise . . . 6.1.6
Textual provisions . . . 6.1.1
South African constitutional protection of property
. . . 6.6

S

SAME-SEX MARRIAGE
Equality . . . 4.5

[References are to sections.]

SOCIAL AND ECONOMIC RIGHTS
Generally . . . 5.1
Australian government to international obligations, non-constitutional response of . . . 5.6
International and American roots . . . 5.1.1
Judicially enforceable protection under South African Constitution
    Generally . . . 5.2
    Health care, allocation of scarce resources for . . . 5.2.1
    Housing, right to . . . 5.2.2
    Medicines, access to . . . 5.2.3
    Right to housing . . . 5.2.2
    Scarce resources for health care, allocation of . . . 5.2.1
Non-constitutional response of Australian government to international obligations . . . 5.6
Reasonableness . . . 5.3
"Security of the person" under Section 7 of Canadian Charter . . . 5.5; 5.5.1
South Africa
    Generally . . . 5.1.2
    Approaches
        Generally . . . 5.1.3
        Comparative analysis, for . . . 5.1.3
    Judicially enforceable protection under South African Constitution (See subhead: Judicially enforceable protection under South African Constitution)
United States
    Constitutional interpretation, possibilities for inclusion through . . . 5.4.1
    Poverty rights, American recognition of . . . 5.4.2
    Rejection of social and economic rights . . . 5.4.3; 5.4.4

SOUTH AFRICA
Bill of Rights, provisions of South African Constitution and . . . 2.4
Close judicial scrutiny . . . 4.3.3
Constitution
    Constitutional law comparative study . . . Intro.1
    Convention, constitutional . . . 8.3.6
    Enactment of . . . Intro. 2.4
    New Constitution . . . 4.1.1.2.3
Democracy and human rights, protection of . . . 9.5
Economic rights, social and (See SOCIAL AND ECONOMIC RIGHTS, subhead: South Africa)
Election spending, regulation of . . . 3.5.4
Enactment of constitution . . . Intro. 2.4
Federalism (See FEDERALISM, subhead: South African co-operative government)
Free speech, approach to . . . 3.2.4
Hate speech . . . 3.3.3
Human rights, protection of democracy and . . . 9.5
Legislative process in political context, comparison of . . . Intro. 4.4
New Constitution . . . 4.1.1.2.3

SOUTH AFRICA—Cont.
Pornography, regulation of . . . 3.4.3
Provisions of South African Constitution and Bill of Rights . . . 2.4
Right to property . . . 6.1.6
Social and economic rights (See SOCIAL AND ECONOMIC RIGHTS, subhead: South Africa)

SPEECH AND EXPRESSION, FREEDOM OF
(See FREEDOM OF SPEECH AND EXPRESSION)

T

TENTH AMENDMENT
Federal legislative power of United States, as limits on . . . 1.4.4

U

UNITED STATES
Civil War amendments . . . 4.1.1.2.1
Close judicial scrutiny: suspect classifications and fundamental rights . . . 4.3.1
Constitution
    Constitutional law comparative study . . . Intro.1
    Enactment of . . . Intro. 2.1
Economic rights, social and (See SOCIAL AND ECONOMIC RIGHTS, subhead: United States)
Election spending, regulation of . . . 3.5.1
Enactment of constitution . . . Intro. 2.1
Federalism (See FEDERALISM, subhead: United States)
Free speech, approach to (See FREEDOM OF SPEECH AND EXPRESSION, subhead: U.S. approach to free speech)
Legislative process in political context, comparison of . . . Intro. 4.1
Pornography, regulation of . . . 3.4.2
Racial minorities, judicial protection of
    Ameliorative practices, contrasting Canadian doctrine regarding . . . 9.4.3
    Brown's legacy . . . 9.4.4
    Canadian doctrine regarding ameliorative practices, contrasting . . . 9.4.3
    Race-conscious policies designed to benefit minorities, judicial review of . . . 9.4.2
    Unconstitutional racial discrimination, proof of . . . 9.4.1
Right to property: American foundations . . . 6.1.3
Social and economic rights (See SOCIAL AND ECONOMIC RIGHTS, subhead: United States)

W

WHITLAM AFFAIR
Generally . . . 8.3.3